THE AFRICAN-AMERICAN EXPERIENCE

BLACK HISTORY AND CULTURE
THROUGH SPEECHES, LETTERS, EDITORIALS,
POEMS, SONGS, AND STORIES

THE
AFRICAN-AMERICAN
EXPERIENCE

BLACK HISTORY AND CULTURE
THROUGH SPEECHES, LETTERS, EDITORIALS,
POEMS, SONGS, AND STORIES

EDITED BY KAI WRIGHT

BLACK DOG
& LEVENTHAL
PUBLISHERS
NEW YORK

Published by Black Dog & Leventhal Publishers, Inc.
151 West 19th Street, New York, NY 10011

Distributed by Workman Publishing Company
225 Varick Street, New York, NY 10014

Manufactured in the United States of America

Cover design by Elizabeth Driesbach
Interior design by 27.12 Design, Ltd.

Quilt on front cover designed and sewn by
Mary Ann Pettway, Gee's Bend Quilters Collective, 2008

ISBN-13: 978-1-57912-773-2

h g f e d c b a

Library of Congress Cataloging-in-Publication Data available upon request.

Previously published as *The African-American Archive*

pp. 722-724 constitute a continuation of this copyright page

CONTENTS

3. I WILL BE HEARD: *Abolition And The Build Up to Civil War*

7. A DREAM NO LONGER DEFERRED:
The Civil Rights Movement

INTRODUCTION

Along with all that Barack Obama had done by the summer of 2008 to revive America's conversation about race, his campaign for president also provided one of our time's most arresting metaphors for how maddening that discussion often feels.

Obama spent much of the Democratic primaries basking in the media glow generated by his stunning upset of establishment candidate Hillary Clinton in the Iowa caucuses. His victory speech that night, presented here, offered a hair-raising moment not only for America but for the world—one from which Clinton would never recover and one that would propel Obama to the Democratic nomination for president. As Obama stood before a crowd of thousands roaring his signature campaign phrase—"Yes we can!"—it was, for the first time, possible to see the young, charismatic leader succeeding in his quixotic bid to become America's first black president, forever changing the course of American history in the process. If a record-setting turnout of largely white Iowans could elect Obama, couldn't it be possible that white supremacy was on the ropes? Couldn't it be possible that our long-awaited racial reconciliation had finally begun in earnest? Weeks later, when Obama claimed another massive victory in South Carolina's heavily African American Democratic primary, his supporters chanted everyone's wish: "Race doesn't matter!"

If only it were so. While the primaries showed us that a skilled black politician could overcome race to win his party's nomination for the presidency, they also offered stark reminders of just how much race continues to shape American life and culture. After months of deftly avoiding the quagmire of racial politics, by spring of 2008, Obama finally found himself mired in it. His former pastor, Rev. Jeremiah Wright, had long been known inside the black community as a provocative orator. His fiery sermons were part of a long African American tradition of exhortations on racial injustice, such as those found throughout the pages of this book. But modern America remains such a deeply segregated nation that most whites are ignorant of both the tradition behind Wright's oratorical style and, sadly, the link he sought to draw between black life today and America's violent history of racial oppression. So when clips of his sermons began circulating on the Internet, they rocked Obama's campaign, generating constant negative press and shaking many white would-be supporters. Suddenly, race mattered again.

Obama faced the political crisis head-on. But rather than immediately disavowing his pastor, Obama first sought to give a teaching moment. He went to Philadelphia, Pennsylvania, the hallowed birthplace of American liberty, where he offered what may have been the most honest speech about race a national politician has ever made. He compared Wright's sentiments to that of his white grandmother—a woman who loved him and helped raise him, but who nonetheless maintained racist stereotypes and a fear of black men. Both Wright and his grandmother, said Obama, are emotionally scarred and mentally boxed-in by America's racial divide and by the history of oppression that created it. To move forward, he declared, Americans of all races would have to stop demonizing one another, seek understanding, and create genuine equal opportunity.

It was a moving message, but one which viewers literally had to strain to hear. The speech was delayed forty-five minutes because the sound system didn't work, and the worldwide broadcast of Obama's masterful effort to bridge the racial divide ended up muffled and faint. Most Americans consumed the speech only through the skewed translation of news sound bites and mainstream media punditry. Within days it had been overshadowed by all-too-familiar racial sniping. Former president Bill Clinton accused Obama of playing the much-discussed "race card." Obama made a subsequent gaffe by calling his grandmother's reflexive fear of black men she encountered in the street "typical" of white people, prompting a defensive—and convenient—backlash against his effort to elevate the conversation. He would ultimately denounce Wright in order to end the controversy, leaving his Philadelphia speech drowned out by America's age-old racial dissonance.

As the documents collected here recount, America's history is defined by similar missed opportunities to honestly confront racial demons. Obama's life itself may offer a more telling anecdote than his political career. He recounts in his autobiography, *Dreams from My Father*, a yarn his white grandfather used to spin, a story about racism and how he boldly rejected it in Jim Crow Texas. Barack's white mom was a grade-schooler at the time—a bookworm who didn't make friends easily but who found a companion in a black girl her age. One day, as the pair lay reading in the family's yard, a bunch of ruffians passed by. "Nigger lover!" they shouted and taunted, paralyzing the girls with fear. Obama's grandfather said the attack so disgusted him that he dropped his whole Texas life and moved the family to Seattle.

Inspiring, but not all true. Obama later discovered that the family had actually moved because work dried up and a friend in Seattle found a job for his grandpa. "I don't entirely dismiss Gramps' recollection of events as a convenient bit of puffery, another act of white revisionism," Obama writes in his memoir. "I can't, precisely because I know how strongly Gramps believed in his fictions, how badly he wanted them to be true, even if he didn't always know how to make them so."

That is searing insight on white America's racial dilemma—the uncomfortable gap between the equality most genuinely want and the amount of racial privilege they're willing to cede to get it. Obama's stunning political success is at least in part due to his keen understanding of that gap, and to his ability—honed over a lifetime of being mixed-race—to transform white racial unease into something hopeful.

But that skill begs us to ask not just why white voters so enthusiastically embraced this black man but also what their group hug means for the future of race in America. Since the close of the civil rights movement, the right has worked tirelessly to redefine our understanding of racism. The argument underpinning the aggressive— and successful—attack on racially conscious policy making, from affirmative action to the social safety net, goes thusly: In post–civil rights America, the playing field has been legally leveled; Martin Luther King, Jr.'s, dream has become reality. In this new utopia, racism is narrowly understood as an individual personality problem rather than a broad, structural concern.

Like the "fictions" of Obama's grandfather, it's an all-too-convenient setup. It means no white person has to actually sacrifice to achieve equality. If we all just get our hearts and minds right, everything will be okay. And what better proof that this fantasy is reality than a post-race black president? What could be more hopeful than a man who bridges the emotional gap between America's dream of equality and its reality of vast, deep disparity?

The Jeremiah Wright episode notwithstanding, that hope has spawned much commentary about the post-race era Obama's remarkable campaign may herald. It remains to be seen whether he and the fast-growing ranks of post–civil rights black leaders—both inside and outside the political sphere—and their white allies will help us find the promised land. But to get there, America must first have an honest, informed conversation about its past and about how that past relates to life today and tomorrow. It is my hope that the documents collected here offer readers a gateway into that process.

For four centuries, people of African descent in the United States have asserted our existence and our humanity in the face of systematic efforts to obscure both. That assertion has taken countless forms—from a 1773 petition circulated by the slaves of Thompson, Massachusetts, in which they asked the state legislature to grant them freedom, to the angry missive "Fuck tha Police" recorded by the 1980s hip-hop group N.W.A. Through literature, poetry, music, and politics, African Americans have transformed the captivity from which we were born and the subhuman caste created for us into a proud community defined by its members rather than its oppressors. This collection illustrates the process through which that transformation occurred.

At the same time, the documents presented here reveal how and why the United States has failed to genuinely wrestle with its dual legacy of freedom and oppression. Racial division has repeatedly driven this nation to the brink of chaos—from the colonial era's slave uprisings to the Civil War to the Southern unrest of the civil rights movement to the urban rioting seen in the late 1960s and early 1990s. Yet, at each juncture, we have resolved the immediate conflict without addressing the divide that created it. We have passed laws outlawing discrimination in society but failed to acknowledge the defining role racism has played in establishing social order. Rather than face the past as a nation, Americans assumed that by simply dismantling the infrastructure of Jim Crow, we could wipe away the spirit that allowed it to exist in the first place. More than a generation later, we continue to stumble over our history.

No two documents in this book better embody America's conflicted past than those contributed by founding hero Thomas Jefferson. The great statesman penned one of the world's most ringing cries for freedom in the Declaration of Independence, then offered one of the most viciously racist tracts ever added to the public record with his "Notes on Virginia." As abolitionist firebrand William Lloyd Garrison often complained, our nation blindly celebrates one half of this legacy without stopping to offer substantive consideration of the other. Black journalist and activist David Walker warned in his 1829 "Appeal to the Coloured Citizens of the World" that if America did not face the white supremacy so explicitly articulated by Jefferson, such ideology would forever ingrain itself in the national psyche. As we read the Congressional Black Caucus's 2001 objection to the election of President George W. Bush, on the grounds that African Americans were systematically denied the right to vote in the Deep South, it is instructive to recall Walker's prophecy.

Scholars by and large agree that the first Africans arrived in the land that would become the United States with Spanish conquerors in the early sixteenth century. Exactly who those Africans were is, unfortunately, left to historical speculation. Spain had begun shipping captured men and women from the West Coast of Africa to Europe and the Americas in 1481, when it established Fort Elmina on the Gold Coast—the first permanent European structure in sub-Saharan Africa. Half a century later, in 1526, an expedition of more than five hundred Spaniards, Native Americans, and Africans set sail from the Spanish West Indies in search of a route to Asia. They made it only as far as the southeastern tip of North America, settling just below today's Savannah, Georgia, and establishing San Miguel de Guadalupe.

Facing food shortages, disease, the desertion of its Native American translators, and the death of its leader shortly after the settlers' arrival, the colony floundered. A secession struggle erupted, and in the midst of the chaos, the Africans staged the first slave revolt on American soil. Although colonists quelled the uprising, historians speculate that a number of Africans escaped into the frontier to live within Native American communities. These renegades were the first Africans to become Americans.

While violence remains an all-too-common element of the black experience today, the early period of black history—from the first Africans' arrival at Jamestown in 1619, through the end of the slave trade—witnessed some of the worst. Horrific violence typified not only the Atlantic slave trade itself but also the wars the slave trade sparked among African communities, the physical and psychological torture slave holders employed, and, ultimately, the many revolts of slaves attempting to break free. White hysteria from these uprisings hastened the institutionalization of barbarities designed to cement slavery and the caste system that justified it.

Among the slave holders' most valued tools for preventing uprisings was illiteracy, and they erected elabo-

rate barriers to block blacks from obtaining the knowledge necessary to navigate the new world in which they found themselves. As a result, most of the surviving accounts of how Africans held captive in the Americas dealt with their new realities come through white voices—transcripts of court proceedings, treatises supporting or objecting to slavery, diaries of slave traders. Not until the nineteenth century and the onset of the abolition movement did the nearly six thousand slave narratives that have been published over the years begin to proliferate.

Through those narratives and the speeches and writings of self-educated free blacks and escaped slaves, the African-American voice emerges. In these documents we follow the post–Revolutionary War attempt of free blacks to reconcile themselves with the longevity of their subjugation. Many had believed the ethos of freedom articulated in Jefferson's Declaration of Independence would extend to them. When the new Constitution made it clear it would not, free blacks began to consider everything from repatriation to Africa to sustained armed revolt. As Southern slaves escaped to the North and told their stories, their writings and speeches revealed the depth of Southern white cruelty. Reading these works, we can watch as their influence radicalizes the movement to end slavery.

Meanwhile, through the writings of black and white religious pioneers, we witness the massive Methodist and Baptist conversion of Africans in the eighteenth century as it leads to the founding of Richard Allen's and Absalom Jones's African Methodist Episcopal Church and to the creation of megacongregations of Southern black Baptists such as that of Andrew Bryan's turn-of-the-century First African Baptist Church. These institutions formed the foundation of black American religion today.

We can watch how, as the abolition movement built steam, black literature—glimpses of which were first visible in the eighteenth-century poetry of Phillis Wheatley, Jupiter Hammon, and Lucy Terry Prince—blossomed with the writings of George Moses Horten, Frances Harper, and Harriet Wilson, among others. As the century progressed, black female writers proliferated with the work of Alice Dunbar-Nelson, Amelia Johnson, and Anna Julia Cooper. The Harlem Renaissance brought us the poetry of Langston Hughes and Claude McKay, the short stories of Zora Neale Hurston, Billie Holiday's bittersweet jazz, and Bessie Smith's defiantly rambunctious blues. Even after this definitive period in black art passed, African American literature continued to expand with the works of Ralph Ellison, James Baldwin, Lorraine Hansberry, Nikki Giovanni, and Maya Angelou, to name just a few of those represented in this collection. Today, the black literary tradition goes on developing with Alice Walker, Toni Morrison, and the musical poets of the hip-hop generation.

The abolition movement also gave birth to black America's tradition of masterful political oratory. Frederick Douglass, Mary Stewart, and Sojourner Truth began a line of great orators that stretches to the present, echoing in Obama's rousing campaign speeches. The abolitionists' fiery rhetoric deliberately deepened the national division over slavery, until, in President Abraham Lincoln's words, the divided house could no longer stand. Again, America's racial stain drove it to violence.

As in the Revolutionary War, blacks, both free and enslaved, fought in order to help achieve the Civil War's promise of liberty. And again those hopes were dashed when the carnage ended and Reconstruction devolved into a retrenched Southern caste system based on race. Slavery was gone, and the Constitution had been amended to embrace black citizenship, but the realities

of sharecropping, Jim Crow, and anti-black violence meant that little had changed. From Booker T. Washington's doctrine of self-help, through the mastery of farming and artisanship, through the civil rights movement and into today's efforts to confront economic inequality, the central question of modern black politics is, How we can reorder the world that Reconstruction's failure left behind?

With the exception of grammatical errors that obscured meaning, the text of the documents in this collection are presented as originally published. In some cases, rare documents and oral texts never published by the author are reproduced as they were published in other volumes. Thus, as a collection of primary sources, *The African American Experience* allows readers to witness firsthand as generation after generation of black Americans stands resolutely against efforts to subjugate and erase them. From the travel logs of slave traders to the political tracts of great minds like Douglass, DuBois, and King, the voices collected here narrate America's tortured journey from a slave nation to one that could nominate a black man for president. In them we find not just our national history but the truths we must face in order to build a better future.

I

'20 and Odd Negroes':
A VIOLENT BEGINNING

'THEY WILL DISPLAY DILIGENCE'
Spanish Council of the Indies

Throughout the 16th century, Spanish explorers pushed northward from their South American and Caribbean colonies into Florida. Africans were present on many of those forays into North America, including Hernando De Soto's 1540 trek through Cherokee land. The Spanish, as would all succeeding European pioneers, considered African labor a central ingredient for success in conquering the New World. In their correspondence, Colonial officials often praised what they perceived to be Herculean survival skills exhibited by African slaves—skills that reduced the cost of caring for and feeding their indispensable capital. Founders of the Spanish colony of St. Augustine (begun as a fort in 1565, it was the first lasting settlement in Florida) drew heavily on African labor. As they went about the arduous task of establishing Augustine, they filed petitions such as the one below, begging the royal government in Spain to allow them to import still more Africans. As a result, historians estimate, ten percent of the settlement's ultimate population was African, both free and bonded.

...The officials of the royal treasury of the province of Florida state in a letter to your Majesty of the 5th of last January that the fort of St. Augustine was in a state of defense, and although the whole fort could be quickly finished as it is of wood, there would always be something to do in it, and the soldiers were tired out with its building and dragging in wood on their shoulders from the forests. Besides this there was heavy expense with the sawyers, which would cease if some of the slaves belonging to your Majesty in Havana were to be sent there. With regard to their food, they will display diligence as they seek it in the country, without any cost to the royal treasury. With respect to this, it appears to the Council that a cédula could be issued ordering the governor of Havana, without causing or making lack of labor in that fortress, that he immediately send to the governor and officials of Florida thirty slaves from those belonging to your Majesty there for the purpose that they ask. He should charge them to be careful to them and treat them well, and see that they do not cause any expense to the royal treasury. He should be advised of what is done and when the need of them there should cease so that he might order and command them as to what is to be done. ... Will your Majesty please order what you consider best? Madrid, June IIII, in the year MDLXXX.

S.R.C.M.

The humble servants of your Majesty who kiss your royal hands

Licentiate Don Gomez de Santillian.

Licentiate Alsonso Martinez Espadero.

Licentiate Don Diego de Cun(tilda)iga.

Don Lope de Vaillo.

Licentiate Henao.

Licentiate Geronimo José.

1.2

'NEGROS MIGHT EASILY BE HAD ON THE COAST OF GUINEA'

Richard Hakluyt

The British were slow to join in the African slave trade, but they eventually began dabbling in it during the early-to-middle 16th century. John Hawkins was the first Englishman to capture and trade human beings from the African coast. In 1533, he brought a reported 24 Africans to England and sold them as slaves. Richard Hakluyt, a contemporary campaigner for transatlantic trade and investment in colonies in America, stirred the public fascination with Hawkins's travels. In the 1600 pamphlet excerpted below, Hakluyt dazzled readers with stories of Hawkins's adventures—and, more important, his financial gain. Hakluyt's campaign helped spark the royal government's eventual issuance of private charters for trading in slaves.

John Hawkins having made divers voyages to the Isles of the Canaries, and there, by his good and upright dealing, being growen in love and favour with the people, informed himselfe amongst them by diligent inquisition of the state of the West India, whereof he has received some knowledge by the instructions of his father, but increased the same by the advertisements and reports of that people. And being amongst other particulars assured that Negros might easily be had on the coast of Guinea, resolved with himselfe to make triall thereof, and communicated that devise with his worshipfull friends of London, namely, with Sir Lionell Duckett, Sir Thomas Lodge, M. Gunson, his father-in-law, Sir William Winter, M. Bromfield and others. All which persons liked so well of his intention that they become liberall contributors and adventureres in the action. For which purpose there were three good ships immediately prouided. The one called the Salomon of the burthen of 120 tunne, wherein Mr. Hawkins himselfe went as Generall; The second, the Swallow of 100 tunnes, wherein went for Captain Mr. Thomas Hampton; and the third

the Ianus a barke of 40 tunnes, wherein the Master supplied the Captaine's roome; in which small fleete M. Hawkins tooke with him not above 100 men, for feare of sickness and other inconveniences, whereunto men on long voyages are commonly subjeck. With this companie he put off and departed from the coast of England in the moneth of October, 1562, and in his course touched first at Teneriffe, where he received friendly entertainment. From thence he passed to Sierre Leona, upon the coast of Guinea which place by the people of the country is called Tagarin, where he stayed some good time and got into his possession, partly by the sworde, and partly by other meanes, to the number of 300 Negros at the least, besides other merchandises which that countrey yieldeth. With this praye he sayled over the Ocean sea unto the Island of Hispaniola, and arrived first at the port of Isabella; and there he had reasonable utterance of his English commodities, as also of some part of his Negros, trusting the Spanyards no further then that by his owne strength he was able to still master them. From the port of Isabella he went to Puerto de Plata where he made like sayles standing alwaies upon his guard; from thence also he sayled to Monte Christo, another port on the North side of Hispaniola, and the last place of his touching, where he had peacable traffique and made vent of the whole number of his Negros; for which he recieued in those three places by way of exchange, such quantitie of marchandise that he did not only lade his owne three shippes with hides, ginger sugars, and some quantitie of pearles, but he fraighted also two other hulkes with hides and other like commodities which he sent into Spaine. And thus leaving the Island, he returned and disembarqued, passing out by the Islands of the Caycos without further entering into the Bay of Mexico in this his first voyage to the West India. And so with prospering successe and much gaine to himselfe and the aforesayde aduenturers, he came home and arrived in the moneth of September, 1653.

───── 1.3 ─────
'20 AND ODD NEGROES'
John Rolfe

The first Africans to permanently land in a British colony arrived aboard a Dutch pirate ship near Jamestown, Virginia, in 1619. Though European traders and explorers had forcibly transported some 200,000 Africans to the New World by this time, these men and women were the first to arrive in one of the colonies that would eventually form the United States, and were thus arguably the first African Americans.

Historians have hotly disputed the details of this landing, including whether the ship ever made it to Jamestown or merely remained where it originally came ashore, in nearby Port Comfort. More important, there remains considerable debate about whether the Africans were sold as slaves or indentured servants—as many Europeans in the settlement had been—and thereby allowed the chance to eventually obtain freedom. The number of Africans who arrived aboard the ship is also in dispute, having been cited most often as 20. (A 1623 census notes 22 "negors" in the colony.)

The Dutch pirate ship's crew had set sail from the West Indies, and arrived in Port Comfort searching for food. One of the Jamestown colonial officials, John Rolfe, husband of Pocahontas, provides the only eyewitness record of the event when he briefly mentions it in a January 1620 letter detailing all of the previous year's activities.

…About the latter end of August, a Dutch man of Warr of the burden of a 160 tunes arrived at Point-Comfort, the Comandor's name Capt Jope, his Pilott for the West Indies one Mr. Marmaduke an Englishman. They met with the Treasurer [an English ship] in the West Indyes, and determyned to hold consort shipp hetherward, but in their passage lost one another. He brought not any thing but 20 and odd Negroes, which the Governor and Cape Merchant bought for victualls (whereof he was in greate need as he portended) at the best and easyest rate they could. He hadd a lardge and ample Comyssion from his Excellency to range and to take purchase in the West Indyes.

───── 1.4 ─────
'THE ONE WHOSE NAME IS ELIZABETH IS TO SERVE THIRTEENE YEARS'
Capt. Francis Pott

At their outset in the early 1600s, Britain's American colonies did not immediately embrace the sort of race-based slave labor system the Spanish had developed over the past centuries. Rather, bonded labor took the same form it had in societies around the globe throughout history: indentured service. Under such a system, class and debt are more relevant than race. The movement from this system to lifelong, race-based bondage was gradual, and Virginia's colonial records show that some blacks in the early to mid 17th century were in fact completely free. Having completed their period of indenture, these new African Americans owned property, paid taxes, brought disputes before the court and even contracted with indentured servants of their own. Those indentured, white and black, were bound by contracts with their owner-employers to serve for a definitive time period under specified conditions, such as in this indenture contract cited by historian John Russell in his study of free blacks in the early colonial period.

This Indenture witnesseth that I Capt. Francis Pott have taken to service two Daughters of my negro Emanuell Dregis to serve & bee to me my heyers Exors. Adms. or Assigns. The one whose name is Elizabeth is to serve thirteene years which will be compleat & ended in the first part of March in the yeare of our Lord God one thousand six hundred Fifty & eight. … And the other child whose name is Jane Dregis (being about one yeare old) is to serve the said Capt. Pott as aforesaid untill she arrive to the age of thirty years old which will be complete & ended … And I the said Francis Pott doe promise to give them sufficient meate, drinke, Apparal & Lodging and to use my best endeavor to bring them up in the feare of God and in the knowledge of our Saviour Christ Jesus. And I doe further testify that the Eldest daughter was given to my negro by one who brought her upp by the space of eight years and the younger he bought and paid for to Capt.

Robert Shephard (as maye bee made appear). In witness whereof have hereunto sett my hand & seale in the 27th of May one thousand six hundred forty & five. Mr. Francis Pott.

--- 1.5 ---

THE FREEMAN ANTHONY JOHNSON AND HIS FAMILY
Northampton County Court Records

Anthony and Mary Johnson were among the first Africans to arrive in Britain's colonies. While they were not likely among John Rolfe's "20 and odd Negroes" who landed in 1619, they did come soon thereafter. Their names appear in census records as far back as 1624, and this 1652 court ruling states that both had been in the Virginia colony for "above thirty years" by that point. Many of the details of the Johnson family's life are unfortunately lost to history—such as the circumstances surrounding the fire that caused their "great Llosse" discussed in this order. What the order does tell us, by implication, is that the Johnson family was then free (as it was able to petition the court) and owned property—something that was not common for former servants whether black or white.

Upon the humble pet of Anth. Johnson Negro; & Mary his wife; & their Information to the Court that they have been Inhabitants in Virginia above thirty years consideration being taken of their hard labor and honoured service performed by the petitioners in this County, for the obtayneing of their Livelyhood And the great Llosse they have sustained by an unfortunate fire wth their present charge to provide for, Be it therefore fitt and ordered that from the day of the date hearof (during their natural lives) the said Mary Johnson & two daughters of Anthony Johnson Negro be disingaged and freed from payment of Taxes and leavyes in Northampton County for public use.

--- 1.6 ---

BLACK CHILDREN TO SERVE 'ACCORDING TO THE CONDITION OF THE MOTHER'
Virginia General Assembly

Gradually, colonial legislatures and courts began passing laws and issuing rulings that recognized slavery as a legal institution. Massachusetts was the first, in 1641. And after Georgia legalized it in 1750, the "peculiar institution" spanned all 13 colonies. For most, absolute subjugation of blacks came in increments, through a series of race laws distinguishing between the rights of white and black, free and bonded.

The Anglican missionaries who had been sent to watch over the British colonists' souls were uneasy with slavery as it took hold in the New World. Their concern, in most cases, was not so much with the well-being of the African, but with the sins slavery forced whites to commit. The brutal subjugation of fellow mankind needed a justification. And the first to arise was simple: Africans are not the same sort of being as Europeans; they are somehow lesser forms. So, the colonial race laws' primary purpose was to institutionalize this notion. Interaction between white and black society became closely regulated.

Virginia's experience was typical. The first race law passed by the Virginia Assembly, in 1662, reversed precedent in ordering that the status of a child conceived by a white man and a black woman would be determined by that of its birth mother—at this point, not always, but most likely, a slave. The act also increased the penalty upon white men and women caught in an act of fornication when their partners were black. If the ideology underpinning and justifying slavery questioned the humanity of Africans as compared to Europeans, shared sexuality presented a dangerous challenge to and particular offense against this principle.

WHEREAS some doubts have arisen whether children got by any Englishman upon a negro woman should be slave or free, Be it therefore enacted and declared by this present grand assembly, that all children borne in this country shalbe held bond or free only according to the condition of the mother, And that if any christian shall committ fornication with a negro man or woman, hee or shee soe offending shall pay double the fines imposed by the former act.

———— 1.7 ————

BAPTISM IS NO EXEMPTION
Virginia Assembly

Along with their humanity, bonded blacks lost the associated protections offered by society and, eventually, their chance to ever achieve freedom. Officials lessened the penalty meted out to planters who killed impudent slaves, barred slaves from carrying weapons of any sort and widely restricted the rights of blacks already free.

Missionaries accepted this logic. Africans were heathens, of course, and thus not fully human. But they countered by arguing that slaves must be baptized, and thus made human. For years, planters fought against it. But, eventually they simply worked around the loophole. Colonial officials began passing laws such as this 1667 Virginia act removing baptism as a route to freedom for blacks.

WHEREAS some doubts have risen whether children that are slaves by birth, and by the charity and piety of their owners made pertakers of the blessed sacrament of baptisme, should by vertue of their baptisme be made free; It is enacted and declared by this grand assembly, and the authority thereof, that the conferring of baptisme doth not alter the condition of the person as to his bondage or freedome; that diverse masters, freed from this doubt, may more carefully endeavour the propagation of christianity by permitting children, though slaves, or those of greater growth if capable to be admitted to that sacrament.

———— 1.8 ————

AN ACT CONCERNING NEGROES AND OTHER SLAVES
Maryland General Assembly

Maryland's 1664 law establishing slavery as a legal institution, and damning all blacks to it for life, was one of the more thorough slave laws inasmuch as it spelled out, and blocked, every route by which slaves might have hoped to gain their freedom. Further, it not only mandated that all

Africans coming to Maryland in the future would be slaves, but grandfathered all those already in the colony to lifelong slavery. The gravity of the Maryland statute's anti-miscegenation language again shows the colonial officials' strong distaste for interracial coupling.

Be it enacted by the Right Honorable the Lord Proprietary by the advise and consent of the upper and lower house of this present Generall Assembly, that all Negroes or other slaves already within the province, and all Negroes and other slaves to be hereafter imported into the province, shall serve durante vita. And all children born of any Negro or other slave shall be slaves as their fathers were, for the term of their lives. And forasmuch as divers freeborn English women, forgetful of their free condition and to the disgrace of our nation, marry Negro slaves, by which also divers suits may arise touching the issue of such women, and a great damage befalls the masters of such Negroes for prevention whereof, for deterring such freeborn woman from such shameful matches. Be it further enacted by the authority, advice, and consent aforesaid, that whatsoever freeborn woman shall marry any slave from and after the last day of this present Assembly shall serve the master of such slave during the life of her husband. And that all the issue of such freeborn women so married shall be slaves as their fathers were. And be it further enacted, that all the issues of English or other freeborn women that have already married Negroes shall serve the masters of their parents till they be thirty years of age and no longer.

———— 1.9 ————

150 ACRES FOR 'NEGROES AS WELL AS CHRISTIANS'
Proprietors of South Carolina

Over the course of the Atlantic Slave Trade, more than a third of all Africans shipped to the British colonies would come ashore at, and remain in, the Carolina region. Spurred by the South Carolina colony's mass production of rice, the African population of Charleston would ultimately outnumber those of European descent by the 18th century and fully double by the Revolutionary War.

Established in 1670, the British colony in South Carolina originally drew both settlers and slaves from other colonies, Barbados in particular. With the Caribbean island overcrowding, and migration among American colonies on the rise, British proprietors of the land just below Virginia saw encouraging New World pioneers to take their chances in the Carolinas as a chance to establish a trading settlement with little investment. But the settlement process was held up throughout the 1660s, as the London proprietors and a group of "Barbados Adventurers" wrestled over "headrights"—or how much land each person in their party was to receive.

A key sticking point in the headright negotiations was how many acres an African slave earned his or her owner. The issue was a significant one because Barbados planters had invested heavily in African slaves, which, as a result, formed the lion's share of their capital. At the same time, the London proprietors knew that success hinged largely on a rapid populating of the area. With this in mind, in 1670, the proprietors sent a letter to a leading official in Barbados announcing that all servants, black or white, would earn for their owner the maximum number of acres proposed. The letter opened the door for a mass forced migration of already-captive Africans from the Caribbean to South Carolina. By 1672, the colony was approximately 30 percent black, and by the turn of the century, 40 percent of the Africans shipped to the British colonies landed in Carolina.

Sir,

Your letters of the 28th of November we have received, by which we perceive the effectual paines you have taken in our Port Royall designe for which we give you many thanks, We find you are mistaken in our Concessions that wee have not made provision of Land for negroes by saying that we grant 150 acres of land for every able man servant in the we meant negroes as well as Christians And the same in other proportions which may cause to be laid out to those who carry negroes.

1.10
THE NEGRO'S AND INDIAN'S ADVOCATE
Morgan Godwyn

Throughout the 17th century, British traders ratcheted up their involvement in the Atlantic Slave Trade. As this trade blossomed, so too did opposition to it. In 1680 an Anglican missionary, stationed in Barbados, penned the first British abolitionist treatise. Addressing his complaint to the Archbishop of Canterbury, Morgan Godwyn was primarily concerned with planters' obstruction of his efforts to proselytize to African slaves. In his objections, however, Godwyn launched a remarkably prescient attack on the developing justifications for enslaving a race of people, critiquing both religious and intellectual perspectives that would shape American racism for centuries to come. His strongest language, perhaps, took aim at the assertion that Africans were somehow less than full humans.

It having been my lot since my arrival upon this island, to fall sometimes into discourses touching the necessity of instructing our Negro's and other heathen in the Christian faith, and of baptizing them (both observed were generally neglected). I seldom or never missed of opposition from one of these three sorts of people: The first, such, as by reason of the difficulty and trouble, affirmed it not only impracticable, but also impossible. The second, such who lookt upon all designs of that nature, as too much favouring of popish supererrogation, and not in the least expedient or necessary. The third, such (and these I found the most numerous) who absolutely condemned the permission and practice thereof, as destructive to their interest, tending to no less mischief than the overthrow of their estates, and the ruine of their lives, threatening the utter subversion of the island. Who therefore have always been watchful to secure that door, and wisely to prevent all such mischief enterprizes. Themselves in the mean time imploying their utmost skill and activity to render the design ridiculous; thereby to affright the better disposed (if any) from ever consenting to an act, which, beyond all peradventure, would so much call their discretion and wisdom into question. …

Now, to represent this more plausible to the world, another no less disingenuous and unmanly position hath been formed; and privately (and as it were in the dark) handed to and again, which is this, that the Negro's, though in their figure they carry some resemblances of manhood, yet are indeed no men. A conceit like unto which I have read, was some time since invented by the Spaniards, to justifie their murthering the Americans. But for this here, I may say, that if atheism and irreligion were the true parents who gave it life, surely sloth and avarice have been no unhandy instruments and assistants to midwife it into the world, and to foster and nurse it up. Under whose protection getting abroad, it hath acquired sufficient strength and reputation to support it self; being now able not only to maintain its ground, but to bid defiance to all its opposers; who in truth are found to be but very few, and those scarcely considerable. The issue whereof is, that as in the Negroe's all pretence to religion is cut off, so their owners are hereby set at liberty, and freed from those importunate scruples, which conscience and better advice might at any time happen to inject into their unsteadie minds. A fiction hardly to be parallel'd throughout the fables of the poets; and which I presume never before found entertainment amongst any, beside those above mentioned; or perhaps our neighbours of Holland, whose religion is also governed by their trade, and (as hath, I fear, been too justly charged upon them) for the sake thereof shall be denied. …

Wherefore it being granted for possible that such wild opinions, by the inducement and instigation of our planters chief deity, profit, may have lodged themselves in the brains of some of us; I shall not fear to betake my self to the refuting of this on which I have spoken of. For the effecting of which, me-thinks, the consideration of the shape and figure of our negro's bodies, their limbs and members; their voice and countenance, in all things according

with other mens; together with their risibility and discourse (man's peculiar faculties) should be sufficient conviction. How should they otherwise be capable of trades, and other no less manly imployments; as also of reading and writing; or shew so much discretion in management of business; eminent in divers of them; but wherein (we know) that many or our own people are deficient, were they not truly men? These being the most clear emanations and results of reason, and therefore the most genuine and perfect characters of homoniety, if I may so speak. Or why should they be tormented and whipt almost (and sometimes quite) to death, upon any, whether small or great miscarriages, it is not material, were they (like brutes) naturally destitute of capacities equal to such undertakings? Or why should their owners, men of reason no doubt, conceive them fit to exercise the place of governours and overseers to their fellow slaves, which is frequently done, if they were but meer brutes? Since nothing beneath the capacity of a man might rationally be presumed proper for those duties and functions, wherein so much of understanding, and a more than ordinary apprehension is required. It would certainly be a pretty kind of comical frenzie, to imploy cattel about business, and to constitute them lieutenants, overseers, and governours, like as Domitian is said to have made his horse consul.

Their objections against this, are poor and trivial; yet because with a great many here, seeming to carry no little weight, (for otherwise they could never both argue and act so absurdly, as they do); And because found serviceable to their great end, which I have before spoken of, not rejected by the wiser; they must not, silly and idle as they be, for these reasons be slighted. They are of divers sorts. The first whereof are certain impertinent and blasphemous distortions of scripture; out of which they would fain bribe four places, to wit, in Genesis 1.27, 28. And 2.7. and 4.15. and lastly, 9.25, 26. to give in evidence for them. Now in the two first of these they strain hard to derive our Negro's from a stock different from Adam's: but by the third, they bespeak them as descendents from Cain, and to carry his Mark: And yet by the last, as if condemned to contradictions, they make them the posterity of that unhappy Son of Noah, who, they say, was, together with his whole family and race, cursed by his father. Of which curse 'tis worth the observing what blessed use they to themselves do make, and what variety of advantages they reap. For from thence, as occasion shall offer, they'll infer their Negro's brutality; justifie their reduction of them under bondage; disable them from all right and clams, even to religion itself, pronounce them reprobates, and upon a sudden (with greater speed and cunning than either the niblest jugler, or witch) transmute them into whatever substance the exigence of their wild reasonings shall drive them to.

… Their specious reasons upon which this pious belief is grounded, do seem to have been drawn from these four pretences; the complexion, bondage, pretended stupidity, and barbarousness of our negro's manners, because different from ours. …

I shall begin with the first, and that is their complexion, which being most obvious to the sight, by which the notion of things doth seem to be most certainly conveyed to the understanding, is apt to make no slight impressions upon rude minds, already prepared to admit of any thing for truth which shall make for interest, especially if supported with but the least shadow of argument: And therefore it may not be so improbable (as I have (elsewhere) heard affirmed) that from so poor a medium, our negro's brutality should be inferred, by such whose affection to so gainful a doctrine, cannot but make the way smooth and easie to their conviction. Such people in these cases being not apt to reflect, (and, probably not caring) how derogatory to the goodness and justice of god it is, to represent him thus idly propitious to empty shadows, and even to white and red, that so out of his infinite regard thereto, he should throw off all respect to the work of his hand, and to unman and unsoul so great a part of the creation, nor yet, (which is more strange, because their own immediate concern) that the argument may come one day to be turned against themselves, and improved to chastise their brutishness, who from thence did at first so maliciously infer that absurd conclusion to the prejudice of so numerous and vast a people. …

But the determination of this point will much depend upon the right understanding and knowledge of Real Beauty, a true standard whereof the nations have not yet pitcht upon. That being deformity with others, which amongst us is the only perfect and compleat figure. As a certain author in a treatise upon this subject, by infinite collections and instances in the practice and behaviour of more distant nations, hath abundantly shewn. So that if the other part of the world should once come to agree upon this particular, without consulting us here (which 'tis possible, when ever they go about it, they may omit), and like unto us, maliciously determine the matter in favour of themselves, they only may be the men, and our selves but beasts.

―――― 1.11 ――――

CORRESPONDENCE FROM FORT JAMES, ACCRA
The Royal African Company

After John Hawkins's adventures drew wide acclaim in England, the royal government issued a series of exclusive charters allowing private companies to engage in the slave trade. The Royal African Company won the final such monopoly right in 1672. While many others joined in—first illegally, and then through the crown's opening of the trade—the Royal African Company represented the face of the British slave trade to the American colonies.

The company's records and correspondence offer insight, albeit through the eyes of Europeans, on the nature and operation of the Atlantic Slave Trade as it blossomed. The European traders were in fact businessmen, and viewed the Africans they bought and sold as capital investments and merchandise, little different from the gold, corn or livestock in which they also dealt.

Dispatches from the chief officer at Fort James in Accra illustrate this perspective and offer details of exchange, such as the prices at which rival African nations sold their captives. The correspondence also illustrates that the captured Africans did not passively accept their lot, but rather immediately began to resist. The second and third dispatches here describe failed efforts to reclaim a group of runaways.

A. January 27, 1681

I have now upwards of 50 slaves in the forte, which easts a chest of corne every day and I cannot gett any for money here. I have once sent my 7 hand canoe to Barracoe for corne and itt costs with charges 3 a chest, which formerly I bought for 2 here. This day I paid 2 paper bralls for 2 chests. And slaves comes in very plenty and I not haveing provisions to supply them, I must send my canoe to windward this night for more corne. They are somewhat deare in their slaves as yett, but the Portugueze nor Dutch buy's none soe I will lower them as much as possible I can. I give now not above 6 pezos for men as your honour has rated goods, and question not but to have itt lower then 6 pezos for men and soe accordingly for woemen, but Ile not buy any but choyce slaves as hitherto have done. I have not now be mee 8 peeces of good sayes and all the green and blew perpetuanos are gone, and Guyney clouts, soe pray a supply of those good and them that are good and all in cases or chests, for all the goods before the last parcell were without any, soe that here are very few good goods (though great quantity) but what are damag'd and of small validity. Itt is thought nay said that Ahenesa will speedily be att home with considerable quantities of slaves and gold which will be brought here, soe shall advise your honour as occasion serves. Mr Wendovers hoggs has come to great mortallity, for within this month of great raines there has dyed 15 breeding sowes, shoats, and 2 very large boars, besides piggs and most of the sowes with pigg, all well over night and dead in the morning. I wrote your honour for a butt of brandy but as yett Captain Shears

is not come, which wee now much want. I have bought att great rates this 2 months out of the Dutchman and cannot be supplyed now; our people humbly beggs your honour to supply them these fogg times, for two are sick now. I had almost forgott to intreate your honour that above all things to send downe 10 paire of strong irons and 20 or 30 paire of short irons, for this day I have borrowed of the Dutchman, and some paper, for I teare my books for this, some iron wedges and a maule to cleave rock's.

B. August 5, 1682

I am extremely troubled to informe your honour that on the 26th of July wee lost 13 men and 1 woeman which gott out of prison in the night, although a centry stood att the doore. They undermined the prison walls and gott out, which was the strongest place in all our forte. I shewed the place to Mr Starland and Mr Towgood whoe will render your Honour an account thereof. I have used my uttmost endeavour ever since and have sent to all parts and as yett cannot have any intelligence, which is a dayly and nightly perplexity to mee. I have gott up to flankers as high as the paveing and shall goe forwards with all vigour. Ahenesa will (as is reported) returne to Quomboe the next weeke and then may expect a supply of slaves. For upwards of 5 weeks here has been 3 or 4 interlopers which has given upwards of a bendy a head for slaves in the Cape Coast Briganteen vizt 12 men, 20 woemen and 1 boy. I have now sent May and June's account, and tomorrow or next day another Capo Corsoe Canoe will goe hence and then shall send July's account, this being the last day. If wind and weather permitts the vessell will saile hence to Cape Corsoe. The irons, maule and wedges were lost, the canoe being kickadevood and staved, soe shall want those necessaries. This is all that offers att present, intending to write two dayes hence of all other things that shall in the interim present.

C. August 9, 1682

I wrote your honour of what you desired in yours of the 2nd instant, which beleeve may be with you ere this. Likewise of the loss of the slaves, which I have ever since endeavoured to regaine. I humbly begg your honour not to impute itt any wayes to my negligence, for I will in verryty certifie your honour that duely and truely a good watch both of whites and blacks is kept every night, and for the future if any slaves breaks through the prison I now have built I will be responsible for. Itt is 4 foot thick and 3 foot in foundation deepe. Captain Starland and Mr Towgood is now in the road windbound, they have in all about 100 slaves aboard their vessells, and I supply their wants both with wood and water. If they stay here any time, I immagine Captain Shears may in a manner be up as soone as they with his loading of slaves per what I understand by a conoe last night from Allampo. Ahenesa will be att home this weeke with great quantity of slaves, and then shall render advice what progress hath made in his atcheivments. Hee hath conquered the Commongs, which was a verry greate people. When hee is att home and certaine thereof I will either send or goe my self if the people will admitt mee. I have here inclosed sent your honour my Jully's accounts as your honour demanded.

——— 1.12 ———
'THEY MUST HAVE ALL MY SLAVES AND GOODS'
Thomas Woolman

European traders competed fiercely up and down the West African coast to purchase slaves at low costs from their African middle men. It was a treacherous and violent business, with all parties seeking to rob and, often, attack one another. Thomas Woolman, a Royal African Company merchant, described his misfortune on a trip up the River Gabon in August of 1683, when he encountered one of the strongest communities in the region on Pongo Island.

…The 29th ditto I saild in company with my brother and that night partied with him, and the 8th of July I came into the Gabboone, and the Prince came aboard of mee from a small island and 7 more men, and shewed mee a letter from Captain Anthony Weilden which informed mee that the Prince and the natives were verry civill. I sent a man ashoare while they was aboard, and hee came off and told mee that there was but one man more upon the island. They told mee that the island was the cheifest place of trade, and bid mee fire 2 gunns to give the country people notice. The next day they came aboard and brought a small parcell of teeth and wax with them, which I bought att a reasonable rate, but they told mee I must not expect the trade to be open in less then 2 or 3 dayes. I intended to stay that time there, and then to goe further up the river. I thinking noe harme went ashore with 3 men more, they treaded mee kindly att the first, but after I had been ashoare about 2 hourse, att my comeing away they panyard mee and all the men and beate and cutt us verry much, wee all looking for nothing but death. After a small time why they did soe, they answered that they must have all my slaves and goods, and that an English ship had been there and burnt their towne and kill'd 2 men and carryed off 13 more. I told them that the goods were none of mine and that I could not give them away, but I seeing that here was about a 100 people upon the island that was come over from the maine in a small time, fear'd that they would goe and take the vessell, there being noe more then my mate and one man and a boy aboard. I sent for the slaves and 40 iron barrs and a bunch of beades, but I haveing neither pen nor paper my mate mistooke and sent a chest of beades. After these goods were ashoare, for when they came first aboard I shewed them all my goods, they would have my powder and musketts, kettles, pintado's, booges, soe I sent for 10 kettles, 10 pintado's, 30 musketts, 1 barrell of powder, 3 plaines. After this they would have all the teeth that I bought of them and wax and severall other small things, and after they had kept mee 24 houres, they lett mee goe. I staid three dayes att the rivers mouth to see if I could gett any Negro's off there, but could not. The 21st ditto I came to an anchor att Cape Lopas, where I found my brother Love, Captain Booth and Captain Rickards was verry well but has mett with a greate mortallity with his slaves. The 23rd ditto my brother sailed. There is noe trade, for the Negro's sayes that here has been 30 or 40 saile of ships within this 3 months. They told me that the privateere were here 6 weeks past with 7 saile in company with him. The 25th ditto there came one Captain Serjant that came out of the Bite, and he inform'd mee that Captain Davis was dead and a greate many of his men, and tha thee had but 50 slaves when hee came away. This Serjant is an interloper and was panyard att the Gabboones 9 dayes before mee, and that they made him pay to the vallue of 150 pounds in teeth and goods, before they lett him goe, upon which Captain How and I agreed to goe downe againe to see if I could recover satisfaction. The 26th wee sailed and mett Captain Clarke, but wee put him to a greate deale of charge, for hee tooke us to be the pyrate. Captain Thompson has tooke his passage upon Captain Howe. The 22nd ditto I came to an anchor att the rivers mouth and went up the river in Captain Howe. The 30th ditto the Prince and about 30 people more came aboard, and after they had been a small time aboard I came in sight and wee panyard the Prince and 8 men more and killed and wounded 10, and the rest leap'd over the board. We kept then 6 dayes and I have gott all my owne slaves and part of my goods, but could not possibly gett all by reason of itt's being distributed up in the country, but I have gott 4 slaves and 160 weight of teeth besides my own teeth for the goods and wee lett the Prince and 2 more goe. The 11th of August I came to an anchor att Cape Lopas againe, where I found Captain Lumley's pink, but hee has been dead this 15 dayes. They have parcell of verry good slaves

and has buried but 2 since they came off the coast. The 13th ditto waid againe and the 17th ditto came unto St Thoma, where Captain How and I was clapt in prison under the pretence of our selling goods and not paying the Kings custome, but I understand better since, for they would force Captain Howe to take his provisions of the Governour and Captain and att what price they would, but I was quickly lett out againe, but Captain Howethey made him come to their price. Since I have been here I understand there has been 2 Portugeeze taken at the Gabboones after the same manner as I was, one had 60 slaves and the other 9 and they tooke all from them both and then lett them goe. I hope to find a better trade att Sherbera to make up my loss time. For neither att the Gabboones nor Cape Lopas is there any trade, soe I hope your honour will not think ill of.

———— 1.13 ————

THE FUNDAMENTAL CONSTITUTIONS OF CAROLINA
Founders of the South Carolina Colony

The debate about whether and how to bring Africans into the Christian fold raged in Britain's North American and Caribbean colonies. The value in spreading European civilization around the globe, primarily through religion, was a central intellectual and moral justification for the colonial effort. But as Morgan Godwyn's treatise charges, that missionary zeal regularly clashed with the more worldly goals of economic gain sought by traders and planters. When the founding principles of the Carolina colony were eventually drawn up, colonial officials (many of whom were the same men Godwyn criticized in Barbados) and London proprietors settled the matter, paper at least.

At length, the document makes clear the import of religion in the colony by mandating the observance of it for white men and granting slaves access to it. However, it also makes clear that the Africans' spiritual salvation would have no impact on their temporal state. In an indication of the colony's eagerness to avoid overly aggravating Native Americans, and thereby not prompt war with them, the document allows for some diversity of religious belief for "natives" ignorant to Christianity. Historians speculate that John Locke, working as secretary to the proprietors of the Carolina territory, wrote early drafts of the document and that his ideas of religious toleration thus informed its treatment of religion among slaves and Native Americans.

... 94. No man shall be permitted to be a Freeman of Carolina or to have any estate or habitation within it that doth not acknowledge a God and that God is publickly and solemnly to be worshiped and that there is a future being after this Life.

95. As the country comes to be sufficiently Planted and distributed into fitt divisions it shall belong to the parliament to take care for the Building of Churches and for the public maintenance of Divines to be implyed In the exercise of Religion according to the Church of England which being the Religion of the Government of England it alone shall be alowed to receive public maintenance by the grant of the parliament. But since the natives of that place who will be concerned in our Plantation are utterly strangers to Christianity whose Idolatry Ignorance or Mistake gives us no right to expel or use them ill and those who remove from other parts to plant there will unavoidably be of different opinions concerning matters of Religion the liberty whereof they will expect to have allowed them and it will not be reasonable for us on this account to keep them out that Civill peace may be maintained amidst the divercety of opinions...

106. Since charity obliges us to wish well to the Souls of all men and Religion ought to alter nothing in any mans Civill Estate or right it shall be Lawful for Slaves as well as others to enter themselves and be of what Church or profession any of them shall think best and thereof be as fully members as any freeman but yet no slave shall hereby be exempted from that civil dominion his master hath over him but in all other things in the same state and condition he was in before.

107. Assemblies upon what pretence soever of Religion not observing and performing the above said rules shall not be estemed as churches but unlawful meetings and be punished as other Ryots.

108. No person whatsoever shall disturb molest or persecute another for his speculative opinions in Religion or his way of worship.

109. Every Freeman of Carolina shall have absolute power and authority over Negro Slaves of what opinion or Religion soever. ...

----------- 1.14 -----------

'SHEEP JUMP, JUMP FOR JOY'
Carolina rice beating songs

The disinterest of contemporary Europeans in chronicling the black experience, combined with the inability of Africans to write in English, has left us with few written examples of early African American culture and society—and less still from slaves' perspectives. But one element of black culture that did stand out to Europeans was music. While historians did not begin asking African Americans to relate their songs from work and worship until the Civil War, the songs then transcribed had been preserved within slave culture since the 17th century. In one project, white music historian Lydia Parrish documented songs such as the ones below, which were used for rice beating in Carolina and Georgia.

The turn of the century rice boom in the southern colonies drove the slave trade's growth more than anything else in the colonial period. It was one more reason the Carolina colony, a premier rice producer, would draw such a disproportionate number of African slaves. Work in the rice fields was some of the most grueling slaves faced in the Americas. They toiled long hours, literally working in swamps, to grow the product, and then set about the arduous and tedious task of beating it into a grain. When doing so, they sang. With its high concentration of slaves, the low country was also a center for proselytizing efforts towards slaves. Christian themes, therefore, begin to appear in the slave songs from that period. They are considered predecessors to African American spirituals of latter years.

A. Sheep jump, jump for joy

Sheep know his shepherd's voice
   Yes Lord, I know the way.
Sheep know his shepherd's voice
   Yes Lord, I know the way.
You know the way an' you wouldn't
come home
   Yes Lord, I know the way.
Every sheep know his shepherd's voice
   Yes Lord, I know the way.
Make a jump, jump for joy!
Make a jump, jump for joy!
Sheep jump, jump for joy!
Sheep jump, jump for joy!
Sheep jump, jump for joy! ...

B. Turn sinner turn

Turn sinner turn—sinner wouldn't turn
Turn sinner turn—sinner wouldn't turn
My Lord call you—wouldn't come
I know sinner too late, too late
O too late I know, sinner, too late.
Church bell ring—you wouldn't come
Preacher preach—and you wouldn't come
My Lord call you—and you wouldn't come
I know sinner too late, too late
O too late, sinner, too late.

———— 1.15 ————

THE SELLING OF JOSEPH
Samuel Sewall

Opposition to slavery and the slave trade existed, if thinly, among the European colonialists from the outset. As mentioned earlier, the settlers at Jamestown, Virginia, only gradually embraced the slave-labor system, and other colonies placed legal limits on its growth early on. However, the colonists' reluctance had little to do with principled objections to slavery. Rather, they by and large feared that the use of a chattel slavery system would lead to an undesirably large population of Africans as opposed to Europeans.

Still, principled opposition to slavery did exist. Boston judge Samuel Sewall—who also presided over the Salem witch trials—was one of the first colonial leaders to explicitly call for the abolition of slavery on moral grounds. In this 1700 pamphlet, Sewall invoked Biblical arguments to challenge the sale and purchase of human liberty as "the most atrocious of capital crimes."

Forasmuch as Liberty is in real
value next unto Life: None ought
to part with it themselves, or
deprive others of it, but
upon most mature
Consideration

The Numerousness of Slaves at this day in the Province, and the Uneasiness of them under their Slavery, hath put many upon thinking whether the Foundation of it be firmly and well laid; so as to sustain the Vast Weight that is built upon it. It is most certain that all Men, as they are the Sons of Adam, are; and have equal Right unto Liberty, and all other outward Comforts of Life. God hat the Earth [with all its Commodities] unto the Sons of Adam, Pal 115.16. And hat made of One Blood, all Nations of Men, for to dwell on all the face of the earth, and hat determined the Times before appointed, and the bounds of their habitation: That they should seek the Lord. Forasmuch then as we are the Offspring of GOD &c. Act 17.26, 27, 29. Now although the Title given by the last ADAM, doth infinitely better Mens Estates, respecting GOD and themselves; and grants them a most beneficial and inviolable Lease under the Broad Seal of Heaven, who were before only Tenants at Will: Yet through the Indulgence of GOD to our First Parents after the Fall, the outward Estate of all and every of the children, remains the same, as to one another. So that Originally, and Naturally, there is no such thing as Slavery. Joseph was rightfully no more a Slave to his Brethren, then they were to him: and they had no more Authority to Sell him, than they had to Slay him. And if they had nothing to do to Sell him; the Ishmaelites bargaining with them, and paying down Twenty pieces of

Silver, could not make a Title. Neither could Potiphar have any better Interest in him than the Ishmaelites had, Gen. 37, 20, 27, 28. For he that shall in this case plead Alteration of Property, seems to have forfeited a great part of his own claim to Humanity. There is no proportion between Twenty Pieces of Silver, and LIBERTY. The Commodity it self is the Claimer. If Arabian Gold be imported in any quantities, most are afraid to meddle with it, though they might have it at easy rates; lest if it should have been wrongfully taken from the Owners, it should kindle a fire to the Consumption of their whole estate. 'Tis pity there should be more Caution used in buying a Horse, or a little lifeless dust; than there is in purchasing Men and Women: Whenas they are the Offspring of GOD, and their Liberty is, ... Auro pretiosior Omni.

And seeing GOD hat said, He that stealeth a Man and Selleth him, or if he be found in his hand, he shall surely be put to Death. Exod. 12.16. This Law being of Everlasting Equity, wherein Man Stealing is ranked amongst the most atrocious of Capital Crimes: What louder Cry can there be made of the Celebrated Warning, Caveat Emptor!

And all thing considered, it would conduce more to the Welfare of the Province, to have White Servants for a Term of Years, than to have Slaves for Life. Few can endure to hear of a Negro's being made free; and indeed they can seldom use their freedom well; yet their continual aspiring after their forbidden, renders them Unwilling Servants. And there is such a disparity in their Conditions, Color & Hair, that they can never embody with us, and grow up into orderly Families, to the Peopling of the Land: but still remain in our Body Politic as a kind of extravasat Blood. As many Negro men as there are among us, so many empty places there are in our Train Bands, and the places taken up of Men that might make Husbands for our Daughters. And the Sons and Daughters of New England would become more like Jacob, and Rachel, if this Slavery

were thrust quite out of doors. Moreover it is too well known what Temptations Masters are under, to connive at the Fornification of their Slaves; lest they should be obliged to find them Wives, or pay their Fines. It seems to be practically pleaded that they might be Lawless; 'Tis thought much so, that the Law should have Satisfaction for their Thefts, and other Immoralities; by which means, Holiness to the Lord, is more rarely engraven upon this sort of Servitude. It is likewise most lamentable to thin, how in taking Negros out of Africa, and selling of them here, That which GOD has joined together men to boldly rend asunder; Men from their Country, Husbands from their Wives, Parents from their Children. How horrible is the Uncleanness, Mortality, if not Murder, that the Ships are guilty of that bring great Crouds of these miserable Men, and Women. Methinks, when we are bemoaning the barbarous Usage of our Friends and Kinsfolk in Africa: it might not be unseasonable to enquire whether we are not culpable in forcing the Africans to become Slaves amongst our selves. And it may be a questions whether all the Benefit received by Negro Slaves, will balance the Accompt of Cash laid out upon them; and for the Redemption of our own enslaved Friends out of Africa. Besides all the Persons and Estates that have perished there.

Obj. 1 These Blackamores are of the Posterity of Cham, and therefore are under the Curse of Slavery. Gen. 9.25, 26, 27.

Answ. Of all Offices, one would not begg this; viz. Uncall'd for, to be an Executioner for the Vindictive Wrath of God; the extent and duration of which is to us uncertain. If this ever was a Commission; How do we know but that it is long since out of date? Many have found it to their Cost, that a Prophetical Denunciation of Judgement against a Person or People, would not warrant them to inflict that evil. If it would, Hazael might justify himself in all he did against his Master, and the Israelites, from 2 Kings 8.10, 12.

But it is possible that by cursory reading, this Text may have been mistaken. For Canaan is the Person Cursed three times over, without the mentioning of Cham. Good Expositors suppose the Curse entailed on him, and that this Prophesie was accomplished in the Extirpation of the Canaanites, and in the Servitude of the Gibeonites. Vide Pareum. Whereas the Balckmores are not descended of Canaan, but of Cush. Psal. 68.31. Princes shall come out to Egypt. Ethiopia shall soon stretch out her hands unto God. Under which Names, all Africa may be comprehended; and the Promised Conversion ought to be prayed for. Jer. 13,23. Can the Ethiopian change his skin? This shows that Black Men are the Posterity of Cush: who time out of mind have been distinguished by their Colour. And for want of the true, Ovid assigns a fabulous cause of it.

Sanguine tum credunt in corpora cumma vacato Aethiopum populous nigrum traxisse coleorm. Metomorph. lib.2.

Obj. 2. The Nigers are brought out of a pagan country, into places where the Gospel is Preached.

Answ. Evil must not be done, that good may come of it. The extraordinary and comprehensive Benefit accruing to the Church of God, and to Joseph personally, did not rectify his brethrens Sale of him.

Obj. 3 The Africans have Wars with one another: our Ships bring lawful Captives taken in those Wars.

Answ. For ought is known, their Wars are much such as were between Jacob's Sons and their brother Joseph. If they be between Town and Town; Provincial, or National: Every War is upon one side Unjust. As Unlawful War can't make lawful Captives. And by Receiving, we are in danger to promote, and partake in their Barbarous Cruelties. I am sure, if some Gentlemen should go down to the Brewsters to take the Air and Fish: And a stronger party from Hull should Surprise them, and Sell them for Slaves to a Ship outward bound: they would think themselves unjustly dealt with; both by Sellers and Buyers. And yet Stil to be feared, we have no other kind of Title to our Nigers. Therefore all things whatsoever ye

would that men should do to you, do ye even so to them: for this is the Law and the Prophets. Matt. 7.12.

Obj. 4 Abraham had servants bought with his Money, and born in his House.

Answ. Until the Circumstances of Abraham's purchase be recorded, no Argument can be drawn from it. In the mean time, Charity obliges us to conclude, that He knew it was lawful and good.

It is Observable that the Israelites were strictly forbidden the buying, or selling of one another for Slaves. Livit. 25.39, 46. Jer. 34.8 ....22. And GOD gages His Blessing in lieu of any loss they might conceipt they suffered thereby. Deut. 15.18. And since the partition Wall is broken down, inordinate Self love should likewise be demolished. GOD expects that Christians should be of a more Ingenuous and benign frame of spirit.

Christians should carry it to all the World, as the Israelites were to carry it one towards another. And for men obstinately to persist in holding their Neighbours and Brethren under the Rigor of perpetual Bondage, seems to be no proper way of gaining Assurance that God has given them Spiritual Freedom. Our Blessed Saviour has altered the Measures of the Ancient Love-Song, and set it to a most Excellent New Tune, which all ought to be ambitious of Learning. Matt. 5, 43, 44. John 13, 34. These Ethiopians, as black as they are; seeing they are the Sons and Daughters of the First Adam, the Brethren and Sister of the Last ADAM, and the Offspring of GOD; They ought to be treated with Respect agreeable.

Servitus perfect voluntaria, inter Christianum & Christiainum, ex parte servi patientis saepe est licita quia est necessaria; sed ex parte domini agentis, & prcodurando & exercendo, vis potestesse licita; quia non convenit regulae illi generali: Quecunque volueritis ut faciant vobis homines, ita & vos facite eis. Matt. 7.12.

Perfecta servitus poenae, non potest jure locim havere, nisi ex delicto gravi quod ultimum supplicum aliquo modo meretur; quia

Libertas ex naturali aestimatione proxime accedit ad vitam ipsam, & eidem a multis prae-ferri solet.

Ames. Cas. Consc. Lib. 5

Cap. 23 Thes. 2, 3

BOSTON of the Massachusets

Printed by Bartholomew Green, and John Allen, June 24th, 1700.

———— 1.16 ————

NEW YORK CITY REVOLT OF 1712
Governor Robert Hunter

At the turn of the century, New York City's slave population was dwarfed only by that of Charlestown, South Carolina. Thus, as would be the case in Charlestown, New York City became a flash point in the conflict between white colonists and the Africans they enslaved. Slaves continually attempted to run away, some successfully, and whites existed in a constant state of paranoia about slave conspiracies.

In the midnight hours of April 6, 1712, an estimated 23 slaves confirmed the colonists' worst fears. They lit an outhouse on fire, hid themselves and, when the towns-people came to extinguish the blaze, attacked. They killed somewhere between five and nine whites before being subdued. The relatively minor plot upset the whole of the British colonies for decades. Both Massachusetts and Pennsylvania eventually limited or banned the importation of African slaves for fear of being overrun like New York City. Laws that had allowed for the manumission of slaves in New York were rewritten to discourage the practice.

In the immediate aftermath of the uprising, white paranoia of slave conspiracies in New York peaked. A hunt for potential conspirators spread so far that the *Boston News Letter* compared it to the Salem witch trials. New York Gov. Robert Hunter, as he mentions in his com-muniqué to London below, in which he describes the revolt, ultimately had to step in and pardon a number of slaves who were falsely accused. Those who were con-victed suffered gruesome public executions.

…I must now give your Lordship an account of a bloody conspiracy of some of the slaves of this place, to destroy as many of the Inhabitants as they could, It was put in execution in this man-ner, when they had resolved to revenge them-selves, for some hard usage, they apprehended to have received from their masters (for I can find no other cause) they agreed to meet in the orchard of Mr Cook the middle of the Town, some provided with fire arms, some with swords and others with knives and hatchets, this was the sixth day of April, the time of meeting was about twelve or one o'clock in the night, when about three and twenty of them were got togeather, one coffee and Negroe slave to one Vantilburgh set fire to an out house of his Masters, and then repairing to the place where the rest were they all sallyed out together with their arm's and marched to the fire, by this time the noise of a fire spreeding through the town, the people began to flock to it upon the approach of severall the slaves fired and killed them, the noise of the guns gave the allarm, and some escaping their shot soon published the cause of the fire, which was the reason, that not above nine Christians were killed, and about five or six wounded, upon the first notice which was very soon after the mischeif was begun, I ordered centries the next day in the most proper places on the Island to prevent their escape, I caused the day following the Militia of this town and of the country of west Chester to drive the Island, and by this means and strict searches in the town, we found all that put the design in execution, six of these having first laid violent hands upon themselves, the rest were forthwith brought to their tryal before the Justices of this place who are authorized by Act of Assembly, to hold a Court in such cases. In that Court were twenty seven condemned whereof twenty one were executed, one being a woman with child, her execution by that meanes suspended, some were burnt, others hanged, one broke on the wheele, and one hung a live in chains in the town, so that there has been the most exemplary punishment inflicted that could be possibly thought of, and which only this act of assembly could Justify, among these guilty persons sever-all others were apprehended, and again acquit-ted by the Court, for want of sufficient evidence … I am informed that in the West Indies where their laws against their slaves are most severe, that in case of a conspiracy in which many are engaged a few only are executed for an example, In this case 21 are executed, and six having done that Justice on themselves more have suffered than we can find were active in this bloody affair which are reasons for my reprieving these, and if your Lordships think them of sufficient weight, I beg you will procure Her Majesty's pleasure to be signifyed to me for their pardon...

Rob: Hunter
New York
June 23rd 1712

—————— 1.17 ——————

RISING TENSIONS AND CLASHING CULTURES

Dr. Francis Le Jau

Dr. Francis Le Jau arrived in Charlestown, South Carolina, in 1706 and worked there on behalf of the Society for the Propagation of the Gospel in Foreign Parts until his death in 1717. He was among countless missionaries sent to the colonies with the dual mission of helping settlers keep their religion and bringing Christianity's "civilizing" grace to Africans and Native Americans. As Morgan Godwyn described in his earlier treatise, planters often objected to the latter of those goals. In his correspondence, Le Jau reiterates the resistance Godwyn described. But Le Jau also writes at a time of heightening tension in British colonies, as planters began to fear, with good reason, the discontent of bonded Africans. Le Jau provides vivid accounts of the brutal torture planters employed in attempts to calm those fears, discourage runaways and forestall rebellion. In alluding to the New York City slave revolt, he reveals how far south the anxiety resulting from that event reached.

Additionally, Le Jau's writings offer a window into the culture clash between Europeans and Africans in the colonies. He describes his efforts to force the Africans to change customs he doesn't understand and that he labels blasphemous or immoral. Unfortunately, contemporary African perspectives have been lost to history. We can imagine, however, that they may have found many of the European behaviors equally odd and offensive.

South Carolina Parish of St. James Goose Creek
Feby. 20th 1711/12
Sr.
...The Mortality that begun to rage in Augt. is not yet over, especially in Towne where the Commissary has attended with much zeal, and I thank God he has been preserved from dangerous sickness, the number of White People dead of late in the Province is near 200, and the slaves as many again, which is a Considerable loss for a place, so thin Inhabited we have allso wanted Salt, and Provisions are very scarce chiefly in Towne where no Body durst go from the Country. The Surgeons are of opinion that the Aire has been infected these 14 years. I look upon a more immediat Cause that is the Irreligion and Lewdness of too many Persons, but chiefly the Barberous usage of the poor Slaves. I endeavour to urge the dutyes of mercy towards them as much as I am able, and I bless God things are upon a better foot in that respect about me—but still I am Contradicted by several Masters, but I trust in God these visitations will serve to make them mind better things than worldly advantages—

I have had of late an opportunity to oppose with all my might the putting of a very unhumane Law and in my Judgmt. very unjust it is in Execution, in Relation to run away Negroes, by a Law Enacted in this Province some years before I came; such an Negroe must be mutilated by amputation of Testicles if it be a man. and of Ears if a Woman. I have openly declared against such punishment grounded upon the Law of God, which setts a slave at liberty if he should loose an Eye or a tooth when he is Corrected. Exod. 21. and some good Planters are of my opinion. I must Informe you of a most Cruel Contrivance a man has Invented to punish small faults in slaves. he puts them in a Coffin where they are crushed almost to death, and he keeps them in that hellish Machine for 24 hours commonly with their feet Chained off, and a Led pressing upon their stomack, this is a matter of fact universally knowen, when I look upon the ordinary cause that makes these pour Souls run away, and almost dispaire I find it is imoderate labour and want of Victualls and rest. God Alm: inspire the Honourable Society my Illustrious Patrons to Consider those things so that they may be remedyed for the Encouragemt. of poor Creatures...

August 30th 1712
Sr.
... I hope through the mercy of God there will be in a Short time Some more Negroe Slaves Baptized: I take all the care I can that they Instruct one another when they have time; there are a few men in Sewall plantations to whom I have recommended to do that Good Service to the others, those men are Religious zealous, honest, they can read well, and by them I am inform'd when there is any disorder among their fellows slaves that it may be remedyed. I discountenance the changing of wives as much as it lyes in my power and I hope the Danceings upon Sundays are quite over in this Neighbourhood. There has been a very severe Act, to punish our Slaves, lately past in this province. Runaway Slaves are to be Mutilated; and at last put to death if they absent themselves for the fourth time for fourteen days. I have taken the Liberty to say Mutilation and Death too Great punishments in that respect But what I most complaine of is that upon Sundays they are Confin'd at home by they Letter of the Act I urg'd to the Magistrates in this parish these poor souls should have the liberty to come to Church. I was answered that it was so Implyed with their Masters leave, but I fear as the greatest part of the Masters is against their Slaves being Instructed they'll take an Advantage of the Tenour of the Act. ...

There was an Insurrection of Slaves in New York which undoubtedly you are better inform'd of than our Selves, what we know is Generall, I believe it was upon that account and to prevent the like that our Assembly has made or rather renew'd the Act I mentioned in this Letter.

February 23th 1712/13
Sr.
... But indeed few Masters appear Zealous or even pleased with what the Missionaries try to do for the Good of their Slaves, they are more Cruel Some of them of late Dayes than before, They hamstring maim & unlimb those poor Creatures for Small faults, A man within this Month had a very fine Negroe batized, Sensible Carefull & good in all Respects who being wearyed with Labour & fallen asleep had the Mischance to loose a parcell of Rice wch by the Oversetting of a Periogua fell into a River. The man tho Intreated by the Minister of the Parish, who is Brother Maule and some Persons of the best Consideration among us to forgive the Negroe, who had Offended only through Neglect without Malice, thought fit to keep him for several Dayes in Chains, & I am told muffled up that he might not Eat, & Scourge him twice Day, and at Night to put him into a hellish Machine contrived by him into the Shape of a Coffin where could not Stirr, The punishment having continued Several Dayes & Nights and there being no Appearance when it should End, the poor Negroe through Despair Ask't one of his Children for a knife & manacled as he was Stabb'd himself with it; I am told this is the 5th Slave that Same man has destroyed by his Cruelty within 2 or 3 Yeares, but he is onely an hired Overseer the Owner of the Slaves lives out of this Province, I own I See everybody almost angry at So much Barbarity, Yet he pretends to go to Church, and they look upon the Man as Guilty of Murder, and So do great many of my Acquaintance who tho not so Barbarous take no Care at all of the Souls of their Slaves, and as little as the can of their bodies I am at a loss when I see them in a praying posture knowing that at the same time they do not love their Neighbour, and what is most Amazing I cannot make them Comprehend that their Neglect is an habitual state of Sin, I have Seen very Severe Judgemts. Since I came, Nothing Else almost but Judgemts and I don't admire at it. ...

January 22th 1713/4
Sr.

… About Christmas last past there was a rumour spread of an Intended Conspiracy of the Negro's against us all like that of New York. I was told that the Plot had been form'd in Goose Creek where there is a good number of fine Negro's. This News made me Inquire and observe being resolved to find out how true the thing might be. The matter has been examined very diligently by our Government this very week. 12 or 15 Negroes living on the North side of Cooper River, having been apprehended under suspicion it has appeared upon good evidence that a Negroe fellow brought hither some years ago from Martineco, and of a very stubborn temper, had Inticed some Slaves to joyn with him that they might get their liberty by force. the thing being proved against him he has been put to death for it, two more Slaves have been very severely chastis'd for hearkening to him, but there was not any sufficient proof to take their life and all denied the Crime, the other prisoners have been acquitted but what I consider as a singular Providence there has not been so much as one of our Goose Creek Negroes accused of having knowledge of the Plot, far from having consented to so great a Crime. The most sensible of our Slaves whom I have admitted to the holy Sacrament have solemnly protested to me that if ever they hear of any Ill design of the Slaves I shall know it from them that it may be prevented, and I can't but depend upon the truth of their words, knowing them to be Exemplarily Pious and Honest.

--------- 1.18 ---------

A VOYAGE TO GUINEA, BRASIL, AND THE WEST INDIES
John Atkins

John Atkins was a surgeon in the British Royal Navy in the early 1700s. In 1735 he published a lengthy account of his voyage around the notorious slave triangle—from Europe, through West Africa, to the Americas and back again. He describes, in exacting detail, everything from the ecology to the local customs of West Africa during that time. And he offers detailed looks at the day-to-day business of the slave trade. Historians have mined his work as an invaluable original source ever since.

Atkins speaks from a jarringly condescending contemporary perspective in discussing Africans and their way of life. Nevertheless, he ultimately condemns the Atlantic Slave Trade as "offending against the laws of natural justice and humanity," and thereby becomes one of Britain's early abolitionist voices. In the passages below, Atkins provides examples of African captives' efforts to resist their enslavement and European traders' barbarous methods of quelling that resistance. He then dissects an argument in support of the trade that asserts Europeans are helping those they ship to the Americas by introducing them to civilized societies.

… The Trade for our African Company here, is carried on from Bense or Brent Island, about 5 Leagues distance from our Anchorage, by Factors, of whom Mr. Plunket is chief. The private Traders are about 30 in number, settled on the Starboard side of the River: loose privateering Blades, that if they cannot trade fairly with the Natives, will rob; but then don't do it so much in pursuance of that trading Advice, (Amass Riches, my Son,) as to put themselves in a Capacity of living well, and treating their Friends, being always well pleased if they can keep Stock at Par, and with their Profits purchase from time to time, Strong-beer, Wine, Cyder, and such Necessaries, of Bristol Ships, that more frequently than others put in there; of these, John Leadstine, commonly called old Cracker, is reckoned the most thriving.

They all keep Gromettas (Negro Servants) which they hire from Sherbro River, at two Accys or Bars a Month. The Women keep House, and are obedient to any Prostitutions their Masters command. The Menservants work in the Boats and Periagoes, which go a trading in turns with Coral, Brass, Pewter Pans, Pots, Arms, English Spirits, &c. and bring back from Rio Nunes, Slaves, and Teeth; and from Sherbro, Camwood for Dyers; a Sloop or two is the most that is loaded from the latter Place in a Year, and that with difficulty; being obliged to go far up the River, narrow and beset with Mangroves, which makes it sickly.

The Ivory here is of the Elephant or Sea Horse, great and small; the former sold at about 40 Accys per Quintal in Exchange; the other at half Price.

The Slaves when brought here, have Chains put on, three or four linked together, under the Care of their Gromettas, till Opportunity of Sale; and then go at about 15 Pounds a good Slave, allowing the Buyer 40 or 50 per Ct. Advance on his Goods.

As the Slaves are placed under Lodges near the Owner's House, for Air, Cleanliness, and Customers better viewing them, I had every day the Curiosity of observing their Behaviour, which with most of them was very dejected. Once, on looking over some of the old Cracker's Slaves, I could not help taking notice of one Fellow among the rest, of a tall, strong Make, and bold, stern aspect. As he imagined we were viewing them with a design to buy, he seemed to disdain his Fellow-Slaves for their Readiness to be examined, and as it were scorned looking at us, refusing to rise or stretch out his Limbs, as the Master commanded; which got him an unmerciful Whipping from Cracker's own Hand, with a cutting Manatea Strap, and had certainly killed him but for the loss he himself must sustain by it; all which the Negro bore with Magnanimity, shrinking very little, and shedding a Tear or two, which he endeavoured to hide as too ashamed of. All the Company grew curious at his Courage, and wanted to know of Cracker, how he came by him; who told us, that this same Fellow, called Captain Tomba, was a Leader of some Country Villages that opposed them, and their Trade, at the River Nunes; killing our Friends there and firing their Cottages. The Sufferers this way, by the Help of my Men, (says Cracker) surprized, and bound him in the Night, about a Month ago, he having killed two in his Defence, before they could secure him, and from thence he was brought hither, and made my Property. ...

To return to Jaque a Jaques; we met there the Robert of Bristol, Captain Harding, who sailed from Sierraleon before us, having purchased thirty Slaves, whereof Captain Tomba mentioned there was one; he gave us the following melancholly Story. That this Tomba, about a Week before, had combined with three or four of the stoutest of his Country-men to kill the Ship's Company, and attempt their Escapes, while they had a Shore to fly to, and had near effected it by means of a Woman-Slave, who being more at large, was to watch the proper Opportunity. She brought him word one night that there were no more than five white Men upon the Deck, and they asleep, bringing him a Hammer at the same time (all the Weapons that she could find) to execute the Treachery. He encouraged the Accomplices what he could do, with the Prospect of Liberty, but could now at the Push, engage only one more and the Woman to follow him upon Deck. He found three Sailors sleeping on the Fore-castle, two of which he presently dispatched, with single Strokes upon the Temples; the other rouzing with the Noise, his Companions seized; Tomba coming soon to their Alliance, and murdering him in the same manner. Going after to finish the work, they found very luckily for the rest of the Company, that these other two of the Watch were with the Confusion already made awake, and upon their Guard, and their Defence soon awakened the Master underneath them, who running up and finding his Men contending for their Lives, took a Hand-spike, the first thing he met with in the Surprize, and redoubling his Strokes home upon Tomba, laid him at length flat upon the Deck, securing them all in Irons.

The Reader may be curious to know their Punishment: Why, Captain Harding weighing the Stoutest and Worth of the two Slaves, did, as in other Countries they do by Rogues of Dignity, whip and scarify them only; while three others, Abettors, but not Actors, nor of Strength for it, he sentenced to cruel Deaths; making them first to eat the Hearts and Liver of one of them killed. The Woman he hoisted up by the Thumbs, whipp'd, and slashed her with Knives, before the other Slaves till she died. ...

Slaves become so (we are told) in this

Country, by War, by Mulcts on some particular Crimes, or Debts which they are unable to discharge; and they are bought by us (some say) not as Merchants, but Christians, to preserve them from Sacrifice and Cannibals, to convey them to a Land flowing with more Milk and Honey, to a better Living, better Manners, Virtue, and Religion; let us examine each of these Pretences.

First, the Negroes. By War for the most part is meant Robbery of inland, defenceless Creatures, who are hurried down to the Coast with the greater Cruelty, as it is from a contented, tho' a very poor Life. Trade has improved the Robbers, but as all are not alike expert, or alike Villains, it is alterable, ebbs and flows, and at some places we have never yet had any.

2. The Negroes become Slaves to one another, by Mulcts imposed on some sort of Crimes, or Debts contracted beyond their Ability to discharge. Few come to us this way; for tho' much Artifice and Revenge might mix in their Palaavers (Judiciary Courts) yet their Jurisdiction extends not beyond their own Towns, when Self-preservation will teach them more regard to Justice for their own sakes, lest the Relations of those sentenced should revenge it, and also because the Barbarity would encrease an Enmity to the Rulers, the Punishment falling on Neighbours of the same Country, Complexion, Language, and Religion.

We who buy Slaves, say we confer Good, removing them to a better state both Temporals and Spirituals; the latter, few have the Hypocrisy (among us) to own, and therefore I shall only touch on the former.

They live indeed, according to our European Phrase, very poor and mean, destitute almost of the common Necessaries of Life; but never starve, that is peculiar to trading Republicks; then who is judge of their Wants, themselves or we? Or what does Poorness mean? More than a sound, to signify we have that which another does not want. Do not many men in politer Nations, renounce the World for Cloisters and Desarts, and place a greater happiness in preserving their Innocence, than enjoying even the Necessaries of Life; nay, often ravished with the neglect of them. Wherever therefore Contentment can dwell, tho' under the meanest of Circum-stances, it is a barbarous Corruption to stile such poor, for they have every thing they desire, or, which is much the same, are happily ignorant of any thing more desirable.

To remove the Negroes then from their Homes and Friends, where they are at ease, to a strange Country, People, and Language, must be highly offending against the Laws of natural Justice and Humanity; and especially when this charge is to hard Labour, corporal Punishment, and for Masters they wish at the D—l.

--------- 1.19 ---------

'THE MOST FIERCE ENEMIES OF THE ENGLISH'
Black fugitives of the English plantations

After the establishment of the Carolina colony, Spanish forces in Florida clashed with British forces near Carolina with regularity. Neither side hesitated to use Native American and African slave posses as surrogate combatants, or at least as laborers supporting militiamen in battle. The frequent clashes thus familiarized Carolina slaves with the route to St. Augustine. In 1693, hoping to destabilize British colonies, the Spanish Crown issued an order granting "liberty to all" slave refugees entering Florida.

Carolina slaves, already familiar with the route, began using it as a path to freedom. The Crown order sparked still more military skirmishes, and Carolina attacked St. Augustine in 1728. The city's black militia fought bravely as part of a defense that successfully repulsed the raid and earned a commendation from the Spanish Crown in 1733. That same year, the Crown strongly reiterated its refugee policy. It would mark the beginning of a violent escalation in the Spanish-British conflict over North America, and spark waves of runaways.

Despite the offers of freedom to British slaves, many St. Augustine blacks were still in bondage. Under the leadership of Captain Francisco Menendez, the black commander of the Spanish slave militia, those slaves petitioned the governor for their promised freedom. In 1738, the Spanish Crown granted freedom not only to all escaped slaves already in Florida, but also to all who would come in the future. The freed slaves established the community of Gracia Real de Santa Teresa de Mose.

Known as Fort Mose, or the "Negro Fort" to the British, the community housed around 40 families of free blacks at its outset and would be led by Capt. Menendez for the next four decades. Spanish officials considered Fort Mose, located two miles north of St. Augustine, and the black militia that was based there its first line of defense against future British incursions. The free men and women who lived there understood and embraced that role, as they made clear in this 1738 pledge to Spanish officials.

Sir.

All black fugitives from the English plantations, we are obedient and loyal slaves to His Majesty, and we state that His Majesty did a Royal Charity when He ordered that freedom was granted to us for having come to this country to embrace Christianity and to follow the true religion in which we will get saved, and without which we have been held slaves for many years and we have suffered misery and starvation.

In slavery and obeying the Royal Mandates of His Majesty, the present governor Don Manuel de Montiano has granted us freedom, and we are very grateful for such a benefit to His Majesty, who also has offered and guaranteed to us that we will build a place called Gracia Real where we will be able to serve God and His Majesty and to harvest the land so that this country bears fruits.

And we promise His Majesty that whenever necessary we will be the most fierce enemies of the English and that we will risk our lives in service of His Majesty to the last drop of blood, always defending the Greater Spanish Crown and our Saint Faith, and therefore His Majesty can always send us any task we, his servants, are supposed to do in order to prove we are loyal slaves for life, and that we will always pray to God for His Majesty's life, so that our Lord takes care of it and of the ones of the Royal House for all the necessary years to come.

San Augustine
La Florida
10th of June of 1738

1.20

PROHIBITING THE IMPORTATION AND USE OF BLACK SLAVES OR NEGROES
The Trustees of the Georgia Colony

The slave trade was booming by the time King George II granted a charter for Georgia to James Oglethorpe and his fellow Trustees in 1732. English slavers were shipping nearly 5,000 Africans a year to Europe and the Americas, generating unprecedented wealth in London and supplying crucial labor in the American colonies. But Oglethorpe's group wasn't interested in this economic windfall. They dreamed of creating a sort of utopian community in Georgia, established for its own sake rather than as a source of commerce. It would be a place where poor families from London could get a new start, where persecuted Protestants in other parts of Europe could seek refuge, where small farms would supplant plantations and noble frontiersmen would reign. For the Royal Government, such a colony was a perfect fit. Spanish and Native American raids were gaining in frequency, and a colony of self-sufficient frontiersmen would make a useful first line of defense.

But the one thing that could destabilize all of this would be the presence of African slaves. Colonies from New York to South Carolina were struggling to contain runaways, rebellions and growing discontent from religious leaders. In some cities, such as Charlestown, blacks now far outnumbered whites—a source of considerable unease. And so, Georgia became the first colony to ban slavery. The ban would stand for nearly 20 years before the colony passed from the Trustees' control to the Royal Government and slavery was permitted.

AN ACT for rendering the Colony of Georgia more Defencible by Prohibiting the Importation and use of Black Slaves or Negroes in the same.

WHEREAS Experience hath Shewn that the manner of Settling Colonys and Plantations with Black Slaves or Negroes hath Obstructed the Increase of English and Christian Inhabitants therein who alone can in case of a War be relyed on for the Defence and Security of the same, and hath Exposed the Colonys so settled to the Insurrections Tumults and Rebellions of such Slaves & Negroes and in Case of a

Rupture with any Foreign State who should Encourage and Support such Rebellions might Occasion the utter Ruin and loss of such Colonys, For the preventing therefore of so great inconveniences in the said Colony of Georgia We the Trustees for Establishing the Colony of Georgia in America humbly beseech Your Majesty THAT it may be ENACTED AND be it ENACTED that from and after the four and twentieth day of June which shall be in the Year of Our Lord One thousand Seven hundred and thirty five if any Person or Persons whatsoever shall import or bring or shall cause to be imported or brought or shall sell or Barter or use in any Part or Place therein and Black or Blacks Negroe or Negroes such Person or Persons for every such Black or Blacks Negroe or Negroes so imported or brought or caused to be imported or brought or sold Bartered or used within the said Province Contrary to the intent and meaning of this Act shall forfeit and lose the Sum of fifty pounds Sterling Money of Great Britain to be recovered in manner hereafter mentioned one half to the said Trustees for Establishing the Colony of Georgia in America to be applied for the Benefit of the said Colony as the Common Council of the said Trustees or the Major part of them for that purpose present and assembled shall think fit and proper and the other half to such person or persons as shall sue for the same AND be it further ENACTED that from and after the said four and twentieth day of June in the Year of Our Lord One thousand Seven hundred and thirty five all and every the Black or Blacks Negroe or Negroes which shall at any time then after be found in the said Province of Georgia or within any Part of Place thereof in the Custody house or Possession of whomsoever the same may be shall and may be Seized and taken by such person or persons as for that purpose shall be authorized and Impowered by the said Common Council of the said Trustees of the Major part or them who shall for that purpose be present and Assembled and the said Black or Black Negroe or Negroes so seized and taken shall be deemed and adjudged and are hereby

declared to be the Sole property of and to belong only to the said Trustees and their Successors and shall and may be Exported Sold and disposed of in such a manner as the said Common Council of the said Trustees of the Major part of them for that purpose present and Assembled shall think most for the benefit and good of the said Colony PROVIDED ALWAYS That if any Black or Blacks Negroe or Negroes shall run away from his Master or Mistress in Carolina or any other of His Majesty's Dominions into the said Province of Georgia if the person or persons to whom such Black or Blacks Negroe or Negroes shall belong shall within the Space of three months next after such Black or Blacks Negroe or Negroes shall have been seized and taken as aforesaid enter his or their Claim or Claims to such Black or Blacks Negroe or Negroes in the Court of the Town of Savanah and shall pay all such Costs and Charges as shall have been expended in apprehending or taking such Black or Blacks Negroe or Negroes and shall make Satisfaction for such Damages and Mischiefs as they or any of them shall have done or Committed on the persons or possessions of any of the Inhabitants whilst within the said Province of Georgia That then and in every Case the said Court of the Town of Savanah shall and are hereby directed to restore to such owner or owners so claiming as aforesaid all and every such Black or Blacks Negroe or Negroes.

———— 1.21 ————

THE DARIEN ANTISLAVERY PETITION
Eighteen Freeholders of New Inverness

The Trustees' original decision to ban slaves from Georgia set the stage for one of America's first intensive debates about the wisdom and morality of slavery. From the beginning, settlers fought bitterly over whether or not the ban should be lifted. The loudest critics of the Trustees and their antislavery policy was a group of wealthy Savannah-based entrepreneurs who became known as the "malcontents." They immediately began campaigning for the slavery ban's repeal, and by the end of 1738 had gathered considerable backing. General James Oglethorpe, who oversaw the colony and felt strongly that slavery would destabilize it, turned for support to a band of Scotsmen whom the Trustees had set up as a military community on Georgia's frontline with Spanish Florida. This group, based in Darien, had thus far proven the most self-sufficient of Georgia's noble frontiersmen, and had therefore won doubly high standing in the eyes of the Trustees in Britain. Oglethorpe brought them into his camp, and in January of 1739, the Darien Scots penned one of the time's most forceful condemnations of the slave-labor system.

To his Excellency General Oglethorpe.
The Petition of the Inhabitants of New Inverness

We are informed, that our Neighbors of Savannah have petitioned your Excellency for the Liberty of having Slaves: We hope, and earnestly intreat, that before such Proposals are hearkened unto, your Excellency will consider our Situation, and what dangerous and bad consequence such Liberty would be of to us, for many Reasons.

The Nearness of the Spaniards, who have proclaimed Freedom to all Slaves, who run away from their Masters, makes it impossible for us to keep them, without more Labour in guarding them, than what we would be at to do their Work.

We are laborious, and know a white Man may be, by the Year, more usefully employed than a Negroe.

We are not rich, and becoming Debtors for Slaves, in Case of their running away or dying, would inevitably ruin the poor Master, and he become a greater Slave to the Negroe-Merchant, than the Slave he bought could be to him.

It would oblige us to keep a Guard Duty at least as severe, as when we expected a daily Invasion: And if that was the Case, how miserable would it be to us, and our Wives and Families, to have one enemy without, and a more dangerous one in our Bosoms!

It is shocking to human Nature, that any Race of Mankind and their Posterity should be sentenc'd to perpetual Slavery; nor in Justice can we think otherwise of it, than that they are thrown amongst us to be our Scourge one Day or other for our Sins: And as Freedom must be as dear to them as to us, what a Scene of Horror must it bring about! And the longer it is unexecuted, the bloody Scene must be the greater. We therefore for our own Sakes, our Wives and Children, and our Posterity, beg your Consideration, and intreat, that instead of introducing Slaves, you'll put us in the Way to get us some of our Countrymen, who, with their Labour in Time of Peace, and our Vigilance, if we are invaded, with the Help of those, will render it a difficult Thing to hurt us, or that Part of the Province we posses. We will for ever pray for your Excellency, and are with all Submission, etc.

Signed by eighteen Freeholders of New Inverness, in the District of Darien

––––––––– 1.22 –––––––––
'HE MADE YOU TO LIVE WITH HIMSELF ABOVE THE SKY. AND SO YOU WILL.'
John Wesley

Anglican attempts to convert Africans in the Americas to Christianity largely failed. By contrast, the evangelical Protestantism that John Wesley would shepherd into the Americas and use to transform southern religion reached far and wide into black populations, slave and free. Ultimately, scores of African Americans would join his Methodist Church, and, along with those who became Baptists, lay the groundwork for black religion as we know it today.

When Wesley arrived in Georgia in the mid 1730s, then still an Anglican missionary, he soon noticed the Anglicans' failure to reach blacks in the colonies. In his journal, he described two chance encounters with slave women in Charlestown, South Carolina, that inspired his determination to bring African Americans into the Christian fold. Following these encounters, Wesley began plotting with supportive planters to find ways to encourage ministry to and among slaves.

A. Saturday, July 31, 1736

…We came to Charlestown. The church is of brick, but plastered over like stone. I believe it would contain three or four thousand persons. About three hundred were present at the morning service the next day, when Mr. Garden desired me to preach; about fifty at the Holy Communion. I was glad to see several negroes at church, one of whom told me she was there constantly, and that her old mistress (now dead) had many times instructed her in the Christian religion. I asked her what religion was. She said she could not tell. I asked if she knew what a soul was. She answered, 'No.' I said, 'Do not you know there is something in you different from your body? Something you cannot see or feel?' She replied, 'I never heard so much before.' I added, 'Do you think, then, a man dies altogether as a horse dies?' She said, 'Yes, to be sure.' O God, where are Thy tender mercies? Are they not over all Thy works? When shall the Sun of Righteousness arise on these outcasts of men, with healing in His wings!

B. Saturday, April 23, 1737

… Mentioning to Mr. Thompson, minister of St. Bartholomew's, near Ponpon, my being disappointed of a passage home by water, he offered me one of his horses if I would go by land, which I gladly accepted of. He went with me twenty miles, and sent his servant to guide me the other twenty to his house. Finding a young negro there, who seemed more sensible than the rest, I asked her how long she had been in Carolina. She said two or three years; but that she was born in Barbados, and had lived there in a minister's family from a child. I asked whether she went to church there. She said, 'Yes, every Sunday, to carry my mistress's children.' I asked what she had learned at church. She said, 'Nothing; I heard a deal, but did not understand it.' 'But what did your master teach you at home?' 'Nothing.' 'Nor your mistress?' 'No.' I asked, 'But don't you know that your hands and feet, and this you call your body, will turn to dust in a little time?' She answered, 'Yes.' 'But there is something in you that will not turn to dust, and this is what they call your soul. Indeed, you cannot see your soul, though it is within you; as you cannot see the wind, though it is all about you. But if you had not a soul in you, you could no more see, or hear, or feel, than this table can. What do you think will become of your soul when your body turns to dust?' 'I don't know.' 'Why, it will go out of your body, and go up there, above the sky, and live always. God lives there. Do you know who God is?' 'No.' 'You cannot see Him, any more than you can see your own soul. It is He that made you and me, and all men and women, and all beasts and birds, and all the world. It is He that makes the sun shine, and rain fall, and corn and fruits grow out of the ground. He makes all these for us. But why do you think He made us? What did He make you and me for?' 'I can't tell.' 'He made you to live with Himself above the sky. And so you will, in a little time, if you are good. If you are good, when your body dies your soul will go up, and want nothing, and have whatever you can desire. No one will beat or hurt you there. You will never be sick. You will never be sorry any more, nor afraid of anything. I can't tell you, I don't know how happy you will be; for you will be with God.'

The attention with which this poor creature listened to instruction is inexpressible. The next day she remembered all, readily answered every question; and said she would ask Him that made her to show her how to be good.

--------- 1.23 ---------

'SHE COULD NOT HELP PRAISING AND BLESSING GOD'
George Whitefield

Just before John Wesley left Georgia amid controversy over his preaching style and efforts to minister to slaves, he wrote to his friend George Whitefield in Britain, asking for help spreading the gospel in the Americas. Whitefield immediately came to Georgia, and launched over three decades of ministry. Whitefield toured the colonies, hosting a circuit of revivals that would come to signify Methodist worship. While he initially received a cool reception from whites, blacks attended in droves. The focus on instant conversion and divine justice, as well as the implied equality of the meetings—whites and blacks worshipped, and found salvation, together—resonated with slaves. The services were spirited, with worshipers often declaring they had been visited by the Holy Ghost. In his journal, Whitefield described one such service, led by a Baptist preacher, in which a slave was "visited."

May 8, 1740

… I conversed also with a poor negro woman, who has been visited in a very remarkable manner. God was pleased to convert her by my preaching last autumn; but being under dejections on Sunday morning, she prayed that salvation might come to her heart, and that the Lord would be pleased to manifest Himself to her soul that day. Whilst she was at meeting, hearing Mr. M—n, a Baptist preacher, the Word came with such power to her heart, that at last she was obliged to cry out; and a great concern fell upon many in the congregation. The minister stopped, and several persuaded her to hold her peace; but she could not help praising and blessing God. Many since this, have called her mad, and said she was full of new wine; but the account she gave me was rational and solid, and, I believe in that hour the Lord Jesus took a great possession of her soul. Such cases, indeed, have not been very common; but when an extraordinary work is being carried on, God generally manifests Himself to some souls in this extraordinary manner. I doubt not, when the poor negroes are to be called, God will highly favour them, to wipe off their approach, and shew that He is no respecter of persons, but that whosoever believeth in Him shall be saved.

Preached, at eleven, to six or seven thousand people, and cleared myself from some aspersions that had been cast upon my doctrine, as though it tended to Antinomianism. I believe God had much people in the city of Philadelphia. The congregations are very large and serious, and I have scarce preached this time amongst them without seeing a stirring amongst the dry bones. At five in the evening, I preached again, but to a rather larger audience; and, after sermon, rode ten miles to a friend's house, that I might be in readiness to preach the next morning, according to appointment. How differently am I treated from my Master? He taught the people by day, and abode all night upon the Mount of Olives. He had not where to lay His head; but go where I will, I find people receiving me into their houses with great gladness.

——— 1.24 ———

REPORT OF THE COMMITTEE OF CONFERENCE ON THE CASE OF THE NEGROES' DESERTION TO ST. AUGUSTINE
South Carolina Assembly

The Spanish offer of freedom to refugees from British slavery had exactly the intended effect. Low country British slaves attempted to flee in increasing numbers, and it drove the colonists in Carolina to distraction. They responded with still more repressive measures to keep slaves in line. The legislative assembly appointed a special commission to study the problem and recommend methods to both stem the flow of escaping slaves and strike back at St. Augustine. In 1739, the committee delivered the report below, suggesting that the colony offer bounties to man-hunters who bring in escaped slaves—or the scalps of those that could not be taken alive. A slave scalp, with the requisite two ears still attached, would earn £20.

The Committee report that having taken the Case under Consideration are of Opinion that the most effectual Method to remedy the Evil for the Future and to obtain a Recompence and Satisfaction for what is past, will be in the first Place to make an humble Representation of the Case to his Majesty to pray such Relief and Assistance in the Premises as to his Majesty shall seem meet.

That a Scout Boat with 10 Men be employed to guard the Water Passages to the Southward.

That an Encouragement be given to white Men and free Indians for taking up and bringing in all Negro Slaves that are already deserted or shall hereafter desert from the Province according to the Rates and Proportions following, to wit,

For Negro Men taken up beyond Savanna River and brought home alive the Sum of £40, a piece,

For Women taken and brought as above £25 each,

For Children under 12 Years of Age £10 each, which Sums shall be paid by their respective Owners.

And that an Encouragement be given for bringing in the Scalps of such Men or Women Negro Slaves that are already deserted or shall hereafter desert who shall be found beyond Savanna River and cannot be taken and brought home alive, to wit, for each Scalp with the two Ears £20 to be paid out of the Publick Treasury.

That a Bill be brought in for this Purpose.

The above Report was again read and debated as usual Paragraph by Paragraph, and the House agreed to the first Paragraph of the said Report wherein it is recommended that the Representation of the Case be made to his Majesty.

On the second Paragraph relating to the Scout Boat the Question was put whether the House would agree to that Paragraph which was carried in the Affirmative.

A Motion was then made that there might be two Scout Boats with a Commander and seven Men in each Boat; which being opposed the Question was put on the Motion, and was carried in the Affirmative.

And it was resolved that the said Boats be continued for a Term not exceeding nine Months.

The rest of the said Report was then agreed to and the Committee who made the said Report were directed to prepare a Bill accordingly.

——— 1.25 ———
'THE SAID CAESAR WAS EXECUTED AT THE USUAL PLACE, AND AFTERWARDS HUNG IN CHAINS'
South Carolina Gazette

As happened after the New York revolt of 1712, colonial officials in the southern colonies became obsessed with carrying out public executions of slaves caught fleeing to St. Augustine. They believed such brutal displays of the law's unforgiving hand would act as a deterrent to those slaves enticed by the Spaniards' offer of liberty. Newspaper reports throughout the 1730s, such as these in the *South Carolina Gazette*, triumphantly describe public executions and broadcast government officials' encouragement of vigilante justice—which formed the second half of a two-part system of violence the whites hoped would crush slave aspirations of freedom. It was a formula white America would continue to use to suppress black discontent as late as the 1960s.

A. January 29, 1732

One Day last Week, Mr. Charles Jones pursuing a Runaway Negro, who had robb'd him, and coming up with the Negro, he resisted and fought him; and he struck the Lock of his Musket into the Negro's Scull and kill'd him. He went and told a Justice what he had done, who ordered him to cut his Head off, fix it on a Pole, and set it up in a Cross-Road; which was done accordingly near Ashley Ferry.

B. April 12, 1739

On Thursday last two Negro-Men named Caesar and Alleboy belonging to Mr. Wm. Romsey and Company, wer tried by Thomas Dale and Robert Austin Esq; and Mr. John Fraser, Capt. Isaac Holmes and Mr. Henry Perroneau jun. being three Freeholders associated with the said Magistrates persuant to an Act of the Assembly, entituled an Act for the better ordering of Negroes and other Slaves. They were charged by Mr. Attorney General with deserting from their Master's Service, and attempting, with several other Slaves, to run-away off this Province either to Augustine or some other Place, which Charge being fully proved, the former was sentenced to die, and the latter to be whipt. Accordingly on Saturday last the said Caesar was executed at the usual Place, and afterwards hung in Chains at Hang-man's Point opposite this Town, in sight of all Negroes passing and repassing by Water: Before he was turned off he made a very sensi-ble Speech to those of his own Colour, exhort-ing them to be just, honest and virtuous, and to take warning by his unhappy Example; after which he begged the Prayers of all Christian People, himself repeating the Lord's Prayer and several others in a fervent and devout Manner.

————— 1.26 —————

'ST. AUGUSTINE ... THAT DEN OF THIEVES AND RUFFIANS!'
South Carolina Assembly

None of the colonists' efforts to stem the flow of runaway slaves to Spanish Florida worked. Spanish officials con-tinued to provoke the British colonies with further efforts to stir discontent among the slave population; Carolina colonists responded with raids. Ultimately, a war of skir-mishes developed between Spain and Britain. Following a particularly bloody battle in the on-and-off conflict that burned throughout the first half of the 1700s, the South Carolina Assembly ordered an investigation of the affair. In this passage from the 1741 report that grew out of that investigation, colonial officials reveal the intensity of their frustration with the Spanish effort to foment unrest among British slaves and describe the manner in which the Spanish spread the word of their offer for freedom.

... In 1738, although Peace subsisted, and Governour Johnson after his Arrival here had in 1733 renewed the before mentioned Stipulation, another Method was taken by the Spaniards to answer their Ends. Hitherto the Government of St. Augustine had not dared to acknowledge, much less to justify, the little Villainies and Violences offered to our Properties; but now an Edict of his Catholic Majesty himself, bearing Date in November 1733, was published by Beat of Drum round the Town of St. Augustine (where many Negroes belonging to English Vessels that car-ried thither Supplies of Provisions &c. had the Opportunity of hearing it) promising Liberty and Protection to all Slaves that should desert thither from any of the English Colonies but more especially from this. And, lest that should not prove sufficient of itself, secret Measures were taken to make it known to our Slaves in general. In Consequences of which Numbers of Slaves did from Time to Time by Land and Water desert to St. Augustine; and the better to facilitate their Escape carried off their Master's Horses, Boats &c., some of them first commit-ting Murder; and were accordingly received and declared free. Our Present Lieutenant Governour by Deputies sent from hence on that Occasion to Seignior Don Manuel de Montiana, the present Governour of St. Augustine, set forth the Manner in which those Slaves had escaped and re-demanded them pursuant to the Stipulation between the two Governments, and to the Peace subsisting between the Crowns. Notwithstanding which, though that Governour acknowledged those Slaves to be there, yet producing the King of Spain's said Edict he declared that he could not deliver them up without a positive Order for that Purpose from the King, and that he should continue to receive all others that should resort thither, it having been an Article of Complaint against his Predecessor that he had not put the said Edict in Force sooner. The Success of those Deputies being too well known at their Return, Conspiracies were formed and Attempts made by more Slaves to desert to St. Augustine, but as every one was by that Time alarmed with Apprehensions of that Nature, by great Vigilance they were prevented from succeeding. ...

The General acquainted our Lieutenant Governour by Letter that the Magistrates of Georgia had seized a Spaniard whom he took to be a Priest, and that they thought from what they had discovered that he was employed by the Spaniards to procure a general Insurrection of the Negroes.

On this Occasion every Breast was filled with Concern. Evil brought Home to us within our very Doors awakened the Attention of the most Unthinking. Every one that had any Relation, any Tie of Nature; every one that had a Life to lose were in the most sensible Manner shocked at such Danger daily hanging over their Heads. With Regret we bewailed our peculiar Case, that we could not enjoy the Benefits of Peace like the rest of Mankind and that our own Industry should be the Means of taking from us all the Sweets of Life and of rendering us liable to the Loss of our Lives and Fortunes. With Indignation we looked at St. Augustine (like another Sallee) that Den of Thieves and Ruffians! Receptacle of Debtors, Servants and Slaves! Bane of Industry and Society! And revolved in our Minds all the Injuries this Province had received from thence ever since it first Settlement, that they had from first to last, in Times of profoundest Peace, both publickly and privately, by themselves and Indians and Negroes, in every Shape molested us not without some Instances of uncommon Cruelty. And what aggravated the same was, that this Government on the contrary had never been wanting in its good Offices with our Indians in their Behalf. And even during Queen Anne's War had exercised so much Humanity towards them that in order to prevent those Indians from scalping them according to their Custom when they should take any of them Prisoners, a Law was passed to give them £5:0:0 Proclamation Money for every one that they should bring in alive. And accordingly a great Number of the Spaniards by that Means were brought in alive and the said Reward paid for them.

St. Augustine having thus at last obtained the Royal Sanction for its mischievous Designs, the Matter was fully represented to his Majesty, from whom we waited with Patience for Redress.

At this melancholy Juncture his Majesty's Proclamation came over with Orders to the Lieutenant Governour to grant Letters of Marque and Reprizal against the Subjects of the Crown of Spain; and War between the two Crowns appeared inevitable.

1.27
'THEY CALLING OUT LIBERTY, MARCHED ON WITH COLOURS DISPLAYED'
The Stono Rebellion

Ultimately, tensions in Carolina erupted in America's second major slave revolt. On Sunday, September 9, 1739, a group of 20 slaves believed to have been from Angola gathered near the Stono River, about 20 miles outside of Charleston, and began what was likely an attempt to flee to St. Augustine's Fort Mose. They stormed a nearby storehouse, acquired weapons and gunpowder, killed the proprietors and left their severed heads on the front steps. Under the leadership of a slave named Jimmy, they marched southward down the main road to Georgia and Florida, killing whites they encountered along the way. They grew in number with each stop, finally reaching what may have been as many as 100 slaves.

Historians have fiercely debated the slaves' decision to stop their march that afternoon, after having made it only about ten miles. Most contemporary accounts, such as the one below asserted that the group was drunk, having stolen liquor along their route. More recent accounts, however, note that the group was acting in line with Central African war customs when it stopped to gather in an open field and raise its flag. Other scholars have speculated that, having grown to a considerable force, the slaves paused to draw still more to their group before marching into Georgia. Whatever the reason, their halt gave the colonial militia an opportunity to catch up and, ultimately, subdue them. Many slaves escaped the battle however, and a prolonged manhunt ensued. It was a full week later before the colonial militia defeated the largest splinter group in a battle about 30 miles further south. It is likely that at least a portion of the rebels at Stono made it to Fort Mose. The rebellion drew such concern among the colonists that reports spread across the Atlantic. London's popular *Gentleman's Magazine* published the account below, which it identified as extracted from a letter sent by a South Carolina colonist.

THE AFRICAN-AMERICAN EXPERIENCE: CHAPTER 1

Extract of a Letter from S. Carolina, dated October 2

Sometime since a Proclamation was publish'd at Augustine, in which the King of Spain (then at Peace with Great Britain) promised Protection and Freedom to all Negroe Slaves, who would resort thither. Certain Negroes belonging to Capt. Davis escaped to Augustine, and were receiv'd there; they were demanded by General Ogelthorpe, who sent Lieut. Demere to Augustine, and the Governor assured the General of his sincere Friendship; but at the same time, shewed his Orders from the Court of Spain, by which he was to receive all Runaway Negroes. Of this other Negroes having Notice, as it is believed, from the Spanish Emissaries, four or five, who were Cattle Hunters, and knew the Woods, some of whom belong'd to Captain Mackpherson, run away with his Horses, wounded his Son, and Kill'd another Man. These marched for Georgia, and were pursued, but the Rangers being then newly reduced, the Country People could not overtake them, tho' they were discovered by the Salizburghers, as they pass'd by Ebenezer. They reach'd Augustine, one being kill'd, and another wounded by the Indians in their Flight. They were received there with great Honours, one of them had a Commission given to him, and a Coat faced with Velvet; amongst the Negroes Slaves, thee are People brought from the Kingdom of Angola in Africa, many of these speak Portugeuze (which Language is as near Spanish as Scotch is to English) by reason that the Portugueze have considerable Settlements, and the Jesuits have a Mission and School in that Kingdom, and many Thousands of Negroes there profess the Roman Catholick Religion. Several Spaniards, upon diverse Pretences, have some time past been strolling about Carolina, two of them, who will give no Account of themselves, have been taken up and committed to Gaol in Georgia. Since the good Reception of the Negroes at Augustine was spread about, several attempted to escape to the Spaniards, and were taken, one of them was hang'd at Charles-Town. In the latter End of July last Don Pedro, Colonel of the Spanish Horse, went in a Launch to Charles Town, under Pretence of a Message to General Oglethorpe, and the Lieutenant-Governor.

On the 9th Day of September last, being Sunday, which is the Day the Planters allow them to work for themselves, some Angola Negroes assembled, to the Number of Twenty, and one, who was called Jimmy, was their Captain, they surpriz'd a Warehouse belonging to Mr. Hutchenson, at a Place called Stone how; they there killed Mr. Robert Bathurst and Mr. Gibbs, plunder'd the House, and took a pretty many small Arms and Powder, which were there for Sale. Next they plunder'd and burnt Mr Godfrey's House, and killed him, his Daughter and Son. They then turned back, and marched Southward along Pons Pons, which is the road thro' Georgia to Augustine; they passed Mr Wallace's tavern about Day break, and said they would not hurt him for he was a good Man and kind to his Slaves; but they broke open and plunder'd Mr Lemy's House and kill'd him, his Wife, and Child. They marched on towards Mr Rose's, resolving to kill him; but he was saved by a Negroe, who having hid him, went out and pacified the others. Several Negroes joined them, they calling out Liberty, marched on with Colours displayed, and two Drums beating, pursuing all the white People they met with, and killing Man, Woman and Child, when they could come up to them. Colonel Bull, Lieutenant-Colonel of South Carolina, who was then riding along the Road, discovered them, was pursued, and with much Difficulty escaped, and raised the Country. They burnt Co. Hext's House, and killed his Overseer and his Wife. They then burnt Mr Sprey's House, then Mr Sacheverell's, and then Mr Nash's House all lying upon the Pons Pons Road, and killed all the white People they found in them. Mr Bullock got off, but they burnt his House. By this time many of them were drunk with the Rum they had taken in the Houses. They increased every Minute by new Negroes coming to them; so that they were above Sixty, some say a Hundred; on which they halted in a Field, and set to Dancing, Singing, and beating Drums, to draw more Negroes to them, thinking they were now victorious over the whole Province, having marched ten Miles, and burnt all before them without Opposition: But the Militia being raised, the Planters with great Briskness pursued them, and when they came up, dismounting, charged them on Foot. The Negroes were soon routed, though they behaved boldly; several being killed on the Spot, many ran back to their Plantations, thinking they had not been missed; but they were there taken and shot; such as were taken in the Field also, were, after being examined, shot on the Spot; and this is to be said to the Honour of the Carolina Planters that, notwithstanding the Provocation they had received from so many Murders, they did not torture one Negroe, but only put them to an easy Death. All who proved to be forced, and were not concerned in the Murders and Burnings, were pardon'd; and this sudden Courage in the Field, and the Humanity afterwards, have had so good an Effect, that there has been no farther Attempt, and the very Spirit of Revolt seems over. About 30 escaped from the Fight, of which ten marched about 30 Miles Southward, and being overtaken by the Planters on Horseback fought stoutly for some time, and were al killed on the Spot, the rest are yet untaken; and in that whole Action about 40 Negroes and 20 Whites were kill'd. The Lieutenant Governor sent an Account of this to General Oglethorpe, who met his Advices in his Return from the Indian Nation. He immediately order'd a Troop of Rangers to be raised, to patrole thro' Georgia, placed some Men in the Garrison at Padchocolas, which was before abandoned, and near which the Negroes formerly passed, being the Place where Horses can come to swim over the River Savannah for near 100 Miles, order'd out the Indians in Pursuit, and a Detachment of the Garrison at Port-Royal to assist the Planters on any Occasion, and publish'd a Proclamation,

ordering all the Constables, &c. of Georgia to pursue and seize all Negroes, with Reward for any who should be taken. It is hoped, these Measures will prevent any Negroes from getting down to the Spaniards.

──────── 1.28 ────────

'AT LEAST A HUNDRED AND FIFTY WERE GOT TOGETHER IN DEFIANCE'
William Stephens

Following Stono, slave revolts, and rumors of such, plagued Carolina and, in fact, spread throughout the rest of the colonies. The paranoid state of the white colonists, and the emboldened spirit of many slaves, conspired to produce one report after another of small and large insurrections. The most significant of those came less than a year later in June 1740, when an estimated 150 slaves gathered near Charlestown with a plan to storm a storehouse in town and acquire weapons. But one of the slaves who knew of the plan revealed it to his owner, for unknown reasons, and the insurrection was usurped. As William Stephens, then treasurer of Georgia, describes in his journal, officials hung the conspirators at the rate of 10 a day.

Wednesday. This Day we had Intelligence again of another Rising of the Negroes in Carolina, which, unless soon suppressed, has the Appearance of greater Danger than any of the former; forasmuch as this broke out near Charles-Town itself, about Ashley River, Dorchester, and the circumjacent Parts, where at least a hundred and fifty were got together in Defiance: But as they were yet unprovided with Arms, and there was no Corn on the Ground ripe, for their Subsistence, it was hoped they would quickly be dispersed: And the Country being all alarmed and in Pursuit of them, they had already taken about fifty, whom they were daily hanging, ten in a Day. Such dreadful Work, it is to be feared, we may hear more of in Time, in case they come to breaking open Stores to find Arms, as they did last Year; and are able to keep the Field, with Plenty of Corn and Potatoes every where; and above all, if it is considered how vastly disproportionate the Number of white Men is to theirs: So that at best, the Inhabitants cannot live without perpetually guarding their own Safety, now become so precarious. What Inference may be drawn from hence, with relation to this Colony, will be best done by the honourable Persons who make the Welfare of Georgia their Study. I had this Afternoon the Pleasure of seeing a Beginning made, of Work long wished for, viz. building a Church at the Town: a few Load of Stones being brought, and laid down in the Place where it is intended to stand.

——— 1.29 ———
PROHIBITING EDUCATION TO SLAVES
South Carolina Assembly

In the wake of Stono, South Carolina also became the first state to prohibit teaching slaves to write—others would follow suit. Such laws mainly only formalized an existing reality. From the onset of the British colonies, planters had resisted education efforts by missionaries, who pushed for literacy so that slaves could read the Bible. As slave revolts grew in frequency, however, few colonists, religious or otherwise, thought it wise to allow slaves too much education.

And whereas, the having of slaves taught to write, or suffering them to be employed in writing, may be attended with great inconveniences; Be it therefore enacted…that all and every person and persons whatsoever, who shall hereafter teach, or cause any slave or slaves to be taught, to write, or shall use or employ any slave as a scribe in any manner of writing whatsoever, hereafter taught to write, every such person and persons, shall, for every such offence, forfeit the sum of one hundred pounds current money.

——— 1.30 ———
THE TRIAL OF CUFFE AND QUACK
Judge Daniel Horsmanden

Southern colonists' unease in the wake of the Stono Rebellion migrated North. New York City, which shared Carolina's slave-heavy demographics, was once again gripped with fear of slave conspiracies. Unlike in 1712, however, it didn't take an actual revolt to set off a massacre of slaves. In 1741, as law enforcement officials questioned Mary Burton, an indentured servant, about what she knew of a routine burglary, she insinuated that she could uncover the cause of a recent series of fires in the city. She told a story that implicated several slaves, along with the family to which she was indentured, in a plot to burn down the city. Based solely on her ever changing and often conflicting tale, officials tried and convicted one slave after another for the plot. As no member of the New York bar would agree to represent the defendants, all were tried without a lawyer. Eventually, Burton began tossing accusations at respected white citizens as well, causing officials to abruptly drop the investigation. When the dust finally settled, however, 14 slaves had been burned alive, 18 hanged, 72 deported from the colony and at least another 50 were still in jail awaiting trial. Here, the judge who presided over the largely illegal trials describes the first one, at which two slaves are charged as the conspiracy's ringleaders.

Friday, May 29.
    Present, the second and third justices.
    The king against (Roosevelt's) Quack, and (Philipse's) Cuffee, Negroes, on trial upon two indictments.
    The prisoners brought to the bar. Jury called and sworn…
    Evidence against Cuffee.—Mary Burton said, "That Cuffee, with Caesar and Prince, the two negroes hanged, used frequently to meet at her master's (Hughson's) house, and that she heard them often talk of burning the fort, and that they would go down to the fly and burn the whole town; and that her master and mistress said they would aid and assist them as much as they could.

"That in their common conversation the used to say, that when all this was done, Caesar should be governor, and Hughson (her master) king.

"That Cuffee used to say, that a great many people had too much, and others too little; that his old master had a great deal of money, but that in a short time, his master would have less and himself have more.

"That at the meetings of the said three negroes, Cuffee, Caesar and Prince, at her master's house, they used to say in their conversations, that when they set fire to the town, they would do it in the night; and as the white people came to extinguish it, they would kill and destroy them.

"That she has known at times, seven or eight guns in her master's house, and some swords; and has seen twenty or thirty negroes at one time there; and that at such large meetings the three aforesaid negroes Cuffee, Caesar and Prince, were generally present and most active; and used to say, that the other negroes durst not refuse to do what they commanded them; and that they were sure they had a number sufficient to stand by them: that the negroes swore, that if ever she published or discovered their design of burning the town, they would burn her whenever them met her."

Court. Did the prisoner Cuffee ever threaten you so?

M. Burton. Yes, he, Caesar and Prince, and the rest.

"That about three weeks after she came to Hughson's, which was about midsummer last, the negroes were there talking of the plot and some of them said perhaps she would tell; and Cuffee said no, she would not, he intended to have her for a wife; and then run up to her; and she had a dishclout in her hand, which she dabbed in his face, and he ran away.

"That at a meeting of the negroes at Hughson's house, Hughson said they were all sworn, negroes and white people present, as she understood; that is, Hughson, his wife, daughter Sarah, and Peggy, and that the pur-

port of the oath was, that they were not to discover the secrets about firing the fort, the houses at the Fly, and the whole town, and about murdering white people; and Hughson said to the negroes present, which were Cuffee, Caesar and Prince, now you must take care, for you are all sworn; and at the same time the witness saw a bible, as she took it to be, in Hughson's hand, and when the witness came into the room he laid it upon the table; and then Caesar spoke to the witness and cautioned her not to tell, and Hughson made answer that she dared not; and Cuffee said, d—n his bl—d, if he would tell of any, if he was burnt; and so said the other two negroes, and so said Hughson, his wife, daughter Sarah, and Peggy." …

Mr. Murray observed, that by an act of assembly of this province, as in all other of his majesty's colonies where there are negroes, the negro evidence is good against each other; and he read the particular clauses in the act to this purpose, and further remarked upon the reasonableness and necessity of this law.

Negro evidence affecting Cuffee.—Fortune (Wilkins' negro) said, "That on Sunday, the day before col. Philipse's storehouse in New-street was set on fire, being sent by his master, towards evening on an errand to their apprentice boy, who lived in the Broadway, he went by the way of New-street, where he saw Cuffee and spoke with him, and that he said he was going to one of his master's storehouses, on which they parted, and the witness went to the Broadway, and tarried there till it was darkish; that he returned the same way, and as he came by the house of Captain Phoenix, at the corner of New-street, he saw Cuffee again, and two negroes more at some small distance from him, but who they were knew not: that he spoke with Cuffee, and asked him what he did there so late? he answered, he waited there for his master, who wanted something out of the storehouse, and that he was to come and bring the key with him, on which they parted again, but the witness believed one of the other two negroes was a

Spaniard, because when he left Cuffee, he heard one of them call him, *venez* a *qui seignior*.

The witness said, "That he had been often asked by Caesar (Vaarck's) Prince (Auboyneau's) and Cuffee, the prisoner, to go with them to Hughson's, but that he never did, but was told they had a dance there every other night."

Negro evidence affecting Quack and Cuffee.—Sandy said, "That he heard Quack and Cuffee say, they would set fire to Mr. Philipse's storehouse.

"That Cuffee said, d—n him, that hang him or burn him, he would set fire to the town." ...

The Prisoners being asked what they had to offer in their defence, they offered nothing but peremptory denials of what had been testified against them, and protestations of their innocency.

Mr. Smith then proceeded to sum up and remark upon the evidence, and spoke as followeth:

...Gentlemen, no scheme more monstrous could have been invented; nor can any thing be thought of more foolish, than the motives that induced these wretches to enter into it! What more ridiculous than that Hughson, in consequence of this scheme, should become King! Caesar, now in gibbets, a Governor! That the white men should be all killed, and the women become prey to the rapacious lust of these villains! That these slaves should thereby establish themselves in peace and freedom in the plundered wealth of their slaughtered masters! It is hard to say whether the wickedness or the folly of this design is the greater; and had it not been in part executed before it was discovered, we should with great difficulty have been persuaded to believe it possible, that such a wicked and foolish plot could be contrived by any creatures in human shape.

Yet, gentlemen, incredible as such a plot would have seemed to have been, the event has in part proved it to be real. Whence else could so many fires have been lighted up all around

you in so short a time, with evident marks of wilful design? A design that could not be executed but by several hands. ...

Thus, gentlemen, I have distinguished the several points of the evidence against the prisoners, and have repeated the substance of what each witness has said to each point, and shall leave it to you to determine whether the prisoners are guilty or not. I have endeavoured to lay no more weight upon any part of the evidence, than it will bear; and I hope I have not urged any consequence which the fact proved will not fairly warrant.

Gentlemen, the prisoners have been indulged with the same kind of trial as is due to free men, though they might have been proceeded against in a more summary and less favourable way. The negro evidence, in the manner in which it has been produced is warranted by the act of the assembly that has been read to you; the law requires no oath to be administered to them, and indeed it would seem to be a profanation of it, to administer it to a Heathen in the legal form. You have seen that the court has put them under the most solemn caution, that their small knowledge of religion can render them capable of. The being and perfections of an Almighty, all knowing, and just God, and the terrors of an eternal world, have been plainly laid before them, and strongly pressed upon them. Unless they were professed Christians, and had taken upon them the bonds and obligations of that religion, their word, with the cautions that have been used, I suppose will be thought by you, as satisfactory as any oath that could have been devised. But, gentlemen, the court has no power to administer an oath, but in the common form, and if Pagan negroes could not be received as witnesses against each other, without an oath in legal form, it is easy to perceive that the greatest villanies would often pass with impunity.

Before I conclude, I cannot help observing to you, gentlemen, that by divers parts of the evidence, it appears that this horrid scene of iniquity has been chiefly contrived and promoted at meetings of negroes in great numbers on Sundays. This instructive circumstance may teach us many lessons, both of reproof and caution, which I only hint at, and shall leave the deduction of the particulars to every one's reflection.

Gentlemen, the monstrous ingratitude of this black tribe, is what exceedingly aggravated their guilt. Their slavery among us is generally softened with great indulgence; they live without care, and are commonly better fed and clothed, and put to less labour, than the poor of most Christian countries. They are indeed slaves, but under the protection of the law, none can hurt them with impunity: they are really more happy in this place, than in the midst of the continual plunder, cruelty, and rapine of their native countries; but notwithstanding all the kindness and tenderness with which they have been treated amongst us, yet this is the second attempt of the same kind, that this brutish and bloody species of mankind have made within one age. That justice that was provoked by former fires, and the innocent blood that was spilt in your streets, should have been a perpetual terror to the negroes that survived the vengeance of that day, and should have been a warning to all that had come after them. But I fear, gentleman, that we shall never be quite safe, till that wicked race are under more restraint, or their number greatly reduced within this city. But I shall not insist further, but refer you, gentlemen, to the direction of the court; and if the evidence against these prisoners proves sufficient in your judgment to convict them, I make no doubt but you will bring in a verdict accordingly, and do what in you lies to rid this country of the vilest creatures in it.

───── 1.31 ─────
'BARS FIGHT'
Lucy Terry Prince

Lucy Terry Prince is credited as the first African American to write a poem. While such grand claims are impossible to substantiate, we can say hers was the first to receive widespread attention from whites. Brought to Rhode Island as an infant by slave traders, Lucy Terry was purchased by a Deerfield, Massachusetts, man. In 1756 a free black landowner named Abijah Prince purchased her freedom and the two married. Her oratorical skills were renowned, and she would go on to use them in a landmark civil rights case before the Supreme Court of the United States at the close of the 18th century. The original 1746 manuscript of her poem, "Bars Fight," was lost. But the poem endured through the oral history of Deerfield, and was eventually transcribed and published in the mid 1800s. The poem is an account and memorial of a battle between a group of Native Americans and some Deerfield residents. Lucy Terry Prince was 16 when she wrote it.

August 'twas the twenty-fifth,
Seventeen hundred forty-six;
The Indians did in ambush lay,
Some very valiant men to slay,
The names of whom I'll not leave out.
Samuel Allen like a hero fout,
And though he was so brave and bold,
His face no more shalt we behold
Eteazer Hawks was killed outright,
Before he had time to fight,—
Before he did the Indians see,
Was shot and killed immediately.
Oliver Amsden he was slain,
Which caused his friends much grief and pain.
Simeon Amsden they found dead,
Not many rods distant from his head.
Adonijah Gillett we do hear
Did lose his life which was so dear.
John Sadler fled across the water,
And thus escaped the dreadful slaughter.
Eunice Allen see the Indians coming,
And hopes to save herself by running,
And had not her petticoats stopped her,
The awful creatures had not catched her,

Nor tommy hawked her on the head,
And left her on the ground for dead.
Young Samuel Allen, Oh lack-a-day!
Was taken and carried to Canada.

——— 1.32 ———

'AN EVENING THOUGHT'
Jupiter Hammon

At the close of the American colonial period, African slaves in the British colonies were gradually becoming African Americans. While the slave trade was still booming, and had years left in it, many of the black slaves of that time had been born and lived their entire lives in the Americas. Jupiter Hammon was one such person. Historians believe Hammon was born in the early 1700s in New York City. He spent the majority of his life as a slave on Long Island's North Shore at Lloyd Manor—the historic home of famed patriot Henry Lloyd and his descendents. In 1760, Hammon became the first African American to publish a poem. His liturgical "An Evening Thought" was released on Christmas Day that year. Hammond was deeply religious, reflecting the general mood of the time, and his poetry dwelled on Christian spirituality. He would publish three more poems and four works of prose before his death sometime after 1790.

An Evening THOUGHT
Salvation by Christ,
with PENETENTIAL CRIES:
Composed by Jupiter Hammon, a Negro belonging to Mr Lloyd, of Queen's-Village, on Long-Island, the 25th of December, 1760.

Salvation comes by Jesus Christ alone,
    The only Son of God;
Redemption now to every one,
    That love his holy Word.
Dear Jesus we would fly to Thee,
    And leave off every Sin,
Thy tender Mercy well agree;
    Salvation from our King.
Salvation comes now from the Lord,
    Our victorious King;
His holy Name be well ador'd,
    Salvation surely bring.
Dear Jesus give they Spirit now,

Thy Grace to every Nation,
That han't the Lord to whom we bow,
    The Author of Salvation.
Dear Jesus unto Thee we cry,
    Give us the Preparation;
Turn not away thy tender Eye;
    We seek thy true Salvation.
Salvation comes from God we know,
    The true and only One;
It's well agreed and certain true,
    He gave his only Son.
Lord hear our penetential Cry:
    Salvation from above;
It is the Lord that doth supply,
    With his Redeeming Love.
Dear Jesus by thy precious Blood,
    The World Redemption have:
Salvation comes now from the Lord,
    He being they captive slave.
Dear Jesus let the Nations cry,
    And all the People say,
Salvation comes from Christ on high,
    Haste on Tribunal Day.
We cry as Sinners to the Lord,
    Salvation to obtain;
It is firmly fixt his holy Word,
    Ye shall not cry in vain.
Dear Jesus unto Thee we cry,
    And make our Lamentation:
O let our Prayers ascend on high;
    We felt thy Salvation.
Lord turn our dark benighted Souls;
    Give us a true Motion,
And let the Hearts of all the World,
    Make Christ their Salvation.
Ten Thousand Angels cry to Thee,
    Yea louder than the Ocean.
Thou art the Lord, we plainly see;
    Thou art the true Salvation.
Now is the Day, excepted Time;
    The Day of Salvation;
Increase your Faith, do not repine:
    Awake ye every Nation.
Lord unto whom now shall we go,
    Or seek a safe Abode;
Thou hast the Word Salvation too
    The only Son of God.

Ho! every one that hunger hath,
  Or pineth after me,
Salvation be thy leading Staff,
  To set the Sinner free.
Dear Jesus unto Thee we fly;
  Depart, depart from Sin,
Salvation doth at length supply,
  The Glory of our King.
Come ye Blessed of the Lord,
  Salvation greatly given;
O turn your Hearts, accept the Word,
  Your Souls are fit for Heaven.
Dear Jesus we now turn to Thee,
  Salvation to obtain;
Our Hearts and Souls do meet again,
  To magnify thy Name.
Come holy Spirit, Heavenly Dove,
  The Object of our Care;
Salvation doth increase our Love;
  Our Hearts hath felt they fear.
Now Glory be to God on High,
  Salvation high and low;
And thus the Soul on Christ rely,
  To Heaven surely go.
Come Blessed Jesus, Heavenly Dove,
  Accept Repentance here;
Salvation give, with tender Love;
  Let us with Angels share.

———— 1.33 ————

SOME MEMOIRS OF THE LIFE OF JOB
Thomas Bluett

Slave narratives, autobiographical stories about the lives of African Americans living in bondage, did not explode as a significant American literary genre until the Abolition Movement spurred their proliferation in the 19th century. However, as early as the middle-1700s these unique stories began to appear. Slave narratives formed the backbone of African-American literature from its outset, and those roots continued to influence black arts and letters throughout their history. Today, black autobiography stretches far beyond the bounds of nonfiction, with self-reflection and personal experience significantly informing most of the community's seminal works of art and literature—from poetry and prose to music and film.

One of the first slave narratives published was the story of a Gambian aristocrat named Job. As with most of the early narratives, Job's was actually *biographical*, written by a white author named Thomas Bluett. Later narratives would be "related" to white authors by slaves who did not write in English, until eventually self-educated slaves who had escaped began writing their own stories. Bluett's touching tale describes Job's life in Gambia as the son of a high priest, his capture and sale into slavery in Maryland, and his ensuing struggle to return home. With Bluett's aide, Job does finally make it back to Gambia.

IN *February*, 1730, JOB's Father hearing of an *English* Ship at *Gambia* River, sent him, with two Servants to attend him, to sell two Negroes and to buy Paper, and some other Necessaries; but desired him not to venture over the River, because the Country of the *Mandingoes*, who are Enemies to the People of *Futa*, lies on the other side. JOB not agreeing with Captain *Pike* (who commanded the Ship, lying then at *Gambia*, in the Service of Captain *Henry Hunt*, Brother to Mr. *William Hunt*, Merchant, in *Little Tower-Street, London*) sent back the two Servants to acquaint his Father with it, and to let him know that he intended to go farther. Accordingly, having agreed with another Man, named *Loumein Yoas*, who understood the *Mandingoe* Language, to go with him as his Interpreter, he crossed the River *Gambia*, and disposed of his Negroes for some Cows. As he was returning Home, he stopp'd for some Refreshment at the House of an old Acquaintance; and the Weather being hot, he hung up his Arms in the House, while he refresh'd himself. Those Arms were very valuable; consisting of a Gold-hilted Sword, a Gold Knife, which they wear by their Side, and a rich Quiver of Arrows, which King *Sambo* had made him a Present of. It happened that a Company of the *Mandingoes*, who live upon Plunder, passing by at that Time, and observing him unarmed, rush'd in, to the Number of seven or eight at once, at a back Door, and pinioned JOB, before he could get to his Arms, together with his Interpreter, who is a Slave in

Maryland still. They then shaved their Heads and Beards, which JOB and his Man resented as the highest Indignity; tho' the *Mandingoes* meant no more by it, than to make them appear like Slaves taken in War. On the 27th of *February*, 1730. They carried them to Captain *Pike* at *Gambia*, who purchased them; and on the first of *March* they were put on Board. Soon after JOB found means to acquaint Captain *Pike* that he was the same Person that came to trade with him a few Days before, and after what Manner he had been taken. Upon this Captain *Pike* gave him leave to redeem himself and his Man; and JOB sent to an Acquaintance of his Father's, near *Gambia*, who promised to send to JOB's Father, to inform him of what had happened, that he might take some Course to have him set at Liberty. But it being a Fortnight's journey between that Friend's House and his Father's, and the Ship failing in about a Week after, JOB was brought with the rest of the Slaves to *Annapolis* in *Maryland*, and delivered to Mr. *Vachell Denton*, Factor to Mr. *Hunt*, before mentioned. JOB heard since, by Vessels that came from *Gambia*, that his Father sent down several Slaves, a little after Captain *Pike* failed, in order to procure his Redemption; and that *Sambo*, King of *Futa*, had made War upon the *Mandingoes*, and cut off great Numbers of them, upon account of the Injury they had done to his Schoolfellow.

Mr. *Vachell Denton* sold JOB to one Mr. *Tolsey* in *Kent* Island in *Maryland*, who put him to work in making Tobacco; but he was soon convinced that JOB had never been used to such Labour. He every Day shewed more and more Uneasiness under this Exercise, and at last grew sick, being no way able to bear it; so that his Master was obliged to find easier Work for him, and therefore put him to tend the Cattle. JOB would often leave the Cattle, and withdraw into the Woods to pray; but a white Boy frequently watched him, and whilst he was at his Devotion would mock him, and throw Dirt in his Face. This very much disturbed JOB, and added to his other Misfortunes; all

which were increased by his Ignorance of the *English* Language, which prevented his complaining, or telling his Case to any Person about him. Grown in some measure desperate, by reason of his present Hardships, he resolved to travel at a Venture; thinking he might possibly be taken up by some Master, who would use him better, or otherwise meet with some lucky Accident, to divert or abate his Grief. Accordingly, he travelled thro' the Woods, till he came to the County of *Kent*, upon *Delaware Bay*, now esteemed Part of *Pensilvania*; altho' it is properly a Part of *Maryland*, and belongs to my Lord *Baltimore*. There is a Law in force, throughout the Colonies of *Virginia*, *Maryland*, *Pensilvania*, &c. as far as *Boston* in *New England*, viz. That any Negroe, or white Servant who is not known in the County, or has no Pass, may be secured by any Person, and kept in the common Goal, till the Master of such Servant shall fetch him. Therefore JOB being able to give no Account of himself, was put in Prison there.

This happened about the Beginning of *June*, 1731 when I, who was attending the Courts there, and had heard of JOB, went with several Gentlemen to the Goaler's House, being a Tavern, and desired to see him. He was brought into the Tavern to us, but could not speak one Word of *English*. Upon our Talking and making Signs to him, he wrote a Line or two before us, and when he read it, pronounced the Words *Allah* and *Mahommed*; by which, and his refusing a Glass of Wine we offered him, we perceived he was a *Mahometan*, but could not imagine of what Country he was, or how he got thither; for by his affable Carriage, and the easy Composure of his Countenance, we could perceive he was no common Slave.

When JOB had been some time confined, an old Negroe Man, who lived in that Neighbourhood, and could speak the *Jalloff* Language, which JOB also understood, went to him, and conversed with him. By this Negroe the Keeper was informed to whom JOB belonged, and what was the Cause of his leaving his Master. The Keeper thereupon wrote to his Master, who soon after fetch'd him home, and was much kinder to him than before; allowing him a Place to pray in, and some other Conveniencies, in order to make his Slavery as easy as possible. Yet Slavery and Confinement was by no means agreeable to JOB, who had never been used to it; he therefore wrote a Letter in *Arabick* to his Father, acquainting him with his Misfortunes, hoping he might yet find Means to redeem him. This Letter he sent to Mr. *Vachell Denton*, desiring it might be sent to *Africa* by Captain *Pike*; but he being gone to *England*, Mr. *Denton* sent the Letter inclosed to Mr. *Hunt*, in order to be sent to *Africa* by Captain *Pike* from England; but Captain *Pike* had sailed for *Africa* before the Letter came to Mr. *Hunt*, who therefore kept it in his own Hands, till he should have a proper Opportunity of sending it. It happened that this Letter was seen by *James Oglethorpe*, Esq; who, according to his usual Goodness and Generosity, took Compassion on JOB, and gave his Bond to Mr. *Hunt* for the Payment of a certain Sum, upon the Delivery of JOB here in *England*. Mr. *Hunt* upon this sent to Mr. *Denton*, who purchas'd him again of his Master for the same Money which Mr. *Denton* had formerly received for him; his Master being very willing to part with him, as finding him no ways fit for his Business.

He lived some time with Mr. *Denton* at *Annapolis*, before any Ship could stir out, upon account of the Ice that lay in all the Rivers of *Maryland* at that Time. In this Interval he became acquainted with the Reverend Mr. *Henderson*, a Gentleman of great Learning, Minister of *Annapolis*, and Commissary to the Bishop of *London*, who gave JOB the Character of a Person of great Piety and Learning; and indeed his good Nature and Affability gain'd him many Friends besides in that Place.

In *March*, 1733 he set sail in the *William*, Captain *George Uriel* Commander; in which Ship I was also a Passenger. The Character which the Captain and I had of him at *Annapolis*, induced us to teach him as much of the *English* Language as we could, he being

then able to speak but few Words of it, and those hardly intelligible. This we set about as soon as we were out at Sea, and in about a Fortnight's Time taught him all his Letters, and to spell almost any single Syllable, when distinctly pronounced to him; but JOB and my self falling sick, we were hindered from making any greater Progress at that Time. However, by the Time that we arrived in *England*, which was the latter End of *April*, 1733. he had learned so much of our Language, that he was able to understand most of what we said in common Conversation; and we that were used to his Manner of Speaking, could make shift to understand him tolerably well. During the Voyage, he was very constant in his Devotions; which he never omitted, on any Pretence, notwithstanding we had exceeding bad Weather all the time we were at Sea. We often permitted him to kill our fresh Stock, that he might eat of it himself; for he eats no Flesh, unless he has killed the Animal with his own Hands, or knows that it has been killed by some *Mussulman*. He has no Scruple about Fish; but won't touch a bit of Pork, it being expresly forbidden by their Law. By his good Nature and Affability he gained the good Will of all the Sailors, who (not to mention other kind Offices) all the way up the Channel shewed him the Head Lands and remarkable Places; the Names of which JOB wrote down carefully, together with the Accounts that were given him about them. His Reason for so doing, he told me, was, that if he met with any *Englishman* in his Country, he might by these Marks be able to convince him that he had been in England.

On our Arrival in *England*, we heard that Mr. *Oglethorpe* was gone to *Georgia*, and that Mr. Hunt had provided a Lodging for JOB at *Limehouse*. After I had visited my Friends in the Country, I went up on purpose to see JOB. He was, very sorrowful, and told me, that Mr. *Hunt* had been applied to by some Persons to sell him, who pretended they would send him home; but he feared they would either sell him again as a Slave, or if they sent him home would expect an unreasonable Ransom for him. I took him to *London* with me, and waited on Mr. *Hunt*, to desire leave to carry him to *Cheshunt* in *Hartfordshire*; which Mr. *Hunt* comply'd with. He told me he had been apply'd to, as JOB had suggested, but did not intend to part with him without his own Consent; but as Mr. *Oglethorpe* was out of *England*, if any of JOB's Friends would pay the Money, he would accept of it, provided they would undertake to send him home safely to his own Country. I also obtained his Promise that he would not dispose of him till he heard farther from me.

JOB, while he was at *Cheshunt*, had the Honour to be sent for by most of the Gentry of that Place, who were mightily pleased with his Company, and concerned for his Misfortunes. They made him several handsome Presents, and proposed that a Subscription should be made for the Payment of the Money to Mr. *Hunt*. The Night before we set out for *London* from *Cheshunt*, a Footman belonging to *Samuel Holden*, Esq; brought a Letter to JOB, which was, I think, directed to Sir *Byby Lake*. The Letter was delivered at the *African* House; upon which the House was pleased to order that Mr. *Hunt* should bring in a Bill of the whole Charges which he had been at about JOB, and be there paid; which was accordingly done, and the Sum amounted to Fifty-nine Pounds, Six Shillings, and eleven Pence Half-penny. This Sum being paid, Mr. *Oglethorpe's* Bond was deliver'd up to the Company. JOB's Fears were now over, with respect to his being sold again as a Slave; yet he could not be persuaded but that he must pay an extravagant Ransom, when he got home. I confess, I doubted much of the Success of a Subscription, the Sum being great, and JOB's Acquaintance in *England* being so small; therefore, to ease JOB's Mind, I spoke to a Gentleman about the Affair, who has all along been JOB's Friend in a very remarkable Manner. This Gentleman was so far from discouraging the Thing, that he began the Subscription himself with a handsome Sum, and promised his further Assistance at a

dead Lift. Not to be tedious: Several Friends, both in *London* and in the Country, gave in their charitable Contributions very readily; yet the Sum was so large, that the Subscription was about twenty Pounds short of it; but that generous and worthy Gentleman before mentioned, was pleased to make up the Defect, and the whole Sum was compleated.

I went (being desired) to propose the Matter to the *African* Company; who, after having heard what I had to say, shew'd me the Orders that the House had made; which were, that JOB should be accommodated at the *African* House at the Company's Expence, till one of the Company's Ships should go to *Gambia*, in which he should be sent back to his Friends without any Ransom. The Company then ask'd me, if they could do any Thing more to make JOB easy; and upon my Desire, they order'd, that Mr. *Oglethorpe's* Bond should be cancelled, which was presently done, and that JOB should have his Freedom in Form, which he received handsomely engross'd with the Company's Seal affixed; after which the full Sum of the whole Charges (*viz.* Fifty-nine Pounds, Six Shillings, and eleven Pence Half-penny) was paid in to their Clerk, as was before proposed.

JOB's Mind being now perfectly easy, and being himself more known, he went chearfully among his Friends to several Places, both in Town and Country, One Day being at Sir *Hans Sloan's*, he expressed his great Desire to see the Royal Family. Sir *Hans* promised to get him introduced, when he had Clothes proper to go in. JOB knew how kind a Friend he had to apply to upon occasion; and he was soon cloathed in a rich silk Dress, made up after his own Country Fashion, and introduced to their Majesties, and the rest of the Royal Family. Her Majesty was pleased to present him with a rich Gold Watch; and the same Day he had the Honour to dine with his Grace the Duke of *Mountague*, and some others of the Nobility, who were pleased to make him a handsome Present after Dinner. His Grace, after that, was pleased to take JOB often into the Country with him, and shew him the Tools that are necessary for Tilling the Ground, both in Gardens and Fields, and made his Servants shew him how to use them; and afterwards his Grace furnished JOB with all Sorts of such Instruments, and several other rich Presents, which he ordered to be carefully done up in Chests, and put on Board for his Use. 'Tis not possible for me to recollect the many Favours he received from his Grace, and several other Noblemen and Gentlemen, who shewed a singular Generosity towards him; only, I may say in general, that the Goods which were given him, and which he carried over with him, were worth upwards of 500 Pounds; besides which, he was well furnished with Money, in case any Accident should oblige him to go on Shore, or occasion particular Charges at Sea. About the latter End of *July* last he embark'd on Board one of the *African* Company's Ships, bound for *Gambia*; where we hope he is safely arrived, to the great Joy of his Friends, and the Honour of the *English* Nation.

——— 1.34 ———

'UNCOMMON SUFFERINGS AND SURPRIZING DELIVERANCE'

Briton Hammon

In 1760, a slave named Briton Hammon authored the first slave narrative printed by a North American publisher. *A Narrative of the Uncommon Sufferings and Surprizing Deliverance of Briton Hammon* is also believed to be the first work of prose published by an African-American writer. Hammon's narrative is distinct from most of the genre in that it does not recount his life as a slave or his deliverance from that bondage. His is actually a travelogue describing the harrowing events surrounding his capture by Native American hunters in the Caribbean and subsequent journeys as he attempts to make his way home to Massachusetts. He expresses no distaste for his position as a slave, but rather presents his story as one of longing to reunite with his master. In the process, he encounters and escapes from pirates in Cuba, lives four years in a "close dungeon" and serves on a British gunboat during a battle with the French.

To THE READER,

AS my Capacities and Condition of Life are very low, it cannot be expected that I should make those Remarks on the Sufferings I have met with, or the kind Providence of a good GOD for my Preservation, as one in a higher Station; but shall leave that to the Reader as he goes along, and so I shall only relate Matters of Fact as they occur to my Mind —

ON Monday, 25th Day of *December*, 1747, with the leave of my Master, I went from Marshfield, with an Intention to go a Voyage to Sea, and the next Day, the 26th, got to Plymouth, where I immediately ship'd myself on board of a Sloop, Capt. John Howland, Master, bound to Jamaica and the *Bay*.—We sailed from Plymouth in a short Time, and after a pleasant Passage of about 30 Days, arrived at Jamaica; we was detain'd at Jamaica only 5 Days, from whence we sailed for the *Bay*, where we arrived safe in 10 Days. We loaded our Vessel with Logwood, and sailed from the Bay the 25th Day of *May* following, and the 15th Day of *June*, we were cast away on Cape-Florida, about 5 Leagues from the Shore; being now destitute of every Help, we knew not what to do or what Course to take in this our sad Condition:—The Captain was advised, intreated, and beg'd on, by every Person on board, to heave over but only 20 Ton of the *Wood*, and we should get clear, which if he had done, might have sav'd his Vessel and Cargo, and not only so, but his own Life, as well as the Lives of the Mate and Nine Hands, as I shall presently relate.

After being upon this Reef two Days, the Captain order'd the Boat to be hoisted out, and then ask'd who were willing to tarry on board? The whole Crew was for going on Shore at this Time, but as the Boat would not carry 12 Persons at once, and to prevent any Uneasiness, the Captain, a Passenger, and one Hand tarry'd on board, while the Mate, with Seven Hands besides myself, were order'd to go on Shore in the Boat, which as soon as we had reached, one half were to be Landed, and the other four to return to the Sloop, to fetch the Captain and the others on Shore. The Captain order'd us to take with us our Arms, Ammunition, Provisions and Necessaries for Cooking, as also a Sail to make a Tent of, to shelter us from the Weather; after having left the Sloop we stood towards the Shore, and being within Two Leagues of the same, we espy'd a Number of Canoes, which we at first took to be Rocks, but soon found our Mistake, for we perceiv'd they moved towards us; we presently saw an English Colour hoisted in one of the Canoes, at the Sight of which we were not a little rejoiced, but on our advancing yet nearer, we found them, to our very great Surprize, to be Indians of which there were Sixty; being now so near them we could not possibly make our Escape; they soon came up with and boarded us, took away all our Arms Ammunition, and Provision.

The whole Number of Canoes (being about Twenty,) then made for the Sloop, except Two which they left to guard us, who order'd us to follow on with them; the Eighteen which made for the Sloop, went so much faster than we that they got on board above Three Hours before we came along side, and had kill'd Captain *Howland*, the Passenger and the other hand; we came to the Larboard side of the Sloop, and they order'd us round to the Starboard, and as we were passing round the Bow, we saw the whole Number of Indians, advancing forward and loading their Guns, upon which the Mate said, "*my Lads we are all dead Men*," and before we had got round, they discharged their Small Arms upon us, and kill'd Three of our hands, viz. *Reuben Young of Cape-Cod*, Mate; Joseph Little and *Lemuel Doty* of Plymouth, upon which I immediately jump'd overboard, chusing rather to be drowned, than to be kill'd by those barbarous and inhuman Savages.

In three or four Minutes after, I heard another Volley which dispatched the other five, viz. John Nowland, and Nathaniel Rich, both belonging to Plymouth, and Elkanah Collymore, and *James Webb*, Strangers, and Moses Newmock, Molatto. As soon as they had kill'd the whole of the People, one of the Canoes padled after me, and soon came up

with me, hawled me into the Canoe, and beat me most terribly with a Cutlass, after that they ty'd me down, then this Canoe stood for the Sloop again and as soon as she came along side, the Indians on board the Sloop betook themselves to their Canoes, then set the Vessel on Fire, making a prodigious shouting and hallowing like so many Devils. As soon as the Vessel was burnt down to the Water's edge, the Indians stood for the Shore, together with our Boat, on board of which they put 5 hands. After we came to the Shore, they led me to their Hutts, where I expected nothing but immediate Death, and as they spoke broken English, were often telling me, while coming from the Sloop to the Shore, that they intended to roast me alive. But the Providence of God order'd it otherways, for He appeared for my Help, in this Mount of Difficulty, and they were better to me then my Fears, and soon unbound me, but set a Guard over me every Night. They kept me with them about five Weeks, during which Time they us'd me pretty well, and gave me boil'd Corn, which was what they often eat themselves. The Way I made my Escape from these Villains was this; A Spanish Schooner arriving there from St. Augustine, the Master of which, whose Name was *Romond*, asked the Indians to let me go on board his Vessel, which they granted, and the Captain knowing me very well, weigh'd Anchor and carry'd me off to the *Havanna*, and after being there four Days the Indians came after me, and insisted on having me again, as I was their Prisoner;—They made Application to the Governor, and demanded me again from him; in answer to which the Governor told them, that as they had put the whole Crew to Death, they should not have me again, and so paid them Ten Dollars for me, adding, that he would not have them kill any Person hereafter, but take as many of them as they could, of those that should be cast away, and bring them to him, for which he would pay them Ten Dollars a-head. At the *Havanna* I lived with the Governor in the Castle about a Twelvemonth, where I was walking thro' the Street, I met with a Press-Gang who immediately prest me, and put me into Goal, and with a Number of others I was confin'd till next Morning, when we were all brought out, and ask'd who would go on board the King's Ships, four of which having been lately built, were bound to Old-Spain, and on my refusing to serve on board, they put me in a close Dungeon, where I was confin'd Four Years and seven months; during which Time I often made application to the Governor, by Persons who came to see the Prisoners, but they never acquainted him with it, nor did he know all this Time what became of me, which was the means of my being confin'd there so long. But kind Providence so order'd it, that after I had been in this Place so long as the Time mention'd above the Captain of a Merchantman, belonging to *Boston*, having sprung a Leak was obliged to put into the Havanna to refit, and while he was at Dinner at *Mrs. Betty Howard's*, she told the Captain of my deplorable Condition, and said she would be glad, if he could by some means or other relieve me; The Captain told *Mrs. Howard* he would use his best Endeavours for my Relief and Enlargement.

Accordingly, after Dinner, came to the Prison, and ask'd the Keeper if he might see me; upon his Request I was brought out of the Dungeon, and after the Captain had Interrogated me, told me, he would intercede with the Governor for my Relief out of that miserable Place, which he did, and the next Day the Governor sent an Order to release me; I lived with the Governor about a Year after I was delivered from the Dungeon, in which Time I endeavour'd three Times to make my Escape, the last of which proved effectual; the first Time I got on board of Captain Marsh, an English Twenty Gun Ship, with a Number of others, and lay on board conceal'd that Night; and the next Day the Ship being under sail, I thought myself safe, and so made my Appearance upon Deck, but as soon as we were discovered the Captain ordered the Boat out, and sent us all on Shore—I intreated the Captain to let me, in particular, stay on board,

begging, and crying to him, to commiserate my unhappy Condition, and added, that I had been confin'd almost five Years in a close Dungeon, but the Captain would not hearken to any Intreaties, for fear of having the Governor's Displeasure, and so was obliged to go on Shore,

After being on Shore another Twelvemonth, I endeavour'd to make my Escape the second Time, by trying to get on board of a Sloop bound to Jamaica, and as I was going from the City to the Sloop, was unhappily taken by the Guard, and ordered back to the Castle, and there confined.—However, in a short Time I was set at Liberty, and order'd with a Number of others to carry the Bishop from the Castle, thro' the Country, to confirm the old People, baptize Children, &c. for which he receives large Sums of Money.—I was employ'd in this Service about Seven Months, during which Time I lived very well, and then returned to the Castle again, where I had my Liberty to walk about the City, and do Work for my self;—*The Beaver*, an English Man of War then lay in the Harbour, and having been informed by some of the Ship's Crew that she was to sail in a few Days, I had nothing now to do, but to seek an Opportunity how I should make my Escape.

Accordingly one Sunday Night the Lieutenant of the Ship with a Number of the Barge Crew were in a Tavern, and Mrs. *Howara* who had before been a Friend to me, interceded with the Lieutenant to carry me on board: the Lieutenant said he would with all his Heart, and immediately I went on board in the Barge. The next Day the Spaniards came along side the *Beaver*, and demanded me again, with a Number of others who had made their Escape from them, and got on board the Ship, but just before I did; but the Captain, who was a true Englishman, refus'd them, and said he could not answer it, to deliver up any Englishmen under English Colours.—In a few Days we set Sail for Jamaica, where we arrived safe, after a short and pleasant Passage.

After being at Jamaica a short Time we sail'd for *London*, as convoy to a Fleet of Merchantmen, who all arrived safe in the *Downs*, I was turned over to another Ship, the Arcenceil, and there remained about a Month. From this Ship I went on board the Sandwich of 90 Guns; on board the Sandwich, I tarry'd 6 Weeks, and then was order'd on board the *Hercules*, Capt. John Porter, a 74 Gun Ship, we sail'd on a Cruize, and met with a French 84 Gun Ship, and had a very smart Engagement, in which about 70 of our Hands were Kill'd and Wounded, the Captain lost his Leg in the Engagement, and I was Wounded in the Head by a small Shot. We should have taken this Ship, if they had not cut away the most of our Rigging; however, in about three Hours after, a 64 Gun Ship, came up with and took her.—I was discharged from the *Hercules* the 12th Day of *May* 1759 (having been on board of that Ship 3 Months) on account of my being disabled in the Arm, and render'd incapable of Service, after being honourably paid the Wages due to me. I was put into the Greenwich Hospital where I stay'd and soon recovered.—I then ship'd myself a Cook on board Captain *Martyn*, an arm'd Ship in the King's Service. I was on board this Ship almost Two Months, and after being paid my Wages, was discharg'd in the Month of *October*.—After my discharge from Captain *Martyn*, I was taken sick in *London* of a Fever, and was confin'd about 6 Weeks, where I expended all my Money, and left in very poor Circumstances; and unhappy for me I knew nothing of my *good Master's* being in *London* at this my very difficult Time. After I got well of my sickness, I ship'd myself on board of a large Ship bound to Guinea, and being in a publick House one Evening, I overheard a Number of Persons talking about Rigging a Vessel bound to *New-England*, I ask'd them to what Part of New-England this Vessel was bound? they told me, to *Boston*; and having ask'd them who was Commander? they told me, Capt. *Watt*; in a few Minutes after this the Mate of the Ship came in, and I ask'd him if Captain *Watt* did not want a Cook, who told me he did, and that the Captain would be in, in a few Minutes; and in about half an Hour the Captain came in, and then I ship'd myself at once, after begging off from the Ship bound to Guinea; I work'd on board Captain *Watt's* Ship almost Three Months, before she sail'd, and one Day being at Work in the Hold, I overheard some Persons on board mention the Name of Winslow, at the Name of which I was very inquisitive, and having ask'd what Winslow they were talking about? They told me it was General Winslow; and that he was one of the Passengers, I ask'd them what General Winslow? For I never knew *my good Master*, by that Title before; but after enquiring more particularly I found it must be *Master*, and in a few Days Time the Truth was joyfully verify'd by a happy Sight of his Person, which so overcome me, that I could not speak to him for some Time—*My good Master* was exceeding glad to see me, telling me that I was like one arose from the Dead, for he thought I had been Dead a great many Years, having heard nothing of me for almost Thirteen Years.

I think I have not deviated from Truth, in any particular of this my Narrative, and tho' I have omitted a great many Things, yet what is wrote may suffice to convince the Reader, that I have been most grievously afflicted, and yet thro' the Divine Goodness, as miraculously preserved, and delivered out of many Dangers; of which I desire to retain a *grateful Remembrance*, as long as I live in the World.

And now, That in the Providence of that GOD, who delivered his Servant David out of the Paw of the Lion and out of the Paw of the Bear, *I am freed from a* long *and* dreadful Captivity, among worse Savages than they; *And am return'd to my* own Native Land, to Shew how Great Things the Lord hoth done for Me; *I would call upon all Men, and Say*, O Magnifie the Lord with Me, and let us Exalt his Name together!—— O that Men would Praise the Lord for His Goodness, and for his Wonderful Works to the Children of Men.

I.35

THE INTERESTING NARATIVE OF THE LIFE OF OLAUDAH EQUIANO
Olaudah Equiano

Olaudah Equiano was abducted from his home in Benin, near the Niger River, when he was 11 years old, around the middle of the 18th century. After arriving in Virginia, Equiano was purchased by a lieutenant in the British Royal Navy, who brought him to England. There, Equiano educated himself and ultimately purchased his freedom. Years later, he wrote and published a slave narrative describing his experiences. In addition to being an important American and British abolitionist text, the book offers an invaluable first person account of the Atlantic Slave Trade from an African perspective. The excerpts here, from chapter two of the book, describe Equiano's ordeal from the time of his capture until his arrival in the New World. It is one of few African accounts of the infamous "middle passage" of a slave ship's standard voyage—the leg between Africa's western coast and the Americas, during which Africans were stowed as cargo in the ship's hull.

CHAP II.

…As I was the youngest of the sons, I became, of course, the greatest favourite with my mother, and was always with her; and she used to take particular pains to form my mind. I was trained up from my earliest years in the art of war: my daily exercise was shooting and throwing javelins; and my mother adorned me with emblems, after the manner of our greatest warriors. In this way I grew up till I was turned the age of eleven, when an end was put to my happiness in the following manner:—Generally when the grown people in the neighbourhood were gone far in the fields to labour, the children assembled together in some of the neighbour's premises to play; and commonly some of us used to get up a tree to look out for any assailant, or kidnapper, that might come upon us; for they sometimes took those opportunities of our parents absence to attack and carry off as many as they could seize. One day as I was watching at the top of a tree in our yard, I saw one of those people come into the yard of our next neighbour but one, to kidnap, there being many stout young people in it. Immediately on this I gave the alarm of the rogue, and he was surrounded by the stoutest of them, who entangled him with cords, so that he could not escape till some of the grown people came and secured him. But, alas! ere long it was my fate to be thus attacked, and to be carried off, when none of the grown people were nigh. One day, when all our people were gone out to their works as usual, and only I and my dear sister were left to mind the house, two men and a woman got over our walls, and in a moment seized us both, and, without giving us time to cry out, or make resistance, they stopped our mouths, and ran off with us, into the nearest wood. Here they ties our hands, and continued to carry us as far as they could, till night came on, when we reached a small house, where the robbers halted for refreshment and spent the night. We were then unbound, but were unable to take any food; and, being quite overpowered by fatigue and grief, our only relief was some sleep, which allayed our misfortune for a short time. The next morning we left the house, and continued travelling all the day. For a long time we had kept the woods, but at last we came into a road which I believed I knew. I had now some hopes of being delivered; for we had covered but a little way before I discovered some people at a distance, on which I began to cry out for their assistance; but my cries had no other effect than to make them tie me faster and stop my mouth, and then they put me into a large sack. They also stopped my sister's mouth, and tied her hands; and in this manner we proceeded till we were out of the sight of these people. When we went to rest the following night they offered us some victuals; but we refused it; and the only comfort we had was in being in one another's arms all that night, and bathing each other with our tears. But alas! we were soon deprived of even the small comfort of weeping together. The next day proved of greater sorrow than I had yet experienced; for my sister and I were separated, while we lay clasped in each others arms. It was in vain that we besought them not to part us; she was torn from me and immediately carried away, while I was left in a state of distraction not to be described. I cried and grieved continually; and for several days did not eat anything but what they forced into my mouth. …

The first object which saluted my eyes when I arrive on the coast was the sea, and a slave ship, which was then riding anchor, and waiting for its cargo. These filled me with astonishment, which was soon converted into terror when I was carried on board. I was immediately handled, and tossed up to see if I were sound, by some of the crew; and I was now persuaded that I had gotten into a world of bad spirits, and that they were going to kill me. Their complexions too differing so much from ours, their long hair, and the language they spoke (which was very different from any I had ever heard) united to confirm me in this belief. Indeed such were the horrors of my views and fears at the moment, that, if ten thousand worlds had been my own, I would have freely parted with them all to have exchanged my condition with that of the meanest slave in my own country. When I looked round the ship too and saw a large furnace or copper-boiling, and a multitude of black people of every description chained together, every one of their countenances expressing dejection and sorrow, I no longer doubted of my fate; and, quite over-powered with horror and anguish, I fell motionless on the deck and fainted. When I recovered a little I found some black people about me, who I believed were some of those who had brought me on board, and had been receiving their pay; they talked to me in order to cheer me, but all in vain. I asked them if we were not to be eaten by those white men with horrible looks, red faces and long hair. They told me I was not: and one of the crew brought me a small portion of spirituous liquor in a wine glass; but being afraid of him, I would not take it out of his hand. One of the blacks therefore took it from him and gave it to me, and I took a little down my palate, which, instead of reviving me, as they thought it would, threw me into the greatest consternation at the strange feeling it produced, having never tasted any such liquor before. Soon after this the blacks who brought me on board went off, and left me abandoned to despair. I now saw myself deprived of all chance of returning to my native country, or even the least glimpse of hope of gaining the shore, which I now considered as friendly; and I even wished for my former slav-ery in preference to my present situation, which was filled with horrors of every kind, still heightened by my ignorance of what I was to undergo. I was not long suffered to indulge my grief; I was soon put down under the decks, and there I received such a salutation in my nostrils I had never experienced in my life: so that with the loathsomness of the stench, and crying together, I became so sick and low that I was not able to eat, nor had I the least desire to taste any thing. I now wished the last friend, death, to relieve me; but soon, to my grief, two of the white men offered me eatables; and, on my refusing to eat, one of them held me fast by the hands, and laid me across, I think the windlass, and tied my feet, while the other flogged me severely. I had never experienced any thing of this kind before: and although not being used to the water, I naturally feared that element the first time I saw it, yet nevertheless, could I have got over the nettings, I would have jumped over the side, but I could not; and, besides, the crew used to watch us very closely who were not chained down to the decks, lest we should leap into the water: and I have seen some of these poor African prisoners most severely cut for attempting to do so, and hourly whipped for not eating. This indeed was often the case with myself. In a little time after, amongst the poor chained men, I found some of my own nation, which in a small degree gave ease to my mind. I inquired of these what was to be done with us? They gave me to understand we were to be car-ried to these white people's country to work for them. I then was a little revived, and though, if it were no worse than working, my situation was not so desperate: but still I feared I should be put to death, the white people looked and acted, as I thought, in so savage a manner; for I had never seen among any people such instances of brutal cruelty. ...

At last, when the ship we were in, had got in all her cargo, they made ready with many fearful noises, and we were all put under deck, so that we could not see how they managed the vessel. But this disappointment was the least of my sorrow. The stench of the hold while we were on the coast was so intolerably loathsome, that it was dangerous to remain there for any time, and some of us had been permitted to stay on the deck for the fresh air; but now that the whole ship's cargo were confined together, it became absolutely pestilential. The closeness of the place, and the heat of the climate, added to the number in the ship, which was so crowded that each had scarcely room to turn himself, almost suffocated us. This produced copious peripirations, so that the air soon became unfit for respiration, from a variety of loathsome smells, and brought on a sickness among the slaves, of which many died, this falling victims to the improvident avarice, as I may call it, of their purchasers. This wretched situation was again aggravated by the galling of the chains, now become insupportable, and the filth of the necessary tubs, into which the children often fell, and were almost suffocated. The shrieks of the women, and the groans of the dying, rendered the whole scene of horror almost inconceivable. Happily perhaps for myself I was soon reduced so low here that it was thought necessary to keep me almost always on deck; and from my extreme youth I was not put in fetters. In this situation I expected every hour to share the fate of my companions, some of whom were already daily brought upon deck at the point of death, which I began to hope would soon put an end to my miseries. Often did I think many of the inhabitants of the deep much more happy than myself, I envied them the freedom they enjoyed, and as often wished I could change my condition for theirs. Every circumstance I met with served only to render my state more painful, and heightened my apprehensions, and my opinion of the cruelty of the whites. One day they had taken a number fishes; and when they had killed and satisfied themselves with as many as they thought fit, to our astonishment who were on the deck, rather than give any of them to us to eat, as we expected, they tossed the remaining fish into the sea again, although we begged and prayed for some as well as we could, but in vain; and some of my countrymen, being pressed by hunger, took an opportunity, when they thought no one saw them, of trying to get a little privately; but they were discovered, and the attempt procured them some very severe floggings. One day, when we had a smooth sea and moderate wind, two of my wearied countrymen who were chained together (I was near them at the time), preferring death to such a life of misery, somehow made through the nettings and jumped into the sea: immediately another quite dejected fellow, who on account of his illness, was suffered to be out of irons, also followed their example; and I believe many more would very soon have done the same if they had not been prevented by the ship's crew who were instantly alarmed. Those of us that were the most active were in a moment put down under the deck, and there was such a noise and confusion amongst the people of the ship as I never heard before, to stop her, and get the boat out to go after the slaves. However two of the wretches were drowned, but they got the other, and afterwards flogged him unmercifully for thus attempting to prefer death to slavery. ...

2

The Birth of African America:
FROM RELIGION TO REVOLUTION

'A MULLATO MAN, NAMED CRISPUS ATTUCKS ... KILLED INSTANTLY'
Samuel Adams

As the Revolutionary Era set in, northern blacks were no less moved than whites by the rhetoric of freedom and independence that typified the time's political discourse. The slave-labor system, after all, belonged to the British, and many blacks believed that the colonists' demands for liberty would ultimately extend to them as well. For this reason, free blacks participated in many of the skirmishes that flared up between British troops and colonists prior to the outbreak of war.

On the night of what would become known as the Boston Massacre, a mixed-race sailor and runaway slave by the name of Crispus Attucks was a primary combatant in the scuffle between dockworkers and troops. And when the scuffle turned into a riot, Attucks was the first to be shot and killed. He and the four men who were slain after him that night became the first martyrs of the American Revolution. In a campaign led by vocal Boston patriot Samuel Adams, pamphleteers depicted the British troops as murderous occupiers and dubbed the event a massacre. In this March 12, 1770, write up in the *Boston Gazette*, Adams describes the skirmish, which took place a little more than a week earlier, and Attucks's death. Two decades previously, an ad in the same newspaper offered a reward for Attucks's return to the planter from whose captivity he had escaped.

...On the Evening of Monday, being the 5th Current, several Soldiers of the 29th Regiment were seen parading the Streets with their drawn Cutlasses and Bayonets, abusing and wounding Numbers of the Inhabitants.

A few minutes after nine o'clock, four youths, named Edward Archbald, William Merchant, Francis Archbald, and John Leech, jun. came down Cornhill together, and separating at Doctor Loring's corner, the two former were passing the narrow alley leading to Murray's barrack, in which was a soldier brandishing a broad sword of an uncommon size against the walls, out of which he struck fire plentifully. A person of a mean countenance armed with a large cudgel bore him company. Edward Archbald admonished Mr. Merchant to take care of the sword, on which the soldier turned round and struck Archbald on the arm, then pushed at Merchant and pierced thro' his cloaths inside the arm close to the arm-pit and grazed the skin. Merchant then struck the soldier with a short stick he had, & the other Person ran to the barrack and bro't with him two soldiers, one armed with a pair of tongs the other with a shovel: he with the tongs pursued Archbald back thro' the alley, collar'd and laid him over the head with the tongs. The noise bro't people together, and John Hicks, a young lad, coming up, knock'd the soldier down, but let him get up again; and more lads gathering, drove them back to the barrack, where the boys stood some time as it were to keep them in. In less than a minute 10 or 12 of them came out with drawn cutlasses, clubs and bayonets, and set upon the unarmed boys and young folks, who stood them a little while, but finding the inequality of their equipment dispersed.—On hearing the noise, one Samuel Atwood, came up to see what was the matter, and entering the alley from dock-square, heard the latter part of the combat, and when the boys dispersed he met the 10 or 12 soldiers aforesaid rushing down the alley towards the square, and asked them if they intended to murder people? They answered Yes, by G-d, root and branch! With that one of them struck Mr. Atwood with a club, which was repeated by another, and being unarmed he turned to go off, and received a wound on the left shoulder which reached the bone and gave him much pain. Retreating a few steps, Mr. Atwood met two officers and said, Gentlemen, what is the matter? They answered, you'll see by and by. Immediately after, those heroes appeared in the square, asking where were the boogers? where were the cowards? But notwithstanding their fierceness to nakedmen, one of them advanced towards a youth who had a split of a raw stave in his hand, and said damn them here is one of them; but the young man seeing a person near him with a drawn sword and good cane ready to support him, held up his stave in defiance, and they quietly passed by him up the little alley by Mr. Silsby's to Kingstreet, where they attacked single and unarmed persons till they raised much clamor, and then turned down Cornhill street, insulting all they met in like manner, and pursuing some to their very doors. Thirty of forty persons, mostly lads, being by this means gathered in Kingstreet, Capt. Preston, with a party of men with charged bayonets, came from the main guard to the Commissioners house, the soldiers pushing their bayonets, crying, Make way! They took place by the custom house, and continuing to push to drive the people off,

pricked some in several places; on which they were clamorous, and it is said, threw snow-balls. On this, the Captain commanded them to fire, and more snow-balls coming, he said, Damn you, Fire, be the consequence what it will! One soldier then fired, and a townsman with a cudgel struck him over the hands with such force that he dropt his firelock; and rushing forward aimed a blow at the Captain's head, which graz'd his hat and fell pretty heavy upon his arm: However, the soldiers continued the fire, successively, till 7 or 8, or as some say 11 guns were discharged.

By this fatal maneuvre, three men were laid dead on the spot, and two more struggling for life; but what shewed a degree of cruelty unknown to British troops, at least since the house of Hanover has directed their operations, was an attempt to fire upon or push with their bayonets the persons who undertook to remove the slain and wounded!

Mr. Benjamin Leigh, now undertaker in the Delph Manufactory, came up, and after some conversation with Capt. Preston relative to his conduct in this affair, advised him to draw off his men, with which he complied.

The dead are Mr. Samuel Gray, killed on the spot, the ball entering his head and beating off a large portion of his skull.

A mulatto man, named Crispus Attucks, who was born in Framingham, but lately belonged to New Providence and was here in order to go for North Carolina, also killed instantly; two balls entering his breast, one of them in special goring the right lobe of the lungs, and a great part of the liver most horribly.

Mr. James Caldwell, mate of Capt. Morton's vessel, in like manner killed by two balls entering his back.

Mr. Samuel Maverick, a promising youth of 17 years of age, son of the widow Maverick, and an apprentice to Mr. Greenwood, Ivory-Turner, mortally wounded, a ball went through his belly, & was cut out at his back: He died the next morning.

——— 2.2 ———
'SUCH A RABBLE OF NEGROES, &C.'
John Adams

Prominent Boston lawyer John Adams, who would become the second United States president, took on the undesirable task of defending the British troops who shot Attucks and his compatriots. In an argument credited as one of legal history's finest, Adams successfully walked the line between damning the British troops' occupying presence and defending their actions enough to spare them the gallows. However, the core of Adams's argument was his assertion that the troops acted in understandable self-defense given the "mad behaviour" of Crispus Attucks and the mob he led. In his closing argument, Adams played to paranoid fears of free blacks, depicting Attucks as a beastly and terrifying "stout Mullatto" leading "a rabble of negroes, &c." It was the American legal system's first example of race baiting.

… The next witness that knows anything was James Bailey, he was Carrol, Montgomery and White, he saw some round the sentry, heaving pieces of ice, large and hard enough to hurt any man, as big as your fist: one question is whether the sentinel was attacked or not. If you want evidence of an attack upon him there is enough of it, here is a witness, an inhabitant of the town, surely no friend to the soldiers, for he was enraged against them at the Ropewalks; he says he saw twenty or thirty round the sentry, pelting with cakes of ice as big as one's fist; certainly cakes of ice of this size may kill a man, if they happen to hit some part of the head. So that here was an attack on the sentinel, the consequences of which he had reason to dread, and it was prudent in him to call for the main guard: he retreated as far as he could, he attempted to get into the Custom House, but could not; then he called to the guard, and he had a good right to call for their assistance; he did not know, he told the witness, what was the matter, but he was afraid there would be mischief by and by; and well he might, with so many shavers and geniuses round him capable of throwing such dangerous things. Bailey swears, Montgomery fired the first gun, and that he stood at the right, "the next man to me, I stood behind him, &c." This witness certainly is not prejudiced in favour of the soldiers, he swears he saw a man come up to Montgomery with a club, and knock him down before he fired, and that he not only fell himself, but his gun flew out of his hand, and as soon as he rose he took it up and fired. If he was knocked down on his station, had he not reason to think his life in danger, or did it not raise his passions and put him off his guard; so that it cannot be more than manslaughter?

When the multitude was shouting and huzzaing, and threatening life, the bells ringing, the mob whistling, screaming and rending like an Indian yell, the people from all quarters throwing every species of rubbish they could pick up in the street, and some who were quite on the other side of the street throwing clubs at the whole party, Montgomery in particular smote with a club and knocked down, and as soon as he could rise and take up his firelock, another club from afar struck his breast or shoulder, what could he do? Do you expect he should behave like a stoic philosopher lost in apathy? Patient as Epictatus while his master was breaking his legs with a cudgel?—It is impossible you should find him guilty of murder. You must suppose him divested of all human passions, if you don't think him at the least provoked, thrown off his guard, and into the *furor brevis*, by such treatment as this.

Bailey "saw the Mulatto seven or eight minutes before the firing, at the head of twenty or thirty sailors in Cornhill, and he had a large cordwood stick." So that this Attucks, by this testimony of Bailey compared with that of Andrew and some others, appears to have undertaken to be the hero of the night; and to lead this army with banners, to form them in the first place in Dock square, and march them up to King-street with their clubs; they passed through the main street up to the main guard, in order to make the attack. If this was not an unlawful assembly, there never was one in the world. Attucks with his myrmidons comes round Jackson's corner, and down to the party by the sentry-box; when the soldiers pushed the people off, this man with his party cried, do not be afraid of them, they dare not fire, kill them! kill them! knock them over!—and he tried to knock their brains out. It is plain the soldiers did not leave their station, but cried to the people, stand off: now to have this reinforcement coming down under the command of a stout Mulatto fellow, whose very looks was enough to terrify any person, what had not the soldiers then to fear? He had hardiness enough to fall in upon them, and with one hand took hold of a bayonet, and with the other knocked the man down: This was the behaviour of Attucks; to whose mad behaviour, in all probability, the dreadful carnage of that night is chiefly to be ascribed. And it is in this manner, this town has been often treated; a Carr from Ireland, and an Attucks from Framingham, happening to be here, shall sally out upon their thoughtless enterprises, at the head of such a rabble of negroes, &c. as they can collect together, and then there are not wanting persons to ascribe all their doings to the good people of the town.

2.3

A 'PEACEABLE AND LAWFUL' PETITION FOR FREEDOM
Slaves of the town of Thompson, Massachusetts

As the revolutionary spirit spread through the colonies, African Americans launched their first efforts to win rights—at this stage simply freedom—by invoking the American ethos of liberty and utilizing the channels of government designed to protect it. Groups of both free and bonded blacks began petitioning governors and state legislative bodies for their freedom, making appeals to the ideals put forth by the patriots. In 1773, four slaves in Thompson, Massachusetts, signed and distributed an open letter to the town's delegate to the state legislature. The letter asked that slaves be granted one day of freedom per week, so that they may earn wages and ultimately buy their freedom from their owners. The letter also states the slaves' intention to return to the coast of

Africa once freed—a reference that predates the turn-of-the-century colonization movement.

BOSTON, April 20th, 1773.
SIR,

The efforts made by the legislative of this province in their last session to free themselves from slavery, gave us, who are in that deplorable state, a high degree of satisfaction. We expect great things from men who have made such a noble stand against the designs of their *fellow*-men to enslave them. We cannot but wish and hope Sir, that you will have the same grand object, we mean civil and religious liberty, in view in your next session. The divine spirit of *freedom*, seems to fire every humane breast on this continent, except such as are bribed to assist in executing the execrable plan.

We are very sensible that it would be highly detrimental to our present masters, if we were allowed to demand all that of *right* belongs to us for past services; this we disclaim. Even the *Spaniards*, who have not those sublime ideas of freedom that English men have, are conscious that they have no right to all the services of their fellow-men, we mean the *Africans*, whom they have purchased with their money: therefore they allow them one day in a week to work for themselves, to enable them to earn money to purchase the residue of their time, which they have a right to demand in such portions as they are able to pay for (a due appraizment of their services being first made, which always stands at the purchase money.) We do not pretend to dictate to you Sir, or to the honorable Assembly, of which you are a member: We acknowledge our obligations to you for what you have already done, but as the people of this province seem to be actuated by the principles of equity and justice, we cannot but expect your house will again take our deplorable case into serious consideration, and give us that ample relief which, as men, we have a right to.

But since the wise and righteous governor of the universe, has permitted our fellow men to make us slaves, we bow in submission to him, and determine to behave in such a manner, as that we may have reason to expect the divine approbation of, and assistance in, our peaceable and lawful attempts to gain our freedom.

We are willing to submit to such regulations and laws, as may be made relative to us, until we leave the province, which we determine to do as soon as we can from our joynt labours procure money to transport ourselves to some part of the coast of *Africa*, where we propose a settlement. We are very desirous that you should have instructions relative to us, from your town, therefore we pray you to communicate this letter to them, and ask this favor for us.

In behalf of our fellow slaves in this province,
And by order of their Committee.
Peter Bestes,
Sambo Freeman,
Felix Holbrook,
Chester Joie.
For the Representative of the town of
Thompson.

———— 2.4 ————

THOUGHTS UPON SLAVERY
John Wesley

In addition to his quest to Christianize slaves in America, Methodist Church founder John Wesley was personally tireless in his crusade against slavery. His widely distributed 1774 treatise *Thoughts Upon Slavery* is one of history's most stinging critiques of the slave-labor system. In it, Wesley first debunks the idea that traders plucked slaves from destitute and savage lands. At length, he describes the geography, culture and people of the West African coast in glowing, if slightly romanticized, language. He then uses equally dramatic language to provide a damning description of the process by which traders capture, transport and ultimately sell Africans. Having set the stage, Wesley goes on to confront what he sees as the key points of the pro-slavery argument of the day. Setting aside theology, he confronts each on the grounds of logic. Wesley compellingly turns the lens from the Africans to the slaveholders, concluding that the actions of those who promote slave labor are simply inhuman.

... I would now inquire whether these things can be defended on the principles of even heathen honesty;—whether they can be reconciled (setting the Bible out of the question) with any degree of either justice or mercy.

2. The grand plea is, "They are authorized by law." But can law, human law, change the nature of things? Can it turn darkness into light, or evil into good? By no means. Notwithstanding ten thousand laws, right is right and wrong is wrong still; there must still remain an essential difference between justice and injustice, cruelty and mercy: so that still I ask, Who can reconcile this treatment of the Negroes, first and last, with either mercy or justice?

Where is the justice of inflicting the severest evils on those that have done us no wrong? of depriving those that never injured us, in word or deed, of every comfort of life? of tearing them from their native country, and depriving them of liberty itself,—to which an Angolan has the same natural right as an Englishman, and on which he sets as high a value? Yea, where is the justice of taking away the lives of innocent, inoffensive men? murdering thousands of them in their own land, by the hands of their own countrymen, many thousands year after year on shipboard, and then casting them like dung into the sea, and tens of thousands in that cruel slavery to which they are so unjustly reduced?

3. That slave-holding is utterly inconsistent with mercy is almost too plain to need a proof. Indeed, it is said, "That these negroes, being prisoners of war, our captains and factors buy them merely to save them from being put to death. And is not this mercy?" I answer, 1, Did Sir John Hawkins and many others seize upon men, women, and children, who were at peace in their own fields and houses, merely to save them from death? 2. Was it to save them from death that they knocked out the brains of those they could not bring away? 3. Who occasioned and fomented those wars wherein these poor creatures were taken prisoners? Was it not themselves? They know in their own con-

science it was, if they have any conscience left. But, 4, To bring the matter to a short issue, can they say before God that they never took a single voyage or bought a single negro from this motive? They cannot: they well know to get money, not to save lives, was the whole and sole spring of their motions.

4. But if this manner of procuring and treating negroes is not consistent either with mercy or justice, yet there is a plea for it which every man of business will acknowledge to be quite sufficient. Fifty years ago, one meeting an eminent statesman in the lobby of the House of Commons said, "You have been long talking about justice and equity: pray, which is this bill, equity or justice?" He answered, very short and plain, "It is necessary." Here also the slaveholder fixes his foot; here he rests the strength of his cause. "If it is not quite right, yet it must be so; there is an absolute necessity for it; it is necessary we should procure slaves, and when we have procured them it is necessary to use them with severity, considering their stupidity, stubbornness, and wickedness."

I answer, You stumble at the threshold. I deny that villainy is ever necessary. It is impossible that it should ever be necessary for any reasonable creature to violate all the laws of justice, mercy, and truth. No circumstances can make it necessary for a man to burst in sunder all the ties of humanity. It can never be necessary for a rational being to sink himself below a brute. A man can be under no necessity of degrading himself into a wolf. The absurdity of the supposition is so glaring that one would wonder any one can help seeing it.

5. This in general. But, to be more particular, I ask, first, what is necessary? and, secondly, to what end? It may be answered, "The whole method now used by the original purchasers of negroes is necessary to the furnishing our colonies yearly with a hundred thousand slaves." I grant this is necessary to that end. But how is that end necessary? How will you prove it necessary that one hundred, that one, of those slaves should be procured? "Why, it is necessary to my gaining a hundred thousand

pounds." Perhaps so, but how is this necessary? It is very possible you might be both a better and a happier man if you had not a quarter of it. I deny that your gaining one thousand is necessary either to your present or eternal happiness. "But, however, you must allow these slaves are necessary for the cultivation of our islands, inasmuch as white men are not able to labor in hot climates." I answer, first, it were better that all those islands should remain uncultivated forever, yea, it were more desirable that they were altogether sunk in the depth of the sea, than that they should be cultivated at so high a price as the violation of justice, mercy, and truth. But, secondly, the supposition on which you ground your argument is false; for white men, even Englishmen, are well able to labor in hot climates, provided they are temperate both in meat and drink, and that they inure themselves to it by degrees. I speak no more than I know by experience. It appears from the thermometer that the summer heat in Georgia is frequently equal to that in Barbadoes, yea, to that under the line; and yet I and my family, eight in number, did employ all our spare time there in felling of trees and clearing of ground,—as hard labor as any negro need be employed in. The German family, likewise, forty in number, were employed in all manner of labor; and this was so far from impairing our health, that we all continued perfectly well, while the idle ones all round about us were swept away as with a pestilence. It is not true, therefore, that white men are not able to labor, even in hot climates, full as well, as black. But, if they were not, it would be better that none should labor there, that the work should be left undone, than that myriads of innocent men should be murdered, and myriads more dragged into the basest slavery.

6. "But the furnishing us with slaves is necessary for the trade, and wealth, and glory of our nation." Here are several mistakes; for, first, wealth is not necessary to the glory of any nation, but wisdom, virtue, justice, mercy, generosity, public spirit, love of our country: these are necessary to the real glory of a nation,

but abundance of wealth is not. Men of understanding allow that the glory of England was full as high in Queen Elizabeth's time as it is now, although our riches and trade were then as much smaller as our virtue was greater. But, secondly, it is not clear that we should have either less money or trade (only less of that detestable trade of manstealing) if there was not a negro in all of our islands, or in all English America. It is demonstrable white men, inured to it by degrees, can work as well as them, and they would do it were negroes out of the way, and proper encouragement given them. However, thirdly, I come back to the same point: better no trade that trade procured by villainy; it is far better to have not wealth than to gain wealth at the expense of virtue. Better is honest poverty than all the riches bought by the tears, and sweat, and blood of our fellow-creatures.

7. "However this be, it is necessary when we have slaves to use them with severity." I pray, to what end is this usage necessary? "Why, to prevent their running away, and to keep them constantly to their labor, that they may not idle away their time, so miserably stupid is this race of men, yea, so stubborn and so wicked." Allowing them to be as stupid as you say, to whom is that stupidity owing? Without question it lies altogether at the door of their inhuman masters, who give them no means, no opportunity of improving their understanding, and, indeed, leave them no motive, either from hope or fear, to attempt any such thing. They were no way remarkable for stupidity while they remained in their own country. The inhabitants of Africa, where they have equal motives and equal means of improvement, are not inferior to the inhabitants of Europe; to some of them they are greatly superior. Impartially survey, in their own country, the natives of Benin and natives of Lapland. Compare (setting prejudice aside) the Samoeids and the Angolans; and on which side does the advantage lie in point of understanding? Certainly the African is in no respect inferior to the European. Their stupidity, therefore, in our plantations is not natural, otherwise than

it is the natural effect of their condition: consequently, it is not their fault, but yours; you must answer for it before God and man.

8. "But their stupidity is not the only reason of our treating them with severity, for it is hard to say which is the greatest, this, or their stubbornness and wickedness." It may be so; but do not these as well as the other lie at your door? Are not stubbornness, cunning, pilfering, and divers other vices, the natural, necessary fruits of slavery? Is not this an observation which has been made in every age and nation? And what means have you used to remove this stubbornness? Have you tried what mildness and gentleness would do? I knew one that did,—that had prudence and patience to make the expirement,—Mr. Hugh Bryan, who then lived on the borders of South Carolina. And what was the effect? Why, that all his negroes (and he had no small number of them) loved and reverenced him as a father, and cheerfully obeyed him out of love: yea, they were more afraid of a frown from him than of many blows from an overseer. And what pains have you taken, what method have you used, to reclaim them from their wickedness? Have you carefully taught them "that there is a God, a wise, powerful, merciful Being, the Creator and Governor of heaven and earth? that he has appointed a day wherein he will judge the world, will take an account of all our thoughts, words, and actions? That in that day he will reward every child of man according to his works"? That "then the righteous shall inherit the kingdom prepared for them from the foundation of the world, and the wicked shall be cast into everlasting fire, prepared for the devil and his angels"? If you have not done this, if you have taken no pains or thought about the matter, can you wonder at their wickedness? You first acted the villain in making them slaves, whether you stole or bought them. You kept them stupid and wicked by cutting them off from all opportunities of improving either in knowledge or virtue; and now you assign their want of wisdom and goodness as the reason for using them worse than brutes!

———— 2.5 ————

'THIS LAND WILL BECOME A FIELD OF BLOOD'
Thomas Rankin

John Wesley and George Whitefield's efforts to attract slaves to Methodism (see Chapter One) were successful in large part because the denomination's equalizing style of worship and message of divine justice resonated with African Americans. But another reason slaves gravitated to the new denomination was that it became home to many vocal anti-slavery preachers. While Wesley and other individual Methodists had long been outspoken in their personal objections to slavery, it wasn't until the Revolutionary War began that the denomination threw its growing weight behind the anti-slavery cause. Historian Betty Wood has credited Thomas Rankin, a circuit preacher in Virginia, with delivering the first anti-slavery sermon from a Methodist pulpit. In extracts from his journal below, he describes the interracial nature of the Methodist "camp meetings" of the time, as well as the 1775 meeting at which he delivered his sermon warning of the divine justice awaiting those who participate in the slave-labor system.

A. Tuesday, November 8, 1774

When I rose this morning my mind was oppressed, but I was enabled to look to Jesus. After an early breakfast we spent about two hours in the affairs of the circuits. At ten our general love-feast began. There were such a number of whites and blacks as never had attended on such an occasion before. After we had sung and prayed, the cloud burst from my mind, and the power of the Lord descended in such an extraordinary manner as I had never seen since my landing at Philadelphia. All the preachers were so overcome with the divine presence, that they could scarce address the people; but only in broken accents saying, "This is none other than the house of God, and the gate of heaven!" When any of the people stood up to declare the loving-kindness of God, they were so overwhelmed with the divine presence, that they were obliged to sit down, and let silence speak his praise. Near the close of our meeting I stood up, and called upon the poor people to look toward that part of the chapel where all the blacks were. I then said, "See the number of the black Africans who have stretched out their hands and hearts to God!" While I was addressing the people thus, it seemed as if the very house shook with the mighty power and glory of Sinai's God. Many of the people were so overcome, that they were ready to faint and die under his almighty hand. For about three hours the gale of the Spirit thus continued to breathe upon the dry bones; and they did live the life of glorious love! As for myself, I scarce knew whether I was in the body or not; and so it was with all my brethren. We did not know how to break up the meeting or part asunder. Surely the fruits of this season will remain to all eternity.

For some time past my mind has been much affected, and my spirit not a little pressed down, at the prospect of public affairs in this country. Matters look extremely gloomy; and what the end of these things will be, who can tell? This I am fully certain of, that, to all human appearance, this land will become a field of blood. My soul laments that so few seem to lay it to heart, or turn to the Hand who shakes his rod over them. Most appear to put their trust in man, and make flesh their arm; but, alas! their hearts do not cleave to the living God.

B. Thursday, July 20, 1775

I rode to the chapel at the forks of Gunpowder Falls, and preached to a numerous congregation. This being the day set apart for a general fast, by the Congress, throughout all the British provinces, all the serious part of the inhabitants paid a particular attention to the same. I endeavoured to open up, and enforce, the cause of all our misery. I told them that the sins of Great Britain and her colonies had long called aloud for vengeance; and in a peculiar manner, the dreadful sin of buying and selling the souls and bodies of the poor Africans, the sons and daughters of Ham. I felt but poorly when I began to preach, but the Lord was my strength, and enabled me to speak with power, and to meet the society afterwards. After the service was over, I rode to Mr. Gough's, at Perry Hall, He and his wife had, by the mercy of God, lately found a sense of the divine favour, and now cheerfully opened their house and hearts to receive the ministers and children of God. I spent a most agreeable evening with Mr. and Mrs. Gough, and the rest of the family. A numerous family of the servants were called in to prayer and exhortation; so that with them, and the rest of the house, we had a little congregation. The Lord was in the midst, and we praised him with joyful lips.

——— 2.6 ———

'THE EXECUTIONER WAS SAVINGLY CONVERTED TO GOD'

John Marrant

Young John Marrant was one of the countless African Americans who joined the Methodist Church as a result of George Whitefield and his fellow evangelists' outreach. In 1785, Marrant published a "conversion narrative" of his spiritual journey, which became one of the most popular works of the genre. Marrant was born free, and his father's death sent his family on a migratory path around the South during his childhood years. While living in Charleston, South Carolina, in his pre-teen years, and working as an indentured servant, he developed a love for music and mastered the French horn. One day, while running an errand, Marrant stumbled across a revival at which Whitefield was preaching. On a dare, he entered the meeting intending to dazzle the attendees with his horn. There, his conversion to evangelical Methodism began. In the following excerpt from his fantastic narrative, Marrant recounts the trials he faced in cementing his faith. When Marrant's family rejects and mocks his newfound spirituality, the young man strikes out into the wilderness where he faces challenges of Biblical proportions before being delivered to safety by God. Marrant leaves the wilderness with a Cherokee man he encounters, only to discover he has broken a law by entering the man's settlement. He faces certain execution until he successfully converts the Native Americans to Christianity.

Marrant went on to live in the Cherokee settlement for months. There he began his ministry to convert Native Americans, and later traveled among the area's nations for some time before returning to colonial South Carolina. Later, Marrant would serve in the British army during the Revolutionary War and, after its resolution, became a leader in Boston's free black community. Eventually, he followed the migration of black British Loyalists to Nova Scotia, Canada, where he established his most lasting ministry.

… Satan began to stir up my two sisters and brother, who were then at home with my mother; they called me every name but that which was good. The more they persecuted me, the stronger I grew in grace. At length my mother turned against me also, and the neighbours joined her, and there was not a friend to assist me, or that I could speak to; this made me earnest with God. In these circumstances, being the youngest but one of our family, and young in Christian experience, I was tempted so far as to threaten my life; but reading my Bible one day, and finding that if I did destroy myself I could not come where God was, I betook myself to the fields, and some days staid out from morning to night to avoid the persecutors. I staid one time two days without any food, but seemed to have clearer views into the spiritual things of God. Not long after this I was sharply tried, and reasoned the matter within myself, whether I should turn to my old courses of sin and vice, or serve and cleave to the Lord; after prayer to God, I was fully persuaded in my mind that if I turned to my old ways I should perish eternally. Upon this I went home, and finding them all as hardened, or worse than before, and everybody saying I was crazy; but a little sister I had, about nine years of age, used to cry when she saw them persecute me, and continuing so about five weeks and three days, I thought it was better for me to die than to live among such people. I rose one morning very early, to get a little quietness and retirement. I went into the woods, and staid till eight o'clock in the morning; upon my return I found them all at breakfast; I passed by them, and went upstairs without any interruption; I went upon my knees to the Lord, and returned him thanks; then I took up a small pocket Bible and one of Dr. Watts's hymnbooks, and passing by them went out without one word spoken by any of us. After spending some time in the fields I was persuaded to go from home altogether. Accordingly I went over the fence, about half a mile from our house, which divided the inhabited and cultivated parts of the country from the wilderness. I continued travelling in the desert all day without the least inclination of returning back. About evening I began to be surrounded with wolves; I took refuge from them on a tree, and remained there all night. About eight o'clock next morning I descended from the tree, and returned God thanks for the mercies of the night. I went on all this day without anything to eat or drink. The third day, taking my Bible out of my pocket, I read and walked for some time, and then being wearied and almost spent I sat down, and after resting awhile I rose to go forward; but had not gone above a hundred yards when something tripped me up, and I fell down; I prayed to the Lord upon the ground that he would command the wild beasts to devour me, that I might be with him in glory. I made this request to God the third and part of the fourth day. The fourth day in the morning, descending from my usual lodging, a tree, and having nothing all this time to eat, and but a little water to drink, I was so feeble that I tumbled half way down the tree, not being able to support myself, and lay upon my back on the ground an hour and a half, praying and crying; after which getting a little strength, and trying to stand upright to walk, I found myself not able; then I went upon my hands and knees, and so crawled till I reached a tree that was tumbled down, in order to get across it, and there I prayed with my body leaning upon it above an hour, that the Lord would take me to himself. Such nearness to God I then enjoyed, that I willingly resigned myself into his hands. After some time I thought I was strengthened,

so I got across the tree without my feet or hands touching the ground; but struggling I fell over on the other side, and then thought the Lord will now answer my prayer, and take me home. But the time was not come. After laying there a little, I rose, and looking about, saw at some distance bunches of grass, called deer-grass; I felt a strong desire to get at it; though I rose, yet it was only on my hands and knees, being so feeble, and in this manner I reached the grass. I was three quarters of an hour going in this form twenty yards. When I reached it I was unable to pull it up, so I bit it off like a horse, and prayed the Lord to bless it to me, and I thought it the best meal I ever had in my life, and I think so still, it was so sweet. … I rose from my knees and walked on, singing hymns of praise to God, about five o'clock in the afternoon, and about 55 miles from home, right through the wilderness. As I was going on, and musing upon the goodness of the Lord, an Indian hunter, who stood some distance, saw me; he hid himself behind a tree; but as I passed along he bolted out, and put his hands on my breast, which surprised me a few moments. He then asked me where I was going? I answered I did not know, but where the Lord was pleased to guide me. Having heard me praising God before I came up to him, he enquired who I was talking to? I told him I was talking to my Lord Jesus; he seemed surprised, and asked me where he was? for he did not see him there. I told him he could not be seen with bodily eyes. After a little more talk, he insisted upon taking me home; but I refused, and added, that I would die rather than return home. He then asked me if I knew how far I was from home? I answered, I did not know. You are 55 miles and a half, says he, from home. He farther asked me how I did to live? I said I was supported by the Lord. He asked me how I slept? I answered, the Lord provided me with a bed every night; he further enquired what preserved me from being devoured by the wild beasts? I replied, the Lord Jesus Christ kept me from them. He stood astonished, and said, you say the Lord Jesus Christ do this, and do that, and do every thing for you, he must be a very fine man, where is he? I replied, he is here present. To this he made me no answer, only said, I know you, and your mother and sister, and upon a little further conversation I found he did know them, having been used in winter to sell skins in our town. This alarmed me, and I wept for fear he would take me home by force; but when he saw me so affected, he said he would not take me home if I would go with him. I objected against that, for fear he would rob me of my comfort and communion with God: But at last, being much pressed, I consented to go. ...

By constant conversation with the hunter, I acquired a fuller knowledge of the Indian tongue: This, together with the sweet communion I enjoyed with God, I have considered as a preparation for the great trial I was soon after to pass through.

The hunting season being now at an end, we left the woods, and directed our course towards a large Indian town, belonging to the Cherokee nation; and having reached it, I said to the hunter, they will not suffer me to enter in. He replied, as I was with him, nobody would interrupt me.

There was an Indian fortification all round the town, and a guard placed at each entrance. The hunter passed one of these without molestation, but I was stopped by the guard and examined. They asked me where I came from, and what was my business there? My companion of the woods attempted to speak for me, but was not permitted; he was taken away, and I saw him no more. I was now surrounded by about 50 men, and carried to one of their chiefs to be examined by him. When I came before him, he asked me what was my business there? I told him I came there with a hunter, whom I met with in the woods. He replied, "Did I not know that whoever came there without giving a better account of themselves than I did, was to be put to death?" I said I did not know it. Observing that I answered him so readily in his own language, he asked me where I learnt it? To this I returned no answer, but burst out into a flood of tears, and

calling upon my Lord Jesus. At this he stood astonished, and expressed a concern for me, and said I was young. He asked me who my Lord Jesus was? To this I gave him no answer, but continued praying and weeping. Addressing himself to the officer who stood by him, he said he was sorry; but it was the law, and it must not be broken. I was then ordered to be taken away, and put into a place of confinement. They led me from their court into a low dark place, and thrust me into it, very dreary and dismal; they made fast the door, and set a watch. The judge sent for the executioner, and gave him his warrant for my execution in the afternoon of the next day. The executioner came, and gave me notice of it, which made me very happy, as the near prospect of death made me hope for a speedy deliverance from the body. And truly this dungeon became my chapel, for the Lord Jesus did not leave me in this great trouble, but was very present, so that I continued blessing him, and singing his praises all night without ceasing. The watch hearing the noise, informed the executioner that somebody had been in the dungeon with me all night; upon which he came in to see and examine, with a great torch lighted in his hand, who it was I had with me; but finding nobody, he turned round, and asked me who it was? I told him it was the Lord Jesus Christ; but he made no answer, turned away, went out, and locked the door. At the hour appointed for my execution I was taken out, and led to the destined spot, amidst a vast number of people. I praised the Lord all the way we went, and when we arrived at the place I understood the kind of death I was to suffer, yet, blessed be God, none of those things moved me. The executioner shewed me a basket of turpentine-wood, stuck full of small pieces, like skewers; he told me I was to be stripped naked, and laid down in the basket, and these sharp pegs were to be stuck into me, and then set on fire, and when they had burnt to my body, I was to be turned on the other side, and served in the same manner, and then to be taken by four men and thrown into the flame, which was to finish the execution. I burst into tears, and asked what I had done to deserve so cruel a death! To this he gave me no answer. I cried out, Lord, if it be thy will that it should be so, thy will be done: I then asked the executioner to let me go to prayer; he asked me to whom? I answered, to the Lord my God; he seemed surprised, and asked me where he was? I told him he was present; upon which he gave me leave. I desired them all to do as I did, so I fell down upon my knees, and mentioned to the Lord his delivering of the three children in the fiery furnace, and of Daniel in the lion's den, and had close communion with God. I prayed in English a considerable time, and about the middle of my prayer, the Lord impressed a strong desire upon my mind to turn into their language, and pray in their tongue. I did so, and with remarkable liberty, which wonderfully affected the people. One circumstance was very singular, and strikingly displays the power and grace of God. I believe the executioner was savingly converted to God. He rose from his knees, and embraced me round the middle, and was unable to speak for about five minutes; the first words he expressed, when he had utterance, were, "No man shall hurt thee till thou hast been to the king."

——— 2.7 ———
'ROLL, JORDAN, ROLL'
Revival songs

The songs that rang through the Methodists' revivals, called "camp meetings," were the first African American spirituals, and the outgrowth of the early rice beating songs of South Carolina and Georgia. Music historians have noted that many of the tunes, which doubled as work songs, also served as a sort of harmonic Morse Code. Slaves plotting escape would designate a particular song as a signal or embed messages in free verses, allowing them to shape and carry out their plans while under the ever-present eye of the overseer. The songs below are two common ones heard at revival meetings and on the plantation.

A. Roll, Jordan, Roll

My brother sittin' on the tree of life,
An' he heard when Jordan roll

Roll, Jordan,
Roll, Jordan,
Roll, Jordan, Roll

[chorus]

O march the angel, march
O march the angel, march

O my soul, arise in heaven, Lord,
For to heard when Jordan roll

Little children, learn to fear the Lord,
And let your days be long;

[chorus]

O let no false nor spiteful word
Be found upon your tongue;

[chorus]

B. Blow Your Trumpet, Gabriel

The tallest tree in paradise
The Christian call the tree of life;

And I hope that trumpet might blow
me home to the new Jerusalem.
Blow your trumpet, Gabriel,
Blow louder, louder
And I hope that trumpet might blow
me home to the new Jerusalem

[chorus]

Paul and Silas, bound in jail,
Sing God's praise both night and day;

[chorus]

——— 2.8 ———

THE BRITISH OFFER FREEDOM FOR SERVICE
Lord Dunmore

When the Revolutionary War finally erupted, blacks throughout the colonies supported and fought for both the British forces and the rebels—whichever side they judged would most likely offer them freedom. At the war's outset, Gen. George Washington was reluctant to allow slaves to join his forces. The British, on the other hand—following the example set by Spanish Florida during its conflict with Britain's southern colonies (see Chapter One)—eagerly accepted and recruited slaves, hoping to not only bolster their forces but also to destabilize the colonies.

The British Governor of Virginia, Lord Dunmore, was the first to recruit slaves with his now infamous November 7, 1775, proclamation that, along with declaring martial law, offered freedom to any escaped male slave who volunteered to fight in the British forces. The proclamation angered and frightened the southern colonists (who, in some places, were now an uncomfortable minority to the slave population) inflaming their anxieties about the threat of massive slave insurrections. It also inspired thousands of slaves to flee and join the British war effort.

By His Excellency the Right Honorable JOHN Earl of DUNMORE, His MAJESTY'S Lieutenant and Governor General of the Colony and Dominion of VIRGINIA, and Vice Admiral of the fame.

A PROCLAMATION.

As I have ever entertained Hopes that an Accommodation might have taken Place between GREAT-BRITAIN and this colony, without being compelled by my Duty to this most disagreeable but now absolutely necessary Step, rendered so by a Body of armed Men unlawfully assembled, bring on His MAJESTY'S Tenders, and the formation of an Army, and that Army now on their March to attack His MAJESTY'S troops and destroy the well disposed Subjects of this Colony. To defeat such unreasonable Purposes, and that all such Traitors, and their Abetters, may be brought to Justice, and that the Peace, and good Order of this Colony may be again restored, which the ordinary Course of the Civil Law is unable to effect; I have thought fit to issue this my Proclamation, hereby declaring, that until the aforesaid good Purposes can be obtained, I do in Virtue of the Power and Authority to ME given, by His MAJESTY, determine to execute Martial Law, and cause the same to be executed throughout this Colony: and to the end that Peace and good Order may the sooner be effected, I do require every Person capable of bearing Arms, to resort to His MAJESTY'S STANDARD, or be looked upon as Traitors to His MAJESTY'S Crown and Government, and thereby become liable to the Penalty the Law inflicts upon such Offences; such as forfeiture of Life, confiscation of Lands, &c. &c. And I do hereby further declare all indentured Servants, Negroes, or others, (appertaining to Rebels,) free that are able and willing to bear Arms, they joining His MAJESTY'S Troops as soon as may be, for the more speedily reducing this Colony to a proper Sense of their Duty, to His MAJESTY'S Leige Subjects, to retain their Quitrents, or any other Taxes due or that may become due, in their own Custody, till such Time as Peace may be again restored to this at present most unhappy Country, or demanded of them for their former salutary Purposes, by Officers properly authorised to receive the same.

GIVEN under my Hand on board the ship WILLIAM, off NORPOLE, the 7th Day of NOVEMBER, in the SIXTEENTH Year of His MAJESTY'S Reign.

DUNMORE.

(GOD save the KING.)

——— 2.9 ———

JOURNAL OF A BLACK LOYALIST SOLDIER
Boston King

Boston King was among those slaves who escaped to join the British forces following Lord Dunmore's proclamation. King, who had been a slave in South Carolina, was also among thousands of slaves the British interred in New York in the late stages of the war, and, eventually, settled in Nova Scotia at its end. The Americans tried to reclaim all of the slaves who had fled to join British forces, but Britain refused to return those who had joined them before the signing of the peace accords. King was one of those people, and he eventually traveled with other Loyalist former slaves to Sierra Leone. King, who became a Methodist minister, later published his journal describing his life experiences in the *Methodist Magazine*. In the excerpts below, he describes his escape from slavery and his harrowing travels with the British regiments he joined.

… Having obtained leave one day to see my parents, who lived about 12 miles off, and it being late before I could go, I was obliged to borrow one of Mr. Waters's horses; but a servant of my master's, took the horse from me to go a little journey, and stayed two or three days longer than he ought. This involved me in the greatest perplexity, and I expected the severest punishment, because the gentleman to whom the horse belonged was a very bad man, and knew not how to shew mercy. To escape his cruelty, I determined to go to Charles-Town, and throw myself into the hands of the English. They received me readily, and I began to feel the happiness of liberty, of which I knew nothing before, altho' I was much grieved at first, to be obliged to leave my friends, and reside among strangers. In this situation I was seized with the small-pox, and suffered great hardships; for all the Blacks affected with that disease, were ordered to be carried a mile from the camp, lest the soldiers should be infected, and disabled from marching. This was a grievous circumstance to me and many others. We lay sometimes a whole day without any thing to eat or drink; but Providence sent a man, who belonged to the York volunteers whom I was acquainted with, to my relief. He brought me such things as I stood in the need of; and by the blessing of the Lord I began to recover.

By this time, the English left the place; but as I was unable to march with the army, I expected to be taken by the enemy. However when they came, and understood that we were ill of the small-pox, they precipitately left us

for fear of the infection. Two days after, the waggons were sent to convey us to the English Army and we were put into a little cottage, (being 25 in number) about a quarter of a mile from the Hospital.

Being recovered, I marched with the army to Chamblem. When we came to the head-quarters, our regiment was 35 miles off. I stayed at the head-quarters three weeks, during which time our regiment had an engagement with the Americans, and the man who relieved me when I was ill of the small-pox, was wounded in the battle, and brought to the hospital. As soon as I heard of his misfortune, I went to see him, and tarried with him in the hospital six weeks, till he recovered; rejoicing that it was in my power to return him the kindness he had shewed me. From thence I went to a place about 35 miles off, where we stayed two months: at the expiration of which, an express came to the Colonel to decamp in fifteen minutes. When these orders arrived I was at a distance from the camp, catching some fish for the captain I waited upon; upon returning to the camp, to my great astonishment, I found all the English were gone, and had left only a few militia. I felt my mind greatly alarmed, but Captain Lewes, who commanded the militia, said, "You need not be uneasy, for you will see your regiment before 7 o'clock to-night." This satisfied me for the present, and in two hours we set off. As we were on the march, the Captain asked, "How will you like me to be your master?" I answered, that I was Captain Grey's servant. "Yes," said he; "but I expect they are all taken prisoners before now; and I have been long enough in the English service, and am determined to leave them." These words roused my indignation, and I spoke some sharp things to him. But he calmly replied, "If you do not behave well, I will put you in irons, and give you a dozen stripes every morning." I now perceived that my case was desperate, and that I had nothing to trust to but to wait the first opportunity for making my escape. The next morning, I was sent with a little boy over the river to an island to fetch the Captain some horses. When we came to the Island we found about fifty of the English horses, that Captain Lewes had stolen from them at different times while they were at Rockmount. Upon our return to the Captain with the horses we were sent for, he immediately set off by himself. I stayed till about 10 o'clock, and then resolved to go to the English army. After travelling 24 miles, I came to a farmer's house, where I tarried all night, and was well used. Early in the morning I continued my journey till I came to the ferry, and found all the boats were on the other side of the river: After anxiously waiting some hours, Major Dial crossed the river, and asked me many questions concerning the regiment to which I belonged. I gave him satisfactory answers, and he ordered the boat to put me over. Being arrived at the head-quarters, I informed my Captain that Mr. Lewes had deserted. I also told him of the horses which Lewes had conveyed to the Island. Three weeks after, our Light-horse went to the Island and burnt his house; they likewise brought back forty of the horses, but he escaped. I tarried with Captain Grey about a year, and then left him, and came to Nelson's-ferry. Here I entered into the service of the commanding officer of that place. But our situation was very precarious, and we expected to be made prisoners every day; for the Americans had 1600 men, not far off, whereas our whole number amounted only to 250: But there were 1200 English about 30 miles off; only we knew not how to inform them of our danger, as the Americans were in possession of the country. Our commander at length determined to send me with a letter, promising me great rewards, if I was successful in the business. I refused going on horse-back, and set off on foot about 3 o'clock in the afternoon; I expected every moment to fall in with the enemy, whom I well knew would shew me no mercy. I went on without interruption, till I got within six miles of my journey's end, and then was alarmed with a great noise a little before me. But I stepped out of the road, and fell flat upon my

face till they were gone by. I then arose, and praised the Name of the Lord for his great mercy, and again pursued my journey, till I came to Mums-corner tavern. I knocked at the door, but they blew out the candle. I knocked again, and intreated the master to open the door. At last he came with a frightful countenance, and said, "I thought it was the Americans; for they were here about an hour ago, and I thought they were returned again." I asked, How many were there? he answered, "about one hundred." I desired him to saddle his horse for me, which he did, and went with me himself. When we had gone about two miles, we were stopped by the picket-guard, till the Captain came out with 30 men: As soon as he knew that I had brought an express from Nelson's-ferry, he received me with great kindness, and expressed his approbation of my courage and conduct in this dangerous business. Next morning, Colonel Small gave me three shillings, and my fine promises, which were all that I ever received for this service from him. However he sent 600 men to relieve the troops at Nelson's-ferry.

―――――― 2.10 ――――――

SALEM POOR AT BUNKER HILL
Colonel William Prescott

Historians have debated just how many African Americans, slave or free, fought for the British versus the rebel Continental Army. The reluctance of George Washington and individual state militias to enlist blacks deterred their participation on the American side at first. But some states, such as Massachusetts and Rhode Island, embraced black soldiers and even raised all black regiments. Following Lord Dunmore's proclamation, Washington tacitly endorsed the recruitment of African Americans as well. In one of the war's earliest and bloodiest battles, the 1775 Battle of Bunker Hill, several black soldiers served and have been counted as heroes. One of those men was 28-year-old Salem Poor, a freeman and volunteer. Poor was credited with valor in the battle, so much so that the officers who led the rebel charge submitted a petition to the General Court of Massachusetts requesting that the Continental Congress honor him with a reward.

The Subscribers begg leave to Report to your Honorable House, (which Wee do in justice to the Caracter of so Brave a Man) that under Our Own observation, We declare that a Negro Man Called Salem Poor of Col. Frye's Regiment—Capt. Ames. Company—in the late Battle of Charlestown, behaved like an Experienced officer, as Well as an Excellent Soldier, to Set forth Particulars of his conduct Would be Tedious. Wee would Only begg leave to Say in the Person of this said Negro Centers a Brave & gallant Soldier. The Reward due to so great and Distinguished a Caracter, Wee Submit to the Congress.

Cambridge, Dec 5th 1775

——— 2.11 ———

THE BATTLE OF GROTON HEIGHTS

An unnamed source

On September 6, 1781, the British sent a force under the command of Benedict Arnold to take the port of New London in Connecticut. The bloody Battle of Groton Heights ensued, and Arnold's troops ultimately prevailed. Two black soldiers emerged as heroes in the battle, in which the American forces were decimated. Their role went largely undocumented until the middle 1800s when African-American historian William Nell resurrected them in his seminal study on black Patriot fighters. Nell quotes an account given to him by a black man who said he had, in turn, received the account from "two veterans who were present at the battle."

September 6th, 1781, New London was taken by the British, under the command of that traitor, Arnold. The small band composing the garrison retreated to the fort opposite, in the town of Groton, and there resolved either to gain a victory or die for their country. The latter pledge was faithfully redeemed, and by none more gallantly than the two colored men; and, if the survivors of that day's carnage tell truly, they fought like tigers, and were butchered after the gates were burst open. One of these men was the brother of my grandmother, by the name of Lambert, but called Lambo,— since chiselled on the marble monument by the *American classic appellation of 'Sambo.'* The name of the other man was Jordan Freeman. Lambert was living with a gentleman in Groton, by the name of Latham, so, of course, he was called Lambert Latham. Mr. Latham and Lambert, on the day of the massacre, were at work in the field, at a distance from the house. On hearing the alarm upon the approach of the enemy, Mr. Latham started for home, leaving Lambert to drive the team up to the house. On arriving at the house, Lambert was told that Mr. Latham had gone up to the fort. Lambert took the cattle from the team, and, making all secure, started for the point of defence, where he arrived before the British began the attack. And here let me say, my dear friend, that there was not any negro pew in that fort, although there was some praying as well as fighting. But there they stood, side by side, and shoulder to shoulder, and, after a few rounds of firing, each man's visage was so blackened by the smoke of powder, that Lambert and Jordan had but little to boast of on the score of color.

The assault on the part of the British was a deadly one, and manfully resisted by the Americans, even to the clubbing of their muskets after their ammunition was expended; but finally, the little garrison was overcome, and, on the entrance of the enemy, the British officer inquired, "Who commands this fort?" The gallant Ledyard replied, "I once did; you do now,"—at the same time handing his sword, which was immediately run through his body to the hilt by the officer. This was the commencement of an unparalleled slaughter. Lambert, being near Col. Ledyard when he was slain, retaliated upon the officer by thrusting his bayonet through his body. Lambert, in return, received from the enemy *thirty-three* bayonet wounds, and thus fell, nobly avenging the death of his commander.

——— 2.12 ———
'A POEM OF THE INHUMAN TRAGEDY' AT LEXINGTON
Lemuel Haynes

Lemuel Haynes, a mixed-race man, grew up as an indentured servant to a Congregationalist family in New England. Launching a course of self-education at an early age, driven by religion and scripture, Haynes began delivering sermons at the church of the family to whom he was indentured while still a teenager. When his indenture ended in 1774, the 21-year-old, enamored with the ideology of the American Revolution, volunteered to serve in the Continental Army. While serving in the army, he wrote and published a poem memorializing the Battle of Lexington, which received widespread acclaim. He published countless sermons and essays throughout his life as a leading African-American religious figure and orator.

1
Some Seraph now my Breast inspire
whilst my Urania sings
while She would try her solemn Lyre
Upon poetic Strings.

2
Some gloomy Vale or gloomy Scat
where Sable veils the sky
Become that Tongue that wd repeat
The dreadfull Tragedy

3
The Nineteenth Day of April last
We ever shall retain
As monumental of the past
most bloody shocking Scene

4
Then Tyrants fill'd wth horrid Rage
A fatal Journey went
& Unmolested. to engage
And slay the innocent

5
Then did we see old Bonner rise
And, borrowing Spite from Hell
They stride along with magic Eyes
where Sons of Freedom dwell

6
At Lexington they did appear
Array'd in hostile Form

And tho our Friends were peacefull there
Yet on them fell the Storm

7
Eight most unhappy Victims fell
Into the Arms of Death
unpitied by those Tribes of Hell
who cursd them wth their Breath

8
The Savage Band still march along
For Concord they were bound
while Oaths & Curses from their Tongue
Accent with hellish Sound

9
To prosecute their full Desire
At Concord they unite
Two Sons of Freedom there expire
By their tyrannic Spite

10
Thus did our Friends endure their Rage
without a murm'ring Word
Till die they must or else engage
and join with one Accord

11
Such Pity did their Breath inspire
That long they bore the Rod
And with Reluctance they conspire
to shed the human Blood

12
But Pity could no longer sway
Tho' 't is a pow'rfull Band
For Liberty now bleeding lay
And call'd them to withstand

13
The Awfull Conflict now begun
To rage with furious Pride
And Blood in great Effusion run
From many a wounded Side

14
For Liberty, each Freeman Strives
As its a Gift of God
And for it willing yield their Lives
And Seal it with their Blood

15
Thrice happy they who thus resign
Into the peacefull Grave
Much better there, in Death Confin'd
Than a Surviving Slave

16

This Motto may adorn their Tombs,
(Let tyrants come and view)
"We rather seek these silent Rooms
"Than live as Slaves to You"

17

Now let us view our Foes awhile
who thus for blood did thirst
See: stately Buildings fall a Spoil
To their unstoick Lust

18

Many whom Sickness did compel
To seek some Safe Retreat
Were dragged from their sheltering Cell
And mangled in the Street

19

Nor were our aged Gransires free
From their vindictive Pow'r
On yonder Ground lo: there you see
Them weltering in their Gore

20

Mothers with helpless Infants strive
T' avoid the tragic Sight
All fearfull wether yet alive
Remain'd their Soul's delight

21

Such awefull Scenes have not had Vent
Since Phillip's War begun
Nay sure a Phillip would relent
And such vile Deeds would shun

22

But Stop and see the Pow'r of God
Who lifts his Banner high
Jehovah now extends his Rod
And makes our Foes to fly

23

Altho our Numbers were but few
And they a Num'rous Throng
Yet we their Armies do pursue
And drive their Hosts along

24

One Son of Freedom could annoy
A Thousand Tyrant Fiends
And their despotick Tribe destroy
And chace them to their Dens

25

Thus did the Sons of Brittain's King
Receive a sore Disgrace
Whilst Sons of Freedom join to sing
The vicery they Imbrace

26

Oh! Brittain how art thou become
Infamous in our Eye
Nearly allied to antient Rome
That Seat of Popery

27

Our Fathers, tho a feeble Band
Did leave their native Place
Exiled to a desert Land
This howling Wilderness

28

A Num'rous Train of savage Brood
Did then attack them round
But still they trusted in their God
Who did their Foes confound

29

Our Fathers Blood did freely flow
To buy our Freedom here
Nor will we let our freedom go
The Price was much too dear

30

Freedom & Life, O precious Sounds
yet Freedom does excell
and we will Need upon the ground
or keep our Freedom still

31

But oh! how can we draw the Sword
Against our native kin
Nature recoils at such a Word
And fain would quit the Scene

32

We feel compassion in our Hearts
That captivating Thing
Nor shall Compassion once depart
While Life retains her String

33

Oh England let thy Fury cease
At this convulsive Hour
Consult those Things that make for Peace
Nor foster haughty Power

34
Let Brittain's king call home his Band
of Soldiers armed to fight
To see a Tyrant in our Land
Is not a pleasing Sight
35
Allegiance to our King we own
And will due Homage pay
As does become his royal Throne
Yet in a legal Way
36
Oh Earth prepare for solemn Things
Behold an angry god
Beware to meet the King of Kings
Arm'd with an awefull Rod
37
Sin is the Cause of all our Woe
That sweet deluding ill
And till we let this darling go
There's greater Trouble still

——— 2.13 ———
POEMS ON
VARIOUS SUBJECTS
Phillis Wheatley

In 1773, a young slave named Phillis Wheatley published a collection of 38 poems under the title *Poems on Various Subjects, Religious and Moral*. Wheatley's groundbreaking collection was the first book published by an African American; she had published her first poem six years earlier, at the age of 14. Throughout her life, Wheatley's poetry invoked the themes of the Revolutionary Era, and often directly addressed an event or hero of the American Revolution—as was the case in her 1772 poem memorializing the Boston Massacre. Wheatley also regularly alluded to the injustice of the slave trade, if only indirectly, as she does in two of the poems presented here.

The Bostonian couple who owned Wheatley maintained influential ties in London, and they found a British publisher for *Poems*. Boston publishers had refused the book owing to doubts that a black woman could have actually authored it. The British publisher included in the book a foreword "To the PUBLIC," in which a panel of Boston's most prominent citizens attested to Wheatley's authorship.

A. To the PUBLIC.

As it has been repeatedly suggested to the Publisher, by Persons, who have seen the Manuscript, that Numbers would be ready to suspect they were not really the Writings of PHILLIS, he has procured the following Attestation, from the most respectable Characters in Boston, that none might have the least Ground for disputing their Original.

WE whose Names are under-written, do assure the World, that the POEMS specified in the following Page, were (as we verily believe) written by Phillis, a young Negro Girl, who was but a few Years since, brought an uncultivated Barbarian from Africa, and has ever since been, and now is, under the Disadvantage of serving as a Slave in a Family in this Town. She has been examined by some of the best Judges, and is thought qualified to write them.

B. "To the Right Honourable WILLIAM, Earl of Darthmouth, His Majesty's Principal Secretary of State for North America, &c."

HAIL, happy day, when, smiling like the morn,
Fair *Freedom* rose *New-England* to adorn:
The northern clime beneath her genial ray,
Darmouth, congratulates thy blissful sway:
Elate with hope her race no longer mourns,
Each soul expands, each grateful bosom burns,
While in thine hand with pleasure we behold
The silken reins, and *Freedom's* charms unfold.
Long lost to realms beneath the northern skies
She shines supreme, while hated *faction* dies:
Soon as appear'd the *Goddess* long desir'd,
Sick at the view, she languish'd and expir'd;
Thus from the splendors of the morning light
The owl in sadness seeks the caves of night.
No more, *America*, in mournful strain
Of wrongs, and grievance unredress'd complain,
No longer shalt thou dread the iron chain,
Which wanton *Tyranny* with lawless hand
Had made, and with it meant t' enslave the land.
Should you, my lord, while you peruse my song,
Wonder from whence my love of *Freedom*
sprung,

Whence flow these wishes for the common good,
By feeling hearts alone best understood,
I, young in life, by seeming cruel fate
Was snatch'd from *Afric's* fancy'd happy feat:
What pangs excruciating must molest,
What sorrows labour in my parent's breast?
Steel'd was that soul and by no misery mov'd
That from a father seiz'd his babe belov'd:
Such, such my case. And can I then but pray
Others may never feel tyrannic sway?
For favours past, great Sir, our thanks are due,
And thee we ask thy favours to renew,
Since in they pow'r, as in they will before,
To sooth the griefs, which thou did'st once deplore.
May heav'nly grace the sacred sanction give
To all they works, and thou for ever live
Not only on the wings of fleeting *Fame*,
Though praise immortal crowns the patriot's name,
But to conduct to heav'ns resulgent sane,
May fiery coursers sweep th' ethereal plain,
And bear thee upwards to that blest abode,
Where, like the prophet, thou shalt find thy God.

C. "On being brought from *Africa* to *America*."

'TWAS mercy brought me from my *Pagan* land,
Taught my benighted soul to understand
That there's a God, that there's a *Saviour* too:
Once I redemption neither sought nor knew,
Some view our sable race with scornful eye,
"Their colour is a diabolic die."
Remember, *Christians*, *Negroes*, black as *Cain*,
May be refin'd, and join th' angelic train.

D. "On the Death of the Rev. Dr. Sewell, 1769."

ERE yet the morn its lovely blushes spread,
See *Sewell* number'd with the happy dead.
Hail, holy man, arriv'd th' immortal shore,
Though we shall hear thy warning voice no more.
Come, let us all behold with wishful eyes
The saint ascending to his native skies;

From hence the prophet wing'd his rapt'rous way
To the blest mansions in eternal day.
Then begging for the Spirit of our God,
And panting eager for the same abode,
Come, let us all with the same vigour rise,
And take a prospect of the blissful skies;
While on our minds *Christ's* image is imprest,
And the dear Saviour glows in ev'ry breast.
Thrice happy saint! to find thy heav'n at last,
What compensation for the evils past!
Great God, incomprehensible, unknown
By sense, we bow at thine exalted throne.
O, while we beg thine excellence to feel,
They sacred Spirit to our hearts reveal,
And give us of that mercy to partake,
Which thou hast promis'd for the *Saviour's* sake!
"*Sewell* is dead." Swift-pinion'd *Fame* thus cry'd.
"Is *Sewell* dead," my trembling tongue reply'd,
O what a blessing in his flight deny'd!
How oft for us the holy prophet pray'd!
How oft to us the Word of Life convey'd!
By duty urg'd my mournful verse to close,
I for his tomb this epitaph compose.
"Lo, here a man, redeem'd by Jesus's blood,
"A sinner once, but now a saint with God;
"Behold ye rich, ye poor, ye fools, ye wife,
"Nor let his monument your heart surprise;
"Twill tell you what this holy man has done,
"Which gives him brighter lustre than the sun.
"Listen, ye happy, from your seats above.
"I speak sincerely, while I speak and love,
"He sought the paths of piety and truth,
"By these made happy from his early youth;
"In blooming years that grace divine he felt,
"Which rescues sinners from the chains of guilt.
"Mourn him, ye indigent, whom he has fed,
"And henceforth seek, like him, for living bread;
"Ev'n *Christ*, the bread descending from above,
"And ask an int'rest in his saving love.
"Mourn him, ye youth, to whom he oft has told
"God's gracious wonders from the times of old.
"I too have cause this mighty loss to mourn,
"For he my monitor will not return.
"O when shall we to his blest state arrive?
"When the same graces in our bosoms thrive."

—— 2.14 ——
'TO HIS EXCELLENCY GENERAL WASHINGTON'
Phillis Wheatley

Phillis Wheatley's support for the Patriot cause was perhaps most visible in a 1775 poem she wrote as a tribute to General George Washington. Wheatley sent the poem to Washington, who, after a year's delay, responded in a brief letter praising the piece as "striking proof of your poetical talents." Historian Matthew Mellon cites Washington's respectful praise in his reply to Wheatley's unsolicited correspondence as proof of the gradual erosion of his support for slavery (and of his increasing belief in the humanity of African Americans) during the course of the war.

A. Wheatley's letter and poem

Providence, October 26, 1775
Sir,

I have taken the freedom to address your Excellency in the enclosed poem, and entreat your acceptance, though I am not insensible of its inaccuracies. Your being appointed by the Grand Continental Congress to be Generalissimo of the armies of North America, together with the fame of your virtues, excite sensations not easy to suppress. Your generosity, therefore, I presume, will pardon the attempt. Wishing your Excellency all possible success in the great cause you are so generously engaged in. I am,

Your Excellency's most obedient humble servant,

Phillis Wheatley

To His Excellency General Washington

Celestial choir! entron'd in realms of light,
Columbia's scenes of glorious toils I write.
While freedom's cause her anxious breast alarms,
She flashes dreadful in resulgent arms.
See mother earth her offspring's fate bemoan,
And nations gaze at scenes before unknown!
See the bright beams of heaven's revolving light
Involved in sorrows and veil of night!

The goddess comes, she moves divinely fair,
Olive and laurel bind her golden hair:
Wherever shines this native of the skies,
Unnumber'd charms and recent rise.

Muse! bow propitious while my pen relates
How pour her armies through a thousand gates,
As when Eolus heaven's fair face deforms,
Enwrapp'd in tempest and a night of storms;
Astonish'd ocean feels the wild uproar,
The refluent surges beat the sounding shore;
Or thick as leaves in Autumn's golden
 reign,
Such, and so many, moves the warrior's train.
In bright array they seek the work of war,
Where high unfurl'd the ensign waves in the air.
Shall I to Washington their praise recite?
Enough thou know'st them in the fields of fight.
Thee, first in peace and honours,—we demand
The grace and glory of thy martial band.
Fam'd for thy valour, for thy virtues more,
Hear every tongue thy guardian aid implore!
One century scarce perform'd its destined round,
When Gallic powers Columbia's fury found;
And so may you, whoever dares disgrace
The land of freedom's heaven-defended race!
Fix'd are the eyes of nations on the scales,
For in their hopes Columbia's arm prevails.
Anon Britannia droops the pensive head,
While round increase the rising hills of dead,
Ah! cruel blindness to Columbia's state!
Lament they thirst of boundless power to late.

Proceed, great chief, with virtue on they side,
Thy ev'ry action let the goddess guide.
A crown, a mansion, and a throne that shine,
With gold unfading, WASHINGTON! be
 thine.

B. Washington's Response

February 28, 1776
Miss Phillis:—Your favor of the 26th of October did not reach my hands till the middle of December. Time enough, you will say, to have given an answer ere this. Granted. But a variety of important occurances, continually

interposing to distract the mind and withdraw the attention, I hope will apologize for the delay, and plead my excuse for the seeming, but not real neglect. I thank you most sincerely for your polite notice of me in the elegant lines you enclosed; and however undeserving I may be of such encomium and panegyric, the style and manner exhibit a striking proof of your poetical talents; in honor of which, and as a tribute justly due your genius, I might have incurred the imputation of vanity. This, and nothing else, determined me not to give it a place in the public prints.

If you ever come to Cambridge, or near headquarters, I shall be happy to see a person favored by the Muses, and to whom nature has been so liberal and beneficient in her dispensations. I am, with great respect, your obedient, humble servant.

——— 2.15 ———

AN ADDRESS TO MISS PHILLIS WHEATLY
Jupiter Hammon

When Jupiter Hammon published his second poem, he chose to honor Phillis Wheatley. Hammon's 1778 memorial was one of the first recognitions of Wheatley as the originator of African-American literature. As with his previous work (see Chapter 1), the liturgical poem is packed with Biblical references and reflects Hammon's deep spirituality.

I

O come you pious youth! Adore
    The wisdom of thy God,
In bringing thee from distant shore,
    To learn His holy word.
                Eccles. xii.

II

Thou mightst been left behind
    Amidst a dark abode;
God's tender mercy still combin'd,
    Thou hast the holy word.
              Psal. cxxxv, 2, 3.

III

Fair wisdom's ways are paths of peace,
    And they that walk therein,
Shall reap the joys that never cease,
    And Christ shall be their king.
         Psal. i. 1, 2; Prov. iii, 7.

IV

God's tender mercy brought thee here;
    Tost o'er the ranging main;
In Christian faith thou hast a share,
    Worth all the gold of Spain.
           Psal. ciii, 1, 3, 4.

V

While thousands tossed by the sea,
    And others settled down,
God's tender mercy set thee free,
    From dangers that come down.
                Death.

VI

That thou a pattern still might be,
    To youth of Boston town,
The blessed Jesus set thee free,
    From every sinful wound.
            2 Cor. v, 10.

VII

The blessed Jesus, who came down,
    Unvail'd his sacred face,
To cleanse the soul of every wound,
    And give repenting grace.
           Rom. v, 21.

VIII

That we poor sinners may obtain,
    The pardon of our sin;
Dear blessed Jesus now constrain,
    And bring us flocking in.
         Psal. xxxiv, 6, 7, 8.

IX

Come you, Phillis, now aspire,
    And seek the living God,
So step by step thou mayst go higher,
    Till perfect in the word.
           Matth. vii, 7, 8.

X

While thousands mov'd to distant shore,
    And others left behind,

The blessed Jesus still adore,
    Implant this in thy mind.
           Psal. lxxxix, 1.

XI
Thou hast left the heathen shore;
    Thro' mercy of the Lord,
Among the heathen live no more,
    Come magnify thy God.
           Psal. xxxiv, 1, 2, 3.

XII
I pray the living God may be,
    The shepherd of thy soul;
His tender mercies still are free,
    His mysteries to unfold.
           Psal. lxxx. 1, 2, 3.

XIII
Thou, Phillis, when thou hunger hast,
    Or pantest for thy God;
Jesus Christ is thy relief,
    Thou hast the holy word.
           Psal. x2i. 1, 2, 3.

XIV
The bounteous mercies of the Lord,
    Are hid beyond the sky,
And holy souls that love His word,
    Shall taste them when they die.
           Psal. xvi. 10, 11.

XV
These bounteous mercies are from God,
    The merits of His Son;
The humble soul that loves His word,
    He chooses for his own.
           Psal. xxxiv. 15.

XVI
Come, dear Phillis, be advis'd,
    To drink Samaria's flood;
There nothing that shall suffice
    But Christ's redeeming blood.
           John iv. 13, 14.

XVII
While thousands muse with earthly toys;
    And range about the street,
Dear Phillis, seek for heaven's joys,
    Where we do hope to meet.
           Matth. vi. 33.

XVIII
When God shall send his summons down,
    And number saints together,
Blest angels chant, (triumphant sound),
    Come live with me forever.
           Psal. cxvi. 15.

XIX
The humble soul shall fly to God,
    And leave the things of time,
Start forth as 'twere at the first word,
    To taste things more divine.
           Matth. v. 3, 8.

XX
Behold! the soul shall waft away,
    Whene'er we come to die,
And leave its cottage made of clay,
    In twinkling of an eye.
           Cor. xv. 51, 52, 53

XXI
Now glory beto the Most High,
    United praises given,
By all on earth, incessantly,
    And all the host of heav'n.
           Psal. cl, 6

—————— 2.16 ——————

ROUGH DRAFT OF DECLARATION OF INDEPENDENCE
Thomas Jefferson

When Thomas Jefferson presented his draft of the Declaration of Independence to the Continental Congress on July 1, 1776, the document included a stinging rebuke of slavery. Jefferson listed Britain's propagation of the slave trade among King George II's crimes, and concluded that it was made all the more treacherous by Lord Dunmore's proclamation granting freedom to runaway slaves who joined the British forces. The offer, in Jefferson's view, was meant to spur slave insurrections, "thus paying off former crimes committed against the liberties of one people, with crimes which he urges them to commit against the lives of another." Representatives at the Congress, however, bristled at the implied abolitionist statement and struck it from the final document, replacing it with a less direct objection solely to Dunmore's proclamation.

When in the course of human events it becomes necessary for one people to dissolve the political bands which have connected them with another, and to assume among the powers of the earth the separate & equal station to which the laws of nature and of nature's God entitle them, a decent respect to the opinions of mankind requires that they should declare the causes which impel them to the separation.

We hold these truths to be self-evident: that all men are created equal; that they are endowed by their creator with inherent and inalienable rights; that among these are life, liberty, & the pursuit of happiness: that to secure these rights, governments are instituted among men, deriving their just powers from the consent of the governed; that whenever any form of government becomes destructive of these ends, it is the right of the people to alter or abolish it, & to institute new government, laying it's foundation on such principles, & organizing it's powers in such form, as to them shall seem most likely to effect their safety & happiness. Prudence indeed will dictate that governments long established should not be changed for light & transient causes; and accordingly all experience hath shown that mankind are more disposed to suffer while evils are sufferable, than to right themselves by abolishing the forms to which they are accustomed. But when a long train of abuses & usurpations begun at a distinguished period and pursuing invariably the same object, evinces a design to reduce them under absolute despotism, it is their right, it is their duty to throw off such government, & to provide new guards for their future security. Such has been the patient sufferance of these colonies; & such is now the necessity which constrains them to expunge their former systems of government. The history of the present king of Great Britain is a history of unremitting injuries & usurpations, among which appears no solitary fact to contradict the uniform tenor of the rest but all have in direct object the establishment of an absolute tyranny over these states. To prove this let facts be submitted to a candid

world for the truth of which we pledge a faith yet unsullied by falsehood.

He has refused his assent to laws the most wholesome & necessary for the public good.

He has forbidden his governors to pass laws of immediate & pressing importance, unless suspended in their operation till his assent should be obtained; & when so suspended, he has utterly neglected to attend to them.

He has refused to pass other laws for the accommodation of large districts of people, unless those people would relinquish the right of representation in the legislature, a right inestimable to them, & formidable to tyrants only.

He has called together legislative bodies at places unusual, uncomfortable, and distant from the depository of their public records, for the sole purpose of fatiguing them into compliance with his measures.

He has dissolved representative houses repeatedly & continually for opposing with manly firmness his invasions on the rights of the people.

He has refused for a long time after such dissolutions to cause others to be elected, whereby the legislative powers, incapable of annihilation, have returned to the people at large for their exercise, the state remaining in the meantime exposed to all the dangers of invasion from without & convulsions within.

He has endeavored to prevent the population of these states; for that purpose obstructing the laws for naturalization of foreigners, refusing to pass others to encourage their migrations hither, & raising the conditions of new appropriations of lands.

He has suffered the administration of justice totally to cease in some of these states refusing his assent to laws for establishing judiciary powers.

He has made our judges dependant on his will alone, for the tenure of their offices, & the amount & paiment of their salaries.

He has erected a multitude of new offices by a self assumed power and sent hither swarms of new officers to harass our people and eat out their substance.

He has kept among us in times of peace standing armies and ships of war without the consent of our legislatures.

He has affected to render the military independent of, & superior to the civil power.

He has combined with others to subject us to a jurisdiction foreign to our constitutions & unacknowledged by our laws, giving his assent to their acts of pretended legislation for quartering large bodies of armed troops among us; for protecting them by a mock-trial from punishment for any murders which they should commit on the inhabitants of these states; for cutting off our trade with all parts of the world; for imposing taxes on us without our consent; for depriving us [in many cases] of the benefits of trial by jury; for transporting us beyond seas to be tried for pretended offences; for abolishing the free system of English laws in a neighboring province, establishing therein an arbitrary government, and enlarging it's boundaries, so as to render it at once an example and fit instrument for introducing the same absolute rule into these states; for taking away our charters, abolishing our most valuable laws, and altering fundamentally the forms of our governments; for suspending our own legislatures, & declaring themselves invested with power to legislate for us in all cases whatsoever.

He has abdicated government here withdrawing his governors, and declaring us out of his allegiance & protection.

He has plundered our seas, ravaged our coasts, burnt our towns, & destroyed the lives of our people.

He is at this time transporting large armies of foreign mercenaries to compleat the works of death, desolation & tyranny already begun with circumstance of cruelty and perfidy unworthy the head of a civilized nation.

He has constrained our fellow citizens taken captive on the high seas to bear arms against their country, to become the executioners of their friends & brethren, or to fall themselves by their hands.

He has endeavored to bring on the inhabitants of our frontiers the merciless Indian sav-ages, whose known rule of warfare is an undistinguished destruction of all ages, sexes, & conditions of existence.

He has incited treasonable insurrections of our fellow-citizens, with the allurements of forfeiture & confiscation of our property.

He has waged cruel war against human nature itself, violating it's most sacred rights of life and liberty in the persons of a distant people who never offended him, captivating & carrying them into slavery in another hemisphere, or to incur miserable death in their transportation thither. This piratical warfare, the opprobrium of INFIDEL Powers, is the warfare of the CHRISTIAN king of Great Britain. Determined to keep open a market where MEN should be bought & sold, he has prostituted his negative for suppressing every legislative attempt to prohibit or to restrain this execrable commerce. And that this assemblage of horrors might want no fact of distinguished die, he is now exciting those very people to rise in arms among us, and to purchase that liberty of which he has deprived them, by murdering the people on whom he also obtruded them: thus paying off former crimes committed against the LIBERTIES of one people, with crimes which he urges them to commit against the LIVES of another.

In every stage of these oppressions we have petitioned for redress in the most humble terms: our repeated petitions have been answered only by repeated injuries.

A prince whose character is thus marked by every act which may define a tyrant is unfit to be the ruler of a people who mean to be free. Future ages will scarcely believe that the hardiness of one man adventured, within the short compass of twelve years only, to lay a foundation so broad & so undisguised for tyranny over a people fostered & fixed in principles of freedom.

Nor have we been wanting in attentions to our British brethren. We have warned them from time to time of attempts by their legislature to extend a jurisdiction over these our states. We have reminded them of the circumstances of our emigration & settlement here, no one of which could warrant so strange a pretension: that these were effected at the expense of our own blood & treasure, unassisted by the wealth or the strength of Great Britain: that in constituting indeed our several forms of government, we had adopted one common king, thereby laying a foundation for perpetual league & amity with them: but that submission to their parliament was no part of our constitution, nor ever in idea, if history may be credited: and, we appealed to their native justice and magnanimity as well as to the ties of our common kindred to disavow these usurpations which were likely to interrupt our connection and correspondence. They too have been deaf to the voice of justice & of consanguinity, and when occasions have been given them, by the regular course of their laws, of removing from their councils the disturbers of our harmony, they have, by their free election, re-established them in power. At this very time too they are permitting their chief magistrate to send over not only soldiers of our common blood, but Scotch & foreign mercenaries to invade & destroy us. These facts have given the last stab to agonizing affection, and manly spirit bids us to renounce forever these unfeeling brethren. We must endeavor to forget our former love for them, and hold them as we hold the rest of mankind, enemies in war, in peace friends. We might have been a free and a great people together; but a communication of grandeur & of freedom it seems is below their dignity. Be it so, since they will have it. The road to happiness & to glory is open to us too. We will tread it apart from them, and acquiesce in the necessity which denounces our eternal separation!

We therefore the representatives of the United States of America in General Congress assembled do in the name & by authority of the good people of these states reject & renounce all allegiance & subjection to the kings of Great Britain & all others who may hereafter claim by, through or under them: we utterly dissolve all political connection which may heretofore

have subsisted between us & the people or parliament of Great Britain: & finally we do assert & declare these colonies to be free & independent states, & that as free & independent states, they have full power to levy war, conclude peace, contract alliances, establish commerce, & to do all other acts & things which independent states may of right do.

And for the support of this declaration we mutually pledge to each other our lives, our fortunes, & our sacred honor.

——— 2.17 ———
NOTES ON THE STATE OF VIRGINIA
Thomas Jefferson

The great paradox of Thomas Jefferson's contribution to African-American history is that he authored both one of the most ringing cries for freedom, in his draft of the Declaration of Independence, and one of the most racist documents of American history, in his *Notes on the State of Virginia*. In the section of his 1784 book in which he advocates returning slaves to Africa—and, notably, the end of slavery—Jefferson argues at length the physical, intellectual and emotional inferiority of Africans. He predates 20th century calls for European racial purity by warning of the ills that could come from allowing too great mixture of the races. He dismisses Phillis Wheatley's work as "below the dignity of criticism," and rebuffs even the argument that slavery itself has caused the inferiority, concluding, "It is not their condition then, but nature, which has produced the distinction." Some historians have defended the hotly debated work by insisting that Jefferson must only be judged by the standards of his own time. Indeed, when compared to the abolitionist writings of his contemporaries John Wesley and Benjamin Franklin, or even that of Morgan Goodwyn a century earlier, Jefferson's thoughts on African Americans provide a striking contrast.

… The first difference which strikes us is that of colour. Whether the black of the negro resides in the reticular membrane between the skin and scarf-skin, or in the scarf-skin itself; whether it proceeds from the colour of the blood, the colour of the bile, or from that of some other secretion, the difference is fixed in nature, and is as real as if its seat and cause were better known to us. And is this difference of no importance? Is it not the foundation of a greater or less share of beauty in the two races? Are not the fine mixtures of red and white, the expressions of every passion by greater or less suffusions of colour in the one, preferable to that eternal monotony, which reigns in the countenances, that immoveable veil of black which covers all the emotions of the other race? Add to these, flowing hair, a more elegant symmetry of form, their own judgment in favour of the whites, declared by their preference of them, as uniformly as is the preference of the Oran-ootan for the black women over those of his own species. The circumstance of superior beauty, is thought worthy attention in the propagation of our horses, dogs, and other domestic animals; why not in that of man? Besides those of colour, figure, and hair, there are other physical distinctions proving a difference of race. They have less hair on the face and body. They secrete less by the kidnies, and more by the glands of the skin, which gives them a very strong and disagreeable odour. This greater degree of transpiration renders them more tolerant of heat, and less so of cold, than the whites. Perhaps too a difference of structure in the pulmonary apparatus, which a late ingenious experimentalist has discovered to be the principal regulator of animal heat, may have disabled them from extricating, in the act of inspiration, so much of that fluid from the outer air, or obliged them in expiration, to part with more of it. They seem to require less sleep. A black, after hard labour through the day, will be induced by the slightest amusements to sit up till midnight, or later, though knowing he must be out with the first dawn of the morning. They are at least as brave, and more adventurous. But this may perhaps proceed from a want of forethought, which prevents their seeing a danger till it be present. When present, they do not go through it with more coolness or steadiness than the whites. They are more ardent after their female: but love seems with them to be more

an eager desire, than a tender delicate mixture of sentiment and sensation. Their griefs are transient. Those numberless afflictions, which render it doubtful whether heaven has given life to us in mercy or in wrath, are less felt, and sooner forgotten with them. In general, their existence appears to participate more of sensation than reflection. To this must be ascribed their disposition to sleep when abstracted from their diversions, and unemployed in labour. An animal whose body is at rest, and who does not reflect, must be disposed to sleep of course. Comparing them by their faculties of memory, reason, and imagination, it appears to me, that in memory they are equal to whites; in reason much inferior, as I think one could scarcely be found capable of tracing and comprehending the investigations of Euclid; and that in imagination they are dull, tasteless, and anomalous. It would be unfair to follow them to Africa for this investigation. We will consider them here, on the same stage with the whites, and where the facts are not apocryphal on which a judgment is to be formed. It will be right to make great allowances for the difference of condition, of education, of conversation, of the sphere in which they move. Many millions of them have been brought to, and born in America. Most of them have been confined to tillage, to their own homes, and their own society: yet many have been so situated, that they might have availed themselves of the conversation of their masters; many have been brought up to the handicraft arts, and from that circumstance have always been associated with the whites. Some have been liberally educated, and all have lived in countries where the arts and sciences are cultivated to a considerable degree, and have had before their eyes samples of the best works from abroad. The Indians, with no advantages of this kind, will often carve figures on their pipes not destitute of design and merit. They will crayon out an animal, a plant, or a country, so as to prove the existence of a germ in their minds which only wants cultivation. They astonish you with strokes of the most sublime oratory; such as prove their reason and sentiment strong, their imagination glowing and elevated. But never yet could I find that a black had uttered a thought above the lever of plain narration; never see even an elementary trait of painting or sculpture. In music they are more generally gifted than the whites with accurate ears for tune and time, and they have been found capable of imagining a small catch. Whether they will be equal to composition of a more extensive run of melody, or of complicated harmony, is yet to be proved. Misery is often the parent of the most affecting touches in poetry.—Among the blacks is misery enough, God knows, but no poetry. Love is the peculiar estrum of the poet. Their love is ardent, but it kindles the senses only, not the imagination. Religion indeed has produced a Phyllis Whately; but it could not produce a poet. The compositions published under her name are below the dignity of criticism. The heroes of the Dunciad are to her, as Hercules to the author of that poem. Ignatius Sancho has approached nearer the merit in composition; yet his letters do more honour to the heart than the head. They breathe the purest effusions of friendship and general philanthropy, and shew how great a degree of the latter may be compounded with strong religious zeal. He is often happy in the turn of his compliments, and his stile is easy and familiar, except when he affects a Shandean fabrication of words. But his imagination is wild and extravagant, escapes incessantly from every restraint of reason and taste, and, in the course of its vagaries, leaves a tract of thought as incoherent and eccentric, as is the course of a meteor through the sky. His subjects should often have led him to a process of sober reasoning: yet we find him always substituting sentiment for demonstration. Upon the whole, though we admit him to the first place among those of his own colour who have presented themselves to the public judgment, yet when we compare him with the writers of the race among whom he lived, and particularly with the epistolary class, in which he has taken his own stand, we are compelled to enroll him at the bottom of the column. This criticism supposes the letters published under his name to be genuine, and to have received amendment from no other hand; points which would not be of easy investigation. The improvement of the blacks in body and mind, in the first instance of their mixture with the whites, has been observed by every one, and proves that their inferiority is not the effect of merely their condition of life. We know that among the Romans, about the Augustan age especially, the condition of their slaves was much more deplorable than that of the blacks on the continent of America. The two sexes were confined in separate apartments, because to raise a child cost the master more than to buy one. Cato, for a very restricted indulgence to his slaves in this particular, took from them a certain price. But in this country the slaves multiply as fast as the free inhabitants. Their situation and manners place the commerce between the two sexes almost without restraint.—The same Cato, on a principle of economy, always sold his sick and superannuated slaves. He gives it as a standing precept to a master visiting his farm, to sell his old oxen, old waggons, old tools, old and diseased servants, and every thing else become useless. "Vendat boves vetulos, plaustrum vetus, ferramenta, vetera, servum senem, servum morbosum, & si quid aliud supersit vendat." The American slaves cannot enumerate this among the injuries and insults they receive. It was the common practice to expose in the island of Esculapius, in the Tyber, diseased slaves, whose cue was like to become tedious. The Emperor Claudius, by an edict, gave freedom to such of them as should recover, and first declared, that if any person chose to kill rather than to expose them, it should be deemed homicide. The exposing them is a crime of which no instance has existed with us; and were it to be followed by death, it would be punished capitally. We are told of certain Vedius Pollio, who, in the presence of Augustus, would have given a slave as food to his fish, for having broken a glass. With the Romans, the regular method of taking the evidence of their slaves was under torture. Here it has been thought better never to resort to their evidence. When a master was murdered, all his slaves, in the same house, or within hearing, were condemned to death. Here punishment falls on the guilty only, and as precise proof is required against him as against a freeman. Yet notwithstanding these and other discouraging circumstances among the Romans, their slaves were often their artists. They excelled too in science, insomuch as to be usually employed as tutors to their master's children. Epictetus, (Diogenes, Phaedon), Terence, and Phaedrus, were slaves. But they were of the race of whites. It is not their condition then, but nature, which has produced the distinction.

———— 2.18 ————

'THREE FIFTHS OF ALL OTHER PERSONS'
The United States Constitution

When the delegates to the Constitutional Convention arrived in Philadelphia in May 1787 to design a stronger central government, one of the key points of division among the confederated states was whether or not the new nation should continue to participate in what was seen as Britain's slave trade. Georgia, which had finally legalized slavery in 1751, joined South Carolina in a strong protest against Northern delegates' moves to ban the further importation of slaves. Virginia delegate James Madison opposed any tax on the ownership of slaves, as it recognized them as property. Madison, as well as Benjamin Franklin, also emerged as critics of the ultimate compromise. Delegates agreed that the Constitution would block the federal government from ending the international slave trade for 20 years, empowering Congress to do so only after 1808. They also decided to continue considering slaves property and, for the purpose of calculating the size of a state's congressional delegation, they agreed that each slave would represent three-fifths of a person.

Article I

Section 2, Clause 3—Representatives and direct Taxes shall be apportioned among the several States which may be included within this Union, according to their respective Numbers, which shall be determined by adding to the whole Number of free Persons, including those bound to Service for a Term of Years, and excluding Indians not taxed, three fifths of all other Persons. The actual Enumeration shall be made within three Years after the first Meeting of the Congress of the United States, and within every subsequent Term of ten Years, in such Manner as they shall by Law direct. The Number of Representatives shall not exceed one for every thirty Thousand, but each State shall have at Least one Representative; and until such enumeration shall be made, the State of New Hampshire shall be entitled to chuse three, Massachusetts eight, Rhode-Island and Providence Plantations one, Connecticut five, New-York six, New Jersey four, Pennsylvania eight, Delaware one, Maryland six, Virginia ten, North Carolina five, South Carolina five, and Georgia three. …

Section 9, Clause 1—The Migration or Importation of such Persons as any of the states now existing shall think proper to admit, shall not be prohibited by the Congress prior to the Year one thousand eight hundred and eight, but a Tax or Duty may be imposed on such Importation, not exceeding ten dollars for each person.

———— 2.19 ————

'PROVIDENCE PUNISHES NATIONAL SINS, BY NATIONAL CALAMITIES'
Constitutional Convention Debate on Slavery

James Madison recorded the debates and conversations of the Constitutional Convention in his notes on the gathering. The meeting was conducted in absolute confidence, with the windows to the chambers barred and guards placed at the doors. Delegates were urged to keep the discussion within the hall and among the participants. For this reason, Madison kept his notes secret and swore to only publish them after all delegates to the Convention had died. When they were finally published, following his own death, they proved to be the most detailed account available of the caucus's deliberations.

The excerpts below formed part of the heated debate about whether and how the new Constitution should limit the slave trade. The issues raised eerily foreshadow the national debate that would ultimately spark a civil war.

Col. Mason. This infernal traffic originated in the avarice of British Merchants. The British Government constantly checked the attempts of Virginia to put a stop to it. The present question concerns not the importing of Slaves alone but the whole Union. The evil of having slaves was experienced during the late war. Had slaves been treated as they might have been by the Enemy, they would have proved dangerous instruments in their hands. But their folly dealt the slaves, as it did by the Tories. He mentioned the dangerous insurrections of the slaves in Greece and Sicily; and the instructions given by Cromwell to the Commissioners sent to Virginia, to arm the servants & slaves, in case other means of obtaining its submission should fail. Maryland & Virginia he said had already prohibited the importation of slaves expressly. N. Carolina had done the same in substance. All this would be in vain if S. Carolina & Georgia be at liberty to import. The Western people are already calling out for slaves for their new lands, and will fill that Country with slaves if they can be got thro' S. Carolina & Georgia. Slavery discourages arts & manufactures. The poor despise labor when performed by slaves. They prevent the immigration of Whites, who really enrich & strengthen a Country. They produce the most pernicious effect on manners. Every master of slaves is born a petty tyrant. They bring the judgment of heaven on a Country. As nations can not be rewarded or punished in the next world they must be in this. By an inevitable chain of causes & effects providence punishes national sins, by national calamities. He lamented that some of our Eastern brethren had from a lust of gain embarked in this nefarious traffic. As to the States being in possession of the Right to import, this was the case with many other rights, now to be properly given up. He held it essential in every point of view that the General Government should have power to prevent the increase of slavery.

Mr. Elsworth. As he had never owned a slave could not judge of the effects of slavery on character: He said however that if it was to be considered in a moral light we ought to go farther and free those already in the Country.—As slaves also multiply so fast in Virginia & Maryland that it is cheaper to raise than import them, whilst in sickly rice swamps foreign supplies are necessary, if we go no farther than is urged, we shall be unjust towards S. Carolina & Georgia. Let us not intermeddle. As population increases poor laborers will be so plenty as to render slaves useless. Slavery in time will not be a speck in our Country. Provision is already made in Connecticut for abolishing it. And the abolition has already take place in Massachusetts. As to the danger of insurrections from foreign influence, that will become a motive to kind treatment of slaves.

Mr. Pinkney. If slavery be wrong, it is justified by the example of all the world. He cited the case of Greece Rome & other antient States; the sanction given by France England, Holland & other modern States. In all ages on half of mankind have been slaves. If the S. States were let alone they will probably of themselves stop importations. He would himself as a Citizen of S. Carolina vote for it. An attempt to take away the right as proposed will produce serious objections to the Constitution which he wished to see adopted.

General Pinkney declared it to be his firm opinion that if himself & all his colleagues were to sign the Constitution & use their personal influence, it would be of no avail towards obtaining the assent of their Constituents. S. Carolina & Georgia cannot do without slaves. As to Virginia she will gain by stopping importations. Her slaves will rise in value, & she has more than she wants. It would be unequal to require S.C. & Georgia to confederate on such unequal terms. He said the Royal assent before the Revolution had never been refused to S. Carolina as to Virginia. He contended that the importation of slaves would be for the interest of the whole Union. The more slaves, the more produce to employ the carrying trade; the more consumption also, and the more of this, the more of revenue for the common treasury. He admitted it to be reasonable that slave should be duties like other imports, but should consider a rejection of the clause an exclusion of S. Carolina from the Union.

—————— 2.20 ——————

PETITION FOR REPATRIATION TO AFRICA
Prince Hall and African Lodge No. 1

As the founder of the first African American Freemason lodge, Prince Hall became one of the time's most influential black leaders. Born a slave, but freed by his owner at the outset of the Revolutionary War, some historians have argued that Hall was among the black soldiers at the Battle of Bunker Hill. Whether he was or not, he made his place in history in the years following the war. As the inaugural "Grand Master" of the African Lodge No. 1, Hall became a primary spokesperson for Boston's black community. He led his fellow lodgers in repeatedly sending petitions to the government of Massachusetts asking for the abolition of slavery—all of which were readily accepted and subsequently ignored by the legislature.

On January 4, 1787, Hall and his colleagues submitted a petition to the legislature that revealed their weariness with attempts to find a place within the new American nation. The petition stated their desire to return to Africa, along with all of the state's blacks. Signed by 73 people, it laid out a plan by which the legislature could work with them to accomplish that goal, arguing its mutual benefit. It was the strongest call for colonization to date, an idea that would gain popularity among abolitionists in coming years. Historian Sidney Kaplan reprinted the petition, in part, in his recent study of African Americans of the Revolutionary Era.

… We, or our ancestors have been taken from all our dear connections, and brought from Africa and put into a state of slavery in this country; from which unhappy situation we have been lately in some measure delivered by the new constitution which has been adopted by this State, or by a free act of our former masters. But we yet find ourselves, in many respects, in very disagreeable and disadvantageous circumstances; most of which must attend us, so long as we and our children live in America.

This, and other consideration, which we need not here particularly mention, induce us earnestly to desire to return to Africa, our native country, which warm climate is much more natural and agreable to us; and, for which the God of nature has formed us; and, where we shall live among our equals, and be more comfortable and happy, than we can be in our present situation; and, at the same time, may have a prospect of usefulness to our brethren there.

This leads us humbly to propose the following plan to the consideration of this honourable Court. The soil of our native country is good, and produces the necessaries of life in great abundance. There are large tracts of uncultivated lands, which, if proper application were made for them, it is presumed, might be obtained, and would be freely given for those to settle upon, who shall be disposed to return to them. When this shall be effected by a number of Blacks, sent there for this purpose, who shall be thought most capable of making such an application, and transacting this business; then they who are disposed to go and settle there shall form themselves into a civil society, united by a political constitution, in which they shall agree. And those who are disposed, and shall be thought qualified, shall unite, and be formed into a religious society, or christian church; and have one or more blacks ordained as their pastors or Bishops: And being thus formed, shall remove to Africa, and settle on said lands.

These must be furnished with necessary provisions for the voyage; and with farming utensils necessary to cultivate the land; and with the materials which cannot at present be obtained there, and which will be needed to build houses and mills.

The execution of this plan will, we hope, be the means of inlightening and civilizing those nations, who are now sunk in ignorance and barbarity; and may give opportunity to those who shall be disposed, and engaged to promote the salvation of their heathen brethren, to spread the knowledge of Christianity among them, and perswade them to embrace it. And schools may be formed to instruct their youth and children, and christian knowledge be spread through many nations who now are in gross darkness; and christian churches be formed, and the only true God and Saviour be worshiped and honoured through that vast extent of country, where are now the habitations of cruelty under the reign of the prince of darkness.

This may also lay a happy foundation for a friendly and lasting connection between that country and the united States of America, by a mutual intercourse and profitable commerce, which may much more than overbalance all the expence which is now necessary in order to carry this plan into effect.

This leads us to observe, that we are poor and utterly unable to prosecute this scheme or to return to Africa, without assistance. Money is wanted to enable those who shall be appointed, to go to Africa, and procure lands to settle upon; and to obtain a passage for us and our families; and to furnish us with necessary provisions, and the utensils and articles that have been mentioned.

We therefore humbly and earnestly apply to this honourable Court, hoping and praying that in your wisdom and goodness, you concert and prosecute the best method to relieve and assist us either by granting a brief for a collection in all the congregations in this State, or in any other way, which shall to your wisdom appear most expedient.

———— 2.21 ————
'THE SLAVISH FEAR OF MAN'
Prince Hall

Prince Hall is judged to have been one of the great orators of African-American history. In addition to his petitions to the Massachusetts legislature, he regularly addressed the African Lodge No. 1. Two of his most famous speeches were his charges to the lodge in 1792 and 1797. In the latter, he challenges the black Masons to seek patience in the face of their troubles as African Americans and rails against the "slavish fear of man" and the oppression men can create. That oppression, Hall exhorts, is meager compared to the strength of God, and thus only God's powers should provoke fear.

… Now my brethren, as we see and experience that all things here are frail and changeable and nothing here to be depended upon: Let us seek those things which are above, which are sure, and steadfast, and unchangeable, and at the same time let us pray to Almighty God, while we remain in the tabernacle, that he would give us the grace of patience and strength to bear up under all our troubles, which at this day God knows we have our share. Patience I say, for were we not possess'd of a great measure of it you could not bear up under the daily insults you meet with in the streets of Boston; much more on public days of recreation, how are you shamefully abus'd, and that at such a degree that you may truly be said to carry your lives in your hands, and the arrows of death are flying about your heads; helpless old women have their clothes torn off their backs, even to the exposing of their nakedness; and by whom are these disgraceful and abusive actions committed, not by the men born and bred in Boston, for they are better bred; but by a mob or horde of shameless, low-lived, envious, spiteful persons, some of them not long since, servants in gentlemen's kitchens, scouring knives, tending horses, and driving chaise. 'Twas said by a gentleman who saw that filthy behaviour in the common, that in all the place he had been in, he never saw so cruel behaviour in all his life, and that a slave in the West-Indies, on Sunday or holidays enjoys himself and friends without any molestation. Not only this man, but many in town who hath seen their behaviour to you, and that without any provocation—twenty or thirty cowards fall upon one man—have wonder'd at the patience of the Blacks: 'tis not for want of courage in you, for they know that they dare not face you man for man, but in a mob, which we despise, and had rather suffer wrong than to do wrong, to the disturbance of the community and the disgrace of our reputation: for every good citizen doth honor to the laws of the State where he resides.

My brethren, let us not be cast down under these and many other abuses we at present labour under: for the darkest is before the break of day. My brethren, let us remember what a dark day it was with our African brethren six years ago, in the French West Indies. Nothing but the snap of a whip was heard from morning to evening; hanging, broken on the wheel, burning, and all manner of tortures inflicted on those unhappy people for nothing else but to gratify their masters pride, wantonness, and cruelty: but blessed be God, the scene is changed; they now confess that God hath no respect of persons, and therefore receive them as their friends, and treat them as brothers. Thus doth Ethiopia begin to stretch forth her hand, from a sink of slavery to freedom and equality.

Although you are deprived of the means of education, yet you are not deprived of the means of meditation; by which I mean thinking, hearing and weighing matters, men, and things in your own mind, and making that judgment of them as you think reasonable to satisfy your minds and give an answer to those who may ask you a question. This nature hath furnished you with, without letter learning; and some have made great progress therein, some of those I have heard repeat psalms and hymns, and a great part of a sermon, only by hearing it read or preached and why not in other things in nature: how many of this class of our brethren that follow the seas can foretell a storm some days before it comes; whether it will be a heavy or light, a long or short one; foretell a hurricane, whether it will be destructive or moderate, without any other means than observation and consideration.

So in the observation of the heavenly bodies, this same class without a telescope or other apparatus have through a smoak'd glass observed the eclipse of the sun: One being ask'd what he saw through his smoaked glass, said, Saw, saw, de clipsey, or de clipseys. And what do you think of it?—Stop, dere be two. Right, and what do they look like?—Look like, why, if I tell you, they look like two ships sailing one bigger than tohter; so they sail by one another, and make no noise. As simple as the answers are they have a meaning, and shew that God can out of the mouth of babes and Africans shew forth his glory; let us then love and adore him as the God who defends us and supports us and will support us under our pressures, let them be ever so heavy and pressing. Let us by the blessing of God, in whatsoever state we are, or may be in, to be content; for clouds and darkness are about him; but justice and truth is his habitation; who hath said, Vengeance is mine and I will repay it, therefore let us kiss the rod and be still, and see the works of the Lord.

Another thing I would warn you against, is the slavish fear of man, which bringest a snare, saith Solomon. This passion of fear, like pride and envy, hath slain its thousands.—What but this makes so many perjure themselves; for fear of offending them at home they are little depending on for some trifles: A man that is under a panic or fear, is afraid to be alone; you cannot hear of a robbery or house broke open or set on fire, but he hath an accomplice with him, who must share the spoil with him; whereas if he was truly bold, and void of fear, he would keep the whole plunder to himself: so when either of them is detected and not the other, he may be call'd to oath to keep it secret, but through fear, (and that passion is so strong) he will not confess, till the fatal cord is put on his neck; then death will deliver him from the fear of man, and he will confess the truth when it will not be of any good to himself or the community: nor is this passion of fear only to be found in this class of men, but among the great.

What was the reason that our African kings and princes have plunged themselves and their peaceable kingdoms into bloody wars, to the destroying of towns and kingdoms, but the fear of the report of a great gun or the glittering of arms and swords, which struck these kings near the seaports with such a panic of fear, as not only to destroy the peace and happiness of their inland brethren, but plung'd millions of their fellow countrymen into slavery and cruel bondage.

So in other countries; see Felix trembling on his throne. How many Emperors and kings have left their kingdoms and best friends at the sight of a handful of men in arms: how many have we seen that have left their estates and their friends and ran over to the stronger side as they thought; all through the fear of men, who is but a worm, and hath no more power to hurt his fellow worm, without the permission of God, than a real worm.

Thus we see, my brethren, what a miserable condition it is to be under the slavish fear of men; it is of such a destructive nature to mankind, that the scriptures every where from Genesis to the Revelation warns us against it; and even our blessed Saviour himself forbids us from this slavish fear of man, in his sermon on the mount; and the only way to avoid it is to be in the fear of God: let a man consider the greatness of his power, as the maker and upholder of all things here below, and that in Him we live, and move, and have our being, the giver of the mercies we enjoy here from day to day, and that our lives are in his hands, and that he made the heavens, the sun, moon and stars to move in their various orders; let us view the greatness of God, and then turn our eyes on mortal man, a worm, a shade, a wafer, and see whether he is an object of fear or not; on the contrary, you will think him in his best estate to be but vanity, feeble and a dependent mortal, and stands in need of your help, and

cannot do without your assistance, in some way or other; and yet some of these poor mortals will try to make you believe they are Gods, but worship them not. My brethren, let us pay all due respect to all whom God hath put in places of honor over us: do justly be faithful to them that hire you, and treat them with that respect they may deserve; but worship no man. Worship God, this much is your duty as christians and as masons. ...

——— 2.22 ———

'IN WHAT SINGLE CIRCUMSTANCE ARE WE DIFFERENT FROM THEREST OF MANKIND?'
A Free Negro

Published speeches and essays by free blacks and slaves proliferated in the height of the Revolutionary Era. As the anti-slavery movement grew in number and strength, individuals and organizations circulated essays such as this one, in which blacks argued for their freedom, usually in the rhetoric of the American Revolution. Originally published in England, but circulated widely in America, this essay is believed to have been authored by a West Indian former slave in the late 1780s.

I am one of that unfortunate race of men who are distinguished from the rest of the human species by a black skin and wooly hair—disadvantages of very little moment in themselves, but which prove to us a source of greatest misery, because there are men who will not be persuaded that it is possible for a human soul to be lodged within a sable body. The West Indian planters could not, if they thought us men, so wantonly spill our blood; nor could they natives of this land of liberty, deeming us of the same species with themselves, submit to be instrumental in enslaving us, or think us proper subjects of sordid commerce. Yet, strong as the prejudices against us are, it will not, I hope on this side of the Atlantic, be considered as a crime for a poor African not to confess himself a being of an inferior order to those who happen to be of a different color from himself, or be thought very presumptuous in one who is but a Negro to offer to the happy subjects of this free government some reflection upon the wretched condition of his countrymen. They will not, I trust, think worse of my brethren for being discontented with so hard a lot as that of slavery, nor disown me for their fellow-creature merely because I deeply feel the unmerited sufferings which my countrymen endure.

It is neither the vanity of being an author, nor a sudden and capricious gust of humanity, which has prompted this present design. It has long been conceived and long been the principal subject of my thoughts. Ever since an indulgent master rewarded my youthful services with freedom and supplied me at a very early age with the means of acquiring knowledge, I have labored to understand the true principles on which the liberties of mankind are founded, and to possess myself of the language of this country in order to plead the cause of those who were once my fellow slaves, and if possible to make my freedom, in some degree, the instrument of their deliverance.

The first thing, then, which seems necessary in order to remove those prejudices which are so unjustly entertained against us is to prove that we are men—a truth which is difficult of proof only because it is difficult to imagine by what argument it can be combated. Can it be contended that a difference of color alone can constitute a difference of species?—If not, in what single circumstance are we different from the rest of mankind? What variety is there in our organization? What imperfection in the faculties of our minds?—Has not a Negro eyes? has not a Negro hands, organs, dimensions, senses, affections, passions?—fed with the same food; hurt with the same weapons; subject to the same diseases; healed by the same means; warmed and cooled by the same summer and winter as a white man? If you prick us, do we not bleed? If you poison us, do we not die? Are we not exposed to all the same wants? Do we not feel all the same sentiments—are we not capable of all the same exertions—and are

we not entitled to all the same rights as other men?

Yes—and it is said we are men, it is true; but that we are men addicted to more and worse vices than those of any other complexion; and such is the innate perverseness of our minds that nature seems to have marked us out for slavery.—Such is the apology perpetually made for our masters and the justification offered for that universal proscription under which we labor.

But I supplicate our enemies to be, though for the first time, just in their proceedings toward us, and to establish the fact before they attempt to draw any conclusions from it. Nor let them imagine that this can be done by merely asserting that such is our universal character. It is the character, I grant, that our inhuman masters have agreed to give us and which they have so industriously and too successfully propagated in order to palliate their own guilt by blackening the helpless victim of it and to disguise their own cruelty under the semblance of justice. Let the natural depravity of our character be proven—not by appealing to declamatory invectives and interest representations, but by showing that a greater proportion of crimes have been committed by the wronged slaves of the plantation than by the luxurious inhabitants of Europe, who are happily strangers to those aggravated provocations by which our passions are every day irritated and incensed. Show us that, of the multitude of Negroes who have within a few years transported themselves to this country, and who are abandoned to themselves; who are corrupted by example, prompted by penury, and instigated by the memory of their wrongs to the commission of crimes—show us, I say (and the demonstration, if it be possible, cannot be difficult), that a greater proportion of these than of white men have fallen under the animadversions of justice and have been sacrificed to your laws. Though avarice may slander and insult our misery, and though poets heighten the horror of their fables by representing us as monsters of vice—that fact is that, if treated like other men, and admitted to a participation of their rights, we should differ from them in nothing, perhaps but in our possessing stronger passions, nicer sensibilities, and more enthusiastic virtue.

Before so harsh a decision was pronounced upon our nature, we might have expected—if sad experience had not taught us to expect nothing but injustice form our adversaries— that some pains would have been taken to ascertain what our nature is; and that we should have been considered as we are found in our native woods and not as we now are— altered and perverted by an inhuman political institution. But instead of this, we are examined, not by philosophers, but by interested traders; not as nature formed us, but as man has depraved us—and from such an inquiry, prosecuted under such circumstances, the perverseness of our dispositions is said to be established. Cruel that you are! you make us slaves; you implant in our minds all the vices which are in some degree inseparable from that condition; and you then impiously impute to nature, and to God, the origin of those vices, to which you alone have given birth; and punish in us the crimes of which you are yourselves the authors.

The condition of the slave is on nothing more deplorable than in its being so unfavorable to the practice of every virtue. The surest foundation of virtue is love of our fellow-creatures; and that affection takes its birth in the social relations of men to one another. But to a slave these are all denied. He never pays or receives the grateful duties of a son—he never knows or experiences the found solicitude of a father— the tender names of husband, of brother, and of friend, are to him unknown. He has no country to defend and bleed for—he can relieve no sufferings—for he looks around in vain to find a being more wretched than himself. He can indulge no generous sentiment— for he sees himself every hour treated with contempt and   ridiculed, and distinguished from irrational brutes by nothing but the severity of punishment. Would it be surprising

if a slave, laboring under all these disadvantages—oppressed, insulted, scorned, trampled on—should come at last to despise himself— to believe the calumnies of his oppressors— and to persuade himself that it would be against his nature to cherish any honorable sentiment or attempt any virtuous action? Before you boast of your superiority over us, place some of your own color (if you have the heart to do it) in the same situation with us and see whether they have such innate virtue, and such unconquerable vigor of mind, as to be capable of surmounting such multiplied difficulties, and of keeping their minds free from infection of every vice, even under the oppressive yoke of such a servitude.

But, not satisfied with denying us that indulgence, to which the misery of our condition gives us so just a claim, our enemies have laid down other and stricter rules of morality to judge our actions by than those by which the conduct of all other men is tried. Habits, which in all human beings except ourselves are thought innocent, are, in us, deemed criminal—and actions, which are even laudable in white men, become enormous crimes in Negroes. In proportion to our weakness, the strictness of censure is increased upon us; and as resources are withheld from us, our duties are multiplied. The terror of punishment is perpetually before our eyes; but we know not how to avert, what rules to act by, or what guides to follow. We have written laws, indeed, composed in a language we do not understand and never promulgated: but what avail written laws, when the supreme law, with us, is the capricious will of our overseers? To obey the dictates of our own hearts, and to yield to the strong propensies of nature, is often to incur severe punishment; and by emulating examples which we find applauded and revered among Europeans, we risk inflaming the wildest wrath of our inhuman tyrants.

To judge the truth of these assertions, consult even those milder subordinate rules for our conduct, the various codes of your West India laws—those laws which allow us to be men, whenever they consider us as victims of their vengeance, but treat us only like a species of living property, as often as we are able to be the objects of their protection—those laws by which (it may be truly said) that we are bound to suffer and be miserable under pain of death. To resent an injury received from a white man, though of the lowest rank, and to dare to strike him, though upon the grossest provocation, is an enormous crime. To attempt to escape from the cruelties exercised upon us by flight is punished with mutilation, and sometimes with death. To take arms against masters, whose cruelties no submission can mitigate, no patience exhaust, and for whom no other means of deliverance are left, is the most atrocious of all crimes, and is punished by a gradual death, lengthened out by torments so exquisite that none but those who have been long familiarized with West Indian barbarity can hear the bare recital of them without horror. And yet I learn from writers, whom the Europeans hold in the highest esteem, that treason is a crime which cannot be committed by a slave against his master; that a slave stands in no civil relation towards his master, and owes him no allegiance; that master and slave are in a state of war; and if the slave take up arms for his deliverance, he acts not only justifiably but in obedience to a natural duty, the duty of self-preservation. I read in authors whom I find venerated by our oppressors, that to deliver one's self and one's countrymen from tyranny is an act of the sublimest heroism. I hear Europeans exalted as the martyrs of public liberty, the saviors of their country, and the deliverers of mankind—I see other memories honored with statues, and their names immortalized in poetry—and yet when a generous Negro is animated by the same passion which ennobled them—when he feels the wrongs of his countrymen as deeply, and attempts to avenge them as boldly—I see him treated by those same Europeans as the most execrable of mankind, and let out, amidst curses and insults, to undergo a painful, gradual and ignominious death. And thus the same Briton, who

applauds his own ancestors for attempting to throw off the easy yoke imposed on them by the Romans, punishes us, as detested parricides, for seeking to get free from the cruelest of all tyrannies, and yielding to the irresistible eloquence of an African Galgacus or Boadicea.

Are then the reasons and morality, for which Europeans so highly value themselves, of a nature so variable and fluctuating as to change with the complexion of those to whom they are applied?—Do rights of nature cease to be such when a Negro is to enjoy them?—Or does patriotism in the heart of an African rankle into treason?

——— 2.23 ———

AN ADDRESS TO THE NEGROES OF THE STATE OF NEW-YORK
Jupiter Hammon

In the twilight of his life, Jupiter Hammon published an essay ostensibly aimed at his fellow African Americans, both slave and free. The 1787 essay, characteristically laden with Christian appeals, both uplifts and scolds the new nation's black population. Hammon warns slaves not to be overly concerned with attaining temporal freedom, but rather to focus on salvation in the Christian afterlife. He urges both free and bonded blacks to remember Christian principles, and to mind their behavior in the face of the oppression of slavery. Yet, he also assures his audience of the divine justice white slave owners will ultimately face and prays for emancipation, though he states that he believes himself to be too elderly to handle freedom.

…When I am writing to you with a design to say something to you for your good, and with a view to promote your happiness, I can with truth and sincerity join with the apostle Paul, when speaking of his own nation the Jews, and say: "*That I have great heaviness and continual sorrow in my heart for my brethren, my kinsmen according to the flesh.*" Yes my dear brethren, when I think of you, which is very often, and of the poor, despised and miserable state you are in, as to the things of this world, and when I think of your ignorance and stupidity, and the great wickedness of the most of you, I am pained to the heart. It is at times, almost too much for human nature to bear, and I am obliged to turn my thoughts from the subject or endeavour to still my mind, by considering that it is permitted thus to be, by that God who governs all things, who setteth up one and pulleth down another. While I have been thinking on this subject, I have frequently had great struggles in my own mind, and have been at a loss to know what to do. I have wanted exceedingly to say something to you, to call upon you with the tenderness of a father and friend, and to give you the last, and I may say dying advice, of an old man, who wishes your best good in this world to come. But while I have had such desires, a sense of my own ignorance, and unfitness to teach others, has frequently discouraged me from attempting to say any thing to you; yet when I thought of our situation, I could not rest easy.

When I was at Hartford in Connecticut, where I lived during the war, I published several pieces which were well received, not only by those of my own colour, but by a number of the white people, who thought they might do good among their servants. This is one consideration, among others, that emboldens me now to publish what I have written to you. Another is, I think you will be more likely to listen to what is said, when you know it comes from a negro, one of your own nation and colour, and therefore can have no interest in deceiving you, or in saying any thing to you, but what he really thinks is your interest, and duty to comply with. My age, I think, gives me some right to speak to you, and reason to expect you will hearken to my advice. I am now upwards of seventy years old, and cannot expect, though I am well, and able to do almost any kind of business, to live much longer. I have passed the common bounds set for man, and must soon go the way of all the earth. I have had more experience in the world than most of you, and I have seen a great deal of the vanity and wickedness of it, I have great reason to be thankful that my lot has been so much better than most slaves have had. I suppose I have had more advantages and privileges than most of you, who are slaves, have ever known, and I believe more than many white people have enjoyed, for which I desire to bless God, and pray that he may bless those who have given them to me. I do not, my dear friends, say these things about myself, to make you think that I am wiser or better than others; but that you might hearken, without prejudice, to what I have to say to you on the following particulars.

1st. Respecting obedience to masters.
Now whether it is right, and lawful, in the sight of God, for them to make slaves of us or not. I am certain that while we are slaves, it is our duty to obey our masters, in all their lawful commands, and mind them unless we are bid to do that which we know to be sin, or forbidden in God's word. The apostle Paul says: "Servants be obedient to them that are your masters according to the flesh, with fear and trembling in singleness in your heart as unto Christ: Not with eye service, as men pleasers, but as the servants of Christ doing the will of God from the heart: With good will doing service to the Lord, and not to men: Knowing that whatever thing a man doeth the same shall he receive of the Lord, whether he be bond or free."—Here is a plain command of God for us to obey our masters. It may seem hard for us, if we think our masters wrong in holding us slaves, to obey in all things, but who of us dare dispute with God! He has commanded us to obey, and we ought to do it cheerfully, and freely. This should be done by us, not only because God commands, but because our own peace and comfort depend upon it. As we depend upon our masters, for what we eat and drink and wear, and for all our comfortable things in this world, we cannot be happay, unless we please them. This we cannot do without obeying them freely, without muttering or finding fault. If a servant strives to please his master and studies and takes pains to do it, I believe there are but few masters who would

use such a servant cruelly. Good servants frequently make good masters. If your master is really hard, unreasonable and cruel, there is no way so likely for you to convince him of it, as always to obey his commands, and try to serve him, and take care of his interest, and try to promote it all in your power. If you are proud and stubborn and always finding fault, your master will think the fault lies wholly on your side; but if you are humble, and meek, and bear all things patiently, your master may think he is wrong; if he does not, his neighbours will be apt to see it, and will befriend you, and try to alter his conduct. If this does not do, you must cry to him, who has the hearts of all men in his hands, and turneth them as the rivers of waters are turned.

2nd. The particular I would mention, is honesty and faithfulness.
You must suffer me now to deal plainly with you, my dear brethren, for I do not mean to flatter or omit speaking the truth, whether it is for you, or against you. How many of you are there, who allow yourselves in stealing from your masters. It is very wicked for you not to take care of your masters' goods; but how much worse is it to pilfer and and steal from them, whenever you think you shall not be found out. This you must know is very wicked and provoking to God. There are none of you so ignorant but that you must know that this is wrong. Though you may try to excuse yourselves by saying that your masters are unjust to you, and though you may try to quiet your consciences in this way, yet if you are honest in owning the truth, you must think it is as wicked, and on some accounts more wicked to steal from your masters, than from others.

We cannot certainly have any excuse, either for taking any thing that belongs to our masters, without their leave, of for being unfaithful in their business. It is our duty to be faithful, *not with eye service as men pleasers.* We have no right to stay, when we are sent on errands, any longer than to do the business we were sent upon. All the time spent idly is spent

wickedly, and is unfaithfulness to our masters. In these things I must say, that I think many of you are guilty. I know that many of you endeavour to excuse yourselves, and say that you have nothing that you can call your own, and that you are under great temptations to be unfaithful and take from your masters. But this will not do; God will certainly punish you for stealing, and for being unfaithful. All that we have to mind, is our own duty. If God has put us in bad circumstances, that is not our fault, and he will not punish us for it. If any are wicked in keeping us so, we cannot help it; they must answer to God for it. Nothing will serve as an excuse to us for not doing our duty. The same God will judge both them and us. Pray then, my dear friends, fear to offend in this way, but be faithful to God, to your masters, and to your own souls. ...

Now I acknowledge that liberty is a great thing, and worth seeking for, if we can get it honestly; and by our good conduct prevail on our masters to set us free: though for my own part I do not wish to be free, yet I should be glad if others, especially the young Negroes, were to be free; for many of us who are grown up slaves, and have always had masters to take care of us, should hardly know how to take care of ourselves; and it may be more for our own comfort to remain as we are. That liberty is a great thing, we may know from our own feelings, and we may likewise judge so from the conduct of the white people in the late war. How much money has been spent, and how many lives have been lost to defend their liberty! I must say that I have hoped that God would open their eyes, when they were so much engaged for liberty, to think of the state of the poor blacks, and to pity us. He has done it in some measure, and has raised us up many friends; for which we have reason to be thankful, and to hope in his mercy. What may be done further, he only knows, for *known unto God are all his ways from the beginning.* But this, my dear brethren, is by no means the greatest thing we have to be concerned about. Getting our liberty in this world is nothing to our having the liberty of the children of God. Now the Bible tells us that we are all, by nature, sinners; that we are slaves to sin and Satan, and that unless we are converted, or born again, we must be miserable for ever. Christ says, except a man be born again, he cannot see the kingdom of God, must be in the kingdom of darkness. There are but two places where all go after death, white and black, rich and poor; those places are Heaven and Hell. ...

I will conclude what I have to say with a few words to those Negroes who have their liberty. The most of what I have said to those who are slaves, may be of use to you; but you have more advantages, on some accounts, if you will improve your freedom, as you may do, than they. You have more time to read God's holy word, and to take care of the salvation of your souls. Let me beg of you to spend your time in this way, or it will be better for you if you had always been slaves. if you think seriously of the matter, you must conclude that if you do not use your freedom to promote the salvation of your souls, it will not be of any lasting good to you. Besides all this, if you are idle, and take to bad courses, you will hurt those of your brethren who are slaves, and do all in your power to prevent their being free. One great reason that is given by some for not freeing us, I understand, is, that we should not know how to take care of ourselves, and should take to bad courses; that we should be lazy and idle, and get drunk and steal. Now all those of you who follow any bad courses, and who do not take care to get an honest living by your labour and industry, are doing more to prevent our being free than any body else. Let me beg of you then, for the sake of your own good and happiness, in time, and for eternity, and for the sake of your poor brethren, who are still in bondage, "*to lead quiet and peaceable lives in all Godliness and honesty*," and may God bless you, and bring you to his kingdom, for Christ's sake, Amen.

--------- 2.24 ---------

'I FREELY AND CHEERFULLY ACKNOWLEDGE, THAT I AM OF THE AFRICAN RACE'
Benjamin Banneker

Benjamin Banneker grew up free in Baltimore County, Maryland. At an early age, he began studying under his English grandmother and in Quaker schools. As he matured, he found a passion for and excellence in mathematics. He befriended a prominent local white mathematician and, in 1791, helped the man survey Washington, D.C. The following year, Banneker published the first of six almanacs. Prior to the first almanac's publication, Banneker sent a copy to Thomas Jefferson. He introduced the volume with a polite but pointed letter in which he challenged Jefferson's assertions, published in *Notes on the State of Virginia*, that African Americans were an inferior race to whites and Native Americans.

A. Banneker's letter

SIR,

I AM fully sensible of the greatness of that freedom, which I take with you on the present occasion; a liberty which seemed to me scarcely allowable, when I reflected on that distinguished and dignified station in which you stand, and the almost general prejudice and prepossession, which is so prevalent in the world against those of my complexion.

I suppose it is a truth too well attested to you, to need a proof here, that we are a race of beings, who have long labored under the abuse and censure of the world; that we have long been looked upon with an eye of contempt; and that we have long been considered rather as brutish than human, and scarcely capable of mental endowments.

Sir, I hope I may safely admit, in consequence of that report which hath reached me, that you are a man far less inflexible in sentiments of this nature, than many others; that you are measurably friendly, and well disposed towards us; and that you are willing and ready to lend your aid and assistance to our relief, from those many distresses, and numerous calamities, to which we are reduced. Now Sir, if this is founded in truth, I apprehend you will embrace every opportunity, to eradicate that train of absurd and false ideas and opinions, which so generally prevails with respect to us; and that your sentiments are concurrent with mine, which are, that one universal Father hath given being to us all; and that he hath not only made us all of one flesh, but that he hath also, without partiality, afforded us all the same sensations and endowed us all with the same faculties; and that however variable we may be in society or religion, however diversified in situation or color, we are all of the same family, and stand in the same relation to him.

Sir, if these are sentiments of which you are fully persuaded, I hope you cannot but acknowledge, that it is the indispensible duty of those, who maintain for themselves the rights of human nature, and who possess the obligations of Christianity, to extend their power and influence to the relief of every part of the human race, from whatever burden or oppression they may unjustly labor under; and this, I apprehend, a full conviction of the truth and obligation of these principles should lead all to. Sir, I have long been convinced, that if your love for yourselves, and for those inestimable laws, which preserved to you the rights of human nature, was founded on sincerity, you could not but be solicitous, that every individual, of whatever rank or distinction, might with you equally enjoy the blessings thereof; neither could you rest satisfied short of the most active effusion of your exertions, in order to their promotion from any state of degradation, to which the unjustifiable cruelty and barbarism of men may have reduced them.

Sir, I freely and cheerfully acknowledge, that I am of the African race, and in that color which is natural to them of the deepest dye; and it is under a sense of the most profound gratitude to the Supreme Ruler of the Universe, that I now confess to you, that I am not under that state of tyrannical thraldom, and inhuman captivity, to which too many of my brethren are doomed, but that I have abun-

dantly tasted of the fruition of those blessings, which proceed from that free and unequalled liberty with which you are favored; and which, I hope, you will willingly allow you have mercifully received, from the immediate hand of that Being, from whom proceedeth every good and perfect Gift.

Sir, suffer me to recal to your mind that time, in which the arms and tyranny of the British crown were exerted, with every powerful effort, in order to reduce you to a state of servitude: look back, I entreat you, on the variety of dangers to which you were exposed; reflect on that time, in which every human aid appeared unavailable, and in which even hope and fortitude wore the aspect of inability to the conflict, and you cannot but be led to a serious and grateful sense of your miraculous and providential preservation; you cannot but acknowledge, that the present freedom and tranquility which you enjoy you have mercifully received, and that it is the peculiar blessing of Heaven.

This, Sir, was a time when you clearly saw into the injustice of a state of slavery, and in which you had just apprehensions of the horrors of its condition. It was now that your abhorrence thereof was so excited, that you publicly held forth this true and invaluable doctrine, which is worthy to be recorded and remembered in all succeeding ages: "We hold these truths to be self-evident, that all men are created equal; that they are endowed by their Creator with certain unalienable rights, and that among these are, life, liberty, and the pursuit of happiness." Here was a time, in which your tender feelings for yourselves had engaged you thus to declare, you were then impressed with proper ideas of the great violation of liberty, and the free possession of those blessings, to which you were entitled by nature; but, Sir, how pitiable is it to reflect, that although you were so fully convinced of the benevolence of the Father of Mankind, and of his equal and impartial distribution of these rights and privileges, which he hath conferred upon them, that you should at the same time counteract his mercies, in detaining by fraud and violence so numerous a part of my brethren, under groaning captivity and cruel oppression, that you should at the same time be found guilty of that most criminal act, which you professedly detested in others, with respect to yourselves.

I suppose that your knowledge of the situation of my brethren, is too extensive to need a recital here; neither shall I presume to prescribe methods by which they may be relieved, otherwise than by recommending to you and all others, to wean yourselves from those narrow prejudices which you have imbibed with respect to them, and as Job proposed to his friends, "put your soul in their souls' stead;" thus shall your hearts be enlarged with kindness and benevolence towards them; and thus shall you need neither the direction of myself or others, in what manner to proceed herein. And now, Sir, although my sympathy and affection for my brethren hath caused my enlargement thus far, I ardently hope, that your candor and generosity will plead with you in my behalf, when I make known to you, that it was not originally my design; but having taken up my pen in order to direct to you, as a present, a copy of an Almanac, which I have calculated for the succeeding year, I was unexpectedly and unavoidably led thereto.

This calculation is the production of my arduous study, in this my advanced stage of life; for having long had unbounded desires to become acquainted with the secrets of nature, I have had to gratify my curiosity herein, through my own assiduous application to Astronomical Study, in which I need not recount to you the many difficulties and disadvantages, which I have had to encounter.

And although I had almost declined to make my calculation for the ensuing year, in consequence of that time which I had allotted therefor, being taken up at the Federal Territory, by the request of Mr. Andrew Ellicott, yet finding myself under several engagements to Printers of this state, to whom I had communicated my design, on my return to my place of residence, I industriously applied myself thereto, which I hope I have accomplished with correctness and accuracy; a copy of which I have taken the liberty to direct to you, and which I humbly request you will favorably receive; and although you may have the opportunity of perusing it after its publication, yet I choose to send it to you in manuscript previous thereto, that thereby you might not only have an earlier inspection, but that you might also view it in my own hand writing.

And now, Sir, I shall conclude, and subscribe myself, with the most profound respect, Your most obedient humble servant,

BENJAMIN BANNEKER.

B. Jefferson's Reply

To Mr. BENJAMIN BANNEKER.
Philadelphia, August 30, 1791.

SIR,

I THANK you, sincerely, for your letter of the 19th instant, and for the Almanac it contained. No body wishes more than I do, to see such proofs as you exhibit, that nature has given to our black brethren talents equal to those of the other colors of men; and that the appearance of the want of them, is owing merely to the degraded condition of their existence, both in Africa and America. I can add with truth, that no body wishes more ardently to see a good system commenced, for raising the condition, both of their body and mind, to what it ought to be, as far as the imbecility of their present existence, and other circumstances, which cannot be neglected, will admit.

I have taken the liberty of sending your Almanac to Monsieur de Condozett, Secretary of the Academy of Sciences at Paris, and Member of the Philanthropic Society, because I considered it as a document, to which your whole color had a right for their justification, against the doubts which have been entertained of them.

I am with great esteem, Sir, Your most obedient Humble Servant,

THOMAS JEFFERSON.

——— 2.25 ———

A PLAN TO AIDE 'OUR HITHERTO TOO MUCH NEGLECTED FELLOW CREATURES'
Benjamin Franklin

Late in his life, following the Revolutionary War, Benjamin Franklin emerged as one of the young nation's most ardent critics of slavery. He quietly, and presciently, warned his colleagues that the compromises on slavery they wedged into the new Constitution would not hold. That same year, 1787, Franklin took over the presidency of the revived Pennsylvania Abolition Society—a pre-war organization believed to have been the first anti-slavery group. In November 1789, Franklin published "An Address to the Public" in which he explained that the Society had broadened its mission to include providing aid to freed slaves. In explaining the need, Franklin—albeit, in the condescending tone of his time—articulates an argument akin to those made today in support of affirmative action.

An Address to the Public
From the Pennsylvania society for Promoting the Abolition of Slavery, and the Relief of Free Negroes unlawfully held in Bondage.

It is with peculiar satisfaction we assure the friends of humanity, that, in prosecuting the design of our association, our endeavors have proved successful, far beyond our most sanguine expectations.

Encouraged by this success, and by the daily progress of that luminous and benign spirit of liberty which is diffusing itself throughout the world, and humbly hoping for the continuance of the divine blessing our labors, we have ventured to make an important addition to our original plan; and do therefore earnestly solicit the support and assistance of all who can feel the tender emotions of sympathy and compassion, or relish the exalted pleasure of benificence.

Slavery is such an atrocious debasement of human nature, that its very extirpation, if not performed with solicitous care, may sometimes open a source of serious evils.

The unhappy man, who has long been treated as a brute animal, too frequently sinks beneath the common standard of the human species. The galling chains that bind his body do also fetter his intellectual faculties, and impair the social affections of his heart. Accustomed to move like a mere machine, by the will of a master, reflection is suspended; he has not the power of choice; and reason and conscience have but little influence over his conduct, because he is chiefly governed by the passion of fear. He is poor and friendless; perhaps worn out by extreme labor, age, and disease.

Under such circumstances, freedom may often prove a misfortune to himself, and prejudicial to society.

Attention to emancipated black people, it is therefore to be hoped, will become a branch of our national policy; but, as far as we contribute to promote this emancipation, so far that attention is evidently a serious duty encumbent on us, which we mean to discharge to the best of our judgment and abilities.

To instruct, to advise, to qualify those who have been restored to freedom, for the exercise and enjoyment of civil liberty; to promote in them habits of industry; to furnish them with employments suited to their age, sex, talents, and other circumstances; and to procure their children an education calculated for their future situation in life,—these are the great outlines of the annexed plan, which we have adopted, and which we conceive will essentially promote the public good, and the happiness of these our hitherto too much neglected fellow creatures.

A plan so extensive cannot be carried into execution without considerable pecuniary resources, beyond the present ordinary funds of the society. We hope much from the generosity of enlightened and benevolent freemen, and will gratefully receive any donations or subscriptions for this purpose which may be made to our Treasurer, James Stars, or to James Pemberton, Chairman of our Committee of Correspondence.

Signed by order of the Society,
B. Franklin, *President*
Phila., 9th of November 1789

——— 2.26 ———
'EQUAL LIBERTY WAS ORIGINALLY THE PORTION, AND IS STILL THE BIRTH-RIGHT, OF ALL MEN'
Benjamin Franklin

In the last public act of his life, in 1790, Benjamin Franklin petitioned Congress to end the slave trade—despite the Constitutional compromise that permitted them from doing so until 1808. His petition, along with one submitted just days before by the Society of the Quakers, uncovered old wounds from the Constitutional Convention and sparked a heated month-long debate. Ultimately, Congress, and President George Washington, again bridged the dangerous rift by reaffirming the original compromise and punting the issue until 1808—by which time, many, including Washington, hoped slavery would have fizzled on its own. About two months after submitting the petition, Franklin died.

The memorial respectfully showeth,—

That, from a regard for the happiness of mankind, an association was formed several years since in this state, by a number of her citizens of various religious denominations, for promoting the abolition of slavery, and for the relief of those unlawfully held in bondage. A just and acute conception of the true principles of liberty, as it spread through the land, produced accessions to their numbers, many friends to their cause, and a legislative co-operation with their views, which, by the blessing of Divine Providence, have been successfully directed to relieving from bondage a large number of their fellow-creatures of the African race. They have also the satisfaction to observe, that, in consequence of that spirit of philanthropy and genuine liberty which is generally diffusing its beneficial influence, similar institutions are forming at home and abroad.

That mankind are all formed by the same Almighty Being, alike objects of his care, and equally designed for the enjoyment of happiness, the Christian religion teaches us to believe, and the political creed of Americans fully coincides with the position. Your memorialists, particularly engaged in attending to the distresses arising from slavery, believe it their indispensable duty to present this subject to your notice. They have observed, with real satisfaction, that many important and salutary powers are vested in you for 'promoting the welfare and securing the blessings of liberty to the people of the United States'; and as they conceive that these blessings ought rightfully to be administered, without distinction of color, to all descriptions of people, so they indulge themselves in the pleasing expectation, that nothing which can be done for the relief of the unhappy objects of their care, will be either omitted or delayed.

From a persuasion that equal liberty was originally the portion, and is still the birth-right, of all men; and influenced by the strong ties of humanity, and the principles of their institution, your memorialists conceive themselves bound to loosen the bands of slavery, and promote a general enjoyment of the blessings of freedom. Under these impressions, they earnestly entreat your serious attention to the subject of slavery; that you will be pleased to countenance the restoration of liberty to those unhappy men, who alone, in this land of freedom, are degraded to perpetual bondage, and who, amidst the general joy of surrounding freemen, are groaning in servile subjection; that you will devise means for removing this inconsistency from the character of the American people; that you will promote mercy and justice toward this distressed race; and that you will step to the very verge of the power vested in you for discouraging every species of traffic in the persons of our fellow-men.

Benjamin Franklin, *President*
Philadelphia, February 3, 1790

—————— 2.27 ——————

'IT INTRODUCES MORE EVILS THAN IT CAN CURE'
George Washington

When the delegates to the Constitutional Convention debated how the new nation should handle slavery and the slave trade, George Washington, presiding over the meeting, remained silent on the topic. But in a 1786 letter to Robert Morris, Washington made it clear his opinion on the topic had developed into a full objection to slavery—though he continued to own slaves to the end of his life. In the letter, however, Washington logs his equally strong objection to the activity of the Society of the Quakers. The Quakers and communities of free blacks had begun actively aiding slaves in their escape and flight north towards Canada through a patchwork of homes and businesses that came to be known as the Underground Railroad. Washington's letter to Morris is believed to be the first documented reference to the famous network.

Dear Sir

I give you the trouble of this letter at the instance of Mr. Dalby of Alexandria; who is called to Philadelphia to attend what he conceives to be a vexatious lawsuit respecting a slave of his, whom a Society of Quakers in the city (formed for such purposes) have attempted to liberate. . . . And if the practice of this Society of which Mr. Dalby speaks, is not discountenanced, none of those whose misfortune it is to have slaves as attendants, will visit the City if they can possibly avoid it; because by so doing they hazard their property; or they must be at the expence (and this will not always succeed) of providing servants of another description for the trip.

I hope it will not be conceived from these observations, that it is my wish to hold the unhappy people, who are the subject of this letter, in slavery. I can only say that there is not a man living who wishes more sincerely than I do, to see a plan adopted for the abolition of it; but there is only one proper and effectual mode by which it can be accomplished and that is by Legislative authority; and this, as far as my suffrage will go, shall never be wanting. But when slaves who are happy and contented with their present masters, are tampered with and seduced to leave; when a conduct of this sort begets discontent on one side and resentment on the other, and when it happens to fall on a man, whose purse will not measure with that of the Society, he looses his property for want of means to defend it; it is oppression in the latter case, and not humanity in any, because it introduces more evils than it can cure.

—————— 2.28 ——————

FUGITIVE ACT OF 1793
United States Congress

Because of the Underground Railroad and the increased sense of urgency among slaves following the war's cessation, the tide of runaways continued to grow as the 18th century drew to a close. In response, the 2nd Congress moved to empower planters in their attempts to reclaim lost slaves. The Constitution had actually already authorized slaveholders to track down and reclaim escaped slaves across state lines, but it did not spell out the limits and means of that authority. The Fugitive Act of 1793 did so. It not only bound states, regardless of their own slave laws, to return "fugitives from labor," but it established a fine for those, such as the Quakers and their Underground Railroad operators, who harbored runaways or interfered with their return.

An Act respecting Fugitives from Justice, and persons escaping from the service of their Masters.

Sec. 1. *Be it enacted by the Senate and House of Representatives of the United States of America in Congress assembled*, That whenever the executive authority of any State in the Union, or of either of the territories northwest or south of the river Ohio, shall demand any person as a fugitive from justice, of the executive authority of any such state or territory to which such person shall have fled, and shall moreover produce the copy of an indictment found, or an affidavit made before a magistrate of any state or territory as aforesaid, charging the person so demanded, with having committed treason, felony or other crime, certified as authentic by the governor or chief magistrate of the state or territory from whence the person so charged, fled, it shall be the duty of the executive authority of the state or territory to which such persons shall have fled, to cause him or her to be arrested and secured, and notice of the arrest to be given to the executive authority making such demand, or to the agent of such authority appointed to receive the fugitive, and to cause the fugitive to be delivered to such agent when he shall appear: But if no such agent shall appear within six months from the time of the arrest, the prisoner may be discharged. And all costs or expenses incurred in the apprehending, securing, and transmitting such fugitive to the state or territory making such demand, shall be paid by such state or territory.

Sec. 2. *And be it further enacted*, That any agent appointed as aforesaid, who shall receive the fugitive into his custody, shall be empowered to transport him or her to the state or territory from which he or she shall have fled. And if any person or persons shall by force set at liberty, or rescue the fugitive from such agent while transporting, as aforesaid, the person or persons so offending shall, on conviction, be fined not exceeding five hundred dollars, and be imprisoned not exceeding one year.

Sec. 3. *And be it also enacted*, That when a person held to labor in any of the United States, or in either of the territories on the northwest or south of the river Ohio, under the laws thereof, shall escape into any other of the said states or territory, the person to whom such labor or service may be due, his agent or attorney, is hereby empowered to seize or arrest such fugitive from labor, and to take him or her before any judge of the Circuit or District Courts of the United States, residing or being within the state, or before any magistrate of a county, city or town corporate, wherein such seizure or arrest shall be made, and upon proof to the satisfaction of such judge or magistrate, either by oral testimony or affidavit taken before and certified by a magistrate of any such state or territory that the person so seized or arrested, doth, under the laws of the state or territory form which he or she fled, owe service or labor to the person claiming him or her, it shall be the duty of such judge or magistrate to give a certificate thereof to such claimant, his agent or attorney, which shall be sufficient warrant for removing the said fugitive from labor, to the state or territory from which he or she fled.

Sec. 4. *And be it further enacted*, That any person who shall knowingly and willingly obstruct or hinder such claimant, his agent or attorney when so arrested pursuant to the authority herein given or declared: or shall harbor or conceal such person after notice that he or she was a fugitive from labor, as aforesaid, shall, for either of the said offences, forfeit and pay the sum of five hundred dollars. Which penalty may be recovered by and for the benefit of such claimant, by action of debt, in any court proper to try the same; saving moreover to the person claiming such labor or service, his right of action for or on account of the said injuries or either of them.

--------- 2.29 ---------

'IT IS MY WILL AND DESIRE THAT ALL SLAVES WHOM I HOLD...RECEIVE THEIR FREEDOM'
George Washington

By the time of his death in 1799, George Washington had come to abhor the slave system. Washington's was a life-long journey from a southern planter who considered slavery a simple economic necessity, to a reluctant general who saw no choice but to bolster his forces with black soldiers, to a prescient president who foresaw the issue's dangerously divisive nature and avoided confronting it. In a letter written shortly before his death, Washington expressed frustration with owning so many slaves but feeling financially unable to set them free and unwilling to sell them off. At his death, he and his wife still owned 277 slaves. In his will, Washington freed them all—an increasingly common practice among northern slaveholders as the 19th century dawned. He also honored William Lee, his storied slave attendant throughout the Revolutionary War.

...Upon the decease of my wife, it is my will and desire that all slaves whom I hold in my own right shall receive their freedom. To emancipate them during her life, would, though earnestly wished by me, be attended with such insuperable difficulties, on account of their intermixture by marriage with the Dower Negroes, as to excite the most painful sensations, if not disagreeable consequences to the latter, while both descriptions are in the occupancy of the same proprietor; it not being in my power, under the tenure by which the Dower Negroes are held, to manumit them. And whereas, among those who will receive freedom according to this devise, there may be some, who from old age or bodily infirmities, and others, who, on account of their infancy, will be unable to support themselves, it is my will and desire, that all who come under the first and second description shall be comfortably clothed and fed by my heirs while they live; and that such of the latter description as have no parents living, or, if living, are unable or unwilling to provide for them, shall be bound by the court until they shall arrive at the age of twenty-five years; and in cases where no record can be produced, whereby their ages can be ascertained, the judgment of the court, upon its view of the subject, shall be adequate and final. The Negroes thus bound are (by their masters and mistresses) to be taught to read and write, and to be brought up to some useful occupation, agreeably to the laws of the Commonwealth of Virginia providing for the support of orphan and other poor children. And I do hereby expressly forbid the sale or transportation out of the said Commonwealth, of any slave I may die possessed of, under any pretence whatsoever. And I do, moreover, most pointedly and most solemnly enjoin it upon my executors hereafter named, or the survivors of them, to see that this clause respecting slaves, and every part thereof, be religiously fulfilled at the epoch it is directed to take place, without evasion, neglect, or delay, after the crops which may then be on the ground be harvested, particularly as it respects the aged and infirm; seeing that a regular and permanent fund be established for their support, as long as there are subjects requiring it; not trusting to the uncertain provision to be made by individuals. And to my mulatto man, William, calling himself William Lee, I give immediate freedom; or, if he should prefer it (on account of the accidents which have befallen him, and which have rendered him incapable of walking or of any active employment), to remain in the situation he now is, it shall be optional in him to do so; in either case, however, I allow him an annuity of thirty dollars, during his natural life, which shall be independent of the victuals and clothes he has been accustomed to receive, if he chooses the last alternative; but in full with his freedom if he prefers the first. And this I give him as a testimony of my sense of his attachment to me, and for his faithful service during the Revolutionary War.

——— 2.30 ———

'WE BELIEVE HEAVEN IS FREE FOR ALL WHO WORSHIP IN SPIRIT AND TRUTH'
Richard Allen

With time, the once open arms of the Methodist Church grew less welcoming to African Americans. While blacks still attended camp meetings and church services by the thousands, individual officials and clergy began to bristle at the equalizing style of worship once typical of Methodism. They began more formally segregating black worship space, and otherwise putting African Americans at arms length.

In Philadelphia, Richard Allen and Absalom Jones, both free black Methodist preachers, were spiritual and civic leaders among the black population following the war. One Sunday, the church at which the men and scores of other blacks worshipped attempted to segregate them during prayer. Angered, Allen and Jones led black members in walking out from the church. With the support of noted abolitionist Benjamin Rush, the group founded the First African Church of Philadelphia two years later in 1794. Methodist officials fought and harassed the church for years, trying to force the black congregation back into a white-led Methodist church. In an attempt to assert control over the black splinter group, the denomination unilaterally declared itself the owner of First African, sparking a legal battle that went all the way to the Supreme Court. In 1816, the court ruled in favor of the black Methodists, declaring their church legally independent and owned by its congregation. That spring, members met with other black Methodists from surrounding states and founded the African Methodist Episcopal Church.

Years later, Richard Allen published the following account of the origins of AME, which today remains a black-led denomination with congregations spread around the world. AME's churches would be the nexus of civic life in black communities around the country for decades. Moreover, as the 19th century began, the denomination would also be the breeding ground for slowly radicalizing black political thought and organization.

...A number of us usually attended St. George's church in Fourth street; and when the colored people began to get numerous in attending the church, they moved us from the seats we usually sat on, and place us around the wall, and on Sabbath morning we went to church and the sexton stood at the door, and told us to go in the gallery. He told us to go, and we would see where to sit. We expected to take the seats over the ones we formerly occupied below, not knowing any better. We took those seats. Meeting had begun, and they were nearly done singing, and just as we got to the seats, the elder said, "Let us pray." We had not been long upon our knees before I heard considerable scuffling and low talking. I raised my head up and saw one of the trustees, H——— M———, having hold of the Rev. Absalom Jones, pulling him up off of his knees, and saying, "You must get up—you must not kneel here." Mr. Jones replied, "Wait until prayer is over." Mr. H——— M——— said "No, you must get up now, or I will call for aid and force you away." Mr. Jones said, "Wait until prayer is over, and I will get up and trouble you no more." With that he beckoned to one of the other trustees, Mr. L——— S——— to come to his assistance. He came, and went to William White to pull him up. By this time prayer was

over, and we all went out of the church in a body, and they were no more plagued with us in the church. This raised a great excitement and inquiry among the citizens, in so much that I believe they were ashamed of their conduct. But my dear Lord was with us, and we were filled with fresh vigor to get a house erected to worship God in seeing our forlorn and distressed situation, many of the hearts of our citizens were moved to urge us forward; notwithstanding we had subscribe largely towards finishing St. George's church, in building the gallery and laying new floors, and just as the house was made comfortable, we were turned out from enjoying the comforts of worship therein. We then hired a store-room, and held worship by ourselves. Here we were pursued with threats of being disowned, and read publicly out of meeting if we did continue worship in the place we had hired; but we believed the Lord would be our friend. We got subscription papers out to raise money to build the house of the Lord. By this time we had waited on Dr. Rush and Mr. Robert Ralston, and told them or our distressing situation. We considered it a blessing that the Lord had put it into our hearts to wait upon those gentlemen. They pitied our situation, and subscribed largely towards the church, and were very friendly towards us, and advised us to go on. We appointed Mr. Ralston our treasurer. Dr. Rush did much for us in public by his influence. I hope the name of Dr. Benjamin Rush and Robert Ralston will never be forgotten among us. They were the first two gentlemen who espoused the cause of the oppressed, and aided us in building the house of the Lord for the poor Africans to worship in. Here was the beginning and rise of the first African church in America. But the elder of the Methodist Church still pursued us. Mr. John McClaskey called upon us and told us if we did not erase our names from the subscription paper, and give up the paper, we would be publicly turned out of meeting. We asked him if we had violated any rules of discipline by so doing. He replied, "I have the charge given to me by the

Conference, and unless you submit I will read you publicly out of meeting." We told him we were willing to abide by the discipline of the Methodist Church, "And if you will show us where we have violated any law of discipline of the Methodist Church, we will submit; and if there is no rule violated in the discipline we will proceed on." He replied, "I will read you all out." We told him if he turned us out contrary to rule of discipline, we should seek further redress. We told him we were dragged off of our knees in St. George's church, and treated worse than heathens; and we were determined to seek out for ourselves, the Lord being our helper. He told us we were not Methodists, and left us. Finding we would go on in raising money to build the church, he called upon us again, and wished to see us all together. We met him. He told us that he wished us well, that he was a friend to us, and used many arguments to convince us that we were wrong in building a church. We told him we had no place of worship; and we did not mean to go to St. George's church anymore, as we were so scandalously treated in the presence of all the congregation present; "and if you deny us your name, you cannot seal up the scriptures from us, and deny us a name in heaven. We believe heaven is free for all who worship in spirit and truth." And he said, "So you are determined to go on." We told him "Yes, God being our helper." He then replied, "We will disown you all from the Methodist connection." We believed if we put our trust in the Lord, he would stand by us. Thus was a trial that I never had to pass through before.

…We then held an election, to know what religious denomination we should unite with. At the election it was determined—there were two in favor of the Methodist, the Rev. Absalom Jones and myself, and large majority in favor of the Church of England. The majority carried. Notwithstanding we had been so violently persecuted by the elder, we were in favor of being attached to the Methodist connection; for I was confident that there was no religious sect or denomination would suit the capacity of the colored people as well as the Methodist; for the plain and simple gospel suits best for any people; for the unlearned can understand, and the learned are sure to understand; and the reason that the Methodist is so successful in the awakening and conversion of the colored people, the plain doctrine and having a good discipline. But in many cases the preachers would act to please their own fancy, without discipline, till some of them became such tyrants, and more especially to the colored people. They would turn them out of society, giving them no trial, for the smallest offense, perhaps only hearsay. They would frequently, in meeting the class, impeach some of the members of whom they had heard an ill report, and turn them out, saying, "I have heard thus and thus of you, and you are no more a member of society"—without witness on either side. This has been frequently done, notwithstanding in the first rise and progress in Delaware state, and elsewhere, the colored people were their greatest support; for there were but few of us free; but the slaves would toil in their little patches many a night until midnight to raise their little truck and sell to get something to support them more than what their masters gave them, but we used often to divide our little support among the white preachers of the Gospel. This was once a quarter. It was in the time of the old Revolutionary War between Great Britain and the United States. The Methodists were the first people that brought glad tidings to the colored people. I feel thankful that ever I heard a Methodist preach. We are beholden to the Methodists, under God, for the light of the Gospel we enjoy; for all other denominations preached so high-flown that we were not able to comprehend their doctrine. Sure am I that reading sermons will never prove so beneficial to the colored people as spiritual or extempore preaching. I am well convinced that the Methodist has proved beneficial to thousands and ten times thousands. It is to be awfully feared that the simplicity of the Gospel that was among them fifty years ago, and that they conform more to the world and the fashions thereof, they would fare very little better than the people of the world. The discipline is altered considerably from what it was. We would ask for the good old way, and desire to walk therein.

...Many of the colored people in other places were in a situation nearly like those of Philadelphia and Baltimore, which induced us, in April 1816, to call a general meeting, by way of Conference. Delegates from Baltimore and other places which met those of Philadelphia, and taking into consideration their grievances, and in order to secure the privileges, promote union and harmony among themselves, it was resolved: "That the people of Philadelphia, Baltimore, etc., etc., should become one body, under the name the African Methodist Episcopal Church." We deemed it expedient to have a form of discipline, whereby we may guide our people in the fear of God, in the unity of the Spirit, and in the bonds of peace, and preserve us from that spiritual despotism which we have so recently experienced—remembering that we are not to lord it over God's heritage, as greedy dogs that can never have enough. But with long suffering and bowels of compassion, to bear each other's burdens, and so fulfill the Law of Christ, praying that our mutual striving together for the promulgation of the Gospel may be crowned with abundant success.

The God of Bethel heard her cries,
He let his power be seen;
He stopp'd the proud oppressor's frown,
And proved himself a King.

Thou sav'd them in the trying hour,
Ministers and councils joined,
And all stood ready to retain
That helpless church of Thine.

Bethel surrounded by her foes,
But not yet in despair,
Christ heard her supplication cries;
The God of Bethel heard.

——— 2.31 ———
'IT IS UNPLEASANT FOR US TO MAKE THESE REMARKS, BUT JUSTICE TO OUR COLOR DEMANDS IT'
Richard Allen and Absalom Jones

In the summer of 1793 a yellow fever epidemic hit Philadelphia, killing thousands. White doctors believed blacks were immune to the disease and, at the urging of Dr. Benjamin Rush, their patron, Richard Allen, Absalom Jones and William Gray helped coordinate a troop of African-American nurses to aid the sick and dying. Presumably, they were motivated by a mixture of their spiritual beliefs and a desire to showcase black intellect, compassion and morality. Philadelphia's black population, however, was in fact not immune and hundreds fell ill and died. Then, as the plague lifted, whites began to charge that the black nurses had taken advantage by either overcharging or outright robbing their patients. Journalist Matthew Carey led the outcry, issuing the charges in his widely read account of the epidemic. Indignant, Allen and Jones published an angry rebuttal in which they detailed the fees charged, stressed that all were set by the white patients and characterized white society as morally bankrupt for having left the work to blacks in the first place.

A. Matthew Carey's charges

...When the yellow fever prevailed in South Carolina, the negroes, according to that accurate observer, dr. Lining, were wholly free from it. "There is something very singular in the constitution of the negroes," says he, "which renders them not liable to this fever; for though many of them were as much exposed as the nurses to this infection, yet I never knew one instance of this fever among them, though they are equally subject with the white people to the bilious fever." The same idea prevailed for a considerable time in Philadelphia; but it was erroneous. They did not escape the disorder; however, there were scarcely any of them seized at first, and the number that were finally affected, was not great; and, as I am informed by an eminent doctor, "it yielded to the power of medicine in them more easily than in the whites." The error that prevailed on this subject had a very salutary effect; for at an early period of the disorder, hardly any white nurses could be procured; and, had the negroes been equally terrified, the sufferings of the sick, great as they actually were, would have been exceedingly aggravated. At the period alluded to, the elders of the African church met, and offered their assistance to, the mayor, to procure nurses for the sick, and to assist in burying the dead. Their offers were accepted; and Absalom Jones, Richard Allen, and William Gray, undertook the management of these two several services. The great demand for nurses afforded an opportunity for imposition, which was eagerly seized by some of the vilest of the blacks. They extorted two, three, four, and even five dollars a night for such attendance, as would have been well paid by a single dollar. Some of them were even detected in plundering the houses of the sick. But it is unjust to call a censure on the whole for this sort of conduct, as many people have done. The services of Jones, Allen, and Gray, and others of their colour, have been very great, and demand public gratitude.

B. Richard Allen and Absalom Jones respond

The bad consequence many of our color apprehend form a partial relation of our conduct are, that it will prejudice the minds of the people in general against us; because it is impossible that one individual can have knowledge of all; therefore at some future day, when some of the most virtuous that were upon most praiseworthy motives, induced to serve the sick, may fall into the service of a family that are strangers to him or her, and it is discovered that it is one of those stigmatized wretches, what may we suppose will be the consequence? Is it not reasonable to think the person will be abhorred, despised and perhaps dismissed from employment, to their great disadvantage? would not this be hard? and have we not therefore sufficient reason to seek for redress? We can with

certainty assure the public that we have seen more humanity, more real sensibility form the poor colored than from the poor whites. When many of the former, of their own accord, rendered services where extreme necessity called for it, the general part of the poor white people were so dismayed, that instead of attempting to be useful, they, in a manner, hid themselves. A remarkable instance of this: A poor, afflicted, dying man stood at his chamber window, praying and beseeching every one that passed by to help him to a drink of water. A number of white people passed, and instead of being moved by the poor man's distress, they hurried, as fast as they could, out of the sound of his cries, until at length a gentleman, who seemed to be a foreigner, came up. He could not pass by, but had not resolution enough to go into the house. He held eight dollars in his hand, and offered it to several as a reward for giving the poor man a drink of water, but was refused by every one, until a poor colored man came up. The gentleman offered the eight dollars to him, if he would relieve the poor man with a little water. "Master," replied the good-natured fellow, "I will supply the gentleman with water, but surely I will not take your money for it," nor could he be prevailed upon to accept his bounty. He went in, supplied the poor subject with water, and rendered him every service he could.

A poor colored man, named Sampson, went constantly from house to house where distress was, and no assistance, without fee or reward. He was smitten with the disorder, and died. After his death, his family was neglected by those he had served.

Sarah Bass, a colored widow woman, gave all the assistance she could in several families, for which she did not receive anything; and when anything was offered her, she left it to the option of those she served.

A colored woman nursed Richard Mason and son. They died. Richard's widow, considering the risk the poor woman had run, and from observing the fears that sometimes rested on her mind, expected she would have demanded something considerable; but upon asking her what she demanded, her reply was, "fifty cents per day." Mrs. Mason intimated it was not sufficient for her attendance. She replied, that it was enough for what she had done, and would take no more. Mrs. Mason's feelings were such, that she settled an annuity of 6£ a year on her for life. Her name was Mary Scott.

An elderly, colored woman nursed—with great diligence and attention. When recovered, he asked what he must give her for her services—she replied, "a dinner, master, on a cold winter's day." And thus she went from place to place, rendering every service in her power, without an eye to reward.

A young colored woman was requested to attend one night upon a white man and his wife, who were very ill. No other person could be had. Great wages were offered her—she replied, "I will not go for money, if I go for money, God will see it and may make me take the disorder and die; but if I go and take no money, he may spare my life. She went about 9 o'clock, and found them both on the floor. She could procure no candle or other light, but stayed with them about two hours, and then left them. They both died that night. She was afterwards very ill with the fever. Her life was spared.

Caesar Cranchal, a man of color, offered his services to attend the sick, and said, "I will not take your money; I will not sell my life for money." It is said he died with the flux.

A colored lad, at the widow Gilpin's, was intrusted with his young master's keys, on his leaving the city, and transacted his business with the greatest honest and despatch; having unloaded a vessel for him in the time, and loaded it again.

A woman that nursed David Bacon charged with exemplary moderation, and said she would not have any more.

It may be said in vindication of the conduct of those who discovered ignorance or incapacity in nursing, that it is, in itself, a considerable art derived from experience as well as the exercise of the finer feelings of humanity. This experience nine-tenths of those employed, it is possible, were wholly strangers to.

We do not recollect such acts of humanity from the poor, white people, in all the round we have been engaged in. we could mention many other instances of the like nature, but think it needless.

It is unpleasant for us to make these remarks, but justice to our color demands it. Mr. Carey pays William Gray and us a compliment; he says, our services and others of our color have been very great, etc. By naming us, he leaves those others in the hazardous state of being classed with those who are called the "vilest." The few that were discovered to merit public censure were brought to justice, which ought to have sufficed, without being canvassed over in his "Trifle" of a pamphlet; which cause us to be more particular, and endeavor to recall the esteem of the public for our friends and the people of color, as far as may be found worthy; for we conceive, and experience proves it, that an ill name is easier given than taken away. We have many unprovoked enemies who begrudge us the liberty we enjoy, and are glad to hear of any complaint against our color, be it just or unjust; in consequence of which we are more earnestly endeavoring all in our power, to warn, rebuke and exhort our African friends to keep a conscience void of offense towards God and man; and at the same time, would not be backward to interfere, when stigmas or oppression appear pointed at or attempted against them unjustly; and we are confident we shall stand justified in the sight of the candid and judicious.

We can assure the public that there were as many white as black people detected in pilfering, although the number of the latter, employed as nurses, was twenty times as great as the former, and that there is, in our opinion, as great a proportion of white as of black inclined to such practices; and it is rather to be admired that so few instances of pilfering and robbery happened, considering the great opportunities there were for such things. We do not know of more than five colored people suspected of anything clandestine, out of the great number employed. The people were glad to get any person to assist them. A colored person was preferred, because it was supposed they were not so likely to take the disorder. The most worthless were acceptable; so that it would have been no cause of wonder if twenty causes of complaint had occurred for every one that hath. It has been alleged that many of the sick were neglected by the nurses; we do not wonder at it, considering their situation; in many instances up night and day, without any one to relieve them; worn down with fatigue and want of sleep they could not, in many cases, render that assistance which was needful. Where we visited, the causes of complaint on this score were not numerous. The case of the nurses, in many instances, were deserving of commiseration; the patient raging and frightful to behold. It has frequently required two persons to hold them from running away; others have made attempts to jump out of a window, in many chambers they were nailed down and the door kept locked to prevent them from running away or breaking their necks; others lay vomiting blood and screaming enough to chill them with horror. Thus were many of the nurses circumstanced, alone, until the patient died; then called away to another scene of distress, and thus have been, for a week or ten days, left to do the best they could, without any sufficient rest, many of them having some of the dearest connections sick at the time an suffering for want, while their husband, wife, father, mother, etc., have been engaged in the service of the white people. We mention this to show the difference between this and nursing in common cases. We have suffered equally with the whites; our distress hath been very great, but much unknown to the white people. Few have been the whites that paid attention to us, while the colored persons were engaged in others' service. We can assure the public that we have taken four and five colored people in a day to be buried. In several instances, when they have been seized with the sickness, while nursing, they have been turned out of the house, wandering destitute, until they found shelter wherever they could (as many of them

would not be admitted to their former homes), they have languished alone, and we know of one who even died in a stable. Others acted with more tenderness; when their nurses were taken sick, they had proper care taken of them at their houses. We know of two instances of this. It is even to this day a generally received opinion in this city, that our color was not so liable to the sickness as the whites. We hope our friends will pardon us for setting this matter in its true state.

The public was informed that in the West Indies and other places, where this terrible malady had been, it was observed that the blacks were not affected with it. Happy would it have been for you, and much more so for us, if this observation had been verified by our experience.

When the people of color had the sickness and died, we were imposed upon, and told it was not with the prevailing sickness, until it became too notorious to be denied; then we were told some few died, but not many. Thus were our services extorted at the peril of our lives. Yet you accuse us of extorting a little money from you. …

We shall now conclude with the following proverb, which we think applicable to those of our color, who exposed their lives in the late afflicting dispensation:

God and a soldier all men do adore
In time of war and not before;
When the war is over, and all things righted,
God is forgotten, and the soldier slighted.

———— 2.32 ————

THE FIRST BAPTIST CHURCH OF SAVANNAH, GA.

Andrew Bryan

Just as Methodism's revivalist style and message of divine justice attracted blacks, so too did that of Baptists. In 1775, George Liele founded the first independent black Baptist church, in Savannah, Georgia. Liele was himself the first officially ordained African-American Baptist preacher—though, as with Methodists, countless black preachers "exhorted" to gatherings without official sanction. The Revolutionary War spread Liele's disciples literally throughout the Americas, and sent him to Jamaica with other Loyalist refugees. Andrew Bryan, a Liele protégé, remained in Georgia and built the Savannah church into a mammoth congregation in the opening years of the 19th century, spawning two sister churches and attracting nearly 4,000 members. In the 1800 letter below, Bryan describes the church's growth.

…With much pleasure, I inform you, dear sir, that I enjoy good health, and am strong in body, tho' sixty-three years old, and am blessed with a pious wife, whose freedom I have obtained, and an only daughter and child who is married to a free man, tho' she, and consequently, under our laws, her seven children, five sons and two daughters, are slaves. By a kind Providence I am well provided for, as to worldly comforts, (tho' I have had very little given me as a minister) having a house and lot in this city, besides the land on which several buildings stand, for which I receive a small rent, and a fifty-six acre tract of land, with all necessary buildings, four miles in the country, and eight slaves; for whose education and happiness, I am enabled thro' mercy to provide.

But what will be infinitely more interesting to my friend, and is so much more prized by myself, we enjoy the rights of conscience to a valuable extent, worshipping in our families and preaching three times every Lord's-day, baptizing frequently from ten to thirty at a time in the Savannah, and administering the sacred supper, not only without molestation, but in the presence, and with the approbation and encouragement of many of the white people. We are now about seven hundred in number, and the work of the Lord goes on prosperously.

An event which has had a happy influence on our affairs was the coming of Mr. Holcombe, late pastor of Euhaw Church, to this place at the call of the heads of the city, of all denominations, who have remained for the thirteen months he has been here among his constant hearers and his liberal supporters. His salary is 2000 a year. He has just had a baptistery, with

convenient appendages, build in his place of worship, and has commenced baptizing.

Another dispensation of Providence has much strengthened our hands, and increased our means of information; Henry Francis, lately a slave to the widow of the late Colonel Leroy Hammond, of Augusta, has been purchased by a few humane gentlemen of this place, and liberated to exercise the handsome ministerial gifts he possesses amongst us, and teach our youth to read and write. He is a strong man about forty-nine years of age, whose mother was white and whose father was an Indian. His wife and only son are slaves.

Brother Francis has been in the ministry fifteen years, and will soon receive ordination, and will probably become the pastor of a branch of my large church, which is getting too unwieldy for one body. Should this event take place, and his charge receive constitution, it will take the rank and title of the 3rd Baptist Church in Savannah.

With the most sincere and ardent prayers to God for your temporal and eternal welfare, and with the most unfeigned gratitude, I remain, reverend and dear sir, your obliged servant in the gospel.

――――― 2.33 ―――――

A NARRATIVE OF THE LIFE AND ADVENTURES OF VENTURE
Venture Smith

Venture Smith's 1798 slave narrative tells the life story of a slave abducted in Guinea at the age of eight and sold in the British colonies. As an adult, Smith is described as a mammoth man, and the story is filled with fantastic tales of his strength. It portrays him as larger-than-life—and certainly more grand than the people that sought to hold him in bondage. He was as obstinate as he was strong, and could not be kept as a slave. The excerpts below describe the difficulty his owner had in selling him due to his refusal to mind the overseer's orders or accept physical abuse. Eventually, Smith purchased both his own freedom and that of his family. He was nearly 70 years old when his narrative was published.

A Narrative of the Life and Adventures of Venture, A Native of Africa:

But resident above sixty years in the United State of America.

Related by Himself.

...Towards the close of the time that I resided with this master I had a falling out with my mistress. This happened one time when my master was gone to Long Island a-gunning. At first the quarrel began between my wife and her mistress. I was then at work in the barn, and hearing a racket in the house induced me to run there and see what had broken out. When I entered the house, I found my mistress in a violent passion with my wife, for what she informed me was a mere trifle; such a small affair that I forbear to put my mistress to the shame of having it known. I earnestly requested my wife to beg pardon of her mistress for the sake of peace, even if she had given no just occasion for offence. But whilst I was thus saying my mistress turned the blows which she was repeating on my wife to me. She took down her horsewhip, and while she was glutting her fury with it, I reached out my great black hand, raised it up and received the blows of the whip on it which were designed for my head. Then I immediately committed the whip to the devouring fire.

When my master returned from the island, his wife told him of the affair, but for the present he seemed to take no notice of it, and mentioned not a word about it to me. Some days after his return, in the morning as I was putting on a log in the fireplace, not suspecting harm from any one, I received a most violent stroke on the crown of my head with a club two feet long and as large round as a chairpost. This blow very badly wounded my head, and the scar of it remains to this day. The first blow made me have my wits about me you may suppose, for as soon as he went to renew it, I snatched the club out of his hands and dragged him out of the door. He then sent for his brother to come and assist him, but I presently left my master, took the club he

wounded me with, carried it to a neighboring Justice of the Peace, and complained of my master. He finally advised me to return to my master, and live contented with him till he abused me again, and then complain. I consented to do accordingly. But before I set out for my master's, up he come, and his brother Robert, after me. The Justice improved this convenient opportunity to caution my master. He asked him for what he treated his slave thus hastily and unjustly, and told him what would be the consequence if he continued the same treatment towards me. After the Justice had ended his discourse with my master, he and his brother set out with me for home, one before and the other behind me. When they had come to a bye place, they both dismounted their respective horses and fell to beating me with great violence. I became enraged at this and immediately turned them both under me, laid one of them across the other, and stamped both with my feet what I would.

This occasioned my master's brother to advise him to put me off. A short time after this I was taken by a constable and two men. They carried me to a blacksmith's shop and had me handcuffed. When I returned home my mistress enquired much of her waiters whether Venture was handcuffed. When she was informed that I was, she appeared to be very contented and was much transported with the news. In the midst of this content and joy, I presented myself before my mistress, showed her my handcuffs, and gave her thanks for my gold rings. For this my master commanded a negro of his to fetch him a large ox chain. This my master locked on my legs with two padlocks. I continued to wear the chain peaceably for two or three days, when my master asked me with contemptuous hard names whether I had not better be freed from my chains and go to work. I answered him, No. Well then, said he, I will send you to the West Indies or banish you, for I am resolved not to keep you. I answered him I crossed the waters to come here, and I am willing to cross them to return.

For a day or two after this not any one said much to me, until one Hempstead Miner, of Stonington, asked me if I would live with him. I answered him that I would. He then requested me to make myself discontented and to appear as unreconciled to my master as I could before that he bargained with him for me; and that in return he would give me a good chance to gain my freedom when I came to live with him. I did as he requested me. Not long after Hempstead Miner purchased me of my master for fifty-six pounds lawful. He took the chain and padlocks from off me immediately after.

It may here be remembered, that I related a few pages back, that I hired out a sum of money to Mr. Robert Stanton, and took his note for it. In the fray between my master Stanton and myself, he broke upon my chest containing his brother's note to me, and destroyed it. Immediately after my present master bought me, he determined to sell me at Hartford. As soon as I became apprised of it, I bethought myself that I would secure a certain sum of money which lay by me; safer than hire it out to a Stanton. Accordingly, I buried it in the earth a little distance from Thomas Stanton's, in the road over which he passed daily. A short time after, my master carried me to Hartford, and first proposed to sell me to one William Hooker of that place. Hooker asked whether I would go to the German Flats with him. I answered, No. He said I should, if not by fair mean I should by foul. If you will go by no other measures, I will tie you down in my sleigh. I replied to him that if he carried me in that manner no person would purchase me, for it would be thought that he had a murderer for sale. After this he tried no more, and said he would not have me as a gift.

——— 2.34 ———

THANKSGIVING SERMON
Absalom Jones

In 1808 Congress banned the further importation of slaves, one year after Britain likewise abolished the international slave trade. In the years preceding these steps, southern planters and slave traders, anticipating the coming ban, stepped up their pace of importing slaves. Tens of thousands of slaves came to America during the period between the ratification of the Constitution and 1808.

On January 1st, 1808, free blacks celebrated and memorialized the "first fruits of peace upon earth." At his St. Thomas's AME Church in Philadelphia, Rev. Absalom Jones delivered a "Thanksgiving Sermon" in which he instructed the congregation on ways to give thanks for the momentous occasion. He opened the sermon by comparing the end of the slave trade to the Biblical deliverance of the Jews from Egypt.

... The history of the world shows us that the deliverance of the children of Isreale from their bondage is not the only instance in which it has pleased God to appear in behalf of oppressed and distressed nations, as the deliverance of the innocent, and of those who call upon his name. He is as unchangeable in his nature and character as he is in his wisdom and power. The great and blessed event, which we have this day met to celebrate, is a striking proof that the God of heaven and earth is the same, yesterday, and today, and descended, and the country in which some of us were born, have been visited by the tender mercy of the Common Father of the human race. He has seen the affliction of our countrymen, with an eye of pity. He has seen such of them as wicked arts, by which wars have been fomented among the different tribe of the Africans, in order to procure captives for the purpose of selling them for slaves. He has seen ships fitted out from different ports in Europe and America, and freighted with trinkets to be exchanged for the bodies and souls of men. He has seen the anguish which has taken place when parents have been torn from their children, and children from their parents, and conveyed, with their hands and feet bound in fetters, on board of ships prepared to receive them. He has seen them thrust in crowds into the holds of those ships, where many of them have perished from the want of air. He has seen such of them as have escaped from that noxious place of confinement, leap into the ocean, with faint hope of swimming back to their native shore, or a determination to seek an early retreat from their impending misery, in a watery grave. He has seen them exposed for sale, like horses and cattle, upon the wharves; or, like bales of good, in warehouses of West India and American sea ports. He has seen the pangs of separation between members of the same family. He has seen them driven into the sugar, the rice, and tobacco fields, and compelled to work—in spite of the habits of ease which they derived from the natural fertility of their own country—in the open air, beneath a burning sun, with scarcely as much clothing upon them as modesty required. He has seen them faint beneath the pressure of their labours. He has seen them return to their smoky huts in the evening, with nothing to satisfy their hunger but a scanty allowance of roots; and these, cultivated for themselves, on that day only, which God ordained as a day of rest for man and beast. He has seen the neglect with which their masters have treated their immortal souls; not only in withholding religious instructions from them, but, in some instances, depriving them of access to the means of obtaining it. He has seen all the different modes of turture, by means of the whip, the screw, the pincers, and the red-hot iron, which have been exercised upon their bodies, by inhuman overseers: overseers, did I say? Yes: but not by these only. Our God has seen masters and mistresses, educated in fashionable life, sometimes take the instruments of torture into their own hands, and, deaf to the cries and shrieks of their agonizing slaves, exceed even their overseers in cruelty. Inhuman wretches! though You have been deaf to their cries and shrieks, they have been heard in Heaven. The ears of Jehovah have been constantly open to

them: He has heard the prayers that have ascended from the hearts of his people; and he has, as in the case of his ancient and chosen people the Jews, come down to deliver our suffering countrymen from the hands of their oppressors. He came down into the United States, when they declared, in the constitution which they framed in 1788, that trade in our African fellowmen should cease in the year 1808: He came down into the British Parliament, when they passed a law to put an end to the same iniquitous trade in May 1807: He came down into the Congress of the United States, the last winter, when they passed a similar law, the operation of which commences on this happy day. Dear land of our ancestors! thou shalt no more be stained with the blood of thy children, shed by British and American hands: the ocean shall no more afford a refuge to their bodies, from impending slavery: nor shall the shores of the British West India islands, and of the United States, any more witness the anguish of families, parted for ever by a publick sale. For this signal interposition of the God of mercies, in behalf of our brethren, it becomes us this day to offer up our united thanks. Let the song of angels, which was first heard in the air at the birth of our Saviour, be heard this day in our assembly: Glory to God in the highest, for these first fruits of peace upon earth, and good-will to man: O! let us give thanks unto the Lord: let us call upon his name, and make known his deeds among the people. Let us sing psalms unto him and talk of all his wondrous works. …

———— 2.35 ————
'THE SWEETS OF LIBERTY'
African Methodist Episcopal Church Hymn

During the January 1, 1808, celebration at St. Thomas AME in Philadelphia, the congregation sang an anthem written for the occasion by Michael Fortune.

To Thee, Almighty, gracious power,
Who sit'st enthron'd, in radiant heaven;
On this bless'd morn, this hallow'd hour,

The homage of the heart be given!
Lift up your souls to God on high,
The fountain of eternal grace,
Who, with a tender father's eye,
Looked down on Afric's helpless race!

The nations heard His stern commands!
Britannia kindly set us free;
Colombia tears the galling bands,
And gives the sweets of Liberty.

Then strike the lyre! your voices raise!
Let gratitude inspire your song!
Pursue religion's holy ways,
Shun sinful Pleasure's giddy throng!

From Mercy's seat may grace descend,
To wake contrition's heartfelt sighs!
O! may our pious strains ascend,
Where ne'er the sainted spirit dies!

Then, we our freedom shall retain,
In peace and love, and cheerful toil:
Plenty shall flow from the wide main,
And golden harvests from the soil.

Ye nations that to us restore
The rights which God bestow'd on all;
For you His blessing we implore:
O! listen further to His call!

From one parental stem ye spring,
A kindred blood your bosoms own;
Your kindred tongues God's praises sing,
And beg forgiveness at his throne:

O, then, your mutual wrongs forgive,
Unlock your hearts to social love!
So shall ye safe and happy live,
By grace and blessings from above.

3

I Will Be Heard:

ABOLITION AND THE BUILD UP TO CIVIL WAR

——— 3.1 ———

'NO BLACK OR MULATTO PERSON SHALL BE PERMITTED TO SETTLE OR RESIDE IN THIS STATE, UNLESS HE OR SHE SHALL FIRST PRODUCE A FAIR CERTIFICATE...OF HIS OR HER ACTUAL FREEDOM'

Manumission Certificates

At the turn of the 19th century, around 60,000 free black people lived in the United States. Many were escaped slaves who had fled to northern states via the Underground Railroad. Just as many remained in the South — though living with much less freedom of movement than those in the North. But a number of these free blacks had been liberated, or manumitted, by former slaveholders who had been persuaded that slavery was either morally wrong or generally bad for the nation. Many slaveholders, such as President Washington (see Chapter One), manumitted their slaves in their wills rather than allowing them to be sold as part of an estate. Determining who was free and who was fugitive became an issue in the eyes of a number of state legislators. Many states passed laws, such as this 1804 Ohio statute, requiring African Americans to be able to produce proof of their freedom if called upon to do so. So, when they freed their slaves, owners would obtain official documentation from the courts stating such. Free blacks, then, would keep these manumission certificates as the guarantors of their freedom.

Sec. 1. *Be it enacted by the General Assembly of the State of Ohio,* That from and after the first day of June next no black or mulatto person shall be permitted to settle or reside in this state, unless he or she shall first produce a fair certificate from some court within the United States, of his or her actual freedom, which certificate shall be attested by the clerk of said court, and the seal thereof annexed thereto, by said clerk.

Sec. 2. *And be it further enacted,* That every black or mulatto person residing within this state, on or before the fifth day of June, one thousand eight hundred and four, shall enter his or her name, together with the name or names of his or her children, in the clerk's office in the county in which he, she or they reside, which shall be entered on record by said clerk, and thereafter the clerk's certificate of such record shall be sufficient evidence of his, her or their freedom; and for every entry and certificate, the person obtaining the same shall pay to the clerk twelve and an half cents. Provided nevertheless, That nothing in this act contained shall bar the lawful claim to any black or mulatto person.

Sec. 3. *And be it further enacted,* That no person or persons residents of this state, shall be permitted to hire, or in any way employ any black or mulatto person, unless such black or mulatto person shall have one of the certificates as aforesaid, under pain of forfeiting and paying any sum not less than ten nor more than fifty dollars, at the discretion of the court, for every such offense, one-half thereof for the use of the informer and the other half for the use of the state; and shall moreover pay to the owner, if any there be, of such black or mulatto person, the sum of fifty cents for every day he, she or they shall in any wise employ, harbour or secret such black or mulatto person, which sum or sums shall be recoverable before any court having cognizance thereof.

Sec. 4. *And be it further enacted*, That if any person or persons shall harbour or secret any black or mulatto person, the property of any person whatever, or shall in any wise hinder or prevent the lawful owner or owners from retaking and possessing his or her black or mulatto servant or servants, shall, upon conviction thereof, by indictment or information, be fined in any sum not less than ten nor more than fifty dollars, at the discretion of the court, one-half thereof for the use of the informer and the other half for the use of the state.

Sec. 5. *And be it further enacted*, That every black or mulatto person who shall come to reside in this state with such certificate as is required in the first section of this act, shall, within two years, have the same recorded in the clerk's office, in the county in which he or she means to reside, for which he or she shall pay to the clerk twelve and an half cents, and the clerk shall give him or her a certificate of such record.

Sec. 6. *And be it further enacted*, That in case any person or persons, his or their agent or agents, claiming any black or mulatto person that now are or hereafter may be in this state, may apply, upon making satisfactory proof that such black or mulatto person or persons is the property of him or her who applies, to any associate judge or justice of the peace within this state, the associate judge or justice is hereby empowered and required, by his precept, to direct the sheriff or constable to arrest such black or mulatto person or persons and deliver the same in the county or township where such officers shall reside, to the claimant

or claimants or his or their agent or agents, for which service the sheriff or constable shall receive such compensation as they are entitled to receive in other cases for similar services.

Sec. 7. *And be it further enacted*, That any person or persons who shall attempt to remove, or shall remove from this state, or who shall aid and assist in removing, contrary to the provisions of this act, any black or mulatto person or persons, without first proving as hereinbefore directed, that he, she or they, is or are legally entitled so to do, shall, on conviction thereof before any court having cognizance of the same, forfeit and pay the sum of one thousand dollars, one-half to the use of the informer and the other half to the use of the state, to be recovered by action of debt, qui tam, or indictment, and shall moreover be liable to the action of the party injured.

─────── 3.2 ───────

'WE WILL WADE TO OUR KNEES IN BLOOD SOONER THAN FAIL IN THE ATTEMPT'

Gabriel's Conspiracy to Rebellion

While legislatures were busy attempting to limit the liberties of free blacks, some slaveholders had begun allowing a certain amount of freedom to select slaves. Driven, of course, by economics, owners hired out slaves seen as trustworthy or possessing a particularly marketable skill. In some cases, exceptionally loose overseers allowed slaves to hire themselves out one day a week in order to make money. Many white community leaders discouraged the practice, but slaves offered cheap labor even to those willing to pay for it, and thus it continued. Those who opposed it were concerned about the contact it allowed slaves to have with free blacks and working class whites — contact that could lead to ideas on how to obtain their liberty. Young Gabriel, slave of Thomas Prosser, was exactly the sort of person they feared.

Most of his fellow slaves in Richmond, Virginia, considered Gabriel a leader. Prosser allowed Gabriel to hire himself out, and historians speculate his increasingly radical ideas were culled from conversations and interactions with the free blacks and white laborers he met. In the fall of

1799, he was publicly branded as punishment for an altercation with a white man, in which he bit the man's ear off. Shortly thereafter, inspired by the success of the slave rebellion in Haiti, he began organizing other slaves for a planned revolt. They intended to storm the state capital and, with the help of a guard there, acquire arms and take Governor James Monroe hostage. They would then rally support from nearby Native American nations and a French navy vessel believed to be docked in the vicinity. Gabriel and his co-conspirators spread the plan throughout surrounding counties and began slowly stowing away weapons. On August 31, 1800, the eve of the date set for the uprising, two slaves betrayed rumors of it to their owners.

Prosecutors in the jury-less court that tried all of the conspirators offered amnesty to two participants for testifying against the rest. Ben Woolfolk and another of Prosser's slaves, also named Ben, offered testimony that led to the execution of 27 people, including Gabriel. The court's notes on the men's testimony and Gabriel's trial are excerpted below. In Gabriel's trial, the witnesses claim that Gabriel had gathered support of over 1,500 people in and around Richmond — by far the largest planned revolt in America's history to that point.

A. Trial of September 15, 1800

CommonWealth against Sundry Negroes Sept 15 1800

Commonwealth against Jupiter the property of Colo Wilkinson—the evidence of Prossers Ben against him—The prisoner told Gabriel he would enlist people in town, that he had done very well in Town, he had enlisted a number—That he expected to enlist more—he enquired of Gabriel how he came on in the Country—Gabriel replied he could make out some arms but not sufficient— The prisoner said he could contrive to let him into the Capitol to get Arms &c That the man who kept the Key would let them into the Capitol to take the Arms —which were there— This conversation took place on the day of raising a new Barn at Mr Prossers—and was the day after Mr Prosser left home to go to Amherst

Thomas H Prosser Deposes: That he left home on his Journey to Amherst about the seventh of August last —

Commonwealth against Sam the property of Colo Wilkinson; The Evidence of Prossers Ben against him—I saw him at our great house about a fortnight before they were to meet— In a conversation in presence of the Deponent, Sam the prisoner observed that if he had a 100 men as valuable as himself, that he would venture to town—That they were to fight with Scythe Blades in the beginning but that they would get Arms from the Capitol—Sam said, that if they had men enough to fill up the Capitol square; they would drive all the White people into the River—He agreed to meet Gabriel on the night appointed— …

CommonWealth v Daniel property of Nathl Wilkinson

Prossers Ben—On Monday the preceeding the Saturday appointed for the Insurrection the prisoner was at Mr Prossers Blacksmith Shop — Prossers Solomon asked the prisoner how all the Boys in Town were The prisoners replied the boys in Town are well and nearly ready to do the Business—from Solomons usual way of addressing persons concerned in the plott the Witness supposed the prisoner to understand the Enquiry from Solomon as alluding to the Insurrection of the Negroes the Witness has heard Gabriel say the prisoner was one of his party but never directly heard the prisoner make any acknowledgement to that effect (acquitted)

CommonWealth v Isham belonging to Wm Burton

Ben—On a Sunday on which the last Barbacue took place amongst the blacks The prisoner went to the Bridge (Brook) about 12 OClock as he believes where he found the prisoner at the Bar & Sundry other Negroes named by him, gaming with quoits pitching —The Witness went below the bridge afishing and was shortly after joined by Gabriel, the prisoner, and a brother of his by name George from hence he the Witness went to the Barbacue where the prisoner Gabriel & some other Negroes whom he saw at the Bridge were also present. That Gabriel, the prisoner, said George the Witness & some other Negroes went home with Gabriel. Gabriel had asked the prisoner &

his brother George to Join him at the Barbacue, after being sometime at Gabriels house he explained to the prisoner & George for what purpose he wished them to join him both agreed they would and each shaking the other by the hand exclaimed here are our hands & hearts. We will wade to our Knees in blood sooner than fail in the attempt ...

B. Gabriel's trial, October 6, 1800

Prossers Ben — Gabriel was appointed Captain at first consultation respecting the Insurrection and afterwards when he had enlisted a number of men was appointed General — That they were to kill Mr. Prosser Mr. Mosby and all the neighbours, and then proceed to Richmond, where they would kill every body, take the treasury, and divide the money amongst his Soldiers after which he would fortify Richmond, and proceed to discipline his men, as he apprehended force would be raised elsewhere to repel him — That if the White people agreed to their freedom they would then hoist a White flag, and He would dine and drink with the merchants of the City, on the day when it should be so agreed to — Gabriel enlisted a number of Negroes — the prisoner went with the Witness to Mr. Youngs to see Ben Woolfolk who was going to Caroline to enlist men, there he gave three shillings for himself and three other Negroes, to be expended in recruiting men — The prisoner made the handles to the swords which were made by Solomon — The prisoner shewed the Witness a quantity of bullets nearly a peck, which he and Martin had run, and some lead then on Hand, and he said he had 10 pounds of powder which he had purchased. Gabriel said he had nearly 10,000 Men — He had 1000 in Richmond, about 600 in Caroline and nearly 500 at the Coal pits, besides others at different places, and that he expected the poor White people would also join him, and that 2 frenchmen had actually joined whom he said Jack Ditcher knew, but whose names he would not mention to the Witness — That the prisoner had enlisted nearly all the Negroes in town as he said, and amongst them had 400 Horsemen — That in consequence of the bad weather on Saturday night an agreement was made to meet at the Tobacco House of Mr Prossers the ensuing night — Gabriel said all the negroes from Petersburg were to join him after he had commenced the Insurrection—

Mrs Prices John—

He saw the prisoner at a meeting who gave a general invitation to the negro men to attend at the Spring to drink Grog — That when there he mentioned the Insurrection, and proposed that all present should join him in the same, and meet in 3 weeks for the purpose of carrying the same into effect, and injoined several of the negroes then present to use the best of their endeavours in enlisting men, and to meeting according to the time appointed —

Ben Woolfolk—

The prisoner was present at the meeting at Mr Youngs who came to get persons to join him to carry on the War against the white people—That after meeting they adjourned to the spring and held a consultation when it was concluded that in 3 Weeks the business should commence—Gabriel said he had 12 dozen of swords made, and had worn out 2 pair of Bullet moulds in running bullets, and pulling a third pair of his pocket observed that was nearly worn out—That Bob Cooley and Mr Tinsleys Jim was to let them into the Capitol to get the arms out — That the lower part of the town towards Rocketts was to be fired, which would draw forth the Citizens (that part of the town being of little value) this would give an opportunity to the negro's to seize on the arms and ammunition, and then they would commence the attack upon them — After the Assembling of the negroes near Prossers and previous to their coming to Richmond a Company was to be sent to Gregories Tavern to take possession of some arms there Deposited — The prisoner said at the time of meeting the witness at Mr. Youngs, that he had the evening before received six Guns, one of which he had delivered to

Colonel Wilkinson's Sam — That he was present when Gabriel was appointed General and George Smith second in Command That none were to be spared of the Whites, except quakers Methodists and French people — The prisoner and Gilbert concluded to purchase a piece of Silk for a flag on which they would have written <u>death or liberty</u>, and they would kill all except as before excepted unless they agreed to the freedom of the Blacks, in which case they would at least cut off one of their Arms — That the prisoner told the Witness that Bob Cooley had told him if he would call on him about a week before the time of the Insurrection, he would untie the Key of the room in which the Arms and Ammunition were kept at the Capitol and give it to him or if he did not come, then on the night of the Insurrection being commenced he would hand him Arms out as fast as he could arm his men, and that he had on Sunday previous to this been shown by Cooley every room in the Capitol. …

──────── 3.3 ────────

BACK TO AFRICA
Paul Cuffe

Over a century before the "back to Africa" movements of the 1900s, free black merchant Paul Cuffe instigated a drive for African Americans to return to their native land. The idea had floated around in antislavery circles and among politically engaged slaves since the American Revolution, but it never took hold as a practical policy recommendation. At the start of the 19th century, however, it would become the leading solution to the problem of where to place freed blacks among antislavery whites. Its legitimate consideration started with Cuffe's advocacy; Cuffe believed black people, free or otherwise, would never win full rights in America. Their only hope for regaining human liberty was to return to West Africa and, with the support of the American government, establish a colony. Britain had already done this when it established Sierra Leone in 1791. So, as part of his advocacy, Cuffe set sail on a fact-finding mission about the British colony of freed slaves. In 1811, he and a crew of nine black men went first to England and then to Sierra

Leone. There, he meticulously recorded the details of the colony's government and composition. In 1812, he published the following pamphlet, *A Brief Account of the Settlement and Present Situation of the Colony of Sierra Leone, in Africa.*

… Sierra Leone is a country on the west coast of Africa. Its situation is inviting, and its soil generally very productive. A river of the same name passes through the country, and the land for a great extent on each side is peculiarly fertile, and with the climate well calculated for the cultivation of West India and other tropical productions. In the year 1791 an act passed the British parliament incorporating a company called the Sierra Leone Company, whose object was to settle and cultivate these lands, and open a trade with other countries in the products of the soil. The first settlers amounted to about 200 white persons, and a number of free blacks or people of colour from North America; and their experiments in sugar, cotton, &c. soon convinced them that they would be abundantly rewarded for their labour. The promising appearance of the settlement soon attracted the attention of the neighboring chiefs, who with their subjects generally, became very friendly. The colony is now considerably increased, and continues to be in a flourishing situation. The population at present as taken by order of Governor Columbine in the 4th. mo. 1811, is as follows, viz.

Europeans,	22	4	2
Nova Scotians,	188	295	499
Maroons,	165	195	447
Africans,	20	43	37
	395	537	985
Making together,			1917

Besides which there are 601 Crue Men, so called from their being natives of the part called Crue Country, from which they have emigrated since the establishment of this colony.

These people have not yet been enrolled in the list of citizens, but are generally hired by the inhabitants as labourers. The disposition prevails very generally to encourage new settlers who may come amongst theme either for the purpose of cultivating the land, or engaging in commercial enterprise. A petition, of which the following is an outline, was lately presented to his excellency governor Columbine, and signed by several of the most respectable inhabitants, viz.

1st. That encouragement may be give to all our brethren, who may come from the British colonies or from America, in order to become farmers, or to assist us in the cultivation of our land.

2d. That encouragement may be given to our foreign brethren who have vessels for the purpose, to establish commerce in Sierra Leone.

3d. That those who may undertake to establish the whale fishery in the colony may be encouraged to persevere in that useful and laudable enterprise.

There are at this time 7 or 8 schools established throughout the colony. One of these is for the instruction of grown persons, and the others contain together about 230 children, who are instructed in all the necessary branches of education.

The inhabitants have likewise six places of public worship, which are generally well attended. Their times for meeting on the sabbath are at 5 and 10 o'clock in the morning, and at 2 and 6 o'clock in the evening. Also, the week through, many of their meetings are attended at 5 in the morning and 6 in the evening. There was also a society formed here some time since for the further promotion of the Christian religion. I have met with one of their epistles, which I shall insert at the close of my communications.

An institution was formed on the 1st of the 12th mo. last for the relief of the poor and disabled. It is now regularly held on the 1st second day in every month, at which time proper persons are appointed to take charge of those under the care of the institution. A general meeting is held once every six months. Everyone can judge of the happy effect of such institutions as these in improving the dispositions and softening the manners of our native brethren.

The colonists have instituted 5 courts, consisting, first, of the Court of Quarter Sessions, which is held four times in the course of the year. The governor always presides as the judge, and is attended by a justice of the peace, sheriff's clerk, messengers of the bailiff and constables. The petit jury consists of 12 men selected from the Europeans, Nova-Scotians, and Maroons.

2d. Mayor's Court. This formerly sat on the 5th day of every week; but the time for holding it has since been prolonged to every three months.

3d. The Court of Requests which is held on the 7th day of every week. The power of this court is confined to the trial of debts not exceeding two pounds. 12 men are selected for this purpose, and four out of the number transact the business of a sitting.

4th. The Police Court, which is likewise held on the 7th day of every week, and is constituted on the same number of persons as the court of requests. Their business is confined to the trial of persons for disorderly conduct.

5th. The Court of Vice Admiralty, which is held as occasion may require.

The inhabitants are governed entirely by the British law, and are generally peaceable and willing to abide by the decisions of their civil magistrates. Governor Columbine lately issues a proclamation in which he offers the protection of these laws to any slave who may arrive in the colony with the consent of his or her owners, and leaves them at liberty to remain or go elsewhere, as they may think proper.

On the 18th of the 3d month, I travelled in amongst the natives of Africa. The first tribe I met was the Bullone Tribe. Their king, whose name is George, appeared to be very friendly. He could speak but little English himself, but had a young man with him by the name of

Peter Wilson, who had received his education in England, and appeared to be a man of very good information. This tribe, from what I could gather, have adopted the mode of circumcision, and seem to acknowledge by the words the existence of a Deity. So accustomed are they to wars and slavery that I apprehend it would be difficult to convinced them of the impropriety of these pernicious practices. I gave the king a Testament and several other books, and let him know by the interpreter the useful records contained in those books, and the great fountain they pointed unto.

The Mendigo Tribe professess Mahometanism. I became acquainted with two men of thse tribe who were apparently men of considerable learning; indeed this tribe generally, appeared to be a people of some education. Their learning appeared to be the Arabic. They do not allow spirituous liquors to be made use of in this tribe.

They have declined the practice of selling their own tribe; but notwithstanding this, they continue to sell those of other tribes, and thought it hard that the traffic in slaves should be abolished, as they were made poor in the consequence thereof. As they themselves were not willing to submit to the bonds of slavery, I endeavoured to hold this out as a light to convince them of their error. But the prejudice of education had taken too firm a hold of their minds to admit of much effect from reason on this subject.

―――――― 3.4 ――――――

'IT IS NOT ASKED FOR BY US'

James Forten and Russell Perrott

Eventually the idea of colonization became quite attractive to antislavery whites. It solved the central conundrum they faced: they felt slavery was bad for the nation and wanted it abolished, but they could not figure out what to do with all of the slaves they would free. Certainly they could not simply introduce freed slaves to American society as equals to whites — the increasing irritation of whites in northern cities with the growing and vocal free

black populations was proof enough that this would not work. Shipping them to Africa, at least in name as missionaries of Christianity, seemed the perfect solution. In 1816, a group of prominent antislavery whites — including "Star Spangled Banner" composer Francis Scott Key — established the American Colonization Society to advocate the creation of an American colony on the coast of Africa for free blacks. They recruited Cuffe to help rally black support.

Cuffe and the ACS originally found black leaders in his hometown, Philadelphia, receptive, including such figures as AME founders Richard Allen and Absalom Jones (see Chapter Two). But no one had yet asked the community at-large how it felt about the matter. So, on January 15, 1817, approximately 3,000 free blacks met at AME Bethel in Philadelphia to discuss the matter. The community's sentiment was clear: not interested. The same answer came from other free black communities, and black leaders began to ardently oppose the scheme. In a carefully worded "Address to the Humane and Benevolent Inhabitants of the City," James Forten, a Philadelphia entrepreneur and Cuffe confidant, explained black resistance to colonization. Emigrating would mean abandoning those still in slavery — many of whom were family and friends of those already free. Their departure, moreover, would silence the increasing demand for an end to slavery in America (a not so subtle reason many southern whites soon joined the ACS). And, finally, blacks in America knew nothing about Africa or the rigors of life there. They were American, and their fates were tied to this land.

The free people of colour, assembled together, under circumstances of deep interest to their happiness and welfare, humbly and respectfully lay before you this expression of their feelings and apprehensions.

Relieved from the miseries of slavery, many of us by your aid, possesesing the benefits which industry and integrity in this prosperous country assure to all its inhabitants, enjoying the rich blessings of religion, by opportunities of worshipping the only true God, under the light of Christianity, each of us according to his understanding; and having afforded to us and to our children the means of education and improvement; we have no wish to separate from our present homes, for any purpose whatever. Contented with our present situation and condition we are not desirous of increasing their prosperity, but by honest efforts and by the use of those opportunities for their improvement, which the constitution and laws allow to all. It is therefore with painful solicitude, and sorrowing regret, we have seen a plan for colonizing the free people of colour of the United States on the coast of Africa, brought forward under the auspices and sanction of gentlemen whose names give value to all they recommend, and who certainly are among the wisest, the best, and the most benevolent of men, in this great nation.

If the plan of colonizing is intended for our benefit and those who now promote it, will never seek our injury; we humbly and respectfully urge that it is not asked for by us; nor will it be required by any circumstances, in our present and future condition; as long as we shall be permitted to share the protection of the excellent laws, and just government which we now enjoy, in common with every individual of the community.

We therefore, a portion of those, who are objects of this plan, and among those whose happiness, with that of others of our colour, it is intended to promote, with humble and grateful acknowledgements to those who have devised it, renounce, and disclaim every connection with it, and respectfully but firmly declare our determination not to participate in any part of it.

If this plan of colonization now proposed is intended to provide a refuge and a dwelling for a portion of our brethren, who are now held in slavery in the south, we have other and stronger objections to it, and we entreat your consideration of them.

The ultimate and final abolition of slavery in the United States is, under the guidance and protection of a just God, progressing. Every year witnesses the release of numbers of the victims of oppression, and affords new and safe assurances that the freedom of all will in the end be accomplished. As they are thus, by degrees

relieved from bondage, our brethren have opportunities for instruction and improvement; and thus they become in some measure fitted for their liberty.—Every year, many of us have restored to us by the gradual, but certain march of the cause of abolition— parents, from whom we have been long separated—wives and children, whom we have left in servitude—and brothers, in blood as well as in early sufferings, from whom we had long been parted.

But if the emancipations of our kindred shall, when the plan of colonization shall go into effect, be attended with transportation to a distant land, and shall be granted on no other condition; the consolation for our past sufferings and of those of our colour, who are in slavery, which have hitherto been, and under the present situation of things, would continue to be afforded to us and to them, will cease for ever. The cords, which now connect them with us will be stretched by the distance to which their ends will be carried until they break; and all the sources of happiness, which affection and connection, and blood bestow, will be ours or theirs no more.

Nor do we view the colonization of those who may become emancipated by its operation among our southern brethren, as capable of producing their happiness. Unprepared by education, and a knowledge of the truths of our blessed religion, for their new situation, those who will thus become colonists will themselves be surrounded by every suffering which can afflict the members of the human family.

Without arts, without habits of industry, and unaccustomed to provide by their own exertions and foresight for their wants, the colony will soon become the abode of every vice and the home of every misery. Soon will the light of Christianity, which now dawns among that section of our species, be shut out by the clouds of ignorance, and their day of life be closed, without the illuminations of the Gospel.

To those of our brethren who shall be left behind, there will be assured perpetual slavery and augmented sufferings. — Diminished in numbers the slave population of the southern states, which by its magnitude alarms its proprietors, will be easily secured. Those among their bondmen, who feel that they should be free, by rights which all mankind have from God and from nature, and who thus may become dangerous to the quiet of their masters, will be sent to the colony; and the tame and submissive will be retained, and subjected to increased rigour. Year after year will witness these means to assure safety and submission among their slaves; and the southern masters will colonize only those whom it may be dangerous to keep them. The bondage of a large portion of our brethren will thus be rendered perpetual.

Should the anticipations of misery and want among the colonists, which with great deference we have submitted to your better judgement, be realized; to emancipate and transport to the colony, will be held forth by slave-holders as the worst and heaviest of punishments, and they will be threatened and successfully used to enforce increased submission to their wishes and subjection to their commands.

Nor ought the sufferings and sorrows, which must be produced by an exercise of the right to transport and colonize such only of their slaves as may be selected by the slave-holders escape the attention and consideration of those whom with all humility we now address. Parents will be torn from their children — husbands from their wives — brothers from brothers — and all the heart-rending agonies which were endured by our forefathers when they were dragged into bondage from Africa will again be renewed, and with increased anguish. The shores of America will like the sands of Africa be watered by the tears of those who will be left behind. Those who shall be carried away will roam childless, widowed, and alone, over the burning plains of Guinea.

Disclaiming, as we emphatically do, a wish or desire to interpose our opinions and feelings between all plans of colonization, and the judgement of those whose wisdom as far exceeds ours, as their situations are exalted above ours; We humbly, respectfully, and fervently entreat and beseech your disapprobation of the plan of colonization now offered by "the American society for colonizing the free people of colour in the United States." — Here, in the city of Philadelphia, where the voice of the suffering sons of Africa was first heard; where was first commenced the work of abolition, on which Heaven hath smiled, for it could have had success only from the Great Maker; let not a purpose be assisted which will stay the cause of the entire abolition of slavery in the United States, and which may defeat it altogether; which proffers to those who do not ask for them what it calls benefits, but which they consider injuries; and which must insure to the multitudes whose prayers can only reach you through us, *misery, and sufferings, and perpetual slavery.*

—————— 3.5 ——————

ESTABLISHING THE LIBERIA COLONY
President James Monroe

Despite the opposition of free blacks, the colonization plans of white antislavery advocates, joined by some southern slaveholders, barreled ahead. In March 1819, as an outgrowth of the ban on the international slave trade, Congress passed an act empowering the president to spend $100,000 to repatriate Africans rescued from intercepted slave ships. The act also empowered the president to appoint an "agent" for receiving those refugees upon their return to the African coast. The American Colonization Society set out to be named that agent, and to use the money to establish a colony. Attorney General William Witt, in a harshly worded analysis, advised President James Monroe that to do so would be overreaching the purpose of the law. A strong supporter of colonization, Monroe ignored his attorney general. In a December 1819 message to Congress, he stated his intent to create a government station on the coast of Africa and appoint agents to be stationed there, with all the supplies necessary to sustain them and the repatriated Africans. Despite language forbidding the agents from colluding with colonizationists, Monroe conspired with the ACS to establish its colony at the same site, and the road to Liberia was paved. The Society would go on to successfully petition Congress to fund the emigration of free blacks to the colony, both as missionaries to aid in the repatriation of refugees and as a "civilizing" force to help end the slave trade. Driven by the ACS and its prominent supporters, nearly 20,000 blacks would emigrate to Liberia by the start of the Civil War.

A. James Monroe's 1819 order

It is enjoined on the Executive to cause all negroes, mulattoes, or persons of color, who may be taken under the act, to be removed to Africa. It is the obvious import of the law, that none of the persons thus taken should remain within the United States; and no place other than the coast of Africa being designated, their removal or delivery, whether carried from the United States or landed immediately from the vessels in which they were taken, was supposed to be confined to that coast. No settlement or station being specified, the whole coast was thought to be left open for the selection of the proper place at which the persons thus taken should be delivered. The Executive is authorized to appoint one or more agents, residing there to receive such persons, and $100,000 are appropriated for the general purposes of the law.

On due consideration of the several sections of the act, and of its humane policy, it was supposed to be the intention of Congress that all the persons above described, who might be taken under it, and landed in Africa, should be aided in their return to their former homes, or in their establishment at or near the place where landed. Some shelter or food would be necessary for them there as soon as landed, let their subsequent disposition be what it might. Should they be landed without such provision having been previously made, they might perish. It was supposed, by the authority given to the Executive to appoint agents residing on that coast, that they should provide such shelter and food, and perform the other beneficent and charitable offices contemplated by the act.

The coast of Africa having been little explored, and no persons residing there, who possessed the requisite qualifications to entitle them to the trust, being known to the Executive, to none such could it be committed. It was believed that citizens only who would go hence, well instructed in the views of their Government, and zealous to give them effect, would be competent to these duties, and that it was not the intention of the law to preclude their appointment. It was obvious that the longer these persons should be detained in the United States in the hands of the marshals, the greater would be the expense, and that for the same term would the main purpose of the law be suspended. It seemed, therefore, to be incumbent on me to make the necessary arrangements for carrying this act into effect in Africa in time to meet the delivery of any persons who might be taken by the public vessels, and landed there under it.

On this view of the policy and sanctions of the law, it has been decided to send a public ship to the coast of Africa, with two such agents, who will take with them tools and other implements necessary for the purpose of the above mentioned. To each of these agents a small salary has been allowed; $1,500 to the principal, and $1,200 to the other. All our public agents on the coast of Africa receive salaries for their services, and it was understood that none of our citizens, possessing the necessary qualifications, would accept these trusts, by which they would be confinedto parts the least frequented and civilized, without a reasonable compensation. Such allowance, therefore, seemed to be indispensable to the execution of the act. It is intended also to subject a portion of the sum appropriated to the order of the principal agent, for the special objects above stated, amounting in the whole, including the salaries of the agents for one year, to rather less than one-third of the appropriation. Special instructions will be given to these agents, defining, in precise terms, their duties in regard to the persons thus delivered to them; the disbursement of the money by the principal agent, and his accountability for the same. They will also have power to select the most suitable place on the coast of Africa, at which all persons who may be taken under this act shall be delivered to them, with an express injunction to exercise no power founded on the principle of colonization, or other power than that of performing the benevolent offices above recited, by the permission and sanction of the exiting Government under which they may establish themselves. Orders will be give to the commander of the public ship in which they will sail to cruise along the coast, to give the more complete effect to the principle object of the act.

B. 1820 American Colonization Society petition to Congress

… The last census shows the number of free people of color of the United States, and their rapid increase. Supposing them to increase in the same ratio, it will appear how large a proportion of our population will, in the course of even a few years, consist of persons of that description.

No argument is necessary to show that this is very far indeed from constituting an increase of our physical strength; nor can there be a population, in any country, neutral as to its effects upon society. The least observation shows that this description of persons are not, and cannot be, either useful or happy among us; and many considerations, which need not be mentioned, prove, beyond dispute, that it is best, for all the parties interested, that there should be a separation; that those who are now free, and those who hereafter may become so, should be provided with the means of attaining to a state of respectability and happiness, which, it is certain, they have never yet reached, and, therefore, can never be likely to reach, in this country.

The two last reports of the Society, to which your memorialists beg leave to refer, show the success of their mission to Africa, and the result of their inquiries upon that continent. From those it is manifest that a situation can be readily obtained, favorable to commerce and agriculture, in a healthy and fertile country, and that the natives are well disposed to give every encouragement to the establishment of such a settlement among them. Thus, it appears, that an object of great national concern, already expressly desired by some of the States, and truly desirable to all, receiving, also, the approbation of those upon whom it is more immediately to operate, is brought within our reach.

But this subject derives, perhaps, its chief interest from its connexion with a measure which has, already, to the honor of our country, occupied the deliberations of the Congress of the United States.

Your memorialists refer, with pleasure, to the act, passed at the last session of Congress, supplementary to the act formerly passed for the suppression of the slave trade. The means afforded, by the provisions of that act, for the accomplishment of its object are certainly great; but the total extirpation of this disgraceful trade cannot, perhaps, be expected from any measures which rely alone upon the employment of a maritime force, however considerable.

The profits attending it are so extraordinary, that the cupidity of the unprincipled will still be tempted to continue it, as long as there is any chance of escaping the vigilance of the cruisers engaged against them. From the best information your memorialists have been able to obtain, of the nature, causes, and course of this trade, and of the present situation of the coast of Africa, and the habits and dispositions of the natives, they are well assured that the suppression of the African slave trade, and the civilization of the natives, are measures of indispensable connexion. …

No nation has it so much in its power to furnish proper settlers for such establishments as this; no nation has so deep an interest in thus disposing of them. By the law passed at the last session, and before referred to, the captives who may be taken by our cruisers, from the slave ships are to be taken to Africa, and delivered to the custody of agents appointed by the President.

There will then be a settlement of captured negroes upon the coast, in consequence of the measures already adopted. And it is evidently most important, if not necessary, to such a settlement, that the Civilized people of color of this country, whose industry, enterprise, and knowledge of agriculture and the arts, would render them most useful assistants, should be connected with such an establishment. ...

When, therefore, the object of the Colonization Society is viewed in connection with that entire suppression of the slave trade which your memorialists trust it is resolved shall be effected, its importance becomes obvious in the extreme.

The beneficial consequences resulting from success in such a measure, it is impossible to calculate. To the general cause of humanity it will afford the most rich and noble contribution, and for the nation that regards that cause, that employs its power in its behalf, it cannot fail to procure a proportionate reward. It is by such a course that a nation insures to itself the protection and favor of the Governor of the World. Nor are there wanting views and considerations, arising from our peculiar political institutions, which would justify the sure expectation of the most signal blessings to ourselves from the accomplishment of such an object. If one of these consequences shall be the gradual and almost imperceptible removal of a national evil, which all unite in lamenting, and for which, with the most intense, but, hitherto, hopeless anxiety, the patriots and statesmen of our country have labored to discover a remedy, who can doubt, that, of all the blessings we may be permitted to bequeath to our descendants, this will receive the richest tribute of their thanks and veneration? ...

Your memorialists beg leave to state that, having expended considerable funds in prosecuting their inquiries and making preparations, they are now about to send out a colony, and complete the purchase, already stipulated for with the native kings and chiefs of Sherbro, of a suitable territory for their establishment. The number they are now enabled to transport and provide for, is but a small proportion of the people of color who have expressed their desire to go; and without a larger and more sudden increase of their funds than can be expected from the voluntary contributions of individuals, their progress must be slow and uncertain. They have always flattered themselves with the hope that when it was seen they had surmounted the difficulties of preparation, and shown that means applied to the execution of their design would lead directly and evidently to its accomplishment, they would be able to obtain for it the national countenance and assistance. To this point they have arrived; and they, therefore, respectfully request that this interesting subject may receive the consideration of your honorable body, and that the Executive Department may be authorized, in such way as may meet your approbation, to extend to this object such pecuniary and other aid as it may be thought to require and deserve. ...

——— 3.6 ———

36 DEGREES 30 MINUTES
Missouri Compromise

The Louisiana Purchase of western territory from France threatened to upset the tenuous balance and agreement on slavery between the northern and southern states. In 1819, the Missouri Territory, where slavery was thriving, applied to become a state. A controversy erupted in Congress over how to admit Missouri without destroying the even distribution of slave versus free states. Kentucky Senator Henry Clay led the way to a compromise. Northern Massachusetts would become Maine, and be admitted as a free state; Missouri would enter as a slave state. In addition, as an attempt to prevent future conflicts over territories that apply for statehood, a line was drawn across the continent at 36 degrees 30 minutes north latitude. States above it would be free; states below it would be slave. The compromise would hold only 30 years, until a dispute over the status of the Kansas Territory would bring the nation to the brink of civil war.

Be it enacted by the Senate and House of Representatives of the United States of

America, in Congress assembled, That the inhabitants of that portion of the Missouri territory included within the boundaries hereinafter designated, be, and they are hereby, authorized to form for themselves a constitution and state government, and to assume such name as they shall deem proper; and the said state, when formed, shall be admitted into the Union, upon an equal footing with the original states, in all respects whatsoever.

Section 2. *And be it further enacted*, That the said state shall consist of all the territory included within the following boundaries, to wit: Beginning in the middle of the Mississippi river, on the parallel of thirty-six degrees of north latitude; thence west, along that parallel of latitude, to the St. Francois river; thence up, and following the course of that river, in the middle of the main channel thereof, to the parallel of latitude of thirty-six degrees and thirty minutes; thence west, along the same, to a point where the said parallel is intersected by a meridian line passing through the middle of the mouth of the Kansas river, where the same empties into the Missouri river, thence, from the point aforesaid north, along the said meridian line, to the intersection of the parallel of latitude which passes through the rapids of the river Des Moines, making the said line to correspond with the Indian boundary line; thence east, from the point of intersection last aforesaid, along the said parallel of latitude, to the middle of the channel of the main fork of the said river Des Moines; thence down and along the middle of the main channel of the said river Des Moines, to the mouth of the same, where it empties into the Mississippi river; thence, due east, to the middle of the main channel of the Mississippi river; thence down, and following the course of the Mississippi river, in the middle of the main channel thereof, to the place of beginning: Provided, The said state shall ratify the boundaries aforesaid; And Provided also, That the said state shall have concurrent jurisdiction on the river Mississippi, and every other river bordering on the said state, so far as the said rivers

shall form a common boundary to the said state; and any other state or states, now or hereafter to be formed and bounded by the same, such rivers to be common to both; and that the river Mississippi, and the navigable rivers and waters leading into the same, shall be common highways, and for ever free, as well to the inhabitants of the said state as to other citizens of the United States, without any tax, duty, impost, or toll, therefor, imposed by the said state. ...

Section 4. *And be it further enacted*, That the members of the convention thus duly elected, shall be, and they are hereby authorized to meet at the seat of government of said territory on the second Monday of the month of June next; and the said convention, when so assembled, shall have power and authority to adjourn to any other place in the said territory, which to them shall seem best for the convenient transaction of their business; and which convention, when so met, shall first determine by a majority of the whole number elected, whether it be, or be not, expedient at that time to form a constitution and state government for the people within the said territory, as included within the boundaries above designated....

Section 5. *And be it further enacted*, That until the next general census shall be taken, the said state shall be entitled to one representative in the House of Representatives of the United States.

Second. That all salt springs, not exceeding twelve in number, with six sections of land adjoining to each, shall be granted to the said state for the use of said state....

Fifth. That thirty-six sections, or one entire township, which shall be designated by the President of the United States, together with the other lands heretofore reserved for that purpose, shall be reserved for the use of a seminary of learning, and vested in the legislature of said state, to be appropriated solely to the use of such seminary by the said legislature....

Section 8. *And be it further enacted*, That in all that territory ceded by France to the United

States, under the name of Louisiana, which lies north of thirty-six degrees and thirty minutes north latitude, not included within the limits of the state, contemplated by this act, slavery and involuntary servitude, otherwise than in the punishment of crimes, whereof the parties shall have been duly convicted, shall be, and is hereby, forever prohibited: Provided always, That any person escaping into the same, from whom labour or service is lawfully claimed, in any state or territory of the United States, such fugitive may be lawfully reclaimed and conveyed to the person claiming his or her labour or service as aforesaid.

——— 3.7 ———

'YOUR PROFESSED DESIGN WAS TO TRAMPLE ON ALL LAWS, HUMAN AND DIVINE; TO RIOT IN BLOOD, OUTRAGE, RAPINE, AND CONFLAGRATION'

Denmark Vesey's Revolt

Denmark Vesey had been known in town as "uppity" from the time he arrived in Charleston, South Carolina, as a slave in service to a sea merchant, in 1783. In 1800, he bought his freedom with gambling winnings, and immediately became obsessed with the question of how slavery could be ended. An active participant in the local AME church, he was considered a rabble-rouser, constantly preaching about liberty and biblical mandates for slaves to revolt. Finally, in 1821, he gathered six fellow conspirators and began plotting an uprising. Slowly, they spread the word about a plan to take the town of Charleston on a Sunday morning, when whites would be out of town and blacks coming in wouldn't be conspicuous. Some reports argue they recruited as many as 9,000 participants, dwarfing even Gabriel's conspiracy in Richmond, Virginia. But, once again, one of the recruits betrayed their plans.

When white officials began to investigate, they were horrified to discover the breadth of participation. They set up a tribunal and, in the short course of five days, tried nearly 100 people, convicting most. Thirty-five people were hung, another 40 were expelled from the state. White leaders left the bodies of Vesey and his co-conspirators hanging for days, as a threat to blacks and a salve for the unsettled nerves of whites. As had been the case after the Stono Rebellion (see Chapter One), the backlash was intense. Legislators even toyed with the idea of ending slavery. Ultimately, countless free blacks fled the state to avoid new, harsh laws designed to curtail their freedom of movement. Below are excerpts from Vesey's trial and sentencing, as well as that of Gullah Jack. Jack was one of the original conspirators and sparked particular anger among whites. As a medicinal priest, he had declared bullets could not kill him and assured Vesey's followers that he would give them similar protection.

THE TRIAL OF DENMARK VESEY, a free black man — Col. G. W. Cross attending as his counsel.

Evidence

William, the slave of Mr. Paul, testified as follows: Mingo Harth told me *that Denmark Vesey was the chief man, and more concerned than anyone else.* Denmark Vesey is an old man in whose yard my master's Negro woman Sarah cooks. He was her father-in-law, having married her mother Beck, and though they have been parted some time, yet he visited her at her house near the Intendant's (Major Hamilton), where I have often heard him speak of the rising. *He said he would not like to have a white man in his presence—that he had a great hatred for the whites*, and that if all were like him they would resist the whites. He studied all he could to put it into the heads of the blacks to have a rising against the whites, and tried to induce me to join. He tried to induce all his acquaintances— this has been his chief study and delight for a considerable time. My last conversation with him was in April. He studied the Bible a great deal and tried to prove from it that slavery and bondage is against the Bible. I am persuaded that Denmark Vesey was chiefly in this business.

WITNESS NO. 1, gave the following testimony: I know Denmark Vesey. I was one day on horseback going to market when I met him on foot; he asked me if I was satisfied in my present situation; if I remembered the fable of Hercules and the Wagoner whose waggon was stalled, and he began to pray, and Hercules said, you fool put your shoulder on the wheel, whip up the horses and your waggon will be pulled out; that if we did not put our hand to the work and deliver ourselves, we should never come out of slavery; *that Congress had made us free*. I know that he is intimately aquatinted with Rolla — Rolla told me that there had been a sort of disagreement and confusion at their place of meeting, and that they meant to meet at Vesey's. Vesey told me that a large army from Santo Domingo and Africa were coming to help us, and we must not stand with our hands in our pockets; he was bitter towards the whites.

FRANK, Mrs. Ferguson's slave gave the following evidence: I know Denmark Vesey and have been to his house. I have heard him say the Negro's situation was so bad he did not know how they could endure it, and was astonished they did not rise and fend for themselves, and he advised me to join and rise. He said he was going about to see different people, and mentioned the names of Ned Bennett and Peter Poyas as concerned with him — that he had spoken to Ned and Peter on this subject, and that they were to go and tell the blacks that they were free, and *must rise and fight for themselves* — that they would take the Magazines and Guard Houses, and the city and would be free — that he was going to send *into the country* to inform the people there too. He said he wanted me to join them — I said I could not answer — he said if I would not go into the country for him he could get others. He said himself, Ned Bennett, Peter Poyas, and Monday Gell were the principal men and himself the head man. He said they were the principal men to go about and inform the people and fix them, — that *one party would land on South Bay, one about Wappoo, and about the farms* — that the party which was to land on South Bay was to take the Guard House and get arms and then they would be able to go on — that the attack was to commence about twelve o'clock at night — *that great numbers would come from all about*, and it must succeed as so many were engaged in — that they would kill all the whites — that they would leave their

master's house and assemble together near the liens, march down and meet the party which would land on South Bay — that he was going to *send a man into the country on a horse to bring down the country people* and that he would pay for the horse. He gave $2 to Jesse to get the horse on Saturday week last (15th June), about one o'clock in the day, and myself and No. 3, also put in 25 cents a piece, and he told Jesse, if he could not go he must send someone wise. I have seen Ned Bennett at Vesey's. One night, I met at Vesey's a great number of men, and as they came in each handed him some money. Vesey said there was a *little man named Jack* who could not be killed, and who would furnish them with arms, he had a charm and he would lead them — that Charles Drayton had promised to be engaged with them. Vesey said the Negroes were living such an abominable life, they ought to rise. I said I was living well — he said though I was, others were not and that 'twas such fools as I, that were in they and would not help them, and that after all things were well he would mark me. He said he did not go with *Creighton to Africa, because he had not a will, he wanted to stay and see what he could* do for his fellow creatures. I met Ned, Monday, and others at Denmark Vesey's where they were talking about the business. The first time I spoke with Monday Gell 'twas one night about Denmark Vesey's house, where I heard Vesey tell Monday that he must *send someone into the country to bring the people down*. Monday said *he had sent up Jack and told him to tell the people to come down and join in the fight* against the whites and also to ascertain and inform him how many people he could get. A few days after I met Vesey, Monday, and Jack, in the streets under Mr. Duncan's trees at night, where *Jack stated that he had been into the country round by Goose Creek and Dorchester*, and that he had spoken to 6,600 persons who had agreed to join. Monday said to Vesey, that if Jack had so many men they had better wait no longer but begin the business at once, and others would join. The first time I saw Monday at Vesey's, he was going away early, when Vesey asked him to stay, to which Monday replied, he expected that night a meeting at his house to fix upon and mature the plan, and that he could stay no longer. I afterwards conversed with Monday in his shop, where he asked me if I had heard that Bennett's and Poyas' people were taken up, that 'twas a great pity — he said he had joined in the business — I told him to take care he was not taken up. Whenever I talked with Vesey, he always spoke of Monday Gell as being his principal and active man in the business.

ADAM, a Negro man belonging to Mr. Ferguson testified as follows: Denmark Vesey one day asked me to walk to his house, and there asked me for 25 cents to hire a horse to send up into the country. I put down the money on the table and asked what he was going to send into the country for — he said 'twould be for my benefit. As he would tell me no more I took up the money and put it back into my pocket again. I afterwards met the man who was to go into the country, who told me he had set off, but had been brought back by the Patrol; *that he was going up to bring down the black people to take this country from the whites.* I have been at Vesey's house and there it was I met the man who was to go into the country, he was a yellowish man — the witness pointing at Jesse said, that is the man who was to go into the country.

BENJAMIN FORD, a white lad, about 15 or 16 years of age, deposed as follows: Denmark Vesey frequently came into our shop which is near his house, and always complained of the hardships of the blacks. He said the laws were very rigid and strict and that the blacks had not their rights — that everyone had his time, and that his would come round too. *His general conversation was about religion which he would apply to slavery,* as for instance, he would speak of the creation of the world, in which he would say all men had equal rights, black as well as whites, — *all his religious remarks were mingled with slavery.* …

SENTENCE ON DENMARK VESEY, a free black man — Denmark Vesey: the Court,

on mature consideration, have pronounced you guilty. You have enjoyed the advantage of able Counsel, and were also heard in your own defense, in which you endeavored, with great art and plausibility, to impress a belief of your innocence. After the most patient deliberation, however, the Court were not only satisfied with your guilt, but that you were the author and original investigator of this diabolical plot. Your professed design was to trample on all laws, human and divine; to riot in blood, outrage, rapine, and conflagration, and to introduce anarchy and confusion in their most horrid forms. Your life has become, therefore, a just and necessary sacrifice, at the shrine of indignant justice. It is difficult to imagine what *infatuation* could have prompted you to attempt an enterprise so wild and visionary. You were a free man; were comparatively wealthy; and enjoyed every comfort compatible with your situation. You had, therefore, much to risk, and little to gain. From your age and experience, you *ought* to have known, that success was impracticable.

A moment's reflection must have convinced you, that the ruin of *your race*, would have been the probable result, and that years would have rolled away, before they could have recovered that confidence which they once enjoyed in this community. The only reparation in your power is full disclosure of the truth. In addition to treason, you have committed the grossest impiety, in attempted to pervert the sacred words of God into a sanction for crimes of the blackest hue. It is evident, that you are totally insensible to the divine influence of that Gospel, "all whose paths are peace." It as to reconcile us to our destinies on earth, and to enable us to discharge with fidelity, all the duties of life, that those holy precepts were imparted by Heaven to fallen man.

If you had searched them with sincerity, you would have discovered instructions, immediately applicable to the victims of your artful wiles — "Servants (says Saint Paul) obey in all things your masters, according to the flesh, not with eyeservice, as menpleasers, but in singleness of heart, fearing God." And again "Servants (says Saint Peter) be subject to your masters with all fear, not only to be good and gentle, but also to the forward." On such texts comment is necessary.

Your "lamp of life" is nearly extinguished; your race is run, and you must shortly pass "from time to eternity." Let me then conjure you to devote the remnant of your existence in solemn preparation for the awful doom that awaits you. Your situation is deplorable, but not destitute of spiritual consolation. To that Almighty Being alone, whose Holy Ordinances you have trampled in the dust, can you know look for mercy, and although "your sins be as scarlet," the tears of sincere penitence may obtain forgiveness at the "Throne of Grace." You cannot have forgotten the history of the malefactor of the Cross, who, like yourself, was the wretched and deluded victim of offended justice. His conscience was awakened in the pangs of dissolution, and yet there is reason to believe, that his spirit was received into the realms of bliss. May you imitate his example, and may your last moments prove you like his! …

SENTENCE ON JACK, a slave belonging to Paul Pritchard, commonly called Gullah Jack, and sometimes Cooter Jack—Gullah Jack: the Court after deliberately considering all the circumstances of your case, are perfectly satisfied of your guilt. In the prosecution of your wicked designs, you were not satisfied with resorting to natural and ordinary means, but endeavored to enlist on your behalf, all the powers of darkness, and employed for that purpose, the most disgusting mummery and superstition. You represented yourself as invulnerable; that you culled neither be taken nor destroyed, and that all who fought under your banners would be invincible. While such wretched expedients are calculated to excite the confidence, or to alarm the fears of the ignorant and credulous, they produce no other emotion in the minds of the intelligent and enlightened, but contempt and disgust. Your boasted charms have not preserved yourself, and of course could not protect others. Your

altars and your Gods have sunk together in the dust. The airy spectres, conjured by you, have been chased away by the superior light of Truth, and you stand exposed, the miserable and deluded victim of offended justice. Your days are literally numbered. You will shortly be consigned to the cold and silent grave; and all the Powers of Darkness cannot rescue you from your approaching Fate! Let me then, conjure you to devote the remnant of your miserable existence, in fleeing from the wrath to come. This can only be done by a full disclosure of the truth. The Court are willing to afford you all the aid in their power, and to permit any Minister of the Gospel, whom you may select to have free access to you. To him you may unburden your guilty conscience. Neglect not the opportunity, for there is not device nor art in the grave, to which you must shortly be consigned.

———— 3.8 ————
'I ASK YOU, O MY BRETHREN!, ARE WE MEN?'
David Walker's Appeal

Historians believe David Walker, a self-proclaimed wanderer, was among those free blacks who fled Charleston following Denmark Vesey's revolt. If so, he was likely among the conspirators. He arrived in Boston in the early 1820s and became an active participant in black civic society. He joined the AME church and was among those who helped finance the establishment of the nation's first black-owned newspaper, *Freedom's Journal*, in 1827. It was in Boston that Walker came to the conclusion that African Americans were the "most degraded, wretched and abject set of beings that ever lived." This was so, he wrote, not just because of the horrid abuse heaped upon them by whites, but because they had allowed it to go on. Black people needed to awaken and steal their liberty by whatever means available to them. In an effort to spark that enlightenment, Walker penned his *Appeal to the Colored Citizens of the World*.

It is a remarkable document for any time period, let alone the early 19th century. It wholly turns American racist thought on its head, placing European civilizations under the microscope of judgment rather than Africans, and in so doing articulates some of the central themes of the Black Power Movement's political philosophy, 150 years before its zenith (see Chapter Eight). A four-part treatise, Walker's *Appeal* argues the criminality of white supremacy and exhorts blacks to rise up against it. In part one, he focuses on slavery as the principle cause of the African American's "wretchedness" and the principle example of white inhumanity. White Americans, he argues, had refined barbarity beyond the limits of any prior civilization. Worse, they had done so in the name of Christianity. He took particular aim at Thomas Jefferson, arguing that his racist ideology represented the foundation of the nation's collective ideology. Presciently, he warned that if blacks did not directly challenge that line of thought, it would soon irrevocably ingrain itself in the national psyche. Walker did not intend for the text to be another conversation between free blacks of the North, but rather hoped it would reach those in slavery. He smuggled it South with black seamen and encouraged those who were literate to hold meetings and read it to others. White southerners, of course, were infuriated when they discovered it in circulation and tried everything to suppress it, including barring black sailors from leaving port.

My dearly beloved Brethren and Fellow Citizens.

Having travelled over a considerable portion of these United States, and having, in the course of my travels, taken the most accurate observations of things as they exist — the result of my observations has warranted the full and unshaken conviction, that we, (coloured people of these United States,) are the most degraded, wretched, and abject set of beings that ever lived since the world began; and I pray God that none like us ever may live again until time shall be no more. They tell us of the Israelites in Egypt, the Helots in Sparta, and of the Roman Slaves, which last were made up from almost every nation under heaven, whose sufferings under those ancient and heathen nations, were, in comparison with ours, under this enlightened and Christian nation, no more than a cipher — or, in other words, those heathen nations of antiquity, had but little more among them than the name and form of slavery; while wretchedness and endless miseries were reserved, apparently in a phial, to be poured out upon our fathers, ourselves and our children, by Christian Americans!

These positions I shall endeavour, by the help of the Lord, to demonstrate in the course of this Appeal, to the satisfaction of the most incredulous mind — and may God Almighty, who is the Father of our Lord Jesus Christ, open your hearts to understand and believe the truth.

The causes, my brethren, which produce our wretchedness and miseries, are so very numerous and aggravating, that I believe the pen only of a Josephus or a Plutarch, can well enumerate and objects, then, of such incomprehensible magnitude, so impenetrable, and so notorious, I shall be obliged to omit a large class of, and content myself with giving you an exposition of a few of those, which do indeed rage to such an alarming pitch, that they cannot but be a perpetual source of terror and dismay to every reflecting mind.

I am fully aware, in making this appeal to my much afflicted and suffering brethren, that I shall not only be assailed by those whose greatest earthly desires are, to keep us in abject ignorance and wretchedness, and who are of the firm conviction that Heaven has designed us and our children to be slaves and beasts of burden to them and their children. I say, I do not only expect to be held up to the public as an ignorant, impudent and restless disturber of the public peace, by such avaricious creatures, as well as a mover of insubordination — and perhaps put in prison or to death, for giving a superficial exposition of our miseries, and exposing tyrants. But I am persuaded, that many of my brethren, particularly those who are ignorantly in league with slave-holders or tyrants, who acquire their daily bread by the blood and sweat of their more ignorant brethren — and not a few of those too, who are too ignorant to see an inch beyond their noses, will rise up and call me cursed —Yea, the jealous ones among us will perhaps use more abject subtlety, by affirming that this work is not worth perusing, that we are well situated, and there is no use in trying to better our condition, for we cannot. I will ask one question here. — Can our condition be any worse? — Can it be more mean and abject? If there are any changes, will they not be for the better, though they may appear for the worst at first? Can they get us any lower? Where can they get us? They are afraid to treat us worse, for they know well, the day they do it they are gone. But against all accusations which may or can be preferred against me, I appeal to Heaven for my motive in writing — who knows that my object is, if possible, to awaken in the breasts of my afflicted, degraded and slumbering brethren, a spirit of inquiry and investigation respecting our miseries and wretchedness in this Republican Land of Liberty!

The sources from which our miseries are derived, and on which I shall comment, I shall not combine in one, but shall put them under distinct heads and expose them in their turn; in doing which, keeping truth on my side, and not departing from the strictest rules of morality, I shall endeavour to penetrate, search out, and lay them open for your inspection. If you cannot or will not profit by them, I shall have done my duty to you, my country and my God.

And as the inhuman system of slavery, is the source from which most of our miseries proceed, I shall begin with that curse to nations, which has spread terror and devastation through so many nations of antiquity, and which is raging to such a pitch at the present day in Spain and in Portugal. ...

Article I
Our Wretchedness in Consequence of Slavery.

My beloved brethren: — The Indians of North and of South America — the Greeks — the Irish, subjected under the king of Great Britain — the Jews, that ancient people of the Lord — the inhabitants of the islands of the sea — in fine, all the inhabitants of the earth, (except however, the sons of Africa) are called men, and of course are, and ought to be free. But we,

(coloured people) and our children are *brutes*! And of course are, and *ought to be* SLAVES to the American people and their children forever to dig their mines and work their farms; and thus go on enriching them, from one generation to another with our *blood* and our *tears*!

I promised in a preceding page to demonstrate to the satisfaction of the most incredulous, that we, (coloured people of these United States of America) are the *most wretched*, *degraded* and *abject* set of beings that ever lived since the world began, and that the white Americans having reduced us to the wretched state of *slavery*, treat us in that condition *more cruel* (they being an enlightened and Christian people,) than any heathen nation did any people whom it had reduced to our condition. These affirmations are so well confirmed in the minds of all unprejudiced men, who have taken the trouble to read histories that they need no elucidation from me. But to put them beyond all doubt, I refer you in the first place to the children of Jacob, or of Israel in Egypt, under Pharaoh and his people. Some of my brethren do not know who Pharaoh and the Egyptians were — I know it to be a fact, that some of them take the Egyptians to have been a gang — of *devils*, not knowing any better, and that they (Egyptians) having got possession of the Lord's people, treated them *nearly* as cruel as *Christian Americans* do us, at the present day. For the information of such, I would only mention that the Egyptians, were Africans or coloured people, such as we are — some of them yellow and others dark — a mixture of Ethiopians and the natives of Egypt — about the same as you see the coloured people of the United States at the present day. — I say, I call your attention then, to the children of Jacob, while I point out particularly to you his son Joseph, among the rest, in Egypt.

"And Pharaoh said unto Joseph . . . thou shalt be over my house, and according unto thy word shall all my people be ruled: only in the throne will I be greater than thou."

"And Pharaoh said unto Joseph, see, I have set thee over all the land of Egypt."

"And Pharaoh said unto Joseph, I am Pharaoh, and without thee shall no man lift up his hand or foot in all the land of Egypt."

Now I appeal to heaven and to earth, and particularly to the American people themselves, who cease not to declare that our condition is not *hard*, and that we are comparatively satisfied to rest in wretchedness and misery, under them and their children. Not, indeed, to show me a coloured President, a Governor, a Legislator, a Senator, a Mayor, or an Attorney at the Bar. — But to show me a man of colour, who holds the low office of a Constable, or one who sits in a juror Box, even on a case of one of his wretched brethren, throughout this great Republic!! — But let us pass Joseph the son of Israel a little farther in review, as he existed with that heathen nation.

"And Pharaoh called Joseph's name Zaphnathpaaneah; and he gave him to wife Asenath the daughter of Potipherah priest of ON. And Joseph went out over all the land of Egypt."

Compare the above, with the American institutions. Do they not institute laws to inhibit us from marrying among the whites? I would wish, candidly, however, before the Lord, to be understood, that I would not give a *pinch of snuff* to be married to any white person I ever saw in all the days of my life. And I do say it, that the black man, or man of colour, who will leave his own colour (provided he can get one, who is good for any thing) and marry a white woman, to be a double slave to her, just because she is white, ought to be treated by her as he surely will be, viz: as a NIGGER! It is not, indeed, what I care about inter-marriages with the whites, which induced me to pass this subject in review; for the Lord knows, that there is a day coming when they will be glad enough to get into the company of the blacks, notwithstanding, we are, in this generation, leveled by them, almost on a level with the brute creation: and some of us they treat even worse than they do the brutes that perish. I only made this extract to show how much lower we are held, and how much more cruel we are treated by the Americans, than were the children of Jacob, by the Egyptians. We will notice the sufferings of Israel some further, under *heathen Pharaoh*, compared with ours under the *enlightened Christians of America*.

"And Pharaoh spoke unto Joseph, saying, thy father and thy brethren are come unto thee:

"The land of Egypt is before thee: in the best of the land make thy father and brethren to dwell; in the land of Goshen let them dwell: and if thou knowest any men of activity among them, then make them rulers over my cattle."

I ask those people who treat us so well, Oh! I ask them, where is the most barren spot of land that they have given unto us? Israel had the most fertile land in all Egypt. Need I mention the very notorious fact, that I have known a poor man of colour, who labored night and day, to acquire a little money, and having acquired it, be vested it in a small piece of land, and got him a house erected thereon, and having paid for the whole, he moved his family into it, where he was suffered to remain but nine months, when he was cheated out of his property by a white man, Genesis, chap. xlvii. 5, 6. and driven out of door! And is not this the case generally? Can a man of colour buy a piece of land and keep it peaceably? Will not some white man try to get it from him, even if it is in a *mud hole*? I need not comment any farther on a subject, which all, both black and white, will readily admit. But I must, really, observe that in this very city, when a man of colour dies, if he owned any real estate it most generally falls into the hands of some white person. The wife and children of the deceased may weep and lament if they please, but the estate will be kept snug enough by its white possessor.

But to prove farther that the condition of the Israelites was better under the Egyptians than ours is under the whites. I call upon the professing Christians, I call upon the philanthropist, I call upon the very tyrant himself, to show me a page of history, either sacred or profane, on which a verse can be found, which maintains, that the Egyptians heaped the *insupportable insult* upon the children of Israel, by telling them that they were not of the *human family*. Can the whites deny this charge? Have they not, after having, reduced us to the deplorable condition of slaves under their feet, held us up as descending originally from the tribes of *Monkeys* or *Orang-Outangs*? O! my God! I appeal to every man of feeling — is not this insupportable? Is it not heaping the grossest insult upon our miseries, because they have got us under their feet and we cannot help ourselves? Oh! pity us we pray thee, Lord Jesus, Master. — Has Mr. Jefferson declared to the world, that we are inferior to the whites, both in the endowments of our bodies and our minds? It is indeed surprising, that a man of such great learning, combined with such excellent natural parts, should speak so of a set of men in chains. I do not know what to compare it to, unless, like putting one wild deer in an iron cage, where it will be secured, and hold another by the side of the same, then let it go, and expect the one in the cage to run as fast as the one at liberty. So far, my brethren, were the Egyptians from heaping these insults upon their slaves that Pharaoh's daughter took Moses, a son of Israel for her own, as will appear by the following.

"And Pharaoh's daughter said unto her, [Moses' mother] take this child away, and nurse it for me and I will pay thee thy wages. And the woman took the child [Moses] and nursed it.

"And the child grew, and she brought him unto Pharaoh's daughter and he became her son. And she called his name Moses: and she said because I drew him out of the water."

In all probability, Moses would have become Prince Regent to the throne, and no doubt, in process of time but he would have been seated on the throne of Egypt. But he had rather suffer shame with the people of God, than to enjoy pleasures with that wicked people for a season. O! that the Coloured people were long since of Moses' excellent disposition, instead of courting favour with, and telling news and lies to our *natural enemies*, against each other — aiding them to keep their hellish chains of slavery upon us. Would we not long

before this time, have been respectable men, instead of such wretched victims of oppression as we are? Would they be able to drag our mothers, our fathers, our wives, our children and us, around the world in chains and handcuffs as they do, to dig up gold and silver for them and theirs? This question, my brethren, I leave for you to digest; and may God Almighty force it home to your hearts. Remember that unless you are united, keeping your tongues within your teeth, you will be afraid to trust your secrets to each other, and thus perpetuate our miseries under the *Christians*! In addition, remember, also to lay humble at the feet of our Lord and Master Jesus Christ, with prayers and fastings. Let our enemies go on with their butcheries and at once fill up their cup. Never make an attempt to gain our freedom or *natural right*, from under our cruel oppressors and murderers, until you see your way clear — when that hour arrives and you move, be not afraid or dismayed; for be you assured that Jesus Christ the King of heaven and of earth who is the God of justice and of armies, will surely go before you. And those enemies who have for hundreds of year, stolen our *rights*, and kept us ignorant of Him and His divine worship, he will remove. Millions who, are this day, so ignorant and avaricious, that they cannot conceive how God can have an attribute of justice, and show mercy to us because it pleased Him to make us *black* — which colour, Mr. Jefferson calls unfortunate!! As though we are not as thankful to our God, for having made us as it pleased himself, as they, (the whites,) are for having made them white. They think because they hold us in their infernal chains of slavery, that we wish to be white, or of their color — but they are dreadfully deceived — we wish to be just as it pleased our Creator to have made us, and no avaricious and unmerciful wretches, have any business to make slaves of, or hold us in slavery. How would they like for us to make slaves of, and hold them in cruel slavery, and murder them as they do us? — But is Mr. Jefferson's assertions true? viz. "that it is unfortunate for us that our

Creator has been pleased to make us black." We will not take his say so, for the fact. The world will have an opportunity to see whether it is unfortunate for us, which our Creator *has made* us darker than the *whites*.

Fear not the number and education of our *enemies*, against whom we shall have to contend for our lawful right; guaranteed to us by our Maker; for why should we be afraid, when God is, and will continue, (if we continue humble) to be on our side?

The man who would not fight under our Lord and Master Jesus Christ, in the glorious and heavenly cause of freedom and of God — to be delivered from the most wretched, abject and servile slavery, that ever a people was afflicted with since the foundation of the world, to the present day — ought to be kept with all of his children or family, in slavery, or in chains, to be butchered by his *cruel enemies*.

I saw a paragraph, a few years since, in a South Carolina paper, which, speaking of the barbarity of the Turks, it said: "The Turks are the most barbarous people in the world — they treat the Greeks more like *brutes* than human beings." And in the same paper was an advertisement, which said: "Eight well built Virginia and Maryland *Negro fellows* and four *wenches* will positively be *sold* this day, *to the highest bidder*!" And what astonished me still more was to see in this same humane paper the cuts of three men, with clubs and budgets on their backs, and an advertisement offering a considerable sum of money for their apprehension and delivery. I declare, it is really so amusing to hear the Southerners and Westerners of this country talk about *barbarity*, that it is positively, enough to make a man *smile*.

The sufferings of the Helots among the Spartans, were somewhat severe, it is true, but to say that theirs, were as severe as ours among the Americans, I do most strenuously deny — for instance, can any man show me an article on a page of ancient history which specifies, that, the Spartans chained, and handcuffed the Helots, and dragged them from their wives and children, children from their parents, mothers from their suckling babes, wives from their husbands, driving them from one end of the country to the other? Notice the Spartans were heathens, who lived long before our Divine Master made his appearance in the flesh.

Can Christian Americans deny these barbarous cruelties? Have you not, Americans, having subjected us under you, added to these miseries, by insulting us in telling us to our face, because we are helpless, that we are not of the human family? I ask you, O! Americans, I ask you, in the name of the Lord, can you deny these charges? Some perhaps may deny, by saying, that they never thought or said that we were not men. But do not actions speak louder than *words*? — have they not made provisions for the Greeks, and Irish? Nations who have never done the least thing for them, while we, who have enriched their country with our blood and tears — have dug up gold and silver for them and their children, from generation to generation, and are in more miseries than any other people under heaven, are not seen, but by comparatively, a handful of the American people? There are indeed, more ways to kill a dog, besides choking it to death with butter. Further — The Spartans or Lacedaemonians, had some frivolous pretext, for enslaving the Helots, for they (Helots) while being free inhabitants of Sparta, stirred up an intestine commotion, and were, by the Spartans subdued, and made prisoners of war. Consequently they and their children were condemned to perpetual slavery.

I have been for years troubling the pages of historians, to find out what our fathers have done to the *white Christians of America*, to merit such condign punishment as they have inflicted on them, and do continue to inflict on us their children. But I must aver, that my researches have hitherto been to no effect. I have therefore, come to the immoveable conclusion, that they (Americans) have, and do continue to punish us for nothing else, but for enriching them and their country. For I cannot conceive of anything else. Nor will I ever believe otherwise, until the Lord shall convince me.

The world knows, that slavery as it existed among, the Romans, (which was the primary cause of their destruction) was, comparatively speaking, no more than a *cypher*, when compared with ours under the Americans. Indeed I should not have noticed the Roman slaves, had not the very learned and penetrating Mr. Jefferson said, "when a master was murdered, all his slaves in the same house, or within hearing, were condemned to death." — Here let me ask Mr. Jefferson, (but he is gone to answer at the bar of God, for the deeds done in his body while living,) I therefore ask the whole American people, had I not rather die, or be put to death, than to be a slave to any tyrant, who takes not only my own, but my wife and children's lives by the inches? Yea, would I meet death with avidity far! far!! in preference to such servile submission to the murderous hands of tyrants. Mr. Jefferson's very severe remarks on us have been so extensively argued upon by men whose attainments in literature, I shall never be able to reach, that I would not have meddled with it, were it not to solicit each of my brethren, who has the spirit of a man, to buy a copy of Mr. Jefferson's "Notes on Virginia," and put it in the hand of his son. For let no one of us suppose that the refutations which have been written by our white friends are enough — they are whites — we are blacks.

We, and the world wish to see the charges of Mr. Jefferson refuted by the blacks *themselves*, according to their chance; for we must remember that what the whites have written respecting this subject, is other men's labours, and did not emanate from the blacks. I know well, that there are some talents and learning among the Coloured people of this country, which we have not a chance to develop in consequence of oppression; but our oppression ought not to hinder us from acquiring all we can. For we will have a chance to develop them by and by. God will not suffer us, always to be oppressed. Our sufferings will come to an end, in spite of all the Americans this side of *eternity*. Then we will want all the learning and talents among ourselves, and perhaps more, to

govern ourselves. — "Every dog must have its day," the American's is coming to an end.

But let us review Mr. Jefferson's remarks respecting us some further. Comparing our miserable fathers, with the learned philosophers of Greece, he says: "Yet notwithstanding these and other discouraging circumstances among the Romans, their slaves were often their rarest artists. They excelled too, in science, insomuch as to be usually employed as tutors to their master's children; Epictetus, Terence and Phaedrus, were slaves, — but they were of the race of whites. It is not their *condition* then, but *nature*, which has produced the distinction." See this, my brethren! Do you believe that this assertion is swallowed by millions of the whites? Do you know that Mr. Jefferson was one of as great characters as ever lived among the whites? See his writings for the world, and public labours for the United States of America. Do you believe that the assertions of such a man, will pass away into oblivion unobserved by this people and the world? If you do you are much mistaken — See how the American people treat us — have we souls in our bodies? Are we men who have any spirits at all? I know that there are many *swell-bellied* fellows among us, whose greatest object is to fill their stomachs. Such I do not mean — I am after those who know and feel, that we are MEN, as well as other people; to them, I say, that unless we try to refute Mr. Jefferson's arguments respecting us, we will only establish them.

But the slaves among the Romans. Every body who has read history, knows, that as soon as a slave among the Romans obtained his freedom, he could rise to the greatest eminence in the State, and there was no law instituted to hinder a slave from buying his freedom. Have not the Americans instituted laws to hinder us from obtaining our freedom? Do any deny this charge? Read the laws of Virginia, North Carolina, &c. Further: have not the Americans instituted laws to prohibit a man of colour from obtaining and holding any office whatever, under the government of the United States of America? Now, Mr. Jefferson tells us, that our condition is not so hard, as the slaves were under the Romans!

It is time for me to bring this article to a close. But before I close it, I must observe to my brethren that at the close of the first Revolution in this country, with Great Britain, there were but thirteen States in the Union, now there are twenty-four, most of which are slave-holding States, and the whites are dragging us around in chains and in handcuffs, to their new States and Territories to work their mines and farms, to enrich them and their children — and millions of them believing firmly that we being a little darker than they, were made by our Creator to be an inheritance to them and their children for even — the same as a parcel of *brutes*.

Are we MEN!! — I ask you, O my brethren! are we *MEN*? Did our Creator make us to be slaves to dust and ashes like ourselves? Are they not dying worms as well as we? Have they not to make their appearance before the tribunal of Heaven, to answer for the deeds done in the body, as well as we? Have we any other Master but Jesus Christ alone? Is he not their Master as well as ours? — What right then, have we to obey and call any other Master, but Himself? How we could be so submissive to a gang of men, whom we cannot tell whether they are as good as ourselves or not, I never could conceive. However, this is shut up with the Lord, and we cannot precisely tell — but I declare, we judge men by their works.

The whites have always been an unjust, jealous, unmerciful, avaricious and blood-thirsty set of beings, always seeking after power and authority. — We view them all over the confederacy of Greece, where then were first known to be any thing, (in consequence of education) we see them there, cutting each other's throats — trying to subject each other to wretchedness and misery — to effect which, they used all kinds of deceitful, unfair, and unmerciful means. We view them next in Rome, where the spirit of tyranny and deceit raged still higher. We view them in Gaul, Spain, and in Britain. — In fine, we view them all over Europe, together with what were scattered about in Asia and Africa, as heathens, and we see them acting more like devils than accountable men. But some may ask, did not the blacks of Africa, and the mulattoes of Asia, go on in the same way as did the whites of Europe. I answer, no — they never were half so avaricious, deceitful and unmerciful as the whites, according to their knowledge.

But we will leave the whites or Europeans as heathens, and take a view of them as Christians, in which capacity we see them as cruel, if not more so than ever. In fact, take them as a body, they are ten times more cruel, avaricious and unmerciful than ever they were; for while they were heathens, they were bad enough it is true, but it is positively a fact that they were not quite so audacious as to go and take vessel loads of men, women and children, and in cold blood, and through devilishness, throw them into the sea and murder them in all kind of ways. While they were heathens they were too ignorant for such barbarity. But being Christians enlightened and sensible, they are completely prepared for such hellish cruelties.

Now suppose God were to give them more sense, what would they do? If it were possible, would they, not dethrone Jehovah and seat themselves upon his throne? I therefore, in the name and fear of the Lord God of Heaven and of earth, divested of prejudice either on the side of my colour or that of the whites, advance my suspicion of them, whether they are *as good by nature* as we are or not. Their actions, since they were known as a people, have been the reverse, I do not indeed suspect them, but this, as I before observed, is shut up with the Lord, we cannot exactly tell, it will be proved in succeeding generations. — The whites have had the essence of the gospel as it was preached by my master and his apostles — the Ethiopians have not, who are to have it in its meridian splendor — the Lord will give it to them to their satisfaction. I hope and pray my God that they will make good use of it, so that it may be well with them.

—— 3.9 ——

'I SHOULD ARISE AND PREPARE MYSELF, AND SLAY MY ENEMIES WITH THEIR OWN WEAPONS'

Nat Turner's Confession

While still a child in South Hampton County, Virginia, young Nat Turner came to believe he had a special gift for prophecy. As he grew older, a reclusive Turner single-mindedly focused on his religious and spiritual studies. In the late 1820s, he began to receive visions from God telling him that he was to lead a violent revolt of his people. In August of 1830, there was a full eclipse of the moon, and Turner took this to be his signal that the time had come. He gathered a handful of confidants and, together, the men plotted revolution. Weeks later, in the middle of the night, the six men gathered, killed Turner's owner and his family in their sleep, and rode from plantation to plantation doing the same. Turner's force grew to nearly 50 slaves, and they slew nearly 60 whites before being confronted by a militia. Most were captured, but Turner escaped and remained on the run for weeks before being taken. As with all previous slave uprisings, white Virginians responded with massive counter-violence. The courts executed scores of slaves believed to be involved and mobs lynched countless more in the weeks to come, many of which had nothing to do with the uprising. As Turner sat in jail awaiting his own trial and execution, white journalist *Thomas Gray* interviewed him. He published that interview as the famous "Confessions of Nat Turner." In the excerpt below, Turner describes the visions that guided him.

…Growing up among them, with this confidence in my superior judgment, and when this, in their opinions, was perfected by Divine inspiration, from the circumstances already alluded to in my infancy, and which belief was ever afterwards zealously inculcated by the austerity of my life and manners, which became the subject of remark by white and black. — Having soon discovered to be great, I must appear so, and therefore studiously avoided mixing in society, and wrapped myself in mystery, devoting my time to fasting and prayer — By this time, having arrived to man's estate,

and hearing the scriptures commented on at meetings, I was struck with that particular passage which says : "Seek ye the kingdom of Heaven and all things shall be added unto you." I reflected much on this passage, and prayed daily for light on this subject — As I was praying one day at my plough, the spirit spoke to me, saying "Seek ye the kingdom of Heaven and all things shall be added unto you." *Question* — what do you mean by the Spirit. Ans. The Spirit that spoke to the prophets in former days — and I was greatly astonished, and for two years prayed continually, whenever my duty would permit — and then again I had the same revelation, which fully confirmed me in the impression that I was ordained for some great purpose in the hands of the Almighty. Several years rolled round, in which many events occurred to strengthen me in this my belief. At this time I reverted in my mind to the remarks made of me in my childhood, and the things that had been shewn me — and as it had been said of me in my childhood by those by whom I had been taught to pray, both white and black, and in whom I had the greatest confidence, that I had too much sense to be raised, and if I was, I would never be of any use to any one as a slave. Now finding I had arrived to man's estate, and was a slave, and these revelations being made known to me, I began to direct my attention to this great object, to fulfil the purpose for which, by this time, I felt assured I was intended. Knowing the influence I had obtained over the minds of my fellow servants, (not by the means of conjuring and such like tricks — for to them I always spoke of such things with contempt) but by the communion of the Spirit whose revelations I often communicated to them, and they believed and said my wisdom came from God. I now began to prepare them for my purpose, by telling them something was about to happen that would terminate in fulfilling the great promise that had been made to me — About this time I was placed under an overseer, from whom I ran-away — and after remaining in the woods thirty days, I returned, to the astonishment of the negroes on the plantation, who thought I had made my escape to some other part of the country, as my father had done before. But the reason of my return was, that the Spirit appeared to me and said I had my wishes directed to the things of this world, and not to the kingdom of Heaven, and that I should return to the service of my earthly master — "For he who knoweth his Master's will, and doeth it not, shall be beaten with many stripes, and thus, have I chastened you." And the negroes found fault, and murmured against me, saying that if they had my sense they would not serve any master in the world. And about this time I had a vision — and I saw white spirits and black spirits engaged in battle, and the sun was darkened — the thunder rolled in the Heavens, and blood flowed in streams — and I heard a voice saying, "Such is your luck, such you are called to see, and let it come rough or smooth, you must surely bare it." I now withdrew myself as much as my situation would permit, from the intercourse of my fellow servants, for the avowed purpose of serving the Spirit more fully — and it appeared to me, and reminded me of the things it had already shown me, and that it would then reveal to me the knowledge of the elements, the revolution of the planets, the operation of tides, and changes of the seasons. After this revelation in the year 1825, and the knowledge of the elements being made known to me, I sought more than ever to obtain true holiness before the great day of judgment should appear, and then I began to receive the true knowledge of faith. And from the first steps of righteousness until the last, was I made perfect; and the Holy Ghost was with me, and said, "Behold me as I stand in the Heavens" — and I looked and saw the forms of men in different attitudes — and there were lights in the sky to which the children of darkness gave other names than what they really were — for they were the lights of the Saviour's hands, stretched forth from east to west, even as they were extended on the cross on Calvary for the redemption of sinners. And I wondered greatly at these miracles, and prayed to be informed of a certainty of the meaning thereof — and shortly afterwards, while laboring in the field, I discovered drops of blood on the corn as though it were dew from heaven — and I communicated it to many, both white and black, in the neighborhood — and I then found on the leaves in the woods hieroglyphic characters, and numbers, with the forms of men in different attitudes, portrayed in blood, and representing the figures I had seen before in the heavens. And now the Holy Ghost had revealed itself to me, and made plain the miracles it had shown me — For as the blood of Christ had been shed on this earth, and had ascended to heaven for the salvation of sinners, and was now returning to earth again in the form of dew — and as the leaves on the trees bore the impression of the figures I had seen in the heavens, it was plain to me that the Saviour was about to lay down the yoke he had borne for the sins of men, and the great day of judgment was at hand. About this time I told these things to a white man, (Etheldred T. Brantley) on whom it had a wonderful effect — and he ceased from his wickedness, and was attacked immediately with a cutaneous eruption, and blood oozed from the pores of his skin, and after praying and fasting nine days, he was healed, and the Spirit appeared to me again, and said, as the Saviour had been baptised so should we be also — and when the white people would not let us be baptised by the church, we went down into the water together, in the sight of many who reviled us, and were baptised by the Spirit — After this I rejoiced greatly, and gave thanks to God. And on the 12th of May, 1828, I heard a loud noise in the heavens, and the Spirit instantly appeared to me and said the Serpent was loosened, and Christ had laid down the yoke he had borne for the sins of men, and that I should take it on and fight against the Serpent, for the time was fast approaching when the first should be last and the last should be first. *Ques.* Do you not find yourself mistaken now? *Ans.* Was not

Christ crucified. And by signs in the heavens that it would make known to me when I should commence the great work — and until the first sign appeared, I should conceal it from the knowledge of men — And on the appearance of the sign, (the eclipse of the sun last February) I should arise and prepare myself, and slay my enemies with their own weapons. And immediately on the sign appearing in the heavens, the seal was removed from my lips, and I communicated the great work laid out for me to do, to four in whom I had the greatest confidence, (Henry, Hark, Nelson, and Sam) — It was intended by us to have begun the work of death on the 4th July last — Many were the plans formed and rejected by us, and it affected my mind to such a degree, that I fell sick, and the time passed without our coming to any determination how to commence — Still forming new schemes and rejecting them, when the sign appeared again, which determined me not to wait longer.

Since the commencement of 1830, I had been living with Mr. Joseph Travis, who was to me a kind master, and placed the greatest confidence in me; in fact, I had no cause to complain of his treatment to me. On Saturday evening, the 20th of August, it was agreed between Henry, Hark and myself, to prepare a dinner the next day for the men we expected, and then to concert a plan, as we had not yet determined on any. Hark, on the following morning, brought a pig, and Henry brandy, and being joined by Sam, Nelson, Will and Jack, they prepared in the woods a dinner, where, about three

Q. Why were you so backward in joining them.

A. The same reason that had caused me not to mix with them for years before.

I saluted them on coming up, and asked Will how came he there, he answered, his life was worth no more than others, and his liberty as dear to him. I asked him if he thought to obtain it? He said he would, or loose his life. This was enough to put him in full confidence. Jack, I knew, was only a tool in the hands of

Hark, it was quickly agreed we should commence at home (Mr. J. Travis') on that night, and until we had armed and equipped ourselves, and gathered sufficient force, neither age nor sex was to be spared, (which was invariably adhered to.) We remained at the feast until about two hours in the night, when we went to the house and found Austin; they all went to the cider press and drank, except myself. On returning to the house, Hark went to the door with an axe, for the purpose of breaking it open, as we knew we were strong enough to murder the family, if they were awaked by the noise; but reflecting that it might create an alarm in the neighborhood, we determined to enter the house secretly, and murder them whilst sleeping. Hark got a ladder and set it against the chimney, on which I ascended, and hoisting a window, entered and came down stairs, unbarred the door, and removed the guns from their places. It was then observed that I must spill the first blood. On which, armed with a hatchet, and accompanied by Will, I entered my master's chamber, it being dark, I could not give a death blow, the hatchet glanced from his head, he sprang from the bed and called his wife, it was his last word, Will laid him dead, with a blow of his axe, and Mrs. Travis shared the same fate, as she lay in bed. The murder of this family, five in number, was the work of a moment, not one of them awoke; there was a little infant sleeping in a cradle, that was forgotten, until we had left the house and gone some distance, when Henry and Will returned and killed it; we got here, four guns that would shoot, and several old muskets, with a pound or two of powder. We remained some time at the barn, where we paraded; I formed them in a line as soldiers, and after carrying them through all the manoeuvres I was master of, marched them off to Mr. Salathul Francis', about six hundred yards distant. ...

——— 3.10 ———

'ADDRESS TO THE FREE PEOPLE OF COLOUR OF THE UNITED STATES'

Richard Allen

After receiving a letter from a young man who inquired whether it would be possible to organize a mass migration of blacks to Canada, Richard Allen and his Philadelphia cohorts decided to call a national convention of free blacks to discuss the matter. So in September 1830, delegates representing the black communities of Connecticut, Delaware, Maryland, New York and Pennsylvania met at AME Bethel to ponder migrating to "Upper Canada." They resolved only to study the matter, and that they considered it a desirable plan. But of more importance, they established the American Society of Free Persons of Color — the first national black political organization. They agreed to hold another convention the following year, and to invite delegates from still more communities. Further, each community was to be encouraged to hold their own conventions, and consider themselves a chapter of the larger "Parent Society." It was the beginning of what became known as the "convention movement." The national meetings would be held annually for decades, and the local meetings would proliferate nationwide. These conventions became a primary breeding ground and platform for black political thought in general and the abolition movement in particular, throughout the 18th century. At that first gathering, Allen, the elected president of the group (and, at the time, likely the most prominent black person in the nation), delivered his "Address to the Free People of Colour of the United States."

Brethren,

Impressed with a firm and settled conviction, and more especially being thought by that inestimable and invaluable instrument, namely, the Declaration of Independence, that all men are born free and equal, and consequently are endowed with unalienable rights, among which are the enjoyments of life, liberty, and the pursuits of happiness.

Viewing these as incontrovertible facts, we have been led to the following conclusions; that our forlorn and deplorable situation earnestly and loudly demand of us to devise and pursue all legal means for the speedy elevation of ourselves and brethren to the scale and standing of men.

And in pursuit of this great object, various ways and means have been resorted to; among others, the African Colonization Society is the most prominent. Not doubting the sincerity of many friends who are engaged in that cause; yet we beg leave to say, that it does not meet with our approbation. However great the debt which these United States may owe to injured Africa, and however unjustly her sons have been made to bleed, and her daughters to drink of the cup of affliction, still we who have been born and nurtured on this soil, we, whose habits, manners, and customs are the same in common with other Americans, can never consent to take our lives in our hands, and be the bearers of the redress offered by that Society to that much afflicted country.

Tell it not to barbarians, lest they refuse to be civilised, and eject our christian missionaries from among them, that in the nineteenth century of the christian era, laws have been enacted in some of the states of this great republic, to compel an unprotected and harmless portion of our brethren to leave their homes and seek an asylum in foreign climes: and in taking a view of the unhappy situation of many of these, whom the oppressive laws alluded to, continually crowd into the Atlantic cities, dependent of their support upon their daily labour, and who often suffer for want of employment, we have had to lament that no means have yet been devised for their relief.

These considerations have led us to the conclusion, that the formation of a settlement in the British province of Upper Canada, would be a great advantage of the people of colour. In accordance with these views, we pledge ourselves to aid each other by all honourable means, to plant and support one in that country, and therefore we earnestly and most feelingly appeal to our coloured brethren, and to all philanthropists here and elsewhere, to assist in this benevolent and important work.

To encourage our brethren earnestly to co-operate with us, we offer the following, viz. 1st. Under that government no invidious distinction of colour is recognised, but there we shall be entitled to all the rights, privileges, and immunities of other citizens. 2nd. That the language, climate, soil, and productions are similar to those in this country. 3rd. That land of the best quality can be purchased at the moderate price of one dollar and fifty cents per acre, by the one hundred acres. 4th. The market for different kinds of produce raised in that colony, is such as to render a suitable reward to the industrious farmer, equal in our opinion to that of the United States. And lastly, as the erection of buildings must necessarily claim the attention of the emigrants, we would invite the mechanics from our large cities to embark in the enterpirse; the advancement of architecture depending much on their exertions, as they must consequently take with them the arts and improvements of our well regulated communities.

It will be much to the advantage of those who have large families, and desire to see them happy and respected, to locate themselves in a land where the laws and prejudices of society will have no effect in retarding their advancement to the summit of civil and religious improvement. There the diligent student will have ample opportunity to reap the reward due to industry and perserverence; whilst those of moderate attainments, if properly nurtured, may be enabled to take their stand as men in the several offices and situations necessary to promote union, peace, order and tranquility. It is to these we must look for the strength and spirit of our future prosperity.

Before we close, we would just remark, that it has been a subject of deep regret to this convention, that we as a people, have not availingly appreciated every opportunity placed within our power by the benevolent efforts of the friends of humanity, in elevating our condition to the rank of freemen. That our mental and physical qualities have not been more actively engaged in pursuits more lasting, is attributable in a great measure to a want of unity among ourselves; whilst our only stimulus to action has been to become domestics, which at best is but a precarious and degraded situation.

It is to obviate these evils, that we have recommended our views to our fellow-citizens in the foregoing instrument, with a desire of raising the moral and political standing of ourselves; and we cannot devise any plan more likely to accomplish this end, than by encouraging agriculture and mechanical arts: for by the first, we shall be enabled to act with a degree of independence, which as yet has fallen to the lot of but few among us; and the faithful pursuit of the latter, in connection with the sciences, which expand and ennoble the mind, will eventually give us the standing and condition we desire.

To effect these great objects, we would earnestly request our brethren throughout the United States, to co-operate with us, by forming societies auxiliary to the Parent Institution, about being established in the city of Philadelphia, under the patronage of the General Convention. And we further recommend to our friends and brethren, who reside in places where, at present, this may be impracticable, so far to aid us, by contributing to the funds of the Parent Institution; and, if disposed, to appoint one delegate to represent them in the next Convention, to be held in Philadelphia the first Monday of June next, it being fully understood, that organized societies be at liberty to send any number of delegates not exceeding five.

――――― 3.11 ―――――

THE HOPE OF LIBERTY
George Moses Horton

George Moses Horton's 1929 *The Hope of Liberty* was the second poetry collection published by an African American. As a young slave in Chatham County, North Carolina, the self-educated Horton wrote poetry in his head while working in the field. On Sundays, he sold fruit at the college campus in Chapel Hill. The students there discovered his wit, and encouraged him to "spout" for them. "I would stand forth and address myself extempore before them," Horton later wrote, "as an orator of inspired promptitude." Eventually, however, he came to understand the whole business to be a way of mocking him. Angered, he changed tack and instead began to recite poetry. Eventually, he developed a business by selling love poems to the awed students for 25 cents a piece. A visiting professor from Boston noticed Horton, and used her connections to have his poems published in a northern newspaper. From that opportunity grew his 1829 collection.

A. "On Liberty and Slavery"

Alas! and am I born for this,
    To wear this slavish chain?
Deprived of all created bliss,
    Through hardship, toil and pain!

How long have I in bondage lain,
    And languished to be free!
Alas! and must I still complain—
    Deprived of liberty.

Oh, Heaven! And is there no relief
    This side of the silent grave—
To soothe the pain—to quell the grief
    And anguish of a slave?

Come Liberty, thou cheerful sound,
    Roll through my ravished ears!
Come, let my grief in joys be drowned,
    And drive away my fears.

Say unto foul oppression, Cease:
    Ye tyrants rage no more,
And let the joyful trump of peace,
    Now bid the vassal soar.

Soar on the pinions of that dove
    Which long has cooed for thee,
And breathed her notes from Afric's grove,
    The sound of Liberty.

Oh, Liberty! thou golden prize,
    So often sought by blood—
We crave thy sacred sun to rise,
    The gift of nature's God!

Bid slavery hide her haggard face,
    And barbarism fly:

I scorn to see the sad disgrace
    In which enslaved I lie.

Dear Liberty! upon thy breast,
    I languish to respire;
And like the Swan unto her nest,
    I'd like to thy smiles retire.

Oh, blest asylum—heavenly balm!
    Unto thy boughs I flee—
And in thy shades the storm shall calm,
    With songs of Liberty!

B. "On hearing of the intention of a gentlemen to purchase the Poet's freedom"

When on life's ocean first I spread my sail,
I then implored a mild auspicious gale;
And from the slippery strand I took my flight,
And sought the peaceful haven of delight.

Tyrannic storms arose upon my soul,
And dreadful did their mad'ning thunders roll;
The pensive muse was shaken from her sphere,
And hope, it vanish'd in the clouds of fear.

At length a golden sun broke thro' the gloom,
And from his smiles arose a sweet perfume—
A calm ensued, and birds began to sing,
And lo! the sacred muse resumed her wing.

With frantic joy she chaunted as she flew,
And kiss'd the clement hand that bore her thro'
Her envious foes did from her sight retreat,
Or prostrate fall beneath her burning feet.

'Twas like a proselyte, allied to Heaven—
Or rising spirits' boast of sins forgiven,
Whose shout dissolves the adamant away
Whose melting voice the stubborn rocks obey.
'Twas like the salutation of the dove,
Borne on the zephyr thro' some
        lonesome grove,
When Spring returns, and Winter's
        chill is past,
And vegetation smiles above the blast.

'Twas like the evening of a nuptial pair,
When love pervades the hour of sad despair—
'Twas like fair Helen's sweet return to Troy,
When every Grecian bosom swell'd with joy.

The silent harp which on the osiers hung,
Was then attuned, and manumission sung:
Away by hope the clouds of fear were driven,
And music breathed my gratitude to heaven.

Hard was the race to reach the distant goal,
The needle oft was shaken from the pole;
In such distress, who could forbear to weep?
Toss'd by the headlong billows of the deep!

The tantalizing beams which shone so plain,
Which turn'd my former pleasures into pain—
Which falsely promised all the joys of fame,
Gave way, and to a more substantial flame.

Some philanthropic souls as from afar,
With pity strove to break the slavish bar;
To whom my floods of gratitude shall roll,
And yield with pleasure to their soft control.

And sure of Providence his work begun—
He shod my feet this rugged race to run;
And in despite of all the swelling tide,
Along the dismal path will prove my guide.

Thus on the dusky verge of deep despair,
Eternal Providence was with me there;
When pleasure seemed to fade on life's
    gay dawn,
And the last beam of hope was almost gone.

——— 3.12 ———
'THE SLAVE AUCTION'
Frances E. W. Harper

Frances Ellen Watkins Harper, dubbed "The Bronze Muse," grew up a free orphan in Baltimore, Maryland. As a teenager, she worked for a white bookstore owner and, it is said, there she developed a love for writing. She published her first book of poetry in 1846, and would go on to publish several collections throughout the 19th century. Watkins was also a novelist and short story writer, and

her 1892 Iola Leroy was until recently believed to be the first novel published by a black woman (see Chapter Five). She was actively involved in the time's politics as well, participating in both the Abolition and Women's Movements and working as a "conductor" on the Underground Railroad. Harper's most famous poem is "The Slave Auction," published in an 1854 collection.

The sale began — young girls were there,
    Defenceless in their wretchedness,
Whose stifled sobs of deep despair
    Revealed their anguish and distress.
And mothers stood with streaming eyes,
    And saw their dearest children sold;
Unheeded rose their bitter cries,
    While tyrants bartered them for gold.
And woman, with her love and truth —
    For these in sable forms may dwell —
Gaz'd on the husband of her youth,
    With anguish none may paint or tell.
And men, whose sole crime was their hue,
    The impress of their Maker's hand,
And frail and shrinking children, too,
    Were gathered in that mournful band.
Ye who have laid your love to rest,
    And wept above their lifeless clay,
Know not the anguish of that breast,
    Whose lov'd are rudely torn away.
Ye may not know how desolate
    Are bosoms rudely forced to part,
And how a dull and heavy weight
    Will press the life drops from the heart.

——— 3.13 ———
'I AM SICK OF OUR UNMEANING DECLAMATION IN PRAISE OF LIBERTY AND EQUALITY; OF OUR HYPOCRITICAL CANT ABOUT THE UNALIENABLE RIGHTS OF MAN'
William Lloyd Garrison

At the end of the 1820s, the primary institutional vehicle — and primary line of thought — for slavery's white critics was the American Colonization Society. And so that was where William Lloyd Garrison first became involved with the drive to end slavery. At the time, he was editing an anti–Andrew Jackson paper in Vermont, and developed a respect for Quaker writer Benjamin Lundy. Lundy roamed the South — nominally searching for a place where freed slaves could establish an independent settlement — and filed reports of the institution's horrors in his *Genius of Universal Emancipation*, a journal based in Baltimore, Maryland. Garrison ran an article praising Lundy; Lundy noticed it and invited Garrison to edit his paper.

The marriage immediately fell on hard times, however, as Garrison developed the radical and uncompromising voice he would come to be known for. As his thoughts quickly matured on the topic, he rejected both colonization and the Quakers' call for gradual emancipation. To this point, even the most ardent of antislavery activists believed universal and immediate emancipation of slaves to be foolhardy. Both the slaves and the white society, they reasoned, would need some sort of transition. But to Garrison, this was not a subject for slow and measured deliberation — slavery was the worst of all history's moral crimes and needed to be abolished completely and immediately. By delivering fiery and uncompromising speeches promoting this doctrine, such as the 1829 Independence Day address below, he quickly became one of America's most controversial figures. But it was Garrison, later joined by fugitive slave Frederick Douglass, who would bring black and white antislavery voices together to build the 19th century abolitionist movement into an influential voice in American politics.

...Every Fourth of July, our Declaration of Independence is produced, with a sublime indignation, to set forth the tyranny of the mother country, and to challenge the admiration of the world. But what a pitiful detail of grievances does this document present, in comparison with the wrongs which our slaves endure! In the one case, it is hardly the plucking of a hair from the head; in the other, it is the crushing of a live body on the wheel; the stings of the wasp contrasted with the tortures of the inquisition. Before God, I must say, that such a glaring contradiction, as exists between our creed and practice, the annals of six thousand years cannot parallel. In view of it, I am ashamed of my country. I am sick of our unmeaning declamation in praise of liberty and equality; of our hypocritical cant about the unalienable rights of man. I could not, for my right hand, stand up before a European assembly, and exult that I am an American citizen, and denounce the usurpations of a kingly government as wicked and unjust; or, should I make the attempt, the recollection of my country's barbarity and despotism would blister my lips, and cover my cheeks with burning blushes of shame.

Will this be termed a rhetorical flourish? Will any man coldly accuse me of intemperate zeal? I will borrow, then, a ray of humanity from one of the brightest stars in our American galaxy, whose light will gather new effulgence to the end of time. 'This, sirs, is a cause, that would be dishonored and betrayed, if I contented myself with appealing only to the understanding. It is too cold, and its processes are too slow for the occasion. I desire to thank God, that, since he has given me an intellect so fallible, he has impressed upon me an instinct that is sure. On a question of shame and honor — liberty and oppression — reasoning is sometimes useless, and worse. I feel the decision in my pulse: if it throws no light upon the brain, it kindles a fire at the heart.'

Let us suppose that endurance has passed its bounds, and that the slaves, goaded to desperation by the cruelty of their oppressors, have girded on the armor of vengeance. Let us endeavor to imagine the appeal which they would publish to the world, in extenuation of their revolt. The preamble might be taken from our own Declaration of Independence, with a few slight alterations. Then what a detail of wrongs would follow! Speaking at first from the shores of Africa, and changing their situation with the course of events, they would say:

'They, (the American people,) arrogantly styling themselves champions of freedom, for a long course of years have been guilty of the most cruel and protracted tyranny. They have invaded our territories, depopulated our villages, and kindled among us the flames of an exterminating war. They have wedged us into the holds of their 'floating hells,' with suffocating compactness, and without the distinction of age or sex—allowing us neither to inhale the invigorating air of heaven, nor to witness the cheering light of the sun, neither wholesome food nor change of raiment — by which treatment thousands have expired under the most horrible sufferings. They have brought us to a free and Christian land, (so called,) and sold us into their market-places like cattle — even in the proud Capital of their Union, and within sight of their legislative halls, where Tyranny struts in the semblance of Liberty. They have cruelly torn the wife from her husband, the mother from her daughter, and children from their parents, and sold them into perpetual exile. They have confined us in loathsome cells and secret prisons — driven us in large droves from State to State, beneath a burning sky, half naked, and heavily manacled — nay, retaken and sold many, who had by years of toil obtained their liberation. They have compelled us 'to till their ground, to carry them, to fan them when they sleep, and tremble when they wake,' and rewarded us only with stripes, and hunger, and nakedness. They have lacerated our bodies with whips, and brands, and knives, for the most innocent and trifling offences, and often solely to gratify their malignant propensities; nor do they esteem it a crime worthy of death to murder us at will. Nor have they deprived us merely of our liberties. They would destroy our souls, by endeavoring to deprive us of the means of instruction — of a knowledge of God, and Jesus Christ, and the Holy Spirit, and a way of salvation: at the same time, they have taxed the whole country (our own labor among other things) to instruct and enlighten those who are at a great remove from them, whom they never fettered nor maimed, whose condition is not so dark or pitiable as our own. They have —

But why need I proceed? My powers of description are inadequate to the task. A greater than Jefferson would fail. Only the pen of the recording angel can declare their manifold wrongs and sufferings; and the revelation will not be made till the day of judgment.

We say, that the disabilities imposed upon our fathers, by the mother country, furnished just cause for rebellion; that their removal was paramount to every other consideration; and that the slaughter of our oppressors was a justifiable act; for we should resist unto blood to save our liberties. Suppose that to-morrow should bring us tidings that the slaves at the South had revolted, en masse, and were spreading devastation and death to the white population? Should we celebrate their achievements in song, and justify their terrible excesses? And why not, if our creed be right? Their wrongs are unspeakably grievous, and liberty is the birthright of every man.

We say, that France was justified in assisting our fathers to maintain their independence; and that, as a nation, we owe her our liveliest gratitude for her timely interference. Suppose, in case of a revolt, that she, or some other European power, should furnish our slaves with guns and ammunition, and pour her troops into our land. Would it be treacherous or cruel? Why, according to our revolutionary credenda? The argument, tremendous as it is, is against us! WELL, IT MAY BE DONE. At a fit moment, a foreign foe may stir up a rebellion, and arm every black, and take the lead in the enterprise. The attempt would not be difficult; the result can be easily imagined.

We say, that the imprisonment of an inconsiderable number of our seamen, by Great Britain, authorized the late war; and we boast of our promptitude to redress their wrongs. More than a million of native-born citizens are at this moment enduring the galling yoke of slavery. Who cries for justice? None. 'But they are blacks!' True, and they are also men; and, moreover, they are American's by birth. …

——— 3.14 ———
'I WILL BE HEARD!'
William Lloyd Garrison

Despite the Quakers' unease with William Lloyd Garrison's vocal demand for immediate emancipation, Benjamin Lundy allowed him to go on editing his *Genius of Universal Emancipation*. In the paper's pages, Garrison did what he could to keep the flames of controversy lit. In

1829, he published an editorial accusing a prominent merchant of using his ships to illegally transport captured Africans into slavery. The merchant sued for libel and won. Garrison refused to pay the fine and, instead, chose to spend 45 days in jail. When he got out, he went on a speaking tour to drum up support for his Immediacy Doctrine. But he was sorely disappointed to find that few antislavery whites wanted anything to do with him. Furious, he launched a newspaper of his own, conceived as a platform to attack northern racism and acceptance of slavery. In the first issue of his *Liberator*, he reprinted the charges for which he had been jailed.

For the remainder of the abolitionist movement, the *Liberator* would be a key voice, providing black and white thinkers, activists, poets and fiction writers who opposed slavery with a platform to air their views and showcase their work. In the opening editorial, Garrison penned the words that would define his life. As a pacifist — or at least someone asserting to be one — he rejected the idea of a revolution. He felt that the nation could be convinced, through relentless and confrontational moral persuasion, that slavery was an affront to Christianity and humanity. Therefore, he wrote, regardless of how much contempt the publication stirred, he would shout his message from the top of his lungs until the world took notice. Famously, he promised, "I will be heard!"

TO THE PUBLIC

In the month of August, I issued proposals for publishing "The Liberator" in Washington City; but the enterprise, though hailed in different sections of the country, was palsied by public indifference. Since that time, the removal of the Genius of Universal Emancipation to the Seat of Government has rendered less imperious the establishment of a similar periodical in that quarter.

During my recent tour for the purpose of exciting the minds of the people by a series of discourses on the subject of slavery, every place that I visited gave fresh evidence of the fact, that a greater revolution in public sentiment was to be effected in the free States — and particularly in New-England — than at the South. I found contempt more bitter, opposition more active, detraction more relentless, prejudice more stubborn, and apathy more frozen, than among slave-owners themselves. Of course, there were individual exceptions to the contrary. This state of things afflicted, but did not dishearten me. I determined, at every hazard, to lift up the standard of emancipation in the eyes of the nation, within sight of Bunker Hill and in the birthplace of liberty. That standard is now unfurled; and long may it float, unhurt by the spoilations of time or the missiles of a desperate foe — yea, till every chain be broken, and every bondman set free! Let Southern oppressors tremble — let their secret abettors tremble — let their Northern apologists tremble — let all the enemies of the persecuted blacks tremble.

I deem the publication of my original Prospectus unnecessary, as it has obtained a wide circulation. The principles therein inculcated will be steadily pursued in this paper, excepting that I shall not array myself as the political partisan of any man. In defending the great cause of human rights, I wish to derive the assistance of all religions and of all parties.

Assenting to the "self-evident truth" maintained in the American Declaration of Independence, "that all men are created equal, and endowed by their Creator with certain inalienable rights — among which are life, liberty and the pursuit of happiness," I shall strenuously contend for the immediate enfranchisement of our slave population. In Park-Street Church, on the Fourth of July, 1829, I unreflectingly assented to the popular but pernicious doctrine of gradual abolition. I seize this moment to make a full and unequivocal recantation, and thus publicly to ask pardon of my God, of my country, and of my brethren the poor slaves, for having uttered a sentiment so full of timidity, injustice, and absurdity. A similar recantation, from my pen, was published in the *Genius of Universal Emancipation* at Baltimore, in September, 1829. My conscience is now satisfied.

I am aware that many object to the severity of my language; but is there not cause for severity? I will be as harsh as truth, and as uncompromising as justice. On this subject, I do not wish to think, or to speak, or write, with moderation. No! no! Tell a man whose house is on fire to give a moderate alarm; tell him to moderately rescue his wife from the hands of the ravisher; tell the mother to gradually extricate her babe from the fire into which it has fallen; — but urge me not to use moderation in a cause like the present. I am in earnest — I will not equivocate — I will not excuse — I will not retreat a single inch — AND I WILL BE HEARD. The apathy of the people is enough to make every statue leap from its pedestal, and to hasten the resurrection of the dead.

It is pretended, that I am retarding the cause of emancipation by the coarseness of my invective and the precipitancy of my measures. The charge is not true. On this question of my influence, — humble as it is, — is felt at this moment to a considerable extent, and shall be felt in coming years , — not perniciously, but beneficially — not as a curse, but as a blessing; and posterity will bear testimony that I was right. I desire to thank God, that he enables me to disregard "the fear of man which bringeth a snare," and to speak his truth in its simplicity and power. And here I close with this fresh dedication:

"Oppression! I have seen thee, face to face,
And met thy cruel eye and cloudy brow,
But thy soul-withering glance I fear not now—
For dread to prouder feelings doth give place
Of deep abhorrence! Scorning the disgrace
Of slavish knees that at thy footstool bow,
I also kneel — but with far other vow
Do hail thee and thy herd of hirelings base:—
I swear, while life-blood warms my throbbing
        veins,
Still to oppose and thwart, with heart and
        hand,
Thy brutalising sway — till Afric's chains
Are burst, and Freedom rules the rescued
        land, —
Trampling Oppression and his iron rod:
Such is the vow I take — SO HELP ME
        GOD!"
[by the Scottish poet *Thomas Pringle*]

—————— 3.15 ——————
DECLARATION OF SENTIMENTS
The American Anti-Slavery Society

The *Liberator* found tremendous popularity among free blacks in the North, but whites were initially cool to it. As a result, the subscriptions were relatively small and the paper foundered financially. In part to develop a foundation to support the paper, and in part to give the growing abolitionist movement an institutional backbone, Garrison started the New England Anti-Slavery Society. In December 1833, the organization led a national convention of anti-slavery advocates at which delegates established the American Anti-Slavery Society, based on the principles published in its "Declaration of Sentiments" below. This organization, which was biracial, with six African Americans on its founding board, was the central anti-slavery organizing vehicle for the remainder of the abolitionist movement. Its local societies proliferated, and by the end of the decade there were 2,000 local antislavery societies with a cumulative membership of over 200,000.

The convention assembled in the city of Philadelphia, to organize a National Anti-Slavery Society, promptly seize the opportunity to promulgate the following Declaration of Sentiments, as cherished by them in relation to the enslavement of one-sixth portion of the American people.

More than fifty-seven years have elapsed, since a band of patriots convened in this place, to devise measures for the deliverance of this country from a foreign yoke. The corner-stone upon which they founded the Temple of Freedom was broadly this — 'that all men are created equal; that they are endowed by their Creator with certain inalienable rights; that among these are life, LIBERTY, and the pursuit of happiness.' At the sound of their trumpet-call, three millions of people rose up as from the sleep of death, and rushed to the strife of blood; deeming it more glorious to die instantly as freemen, than desirable to live one hour as slaves. They were few in number — poor in resources; but the honest conviction that Truth, Justice and Right were on their side, made them invincible.

We have met together for the achievement of an enterprise, without that of our fathers is incomplete; and which, for its magnitude, solemnity, and probably results upon the destiny of the world, as far transcends theirs as moral truth does physical force.

In purity of motive, in earnestness of zeal, in decision of purpose, in intrepidity of action, in steadfastness of faith, in sincerity of spirit, we would not be inferior to them.

Their principles led them to wage war against their oppressors, and to spill human blood like water, in order to be free. Ours forbid the doing of evil that good may come, and lead us to reject, and to entreat the oppressed to reject, the use of all carnal weapons for deliverance from bondage; relying solely upon those which are spiritual, and mighty through God to the pulling down of strong holds.

Their measures were physical resistance — the marshalling in arms — the hostile array — the mortal encounter. Ours shall be such only as the opposition of moral purity to moral corruption — the destruction of error by the potency of truth — the overthrow of prejudice by the power of love — and the abolition of slavery by the spirit of repentance.

Their grievances, great as they were, were trifling in comparison with the wrongs and sufferings of those for whom we plead. Our fathers were never slaves — never bought and sold like cattle — never shut out from the light of knowledge and religion — never subjected to the lash of brutal taskmasters.

But those, for whose emancipation we are striving — constituting at the present time at least one-sixth part of our countrymen — are recognized by law, and treated by their fellow-beings, as marketable commodities, as goods and chattels, as brute beasts; are plundered daily of the fruits of their toil without redress; really enjoy no constitutional nor legal protection from licentious and murderous outrages upon their persons; and are ruthlessly torn asunder — the tender babe from the arms of its frantic mother — the heart-broken wife from her weeping husband — at the caprice or pleasure of irresponsible tyrants. For the crime of having a dark complexion, they suffer the pangs of hunger, the infliction of stripes, the ignominy of brutal servitude. They are kept in heathenish darkness by laws expressly enacted to make their instruction a criminal offence.

These are the prominent circumstances in the condition of more than two million of our people, the proof of which may be found in thousands of indisputable facts, and in the laws of the slaveholding States.

Hence we maintain — that, in view of the civil and religious privileges of this nation, the guilt of its oppression is unequalled by any other on the face of the earth; and, therefore, that it is bound to repent instantly, to undo the heavy burdens, and to let the oppressed go free.

We further maintain — that not man has a right to enslave or imbrute his brother — to hold or acknowledge him, for one moment, as a piece of merchandise — to keep back his hire by fraud — or to brutalize his mind, by denying him the means of intellectual, social and moral improvement.

The right to enjoy liberty is inalienable. To invade it is to usurp the prerogative of Jehovah. Every man has a right to his own body — to the products of his own labor — to the protection of law — and to the common advantages of society. It is piracy to buy or steal a native African, and subject him to servitude. Surely, the sin is as great to enslave an American as an African.

Therefore we believe and affirm — that there is no difference, in principle, between the African slave trade and American slavery:

That every American citizen, who detains a human being in involuntary bondage as his property, is, according to Scripture, (Ex. Xxi. 16,) a man-stealer:

That the slaves ought instantly to be set free, and brought under the protection of law:

That if they had lived from the time of Pharaoh down to the present period, and had been entailed through successive generations, their right to be free could never have been alienated, but their claims would have constantly risen in solemnity:

That all those laws which are now in force, admitting the right of slavery, are therefor, before God, utterly null and void; being an audacious usurpation of the Divine prerogative, a daring infringement on the law of nature, a base overthrow of the very foundations of the social compact, a complete extinction of all the relations, endearments and obligations of mankind, and a presumptuous transgression of all the holy commandments; and that therefore they ought instantly to be abrogated.

We further believe and affirm — that all persons of color, who possess the qualifications which are demanded of others, ought to be admitted forthwith to the enjoyment of the same privileges, and the exercise of the same prerogatives, as others; and that the paths of preferment, of wealth, and of intelligence, should be opened as widely to them as to persons of a white complexion.

We maintain that no compensation should be give to the planters emancipating their slaves:

Because it would be a surrender of the great fundamental principle, that man cannot hold property in man:

Because slavery is a crime, and therefore is not an article to be sold:

Because the holders of slaves are not the just proprietors of what they claim; freeing the slave is not depriving them of property, but restoring it to its rightful owner; it is not wrong the master, but righting the slave — restoring him to himself:

Because immediate and general emancipation would only destroy nominal, not real property; it would not amputate a limb or break a bone of the slaves, but by infusing motives into their breasts, would make them doubly valuable to the masters as free laborers; and

Because, if compensation is to be given at all, it should be given to the outraged and guiltless slaves, and not to those who have plundered and abused them.

We regard as delusive, cruel and dangerous, any scheme of expatriation which pretends to aid, either directly or indirectly, in the emancipation of the slaves, or to be a substitute for he immediate and total abolition of slavery.

We fully and unanimously recognise the sovereignty of each State, to legislate exclusively on the subject of the slavery which is tolerated within its limits; we concede that Congress, under the present national compact, has no right to interfere with any of the slave States, in relation to this momentous subject:

But we maintain that Congress has a right, and is solemnly bound, to suppress the domestic slave trade between the several States, and to abolish slavery in those portions of our territory which the Constitution has placed under its exclusive jurisdiction.

We also maintain that there are, at the present time, the highest obligations resting upon the people of the free States to remove slavery by moral and political action, as prescribed in the Constitution of the United States. They are now living under a pledge of their tremendous physical force, to fasten the galling fetters of tyranny upon the limbs of millions in the Southern States; they are liable to be called at any moment to suppress a general insurrection of the slaves; they authorize the slave owner to vote for three-fifths of his slaves as property, and thus enable him to perpetuate his oppression; they support a standing army at the South for its protection; and they seize the slave, who has escaped into their territories, and send him back to be tortured by an enraged master or brutal driver. This relation to slavery is criminal, and full of danger: IT MUST BE BROKEN UP.

These are our views and principles — these our designs and measures. With entire confidence in the overruling justice of God, we plant ourselves upon the Declaration of our Independence and the truths of Divine Revelation, as upon the Everlasting Rock.

We shall organize Anti-Slavery Societies, if possible, in every city, town and village in our land.

We shall send forth agents to lift up the voice of remonstrance, of warning, of entreaty, and of rebuke.

We shall circulate, unsparingly and extensively, anti-slavery tracts and periodicals.

We shall enlist the pulpit and the press in the cause of the suffering and the dumb.

We shall aim at the purification of the churches from all participation in the guilt of slavery.

We shall encourage the labor of freemen rather than that of slaves, by giving a preference to their productions: and

We shall spare no exertions nor means to bring the whole nation to speedy repentance.

Our trust for victory is solely in God. We may be personally defeated, but our principles never. Truth, Justice, Reason, Humanity, must and will gloriously triumph. Already a host is coming up to the help of the Lord against the mighty, and the prospect before us is full of encouragement.

Submitting this Declaration to the candid examination of the people of this country, and of the fields of liberty throughout the world, we hereby affix our signatures to it; pledging ourselves that, under the guidance and by the help of Almighty God, we will do all that in us lies, consistently with this Declaration of our principles, to overthrow the most execrable system of slavery that has ever been witnessed upon earth; to deliver our land from its deadliest curse; to wipe out the foulest stain which rests upon our national escutcheon; and to secure to the colored population of the United States, all the rights and privileges which belong to them as men, and as Americans — come what may to our persons, our interests, our reputation — whether we live to witness the triumph of Liberty, Justice and Humanity, or perish untimely as martyrs in this great, benevolent, and holy cause.

Done at Philadelphia, December 6th, A.D. 1833.

3.16

'THOUGHTS ON AFRICAN COLONIZATION'
William Lloyd Garrison

As the abolitionist movement blossomed, a feud developed between it and the American Colonization Society. In many ways, the two movements competed for the support of influential liberal whites seeking an end to slavery. Abolitionists galvanized diffuse opposition to colonization, started by free black leaders earlier in the century, into an identifiable force. The criticism of William Lloyd Garrison, of course, drew the most attention. He, as had James Forten and Russell Perrott years earlier noted that the motives of many ACS members were less than pure. The group's increased popularity in Congress was due in no small part to the addition of southern slaveholders into its fold. They, as Forten and Perrot predicted, saw the scheme as a way to siphon off unbreakable slaves who stirred the proliferating uprisings and to silence the calls for slavery's end — colonization was to stand in for abolition. Garrison took aim in a lengthy and impassioned essay he published in an 1832 pamphlet attacking the ACS.

… I am constrained to declare, with the utmost sincerity, that I look upon the Colonization scheme as inadequate in its design, injurious in its operation, and contrary to sound principle; and the more scrupulously I examine its pretensions, the stronger is my conviction of its sinfulness. Nay, were Jehovah to speak in an audible voice from his holy habitation, I am persuaded that his language would be, 'Who hath required this at your hands?'

It consoles me to believe that no man, who knows me personally or by reputation, will suspect the honesty of my skepticism. If I were politic, and intent only on my own preferment or pecuniary interest, I should swim with the strong tide of public sentiment, instead of breasting its powerful influence. The hazard is too great, the labor too burdensome, the remuneration too uncertain, the contest too unequal, to induce a selfish adventurer to assail a combination so formidable. Disinterested opposition and sincere conviction, however, are not conclusive proofs of individual rectitude; for a man may very honestly do mischief, and not be aware of his error. Indeed, it is in this light I view many of the friends of African colonization. I concede to them benevolence of purpose and expansiveness of heart; but, in my opinion, they are laboring under the same delusion as that which swayed Saul of Tarsus — persecuting the blacks even unto a strange country and verily believing that they are doing God service. I blame them, nevertheless, for taking this mighty scheme upon trust; for not perceiving and rejecting the monstrous doctrines avowed by the master spirits in this crusade; and for feeling so indifferent to the moral, political and social advancement of the free people of color in this, their only legitimate home. ...

I should oppose this Society, even were its doctrines harmless. It imperatively and effectually seals the lips of a vast number of influential and pious men, who, for fear of giving offence to those slaveholders with whom they associate, and thereby leading to a dissolution of the compact, dare not expose the flagrant enormities of the system of slavery, nor denounce the crime of holding human beings in bondage. They dare not lead to the onset against the forces of tyranny; and if *they* shrink from the conflict, how shall the victory be won? I do not mean to aver, that, in their sermons, or addresses, or private conversations, they never allude to the subject of slavery; for they do so frequently, or at least every Fourth of July. But my complaint is, that they content themselves with representing slavery as an evil, — a misfortune, — calamity which has been entailed upon us by former generations, — *and not as an individual* CRIME, embracing in its folds robbery, cruelty, oppression and piracy. They do not identify the criminals; they make no direct, pungent, earnest appeal to the consciences of menstealers; by consenting to walk arm-in-arm with them, they virtually agree to abstain from all offensive remarks, and to aim entirely at the expulsion of the free people of color; their lugubrious exclamations, and solemn animadversions, and reproachful reflections, are alto-

gether indefinite; they 'go about, and about, and all the way round to nothing;' they generalize, they shoot into the air, they do not disturb the repose nor wound the complacency of the sinner; 'they have put no difference between the holy and profane, neither have they shewed difference between the unclean and the clean.' Thus has free inquiry been suppressed, and a universal fear created, and the tongue of the boldest silenced, and the sleep of death fastened upon the nation. 'Truth has fallen in the streets, and equity cannot enter.' The plague is raging with unwonted fatality; but no *cordon sanitaire* is established — no adequate remedy sought. The tide of moral death is constantly rising and widening; but no efforts are made to stay its desolating career. The fire of God's indignation is kindling against us, and thick darkness covers the heavens, and the hour of retribution is at hand; but we impiously throw the burden of our guilt upon our predecessors, we affect resignation to our unfortunate lot, we descant upon the mysterious dispensations of Providence, and we deem ourselves the objects of God's compassion rather than his displeasure!

Were the American Colonization Society bending its energies directly to the immediate abolition of slavery; seeking to enlighten and consolidate public opinion, on this momentous subject; faithfully exposed the awful guilt of the owners of slaves; manfully contending for the bestowal of equal rights upon our free colored population in this their native land; assiduously endeavoring to uproot the prejudices of society; and holding no fellowship with oppressors; my opposition would cease. It might continue, without censure, to bestow its charities upon such as spontaneously desire to remove to Africa, whether animated by religious, or the hope of bettering their temporal condition. But, alas! it's governing spirit and purpose are of an opposite character.

The popularity of the Society is not attributable to its merits, but exclusively to its congeniality with those unchristian prejudices which have so long been cherished against a sable complexion. It is agreeable to slaveholders, because it is striving to remove a class of persons who they fear may stir up their slaves to rebellion. All who avow undying hostility to the people of color are in favor of it; all who shrink from acknowledging them as brethren and friends, or who make them a distinct and inferior caste, or who deny the possibility of elevating them in the scale of improvement here, most heartily embrace it. …

--------- 3.17 ---------

'WE KNOW NOTHING OF THAT DEBASING INFERIORITY WITH WHICH OUR VERY COLOUR STAMPED US IN AMERICA'
Letters from Liberia

The American Colonization Society had to counter the public attacks on it. One critique of the colonization effort charged that the emigrants in Liberia were miserable. Reports filtered back to the States of trouble growing crops, of rampant disease and of hostility between them and the local African communities. The ACS had to respond to these charges, particularly if it hoped to maintain the support of northern whites and convince free blacks to participate. In one pamphlet, journalist Matthew Carey published a letter from the colonists in Liberia declaring the reports of misery to be patent lies. Things were fine, the author assured supporters, and the emigrants enjoyed a liberty that free blacks in America could only dream of. Other letters, however, reported a much different world. Historian Bell Wiley recently published a volume of letters written by colonists to their former owners (actually, to their friends and families via their owners). The correspondent below, Peyton Skipwith, describes his travails and his hope to either move to Sierra Leone or return to America.

A. Letter from colonists in Matthew Carey's pamphlet

As much speculation and uncertainty continues to prevail among the people of colour in the United States, respecting our situation and prospects in Africa; and many misrepresentations have been put in circulation there, of a nature slanderous to us, and, in their effects, injurious to them; we felt it our duty, by a true statement of our circumstances, to endeavor to correct them.

The first consideration which caused our voluntary removal to this country, and the object, which we still regard with the deepest concern, is liberty — liberty, in the sober, simple, but complete sense of the word; not a licentious liberty, nor a liberty without government, or which should place us without government, or which should place us without the restraint of salutary laws — but that liberty of speech, action and conscience, which distinguishes the free, enfranchised citizens of a free state. *We did not enjoy that freedom in our native country; and, from causes which, as respects ourselves, we shall soon forget forever, we were certain it was not there attainable for ourselves or our children.* This, then, being the first object of our pursuit in coming to Africa, is probably the first object on which you will ask for information. And we must truly declare to you, that our expectations and hopes, in this respect, have been realized. Our constitution secures to us, so far as our condition allows, "all the rights and privileges enjoyed by the citizens of the United States;" and these rights and privileges are ours: — *we are the proprietors of the soil we live on, and possess the rights of freeholders. Our suffrages, and, what is of more importance, our sentiments and our opinions, have their due weight in the government we live under. Our laws are altogether our own: they grow out of our circumstances; are framed for our exclusive benefit, and administered either by officers of our own appointment, or such as possess our confidence.* We have a judiciary, chosen from among ourselves; we serve as jurors in the trial of others; and are liable to be tried only by juries of our fellow-citizens ourselves. *We have all that is meant by liberty of conscience.* The time and mode of worshipping God, as prescribed to us in the word, and dictated by our conscience, we are not only free to follow, but are protected in following.

Forming a community of our own, in the land of our forefathers; having the commerce, and soil, and resources of the country, at our disposal; *we know nothing of that debasing inferiority with which our very colour stamped us in America: there is nothing here to create the feeling on our part — nothing to cherish the feeling of superiority on the minds of foreigners who visit us. It is this moral emancipation — this liberation of the mind from worse than iron fetters — that repays us ten thousand times over, for all that is has cost us, and makes us grateful to God and our American patrons, for the happy change that has taken place in our situation.* We are not so self-complacent as to rest satisfied with our improvement, either as regards our minds or our circumstances. We do not expect to remain stationary. Far from it. But we certainly feel ourselves, for the first time, in a state to improve either, to any purpose. The burden is now gone from our shoulders; we now breathe and move freely; and know not, (in surveying your present state) for which to pity you most — in the name of liberty, which you endeavour to content yourselves with, in a country that is not yours, or the delusion which makes you hope for ampler privileges in that country hereafter. Tell us, which is the white man, who, with a prudent regard to his own character, can associate with one of you, on terms of equality? Ask us, which is the white man who would decline such association with one of our number, whose intellectual and moral qualities are not an objection? To both these questions, we unhesitatingly make the same answer: — There is no such white man.

We solicit none of you to emigrate to this country: for we know not who among you prefers rational independence, and the honest respect of his fellow men, to that mental sloth and careless poverty which you already possess, and your children will inherit after you, in America. But if your views and aspirations rise to a degree higher — if your minds are not as servile as your present condition — we can decide the question at once; and with confidence say, that you will bless the day, and your children after you, when you determined to become citizens of Liberia.

But we do not hold this language on the blessings of liberty, for the purpose of consoling ourselves for the sacrifice of health, or the suffering of want, in consequence to our removal to Africa. We enjoy health, after a few months' residence in the country, as uniformly, and in as perfect a degree, as we possessed that blessing in our native country. And a distressing scarcity of provisions, or any of the comforts of life, has, for the last two years, been this entirely unknown, even to the poorest persons in this community. On these points there are, and have been much misconception, and some malicious misrepresentations in the U. States.

The true character of the African climate is not well understood in other countries. Its inhabitants are as robust, as healthy, as long lived, to say the least, as those of any other country. Nothing like an epidemic has ever appeared in this colony; nor can we learn from the natives, that the calamity of a sweeping sickness ever yet visited this part of the continent. But the change from a temperate to a tropical country is a great one — too great not to affect the health more or less — and, in the cases of old people, and the very young children, it often causes death. In the early years of the colony, want of good houses, the great fatigues and dangers of the settlers, their irregular mode of living, and the hardships and discouragement they met with, greatly helped the other causes of sickness, which prevailed to an alarming extent, and were attended with great mortality. But we look back to those times as a season of trial long past, and nearly forgotten. Our houses and circumstances are now comfortable; and, for the last two or three years, not one person in forty, from the middle and southern states, has died from the change of climate. The disastrous fate of the company of settlers who came out from Boston in the brig Vine, eighteen months ago, is an exception to the common lot of emigrants; and the causes of it ought to be explained. Those people left a cold region in the coldest part of winter, and arrived here in the hottest season of our year. Many of them were too old to have survived long in any country. They most imprudently neglected the prescriptions of our very successful physician, the Rev. Lott Cary, who has great experience and great skill in the fevers of the country; and depended on medicines brought with them, which could not fail to prove injurious. And, in consequence of all those unfortunate circumstances, their sufferings were severe, and many died. But we are not apprehensive that a similar calamity will befall any future emigrants, except under similar disadvantages.

People now arriving, have comfortable houses to receive them; will enjoy the regular attendance of a physician in the slight sickness that may await them, will be surrounded and attended by healthy and happy people, who will have borne the effects of the climate, who will encourage and fortify them against that despondency which, alone, has carried off several in the first years of the colony.

But you may say, that even health and freedom, as good as they are, are still dearly paid for, when they cost you the common comforts of life, and expose your wives and children to famine, and all the evils of want and poverty. We do not dispute the soundness of this conclusion either; but we utterly deny that is has any application to the people of Liberia.

Away with all the false notions that are circulating about the barrenness of this country: they are the observations of such ignorant and designing men, as would injure both it and you. *A more fertile soil, and a more productive country so far as it is cultivated, there is not, we believe, on the face of this earth.* Its hills and plains are covered with a verdure which never fades: the productions of nature keep on in their growth through all the seasons of the year. Even the natives for the country, almost without farming tools, without skill, and with very little labour, make more grain and vegetables than they can consume, and often more than they can sell.

Cattle, swine, fowls, ducks, goats, and sheep, thrive without feeding, and require no other care than to keep them from straying. Cotton, coffee, indigo, and the sugar cane, are all the spontaneous growth of our forests; and may be cultivated, at pleasure, to any extent, by such as they are disposed. The same may be said of rice, Indian corn, guinea corn, millet, and too many species of fruits and vegetables to be enumerated. Add to all this, *we have no dreary winter here, for one half of the year to consume the productions of the other half.* Nature is constantly renewing herself, and constantly pouring her treasures, all the year round, into the laps of the industrious. We could say, on this subject, more; but we are afraid of exciting, too highly, the hopes of the imprudent. Such persons, we think, will to well to keep their rented cellars, and earn their twenty-five cents at the wheelbarrow, in the commercial towns of America, and stay where they are. *It is only the industrious and virtuous that we can point to independence, and plenty, and happiness, in this country.* Such people are nearly sure to attain, in a very few years, to a style of comfortable living, which they may in vain hope for in the United States; and, however short we come of this character ourselves, it is only a due acknowledgement of the bounty of Divine Providence to say, that we generally enjoy the good things of this life to our entire satisfaction.

Our trade is chiefly confined to the coast, to the interior parts of the continent, and to foreign vessels. It is already valuable and fast increasing. It is carried on in the productions of the country, consisting of rice, palm oil, ivory, tortoise shell, dye-woods, gold, hides, wax, and a small portion of coffee: and it brings us, in return, the products of manufacturers of the four quarters of the world. Seldom, indeed, is our harbour clear of European and American shipping; and the bustle and thronging of our streets, show something, already, of the activity of the smaller seaports of the United States.

Mechanics of nearly every trade, are carrying on their various occupations; their wages are high, and a large number would be sure of constant and profitable employment.

Not a child or youth in the colony, but is provided with an appropriate school. We have numerous public library, and a court house, meeting houses, school houses, and fortifications sufficient, or nearly so, for the colony, in its present state.

Our houses are constructed of these same materials, and finished in the same style, as in the towns of America. We have abundance of good building stone, shells for lime, and clay, of an excellent quality, for bricks. Timber is plentiful, of various kinds, and fit for all the different purposes of building and fencing.

Truly we have a goodly heritage: and if there is anything lacking in the character or condition of the people in this colony, it never can be charged to the account of this colony, it must be the fruit of our own mismanagement, or slothfulness, or vices. But from these evils we confide in Him, to whom we are indebted for all our blessings, to preserve us. It is the topic of our weekly and daily thanksgiving to Almighty God, both in public and in private, and He knows with what sincerity, that we were ever conducted, by his Providence, to this shore. Such great favours, in so short a time, and mixed with so few trails, are to be ascribed to nothing but his special blessing. This we acknowledge. We only want the gratitude which such signal favours call for. Nor are we willing to close this paper, without adding a heartfelt testimonial of the deep obligations we owe to our American patrons and best earthly benefactors, whose wisdom pointed us to this home of our nation, and whose active and persevering benevolence enabled us to reach it. Judge, then, of the feelings, with which we hear the motives and doings of the Colonizations Society traduced; and that, too, by men too ignorant to know what the Society has accomplished; too weak to look through its plans and intentions; or too dishonest to acknowledge either. But, without pretending to any prophetic sagacity, we can certainly predict to that society, the ultimate triumph of their hopes and labours, and disappointment and defeat to all who opposed them. Men may theorize, and speculate about their plans in America, but there can be no speculation here. The cheerful abodes of civilization and happiness which are scattered over this verdant mountain — the flourishing settlements which are spreading around it — this sound of christian instruction, and scenes of christian worship, which are heard, and seen in this land of brooding pagan darkness — a thousand contented freemen, uniting in forming a new christian empire, happy themselves, and instruments of happiness to others — every object, every individual, is an argument, is demonstration, of the wisdom and goodness of the plan of colonization.

Where is the argument that shall refute facts like these? And where is the man hardy enough to deny them?

B. Peyton Skipwith's letters

Monrovia, March 6th, 1835
Dear Sir:

I embrace this opportunity to write you these few lines to inform you that I am not well with a blindness of nights so that I cannot see. All the information that I can get from the doctors is that must stop laying stone. I have lost my wife. She died on July 2d, 1834. The rest of my family are tolerable well. Sir This is the third letter that I have wrote to you and have received no answer and would be thankful if you would write by the first chance and I do not know of any better chance than to write by Mr. Jos. J. Roberts. I wonce had the notion of coming home and still have a notion but I want to go up to Sirralione as I am advised by the doctors to quit laying s[t]one for it is injurious to my health & if I get my health by going there I will s[t]ay there. If not will return back to America. Give my respects to your family, also to the people. Let my Mother know that you have received a letter from me. I don't want to you say any thing to [her] about my being blind but let her know that I will return. Dianah send her love to Miss Sally and all of the family is very desirous of returning back again. She wants to write her word also by the first opportunity. Let her know how Miss Nancy Cavil and her family. I have put myself to a gread deal of truble of searching the servant of Mr. Cavil and also that of Mr. Harris but I can't find eather of them. Nothing more but I remain yours truly,

Peyton Skipworth

Lucy Nichols
May 10, Monrovia, Liberia
Dear Mother:

I rite to you theas fue lines to inform you that I am verry unwell but the rest of the family is quit wel and I hope that these fue lines will find you in good health; I am in hopes that you will not greav after Father because I beleav if he keep the faith he is gone to beter world than this. All that you wil have to do mother is to prepare to meat death for the Lord giveth and the Lor Takeeth and blessed is the nam of the lord. I have not greve after my father for I be leav that he is gone to a better world than thihs. I was more shock when I heard the death of Cussan Charls be caus you did not rite me whither he maid his peace with god or not. Tell my brother Erasmus deal fair with his self for I know that if the love of god ever was applied to his troubleed contion he know it. You wish to see me but cant be more disires to see me that I am to see you all. I Calculate to come and see your all this year but this wound have thrown me so far back I dont know when I shal be able to come and this mother I hope wil give you consolation: if you never see me no more in this world, I am triing to meat you in a better world this this whare we Shal part no more. Tell Brother Georg that I hope his faith has not fail. Ask him if he a solder. Do he mean to fite in the indureing of the war? If you dos you go on for I am bound to meat you. Tell uncle ned that I am verry glad that he got his famiy and that he is living well but I am verry much Surprise that he have not rote me a letter Since I have bin hear. Ask brother Gerry do he mean to dy a Sinner or what is calculation. Tel him to write me for I feel consurned bout situation. Tell Lavinia that I Shant say much to her because she told me when I cam home that nothing Should Seperrate her from the love of god. Tel

me by your next letter if all the mebres of the temperanse Sosiety that I leav is hold out faith ful. I wil tel you uppon the oner of a man that I have ceep my pleg for I have not baught one gil of Spirrit since I leave ameeria nor use it in no way. Tell Charls most that I wish to se him verry much.

It is so teagest for me to call all of people naim but give my love to Cissiah and her children to Sam Kello and to all of my inquireing friends fer and near. The children all send thire lve to every body. Matilda send her love to ned and aunt Luvina and to the rest of the family. I get the ribbons and hankerchief and one pare of socks. I have not sene mr. Minor yet but if my health wil admit I expect to go to Capepalamos for to work nax dries and thire I Shal Se him if he dont leave for emmerica before that time. I have nothing more to say.

Peyton Skipworth

——— 3.18 ———

'ALL WE WANT IS MAKE US FREE'
The Amistad Africans

In the early morning hours of July 2, 1839, a captured African stowed in the hull of a slave ship freed himself and his 52 fellow prisoners, then led a revolt. The ship had set sail just days earlier from Havana, Cuba en route to Puerto Principe. The Africans spared the lives of the Spanish captains, who had illegally taken them into slavery, and ordered them to guide the ship to Africa instead. The Spaniards sailed east by day, but north by night, and two months later the "long, low black schooner" pulled into port at Long Island, seeking food and supplies. The arrival of a ship full of Africans sparked intense curiosity, and eventually officials boarded the ship to investigate. On board, they learned of the revolt from the Spaniards, seized the vessel and took the Africans into custody. The trial of the 19th century followed.

Abolitionists quickly rallied around the Africans, demanding they be set free since their captivity violated several legal bans on the international slave trade. Opposing them were Spanish diplomats, represented by the U.S. government, who demanded the Africans be extradited to Spain where they could be tried for murder and treason. Throughout the series of trials — a rushed District Court ruling, a Circuit Court order and eventually a Supreme Court decision — abolitionists provided a translator for the Africans and kept up a steady public campaign on their behalf. Missionaries swarmed the jails hoping to convert them (and the Africans soon realized the value of at least offering lip service to their discovery of Christianity and intent to spread its gospel if returned home). The story captured popular imagination, spawning a hit play and countless journalistic investigations and narratives of the events. Observers were particularly fascinated with the revolt's leader, Joseph Cinque. He became a savage superhero to abolitionists, a murderous beast to those who supported his extradition.

A. The *Colored American* on Cinque

The *Colored American* was among the nation's leading black newspapers at the time of the Amistad case. As they did with other blacks, the paper lionized Cinque, morphing him into a figure of Herculean stature. Shortly after the affair began, in October of 1839, the paper ran the following editorial discussing Cinque. Emphasizing — and glorifying — his African features, the article compares Cinque to popular New York Senator Daniel Webster, and argues that no supposedly inferior race could produce such an awe-inspiring man.

CINGUES.
We are inclined to call the noble African by this name, although he is called by as many different titles as our republicanism offers reasons for enslaving his people. We have seen a wood-cut representation of the royal fellow. It looks as we think it would. It answers well to his lion-like character. — The head has the towering front of Webster, and though some shades darker than our great country-man, we are struck at first sight, with his resemblance to him. He has Webster's lion aspect. — His majestic, quiet, uninterested cast of expression, looking, when at rest, as if there was nobody and nothing about him to care about or look at. His eye is deep, heavy — the cloudy iris extending up behind the brow almost inexpressive, and yet as

if volcanoes of action might be asleep behind it. It looks like the black sea or the ocean in a calm — an unenlightened eye, as Webster's would have looked, had he been bred in the desert, among the lions, as Cingues was, and if instead of pouring upon Homer and Shakespeare, and Coke and the Bible (for Webster read the Bible when he was young, and got his *regal* style there) it had rested, from savage boyhood, on the sands and sky of Africa. It looks like a wilderness, a grand, but uninhabited land, or, if peopled, the abode of aboriginal man. Webster's eye like a civilized and cultivated country — *country* rather than city — more on the whole like woods and wilderness than fields or villages. For after all, nature predominates greatly in the eye of our majestic countryman.

The nose and mouth of Cingues are African. We discover the expanded and powerful nostrils mentioned in the description, and can fancy readily its contractions and dilations, as he made those addresses to his countrymen and called upon them to rush, with a greater than Spartan spirit, upon the countless white people, who he apprehended would doom them to a life of slavery. He has none of the look of an Indian — nothing of the savage. It is a gentle, magnanimous, generous look, not so much of the warrior as the sage — a sparing and not a destructive look, like the lion's when unaroused by hunger or the spear of the huntsman. It must have flashed terribly upon that midnight deck, when he was dealing with the wretched Ramonflues.

We bid pro-slavery look upon Cingues and behold in him the race we are enslaving. He is a sample. Every Congolese or Mandingan is not, be sure, a Cingues. Nor was every Corsican a Napolian, or every Yankee a Webster. "Giants are rare," said Ames, "and it is forbidden that there should be races of them." But call not the race inferior, which in now and then an age produces such men.

Our shameless people have made merchandise of the likeness of Cingues — as they have of the originals of his (and their own) countrymen. They had the effrontery to look him in the face long enough to delineate it, and at his eye long enough to copy its wonderful expression.

By the way, Webster ought to come home to defend Cingues. He ought to have no counsel short of his twin spirit. His defence were a nobler subject for Webster's giant intellect, than the Foote resolutions or Calhoun's nullification. There is indeed no defence to make. It would give Webster occasion to strike at the slave trade and at our people for imprisoning and trying a man admitted to have risen only against the worst of pirates, and for more than life — for liberty, for country and for home.

Webster should vindicate him if he must be tried. Old Marshall would be the man to try him. And after his most honorable acquittal and triumph, a ship should be sent to convey him to his country — not an American ship. They are all too near a kin to the "*low, long, black schooner.*" A British ship — old Nelson's line of battle, if it is yet afloat, the one he had at Trafalgar; and Hardy, Nelson's captain, were a worthy sailor to command it to Africa. He would steer more honestly than the treacherous old Spaniard. He would steer them toward the sunrise, by night as well as by day. An old British sea captain would have scorned to betray the noble Cinques. He would have been as faithful as the compass.

We wait to see the fate of the African hero. We feel no anxiety for him. The country can't reach him. He is above their reach and above death. He has conquered death. But his wife and children — they who

"Weep beside the cocoa tree —"

And we wait to see the bearings of this providential event upon American Slavery.— *Herald of Freedom*

B. Africans write to John Quincy Adams

President Martin Van Buren's administration promised the Spanish government it would deliver the Africans, and laid preparations for their extradition. But the Circuit Court in Connecticut frustrated the administration's plans by ruling that the Africans should be set free. When the government appealed the case to the Supreme Court, the Africans' abolitionist supporters, led by Lewis Tappan, became concerned about their chances. They knew they needed an attorney both experienced in the court and respected by it. They asked then–U.S. Representative and former president John Quincy Adams to take the case. Adams was an abolitionist champion. Nevertheless, he was at first reluctant to become involved in the Amistad affair. Late in his life and career, the 73-year-old Adams likely cringed at the idea of such a high-profile dispute. Eventually, however, he relented. Several of the Africans wrote him letters thanking him for his support and pleading with him to do everything he could to secure their freedom.

Westville, Jan. 4, 1841
Dear Friend Mr. Adams:
I want to write a letter to you because you love Mendi people, and you talk to the grand court. We want to tell you one thing. Jose Ruiz say we born in Havana, he tell lie. We stay in Havana 10 days and 10 nights. We stay no more. We all born in Mendi — we no understand the Spanish language. Mendi people been in America 17 moons. We talk America language a little, not very good. We write every day; we write plenty letters. We read most all time. We read all Matthew, and Mark, and Luke, and John, and plenty of little books. We love books very much. We want you to ask the Court what we have done wrong. What for Americans keep us in prison. Some people say Mendi people crazy, Mendi people dolt, because we no talk America language. America people no talk Mendi language. American people crazy dolts? They tell bad things about Mendi people and we no understand. Some men say Mendi people very happy because they laugh and have plenty to eat. Mr. Pendleton come and Mendi people all look sorry because they think about Mendiland and friends we no see now. Mr. Pendleton say we feel anger and white men afraid of us. Then we no look sorry again. That's why we laugh. But Mendi people feel bad. O, we can't tell how bad. Some people say, Mendi people no have

souls. Why we feel bad, we no have no souls? We want to be free very much.

Dear friend Mr. Adams, you have children, you have friends, you love them, you feel very sorry if Mendi people come and take all to Africa. We feel bad for our friends, and our friends all feel bad for us. Americans not take us in ship. We were on shore and Americans tell us slave ship catch us. They say we make you free. If they make us free they tell truth, if they not make us free they tell lie. If America give us free we glad, if they no give us free we sorry — we sorry for Mendi people little, we sorry for America people great deal because God punish liars. We want you to tell court that Mendi people no want to go back to Havana, we no want to be killed. Dear friend, we want you to know how we feel. Mendi people think, think, think. nobody know. Teacher, he know, we tell him some. Mendi people have got souls. We think we know God punish us if we tell lie. We never tell lie; we speak the truth. What for Mendi people afraid? Because they have got souls. Cook say he kill, he eat Mendi people — we afraid — we kill cook. Then captain kill one man with knife, and cut Mendi people plenty. We never kill captain if he no kill us. If Court ask who bring Mendi people to America, we bring ourselves. Ceci hold the rudder. All we want is make us free, not send us to Havanna. Send us home. Give us Missionary. We tell Mendi people Americans spoke truth. We give them good tidings. We tell them there is one god. You must worship him. Make us free and we will bless you and all Mendi people will bless you, Dear friend Mr.Adams.

Your friend,

Kale

C. Colored American on Adams' Supreme Court argument

John Quincy Adams argued before the Supreme Court that the Amistad Africans could not be tried for any crime by Spain or by the United States or by any other government besides their own. They had been illegally kidnapped, in contradiction of both the laws of the U.S. and treaties signed by Spain, and their mutiny was an attempt to free themselves from that illegal action. They had never been slaves, but were rather citizens of Africa and should be returned there immediately. He relentlessly attacked the Van Buren administration, declaring that he was ashamed as an American at its willingness to aid Spain in violating international law and trampling on American values of justice and fairness.

During the course of Adams's collective seven hours worth of argument, Justice Philip Barbour died. The court adjourned for three days, and then returned to hear the rest of Adams's presentation. In the report below, the *Colored American* correspondent describes Adams's argument and speculates that the pause in deliberations may work to the Africans' advantage. The Van Buren administration was nearing a close, and the Africans' supporters hoped that, even should they lose the case, a new administration would take a less hard-line stance on their extradition. The point became moot, as the Supreme Court agreed with Adams. It ordered the Africans freed, but ruled the president had no responsibility to send them home. Abolitionists then organized a speaking tour for the group, in which they raised money to transport themselves home.

FROM OUR WASHINGTON CORRESPONDENT. U.S. Representatives' Hall. Washington, D.C., March 1, 1841.

Mr. Editor: …Mr. Adams commenced his plea in behalf of the Amistad captives, on Wednesday last. There was a well filled Court room, and, among the auditors, I noticed Mr. Clay, Mr. Crittenden, &c. He occupied four hours, and not having finished, the Court adjourned. During the night, Judge Barbour, one of the judges of the Supreme Court, expired. On the meeting of the Court the next day, his death was announced, and they immediately adjourned over till today. The funeral solemnities of the Judge were attended on Friday, and his remains were conveyed to his family residence in Virginia. Today, Mr. Adams has finished his plea, having occupied about three hours more. Of course you will not expect me to give you a sketch of a seven hours' speech, in a letter of this nature. Suffice it to say, that he took the ground that no law was applicable to the case of his clients, save that contained in our Declaration of Independence, two copies of which always hung in that room; that they had gained their Independence, and we had no right to interfere with them, nor the Spanish Government the right to demand them of us; that those who caused the arrest of Montez and Ruiz, though by some denominated fanatics, were, in his opinion, friends of human kind, friends of human liberty, unwilling to see forty of their fellow beings deprived of their liberty, and burnt at the stake, without an effort to save them; that the ghosts of the sixteen victims of Montea, sent by his ill treatment to premature graves, would pass by his couch in his dying hour, at which fearful sight he would exclaim, "O! how will they press upon my soul tomorrow!" that the conduct of our Government, during the whole progress of this Amistad business, had been partial, unjust, despotic, and outrages; that he felt ashamed to have it said, that the country to which he belonged was thus disgraced by such management on the part of its Executive and his Attorney General; and that the time was, when the United States Government sympathized with the *victims* of the slave traders, and not with *those traders themselves*. The closing part of his speech was the most touching and affecting of anything of the kind to which I ever listened. "Thirty-seven years ago," said he, "I was admitted as an Attorney and Counsellor at the bar of this Court. A few years after, I appeared here to plead the cause of the oppressed. I now appear here again, to plead a similar cause, and in all probability for the last time. But where are the Judges who formerly sat here? Where is Marshall and where are his associates? They are gone — gone, I hope, to a blessed reward. And where's the Judge who sat in that vacant seat at the commencement of the plea which I am now about to close? He too has gone to take his own trial before another tribunal, higher than this. And I do most fervently ejaculate the prayer, that you may so act your part, that it shall be said to each one of you, when you go

hence. 'Well done, good and faithful servant, enter thou into the joy of thy Lord.' "In uttering the last sentence or two, Mr. Adams' voice almost failed him, through the force of his feelings, and as he sat down, the tears started from his eyes, as they did likewise from the eyes of others, (your correspondent's among the rest.) And when an acquaintance at that moment asked me what I thought of it, I was unable to reply, so deeply were my feelings affected. I was informed that the Clerk of the Court shed tears. I did not observe the Judges being absorbed with my own emotions; but I doubt not they were deeply affected likewise. How could they be otherwise? As to Mr. Adams, the nation will mourn his loss when he dies. He is highly valued now, but he will be still more highly prized when we are deprived of him. God preserve him to us many years to come.

It *may* prove to be a providential interference in behalf of the captives, that Judge Barbour's death took place as it did. God smote him down from his high seat, in consequence of which, the Court adjourned for three days, so that the Amistad case was delayed. It is still on hand. The present administration have but two days more to rule. By the delay of that case, it will now probably not be decided by the Court till this administration shall end, for the Attorney General is to make his closing plea tomorrow, after which, the Judges will have to hold a consultation on the subject. They will probably decide, that they have no jurisdiction in the case. Were this decision to be made before the end of Mr. Van Buren's *reign*, the poor captives would be instantly seized and delivered to the Spanish authorities. But should it not be made till his career has terminated, they will no doubt be set at liberty.

D. John Barber's descriptions of the Amistad Africans

On November 27, 1841, two years after their revolt, the 35 survivors set sail for home. Earlier, in 1840, John Barber compiled and published documents and descriptions relative to the famous case. He included descriptions and brief biographies of the 36 Africans alive at that time.

SING-BE [Cin-gue] (generally spelt *Cinquez*) was born in Ma-ni, in Dzho-poa, *i. e.* in the *open land*, in the Mendi county. The distance from Mani to Lomboko, he says is ten suns, or days. His mother is dead, and he lived with his father. He has a wife and three children, one son and two daughters. His son's name is *Ge-waw*, (God). His king, Ka-lum-bo, lived at Kaw-men-di, a large town in the Mendi country. He is a planter of rice, and never owned or sold slaves. He was seized by four men, when traveling in the road, and his right hand tied to his neck. Ma-ya-gi-la-lo sold him to Ba-ma-dzha, son of Shaka, king of Gen-du-ma, in the Vai country. Bamadzha carried him to Lomboko and sold him to a Spaniard. He was with Mayhagila three nights; with Bamadzha one month, and at Lomboko two months. He had heard of Pedro Blanco, who lived at Te-i-lu, near Lomboko.

2. GI-LA-BA-RU, [Grab-eau] (*have mercy on me*) was born at Fu-lu, in the Mendi country, two moons' journey into the interior. His name in the public prints is generally spelt GRABEAU. He was the next after Cinque in command of the Amistad. His parents are dead, one brother and one sister living. He is married, but no children; he is a planter of rice. His king Baw-baw, lived at Fu-lu. He saw Cingue at Fu-lu and Fadzhinna, in Bombali. He was caught on the road when going to Taurang, in the Bandi country, to buy clothes. His uncle had bought two slaves in Bandi, and gave them in payment for a debt; one of them ran away, and he (Grabeau) was taken for him. He was sold to a Vai-man, who sold him to Laigo, a Spaniard, at Lomboko. Slaves in this place are put into a prison, two are chained together by the legs, and the Spaniards give them rice and fish to eat. In his country has seen people write — they wrote from right to left. They have cows, sheep and goats, and wear cotton cloth. Smoking tobacco is a common practice. None but the rich eat salt, it

costs so much. Has seen leopards and elephants, the latter of which, are hunted for ivory. Grabeau is four feet eleven inches in height; very active, especially in turning somersets. Besides Mendi, he speaks Vai, Kon-no and Gissi. He aided John Ferry by his knowledge of Gissi, in the examination at Hartford.

3. KIMBO, (cricket) is 5 ft. 6 in. in height, with mustaches and long beard; in middle life, and is intelligent. He was born at Maw-ko-ba, a town in the Mendi country; his father was a gentleman, and after his death, his king took him for his slave, and gave him to his son Ban-ga, residing in the Bullom country. He was sold to a Bullom man, who sold him to a Spaniard at Lomboko. He counts thus: 1, eta; 2, fili; 3, kiau-wa; 4, naeni; 5, loelu; 6, weta; 7, wafura; 8, wayapa; 9, ta-u; 10, pu. — Never saw any books in his country. When people die in his country, they suppose the spirit lives, but where, they cannot tell.

4. NAZHA-U-LU (*a water stick*) also called from his country, KON-NO-MA, is 5 ft. 4 in. in height, has large lips, and projecting mouth, his incisor teeth pressed outward and filed, giving him rather a savage appearance; he is the one who was supposed to be a cannibal, tattooed in the forehead with a diamond shaped figure. He was born in the Konno country: his language is not readily understood by Covey, the interpreter. Kon-no-ma recognizes many words in Mungo Plark's Mandingo vocabulary.

5. BUR-NA, the younger, height 5 ft. 2 in., lived in a small town in the Mendi country. He counts in Tim-ma-ni and Bullom. He was a blacksmith in his native village, and made hoes, axes, and knives; he also planted rice. He was sold for crim. con. to a Spaniard at Lomboko. He was taken in the road, and was four days in traveling to Lomboko. Has a wife and one child, a father, three sisters and brother living.

6. GBA-TU, [Bar-tu] (*a club or sword*) height 5 ft. 6 in. with a tattooed breast, was born in the country of Tu-ma, near a large body of fresh water, called Ma-wu-a. His father is a gentleman and does no work. His king,

named Da-be, resided in the town of Tu-ma. He was sent by his father to a village to buy clothes; on his return, he was seized by six men, and his hands tied behind; was ten days in going to Lomboko. There are high mountains in his country, rice is cultivated, people have guns; has seen elephants. *Remark.* — There is a village called Tu-ma, in the Timmani country, 60 miles from Sierra Leone, visited by Major Laing.

7. GNA-KWOI (in *Ba-lu* dialect, *second born*) was born at Kong-go-la-hung, the largest town in the Balu country. This town is situated on a large river called in Balu, *Za-li-ba*; and in Mendi, *Kal-wa-ra*: fish are caught in this river as large as a man's body — they are caught in nets and sometimes shot with guns. When going to the gold country to buy clothes, he was taken and sold to a Vai man who sold him to a Spaniard named Peli. Gna-kwoi has a wife and one child; he calls himself a Balu-man; has learned the Mendi language since he was a slave; 5 ft. 6 in. in height.

8. KWONG was born at Mam-bui, a town in the Mendi country. When a boy he was called Ka-gnwaw-ni. Kwong is a Bullom name. He was sold by a Timmani gentleman in the Du-bu country, for crim. con. with his wife, to Luisi, a Spaniard, at Lomboko. He is in middle life, 5 ft. 6 in. high

9. FU-LI-WA, Fu-li, (sun) called by his fellow prisoners Fuliwa, (great Fuli) to distinguish him from Fu-li-wu-lu, (little Fuli), was born at Ma-no, a town in the Mendi country, where his king, Ti-kba, resided. He lived with his parents, and has five brothers. His town was surrounded by soldiers, some were killed, and he with the rest were taken prisoners. He passed through the Vai country, when taken to Lomboko, and was one month on the journey. He is in middle life, 5 ft. 3 in. high, face broad in the middle, with a slight beard. It was this Fuli who instituted the suit against Ruiz and Montez.

10. P-IE, Pi-e or Bi-a (5 ft. 4 1/2 in. high) calls himself a Timmani, and the father of Fu-li-wu-lu. He appears to have been distin-

guished for hunting in his country: says he has killed 5 leopards, 3 on the land, and 2 in the water; has killed three elephants. He has a very pleasant countenance; his hands are whitened by wounds received from the bursting of a gun barrel which he had overloaded when showing his dexterity. He had a leopard's skin hung up on his hut to show that he was a hunter. He has a wife and four children. He recognizes with great readiness the Timmani words and phrases contained in Winterbottom's account of Sierra Leone. He and his son, seemed overjoyed to find an American who could articulate the sound of their native tongue.

11. PU-GNWAW-NI [Pung-wu-ni] (*a duck*) 5 ft. 1 in. high, body tatooed, teeth filed, was born at Fe-baw, in Sando, between Mendi and Konno. His mother's brother sold him for a coat. He was taken in the night, and was taken a six days' journey, and sold to Garloba, who had four wives. He staid with this man two years, and was employed in cultivating rice: His master's wives and children were employed in the same manner, and no distinction made in regard to labor.

12. SES-SI, 5 ft. 7 1/2 in. with a sly and mirthful countenance, was born in Mas-sa-kum, in the Bandi country, where his king, Pa-ma-sa, resided. He has three brothers, two sisters, a wife, and three children. He is a blacksmith, having learnt that trade of his brother; he made axes, hoes, and knives from iron obtained in the Mendi country. He was taken captive by soldiers and wounded in the leg. He was sold twice before he arrived at Lomboko, where he was kept about a month: Although a Bandi, he appears to have been able to talk in Mendi.

13. MO-RU, middle age, 5 ft. 8 1/2 in. with full negro features, was born at Sanka, in the Bandi country. His parents died when he was a child. His master, Margona, who sold him, had ten wives and many houses; he was twenty days on his journey to Lomboko. He was sold to Be-le-wa (*great wiskers*) i.e. to a Spaniard.

14. NDAM-MA (*put on, or up*) 5 ft. 3 in., a stout built youth, born in the Mendi country,

on the river Ma-le. His father is dead, and he lived with his mother; has a brother and sister. He was taken in the road by twenty men, and was many days in traveling to Lomboko.

15. FU-LI-WU-LU — *Fuli* or as the name has been written, Furie (*sun*), called Fuliwulu, to distinguish him from Fuliwa (great Fuli) lived with his parents in the Timmani near the Mendi country. He is the son of Pie (No. 10). He was taken with his father, by an African, who sold him to a Bullom man, who sold him to Luis, a Spaniard at Lomboko. He has a depression in the skull from a wound in the forehead. 5 ft. 2 1/2 in. in height.

16. BA-U (*broke*) 5 ft. 5 in. high, sober, intelligent looking, and rather slightly built. Has a wife and three children. He was caught in the bush by 4 men as he was going to plant rice; his left hand was tied to his neck; was ten days in going to Lomboko. He lived near a large river named Wo-wa. In his country all have to pay for their wives; for his, he had to pay 10 clothes, 1 goat, 1 gun, and plenty of mats; his mother made the cloth for him.

17. BA (*have none*) 5 ft. 4 1/2 in. with a narrow and high head; in middle life. Parents living, 4 brothers and 4 sisters; has got a wife and child. He is a planter of rice. He was seized by two men in the road, and was sold to a Gallina Vai man, who sold him to a Spaniard. High mountains in his country, but small streams; cotton cloth is manufactured, and hens, sheep, goats, cows and wild hogs are common.

18. SHU-LE (*water fall*) 5 ft. 4 in. the oldest of the Amistad captives, and the fourth in command, when on board the schooner. He was born at Konabu, in the open land, in the Mendi country. He was taken for a slave by Ma-ya, for crim. con. with his wife. Momawru caught both him and his master Ma-ya, and made them slaves, and sold them to a man who sold him to the Spaniards at Lomboko. There is a large river in his country named Wu-wa, which runs from Gissi, passes through Mendi, and runs south into the Konno country.

19. KA-LE (*bone*) 5 ft. 4 in., small head and large under lip, young and pleasant. His par-

ents living; has two sisters. He was taken while going to a town to buy rice. He was two months in traveling to Lomboko.

20. BA-GNA (*sand* or *gravel*) 5 ft. 3 in., was born at Du-gau-na, in the Konno country, where his king, Da-ga, lived. His parents are dead, and he lived with his brother, a planter of rice.

21. SA, 5 ft. 2 in., a youth with a long narrow head. He was the only child of his parents, and was stolen when walking in the road by two men. He was two months in traveling to Lomboko.

22. KIN-NA (*man* or *big man*) 5 ft. 5 1/2 in., has a bright countenance, is young, and, since he has been in New Haven, has been a good scholar. His parents and grandparents were living; has four brothers and one sister. He was born at Si-ma-bu, in the Mendi country; his king, Sa-mang, resided at the same place. He was seized when going to Kon-gol-li, by a Bullom man, who sold him to Luiz, at Lomboko.

23. NDZHA-GNWAW-NI [Nga-ho-ni] (*water bird*) 5 ft. 9 in. with a large head, high cheek bones, in middle life. He has a wife and one child; he gave twenty clothes and one shawl for his wife. He lived in a mountainous country; his town was formerly fenced around, but now broken down. He was seized by four men when in a rice field, and was two weeks in traveling to Lomboko.

24. FANG [Fa-kin-na] 5 ft. 4 in., head elevated in the middle, stout built, and middle aged. He was born at Dzho-po-a-hu, in the Mendi country, at which place his father, Bawnge, is chief or king. He has a wife and two children; was caught in the bushes by a Mendi man, belonging to a party with guns,and says he was ten days in traveling to Lomboko after being a slave to the man that took him, less than a month.

25. FAHI-DZHIN-NI [Fa-gin-na] (*twin*) 5 ft. 4 in., marked on the face with the small pox; was born at Tom-bo-lu, a town Bombali, in the Mendi country. He was made a slave by a Tamu for crim. con. with his wife. Tamu sold

him to a Mendi man, who sold him to Laigo, a Spaniard, the same who purchased Grabeau. He says many people in his country have the small pox, to cure which, they oil their bodies.

26. YA-BOI, 5 ft. 7 in., large head, stout built, and in middle life; was born at Kon-do-wa-lu, where his king, Ka-kbe-ni (*lazy*) resided. His village was surrounded by soldiers, and he was taken by Gillewa, a Mendi man, to whom he was a slave ten years. Had a wife and one child. Gillewa sold him to Luiz, the Spaniard.

27. FA-BAN-NA (*remember*) 5 ft. 5 in., large round head, tattooed on the breast; in middle life; he and Grabeau were from the same country, both having the same king. He has two wives and one child; all lived in one house. His village was surrounded by soldiers: he was taken prisoner, sold twice, the last time to a Spaniard at Lomboko.

28. TSU-KA-MA (*a learner*) 5 ft. 5 1/2 in., young, with a pleasant countenance; was born at Sun-ga-ru, in the Mendi country; where his king, Gnam-be, resided; has parents living, 3 sisters, and 4 brothers. He was taken and sold into the Bullom country, where he lived for a time with his master, who sold him to Luiz, at Lomboko.

29. BE-RI [Ber-ri] (*stick*) 5 ft. 3 in., with mustaches and beard, broadnose; in middle life. He was born at Fang-te, in Gula, a large fenced town, where his king, Ge-la-wa, resided. He was taken by soldiers, and was sold to Shaka, king of Genduma, in the Vai or Gallina country, who sold him to a Spaniard. Genduma is on a fresh water river called Boba. It is three or four miles from the river, and nine from the sea.

30. FAW-NI [Fo-ni] 5 ft. 2 in., stout built; in middle life. He was born at Bum-be, a large town in the Mendi country: the name of his king was Ka-ban-du. He is married, and has parents, brothers, and sisters living. He was seized by two men as he was going to plant rice. He was carried to Bem-be-law, in the Vai country, and sold to Luiz, who kept him there two months before he took him to Lomboko. From Bem-be-law to Lomboko is one day's walk.

31. BUR-NA, (*twin*) the elder, has a cast in the eye; was taken when going to the next town, by three men. His father is dead, and he lived with his mother; has four sisters and two brothers. When his father died his brother married; all lived in the same house. In his country are high mountains, but no rivers; has seen elephants and leopards. He was six weeks in traveling to Lomboko, where he was kept three and a half moons.

32. SHUMA (*falling water*) 5 ft. 6 in., with mustaches and beard; in middle life. He can count in the Mendi, Timmani, and Bullom. His parents have been dead a long time; has a wife and one child, was taken prisoner in war, and it was four moons after he was taken before he arrived at Lomboko. Shuma spoke over the corpse of Tua, after the Rev. Mr. Bacon's prayer. The substance of what he said, as translated by Covey, was "Now Tua dead, God takes Tua, — we are left behind. No one can die but once," &c.

33. KA-LI (*bone*) 4 ft. 3 in., a small boy with a large head, flat and broad nose, stout built. He says his parents are living; has a sister and brother; was stolen when in the street and was about a month in traveling to Lomboko.

34. TE-ME (*frog*) 4 ft. 3 in., a young girl, says she lived with her mother, with an elder brother and sister; her father was dead. A party of men in the night broke into her mother's house and made them prisoners; she never saw her mother or brother afterwards, and was a long time in traveling to Lomboko.

35. KA-GNE (*country*) 4 ft. 3 in., a young girl. She counts in Mendi like Kwong, she also counts in Fai or Gallina, imperfectly. She says her parents are living, and has four brothers and four sisters; she was put in pawn for a debt by her father which not being paid, she was sold into slavery, and was many days in going to Lomboko.

36. MAR-GRU (*black snake*) 4 ft. 3 in., a young girl with a large high forehead; her parents were living; she had four sisters and two brothers; she was pawned by her father for a debt, which being unpaid, she was sold into slavery.

The foregoing list comprises all the Africans now, May, 1840, living. Six have died while they have been in New Haven; viz. 1. Fa, Sept. 3d, 1839; 2, Tua (a Bullom name) died Sept. 11th; 3, We-lu-wa (a Bandi name) died Sept. 14th; 4, Ka-ba, a Mendi man, died Dec. 31; 5, Ka-pe-lio, a Mendi youth, died Oct. 30; 6, Yam-mo-ni, in middle life, died Nov. 4th.

—————— 3.19 ——————

'IF THE MAN MAY PREACH... WHY NOT THE WOMAN?'
Jarena Lee

At its outset, the African Methodist Episcopal Church did not allow women to take the pulpit. Bishop and founder Richard Allen did however encourage particularly inspired women to "exhort" in private prayer meetings for other women at their homes, and that is what he advised Jarena Lee to do when she first approached him. Lee had come to Allen's AME Bethel in Philadelphia during a period of emotional crisis in which she had tried to commit suicide. After a long and tortuous process, she later wrote, Lee found happiness in the "salvation" of God and Methodism. And, soon, she was struck with the call to preach. She dutifully accepted Allen's offer to exhort, until one day she rose in service and gave an extemporaneous exhortation. Allen was so impressed, he allowed her to be ordained as a preacher. She went on to become a wildly popular itinerant preacher throughout the northern part of the country. In 1936 she published her religious journal. In the excerpt below, she describes her call to preach and argues that it is as legitimate as that of a man.

... Between four and five years after my sanctification, on a certain time, an impressive silence fell upon me, and I stood as if some one was about to speak to me, yet I had no such thought in my heart. — But to my utter surprise there seemed to sound a voice which I thought I distinctly heard, and most certainly understand, which said to me, "Go preach the Gospel!" I immediately replied aloud, "No one will believe me," Again I listened, and again the same voice seemed to say— "Preach the Gospel; I will put words in your mouth, and will turn your enemies to become your friends."

At first I supposed that Satan had spoken to me, for I had read that he could transform himself into an angel of light for the purpose of deception. Immediately I went into a secret place, and called upon the Lord to know if he had called me to preach, and whether I was deceived or not; when there appeared to my view the form and figure of a pulpit, with a Bible lying thereon, the back of which was presented to me as plainly as if it had been a literal fact.

In consequence of this, my mind became so exercised, that during the night following, I took a text and preached in my sleep. I thought there stood before me a great multitude, while I expounded to them the things of religion. So violent were my exertions and so loud were my exclamations, that I awoke from the sound of my own voice, which also awoke the family of the house where I resided. Two days after I went to see the preacher in charge of the African Society, who was the Rev. Richard Allen, the same before named in these page, to tell him that I felt it my duty to preach the gospel. But as I drew near the street in which his house was, which was in the city of Philadelphia, my courage began to fail me; so terrible did the cross appear, it seamed that I should not be able to bear it. Previous to my setting out to go to see him, so agitated was my mind, that my appetite for my daily food failed me entirely. Several times on my way there, I turned back again; but as often I felt my strength again renewed, and I soon found that the nearer I approached to the house of the minister, the less was my fear. Accordingly, as soon as I came to the door, my fears subsided, the cross was removed, all things appeared pleasant — I was tranquil.

I now told him, that the Lord had revealed it to me, that I must preach the gospel. He replied, by asking, in what sphere I wished to move in? I said, among the Methodists. He then replied, that a Mrs. Cook, a Methodist lady, had also some time before requested the same privilege; who, it was believed, had done much good in the way of exhortation, and holding prayer meetings; and who had been permitted to do so by the verbal licence of the preacher in charge at the time. But as to women preaching, he said that our Discipline knew nothing at all about it — that it did not call for women preachers. This I was glad to hear, because it removed the fear of the cross — but no sooner did this feeling cross my mind, than I found that a love of souls had in measure departed from me; that holy energy which burned within me, as a fire, began to be smothered. This I soon perceived.

O how careful ought we to be, lest through our by-laws of church government and discipline, we bring into disrepute even the word of life. For as unseemly as it may appear now-a-days for a woman to preach, it should be remembered that nothing is impossible, with God. And why should it be thought impossible, heterodox, or improper for a woman to preach? seeing the Saviour died for the woman as well as for the man.

If the man may preach, because the Saviour died for him, why not the woman? seeing he died for her also. Is he not a whole Saviour, instead of a half one? as those who hold it wrong for a woman to preach, would seem to make it appear.

Did not Mary first preach the risen Saviour, and is not the doctrine of the resurrection the very climax of Christianity — hangs not all our hope on this, as argued by St. Paul? Then did not Mary, a woman, preach the gospel? for she preached the resurrection of the crucified Son of God.

But some will say that Mary did not expound the Scripture, therefore, she did not preach, in the proper sense of the term. To this I reply, it may be that the term preach in those primitive times, did not mean exactly what it is now made to mean; perhaps it was a great deal more simple then, than it is now — if it were not, the unlearned fishermen could not have preached the gospel at all, as they had no learning.

To this it may be replied, by those who are determined not to believe that it is right for a woman to preach, that the disciples, though they were fishermen and ignorant of letters too, were inspired so to do. To which I would reply, that though they were inspired, yet that inspiration did not save them from showing their ignorance of letters, and man's wisdom this the multitude soon found out, by listening to the remarks of the envious Jewish priests. If then, to preach the gospel, by the gift of heaven, comes by inspiration solely, is God straitened; must he take the man exclusively? May he not, did he not, and can he not inspire a female to preach the simple story of the birth, life, death and resurrection of our Lord, and accompany it too with power to the sinner's heart. As for me, I am fully persuaded that the Lord called me to labor according to what I have received, in his vineyard. If he has not, how could he consistently bear testimony in favor of my poor labors, in awakening and converting sinners? In my wanderings up and down among men, preaching according to my ability, I have frequently found families who told me that they had not for several years been to a meeting, and yet, while listening to hear what God would say by his poor female instrument, have believed with trembling — tears rolling down their cheeks, the signs of contrition and repentance towards God. I firmly believe that I have sown seed, in the name of the Lord, which shall appear with its increase at the great day of accounts, when Christ shall come to make up his jewels.

At a certain time, I was beset with the idea, that soon or late I should fall from grace and lose my soul at last. I was frequently called to the throne of grace about this matter, but found no relief; the temptation pursued me still. Being more and more affected with it, till at a certain time, when the spirit strongly impressed it on my mind to enter into my closet and carry my case once more to the Lord; the Lord enabled me to draw nigh to him, and to his mercy seat, at this time, in an extraordinary manner; for while I wrestled with him for the victory over this disposition to doubt whether I should persevere, there appeared a form of fire, about the size of a man's hand, as I was on my knees; at the same moment there appeared to the eye of faith a man robed in a white garment, from the shoulders down to the feet; from him a voice proceeded, saying: "Thou shalt never return from the cross." Since that time I have never doubted, believe that God will keep me until the day of redemption. Now I could adopt the very language of St. Paul, and say, that nothing could have a separated me from the love of God, which is in Christ Jesus. Since that time, 1807, until the present, 1833, I have not even doubted the power and goodness of God to keep me from failing, through the sanctification of the spirit and belief of the truth. …

—————— 3.20 ——————

'THERE ARE NO CHAINS SO GALLING AS THE CHAINS OF IGNORANCE'

Maria Stewart

Maria Stewart had been a prominent member of Boston's black middle class society when her husband died. A white associate conned her out of her inheritance, and she was forced to return to domestic work for a period. But, while working, she began to develop her political thoughts and writings. In 1831, William Lloyd Garrison issued a call for submissions from black women to his Liberator. Stewart responded, and began regularly contributing to the paper. Eventually, her writing led to speaking as well. And on September 21, 1832, she addressed a gathering of the New England Anti-Slavery Society in Boston. Her speech was the first given by a woman of any color on a political matter before a mixed-gender crowd. At the time, American society supposed women should not become involved in political matters, and the increasing numbers of women joining the abolitionist cause became a point of tension within the movement. Nevertheless, women became vocal leaders in the drive to end slavery.

Why sit ye here and die? If we say we will go to a foreign land, the famine and the pestilence are there, and there we shall die. If we sit here, we shall die. Come let us plead our cause before the whites: if they save us alive, we shall live — and if they kill us, we shall but die.

Methinks I heard a spiritual interrogation — 'Who shall go forward, and take off the reproach that is cast upon the people of color? Shall it be a woman? And my heart made this reply — 'If it is thy will, be it even so, Lord Jesus!'

I have heard much respecting the horrors of slavery; but may Heaven forbid that the generality of my color throughout these United States should experience any more of its horrors than to be a servant of servants, or hewers of wood and drawers of water! Tell us no more of southern slavery; for with few exceptions, although I may be very erroneous in my opinion, yet I consider our condition but little better than that. Yet, after all, methinks there are no chains so galling as the chains of ignorance — no fetters so binding as those that bind the soul, and exclude it from the vast field of useful and scientific knowledge. O, had I received the advantages of early education, my ideas would, ere now, have expanded far and wide; but, alas! I possess nothing but moral capability — no teachings but the teachings of the Holy spirit.

I have asked several individuals of my sex, who transact business for themselves, if providing our girls were to give them the most satisfactory references, they would not be willing to grant them an equal opportunity with others? Their reply has been — for their own part, they had no objection; but as it was not the custom, were they to take them into their employ, they would be in danger of losing the public patronage.

And such is the powerful force of prejudice. Let our girls possess what amiable qualities of soul they may; let their characters be fair and spotless as innocence itself; let their natural taste and ingenuity be what they may; it is impossible for scarce an individual of them to rise above the condition of servants. Ah! why is this cruel and unfeeling distinction? Is it merely because God has made our complexion to vary? If it be, O shame to soft, relenting humanity! "Tell it not in Gath! publish it not in the streets of Askelon!" Yet, after all, methinks were the American free people of color to turn their attention more assiduously to moral worth and intellectual improvement, this would be the result: prejudice would gradually diminish, and the whites would be compelled to say, unloose those fetters!

Though black their skins as shades of night,
Their hearts are pure, their souls are white.

Few white persons of either sex, who are calculated for any thing else, are willing to spend their lives and bury their talents in performing mean, servile labor. And such is the horrible idea that I entertain respecting a life of servitude, that if I conceived of there being no possibility of my rising above the condition of a servant, I would gladly hail death as a welcome messenger. O, horrible idea, indeed! to possess noble souls aspiring after high and honorable acquirements, yet confined by the chains of ignorance and poverty to lives of continual drudgery and toil. Neither do I know of any who have enriched themselves by spending their lives as house-domestics, washing windows, shaking carpets, brushing boots, or tending upon gentlemen's tables. I can but die for expressing my sentiments; and I am as willing to die by the sword as the pestilence; for I am a true born American; your blood flows in my veins, and your spirit fires my breast.

I observed a piece in the Liberator a few months since, stating that the colonizationists had published a work respecting us, asserting that we were lazy and idle. I confute them on that point. Take us generally as a people, we are neither lazy nor idle; and considering how little we have to excite or stimulate us, I am almost astonished that there are so many industrious and ambitious ones to be found; although I acknowledge, with extreme sorrow, that there are some who never were and never

will be serviceable to society. And have you not a similar class among yourselves?

Again. It was asserted that we were "a ragged set, crying for liberty." I reply to it, the whites have so long and so loudly proclaimed the theme of equal rights and privileges, that our souls have caught the flame also, ragged as we are. As far as our merit deserves, we feel a common desire to rise above the condition of servants and drudges. I have learnt, by bitter experience, that continual hard labor deadens the energies of the soul, and benumbs the faculties of the mind; the ideas become confined, the mind barren, and, like the scorching sands of Arabia, produces nothing; or, like the uncultivated soil, brings forth thorns and thistles.

Again, continual hard labor irritates our tempers and sours our dispositions; the whole system becomes worn out with toil and failure; nature herself becomes almost exhausted, and we care but little whether we live or die. It is true, that the free people of color throughout these United States are neither bought nor sold, nor under the lash of the cruel driver; many obtain a comfortable support; but few, if any, have an opportunity of becoming rich and independent; and the employments we most pursue are as unprofitable to us as the spider's web or the floating bubbles that vanish into air. As servants, we are respected; but let us presume to aspire any higher, our employer regards us no longer. And were it not that the King eternal has declared that Ethiopia shall stretch forth her hands unto God, I should indeed despair.

I do not consider it derogatory, my friends, for persons to live out to service. There are many whose inclination leads them to aspire no higher; and I would highly commend the performance of almost any thing for an honest livelihood; but where constitutional strength is wanting, labor of this kind, in its mildest form, is painful. And doubtless many are the prayers that have ascended to Heaven from Africa's daughters for strength to perform their work. Oh, many are the tears that have been shed for the want of that strength! Most of our color have dragged out a miserable existence of servitude from the cradle to the grave. And what literary acquirements can be made, or useful knowledge derived, from either maps, books or charm, by those who continually drudge from Monday morning until Sunday noon? O, ye fairer sisters, whose hands are never soiled, whose nerves and muscles are never strained, go learn by experience! Had we had the opportunity that you have had, to improve our moral and mental faculties, what would have hindered our intellects from being as bright, and our manners from being as dignified as yours? Had it been our lot to have been nursed in the lap of affluence and ease, and to have basked beneath the smiles and sunshine of fortune, should we not have naturally supposed that we were never made to toil? And why are not our forms as delicate, and our constitutions as slender, as yours? Is not the workmanship as curious and complete? Have pity upon us, have pity upon us, O ye who have hearts to feel for other's woes; for the hand of God has touched us. Owing to the disadvantages under which we labor, there are many flowers among us that are

"—born to bloom unseen,
And waste their fragrance on the desert air."

My beloved brethren, as Christ has died in vain for those who will not accept of offered mercy, so will it be vain for the advocates of freedom to spend their breath in our behalf, unless with united hearts and souls you make some mighty efforts to raise your sons, and daughters from the horrible state of servitude and degradation in which they are placed. It is upon you that woman depends; she can do but little besides using her influence; and it is for her sake and yours that I have come forward and made myself a hissing and a reproach among the people; for I am also one of the wretched and miserable daughters of the descendants of fallen Africa. Do you ask, why are you wretched and miserable? I reply, look at many of the most worthy and interesting of us

doomed to spend our lives in gentlemen's kitchens. Look at our young men, smart, active and energetic, with souls filled with ambitious fire; if they look forward, alas! what are their prospects? They can be nothing but the humblest laborers, on account of their dark complexions; hence many of them lose their ambition, and become worthless. Look at our middle-aged men, clad in their rusty plaids and coats; in winter, every cent they earn goes to buy their wood and pay their rents; their poor wives also toil beyond their strength, to help support their families. Look at our aged sires, whose heads are whitened with the front of seventy winters, with their old wood-saws on their backs. Alas, what keeps us so? Prejudice, ignorance and poverty. But ah! methinks our oppression is soon to come to an end; yes, before the Majesty of heaven, our groans and cries have reached the ears of the Lord of Sabaoth. As the prayers and tears of Christians will avail the finally impenitent nothing; neither will the prayers and tears of the friends of humanity avail us any thing, unless we possess a spirit of virtuous emulation within our breasts. Did the pilgrims, when they first landed on these shores, quietly compose themselves, and say, "the Britons have all the money and all the power, and we must continue their servants forever?" Did they sluggishly sigh and say, "our lot is hard, the Indians own the soil, and we cannot cultivate it?" No; they first made powerful efforts to raise themselves and then God raised up those illustrious patriots Washington and Lafayette to assist and defend them. And, my brethren, have you made a powerful effort? Have you prayed the Legislature for mercy's sake to grant you all the rights and privileges of free citizens, that your daughters may raise to that degree of respectability which true merit deserves, and your sons above the servile situations which most of them fill?

——— 3.21 ———

'LIKE OUR BRETHREN IN BONDS, WE MUST SEAL OUR LIPS IN SILENCE AND DESPAIR'

Anti-Slavery Convention of American Women

In May 1837, five years after Maria Stewart gave her historic address, 200 women, black and white, gathered in New York City for a three-day conference on the role of women in the abolitionist movement. It was America's first large, public gathering of women to discuss a political issue. The organizers barred men from the gathering, frustrating reporters who scoffed at what they perceived as the women's arrogance. The Women's Movement lay in the not-too-distant future, and many of the same women who would launch that effort were leaders at this meeting. The delegates agreed to undertake a campaign to petition Congress for an end to slavery in the District of Columbia, and raised funds to publish a series of abolitionist pamphlets. In the one excerpted below, the authors rebut arguments that women should not be involved in politics.

SLAVERY A POLTICAL SUBJECT.

I. Let us first look at it as a *political* subject. Such incongruous elements as freedom and slavery, republicanism and despotism, cannot exist together; the unnatural and unhallowed union between these things must sooner or later be broken. Not only are one-sixth part of the inhabitants of this republic held in abject slavery, but the free and the slave States are unequally yoked together — they do not enjoy equal privileges. In the former, persons only are represented in our National Congress; in the latter, *property* as well as persons send their representatives there. The slaveholding and non-slaveholding States have antagonist interests, which are continually conflicting, and producing jealousies and heart-burnings between the contending parties. Our Congressional debates have presented one unvaried scene of unreasonable demands and haughty threats on the one hand — of tame compromise, and unmanly, and in many cases most *unprincipled* submis-

sion on the other. Slavery not only robs the slave of all his rights as a man in thirteen of the States of the Confederacy, but it vaults over the barrier of Mason's and Dixon's line, swims the Ohio and the Potomac, and bribes Northern citizens to kidnap and enslave freemen of the North — drags them into hopeless bondage, and sells them under the hammer of the auctioneer. Not only so — it outlaws every Northerner who openly avows the sentiments of the Declaration of Independence, and destroys the free communication of our sentiments through the medium of the mail, so that the daughter of America cannot now send the productions of their pen to the parent who resides in a slaveholding State. It threatens even our Representatives in Congress with assassination, if they dare to open their lips in defense of the oppressed and the dumb — tramples in the dust the right of petition, when exercised by free men and free women — brands them with the opprobrious epithets of "white slaves" and "devils," and rides triumphantly over the bowed heads of the senators and representatives of our free States. Slavery nurses within the bosom of our country her deadliest foes, and threatens to bring down the "exterminating thunders" of divine vengeance on our guilty heads. "The dark spirit of slavery rules in our national councils, and menaces the severance, of the bonds which bind together these United States, and to shake from our star-spangled banner, as with a mighty wind, those glittering emblems of our country's pre-eminence among the nations of the earth, and to burn our Declaration as a "splendid absurdity," a "rhetorical flourish;" to offer the glorious charter of our constitutional liberties and alliance upon the same- altar — to the horns of which the bleeding slave is, now bound by the chain of his servitude, and the colored, freeman by "the cord of caste."

This is a very imperfect outline of the political bearings of this great question; and it is gravely urged, that as it is a *political subject*, women have no concernment with it: this doctrine of the North is a sycophantic response to the declaration of a Southern representative, that women have no right to send up petitions to Congress, We know, dear sisters, that the open and the secret enemies of freedom in our country have dreaded our influence, and therefore have reprobated our interference; and in order to blind us to our responsibilities, have thrown dust into our eyes, well knowing that if the organ of vision is only clear, the whole body the moving and acting faculties will become full of light, and will soon be thrown into powerful action. Some, who pretend to be very jealous for the honor of our sex, and are very anxious that we should scrupulously maintain the dignity and delicacy of female propriety, continually urge this objection to female effort. We grant thatit is a political, as well as a moral subject: does this exonerate women *from* their duties as subjects of the government, as members of the great human family? Have women never wisely and laudably exercised political responsibilities?

When the Lord led out his chosen people like a flock into the wilderness, from the house of bondage, was it not a WOMAN whom He sent before them with Moses and Aaron? Did she not lead her manumitted sisters in that sublime peon of thanksgiving and praise which ascended from their grateful hearts as they answered the chorus of their brethren with the inspired words, "Sing ye to the Lord — for he hath triumphed gloriously: the horse and his rider hath he thrown into the sea." And was not the deliverance of Israel from Egyptian bondage a *political concern*? Did it not shake the throne of the Pharaohs, desolate the land of Egypt, and strike terror into the stubborn hearts of subtle politicians. Miriam then interfered with the *political concerns* of Egypt; and we doubt not had the monarch been permitted to lay his hand upon the sister of Moses, she would have suffered as a leader in this daring attempt to lead out her sisters from the house of bondage. Would not her fate have been similar to that of the heroine of the fifteenth century?

When Barak received the divine command to go down to Mount Tabor, and the promise

that with ten thousand men he should overcome the hosts of Sisera with their iron chariots, to whom did he appeal in those memorable words — "*If thou* wilt go with me, then I will go; but if thou wilt not go with me, then I will not go?" It was to Deborah; and this woman intermeddled so far with the political concerns of Israel as to go up with him to the battle; and when, as she predicted, Sisera was sold into the hands of a woman, she united with Barak in a song of triumphant praise, that the ancient Kishon hid swept down in the current of its waters the lifeless bodies of the Canaanitish warriors.

But many seem to think, that although women may have been called to the performance of extraordinary duties in the days of miracle and of inspiration, that under no other circumstances could such conduct have been warranted. Let us turn, then, to the history of Rome. When Coriolanus, who had been banished by the Roman Senate, returned with a host of barbarians to wreak his vengeance upon the proud mistress of the world, and after the embassies of senators, and priests, and augurs, had failed to move his unrelenting heart, who were sent out to try the magic power of their tears and prayers? Were they not the wife and mother of the Roman warrior, and were they not followed by a train of matrons, who approached the Volscian camp to plead their country's cause? And what was the success of this embassage of mercy and love? The hero's icy heart was melted by the tears and pleadings of these feebler ones: he bowed his stubborn will to theirs, turned back his disappointed free-booters from the gates of Rome, and sent these women home with the glad tiding of peace upon their trembling lips.

But perhaps the sage objector may say, "True; but these women were delegated by the Roman Senate — *they* were vested with authority by 'the powers that be' — they did not rush uncalled into the field of action." Was this, then, their commission for intermeddling with the *political concerns* of their country? Where, then, was the commission of those

Sabine women, who threw themselves between the hostile armies, when they were just about plunging their javelins into the hearts of their own fathers, brothers, and sons? Were *they* deputed by the Roman Senate? No! they held higher credentials. The angel of mercy commissioned them each to do and to dare all that might become a woman, in such a fearful hour of agony and boding. They rushed between the embattled hosts. At the sight of their tears and prayers, the iron grasp relaxed — the weapons fell — and they who met in hate to kill, embraced in love, and thenceforth mingled into one. These *women* poured the assuasive oil over the troubled waters of strife. *Woman* became the healer of breaches — the restorer of paths to dwell in. ...

But let us turn over the pages of our own history. When the British army had taken possession of our beautiful city of brotherly love, who arose at midnight to listen to the plots which were laid in an upper chamber, by General Howe in his council of war? It was a *woman*: and when she stole the secret from their unconscious lips, she kept it locked within her own bosom, until under an ingenious pretext she repaired to Frankford, gained an interview with Washington, and disclosed to him the important intelligence which saved the lives of her countrymen. Did Lydia Darrah confer a benefit upon the American army — did she perform the duties of an American citizen? Or, was this act an impertinent intermeddling with the political concerns of her country, with which, as a woman, she had nothing to do? Let the daughters of this republic answer the question.

It is related of Buonaparte, that he one day rebuked a French lady for busying herself with politics. "Sire," replied she, "in a country where *women* are put to death, it is very natural that *women* should wish to know the reason why." And, dear sisters, in a country where women are degraded and brutalized, and where their exposed persons bleed under the lash — where they are sold in the shambles of "negro brokers" — robbed of their hard earnings —

torn from their husbands, and forcibly plundered of their virtue and their offspring; surely in such a country, it is very natural that *women* should wish to know "the reason why" — especially when these outrages of blood and nameless horror are practiced in violation of the principles of our national Bill of Rights and the Preamble of our Constitution. We do not, then, and cannot concede the position, that because this is a *political subject* women ought to fold their hands in idleness, and close their eyes and ears to "horrible things" that are practiced in our land. The denial of our duty to act, is a bold denial of our right to act; and if we have no right to act, then may we well be termed "the white slaves of the North" — for, like our brethren in bonds, we must seal our lips in silence and despair.

———— 3.22 ————
'WHAT IS A MOB? ...
ANY EVIDENCE THAT WE
ARE WRONG?'
Angela Grimké Weld

Mob attacks on those who spoke out against slavery in the early 19th century were not uncommon. William Lloyd Garrison had been attacked and dragged through the streets of Boston in 1835. But the second Anti-Slavery Convention of American Women was the scene of some of the worst of the era's violence against abolitionists. The combination of women speaking on politics, in a mixed race setting and against slavery was too much for the Philadelphia public to take.

In 1838, abolitionists, seeking a way around the common annoyance of being refused the use of meeting spaces, raised funds to erect their own facility. Stately Pennsylvania Hall was one of the most ornate buildings of its time, and its very existence angered many pro-slavery whites. The first meeting held in the building was the ACAW's second annual convention. Flyers had been circulating encouraging mob violence, but 3,000 women gathered for the first day of the convention nonetheless. A mob indeed formed, and began shouting and throwing stones. Eventually they burst into the building and disrupted the meeting. After the rioters dispersed, Angela Grimké Weld took the podium to urge the women to stay and continue their meeting in defiance. As she began her speech, the mob again erupted outside, throwing stones and chanting taunts. Weld, undeterred, shouted over them, and eventually delivered her speech, below, in its entirety. In a few years, the bold abolitionist woman would be among the pioneers of the Women's Movement as well.

After the first day of the convention, the mayor confiscated the keys to Pennsylvania Hall and forbade the women from returning. The mob gathered just the same, stormed the building and destroyed it. The mob then proceeded to rampage for several days, attacking black institutions around the city.

Men, brethren and fathers — mothers, daughters and sisters, what came ye out for to see? A reed shaken with the wind? Is it curiosity merely, or a deep sympathy with the perishing slave, that has brought this large audience together? [A yell from the mob without the building.] Those voices without ought to awaken and call out our warmest sympathies. Deluded beings! "they know not what they do." They know not that they are undermining their own rights and their own happiness, temporal and eternal. Do you ask, "what has the North to do with slavery?" Hear it — hear it. Those voices without tell us that the spirit of slavery is here, and has been roused to wrath by our abolition speeches and conventions: for surely liberty would not foam and tear herself with rage, because her friends are multiplied daily, and meetings are held in quick succession to set forth her virtues and extend her peaceful kingdom. This opposition shows that slavery has done its deadliest work in the hearts of our citizens. Do you ask, then, "what has the North to do?" I answer, cast out first the spirit of slavery from your own hearts, and then lend your aid to convert the South. Each one present has a work to do, be his or her situation what it may, however limited their means, or insignificant their supposed influence. The great men of this country will not do this work; the church will never do it. A desire to please the world, to keep the favor of all parties and of all conditions, makes them dumb on this and every other unpopular subject. They have become worldly-wise, and therefore God, in his wisdom, employs them not to carry on his plans of reformation and salvation. He hath chosen the foolish things of the world to confound the wise, and the weak to overcome the mighty.

As a Southerner I feel that it is my duty to stand up here tonight and bear testimony against slavery. I have seen it — I have seen it. I know it has horrors that can never be described. I was brought up under its wing: I witnessed for many years its demoralizing influences, and its destructiveness to human happiness. It is admitted by some that the slave is not happy under the worst forms of slavery. But I have never seen a happy slave. I have seen him dance in his chains, it is true; but he was not happy. There is a wide difference between happiness and mirth. Man cannot enjoy the former while his manhood is destroyed, and that part of the being which is necessary to the making, and to the enjoyment of happiness, is completely blotted out. The slaves, however, may be, and sometimes are, mirthful. When hope is extinguished, they say, "let us eat and drink, for tomorrow we die." [Just then stones were thrown at the windows, — a great noise without, and commotion within.] What is a mob? What would the breaking of every window be? What would the levelling of this Hall be? Any evidence that we are wrong, or that slavery is a good and wholesome institution? What if the mob should now burst in upon us, break up our meeting and commit violence upon our persons — would this be any thing compared with what the slaves endure? No, no: and we do not remember them "as bound with them," if we shrink in the time of peril, or feel unwilling to sacrifice ourselves, if need be, for their sake. [Great noise.] I thank the Lord that there is yet life left enough to feel the truth, even though it rages at it — that conscience is not so completely seared as to be unmoved by the truth of the living God.

Many persons go to the South for a season, and are hospitably entertained in the parlor and at the table of the slave-holder. They never enter the huts of the slaves; they know nothing of the dark side of the picture, and they return home with praises on their lips of the generous character of those with whom they had tarried. Or if they have witnessed the cruelties of slavery, by remaining silent spectators they have naturally become callous — an insensibility has ensued which prepares them to apologize even for barbarity. Nothing but the corrupting influence of slavery on the hearts of the Northern people can induce them to apologize for it; and much will have been done for the destruction of Southern slavery when we have so reformed the North that no one here will be willing to risk his reputation by advocating or even excusing the holding of men as property. The South know it, and acknowledge that as fast as our principles prevail, the hold of the master must be relaxed. [Another outbreak of mobocratic spirit, and some confusion in the house.]

How wonderfully constituted is the human mind! How it resists, as long as it can, all efforts made to reclaim from error! I feel that all this disturbance is but an evidence that our efforts are the best that could have been adopted, or else the friends of slavery would not care for what we say and do. The South know what we do. I am thankful that they are reached by our efforts. Many times have I wept in the land of my birth, over the system of slavery. I knew of none who sympathized in my feelings — I was unaware that any efforts were made to deliver the oppressed — no voice in the wilderness was heard calling on the people to repent and do works meet for repentance — and my heart sickened within me. Oh, how should I have rejoiced to know that such efforts as these were being made. I only wonder that I had such feelings. I wonder when I reflect under what influence I was brought up that my heart is not harder than the nether millstone. But in the midst of temptation I was preserved, and my sympathy grew warmer, and my hatred of slavery more inveterate, until at last I have exiled myself from my native land because I could no longer endure to hear the wailing of the slave. I fled to the land of Penn; for here, thought I, sympathy for the slave will

surely be found. But I found it not. The people were kind and hospitable, but the slave had no place in their thoughts. Whenever questions were put to me as to his condition, I felt that they were dictated by an idle curiosity, rather than by that deep feeling which would lead to effort for his rescue. I therefore shut up my grief in my own heart. I remembered that I was a Carolinian, from a state which framed this iniquity by law. I knew that throughout her territory was continual suffering, on the one part, and continual brutality and sin on the other. Every Southern breeze wafted to me the discordant tones of weeping and wailing, shrieks and groans, mingled with prayers and blasphemous curses. I thought there was no hope; that the wicked would go on in his wickedness, until he had destroyed both himself and his country. My heart sunk within me at the abominations in the midst of which I had been born and educated. What will it avail, cried I in bitterness of spirit, to expose to the gaze of strangers the horrors and pollutions of slavery, when there is no ear to hear nor heart to feel and pray for the slave. The language of my soul was, "Oh tell it not in Gath, publish it not in the streets of Askelon." But how different do I feel now! Animated with hope, nay, with an assurance of the triumph of liberty and good will to man, I will lift up my voice like a trumpet, and show this people their transgression, their sins of omission towards the slave, and what they can do towards affecting Southern mind, and overthrowing Southern oppression.

We may talk of occupying neutral ground, but on this subject, in its present attitude, there is no such thing as neutral ground. He that is not for us is against us, and he that gathereth not with us, scattereth abroad. If you are on what you suppose to be neutral ground, the South look upon you as on the side of the oppressor. And is there one who loves his country willing to give his influence, even indirectly, in favor of slavery — that curse of nations ? God swept Egypt with the besom of destruction, and punished Judea also with a sore punishment, because of slavery. And have we any reason to believe that he is less just now? — or that he will be more favorable to us than to his own "peculiar people?" [Shoutings, stones thrown against the windows, &c.]

There is nothing to be feared from those who would stop our mouths, but they themselves should fear and tremble. The current is even now setting fast against them. If the arm of the North had not caused the Bastile of slavery to totter to its foundation, you would not hear those cries. A few years ago, and the South felt secure, and with a contemptuous sneer asked, "Who are the abolitionists? The abolitionists are nothing?" — Ay, in one sense they were nothing, and they are nothing still. But in this we rejoice, that "God has chosen things that are not to bring to nought things that are." [Mob again disturbed the meeting.]

We often hear the question asked, "What shall we do?" Here is an opportunity for doing something now. Every man and every woman present may do something by showing that we fear not a mob, and, in the midst of threatenings and revilings, by opening our mouths for the dumb and pleading the cause of those who are ready to perish.

To work as we should in this cause, we must know what Slavery is. Let me urge you then to buy the books which have been written on this subject and read them, and then lend them to your neighbors. Give your money no longer for things which pander to pride and lust, but aid in scattering "the living coals of truth" upon the naked heart of this nation, — in circulating appeals to the sympathies of Christians in behalf of the outraged and suffering slave. But, it is said by some, our "books and papers do not speak the truth." Why, then, do they not contradict what we say? They cannot. Moreover the South has entreated, nay commanded us to be silent; and what greater evidence of the truth of our publications could be desired?

Women of Philadelphia! allow me as a Southern woman, with much attachment to the land of my birth, to entreat you to come up to this work. Especially let me urge you to petition. Men may settle this and other questions at the ballot-box, but you have no such right; it is only through petitions that you can reach the Legislature. It is therefore peculiarly *your duty* to petition. Do you say, "It does no good?" The South already turns pale at the number sent. They have read the reports of the proceedings of Congress, and there have seen that among other petitions were very many from the women of the North on the subject of slavery. This fact has called the attention of the South to the subject. How could we expect to have done more as yet? Men who hold the rod over slaves, rule in the councils of the nation: and they deny our right to petition and to remonstrate against abuses of our sex and of our kind. We have these rights, however, from our God. Only let us exercise them: and though often turned away unanswered, let us remember the influence of importunity upon the unjust judge, and act accordingly. The fact that the South look with jealousy upon our measures shows that they are effectual. There is, therefore, no cause for doubting or despair, but rather for rejoicing.

It was remarked in England that women did much to abolish Slavery in her colonies. Nor are they now idle. Numerous petitions from them have recently been presented to the Queen, to abolish the apprenticeship with its cruelties nearly equal to those of the system whose place it supplies. One petition two miles and a quarter long has been presented. And do you think these labors will be in vain ? Let the history of the past answer. When the women of these States send up to Congress such a petition, our legislators will arise as did those of England, and say, "When all the maids and matrons of the land are knocking at our doors we must legislate." Let the zeal and love, the faith and works of our English sisters quicken ours — that while the slaves continue to suffer, and when they shout deliverance, we may feel the satisfaction of *having done what we could*.

——— 3.23 ———

'TO INSTRUCT OTHERS IS BENEFICIAL TO THE MIND'

Ann Plato

Until recently, the writings of Ann Plato were largely over-looked by literary historians, as much of the 19th and early 20th century work of African-American women has been. Contemporary scholarship has strived to make up for that omission, and, as a result, Plato's 1841 *Essays* has assumed its important place in history as only the second book published by an African-American woman. A devout Congregationalist, Plato intended *Essays* to be a series of charges urging people to lead holy lives. Each of the 16 essays, written in plain, unornamented prose, takes up a different aspect of daily life through which one can exhibit Christian values. The essays are reminiscent of that of Jupiter Hammon's 18th century poetry and prose (see Chapters One and Two) in that they focus on spiritual rather than temporal salvation, and still more unusual in that they do not confront southern slavery or northern racism. Given the understandably overwhelming interest in these topics of most black writers and commentators of the time, *Essays* raises many questions about the perspective from which Plato wrote. Unfortunately, however, owing to the gap in research on black women writers, we know little about Plato herself, beyond the fact that, at the time of the book's publication, she lived in Hartford, Connecticut, and was an active participant in the First Congregational Church of Old Lyme. Historians do not believe Plato published again.

OBEDIENCE.

Obedience to parents is the BASIS of all order and improvement, and is not only pre-emptorily and repeatedly enjoined by Scripture, but even the heathen laid great stress upon the due performance of obedience to parents and other superiors. The young rose up and gave place to them. They solicited their opinion, and listened attentively until they had done speaking. They bowed down reverently before them, and sought opinions of their hoary men; and withheld not the reverence from them that was their due.

We read, indeed, that the Romans gave to parents unlimited jurisdiction over their chil-dren; and fathers were empowered to (and frequently did) punish filial disobedience with stripes, slavery, and even Death. "Honor thy father and thy mother, that thy days may be long on the land which the Lord thy God giveth thee," is the solemn command of the Most High; and we may safely assure ourselves that God will not only bless the dutiful here, and hereafter, but that he will punish, in the most signal and terrible manner, all those who, by parental neglect and unfilial conduct, set at defiance his written law, and violate that holy and ust principle which he has implanted in every human breast.

Youth, in particular, should constantly bear in mind, that every comfort they enjoy, all the intellectual attainments which render them superior to the savage, they owe to their parents. Think of the miseries of orphanage. The greatest loss that can befall a child, is to be deprived of pious and affectionate parents. While you are surrounded by such blessings, never be so ungrateful as to injure them by disobedience.

In their absence, their commands ought always to be observed the same as in their presence. To obey willingly, is a love of obedience. Who would not doubt the obedience of a child, when told by his superior to do as he was bid; when some minutes after, to be asked, if he had done as he was bade? I should doubt its obedience when I heard the command.

It is a great duty of the young to treat old persons with respect. The Bible commands them "to rise up before the face of the old man, and to honor the hoary head." This is too often forgotten, although a command from the Bible. You remember the scenes of a hoary headed man, while in an assembly at Athens, but again in Sparta, he was in a similar situation, but was treated with respect. "The Athenians KNOW what is right," said he, "but the Spartans PRACTICE it."

May it never be said of us, that we understand our duties, yet fail in regarding them. In walking I have often observed a want of reverence which is due to the aged. Years have given them experience which is worthy of honor. If the Bible were not disregarded in this, they would at once receive the respect which is due to them. If in nations the laws are disregarded, what safety is there for the people?

When you are in school, consider it a privilege to be there, and give your time and thought to the employment which is marked for you, by your teacher. Those who think thus will keep all the rules, and consider it improper to break them. If pupils refuse to obey the directions of their teacher, no benefit can be received from their instructions.

If persons know not obedience how can they teach it to others, which may in time be their lot? A person who will not obey, is not capable of commanding obedience. They know not how to estimate a duty so valuable. Those who are distinguished by faithfully discharging their first and earliest obligations, will be prepared to act well their part in future life. They will maintain good order in their own families, and honor just government in the land.

It is, however, certain, that in whatever situation of life a person is placed in, from the cradle to the grave, a spirit of obedience and submission, pliability of temper, and humility of mind, are required from, them; and the most highly gifted cannot pass over it, without injury to their character. Let us ever live with principles of obedience; and that with us we may carry it to our graves; and when we lay upon our beds of death, may we say to the living — live with this great duty — Obedience.

EMPLOYMENT OF TIME.

To make a good use of time, each minute must be well spent. It is well said, by a celebrated author, that many persons lose two or three hours every day for the want of employing odd minutes. A certain regularity is absolutely necessary, to make a proper use of time.

In the distribution of your time, let the first hour of the day be devoted to the service of God. Accustom yourselves to the practice of religious duties, as a natural expression of gratitude to Him for all his bounty and benevolence. Consider it as the service of the God of your fathers; of Him to whom your parents devoted you; of Him whom, in former ages, your ancestors honored, and by whom they are now rewarded and blessed in heaven.

Time to you is every thing, if well improved. "Time," said Dr. Franklin, "is money." An Italian Philosopher said that "time was his estate." In employing your time, consider it your privilege to spend your leisure hours in deepening the mind, and preparing yourselves for future action.

The human mind was made for action. In virtuous action consists its highest enjoyment. Reading is good employment, and very useful, if well understood. Some books are injurious to the mind, as well as useful. Books have a silent, but powerful influence in the formation of character. Says a distinguished clergyman, "let me see the private books of an individual, and I will tell you his character." Says another, "let me write the private books of a nation, and I care not who makes the laws."

The poems of Homer inspired Alexander with an insatiable thirst for fame and military glory, and they were the foundation of the superstructure that covered the world. The memoirs of this conqueror stamped a like character upon Cæsar these, and similar ones, made Napoleon a second Alexander.

Whatever you pretend to learn, be sure and have ambition enough to desire to excel in; for mediocrity is a proof of weakness; and perfection may always be purchased by application. "Knowledge," says an elegant writer, "is a comfortable and necessary shelter for us in an advanced age;" but if you do not plant it while young it will afford you no shade when you become old.

To instruct others is beneficial to the mind. It deepens the knowledge which it already possesses, and quickens it to acquire more. It is beneficial to the moral habits.

It teaches self-control. It moves to set a good example. It improves the affections. For we love those whom we make wiser and better, and their gratitude is a sweet reward.

Time is more valuable than money. If you hinder a scholar from studying, you commit a robbery against him; for robbers of time, are more guilty, than robbers of money. The young are not apt to value the importance of time. They forget that time is money! If time was more improved, there would be more happiness, and less discontentment, than there is at this present date.

Perhaps many consider that their station in life is too high, to admit of having employment. I think some will say that none are in too high station, be their knowledge ever so deep, to make a proper use of time.

When the unfortunate Greeks stood in need of assistance, ladies of the greatest wealth, plied their needles industriously that the unfortunate people might be clothed. Their servants also came offering a part of their wages. They sat down by their side, working for the same charity; while the young ones said to each other, "Greece hungered, and we gave her food; she was naked, and we clothed her."

May we not rest in our beds until we have made up our minds to ask God for assistance, in making a proper use of time. It will be for our edification, and for memorable thoughts, in our declining years of life.

3.24

'I HAVE COME TO TELL YOU SOMETHING ABOUT SLAVERY — WHAT I KNOW OF IT, AS I HAVE FELT IT.'
Frederick Douglass

William Lloyd Garrison provided the abolitionist movement with a national personality. His Anti-Slavery Society provided a centralizing institution. Frederick Douglass brought to the movement the moral weight of black America and a practical approach that engaged and manipulated the political system rather than merely damning its hypocrisy or appealing to its generosity.

Douglass credited Garrison with mentoring his abolitionist views. But the two men would ultimately come to represent competing factions in the movement — the radical Garrison, convinced the nation would first need to be torn apart to end slavery; the practical Douglass, certain that the slaves' only route to salvation would be through the nation's supposed tools of liberty. To Douglass, the problem lay in the hypocritical failure of the nation's white leaders to implement their ideologically sound system of government, not in the system itself. Douglass also believed that dissolution of the nation would ultimately damn the slaves in the southern states to bondage forever.

Douglass delivered the first of countless stirring abolitionist lectures in 1841, barely three years after his own escape from slavery in Baltimore. Attending a meeting of the Massachusetts Anti-Slavery Society in Nantucket, he was asked to say a few extemporaneous words about life as a slave. Impressed with his eloquence, the group hired him to tour the state. And with that, at age 23 and still a fugitive, Douglass joined Garrison at the forefront of the abolitionist movement. His name would soon become synonymous with the fight against slavery. Below is a speech he delivered in October 1841 in Lynn, Massachusetts, again offering his perspective as a former slave on behalf of the Society.

I feel greatly embarrassed when I attempt to address an audience of white people. I am not used to speak to them, and it makes me tremble when I do so, because I have always looked up to them with fear. My friends, I have come to tell you something about slavery — what I *know* of it, as I have *felt* it. When I came North, I was astonished to find that the abolitionists knew so much about it, that they were acquainted with effects as well as if they had lived in its midst. But though they can give you its history — though they can depict its horrors, they cannot speak as I can from experience; they cannot refer you to a back red with scars, as I can; for I have felt these wounds; I have suffered under the lash without the power of resisting. Yes, my blood has sprung out as the lash embedded itself in my flesh. And yet my master has the reputation of being a pious man and a good Christian. He was a leader in the Methodist church. I have seen this pious class leader cross and tie the hands of one of his young female slaves, and lash her bare skin and justify the deed by the quotation from the Bible, "he who knoweth his master's will and doeth it not, shall be beaten with many stripes."

Our masters do not hesitate to prove from the Bible that slavery is right, and ministers of the Gospel tell us that we were born to be slaves: — to look at our hard hands, and see how wisely Providence has them to do the labor; and then tell us, holding up their delicate white hands, that theirs are not fit to work. Some of us know very well that we have not time to cease from labor, or ours would get soft too; but I have heard the superstitious ones exclaim — and ignorant people are always superstitious — that "if ever a man told the truth, that one did."

A large portion of the slaves know that they have a right to their liberty. — It is often talked about and read of, for some of us know how to read, although all our knowledge is gained in secret.

I well remember getting possession of a speech by John Quincy Adams, made in Congress about slavery and freedom, and reading it to my fellow slaves. Oh! what joy and gladness it produced to know that so great, so good a man was pleading for us, and further, to know that there was a large and growing class of people in the north called abolitionists, who were moving for our freedom. This is known all through the south, and cherished with gratitude. It has increased the slaves' hope for liberty. Without it his heart would faint within him; his patience would be exhausted. On the agitation of this subject he has built his highest hopes. My friends let it not be quieted, for upon you the slaves look for help. There will be no outbreaks, no insurrections, whilst you continue this excitement: let it cease, and the crimes that would follow cannot be told.

Emancipation, my friends, is that cure for slavery and its evils. It alone will give to the south peace and quietness. It will blot out the insults we have borne, will heal the wounds we have endured, and are even now groaning under, will pacify the resentment which would kindle to a blaze were it not for your exertions, and, though it may never unite the many kindred and dear friends which slavery has torn asunder, it will be received with gratitude and a forgiving spirit. Ah! how the slave yearns for it, that he may be secure from the lash, that he may enjoy his family, and no more be tortured with the worst feature of slavery, the separation of friends and families. The whip we can bear without a murmur, compared to the idea of separation. Oh, my friends, you cannot feel the slave's misery, when he is separated from his kindred. The agony of the mother when parting from her children cannot be told. There is nothing we so much dread as to be sold farther south. My friends, we are not taught from books; there is a law against teaching although I have heard some folks say we could not learn if we had a chance. The northern people say so, but the south do not believe it, or they would not have laws with heavy penalties to prevent it. The northern people think that if slavery were abolished, we would all come. They may be more afraid of the free colored people and the runaway slaves going South. We would all seek our home and our friends, but, more than all, to escape from northern prejudice, would we go to the south. Prejudice against color is stronger north than south; it hangs around my neck like a heavy weight. It presses me out from among my men, and, although I have met it at every step the three years I have been out of southern slavery, I have been able, in spite of its influence, "to take good care of myself."

———— 3.25 ————

'BRETHREN, ARISE! ARISE! STRIKE FOR YOUR LIVES AND LIBERTIES'
Henry Highland Garnet

As more escaped slaves took the podium at abolitionist meetings and conventions, the movement's spirit became increasingly radical. Often fresh from the Underground Railroad, these former slaves knew personally of the system's horrors and rallied around William Lloyd Garrison's doctrine of immediate and universal abolition. While Garrison claimed pacifism, and Frederick Douglass and free blacks sought strategic political engagement, many ex-slave voices predated the 20th century demand for freedom by whatever means necessary. One such person was Henry Highland Garnet. At the 1843 National Negro Convention in Buffalo, New York, Garnet delivered a speech that symbolized the more radical, ex-slave voice of the time. His "Call to Rebellion," as it has been dubbed, eulogized fallen revolutionaries from Denmark Vesey to Joseph Cinque of the Amistad Africans. Addressing the slave population directly, Garnet charged that they have a Christian responsibility to fight for their freedom. Proclaiming it "sinful in the extreme for you to voluntarily submit," Garnet urged them to "use every means, both moral, intellectual, and physical that promises success."

The speech sparked heated controversy at the convention. Douglass rose and opposed Garnet's views. And even after Garnet agreed to tone it down, the convention refused to endorse it.

BRETHREN AND FELLOW CITIZENS: — Your brethren of the North, East, and West have been accustomed to meet together in National Conventions, to sympathize with each Other, and to weep over your unhappy condition. In these meetings we have addressed all classes of the free, but we have never until this time, sent a word of consolation and advice to you. We have been contented in sitting still and mourning over your sorrows, earnestly hoping that before this day your sacred liberty would have been restored. But, we have hoped in vain. Years have rolled on, and tens of thousands have been borne on streams of blood and tears, to the shores of eternity. While you have been oppressed, we have also been partakers with you; nor can we be free while you are enslaved. We, therefore, write to you as being bound with you.

Many of you are bound to us, not only by the ties of a common humanity, but we are connected by the more tender relations of parents, wives, husbands, children, brothers, and sisters, and friends. As such we most affectionately address you.

Slavery has fixed a deep gulf between you and us, and while it shuts out from you the relief and consolation which your friends would willingly render, it affects and persecutes you with a fierceness which we might not expect to see in the fiends of hell. But still the Almighty Father of mercies has left to us a glimmering ray of hope, which shines out like a lone star in a cloudy sky. Mankind are becoming wiser, and better — the oppressor's power is fading, and you, every day, are becoming better informed, and more numerous. Your grievances, brethren, are many. We shall not attempt, in this short address, to present to the world all the dark catalogue of this nation's sins, which have been committed upon an innocent people. Nor is it indeed necessary, for you feel them from day to day, and all the civilized world look upon them with amazement.

Two hundred and twenty-seven years ago, the first of our injured race were brought to the shores of America. They came not with glad spirits to select their homes in the New World. They came not with their own consent, to find an unmolested enjoyment of the blessings of this fruitful soil. The first dealings they had with men calling themselves Christians, exhibited to them the worst features of corrupt and sordid hearts; and convinced them that no cruelty is too great, no villainy and no robbery too abhorrent for even enlightened men to perform, when influenced by avarice and lust.

Neither did they come flying upon the wings of Liberty, to a land of freedom. But they came with broken hearts, from their beloved native land, and were doomed to unrequited toil and deep degradation. Nor did the evil of their bondage end at their emancipation by death. Succeeding generations inherited their chains, and millions have come from eternity into time, and have returned again to the world of spirits, cursed and ruined by American slavery.

The propagators of the system, or their immediate ancestors, very soon discovered its growing evil, and its tremendous wickedness, and secret promises were made to destroy it.

The gross inconsistency of a people holding slaves, who had themselves "ferried o'er the wave" for freedom's sake, was too apparent to be entirely overlooked. The voice of Freedom cried, "Emancipate your slaves." Humanity supplicated with tears for the deliverance of the children of Africa. Wisdom urged her solemn plea. The bleeding captive pled his innocence, and pointed to Christianity who stood weeping at the cross. Jehovah frowned upon the nefarious institution, and thunderbolts, red with vengeance, struggled to leap forth to blast the guilty wretches who maintained it. But all was in vain. Slavery had stretched its dark wings of death over the land, the Church stood silently by — the priests prophesied falsely, and the people loved to have it so. Its throne is established, and now it reigns triumphant.

Nearly three millions of your fellow-citizens are prohibited by law and public opinion, (which in this country is stronger than law,) from reading the Book of Life. Your intellect has been destroyed as much as possible, and every ray of light they have attempted to shut out from your minds. The oppressors themselves have become involved in the ruin. They have become weak, sensual, and rapacious — they have cursed you — they have cursed themselves — they have cursed the earth which they have trod.

The colonists threw the blame upon England. They said that the mother country entailed the evil upon them, and that they would rid themselves of it if they could. The world thought they were sincere, and the philanthropic pitied them. But time soon tested their sincerity.

In a few years the colonists grew strong, and severed themselves from the British Government. Their independence was declared, and they took their station among the sovereign powers of the earth. The declaration was a glorious document. Sages admired it, and the patriotic of every nation reverenced the God-like sentiments which it contained. When the power of Government returned to their hands, did they emancipate the slaves? No; they rather added new links to our chains. Were they ignorant of the principles of Liberty? Certainly they were not. The sentiments of their revolutionary orators fell in burning eloquence upon their hearts, and with one voice they cried, LIBERTY OR DEATH. Oh what a sentence was that! It ran from soul to soul like electric fire, and nerved the arm of thousands to fight in the holy cause of Freedom. Among the diversity of opinions that are entertained in regard to physical resistance, there are but a few found to gainsay that stern declaration. We are among those who do not.

SLAVERY! How much misery is comprehended in that single word? What mind is there that does not shrink from its direful effects? Unless the image of God be obliterated from the soul, all men cherish the love of Liberty. The nice discerning political economist does not regard the sacred right more than the untutored African who roams in the wilds of Congo. Nor has the one more right to the full enjoyment of his freedom than the other. In every man's mind the good seeds of liberty are planted, and he who brings his fellow down so low, as to make him contented with a condition of slavery, commits the highest crime against God and man. Brethren, your oppressors aim to do this. They endeavor to make you as much like brutes as possible. When they have blinded the eyes of your mind — when they have embittered the sweet waters of life — then, and not till then, has American slavery done its perfect work.

TO SUCH DEGRADATION IT IS SINFUL IN THE EXTREME FOR YOU TO MAKE VOLUNTARY SUBMISSION. The divine commandments you are in duty bound to reverence and obey. If you do not obey them, you will surely meet with the displeasure of the Almighty. He requires you to love him supremely, and your neighbor as yourself — to keep the Sabbath day holy — to search the Scriptures — and bring up your children with respect for his laws, and to worship no other God but him. But slavery sets all these at nought, and hurls defiance in the face of

Jehovah. The forlorn condition in which you are placed, does not destroy your moral obligation to God. You are not certain of heaven, because you suffer yourselves to remain in a state of slavery, where you cannot obey the commandments of the Sovereign of the universe. If the ignorance of slavery is a passport to heaven, then it is a blessing, and no curse, and you should rather desire its perpetuity than its abolition. God will not receive slavery, nor ignorance, nor any other state of mind, for love and obedience to him. Your condition does not absolve you from your moral obligation. The diabolical injustice by which your liberties are cloven down, NEITHER GOD, NOR ANGELS, OR JUST MEN, COMMAND YOU TO SUFFER FOR A SINGLE MOMENT. THEREFORE IT IS YOUR SOLEMN AND IMPERATIVE DUTY TO USE EVERY MEANS, BOTH MORAL, INTELLECTUAL, AND PHYSICAL THAT PROMISES SUCCESS. If a band of heathen men should attempt to enslave a race of Christians, and to place their children under the influence of some false religion, surely Heaven would frown upon the men who would not resist such aggression, even to death. If, on the other hand, a band of Christians should attempt to enslave a race of heathen men, and to entail slavery upon them, and to keep them in heathenism in the midst of Christianity, the God of heaven would smile upon every effort which the injured might make to disenthral themselves.

Brethren, it is as wrong for your lordly oppressors to keep you in slavery as it was for the man thief to steal our ancestors from the coast of Africa. You should therefore now use the same manner of resistance, as would have been just in our ancestors when the bloody footprints of the first remorseless soul-thief was placed upon the shores of our fatherland. The humblest peasant is as free in the sight of God as the proudest monarch that ever swayed a sceptre. Liberty is a spirit sent out from God, and like its great Author, is no respecter of persons.

Brethren, the time has come when you must act for yourselves. It is an old and true saying that, "if hereditary bondmen would be free, they must themselves strike the blow." You can plead your own cause, and do the work of emancipation better than any others. The nations of the world are moving in the great cause of universal freedom, and some of them at least will, ere long, do you justice. The combined powers of Europe have placed their broad seal of disapprobation upon the African slave-trade. But in the slaveholding parts of the United States, the trade is as brisk as ever. They buy and sell you as though you were brute beasts. The North has done much — her opinion of slavery in the abstract is known. But in regard to the South, we adopt the opinion of the *New York Evangelist* — We have advanced so far, that the cause apparently waits for a more effectual door to be thrown open than has been yet. We are about to point out that more effectual door. Look around you, and behold the bosoms of your loving wives heaving with untold agonies! Hear the cries of your poor children! Remember the stripes your fathers bore. Think of the torture and disgrace of your noble mothers. Think of your wretched sisters, loving virtue and purity, as they are driven into concubinage and are exposed to the unbridled lusts of incarnate devils. Think of the undying glory that hangs around the ancient name of Africa — and forget not that you are native born American citizens, and as such, you are justly entitled to all the rights that are granted to the freest. Think how many tears you have poured out upon the soil which you have cultivated with unrequited toil and enriched with your blood; and then go to your lordly enslavers and tell them plainly, that you are *determined to be free*. Appeal to their sense of justice, and tell them that they have no more right to oppress you, than you have to enslave them. Entreat them to remove the grievous burdens which they have imposed upon you, and to remunerate you for your labor. Promise them renewed diligence in the cultivation of the soil, if they will render to you an equivalent for your services. Point them to the increase of happiness and prosperity in the British West Indies since the Act of Emancipation. Tell them in language which they cannot misunderstand, of the exceeding sinfulness of slavery, and of a future judgment, and of the righteous retributions of an indignant God. Inform them that all you desire is FREEDOM, and that nothing else will suffice. Do this, and for ever after cease to toil for the heartless tyrants, who give you no other reward but stripes and abuse. If they then commence the work of death, they, and not you, will be responsible for the consequences. You had better all die — *die immediately*, than live slaves and entail your wretchedness upon your posterity. If you would be free in this generation, here is your only hope. However much you and all of us may desire it, there is not much hope of redemption without the shedding of blood. If you must bleed, let it all come at once rather *die freemen, than live to be slaves*. It is impossible like the children of Israel, to make a grand exodus from the land of bondage. The Pharaohs are on both sides of the blood-red waters! You cannot move en masse, to the dominions of the British Queen — nor can you pass through Florida and overrun Texas, and at last find peace in Mexico. The propagators of American slavery are spending their blood and treasure, that they may plant the black flag in the heart of Mexico and riot in the halls of the Montezumas. In the language of the Rev. Robert Hall, when addressing the volunteers of Bristol, who were rushing forth to repel the invasion of Napoleon, who threatened to lay waste the fair homes of England, "Religion is too much interested in your behalf, not to shed over you her most gracious influences."

You will not be compelled to spend much time in order to become inured to hardships. From the first moment that you breathed the air of heaven, you have been accustomed to nothing else but hardships. The heroes of the American Revolution were never put upon harder fare than a peck of corn and a few herrings per week. You have not become enervated by the luxuries of life. Your sternest energies

have been beaten out upon the anvil of severe trial. Slavery has done this, to make you subservient, to its own purposes; but it has done more than this, it has prepared you for any emergency. If you receive good treatment, it is what you could hardly expect; if you meet with pain, sorrow, and even death, these are the common *lot of slaves*.

Fellow men! Patient sufferers! behold your dearest rights crushed to the earth! See your sons murdered, and your wives, mothers and sisters doomed to prostitution. In the name of the merciful God, and by all that life is worth, let it no longer be a debatable question whether it is better to choose Liberty or death.

In 1822, Denmark Veazie, of South Carolina, formed a plan for the liberation of his fellow men. In the whole history of human efforts to overthrow slavery, a more complicated and tremendous plan was never formed. He was betrayed by the treachery of his own people, and died a martyr to freedom. Many a brave hero fell, but history, faithful to her high trust, will transcribe his name on the same monument with Moses, Hampden, Tell, Bruce and Wallace, Toussaint L'Ouverture, Lafayette and Washington. That tremendous movement shook the whole empire of slavery. The guilty soulthieves were overwhelmed with fear. It is a matter of fact, that at that time, and in consequence of the threatened revolution, the slave States talked strongly of emancipation. But they blew but one blast of the trumpet of freedom and then laid it aside. As these men became quiet, the slaveholders ceased to talk about emancipation; and now behold your condition today! Angels sigh over it, and humanity has long since exhausted her tears in weeping on your account!

The patriotic Nathaniel Turner followed Denmark Veazie. He was goaded to desperation by wrong and injustice. By despotism, his name has been recorded on the list of infamy, and future generations will remember him among the noble and brave.

Next arose the immortal Joseph Cinque, the hero of the Amistad. He was a native

African, and by the help of God he emancipated a whole shipload of his fellow men on the high seas. And he now sings of liberty on the sunny hills of Africa and beneath his native palm-trees, where he hears the lion roar and feels himself as free as that king of the forest.

Next arose Madison Washington that bright star of freedom, and took his station in the constellation of true heroism. He was a slave on board the brig Creole, of Richmond, bound to New Orleans, that great slave mart, with a hundred and four others. Nineteen struck for liberty or death. But one life was taken, and the whole were emancipated, and the vessel was carried into Nassau, New Providence.

Noble men! Those who have fallen in freedom's conflict, their memories will be cherished by the true-hearted and the God-fearing in all future generations; those who are living, their names are surrounded by a halo of glory.

Brethren, arise, arise! Strike for your lives and liberties. Now is the day and the hour. Let every slave throughout the land do this and the days of slavery are numbered. You cannot be more oppressed than you have been — you cannot suffer greater cruelties than you have already. *Rather die freemen than live to be slaves.* Remember that you are FOUR MILLIONS!

It is in your power so to torment the God-cursed slaveholders that they will be glad to let you go free. If the scale was turned, and black men were the masters and white men the slaves, every destructive agent and element would be employed to lay the oppressor low. Danger and death would hang over their heads day and night. Yes, the tyrants would meet with plagues more terrible than those of Pharaoh. But you are a patient people. You act as though you were made for the special use of these devils. You act as though your daughters were born to pamper the lusts of your masters and overseers. And worse than all, you tamely submit while your lords tear your wives from your embraces and defile them before your eyes. In the name of God, we ask you, are you men? Where is the blood of your fathers? Has

it all run out of your veins? Awake, awake; millions of voices are calling you! Your dead fathers speak to you from their graves. Heaven, as with a voice of thunder, calls on you to arise from the dust.

Let your motto be resistance! *resistance!* RESISTANCE! No oppressed people have ever secured their liberty without resistance. What kind of resistance you had better make, you must decide by the circumstances that surround you, and according to the suggestion of expediency. Brethren, adieu! Trust in the living God. Labor for the peace of the human race, and remember that you are FOUR MILLIONS.

————— 3.26 —————

'THE LIGHT BROKE IN UPON ME BY DEGREES'
Frederick Douglass

Having established himself as a premier orator and movement leader, in 1845 Frederick Douglass published the first of three autobiographical works, *Narrative of the Life of Frederick Douglass, An American Slave. Written by Himself.* His work is perhaps the grandest of the slave narrative genre, hailed as both an important political document and a literary masterpiece, it sold 30,000 copies in 15 years and became an international hit. In it, among other things, Douglass describes his escape via the Underground Railroad. Given Douglass's fugitive status, this was a significantly brash act. In the excerpt below, he explains his successful scheme to teach himself to read and write at age 12, as well as how he developed his resolve to run away.

CHAPTER VII.

I LIVED in Master Hugh's family about seven years. During this time, I succeeded in learning to read and write. In accomplishing this, I was compelled to resort to various stratagems. I had no regular teacher. My mistress, who had kindly commenced to instruct me, had, in compliance with the advice and direction of her husband, not only ceased to instruct, but had set her face against my being instructed by any one else. It is due, however, to my mistress to say of her, that she did not adopt this course of treatment immediately. She at first lacked the depravity indispensable to shutting me up in mental darkness. It was at least necessary for her to have some training in the exercise of irresponsible power, to make her equal to the task of treating me as though I were a brute.

My mistress was, as I have said, a kind and tender-hearted woman; and in the simplicity of her soul she commenced, when I first went to live with her, to treat me as she supposed one human being ought to treat another. In entering upon the duties of a slaveholder, she did not seem to perceive that I sustained to her the relation of a mere chattel, and that for her to treat me as a human being was not only wrong, but dangerously so. Slavery proved as injurious to her as it did to me. When I went there, she was a pious, warm, and tender-hearted woman. There was no sorrow or suffering for which she had not a tear. She had bread for the hungry, clothes for the naked, and comfort for every mourner that came within her reach. Slavery soon proved its ability to divest her of these heavenly qualities. Under its influence, the tender heart became stone, and the lamblike disposition gave way to one of tiger-like fierceness. The first step in her downward course was in her ceasing to instruct me. She now commenced to practise her husband's precepts. She finally became even more violent in her opposition than her husband himself. She was not satisfied with simply doing as well as he had commanded; she seemed anxious to do better. Nothing seemed to make her more angry than to see me with a newspaper. She seemed to think that here lay the danger. I have had her rush at me with a face made all up of fury, and snatch from me a newspaper, in a manner that fully revealed her apprehension. She was an apt woman; and a little experience soon demonstrated, to her satisfaction, that education and slavery were incompatible with each other.

From this time I was most narrowly watched. If I was in a separate room any considerable length of time, I was sure to be sus-pected of having a book, and was at once called to give an account of myself. All this, however, was too late. The first step had been taken. Mistress, in teaching me the alphabet, had given me the *inch*, and no precaution could prevent me from taking the *ell*.

The plan which I adopted, and the one by which I was most successful, was that of making friends of all the little white boys whom I met in the street. As many of these as I could, I converted into teachers. With their kindly aid, obtained at different times and in different places, I finally succeeded in learning to read. When I was sent of errands, I always took my book with me, and by going one part of my errand quickly, I found time to get a lesson before my return. I used also to carry bread with me, enough of which was always in the house, and to which I was always welcome; for I was much better off in this regard than many of the poor white children in our neighborhood. This bread I used to bestow upon the hungry little urchins, who, in return, would give me that more valuable bread of knowledge. I am strongly tempted to give the names of two or three of those little boys, as a testimonial of the gratitude and affection I bear them; but prudence forbids; — not that it would injure me, but it might embarrass them; for it is almost an unpardonable offence to teach slaves to read in this Christian country. It is enough to say of the dear little fellows, that they lived on Philpot Street, very near Durgin and Bailey's ship-yard. I used to talk this matter of slavery over with them. I would sometimes say to them, I wished I could be as free as they would be when they got to be men. "You will be free as soon as you are twenty-one, *but I am a slave for life*! Have not I as good a right to be free as you have?" These words used to trouble them; they would express for me the liveliest sympathy, and console me with the hope that something would occur by which I might be free.

I was now about twelve years old, and the thought of *being a slave for life* began to bear heavily upon my heart. Just about this time, I got hold of a book entitled "The Columbian

Orator." Every opportunity I got, I used to read this book. Among much of other interesting matter, I found in it a dialogue between a master and his slave. The slave was represented as having run away from his master three times. The dialogue represented the conversation which took place between them, when the slave was retaken the third time. In this dialogue, the whole argument in behalf of slavery was brought forward by the master, all of which was disposed of by the slave. The slave was made to say some very smart as well as impressive things in reply to his master — things which had the desired though unexpected effect; for the conversation resulted in the voluntary emancipation of the slave on the part of the master.

In the same book, I met with one of Sheridan's mighty speeches on and in behalf of Catholic emancipation. These were choice documents to me. I read them over and over again with unabated interest. They gave tongue to interesting thoughts of my own soul, which had frequently flashed through my mind, and died away for want of utterance. The moral which I gained from the dialogue was the power of truth over the conscience of even a slaveholder. What I got from Sheridan was a bold denunciation of slavery, and a powerful vindication of human rights. The reading of these documents enabled me to utter my thoughts, and to meet the arguments brought forward to sustain slavery; but while they relieved me of one difficulty, they brought on another even more painful than the one of which I was relieved. The more I read, the more I was led to abhor and detest my enslavers. I could regard them in no other light than a band of successful robbers, who had left their homes, and gone to Africa, and stolen us from our homes, and in a strange land reduced us to slavery. I loathed them as being the meanest as well as the most wicked of men. As I read and contemplated the subject, behold! that very discontentment which Master Hugh had predicted would follow my learning to read had already come, to torment and sting my soul to unutterable anguish. As I writhed under it, I would at times feel that learning to read had been a curse rather than a blessing. It had given me a view of my wretched condition, without the remedy. It opened my eyes to the horrible pit, but to no ladder upon which to get out. In moments of agony, I envied my fellow-slaves for their stupidity. I have often wished myself a beast. I preferred the condition of the meanest reptile to my own. Any thing, no matter what, to get rid of thinking! It was this everlasting thinking of my condition that tormented me. There was no getting rid of it. It was pressed upon me by every object within sight or hearing, animate or inanimate. The silver trump of freedom had roused my soul to eternal wakefulness. Freedom now appeared, to disappear no more forever. It was heard in every sound, and seen in every thing. It was ever present to torment me with a sense of my wretched condition. I saw nothing without seeing it, I heard nothing without hearing it, and felt nothing without feeling it. It looked from every star, it smiled in every calm, breathed in every wind, and moved in every storm.

I often found myself regretting my own existence, and wishing myself dead; and but for the hope of being free, I have no doubt but that I should have killed myself, or done something for which I should have been killed. While in this state of mind, I was eager to hear any one speak of slavery. I was a ready listener. Every little while, I could hear something about the abolitionists. It was some time before I found what the word meant. It was always used in such connections as to make it an interesting word to me. If a slave ran away and succeeded in getting clear, or if a slave killed his master, set fire to a barn, or did any thing very wrong in the mind of a slaveholder, it was spoken of as the fruit of *abolition*. Hearing the word in this connection very often, I set about learning what it meant. The dictionary afforded me little or no help. I found it was "the act of abolishing;" but then I did not know what was to be abolished. Here I was perplexed. I did not dare to ask any one about its meaning, for I was satisfied that it was something they wanted me to know very little about. After a patient waiting, I got one of our city papers, containing an account of the number of petitions from the north, praying for the abolition of slavery in the District of Columbia, and of the slave trade between the States. From this time I understood the words *abolition* and *abolitionist*, and always drew near when that word was spoken, expecting to hear something of importance to myself and fellow-slaves. The light broke in upon me by degrees. I went one day down on the wharf of Mr. Waters; and seeing two Irishmen unloading a scow of stone, I went, unasked, and helped them. When we had finished, one of them came to me and asked me if I were a slave. I told him I was. He asked, "Are ye a slave for life?" I told him that I was. The good Irishman seemed to be deeply affected by the statement. He said to the other that it was a pity so fine a little fellow as myself should be a slave for life. He said it was a shame to hold me. They both advised me to run away to the north; that I should find friends there, and that I should be free. I pretended not to be interested in what they said, and treated them as if I did not understand them; for I feared they might be treacherous. White men have been known to encourage slaves to escape, and then, to get the reward, catch them and return them to their masters. I was afraid that these seemingly good men might use me so; but I nevertheless remembered their advice, and from that time I resolved to run away. I looked forward to a time at which it would be safe for me to escape. I was too young to think of doing so immediately; besides, I wished to learn how to write, as I might have occasion to write my own pass. I consoled myself with the hope that I should one day find a good chance. Meanwhile, I would learn to write.

The idea as to how I might learn to write was suggested to me by being in Durgin and Bailey's ship-yard, and frequently seeing the ship carpenters, after hewing, and getting a piece of timber ready for use, write on the timber the name of that part of the ship for which

it was intended. When a piece of timber was intended for the larboard side, it would be marked thus — "L." When a piece was for the starboard side, it would be marked thus — "S." A piece for the larboard side forward, would be marked thus — "L. F." When a piece was for starboard side forward, it would be marked thus — "S. F." For larboard aft, it would be marked thus — "L. A." For starboard aft, it would be marked thus — "S. A." I soon learned the names of these letters, and for what they were intended when placed upon a piece of timber in the ship-yard. I immediately commenced copying them, and in a short time was able to make the four letters named. After that, when I met with any boy who I knew could write, I would tell him I could write as well as he. The next word would be, "I don't believe you. Let me see you try it." I would then make the letters which I had been so fortunate as to learn, and ask him to beat that. In this way I got a good many lessons in writing, which it is quite possible I should never have gotten in any other way. During this time, my copy-book was the board fence, brick wall, and pavement; my pen and ink was a lump of chalk. With these, I learned mainly how to write. I then commenced and continued copying the Italics in Webster's Spelling Book, until I could make them all without looking on the book. By this time, my little Master Thomas had gone to school, and learned how to write, and had written over a number of copy-books. These had been brought home, and shown to some of our near neighbors, and then laid aside. My mistress used to go to class meeting at the Wilk Street meeting house every Monday afternoon, and leave me to take care of the house. When left thus, I used to spend the time in writing in the spaces left in Master Thomas's copy-book, copying what he had written. I continued to do this until I could write a hand very similar to that of Master Thomas. Thus, after a long, tedious effort for years, I finally succeeded in learning how to write.

———— 3.27 ————

'WHAT IS AMERICAN SLAVERY?'

Frederick Douglass

After publicizing his escape and his former owner's name in his *Narrative*, Frederick Douglass fled to Britain to avoid slave hunters and allow the storm to blow over. While there, he continued speaking and advocating on behalf of American abolition, touring England, Ireland and Scotland, and building an international following. While in Scotland, he took a central role in a campaign to force the Free Church of Scotland to "Send the Money Back," or return donations from southern American slaveholders. In 1846, a group of British supporters purchased Douglass's freedom. He returned to the States shortly thereafter.

On May 12, 1846, at Moorsfield, England's Finsbury Chapel, Douglass delivered one of his most famous speeches. (He later republished a reporter's transcription of the speech, excerpted below, in his second autobiography.) In it, he attempts to explain to the world the true nature of American slavery, which he argues has been missed by too many overseas observers. But he also lists as a goal his desire "to let the slaveholders of America know that the curtain which conceals their crimes is being lifted abroad." Douglass describes in horrifying detail the 19th century's refined techniques of physical, mental and emotional torture designed to "break" a slave and preserve his or her market value, as well as the sober laws written in slave states legalizing such torture. Finally, he notes the religious justification for slavery, decrying "the woman-whipping, the mind-darkening, the soul-destroying religion that exists in the southern states of America." The speech sparked the passions of British abolitionists, and is perhaps equally instructive for latter American generations, numbed by time to the depth of slavery's crimes against humanity.

Mr. Douglass rose amid loud cheers, and said: I feel exceedingly glad of the opportunity now afforded me of presenting the claims of my brethren in bonds in the United States, to so many in London and from various parts of Britain, who have assembled here on the present occasion. I have nothing to commend me to your consideration in the way of learning, nothing in the way of education, to entitle me to your attention; and you are aware that slavery is a very bad school for rearing teachers of morality and religion. Twenty-one years of my life have been spent in slavery — personal slavery — surrounded by degrading influences, such as can exist now here beyond the pale of slavery; and it will not be strange, if under such circumstances, I should betray, in what I have to say to you, a deficiency of that refinement which is seldom or ever found, except among persons that have experienced superior advantages to those which I have enjoyed. But I will take it for granted that you know something about the degrading influences of slavery, and that you will not expect great things from me this evening, but simply such facts as I may be able to advance immediately in connection with my own experience of slavery.

Now, what is this system of slavery? This is the subject of my lecture this evening — what is the character of this institution? I am about to answer the inquiry, what is American slavery? I do this the more readily, since I have found persons in this country who have identified the term slavery with that which I think it is not, and in some instances, I have feared, in so doing, have rather (unwittingly, I know,) detracted much from the horror with which the term slavery is contemplated. It is common in this country to distinguish every bad thing by the name of slavery. Intemperance is slavery; to be deprived of the right to vote is slavery, says one; to have to work hard is slavery, says another; and I do not know but that if we should let them go on, they would say that to eat when we are hungry, to walk when we desire to have exercise, or to minister to our necessities, or have necessities at all, is slavery. I do not wish for a moment to detract from the horror with which the evil of intemperance is contemplated — not at all; nor do I wish to throw the slightest obstruction in the way of any political freedom that any class of persons in this country may desire to obtain. But I am here to say that I think the term slavery is sometimes abused by identifying it with that which it is not. Slavery in the United States is the granting of that power by which one man exercises and enforces a right of property in the body and soul of another. The condition of a slave is simply that of the brute beast. He is a piece of property — a marketable commodity, in the language of the law, to be bought or sold at the will and caprice of the master who claims him to be his property; he is spoken of, thought of, and treated as property. His own good, his conscience, his intellect, his affections, are all set aside by the master. The will and the wishes of the master are the law of the slave. He is as much a piece of property as a horse. If he is fed, he is fed because he is property. If he is clothed, it is with a view to the increase of his value as property. Whatever of comfort is necessary to him for his body or soul that is inconsistent with his being property, is carefully wrested from him, not only by public opinion, but by the law of the country. He is carefully deprived of everything that tends in the slightest degree to detract from his value as property. He is deprived of education. God has given him an intellect; the slaveholder declares it shall not be cultivated. If his moral perception leads him in a course contrary to his value as property, the slaveholder declares he shall not exercise it. The marriage institution cannot exist among slaves, and one-sixth of the population of democratic America is denied its privileges by the law of the land. What is to be thought of a nation boasting of its liberty, boasting of its humanity, boasting of its christianity, boasting of its love of justice and purity, and yet having within its own borders three millions of persons denied by law the right of marriage? — what must be the condition of that people? I need not lift up the veil by giving you any experience of my own. Every one that can put two ideas together, must see the most fearful results from such a state of things as I have just mentioned. If any of these three millions find for themselves companions, and prove themselves honest, upright, virtuous persons to each other, yet in these cases — few

as I am bound to confess they are — the virtuous live in constant apprehension of being torn asunder by the merciless men-stealers that claim them as their property. This is American slavery; no marriage — no education — the light of the gospel shut out from the dark mind of the bondman — and he forbidden by law to learn to read. If a mother shall teach her children to read, the law in Louisiana proclaims that she may be hanged by the neck. If the father attempt to give his son a knowledge of letters, he may be punished by the whip in one instance, and in another be killed, at the discretion of the court. Three millions of people shut out from the light of knowledge! It is easy for you to conceive the evil that must result from such a state of things.

I now come to the physical evils of slavery. I do not wish to dwell at length upon these, but it seems right to speak of them, not so much to influence your minds on this question, as to let the slaveholders of America know that the curtain which conceals their crimes is being lifted abroad; that we are opening the dark cell, and leading the people into the horrible recesses of what they are pleased to call their domestic institution. We want them to know that a knowledge of their whippings, their scourgings, their brandings, their chainings, is not confined to their plantations, but that some negro of theirs has broken loose from his chains — has burst through the dark incrustation of slavery, and is now exposing their deeds of deep damnation to the gaze of the christian people of England.

The slaveholders resort to all kinds of cruelty. If I were disposed, I have matter enough to interest you on this question for five or six evenings, but I will not dwell at length upon these cruelties. Suffice it to say, that all the peculiar modes of torture that were resorted to in the West India islands, are resorted to, I believe, even more frequently, in the United States of America. Starvation, the bloody whip, the chain, the gag, the thumb-screw, cat-hauling, the cat-o'-nine-tails, the dungeon, the blood-hound, are all in requisition to keep the slave in his condition as a slave in the United States. If any one has a doubt upon this point, I would ask him to read the chapter on slavery in Dickens's *Notes on America*. If any man has a doubt upon it, I have here the "testimony of a thousand witnesses," which I can give at any length, all going to prove the truth of my statement. The blood-hound is regularly trained in the United States, and advertisements are to be found in the southern papers of the Union, from persons advertising themselves as blood-hound trainers, and offering to hunt down slaves at fifteen dollars a piece, recommending their hounds as the fleetest in the neighborhood, never known to fail. Advertisements are from time to time inserted, stating that slaves have escaped with iron collars about their necks, with bands of iron about their feet, marked with the lash, branded with red-hot irons, the initials of their master's name burned into their flesh; and the masters advertise the fact of their being thus branded with their own signature, thereby proving to the world, that, however damning it may appear to non-slaveholders, such practices are not regarded discreditable among the slaveholders themselves. Why, I believe if a man should brand his horse in this country — burn the initials of his name into any of his cattle, and publish the ferocious deed here — that the united execrations of christians in Britain would descend upon him. Yet, in the United States, human beings are thus branded. As Whittier says —

". . . Our countrymen in chains,
The whip on woman's shrinking flesh,
Our soil yet reddening with the stains
Caught from her scourgings warm and fresh."

The slave-dealer boldly publishes his infamous acts to the world. Of all things that have been said of slavery to which exception has been taken by slaveholders, this, the charge of cruelty, stands foremost, and yet there is no charge capable of clearer demonstration, than that of the most barbarous inhumanity on the part of the slaveholders toward their slaves. And all this is necessary; it is necessary to resort to these cruelties, in order to *make the slave a slave*, and to *keep him a slave*. Why, my experience all goes to prove the truth of what you will call a marvelous proposition, that the better you treat a slave, the more you destroy his value *as a slave*, and enhance the probability of his eluding the grasp of the slaveholder; the more kindly you treat him, the more wretched you make him, while you keep him in the condition of a slave. My experience, I say, confirms the truth of this proposition. When I was treated exceedingly ill; when my back was being scourged daily; when I was whipped within an inch of my life — *life* was all I cared for. "Spare my life," was my continual prayer. When I was looking for the blow about to be inflicted upon my head, I was not thinking of my liberty; it was my life. But, as soon as the blow was not to be feared, then came the longing for liberty. If a slave has a bad master, his ambition is to get a better; when he gets a better, he aspires to have the best; and when he gets the best, he aspires to be his own master. But the slave must be brutalized to keep him as a slave. The slaveholder feels this necessity. I admit this necessity. If it be right to hold slaves at all, it is right to hold them in the only way in which they can be held; and this can be done only by shutting out the light of education from their minds, and brutalizing their persons. The whip, the chain, the gag, the thumb-screw, the blood-hound, the stocks, and all the other bloody paraphernalia of the slave system, are indispensably necessary to the relation of master and slave. The slave must be subjected to these, or he ceases to be a slave. Let him know that the whip is burned; that the fetters have been turned to some useful and profitable employment; that the chain is no longer for his limbs; that the bloodhound is no longer to be put upon his track; that his master's authority over him is no longer to be enforced by taking his life — and immediately he walks out from the house of bondage and asserts his freedom as a man. The slaveholder finds it necessary to have these implements to keep the slave in bondage; finds it necessary to be able to say, "Unless you do so and so; unless you do as I bid you — I will take away your life!"

Some of the most awful scenes of cruelty are constantly taking place in the middle states of the Union. We have in those states what are called the slave-breeding states. Allow me to speak plainly. Although it is harrowing to your feelings, it is necessary that the facts of the case should be stated. We have in the United States slave-breeding states. The very state from which the minister from our court to yours comes, is one of these states — Maryland, where men, women, and children are reared for the market, just as horses, sheep, and swine are raised for the market. Slave-rearing is there looked upon as a legitimate trade; the law sanctions it, public opinion upholds it, the church does not condemn it. It goes on in all its bloody horrors, sustained by the auctioneer's block. If you would see the cruelties of this system, hear the following narrative. Not long since the following scene occurred. A slave-woman and a slave-man had united themselves as man and wife in the absence of any law to protect them as man and wife. They had lived together by the permission, not by right, of their master, and they had reared a family. The master found it expedient, and for his interest, to sell them. He did not ask them their wishes in regard to the matter at all; they were not consulted. The man and woman were brought to the auctioneer's block, under the sound of the hammer. The cry was raised, "Here goes; who bids cash?" Think of it — a man and wife to be sold! The woman was placed on the auctioneer's block; her limbs, as is customary, were brutally exposed to the purchasers, who examined her with all the freedom with which they would examine a horse. There stood the husband, powerless; no right to his wife; the master's right preeminent. She was sold. He was next brought to the auctioneer's block. His eyes followed his wife in the distance; and he looked beseechingly, imploringly, to the man that had bought his wife, to buy him also. But he was at length bid off to another person. He

was about to be separated forever from her he loved. No word of his, no work of his, could save him from this separation. He asked permission of his new master to go and take the hand of his wife at parting. It was denied him. In the agony of his soul he rushed from the man who had just bought him, that he might take a farewell of his wife; but his way was obstructed, he was struck over the head with a loaded whip, and was held for a moment; but his agony was too great. When he was let go, he fell a corpse at the feet of his master. His heart was broken. Such scenes are the every-day fruits of American slavery. Some two years since, the Hon. Seth M. Gates, an anti-slavery gentleman of the state of New York, a representative in the congress of the United States, told me he saw with his own eyes the following circumstance. In the national District of Columbia, over which the star-spangled emblem is constantly waving, where orators are ever holding forth on the subject of American liberty, American democracy, American republicanism, there are two slave prisons. When going across a bridge, leading to one of these prisons, he saw a young woman run out, bare-footed and bare-headed, and with very little clothing on. She was running with all speed to the bridge he was approaching. His eye was fixed upon her, and he stopped to see what was the matter. He had not paused long before he saw three men run out after her. He now knew what the nature of the case was; a slave escaping from her chains — a young woman, a sister — escaping from the bondage in which she had been held. She made her way to the bridge, but had not reached it, ere from the Virginia side there came two slaveholders. As soon as they saw them, her pursuers called out, "Stop her!" True to their Virginian instincts, they came to the rescue of their brother kidnappers, across the bridge. The poor girl now saw that there was no chance for her. It was a trying time. She knew if she went back, she must be a slave forever — she must be dragged down to the scenes of pollution which the slaveholders continually provide for most of the poor, sinking, wretched young women, whom they call their property. She formed her resolution; and just as those who were about to take her, were going to put hands upon her, to drag her back, she leaped over the balustrades of the bridge, and down she went to rise no more. She chose death, rather than to go back into the hands of those christian slaveholders from whom she had escaped.

Can it be possible that such things as these exist in the United States? Are not these the exceptions? Are any such scenes as this general? Are not such deeds condemned by the law and denounced by public opinion? Let me read to you a few of the laws of the slaveholding states of America. I think no better exposure of slavery can be made than is made by the laws of the states in which slavery exists. I prefer reading the laws to making any statement in confirmation of what I have said myself; for the slaveholders cannot object to this testimony, since it is the calm, the cool, the deliberate enactment of their wisest heads, of their most clear-sighted, their own constituted representatives. "If more than seven slaves together are found in any road without a white person, twenty lashes a piece; for visiting a plantation without a written pass, ten lashes; for letting loose a boat from where it is made fast, thirty-nine lashes for the first offense; and for the second, shall have cut off from his head one ear; for keeping or carrying a club, thirty-nine lashes; for having any article for sale, without a ticket from his master, ten lashes; for traveling in any other than the most usual and accustomed road, when going alone to any place, forty lashes; for traveling in the night without a pass, forty lashes." I am afraid you do not understand the awful character of these lashes. You must bring it before your mind. A human being in a perfect state of nudity, tied hand and foot to a stake, and a strong man standing behind with a heavy whip, knotted at the end, each blow cutting into the flesh, and leaving the warm blood dripping to the feet; and for these trifles. "For being found in another person's negro-quarters, forty lashes; for hunting

with dogs in the woods, thirty lashes; for being on horseback without the written permission of his master, twenty-five lashes; for riding or going abroad in the night, or riding horses in the day time, without leave, a slave may be whipped, cropped, or branded in the cheek with the letter R, or otherwise punished, such punishment not extending to life, or so as to render him unfit for labor." The laws referred to, may be found by consulting Brevard's Digest; Haywood's Manual; Virginia Revised Code; Prince's Digest; Missouri Laws; Mississippi Revised Code. A man, for going to visit his brethren, without the permission of his master — and in many instances he may not have that permission; his master, from caprice or other reasons, may not be willing to allow it — may be caught on his way, dragged to a post, the branding-iron heated, and the name of his master or the letter R branded into his cheek or on his forehead. They treat slaves thus, on the principle that they must punish for light offenses, in order to prevent the commission of larger ones. I wish you to mark that in the single state of Virginia there are seventy-one crimes for which a colored man may be executed; while there are only three of these crimes, which, when committed by a white man, will subject him to that punishment. There are many of these crimes which if the white man did not commit, he would be regarded as a scoundrel and a coward. In the state of Maryland, there is a law to this effect: that if a slave shall strike his master, he may be hanged, his head severed from his body, his body quartered, and his head and quarters set up in the most prominent places in the neighborhood. If a colored woman, in the defense of her own virtue, in defense of her own person, should shield herself from the brutal attacks of her tyrannical master, or make the slightest resistance, she may be killed on the spot. No law whatever will bring the guilty man to justice for the crime.

But you will ask me, can these things be possible in a land professing christianity? Yes, they are so; and this is not the worst. No; a darker feature is yet to be presented than the mere existence of these facts. I have to inform you that the religion of the southern states, at this time, is the great supporter, the great sanctioner of the bloody atrocities to which I have referred. While America is printing tracts and bibles; sending missionaries abroad to convert the heathen; expending her money in various ways for the promotion of the gospel in foreign lands — the slave not only lies forgotten, uncared for, but is trampled under foot by the very churches of the land. What have we in America? Why, we have slavery made part of the religion of the land. Yes, the pulpit there stands up as the great defender of this cursed *institution*, as it is called. Ministers of religion come forward and torture the hallowed pages of inspired wisdom to sanction the bloody deed. They stand forth as the foremost, the strongest defenders of this "institution." As a proof of this, I need not do more than state the general fact, that slavery has existed under the droppings of the sanctuary of the south for the last two hundred years, and there has not been any war between the *religion* and the *slavery* of the south. Whips, chains, gags, and thumb-screws have all lain under the droppings of the sanctuary, and instead of rusting from off the limbs of the bondman, those droppings have served to preserve them in all their strength. Instead of preaching the gospel against this tyranny, rebuke, and wrong, ministers of religion have sought, by all and every means, to throw in the back-ground whatever in the bible could be construed into opposition to slavery, and to bring forward that which they could torture into its support. This I conceive to be the darkest feature of slavery, and the most difficult to attack, because it is identified with religion, and exposes those who denounce it to the charge of infidelity. Yes, those with whom I have been laboring, namely, the old organization anti-slavery society of America, have been again and again stigmatized as infidels, and for what reason? Why, solely in consequence of the faithfulness of their attacks upon the slaveholding religion of the southern states, and the northern

religion that sympathizes with it. I have found it difficult to speak on this matter without persons coming forward and saying, "Douglass, are you not afraid of injuring the cause of Christ? You do not desire to do so, we know; but are you not undermining religion?" This has been said to me again and again, even since I came to this country, but I cannot be induced to leave off these exposures. I love the religion of our blessed Savior. I love that religion that comes from above, in the "wisdom of God, which is first pure, then peaceable, gentle, and easy to be entreated, full of mercy and good fruits, without partiality and without hypocrisy." I love that religion that sends its votaries to bind up the wounds of him that has fallen among thieves. I love that religion that makes it the duty of its disciples to visit the fatherless and the widow in their affliction. I love that religion that is based upon the glorious principle, of love to God and love to man; which makes its followers do unto others as they themselves would be done by. If you demand liberty to yourself, it says, grant it to your neighbors. If you claim a right to think for yourself, it says, allow your neighbors the same right. If you claim to act for yourself, it says, allow your neighbors the same right. It is because I love this religion that I hate the slaveholding, the woman-whipping, the mind-darkening, the soul-destroying religion that exists in the southern states of America. It is because I regard the one as good, and pure, and holy, that I cannot but regard the other as bad, corrupt, and wicked. Loving the one I must hate the other; holding to the one I must reject the other.

I may be asked, why I am so anxious to bring this subject before the British public — why I do not confine my efforts to the United States? My answer is, first, that slavery is the common enemy of mankind, and all mankind should be made acquainted with its abominable character. My next answer is, that the slave is a man, and, as such, is entitled to your sympathy as a brother. All the feelings, all the susceptibilities, all the capacities, which you have, he has. He is a part of the human family.

He has been the prey — the common prey — of christendom for the last three hundred years, and it is but right, it is but just, it is but proper, that his wrongs should be known throughout the world. I have another reason for bringing this matter before the British public, and it is this: slavery is a system of wrong, so blinding to all around, so hardening to the heart, so corrupting to the morals, so deleterious to religion, so sapping to all the principles of justice in its immediate vicinity, that the community surrounding it lack the moral stamina necessary to its removal. It is a system of such gigantic evil, so strong, so overwhelming in its power, that no one nation is equal to its removal. It requires the humanity of christianity, the morality of the world to remove it. Hence, I call upon the people of Britain to look at this matter, and to exert the influence I am about to show they possess, for the removal of slavery from America. I can appeal to them, as strongly by their regard for the slaveholder as for the slave, to labor in this cause. I am here, because you have an influence on America that no other nation can have. You have been drawn together by the power of steam to a marvelous extent; the distance between London and Boston is now reduced to some twelve or fourteen days, so that the denunciations against slavery, uttered in London this week, may be heard in a fortnight in the streets of Boston, and reverberating amidst the hills of Massachusetts. There is nothing said here against slavery that will not be recorded in the United States. I am here, also, because the slaveholders do not want me to be here; they would rather that I were not here. I have adopted a maxim laid down by Napoleon, never to occupy ground which the enemy would like me to occupy. The slaveholders would much rather have me, if I will denounce slavery, denounce it in the northern states, where their friends and supporters are, who will stand by and mob me for denouncing it. They feel something as the man felt, when he uttered his prayer, in which he made out a most horrible case for himself, and one of his neighbors touched him and said, "My friend, I always had the opinion of you that you have now expressed for yourself — that you are a very great sinner." Coming from himself, it was all very well, but coming from a stranger it was rather cutting. The slaveholders felt that when slavery was denounced among themselves, it was not so bad; but let one of the slaves get loose, let him summon the people of Britain, and make known to them the conduct of the slaveholders toward their slaves, and it cuts them to the quick, and produces a sensation such as would be produced by nothing else. The power I exert now is something like the power that is exerted by the man at the end of the lever; my influence now is just in proportion to the distance that I am from the United States. My exposure of slavery abroad will tell more upon the hearts and consciences of slaveholders, than if I was attacking them in America; for almost every paper that I now receive from the United States, comes teeming with statements about this fugitive negro, calling him a "glib-tongued scoundrel," and saying that he is running out against the institutions and people of America. I deny the charge that I am saying a word against the institutions of America, or the people, as such. What I have to say is against slavery and slaveholders. I feel at liberty to speak on this subject. I have on my back the marks of the lash; I have four sisters and one brother now under the galling chain. I feel it my duty to cry aloud and spare not. I am not averse to having the good opinion of my fellow-creatures. I am not averse to being kindly regarded by all men; but I am bound, even at the hazard of making a large class of religionists in this country hate me, oppose me, and malign me as they have done — I am bound by the prayers, and tears, and entreaties of three millions of kneeling bondsmen, to have no compromise with men who are in any shape or form connected with the slaveholders of America. I expose slavery in this country, because to expose it is to kill it. Slavery is one of those monsters of darkness to whom the light of truth is death. Expose slavery, and it dies. Light is to slavery what the heat of the sun is to the root of a tree; it must die under it. All the slaveholder asks of me is silence. He does not ask me to go abroad and preach *in favor* of slavery; he does not ask any one to do that. He would not say that slavery is a good thing, but the best under the circumstances. The slaveholders want total darkness on the subject. They want the hatchway shut down, that the monster may crawl in his den of darkness, crushing human hopes and happiness, destroying the bondman at will, and having no one to reprove or rebuke him. Slavery shrinks from the light; it hateth the light, neither cometh to the light, lest its deeds should be reproved. To tear off the mask from this abominable system, to expose it to the light of heaven, aye, to the heat of the sun, that it may burn and wither it out of existence, is my object in coming to this country. I want the slaveholder surrounded, as by a wall of anti-slavery fire, so that he may see the condemnation of himself and his system glaring down in letters of light. I want him to feel that he has no sympathy in England, Scotland, or Ireland; that he has none in Canada, none in Mexico, none among the poor wild Indians; that the voice of the civilized, aye, and savage world is against him. I would have condemnation blaze down upon him in every direction, till, stunned and overwhelmed with shame and confusion, he is compelled to let go the grasp he holds upon the persons of his victims, and restore them to their long-lost rights.

--------- 3.28 ---------

THE NORTH STAR
Frederick Douglass and
Martin Delany

When Frederick Douglass returned from Britain in 1847, he teamed with black radical abolitionist Martin Delany to found a weekly newspaper. With money raised during Douglass's travels, the pair began publishing The North Star on December 3, 1847, from Rochester, New York. It would be the first of three abolitionist and civil rights newspapers Douglass established between then and the

end of his journalistic career (each, essentially, the same original paper given a new name). In addition to his continued lecturing, the papers served as Douglass's voice and, like William Lloyd Garrison's *Liberator*, offered a vehicle for the writings of black thinkers, poets and advocates of his time. Its motto proclaimed, "Right is of no Sex - Truth is of no Color - God is the Father of us all, and we are all brethren." The paper, influential beyond its number, circulated 4,000 copies around the world.

From this perch Douglass also expanded his advocacy to include the rights of women, of all races. The Abolitionist and Women's Movements intersected considerably, largely because so many women who were involved in the fight against slavery were also pioneers in the Women's Movement. But female political leadership was still taboo, and many abolitionists were uncomfortable with, if not hostile to, the participation of women. Douglass and Garrison were notable exceptions. They not only embraced female involvement in the abolitionist movement, they championed women's rights as well. Douglass would be the only male in attendance at the first Women's Rights Convention in Seneca Falls in 1838. He published the following item discussing the meeting in the July 28, 1848, *North Star*.

One of the most interesting events of the past week, was the holding of what is technically styled a Woman's Rights Convention at Seneca Falls. The speaking, addresses, and resolutions of this extraordinary meeting was wholly conducted by women; and although they evidently felt themselves in a novel position, it is but simple justice to say that their whole proceedings were characterized by marked ability and dignity. No one present, we think, however much he might be disposed to differ from the views advanced by the leading speakers on that occasion, will fail to give them credit for brilliant talents and excellent dispositions. In this meeting, as in other deliberative assemblies, there were frequent differences of opinion and animated discussion; but in no case was there the slightest absence of good feeling and decorum. Several interesting documents setting forth the rights as well as the grievances of women were read. Among these was a Declaration of Sentiments, to be regarded as the basis of a grand movement for attaining the civil, social, political, and religious rights of women. We should not do justice to our own convictions, or to the excellent persons connected with this infant movement, if we did not in this connection offer a few remarks on the general subject which the Convention met to consider and the objects they seek to attain. In doing so, we are not insensible that the bare mention of this truly important subject in any other than terms of contemptuous ridicule and scornful disfavor, is likely to excite against us the fury of bigotry and the folly of prejudice. A discussion of the rights of animals would be regarded with far more complacency by many of what are called the "wise" and the "good" of our land, than would a discussion of the rights of women. It is, in their estimation to be guilty of evil thoughts, to think that woman is entitled to equal rights with man. Many who have at last made the discovery that the negroes have some rights as well as other members of the human family, have yet to be convinced that women are entitled to any. Eight years ago a number of persons of this description actually abandoned the anti-slavery cause, lest by giving their influence in that direction they might possibly be giving countenance to the dangerous heresy that woman, in respect to rights, stands on an equal footing with man. In the judgment of such persons the American slave system, with all its concomitant horrors, is less to be deplored than this "wicked" idea. It is perhaps needless to say, that we cherish little sympathy for such sentiments or respect for such prejudices. Standing as we do up on the watch-tower of human freedom, we cannot be deterred from an expression of our approbation of any movement, however humble, to improve and elevate the character of any members of the human family. While it is impossible for us to go into this subject at length, and dispose of the various objections which are often urged against such a doctrine as that of female equality, we are free to say that in respect to political rights, we hold woman to be justly entitled to all we claim for man. We go farther, and express our conviction that all political rights which it is expedient for man to exercise, it is equally for woman. All that distinguishes man as an intelligent and accountable being, is equally true of woman, and if that government only is just which governs by the free consent of the governed, there can be no reason in the world for denying to woman the exercise of the elective franchise, or a hand in making and administering the laws of the land. Our doctrine is that "right is of no sex." We therefore bid the women engaged in this movement our humble Godspeed.

—————— 3.29 ——————

'AR'N'T I A WOMAN?'
Sojourner Truth

Born Isabella Baumfree, to Dutch-speaking slave parents, the woman who would become Sojourner Truth was manumitted when New York abolished slavery in 1827. She moved to New York City and, an evangelical Methodist, began preaching at camp meetings. She went on to join a series of religious extremist groups, including the apocalyptic Millerites in the 1840s. In 1843, the year the Millerites predicted as the end of the world, Isabella discarded her past and renamed herself Sojourner Truth.

Shortly thereafter, Truth met Frederick Douglass and other abolitionists and joined their fold as a lecturer. Perhaps more than any other person, Truth embodies the bridge between the Abolitionist and the Women's rights movements. She styled herself a voice of working-class women, black and white, and thus has also become a hero of labor movements over the years. The details of Truth's life and career are shrouded in mystery. Her 1878 autobiography, among the most popular slave narratives ever published, is the sole source of information on her life.

Her most famous speech, delivered at the 1851 Women's Rights Convention in Akron, Ohio, is itself an example of how Truth occupies a space between reality and myth in African-American history. It was in this speech that she supposedly issued her bold inquiry, "Ar'n't I a Woman?" But the original account of the speech, written by her colleague Marcus Robinson for the *Anti-Slavery Buglar*, did not contain the phrase. A decade later, in 1863, the conference's organizer, Frances Dana Gage, published her own account of the meeting in which

Truth speaks in a thick southern dialect and issues the famous question. In both versions, however, the speech's revolutionary message is the same: the days of the white man's rule is numbered, for slaves of the South and women of the North were fed up with his oppression.

A. Original account in the *Anti-Slavery Buglar*

... One of the most unique and interesting speeches of the convention was made by Sojourner Truth, an emancipated slave. It is impossible to transfer it to paper, or convey any adequate idea of the effect it produced upon the audience. Those only can appreciate it who saw her powerful form, her whole-souled, earnest gesture, and listened to her strong and truthful tones. She came forward to the platform and addressing the President said with great simplicity: "May I say a few words?" Receiving an affirmative answer, she proceeded:

I want to say a few words about this matter. I am a woman right? I have as much muscle as any man, and can do as much work as any man. I have plowed and reaped and husked and chopped and mowed, and can any man do more than that? I have heard much about the sexes being equal. I can carry as much as any man, and can eat as much too, if I can get it. I am as strong as any man that is now. As for intellect, all I can say is, if a woman have a pint, and a man a quart — why can't she have her little pint full? You need not be afraid to give us our rights for fear we will take too much, — for we can't take more than our pint'll hold. The poor men seems to be all in confusion, and don't know what to do. Why children, if you have woman's rights, give it to her and you will feel better. You will have your own rights, and they won't be so much trouble. I can't read, but I can hear. I have heard the bible and have learned that Eve caused man to sin. Well, if woman upset the world, do give her a chance to set it right side up again. The Lady has spoken about Jesus, how he never spurned woman from him, and she was right. When Lazarus died, Mary and Martha came to him with faith and love and

besought him to raise their brother. And Jesus wept and Lazarus came forth. And how came Jesus into the world? Through God who created him and the woman who bore him. Man, where was your part? But the women are coming up blessed be God and a few of the men are coming up with them. But man is in a tight place, the poor slave is on him, woman is coming on him, he is surely between a hawk and a buzzard.

B. Frances Dana Gage's version

In Gage's version, the convention had been rocked by the news that Truth, a black woman associated with abolition, might address it. Some believed that the women's movement would damage itself by "mixing up with abolition and niggers." (Abolitionist supporters of the women's movement faced similar complaints from those who feared discrediting their cause by allowing women to be leaders.) Gage, as the president, decided to allow Truth a podium, from which she delivered her famed address.

... slowly from her seat in the corner rose Sojourner Truth, who till now had scarcely lifted her head. "Don't let her speak!" gasped half a dozen in my ear. She moved slowly and solemnly to the front, laid her old bonnet at her feet, and turned her great speaking eyes to me. There was a hissing sound of disapprobation above and below. I rose and announced "Sojourner Truth," and begged the audience to keep silence for a few moments.

The tumult subsided at once, and every eye was fixed on this almost Amazon form, which stood nearly six feet high, head erect, and eyes piercing the upper air like one in a dream. At her first word there was a profound hush. She spoke in deep tones, which, though not loud, reached every ear in the house, and away through the throng at the doors and windows.

"Wall, chilern, whar dar is so much racket dar must be somethin' out o' kilter. I tink dat 'twixt de nigger of de Souf and de womin at de Norf, all talkin' 'bout rights, de white men will be in a fix pretty soon. But what's all dis here talkin' 'bout?

"Dat man ober dar say dat womin needs to be helped into carriages, and lifted ober ditches, and to hab de best place everywhar. Nobody eber halps me into carriages, or ober mudpuddles, or gibs me any best place!"

And raising herself to her full height, and her voice to a pitch like rolling thunder, she asked, "And ar'n't I a woman? Look at me! Look at my arm! [And here she bared her right arm to the shoulder, showing her tremendous muscular power] "I have ploughed, and planted, and gathered into barns, and no man could head me! And ar'n't I a woman? I could work as much and eat as much as a man — when I could get it — and bear de lash as well! And ar'n't' I a woman? I have borne thirteen chilern, and seen 'em mos' all sold off the slavery, and when I cried out with my mother's grief, none but Jesus heard me! And ar'n't I a woman?

"Den dey talks 'bout dis ting in de head; what dis dey call it?" "Intellect," whispered someone near. "Dat's it, honey. What's dat got to do wid womin's rights or nigger's rights? If my cup won't hold but a pint, and yourn holds a quart, wouldn't ye be mean not to let me have my little half-measure full?" And she pointed her significant finger, and sent a keen glance at the minister who had made the argument. The cheering was long and loud.

"Den dat little man in black dar, he say women can't have as much rights as men, 'cause Christ wan't a woman! Whar did your Christ come from?" Rolling thunder couldn't have stilled that crowd, as did those deep, wonderful tones, as she stood there with outstretched arms and eyes of fire. Raising her voice still louder, she repeated, "Whar did your Christ come from? From God and a woman! Man had nothin' to do wid Him." Oh, what a rebuke that was to the little man.

Turning again to another objector, she took up the defense of Mother Eve, I cannot follow her through it all. It was pointed and witty, and solemn; eliciting at almost every sentence deafening applause; and she ended by asserting, "If de fust woman God ever made was strong enough to turn de world upside down all alone, dese women togedder [and she glanced her eye over the platform] ought to be able to turn it back, and get it right side up again! And now dey is asking to do it, de men better let 'em." Long continued cheering greeted this. "Bleeged to ye for hearin' on me, and now ole Sojourner han't got nothin' more to say."

Amid roars of applause, she returned to her corner, leaving more than one of us with streaming eyes, and hearts beating with gratitude. She had taken us up in her strong arms and carried us safely over the slough of difficulty, turning the whole tide in our favor. I have never in my life seen anything like the magical influence that subdued the mobbish spirit of the day, and turned the sneers and jeers of an excited crowd into notes of respect and admiration. Hundreds rushed up to shake hands with her, and congratulate the glorious old mother, and bid her God-speed on her mission of "testifyin' agin concerning the wickedness of this 'ere people."

———— 3.30 ————

'MRS. BRADFORD HAD A SON ABOUT TEN YEARS OLD; SHE USED TO MAKE HIM BEAT ME AND SPIT IN MY FACE'
Leonard Black

Slave narratives provided, then and now, a personalized window into the everyday lives of the men, women and children who lived through, and escaped from, the slave system. They formed the backbone of the abolitionist literary movement, and drove the cause's steady growth among northern whites — who knew little of the lives of black people even in their own communities, let alone of those in slavery.

While the narratives of Frederick Douglass and other renowned African Americans of the time now provide us with useful biographical information on history-makers, others offer descriptions of the equally important, if more pedestrian, average life. In the following excerpts from the 1847 narrative of escaped slave Leonard Black, the author gives a unique look at childhood as a slave.

... At six years of age I was placed with a Mr. Bradford, separated from my father, mother and family. But the eye of God was upon me, and blessed me. My master was a carpenter, and much from home — Mrs. Bradford beat me so much that her husband sent me to his father's. Mrs. Bradford ordered me one day to take a bushel of corn up stairs; but I was unable to do it, upon which she knocked me down with the johnny-cake board, cutting my head so badly that it bled more than a quart. It was then that I thought of my mother. My little friends — who have your liberty and the protecting hand of parents — these are some of the fruits of slavery; let your hearts warm with gratitude to the great Giver of all good, for the blessings you enjoy. Mrs. Bradford had a son about ten years old; she used to make him beat me and spit in my face. Here I was, a poor slave boy, without father or mother to take my part.

At the end of two years, Mrs. Bradford beat me so much, that her husband, fearing she would kill me, placed me at his father's, where I remained until the death of the old gentleman. But old Mr. Bradford was worse than Mrs. Bradford! He had been a professor of religion, a class leader in the Methodist Church, but at this time he was a backslider; yea, a wanderer from God, and as cold as though he had never been warmed by the vivifying power of the religion of Jesus Christ.

I lived in this family seven and a half years, and when I left I was thirteen years old. During this time I had no hat, no pantaloons, but one pair of shoes, and wore a lindsey slip only. I was not allowed to sit down while I ate my meals. For my breakfast I had a pint of pot liquor, half a herring, and a little piece of bread. Whether this would stay the cravings of a young appetite or not, there was no more to be had. For my dinner I had a pint of pot liquor, and the skin off of the pork. I must say as the colored people say at the south, when singing to cheer their hearts while under the burning sun, and the crack of the whip, remembering what is placed before them every day for food — "My old master is a hardhearted man; he eats the meat, and gives poor nigger bones." At night I had a bit of bread for my supper, and a piece of carpet for my bed, spread down on the hearth, winter and summer. In the winter, when the fire got low, I used to burn my feet by getting them into the embers.

My work, in the winter time, was to fetch wood from the swamp up to the house. Being without shoes or hat, and thinly clad, I used to go into the house to warm myself. When in the house for this purpose, at one time, old Mr. Bradford followed me in, and said: "If you want to be warmed, I'll warm you." He took the tongs, heated them in the fire, and branded my legs; and the scars are there to this day. I could not sit down in consequence of the wound. He whipped me also, and used to put my head under the fence.

Christians! I beseech you, do not become backsliders; especially slave-holding Christians! for the terrible effects of backsliding, slave-holding Christianity are awfully developed in my history!

Shortly after this, the death of this man delivered me from his hands. I rejoiced. God only knows whether he went to perdition. With all my heart I have forgiven him. I expect to meet him at the bar of God with the scars and the tongs. Farewell, Mr. Bradford! But this is not all. He left all his property to his daughter Elizabeth; and her brother Nathan, a taxgatherer, was overseer of the farm for her. One year after her father's death, Elizabeth got married to Wm. Gardener, a gentleman from Baltimore, a member of the Methodist Church. I then thought I should have a good master. But oh, my soul! it was worse and worse! All is not gold that shines, nor silver that glitters. He had not been married a great while before my heart beat and my feet burned. He was a collier, engaged in burning charcoal, and used to draw it to the village landing, and sometimes to Baltimore.

One day he left me twenty-five bushels of coal to draw. By being broken of my rest the night previous, engaged in watching the coal pit, I was tired and sleepy. When I had drawn all the coal out, supposing I had put the fire out, I laid down to rest my weary limbs. The coal burned up. Mr. Gardner came into the woods where I lay asleep, hallooed and scared me up; he struck me with the shovel, and cut my head so that I knew nothing for two days. I was so weak from the loss of blood, that he was compelled to carry me home on his shoulders, covering himself with blood. His wife was very much alarmed. We were about a mile from home, and he told me not to speak of it.

At another time, he cut my head with a hoe handle, so that altogether I was sick for a long time. Mr. Gardner had a very quick temper, and would strike me with anything he happened to have in his hand, reckless of consequences.

One day, Eliza (a slave girl of his,) and myself, went into the water-melon patch, procured a melon and ate it. We were compelled to this by the promptings of hunger, for the living had not altered since the death of Mr. Bradford. Eliza was about eighteen years of age. For that offence, our cruel master stripped us and tied us both up together, and whipped us till the blood ran down on the ground in a puddle.

When I was sick, he used to send me into the place where they smoked meat, for fear I should vomit on the floor. On Wednesdays, there were meetings in the meeting-house, and Mr. Gardner used to make me stay away from the house, for the minister would come home with him, and he was fearful I should tell him of his cruel treatment. He did not say as Hagar of old — "Thou, God, seest me."

One day he sent me to drive the horse from the peach tree. The horse kicked me in the head, and I was laid up six months. My head was sewed up; and I also received a great many knocks in the side, from the effects of which I have not yet recovered! On one occasion, he struck me in the mouth with an iron-toothed rake, which knocked out one of my front teeth. All this time, my more fortunate reader, I was a poor slave boy, with no one to pity me, with no

parents to take my part. I had no father; no mother! But God pitied me. The eye of the all-merciful God, without whose notice not a sparrow falls to the ground, was upon me. He it was that bore my feeble spirit up, when my lacerated and quivering frame was writhing under the God-defying curse of slavery. ...

--------- 3.31 ---------

A TALE OF ESCAPE AND BETRAYAL
Henry Bibb

Henry Bibb's 1849 narrative provides a thrilling account of his repeated, and ultimately successful, effort to escape slavery and flee to Canada. Like Leonard Black's, Bibb's narrative lacked the celebrity of a Frederick Douglass or the imprint of an abolitionist organization to propel it to fame upon release. But its detailed descriptions of his escapes later drew the attention of slavery scholars, and the narrative remains an important resource today. In the excerpt below, Bibb describes a failed attempt to escape from Kentucky. He originally made it out of the state, going as far as Michigan. But when he returned for his family, disguised as a peddler and passing for white, he was betrayed by slave catchers posing as abolitionists, some of whom were black. Such bands of hired black slave catchers were common in the middle 19th century, as white slaveholders found them an effective counter to the Underground Railroad.

In the fall or winter of 1837 I formed a resolution that I would escape, if possible, to Canada, for my Liberty. I commenced from that hour making preparations for the dangerous experiment of breaking the chains that bound me as a slave. My preparation for this voyage consisted in the accumulation of a little money, perhaps not exceeding two dollars and fifty cents, and a suit which I had never been seen or known to wear before; this last was to avoid detection.

On the twenty-fifth of December, 1837, my long anticipated time had arrived when I was to put into operation my former resolution, which was to bolt for Liberty or consent to die a Slave. I acted upon the former, although I confess it to be one of the most self-denying acts of my whole life, to take leave of an affectionate wife, who stood before me on my departure with dear little Frances in her arms, and with tears of sorrow in her eyes as she bid me a long farewell. It required all the moral courage that I was master of to suppress my feeling while taking leave of my little family.

Had Malinda known my intention at that time, it would not have been possible for me to have got away, and I might have this day been a slave. Notwithstanding every inducement was held out to me to run away if I would be free, and the voice of liberty was thundering in my very soul, "Be free, oh, man! be free," I was struggling against a thousand obstacles which had clustered around my mind to bind my wounded spirit still in the dark prison of mental degradation. My strong attachments to friends and relatives, with all the love of home and birth-place which is so natural among the human family, twined about my heart and were hard to break away from. And withal, the fear of being pursued with guns and bloodhounds, and of being killed, or captured and taken to the extreme South, to linger out my days in hopeless bondage on some cotton or sugar plantation, all combined to deter me. But I had counted the cost, and was fully prepared to make the sacrifice. The time for fulfilling my pledge was then at hand. I must forsake friends and neighbors, wife and child, or consent to live and die a slave.

By the permission of my keeper, I started out to work for myself on Christmas. I went to the Ohio River, which was but a short distance from Bedford. My excuse for wanting to go there was to get work. High wages were offered for hands to work in a slaughter-house. But in place of my going to work there, according to promise, when I arrived at the river I managed to find a conveyance to cross over into a free state. I was landed in the village of Madison, Indiana, where steamboats were landing every day and night, passing up and down the river, which afforded me a good opportunity of getting a boat passage to Cincinnati. My anticipa-tion being worked up to the highest pitch, no sooner was the curtain of night dropped over the village, than I secreted myself where no one could see me, and changed my suit ready for the passage. Soon I heard the welcome sound of a Steamboat coming up the river Ohio, which was soon to waft me beyond the limits of the human slave markets of Kentucky. When the boat had landed at Madison, notwithstanding my strong desire to get off, my heart trembled within me in view of the great danger to which I was exposed in taking passage on board of a Southern Steamboat; hence before I took passage, I kneeled down before the Great I Am, and prayed for his aid and protection, which He bountifully bestowed even beyond my expectation; for I felt myself to be unworthy. I then stept boldly on the deck of this splendid swift-running Steamer, bound for the city of Cincinnati. This being the first voyage, that I had ever taken on board of a Steamboat, I was filled with fear and excitement, knowing that I was surrounded by the vilest enemies of God and man, liable to be seized and bound hand and foot by any white man, and taken back into captivity. But I crowded myself back from the light among the deck passengers, where it would be difficult to distinguish me from a white man. Every time during the night that the mate came round with a light after the hands, I was afraid he would see I was a colored man, and take me up; hence I kept from the light as much as possible. Some men love darkness rather than light, because their deeds are evil; but this was not the case with myself; it was to avoid detection in doing right. This was one of the instances of my adventures that my affinity with the Anglo-Saxon race, and even slaveholders, worked well for my escape. But no thanks to them for it. While in their midst they have not only robbed me of my labor and liberty, but they have almost entirely robbed me of my dark complexion. Being so near the color of a slaveholder, they could not, or did not find me out that night among the white passengers. There was one of the deck hands on board called out on his watch, whose hammock was swinging up near by me. I asked him if he would let me lie in it. He said if I would pay him twenty-five cents that I might lie in it until day. I readily paid him the price and got into the hammock. No one could see my face to know whether I was white or colored, while I was in the hammock; but I never closed eyes for sleep that night. I had often heard explosions on board of Steamboats; and every time the boat landed, and blowed off steam, I was afraid the boilers had bursted and we should all be killed; but I lived through the night amid the many dangers to which I was exposed. I still maintained my position in the hammock, until the next morning about 8 o'clock, when I heard the passengers saying the boat was near Cincinnati; and by this time I supposed that the attention of the people would be turned to the city, and I might pass off unnoticed.

There were no questions asked me while on board the boat. The boat landed about 9 o'clock in the morning in Cincinnati, and I waited until after most of the passengers had gone off of the boat; I then walked as gracefully up street as if I was not running away, until I had got pretty well up Broadway. My object was to go to Canada, but having no knowledge of the road, it was necessary for me to make some inquiry before I left the city. I was afraid to ask a white person, and I could see no colored person to ask. But fortunately for me I found a company of little boys at play in the street, and through these little boys, by asking them indirect questions, I found the residence of a colored man.

"Boys, can you tell me where that old colored man lives who saws wood, and works at jobs around the streets?"

"What is his name?" said one of the boys,

"I forget."

"Is it old Job Dundy?"

"Is Dundy a colored man?"

"Yes, sir."

"That is the very man I am looking for; will you show me, where he lives?"

"Yes," said the little boy, and pointed me out the house.

Mr. D. invited me in, and I found him to be a true friend. He asked me if I was a slave from Kentucky, and if I ever intended to go back into slavery? Not knowing yet whether he was truly in favor of slaves running away, I told him that I had just come over to spend my christmas holydays, and that I was going back. His reply was, "my son, I would never go back if I was in your place; you have a right to your liberty." I then asked him how I should get my freedom? He referred me to Canada, over which waved freedom's flag, defended by the British Government, upon whose soil there cannot be the foot print of a slave.

He then commenced telling me of the facilities for my escape to Canada; of the Abolitionists; of the Abolition Societies, and of their fidelity to the cause of suffering humanity. This was the first time in my life that ever I had heard of such people being in existence as the Abolitionists. I supposed that they were a different race of people. He conducted me to the house of one of these warm-hearted friends of God and the slave. I found him willing to aid a poor fugitive on his way to Canada, even to the dividing of the last cent, or morsel of bread if necessary.

These kind friends gave me something to eat, and started me on my way to Canada, with a recommendation to a friend on my way. This was the commencement of what was called the under ground rail road to Canada. I walked with bold courage, trusting in the arm of Omnipotence; guided by the unchangable North Star by night, and inspired by an elevated thought that I was fleeing from a land of slavery and oppression, bidding farewell to hand-cuffs, whips, thumb-screws and chains.

I travelled on until I had arrived at the place where I was directed to call on an Abolitionist, but I made no stop: so great were my fears of being pursued by the pro-slavery hunting dogs of the South. I prosecuted my journey vigorously for nearly forty-eight hours without food or rest, struggling against external difficulties such as no one can imagine who has never experienced the same: not knowing what moment I might be captured while travelling among strangers, through cold and fear, breasting the north winds, being thinly clad, pelted by the snow storms through the dark hours of the night, and not a house in which I could enter to shelter me from the storm.

The second night from Cincinnati, about midnight, I thought that I should freeze; my shoes were worn through, and my feet were exposed to the bare ground. I approached a house on the road-side, knocked at the door, and asked admission to their fire, but was refused. I went to the next house, and was refused the privilege of their fire-side, to prevent my freezing. This I thought was hard treatment among the human family. But — "Behind a frowning Providence there was a smiling face," which soon shed beams of light upon unworthy me.

The next morning I was still found struggling on my way, faint, hungry, lame, and rest-broken. I could see people taking breakfast from the road-side, but I did not dare to enter their houses to get my breakfast, for neither love nor money. In passing a low cottage, I saw the breakfast table spread with all its bounties, and I could see no male person about the house; the temptation for food was greater than I could resist.

I saw a lady about the table, and I thought that if she was ever so much disposed to take me up, that she would have to catch and hold me, and that would have been impossible. I stepped up to the door with my hat off, and asked her if she would be good enough to sell me a sixpence worth of bread and meat. She cut off a piece and brought it to me; I thanked her for it, and handed her the pay, but instead of receiving it, she burst into tears, and said "never mind the money," but gently turned away bidding me go on my journey. This was altogether unexpected to me: I had found a friend in the time of need among strangers, and nothing could be more cheering in the day of trouble than this. When I left that place I started with bolder courage. The next night I put up at a tavern, and continued stopping at

public houses until my means were about gone. When I got to the Black Swamp in the county of Wood, Ohio, I stopped one night at a hotel, after travelling all day through mud and snow; but I soon found that I should not be able to pay my bill. This was about the time that the "wild-cat banks" were in a flourishing state, and "shin plasters" in abundance; they would charge a dollar for one night's lodging.

After I had found out this, I slipped out of the bar room into the kitchen where the landlady was getting supper; as she had quite a number of travellers to cook for that night, I told her if she would accept my services, I would assist her in getting supper; that I was a cook. She very readily accepted the offer, and I went to work.

She was very much pleased with my work, and the next morning I helped her to get breakfast. She then wanted to hire me for all winter, but I refused for fear I might be pursued. My excuse to her was that I had a brother living in Detroit, whom I was going to see on some important business, and after I got that business attended to I would come back and work for them all winter.

When I started the second morning they paid me fifty cents beside my board, with the understanding that I was to return; but I have not gone back yet.

I arrived the next morning in the village of Perrysburgh, where I found quite a settlement of colored people, many of whom were fugitive slaves. I made my case known to them and they sympathized with me. I was a stranger, and they took me in and persuaded me to spend the winter in Perrysburgh, where I could get employment and go to Canada the next spring, in a steamboat which run from Perrysburgh, if I thought it proper so to do.

I got a job of chopping wood during that winter which enabled me to purchase myself a suit, and after paying my board the next spring, I had saved fifteen dollars in cash. My intention was to go back to Kentucky after my wife.

When I got ready to start, which was about, the first of May, my friends all persuaded me not to go, but to get some other person to go, for fear I might be caught and sold off from my family into slavery forever. But I could not refrain from going back myself, believing that I could accomplish it better than a stranger.

The money that I had would not pass in the South, and for the purpose of getting it off to a good advantage, I took a steamboat passage to Detroit, Michigan, and there I spent all my money for dry goods, to peddle out on my way back through the State of Ohio. I also purchased myself a pair of false whiskers to put on when I got back to Kentucky, to prevent any one from knowing me after night, should they see me. I then started back after my little family.

CHAPTER V.

I succeeded very well in selling out my goods, and when I arrived in Cincinnati, I called on some of my friends who had aided me on my first escape. They also opposed me in going back only for my own good. But it has ever been characteristic of me to persevere in what I undertake.

I took a Steamboat passage which would bring me to where I should want to land about dark, so as to give me a chance to find my family during the night if possible. The boat landed me at the proper time accordingly. This landing was about six miles from Bedford, where my mother and wife lived, but with different families. My mother was the cook at a tavern, in Bedford. When I approached the house where mother was living, I remembered where she slept in the kitchen; her bed was near the window.

It was a bright moonlight night, and in looking through the kitchen window, I saw a person lying in bed about where my mother had formerly slept. I rapped on the glass which awakened the person, in whom I recognised my dear mother, but she knew me not, as I was dressed in disguise with my false whiskers on; but she came to the window and asked who I was and what I wanted. But when I took off my false whiskers, and spoke to her, she knew

my voice, and quickly sprang to the door, clasping my hand, exclaiming, "Oh! is this my son," drawing me into the room, where I was so fortunate as to find Malinda, and little Frances, my wife and child, whom I had left to find the fair climes of liberty, and whom I was then seeking to rescue from perpetual slavery.

They never expected to see me again in this life. I am entirely unable to describe what my feelings were at that time. It was almost like the return, of the prodigal son. There was weeping and rejoicing. They were filled with surprise and fear; with sadness and joy. The sensation of joy at that moment flashed like lightning over my afflicted mind, mingled with a thousand dreadful apprehensions, that none but a heart wounded slave father and husband like myself can possibly imagine. After talking the matter over, we decided it was not best to start with my family that night, as it was very uncertain whether we should get a boat passage immediately. And in case of failure, if Malinda should get back even before daylight the next morning, it would, have excited suspicion against her, as it was not customary for slaves to leave home at that stage of the week without permission. Hence we thought it would be the most, effectual way for her to escape, to start on Saturday night; this being a night on which the slaves of Kentucky are permitted to visit around among their friends, and are often allowed to stay until the afternoon on Sabbath day.

I gave Malinda money to pay her passage on board of a Steamboat to Cincinnati, as it was not safe for me to wait for her until Saturday night; but she was to meet me in Cincinnati, if possible, the next Sunday. Her father was to go with her to the Ohio River on Saturday night, and if a boat passed up during the night she was to get on board at Madison, and come to Cincinnati. If she should fail in getting off that night, she was to try it the next Saturday night. This was the understanding when we separated. This we thought was the best plan for her escape, as there had been so much excitement caused by my running away.

The owners of my wife were very much

afraid that she would follow me; and to prevent her they had told her and other slaves that I had been persuaded off by the Abolitionists, who had promised to set me free, but had sold me off to New Orleans. They told the slaves to beware of the abolitionists, that their object was to decoy off slaves and then sell them off in New Orleans. Some of them believed this, and others believed it not; and the owners of my wife were more watchful over her than the had ever been before as she was unbelieving.

This was in the month of June, 1838. I left Malinda on a bright but lonesome Wednesday night. When I arrived at the river Ohio, I found a small craft chained to a tree, in which I ferried myself across the stream.

I succeeded in getting a Steamboat passage back to Cincinnati, where I put up with one of my abolition friends who knew that I had gone after my family, and who appeared to be much surprised to see me again. I was soon visited by several friends who knew of my having gone back after my family. They wished to know why I had not brought my family with me; but after they understood the plan, and that my family was expected to be in Cincinnati within a few days, they thought it the best and safest plan for us to take a stage passage out to Lake Erie. But being short of money, I was not able to pay my passage in the stage, even if it would have prevented me from being caught by the slave hunters of Cincinnati, or save me from being taken back into bondage for life.

These friends proposed helping me by subscription; I accepted their kind offer, but in going among friends to solicit aid for me, they happened to get among traitors, and kidnappers, both white and colored men, who made their living by that kind of business. Several persons called on me and made me small donations, and among them two white men came in professing to be my friends. They told me not to be afraid of them, they were abolitionists. They asked me a great many questions. They wanted to know if I needed any help? and they wanted to know if it could be possible that a man so near white as myself could be a slave? Could it be possible that men would make slaves of their own children? They expressed great sympathy for me, and gave me fifty cents each; by this they gained my confidence. They asked my master's name; where he lived, &c. After which they left the room, bidding me God speed. These traitors, or land pirates, took passage on board of the first Steamboat down the river, in search of my owners. When they found them, they got a reward of three hundred dollars offered for the re-capture of this "stray" which they had so long and faithfully been hunting, by day and by night, by land and by water, with dogs and with guns, but all without success. This being the last and only chance for dragging me back into hopeless bondage, time and money was no object when they saw a prospect of my being re-taken.

Mr. Gatewood got two of his slaveholding neighbors to go with him to Cincinnati, for the purpose of swearing to anything which might be necessary to change me back into property. They came on to Cincinnati, and with but little effort they soon rallied a mob of ruffians who were willing to become the watch-dogs of slaveholders, for a dram, in connection with a few slavehunting petty constables.

While I was waiting the arrival of my family, I got a job of digging a cellar for the good lady where I was stopping, and while I was digging under the house, all at once I heard a man enter the house; another stept up to the cellar door to where I was at work; he looked in and saw me with my coat off at work. He then rapped over the cellar door on the house side, to notify the one who had entered the house to look for me that I was in the cellar. This strange conduct soon excited suspicion so strong in me, that I could not stay in the cellar and started to come out, but the man who stood by the door, rapped again on the house side, for the other to come to his aid, and told me to stop. I attempted to pass out by him, and he caught hold of me, and drew a pistol, swearing if I did not stop he would shoot me down. By this time I knew that I was betrayed.

I asked him what crime I had committed that I should be murdered.

"I will let you know, very soon," said he.

By this time there were others coming to his aid, and I could see no way by which I could possibly escape the jaws of that hell upon earth.

All my flattering prospects of enjoying my own fire-side, with my little family, were then blasted and gone; and I must bid farewell to friends and freedom forever.

In vain did I look to the infamous laws of the Commonwealth of Ohio, for that protection against violence and outrage, that even the vilest criminal with a white skin might enjoy. But oh! the dreadful thought that after all my sacrifice and struggling to rescue my family from the hands of the oppressor; that I should be dragged back into cruel bondage to suffer the penalty of a tyrant's law, to endure stripes and imprisonment, and to be shut out from all moral as well as intellectual improvement, and linger out almost a living death.

When I saw a crowd of blood-thirsty, unprincipled slave hunters rushing upon me armed with weapons of death, it was no use for me to undertake to fight my way through against such fearful odds.

But I broke away from the man who stood by with his pistol drawn to shoot me if I should resist, and reached the fence and attempted to jump over it before I was overtaken; but the fence being very high I was caught by my legs before I got over.

I kicked and struggled with all my might to get away, but without success. I kicked a new cloth coat off of his back, while he was holding on to my leg. I kicked another in his eye; but they never let me go until they got more help. By this time, there was a crowd on the out side of the fence with clubs to beat me back. Finally, they succeeded in dragging me from the fence and overpowered me by numbers and choked me almost to death.

These ruffians dragged me through the streets of Cincinnati, to what was called a justice office. But it was more like an office of injustice.

When I entered the room I was introduced to three slaveholders, one of whom was a son of Wm. Gatewood, who claimed me as his property. They pretended to be very glad to see me.

They asked me if I did not want to see my wife and child; but I made no reply to any thing that was said until I was delivered up as a slave. After they were asked a few questions by the court, the old pro-slavery squire very gravely pronounced me to be the property of Mr. Gatewood. ...

———— 3.32 ————

ABOLITION IN THE NATION'S POETRY
Whittier, Lowell and Longfellow

The abolitionist movement invaded more than American politics, it also worked its way into popular culture and arts of the 19th century. Douglass and Garrison were both known for their love of poetry, in particular that which related to the emancipation of slaves. Quaker writer and activist John Greenleaf Whittier became somewhat of the poet laureate of the movement, with his famous 1837 broadside "Our Fellow Countrymen in Chains," and his response to the branding of whites caught helping slaves escape, "The Branded Hand." James Russell Lowell's 1844 "The Present Crisis" also drew praise in the movement, along with Henry Wadsworth Longfellow's 1842 collection *Poems on Slavery*.

A. "Our Fellow Countrymen in Chains,"
John Greenleaf Whittier

OUR FELLOW COUNTRYMEN
      IN CHAINS!
SLAVES — in a land of light and law! —
SLAVES — crouching on the very plains
Where rolled the storm of Freedom's war!
A groan from Eutaw's haunted wood —
      A wail where Camden's martyr's fell —
By every shrine of patriot blood,
      From Moultrie's wall and Jasper's well!

By storied hill and hallowed grot,
      By mossy wood and marshy glen,
Whence rang of old the rifle shot,
      And hurrying shout of Marion's men! —

The groan of breaking hearts is there —
    The falling lash — the fetter's clank! —
Slaves — SLAVES are breathing in that air
    Which old De Kalb and Sumpter drank!

What, ho! — our countrymen in chains! —
    The whip on WOMAN'S shrinking flesh!
Our soil yet reddening with the stains,
    Caught from her scourging, warm and
    fresh!
What! mothers from their children riven! —
    What! God's own image bought and
    sold! —
AMERICANS to market driven,
    And bartered as the brute for gold!
Speak! — shall their agony of prayer
    Come thrilling to our hearts in vain!
To us — whose fathers scorned to bear
    The paltry menace of a chain; —
To us whose boast is loud and long
    Of holy liberty and light —
Say, shall these writhing slaves of Wrong
    Plead vainly for their plundered Right?

What! — shall we send, with lavish breath,
    Our sympathies across the wave,
Where manhood on the field of death
    Strikes for his freedom, or a grave? —
Shall prayers go up — and hymns be sung
    For Greece, the Moslem fetter
    spurning —
And millions hail with pen and tongue
    Our light on all her altars burning!

Shall Belgium feel, and gallant France,
    By Vendome's pile and Schoenbrun's wall
And Poland, gasping on her lance,
    The impulse of our cheering call?
And shall the SLAVE, beneath our eye,
    Clank o'er our fields his hateful chain?
And toss his fettered arm on high,
    And groan for freedom's gift, in vain?

Oh say, shall Prussia's banner be
    A refuge for the stricken slave; —
And shall the Russian serf go free
    By Baikal's lake and Neva's wave; —

And shall the wintry-bosomed Dane
    Relax the iron hand of pride,
And bid his bondmen cast the chain
    From fettered soul and limb, aside?

Shall every flap of England's flag
    Proclaim that all around are free,
From 'fartherst Ind' to each blue crag
    That beetles o'er the Western Sea?
And shall we scoff at Europe's kings,
    When Freedom's fire is dim with us,
And round our country's altar clings
    The damning shade of Slavery's curse?

Go — let us ask of Constantine
    To loose his grasp on Poland's throat —
And beg the lord of Mahmoud's line
    To spare the struggling Suliote.
Will not the scorching answer come
    From turbaned Turk, and fiery Russ —
'Go, loose your fettered slaves at home,
    Then turn and ask the like of us!'

Just God! and shall we calmly rest,
    The christian's scorn — the
    heathen's mirth —
Content to live the lingering jest
    And by word of a mocking earth?
Shall our own glorious land retain
    That curse which Europe seems to bear?
Shall our own brethren drag the chain
    Which not even Russia's menials wear?

Up, then, in Freedom's manly part,
    From gray-beard old to fiery youth,
And on the nation's naked heart
    Scatter the living coals of Truth.
Up — while ye slumber, deeper yet
    The shadow of our fame is growing —
Up — While ye pause, our sun may set
    In blood, around our altars flowing!

Oh rouse ye, ere the storm comes forth —
    The gathered wrath of God and man —
Like that which wasted Egypt's earth,
    When hail and fire above it ran.
Hear ye no warnings in the air?

Feel ye no earthquake underneath?
Up — up — why will ye slumber where
   The sleeper only wakes in death?
Up NOW for Freedom! — not in strife
   Like that your sterner fathers saw
The awful waste of human life —
   The glory and the guilt of war:
But break the chain — the yoke remove
   And smite to earth oppression's rod,
With those mild arms of Truth and Love,
   Made mighty through the living God!

Prone let the shrine of Moloch sink,
   And leave no traces where it stood
Nor longer let its idol drink
   His daily cup of human blood:
Bur rear another altar there,
   To truth and love and mercy given,
And Freedom's gift and Freedom's prayer
   Shall call an answer down from Heaven!

B. "The Present Crisis," James Russell Lowell

WHEN a deed is done for Freedom, through the
   broadearth's aching breast
Runs a thrill of joy prophetic, trembling on
   from east to west,
And the slave, where'er he cowers, feels the
   soul within him climb
To the awful verge of manhood, as the
   energy sublime
Of a century bursts full-blossomed on the
   thorny stem of Time.

Through the walls of hut and palace shoots the
   instantaneous throe,
When the travail of the Ages wrings earth's
   systems to and fro;
At the birth of each new Era, with a recognizing
   start,
Nation wildly looks at a nation, standing with
   mute lips apart,
And glad Truth's yet mightier man-child leaps
   beneath the Future's heart.

So the Evil's triumph sendeth, with a terror
   and a chill,
Under continent to continent, the sense of
   coming ill,
And the slave, where'er he cowers, feels his
   sympathies with God
In hot tear-drops ebbing earthward, to be drunk
   up by the sod,
Till a corpse crawls round unburied, delving in
   the nobler clod.

For mankind are one in sprit, and an instinct
   bears along,
Round the earth's electric circle, the swift flash
   of right or wrong;
Whether conscious or unconscious, yet
   Humanity's vast frame
Through its ocean-sundered fibres feels the
   gush of joy or shame; —
In the gain or loss of one race all the rest have
   equal claim.

Once to every man and nation comes the
   moment to decide,
In the strife of Truth with Falsehood, for the
   good or evil side;
Some great cause, God's new Messiah, offering
   each the bloom or blight,
Parts the goats upon the left hand, and the
   sheep upon the right,
And the choice goes by forever 'twixt that
   darkness and that light.

Hast thou chosen, O my people, on whose
   party thou shalt stand,
Ere the Doom from its worn sandals shakes the
   dust against our land?
Though the cause of Evil prosper, yet 'tis
   Truth alone is strong,
And, albeit she wander outcast now, I see
   around her throng
Troops of beautiful, tall angels, to enshield her
   from all wrong.

Backward look across the ages and the beacon-
   moments see,
That, like peaks of some sunk continent,
   jut through Oblivion's sea;

Not an ear in court or market for the low
    foreboding cry
Of those Crises, God's stern winnowers, from
    whose feet earth's chaff must fly;
Never shows the choice momentous till the
    judgement hath passed by.

Careless seems the great Avenger; history's
    pages but record
One death-grapple in the darkness 'twixt old
    systems and the Word;
Truth forever on the scaffold, Wrong forever on
    the throne, —
Yet that scaffold sways the future, and, behind
    the dim unknown,
Standeth God within the shadow, keeping
    watch above his own.

We see dimly in the Present what is small and
    what is great,
Slow of faith how weak an arm may turn this
    iron helm of fate,
But the soul is still oracular; amid the
    market's din,
List the ominous stern whisper from the
    Delphic cave within, —
"They enslave their children's children who
    make compromise with sin."

Slavery, the earth-born Cyclops, fellest of the
    giant brood,
Sons of brutish Force and Darkness, who have
    drenched the earth with blood,
Famished in his self-made desert, blinded by
    our purer day,
Gropes in yet unblasted regions for his
    miserable prey; —
Shall we guide his gory fingers where our
    helpless children play?

Then to side with Truth is noble when we share
    her wretched crust,
Ere her cause bring fame and profit, and 'tis
    prosperous to be just;
Then it is the brave man chooses, while the
    coward stands aside,

Doubting in his abject sprit, till his Lord
    is crucified,
And the multitude make virtue of the faith
    they had denied.

Count me o'er the earth's chosen heroes,
    — they were souls that stood alone,
While the men they agonized for hurled the
    contume lious stone,
Stood serene, and down the future saw the
    golden beam incline
To the side of perfect justice, mastered by their
    faith divine,
By one man's plain truth to manhood and to
    God's supreme design.

By the light of burning heretics Christ's
    bleeding feet I track,
Toiling up new Calvaries ever with the cross
    that turns not back,
And these mounts of anguish number how
    each generation learned
One new word of that grand Credo which in
    prophet-hearts hath burned
Since the first man stood God-conquered with
    his face to heaven upturned.

For Humanity sweeps onward: where today the
    martyr stands,
On the morrow, crouches Judas with the silver
    in his hands;
Far in front the cross stands ready and the
    crackling fagots burn,
While the hooting mob of yesterday in silent
    awe return
To glean up the scattered ashes into History's
    golden urn.

'Tis as easy to be heroes as to sit the idle slaves
Of a legendary virtue carved upon our
    father's graves,
Worshippers of light ancestral make the
    present light a crime; —
Was the Mayflower launched by cowards,
    steered by men behind their time?
Turn those tracks toward Past or Future,
    that make Plymouth Rock sublime?

They were men of present valor, stalwart
    old iconoclasts,
Unconvinced by axe or gibbet that all
    virtue was the Past's;
But we make their truth our falsehood,
    thinking that hath made us free,
Hoarding it in mouldy parchments, while
    our tender spirits flee
The rude grasp of that great Impulse
    which drove them across the sea.

They have rights who dare maintain
    them; we are traitors to our sires,
Smothering in their holy ashes Freedom's
    new-lit altar-fires;
Shall we make their creed our jailer?
    Shall we, in our haste to slay,
From the tombs of the old prophets steal
    the funeral lamps away
To light up the martry-fagots round the
    prophet of today?
New occasions teach new duties; Time
    makes ancient good uncouth;
They must upward still, and onward,
    who would keep abreast of Truth;
Lo, before us gleam her campfires?
    We ourselves must Pilgrims be,
Launch our Mayflower, and steer boldly
    through the desperate winter sea,
Nor attempt the Future's portal with the
    Past's blood-rusted key.

C. "The Witness," from *Poems on Slavery*,
Henry Wadsworth Longfellow

In Ocean's wide domains,
    Half buried in the sands,
Lie skeletons in chains,
    With shackled feet and hands.
Beyond the fall of dews,
    Deeper than plummet lies,
Float ships, with all their crews,
    No more to sink nor rise.
There the black Slave-ship swims,
    Freighted with human forms,
Whose fettered, fleshless limbs
    Are not the sport of storms.

These are the bones of Slaves;
    They gleam from the abyss;
They cry, from yawning waves,
    "We are the Witnesses!"
Within Earth's wide domains
    Are markets for men's lives;
Their necks are galled with chains,
    Their wrists are cramped with gyves.
Dead bodies, that the kite
    In deserts makes its prey;
Murders, that with affright
    Scare school-boys from their play!
All evil thoughts and deeds;
    Anger, and lust, and pride;
The foulest, rankest weeds,
    That choke Life's groaning tide!
These are the woes of Slaves;
    They glare from the abyss;
They cry, from unknown graves,
    "We are the Witnesses!"

––––––– 3.33 –––––––

FACT MEETS FICTION IN
THE FIRST BLACK NOVEL
William Wells Brown

The prolific William Wells Brown's 1847 slave narrative was one of the genre's most popular. Along with two books chronicling his journeys through Europe, the first travel books published by an African American, and his plays, Brown's narrative established him as a premier black writer of the 19th century. His most fascinating work is likely his 1853 novel, published in Europe, about Thomas Jefferson's daughters. *Clotel* built upon the still-circulating rumors about Jefferson's love affair with one of his slaves — since identified as Sally Hemmings, the half sister of Jefferson's wife Martha. (Brown published three subsequent editions of the book, each under a different title and with significantly different content.) A slave narrative in form, the novel is a fictional account of the life of one of Hemmings' and Jefferson's daughters, who was born a slave to Jefferson. Brown, himself a self-educated escaped slave, published the novel before he legally secured his freedom and was thus still a fugitive.

    In the excerpt below, Brown's heroine, Clotel, escapes from slavery by passing as both male and white. In reality, escaping slaves commonly manipulated preconceptions about race and gender to manage their journeys north unde-tected. Two of Brown's friends, William and Ellen Craft, were famous abolitionist lecturers whose escape from slavery, in technique, closely mirrored that of Brown's fictional Clotel.

… We have seen Clotel sold to Mr. French in Vicksburgh, her hair cut short, and everything done to make her realise her position as a ser-vant. Then we have seen her re-sold, because her owners feared she would die through grief. As yet her new purchaser treated her with respectful gentleness, and sought to win her favour by flattery and presents, knowing that whatever he gave her he could take back again. But she dreaded every moment lest the scene should change, and trembled at the sound of every footfall. At every interview with her new master Clotel stoutly maintained that she had left a husband in Virginia, and would never think of taking another. The gold watch and chain, and other glittering presents which he purchased for her, were all laid aside by the quadroon, as if they were of no value to her. In the same house with her was another servant, a man, who had from time to time hired himself from his master. William was his name. He could feel for Clotel, for he, like her, had been separated from near and dear relatives, and often tried to console the poor woman, One day the quadroon observed to him that her hair was growing out again. "Yes," replied William, "you look a good deal like a man with your short hair." "Oh," rejoined she, "I have often been told that I would make a better looking man than a woman. If I had the money," con-tinued she, "I would bid farewell to this place." In a moment more she feared that she had said too much, and smilingly remarked, "I am always talking nonsense." William was a tall, full-bodied Negro, whose very countenance beamed with intelligence. Being a mechanic, he had, by his own industry, made more than what he paid his owner; this he laid aside, with the hope that some day he might get enough to purchase his freedom. He had in his chest one hundred and fifty dollars. His was a heart that felt for others, and he had again and again

wiped the tears from his eyes as he heard the story of Clotel as related by herself. "If she can get free with a little money, why not give her what I have?" thought he, and then he resolved to do it. An hour after, he came into the quadroon's room, and laid the money in her lap, and said, "There, Miss Clotel, you said if you had the means you would leave this place; there is money enough to take you to England, where you will be free. You are much fairer than many of the white women of the South, and can easily pass for a free white lady." At first Clotel feared that it was a plan by which the Negro wished to try her fidelity to her owner; but she was soon convinced by his earnest man-ner, and the deep feeling with which he spoke, that he was honest. "I will take the money only on one condition," said she; "and that is, that I effect your escape as well as my own." "How can that be done?" he inquired. "I will assume the disguise of a gentleman and you that of a servant, and we will take passage on a steam-boat and go to Cincinnati, and thence to Canada." Here William put in several objec-tions to the plan. He feared detection, and he well knew that, when a slave is once caught when attempting to escape, if returned is sure to be worse treated than before. However, Clotel satisfied him that the plan could be car-ried out if he would only play his part.

The resolution was taken, the clothes for her disguise procured, and before night everything was in readiness for their departure. That night Mr. Cooper, their master, was to attend a party, and this was their opportunity. William went to the wharf to look out for a boat, and had scarcely reached the landing ere he heard the puffing of a steamer. He returned and reported the fact. Clotel had already packed her trunk, and had only to dress and all was ready. In less than an hour they were on board the boat. Under the assumed name of "Mr. Johnson," Clotel went to the clerk's office and took a pri-vate state room for herself, and paid her own and servant's fare. Besides being attired in a neat suit of black, she had a white silk handkerchief tied round her chin, as if she was an invalid. A pair of green glasses covered her eyes; and fearing that she would be talked to too much and thus render her liable to be detected, she assumed to be very ill. On the other hand, William was playing his part well in the servants' hall; he was talking loudly of his master's wealth. Nothing appeared as good on the boat as in his master's fine mansion. "I don't like dees steamboats no how," said William; "I hope when marser goes on a journey agin he will take de carriage and de bosses." Mr. Johnson (for such was the name by which Clotel now went) remained in his room, to avoid, as far as possible, conversation with others. After a passage of seven days they arrived at Louisville, and put up at Gough's Hotel. Here they had to await the departure of another boat for the North. They were now in their most critical position. They were still in a slave state, and John C. Calhoun, a distinguished slave-owner, was a guest at this hotel. They feared, also, that trouble would attend their attempt to leave this place for the North, as all persons taking Negroes with them have to give bail that such Negroes are not runaway slaves. The law upon this point is very stringent: all steamboats and other public conveyances are liable to a fine for every slave that escapes by them, besides paying the full value for the slave. After a delay of four hours, Mr. Johnson and servant took passage on the steamer Rodolph, for Pittsburgh. It is usual, before the departure of the boats, for an officer to examine every part of the vessel to see that no slave secretes himself on board. "'Where are you going?" asked the officer of William, as he was doing his duty on this occasion. "I am going with marser," was the quick reply. "Who is your master?" "Mr. Johnson, sir, a gentleman in the cabin." "You must take him to the office and satisfy that captain that all is right, or you can't go on this boat." William informed his master what the officer had said. The boat was on the eve of going, and no time could be lost, yet they knew not what to do. At last they went to the office, and Mr. Johnson, addressing the captain, said, "I am informed that my boy can't go with me unless I give security that he belongs to me.

"Yes," replied the captain, "that is the law." "A very strange law indeed," rejoined Mr. Johnson, "that one can't take his property with him." After a conversation of some minutes, and a plea on the part of Johnson that he did not wish to be delayed owing to his illness, they were permitted to take their passage without farther trouble, and the boat was soon on its way up the river. The fugitives had now passed the Rubicon, and the next place at which they would land would be in a Free State. Clotel called William to her room, and said to him, "We are now free, you can go on your way to Canada, and I shall go to Virginia in search of my daughter." The announcement that she was going to risk her liberty in a Slave State was unwelcome news to William. With all the eloquence he could command, he tried to persuade Clotel that she could not escape detection, and was only throwing her freedom away. But she had counted the cost, and made up her mind for the worst. In return for the money he had furnished, she had secured for him his liberty, and their engagement was at an end.

After a quick passage the fugitives arrived at Cincinnati, and there separated. William proceeded on his way to Canada, and Clotel again resumed her own apparel, and prepared to start in search of her child. ...

—————— 3.34 ——————

ANOTHER SLAVERY COMPROMISE HOLDS THE UNION
Fugitive Slave Act of 1850

The course to civil war, of course, was set during the Constitutional Convention of 1787 — as both Benjamin Franklin and James Madison noted at the time. But, in the years preceding the South's secession, the most definitive point in the build up to war must be said to be the Compromise of 1850. It began when California, booming with gold, petitioned to join the Union as a free state. Kentucky Senator Henry Clay, determined to hold his 1820 compromise together, offered a new version. There were several issues at stake, but the status of California, and the balance of slave-to-free states, was the primary one. The deal allowed California to join as a free state, and in return gave the slave states what has been termed the Fugitive Slave Act.

The Constitution and the 1793 Fugitive Slave Law already bound state law enforcement officials to return escaped slaves who crossed state lines, and levied a fine against those who aided their escape. But the new 1850 law moved far beyond these provisions, giving slaveholders far-reaching and nearly omnipotent powers in tracking down "fugitives from labor." It reached into northern free states to compel not only law enforcement officials but all citizens to aid in the capture of escaped slaves. It did away with trial by jury and set up "commissioners" who would determine whether or not the person in question was to be delivered to the slaveholder, banning any testimony from the accused "fugitive" in those proceedings. It streamlined the process for slaveholders' claims, and beefed up the federal role in chasing down escaped slaves. And in its effort to drastically broaden the number of people responsible for recovery of escaped slaves, the law empowered marshals to deputize citizens to help track them down — thereby nationally legalizing the slave hunter posses.

The act both terrified black people who had fled slavery to set up a free life and energized abolitionists, who sped up efforts to move escapees through the Underground Railroad. An estimated 20,000 African Americans emigrated to Canada in the decade following the act's passage.

A. Fugitive Slave Act

...Sec. 5. *And be it further enacted*, That it shall be the duty of all marshals and deputy marshals to obey and execute all warrants and precepts issued under the provisions of this act, when to them directed; and should any marshal or deputy marshal refuse to receive such warrant, or other process, when tendered, or to use all proper means diligently to execute the same, he shall, on conviction thereof, be fined in the sum of one thousand dollars, to the use of such claimant, on the motion of such claimant, by the Circuit or District Court for the district of such marshal; and after arrest of such fugitive, by such marshal or his deputy, or whilst at any time in his custody under the provisions of this act, should such fugitive escape, whether with or without the assent of such marshal or his deputy, such marshal shall be liable, on his official bond, to be prosecuted for the benefit of such claimant, for the full value of the service or labor of said fugitive in the State, Territory, or District whence he escaped: and the better to enable the said commissioners, when thus appointed, to execute their duties faithfully and efficiently, in conformity with the requirements of the constitution of the United States and of this act, they are hereby authorized and empowered, within their counties respectively, to appoint, in writing under their hands, any one or more suitable persons, from time to time, to execute all such warrants and other process as may be issued by them in the lawful performance of their respective duties; with authority to such commissioners, or the persons to be appointed by them, to execute process as aforesaid, to summon and call to their aid the bystanders, or posse comitatus of the proper county, when necessary to ensure a faithful observance of the clause of the Constitution referred to, in conformity with the provisions of this act; and all good citizens are hereby commanded to aid and assist in the prompt and efficient execution of this law, whenever their services may be required, as aforesaid, for that purpose; and said warrants shall run, and be executed by said officers, any where in the State within which they are issued.

Sec. 6. *And be it further enacted*, That when a person held to service or labor in any State or Territory of the United States, has heretofore or shall hereafter escape into another State or Territory of the United States, the person or persons to whom such service or labor may be due, or his, her, or their agent or attorney, duly authorized, by power of attorney, in writing, acknowledged and certified under the seal of some legal officer or court of the State or Territory in which the same may be executed, may pursue and reclaim such fugitive person, either by procuring a warrant from some one of the courts, judges, or commissioners aforesaid, of the proper circuit, district, or county, for the apprehension of such fugitive from service or labor, or by seizing and arresting such fugitive, where the same can be done without process, and by taking, or causing such person to be taken, forthwith before such court, judge, or commissioner, whose duty it shall be to hear and determine the case of such claimant in a summary manner; and upon satisfactory proof being made, by deposition or affidavit, in writing, to be taken and certified by such court, judge, or commissioner, or by other satisfactory testimony, duly taken and certified by some court, magistrate, justice of the peace, or other legal officer authorized to administer an oath and take depositions under the laws of the State or Territory from which such person owing service or labor may have escaped. ... In no trial or hearing under this act shall the testimony of such alleged fugitive be admitted in evidence; and the certificates in this and the first [fourth] section mentioned, shall be conclusive of the right of the person or persons in whose favor granted, to remove such fugitive to the State or Territory from which he escaped, and shall prevent all molestation of such person or persons by any process issued by any court, judge, magistrate, or other person whomsoever.

Sec. 7. *And be it further enacted*, That any person who shall knowingly and willingly obstruct, hinder, or prevent such claimant, his agent or attorney, or any person or persons lawfully assisting him, her, or them, from arresting such a fugitive from service or labor, either with or without process as aforesaid, or shall rescue, or attempt to rescue, such fugitive from service or labor, from the custody of such claimant, his or her agent or attorney, or other person or persons lawfully assisting as aforesaid, when so arrested, pursuant to the authority herein given and declared; or shall aid, abet, or assist such person so owing service or labor as aforesaid, directly or indirectly, to escape from such claimant, his agent or attorney, or other person or persons legally authorized as aforesaid; or shall harbor or conceal such fugi-

tive, so as to prevent the discovery and arrest of such person, after notice or knowledge of the fact that such person was a fugitive from service or labor as aforesaid, shall, for either of said offences, be subject to a fine not exceeding one thousand dollars, and imprisonment not exceeding six months ... and shall moreover forfeit and pay, by way of civil damages to the party injured by such illegal conduct, the sum of one thousand dollars for each fugitive so lost as aforesaid, to be recovered by action of debt, in any of the District or Territorial Courts aforesaid, within whose jurisdiction the said offence may have been committed. ...

Sec. 9. *And be it further enacted*, That, upon affidavit made by the claimant of such fugitive, his agent or attorney, after such certificate has been issued, that he has reason to apprehend that such fugitive will be rescued by force from his or their possession before he can be taken beyond the limits of the State in which the arrest is made, it shall be the duty of the officer making the arrest to retain such fugitive in his custody, and to remove him to the State whence he fled, and there to deliver him to said claimant, his agent, or attorney. And to this end, the officer aforesaid is hereby authorized and required to employ so many persons as he may deem necessary to overcome such force, and to retain them in his service so long as circumstances may require. The said officer and his assistants, while so employed, to receive the same compensation, and to be allowed the same expenses, as are now allowed by law for transportation of criminals, to be certified by the judge of the district within which the arrest is made, and paid out of the treasury of the United States. ...

B. Samuel Ward chides Congress

Abolitionists detested the compromise, and fought tirelessly over the course of the eight-month congressional debate to block it. Among the compromise's lead proponents was Massachusetts Senator Daniel Webster. In the speech below, leading New York abolitionist and Presbyterian preacher Samuel Ward, himself a "fugitive from labor" in Maryland, berates Webster, along with other members of Congress who were supporting the compromise. Delivered in Massachusetts in April of 1850, the speech was reprinted in the *Liberator* as it appears here. Ward was among the blacks who fled to Canada following the bill's passage.

I am here to-night simply as a guest. You have met here to speak of the sentiments of a Senator of your State whose remarks you have the honor to repudiate. In the course of the remarks of gentleman who preceded me, he has done us the favor to make honorable mention of a Senator of my own State — Wm. H. Seward.

I thank you for this manifestation of approbation of a man has always stood head and shoulders above his party, and who has never receded from his position on the question of slavery. It was my happiness to receive a letter from him a few days since, in which he said he never would swerve from his position as the friend of freedom.

To be sure, I agree not with Senator Seward in politics, but when an individual stands up for the rights of men against slaveholders, I care not for party distinctions. He is my brother.

We have here much of common cause and interest in this matter. That infamous bill of Mr. Mason, of Virginia, proves itself to be like all other propositions presented by Southern men. It finds just enough of Northern doughfaces who are willing to pledge themselves, if you will pardon the uncouth language of a backwoodsman, to lick up the spittle of the slavocrats, and swear it is delicious.

You of the old Bay State — a State to which many of us are accustomed to look as to our fatherland, just as well look back to England as our mother country — you have a Daniel who has deserted the cause of freedom. We, too, in New York, have a "Daniel who has come to judgment," only he don't come quite fast enough to the right kind of judgment. Daniel S. Dickinson represents some one, I suppose, in the State of New York; God knows, he does-

n't represent me. I can pledge you that our Daniel will stand cheek by jowl with your Daniel. He was never known to surrender slavery, but always to surrender liberty.

The bill of which you most justly complain, concerning the surrender of fugitive slaves, is to apply alike to your State and to our State, if it shall ever apply at all. But we have come here to make a common oath upon a common altar, that that bill shall never take effect. Honorable Senators may record their names in its behalf, and it may have the sanction of the House of Representatives; but we, the people, who are superior to both Houses and the Executive, too, we, the people, will never be human bipeds, to howl upon the track, of the fugitive slave, even though led by the corrupt Daniel of your State, or the degraded one of ours.

Though there are many attempts to get up compromises — and there is no term which I detest more than this, it is always the term which makes right yield to wrong; it has always been accursed since Eve made the first compromise with the devil. [Interrupted by applause.] I was saying, sir, that it is somewhat singular, and yet historically true, that whensoever these compromises are proposed, there are men of the North who seem to foresee that Northern men, who think their constituency will not look into these matters, will seek to do more than the South demands. They seek to prove to Northern men that all is right and all is fair; and this is the game Webster is attempting to play.

"Oh," says Webster, "the will of God has fixed that matter, we will not re-enact the will of God." Sir, you remember the time in 1841, '42, '43 and '44, when it was said that Texas could never be annexed. The design of such dealing was that you should believe it, and then, when you thought yourselves secure, they would spring the trap upon you. And now it is their wish to seduce you into the belief that slavery never will go there, and then the slaveholders will drive slavery there as fast as possible. I think that this is the most contemptible proposition of the whole, except the support of that bill which would attempt to make the whole North the slave-catchers of the South.

You will remember that that bill of Mr. Mason says nothing about color. Mr. Phillips, a man whom I always loved, a man who taught me my horn-book on this subject of slavery, when I was a poor boy, has referred to Marshfield. There is a man who sometimes lives in Marshfield, and who has the reputation of having an honorable dark skin. Who knows but that some postmaster may have to sit upon the very gentleman whose character you have been discussing to-night? "What is sauce for the goose is sauce for the gander." If this bill is to relieve grievances, why not make an application to the immortal Daniel of Marshfield? There is no such thing as complexion mentioned. It is not only true that the colored man of Massachusetts — it is not only true that the fifty thousand colored men of New York may be taken — though I pledge you there is one, whose name is Sam Ward, who will never be taken alive. Not only is it true that the fifty thousand black men in New York may be taken, but any one else also can be captured. My friend Theodore Parker alluded to Ellen Crafts. I had the pleasure of taking tea with her, and accompanied her here to-night. She is far whiter than many who come here slave-catching. This line of distinction is so nice that you cannot tell who is white or black. As Alexander Pope used to say, "White and black soften and blend in so many thousand ways, that it is neither white nor black."

This is the question, Whether a man has a right to himself and his children, his hopes and his happiness, for this world and the world to come. That is a question which, according to this bill, may be decided by any backwoods postmaster in this State or any other. Oh, this is a monstrous proposition; and I do thank God that if the Slave Power has such demands to make on us, that the proposition has come now — now, that the people know what is being done — now that the public mind is turned toward this subject — now that they are trying to find what is the truth on this subject.

Sir, what must be the moral influence of this speech of Mr. Webster on the minds of young men, lawyers and others, here in the North? They turn their eyes towards Daniel Webster as towards a superior mind, and a legal and constitutional oracle. If they shall catch the spirit of this speech, its influence upon them and upon following generations will be so deeply corrupting that it never can be wiped out or purged.

I am thankful that this, my first entrance into Boston, and my first introduction to Faneuil Hall, gives me the pleasure and privilege of uniting with you in uttering my humble voice against the two Daniels, and of declaring, in behalf of our people, that if the fugitive slave is traced to our part of New York State, he shall have the law of Almighty God to protect him, the law which says, "Thou shalt not return to the master the servant that is escaped unto thee, but he shall dwell with thee in thy gates, where it liketh him best." And if our postmasters cannot maintain their constitutional oaths, and cannot live without playing the pander to the slave-hunter, they need not live at all. Such crises as these leave us to the right of Revolution, and if need be, that right we will, at whatever cost, most sacredly maintain.

C. "Slavery in Massachusetts," Henry David Thoreau

In 1854, a 21-year-old Virginia slave named Anthony Burns fled and landed in Boston, Massachusetts. Empowered by the new Fugitive Slave Act, his former owner pursued him and had him arrested. The wounds from the debate over the act still fresh, Boston's free blacks and abolitionist whites found this particular capture to be an affront. Led by free blacks, around 2,000 people marched on the courthouse where Burns was being held. A small group beat the door down and attempted to rescue him, but were turned back by deputies. President Franklin Pierce, seeing the incident as a make-or-break test for the new fugitive law, dispatched federal troops to help guard Burns and ultimately transport him back to Virginia. A crowd of 50,000 lined the streets the day officials marched Burns out of the courthouse, many shouting "kidnappers." A year later, however, black supporters in Boston purchased Burns's freedom and he returned.

The incident revealed how much the fugitive slave law angered northern abolitionists. Slavery, it now seemed, was not an abstract grievance on far-off southern plantations, but could invade the very streets of Boston. At a Fourth of July antislavery rally in Framingham, Massachusetts, in 1854, Henry David Thoreau epitomized the popular resentment in a now-famous "Slavery in Massachusetts" address. At this same rally, William Lloyd Garrison sparked heavy controversy by burning a copy of the U.S. Constitution.

I lately attended a meeting of the citizens of Concord, expecting, as one among many, to speak on the subject of slavery in Massachusetts; but I was surprised and disappointed to find that what had called my townsmen together was the destiny of Nebraska, and not of Massachusetts, and that what I had to say would be entirely out of order. I had thought that the house was on fire, and not the prairie; but though several of the citizens of Massachusetts are now in prison for attempting to rescue a slave from her own clutches, not one of the speakers at that meeting expressed regret for it, not one even referred to it. It was only the disposition of some wild lands a thousand miles off which appeared to concern them. The inhabitants of Concord are not prepared to stand by one of their own bridges, but talk only of taking up a position on the highlands beyond the Yellowstone River. Our Buttricks and Davises and Hosmers are retreating thither, and I fear that they will leave no Lexington Common between them and the enemy. There is not one slave in Nebraska; there are perhaps a million slaves in Massachusetts.

They who have been bred in the school of politics fail now and always to face the facts. Their measures are half measures and makeshifts merely. They put off the day of settlement indefinitely, and meanwhile the debt accumulates. Though the Fugitive Slave Law had not been the subject of discussion on that occasion, it was at length faintly resolved by my townsmen, at an adjourned meeting, as I learn, that the compromise compact of 1820 having been repudiated by one of the parties, "Therefore, ... the Fugitive Slave Law of 1850 must be repealed." But this is not the reason why an iniquitous law should be repealed. The fact which the politician faces is merely that there is less honor among thieves than was supposed, and not the fact that they are thieves.

As I had no opportunity to express my thoughts at that meeting, will you allow me to do so here?

Again it happens that the Boston Court-House is full of armed men, holding prisoner and trying a MAN, to find out if he is not really a SLAVE. Does any one think that justice or God awaits Mr. Loring's decision? For him to sit there deciding still, when this question is already decided from eternity to eternity, and the unlettered slave himself and the multitude around have long since heard and assented to the decision, is simply to make himself ridiculous. We may be tempted to ask from whom he received his commission, and who he is that received it; what novel statutes he obeys, and what precedents are to him of authority. Such an arbiter's very existence is an impertinence. We do not ask him to make up his mind, but to make up his pack.

I listen to hear the voice of a Governor, Commander-in-Chief of the forces of Massachusetts. I hear only the creaking of crickets and the hum of insects which now fill the summer air. The Governor's exploit is to review the troops on muster days. I have seen him on horseback, with his hat off, listening to a chaplain's prayer. It chances that that is all I have ever seen of a Governor. I think that I could manage to get along without one. If *he* is not of the least use to prevent my being kidnapped, pray of what important use is he likely to be to me? When freedom is most endangered, he dwells in the deepest obscurity. A distinguished clergyman told me that he chose the profession of a clergyman because it afforded the most leisure for literary pursuits. I would recommend to him the profession of a Governor.

Three years ago, also, when the Sims tragedy was acted, I said to myself, There is such an officer, if not such a man, as the Governor of Massachusetts — what has he been about the last fortnight? Has he had as much as he could do to keep on the fence during this moral earthquake? It seemed to me that no keener satire could have been aimed at, no more cutting insult have been offered to that man, than just what happened — the absence of all inquiry after him in that crisis. The worst and the most I chance to know of him is that he did not improve that opportunity to make himself known, and worthily known. He could at least have *resigned* himself into fame. It appeared to be forgotten that there was such a man or such an office. Yet no doubt he was endeavoring to fill the gubernatorial chair all the while. He was no Governor of mine. He did not govern me.

But at last, in the present case, the Governor was heard from. After he and the United States government had perfectly succeeded in robbing a poor innocent black man of his liberty for life, and, as far as they could, of his Creator's likeness in his breast, he made a speech to his accomplices, at a congratulatory supper!

I have read a recent law of this State, making it penal for any officer of the "Commonwealth" to "detain or aid in the ... detention," anywhere within its limits, "of any person, for the reason that he is claimed as a fugitive slave." Also, it was a matter of notoriety that a writ of replevin to take the fugitive out of the custody of the United States Marshal could not be served for want of sufficient force to aid the officer.

I had thought that the Governor was, in some sense, the executive officer of the State; that it was his business, as a Governor, to see that the laws of the State were executed; while, as a man, he took care that he did not, by so doing, break the laws of humanity; but when there is any special important use for him, he is useless, or worse than useless, and permits the laws of the State to go unexecuted. Perhaps I do not know what are the duties of a Governor; but if to be a Governor requires to

subject one's self to so much ignominy without remedy, if it is to put a restraint upon my manhood, I shall take care never to be Governor of Massachusetts. I have not read far in the statutes of this Commonwealth. It is not profitable reading. They do not always say what is true; and they do not always mean what they say. What I am concerned to know is, that that man's influence and authority were on the side of the slaveholder, and not of the slave — of the guilty, and not of the innocent — of injustice, and not of justice. I never saw him of whom I speak; indeed, I did not know that he was Governor until this event occurred. I heard of him and Anthony Burns at the same time, and thus, undoubtedly, most will hear of him. So far am I from being governed by him. I do not mean that it was anything to his discredit that I had not heard of him, only that I heard what I did. The worst I shall say of him is, that he proved no better than the majority of his constituents would be likely to prove. In my opinion, he was not equal to the occasion.

The whole military force of the State is at the service of a Mr. Suttle, a slaveholder from Virginia, to enable him to catch a man whom he calls his property; but not a soldier is offered to save a citizen of Massachusetts from being kidnapped! Is this what all these soldiers, all this training, have been for these seventy-nine years past? Have they been trained merely to rob Mexico and carry back fugitive slaves to their masters?

These very nights I heard the sound of a drum in our streets. There were men training still; and for what? I could with an effort pardon the cockerels of Concord for crowing still, for they, perchance, had not been beaten that morning; but I could not excuse this rub-a-dub of the "trainers." The slave was carried back by exactly such as these; i.e., by the soldier, of whom the best you can say in this connection is that he is a fool made conspicuous by a painted coat.

Three years ago, also, just a week after the authorities of Boston assembled to carry back a perfectly innocent man, and one whom they knew to be innocent, into slavery, the inhabitants of Concord caused the bells to be rung and the cannons to be fired, to celebrate their liberty — and the courage and love of liberty of their ancestors who fought at the bridge. As if *those* three millions had fought for the right to be free themselves, but to hold in slavery three million others. Nowadays, men wear a fool's-cap, and call it a liberty-cap. I do not know but there are some who, if they were tied to a whipping-post, and could but get one hand free, would use it to ring the bells and fire the cannons to celebrate their liberty. So some of my townsmen took the liberty to ring and fire. That was the extent of their freedom; and when the sound of the bells died away, their liberty died away also; when the powder was all expended, *their* liberty went off with the smoke.

The joke could be no broader if the inmates of the prisons were to subscribe for all the powder to be used in such salutes, and hire the jailers to do the firing and ringing for them, while they enjoyed it through the grating.

This is what I thought about my neighbors.

Every humane and intelligent inhabitant of Concord, when he or she heard those bells and those cannons, thought not with pride of the events of the 19th of April, 1775, but with shame of the events of the 12th of April, 1851. But now we have half buried that old shame under a new one.

Massachusetts sat waiting Mr. Loring's decision, as if it could in any way affect her own criminality. Her crime, the most conspicuous and fatal crime of all, was permitting him to be the umpire in such a case. It was really the trial of Massachusetts. Every moment that she hesitated to set this man free — every moment that she now hesitates to atone for her crime, she is convicted. The Commissioner on her case is God; not Edward G. God, but simply God.

I wish my countrymen to consider, that whatever the human law may be, neither an individual nor a nation can ever commit the least act of injustice against the obscurest individual without having to pay the penalty for it. A government which deliberately enacts injustice, and persists in it, will at length even become the laughing-stock of the world.

Much has been said about American slavery, but I think that we do not even yet realize what slavery is. If I were seriously to propose to Congress to make mankind into sausages, I have no doubt that most of the members would smile at my proposition, and if any believed me to be in earnest, they would think that I proposed something much worse than Congress had ever done. But if any of them will tell me that to make a man into a sausage would be much worse — would be any worse — than to make him into a slave — than it was to enact the Fugitive Slave Law, I will accuse him of foolishness, of intellectual incapacity, of making a distinction without a difference. The one is just as sensible a proposition as the other.

I hear a good deal said about trampling this law under foot. Why, one need not go out of his way to do that. This law rises not to the level of the head or the reason; its natural habitat is in the dirt. It was born and bred, and has its life, only in the dust and mire, on a level with the feet; and he who walks with freedom, and does not with Hindoo mercy avoid treading on every venomous reptile, will inevitably tread on it, and so trample it under foot — and Webster, its maker, with it, like the dirt-bug and its ball.

Recent events will be valuable as a criticism on the administration of justice in our midst, or, rather, as showing what are the true resources of justice in any community. It has come to this, that the friends of liberty, the friends of the slave, have shuddered when they have understood that his fate was left to the legal tribunals of the country to be decided. Free men have no faith that justice will be awarded in such a case. The judge may decide this way or that; it is a kind of accident, at best. It is evident that he is not a competent authority in so important a case. It is no time, then, to be judging according to his precedents, but to establish a precedent for the future. I would much rather trust to the sentiment of the people. In their vote you would get something of some value, at least, however small; but in the other case, only the trammeled judgment of an individual, of no significance, be it which way it might.

It is to some extent fatal to the courts, when the people are compelled to go behind them. I do not wish to believe that the courts were made for fair weather, and for very civil cases merely; but think of leaving it to any court in the land to decide whether more than three millions of people, in this case a sixth part of a nation, have a right to be freemen or not! But it has been left to the courts of *justice*, so called — to the Supreme Court of the land — and, as you all know, recognizing no authority but the Constitution, it has decided that the three millions are and shall continue to be slaves. Such judges as these are merely the inspectors of a pick-lock and murderer's tools, to tell him whether they are in working order or not, and there they think that their responsibility ends. There was a prior case on the docket, which they, as judges appointed by God, had no right to skip; which having been justly settled, they would have been saved from this humiliation. It was the case of the murderer himself.

The law will never make men free; it is men who have got to make the law free. They are the lovers of law and order who observe the law when the government breaks it.

Among human beings, the judge whose words seal the fate of a man furthest into eternity is not he who merely pronounces the verdict of the law, but he, whoever he may be, who, from a love of truth, and unprejudiced by any custom or enactment of men, utters a true opinion or *sentence* concerning him. He it is that *sentences* him. Whoever can discern truth has received his commission from a higher source than the chiefest justice in the world who can discern only law. He finds himself constituted judge of the judge. Strange that it should be necessary to state such simple truths!

I am more and more convinced that, with reference to any public question, it is more important to know what the country thinks of it than what the city thinks. The city does not *think* much. On any moral question, I would

rather have the opinion of Boxboro' than of Boston and New York put together. When the former speaks, I feel as if somebody *had* spoken, as if *humanity* was yet, and a reasonable being had asserted its rights — as if some unprejudiced men among the country's hills had at length turned their attention to the subject, and by a few sensible words redeemed the reputation of the race. When, in some obscure country town, the farmers come together to a special town-meeting, to express their opinion on some subject which is vexing the land, that, I think, is the true Congress, and the most respectable one that is ever assembled in the United States.

It is evident that there are, in this Commonwealth at least, two parties, becoming more and more distinct — the party of the city, and the party of the country. I know that the country is mean enough, but I am glad to believe that there is a slight difference in her favor. But as yet she has few, if any organs, through which to express herself. The editorials which she reads, like the news, come from the seaboard. Let us, the inhabitants of the country, cultivate self-respect. Let us not send to the city for aught more essential than our broadcloths and groceries; or, if we read the opinions of the city, let us entertain opinions of our own.

Among measures to be adopted, I would suggest to make as earnest and vigorous an assault on the press as has already been made, and with effect, on the church. The church has much improved within a few years; but the press is, almost without exception, corrupt. I believe that in this country the press exerts a greater and a more pernicious influence than the church did in its worst period. We are not a religious people, but we are a nation of politicians. We do not care for the Bible, but we do care for the newspaper. At any meeting of politicians — like that at Concord the other evening, for instance — how impertinent it would be to quote from the Bible! how pertinent to quote from a newspaper or from the Constitution! The newspaper is a Bible which we read every morning and every afternoon, standing and sitting, riding and walking. It is a Bible which every man carries in his pocket, which lies on every table and counter, and which the mail, and thousands of missionaries, are continually dispersing. It is, in short, the only book which America has printed and which America reads. So wide is its influence. The editor is a preacher whom you voluntarily support. Your tax is commonly one cent daily, and it costs nothing for pew hire. But how many of these preachers preach the truth? I repeat the testimony of many an intelligent foreigner, as well as my own convictions, when I say, that probably no country was ever ruled by so mean a class of tyrants as, with a few noble exceptions, are the editors of the periodical press in *this* country. And as they live and rule only by their servility, and appealing to the worse, and not the better, nature of man, the people who read them are in the condition of the dog that returns to his vomit.

The *Liberator* and the *Commonwealth* were the only papers in Boston, as far as I know, which made themselves heard in condemnation of the cowardice and meanness of the authorities of that city, as exhibited in '51. The other journals, almost without exception, by their manner of referring to and speaking of the Fugitive Slave Law, and the carrying back of the slave Sims, insulted the common sense of the country, at least. And, for the most part, they did this, one would say, because they thought so to secure the approbation of their patrons, not being aware that a sounder sentiment prevailed to any extent in the heart of the Commonwealth. I am told that some of them have improved of late; but they are still eminently time-serving. Such is the character they have won.

But, thank fortune, this preacher can be even more easily reached by the weapons of the reformer than could the recreant priest. The free men of New England have only to refrain from purchasing and reading these sheets, have only to withhold their cents, to kill a score of them at once. One whom I respect told me that he purchased Mitchell's *Citizen* in the cars, and then throw it out the window. But

would not his contempt have been more fatally expressed if he had not bought it?

Are they Americans? are they New Englanders? are they inhabitants of Lexington and Concord and Framingham, who read and support the Boston *Post, Mail, Journal, Advertiser, Courier,* and *Times*? Are these the Flags of our Union? I am not a newspaper reader, and may omit to name the worst.

Could slavery suggest a more complete servility than some of these journals exhibit? Is there any dust which their conduct does not lick, and make fouler still with its slime? I do not know whether the Boston *Herald* is still in existence, but I remember to have seen it about the streets when Sims was carried off. Did it not act its part well — serve its master faithfully! How could it have gone lower on its belly? How can a man stoop lower than he is low? do more than put his extremities in the place of the head he has? than make his head his lower extremity? When I have taken up this paper with my cuffs turned up, I have heard the gurgling of the sewer through every column. I have felt that I was handling a paper picked out of the public gutters, a leaf from the gospel of the gambling-house, the groggery, and the brothel, harmonizing with the gospel of the Merchants' Exchange.

The majority of the men of the North, and of the South and East and West, are not men of principle. If they vote, they do not send men to Congress on errands of humanity; but while their brothers and sisters are being scourged and hung for loving liberty, while — I might here insert all that slavery implies and is — it is the mismanagement of wood and iron and stone and gold which concerns them. Do what you will, O Government, with my wife and children, my mother and brother, my father and sister, I will obey your commands to the letter. It will indeed grieve me if you hurt them, if you deliver them to overseers to be hunted by bounds or to be whipped to death; but, nevertheless, I will peaceably pursue my chosen calling on this fair earth, until perchance, one day, when I have put on mourning for them dead, I shall have persuaded you to relent. Such is the attitude, such are the words of Massachusetts.

Rather than do thus, I need not say what match I would touch, what system endeavor to blow up; but as I love my life, I would side with the light, and let the dark earth roll from under me, calling my mother and my brother to follow.

I would remind my countrymen that they are to be men first, and Americans only at a late and convenient hour. No matter how valuable law may be to protect your property, even to keep soul and body together, if it do not keep you and humanity together.

I am sorry to say that I doubt if there is a judge in Massachusetts who is prepared to resign his office, and get his living innocently, whenever it is required of him to pass sentence under a law which is merely contrary to the law of God. I am compelled to see that they put themselves, or rather are by character, in this respect, exactly on a level with the marine who discharges his musket in any direction he is ordered to. They are just as much tools, and as little men. Certainly, they are not the more to be respected, because their master enslaves their understandings and consciences, instead of their bodies.

The judges and lawyers — simply as such, I mean — and all men of expediency, try this case by a very low and incompetent standard. They consider, not whether the Fugitive Slave Law is right, but whether it is what they call *constitutional*. Is virtue constitutional, or vice? Is equity constitutional, or iniquity? In important moral and vital questions, like this, it is just as impertinent to ask whether a law is constitutional or not, as to ask whether it is profitable or not. They persist in being the servants of the worst of men, and not the servants of humanity. The question is, not whether you or your grandfather, seventy years ago, did not enter into an agreement to serve the Devil, and that service is not accordingly now due; but whether you will not now, for once and at last, serve God — in spite of your own past recreancy, or that of your ancestor — by obeying

that eternal and only just CONSTITUTION, which He, and not any Jefferson or Adams, has written in your being.

The amount of it is, if the majority vote the Devil to be God, the minority will live and behave accordingly — and obey the successful candidate, trusting that, some time or other, by some Speaker's casting-vote, perhaps, they may reinstate God. This is the highest principle I can get out or invent for my neighbors. These men act as if they believed that they could safely slide down a hill a little way — or a good way — and would surely come to a place, by and by, where they could begin to slide up again. This is expediency, or choosing that course which offers the slightest obstacles to the feet, that is, a downhill one. But there is no such thing as accomplishing a righteous reform by the use of "expediency." There is no such thing as sliding up hill. In morals the only sliders are backsliders.

Thus we steadily worship Mammon, both school and state and church, and on the seventh day curse God with a tintamar from one end of the Union to the other.

Will mankind never learn that policy is not morality — that it never secures any moral right, but considers merely what is expedient? chooses the available candidate — who is invariably the Devil — and what right have his constituents to be surprised, because the Devil does not behave like an angel of light? What is wanted is men, not of policy, but of probity — who recognize a higher law than the Constitution, or the decision of the majority. The fate of the country does not depend on how you vote at the polls — the worst man is as strong as the best at that game; it does not depend on what kind of paper you drop into the ballot-box once a year, but on what kind of man you drop from your chamber into the street every morning.

What should concern Massachusetts is not the Nebraska Bill, nor the Fugitive Slave Bill, but her own slaveholding and servility. Let the State dissolve her union with the slaveholder. She may wriggle and hesitate, and ask leave to read the Constitution once more; but she can find no respectable law or precedent which sanctions the continuance of such a union for an instant.

Let each inhabitant of the State dissolve his union with her, as long as she delays to do her duty.

The events of the past month teach me to distrust Fame. I see that she does not finely discriminate, but coarsely hurrahs. She considers not the simple heroism of an action, but only as it is connected with its apparent consequences. She praises till she is hoarse the easy exploit of the Boston tea party, but will be comparatively silent about the braver and more disinterestedly heroic attack on the Boston Court-House, simply because it was unsuccessful!

Covered with disgrace, the State has sat down coolly to try for their lives and liberties the men who attempted to do its duty for it. And this is *called* justice! They who have shown that they can behave particularly well may perchance be put under bonds for *their good behavior*. They whom truth requires at present to plead guilty are, of all the inhabitants of the State, preeminently innocent. While the Governor, and the Mayor, and countless officers of the Commonwealth are at large, the champions of liberty are imprisoned.

Only they are guiltless who commit the crime of contempt of such a court. It behooves every man to see that his influence is on the side of justice, and let the courts make their own characters. My sympathies in this case are wholly with the accused, and wholly against their accusers and judges. Justice is sweet and musical; but injustice is harsh and discordant. The judge still sits grinding at his organ, but it yields no music, and we hear only the sound of the handle. He believes that all the music resides in the handle, and the crowd toss him their coppers the same as before.

Do you suppose that that Massachusetts which is now doing these things — which hesitates to crown these men, some of whose lawyers, and even judges, perchance, may be driven to take refuge in some poor quibble, that they may not wholly outrage their instinctive sense of justice — do you suppose that she is anything but base and servile? that she is the champion of liberty?

Show me a free state, and a court truly of justice, and I will fight for them, if need be; but show me Massachusetts, and I refuse her my allegiance, and express contempt for her courts.

The effect of a good government is to make life more valuable — of a bad one, to make it less valuable. We can afford that railroad and all merely material stock should lose some of its value, for that only compels us to live more simply and economically; but suppose that the value of life itself should be diminished! How can we make a less demand on man and nature, how live more economically in respect to virtue and all noble qualities, than we do? I have lived for the last month — and I think that every man in Massachusetts capable of the sentiment of patriotism must have had a similar experience — with the sense of having suffered a vast and indefinite loss. I did not know at first what ailed me. At last it occurred to me that what I had lost was a country. I had never respected the government near to which I lived, but I had foolishly thought that I might manage to live here, minding my private affairs, and forget it. For my part, my old and worthiest pursuits have lost I cannot say how much of their attraction, and I feel that my investment in life here is worth many per cent less since Massachusetts last deliberately sent back an innocent man, Anthony Burns, to slavery. I dwelt before, perhaps, in the illusion that my life passed somewhere only *between* heaven and hell, but now I cannot persuade myself that I do not dwell *wholly within* hell. The site of that political organization called Massachusetts is to me morally covered with volcanic scoriae and cinders, such as Milton describes in the infernal regions. If there is any hell more unprincipled than our rulers, and we, the ruled, I feel curious to see it. Life itself being worth less, all things with it, which minister to it, are worth less. Suppose you have a small library, with pictures to adorn the walls

— a garden laid out around — and contemplate scientific and literary pursuits.&c., and discover all at once that your villa, with all its contents is located in hell, and that the justice of the peace has a cloven foot and a forked tail — do not these things suddenly lose their value in your eyes?

I feel that, to some extent, the State has fatally interfered with my lawful business. It has not only interrupted me in my passage through Court Street on errands of trade, but it has interrupted me and every man on his onward and upward path, on which he had trusted soon to leave Court Street far behind. What right had it to remind me of Court Street? I have found that hollow which even I had relied on for solid.

I am surprised to see men going about their business as if nothing had happened. I say to myself, "Unfortunates! they have not heard the news." I am surprised that the man whom I just met on horseback should be so earnest to overtake his newly bought cows running away — since all property is insecure, and if they do not run away again, they may be taken away from him when he gets them. Fool! does he not know that his seed-corn is worth less this year — that all beneficent harvests fail as you approach the empire of hell? No prudent man will build a stone house under these circumstances, or engage in any peaceful enterprise which it requires a long time to accomplish. Art is as long as ever, but life is more interrupted and less available for a man's proper pursuits. It is not an era of repose. We have used up all our inherited freedom. If we would save our lives, we must fight for them.

I walk toward one of our ponds; but what signifies the beauty of nature when men are base? We walk to lakes to see our serenity reflected in them; when we are not serene, we go not to them. Who can be serene in a country where both the rulers and the ruled are without principle? The remembrance of my country spoils my walk. My thoughts are murder to the State, and involuntarily go plotting against her.

But it chanced the other day that I scented a white water-lily, and a season I had waited for had arrived. It is the emblem of purity. It bursts up so pure and fair to the eye, and so sweet to the scent, as if to show us what purity and sweetness reside in, and can be extracted from, the slime and muck of earth. I think I have plucked the first one that has opened for a mile. What confirmation of our hopes is in the fragrance of this flower! I shall not so soon despair of the world for it, notwithstanding slavery, and the cowardice and want of principle of Northern men. It suggests what kind of laws have prevailed longest and widest, and still prevail, and that the time may come when man's deeds will smell as sweet. Such is the odor which the plant emits. If Nature can compound this fragrance still annually, I shall believe her still young and full of vigor, her integrity and genius unimpaired, and that there is virtue even in man, too, who is fitted to perceive and love it. It reminds me that Nature has been partner to no Missouri Compromise. I scent no compromise in the fragrance of the water-lily. It is not a *Nymphoea Douglasii*. In it, the sweet, and pure, and innocent are wholly sundered from the obscene and baleful. I do not scent in this the time-serving irresolution of a Massachusetts Governor, nor of a Boston Mayor. So behave that the odor of your actions may enhance the general sweetness of the atmosphere, that when we behold or scent a flower, we may not be reminded how inconsistent your deeds are with it; for all odor is but one form of advertisement of a moral quality, and if fair actions had not been performed, the lily would not smell sweet. The foul slime stands for the sloth and vice of man, the decay of humanity; the fragrant flower that springs from it, for the purity and courage which are immortal.

Slavery and servility have produced no sweet-scented flower annually, to charm the senses of men, for they have no real life: they are merely a decaying and a death, offensive to all healthy nostrils. We do not complain that they live, but that they do not get buried. Let the living bury them: even they are good for manure.

——— 3.35 ———
UNCLE TOM'S CABIN
Harriet Beecher Stowe

Harriet Beecher Stowe's novel *Uncle Tom's Cabin* leaves perhaps a more complicated history than any document of the abolition era. Then, as now, it was hated by many African Americans for its depiction of the slave Tom, who endured the barbarity of his owner and responded only with Christian piety and forgiveness. Its most lasting legacy is this signature depiction of liberal white society's image of a servile, humble and helpless black man. But, ironically, no abolitionist text was as hated among southern white proponents of slavery as Stowe's novel. Pro-slavery writers published counter-novels depicting happy and comfortable slaves or kindly slave owners. Moreover, more black abolitionists loved than hated the book, including Frederick Douglass, who was a friend of Stowe's and advised her during its writing.

In 1851, Stowe, a white freelance journalist from an antislavery family, was among those who wanted to respond to the Fugitive Slave Law. She began writing "Uncle Tom's Cabin" as a serial for the *National Era*. The serial, basically a fictional slave narrative, depicted Tom's life as a slave, juxtaposing his simple and pious character against that of his cruel and heartless owner. The story's popularity led Stowe to publish it in book form. The first run sold out in just two days, and the novel sold half a million copies worldwide in its first year. Countless plays, songs and other cultural artifacts continue to spin off from it today. The novel opens with Tom's kindly Kentucky owner breaking up a slave family by selling a few of them, including Tom, to an ominous southern trader. In the excerpt below, Chapter 4, Stowe introduces Tom and his family and pits their merriment together against the scene of their fateful sale. Here, the reader sees the depiction of ignorant and simple slaves that Stowe meant to be heroic but, ultimately, was a condescending caricature.

CHAPTER IV
An Evening in Uncle Tom's Cabin

The cabin of Uncle Tom was a small log building, close adjoining to "the house," as the negro *par excellence* designates his master's dwelling. In front it had a neat garden-patch, where, every summer, strawberries, raspberries, and a variety of fruits and vegetables, flourished under careful tending. The whole front of it was covered by a large scarlet bignonia and a native multiflora rose, which, entwisting and interlacing, left scarce a vestige of the rough logs to be seen. Here, also, in summer, various brilliant annuals, such as marigolds, petunias, four-o'clocks, found an indulgent corner in which to unfold their splendors, and were the delight and pride of Aunt Chloe's heart.

Let us enter the dwelling. The evening meal at the house is over, and Aunt Chloe, who presided over its preparation as head cook, has left to inferior officers in the kitchen the business of clearing away and washing dishes, and come out into her own snug territories, to "get her ole man's supper"; therefore, doubt not that it is her you see by the fire, presiding with anxious interest over certain frizzling items in a stew-pan, and anon with grave consideration lifting the cover of a bake-kettle, from whence steam forth indubitable intimations of "something good." A round, black, shining face is hers, so glossy as to suggest the idea that she might have been washed over with white of eggs, like one of her own tea rusks. Her whole plump countenance beams with satisfaction and contentment from under her well-starched checked turban, bearing on it, however, if we must confess it, a little of that tinge of self-consciousness which becomes the first cook of the neighborhood, as Aunt Chloe was universally held and acknowledged to be.

A cook she certainly was, in the very bone and centre of her soul. Not a chicken or turkey or duck in the barn-yard but looked grave when they saw her approaching, and seemed evidently to be reflecting on their latter end; and certain it was that she was always meditating on trussing, stuffing and roasting, to a degree that was calculated to inspire terror in any reflecting fowl living. Her corn-cake, in all its varieties of hoe-cake, dodgers, muffins, and other species too numerous to mention, was a sublime mystery to all less practised compounders; and she would shake her fat sides with honest pride and merriment, as she would narrate the fruitless efforts that one and another of her compeers had made to attain to her elevation.

The arrival of company at the house, the arranging of dinners and suppers "in style," awoke all the energies of her soul; and no sight was more welcome to her than a pile of travelling trunks launched on the verandah, for then she foresaw fresh efforts and fresh triumphs.

Just at present, however, Aunt Chloe is looking into the bake-pan; in which congenial operation we shall leave her till we finish our picture of the cottage.

In one corner of it stood a bed, covered neatly with a snowy spread; and by the side of it was a piece of carpeting, of some considerable size. On this piece of carpeting Aunt Chloe took her stand, as being decidedly in the upper walks of life; and it and the bed by which it lay, and the whole corner, in fact, were treated with distinguished consideration, and made, so far as possible, sacred from the marauding inroads and desecrations of little folks. In fact, that corner was the drawing-room of the establishment. In the other corner was a bed of much humbler pretensions, and evidently designed for use. The wall over the fireplace was adorned with some very brilliant scriptural prints, and a portrait of General Washington, drawn and colored in a manner which would certainly have astonished that hero, if ever he happened to meet with its like.

On a rough bench in the corner, a couple of woolly-headed boys, with glistening black eyes and fat shining cheeks, were busy in superintending the first walking operations of the baby, which, as is usually the case, consisted in getting up on its feet, balancing a moment, and then tumbling down, — each successive failure being violently cheered, as something decidedly clever.

A table, somewhat rheumatic in its limbs, was drawn out in front of the fire, and covered with a cloth, displaying cups and saucers of a decidedly brilliant pattern, with other symptoms of an approaching meal. At this table was

seated Uncle Tom, Mr. Shelby's best hand, who, as he is to be the hero of our story, we must daguerreotype for our readers. He was a large, broadchested, powerfully-made man, of a full glossy black, and a face whose truly African features were characterized by an expression of grave and steady good sense, united with much kindliness and benevolence. There was something about his whole air self-respecting and dignified, yet united with a confiding and humble simplicity.

He was very busily intent at this moment on a slate lying before him, on which he was carefully and slowly endeavoring to accomplish a copy of some letters, in which operation he was overlooked by young Mas'r George, a smart, bright boy of thirteen, who appeared fully to realize the dignity of his position as instructor.

"Not that way, Uncle Tom, — not that way," said he, briskly, as Uncle Tom laboriously brought up the tail of his g the wrong side out; "that makes a q, you see."

"La sakes, now, does it?" said Uncle Tom, looking with a respectful, admiring air, as his young teacher flourishingly scrawled q's and g's innumerable for his edification; and then, taking the pencil in his big, heavy fingers, he patiently recommenced.

"How easy white folks al'us does things!" said Aunt Chloe, pausing while she was greasing a griddle with a scrap of bacon on her fork, and regarding young Master George with pride. "The way he can write, now! and read, too! and then to come out here evenings and read his lessons to us, — it's mighty interestin'!"

"But, Aunt Chloe, I'm getting mighty hungry," said George. "Isn't that cake in the skillet almost done?"

"Mose done, Mas'r George," said Aunt Chloe, lifting the lid and peeping in, — "browning beautiful — a real lovely brown. Ah! let me alone for dat. Missis let Sally try to make some cake, t' other day, jes to larn her, she said. 'O, go way, Missis,' said I; 'it really hurts my feelin's, now, to see good vittles spilt dat ar way! Cake ris all to one side — no shape at all; no more than my shoe; go way!"

And with this final expression of contempt for Sally's greenness, Aunt Chloe whipped the cover off the bake-kettle, and disclosed to view a neatly-baked pound-cake, of which no city confectioner need to have been ashamed. This being evidently the central point of the entertainment, Aunt Chloe began now to bustle about earnestly in the supper department.

"Here you, Mose and Pete! get out de way, you niggers! Get away, Mericky, honey, — mammy'll give her baby some fin, by and by. Now, Mas'r George, you jest take off dem books, and set down now with my old man, and I'll take up de sausages, and have de first griddle full of cakes on your plates in less dan no time."

"They wanted me to come to supper in the house," said George; "but I knew what was what too well for that, Aunt Chloe."

"So you did — so you did, honey," said Aunt Chloe, heaping the smoking batter-cakes on his plate; "you know'd your old aunty'd keep the best for you. O, let you alone for dat! Go way!" And, with that, aunty gave George a nudge with her finger, designed to be immensely facetious, and turned again to her griddle with great briskness.

"Now for the cake," said Mas'r George, when the activity of the griddle department had somewhat subsided; and, with that, the youngster flourished a large knife over the article in question.

"La bless you, Mas'r George!" said Aunt Chloe, with earnestness, catching his arm, "you wouldn't be for cuttin' it wid dat ar great heavy knife! Smash all down — spile all de pretty rise of it. Here, I've got a thin old knife, I keeps sharp a purpose. Dar now, see! comes apart light as a feather! Now eat away — you won't get anything to beat dat ar."

"Tom Lincon says," said George, speaking with his mouth full, "that their Jinny is a better cook than you."

"Dem Lincons an't much count, no way!" said Aunt Chloe, contemptuously; "I mean, set along side our folks. They's 'spectable folks enough in a kinder plain way; but, as to gettin' up anything in style, they don't begin to have a notion on 't. Set Mas'r Lincon, now, alongside Mas'r Shelby! Good Lor! and Missis Lincon, — can she kinder sweep it into a room like my missis, — so kinder splendid, yer know! O, go way! don't tell me nothin' of dem Lincons!" — and Aunt Chloe tossed her head as one who hoped she did know something of the world.

"Well, though, I've heard you say," said George, "that Jinny was a pretty fair cook."

"So I did," said Aunt Chloe, — "I may say dat. Good, plain, common cookin', Jinny'll do; — make a good pone o' bread, — bile her taters *far*, — her corn cakes isn't extra, not extra now, Jinny's corn cakes isn't, but then they's *far*, — but, Lor, come to de higher branches, and what can she do? Why, she makes pies — sartin she does; but what kinder crust? Can she make your real flecky paste, as melts in your mouth, and lies all up like a puff? Now, I went over thar when Miss Mary was gwine to be married, and Jinny she jest showed me de weddin' pies. Jinny and I is good friends, ye know. I never said nothin'; but go 'long, Mas'r George! Why, I shouldn't sleep a wink for a week, if I had a batch of pies like dem ar. Why, dey wan't no 'count 't all."

"I suppose Jinny thought they were ever so nice," said George.

"Thought so! — didn't she? Thar she was, showing 'em, as innocent — ye see, it's jest here, Jinny *don't know*. Lor, the family an't nothing! She can't be spected to know! 'Ta'nt no fault o' hem. Ah, Mas'r George, you doesn't know half your privileges in yer family and bringin' up!" Here Aunt Chloe sighed, and rolled up her eyes with emotion.

"I'm sure, Aunt Chloe, I understand my pie and pudding privileges," said George. "Ask Tom Lincon if I don't crow over him, every time I meet him."

Aunt Chloe sat back in her chair, and indulged in a hearty guffaw of laughter, at this witticism of young Mas'r's, laughing till the tears rolled down her black, shining cheeks, and varying the exercise with playfully slapping and poking Mas'r Georgey, and telling him to go way, and that he was a case — that he was fit to kill her, and that he sartin would kill her, one of these days; and, between each of these sanguinary predictions, going off into a laugh, each longer and stronger than the other, till George really began to think that he was a very dangerously witty fellow, and that it became him to be careful how he talked "as funny as he could."

"And so ye told Tom, did ye? O, Lor! what young uns will be up ter! Ye crowed over Tom? O, Lor! Mas'r George, if ye wouldn't make a hornbug laugh!"

"Yes," said George, "I says to him, 'Tom, you ought to see some of Aunt Chloe's pies; they're the right sort,' says I."

"Pity, now, Tom couldn't," said Aunt Chloe, on whose benevolent heart the idea of Tom's benighted condition seemed to make a strong impression. "Ye oughter just ask him here to dinner, some o' these times, Mas'r George," she added; "it would look quite pretty of ye. Ye know, Mas'r George, ye oughtenter feel 'bove nobody, on 'count yer privileges, 'cause all our privileges is gi'n to us; we ought al'ays to 'member that," said Aunt Chloe, looking quite serious.

"Well, I mean to ask Tom here, some day next week," said George; "and you do your prettiest, Aunt Chloe, and we'll make him stare. Won't we make him eat so he won't get over it for a fortnight?"

"Yes, yes — sartin," said Aunt Chloe, delighted;

"You'll see. Lor! to think of some of our dinners! Yer mind dat ar great chicken pie I made when we guv de dinner to General Knox? I and Missis, we come pretty near quarrelling about dat ar crust. What does get into ladies sometimes, I don't know; but, sometimes, when a body has de heaviest kind o' 'sponsibility on 'em, as ye may say, and is all kinder 'seris' and taken up, dey takes dat ar time to be hangin' round and kinder interferin'! Now, Missis, she wanted me to do dis way, and she wanted me to do dat way; and, finally, I got kinder sarcy, and, says I, 'Now, Missis, do jist look at dem beautiful white hands o' yourn with long fin-

gers, and all a sparkling with rings, like my white lilies when de dew 's on 'em; and look at my great black stumpin hands. Now, don't ye think dat de Lord must have meant me to make de pie-crust, and you to stay in de parlor? Dar! I was jist so sarcy, Mas'r George."

"And what did mother say?" said George.

"Say? — why, she kinder larfed in her eyes — dem great handsome eyes o' hern; and, says she, 'Well, Aunt Chloe, I think you are about in the right on 't,' says she; and she went off in de parlor. She oughter cracked me over de head for bein' so sarcy; but dar's whar 't is — I can't do nothin' with ladies in de kitchen!"

"Well, you made out well with that dinner, — I remember everybody said so," said George.

"Didn't I? And wan't I behind de dinin'-room door dat bery day? and didn't I see de General pass his plate three times for some more dat bery pie? — and, says he, 'You must have an uncommon cook, Mrs. Shelby.' Lor! I was fit to split myself.

"And de Gineral, he knows what cookin' is," said Aunt Chloe, drawing herself up with an air. "Bery nice man, de Gineral! He comes of one of de bery *fustest* families in Old Virginny! He knows what's what, now, as well as I do — de Gineral. Ye see, there's *pints* in all pies, Mas'r George; but tan't everybody knows what they is, or as orter be. But the Gineral, he knows; I knew by his 'marks he made. Yes, he knows what de pints is!"

By this time, Master George had arrived at that pass to which even a boy can come (under uncommon circumstances, when he really could not eat another morsel), and, therefore, he was at leisure to notice the pile of woolly heads and glistening eyes which were regarding their operations hungrily from the opposite corner.

"Here, you Mose, Pete," he said, breaking off liberal bits, and throwing it at them; "you want some, don't you? Come, Aunt Chloe, bake them some cakes."

And George and Tom moved to a comfortable seat in the chimney-corner, while Aunte

Chloe, after baking a goodly pile of cakes, took her baby on her lap, and began alternately filling its mouth and her own, and distributing to Mose and Pete, who seemed rather to prefer eating theirs as they rolled about on the floor under the table, tickling each other, and occasionally pulling the baby's toes.

"O! go long, will ye?" said the mother, giving now and then a kick, in a kind of general way, under the table, when the movement became too obstreperous. "Can't ye be decent when white folks comes to see ye? Stop dat ar, now, will ye? Better mind yerselves, or I'll take ye down a button-hole lower, when Mas'r George is gone!

What meaning was couched under this terrible threat, it is difficult to say; but certain it is that its awful indistinctness seemed to produce very little impression on the young sinners addressed.

"La, now!" said Uncle Tom, "they are so full of tickle all the while, they can't behave theirselves."

Here the boys emerged from under the table, and, with hands and faces well plastered with molasses, began a vigorous kissing of the baby.

"Get along wid ye!" said the mother, pushing away their woolly heads. "Ye'll all stick together, and never get clar, if ye do dat fashion. Go long to de spring and wash yerselves!" she said, seconding her exhortations by a slap, which resounded very formidably, but which seemed only to knock out so much more laugh from the young ones, as they tumbled precipitately over each other out of doors, where they fairly screamed with merriment.

"Did ye ever see such aggravating young uns?" said Aunt Chloe, rather complacently, as, producing an old towel, kept for such emergencies, she poured a little water out of the cracked tea-pot on it, and began rubbing off the molasses from the baby's face and hands; and, having polished her till she shone, she set her down in Tom's lap, while she busied herself in clearing away supper. The baby employed the intervals in pulling Tom's nose, scratching his face, and burying her fat hands in his woolly hair, which last operation seemed to afford her special content.

"Aint she a peart young un?" said Tom, holding her from him to take a full-length view; then, getting up, he set her on his broad shoulder, and began capering and dancing with her, while Mas'r George snapped at her with his pocket-handkerchief, and Mose and Pete, now returned again, roared after her like bears, till Aunt Chloe declared that they "fairly took her head off" with their noise. As, according to her own statement, this surgical operation was a matter of daily occurrence in the cabin, the declaration no whit abated the merriment, till every one had roared and tumbled and danced themselves down to a state of composure.

"Well, now, I hopes you're done," said Aunt Chloe, who had been busy in pulling out a rude box of a trundle-bed; "and now, you Mose and you Pete, get into thar; for we's goin' to have the meetin'."

"O mother, we don't wanter. We wants to sit up to meetin', — meetin's is so curis. We likes 'em."

"La, Aunt Chloe, shove it under, and let 'em sit up," said Mas'r George, decisively, giving a push to the rude machine.

Aunt Chloe, having thus saved appearances, seemed highly delighted to push the thing under, saying, as she did so, "Well, mebbe 't will do 'em some good."

The house now resolved itself into a committee of the whole, to consider the accommodations and arrangements for the meeting.

"What we's to do for cheers, now, I declar I don't know," said Aunt Chloe. As the meeting had been held at Uncle Tom's weekly, for an indefinite length of time, without any more "cheers," there seemed some encouragement to hope that a way would be discovered at present.

"Old Uncle Peter sung both de legs out of dat oldest cheer, last week," suggested Mose.

"You go long! I'll boun' you pulled 'em out; some o' your shines," said Aunt Chloe.

"Well, it'll stand, if it only keeps jam up agin de wall!" said Mose.

"Den Uncle Peter mus'n't sit in it, cause he al'ays hitches when he gets a singing. He hitched pretty nigh across de room, t' other night," said Pete.

"Good Lor! get him in it, then," said Mose, "and den he'd begin, 'Come saints — and sinners, hear me tell,' and den down he'd go," — and Mose imitated precisely the nasal tones of the old man, tumbling on the floor, to illustrate the supposed catastrophe.

"Come now, be decent, can't ye?" said Aunt Chloe; "an't yer shamed?"

Mas'r George, however, joined the offender in the laugh, and declared decidedly that Mose was a "buster." So the maternal admonition seemed rather to fail of effect.

"Well, ole man," said Aunt Chloe, "you'll have to tote in them ar bar'ls."

"Mother's bar'ls is like dat ar widder's, Mas'r George was reading 'bout, in de good book, — dey never fails," said Mose, aside to Peter.

"I'm sure one on 'em caved in last week," said Pete, "and let 'em all down in de middle of de singin'; dat ar was failin', warnt it?"

During this aside between Mose and Pete, two empty casks had been rolled into the cabin, and being secured from rolling, by stones on each side, boards were laid across them, which arrangement, together with the turning down of certain tubs and pails, and the disposing of the rickety chairs, at last completed the preparation.

"Mas'r George is such a beautiful reader, now, I know he'll stay to read for us," said Aunt Chloe; "'pears like 't will be so much more interestin'."

George very readily consented, for your boy is always ready for anything that makes him of importance.

The room was soon filled with a motley assemblage, from the old gray-headed patriarch of eighty, to the young girl and lad of fifteen. A little harmless gossip ensued on various themes, such as where old Aunt Sally got her new red headkerchief, and how "Missis was a going to give Lizzy that spotted muslin gown, when she'd got her new berage made up;" and

how Mas'r Shelby was thinking of buying a new sorrel colt, that was going to prove an addition to the glories of the place. A few of the worshippers belonged to families hard by, who had got permission to attend, and who brought in various choice scraps of information, about the sayings and doings at the house and on the place, which circulated as freely as the same sort of small change does in higher circles.

After a while the singing commenced, to the evident delight of all present. Not even all the disadvantage of nasal intonation could prevent the effect of the naturally fine voices, in airs at once wild and spirited. The words were sometimes the well-known and common hymns sung in the churches about, and sometimes of a wilder, more indefinite character, picked up at camp-meetings.

The chorus of one of them, which ran as follows, was sung with great energy and unction:

*"Die on the field of battle,
Die on the field of battle,
Glory in my soul."*

Another special favorite had oft repeated the words—

*"O, I'm going to glory, —
won't you come along with me?
Don't you see the angels beck'ning,
and a calling me away?
Don't you see the golden city
and the everlasting day?"*

There were others, which made incessant mention of "Jordan's banks," and "Canaan's fields," and the "New Jerusalem;" for the negro mind, impassioned and imaginative, always attaches itself to hymns and expressions of a vivid and pictorial nature; and, as they sung, some laughed, and some cried, and some clapped hands, or shook hands rejoicingly with each other, as if they had fairly gained the other side of the river.

Various exhortations, or relations of experience, followed, and intermingled with the singing. One old gray-headed woman, long past work, but much revered as a sort of chronicle of the past, rose, and leaning on her staff, said —

"Well, chil'en! Well, I'm mighty glad to hear ye all and see ye all once more, 'cause I don't know when I'll be gone to glory; but I've done got ready, chil'en; 'pears like I'd got my little bundle all tied up, and my bonnet on, jest a waitin' for the stage to come along and take me home; sometimes, in the night, I think I hear the wheels a rattlin', and I'm lookin' out all the time; now, you jest be ready too, for I tell ye all, chil'en," she said striking her staff hard on the floor, "dat ar *glory* is a mighty thing! It's a mighty thing, chil'en, — you don'no nothing about it, — it's *wonderful*." And the old creature sat down, with streaming tears, as wholly overcome, while the whole circle struck up —

"O Canaan, bright Canaan
I'm bound for the land of Canaan."

Mas'r George, by request, read the last chapters of Revelation, often interrupted by such exclamations as "The sakes now!" "Only hear that!" "Jest think on 't!" "Is all that a comin' sure enough?"

George, who was a bright boy, and well trained in religious things by his mother, finding himself an object of general admiration, threw in expositions of his own, from time to time, with a commendable seriousness and gravity, for which he was admired by the young and blessed by the old; and it was agreed, on all hands, that "a minister couldn't lay it off better than he did;" that "'t was reely 'mazin'!"

Uncle Tom was a sort of patriarch in religious matters, in the neighborhood. Having, naturally, an organization in which the morale was strongly predominant, together with a greater breadth and cultivation of mind than obtained among his companions, he was looked up to with great respect, as a sort of minister among them; and the simple, hearty, sincere style of his exhortations might have edified even better educated

persons. But it was in prayer that he especially excelled. Nothing could exceed the touching simplicity, the child-like earnestness, of his prayer, enriched with the language of Scripture, which seemed so entirely to have wrought itself into his being, as to have become a part of himself, and to drop from his lips unconsciously; in the language of a pious old negro, he "prayed right up." And so much did his prayer always work on the devotional feelings of his audiences, that there seemed often a danger that it would be lost altogether in the abundance of the responses which broke out everywhere around him.

While this scene was passing in the cabin of the man, one quite otherwise passed in the halls of the master.

The trader and Mr. Shelby were seated together in the dining room afore-named, at a table covered with papers and writing utensils.

Mr. Shelby was busy in counting some bundles of bills, which, as they were counted, he pushed over to the trader, who counted them likewise.

"All fair," said the trader; "and now for signing these yer."

Mr. Shelby hastily drew the bills of sale towards him, and signed them, like a man that hurries over some disagreeable business, and then pushed them over with the money. Haley produced, from a well-worn valise, a parchment, which, after looking over it a moment, he handed to Mr. Shelby, who took it with a gesture of suppressed eagerness.

"Wal, now, the thing's *done*!" said the trader, getting up.

"It's *done*!" said Mr. Shelby, in a musing tone; and, fetching a long breath, he repeated, "*It's done*!"

"Yer don't seem to feel much pleased with it, 'pears to me," said the trader.

"Haley," said Mr. Shelby, "I hope you'll remember that you promised, on your honor, you wouldn't sell Tom, without knowing what sort of hands he's going into."

"Why, you've just done it sir," said the trader.

"Circumstances, you well know, *obliged* me," said Shelby, haughtily.

"Wal, you know, they may 'blige *me*, too," said the trader. "Howsomever, I'll do the very best I can in gettin' Tom a good berth; as to my treatin' on him bad, you needn't be a grain afeard. If there's anything that I thank the Lord for, it is that I'm never noways cruel."

After the expositions which the trader had previously given of his humane principles, Mr. Shelby did not feel particularly reassured by these declarations; but, as they were the best comfort the case admitted of, he allowed the trader to depart in silence, and betook himself to a solitary cigar.

——— 3.36 ———

AN IDEOLOGICAL RIFT OVER THE U.S. CONSTITUTION AND SLAVERY

Frederick Douglass and William Lloyd Garrison

In the years following the odious Fugitive Slave Act's passage, the simmering intellectual conflict between William Lloyd Garrison and Frederick Douglass boiled over. Garrison had become increasingly radical, and Douglass was among those angered by his Constitution-burning protest at the 1854 rally following Anthony Burns's arrest. A few years earlier, Garrison had come to the conclusion that the Constitution was an instrument of oppression rather than liberty, a pro-slavery document that must be attacked along with the slave system itself. Douglass believed it most politically expedient to use the document to save the slaves of the South. Garrison proclaimed there could be "no union with slavery," and that the nation would have to be dissolved; to do so, Douglass protested, was to abandon southern slaves. The two men would never heal their ideological rift, which exploded in 1851, when Douglass publicly broke with Garrison on the matter, first in a speech and then in an editorial in his *North Star*.

A. Douglass breaks with Garrison in *North Star*.

CHANGE OF OPINION ANNOUNCED

The debate on the resolution relative to anti-slavery newspapers [at the annual meeting of American Anti-Slavery, Society] assumed such a character as to make it our duty to define the position of the *North Star* in respect to the Constitution of the United States. The ground having been distinctly taken, that no paper ought to receive the recommendation of the American Anti-Slavery Society that did not assume the Constitution to be a pro-slavery document, we felt in honor bound to announce at once to our old anti-slavery companions that we no longer possessed the requisite qualification for their official approval and commendation; and to assure them that we had arrived at the firm conviction that the Constitution, construed in the light of well established rules of legal interpretation, might be made consistent in its details with the noble purposes avowed in its preamble; and that hereafter we should insist upon the application of such rules to that instrument, and demand that it be wielded in behalf of emancipation. The change in our opinion on this subject has not been hastily arrived at. A careful study of the writings of Lynsander Spooner, of Gerrit Smith, and of William Goodell, has brought us to our present conclusion. We found, in our former position, that, when debating the question, we were compelled to go behind the letter of the Constitution, and to seek its meaning in the history and practice of the nation under it — a process always attended with disadvantages; and certainly we feel little inclination to shoulder disadvantages of any kind, in order to give slavery the slightest protection. In short, we hold it to be a system of lawless violence; that it *never was lawful*, and never can be made so; and that it is the first duty of every American citizen, whose conscience permits so to do, to use his *political* as well as his *moral* power for its overthrow. Of course, this avowal did not pass without animadversion, and it would have been strange if it had passed without some crimination; for it is hard for any combination or party to attribute good motives to any one who differs from them in what, they deem a vital point. Brother Garrison at once exclaimed, "There is roguery somewhere!" but we can easily forgive this hastily expressed imputation, falling, as it did, from the lips of one to whom we shall never cease to be grateful, and for whom we have cherished (and do now cherish) a veneration only inferior in degree to that which we owe to our conscience and to our God.

B. Garrison's response

There are some very worthy men, who are gravely trying to convince this slaveholding and slave-trading nation, that it has an Anti-Slavery Constitution, if it did but know it — always has had it since it was a nation — and so designed it to be from the beginning! Hence, all slaveholding under it is illegal, and ought in virtue of it to be forthwith abolished by act of Congress. As rationally attempt to convince the American people that they inhabit the moon, and I 'run upon all fours,' as that they have not intelligently deliberately and purposely entered into a covenant, by which three millions of slaves are now held securely in bondage! They are not to be let off so easily, either by indignant Heaven or outraged Earth! To tell them that, for three score years, they have misunderstood and misinterpreted their own Constitution, in a manner gross and distorted beyond any thing known in human history; that Washington, Jefferson, Adams, all who framed that Constitution — the Supreme Court of the United States, and all its branches, and all other Courts — the national Congress and all State Legislatures — have utterly perverted its scope and meaning — is the coolest and absurdest thing ever heard of beneath the stars! No, not thus are they to be allowed to escape hot censure and unsparing condemnation. They have committed no blunder; they have not erred through stupidity; they have not been misled by any legal sophistry. They are verily guilty of the most atrocious crimes, and have sinned against the clearest light ever vouchsafed to any people. They have designedly 'framed mischief by a law,' and consigned to chains and infamy an

inoffensive and helpless race. Hence, it is not an error in legal interpretation that they are to correct, but they are to be arraigned as criminals of the deepest dye, warned of the wrath to come, and urged to the immediate confession and abandonment of this great 'besetting sin.' 'Now, therefore, go to, speak to the men of Judah, and to the inhabitants of Jerusalem, saying, Thus saith the Lord, Behold, I frame evil against you, and devise a device against you; return ye now every one from his evil way, and make your ways and your doings good.'

Some are unwilling to admit the possibility of legalizing slavery, because of its foul and monstrous character. But what iniquity may not men commit by agreement? and what obligations so diabolical, that men may not promise to perform them to the letter? To say that men have no right to do wrong is a truism; to intimate that they have not the power to do so is an absurdity. If they have the power, it is possible for them to use it; and no where do they use it with more alacrity, or on a more gigantic scale, than in the United States. ...

———— 3.37 ————
'WHAT TO THE SLAVE IS THE FOURTH OF JULY?'
Frederick Douglass

Frederick Douglass was such a prolific speaker and writer that to attempt to isolate some works above others is a nearly meaningless task. Nevertheless, it at least seems clear that, as for writing, his *Narrative* not only stands out among his other works, but remains one of history's great autobiographies. Of his oratory, observers have noted two particularly moving speeches: one was his 1846 "What is American Slavery?" speech in Moorsfield, England. The other he delivered at home in Rochester, New York, on July 4, 1852. There, Douglass presented another question, "What to the Slave is the Fourth of July?" The speech encapsulates Douglass's political philosophy, and goes a long way towards explaining his differences with William Lloyd Garrison. On one hand, he ridiculed the hypocritical American ethos of liberty; on the other, he celebrated abolition as a truly American quest for freedom.

... This, for the purpose of this celebration, is the 4th of July. It is the birthday of your National Independence, and of your political freedom. This, to you, is what the Passover was to the emancipated people of God. It carries your minds back to the day, and to the act of your great deliverance; and to the signs, and to the wonders, associated with that act, and that day. This celebration also marks the beginning of another year of your national life; and reminds you that the Republic of America is now 76 years old. I am glad, fellow-citizens, that your nation is so young. Seventy-six years, though a good old age for a man, is but a mere speck in the life of a nation. Three score years and ten is the allotted time for individual men; but nations number their years by thousands. According to this fact, you are, even now, only in the beginning of your national career, still lingering in the period of childhood. I repeat, I am glad this is so. There is hope in the thought, and hope is much needed, under the dark clouds which lower above the horizon. The eye of the reformer is met with angry flashes, portending disastrous times; but his heart may well beat lighter at the thought that America is young, and that she is still in the impressible stage of her existence. May he not hope that high lessons of wisdom, of justice and of truth, will yet give direction to her destiny? Were the nation older, the patriot's heart might be sadder, and the reformer's brow heavier. Its future might be shrouded in gloom, and the hope of its prophets go out in sorrow. There is consolation in the thought that America is young. Great streams are not easily turned from channels, worn deep in the course of ages. They may sometimes rise in quiet and stately majesty, and inundate the land, refreshing and fertilizing the earth with their mysterious properties. They may also rise in wrath and fury, and bear away, on their angry waves, the accumulated wealth of years of toil and hardship. They, however, gradually flow back to the same old channel, and flow on as serenely as ever. But, while the river may not be turned aside, it may dry up, and leave nothing behind but the withered branch, and the unsightly rock, to howl in the abyss-sweeping wind, the sad tale of departed glory. As with rivers so with nations.

Fellow-citizens, I shall not presume to dwell at length on the associations that cluster about this day. The simple story of it is that, 76 years ago, the people of this country were British subjects. The style and title of your "sovereign people" (in which you now glory) was not then born. You were under the British Crown. Your fathers esteemed the English Government as the home government; and England as the fatherland. This home government, you know, although a considerable distance from your home, did, in the exercise of its parental prerogatives, impose upon its colonial children, such restraints, burdens and limitations, as, in its mature judgement, it deemed wise, right and proper.

But, your fathers, who had not adopted the fashionable idea of this day, of the infallibility of government, and the absolute character of its acts, presumed to differ from the home government in respect to the wisdom and the justice of some of those burdens and restraints. They went so far in their excitement as to pronounce the measures of government unjust, unreasonable, and oppressive, and altogether such as ought not to be quietly submitted to. I scarcely need say, fellow-citizens, that my opinion of those measures fully accords with that of your fathers. Such a declaration of agreement on my part would not be worth much to anybody. It would, certainly, prove nothing, as to what part I might have taken, had I lived during the great controversy of 1776. To say now that America was right, and England wrong, is exceedingly easy. Everybody can say it; the dastard, not less than the noble brave, can flippantly discant on the tyranny of England towards the American Colonies. It is fashionable to do so; but there was a time when to pronounce against England, and in favor of the cause of the colonies, tried men's souls. They who did so were accounted in their day, plotters of mischief, agitators and rebels, dangerous men. To side with the right, against the wrong, with the weak against the strong, and with the oppressed against the oppressor! here lies the merit, and the one which, of all others, seems unfashionable in our day. The cause of liberty may be stabbed by the men who glory in the deeds of your fathers. But, to proceed.

Feeling themselves harshly and unjustly treated by the home government, your fathers, like men of honesty, and men of spirit, earnestly sought redress. They petitioned and remonstrated; they did so in a decorous, respectful, and loyal manner. Their conduct was wholly unexceptionable. This, however, did not answer the purpose. They saw themselves treated with sovereign indifference, coldness and scorn. Yet they persevered. They were not the men to look back.

As the sheet anchor takes a firmer hold, when the ship is tossed by the storm, so did the cause of your fathers grow stronger, as it breasted the chilling blasts of kingly displeasure. The greatest and best of British statesmen admitted its justice, and the loftiest eloquence of the British Senate came to its support. But, with that blindness which seems to be the unvarying characteristic of tyrants, since Pharaoh and his hosts were drowned in the Red Sea, the British Government persisted in the exactions complained of.

The madness of this course, we believe, is admitted now, even by England; but we fear the lesson is wholly lost on our present rulers.

Oppression makes a wise man mad. Your fathers were wise men, and if they did not go mad, they became restive under this treatment. They felt themselves the victims of grievous wrongs, wholly incurable in their colonial capacity. With brave men there is always a remedy for oppression. Just here, the idea of a total separation of the colonies from the crown was born! It was a startling idea, much more so, than we, at this distance of time, regard it. The timid and the prudent (as has been intimated) of that day, were, of course, shocked and alarmed by it.

Such people lived then, had lived before, and will, probably, ever have a place on this planet; and their course, in respect to any great change, (no matter how great the good to be attained, or the wrong to be redressed by it), may be calculated with as much precision as can be the course of the stars. They hate all changes, but silver, gold and copper change! Of this sort of change they are always strongly in favor.

These people were called tories in the days of your fathers; and the appellation, probably, conveyed the same idea that is meant by a more modern, though a somewhat less euphonious term, which we often find in our papers, applied to some of our old politicians.

Their opposition to the then dangerous thought was earnest and powerful; but, amid all their terror and affrighted vociferations against it, the alarming and revolutionary idea moved on, and the country with it.

On the 2d of July, 1776, the old Continental Congress, to the dismay of the lovers of ease, and the worshipers of property, clothed that dreadful idea with all the authority of national sanction. They did so in the form of a resolution; and as we seldom hit upon resolutions, drawn up in our day, whose transparency is at all equal to this, it may refresh your minds and help my story if I read it.

"Resolved, That these united colonies are, and of right, ought to be free and Independent States; that they are absolved from all allegiance to the British Crown; and that all political connection between them and the State of Great Britain is, and ought to be, dissolved."

Citizens, your fathers made good that resolution. They succeeded; and to-day you reap the fruits of their success. The freedom gained is yours; and you, therefore, may properly celebrate this anniversary. The 4th of July is the first great fact in your nation's history — the very ring-bolt in the chain of your yet undeveloped destiny.

Pride and patriotism, not less than gratitude, prompt you to celebrate and to hold it in perpetual remembrance. I have said that the

Declaration of Independence is the ring-bolt to the chain of your nation's destiny; so, indeed, I regard it. The principles contained in that instrument are saving principles. Stand by those principles, be true to them on all occasions, in all places, against all foes, and at whatever cost.

From the round top of your ship of state, dark and threatening clouds may be seen. Heavy billows, like mountains in the distance, disclose to the leeward huge forms of flinty rocks! That bolt drawn, that chain broken, and all is lost. Cling to this day — cling to it, and to its principles, with the grasp of a storm-tossed mariner to a spar at midnight.

The coming into being of a nation, in any circumstances, is an interesting event. But, besides general considerations, there were peculiar circumstances which make the advent of this republic an event of special attractiveness.

The whole scene, as I look back to it, was simple, dignified and sublime.

The population of the country, at the time, stood at the insignificant number of three millions. The country was poor in the munitions of war. The population was weak and scattered, and the country a wilderness unsubdued. There were then no means of concert and combination, such as exist now. Neither steam nor lightning had then been reduced to order and discipline. From the Potomac to the Delaware was a journey of many days. Under these, and innumerable other disadvantages, your fathers declared for liberty and independence and triumphed.

Fellow Citizens, I am not wanting in respect for the fathers of this republic. The signers of the Declaration of Independence were brave men. They were great men too — great enough to give fame to a great age. It does not often happen to a nation to raise, at one time, such a number of truly great men. The point from which I am compelled to view them is not, certainly, the most favorable; and yet I cannot contemplate their great deeds with less than admiration. They were statesmen, patri-

ots and heroes, and for the good they did, and the principles they contended for, I will unite with you to honor their memory.

They loved their country better than their own private interests; and, though this is not the highest form of human excellence, all will concede that it is a rare virtue, and that when it is exhibited, it ought to command respect. He who will, intelligently, lay down his life for his country, is a man whom it is not in human nature to despise. Your fathers staked their lives, their fortunes, and their sacred honor, on the cause of their country. In their admiration of liberty, they lost sight of all other interests.

They were peace men; but they preferred revolution to peaceful submission to bondage. They were quiet men; but they did not shrink from agitating against oppression. They showed forbearance; but that they knew its limits. They believed in order; but not in the order of tyranny. With them, nothing was "settled" that was not right. With them, justice, liberty and humanity were "final;" not slavery and oppression. You may well cherish the memory of such men. They were great in their day and generation. Their solid manhood stands out the more as we contrast it with these degenerate times.

How circumspect, exact and proportionate were all their movements! How unlike the politicians of an hour! Their statesmanship looked beyond the passing moment, and stretched away in strength into the distant future. They seized upon eternal principles, and set a glorious example in their defence. Mark them!

Fully appreciating the hardship to be encountered, firmly believing in the right of their cause, honorably inviting the scrutiny of an on-looking world, reverently appealing to heaven to attest their sincerity, soundly comprehending the solemn responsibility they were about to assume, wisely measuring the terrible odds against them, your fathers, the fathers of this republic, did, most deliberately, under the inspiration of a glorious patriotism, and with a sublime faith in the great principles of justice and freedom, lay deep the corner-stone of the national superstructure, which has risen and still rises in grandeur around you.

Of this fundamental work, this day is the anniversary. Our eyes are met with demonstrations of joyous enthusiasm. Banners and pennants wave exultingly on the breeze. The din of business, too, is hushed. Even Mammon seems to have quitted his grasp on this day. The ear-piercing fife and the stirring drum unite their accents with the ascending peal of a thousand church bells. Prayers are made, hymns are sung, and sermons are preached in honor of this day; while the quick martial tramp of a great and multitudinous nation, echoed back by all the hills, valleys and mountains of a vast continent, bespeak the occasion one of thrilling and universal interests nation's jubilee.

Friends and citizens, I need not enter further into the causes which led to this anniversary. Many of you understand them better than I do. You could instruct me in regard to them. That is a branch of knowledge in which you feel, perhaps, a much deeper interest than your speaker. The causes which led to the separation of the colonies from the British crown have never lacked for a tongue. They have all been taught in your common schools, narrated at your firesides, unfolded from your pulpits, and thundered from your legislative halls, and are as familiar to you as household words. They form the staple of your national poetry and eloquence.

I remember, also, that, as a people, Americans are remarkably familiar with all facts which make in their own favor. This is esteemed by some as a national trait — perhaps a national weakness. It is a fact, that whatever makes for the wealth or for the reputation of Americans, and can be had cheap! will be found by Americans. I shall not be charged with slandering Americans, if I say I think the American side of any question may be safely left in American hands.

I leave, therefore, the great deeds of your fathers to other gentlemen whose claim to have been regularly descended will be less likely to be disputed than mine!

THE PRESENT.

My business, if I have any here to-day, is with the present. The accepted time with God and his cause is the ever-living now.

"Trust no future, however pleasant,
Let the dead past bury its dead;
Act, act in the living present,
Heart within, and God overhead."

We have to do with the past only as we can make it useful to the present and to the future. To all inspiring motives, to noble deeds which can be gained from the past, we are welcome. But now is the time, the important time. Your fathers have lived, died, and have done their work, and have done much of it well. You live and must die, and you must do your work. You have no right to enjoy a child's share in the labor of your fathers, unless your children are to be blest by your labors. You have no right to wear out and waste the hard-earned fame of your fathers to cover your indolence. Sydney Smith tells us that men seldom eulogize the wisdom and virtues of their fathers, but to excuse some folly or wickedness of their own. This truth is not a doubtful one. There are illustrations of it near and remote, ancient and modern. It was fashionable, hundreds of years ago, for the children of Jacob to boast, we have "Abraham to our father," when they had long lost Abraham's faith and spirit. That people contented themselves under the shadow of Abraham's great name, while they repudiated the deeds which made his name great. Need I remind you that a similar thing is being done all over this country to-day? Need I tell you that the Jews are not the only people who built the tombs of the prophets, and garnished the sepulchres of the righteous? Washington could not die till he had broken the chains of his slaves. Yet his monument is built up by the price of human blood, and the traders in the bodies and souls of men, shout — "We have Washington to our father." Alas! that it should be so; yet so it is.

"The evil that men do, lives after them,
The good is oft' interred with their bones."

Fellow-citizens, pardon me, allow me to ask, why am I called upon to speak here to-day? What have I, or those I represent, to do with your national independence? Are the great principles of political freedom and of natural justice, embodied in that Declaration of Independence, extended to us? and am I, therefore, called upon to bring our humble offering to the national altar, and to confess the benefits and express devout gratitude for the blessings resulting from your independence to us?

Would to God, both for your sakes and ours, that an affirmative answer could be truthfully returned to these questions! Then would my task be light, and my burden easy and delightful. For who is there so cold, that a nation's sympathy could not warm him? Who so obdurate and dead to the claims of gratitude, that would not thankfully acknowledge such priceless benefits? Who so stolid and selfish, that would not give his voice to swell the hallelujahs of a nation's jubilee, when the chains of servitude had been torn from his limbs? I am not that man. In a case like that, the dumb might eloquently speak, and the "lame man leap as an hart."

But, such is not the state of the case. I say it with a sad sense of the disparity between us. I am not included within the pale of this glorious anniversary! Your high independence only reveals the immeasurable distance between us. The blessings in which you, this day, rejoice, are not enjoyed in common. The rich inheritance of justice, liberty, prosperity and independence, bequeathed by your fathers, is shared by you, not by me. The sunlight that brought life and healing to you, has brought stripes and death to me. This Fourth July is yours, not mine. You may rejoice, I must mourn. To drag a man in fetters into the grand illuminated temple of liberty, and call upon him to join you in joyous anthems, were inhuman mockery and sacrilegious irony. Do you mean, citizens, to mock me, by asking me to speak to-day? If so, there is a parallel to your conduct. And let me warn you that it is dangerous to copy the example of a nation whose crimes, lowering up to heaven, were thrown down by the breath of the Almighty, burying that nation in irrecoverable ruin! I can to-day take up the plaintive lament of a peeled and woe-smitten people!

"By the rivers of Babylon, there we sat down. Yea! we wept when we remembered Zion. We hanged our harps upon the willows in the midst thereof. For there, they that carried us away captive, required of us a song; and they who wasted us required of us mirth, saying, Sing us one of the songs of Zion. How can we sing the Lord's song in a strange land? If I forget thee, O Jerusalem, let my right hand forget her cunning. If I do not remember thee, let my tongue cleave to the roof of my mouth."

Fellow-citizens; above your national, tumultous joy, I hear the mournful wail of millions! whose chains, heavy and grievous yesterday, are, to-day, rendered more intolerable by the jubilee shouts that reach them. If I do forget, if I do not faithfully remember those bleeding children of sorrow this day, "may my right hand forget her cunning, and may my tongue cleave to the roof of my mouth!" To forget them, to pass lightly over their wrongs, and to chime in with the popular theme, would be treason most scandalous and shocking, and would make me a reproach before God and the world. My subject, then fellow-citizens, is AMERICAN SLAVERY. I shall see, this day, and its popular characteristics, from the slave's point of view. Standing, there, identified with the American bondman, making his wrongs mine, I do not hesitate to declare, with all my soul, that the character and conduct of this nation never looked blacker to me than on this 4th of July! Whether we turn to the declarations of the past, or to the professions of the present, the conduct of the nation seems equally hideous and revolting. America is false to the past, false to the present, and solemnly binds herself to be false to the future. Standing with God and the crushed and bleeding slave on this occasion, I will, in the name of humanity which is outraged, in the name of liberty which is fettered, in the name of the constitution and the Bible, which are disregarded and trampled upon, dare to call in question and to denounce, with all the emphasis I can command, everything that serves to perpetuate slavery — the great sin and shame of America! "I will not equivocate; I will not excuse;" I will use the severest language I can command; and yet not one word shall escape me that any man, whose judgement is not blinded by prejudice, or who is not at heart a slaveholder, shall not confess to be right and just.

But I fancy I hear some one of my audience say, it is just in this circumstance that you and your brother abolitionists fail to make a favorable impression on the public mind. Would you argue more, and denounce less, would you persuade more, and rebuke less, your cause would be much more likely to succeed. But, I submit, where all is plain there is nothing to be argued. What point in the anti-slavery creed would you have me argue? On what branch of the subject do the people of this country need light? Must I undertake to prove that the slave is a man? That point is conceded already. Nobody doubts it.

The slaveholders themselves acknowledge it in the enactment of laws for their government. They acknowledge it when they punish disobedience on the part of the slave. There are seventy-two crimes in the State of Virginia, which, if committed by a black man, (no matter how ignorant he be), subject him to the punishment of death; while only two of the same crimes will subject a white man to the like punishment.

What is this but the acknowledgement that the slave is a moral, intellectual and responsible being? The manhood of the slave is conceded. It is admitted in the fact that Southern statute books are covered with enactments forbidding, under severe fines and penalties, the teaching of the slave to read or to write.

When you can point to any such laws, in reference to the beasts of the field, then I may consent to argue the manhood of the slave. When the dogs in your streets, when the fowls of the air, when the cattle on your hills, when the fish of the sea, and the reptiles that crawl, shall be unable to distinguish the slave from a brute, there will I argue with you that the slave is a man!

For the present, it is enough to affirm the equal manhood of the negro race. Is it not astonishing that, while we are ploughing, planting and reaping, using all kinds of mechanical tools, erecting houses, constructing bridges, building ships, working in metals of brass, iron, copper, silver and gold; that, while we are reading, writing and cyphering, acting as clerks, merchants and secretaries, having among us lawyers, doctors, ministers, poets, authors, editors, orators and teachers; that, while we are engaged in all manner of enterprises common to other men, digging gold in California, capturing the whale in the Pacific, feeding sheep and cattle on the hill-side, living, moving, acting, thinking, planning, living in families as husbands, wives and children, and, above all, confessing and worshipping the Christian's God, and looking hopefully for life and immortality beyond the grave, we are called upon to prove that we are men!

Would you have me argue that man is entitled to liberty? that he is the rightful owner of his own body? You have already declared it. Must I argue the wrongfulness of slavery? Is that a question for Republicans? Is it to be settled by the rules of logic and argumentation, as a matter beset with great difficulty, involving a doubtful application of the principle of justice, hard to be understood? How should I look to-day, in the presence of Americans, dividing, and subdividing a discourse, to show that men have a natural right to freedom? speaking of it relatively, and positively, negatively, and affirmatively. To do so, would be to make myself ridiculous, and to offer an insult to your understanding. There is not a man beneath the canopy of heaven, that does not know that slavery is wrong for him.

What, am I to argue that it is wrong to make men brutes, to rob them of their liberty, to work them without wages, to keep them ignorant of their relations to their fellow men, to beat them with sticks, to flay their flesh with the lash, to load their limbs with irons, to hunt them with dogs, to sell them at auction, to sunder their families, to knock out their teeth, to burn their flesh, to starve them into obedience and submission to their masters? Must I argue that a system thus marked with blood, and stained with pollution, is wrong? No! I will not. I have better employments for my time and strength, than such arguments would imply.

What, then, remains to be argued? Is it that slavery is not divine; that God did not establish it; that our doctors of divinity are mistaken? There is blasphemy in the thought. That which is inhuman, cannot be divine! Who can reason on such a proposition? They that can, may; I cannot. The time for such argument is past.

At a time like this, scorching irony, not convincing argument, is needed. O! had I the ability, and could I reach the nation's ear, I would, to-day, pour out a fiery stream of biting ridicule, blasting reproach, withering sarcasm, and stern rebuke. For it is not light that is needed, but fire; it is not the gentle shower, but thunder. We need the storm, the whirlwind, and the earthquake. The feeling of the nation must be quickened; the conscience of the nation must be roused; the propriety of the nation must be startled; the hypocrisy of the nation must be exposed; and its crimes against God and man must be proclaimed and denounced.

What, to the American slave, is your 4th of July? I answer: a day that reveals to him, more than all other days in the year, the gross injustice and cruelty to which he is the constant victim. To him, your celebration is a sham; your boasted liberty, an unholy license; your national greatness, swelling vanity; your sounds of rejoicing are empty and heartless; your denunciations of tyrants, brass fronted impudence; your shouts of liberty and equality, hollow mockery; your prayers and hymns, your sermons and thanksgivings, with all your religious parade, and solemnity, are, to him, mere bombast, fraud, deception, impiety, and hypocrisy — a thin veil to cover up crimes which would disgrace a nation of savages.

There is not a nation on the earth guilty of practices, more shocking and bloody, than are the people of these United States, at this very hour.

Go where you may, search where you will, roam through all the monarchies and despotisms of the old world, travel through South America, search out every abuse, and when you have found the last, lay your facts by the side of the everyday practices of this nation, and you will say with me, that, for revolting barbarity and shameless hypocrisy, America reigns without a rival. …

THE CONSTITUTION.

But it is answered in reply to all this, that precisely what I have now denounced is, in fact, guaranteed and sanctioned by the Constitution of the United States; that the right to hold and to hunt slaves is a part of that Constitution framed by the illustrious Fathers of this Republic.

Then, I dare to affirm, notwithstanding all I have said before, your fathers stooped, basely stooped

"To palter with us in a double sense:
And keep the word of promise to the ear,
But break it to the heart."

And instead of being the honest men I have before declared them to be, they were the veriest imposters that ever practised on mankind. This is the inevitable conclusion, and from it there is no escape. But I differ from those who charge this baseness on the framers of the Constitution of the United States. It is a slander upon their memory, at least, so I believe.

There is not time now to argue the constitutional question at length — nor have I the ability to discuss it as it ought to be discussed. The subject has been handled with masterly power by Lysander Spooner, Esq., by William Goodell, by Samuel E. Sewall, Esq., and last, though not least, by Gerritt Smith, Esq. These gentlemen have, as I think, fully and clearly vindicated the Constitution from any design to support slavery for an hour.

Fellow-citizens! there is no matter in respect to which, the people of the North have allowed themselves to be so ruinously imposed upon, as that of the pro-slavery character of the Constitution. In that instrument I hold there is neither warrant, license, nor sanction of the hateful thing; but, interpreted as it ought to be interpreted, the Constitution is a GLORIOUS LIBERTY DOCUMENT. Read its preamble, consider its purposes. Is slavery among them? Is it at the gateway? or is it in the temple? It is neither. While I do not intend to argue this question on the present occasion, let me ask, if it be not somewhat singular that, if the Constitution were intended to be, by its framers and adopters, a slave-holding instrument, why neither slavery, slaveholding, nor slave can anywhere be found in it. What would be thought of an instrument, drawn up, legally drawn up, for the purpose of entitling the city of Rochester to a track of land, in which no mention of land was made? Now, there are certain rules of interpretation, for the proper understanding of all legal instruments. These rules are well established. They are plain, common-sense rules, such as you and I, and all of us, can understand and apply, without having passed years in the study of law. I scout the idea that the question of the constitutionality or unconstitutionality of slavery is not a question for the people. I hold that every American citizen has a right to form an opinion of the constitution, and to propagate that opinion, and to use all honorable means to make his opinion the prevailing one. Without this fight, the liberty of an American citizen would be as insecure as that of a Frenchman. Ex-Vice-President Dallas tells us that the Constitution is an object to which no American mind can be too attentive, and no American heart too devoted. He further says, the Constitution, in its words, is plain and intelligible, and is meant for the home-bred, unsophisticated understandings of our fellow-citizens. Senator Berrien tell us that the Constitution is the fundamental law, that which controls all others.

The charter of our liberties, which every citizen has a personal interest in understanding thoroughly. The testimony of Senator Breese, Lewis Cass, and many others that might be named, who are everywhere esteemed as sound lawyers, so regard the Con-stitution. I take it, therefore, that it is not presumption in a private citizen to form an opinion of that instrument.

Now, take the Constitution according to its plain reading, and I defy the presentation of a single pro-slavery clause in it. On the other hand it will be found to contain principles and purposes, entirely hostile to the existence of slavery.

I have detained my audience entirely too long already. At some future period I will gladly avail myself of an opportunity to give this subject a full and fair discussion.

Allow me to say, in conclusion, notwithstanding the dark picture I have this day presented of the state of the nation, I do not despair of this country. There are forces in operation, which must inevitably work The downfall of slavery. "The arm of the Lord is not shortened," and the doom of slavery is certain. I, therefore, leave off where I began, with hope. While drawing encouragement from the Declaration of Independence, the great principles it contains, and the genius of American Institutions, my spirit is also cheered by the obvious tendencies of the age. Nations do not now stand in the same relation to each other that they did ages ago. No nation can now shut itself up from the surrounding world, and trot round in the same old path of its fathers without interference. The time was when such could be done. Long established customs of hurtful character could formerly fence themselves in, and do their evil work with social impunity. Knowledge was then confined and enjoyed by the privileged few, and the multitude walked on in mental darkness. But a change has now come over the affairs of mankind. Walled cities and empires have become un-fashionable. The arm of commerce has borne away the gates of the strong city. Intelligence is penetrating the darkest corners of the globe. It makes its pathway over and under the sea, as well as on the earth. Wind, steam, and lightning are its chartered agents. Oceans no longer divide, but link nations together. From Boston to London is now a holiday excursion. Space is comparatively annihilated. Thoughts expressed on one side of the Atlantic are, distinctly heard on the other.

The far off and almost fabulous Pacific rolls in grandeur at our feet. The Celestial Empire, the mystery of ages, is being solved. The fiat of the Almighty, "Let there be Light," has not yet spent its force. No abuse, no outrage whether in taste, sport or avarice, can now hide itself from the all-pervading light. The iron shoe, and crippled foot of China must be seen, in contrast with nature. Africa must rise and put on her yet unwoven garment. "Ethiopia shall stretch out her hand unto God." In the fervent aspirations of William Lloyd Garrison, I say, and let every heart join in saying it:

God speed the year of jubilee
The wide world o'er!
When from their galling chains set free,

Th' oppress'd shall vilely bend the knee,
And wear the yoke of tyranny
Like brutes no more.
That year will come, and freedom's reign,
To man his plundered rights again
Restore.

God speed the day when human blood
Shall cease to flow!
In every clime be understood,
The claims of human brotherhood,
And each return for evil, good,
Not blow for blow;
That day will come all feuds to end
And change into a faithful friend
Each foe.

God speed the hour, the glorious hour,
When none on earth
Shall exercise a lordly power,
Nor in a tyrant's presence cower;
But all to manhood's stature tower,
By equal birth!
THAT HOUR WILL, COME, to each, to all,
And from his prison-house, the thrall
Go forth.

Until that year, day, hour, arrive,
With head, and heart, and hand I'll strive,
To break the rod, and rend the gyve,
The spoiler of his prey deprive —
So witness Heaven!
And never from my chosen post,
Whate'er the peril or the cost,
Be driven.

4

A House Divided:

EMANCIPATION AND THE CIVIL WAR ERA

——— 4.1 ———

THE KANSAS-NEBRASKA ACT
Stephen Douglas and Abraham Lincoln

It didn't take long for the Compromise of 1850 to fall apart. When Manifest Destiny sparked plans for a transcontinental railroad, Illinois Senator Stephen Douglas launched a campaign to make sure the eastern terminal would be built in Chicago, not St. Louis. To do so, he knew the recently acquired Nebraska Territory would have to be organized and made a state. Needing the support of southern senators, Douglas, who had helped draft the 1850 compromise, crafted a bill that split the territory in two and rendered the original 1820 Missouri compromise on slavery in the newly acquired lands "inoperative and void." The bill empowered the people of each new state to determine whether or not slavery would be legal. Again, abolitionists, now joined by northern whites resentful of the slavocracy, were irate with their representatives' unwillingness to stand up to southern planters.

A. The Kansas-Nebraska Act

Be it enacted by the Senate and House of Representatives of the United States of America in Congress assembled, That all that part of the territory of the United States included within the following limits, except such portions thereof as are hereinafter expressly exempted from the operations of this act, to wit: beginning at a point in the Missouri River where the fortieth parallel of north latitude crosses the same; then west on said parallel to the east boundary of the Territory of Utah, the summit of the Rocky Mountains; thence on said summit northwest to the forty-ninth parallel of north latitude; thence east on said parallel to the western boundary of the territory of Minnesota; thence southward on said boundary to the Missouri River; thence down the main channel of said river to the place of beginning, be, and the same is hereby, created into a temporary government by the name of the Territory Nebraska; and when admitted as a State or States, the said Territory or any portion of the same, shall be received into the Union with or without slavery, as their constitution may prescribe at the time of the admission. ...

Sec. 14. *And be it further enacted*, That a delegate to the House of Representatives of the United States, to serve for the term of two years, who shall be a citizen of the United States, may be elected by the voters qualified to elect members of the Legislative Assembly, who shall be entitled to the same rights and privileges as are exercised and enjoyed by the delegates from the several other Territories of the United States to the said House of Representatives, but the delegate first elected shall hold his seat only during the term of the Congress to which he shall be elected. The first election shall be held at such time and places, and be conducted in such manner, as the Governor shall appoint and direct; and at all subsequent elections the times, places, and manner of holding the elections, shall be prescribed by law. The person having the greatest number of votes shall be declared by the Governor to be duly elected; and a certificate thereof shall be given accordingly. That the Constitution, and all Laws of the United States which are not locally inapplicable, shall have the same force and effect within the said Territory of Nebraska as elsewhere within the United States, except the eighth section of the act preparatory to the admission of Missouri into the Union approved March sixth, eighteen hundred and twenty, which, being inconsistent with the principle of non-intervention by Congress with slaves in the States and Territories, as recognized by the legislation of eighteen hundred and fifty, commonly called the Compromise Measures, is hereby declared inoperative and void; it being the true intent and meaning of this act not to legislate slavery into any Territory or State, nor to exclude it therefrom, but to leave the people thereof perfectly free to form and regulate their domestic institutions in their own way, subject only to the Constitution of the United States: Provided, That nothing herein contained shall be construed to revive or put in force any law or regulation which may have existed prior to the act of sixth March, eighteen hundred and twenty, either protecting, establishing, prohibiting, or abolishing slavery.

B. Abraham Lincoln on the Act

The bill passed in May of 1854, but debate over it had just begun. Its approval ripped apart both the Democratic and Whig Parties, and opponents from both joined to form the Republican Party — which many blacks, including Frederick Douglass, heartily embraced. Illinois lawyer and candidate for Senate Abraham Lincoln was among those who opposed the bill. A former member of the state legislature and representative to the U.S. House, Lincoln re-entered politics largely through his opposition to Douglas's act. In October, he was invited to rebut a Douglas speech defending the bill and delivered the address excerpted below.

In an often conflicting speech, Lincoln first offers a lengthy history of the legal prohibition on slavery in the territories, then issues a series of qualifiers to his seemingly abolitionist position: he supports a fugitive slave law, he supports only gradual emancipation, he would prefer freed slaves be colonized in Liberia and he unequivocally opposes making them "politically and socially our equals." He explains that he despises, however, any expansion of the system, and therein lies his opposition to the Act. As he holds forth against it, Lincoln launches a scathing attack on both the slave system and the ideology that underpins it.

… I think, and shall try to show, that it is wrong; wrong in its direct effect, letting slavery into Kansas and Nebraska — and wrong in its prospective principle, allowing it to spread to every other part of the wide world, where men can be found inclined to take it.

This declared indifference, but as I must think, covert real zeal for the spread of slavery, I can not but hate. I hate it because of the monstrous injustice of slavery itself. I hate it because it deprives our republican example of its just influence in the world — enables the enemies of free institutions, with plausibility, to taunt us as hypocrites — causes the real friends of freedom to doubt our sincerity, and especially because it forces so many really good men amongst ourselves into an open war with the very fundamental principles of civil liberty — criticising the Declaration of Independence, and insisting that there is no right principle of action but self-interest.

Before proceeding, let me say that I think I have no prejudice against the Southern people. They are just what we would be in their situation. If slavery did not now exist among us, we should not instantly give it up. This I believe of the masses north and south. Doubtless there are individuals, on both sides, who would not hold slaves under any circumstances; and others who would gladly introduce slavery anew, if it were out of existence. We know that some southern men do free their slaves, go north, and become tip-top abolitionists; while some northern ones go south, and become most cruel slave-masters.

When southern people tell us they are no more responsible for the origin of slavery, than we; I acknowledge the fact. When it is said that the institution exists and that it is very difficult to get rid of it, in any satisfactory way, I can understand and appreciate the saying. I surely will not blame them for not doing what I should know how to do myself. If all earthly power were given to me, I should not know what to do, as to the existing institution. My first impulse would be to free all the slaves, and send them to Liberia, — to their own native land. But a moment's reflection would convince me, that whatever of high hope, (as I think there is) there may be in this, in the long run, its sudden execution is impossible. If they were all landed there in a day, they would all perish in the next ten days; and there are not surplus shipping and surplus money enough in the world to carry them there in many times ten days. What then? Free them all, and keep them among us as underlings? Is it quite certain that this betters their condition? I think I would not hold one in slavery, at any rate; yet the point is not clear enough for me to denounce people upon. What next? Free them, and make them politically and socially our equals? My own feelings would not admit of this; and if mine would, we well know that those of the great mass of white people will not. Whether this feeling accords with justice and sound judgement, is not the sole question, if indeed, it is part of it. A universal feeling, whether well or ill-founded, can not be safely disregarded. We can not, then, make them equals. It does seem to me that systems of gradual emancipation might be adopted; but for their tardiness in this, I will not undertake to judge our brethren of the south.

When they remind us of their constitutional rights, I acknowledge them, not grudgingly, but fully, and fairly; and I would give them any legislation for the reclaiming of their fugitives, which should not, in its stringency, be more likely to carry a free man into slavery, than our ordinary criminal laws are to hang an innocent one.

But all this, to my judgement, furnishes no more excuse for permitting slavery to go into our own free territory, than it would for reviving the African slave trade by law. The law which forbids the bringing of slaves from Africa; and that which has so long forbid the taking of them to Nebraska, can hardly be distinguished on any moral principle; and the repeal of the former could find quite as plausible excuses as that of the latter. …

Equal justice to the south, it is said, requires us to consent to the extending of slavery to new countries. That is to say, inasmuch as you do not object to my taking my hog to Nebraska, therefore I must not object to you taking your slave. Now, I admit this is perfectly logical, if there is no difference between hogs and Negroes. But while you thus require me to deny the humanity of the Negro, I wish to ask whether you of the south yourselves, have ever been willing to do as much? It is kindly provided that of all those who come into the world, only a small percentage are natural tyrants. That percentage is no larger in the slave States than in the free. The great majority, south as well as north, have human sympathies, of which they can no more divest themselves than they can of their sensibility to physical pain. These sympathies in the bosoms of the southern people manifest in many ways, their sense of the wrong of slavery, and their consciousness that, after all, there is humanity in the Negro. If they deny this, let me address them a few plain questions. In 1820 you joined the north, almost unanimously, in declaring the African slave trade piracy, and in annexing to it the punishment of death. Why did you do this? If you did not feel that it was wrong, why did you join in providing that men should be hung for it? The practice was no more than bringing wild Negroes from Africa, to sell to such as would buy them. But you never thought of hanging men for catching and selling wild horses, wild buffaloes or wild bears.

Again, you have amongst you, a sneaking individual, of the class of native tyrants, known as the "SLAVE-DEALER." He watches your necessities, and crawls up to buy your slave, at a speculating price. If you cannot help it, you sell to him; but if you can help it, you drive him from your door. You despise him utterly. You do not recognise him as a friend, or even as an honest man. Your children must not play with his; they may rollick freely with the little Negroes, but not with the "slave-dealers" children. If you are obliged to deal with him, you try to get through the job without so much as touching him. It is common with you to join hands with the men you meet; but with the slave dealer you avoid the ceremony — instinctively shrinking from the snaky contact. If he grows rich and retires from business, you still remember him, and still keep up the ban of non-intercourse upon him and his family. Now why is this? You do not so treat the man who deals in corn, cattle or tobacco.

And yet again; there are in the United States and territories, including the District of Columbia, 433,643 free blacks. At $500 per head they are worth over two hundred millions of dollars. How comes this vast amount of property to be running about without owners? We do not see free horses or free cattle running at large. How is this? All these free blacks are the descendants of slaves, or have been slaves they, and they would be slaves now, but for SOMETHING which has operated on their white owners, inducing them, at vast pecuniary sacrifices, to liberate them. What is that SOMETHING? Is there any mistaking it? In all these cases it is your sense of justice, and human sympathy, continually telling you, that the poor negro has some natural right to himself — that those who deny it, and make mere merchandise of him, deserve kicking, contempt and death.

And now, why will you ask us to deny the humanity of the slave? and estimate him only as the equal of the hog? Why ask us to do what you will not do yourselves? Why ask us to do for nothing, what two hundred million of dollars could not induce you to do?

But one great argument in the support of the repeal of the Missouri Compromise, is still to come. That argument is "the sacred right of self-government." It seems our distinguished Senator has found great difficulty in getting his antagonists, even in the Senate to meet him fairly on this argument — some poet has said, "Fools rush in where angels fear to tread." At the hazard of being thought one of the fools of this quotation, I meet that argument — I rush in, I take that bull by the horns.

I trust I understand, and truly estimate the right of self-government. My faith in the proposition that each man should do precisely as he pleases with all which is exclusively his own, lies at the foundation of the sense of justice there is in me. I extend the principles to communities of men, as well as to individuals. I so extend it, because it is politically wise, as well as naturally just: politically wise, in saving us from broils about matters, which do not concern us. Here, or at Washington, I would not trouble myself with the oyster laws of Virginia, or the cranberry laws of Indiana.

The doctrine of self-government is right — absolutely and eternally right — but it has no just application, as here attempted. Or perhaps I should rather say that whether it has such just application depends upon whether a Negro is not or is a man. If he is not a man, why in that case, he who is a man may, as a matter of self-government, do just as he pleases with him. But if the negro is a man, is it not to that extent, a total destruction of self-government, to say that he too shall not govern himself? When the white man governs himself, and also governs another man, that is more than self-government — that is despotism. If the Negro is a man, why then my ancient faith teaches me that "all men are created equal;" and that there can be no moral right in connection with one man's making a slave of another.

Judge Douglas frequently, with bitter irony and sarcasm, paraphrases our argument by saying "The white people of Nebraska are good enough to govern themselves, but they are not good enough to govern a few miserable Negroes!!"

Well I doubt not that the people of Nebraska are, and will continue to be as good as the average of people elsewhere. I do not say the contrary. What I do say is, that no man is good enough to govern another man, without the other's consent. I say this is the leading principle — the sheet anchor of American republicanism. Our Declaration of Independence says:

"We hold these truths to be self evident: that all men are created equal; that they are endowed by their Creator with certain inalienable rights; that among these are life, liberty and the pursuit of happiness. That to secure these rights, governments are instituted among men, DERIVING THEIR JUST POWERS FROM THE CONSENT OF THE GOVERNED."

I have quoted so much at this time merely to show that according to our ancient faith, the just powers of governments are derived from the consent of the governed. Now the relation of masters and slaves is, PRO TANTO, a total violation of this principle. The master not only governs the slave without his consent; but he governs him by a set of rules altogether different from those, which he prescribes for himself. Allow ALL the governed an equal voices in the government, and that, and that only is self-government.

Let it not be said I am contending for the establishment of political and social equality between the whites and blacks. I have already said the contrary. I am not now combating the argument of NECESSITY, arising from the fact that the blacks are already amongst us; but I am combating what is set up as MORAL argument for allowing them to be taken where they have never yet been — arguing against the EXTENSION of a bad thing, which where it already exists, we must of necessity, manage as we best can.

In support of his application of the doctrine of self-government, Senator Douglas has sought to bring to his aid the opinions and examples of our revolutionary fathers. I am glad he has done this. I love the sentiments of those old-time men; and shall be most happy to abide by their opinions. He shows us that when it was in contemplation for the colonies to break off from Great Britain, and set up a new government for themselves, several of the states instructed their delegates to go for the measure PROVIDED EACH STATE SHOULD BE ALLOWED TO REGULATE ITS DOMESTIC CONCERNS IN ITS OWN WAY. I do not quote; but this in substance. This was right. I see nothing objectionable in it. I also think it probable that it had some reference to the existence of slavery amongst them. I will not deny that it had. But had it, in any reference to the carrying of slavery into NEW COUNTRIES? That is the question; and we will let the fathers themselves answer it.

This same generation of men, and mostly the same individuals of the generation, who declared this principle — who declared independence — who fought the war of the revolution through — who afterwards made the Constitution under which we still live — these same men passed the ordinance of '87, declaring that slavery should never go to the north-west territory. I have no doubt Judge Douglas thinks they were very inconsistent in this. It is a question of discrimination between them and him. But there is not an inch of ground left for his claiming that their opinions — their example — their authority — are on his side in this controversy.

Again, is not Nebraska, while a territory, a part of us? Do we not own the country? And if we surrender the control of it, do we not surrender the right of self-government? It is part of ourselves. If you say we shall not control it because it is ONLY part, the same is true of every other part; and when all the parts are gone, what has become of the whole? What is then left of us? What use for the general government, when there is nothing left for it [to] govern?

But you say this question should be left to the people of Nebraska, because they are more particularly interested. If this be the rule, you must leave it to each individual to say for himself whether he will have slaves. What better moral right have thirty-one citizens of Nebraska to say, that the thirty-second shall not hold slaves, than the people of the thirty-one States have to say that slavery shall not go into the thirty-second State at all?

But if it is a sacred right for the people of Nebraska to take and hold slaves there, it is equally their sacred right to buy them where they can buy them cheapest; and that undoubtedly will be on the coast of Africa; provided you will consent to not hang them for going there to buy them. You must remove this restriction too, from the sacred right of self-government. I am aware you say that taking slaves from the States to Nebraska does not make slaves of freemen; but the African slave-trader can say just as much. He does not catch free Negroes and bring them here. He finds them already slaves in the hands of their black captors, and he honestly buys them at the rate of about a red cotton handkerchief a head. This is very cheap, and it is a great abridgement of the sacred right of self-government to hang men for engaging in this profitable trade!

Another important objection to this application of the right of self-government, is that it enables the first FEW, to deprive the succeeding MANY, of a free exercise of the right of self-government. The first few may get slavery IN, and the subsequent many cannot easily get it OUT. How common is the remark now in the slave States — "If we were only clear of our slaves, how much better it would be for us." They are actually deprived of the privilege of governing themselves as they would, by the action of a very few, in the beginning. The same thing was true of the whole nation at the time our constitution was formed.

Whether slavery shall go into Nebraska, or other new territories, is not a matter of exclusive concern to the people who may go there. The whole nation is interested that the best use shall be made of these territories. We want them for the homes of free white people. This they cannot be, to any considerable extent, if slavery shall be planted within them. Slave States are places for poor white people to remove FROM; not to remove TO. New free States are the places for poor people to go to and better their condition. For this use, the nation needs these territories.

Still further; there are constitutional relations between the slave and free States, which are degrading to the latter. We are under legal obligations to catch and return their runaway slaves to them — a sort of dirty, disagreeable job, which I believe, as a general rule the slaveholders will not perform for one another. Then again, in the control of the government the management of the partnership affairs — they have greatly the advantage of us. By the Constitution, each State has two Senators — each has a number of Representatives; in proportion to the number of its people — and each has a number of presidential electors, equal to the whole number of its Senators and Representatives together. But in ascertaining the number of the people, for this purpose, five slaves are counted as being equal to three whites. The slaves do not vote; they are only counted and so used, as to swell the influence of the white people's votes. The practical effect of this is more aptly shown by a comparison of the States of South Carolina and Maine. South Carolina has six representatives, and so has Maine; South Carolina has eight presidential electors, and so has Maine. This is precise equality so far; and, of course they are equal in Senators, each having two. Thus in the control of the government, the two States are equals precisely. But how are they in the number of their white people? Maine has 581,813 — while South Carolina has 274,567. Maine has twice as many as South Carolina, and 32,679 over. Thus each white man in South Carolina is more than the double of any man in Maine. This is all because South Carolina, besides her free people, has 384,984 slaves. The South Carolinian has precisely the same advantage over the white man in every other free State, as well as in Maine. He is more than the double of any one of us in this crowd. The same advantage, but not to the same extent, is held by all the citizens of the slave States, over those of the free; and it is an absolute truth, without an exception, that there is no voter in any slave State, but who has more legal power in the government, than any voter in any free State. There is no instance of exact equality; and the disadvantage is against us the whole chapter through. This principle, in the aggregate, gives the slave States, in the present Congress, twenty additional representatives — being seven more than the whole majority by which they passed the Nebraska bill.

Now all this is manifestly unfair; yet I do not mention it to complain of it, in so far as it is already settled. It is in the Constitution; and I do not, for that cause, or any other cause, propose to destroy, or alter, or disregard the Constitution. I stand to it, fairly, fully, and firmly.

But when I am told I must leave it altogether to OTHER PEOPLE to say whether new partners are to be bred up and brought into the firm, on the same degrading terms against me, I respectfully demur. I insist, that whether I shall be a whole man, or only, the half of one, in comparison with others, is a question in which I am somewhat concerned; and one which no other man can have a sacred right of deciding for me. If I am wrong in this — if it really be a sacred right of self-government, in the man who shall go to Nebraska, to decide whether he will be the EQUAL of me or the DOUBLE of me, then after he shall have exercised that right, and thereby shall have reduced me to a still smaller fraction of a man than I already am, I should like for some gentleman deeply skilled in the mysteries of sacred rights, to provide himself with a microscope, and peep about, and find out, if he can, what has become of my sacred rights! They will surely be too small for detection with the naked eye.

Finally, I insist, that if there is ANY THING which it is the duty of the WHOLE PEOPLE to never entrust to any hands but their own, that thing is the preservation and perpetuity, of their own liberties, and institutions. And if they shall think, as I do, that the extension of slavery endangers them, more than any, or all other causes, how recreant to themselves, if they submit the question, and with it, the fate of their country, to a mere hand-full of men, bent only on temporary self-interest. If this question of slavery extension were an insignificant one having no power to do harm — it might be shuffled aside in this way. But being, as it is, the great Behemoth of danger, shall the strong grip of the nation be loosened upon him, to entrust him to the hands of such feeble keepers? …

———— 4.2 ————
'CRIMES AGAINST KANSAS'
Charles Sumner

Following the Kansas-Nebraska Act's passage, the southern portion of the territory, Kansas, which sat adjacent to the slave state Missouri, became the area of contention. No one on either side of the battle intended to leave the decision of whether or not the state would be free up to the people of Kansas, as the act's "popular sovereignty" provision decreed. "Free-soilers," who resented southern planters' designs on the new land, joined abolitionists in a rush to settle in the state and cast their vote against slavery; southerners and Missouri proponents of slavery came just as quickly. Ultimately, two opposing governments established themselves and claimed control over the state. President Franklin Pierce acknowledged the pro-slavery government.

Soon, the dispute erupted in violence. Armed bands on both sides began attacking and counterattacking one another. In the most infamous episode, a pro-slavery mob attacked and destroyed a hotel in Lawrence, an antislavery stronghold. In retaliation, white abolitionist John Brown led a posse to Pottawatomie Creek, where they captured and killed five pro-slavery men. Countless more on both sides were slain. The Civil War had already begun in Kansas.

In Congress, the dispute was equally heated. Missouri Senator David Atchinson openly urged violence to defend Kansas's slave status. Others, such as Massachusetts Senator Charles Sumner, railed against the pro-slavery forces. In May 1856, Sumner delivered his "Crimes Against Kansas" speech, a largely personal attack on pro-slavery senators and a relentless demeaning of the state of South Carolina. Afterwards, South Carolina Congressman Preston Brooks — nephew of South Carolina Senator Andrew Butler, who was also much maligned in the speech — rose and attacked Sumner on the Senate floor, beating him with a cane.

… But, before entering upon the argument, I must say something of a general character, particularly in response to what has fallen from Senators who have raised themselves to eminence on this floor in championship of human wrongs. I mean the Senator from South Carolina (Mr. Butler), and the Senator from Illinois (Mr. Douglas), who, though unlike as Don Quixote and Sancho Panza, yet, like this couple, sally forth together in the same adventure. I regret much to miss the elder Senator from his seat; but the cause, against which he has run a tilt, with such activity of animosity, demands that the opportunity of exposing him should not be lost; and it is for the cause that I speak. The Senator from South Carolina has read many books of chivalry, and believes himself a chivalrous knight, with sentiments of honor and courage. Of course he has chosen a mistress to whom he has made his vows, and who, though ugly to others, is always lovely to him; though polluted in the sight of the world, is chaste in his sight I mean the harlot, Slavery. For her, his tongue is always profuse in words. Let her be impeached in character, or any proposition made to shut her out from the extension of her wantonness, and no extravagance of manner or hardihood of assertion is then too great for this Senator. The frenzy of Don Quixote, in behalf of his wench, Dulcinea del Toboso, is all surpassed. The asserted rights of Slavery, which shock equality of all kinds, are cloaked by a fantastic claim of equality. If the slave States cannot enjoy what, in mockery of the great fathers of the Republic, he misnames equality under the Constitution in other words, the full power in the National Territories to compel fellowmen to unpaid toil, to separate husband and wife, and to sell little children at the auction block then, sir, the chivalric Senator will conduct the State of South Carolina out of the Union! Heroic knight! Exalted Senator! A second Moses come for a second exodus!

But not content with this poor menace, which we have been twice told was "measured," the Senator in the unrestrained chivalry of his nature, has undertaken to apply opprobrious words to those who differ from him on this floor. He calls them "sectional and fanatical;" and opposition to the usurpation in Kansas he denounces as "an uncalculating fanaticism." To be sure these charges lack all grace of originality, and all sentiment of truth; but the adventurous Senator does not hesitate. He is the uncompromising, unblushing representative on this floor of a flagrant sectionalism, which now domineers over the Republic, and yet with a ludicrous ignorance of his own position unable to see himself as others see him — or with an effrontery which even his white head ought not to protect from rebuke, he applies to those here who resist his sectionalism the very epithet which designates himself. The men who strive to bring back the Government to its original policy, when Freedom and not Slavery was sectional, he arraigns as sectional. This will not do. It involves too great a perversion of terms. I tell that Senator that it is to himself, and to the "organization" of which he is the "committed advocate," that this epithet belongs. I now fasten it upon them. For myself, I care little for names; but since the question has been raised here, I affirm that the Republican party of the Union is in no just sense sectional, but, more than any other party, national; and that it now goes forth to dislodge from the high places of the Government the tyrannical sectionalism of which the Senator from South Carolina is one of the maddest zealots.

As the Senator from South Carolina is the Don Quixote, the Senator from Illinois (Mr. Douglas) is the Squire of Slavery, its very Sancho Panza, ready to do all its humiliating offices. This Senator, in his labored address, vindicating his labored report — piling one mass of elaborate error upon another mass constrained himself, as you will remember, to unfamiliar decencies of speech. Of that address I have nothing to say at this moment, though before I sit down I shall show something of its fallacies. But I go back now to an earlier occasion, when, true to his native impulses, he threw into this discussion, "for a charm of powerful trouble," personalities most discreditable to this body. I will not stop to repel the imputations which he cast upon myself; but I mention them to remind you of the "sweltered venom sleeping got," which, with other poisoned ingredients, he cast into the caldron of this debate. Of other things I speak. Standing on this floor, the Senator issued his rescript, requiring submission to the Usurped Power of Kansas; and this was accompanied by a manner — all his own — such as befits the tyrannical threat. Very well. Let the Senator try. I tell him now that he cannot enforce any such submission. The Senator, with the slave power at his back, is strong; but he is not strong enough for this purpose. He is bold. He shrinks from nothing. Like Danton, he may cry, "L'audace! L'audace! Toujours L'audace! " but even his audacity cannot compass this work. The Senator copies the British officer who, with boastful swagger, said that with the hilt of his sword he would cram the "stamps" down the throats of the American people, and he will meet a similar failure. He may convulse this country with a civil feud. Like the ancient madman, he may set fire to this Temple of Constitutional Liberty, grander than the Ephesian dome; but he cannot enforce obedience to that Tyrannical Usurpation.

The Senator dreams that he can subdue the North. He disclaims the open threat, but his conduct still implies it. How little that Senator knows himself or the strength of the cause which he persecutes! He is but a mortal man; against him is an immortal principle. With finite power he wrestles with the infinite, and he must fall. Against him are stronger battalions than any marshalled by mortal arm; the inborn, ineradicable, invincible sentiments of the human heart; against him is nature in all

her subtle forces; against him is God. Let him try to subdue these.

With regret, I come again upon the Senator from South Carolina (Mr. Butler), who, omnipresent in this debate, overflowed with rage at the simple suggestion that Kansas had applied for admission as a State and, with incoherent phrases, discharged the loose expectoration of his speech, now upon her representative, and then upon her people. There was no extravagance of the ancient parliamentary debate, which he did not repeat; nor was there any possible deviation from truth which he did not make, with so much of passion, I am glad to add, as to save him from the suspicion of intentional aberration. But the Senator touches nothing which he does not disfigure with error, sometimes of principle, sometimes of fact. He shows an incapacity of accuracy, whether in stating the Constitution, or in stating the law, whether in the details of statistics or the diversions of scholarship. He cannot open his mouth, but out there flies a blunder. ...

But it is against the people of Kansas that the sensibilities of the Senator are particularly aroused. Coming, as he announces, "from a State," ay, sir, from South Carolina, he turns with lordly disgust from this newly-formed community, which he will not recognize even as a "body politic." Pray, sir, by what title does he indulge in this egotism? Has he read the history of "the State" which he represents? He cannot surely have forgotten its shameful imbecility from Slavery, confessed throughout the Revolution, followed by its more shameful assumptions for Slavery since. He cannot have forgotten its wretched persistence in the slave-trade as the very apple of its eye, and the condition of its participation in the Union. He cannot have forgotten its constitution, which is Republican only in name, confirming power in the hands of the few, and founding the qualifications of its legislators on "a settled freehold estate and ten negroes." And yet the Senator, to whom that "State" has in part committed the guardianship of its good name, instead of moving, with backward treading steps, to cover its nakedness, rushes forward in the very ecstasy of madness, to expose it by provoking a comparison with Kansas. South Carolina is old; Kansas is young. South Carolina counts by centuries, where Kansas counts by years. But a beneficent example may be born in a day; and I venture to say, that against the two centuries of the older "State," may be already set the two years of trial, evolving corresponding virtue, in the younger community. In the one, is the long wail of Slavery; in the other, the hymns of Freedom. And if we glance at special achievements, it will be difficult to find any thing in the history of South Carolina which presents so much of heroic spirit in an heroic cause as appears in that repulse of the Missouri invaders by the beleaguered town of Lawrence, where even the women gave their effective efforts to Freedom. The matrons of Rome, who poured their jewels into the treasury for the public defence, the wives of Prussia, who, with delicate fingers, clothed their defenders against French invasion, the mothers of our own Revolution, who sent forth their sons, covered with prayers and blessings, to combat for human rights, did nothing of self-sacrifice truer than did these women on this occasion. Were the whole history of South Carolina blotted out of existence, from its very beginning down to the day of the last election of the Senator to his present seat on this floor, civilization might lose — I do not say how little; but surely less than it has already gained by the example of Kansas, in its valiant struggle against oppression, and in the development of a new science of emigration. Already, in Lawrence alone, there are newspapers and schools, including a High School, and throughout this infant Territory there is more mature scholarship far, in proportion to its inhabitants, than in all South Carolina. Ah, sir, I tell the Senator that Kansas, welcomed as a free State, will be a "ministering angel" to the Republic, when South Carolina, in the cloak of darkness which she hugs, "lies howling." …

4.3

DRED SCOTT V. SANFORD
The United States Supreme Court

Dred Scott was born a slave in Virginia, and lived throughout the new territories and the South as a slave bonded to a series of masters. For part of that time, he lived in Illinois and in Wisconsin Territory, both of which barred slavery and, thus, through which he could have claimed his freedom. He did not do so, however, until several years later, after the death of his last owner. In 1847, while living in St. Louis, Missouri, a slave state, he sued for freedom based on his prior residence in free states. A series of conflicting rulings in state and federal courts set the case up for a hearing before the U.S. Supreme Court in 1856. What followed was the most complete defeat of the legal rights of African Americans in U.S. history. Chief Justice Roger Taney wrote a majority opinion in 1857 that not only refused to free Scott, but did so based on the argument that no African American was or could be a citizen of the United States. The framers of both the Constitution and the Declaration of Independence, Taney wrote, clearly did not intend to include people of African descent in the phrase "we the people." Further, Taney's expansive opinion proclaimed, the Missouri Compromise of 1820 — which barred slavery in the new territories — was wholly unconstitutional. Ironically, his effort to detail how the actions of the nation's forefathers prove their intent to bar the inclusion of blacks often reads like an indictment of the nation's racist past.

…This is certainly a very serious question, and one that now for the first time has been brought for decision before this court. But it is brought here by those who have a right to bring it, and it is our duty to meet it and decide it.

The question is simply this: Can a negro, whose ancestors were imported into this country, and sold as slaves, become a member of the political community formed and brought into existence by the Constitution of the United States, and as such become entitled to all the rights, and privileges, and immunities, guarantied by that instrument to the citizen? One of which rights is the privilege of suing in a court of the United States in the cases specified in the Constitution.

It will be observed, that the plea applies to that class of persons only whose ancestors were negroes of the African race, and imported into this country, and sold and held as slaves. The only matter in issue before the court, therefore, is, whether the descendants of such slaves, when they shall be emancipated, or who are born of parents who had become free before their birth, are citizens of a State, in the sense in which the word citizen is used in the Constitution of the United States. And this being the only matter in dispute on the pleadings, the court must be understood as speaking in this opinion of that class only, that is, of those persons who are the descendants of Africans who were imported into this country, and sold as slaves. …

The words 'people of the United States' and 'citizens' are synonymous terms, and mean the same thing. They both describe the political body who, according to our republican institutions, form the sovereignty, and who hold the power and conduct the Government through their representatives. They are what we familiarly call the 'sovereign people,' and every citizen is one of this people, and a constituent member of this sovereignty. The question before us is, whether the class of persons described in the plea in abatement compose a portion of this people, and are constituent members of this sovereignty? We think they are not, and that they are not included, and were not intended to be included, under the word 'citizens' in the Constitution, and can therefore claim none of the rights and privileges which that instrument provides for and secures to citizens of the United States. On the contrary, they were at that time considered as a subordinate and inferior class of beings, who had been subjugated by the dominant race, and, whether emancipated or not, yet remained subject to their authority, and had no rights or privileges but such as those who held the power and the Government might choose to grant them.

It is not the province of the court to decide upon the justice or injustice, the policy or impolicy, of these laws. The decision of that question belonged to the political or law-making power; to those who formed the sovereignty and framed the Constitution. The duty of the court is, to interpret the instrument they have framed, with the best lights we can obtain on the subject, and to administer it as we find it, according to its true intent and meaning when it was adopted. …

In the opinion of the court, the legislation and histories of the times, and the language used in the Declaration of Independence, show, that neither the class of persons who had been imported as slaves, nor their descendants, whether they had become free or not, were then acknowledged as a part of the people, nor intended to be included in the general words used in that memorable instrument.

It is difficult at this day to realize the state of public opinion in relation to that unfortunate race, which prevailed in the civilized and enlightened portions of the world at the time of the Declaration of Independence, and when the Constitution of the United States was framed and adopted. But the public history of every European nation displays it in a manner too plain to be mistaken.

They had for more than a century before been regarded as beings of an inferior order, and altogether unfit to associate with the white race, either in social or political relations; and so far inferior, that they had no rights which the white man was bound to respect; and that the negro might justly and lawfully be reduced to slavery for his benefit. He was bought and sold, and treated as an ordinary article of merchandise and traffic, whenever a profit could be made by it. This opinion was at that time fixed and universal in the civilized portion of the white race. It was regarded as an axiom in morals as well as in politics, which no one thought of disputing, or supposed to be open to dispute; and men in every grade and position in society daily and habitually acted upon it in their private pursuits, as well as in matters of public concern, without doubting for a moment the correctness of this opinion.

And in no nation was this opinion more firmly fixed or more uniformly acted upon than by the English Government and English people. They not only seized them on the coast of Africa, and sold them or held them in slavery for their own use; but they took them as ordinary articles of merchandise to every country where they could make a profit on them, and were far more extensively engaged in this commerce than any other nation in the world.

The opinion thus entertained and acted upon in England was naturally impressed upon the colonies they founded on this side of the Atlantic. And, accordingly, a negro of the African race was regarded by them as an article of property, and held, and bought and sold as such, in every one of the thirteen colonies which united in the Declaration of Independence, and afterwards formed the Constitution of the United States. The slaves were more or less numerous in the different colonies, as slave labor was found more or less profitable. But no one seems to have doubted the correctness of the prevailing opinion of the time. The legislation of the different colonies furnishes positive and indisputable proof of this fact. ...

The language of the Declaration of Independence is equally conclusive:

It begins by declaring that, 'when in the course of human events it becomes necessary for one people to dissolve the political bands which have connected them with another, and to assume among the powers of the earth the separate and equal station to which the laws of nature and nature's God entitle them, a decent respect for the opinions of mankind requires that they should declare the causes which impel them to the separation.'

It then proceeds to say: 'We hold these truths to be self-evident: that all men are created equal; that they are endowed by their Creator with certain unalienable rights; that among them is life, liberty, and the pursuit of happiness; that to secure these rights, Governments are instituted, deriving their just powers from the consent of the governed.'

The general words above quoted would seem to embrace the whole human family, and if they were used in a similar instrument at this day would be so understood. But it is too clear for dispute, that the enslaved African race were not intended to be included, and formed no part of the people who framed and adopted this declaration; for if the language, as understood in that day, would embrace them, the conduct of the distinguished men who framed the Declaration of Independence would have been utterly and flagrantly inconsistent with the principles they asserted; and instead of the sympathy of mankind, to which they so confidently appealed, they would have deserved and received universal rebuke and reprobation.

Yet the men who framed this declaration were great men-high in literary acquirements-high in their sense of honor, and incapable of asserting principles inconsistent with those on which they were acting. They perfectly understood the meaning of the language they used, and how it would be understood by others; and they knew that it would not in any part of the civilized world be supposed to embrace the negro race, which, by common consent, had been excluded from civilized Governments and the family of nations, and doomed to slavery. They spoke and acted according to the then established doctrines and principles, and in the ordinary language of the day, and no one misunderstood them. The unhappy black race were separated from the white by indelible marks, and laws long before established, and were never thought of or spoken of except as property, and when the claims of the owner or the profit of the trader were supposed to need protection.

This state of public opinion had undergone no change when the Constitution was adopted, as is equally evident from its provisions and language. ...

No one, we presume, supposes that any change in public opinion or feeling, in relation to this unfortunate race, in the civilized nations of Europe or in this country, should induce the court to give to the words of the

Constitution a more liberal construction in their favor than they were intended to bear when the instrument was framed and adopted. Such an argument would be altogether inadmissible in any tribunal called on to interpret it. If any of its provisions are deemed unjust, there is a mode prescribed in the instrument itself by which it may be amended; but while it remains unaltered, it must be construed now as it was understood at the time of its adoption. It is not only the same in words, but the same in meaning, and delegates the same powers to the Government, and reserves and secures the same rights and privileges to the citizen; and as long as it continues to exist in its present form, it speaks not only in the same words, but with the same meaning and intent with which it spoke when it came from the hands of its framers, and was voted on and adopted by the people of the United States. Any other rule of construction would abrogate the judicial character of this court, and make it the mere reflex of the popular opinion or passion of the day. This court was not created by the Constitution for such purposes. Higher and graver trusts have been confided to it, and it must not falter in the path of duty.

What the construction was at that time, we think can hardly admit of doubt. We have the language of the Declaration of Independence and of the Articles of Confederation, in addition to the plain words of the Constitution itself; we have the legislation of the different States, before, about the time, and since, the Constitution was adopted; we have the legislation of Congress, from the time of its adoption to a recent period; and we have the constant and uniform action of the Executive Department, all concurring together, and leading to the same result. And if anything in relation to the construction of the Constitution can be regarded as settled, it is that which we now give to the word 'citizen' and the word 'people.'

And upon a full and careful consideration of the subject, the court is of opinion, that, upon the facts stated in the plea in abatement, Dred Scott was not a citizen of Missouri within

the meaning of the Constitution of the United States, and not entitled as such to sue in its courts; and, consequently, that the Circuit Court had no jurisdiction of the case, and that the judgment on the plea in abatement is erroneous. ...

<hr>

4.4

A HOUSE DIVIDED
Abraham Lincoln

When Abraham Lincoln addressed the Republican Party convention in 1858, launching his bid for the Illinois Senate seat, he took as his text the Dred Scott decision. Lincoln shared a popular fear among abolitionists and others opposing the expansion of slavery that the decision would lead to the institution's legalization nationwide, and he even argued the existence of a conspiracy to that effect. Lincoln ominously warned that the union could not proceed "half slave and half free" — the conflict would have to be settled one way or the other in order to move forward. He then proceeded to argue that the nation was unfortunately barreling in the direction of slavery rather than liberty, and attacked Stephen Douglas, his opponent in the campaign, for his role in upsetting the compromises that had limited slavery's growth.

If we could first know where we are, and whither we are tending, we could better judge what to do, and how to do it. We are now far into the fifth year since a policy was initiated with the avowed object, and confident promise, of putting an end to slavery agitation. Under the operation of that policy, that agitation has not only not ceased, but has constantly augmented. In my opinion, it will not cease, until a crisis shall have been reached and passed. "A house divided against itself cannot stand." I believe this government cannot endure permanently half slave and half free. I do not expect the Union to be dissolved — I do not expect the house to fall — but I do expect it will cease to be divided. It will become all one thing, or all the other. Either the opponents of slavery will arrest the further spread of it, and place it where the public mind shall rest in the belief that it is in the course of ultimate extinction; or its advocates will push it forward, till it shall become alike lawful in all the States, old as well as new — North as well as South.

Have we no tendency to the latter condition?

Let any one who doubts, carefully contemplate that now almost complete legal combination — piece of machinery, so to speak — compounded of the Nebraska doctrine, and the Dred Scott decision. Let him consider not only what work the machinery is adapted to do, and how well adapted; but also, let him study the history of its construction, and trace, if he can, or rather fail, if he can, to trace the evidences of design, and concert of action, among its chief architects, from the beginning.

The new year of 1854 found slavery excluded from more than half the States by State Constitutions, and from most of the national territory by Congressional prohibition. Four days later, commenced the struggle which ended in repealing that Congressional prohibition. This opened all the national territory to slavery, and was the first point gained.

But, so far, Congress only had acted; and an indorsement by the people, real or apparent, was indispensable, to save the point already gained, and give chance for more.

This necessity had not been overlooked; but had been provided for, as well as might be, in the notable argument of "squatter sovereignty," otherwise called "sacred right of self-government," which latter phrase, though expressive of the only rightful basis of any government, was so perverted in this attempted use of it as to amount to just this: That if any one man choose to enslave another, no third man shall be allowed to object. That argument was incorporated into the Nebraska bill itself, in the language which follows: "It being the true intent and meaning of this act not to legislate slavery into any Territory or State, nor to exclude it therefrom; but to leave the people thereof perfectly free to form and regulate their domestic institutions in their own way, subject only to the Constitution of the United States." Then opened the roar of loose declamation in favor of "Squatter Sovereignty," and "sacred right

of self-government." "But," said opposition members, "let us amend the bill so as to expressly declare that the people of the Territory may exclude slavery." "Not we," said the friends of the measure; and down they voted the amendment.

While the Nebraska bill was passing through Congress, a law case involving the question of a negro's freedom, by reason of his owner having voluntarily taken him first into a free State and then into a Territory covered by the Congressional prohibition, and held him as a slave for a long time in each, was passing through the U. S. Circuit Court for the District of Missouri; and both Nebraska bill and law suit were brought to a decision in the same month of May, 1854. The negro's name was "Dred Scott," which name now designates the decision finally made in the case. Before the then next Presidential election, the law case came to, and was argued in, the Supreme Court of the United States; but the decision of it was deferred until after the election. Still, before the election, Senator Trumbull, on the floor of the Senate, requested the leading advocate of the Nebraska bill to state his opinion whether the people of a Territory can constitutionally exclude slavery from their limits; and the latter answers: "That is a question for the Supreme Court."

The election came. Mr. Buchanan was elected, and the endorsement, such as it was, secured. That was the second point gained. The endorsement, however, fell short of a clear popular majority by nearly four hundred thousand votes, and so, perhaps, was not overwhelmingly reliable and satisfactory. The outgoing President, in his last annual message, as impressively as possible echoed back upon the people the weight and authority of the endorsement. The Supreme Court met again; did not announce their decision, but ordered a re-argument. The Presidential inauguration came, and still no decision of the court; but the incoming President in his inaugural address, fervently exhorted the people to abide by the forthcoming decision, whatever it might be. Then, in a few days, came the decision.

The reputed author of the Nebraska bill finds an early occasion to make a speech at this capital endorsing the Dred Scott decision, and vehemently denouncing all opposition to it. The new President, too, seizes the early occasion of the Silliman letter to endorse and strongly construe that decision, and to express his astonishment that any different view had ever been entertained!

At length a squabble springs up between the President and the author of the Nebraska bill, on the mere question of fact, whether the Lecompton Constitution was or was not, in any just sense, made by the people of Kansas; and in that quarrel the latter declares that all he wants is a fair vote for the people, and that he cares not whether slavery be voted down or voted up. I do not understand his declaration that he cares not whether slavery be voted down or voted up, to be intended by him other than as an apt definition of the policy he would impress upon the public mind — the principle for which he declares he has suffered so much, and is ready to suffer to the end. And well may he cling to that principle. If he has any parental feeling, well may he cling to it. That principle is the only shred left of his original Nebraska doctrine. Under the Dred Scott decision "squatter sovereignty" squatted out of existence, tumbled down like temporary scaffolding — like the mould at the foundry served through one blast and fell back into loose sand — helped to carry an election, and then was kicked to the winds. His late joint struggle with the Republicans, against the Lecompton Constitution, involves nothing of the original Nebraska doctrine. That struggle was made on a point — the right of a people to make their own constitution — upon which he and the Republicans have never differed.

The several points of the Dred Scott decision, in connection, with Senator Douglas's "care not" policy, constitute the piece of machinery, in its present state of advancement. This was the third point gained. The working points of that machinery are:

First, that no Negro slave, imported as such from Africa, and no descendant of such slave, can ever be a citizen of any State, in the sense of that term as used in the Constitution of the United States. This point is made in order to deprive the Negro, in every possible event, of the benefit of that provision of the United States Constitution, which declares that "The citizens of each State, shall be entitled to all privileges and immunities of citizens in the several States."

Secondly, that "subject to the Constitution of the United States," neither Congress nor a Territorial Legislature can exclude slavery from any United States territory. This point is made in order that individual men may fill up the Territories with slaves, without danger of losing them as property, and thus to enhance the chances of permanency to the institution through all the future.

Thirdly, that whether the holding a Negro in actual slavery in a free State, makes him free, as against the holder, the United States courts will not decide, but will leave to be decided by the courts of any slave State the Negro may be forced into by the master. This point is made, not to be pressed immediately; but, if acquiesced in for awhile, and apparently endorsed by the people at an election, then to sustain the logical conclusion that what Dred Scott's master might lawfully do with Dred Scott, in the free State of Illinois, every other master may lawfully do with any other one, or one thousand slaves, in Illinois, or in any other free State.

Auxiliary to all this, and working hand in hand with it, the Nebraska doctrine, or what is left of it, is to educate and mould public opinion, at least Northern public opinion, not to care whether slavery is voted down or voted up. This shows exactly where we now are; and partially, also, whither we are tending.

It will throw additional light on the latter, to go back, and run the mind over the string of historical facts already stated. Several things will now appear less dark and mysterious than they did when they were transpiring. The people were to be left "perfectly free," "subject only to the Constitution." What the Constitution had to do with it, outsiders could not then see. Plainly enough now, it was an exactly fitted niche, for the Dred Scott decision to afterward come in, and declare the perfect freedom of the people to be just no freedom at all. Why was the amendment, expressly declaring the right of the people, voted down? Plainly enough now: the adoption of it would have spoiled the niche for the Dred Scott decision. Why was the court decision held up? Why even a Senator's individual opinion withheld, till after the Presidential election? Plainly enough now: the speaking out then would have damaged the perfectly free argument upon which the election was to be carried. Why the outgoing President's felicitation on the endorsement? Why the delay of a re-argument? Why the incoming President's advance exhortation in favor of the decision? These things look like the cautious patting and petting of a spirited horse preparatory to mounting him, when it is dreaded that he may give the rider a fall. And why the hasty after-endorsement of the decision by the President and others?

We cannot absolutely know that all these exact adaptations are the result of pre-concert. But when we see a lot of framed timbers, different portions of which we know have been gotten out at different times and places and by different workmen — Stephen, Franklin, Roger and James, for instance — and when we see these timbers joined together, and see they exactly make the frame of a house or a mill, all the tenons and mortices exactly fitting, and all the lengths and proportions of the different pieces exactly adapted to their respective places, and not a piece too many or too few — not omitting even scaffolding — or, if a single piece be lacking, we see the place in the frame exactly fitted and prepared yet to bring such a piece in — in such a case, we find it impossible not to believe that Stephen and Franklin and Roger and James all understood one another from the beginning, and all worked upon a common plan or draft drawn up before the first blow was struck.

It should not be overlooked that, by the Nebraska bill, the people of a State as well as Territory, were to be left "perfectly free," "subject only to the Constitution." Why mention a State? They were legislating for Territories, and not for or about States. Certainly the people of a State are and ought to be subject to the Constitution of the United States; but why is mention of this lugged into this merely Territorial law? Why are the people of a Territory and the people of a State therein lumped together, and their relation to the Constitution therein treated as being precisely the same? While the opinion of the court, by Chief Justice Taney, in the Dred Scott case, and the separate opinions of all the concurring Judges, expressly declare that the Constitution of the United States neither permits Congress nor a Territorial Legislature to exclude slavery from any United States Territory, they all omit to declare whether or not the same Constitution permits a State, or the people of a State, to exclude it. Possibly, this is a mere omission; but who can be quite sure, if McLean or Curtis had sought to get into the opinion a declaration of unlimited power in the people of a State to exclude slavery from their limits, just as Chase and Mace sought to get such declaration, in behalf of the people of a Territory, into the Nebraska bill; — I ask, who can be quite sure that it would not have been voted down in the one case as it had been in the other? The nearest approach to the point of declaring the power of a State over slavery, is made by Judge Nelson. He approaches it more than once, using the precise idea, and almost the language, too, of the Nebraska act. On one occasion, his exact language is, "except in cases where the power is restrained by the Constitution of the United States, the law of the State is supreme over the subject of slavery within its jurisdiction." In what cases the power of the States is so restrained by the United States Constitution, is left an open question, precisely as the same question, as to the restraint on the power of the Territories, was left open in the Nebraska act. Put this and that together, and we have another nice little niche, which we may, ere long, see filled with another Supreme Court decision, declaring that the Constitution of the United States does not permit a State to exclude slavery from its limits. And this may especially be expected if the doctrine of "care not whether slavery be voted down or voted up," shall gain upon the public mind sufficiently to give promise that such a decision can be maintained when made. Such a decision is all that slavery now lacks of being alike lawful in all the States. Welcome, or unwelcome, such decision is probably coming, and will soon be upon us, unless the power of the present political dynasty shall be met and overthrown. We shall lie down pleasantly dreaming that the people of Missouri are on the verge of making their State free, and we shall awake to the reality instead, that the Supreme Court has made Illinois a slave State. To meet and overthrow the power of that dynasty, is the work now before all those who would prevent that consummation. That is what we have to do. How can we best do it?

There are those who denounce us openly to their own friends, and yet whisper us softly, that Senator Douglas is the aptest instrument there is with which to effect that object. They wish us to infer all, from the fact that he now has a little quarrel with the present head of the dynasty; and that he has regularly voted with us on a single point, upon which he and we have never differed. They remind us that he is a great man, and that the largest of us are very small ones. Let this be granted. But "a living dog is better than a dead lion." Judge Douglas, if not a dead lion, for this work, is at least a caged and toothless one. How can he oppose the advances of slavery? He don't care anything about it. His avowed mission is impressing the "public heart" to care nothing about it. A leading Douglas democratic newspaper thinks Douglas's superior talent will be needed to resist the revival of the African slave trade. Does Douglas believe an effort to revive that trade is approaching? He has not said so. Does he really think so? But if it is, how can he resist it? For years he has

labored to prove it a sacred right of white men to take Negro slaves into the new Territories. Can he possibly show that it is less a sacred right to buy them where they can be bought cheapest? And unquestionably they can be bought cheaper in Africa than in Virginia. He has done all in his power to reduce the whole question of slavery to one of a mere right of property; and as such, how can he oppose the foreign slave trade — how can he refuse that trade in that "property" shall be "perfectly free" — unless he does it as a protection to the home production? And as the home producers will probably not ask the protection, he will be wholly without a ground of opposition.

Senator Douglas holds, we know, that a man may rightfully be wiser today than he was yesterday — that he may rightfully change when he finds himself wrong. But can we, for that reason, run ahead, and infer that he will make any particular change, of which he, himself, has given no intimation? Can we safely base our action upon any such vague inference? Now, as ever, I wish not to misrepresent Judge Douglas's position, question his motives, or do aught that can be personally offensive to him. Whenever, if ever, he and we can come together on principle so that our cause may have assistance from his great ability, I hope to have interposed no adventitious obstacle. But clearly, he is not now with us — he does not pretend to be — he does not promise ever to be.

Our cause, then, must be entrusted to, and conducted by, its own undoubted friends — those whose hands are free, whose hearts are in the work — who do care for the result. Two years ago the Republicans of the nation mustered over thirteen hundred thousand strong. We did this under the single impulse of resistance to a common danger, with every external circumstance against us. Of strange, discordant, and even hostile elements, we gathered from the four winds, and formed and fought the battle through, under the constant hot fire of a disciplined, proud and pampered enemy. Did we brave all then, to falter now? — now, when that same enemy is wavering, dissevered and belligerent? The result is not doubtful. We shall not fail — if we stand firm, we shall not fail. Wise counsels may accelerate, or mistakes delay it, but, sooner or later, the victory is sure to come.

———— 4.5 ————

"HAD I SO INTERFERED IN BEHALF OF THE RICH, THE POWERFUL ... THIS COURT WOULD HAVE DEEMED IT AN ACT WORTHY OF REWARD"
John Brown's Raid

All of the violence and harsh rhetoric of the 1850s surrounding slavery culminated in a brazen attack on the federal armory in Harper's Ferry, Virginia, by white free-soiler and abolitionist John Brown. Brown had long supported military efforts to overturn slavery, and as early as 1847 confided to Frederick Douglass his plans to lead America's slaves in a revolt launched from Virginia. Perhaps emboldened by the bloody battles in Kansas, Brown finally launched his assault on October 16, 1859. His five black and 16 white raiders successfully seized the federal armory and took 60 townspeople hostage. But they were soon overpowered. Douglass, whom Brown tried to recruit to join his 21-member "provisional army," had warned that the men "would never get out alive." He was right. The group successfully took the armory, but held it for only 36 hours before militiamen and U.S. Marines led by Robert E. Lee killed or captured most of them.

Originally, northerners and abolitionists were shocked by the raid, but, in the tradition of the Boston Massacre, it quickly morphed into a heroic strike for liberty. Poets and speakers eulogized Brown as a fallen martyr for the nation and the antislavery cause. Ballads began appearing in popular culture, sung in black churches across the country and, later, by Union soldiers in the Civil War. Today, the ballad "John Brown's Body" is likely the most identifiable cultural artifact of the war.

A. Last words of John Copeland, a black raider

Of the five black members of Brown's provisional army, two were killed at the siege, two were captured and later hanged and one escaped to Canada. John Copeland was one of the two hanged. A free man and student at Oberlin College in Ohio, Copeland impressed the white prosecutor and judge, who commented on Copeland's intelligence and noted "a dignity about him that I could not help liking." Nevertheless, the judge sentenced him to hang, and he was executed on December 16, 1859. A few hours before his death, Copeland wrote the following letter to his family.

Dear Father, Mother, Brothers Henry, William and Freddy and Sisters Sarah and Mary:
The last Sabbath with me on earth has passed away. The last Monday, Tuesday, Wednesday and Thursday that I shall ever see on this earth, have now passed by. God's glorious sun, which he has placed in the heavens to illuminate this earth — whose warm rays make man's home on earth pleasant — whose refulgent beams are watched for by the poor invalid, to enter and make as it were a heaven of the room in which he is confined — I have seen declining behind the western mountains for the last time. Last night, for the last time, I beheld the soft bright moon as it rose, casting its mellow light into my felon's cell, dissipating the darkness, and filling it with that soft pleasant light which causes such thrills of joy to all those in like circumstances with myself. This morning, for the last time, I beheld the glorious sun of yesterday rising in the far-off East, away off in the country where our Lord Jesus Christ first proclaimed salvation to man; and now, as he rises higher and his bright light takes the place of the pale, soft moonlight, I will take my pen, for the last time, to write you who are bound to me by those strong ties, (yea, the strongest that God ever instituted,) the ties of blood and relationship. I am well, both in body and in mind. And now, dear ones, if it were not that I knew your hearts will be filled with sorrow at my fate, I could pass from this earth without a regret. Why should you sorrow? Why should your hearts be wracked with grief? Have I not everything to gain, and nothing to lose by the change? I fully believe that not only myself, but also all three of my poor comrades who are to ascend the same scaffold — (a scaffold already made sacred to the cause of freedom by the death of that great champion of human free-

dom — Captain John Brown) are prepared to meet our God.

I am only leaving a world filled with sorrow and woe, to enter one in which there is but one lasting day of happiness and bliss. I feel that God, in his Mercy, has spoken peace to my soul, and that all my numerous sins are forgiven.

Dear parents, brothers and sisters, it is true that I am now in a few hours to start on a journey from which no traveler returns. Yes, long before this reaches you, I shall, as I sincerely hope, have met our brother and sister who have for years been worshiping God around his throne — singing praises to him and thanking him that he gave his Son to die that they might have eternal life. I pray daily and hourly that I may be fitted to have my home with them, and that you, one and all, may prepare your souls to meet your God, that so, in the end, though we meet no more on earth, we shall meet in heaven, where we shall not be parted by the demands of the cruel and unjust monster Slavery.

But think not that I am complaining, for I feel reconciled to meet my fate. I pray God that his will be done, not mine.

Let me tell you that it is not the mere fact of having to meet death, which I should regret, (if I should express regret I mean) but that such an unjust institution should exist as the one which demands my life, and not my life only, but the lives of those to whom my life bears but the relative value of zero to the infinite. I beg of you, one and all, that you will not grieve about me; but that you will thank God that he spared me to make my peace with him.

And now, dear ones, attach no blame to any one for my coming here, for not any person but myself is to blame.

I have no antipathy against any one. I have freed my mind of all hard feelings against every living being, and I ask all who have any thing against me to do the same.

And now, dear Parents, Brothers and Sisters, I must bid you to serve your God, and meet me in heaven.

I must with a very few words close my correspondence with those who are the most near

and dear to me: but I hope, in the end, we may again commune never more to cease.

Dear ones, he who writes this will, in a few hours, be in this world no longer. Yes, these fingers which hold the pen with which this is written will, before today's sun has reached its meridian, have laid it aside forever, and this poor soul have taken its light to meet its God.

And now, dear ones, I must bid you that last, long, sad farewell. Good by, Father, Mother, Henry, William and Freddy, Sarah and Mary! Serve your God and meet me in heaven.

Your Son and Brother to eternity,
JOHN A. COPELAND

B. Black raider Dangerfield Newby's motivation

Another black raider was 48-year-old Dangerfield Newby, a free man from Virginia who had been manumitted following the deaths of both his owner and his father. Newby was the first to die in the siege, shot through the neck with a six-inch spike, his corpse mutilated by either livestock or townspeople or both afterwards. In his pocket, he carried a letter from his wife, dated August 16 of that year, in which she discussed her expected sale to Louisiana. Her owner had offered to sell her and the youngest of their seven children to Newby for $1,500, but he had been unable to raise the money. Historians believe Newby joined Brown's raiders as a last ditch effort to unite his family. Shortly after the raid, Newby's wife was in fact sold to a Louisiana slave dealer.

Dear Husband — It is said Master is in want of money. If so, I know not what time he may sell me, and then all my bright hopes of the future are blasted, for there has been one bright hope to cheer me in all my troubles, that is to be with you. If I thought I should never see you this earth would have no charms for me. Come this fall without fail money or no money. Do all you can for me, which I have no doubt you will. The children are all well. The baby cannot walk yet. You must write soon and say when you think youcan come.

Your affectionate wife,
Harriet Newby

C. John Brown's last words

In the end, only five of Brown's raiders escaped the siege and survived. The rest were either killed on the spot or arrested and later hanged. During his trial, Brown, having been sentenced to death for murder and treason, was asked by the judge if he had any words. Lying injured on a cot in the courtroom, Brown rose and, while arguing he never intended to murder anyone, declined to apologize for his act. If he had struck on the behalf of "the rich, the powerful, the intelligent, the so-called great, or in behalf of any of their friends," he argued, the court would now declare him a hero.

I have, may it please the court, a few words to say.

In the first place, I deny everything but what I have all along admitted, — the design on my part to free slaves. I intended certainly to have made a clean thing of that matter, as I did last winter, when I went into Missouri and took slaves without the snapping of a gun on either side, moved them through the country, and finally left them in Canada. I designed to do the same thing again, on a larger scale. That was all I intended. I never did intend murder, or treason, or the destruction of property, or to excite or incite slaves to rebellion, or to make insurrection.

I have another objection; and that is, it is unjust that I should suffer such a penalty. Had I interfered in the manner which I admit, and which I admit has been fairly proved (for I admire the truthfulness and candor of the greater portion of the witnesses who have testified in this case), — had I so interfered in behalf of the rich, the powerful, the intelligent, the so-called great, or in behalf of any of their friends — either father, mother, sister, wife, or children, or any of that class — and suffered and sacrificed what I have in this interference, it would have been all right; and every man in this court would have deemed it an act worthy of reward rather than punishment.

The court acknowledges, as I suppose, the validity of the law of God. I see a book kissed here which I suppose to be the Bible, or at least the New Testament. That teaches me that all things whatsoever I would that men should do to me, I should do even so to them. It teaches me further to "remember them that are in bonds, as bound with them." I endeavored to act up to that instruction. I say, I am too young to understand that God is any respecter of persons. I believe that to have interfered as I have done — as I have always freely admitted I have done — in behalf of His despised poor, was not wrong, but right. Now if it is deemed necessary that I should forfeit my life for the furtherance of the ends of justice, and mingle my blood further with the blood of my children and with the blood of millions in this slave country whose rights are disregarded by wicked, cruel, and unjust enactments. — I submit; so let it be done!

Let me say one word further.

I feel entirely satisfied with the treatment I have received on my trial. Considering all the circumstances, it has been more generous than I expected. I feel no consciousness of my guilt. I have stated from the first what was my intention, and what was not. I never had any design against the life of any person, nor any disposition to commit treason, or excite slaves to rebel, or make any general insurrection. I never encouraged any man to do so, but always discouraged any idea of any kind.

Let me say also, a word in regard to the statements made by some to those connected with me. I hear it has been said by some of them that I have induced them to join me. But the contrary is true. I do not say this to injure them, but as regretting their weakness. There is not one of them but joined me of his own accord, and the greater part of them at their own expense. A number of them I never saw, and never had a word of conversation with, till the day they came to me; and that was for the purpose I have stated.

Now I have done.

—————— 4.6 ——————
'HIS TRUTH IS MARCHING ON'
Julia Ward Howe

One of the cultural legacies of John Brown's raid and his subsequent martyrdom is the ballad "John Brown's Body." There are countless versions and interpretations of the song. One of the first incarnations was as a hymn, titled "Say, brothers, will you meet us," sung in black churches and at Methodist camp meetings during the first half of the nineteenth century. Later, with the start of the Civil War, Union soldiers turned the tune into a marching song eulogizing Brown. In both cases, the verses were largely improvised and mingled with the lasting main chorus. Finally, in 1861, Julia Ward Howe wrote the words to the formal "Battle Hymn of the Republic," based on the original "John Brown's Body," which she published in the February 1862 issue of *The Atlantic Monthly*.

A. "Say, brothers, will you meet us"

Say, brothers, will you meet us
Say, brothers, will you meet us
Say, brothers, will you meet us
On Canaan's happy shore.

[Chorus]
Glory, glory, hallelujah
Glory, glory, hallelujah
Glory, glory, hallelujah
For ever, evermore!

By the grace of God we'll meet you (3x)
By the grace of God we'll meet you
By the grace of God we'll meet you
Where parting is no more.

[Chorus]

Jesus lives and reigns forever
Jesus lives and reigns forever
Jesus lives and reigns forever
On Canaan's happy shore.

B. Union Marching song

Old John Brown's body lies a-mouldering
    in the grave,
While weep the sons of bondage whom
    he ventured all to save;
But though he lost his life in struggling for
    the slave,
His truth is marching on.

[Chorus]
Glory, Glory, hallelujah!
Glory, Glory, hallelujah!
Glory, Glory, hallelujah!
His Truth is marching on.

John Brown was a hero, undaunted, true
    and brave;
Kansas knew his valor when he fought her
    rights to save;
And now though the grass grows green
    above his grave,
His truth is marching on.

[Chorus]

He captured Harper's Ferry with his nineteen
    men so few,
And he frightened "Old Virginy" till she
    trembled through and through,
They hung him for a traitor, themselves a
    traitor crew,
But his truth is marching on.

[Chorus]

C. The Battle Hymn of the Republic

Mine eyes have seen the glory of the coming of
    the Lord:
He is trampling out the vinyards where the
    grapes of wrath are stored;
He hath loosed the fateful lightning of His
    terrible swift sword:
His truth is marching on.

I have seen Him in the watch-fires of a hundred
circling camps,
They have builded Him an altar in the evening
dews and damps;
I can read His righteous sentence by the dim
and flaring lamps:
His day is marching on.

I have read a fiery gospel writ in burnished
rows of steel:
"As ye deal with my contemners, so with you
my grace shall deal;
Let the Hero, born of woman, crush the serpent
with his heel,
Since God is marching on."

He has sounded forth the trumpet that shall
never call retreat;
He is sifting out the hearts of men before
His judgment-seat:
Oh, be swift, my soul, to answer Him! be
jubilant, my feet!
Our God is marching on.

In the beauty of the lilies Christ was born acros
the sea,
With a glory in his bosom that transfigures you
and me:
As he died to make men holy, let us die to
make men free,
While God is marching on.

——— 4.7 ———
OUR NIG
Harriet Wilson

As was the case with essayist Ann Plato (see Chapter
Three), very little is known today about the first black
woman to publish a full-length novel. Harriet Wilson
published her jarringly-titled novel *Our Nig* in 1859. In
the preface, she states that she hoped to raise money to
support her child. A single mother, Wilson had struggled
to maintain steady work and lost custody of her son. But
five months after the book's publication, the boy, George,
died of a fever. Owing to the gap in scholarship about
black female writers of her time, that is about the extent
of what we know of Wilson. Her novel itself, in fact, had

been lost to history until noted African-American Studies
scholar Henry Louis Gates, Jr., then an associate professor at Yale, rediscovered it in 1983. It tells the story of
Alfredo, a young mixed-race woman who was raised and
abused by a white family after the death of her black
father and abandonment of her white mother. Later, she
marries a man who abandons her along with their young
son. Written in the form of a slave narrative from
Alfredo's vantage, the book indicts northern white
racism, a unique undertaking for the time's literature. In
the conclusion, excerpted here, Alfredo shows her disgust for the society that has so tortured her.

Chapter XII
The Winding Up of The Matter

"Nothing new under the sun." — Solomon

A few years ago, within the compass of my narrative, there appeared often in some of our New
England villages, professed fugitives from slavery,
who recounted their personal experience in
homely phrase, and awakened the indignation of
non-slaveholders against brother Pro. Such a one
appeared in the new home of Frado; and as people of color were rare there, was it strange she
should attract her dark brother; that he should
inquire her out; succeed in seeing her; feel a
strange sensation in his heart towards her; that he
should toy with her shining curls feel proud to
provoke her to smile and expose the ivory concealed by thin, ruby lips; that her sparkling eyes
should fascinate; that he should propose; that
they should marry? A short acquaintance was
indeed an objection, but she saw him often, and
thought she knew him. He never spoke of his
enslavement to her when alone, but she felt that,
like her own oppression, it was painful to disturb
oftener than was needful.

He was a fine, straight negro, whose back
showed no marks of the lash, erect as if it never
crouched beneath a burden. There was a silent
sympathy which Frado felt attracted her, and
she opened her heart to the presence of love —
that arbitrary and inexorable tyrant.

She removed to Singleton, her former residence, and there was married. Here were Frado's

first feelings of trust and repose on human arm. She realized, for the first time, the relief of looking to another for comfortable support. Occasionally he would leave her to "lecture."

Those tours were prolonged often to weeks. Of course he had little spare money. Frado was again feeling her self-dependence, and was at last compelled to resort alone to that. Samuel was kind to her when at home, but made no provision for his absence, which was at last unprecedented.

He left her to her fate — embarked at sea, with the disclosure that he had never seen the South, and that his illiterate harangues were humbugs for hungry abolitionists. Once more alone! Yet not alone. A still newer companionship would soon force itself upon her. No one wanted her with such prospects. Herself was a burden enough; who would have an additional one?

The horrors of her condition nearly prostrated her, and she was again thrown upon the public for sustenance. Then followed the birth of her child. The long absent Samuel unexpectedly returned, and rescued her from charity. Recovering from her expected illness, she once more commenced toil for herself and child, in a room obtained of a poor woman, but with better fortune. One so well known would not be wholly neglected. Kind friends watched her when Samuel was from home, prevented her from suffering, and when the cold weather pinched the warmly clad, a kind friend took them in, and thus preserved them. At last Samuel's business became very engrossing, and after long desertion, news reached his family that he had become a victim of yellow fever, in New Orleans.

So much toil as was necessary to sustain Frado, was no more than she could endure. As soon as her babe could be nourished without his mother, she left him in charge of a Mrs. Capon, and procured an agency, hoping to recruit her health, and gain an easier livelihood for herself and child. This afforded her better maintenance than she had yet found. She passed into the various towns of the State she lived in, then into Massachusetts. Strange were some of her adventures. Watched by kidnappers, maltreated by professed abolitionists, who didn't want slaves at the South, nor niggers in their own houses, North. Faugh! To lodge one; to eat with one; to admit one through the front door; to sit next one; awful!

Traps slyly laid by the vicious to ensnare her, she resolutely avoided. In one of her tours, Providence favored her with a friend who, pitying her cheerless lot, kindly provided her with a valuable recipe, from which she might herself manufacture a useful article for her maintenance. This provided a more agreeable, and an easier way of sustenance.

And thus, to the present time, may you see her busily employed in preparing her merchandise; then sallying forth to encounter many frowns, but some kind friends and purchasers. Nothing turns her from her steadfast purpose of elevating herself. Reposing on God, she has thus far journeyed securely. Still an invalid, she asks your sympathy, gentle reader. Refuse not, because some part of her history is unknown, save by the Omniscient God. Enough has been unrolled to demand your sympathy and aid. …

——— 4.8 ———

INCIDENTS IN THE LIFE OF A SLAVE GIRL
Harriet Jacobs

Harriet Jacobs's 1859 narrative *Incidents in the Life of a Slave Girl* shocked even her fellow abolitionists. The story painfully chronicles the ordeal Jacobs faced as a teenage slave fighting off the sexual advances of her predatory owner. The tale forced open a taboo discussion about the sexual abuse that was so central a component of slavery. From the age of 14, Jacobs writes, she fought and connived to avoid her owner's determined quest to make her his concubine, often pitting his wife against him and, ultimately, submitting to sexual relations with another white man in an effort to "spoil" herself for her owner. She bore two children as a result of that effort, but still did not deter the man. In the end, she fled. But, unable to leave her children, she merely hid in a crawlspace in the home where her children, property of her lover, lived. She stayed there for seven years, living amongst rodents so that she could peer out of a peephole at her children playing in the yard. She did finally escape to the North, however, and become involved in the abolitionist movement. The topic of sexual abuse of slaves was so sensitive at the time she published her narrative, she had to assume a pseudonym for its original release.

A PERILOUS PASSAGE IN THE SLAVE GIRL'S LIFE.

AFTER my lover went away, Dr. Flint contrived a new plan. He seemed to have an idea that my fear of my mistress was his greatest obstacle. In the blandest tones, he told me that he was going to build a small house for me, in a secluded place, four miles away from the town. I shuddered; but I was constrained to listen, while he talked of his intention to give me a home of my own, and to make a lady of me. Hitherto, I had escaped my dreaded fate, by being in the midst of people. My grandmother had already had high words with my master about me. She had told him pretty plainly what she thought of his character, and there was considerable gossip in the neighborhood about our affairs, to which the open-mouthed jealousy of Mrs. Flint contributed not a little. When my master said he was going to build a house for me, and that he could do it with little trouble and expense, I was in hopes something would happen to frustrate his scheme; but I soon heard that the house was actually begun. I vowed before my Maker that I would never enter it. I had rather toil on the plantation from dawn till dark; I had rather live and die in jail, than drag on, from day to day, through such a living death. I was determined that the master, whom I so hated and loathed, who had blighted the prospects of my youth, and made my life a desert, should not, after my long struggle with him, succeed at last in trampling his victim under his feet. I would do any thing, every thing, for the sake of defeating him. What could I do? I thought and thought, till I became desperate, and made a plunge into the abyss.

And now, reader, I come to a period in my unhappy life, which I would gladly forget if I could. The remembrance fills me with sorrow and shame. It pains me to tell you of it; but I have promised to tell you the truth, and I will do it honestly, let it cost me what it may. I will not try to screen myself behind the plea of compulsion from a master; for it was not so. Neither can I plead ignorance or thoughtlessness. For years, my master had done his utmost to pollute my mind with foul images, and to destroy the pure principles inculcated by my grandmother, and the good mistress of my childhood. The influences of slavery had had the same effect on me that they had on other young girls; they had made me prematurely knowing, concerning the evil ways of the world. I know what I did, and I did it with deliberate calculation.

But, O, ye happy women, whose purity has been sheltered from childhood, who have been free to choose the objects of your affection, whose homes are protected by law, do not judge the poor desolate slave girl too severely! If slavery had been abolished, I, also, could have married the man of my choice; I could have had a home shielded by the laws; and I should have been spared the painful task of confessing what I am now about to relate; but all my prospects had been blighted by slavery. I wanted to keep myself pure; and, under the most adverse circumstances, I tried hard to preserve my self-respect; but I was struggling alone in the powerful grasp of the demon Slavery; and the monster proved too strong for me. I felt as if I was forsaken by God and man; as if all my efforts must be frustrated; and I became reckless in my despair.

I have told you that Dr. Flint's persecutions and his wife's jealousy had given rise to some gossip in the neighborhood. Among others, it chanced that a white unmarried gentleman had obtained some knowledge of the circumstances in which I was placed. He knew my grandmother, and often spoke to me in the street. He became interested for me, and asked questions about my master, which I answered in part. He expressed a great deal of sympathy, and a wish to aid me. He constantly sought opportunities to see me, and wrote to me frequently. I was a poor slave girl, only fifteen years old.

So much attention from a superior person was, of course, flattering; for human nature is the same in all. I also felt grateful for his sympathy, and encouraged by his kind words. It seemed to me a great thing to have such a friend. By degrees, a more tender feeling crept into my heart. He was an educated and eloquent gentleman; too eloquent, alas, for the poor slave girl who trusted in him. Of course I saw whither all this was tending. I knew the impassable gulf between us; but to be an object of interest to a man who is not married, and who is not her master, is agreeable to the pride and feelings of a slave, if her miserable situation has left her any pride or sentiment. It seems less degrading to give one's self, than to submit to compulsion. There is something akin to freedom in having a lover who has no control over you, except that which he gains by kindness and attachment. A master may treat you as rudely as he pleases, and you dare not speak; moreover, the wrong does not seem so great with an unmarried man, as with one who has a wife to be made unhappy. There may be sophistry in all this; but the condition of a slave confuses all principles of morality, and, in fact, renders the practice of them impossible.

When I found that my master had actually begun to build the lonely cottage, other feelings mixed with those I have described. Revenge, and calculations of interest, were added to flattered vanity and sincere gratitude for kindness. I knew nothing would enrage Dr. Flint so much as to know that I favored another; and it was something to triumph over my tyrant even in that small way. I thought he would revenge himself by selling me, and I was sure my friend, Mr. Sands, would buy me. He was a man of more generosity and feeling than my master, and I thought my freedom could be easily obtained from him. The crisis of my fate now came so near that I was desperate. I shuttered to think of being the mother of children that should be owned by my old tyrant. I knew that

as soon as a new fancy took him, his victims were sold far off to get rid of them; especially if they had children. I had seen several women sold, with his babies at the breast. He never allowed his offspring by slaves to remain long in sight of himself and his wife. Of a man who was not my master I could ask to have my children well supported; and in this case, I felt confident I should obtain the boon. I also felt quite sure that they would be made free. With all these thoughts revolving in my mind, and seeing no other way of escaping the doom I so much dreaded, I made a headlong plunge. Pity me, and pardon me, O virtuous reader! You never knew what it is to be a slave; to be entirely unprotected by law or custom; to have the laws reduce you to the condition of a chattel, entirely subject to the will of another. You never exhausted your ingenuity in avoiding the snares, and eluding the power of a hated tyrant; you never shuddered at the sound of his footsteps, and trembled within hearing of his voice. I know I did wrong. No one can feel it more sensibly than I do. The painful and humiliating memory will haunt me to my dying day. Still, in looking back, calmly, on the events of my life, I feel that the slave woman ought not to be judged by the same standard as others.

The months passed on. I had many unhappy hours. I secretly mourned over the sorrow I was bringing on my grandmother, who had so tried to shield me from harm. I knew that I was the greatest comfort of her old age, and that it was a source of pride to her that I had not degraded myself, like most of the slaves. I wanted to confess to her that I was no longer worthy of her love; but I could not utter the dreaded words.

As for Dr. Flint, I had a feeling of satisfaction and triumph in the thought of telling him. From time to time he told me of his intended arrangements, and I was silent. At last, he came and told me the cottage was completed, and ordered me to go to it. I told him I would never enter it. He said, "I have heard enough of such talk as that. You shall go, if you are carried by force; and you shall remain there." I replied, "I will never go there. In a few months I shall be a mother."

He stood and looked at me in dumb amazement, and left the house without a word. I thought I should be happy in my triumph over him. But now that the truth was out, and my relatives would hear of it, I felt wretched. Humble as were their circumstances, they had pride in my good character. Now, how could I look them in the face? My self-respect was gone! I had resolved that I would be virtuous, though I was a slave. I had said, "Let the storm beat! I will brave it till I die." And now, how humiliated I felt!

I went to my grandmother. My lips moved to make confession, but the words stuck in my throat. I sat down in the shade of a tree at her door and began to sew. I think she saw something unusual was the matter with me. The mother of slaves is very watchful. She knows there is no security for her children. After they have entered their teens she lives in daily expectation of trouble. This leads to many questions. If the girl is of a sensitive nature, timidity keeps her from answering truthfully, and this well-meant course has a tendency to drive her from maternal counsels. Presently, in came my mistress, like a mad woman, and accused me concerning her husband. My grandmother, whose suspicions had been previously awakened, believed what she said. She exclaimed, "O Linda! has it come to this? I had rather see you dead than to see you as you now are. You are a disgrace to your dead mother." She tore from my fingers my mother's wedding ring and her silver thimble. "Go away!" she exclaimed, "and never come to my house, again." Her reproaches fell so hot and heavy, that they left me no chance to answer. Bitter tears, such as the eyes never shed but once, were my only answer. I rose from my seat, but fell back again, sobbing. She did not speak to me; but the tears were running down her furrowed cheeks, and they scorched me like fire. She had always been so kind to me! So kind! How I longed to throw myself at her feet, and tell her all the truth! But she had ordered me to

go, and never to come there again. After a few minutes, I mustered strength, and started to obey her. With what feelings did I now close that little gate, which I used to open with such an eager hand in my childhood! It closed upon me with a sound I never heard before.

Where could I go? I was afraid to return to my master's. I walked on recklessly, not caring where I went, or what would become of me. When I had gone four or five miles, fatigue compelled me to stop. I sat down on the stump of an old tree. The stars were shining through the boughs above me. How they mocked me, with their bright, calm light! The hours passed by, and as I sat there alone a chilliness and deadly sickness came over me. I sank on the ground. My mind was full of horrid thoughts. I prayed to die; but the prayer was not answered. At last, with great effort I roused myself, and walked some distance further, to the house of a woman who had been a friend of my mother. When I told her why I was there, she spoke soothingly to me; but I could not be comforted. I thought I could bear my shame if I could only be reconciled to my grandmother. I longed to open my heart to her. I thought if she could know the real state of the case, and all I had been bearing for years, she would perhaps judge me less harshly. My friend advised me to send for her. I did so; but days of agonizing suspense passed before she came. Had she utterly forsaken me? No. She came at last. I knelt before her, and told her the things that had poisoned my life; how long I had been persecuted; that I saw no way of escape; and in an hour of extremity I had become desperate. She listened in silence. I told her I would bear any thing and do any thing, if in time I had hopes of obtaining her forgiveness. I begged of her to pity me, for my dead mother's sake. And she did pity me. She did not say, "I forgive you;" but she looked at me lovingly, with her eyes full of tears. She laid her old hand gently on my head, and murmured, "Poor child! Poor child!"

——— 4.9 ———
A GEORGIA PLANTATION
Mortimer Thompson and
Fanny Kemble

Slave life on antebellum plantations was, of course, phys-ically miserable — long work hours, insufficient food, squalid housing and constant abuse. But it was also emotionally and psychologically tortuous. Family mem-bers lived in steady fear — often eventually realized — of being torn apart due to some economic decision made by men they would likely never meet. Two literary works by white abolitionists brought this aspect of slave life to the broader public eye in the decade before the Civil War.

A. "What became of the Slaves on a Georgia Plantation"

The largest sale of human beings in American history occurred over two days, from March 2nd to 3rd, in 1859. The slaves belonged to Pierce Butler, grandson of a wealthy Senator and Revolutionary War veteran who owned two of the country's largest plantations, located in the Georgia Sea Islands. Butler, with his older brother, inherited those plantations when his grandfather died in 1836 and became one of the largest slave owners of his time. But he famously squandered his wealth, and twenty years later had to sell off his belongings to satisfy his debtors. Over 400 of his slaves (half of those in his pos-session, the other half were transferred to his brother's estate) were loaded into railcars and shipped to a race-track in Savannah, Georgia. Word went out that this mass of humans would be sold off, at good prices, and traders flocked to join the spectacle. But renowned *New York Tribune* journalist Mortimer Thompson — both he and his paper were abolitionists — also came. Thompson filed a long and unforgiving piece describing the sale and the cruel treatment of the Butler slaves. He later published the account as a book.

… None of the Butler slaves have ever been sold before, but have been on these two plan-tations since they were born. Here have they lived their humble lives, and loved their simple loves; here were they born, and here have many of them had children born unto them; here had their parents lived before them, and are now resting in quiet graves on the old planta-tions that these unhappy ones are to see no more forever; here they left not only the well-known scenes dear to them from very baby-hood by a thousand fond memories, and homes as much loved by them, perhaps, as brighter homes by men of brighter faces; but all the clinging ties that bound them to living hearts were torn asunder, for but one-half of each of these two happy little communities was sent to the shambles, to be scattered to the four winds, and the other half was left behind. And who can tell how closely intertwined are the affections of a little band of four hundred per-sons, living isolated from all the world beside, from birth to middle age? Do they not natu-rally become one great family, each man a brother unto each?

It is true that they were sold "in families;" but let us see: a man and his wife were called a "family," their parents and kindred were not taken into account; the man and wife might be sold to the pine woods of North Carolina, their brothers and sisters be scattered through the cotton fields of Alabama and the rice swamps of Louisiana, while the parents might be left out in the old plantation to wear out their weary lives in heavy grief, and lay their heads in far-off graves, over which their children might never weep. And no account could be taken of loves that were as yet unconsummated by marriage; and how many aching hearts have been divorced by this summary proceeding as no man can ever know. And the separation is as utter, and is infinitely more hopeless, than that made by the Angel of Death, for then the loved ones are committed to the care of a merciful Diety; but in the other instance, to the tender mercies of a slave-driver. These dark-skinned unfortunates are perfectly unlettered, and could not communicate by writing even if they should know where to send their missives. And so to each other, and to the old familiar places of their youth, clung all their sympathies and affections, not less strong, perhaps, because they are so few. The blades of grass on all the Butler estates are outnumbered by the tears that are poured out in agony at the wreck that has been wrought in happy homes, and the crushing grief that has been laid on loving hearts.

But, then, what have "niggers" with tears? Besides, didn't Pierce Butler give them a silver dollar a-piece? which will appear in the sequel. And, sad as it is, it was all necessary, because a gentleman was not able to live on the beggardly pittance of half a million, and so must needs enter into speculations which turned out adversely.

HOW THEY WERE TREATED IN SAVANNAH.

The negroes were brought to Savannah in small lots, as many at a time as could be conveniently taken care of, the last of them reaching the city the Friday before the sale. They were consigned to the care of Mr. J. Bryan, Auctioneer and Negro Broker, who was to feed and keep them in condition until disposed of. Immediately on their arrival they were taken to the Race-course, and there quartered in the sheds erected for the accommodation of the horses and carriages of gentlemen attending the races. Into these sheds they were huddled pell-mell, without any more attention to their comfort than was necessary to prevent their becoming ill and unsaleable. Each "family" had one or more boxes or bundles, in which were stowed such scanty articles of their clothing as were not brought into immediate requisition, and their tin dishes and gourds for their food and drink.

It is, perhaps, a fit tribute to large-handed munificence to say that, when the negro man was sold, there was no extra charge for the negro man's clothes; they went with the man, and were not charged in the bill. Nor is this altogether a contemptible idea, for many of them had worldly wealth, in the shape of clothing and other valuables, to the extent of perhaps four or five dollars; and had all these been taken strictly into the account, the sum total of the sale would have been increased, possibly, a thousand dollars. In the North, we

do not necessarily sell the harness with the horse; why, in the South, should the clothes go with the negro?

In these sheds were the chattels huddled together on the floor, there being no sign of bench or table. They eat and slept on the bare boards, their food being rice and beans, with occasionally a bit of bacon and corn bread. Their huge bundles were scattered over the floor, and thereon the slaves sat or reclined, when not restlessly moving about, or gathered into sorrowful groups, discussing the chance of their future fate. On the faces of all was an expression of heavy grief; some appeared to be resigned to the hard stroke of Fortune that had torn them from their homes, and were sadly trying to make the best of it; some sat brooding moodily over their sorrows, their chins resting on their hands, their eyes staring vacantly, and their bodies rocking to and fro, with a restless motion that was never stilled; few wept, the place was too public and the drivers too near, though some occasionally turned aside to give way to a few quiet tears. They were dressed in every possible variety of uncouth and fantastic garb, in every style and of every imaginable color; the texture of the garments was in all cases coarse, most of the men being clothed in the rough cloth that is made expressly for the slaves. The dresses assumed by the negro minstrels, when they give imitations of plantation character, are by no means exaggerated; they are, instead, weak and unable to come up to the original. There was every variety of hats, with every imaginable slouch; and there was every cut and style of coat and pantaloons, made with every conceivable ingenuity of misfit, and tossed on with a general appearance of perfect looseness that is perfectly indescribable, except to say that a Southern negro always looks as if he could shake his clothes off without taking his hands out of his pockets. The women, true to the feminine instinct, had made, in almost every case, some attempt at finery. All wore gorgeous turbans, generally manufactured in an instant out of a gay-colored handkerchief by a sudden and graceful twist of the fingers; though there was occasionally a more elaborate turban, a turban complex and mysterious, got up with care, and ornamented with a few beads or bright bits of ribbon. Their dresses were mostly coarse stuff, though were some gaudy calicoes; a few had ear-rings, and one possessed the treasure of a string of yellow and blue beads. The little children were always better and more carefully dressed than the older ones, the parental pride coming out in a the shape of a yellow cap pointed like a mitre, or a jacket with a strip of red broadcloth round the bottom. The children were all sizes, the youngest being fifteen days old. The babies were generally good-natured; though when one would set up a yell, the complaint soon attacked the others, and a full chorus would result.

The slaves remained at the Race-course, some of them for more than a week, and all of them for four days before the sale. They were brought in thus early that buyers who desired to inspect them might enjoy that privilege, although none of them were sold at private sale. For these preliminary days their shed was constantly visited by speculators. The negroes were examined with as little consideration as if they had been brutes indeed; the buyers pulling their mouths open to see their teeth, pinching their limbs to find how muscular they were, walking them up and down to detect any signs of lameness, making them stoop and bend in different ways that they might be certain there was no concealed rupture or wound; in addition to all this treatment, asking them scores of questions relative to their qualifications and accomplishments. All these humiliations were submitted to without a murmur, and in some instances with good-natured cheerfulness — where the slave liked the appearance of the proposed buyer, and fancies that he might prove a kind "Mas'r."

The following curiously sad scene is the type of a score of others that were enacted:

"Elisha," chattel No. 5 in the catalogue, had taken a fancy to a benevolent-looking middle-aged gentleman, who was inspecting the stock,

and thus used his powers of persuasion to induce the benevolent man to purchase him, with his wife, boy and girl, Molly, Israel and Sevanda, chattels No. 5, 7 and 8. The earnestness with which the poor fellow pressed his suit, knowing, as he did, that perhaps the happiness of his whole life depended on his success, was touching, and the arguments he used most pathetic. He made no appeal to the feelings of the buyer; he rested no hope on his charity and kindness, but only strove to show how well worth his dollars were the bone and blood he was entreating him to buy.

"Look at me, Mas'r; am a prime rice planter; sho' you won't find a better man den me; no better on de whole plantation; not a bit old yet; do mo' work den ever; do carpenter work, too, little; better buy me, Mas'r; I'se be a good sarvant, Ms'r. Mlly, too, my wife, Sa, Fus'rate rice hand; mos as good as me. Stan' ou yer, Molly, and let the gen'lm'n see."

Molly advances, with her hands crossed at her bosom, and makes a quick short curtsy, and stands mute, looking appealingly in the benevolent man's face. But Elisha talks all the faster.

"Show mas'r yer arm, Molly — good arm dat, Mas'r — she do a heap of work mo' with dat arm yet. Let good Mas'r see yer teeth, Molly — see dat Mas'r, teeth all reg'lar, all good — she'm young gal yet. Come out yer, Israel, walk aroun' an' let the gen'lm'n see how spry you be" —

Then, pointing to the three-year-old girl who stood with her chubby hand to her mouth, holding on to her mother's dress, and uncertain what to make of the strange scene.

"Little Vardy's only a chile yet; make prime gal by-and-by. Better buy us, Mas'r, we'm fus' rate bargain" — and so on. But the benevolent gentleman found where he could drive a closer bargain, and so bought somebody else.

Similar scenes were transacting all the while on every side — parents praising the strength and cleverness of their children, and showing off every muscle and sinew to the very best advantage, not with the excusable pride of other parents, but to make them the more desirable in the yes of the man-buyer; and, on the other hand, children excusing and mitigating the age and inability of parents, that they might be marketable and fall, if possible, into kind hands. Not unfrequently these representations, if borne out by the facts, secured a purchaser. The women never spoke to the white men unless spoken to, and then made the conference as short as possible. And not one of them all, during the whole time they were thus exposed to the rude questions of vulgar men, spoke a first unwomanly or indelicate word, or conducted herself in any regard otherwise than as a modest woman should do; their conversation and demeanor were quite as unexceptionable as they would have been had they been the highest ladies in the land, and through all the insults to which there were subjected they conducted themselves with the most perfect decorum and self-respect.

The sentiment of the subjoined characteristic dialogue was heard more than once repeated:

"Well, Colonel, I seen you looking sharp at Shoemaker Bill's Sally. Going to buy her?"

"Well, Major, I think not. Sally's a good, big, strapping gal, and can do a heap o'work; but it's five years since she had any children. *She's done breeding, I reckon.*"

In the intervals of more active labor, the discussion of the reopening of the slave trade was commenced, and the opinion seemed to generally prevail that its reëstablishment is a consummation devoutly to be wished, and one red-faced Major or General or Corporal clinched his remarks with the emphatic assertion that "We'll have all the niggers in Africa over here in three years — we won't leave enough for seed."

B. *Journal of a Residence on a Georgia Plantation*

When Butler originally inherited his plantation, he met British actor Frances Anne Kemble, then on a two-year tour in American theaters. With her tour a booming success, the working-class woman found herself introduced to the upper crust of American society, where she met Butler. Butler courted Kemble and, just prior to inheriting

his plantation, the pair married. Kemble, an opponent of slavery, later claimed she did not know the source of Butler's wealth when they met. Their storied romance soon hit rocky waters, as Kemble's independence and opposition to Butler's business strained their bond. She insisted on being allowed to see his plantation for herself, and spent four months on St. Simon's Island in Georgia with the Butler brothers and their slaves. Appalled, she recorded her observations in her diary, but Butler forbade her from publishing them. Shortly thereafter, with the marriage strained beyond repair, she returned to England and the two divorced in a bitter and public legal feud over the custody of their children. After the Civil War erupted, back in England, Kemble published her diary in 1863, hoping it would build international opposition to the Confederacy. Her detailed account described not only the horrid physical conditions the slaves endured, but the emotional and psychological pain as well, as in the passage below. Also below, Kemble discusses her own sense of responsibility for slavery, and by extension the responsibility of all white Americans and Europeans, slaveholders or not, for allowing it to continue.

PSYCHE'S SADNESS
January 1839
I will tell you a story which has just formed an admirable illustration for my observation of all the mysteries of which this accursed system of slavery is the cause, even under the best and most humane administration of its laws and usages. You will find, in the absence of all voluntary or even conscious cruelty on the part of the master, the best possible comment on a state of things which, without the slightest desire to injure and oppress, produces such intolerable injury and oppression.

We have, as sort of under nursemaid and assistant, a young woman named Psyche, commonly called Sack; she can not be much over twenty, has a very pretty figure, a graceful, gentle deportment, and a face which, but for its color (she is a dingy mulatto), would be pretty, and is extremely pleasing, from the perfect sweetness of its expression; she is always serious, not to say sad and silent, and has always an air of melancholy and timidity. Just in proportion as I have found the slaves on this plantation intelligent and advanced beyond the general brutish level of the majority, have observed this pathetic expression of countenance in them, a mixture of sadness and fear, the involuntary exhibition of the two feelings, which I suppose must be the predominant experience of their whole lives, regret and apprehension, not the less heavy, either of them, for being, in some degree, vague and indefinite — a sense of incalculable past loss and injury, and a dread of incalculable future loss and injury.

I have never questioned Psyche as to her sadness. To my great astonishment, the other day Margery asked me if I knew to whom Psyche belonged, as the poor woman had inquired of her with much hesitation and anguish if she could tell her who owned her and her children. She has two nice little children under six years old, whom she keeps as clean and tidy, and who are sad and as silent as herself. My astonishment at this question was, as you will readily believe, not small, and I forthwith sought out Psyche for an explanation. She was thrown into extreme perturbation at finding that her questions had been referred to me, and it was some time before I could sufficiently reassure her to be able to comprehend, in the midst of her reiterated entreaties for pardon, and hopes that she had not offended me. She was, at one time, the property of Mr. King, the former overseer, of whom I have already spoken to you, and who has just been paying Mr. Butler a visit. Whether she still belonged to Mr. King or not she did not know, and entreated to me, if she did, to endeavor to persuade Mr. Butler to buy her. Now you must know that this poor woman is the wife of one of Mr. Butler's slaves, a fine, intelligent, active, excellent young man, whose whole family are among some of the very best specimens of character and capacity on the estate. I was so astonished at the (to me) extraordinary state of things revealed by poor Sack's petition, that I could only tell her that I had supposed all the negroes on the planta-

tion were Mr. Butler's property, but that I would certainly inquire, and find out for her, if I could, to whom she belonged, and if I could, endeavor to get Mr. Butler to purchase her, if she really was not his.

I did not see Mr. Butler until the evening; but, in the mean time, meeting Mr. O—, the overseeer, with whom, as I believe I have already told you, we are living here, I asked him about Psyche, and who was her proprietor, when, to my infinite surprise, he told me that he had bought her and her children from Mr. King, who had offered them to him, saying that they would be rather troublesome to him where he was going; "and so," said Mr. O—, "as I had no objection to investing a little money that way, I bought them." With a heart much lightened, I flew to tell poor Psyche the news, so that, at any rate, she might be relieved from the dread of any immediate separation from her husband. You can imagine better than I can tell you what her sensations were; but she still renewed her prayer that I would, if possible, induce Mr. Butler to purchase her, and I promised to do so.

Early the next morning, while I was still dressing, I was suddenly startled by hearing voices in loud tones in Mr. Butler's dressing-room, which adjoins my bedroom, and the noise increasing until there was an absolute cry of despair uttered by some man. I could restrain myself no longer, but opened the door of communication and saw Joe, the young man, poor Psyche's husband, raving almost in a state of frenzy, and in a voice broken with sobs and almost inarticulate with passion, reiterating his determination to never leave this plantation, never to go to Alabama, never to leave his old father and mother, his poor wife and children, and dashing his hat, which he was wringing like a cloth in his hands, upon the ground, he declared he would kill himself if he was compelled to follow Mr. King. I glanced from the poor wretch to Mr. Butler, who was standing, leaning against a table with his arms folded, occasionally uttering a few words of counsel to his slave to be quiet and not fret, and not make a fuss about what there was no help for. I retreated immediately from the horrid scene, breathless with surprise and dismay, and stood for some time in my own room, with my heart and temples throbbing to such a degree that I could hardly support myself. As soon as I recovered myself I again sought Mr. O—, and inquired of him if he knew the cause of poor Joe's distress. He then told me that Mr. Butler, who is highly pleased with Mr. King's past administration of his property, wished, on his departure for his newly-acquired slave plantation, to give him some token of his satisfaction, and *had made him a present* of the man Joe, who had just received the intelligence that he was to go down to Alabama with his new owner the next day, leaving father, mother, wife and children behind.

When I saw Mr. Butler after his most wretched story became known to me in all its details, I appealed to him not to commit so great a cruelty. How I cried, and how I adjured, and how all my sense of justice, and of mercy, and of pity for the poor wretch, and of wretchedness at finding myself implicated in such a state of things, broke in torrents of words from my lips and tears from my eyes! Mr. Butler gave me no answer whatsoever, and I have since thought that the intemperate vehemence of my entreaties and expostulations perhaps deserved that he should leave me as he did without one single word of reply; and miserable enough I remained.

Toward evening, as I was sitting along, my children had gone to bed, Mr. O— came into my room. I had but one subject on my mind; I had not been able to eat for it. I could hardly sit still for the nervous distress which every thought of these poor people filled me with. As he sat down looking over some accounts, I said to him, "Have you seen Joe this afternoon, Mr. O—?" "Yes, ma'am; he is a great deal happier that he was this morning." "Why, how is that?" asked I, eagerly. "Oh, he is not going to Alabama. Mr. King heard that he had kicked up a fuss about it, and said that if the fellow wasn't willing to go with him, he did not wish to be bothered with any niggers down there who were to be troublesome, so he might stay behind." "And does Psyche know this?" "Yes, ma'am, I suppose so." I drew a long breath. The man was for the present safe, and I remained silently pondering his deliverance and the whole proceeding, and the conduct of every one engaged in it, and, above all, Mr. Butler's share in the transaction, and I think, for the first time, almost a sense of horrible personal responsibility and implication took hold of my mind, and I felt the weight of an unimagined guilt upon my conscience.

With these agreeable reflections I went to bed. Mr. Butler said not a word to me upon the subject of these poor people the next day, and in the mean time I became very impatient of this reserve on his part, because I was dying to prefer my request that he would purchase Psyche and her children, and so prevent any future separation between her and her husband, as I supposed he would not again attempt to make a present of Joe. In the evening I was again with Mr. O— along in the strange, bare, wooden-walled sort of shanty which is our sitting room, and revolving in my mind the means of rescuing Psyche from her miserable suspense. I suddenly accosted Mr. O—, it was to this effect: "Mr. O—, I have a particular favor to beg of you. Promise me that you will never sell Psyche and her children without first letting me know of your intention to do so, and giving me the option of buying them." Mr. O— laid down a book he was reading, and directed his head and one of his eyes toward me and answered, "Dear me, ma'am, I am very sorry — I have sold them." My work fell down on the ground, and my mouth opened wide, but I could utter no sound, I was so dismayed and surprised; and he deliberately proceeded; "I didn't know, ma'am, you see, at all, that you entertained any idea of making an investment of that nature; for I'm sure, if I had, I would willingly have sold the woman to you; but I sold her and her children this morning to Mr. Butler."

I jumped up and left Mr. O— still speaking, and ran to find Mr. Butler, to thank him for what he had done. Think how it fares with slaves on plantations where there is not crazy English woman to weep, and entreat, and implore, and upbraid for them, and no master willing to listen to such appeals.

——— 4.10 ———

SLAVERY'S EXPANSION 'THE ONLY SUBSTANTIAL DISPUTE'
Abraham Lincoln

When Republican candidate Abraham Lincoln won the 1860 presidential election, most Americans believed it to be slavery's death knell. Both sides of the debate on slavery's expansion had drawn their respective lines in the sand years earlier — with Lincoln standing at the head of one faction, and South Carolina's national representatives at the other. And in the eyes of South Carolina, a Lincoln administration surely meant the eventual end of the state's sole economic engine. The state was thus the first to secede in December of that year. In the proceeding months, six more southern states followed, and they formed the Confederacy. But in his March 1861 inaugural speech, Lincoln held his ground, repeating arguments he had made for the past four years: though he had no designs to roll slavery back, he could not tolerate its expansion. He urged the southern states to willingly remain in the Union, but also refused to recognize their secession. And, seeking to downplay the national divide, he declared that the question of slavery's expansion was the nation's "only substantial dispute."

Fellow citizens of the United States:

In compliance with a custom as old as the government itself, I appear before you to address you briefly, and to take, in your presence, the oath prescribed by the Constitution of the United States, to be taken by the President "before he enters on the execution of his office."

I do not consider it necessary, at present, for me to discuss those matters of administration about which there is no special anxiety, or excitement.

Apprehension seems to exist among the people of the Southern States, that by the accession of a Republican Administration, their property, and their peace, and personal security, are to be endangered. There has never been any reasonable cause for such apprehension. Indeed, the most ample evidence to the contrary has all the while existed, and been open to their inspection. It is found in nearly all the published speeches of him who now addresses you. I do but quote from one of those speeches when I declare that "I have no purpose, directly or indirectly, to interfere with the institution of slavery in the States where it exists. I believe I have no lawful right to do so, and I have no inclination to do so." Those who nominated and elected me did so with full knowledge that I had made this, and many similar declarations, and had never recanted them. And more than this, they placed in the platform, for my acceptance, and as a law to themselves, and to me, the clear and emphatic resolution which I now read:

"Resolved, That the maintenance inviolate of the rights of the States, and especially the right of each State to order and control its own domestic institutions according to its own judgment exclusively, is essential to that balance of power on which the perfection and endurance of our political fabric depend; and we denounce the lawless invasion by armed force of the soil of any State or Territory, no matter under what pretext, as among the gravest of crimes."

I now reiterate these sentiments: and in doing so, I only press upon the public attention the most conclusive evidence of which the case is susceptible, that the property, peace and security of no section are to be in any wise endangered by the now incoming Adminis-tra-tion. I add too, that all the protection which, consistently with the Constitution and the laws, can be given, will be cheerfully given to all the States when lawfully demanded, for whatever cause — as cheerfully to one section, as to another.

There is much controversy about the delivering up of fugitives from service or labor. The clause I now read is as plainly written in the Constitution as any other of its provisions:

"No person held to service or labor in one State under the laws thereof, escaping into another, shall, in consequence of any law or regulation therein, be discharged from such service or labor, but shall be delivered up on claim of the party to whom such service or labor may be due."

It is scarcely questioned that this provision was intended by those who made it, for the reclaiming of what we call fugitive slaves; and the intention of the law-giver is the law. All members of Congress swear their support to the whole constitution — to this provision as much as to any other. To the proposition then, that slaves whose cases come within the terms of this clause, "shall be delivered up," their oaths are unanimous. Now, if they would make the effort in good temper, could they not, with nearly equal unanimity, frame and pass a law, by means of which to keep good that unanimous oath?

There is some difference of opinion whether this clause should be enforced by national or by state authority; but surely that difference is not a very material one. If the slave is to be surrendered, it can be of but little consequence to him, or to others, by which authority it is done. And should any one, in any case, be content that his oath shall go unkept, on a merely unsubstantial controversy as to how it shall be kept?

Again, in any law upon this subject, ought not all the safeguards of liberty known in civilized and humane jurisprudence to be introduced, so that a free man be not, in any case, surrendered as a slave? And might it not be well, at the same time, to provide by law for the enforcement of that clause in the Constitution which guaranties that "The citizens of each State shall be entitled to all privileges and immunities of citizens in the several States?"

I take the official oath to-day, with no mental reservations, and with no purpose to construe the Constitution or laws, by any hypercritical rules. And while I do not choose now to specify particular acts of Congress as proper to be enforced, I do suggest, that it will be much safer for all, both in official and private stations, to conform to, and abide by, all those acts which stand unrepealed, than to violate any of them, trusting to find impunity in having them held to be unconstitutional. …

Before entering upon so grave a matter as the destruction of our national fabric, with all its benefits, its memories, and its hopes, would it not be wise to ascertain precisely why we do it? Will you hazard so desperate a step, while there is any possibility that any portion of the ills you fly from, have no real existence? Will you, while the certain ills you fly to, are greater than all the real ones you fly from? Will you risk the commission of so fearful a mistake?

All profess to be content in the Union, if all constitutional rights can be maintained. Is it true, then, that any right, plainly written in the Constitution, has been denied? I think not. Happily the human mind is so constituted, that no party can reach to the audacity of doing this. Think, if you can, of a single instance in which a plainly written provision of the Constitution has ever been denied. If, by the mere force of numbers, a majority should deprive a minority of any clearly written constitutional right, it might, in a moral point of view, justify revolution — certainly would, if such right were a vital one. But such is not our case. All the vital rights of minorities, and of individuals, are so plainly assured to them, by affirmations and negations, guaranties and prohibitions in the Constitution, that controversies never arise concerning them. But no organic law can ever be framed with a provision specifically applicable to every question which may occur in practical administration. No foresight can anticipate, nor any document of reasonable length contain express provisions for all possible questions. Shall fugitives from labor be surrendered by national or by State authority? The Constitution does not expressly say. May Congress prohibit slavery in the territories? The Constitution does not expressly say. Must Congress protect slavery in the territories? The Constitution does not expressly say.

From questions of this class spring all our constitutional controversies, and we divide upon them into majorities and minorities. If the minority will not acquiesce, the majority must, or the government must cease. There is no other alternative; for continuing the government, is acquiescence on one side or the other. If a minority, in such case, will secede rather than acquiesce, they make a precedent which, in turn, will divide and ruin them; for a minority of their own will secede from them, whenever a majority refuses to be controlled by such minority. For instance, why may not any portion of a new confederacy, a year or two hence, arbitrarily secede again, precisely as portions of the present Union now claim to secede from it? All who cherish disunion sentiments, are now being educated to the exact temper of doing this. Is there such perfect identity of interests among the States to compose a new Union, as to produce harmony only, and prevent renewed secession?

Plainly, the central idea of secession, is the essence of anarchy. A majority, held in restraint by constitutional checks, and limitations, and always changing easily, with deliberate changes of popular opinions and sentiments, is the only true sovereign of a free people. Whoever rejects it, does of necessity, fly to anarchy or to despotism. Unanimity is impossible; the rule of a minority as a permanent arrangement, is wholly inadmissible; so that rejecting the majority principle, anarchy, or despotism in some form, is all that is left. ...

One section of our country believes slavery is right, and ought to be extended, while the other believes it is wrong, and ought not to be extended. This is the only substantial dispute. The fugitive slave clause of the Constitution, and the law for the suppression of the foreign slave trade, are each as well enforced, perhaps, as any law can ever be in a community where the moral sense of the people imperfectly supports the law itself. The great body of the people abide by the dry legal obligation in both cases, and a few break over in each. This, I think, cannot be perfectly cured; and it would be worse in both cases after the separation of the sections, than

before. The foreign slave trade, now imperfectly suppressed, would be ultimately revived without restriction, in one section; while fugitive slaves, now only partially surrendered, would not be surrendered at all, by the other.

Physically speaking, we cannot separate. We cannot, remove our respective sections from each other, nor build an impassable wall between them. A husband and wife may be divorced, and go out of the presence, and beyond the reach of each other; but the different parts of our country cannot do this. They cannot but remain face to face; and intercourse, either amicable or hostile, must continue between them. Is it possible then to make that intercourse more advantageous or more satisfactory, after separation than before? Can aliens make treaties easier than friends can make laws? Can treaties be more faithfully enforced between aliens, than laws can among friends? Suppose you go to war, you cannot fight always; and when, after much loss on both sides, and no gain on either, you cease fighting, the identical old questions, as to terms of intercourse, are again upon you. ...

My countrymen, one and all, think calmly and well, upon this whole subject. Nothing valuable can be lost by taking time. If there be an object to hurry any of you, in hot haste, to a step which you would never take deliberately, that object will be frustrated by taking time; but no good object can be frustrated by it. Such of you as are now dissatisfied, still have the old Constitution unimpaired, and, on the sensitive point, the laws of your own framing under it; while the new administration will have no immediate power, if it would, to change either. If it were admitted that you who are dissatisfied, hold the right side in the dispute, there still is no single good reason for precipitate action. Intelligence, patriotism, Christianity, and a firm reliance on Him, who has never yet forsaken this favored land, are still competent to adjust, in the best way, all our present difficulty.

In your hands, my dissatisfied fellow countrymen, and not in mine, is the momentous issue of civil war. The government will not assail you. You can have no conflict, without being yourselves the aggressors. You have no oath registered in Heaven to destroy the government, while I shall have the most solemn one to "preserve, protect and defend" it.

I am loath to close. We are not enemies, but friends. We must not be enemies. Though passion may have strained, it must not break our bonds of affection. The mystic chords of memory, stretching from every battle-field, and patriot grave, to every living heart and hearthstone, all over this broad land, will yet swell the chorus of the Union, when again touched, as surely they will be, by the better angels of our nature.

--------- 4.11 ---------

A War for Emancipation
Frederick Douglass

The Civil War began in earnest on April 12, 1861, when Confederate troops attacked Fort Sumter in South Carolina. President Lincoln, while calling for volunteers to put down the rebellion, took a cautious public stance. He insisted that the North's military response was not an effort to force slavery's end, but purely a reaction to the illegal secession and rebellion of the southern states. But abolitionists, led by Frederick Douglass, were determined to seize the day. In a series of speeches, such as the one below, delivered in March of 1862 in Rochester, New York, Douglass pressured Lincoln to declare emancipation an aim of the war. He commends the Union army's effort to quell the Confederate uprising thus far, and declares that, having marshaled an effective military response, it is essential that the nation address the larger question of how the seceding states will be governed once the war ends. Douglass lauds Lincoln's steady moves toward emancipation. (The president had just sent a bill to Congress seeking to abolish slavery in the District of Columbia, and a separate bill proposing federal aid to any state that launched a program to gradually abolish slavery.) Douglass then argues that to stop short of universal emancipation is to leave the war unresolved. Echoing Lincoln's "a house divided" speech, Dougalss declares there can be no further compromise on slavery: "The South must put off the yoke of slavery or the North must prepare her neck for that yoke."

… But now a higher and more important problem presses for consideration. It is a problem for statesmen rather than Generals. Soldiers can capture a State, but statesmen must govern a State. It is sometimes hard to pull down a house but it is always harder to build one up.

This is the question now to be decided, having broken down the rebel power in the seceded States, how shall we extend the Constitution and the Union over them? We know how to make war, we know how to conquer, but the question is do we know how to make peace? We can whip the South, but can we make the South loyal? Baltimore is in our hands, but her parlors and drawing rooms are full of Traitors. The army is at Nashville but the people have fled. General Sherman writes loving epistles to erring rebels, but no one will carry them to the rebels, nor will the rebels touch them. The fact is the South hates the north. It hates the Union. The feeling is genuine and all-pervading. Whence comes this hate? This is an imperative inquiry for statesmen, who would place the peace of this government on an immovable foundation. You are of the same race, the same language, the same sacred historic memories. Why do they hate you? Certainly not because you have been in any manner ungenerous or unjust to them. Why do they hate you? Is it because they are naturally worse than other men? Not at all. I hold that the slaveholder is just as good as his slave system will allow him to be. If I were a slaveholder, and was determined to remain such, I would equal the worst, both in cruelty to the slave and in hatred to the North. I should hate the Declaration of Independence, hate the Constitution, hate the Golden rule, hate free schools, free speech, free press, and every other form of freedom. Because in them all, I should see an enemy to my claim of property in man. I should see that the whole North is a point blank and killing condemnation of all my pretensions. The real root of bitterness, that which has generated this intense Southern hate to North, is Slavery. Here is the stone of stumbling and the rock of offence. Once I felt it necessary to argue this point. The time for such argument has past. Slavery stands confessed as the grand cause of the war. It has drilled every rebel soldier, loaded, primed, aimed and fired every rebel cannon since the war began. No other interest, commercial, manufacturing or political, could have wrought such a social earthquake amongst us. It has within itself that which begets a character in all around it favorable to its own continuance. It makes slaves of the negroes, vassals of the poor whites and tyrants of the masters. Pride, injustice, ingratitude, lust of dominion, cruelty, scorn, and contempt are the qualities of this rebellion, and slavery breeds them all. The tyrant wants no law above his own will, no associates but men of his own stamp of baseness. He is willing to administer the laws when he can bend them to his will, but he will break them when he can no longer bend them. Where labor is performed under the lash, justice will be administered under the bowie knife. The south is in this respect just what slavery has made her. She has been breeding thieves, rebels and traitors, and this stupendous conflict is the result. She could not do otherwise and cherish slavery in the midst of her.

Now the great question is what shall be the conditions of peace? What shall be done with slavery? We have gradually drifted to this vital question. Slavery is the pivot on which turns all the machinery of this tremendous war, and upon it will depend the character of the future of our peace or want of it.

It is really wonderful how we have been led along towards this grand issue, and how all efforts to evade, postpone, and prevent its coming, have been mocked and defied by the stupendous sweep of events.

It was oracularly given out from Washington many months ago, that whether this rebellion should succeed or fail, the status of no man in the country would be changed by the result. You know what that meant. Europe knew what that meant. It was an assurance given to the world in general, and the slaveholding states in particular, that no harm

should come to slavery in the prosecution of the war for the Union. It was a last bid for a compromise with the rebels. But despite of diplomatic disclaimers, despite border State influence, despite the earlier proclamation of the President himself, the grand question of Emancipation now compels attention and the most thoughtful consideration of men in high places of the nation.

By the events of this war, Washington has become to the nation what Syracuse was to the State of New York after the rescue of Jerry, the grand centre for abolition meetings. A new Congress has assembled there.

Dr. Cheever, Ralph Waldo Emerson, Gerrit Smith, Wendell Phillips, William Goodell and William Lloyd Garrison may now utter in safety their opinions on slavery in the national capital. Meanwhile Congress has a bill before it for the abolition of slavery in the District of Columbia. Kill slavery at the heart of the nation, and it will certainly die at the extremities. Down with it there, and it is the brick knocked down at the end of the row by which the whole line is prostrate.

More and better, the infernal business of slave catching by our army in Missouri and on the Potomac, is at last peremptorily forbidden under penalty of dismissal from the service. This looks small, but is not so. It is a giant stride toward the grand result.

I thank all the powers of earth and sky, that I am permitted to be a witness to this day's events. That slavery could always live and flourish in this country I have always known to be a foul and guilty heresy. That the vile system must eventually go down I have never doubted, even in the darkest days of my life in slavery. But that I should live to see the President of the United States deliberately advocating Emancipation was more than I ever ventured to hope.

It is true that the President lays down his propositions with many qualifications some of which to my thinking, are unnecessary, unjust and wholly unwise. These are spots on the Sun. A blind man can see where the President's heart is. I read the spaces as well as the lines of that message, I see in them a brave man trying against great odds, to do right. An honest patriot endeavoring to save his country in its day of peril. It is the first utterance, and first utterances are not according to Carlyle the most articulate and perfect. Time and practice will improve the President as they improve other men. He is tall and strong but he is not done growing, he grows as the nation grows. He has managed to say one good word, and to say it so distinctly that all the world may hear. He has dared to say that the highest interest of the country will be promoted by the abolition of slavery. ….

But what shall be the conditions of peace? How shall the Union be reconstructed? To my mind complete Emancipation is the only basis of permanent peace. Any other basis will place us just at the point from which we started. To leave slavery standing in the rebel States, is to leave the eggs of treason in the nest from whence we shall have to meet a larger brood of traitors, and rebels at another time; it is to transmit to posterity the question that ought to be settled to-day. Leave slavery where it is, and you leave the same generator of hate towards the north which has already cost us rivers of blood and millions of treasure. Leave slavery in the south and it will be as dangerous for a Northern man to travel in the south, as for a man to enter a powder magazine with fire. Despots are suspicious, and every slaveholder is an unmitigated despot, a natural foe to every form of freedom. Leave slavery in the south, and you will fill the north with a full fledged breed of servile panderers to slavery, baser than all their predecessors.

Leave slavery where it is and you will hereafter, as heretofore, see in politics a divided, fettered, north, and an united south. You will see the statesmen of the country facing both ways, speaking two languages, assenting to the principles of freedom in the north, and bowing to the malign spirit and practices of slavery at the South. You will see all the pro-slavery elements of the country attracted to the south, giving that section ascendancy again in the counsels of the nation and making them masters of the destinies of the Republic. Restore slavery to its old status in the Union and the same elements of demoralization which have plunged this country into this tremendous war will begin again to dig the grave of free Institutions.

It is the boast of the South that her Institutions are peculiar and homogeneous, and so they are. Her statesmen have had the wit to see that with the free North must either make the North like herself, or that she herself must become like the North. They are right. The South must put off the yoke of slavery or the North must prepare her neck for that yoke, provided the union is restored. There is a middle path — We have pursued that middle path. It is *compromise* and by it we have reached the civil war with all its horrid consequences. The question is shall we start anew in the same old path?

Who wants a repetition of the same event thro' which we are passing? Who wants to see the nation taxed to keep a standing army in the South to maintain respect for the Federal Government and protect the rights of citizens of the United States? To such a man I say, leave slavery still dominant at the South and you shall have all your wants supplied.

On the other hand abolish slavery and the now disjointed nation like kindred drops would speedily mingle into one. Abolish slavery and the last hinderance to a solid nationality is abolished. Abolish slavery and you give conscience a chance to grow, and you will win the respect and admiration of mankind. Abolish slavery and you put an end to all sectional politics founded upon conflicting sectional interests, and imparting strife bitterness to all our general elections, and to the debates on the floor of Congress. Abolish slavery and the citizens of each state will be regarded and treated as equal citizens of the United States, and may travel unchallenged and unmolested in all the states of the Union. Abolish slavery and you put an end to sectional religion and morals, and establish free speech and liberty of conscience throughout your common country.

Abolish slavery and rational, law abiding Liberty will fill the whole land with peace, joy, and permanent safety now and forever.

——— 4.12 ———

'WE ARE READY TO STAND AND DEFEND OUR GOVERNMENT'
Northern Blacks

When war broke out, black men rushed to join the Union Army. But Lincoln feared backlash within the Union and was loath to excessively antagonize the rebels states, lest it be that much harder to reincorporate them. So, despite the fact that blacks had fought in both the Revolutionary War and the War of 1812, Lincoln enforced the 1792 law barring blacks from carrying arms in the U.S. army and refused to accept African-American volunteers. Northern blacks were outraged, and called for their right to fight. Immediately following the Confederate attack on Fort Sumter in 1861, hundreds of free blacks in New Bedford, Massachusetts (where members of the famed Massachusetts 54th black regiment would later be recruited) met and issued a declaration of their willingness to fight — and, moreover, their intent to train for battle so as to be ready if the ban was lifted. Speakers such as Frederick Douglass also once again hounded Lincoln to broaden his public perspective on the war.

A. April 1861 declaration by free blacks of New Bedford, Massachusetts

Whereas, In view of the probable departure from our city within a short time of a large portion of our patriotic military companies, called out for defense of our common country, in which case the citizens of New Bedford would naturally have a feeling of insecurity for their persons and property in the excited state of the public mind incident upon the existence of actual war, therefore,

Resolved, That as true and loyal citizens (although exempt by law from military duty,) we hold ourselves in readiness to organize military companies to be officered and equipped, and to drill regularly for the protection and maintenance of peace and good order, and for the security and defence of our city and State against any and all emergencies.

Resolved, That the proceedings of this meeting be laid before the Mayor of this city and the Governor of this State, and we pledge them four hundred men will fight for liberty, to be ready at any moment to rally to their support wherever our services may be required.

B. "Fighting Rebels with Only One Hand," from September 1861 issue of *Frederick Douglass's Monthly* (successor to *The North Star*)

What on earth is the matter with the American Government and people? Do they really covet the world's ridicule as well as their own social and political ruin? What are they thinking about, or don't they condescend to think at all? So, indeed, it would seem from their blindness in dealing with the tremendous issue now upon them. Was there ever anything like it before? They are sorely pressed on every hand by a vast army of slaveholding rebels, flushed with success, and infuriated by the darkest inspirations of a deadly hate, bound to rule or ruin. Washington, the seat of Government, after ten thousand assurances to the contrary, is now positively in danger of falling before the rebel army. Maryland, a little while ago considered safe for the Union, is now admitted to be studded with the materials for insurrection, and which may flame forth at any moment. — Every resource of the nation, whether of men or money, whether of wisdom or strength, could be well employed to avert the impending ruin. Yet most evidently the demands of the hour are not comprehended by the Cabinet or the crowd. Our Presidents, Governors, Generals and Secretaries are calling, with almost frantic vehemance, for men. — "Men! men! send us men!" they scream, or the cause of the Union is gone, the life of a great nation is ruthlessly sacrificed, and the hopes of a great nation go out in darkness; and yet these very officers, representing the people and Government, steadily and persistently refuse to receive the very class of men which have a deeper interest in the defeat and humiliation of the rebels, than all others. — Men are wanted in Missouri — wanted in Western Virginia, to hold and defend what has been already gained; they are wanted in Texas, and all along the sea coast, and though the Government has at its command a class in the country deeply interested in suppressing the insurrection, it sternly refuses to summon from among the vast multitude a single man, and degrades and insults the whole class by refusing to allow any of their number to defend with their strong arms and brave hearts the national cause. What a spectacle of blind, unreasoning prejudice and pusillanimity is this! The national edifice is on fire. Every man who can carry a bucket of water, or remove a brick, is wanted; but those who have the care of the building, having a profound respect for the feeling of the national burglars who set the building on fire, are determined that the flames shall only be extinguished by Indo-Caucasian hands, and to have the building burnt rather than save it by means of any other. Such is the pride, the stupid prejudice and folly that rules the hour.

Why does the Government reject the Negro? Is he not a man? Can he not wield a sword, fire a gun, march and countermarch, and obey orders like any other? Is there the least reason to believe that a regiment of well-drilled Negroes would deport themselves less soldier-like on the battlefield than the raw troops gathered up generally from the towns and cities of the State of New York? We do believe that such soldiers, if allowed to take up arms in defence of the Government, and made to feel that they are hereafter to be recognized as persons having rights, would set the highest example of order and general good behavior to their fellow soldiers, and in every way add to the national power.

If persons so humble as we can be allowed to speak to the President of the United States, we should ask him if this dark and terrible hour of the nation's extremity is a time for consulting a mere vulgar and unnatural prejudice? We should ask him if national preservation and necessity were not better guides in this emer-

gency than either the tastes of the rebels, or the pride and prejudices of the vulgar? We would tell him that General Jackson in a slave state fought side by side with Negroes at New Orleans, and like a true man, despising meanness, he bore testimony to their bravery at the close of the war. We would tell him that colored men in Rhode Island and Connecticut performed their full share in the war of the Revolution, and that men of the same color, such as the noble Shields Green, Nathaniel Turner and Denmark Vesey stand ready to peril everything at the command of the Government. We would tell him that this is no time to fight with one hand, when both are needed; that this is no time to fight only with your white hand, and allow your black hand to remain tied.

Whatever may be the folly and absurdity of the North, the South at least is true and wise. The Southern papers no longer indulge in the vulgar expression, "free n———rs." That class of bipeds are now called "colored residents." The Charleston papers say:

"The colored residents of this city can challenge comparison with their class, in any city or town, in loyalty or devotion to the cause of the South. Many of them individually, and without ostentation, have been contributing liberally, and on Wednesday evening, the 7th inst., a very large meeting was held by them, and a committee appointed to provide for more efficient aid. The proceedings of the meeting will appear in results hereinafter to be reported."

It is now pretty well established, that there are at the present moment many colored men in the Confederate army doing duty not only as cooks, servants and laborers, but as real soldiers, having muskets on their shoulders, and bullets in their pockets, ready to shoot down loyal troops, and do all that soldiers may to destroy the Federal Government and build up that of the traitors and rebels. There were such soldiers at Manassas, and they are probably there still. There is a Negro in the army as well as in the fence, and our Government is likely to find it out before the war comes to an end. That the Negroes are numerous in the rebel army, and do for that army its heaviest work, is beyond question. They have been the chief laborers upon those temporary defences in which the rebels have been able to mow down our men. Negroes helped to build the batteries at Charleston. They relieve their gentlemanly and military masters from the stiffening drudgery of the camp, and devote them to the nimble and dexterous use of arms. Rising above vulgar prejudice, the slaveholding rebel accepts the aid of the black man as readily as that of any other. If a bad cause can do this, why should a good cause be less wisely conducted? We insist upon it, that one black regiment in such a war as this is, without being any more brave and orderly, would be worth to the Government more than two of any other; and that, while the Government continues to refuse the aid of colored men, thus alienating them from the national cause, and giving the rebels the advantage of them, it will not deserve better fortunes than it has thus far experienced. — Men in earnest don't fight with one hand, when they might fight with two, and a man drowning would not refuse to be saved even by a colored hand.

—————— 4.13 ——————

DEBATING 'THE DUTY OF THE BLACK MAN'
Alfred Green and "R.H.V."

Not all African Americans believed black people should join the war effort. Indeed, some vehemently opposed the idea of sacrificing their lives on behalf of a government that not only allowed slavery to persist but largely barred those that were free from participation in the polity. In the early days of the war, prominent black convention movement figure Alfred Green pushed the debate among African Americans, speaking and writing letters to newspapers urging blacks to join the fight. His opponents responded in kind. One lengthy exchange took place in September 1861 in the pages of the *Anglo-African Magazine*, the first literary journal published wholly by African Americans. An unidentified "R.H.V." argued against black participation; Green defended it. The following year, Green collected his writings, and the letters opposing him, and published them as a pamphlet.

A. R.H.V.'s argument against black participation

September 28, 1861

Mr. Editor:

The duty of the black man at this critical epoch is a question of much importance, deeply interesting to friends of liberty, both white and black. The most imposing feature of this duty, I am told, is in relation to military organizations. This question, I am told, is forced upon us by our eminent, educated, far-sighted leaders, who, anxious for our elevation and zealous for our reputation, in connection with our white brothers would have us write our names side by side with them upon the immortal book of fame, won by well-contested and desperate encounters upon the battle-field. Claiming that any omission on our part to exhibit that patriotism so noticeable in the whites, will, when history shall record the doings of this memorable country, leave our names without one deed of patriotism or expressed desire for the success of the cause of liberty; not one laurel to entwine the brows of those whose valor like blazing stars upon the battle-field would, no doubt, have eclipsed those whom we now are satisfied to acknowledge as superiors and protectors. Is this all wisdom, this mode of reasoning; or is it a mistaken idea, called into existence by a desire for fame? Is it a demanding necessity that the world will decide belongs to us to meet, thus to prove our manhood and love of liberty? Have not two centuries of cruel and unrequited servitude in this country, alone entitled the children of this generation to the rights of men and citizens? Have we not done our share towards creating a national existence for those who now enjoy it to our degradation, ever devising evil for our suffering, heart-crushed race?

Who that will carefully note the many historical reminiscences, made mention of by those who are ready to do justice to us, can doubt our bravery? Who has heard of the many privations, hair-breadth escapes, and the unflinching determination of our enslaved brethren seeking the free shores of Canada, can doubt our love of liberty? True patriotism does not consist in words alone. Neither do patriotic demonstrations always contribute to the end alone, independent of material aid. I do not suppose any people have been taxed heavier or more than the poor colored people for the cause of liberty, with such small results to themselves. Now, if we have contributed our share to support in the benefits thereof, what becomes our duty when that government is menaced by those they have cherished at the expense of our blood, toil and degradation?

Let your own heart answer this questions, and no regiments of black troops will leave their bodies to rot upon this battle-field beneath a Southern sun — to conquer a peace based upon the perpetuity of human bondage — stimulating and encouraging the inveterate prejudice that now bars our progress in the scale of elevation and education.

I claim that the raising of black regiments for the war would be highly impolitic and uncalled for under the present state of affairs, knowing, as we do, the policy of the Government in relation to colored men. It would show our incompetency to comprehend the nature of the differences existing between the two sections now at variance, by leading our aid to either party. By taking such measures we invite injustice at the hands of those we prefer to serve; we would contribute to the African colonization scheme, projected a half century ago, by ridding the country of that element so dangerous to the charming institution of negro slavery.

Entertaining the sentiment and determination that they do, would it not be unjust in them to accept our service? Would we still invite them to cap the climax by forcing us to the cannon's mouth to save the destruction of those whose whole existence should be merged in with their country's weal and woe? That death should be the readiest sacrifice patriotic citizens could offer to uphold the people's hope, the people's palladium, no one should deny. But what do we enjoy, that should inspire us with those feelings toward a government that would sooner consign five millions of human beings to never-ending slavery than wrong one slave master of his human property? Does not the contemplation of so flagrant a wrong cause your blood to boil with Christian indignation, or bring tears to the eyes of your broken-hearted old men, whose heads, now silvered by time or bleached by sorrow, can no longer shoulder the weightier responsibilities of a young man's calling?

Not only that. Any public demonstration (for this could not well be done in a corner) would only embarrass the present administration, by stirring up old party prejudices which would cause the loss of both sympathy and treasure, which the government cannot well afford to lose at present. By weakening the arm of the government, we strengthen that of the slave power, who would soon march through these States without fear of forcible resistance.

It would be contrary to Christian humanity to permit so flagrant an outrage in silence to be perpetuated upon any people, especially a class who have know naught else but wrong at their hands, whom they would so gloriously serve in time of danger to their own liberties and sacred rights, preferring now their services to uphold a Government leagued with perdition, upon which the doom of death is written, unless they repent, in letters so plain that he who runs may read. Let us weigh well this thing before taking steps which will not only prove disastrous to the cause we would help, but bring suffering and sorrows upon those left to mourn unavailingly our loss.

I maintain that the principle of neutrality is the only safe one to govern us at this time. When men's lives are in their hands, and so little inducement as there is for us to cast ourselves into the breach, our work for the present lies in quite a different channel from assuming war responsibilities uninvited, with no promised future in store for us — a dilemma inviting enmity and destruction to the few, both North and South, among our people, enjoying partial freedom.

The slaves' only hope — his only help — is his suffering brother at the North. When we are removed, the beacon light which directs and assists the panting fugitive is darkened and obscured — his once bright hope, that gave comfort to him as he pressed on to liberty's goals, is shadowed o'er forever. Our own precipitous, unwise zeal must never be the cause to stay the car of freedom, but ever let it roll onward and upward until earth and heaven united shall become one garden of paradisal freedom, knowing no color, no clime, but all one people, one language, one Father, Almighty God.

Once under army discipline, subject to the control of government officers or military leaders, could we dictate when and where the blow should be struck? Could we enter upon Quixotic crusades of our own projecting, independent of the constituted authorities, or these military chiefs? Will the satisfaction of again hearing a casual mention of our heroic deeds upon the field of battle, by our own children, doomed for all that we know to the same inveterate, heart-crushing prejudice that we have come up under, and die leaving as a legacy unto our issues — all from those for whom you would so unwittingly face the cannon's mouth to secure to them a heritage denied you and yours?

In this country ready and anxious to intimate a new era for downtrodden humanity, that you know so eagerly propose to make a sacrifice of thousands of our ablest men to encourage and facilitate the great work of regeneration? No! no!! your answer must be: No!!! No black regiments, unless by circumstances over which we have no option, no control; no initiatory war measures, to be adopted or encouraged by us. Our policy must be neutral, ever praying for the success of that party determined to initiate first the policy of justice and equal rights.

Who can say that in another twelve months' time the policy of the South will not change in our favor, if the assistance of England or France will by it be gained, rather than submit to northern dictation of subjugation? Did that idea ever suggest itself to your mind? Strange things happen all the while. Look back for the last twenty-four months, and ask yourself if you could have foretold what to-day you are so well informed has actually transpired when coming events cast their shadows before?

In these days, principle is supplanted by policy, and interest shapes policy, I find by daily observation, both in high and low places. Although to many the above idea may seem ideal and delusory, inconsistent with the present spirit and suicidal of the South, yet I for one would feel justified entertaining it equally with the idea that the north would proclaim a general emancipation so long as she supposed it a possibility to reclaim the disaffected States of the Southern Confederacy.

And, if an impossibility, what would all proclamations to that effect avail?

I believe with the act of emancipation adopted and proclaimed by the South, both England and France, (and in fact I might safely say all Europe,) would not only recognize all of their independence, but would render them indirectly material aid and sympathy.

To get the start of the northern slave-worshippers, as they are sometimes termed, who can say that, as a last resort, these rebel leaders have not had that long in contemplation, knowing that they should succumb to this government through the force of circumstances, or the uncertain chances of war, their lives would be valueless only as a warning to future generations.

Then, why may we not hope that such is their ultimatum in case of a series of defeats — the liberation of four millions of our poor, heart-crushed, enslaved race. One or two large battles will decide the future policy of both the contending parties — the sooner it comes the sooner we will know our fate. It is in that scale it hangs.

Then let us do our duty to each other — use care in all our public measures — be not too precipitous, but in prayer wait and watch the salvation of God.

R. H. V.

B. Alfred Green's rebuttal

October 19, 1861.

MR. EDITOR:

In your issue of September 28th, appears an able and elaborate article on the "Formation of Colored Regiments." I have no desire for contention at a time like this with those who differ honorably from me in opinion; but I think it just, once in a while, to speak out and let the world know where we stand on the great issues of the day, for it is only by this means that we can succeed in arousing our people from a mistaken policy of inactivity, at a time when the world is rushing like a wild tornado in the direction of universal emancipation. The inactivity that is advocated is the principle that has ever had us left behind, and will leave us again, unless we arouse from lethargy and arm ourselves as men and patriots against the common enemy of God and man. For six months I have labored to arouse our people to the necessity of action, and I have the satisfaction to say not without success. I have seen companies organized and under the most proficient modern drill in that time. I have seen men drilled among our sturdy-going colored men of the rural districts of Pennsylvania and New Jersey, in the regular African Zouave drill, that would make the hearts of secession traitors or prejudiced northern Yankees quake and tremble for fear.

Now I maintain that for all practical purposes, whatever be the turn of the war, preparation on our part, by the most efficient knowledge of the military art and discipline, is one of the most positive demands of the times. No nation ever has or ever will be emancipated from slavery, and the result of such a prejudice as we are undergoing in this country, but by the sword, wielded too by their own strong arms. It is a foolish idea for us to be still nursing our past grievances to our own detriment, when we should as one man grasp the sword — grasp this most favorable opportunity of becoming inured to that service that must burst the fetters of the enslaved and enfran-chise the nominally free of the north. We admit all that has been or can be said about the meanness of this government towards us — we are fully aware that there is no more soul in the present administration on the great moral issues involved in the slavery question and the present war, than has characterized previous administrations; but, what of that; it all teaches the necessity of our making ourselves felt as a people, at this extremity of our national government, worthy of consideration, and of being recognized as part of its own strength. Had every State in the Union taken active steps in the direction of forming regiments of about eight thousand five hundred men, have numbered seventy-five thousand — besides awakening an interest at home and abroad, that no vacillating policy of the half-hearted semi-seccessionists of the North could have suppressed.

It would have relieved the administration of so much room for cavil on the slavery questions and colored men's right to bear arms, &c. It is a strange fact that now, when we should be the most united and decided as to our future destiny; when we should all have our shoulders to the wheel in order to enforce the doctrine we have ever taught of self-reliance, and ourselves striking blows for freedom; that we are most divided, most inactive, and in many respects most despondent of any other period of our history. Some are wasting thought and labor, physical and intellectual, in counseling emigration, (which I have nothing against when done with proper motives); others are more foolishly wasting time and means in an unsuccessful war against it; while a third class, and the most unfortunate of the three, counsel sitting still to see the salvation of God. Oh, that we could see that God will help no one that refuses to help himself. Stretch forth thy hand, said the Saviour to the man with a withered handle. He did so and was healed. Take up they bed and walk, said he, and the man arose; go and wash, said he to the blind man, and he did it. How many are the evidences of this kind. God is saying to us to-day, as plainly as events can be pointed out, stretch forth, thy hand; but we sit idly, with our hands folded, while the whole world, even nations thousands of miles distant across the ocean, are maddened by the fierceness of this American strife, which after all is nothing less than God's means of opening the way for us to free ourselves by the assistance of our own enslavers, if we will do it.

Can we be still or idle under such circumstances. If ever colored men plead for rights or fight for liberty, now of all others is the time. The prejudiced white men, North or South, never will respect us until they are forced to do it by deeds of our own. Let us draw upon European sentiment as well as unbiased minds in our own country, by presenting an undaunted front on the side of freedom and equal rights; but we are blindly mistaken if we think to draw influence from any quarter by sitting still at a time like this. The world must know we are here, and that we have aims, objects and interests in the present great struggle.

Without this we will be left a hundred years behind this gigantic age of human progress and development. I never care to reply to such views as those which set up the plea of previous injustice or even of present injustice done to us, as a reason why we should stand still at such a time as this. I have lived long enough to know that men situated like ourselves must accept the least of a combination of difficulties: if, therefore, there is a chance for us to get armed and equipped for active military service, that is one point gained which never could be gained in a time of peace and prosperity in this country: and that could have been done months ago, and can now be done in a few weeks, if we adopt the measure of united effort for its accomplishment.

Does anyone doubt the expediency of our being armed and under military discipline, even if we have always been sufferers at the hands of those claiming superiority? But enough of this. As to public demonstrations of this kind weakening the arm of the Federal Government, I must say that I was prepared to hear that remark among Democratic Union-savers, but I am startled to hear it from among our own ranks of unflinching abolitionists.

Indeed, sir, the longer the government shirks the responsibility of such a measure, the longer time she gives the rebel government to tamper with the free colored people of the South, and prompt and prepare their slaves for shifting the horrors of Saint Domingo from the South to the North; and, in such an event, could we rid ourselves of the responsibility of entering the field, more than any other Northern men whom the government chose to call into active service?

Could we more effectually exercise proper discretion, without arms, without drill, without union, than by availing ourselves of all these at the present time, looking boldly forward to that auspicious moment?

The South (as I have said in an article written for the Philadelphia "Press," and copied into several popular journals) can mean nothing less than emancipation, by the act of her having thousands of free colored men, as well as slaves, even now under the best military discipline. England and France of course would favor such a project, should the South thus snatch the key to a termination of this rebellion from the hands of the Federal Government. But how much better off would we be, sitting here like Egyptian mummies, till all this was done, and then drafted and driven off, undisciplined, to meet well-disciplined troops, who will then truly be fighting for freedom; and while we could have no other motive than to help conquer a peace for the "*Union still*" in its perfidious unregenerate state? Tell me not that it will be optional with us, in the event of emancipation by the South, whether we fight or not. On the contrary, there is no possible way to escape it but either commit suicide or run away to Africa, forever. The climate of Canada, in such an event, would not be cool enough to check the ardor of fighting abolitionists against the hell-born prejudice of the North, and the cowardly black man, would sit here quietly with his arms folded, instead of taking advantage of the times, till even the emancipated slaves of the

South, rigorous in their majesty, force him to rise and flee to Canada to save his unsavory bacon. Let us then, sir, hear no more of these measures of actual necessity inaugurating a "dilemma, inviting emnity, and destruction to the few, both North and South, among our people enjoying partial freedom." That is a work that cannot be accomplished by loyal patriotic efforts to prepare a hundred thousand men to do service for God, for freedom, for themselves. Sitting still, shirking the responsibility God has thrown upon our shoulders, alone can engender such a dilemma.

Your correspondence also asks whether: "Once under army discipline, subject to the control of the government officers or military orders, we could dictate when and where the blow should be struck. Could we enter upon Quixotic crusades of our own projecting, independent of the constituted authorities or these military chiefs?" Sir, it appears to me that, under whatever charges of governmental policy, our favor would be courted more under such circumstances, and our dictation received with more favor and regard, both by the authorities, chiefs, and the people at large, than by our weak, effeminate pleadings for favor on the merits of our noble ancestry, rather than nerving our own arms and hearts for a combat that we have long half-heartedly invited by our much groanings and pleadings at the throne of grace.

The issue is here: let us prepare to meet it with manly spirit; let us say to the demagogues of the North who would prevent us now from proving our manhood and foresight in the midst of all these complicated difficulties, that we will be armed, we will be schooled in military service, and if our fathers were cheated and disfranchised after nobly defending the country, we, their sons, have the manhood to defend the right and the sagacity to detect the wrong; time enough to secure to ourselves the primary interest we have in the great and moving cause of the great American rebellion. I am, as ever, yours, for truth and justice, ALFRED M. GREEN.

——— 4.14 ———

'THE UTERUS PROTRUDING, AS LARGE, YES LARGER THAN MY FIST; IT HAS BEEN SO 10 YEARS'
Life in the Contraband Camps

As Union troops moved through the south, they encountered, and were often sought out by, massive numbers of slaves who had either escaped or who were living on the plantations seized by the army. Transporting these former slaves created a mammoth logistical problem for Union officers as they moved their regiments from battle to battle and were faced with the question of what to do with these men, women and children.

Eventually, officers began creating "contraband camps" to house the freed slaves. The camps varied widely in size and condition. Many were squalid refugee settlements where disease and hunger ran rampant. Others were experimental free-labor communities, where the ex-slaves worked for themselves on tiny parcels of confiscated land. But uniformly, these camps hosted the first substantive interactions between southern blacks and northern whites. Liberal northerners who volunteered in philanthropic societies traveled south to help both soldiers and emancipated slaves at the front and in the camps. They were shocked at the conditions in which the slaves lived and wrote letters home that described the miserable scenes. Their reflections, along with those of the handful of self-educated slaves in the camps, offer contemporary perspectives on this initial encounter between two cultures — cultures that would maintain a delicate coalition as they worked for the next 100 years to combat America's systemic racism.

A. The health of freed slaves

A number of the northern whites who journeyed south to help in contraband camps were physicians and teachers. Healthcare and education (chief among problems faced by the African American community today) emerged as two immediate problems for emancipated slaves — as slaveholders had deliberately withheld both. Not only were work conditions detrimental to slaves' health (not to mention the injuries that overseers inflicted deliberately as a form of torture) plantation owners made macabre economic calculations about how much treatment their chattel would receive for healthcare problems. In a series of letters to his wife, herself a teacher in the Freedmen's Relief Association, Dr. J. Milton Hawks describes some of the injuries and chronic illnesses he discovered in contraband camps as he traveled south with the Union army.

Beaufort, S.C. Aug. 3 1862 …
Dear Ette:

… I will not ask of the Soldier's Aid Society anything for the blacks; it might lessen the zeal of the sisters, and I should be sorry to do that. But if they could see the old half palsied woman in hospital, who had before we took her, involuntary discharges from her bowels, and has no change of clothes, they would be willing to send at least one dress and shirt.

At our hospital folks sleep with their clothes on. These are the part of a new arrival, that came in since the old clothes were all distributed. …

North Edisto Island, S.C.
Saturday Morn., May 17th 1862
My Dear Wife:

… In midwifery here, Drs. are not called. Several births have accured since I have been here, all attended by one of the negro women on the place; these midwives are each known as the "granny." I keep a record of the births, the same as required in New Hampshire only not as many particulars about the parents. When the child is a week old, it is named; then I give every mother a card with the child's name and date of birth on it. In this way the next generation of negroes will be able to know how old they are.

There is one case I have prescribed ointment and tonic for, of complete prolapsas — The uterus protruding, as large, yes larger than my fist; it has been so 10 years. Her master made her work in the field, sometimes till she would drop down at work unable to stand. She does not work now —

Another of my patients was whipped so severely by his driver 6 years ago, that he was left senseless of the field; brought to his house by other negroes, and has never been able to stand since, and appears idiotic. He is not content to be in a cabin with a floor, he has sat on the ground so long; so they took up a part of the floor next to the fire place for him; there he sits in the dirt, covered with an old carpet (the negro, not the dirt) with a pile of sweet potatoes in reach — these he pokes into the fire and roasts and eats as he wants — It is a disgusting sight —

On the same place is a man who had fits; 9 years ago he fell in the fire, and burned his foot and ankle off. — No doctor was ever called — the stump has never healed over, it is a large raw sore. — He was washing it with urine and warm water and bar soap, and sitting on leaves. I gave him some ointment and a piece of castilo soap…

B. Susie King Taylor's *Reminiscences of My Life in Camp*

When Union forces took Fort Polaski near Savannah, Georgia in April 1862, they created a camp nearby for the slaves they liberated. Fourteen-year-old Susie King Taylor was among those slaves. Years later, she published an account of life at the camp. In the section excerpted below, Taylor describes her work starting a school there, incessant rumors about the war's end and the fate of the freed slaves, and the continued danger of recapture by rebels. She also describes the formation of the Union's first black regiment, the First South Carolina Volunteers (later the 33rd Regiment) in May 1862, for which men from King's camp were recruited. General David Hunter formed the regiment in defiance of Lincoln's policy banning blacks from fighting. Taylor further discusses the dissatisfaction that spread in this regiment, and eventually throughout the Union's black soldiers, because of its policy of refusing them equal pay. It was not until June of 1864 that Congress granted the U.S. Colored Troops pay equal to that of whites.

… After I had been on St. Simon's about three days, Commodore Golds-borough heard of me, and came to Gaston Bluff to see me. I found him very cordial. He said Captain Whitmore had spoken to him of me, and that he was pleased to hear of my being so capable, etc., and wished me to take charge of a school for the children on the island. I told him I would gladly do so, if I could have some books. He said I should have them, and in a week or two I received two large boxes of books and testaments from the North. I had about forty children to teach, beside a number of adults who came to me nights, all of them so eager to learn to read, to read above anything else. Chaplain French, of Boston, would come to the school, sometimes, and lecture to the pupils on Boston and the North.

About the first of June we were told that there was going to be a settlement of the war. Those who were on the Union side would remain free, and those in bondage were to work three days for their masters and three for themselves. It was a gloomy time for us all, and we were to be sent to Liberia. Chaplain French asked me would I rather go back to Savannah or go to Liberia. I told him the latter place by all means. We did not know when this would be, but we were prepared in case this settlement should be reached. However, the Confederates would not agree to the arrangement, or else it was one of the many rumors flying about at the time, as we heard nothing further of the matter. There were a number of settlements on this island of St. Simon's, just like little villages, and we would go from one to the other on business, to call, or only for a walk.

One Sunday, two men, Adam Miller and Daniel Spaulding, were chased by some rebels as they were coming from Hope Place (which was between the Beach and Gaston Bluff), but the latter were unable to catch them. When they reached the Beach and told this, all the men on the place, about ninety, armed themselves, and next day (Monday), with Charles O'Neal as their leader, skirmished the island for the "rebs." In a short while they discovered them in the woods, hidden behind a large log, among the thick underbrush. Charles O'Neal was the first to see them, and he was killed; also John Brown, and their bodies were never found. Charles O'Neal was an uncle of Edward King, who later was my husband and a sergeant in Co. E., U. S. I. Another man was shot, but not found for three days. ...

There were about six hundred men, women, and children on St. Simon's, the women and children being in the majority, and we were afraid to go very far from our own quarters in the day time, and at night even to go out of the house for a long time, although the men were on the watch all the time; for there were not any soldiers on the island, only the marines who were on the gunboats along the coast. The rebels, knowing this, could steal by them under cover of the night, and getting on the island would capture any persons venturing out alone and carry them to the mainland. Several of the men disappeared, and as they were never heard from we came to the conclusion they had been carried off in this way.

The latter part of August, 1862, Captain C. T. Trowbridge, with his brother John and Lieutenant Walker, came to St. Simon's Island from Hilton Head, by order of General Hunter, to get all the men possible to finish filling his regiment which he had organized in March, 1862. He had heard of the skirmish on this island, and was very much pleased at the bravery shown by these men. He found me at Gaston Bluff teaching my little school, and was much interested in it. When I knew him better I found him to be a thorough gentleman and a staunch friend to my race.

Captain Trowbridge remained with us until October, when the order was received to evacuate, and so we boarded the Ben-De-Ford, a transport, for Beaufort, S. C. When we arrived in Beaufort, Captain Trowbridge and the men he had onlisted went to camp at Old Fort, which they named "Camp Saxton." I was enrolled as laundress.

The first suits worn by the boys were red coats and pants, which they disliked very much, for, they said, "The rebels see us, miles away."

The first colored troops did not receive any pay for eighteen months, and the men had to depend wholly on what they received from the commissary, established by General Saxton. A great many of these men had large families, and as they had no money to give them, their wives were obliged to support themselves and children by washing for the officers of the gunboats and the soldiers, and making cakes and pies which they sold to the boys in camp. Finally, in 1863, the government decided to give them half pay, but the men would not accept this. They wanted "full pay" or nothing. They preferred rather to give their services to the state, which they did until 1864, when the government granted them full pay, with all the back pay due.

I remember hearing Captain Heasley telling his company, one day, "Boys, stand up for your full pay! I am with you, and so are all the officers." This captain was from Pennsylvania, and was a very good man; all the men liked him. N. G. Parker, our first lieutenant, was from Massachusetts. H. A. Beach was from New York. He was very delicate, and had to resign in 1864 on account of ill health.

I had a number of relatives in this regiment, — several uncles, some cousins, and a husband in Company E, and a number of cousins in other companies. Major Strong, of this regiment, started home on a furlough, but the vessel he was aboard was lost, and he never reached his home. He was one of the best officers we had. After his death, Captain C. T. Trowbridge was promoted major, August, 1863, and filled Major Strong's place until December, 1864, when he was promoted lieutenant-colonel, which he remained until he was mustered out, February 6, 1866.

In February, 1863, several cases of varioloid broke out among the boys, which caused some anxiety in camp. Edward Davis, of Company E (the company I was with), had it very badly. He was put into a tent apart from the rest of the men, and only the doctor and camp steward, James Cummings, were allowed to see or attend him; but I went to see this man every day and nursed him. The last thing at night, I always went in to see that he was comfortable, but in spite of the good care and attention he received, he succumbed to the disease.

I was not in the least afraid of the smallpox. I had been vaccinated, and I drank sassafras tea constantly, which kept my blood purged and prevented me from contracting this dread scourge, and no one need fear getting it if they will only keep their blood in good condition with this sassafras tea, and take it before going where the patient is.

——— 4.15 ———
'LET MY PEOPLE GO!'
African-American Spirituals

Since the first Africans arrived in the Americas, black people had composed their own varied and unique forms of music. In the earliest days of slavery, Africans composed work songs to help pass the tedious but rigorous hours of fieldwork. During the Great Awakenings, as evangelical Protestantism spread among African Americans, black "shout" songs for camp meetings spread. As the Underground Railroad blossomed, and escape from slavery became an organized endeavor, those same shouts and work songs were used as code to communicate discreetly amidst constant observation from plantation overseers. But it wasn't until the Civil War, when northern whites went south to help in contraband camps, that white society began to notice African-American music as legitimate compositions. Soldiers, journalists, missionaries and relief workers "discovered" and began chronicling black music. They took particular notice of the spiritual songs escaping or confiscated slaves sung at the camps, which, appropriately, focused on God's deliverance of his followers from bondage.

A. Go Down Moses

When Israel was in Egypt's land:
Let my people Go!
Oppress'd so hard they could not stand,
Let my people Go!

[CHORUS]

Go down Moses,
'way down in Egypt's land:
Tell ol' Pharoah,
Let my people go.

The Lord told Moses what to do:
Let my people GO!
To lead the children of Israel through,
Let my people Go!

[CHORUS]

Your foes shall not before you stand:
Let my people Go!
And you'll possess fair Canaan's land,
Let my people Go!

[CHORUS]

I believe without a doubt:
Let my people Go!
A Christian has a right to shout,
Let my people Go!

[CHORUS]

B. Down in the Valley

We'll run and never tire,
We'll run and never tire,
We'll run and never tire,
   Jesus set poor sinners free.
Way down in the valley,
   Who will rise and go with me?
You've heern talk of Jesus,
   Who set poor sinners free.

The lightnin' and the flashin'
The lightnin' and the flashin'
The lightnin' and the flashin'
   Jesus set poor sinners free.
I can't stand the fire.
I can't stand the fire.
I can't stand the fire.
   Jesus set poor sinners free.

The green trees a-flamin'.
The green trees a-flamin'.
The green trees a-flamin'.
   Jesus set poor sinners free.

Way down in the valley,
   Who will rise and go with me?
You've heern talk of Jesus,
   Who set poor sinners free.

— 4.16 —

CONFISCATION AND MILITIA ACT

U.S. Congress

Throughout 1862, the movement to transform the war into one for emancipation of the South's slaves gained momentum. Abolitionists and radical Republicans stepped up their drive to cast the war as one for African-American freedom. Manpower shortages drove field officers to clamor for the use of black troops. Prior to Gen. Hunter's attempt to build a black regiment in South Carolina in May 1862 (which Lincoln disbanded), Gen. John Fremont had attempted to do the same thing in August of 1861. Both officers had issued orders emancipating slaves in their regions in conjunction with their efforts to recruit black troops — and Lincoln overruled them on both occasions. But Congress set the ball rolling toward emancipation with a series of actions in 1862. In March, legislators issued an article of war that forbade Union officers from returning escaped slaves to their owners. In April, they abolished slavery in the District of Columbia. And, finally, in July, they took the step that set the stage for emancipation: Congress passed a law that freed all slaves in Union-occupied territory within the South and empowered the president to arm them for combat — reversing the 18th century statute that Lincoln had heretofore used to prevent blacks from serving. At the same time, Lincoln and members of Congress were working with a handful of black leaders in an effort to launch yet another colonization scheme — this time, relocating African Americans to Central America. As with previous plans, most blacks rejected the idea. But, in a July 1862 act, Congress appropriated funds for the project. Lincoln and most white officials still believed that, while slaves should be freed, they could not enter American society as citizens. The best solution they could foresee was the removal of African Americans from the nation.

An Act to suppress Insurrection, to punish Treason and Rebellion, to seize and confiscate the Property of Rebels, and for other Purposes.

Be it enacted by the Senate and House of Representatives of the United States of America in Congress assembled, That every person who shall hereafter commit the crime of treason against the United States, and shall be adjudged guilty thereof, shall suffer death, and all his slaves, if any, shall be declared and made free; or, at the discretion of the court, he shall be imprisoned for not less than five years and fined not less than ten thousand dollars, and all his slaves, if any, shall be declared and made free; said fine shall be levied and collected on any or all of the property, real and personal, excluding slaves, of which the said person so convicted was the owner at the time of committing the said crime, any sale or conveyance to the contrary notwithstanding. ...

SEC. 9. And be it further enacted, That all slaves of persons who shall hereafter be engaged in rebellion against the government of the United States, or who shall in any way give aid or comfort thereto, escaping from such persons and taking refuge within the lines of the army; and all slaves captured from such persons or deserted by them and coming under the control of the government of the United States; and all slaves of such person found on [or] being within any place occupied by rebel forces and afterwards occupied by the forces of the United States, shall be deemed captives of war, and shall be forever free of their servitude, and not again held as slaves.

SEC. 10. And be it further enacted, That no slave escaping into any State, Territory, or the District of Columbia, from any other State, shall be delivered up, or in any way impeded or hindered of his liberty, except for crime, or some offence against the laws, unless the person claiming said fugitive shall first make oath that the person to whom the labor or service of such fugitive is alleged to be due is his lawful owner, and has not borne arms against the United States in the present rebellion, nor in any way given aid and comfort thereto; and no person engaged in the military or naval service of the United States shall, under any pretence whatever, assume to decide on the validity of the claim of any person to the service or labor of any other person, or surrender up any such person to the claimant, on pain of being dismissed from the service.

SEC. 11. And be it further enacted, That the President of the United States is authorized to employ as many persons of African descent as he may deem necessary and proper for the suppression of this rebellion, and for this purpose he may organize and use them in such manner as he may judge best for the public welfare.

SEC. 12. And be it further enacted, That the President of the United States is hereby authorized to make provision for the transportation, colonization, and settlement, in some tropical country beyond the limits of the United States, of such persons of the African race, made free by the provisions of this act, as may be willing to emigrate, having first obtained the consent of the government of said country to their protection and settlement within the same, with all the rights and privileges of freemen. ...

APPROVED, July 17, 1862.

––––––– 4.17 –––––––

'MY PARAMOUNT OBJECT IN THIS STRUGGLE IS TO SAVE THE UNION'

Abraham Lincoln

New York Tribune editor Horace Greeley was among the radicals who had joined Frederick Douglass in an ongoing public campaign pressuring President Lincoln to view the war as one for emancipation of slaves. In an August 1862 open letter to Lincoln, Greeley echoed many of Douglass's arguments for making abolition of slavery a war aim. Greeley argued that to ignore slavery's centrality among the causes for the rebels' secession was not only ridiculous but damned any effort to rebuild the nation later. Moreover, emancipation would be a useful military tool, both boosting conscripts and frustrating the South. Lincoln responded with a letter to the *Tribune* the following week. Here, he made his infamous declaration, "If I could save the Union without freeing *any* slave, I would do it." At the time, however, Lincoln had already drafted an order freeing slaves in the Confederate states and begun discussing the details of its implementation with his Cabinet.

Executive Mansion, Washington, August 22, 1862

Hon. Horace Greeley:

DEAR SIR: I have just read yours of the nineteenth, addressed to myself through the New-York *Tribune*. If there be in it any statements or assumptions of fact which I may know to be erroneous, I do not now and here controvert them. If there be in it any inferences which I may believe to be falsely drawn, I do not now and here argue against them. If there be perceptible in it an impatient and dictatorial tone, I waive it in deference to an old friend, whose heart I have always supposed to be right.

As to the policy I "seem to be pursuing," as you say, I have not meant to leave any one in doubt.

I would save the Union. I would save it the shortest way under the Constitution. The sooner the National authority can be restored, the nearer the Union will be "the Union as it was." If there be those who would not save the Union unless they could at the same time *save* Slavery, I do not agree with them. If there be those who would not save the Union unless they could at the same time *destroy* Slavery, I do not agree with them. My paramount object in this struggle is to save the Union, and is *not* either to save or destroy Slavery. If I could save the Union without freeing *any* slave, I would do it; and if I could save it by freeing *all* the slaves, I would do it; and if I could do it by freeing some and leaving others alone, I would also do that. What I do about Slavery and the colored race, I do because I believe it helps to save this Union; and what I forbear, I forbear because I do not believe it would help to save the Union. I shall do *less* whenever I shall believe what I am doing hurts the cause, and I shall do *more* whenever I shall believe doing more will help the cause. I shall try to correct errors when shown to be errors; and I shall adopt new views so fast as they shall appear to be true views. I have here stated my purpose according to my view of *official* duty, and I intend no modification of my oft-expressed personal wish that all men, everywhere, could be free.

Yours,

A. LINCOLN.

4.18

'ALL PERSONS HELD AS SLAVES WITHIN SAID DESIGNATED STATES ... ARE, AND HENCEFORWARD SHALL BE, FREE'

The Emancipation Proclamation

With Congress having paved the way with its sweeping actions throughout 1862, President Lincoln was prepared to give in to abolitionists and issue an order freeing the slaves. He first drafted an Emancipation Proclamation in the early summer of 1862, and revealed it to his cabinet in July. The reaction was at best mixed, with some, such as Post Master General Montgomery Blair warning of political backlash and others, such as Secretary of War Edwin Stanton embracing it immediately as an effective tool to foment chaos in the South and create access to more troops for the Union army. In September, he issued a preliminary statement warning that slaves would be freed in rebel states that did not return to the Union by January 1st, 1863. On that date, Lincoln issued the momentous document. It was grand in language, but limited in scope. It freed only slaves in rebel states, ignoring the estimated one million slaves in states still in the Union. Lincoln, ever cautious, feared angering the slave-holding states that had not seceded. *The New York Times* praised the order's caution, arguing that Lincoln had only the constitutional power to free those slaves in rebel states, using a war order, and that only Congress could have done anything more broad. The *Times* also noted the sobering reality that the Proclamation would not free a single slave, and that their liberation would come only as Union troops took control of southern territory. But it went further to sound a condescending and foreboding note about the emancipated slaves' future. As did many whites of the era, the paper's editors were deeply concerned that blacks would refuse to work without slavery to force them. That paranoia, based in the same racist assumptions that allowed slavery to exist in the first place, would drive both federal and state government policies in the proceeding years.

A. Emancipation Proclamation

Whereas on the 22nd day of September, A.D. 1862, a proclamation was issued by the

President of the United States, containing, among other things, the following, to wit:

"That on the 1st day of January, A.D. 1863, all persons held as slaves within any State or designated part of a State the people whereof shall then be in rebellion against the United States shall be then, thenceforward, and forever free; and the executive government of the United States, including the military and naval authority thereof, will recognize and maintain the freedom of such persons and will do no act or acts to repress such persons, or any of them, in any efforts they may make for their actual freedom.

"That the executive will on the 1st day of January aforesaid, by proclamation, designate the States and parts of States, if any, in which the people thereof, respectively, shall then be in rebellion against the United States; and the fact that any State or the people thereof shall on that day be in good faith represented in the Congress of the United States by members chosen thereto at elections wherein a majority of the qualified voters of such States shall have participated shall, in the absence of strong countervailing testimony, be deemed conclusive evidence that such State and the people thereof are not then in rebellion against the United States."

Now, therefore, I, Abraham Lincoln, President of the United States, by virtue of the power in me vested as Commander-In-Chief of the Army and Navy of the United States in time of actual armed rebellion against the authority and government of the United States, and as a fit and necessary war measure for supressing said rebellion, do, on this 1st day of January, A.D. 1863, and in accordance with my purpose so to do, publicly proclaim for the full period of one hundred days from the first day above mentioned, order and designate as the States and parts of States wherein the people thereof, respectively, are this day in rebellion against the United States the following, to wit:

Arkansas, Texas, Louisiana (except the parishes of St. Bernard, Palquemines, Jefferson, St. John, St. Charles, St. James, Ascension, Assumption, Terrebone, Lafourche, St. Mary, St. Martin, and Orleans, including the city of New Orleans), Mississippi, Alabama, Florida, Georgia, South Carolina, North Carolina, and Virginia (except the forty-eight counties designated as West Virginia, and also the counties of Berkeley, Accomac, Morthhampton, Elizabeth City, York, Princess Anne, and Norfolk, including the cities of Norfolk and Portsmouth), and which excepted parts are for the present left precisely as if this proclamation were not issued.

And by virtue of the power and for the purpose aforesaid, I do order and declare that all persons held as slaves within said designated States and parts of States are, and henceforward shall be, free; and that the Executive Government of the United States, including the military and naval authorities thereof, will recognize and maintain the freedom of said persons.

And I hereby enjoin upon the people so declared to be free to abstain from all violence, unless in necessary self-defence; and I recommend to them that, in all case when allowed, they labor faithfully for reasonable wages.

And I further declare and make known that such persons of suitable condition will be received into the armed service of the United States to garrison forts, positions, stations, and other places, and to man vessels of all sorts in said service.

And upon this act, sincerely believed to be an act of justice, warranted by the Constitution upon military necessity, I invoke the considerate judgment of mankind and the gracious favor of Almighty God.

B. *New York Times* **editorial on the Proclamation**

The President's Proclamation.

President Lincoln's proclamation, which we publish this morning, marks an era in the history, not only of this war but of this country and world. It is not necessary to assume that it will set free instantly the enslaved blacks of the South, in order to ascribe to it the greatest and most permanent importance. Whatever may be its immediate results, it changes entirely the relations of the National Government to the institution of

Slavery. Hitherto Slavery has been under the protection of the Government; henceforth it is under its ban. The power of the Army and Navy, hitherto employed in hunting and returning to bondage the fugitive from service, are to be employed in maintaining his freedom whenever and wherever he may choose to assert it. This change of attitude is itself a revolution.

President Lincoln takes care, by great precision in his language, to define the basis on which this action rests. He issues the Proclamation "as a fit and necessary war measure for the suppressing of the rebellion." While he sincerely believes it to be an "act of justice warranted by the Constitution," he issues it "upon military necessity." In our judgment it is only upon that ground and for that purpose that he has any right to issue it at all. In his civil capacity as President, he has not the faintest shadow of authority to decree the emancipation of a single slave, either as an "act of justice" or for any other purpose whatever. As Commander-in-Chief of the army he has undoubtedly the right *to deprive the rebels of the aid of their slaves* — just as he has the right to take their horses, and to arrest all persons who may be giving them aid and comfort, "as a war measure" and upon grounds of military necessity.

It may seem at first sight a matter of small importance in what capacity the act is done. But its validity may, in the end, depend upon that very point. Sooner or later his action in this matter will come up for review before the Supreme Court, and it is a matter of the utmost importance to the President, to the slaves, and to the country, that it should come in a form to be sustained. It must be a legal and a constitutional act in form as well as in substance. We wish that for this reason the President had given it the form of a *Military Order*, — addressed to his subordinate Generals, enjoining upon them specific acts in the performance of their military duties, instead of a Proclamation addressed to the world at large, and embodying declarations and announcement instead of commands.

What effect the Proclamation will have remains to be seen. We do not think that it will at once set free any considerable number of slaves beyond the actual and effective jurisdiction of our armies. It will lead to no immediate insurrections, and involve no massacres, except such as the rebels in the blindness of their wrath may themselves set on foot. The slaves have no arms, are without organization, and in dread of the armed and watchful whites. Besides, they evince no disposition to fight for themselves so long as they see that we are fighting for them. They understand, beyond all question, that the tendency of this war is to give them freedom and that the Union armies, whatever may be their motive, are actually and practically fighting for their liberty. If the war should suddenly end, — if they should see the fighting stop, and the Constitution which protects Slavery restored to full vigor in the Slave States, their disappointment would vent itself in the wrathful explosion of insurrection and violence. But so long as the war continues, we look for nothing of that kind. Whenever our armies reach their immediate vicinity, they will doubtless assert their freedom, and call upon us to recognize and maintain it. Until then, they will work for their masters and wait for deliverance.

President Lincoln "recommends" the enfranchisement of slaves, "in all cases, when allowed, to labor faithfully for reasonable wages." That great question, before the end is reached, will demand other treatment than this. If the President supposes that millions of men, who never made a bargain in their lives, who never consulted on any subject affecting their own interest, who never made provision for their own support, or had the slightest charge connected with the maintenance of wives or children, and who have worked all their lives under the pressure of force and fear, can pass suddenly to the condition of free men, — recognizing at once all its responsibilities and performing all its duties, — he must believe the age of miracles is not yet past. If the Proclamation makes the slaves actually free, there will come the further duty of making them work. That the whole negro race is to remain idle if it should *choose* so to do, being free, no one can seriously propose. If the slaves choose to "labor faithfully for reasonable wages" — very well: — they will establish their claim to freedom by the highest of titles, the ability to use and enjoy it. But if they do not, they must be compelled to do it, — not by brute force, nor by being owned like cattle, and denied every human right, but by just and equal laws — such laws as in every community control and forbid vagrancy, mendicancy and all the shapes by which idle vagabondage preys upon industry and thrift.

But still this opens a vast and most difficult subject, with which we do not propose now to deal. In time, however, it will challenge universal attention, and demand for the solution of the problems which it involves the ablest and most patient statesmanship of the land.

────── 4.19 ──────

'HIS BODY WAS LEFT SUSPENDED FOR SEVERAL HOURS'
The New York Draft Riot of 1863

By the time President Lincoln issued the Emancipation Proclamation, tensions in northern cities had already reached the point of danger. Wartime inflation pinched white laborers throughout the North, and their frustration often turned into anti-black violence. In New York City, black laborers had held most of the unskilled jobs in the years before the war. As Irish immigrants began competing for those jobs, many blacks were relegated to "scab" work — shipped in to fill the jobs of striking whites. Employment became a racially-charged issue. With the Proclamation, Democratic politicians began warning that freed slaves would be shipped north to further tighten the labor market. They also fanned whites' fears — such as those articulated in *The New York Times* editorial on the Emancipation Proclamation — that freed slaves wouldn't work, and would instead leech off of philanthropist and government aid.

Into this volatile atmosphere came the Enrollment Act of 1863, creating a draft in the Union. The Act allowed men to pay $300 to exempt themselves, a substantial portion of a year's pay for many laborers of the time. The draft started in June, and that July, in a largely Irish and Democratic area of New York City, one of the era's worst urban riots erupted. The mob first took aim at the draft office, and then wealthy white men presumed to be capable of exempting themselves. But, ultimately, the rioters turned on the city's black population. They seized and lynched men and women in the streets, burnt businesses that employed blacks and even ransacked and burned an orphanage for black children. The riot lasted three days, until troops returning from Gettysburg arrived to quell it — largely by shooting rioters. A committee of merchants raised money to rebuild damaged property for both blacks and whites. That committee published a report, excerpted below, describing varied acts of violence during the riot.

Incidents of the Riot.
ABRAHAM FRANKLIN.

This young man who was murdered by the mob on the corner of Twenty-seventh St., and Seventh avenue, was a quiet, inoffensive man, 23 years of age, of unexceptionable character, and a member of Zion African Church in this city. Although a cripple, he earned a living for himself and his mother by serving a gentleman in the capacity of coachman. A short time previous to the assault upon his person, he called upon his mother to see if anything could be done by him for her safety. The old lady, who is noted for her piety and her Christian deportment, said she considered herself perfectly safe; but if her time to die had come, she was ready to die. Her son then knelt down by her side, and implored the protection of Heaven in behalf of his mother. The old lady was affected to tears, and said to our informant that it seemed to her that good angels were present in the room. Scarcely had the supplicant risen from his knees, when the mob broke down the door, seized him, beat him over the head and face with fists and clubs, and then hanged him in the presence of his mother.

While they were thus engaged, the military came and drove them away, cutting down the body of Franklin, who raised his arm once slightly and gave a few signs of life.

The military then moved on to quell other riots, when the mob returned and again suspended the now probably lifeless body of Franklin, cutting out pieces of flesh and otherwise mutilating it.

AUGUSTUS STUART.

Died at the Hospital, Blackwell's Island July 22d, from the effects of a blow received at the hands of the mob, within one block and a half of the State Arsenal, corner 7th Avenue and 35th street, on Wednesday evening, July 15th. He had been badly beaten previously by a band of rioters and was frightened and insane from the effects of the blows which he had received. He was running towards the Arsenal for safety when he was overtaken by the mob from whom he received his death blow.

Mrs. Stuart, his wife, says that some of the rioters declared that at the second attack upon him he had fired a pistol at his pursuers; but she says that if he did, he must have obtained the weapon from some friend after he had left home, a few minutes before, for he had no weapon then, nor was he ever known to have had one. He was a member of the church.

PETER HEUSTON.

Peter Heuston, sixty-three years of age, a Mohawk Indian, with dark complexion and straight black hair, who has for several years been a resident of this city, at the corner of Rosevelt and Oak streets, and who has obtained a livelihood as a laborer, proved a victim to the late riots.

His wife died about three weeks before the riots, leaving with her husband an only child, a little girl named Lavinia, aged eight years, whom the Merchant's committee have undertaken to adopt with a view of affording her guardianship and an education. Hueston served with the New York Volunteers in the Mexican War, and has always been loyal to our government. He was brutally attacked on the 13th of July by a gang of ruffians who evidently thought him to be of the African race because of his dark complexion. He died within four days at Bellevue Hospital from his injuries.

The end of the Mexican War Heuston received a land warrant from the government, which enabled him to settle on a tract of land at the West, where he lived but a short time previous to his coming to this city.

WILLIAM JONES.

A crowd of rioters in pursuit of a negro, who in self defense had fired on some rowdies who had attacked him, met an innocent colored man returning from a bakery with a loaf of bread under his arm. They instantly set upon him and beat him and after nearly killing him, hanged him to a lamp-post. His body was left suspended for several hours and was much mutilated.

A sad illustration of the painful uncertainty which hung over the minds of the two wives and children of the colored men was found in the fact that two wives and their families, were both mourning the loss of their husbands in the case of this man, for upwards of the two weeks after its occurrence. And so great was the fear inspired by the mob that no white person dared to manifest sufficient interest in the mutilated body of the murdered man while it remained in the neighborhood to be able to testify as to who it was. At the end of the two weeks the husband of one of the mourners to her great joy returned, like one recovered from the grave.

The principal evidence which the widow, Mary Jones, has to identify the murdered man as her husband is the fact of his having a loaf of bread under his arm. He having left the house to get a loaf of bread a few minutes before the attacked.

One of our colored missionaries is still investigating the case. …

BURNING OF THE COLORED ORPHAN ASYLUM.

Our attention was early called to this outrage by a number of letters from the relatives and friends of the children, anxiously inquiring as to the whereabouts of the little ones. It is well known that as soon as the Bull's Head Hotel had been attacked by the mob, their next destination was the Colored Orphan Asylum, on Fifth Avenue, near Forty-third street. The crowd has swelled to an immense number at this locality, and went professionally to work in order to destroy the building, and, at the same time, to make appropriation of any thing of value by which they might aggrandize themselves. About four hundred entered the house at the time, and immediately proceeded to pitch out beds, chairs, tables, and every species of furniture, which were eagerly seized by the crowd below, and carried off. When all was taken, the house was then set on fire, and shared the fate of the others.

While the rioters were clamoring for admittance at the front door, the Matron and Superintendent were quietly and rapidly conducting the children out the back yard, down to the police station. They remained there until Thursday, (the burning of the Asylum occurred on Monday, July 13th, when they were all removed in safety to Blackwell's Island, where they still remain).

There were 230 children between the ages of 4 and 12 years in the home at the time of the riot.

The Asylum was located on the Fifth Avenue, between 43d and 44th streets. The main building was nearly 200 feet in length, three stores and light basement in height, with an hospital 100 feet long, three stories high, connected with the main building, by a covered way. Several work shops were attached, and the residence of the Superintendent, Mr. Wm. Davis, was next door. The buildings were of brick and were substantial and commodious structures. A number of fine shade trees and flowering shrubs adorned the ample play grounds and front court yard, and a well built fence surrounded the whole. The main buildings were burned. The trees girdled by cutting with axes; the shrubs uprooted, and the fence carried away. All was destroyed except the residence of Mr. Davis, which was sacked. ...

—————— 4.20 ——————

'MORTAL MEN COULD NOT STAND SUCH A FIRE'
Massachusetts 54th Regiment

The Emancipation Proclamation lifted the ban on black service members, and Union officers began forming all-African-American units. (Many blacks were already serving in the Navy, which had always allowed them because of the difficulties it faced enlisting men to serve under unpleasant and dangerous conditions at sea.) Of the estimated two million Union soldiers throughout the war, nearly 200,000 of them would be African American. The most celebrated of the black units was the first — the 54th Massachusetts Infantry Regiment. Immediately following the Proclamation, Massachusetts Governor John Andrew, long a proponent of letting blacks serve, began building a black unit. He appointed Col. Robert Gould Shaw, a white man, the commanding officer and appealed to black leaders such as Frederick Douglass and William Wells Brown for help recruiting black soldiers. At a February meeting of free blacks in New Bedford, nearly 200 members of the final 54th regiment, including future Congressional Medal of Honor winner William H. Carney, signed up.

Most northerners inside and out of the military were slow to accept black service members, however, and the 54th was initially assigned mostly to manual labor. Then, on July 18, 1863, came their storied attack on Fort Wagner in Charleston, South Carolina. Capturing the symbolically and strategically significant southern city was a Union priority from day one of the war. But it was heavily defended, and the Union offensive that began that spring had gone poorly. An assault on Fort Wagner, one of several garrisons guarding the city, had ended terribly on the 17th. The 54th arrived the next day from another battle. After three days journey, with little rest, they were sent to lead a second, direct assault on Wagner. It was a massacre, and nearly half of the 600 Union troops involved were killed. Of those, 116 were members of the 54th. However, accounts circulated throughout the north heralding the black troops' performance and bravery in the battle, and public opinion about African Americans' suitability for fighting swung considerably. The battle later inspired the movie *Glory*.

The *New Bedford Mercury* published weekly letters from 54th Regiment Corporal James Henry Gooding throughout the unit's first year of action. In the dispatch below, Gooding describes both the battle at Fort Wagner and their previous, more successful, engagement.

Morris Island, July 20, 1863

Messrs. Editors: — At last we have something stirring to record. The 54th, the past week, has proved itself twice in battle. The first was on James Island on the morning of the 16th. There were four companies of the 54th on picket duty at the time; our picket lines extending to the right of the rebel battery, which commands the approach to Charleston through the Edisto river. About 3 o'clock in the morning, the rebels began harassing our pickets on the right, intending, no doubt, to drive them in, so that by daylight the coast would be clear to rush their main force down on us, and take us by surprise. They did not suppose we had any considerable force to the rear of our pickets on the right, as Gen. Stevenson's brigade was plain in sight on the left; and their plan, I supposed, was to rush down and cut Gen. Stevenson off. They made a mistake — instead of returning fire, the officer in charge of the pickets directed the men to lie down under cover of a hedge, rightly expecting the rebels to advance by degrees toward our lines. As he expected, at daylight they were within 600 yards of the picket line, when our men rose and poured a volley into them. That was something the rebels didn't expect — their line of skirmishers was completely broken; our men then began to fall back gradually on our line of battle, as the rebels were advancing their main force on to them. On they came, with six pieces of artillery and four thousand infantry, leaving a heavy force to drive Gen. Stevenson on the left. As their force advanced on our right, the boys held them in check like veterans; but of course they were falling back all the time, and fighting too. After the officers saw there was no chance for their men, they ordered them to move on to a creek under cover of the gunboats. When the rebels got within 900 yards of our line of battle, the right wing of Gen. Terry's brigade gave them three volleys, which checked their advance. They then made a stand with their artillery and began shelling us, but it had no effect on our forces, as the rebels fired too high. The 6th Connecticut battery then opened fire on them from the right, the John Adams and May Flower from the creek between James and Cole Islands, and the Pawnee and a mortar

schooner from the Edisto, when the rebels began a hasty retreat. It was a warmer reception than they had expected. Our loss in the skirmishing before the battle, so far as we can ascertain, was nine killed, 13 wounded, and 17 missing, either killed or taken prisoners; but more probably they were driven into the creek and drowned. Sergeant Wilson, of Co. H, was called upon to surrender, but would not; he shot four men before he was taken. After he was taken they ordered him to give up his pistol which he refused to do, when he was shot through the head.

The men of the 54th behaved gallantly on the occasion — so the Generals say. It is not for us to blow our horn; but when a regiment of white men gave us three cheers as we were passing them, it shows that we did our duty as men should.

I shall pass over the incidents of that day, as regards individuals, to speak of a greater and more terrible ordeal the 54th regiment has passed through. I shall say nothing now of how we came from James and Morris Island; suffice it to say, on Saturday afternoon we were marched up past our batteries, amid the cheers of the officers and soldiers. We wondered what they were all cheering for, but we soon found out. Gen. Strong rode up, and we halted. Well, you had better believe there was some guessing what we were to do. Gen. Strong asked us if we would follow him into Fort Wagner. Every man said, yes — we were ready to follow wherever we were led. You may all know Fort Wagner is the Sebastopol of the rebels; but we went at it, over the ditch and on to the parapet through a deadly fire, but we could not get into the fort. We met the foe on the parapet of Wagner with the bayonet — we were exposed to a murderous fire from the batteries of the fort, from our Monitors and our land batteries, as they did not cease firing soon enough. Mortal men could not stand such a fire, and the assault on Wagner was a failure. The 9th Me., 10th Conn., 63d Ohio, 48th and 100th N.Y. were to support us in the assault; but after we made the first charge, everything was in such confusion that we could hardly tell where the reserve was. At the first charge the 54th rushed to within twenty yards of the ditches, and, as might be expected of raw recruits, wavered — but at the second advance they gained the parapet. The color bearer of the State colors was killed on the parapet. Col. Shaw seized the staff when the standard bearer fell, and in less than a minute after, the Colonel fell himself. When the men saw their gallant leader fall, they made a desperate effort to get him out, but they were either shot down, or reeled in the ditch below. One man succeeded in getting hold of the State color staff, but the color was completely torn to pieces.

I have no more paper here at present, as all our baggage is at St. Helena yet; so I cannot further particularize this letter. Lieut. Grace was knocked down by a piece of shell, but he is not injured. He showed himself a great deal braver and cooler than any line officer.

J. H. G.

--------- 4.21 ---------

'NIGGERS HAS RIZ IN PUBLIC ESTIMATION AND ARE AT A HIGH PREMIUM'
Christian Abraham Fleetwood

Christian Abraham Fleetwood, born free in 1840 in Baltimore, Maryland, was one of 14 African Americans to receive the Congressional Medal of Honor for their bravery during Civil War battles. A bright young man, Fleetwood began his education early, in the home of a white friend of the family and in the offices of the Maryland Colonization Society. He traveled to both Liberia and Sierra Leone before attending college at Lincoln University (then Ashmun Institute) in Pennsylvania in 1860. With friends, he founded and edited the Baltimore black newspaper *Lyceum Observer*. Following the war, he moved to Washington, D.C., where he became a teacher and black leader who was lauded by both blacks and whites for his service in the community. At the century's close, he wrote a seminal account detailing the contributions of black veterans in the nation's wars.

In 1863, at the age of 23, Fleetwood enlisted as a sergeant in Company G, 4th Regiment, U.S. Colored Volunteer Infantry. He was quickly promoted to Sgt. Major, the highest rank an African American could achieve at the time. Highly literate, Fleetwood was a prolific writer before, during and after the war. As a result, his personal papers include a wealth of first person accounts of black participation in the Civil War.

A. Blacks conscripted for manual labor

Early in the war, and indeed throughout, blacks were often relegated to manual labor or servants' duties for the Union army. Many people, including Fleetwood, were not eager to do such menial work, and troops rounded up and arrested them to force their participation. In June of 1863, Fleetwood wrote to his father describing the conscription of free African Americans in Baltimore to build the city's fortifications.

Balto. June 23, 1863
Dear Pap:

Your letter received yesterday at 11 o'clock, Joe's message from you this morning at 10. It is now 20 min. to one. Here I am by good luck only and providentially in good health. In common with my other colored brudderen, great has been my disgruntlement since I last wrote you. Niggers has riz in public estimation and are at a high premium. Since Saturday Guards, police and "poor white trash" have been running, chasing, catching and impressing every "likely Negro" they could lay eyes on in the house or out of doors. "Niggers is scarce" here now and no mistake. Ditches and entrenchments are being dug and thrown up all around the city, the streets barricaded and every preparation being made to meet a raid from the seceshers, "May the devil admire them." I left the office at a tolerably early hour on Saturday, thinking no evil, and started for Jim Jordan's shop near the watch-house, and had it not been for some boys I would have landed much nearer the watch house than I thought for. A party of them met by the theatre, and attempted to capture me and take me down by force. Not recognizing their authority, I refused to "see it", and executed a flank movement up Lexington street, and down

North. They hung on my flank and rear and raised promiscuous Cain because I would not go. I pursued the even tenor of my way to Saratoga St. Then they reared and yelled for guard and police, but none came, only another boy taller than myself rushed ahead of me and tried to turn my flank. In few but pointed words I expressed my intention not to go for them or any like them, and kept on, meeting with no further molestation. Taking the advice of some friends whom I met, I went home, but not satisfied to "let well enough alone", I must needs start out again and make another effort to reach Jim.

Turned out of Pleasant into Holliday St., and walked down nearly to Jim's door. When four Irishmen charged at me from the rear and left flank simultaneously. To escape by the front was impossible, by the rear ditto, by the left flank ditto. I executed another strategic movement of my entire column by the right flank at a double quick step, through the depot into North St. Cheated a big Irishmen into letting me pass the North St. door, and made a rapid change of base, and after a force march of about a mile, succeeded in running the blockade, passing the barricade, and occupying Fort 48 on Tyson Heights.

I remained in garrison until Sunday morning, intending to march upon the Sunday school at an early hour, but by the time I was up, the police and guards were scouring the neighborhood, and got every black man they could find. Mrs. Williams told them the man who lived in our house had gone to Washington. So they pressed our house. So it was all day. At night I went a little way down the alley, except which I was a close prisoner from Saturday afternoon till near eleven o'clock yesterday morning. I wrote a note to Dr. stating the circumstance, and told him if he needed me to send me a pass, as I would rather go out and work on the fortifications than spend another such day as Sunday in the house.

After much trouble he succeeded in getting one, though hundreds were refused. He being lame, and the Marshall happened to know

him, and his statement that I was his only assistant were the only things that saved me. Mother brought the pass, and I started down town. It was amusing to see the looks of astonishment with which everyone regarded me as I passed, walking in my usual free and easy style, but with a little extra set to my hat, just for the fun of it. John Henry Butler, John M. Brown, Josh Jordan, Jim Jordan, Jesse Jordan, one of our editors named Brown, and in fact, nearly everybody you can think of were out. Jesse came in Sunday. Jim was out only yesterday. Handy was caught, but escaped from the squad while enroute to the works. Leed Matthews took the back fence while the officers were at the front door. He and Handy have been close prisoners ever since. Yesterday afternoon I traversed Baltimore, Eastern, Central and Southern. Wayman was arrested and released five times. Hunter was taken out to the ground and released, after a pleasant walk of ten miles.

Jordan was hid all day Sunday in his shop, though it was searched they did not find him, but getting tired of that, he went over to try to get an exemption on Monday morning, Mahogany head Jackson at the same time. While negotiations were in progress, they were marched out and put to work. Jim's pass was procured at 12 o'clock, but he did not get it until after five, as they could not find Josh was in last night, but out again this morning. None of Joe's people are out. I have written this much of my letter as much for his benefit as yours, so you may read it to him. Ask him whether he does not owe me a letter. It seems to me that I wrote to him some time ago, and have not received any letter since, except this message from you this morning.

Your affectionate son

Christian A. Fleetwood

B. Defending his regiment's reputation

Fleetwood was obviously a proud man. At a mere 5'4", he exuded a stature, by all reports, of a man twice his physical appearance. He joined the 4th Regiment U.S.C.T. in August of 1863, and continued to read and correspond with newspapers throughout his time in the Union Army. In June of 1864, prior to his regiment's entry into the famously prolonged siege of Petersburg, Virginia, Fleetwood wrote a letter to the *Anglo-African* in response to a report on a recent battle published there. The report, also penned by a black soldier, claimed Fleetwood's 4th Regiment had fled "in confusion" during the battle. Fleetwood fired off an indignant defense of their valor, setting the record straight.

Dear Sir,

Permit me to occupy a small space in your paper to correct a misstatement made in your paper by some one writing from the 5th Mass. Cav. over the nom de plume of "Africans." I will do so in as few words as possible. He states that the 4th Regt. being deployed as skirmishers were unable to sustain themselves and fell back upon them (the 5th Cav.) in confusion. Our Regt. advanced through the woods in line of battle, its front covered by skirmishers, two companies deployed, the 22nd U.S.C.T. on our right, the 6th on our left. The 5th Mass. Cav. and the 5th U.S.C.T. forming the reserve.

Our regiment was the first to clear the woods, and received the concentrated fire from the rebel works completely enfilading our lines. Notwith-standing this we charged the works at a double quick until the 5th Mass. Cavalry, our reserve, who were not yet out of the woods nor in sight of the enemy, fired a volley which took effect upon our rear throwing our entire left wing into confusion.

The shot from the rebel battery still mowing us down we were ordered back into the woods to re-form. And back accordingly, re-formed and again advanced in time to lose several more men killed and wounded.

A better and braver regiment than the 5th U.S.C.T. is not in the service. Yet "Honor to whom honor is due." It was the 22nd U.S.C.T. and not the 5th which carried the works after we had fallen back.

One thing more and I close. Africans wonders why the casualties were so small in his Regt. Perhaps the fact that they did not come out of the friendly shelter of the woods until the action was over may partly account for their loss being so small while ours summed up to one hundred and sixty killed and wounded out of less than six hundred, in the short time of ten minutes.

In justice to our boys, I trust you will give this an insertion.

Yours respectfully,
C.A. Fleetwood
Sergt. Major 4th U.S.C.T.

C. Fleetwood leaves the forces angered by inequality

Despite his Congressional recognition, Fleetwood left the U.S. Armed Forces angered by its treatment of black soldiers. He detested policies limiting their rise through the officer ranks, and sought discharge because he believed "continuing to Act in a subordinate capacity" harmed his community. In a letter to his former employer in Baltimore, Fleetwood explained his reasons for quitting the service. He had originally joined to abolish slavery, he explained, to serve his people in the best way he saw at the time. That accomplished, he could now better serve his people as a civilian. In the forces, Fleetwood concluded, no matter what *African Americans* accomplished, "they will shortly be considered as 'lazy nigger sojers.'"

Baltimore June 8th 1865
Dr. James Hall
Dear Sir:

I much regret that you disapprove or rather do not approve of my leaving the service at the expiration of my term of enlistment.

Be assured that in this matter I am actuated by the same motives which induced me to leave your office, and light & agreeable employment and take to the arduous & adventurous duties of the camp — some personal ambition to be sure but mainly from a desire to benefit my race.

From representations made by Col. Birney and from the position assumed by our friends in Congress, you remember we were induced to believe or hope that on evidence of merit and ability to do our duty we should receive promotion, at least to the rank of company & regimental officers. — That I have well performed the duties of the office which I have held the past two years, it becomes me not to say, although I wear a medal conferred for some special acts as a soldier, yet am bold to say that no regiment has performed more active, arduous, & dangerous service than the 4th U.S. Cold. Troops.

Leaving Baltimore in September 1863 we reported at Yorktown Va. and in less than a week were ordered on a raid, making thirty (30) miles per day, with no stragglers. We remained at Yorktown until 1864 engaging in similar expeditions once or twice in every month.

In April we were ordered to Point Lookout, Md. to guard the prisoners there, and remained until the organization of the first division of colored troops in the U.S. service, viz. the 3d Division, 18th Army Corps.

Leaving Fortress Monroe with the "James River Expedition" in May 64 we were the first ashore at City Point, and built works, held them and made reconnaissances from then to June 15th when the first serious demonstration was made upon Petersburg, losing on that day about two hundred and fifty (250) out of less than six hundred (600) men. Assisted in the siege of Petersburg until August when we were transferred to Dutch Gap working in the canal under the shelling of the rebel batteries until the latter part of September when we were ordered to Deep Bottom and under Major Gen. Birney on the 29th September, at the taking of New Market Heights and Fort Harrison, lost two thirds of our available force. Entrenching on the lines before Richmond, we remained until Gen. [Benjamin F.] Butler's Expedition to Fort Fisher, returned to our old camp and in a few days again embarked under Gen. [Alfred H.] Terry upon his successful expedition, and have taken part in all of the marches and fighting encountered by "Terry's Command" until the surrender of [General Joseph E.] Johnston's Army in April last. Upon all our record there is not a single blot, and yet no member of this regiment is considered deserving of a commission or if so cannot receive one. I trust you will understand that I

speak not of and for myself individually, or that the lack of the pay or honor of a commission induces me to quit the service. Not so by any means, but I see no good that will result to our people by continuing to serve, on the contrary it seems to me that our continuing to Act in a subordinate capacity, with no hope of advancement or promotion is an absolute injury to our cause. It is a tacit but telling acknowledgement on our part that we are not fit for promotion, & that we are satisfied to remain in a state of marked and acknowledged subserviency.

A double purpose induced me and most others to enlist, to assist in abolishing slavery and to save the country from ruin. Something in furtherance of both objects we have certainly done, and now it strikes me that more could be done for our welfare in the pursuits of civil life. I think that a camp life would be decidedly an injury to our people. No matter how well and faithfully they may perform their duties they will shortly be considered as "lazy nigger sojers" — as drones in the great hive.

I have trespassed upon your time to a much greater extent than I intended but I wished you correctly to appreciate my motives for leaving the service.

Very truly & respectfully Yours
Christian A. Fleetwood
Sergt. Major 4th U.S. Cold. Troops

———— 4.22 ————

'WE HAVE DONE A SOLDIER'S DUTY. WHY CAN'T WE HAVE A SOLDIER'S PAY?'
Corporal James Henry Gooding

Throughout the first year and a half of black service in the military, African Americans were paid a laborer's wage of $10 a month, of which $3 was subtracted to pay for their clothing. White soldiers, meanwhile, earned $13 a month, almost double the blacks' take-home pay. From the onset, the black soldiers were aware of and angered by the policy. In protest, a large group of them, including both the 54th Massachusetts Infantry Regiment and the First South Carolina Volunteer Regiment, refused to accept any pay at all. Black leaders who had encouraged participation in the war lobbied President Lincoln to equalize the pay. Frederick Douglass, whose two sons fought in the 54th, met with Lincoln at the White House in July of 1863 about the matter. But it wasn't until June of 1864 that Congress finally equalized black and white soldiers' pay, making the policy change retroactive.

In September 1863, two months following the 54th's heroic, if tragic, effort at Fort Wagner, Corporal James Henry Gooding sent as his regular dispatch to the *New Bedford Mercury* an open letter to President Lincoln protesting the uneven pay scale.

Camp of the 54th Massachusetts colored regt.,
Morris Island.
Dept. Of the South. Sept. 28th, 1863.
Your Excellency, Abraham Lincoln:

Your Excellency will pardon the presumption of an humble individual like myself, in addressing you, but the earnest Solicitation of my comrades in Arms beside the genuine interest felt by myself in the matter is my excuse, for placing before the Executive head of the Nation our Common Grievance.

On the 6th day of the last Month, the Paymaster of the department informed us, that if we would decide to receive the sum of $10 per month, he would come and pay us that sum, but that, on the sitting of Congress, the Regt., would, in his opinion, be allowed the other three. He did not give us any guarantee that this would be, as he hoped; certainly he had no authority for making any such guarantee, and we cannot suppose him acting in any way interested.

Now the main question is, Are we Soldiers, or are we Labourers? We are fully armed and equipped, have done all the various Duties pertaining to a Soldier's life, have conducted ourselves to the complete satisfaction of General Officers, who were, if any[thing], prejudiced against us, but who now accord us all the encouragement and honour due us; have shared the perils and Labour of Reducing the first stronghold that flaunted a Traitor Flag; and more, Mr. President. Today the Anglo-Saxon Mother, Wife, or Sister are not alone in tears for departed Sons, Husbands and Brothers. The patient, trusting Descendants of Africa's Clime have dyed the ground with blood, in defense of the Union, and Democracy. Men, too, your Excellency, who know in a measure the cruelties of the Iron heel of oppression, which in years gone by, the very Power their blood is now being spilled to maintain, ever ground them to the dust.

But When the war trumpet sounded o'er the land, when men knew not the Friend from the Traitor, the Black man laid his life at the Altar of the Nation — and he was refused. When the arms of the Union were beaten, in the first year of the War, and the Executive called more food for its ravaging maw, again the black man begged the privilege of aiding his country in her need, to be again refused.

And now he is in the War, and how has he conducted himself? Let their dusky forms rise up, out the mires of James Island, and give the answer. Let the rich mould around Wagner's parapets be upturned, and there will be found an Eloquent answer. Obedient and patient and Solid as a wall as are they. All we lack is a paler hue and a better acquaintance with the Alphabet.

Now your Excellency, we have done a Soldier's Duty. Why Can't we have a Solider's pay? You caution the Rebel Chieftain, that the United States knows no distinction in her Soldiers. She insists on having all her Soldiers of whatever creed or Color, to be treated according to the usages of War. Now if the United States exacts uniformity of treatment of her Soldiers from the Insurgents, would it not be well and consistent to set the example herself by paying all her Soldiers alike?

We of this Regt. were not enlisted under any "contraband" act. But we do not wish to be understood as rating our Service of more Value to the Government than the service of the ex-slave. Their Service is undoubtedly worth much to the Nation, but Congress made express provision touching their case, as slaves freed by military necessity, and assuming the Government to be their temporary Guardian.

Not so with us. Freemen by birth and consequently having the advantage of thinking and acting for ourselves so far as the laws would allow us, we do not consider ourselves fit subject for the Contraband act.

We appeal to you, Sir, as the Executive of the Nation, to have us justly Dealt with. The Regt. do pray that they be assured their service will be fairly appreciated by paying them as American Soldiers, not as menial hirelings. Black men, you may well know, are poor; three dollars per month for a year will supply their needy Wives and little ones with fuel. If you, as Chief magistrate of the Nation, will assure us of our whole pay, we are content. Our Patriotism, our enthusiasm will have a new impetus, to exert our energy more and more to aid our Country. Not that our hearts ever flagged in Devotion, spite the evident apathy displayed in our behalf, but We feel as though our Country spurned us, now that we are sworn to serve her. Please give this a moment's attention.

James Henry Gooding

———— 4.23 ————

'THE LONGOR YOU KEEP MY CHILD FROM ME THE LONGOR YOU WILL HAVE TO BURN IN HELL AND THE QWICER YOULL GET THEIR'
Private Spotswood Rice

Alongside free blacks, many of the emancipated slaves chose to join the ranks of the Union army as well. Even more than northern free blacks, those former slaves who served often fought for reasons that were intensely personal, rather than for the broader designs of the nation. Of course, many longed to contribute to a war they saw as a means of achieving freedom. But a primary motivation was the hunt for or rescue of family members. And for years following the war, this quest — by whatever means available — to find and reunite families ripped apart by slave economics would be the all-encompassing mission for many freed slaves. Private Spotswood Rice, a former slave from Glasgow, Missouri, was one such person. He joined the Union army in February 1864, and months later prepared to march on Glasgow with the North's forces. In

these September 1864 letters, before the planned movement, Rice wrote to his daughters, still captive, and their owner. In the letters, he reassures his daughters that he is on his way to claim their freedom, and warns the woman who holds them in bondage of the wrath headed her way.

A. Spotswood Rice's letter to his daughters

My Children

I take my pen in hand to rite you A few lines to let you know that I have not forgot you and that I want to see you as bad as ever now my Dear Children. I want you to be contented with whatever may be your lots. be assured that I will have you if it cost me my life. on the 28th of the mounth. 8 hundred White and 8 hundred blacke solders expects to start up the rivore to Glasgow and above there thats to be jeneraled by a jeneral that will give me both of you. when they Come I expect to be with, them and expect to get you both in return. Dont be uneasy my children. I expect to have you. If Diggs dont give you up this Government will and I feel confident that I will get you. Your Miss Kaitty said that I tried to steal you. But I'll let her know that god never intended for man to steal his own flesh and blood. If I had no confidence in God I could have confidence in her. But as it is If I ever had any Confidence in her I have none now and never expect to have. And I want her to remember if she meets me with ten thousand soldiers she will meet her enemy. I once thought that I had some respect for them but now my respects is worn out and have no sympathy for Slaveholders. And as for her cristianantty I expect the Devil has Such in hell. You tell her from me that She is the first Christian that I ever hard say that a man could Steal his own child especially out of human bondage

You can tell her that She can hold to you as long as she can. I never would expect to ask her again to let you come to me because I know that the devil has got her hot set againsts that that is write. now my Dear children I am a going to close my letter to you. Give my love to all enquiring friends. tell them all that we are well and want to see them very much and

Corra and Mary receive the greater part of it you sefves and dont think hard of us not sending you any thing. I you father have a plenty for you when I see you. Spott & Noah sends their love to both of you. Oh! My Dear children how I do want to see you

B. Spotswood Rice's letter to his daughter's owner

I received a letter from Cariline telling me that you say I tried to steal to plunder my child away from you. now I want you to understand that mary is my Child and she is a God given rite of my own and you may hold on to her as long as you can but I want you to rembor this one thing that the longor you keep my Child from me the longor you will have to burn in hell and the qwicer youll get their. for we are now making up a bout one thoughsand blacke troops to Come up tharough and wont to come through Glasgow and when we come wo be to Copperhood rabbels and to the Slaveholding rebbels for we dont expect to leave them there root neor branch. but we thinke how ever that we that have Children in the hands of you devels we will trie your vertues the day that we enter Glasgow. I want you to understand kittey diggs that where ever you and I meets we are enmays to each orthere. I offered once to pay you forty dollers for my own Child but I am glad now that you did not accept it. Just hold on now as long as you can and the worse it will be for you. you never in you life befor I came down hear did you give Children any thing not eny thing whatever not even a dollers worth of expencs. now you call my children your property. not so with me. my Children is my own and I expect to get them and when I get ready to come after mary I will have bout a powrer and autherity to bring hear away and to exacute vengencens on them that holds my Child. you will then know how to talke to me. I will assure

that and you will know how to talk rite too. I want you now to just hold on to hear if you want to. iff your conchosence tells thats the road go that road and what it will brig you to kittey digs. I have no fears about geting mary out of your hands. this whole Government gives chear to me and you cannot help your self. Spotswood Rice

————— 4.24 —————

THE END OF SLAVERY
The Thirteenth Amendment

Perhaps the most significant act undertaken by a "lame-duck" Congress in American history was the passage of the 13th Amendment. President Lincoln, goaded on by other abolitionist Republicans, put the issue of a constitutional amendment to ban slavery at the forefront of his 1864 reelection campaign. As *The New York Times* had soberly noted following the Emancipation Proclamation, Lincoln freed only the South's slaves and did so only by the power of a war order. Thus, to end slavery nationally and permanently, Congress would have to act.

After Lincoln won reelection, he pushed the lame-duck Congress to immediately amend the Constitution rather than wait for the members-elect to take their seats in the next session. The leadership agreed, and on January 31, 1865, with the Confederacy's defeat looming, Congress passed the 13th Amendment. Its simplicity provides an ironic end to 200 years' worth of seemingly complicated arguments for and against slavery.

Amendment XIII

Section 1. Neither slavery nor involuntary servitude, except as a punishment for crime whereof the party shall have been duly convicted, shall exist within the United States, or any place subject to their jurisdiction.

Section 2. Congress shall have power to enforce this article by appropriate legislation.

5

Forty Acres and a Mule:
RECONSTRUCTION AND ITS AFTERMATH

'IF HE KNOWS ENOUGH TO BE HANGED, HE KNOWS ENOUGH TO VOTE'
Frederick Douglass

The Emancipation Proclamation brought the abolitionist movement to a fork in the road. Many people, led by William Lloyd Garrison, considered the battle won and urged the Anti-Slavery Society to dissolve itself. But Frederick Douglass harshly disagreed. To Douglass, the fight for the end of slavery was but the beginning of a larger war. At the Society's convention in December 1863, Douglass gave an impassioned speech to this effect. He urged the delegates to understand "our work will not be done until the colored man is admitted a full member in good and regular standing into the American body politic." The end of slavery, Douglass argued, was merely the beginning of the fight for black suffrage. And in that struggle, he predicted, "we shall see the trying time in this country." Indeed, as Reconstruction began, a central argument turned on whether African Americans should be guaranteed the right to vote in the South.

… A mightier work than abolition of slavery now looms up before the Abolitionist. This Society was organized, if I remember rightly, for two distinct objects; one was the emancipation of the slave, and the other the elevation of the colored people. When you have taken the chains off the slave, as I believe we shall do, we shall find a harder resistance to the second purpose of this great association than we have found even upon slavery itself. …

My respected friend, Mr. Purvis, called attention to the existence of prejudice against color in this country. This gives me great cause for apprehension, if not for alarm. I am afraid of this powerful element of prejudice against color. While it exists, I want the voice of the American Anti-Slavery Society to be continually protesting, continually exposing it. While it can be said that in this most anti-slavery city in the Northern States our Union, in the city of Philadelphia, the city of Brotherly Love, in the city of churches, the city of piety, that the most genteel and respectable colored lady or gentleman may be kicked out of your commonest street car, we are in danger of a compromise. While it can be said that black men, fighting bravely for this country, are asked to take $7 per month, while the government lays down as a rule or criterion of pay a complexional one, we are in danger of a compromise. While to be radical is to be unpopular, we are in danger of a compromise. While we have a large minority, called Democratic, in every State of the North, we have a powerful nucleus for a most infernal re-action in favor of slavery. I know it is said that we have recently achieved vast political victories. I am glad of it. I value those victories, however, more for what they have prevented than for what they have actually accomplished. I should have been doubly sad at seeing any one of these States wheel into line with the Peace Democracy. But, however it may be in the State of Pennsylvania, I know that you may look for abolition in the creed of any party in New York with a microscope, and you will not find a single line of anti-slavery (?) there. The victories Union victories, victories to save the Union in such ways as the country may devise to save it. But whatever may have been the meaning of the majorities in regard to the Union, we know one thing, that the minorities at least, mean slavery. They mean submission. They mean the degradation of the colored man. They mean everything but open rebellion against the Federal government in the South. But the mob, the rioters in the city of New York, convert that city into a hell, and its lower orders into demons, and dash out the brains of little children against the curbstones; and they mean anything and everything that the Devil exacts at their hand. While we had in this State a majority of but 15,000 over this pro-slavery Democratic party, they have a mighty minority, a dangerous minority. Keep in mind when these minorities were gotten. Powerful as they are, they were gotten when slavery, with bloody hands, was stabbing at the very heart of the nation itself. With all that disadvantage, they have piled up powerful minorities.

We have work to do, friends and fellow-citizens, to look after these minorities. The day that shall see Jeff Davis fling down his Montgomery Constitution, and call home his Generals, will be the most trying day to the virtue of this people that this country has ever seen. When the slaveholders shall give up the contest, and ask for re-admission into the Union, then, as Mr. Wilson has told us, we shall see the trying time in this country. Your Democracy will clamor for peace and for restoring the old order of things, because that old order of things was the life of the Democratic party. "You do take away mine house, when you take away the prop that sustains my house," and the support of the Democratic party we all know to be slavery. ...

I have said that our work will not be done until the colored are admitted a full member in good and regular standing into the American body politic. Men have very nice ideas about the body politic where I traveled; and they don't like the idea of having the negro in the body politic. He may remain in this country, for he will be useful as a laborer, valuable perhaps in time of trouble as a helper; but to make him a full complete citizen, a legal voter, that would be contaminating the body politic. I was a little curious, some years ago, to find out what sort of a thing this body politic was; and I was very anxious to know especially about what amount of baseness, brutality, coarseness, ignorance, bestiality, could find its way into the body politic; and I was not long in finding it out. I took my stand near the little hole through which the body politic put its votes. And first among the mob, I saw Ignorance, unable to read its vote, asking me to read it, by the way, depositing its vote in the body politic. Next I saw a man stepping up to the body politic, casting in his vote, having a black eye, and another one ready to be blacked, having been engaged in a street fight. I saw again, Pat, fresh from the Emerald Isle, with the delightful brogue peculiar to him, stepping up — not walking, but leaning upon the arms of two of friends, unable to stand, passing into the body politic! I came to the conclusion that this body politic was, after all, not quite so pure as the representation of its friends would lead us to believe.

I know it will be said that I ask you to make the black man a voter in the South. Yet you are for having brutality and ignorance introduced into the ballot-box. It is said that the colored man is ignorant, and therefore he shall not vote. In saying this, you lay down a rule for the black man that apply to no other class of your citizens. I will hear nothing of degradation nor of ignorance against the black man. If he knows enough to be hanged, he knows enough to vote. If he knows an honest man from a thief, he knows much more than some of our white voters. If he knows as much when sober as an Irishman knows when drunk, he knows enough to vote. If he knows enough to take up arms in defence of this government, and bare his breast to the storm of rebel artillery, he knows enough to vote.

Away with this talk of the want of knowledge on the part of the Negro! I am about as big a negro as you will find anywhere about town; and any that does not believe I know enough to vote, let him try it. I think I can convince him that I do. Let him run for office in my district, and solicit my vote, and I will show him.

All I ask, however, in regard to the blacks, is that whatever rule you adopt, whether of intelligence or wealth, as the condition of voting, you should apply it equally to the black man. Do that, and I am satisfied, and eternal justice is satisfied. Liberty, fraternity, equality, are satisfied; and the country will move on harmoniously.

Mr. President, I have a patriotic argument in favor of insisting upon the immediate enfranchisement of the slaves of the South; and it is this. When this rebellion shall have been put down, when the arms shall have fallen from the guilty hand of traitors, you will need the friendship of the slaves of the South, of those millions there. Four or five million men are not of inconsiderable importance at any time; but they will be doubly important when you come to reorganize and reestablish republican institutions in the South. Will you mock those bondmen by breaking their chains with one hand, and with the other giving their rebel masters the elective franchise and robbing them of theirs? ...

For twenty-five years, Mr. President, you know that when I got as far south as Philadelphia, I felt that I was rubbing against my prison wall, and could not go any further. I dared not go over yonder into Delaware. Twenty years ago, when I attended the first Decade meeting of this Society, as I came along the vales and hills of Gettysburg, my good friends; the anti-slavery people along there, warned me to remain in the house during the daytime and travel in the night, lest I should be kidnapped,

and carried over into Maryland. My good friend Dr. Fussell was one of the number who did not think it safe for me to attend an anti-slavery meeting along borders of this State. I can go down there now. I have been to Washington to see the President; and as you were not there, perhaps you may like to know how the President of the United States received a black man at the White House. I will tell you how he received me — just as you have seen one gentleman receive another!; with a hand and a voice well-balanced between a kind cordiality and a respectful reserve. I tell I felt big there. ...

Now you will want to know how I was impressed by him. I will tell you that, too. He impressed me as being just what every one of you have been in the habit of calling him — an honest man. I never met with a man who, on the first blush, impressed me more entirely with his sincerity, with his devotion to his country, and with his determination to save it at all hazards. He told me (I think he did me more honor than I deserve), that I had made a little speech somewhere in New York, and it had got into the papers, and among the things I had said was this: That if I were called upon to state what I regarded as the most sad and most disheartening feature in our present political and military situation, it would not be the various disasters experienced by our armies and our navies, on flood and field, but it would be the tardy, hesitating and vacillating policy of the President of the United States; and the President said to me, "Mr. Douglass, I have been charged with being tardy, and the like;" and he went on, and partly admitted that he might seem slow; but he said, "I am charged with vacillating; but, Mr. Douglass, I do not think that charge can be sustained; I think it cannot be shown that when I have once taken a position, I have ever retreated from it." That I regarded as the most significant point in what he said during our interview. I told him that he had been somewhat slow in proclaiming equal protection to our colored soldiers and prisoners; and he said that the country needed talking up to that point. He hesitated in regard to it when he felt that the country was not ready for it. He knew that the colored man throughout this country was a despised man, a hated man, and he knew that if he at first came out with such a proclamation, all the hatred which is poured on the head of the negro race would be visited on his Administration. He said that there was preparatory work needed, and that that preparatory work had been done. And he added, "Remember this, Mr. Douglass; remember Milliken's Bend, Port Hudson, and Fort Wagner are recent events; these were necessary to prepare the way for this very proclamation of mine." I thought it was reasonable; but I came to the conclusion that while Abraham Lincoln will not go down to posterity as Abraham the Great, or as Abraham the Wise, or as Abraham the Eloquent, although he is all three, wise, great, and eloquent, he will go down to posterity, if the country is saved, as Honest Abraham; and going thus, his name may be written anywhere in this wide world of ours side by side with that of Washington, without disparaging the latter.

But we are not to be saved by the captain this time, but by the crew. We are not to be saved by Abraham Lincoln, but by that power behind the throne, greater than the throne itself. You and I and all of us have this matter in hand. Men talk about saving the Union, and restoring the Union as it was. They delude themselves with the miserable idea that that old Union can be brought to life again. That old Union, whose canonized bones we so quietly inurned under the shattered walls of Sumter, can never come to life again. It is dead, and you cannot put life into it. The first shot fired at the walls of Sumter caused it to fall as dead as the body of Caesar when stabbed by Brutus. We do not want it. We have outlived the old Union. We had outlived it long before the rebellion came to tell us — I mean the Union under the old pro-slavery interpretation of it — and had become ashamed of it. The South hated it with our anti-slavery interpretation, and the North hated it with the Southern interpretation of its requirements. We had already come to think with horror of the idea of being called upon here in our churches and literary societies, to take up arms and go down South, and pour the leaden death into the breasts of the slaves, in case they should rise for liberty; and the better part of the people did not mean to do it. They shuddered at the idea of so sacrilegious a crime. They had already become utterly disgusted with the idea of playing the part of bloodhounds for the slave-masters, and watch-dogs for the plantations. They had come to detest the principle upon which the slaveholding States had a larger representation in Congress than the free States. They had come to think that the little finger of dear old John Brown was worth more to the world than all the slaveholders in Virginia put together. What business, then, have we to fight for the old Union? We are not fighting for it. We are fighting for something incomparably better than the old Union. We are fighting for unity; unity of object, unity of institutions, in which there shall be no North, no South, no East, no West, no black, no white, but a solidarity of the nation, making every slave free, and every free man a voter.

———— 5.2 ————

'I WILL INDEED BE YOUR MOSES'
Andrew Johnson

The period known as Reconstruction, in which the U.S. struggled to reincorporate the seceding states, and do so without a slave labor system, has been assigned many different starting points. One is the end of 1863, when President Lincoln issued his Proclamation on Amnesty and Reconstruction. This announcement laid out the rules by which the Confederates would be reincorporated into the Union. It offered conquered rebel states broad freedom in reconstructing their local government on all but one point: They had to abolish slavery. The reaction in both the North and South was mixed. Many received the policy warmly, but others hated it. Lincoln had conspicuously ignored the question of whether or not blacks should be guaranteed the right to vote in the southern states, and thereby angered some abolitionists.

Andrew Johnson emerged as one of those standing firmly behind the order. When the Union captured Nashville in 1862, Lincoln appointed Johnson military governor of Tennessee. He thus presided over early Reconstruction there, and was believed to be a "radical" who wanted the southern slaveholders' backs broken and the black population embraced. It would later become clear, however, that Johnson, a self-described champion of white yeomanry, was less concerned about the welfare of the slaves than he was about destroying the slaveocracy — as he famously declared, "Damn the Negroes, I am fighting those traitorous aristocrats, their masters." In the fall of 1864, however, he was still styling himself a champion of African Americans, as in this October address, reported by the *Nashville Times and True Union*.

Colored Men of Nashville: You have all heard of the President's Proclamation, by which he announces to the world that the slaves in a large portion of the seceded States were thenceforth and forever free. For certain reasons, which seemed wise to the President, the benefits of that Proclamation did not extend to you or your native State. Many of you consequently were left in bondage. The task-master's scourge was not yet broken, and the fetters still galled your limbs. Gradually this inequity has been passing away; but the hour has come when the last vestiges of it must be removed. Consequently, I, too, with out reference to the President or any person, have a proclamation to make; and, standing here upon the steps of the Capitol, with the past history of the State to witness, the present condition to guide, and its future to encourage me, I, Andrew Johnson, do hereby proclaim freedom, full, broad and unconditional, to every man in Tennessee!

I invoke the colored people to be orderly and law-abiding, but at the same time let them assert their rights, and if traitors and ruffians attack them, while in the discharge of their duties, let them defend themselves as all men have a right to do.

I am no agrarian. I respect the rights of property acquired by honest labor. But I say, nevertheless, that if the great farm of Mark Cockrill, who gave $25,000 to Jeff. Davis's Confederacy, were divided into small farms and sold to fifteen or twenty honest farmers, society would be improved, Nashville mechanics and tradesmen would be enriched, the State would have more good citizens, and our city would have a much better market than it now has.

I am no agrarian, but if the princely plantation of Wm. G. Harding, who boasted that he had disbursed over $5,000,000 for the rebel Confederacy, were parcelled out among fifty loyal, industrious farmers, it would be a blessing to our noble Commonwealth. I speak tonight as a citizen of Tennessee. I am here on my own soil, and mean to remain here and fight this great battle of freedom through to the end. Loyal men, from this day forward, are to be the controllers of Tennessee's grand and sublime destiny, and Rebels must be dumb. We will not listen to their counsels. Nashville is not the place for them to hold their meetings. Let them gather their treasonable conclaves elsewhere; among their friends in the Confederacy. They shall not hold their conspiracies in Nashville.

The representatives of this corrupt (and if you will permit me almost to swear a little) this damnable aristocracy, taunt us with our desire to see justice done, and charge us with favoring negro equality. Of all living men they should be the last to mouth that phrase; and even when uttering in their hearing, it should cause their cheeks to tinge and burn with shame. Negro equality, indeed! Why pass, any day, along the sidewalks of High Street where these aristocrats more particularly dwell — these aristocrats, whose sons are now in the bands of guerillas and cutthroats who prowl and rob and murder around our city — pass by their dwellings, I say, and you will see as many mulatto as negro children, the former bearing an unmistakable resemblance to their aristocratic owners!

Colored men of Tennessee! This too shall cease! Your wives and daughters shall no longer be dragged into a concubinage, compared to which polygamy is a virtue, to satisfy the brutal lusts of slaveholders and overseers! Henceforth the sanctity of God's holy law of marriage shall be respected in your persons, and the great State of Tennessee shall no more give her sanction to your degradation and your shame!

"Thank God! thank God!" came from the lips of a thousand women, who in their own persons had experienced the hellish iniquity of the man-seller's code. "Thank God!" fervently echoed the fathers, husbands, brothers of those women.

And if the law protects you in the possession of your wives and children, if the law shields those whom you hold dear from the unlawful grasp of lust, will you endeavor to be true to yourselves, and shun, as it were death itself, the path of lewdness, crime and vice?

"We will! we will!" cried the assembled thousands; and joining up in a sublime and tearful enthusiasm, another mighty shout went up to heaven.

"Look at this vast crowd of colored people," continued the Governor, "and reflecting through what a storm of persecution and obloquy they are compelled to pass, I am almost induced to wish that, as in the days of old, a Moses might arise who should lead them safely to their promised land of freedom and happiness."

"You are our Moses," shouted several voices and the exclamation was caught up and cheered until the Capitol rung again.

"God," continued the speaker, "no doubt has prepared somewhere an instrument for the great work He designs to perform in behalf of this outraged people, and in due time your leader will come forth; your Moses will be revealed to you."

"We want no Moses but you!" again shouted the crowd.

"Well, then," replied the speaker, "humble and unworthy as I am, if no other better shall be found, I will indeed be your Moses, and lead you through the Red Sea of war and bondage, to a fairer future of liberty and peace. I speak now as one who feels the world his country, and all who love equal rights his friends. I speak, too, as a citizen of Tennessee. I am here on my own soil, and here I mean to stay and fight this great battle of truth and jus-

tice to a triumphant end. Rebellion and slavery shall, by God's good help, no longer pollute our State. Loyal men, whether white or black, shall alone control her destinies: and when this strife in which we are all engaged is past, I trust, I know, we shall have a better state of things, and shall all rejoice that honest labor reaps the fruit of its own industry, and that every man has a fair chance in the race of life."

———— 5.3 ————

THE LAST SPEECH
Abraham Lincoln

Louisiana was the first state to attempt re-entry into the Union via the rules set by President Lincoln's 1863 Reconstruction plan. There, the order's neglect of rights for African Americans drew substantial criticism from "Radical Republicans" — those, like Andrew Johnson, who preferred an unforgiving stance towards the defeated Confederate states. Led by abolitionists, these radicals pushed black suffrage, even at the cost of damaging southern will to reintegrate into the Union. In the last public address he gave before his assassination, Lincoln defended the negotiated terms of Louisiana's re-entry, and urged a more compromising posture towards southerners. The radicals' aims, he argues below, would never be accomplished without some compromise. However, in a notable concession, Lincoln finally announces his qualified support for black suffrage.

We meet this evening, not it sorrow, but in gladness of heart. The evacuation of Petersburg and Richmond, and the surrender of the principal insurgent army, give hope of a righteous and speedy peace whose joyous expression can not be restrained. In the midst of this, however, He from whom all blessings flow, must not be forgotten. A call for a national thanksgiving is being prepared, and will be duly promulgated. Nor must those whose harder part gives us the cause of rejoicing, be overlooked. Their honors must not be parcelled out with others. I myself was near the front, and had the high pleasure of transmitting much of the good news to you; but no part of the honor, for plan or execution, is mine. To Gen. Grant, his skillful officers, and brave men, all belongs. The gallant Navy stood ready, but was not in reach to take active part.

By these recent successes the re-inauguration of the national authority — reconstruction — which has had a large share of thought from the first, is pressed much more closely upon our attention. It is fraught with great difficulty. Unlike a case of a war between independent nations, there is no authorized organ for us to treat with. No one man has authority to give up the rebellion for any other man. We simply must begin with, and mould from, disorganized and discordant elements. Nor is it a small additional embarrassment that we, the loyal people, differ among ourselves as to the mode, manner, and means of reconstruction.

As a general rule, I abstain from reading the reports of attacks upon myself, wishing not to be provoked by that to which I can not properly offer an answer. In spite of this precaution, however, it comes to my knowledge that I am much censured for some supposed agency in setting up, and seeking to sustain, the new State government of Louisiana. In this I have done just so much as, and no more than, the public knows. In the Annual Message of Dec. 1863 and accompanying Proclamation, I presented a plan of re-construction (as the phrase goes) which, I promised, if adopted by any State, should be acceptable to, and sustained by, the Executive government of the nation. I distinctly stated that this was not the only plan which might possibly be acceptable; and I also distinctly protested that the Executive claimed no right to say when, or whether members should be admitted to seats in Congress from such States. This plan was, in advance, submitted to the then Cabinet, and distinctly approved by every member of it. One of them suggested that I should then, and in that connection, apply the Emancipation Proclamation to the theretofore excepted parts of Virginia and Louisiana; that I should drop the suggestion about apprenticeship for freed-people, and that I should omit the protest against my own power, in regard to the admission of members to Congress; but even he approved

every part and parcel of the plan which has since been employed or touched by the action of Louisiana. The new constitution of Louisiana, declaring emancipation for the whole State, practically applies the Proclamation to the part previously excepted. It does not adopt apprenticeship for freed-people; and it is silent, as it could not well be otherwise, about the admission of members to Congress. So that, as it applies to Louisiana, every member of the Cabinet fully approved the plan. The message went to Congress, and I received many commendations of the plan, written and verbal; and not a single objection to it, from any professed emancipationist, came to my knowledge, until after the news reached Washington that the people of Louisiana had begun to move in accordance with it. From about July 1862, I had corresponded with different persons, supposed to be interested, seeking a reconstruction of a State government for Louisiana. When the message of 1863, with the plan before mentioned, reached New-Orleans, Gen. Banks wrote me that he was confident the people, with his military co-operation, would reconstruct, substantially on that plan. I wrote him, and some of them to try it; they tried it, and the result is known. Such only has been my agency in getting up the Louisiana government. As to sustaining it, my promise is out, as before stated. But, as bad promises are better broken than kept, I shall treat this as a bad promise, and break it, whenever I shall be convinced that keeping it is adverse to the public interest. But I have not yet been so convinced.

I have been shown a letter on this subject, supposed to be an able one, in which the writer expresses regret that my mind has not seemed to be definitely fixed on the question whether the seceded States, so called, are in the Union or out of it. It would perhaps, add astonishment to his regret, were he to learn that since I have found professed Union men endeavoring to make that question, I have purposely forborne any public expression upon it. As appears to me that question has not been, nor yet is, a practically material one, and that any discussion of it, while it thus remains practically immaterial, could have no effect other than the mischievous one of dividing our friends. As yet, whatever it may hereafter become, that question is bad, as the basis of a controversy, and good for nothing at all — a merely pernicious abstraction.

We all agree that the seceded States, so called, are out of their proper practical relation with the Union; and that the sole object of the government, civil and military, in regard to those States is to again get them into that proper practical relation. I believe it is not only possible, but in fact, easier to do this, without deciding, or even considering, whether these States have ever been out of the Union, than with it. Finding themselves safely at home, it would be utterly immaterial whether they had ever been abroad. Let us all join in doing the acts necessary to restoring the proper practical relations between these States and the Union; and each forever after, innocently indulge his own opinion whether, in doing the acts, he brought the States from without, into the Union, or only gave them proper assistance, they never having been out of it.

The amount of constituency, so to speak, on which the new Louisiana government rests, would be more satisfactory to all, if it contained fifty, thirty, or even twenty thousand, instead of only about twelve thousand, as it does. It is also unsatisfactory to some that the elective franchise is not given to the colored man. I would myself prefer that it were now conferred on the very intelligent, and on those who serve our cause as soldiers. Still the question is not whether the Louisiana government, as it stands, is quite all that is desirable. The question is, "Will it be wiser to take it as it is, and help to improve it; or to reject, and disperse it?" "Can Louisiana be brought into proper practical relation with the Union sooner by sustaining, or by discarding her new State government?"

Some twelve thousand voters in the heretofore slave-state of Louisiana have sworn allegiance to the Union, assumed to be the rightful political power of the State, held elections, organized a State government, adopted a free-state constitution, giving the benefit of public schools equally to black and white, and empowering the Legislature to confer the elective franchise upon the colored man. Their Legislature has already voted to ratify the constitutional amendment recently passed by Congress, abolishing slavery throughout the nation. These twelve thousand persons are thus fully committed to the Union, and to perpetual freedom in the state — committed to the very things, and nearly all the things the nation wants — and they ask the nation's recognition and its assistance to make good their committal. Now, if we reject, and spurn them, we do our utmost to disorganize and disperse them. We in effect say to the white men "You are worthless, or worse — we will neither help you, nor be helped by you." To the blacks we say "This cup of liberty which these, your old masters, hold to your lips, we will dash from you, and leave you to the chances of gathering the spilled and scattered contents in some vague and undefined when, where, and how." If this course, discouraging and paralyzing both white and black, has any tendency to bring Louisiana into proper practical relations with the Union, I have, so far, been unable to perceive it. If, on the contrary, we recognize, and sustain the new government of Louisiana, the converse of all this is made true. We encourage the hearts, and nerve the arms of the twelve thousand to adhere to their work, and argue for it, and proselyte for it, and fight for it, and feed it, and grow it, and ripen it to a complete success.

The colored man too, in seeing all united for him, is inspired with vigilance, and energy, and daring, to the same end. Grant that he desires the elective franchise, will he not attain it sooner by saving the already advanced steps toward it, than by running backward over them? Concede that the new government of Louisiana is only to what it should be as the egg is to the fowl, shall we sooner have the fowl by hatching the egg than by smashing it? Again, if we reject Louisiana, we also reject one vote in favor of the proposed amendment to the national Constitution. To meet this proposition, it has been argued that no more than three-fourths of those States which have not attempted secession are necessary to validly ratify the amendment. I do not commit myself against this, further than to say that such a ratification would be questionable, and sure to be persistently questioned; while a ratification by three-fourths of all the States would be unquestioned and unquestionable.

I repeat the question. "Can Louisiana be brought into proper practical relation with the Union sooner by sustaining or by discarding her new State Government?"

What has been said of Louisiana will apply generally to other States. And yet so great peculiarities pertain to each state, and such important and sudden changes occur in the same state; and, withal, so new and unprecedented is the whole case, that no exclusive, and inflexible plan can safely be prescribed as to details and collaterals. Such exclusive, and inflexible plan, would surely become a new entanglement. Important principles may, and must, be inflexible.

In the present "situation" as the phrase goes, it may be my duty to make some new announcement to the people of the South. I am considering, and shall not fail to act, when satisfied that action will be proper.

─────── 5.4 ───────

'IN THE MATTER OF GOVERNMENT ... NO NOTICE SHOULD BE TAKEN OF THE COLOR OF MEN'
The National Convention of Colored Men

In the North, the onset of Reconstruction meant renewed efforts to secure civil and political rights for blacks. Many of the laws passed at the century's outset remained on the books, circumscribing the world free blacks could navigate. And black voting rights throughout the North and South were, at best, in question. In October 1864, 145 free black men, many of whom would be representa-

tives in state-level politics just a few years later, gathered in Syracuse, New York, for a national convention to discuss strategies and goals concerning the civil rights of black people. They founded the National Equal Rights League, with chapters in each state, to advance the cause. And they issued the following address, articulating their post-emancipation demands for the rights of African Americans. The address reflects the ongoing intellectual transition from advocating abolition to demanding civil rights (and bears the rhetorical imprint of its believed author, Frederick Douglass). Equating slavery with "prejudice against men on account of their color," the address declares, "The one controls the South and the other controls the North. Both are original sources of power, and generate peculiar sentiments, ideas, and laws concerning us." The delegates were convinced that the Democratic Party aimed to re-institute slavery, and the address condemns Democrats for that. But, more importantly, it also chastises Republicans who had once supported abolition but, having won that fight, were reluctant to join a civil rights struggle.

The new civil rights activism reaped dividends in northern states quickly. The following May, Massachusetts passed the nation's first-ever law banning discrimination based on race in public accommodations. Later, Illinois repealed a law barring blacks from entering the state, and several northern states around this time desegregated public transportation.

... When great and terrible calamities are abroad in the land, men are said to learn righteousness. It would be a mark of unspeakable national depravity, if neither the horrors of this war, nor the dawning prospect of peace, should soften the heart, and dispose the American people to renounce and forsake their evil policy towards the colored race. Assuming the contrary, we deem this a happily chosen hour for calling your attention to our cause. We know that the human mind is so constituted, that all postponement of duty, all refusal to go forward when the right path is once made plain, is dangerous. ...

While joyfully recognizing the vast advances made by our people in popular consideration, and the apparent tendency of events in our favor, we cannot conceal from ourselves, and would not conceal from you, the fact that there are many and powerful influences, constantly operating, intended and calculated to defeat our just hopes, prolong the existence of the source of all our ills, — the system of slavery, —strengthen the slave power, darken the conscience of the North, intensify popular prejudice against color, multiply unequal and discriminating laws, augment the burdens long borne by our race, consign to oblivion the deeds of heroism which have distinguished the colored soldier, deny and despise his claims to the gratitude of his country, scout his pretensions to American citizenship, establish the selfish idea that this is exclusively the white man's country, pass unheeded all the lessons taught by these four years of fire and sword, undo all that has been done towards our freedom and elevation, take the musket from the shoulders of our brave black soldiers, deny them the constitutional right to keep and bear arms, exclude them from the ballot-box where they now possess that right, prohibit the extension of it to those who do not possess it, over-awe free speech in and out of Congress, obstruct the right of peaceably assembling, reenact the Fugitive-slave Bill, revive the internal slave-trade, break up all diplomatic relations with Hayti and Liberia, reopen our broad territories to the introduction of slavery, reverse the entire order and tendency of the events of the last three years, and postpone indefinitely that glorious deliverance from bondage, Which for our sake, and for the sake of the future unity, permanent peace, and highest welfare of all concerned, we had fondly hoped and believed was even now at the door.

In surveying our possible future, so full of interest at this moment, since it may bring to us all the blessings of equal liberty, or all the woes of slavery and continued social degradation, you will not blame us if we manifest anxiety in regard to the position of our recognized friends, as well as that of our open and declared enemies; for our cause may suffer even more from the injudicious concessions and weakness of our friends, than from the machinations and power of our enemies. The weakness of our friends is strength to our foes. When the "Anti-slavery Standard," representing the American Anti-slavery Society, denies that that society asks for the enfranchisement of colored men, and the "Liberator" apologizes for excluding the colored men of Louisiana from the ballot-box, they injure us more vitally than all the ribald jests of the whole proslavery press.

Again: had, for instance, the present Administration, at the beginning of the war, boldly planted itself upon the doctrine of human equality as taught in the Declaration of Independence; proclaimed liberty to all the slaves in all the Slave States; armed every colored man, previously a slave or a freeman, who would or could fight under the loyal flag; recognized black men as soldiers of the Republic; avenged the first act of violence upon colored prisoners, in contravention of the laws of war; sided with the radical emancipation party in Maryland and Missouri; stood by its antislavery generals, instead of casting them aside, — history would never have had to record the scandalous platform adopted at Chicago, nor the immeasurable horrors of Fort Pillow. The weakness and hesitation of our friends, where promptness and vigor were required, have invited the contempt and rigor of our enemies. Seeing that, while perilling every thing for the protection and security of our country, our country did not think itself bound to protect and secure us, the rebels felt a license to treat us as outlaws. Seeing that our Government did not treat us as men, they did not feel bound to treat us as soldiers. It is, therefore, not the malignity of enemies alone we have to fear, but the deflection from the straight line of principle by those who are known throughout the world as our special friends. We may survive the arrows of the known negro-haters of our country; but woe to the colored race when their champions fail to demand, from any reason, equal liberty in every respect!

We have spoken of the existence of powerful re-actionary forces arrayed against us, and of the objects to which they tend. What are these mighty forces? and through what agencies do they operate and reach us? They are many; but we shall detain by no tedious enumeration. The first and most powerful is slavery; and the second, which may be said to be the shadow of slavery, is prejudice against men on account of their color. The one controls the South, and the other controls the North. Both are original sources of power, and generate peculiar sentiments, ideas, and laws concerning us. The agents of these two evil influences are various: but the chief are, first, the Democratic party; and, second, the Republican party. The Democratic party belongs to slavery; and the Republican party is largely under the power of prejudice against color. While gratefully recognizing a vast difference in our favor in the character and composition of the Republican party, and regarding the accession to power of the Democratic party as the heaviest calamity that could befall us in the present juncture of affairs, it cannot be disguised, that, while that party is our bitterest enemy, and is positively and actively re-actionary, the Republican party is negatively and passively so in its tendency. What we have to fear from these two parties, — looking to the future, and especially to the settlement of our present national troubles, — is, alas! only too obvious. The intentions, principles, and policy of both organizations, through their platforms, and the antecedents and the recorded utterances of the men who stand upon their respective platforms, teach us what to expect at their hands, and what kind of a future they are carving out for us, and for the country which they propose to govern. Without using the word "slavery," or "slaves," or "slaveholders," the Democratic party has nonetheless declared, in its platform, its purpose to be the endless perpetuation of slavery. Under the apparently harmless verbiage, "private rights," "basis of the Federal Union," and under the language employed in denouncing the Federal Administration for "disregarding the Constitution in every part," "pretence of military necessity," we see the purpose of the Democratic party to restore slavery to all its

ancient power, and to make this Government just what it was before the rebellion, — simply an instrument of the slave-power. "The basis of the Federal Union" only means the alleged compromises and stipulations, as interpreted by Judge Taney, by which black men are supposed to have no rights which white men are bound to respect; and by which the whole Northern people are bound to protect the cruel masters against the justly deserved violence of the slave, and to do the fiendish work of hell-hounds when slaves make their escape from thraldom. The candidates of that party take their stand upon its platform; and will, if elected, — which Heaven forbid! — carry it out to the letter. From this party we must look only for fierce, malignant, and unmitigated hostility. Our continued oppression and degradation is the law of its life, and its sure passport to power. In the ranks of the Democratic party, all the worst elements of American society fraternize; and we need not expect a single voice from that quarter for justice, mercy, or even decency. To it we are nothing; the slave-holders everything. We have but to consult its press to know that it would willingly enslave the free colored people in the South; and also that it would gladly stir up against us mob-violence at the North, — re-enacting the sanguinary scenes of one year ago in New York and other large cities. We therefore pray, that whatever wrath, curse, or calamity, the future may have in store for us, the accession of the Democratic party to the reins of power may not be one of them; for this to us would comprise the sum of all social woes.

How stands the case with the great Republican party in question? We have already alluded to it as being largely under the influence of the prevailing contempt for the character and rights of the colored race. This is seen by the slowness of our Government to employ the strong arm of the black man in the work of putting down the rebellion: and in its unwillingness, after thus employing him, to invest him with the same incitements to deeds of daring, as white soldiers; neither giving him the same pay, rations, and protection, nor any hope of rising in the service by meritorious conduct. It is also seen in the fact, that in neither of the plans emanating from this party for reconstructing the institutions of the Southern States, are colored men, not even those who had fought for the country, recognized as having any political existence or rights whatever. ...

Do you, then, ask us to state, in plain terms, just what we want of you, and just what we think we ought to receive at your hands? We answer: First of all, the complete abolition of the slavery of our race in the United States. We shall not stop to argue. We feel the terrible sting of this stupendous wrong, and that we cannot be free while our brothers are slaves. ...

There is still one other subject, fellow-citizens,— one other want, — looking to the peace and welfare of our common country, as well as to the interests of our race; and that is, political equality. We want the elective franchise in all the States now in the Union, and the same in all such States as may come into the Union hereafter. We believe that the highest welfare of this great country will be found in erasing from its statute-books all enactments discriminating in favor or against any class of its people, and by establishing one law for the white and colored people alike. Whatever prejudice and taste may be innocently allowed to do or to dictate in social and domestic relations, it is plain, that in the matter of government, the object of which is the protection and security of human rights, prejudice should be allowed no voice whatever. In this department of human relations, no notice should be taken of the color of men; but justice, wisdom, and humanity should weigh alone, and be all-controlling.

Formerly our petitions for the elective franchise were met and denied upon the ground, that, while colored men were protected in person and property, they were not required to perform military duty. Of course this was only a plausible excuse; for we were subject to any call the Government was pleased to make upon us, and we could not properly be made to suf-

fer because the Government did not see fit to impose military duty upon us. The fault was with the Government, not with us.

But now even this frivolous though somewhat decent apology for excluding us from the ballot-box is entirely swept away. Two hundred thousand colored men, according to a recent statement of President Lincoln, are now in the service, upon field and flood, in the army and the navy of the United States; and every day adds to their number. They are there as volunteers, coming forward with other patriotic men at the call of their imperilled country; they are there also as substitutes filling up the quotas which would otherwise have to be filled up by white men who now remain at home; they are also there as drafted men, by a certain law of Congress, which, for once, makes no difference on account of color: and whether they are there as volunteers, as substitutes, or as drafted men, neither ourselves, our cause, nor our country, need be ashamed of their appearance or their action upon the battle-field. Friends and enemies, rebels and loyal men, — each, after their kind, — have borne conscious and unconscious testimony to the gallantry and other noble qualities of the colored troops.

Your fathers laid down the principle, long ago, that universal suffrage is the best foundation of Government. We believe as your fathers believed, and as they practised; for, in eleven States out of the original thirteen, colored men exercised the right to vote at the time of the adoption of the Federal Constitution. The Divine-right Govern-ments of Europe, with their aristocratic and privileged classes of priests and nobles, are little better than cunningly devised conspiracies against the natural rights of the people to govern themselves.

Whether the right to vote is a natural right or not, we are not here to determine. Natural or conventional, in either case we are amply supported in our appeal for its extension to us. If it is, as all the teachings of your Declaration of Independence imply, a natural right, to deny to us its exercise is a wrong done to our human nature. If, on the other hand, the right to vote is simply a conventional right, having no other foundation or significance than a mere conventional arrangement, which may be extended or contracted, given or taken away, upon reasonable grounds, we insist, that, even basing the right upon this uncertain foundation, we may reasonably claim a right to a voice in the election of the men who are to have at their command our time, our services, our property, our persons, and our lives. This command of our persons and lives is no longer theory, but now the positive practice of our Government. We say, therefore, that having required, demanded, and in some instances compelled, us to serve with our time, our property, and our lives, coupling us in all the obligations and duties imposed upon the more highly favored of our fellow-citizens in this war to protect and defend your country from threatened destruction, and having fully established the precedent by which, in all similar and dissimilar cases of need, we may be compelled to respond to a like requisition, — we claim to have fully earned the elective franchise; and that you, the American people, have virtually contracted an obligation to grant it, which has all the sanctions of justice, honor, and magnanimity, in favor of its prompt fulfilment.

Are we good enough to use bullets, and not good enough to use ballots? May we defend rights in time of war, and yet be denied the exercise of those rights in time of peace? Are we citizens when the nation is in peril, and aliens when the nation is in safety? May we shed our blood under the star-spangled banner on the battle-field, and yet be debarred from marching under it to the ballot-box? Will the brave white soldiers, bronzed by the hardships and exposures of repeated campaigns, men who have fought by the side of black men, be ashamed to cast their ballots by the side of their companions-in-arms? May we give our lives, but not our votes, for the good of the republic? Shall we toil with you to win the prize of free government, while you alone shall monopolize all its valued privileges? Against such a conclusion, every sentiment of honor

and manly fraternity utters an indignant protest.

It is quite true, that some part of the American people may, with a show of plausibility, evade the force of this appeal and deny this claim. There are men in all countries who can evade any duty or obligation which is not enforced by the strong arm of the law. Our country is no exception to the rule. They can say in this case, "Colored men, we have done you no wrong. We have purchased nothing at your hands, and owe you nothing. From first to last, we have objected to the measure of employing you to help put down this rebellion; foreseeing the very claim you now set up. Were we to-day invested with the power and authority of this Government, we would instantly disband every colored regiment now in front of Richmond, and everywhere else in the Southern States. We do not believe in making soldiers of black men." To all that, we reply, There need be no doubt whatever. No doubt they would disband the black troops if they had the power; and equally plain is it that they would disband the white troops also if they had the power.

They do not believe in making black men soldiers; but they equally do not believe in making white men soldiers to fight slaveholding rebels. But we do not address ourselves here to particular parties and classes of our countrymen: we would appeal directly to the moral sense, honor, and magnanimity of the whole nation; and, with a cause so good, cannot believe that we shall appeal in vain. Parties and classes rise and fall, combine and dissolve: but the national conscience remains forever; and it is that to which our cause is addressed. It may, however, be said that the colored people enlisted in the service of the country without any promise or stipulation that they would be rewarded with political equality at the end of the war; but all the more, on this very account, do we hold the American people bound in honor thus to reward them. By the measure of confidence reposed in the national honor and generosity, we have the right to measure the obligation of fulfilment. The fact, that, when called into the service of the country, we went forward without exacting terms or conditions, to the mind of the generous man enhances our claims.

But, again, why are we so urgent for the possession of this particular right? We are asked, even by some Abolitionists, why we cannot be satisfied, for the present at least, with personal freedom; the right to testify in courts of law; the right to own, buy, and sell real estate; the right to sue and be sued. We answer, Because in a republican country, where general suffrage is the rule, personal liberty, the right to testify in courts of law, the right to hold, buy, and sell property, and all other rights, become mere privileges, held at the option of others, where we are excepted from the general political liberty. What gives to the newly arrived emigrants, fresh from lands governed by kingcraft and priestcraft, special consequence in the eyes of the American people? It is not their virtue, for they are often depraved; it is not their knowledge, for they are often ignorant; it is not their wealth, for they are often very poor: why, then, are they courted by the leaders of all parties? The answer is, that our institutions clothe them with the elective franchise, and they have a voice in making the laws of the country. Give the colored men of this country the elective franchise, and you will see no violent mobs driving the black laborer from the wharves of large cities, and from the toil elsewhere by which he honestly gains his bread. You will see no influential priest, like the late Bishop Hughes, addressing mobocrats and murderers as "gentlemen;" and no influential politician, like Governor Seymour, addressing the "misguided" rowdies of New York as his "friends." The possession of that right is the keystone to the arch of human liberty: and, without that, the whole may at any moment fall to the ground; while, with it, that liberty may stand forever, — a blessing to us, and no possible injury to you. If you still ask why we want to vote, we answer, Because we don't want to be mobbed from our work, or insulted with impunity at every corner. We are men, and want to be as free in our native country as other men.

Fellow-citizens, let us entreat you, have faith in your own principles. If freedom is good for any, it is good for all. If you need the elective franchise, we need it even more. You are strong, we are weak; you are many, we are few; you are protected, we are exposed. Clothe us with this safeguard of our liberty, and give us an interest in the country to which, in common with you, we have given our lives and poured out our best blood. You cannot need special protection. Our degradation is not essential to your elevation, nor our peril essential to your safety. You are not likely to be outstripped in the race of improvement by persons of African descent; and hence you have no need of superior advantages, nor to burden them with disabilities of any kind. Let your Government be what all governments should be, — a copy of the eternal laws of the universe; before which all men stand equal as to rewards and punishments, life and death, without regard to country, kindred, tongue, or people. ...

But we will not weary you. Our cause is in some measure before you. The power to redress our wrongs, and to grant us our just rights, is in your hands. You can determine our destiny, — blast us by continued degradation, or bless us with the means of gradual elevation. We are among you, and must remain among you; and it is for you to say, whether our presence shall conduce to the general peace and welfare of the country, or be a constant cause of discussion and of irritation, — troubles in the State, troubles in the Church, troubles everywhere.

To avert these troubles, and to place your great country in safety from them, only one word from you, the American people, is needed, and that is JUSTICE: let that magic word once be sounded, and become all-controlling in all your courts of law, subordinate and supreme; let the halls of legislation, state and national, spurn all statesmanship as mischievous and ruinous that has not justice for its foundation; let justice without compromise, without curtailment, and without partiality, be observed with respect to all men, no class of men claiming for themselves any right which they will not grant to another, — then strife and discord will cease; peace will be placed upon enduring foundations; and the American people, now divided and hostile, will dwell together in power and unity.

——— 5.5 ———

'WE WERE AND STILL ARE OPPRESSED; WE ARE NOT DEMORALIZED CRIMINALS'
New Orleans Tribune

The free and emancipated population of New Orleans, Louisiana, offered one of the loudest objections to President Lincoln's (and, later, President Andrew Johnson's) vision of Reconstruction without guarantees of full citizenship — from voting rights to land ownership — for black southerners. In 1864, a group of well-off free blacks of French ancestry, educated in France and heavily influenced by the ideals of the French Revolution, founded the New Orleans Tribune. It immediately became a platform for Radical Republican ideas on how southern government should be rebuilt, and how blacks should be included in it. Its popularity reached not only to the North but across the Atlantic, as well.

A. Our Dormant Partners

Among the paper's favored topics was championing political coalition between free blacks and emancipated slaves, which it argued would provide a bloc strong enough to influence policy. In the August 1864 editorial below, the Tribune's editors warn that prejudice against black people remains, in both the North and South, despite slavery's abolition. Emancipation, they argue, is not a result of that prejudice's end in either section, but rather an indirect result of the war for and against southern independence. The civil rights struggle — the fight to ingrain the idea that "before the law all men are equal" — would have to erase this prejudice. Optimistically, the paper presumes freed slaves will be given the right to vote in Louisiana, and that this, then, will be their weapon against that prejudice.

Our Dormant Partners.

When the present Rebellion became flagrant, the attention of the men of both sections was directed with additional anxiety to the relations of the States, in their capacity of individual members of the Union, towards the Government. Some likened these relations to the contract of marriage under the Catholic church, which tolerated no divorce. Others to the contract of partnership, which, being perpetual, could not be dissolved without good and sufficient cause. In pursuing these analogies, more imaginary than real, a skillful debater very naturally suggested, that in such a partnership as existed between the several States of the Union, the four millions of colored persons in the Southern States were the *dormant partners* in the concern, who, from the very inception of the war were *the real parties in interest*, and whom it would be in vain either to overlook or ignore during hostilities, or in fixing upon the basis for permanent peace.

The suggestion was not only natural, but in all respects true. The war effectually and forever broke all the chains of the slave. The municipal law, under which the man owner controlled five, fifty or five hundred human beings, all indentically like him but in the color of skin, was abrogated by the very fact of the war. The only wonder is, that such municipal law was endured so long; that it progressed so fast; that it grew so rapidly in continually greater antagonism to the spirit of our Government. It was a law contrary to the common conscience of the whole people. It was the opprobrium at the same time both of the nation and each individual citizen; and attached alike in foreign countries to the slave driver and the abolitionist. Such a law required a sharp repealing clause, and got it, as we see. When we see Nature regress; when the fruit becomes a bud; when an infant becomes its own father; when the fetus being expelled gets back into the womb again, then it is possible, but not before then, that we may see this municipal law restored and re-enacted.

Four millions of people, no longer slaves nor serfs, raised into the freedom of citizens of the United States — this is the firm, fixed and immovable fact; and no more clear, or apparent, or felt by us, than by the promoted over-seers holding high carnival in Richmond. It is a fact universally recognized. Fighting may be continued for years; the parties to the conflict may roll up what debt soever they please; no matter what lives may be lost, money spent, material interests destroyed, the men of color on this Continent are and will forever be FREE MEN. "'Tis destiny unshunnable as death."

These, our *dormant partners*, are soon to be *active participants* in our system of self-govern-ment, now on its trial before the tribunal of the world. To their hands, political powers will soon be entrusted. Their votes will be eagerly canvassed and anxiously solicited by the con-tending parties; and it will necessarily happen that on the most important occasions, these votes will be the decisive element in the con-troversy. How important then, that they should be educated up to the requirements of their new position! How necessary that they should fully understand the absolute right and wrong of every question brought before them, that they may known their rights, and know-ing, dare maintain them. …

Slavery was, at one time, the important ele-ment of this Rebellion; but never the only one. The idea of the right of slavery; the idea of "property in man" was the lever, by means of which the Southern statesmen fire the hearts of their people, and appealed to their instincts rather than their reason, for support in this war. That idea is now obsolete; so much so, that even if gradual emancipation were sug-gested as the basis of compromise for a recon-struction of the Union, the Southerners in their Richmond capital would instantly and contumeliously reject it. The darling idea, which has nerved the arms of the rebels and carried them so bravely through many blood fields of strife, is not to be found in a low instinct of owning slaves; though this, it is admitted, was the main, ostensible object in view, at the beginning. Such an instinct could not have animated so many men, for so long a time, and through such perilous circum-stances, had it not been connected with

another idea; the idea of Southern Independ-ence. The two ideas together have made a unit of their people; have made them fight as men have seldom fought before; have nerved their souls to the full heroism of their position, and the resolve to do or die. Grant them this boon of Southern Independence, and they would all become as vehement abolitionists as any of the recent converts in our midst, at the present day. Grant them this, and they will agree to liberate all their slaves and make a peace in the course of a little month.

The men of color, then, of the United States stand under no obligations for their freedom either to the North or South. The war was begun with no such end in view by either party. If they are free it is the result of the war — the inevitable result; the deep-rooted preju-dice against this people still remains in all its pristine strength and vigor, in the North quite as much as in the South, and will so continue, till public opinion be brought up to a higher standard and recognizes the true principle of politics that, *before the law all men are equal.*

No new constitution either State or National is now needed to tell us there can be no property in man. Constitutions embody, but never originate ideas. The proposed Constitution of Louisiana confers no favor upon, grants no boon to the free people of color within her boundaries. Their "certain inalienable rights" were long since fixed, deter-mined and promulgated in the Declaration of Independence; and neither the Rebel nor the Loyalist will ever seek to deprive them of these rights, after this war has ended. And then, *our dormant partners* may hold the controlling political influence in Louisiana.

B. Opposition to military rule

As the war ended, the military took control over southern cities and states, acting as temporary Reconstruction pol-icy makers. But military officers were not solely concerned with forcing southern loyalty to the Union. They also believed it of the utmost urgency that freed slaves be put back to labor. Infected with the national racism, these officers by and large shared the southern belief that, absent the force of slavery, blacks would not voluntarily work and contribute to society. Moreover, they well knew that the sagging national economy's revitalization would depend in no small part on restarting the South's agricultural production. Occupying armies all over the South, thus, issued strict orders punishing black "vagrancy" and even legalizing the same sort of torture practiced by plantation owners to enforce them. Opposition to these military orders sparked the first widespread wave of post-war political organizing among freed blacks. The Tribune led the outcry in Louisiana with editorials such as the one below from August 1865, in which the paper responds to a local white official's letter expressing surprise at blacks' willingness to work thus far. Notably, the editorial criticizes the idea that African Americans are a "fallen race," arguing that they are instead an "oppressed race" — and that any deficiencies they bear have been thrust upon them by slavery and prejudice. The distinction, the editors conclude, is significant because the nature of the aid given to emancipated slaves will depend on the perspective from which those in government approach the issue.

Official Vindication of Freedmen.

The following letter, addressed to the N.O. Times by Assistant Commissioner Conway will speak for itself. It will be read with uncommon interest. The satisfaction that is conferred by this candid and frank statement of facts must not, however, prevent our making a critical remark. Chaplain Conway says that "the small amount of negro vagrancy" which he finds in the State is an item of credit to the race *which he did not expect*. Why did Mr. Conway not expect so small an amount of "negro vagrancy?" There is only one answer; because he was imbued with the common prejudices against us. This always flows from the same idea that the African race in America is a "fallen race," while it is an "oppressed race." The spirit with which comfort is given to the oppressed is very different from the spirit that prompts the benevolent to help fallen creatures to be reconciled with a decent and holy life. Philanthropists are sometimes a strange class of people they love their fellow men, but their first impression is always that these fellowmen, to be worthy of their assistance, must be of an inferior kind. We were and still are oppressed; we are not demoralized criminals.

─────── 5.6 ───────

FORTY ACRES AND A MULE
Gen. William T. Sherman and the Freedmen's Bureau

In September 1864, Gen. William Sherman's army took Atlanta, Georgia, spelling the almost certain defeat of the Confederacy. He then set out on his march to the sea, through Georgia low country. Along the way, thousands of slaves ran to join his forces, escaping, or simply walking away from, slaveholders' abandoned plantations. Sherman considered the slaves a nuisance, to say the least. He was prosecuting a war and felt there was no time to figure out what to do with thousands of refugees. Reports filtered back to Washington that he had begun ordering soldiers to chase the refugees off, which angered administration and Republican Party officials. Secretary of War Edwin Stanton, in part intending to investigate the matter, met Sherman in Savannah. Sherman was equally annoyed with this scrutiny of his actions. To him, "no army ever did more for that race than the one I commanded in Savannah." Indeed, his troops had gone to lengths to provide humanitarian assistance in difficult circumstances. Still, the freed slaves, some of whom were dying from exposure and starvation, understandably asked for a more organized and sustained effort.

While in Savannah, Stanton asked Sherman to arrange a meeting with 20 black leaders in the area, mostly ministers. (Sherman, predicting blacks would soon be granted the vote nationwide, felt Stanton's interest stemmed for the rising political value of African-American support.) The ministers told Sherman and Stanton, among other things, that they "would prefer to live by ourselves, for there is a prejudice in the South that will take years to get over." In response to the meeting, on January 16, 1865, Sherman drafted Field Order No. 15. The order set aside the Georgia Sea Islands and 30 miles of land on the Charleston, South Carolina, coast for black settlements. It forbade any "white person whatever" from settling there and decreed "the sole and exclusive management of affairs will be left to the freed people themselves." It granted each family up to "40 acres of tillable ground," and Sherman later added that the army would loan them mules. Sherman saw it as a temporary solution to his refugee problem; the freed slaves saw it as a permanent repayment for their services to the old plantation owners. Ultimately, the issue of land redistribution would join that of black suffrage as among the most controversial in Reconstruction.

IN THE FIELD, SAVANNAH, GA., January 16th, 1865.
SPECIAL FIELD ORDERS, No. 15.

I. The islands from Charleston, south, the abandoned rice fields along the rivers for thirty miles back from the sea, and the country bordering the St. Johns river, Florida, are reserved and set apart for the settlement of the negroes now made free by the acts of war and the proclamation of the President of the United States.

II. At Beaufort, Hilton Head, Savannah, Fernandina, St. Augustine and Jacksonville, the blacks may remain in their chosen or accustomed vocations — but on the islands, and in the settlements hereafter to be established, no white person whatever, unless military officers and soldiers detailed for duty, will be permitted to reside; and the sole and exclusive management of affairs will be left to the freed people themselves, subject only to the United States military authority and the acts of Congress. By the laws of war, and orders of the President of the United States, the negro is free and must be dealt with as such. He cannot be subjected to conscription or forced military service, save by the written orders of the highest military authority of the Department, under such regulations as the President or Congress may prescribe. Domestic servants, blacksmiths, carpenters and other mechanics, will be free to select their own work and residence, but the young and able-bodied negroes must be encouraged to enlist as soldiers in the service of the United States, to contribute their share towards maintaining their own freedom, and securing their rights as citizens of the United States.

Negroes so enlisted will be organized into companies, battalions and regiments, under the orders of the United States military author-

ities, and will be paid, fed and clothed according to law. The bounties paid on enlistment may, with the consent of the recruit, go to assist his family and settlement in procuring agricultural implements, seed, tools, boots, clothing, and other articles necessary for their livelihood.

III. Whenever three respectable negroes, heads of families, shall desire to settle on land, and shall have selected for that purpose an island or a locality clearly defined, within the limits above designated, the Inspector of Settlements and Plantations will himself, or by such subordinate officer as he may appoint, give them a license to settle such island or district, and afford them such assistance as he can to enable them to establish a peaceable agricultural settlement. The three parties named will subdivide the land, under the supervision of the Inspector, among themselves and such others as may choose to settle near them, so that each family shall have a plot of not more than (40) forty acres of tillable ground, and when it borders on some water channel, with not more than 800 feet water front, in the possession of which land the military authorities will afford them protection, until such time as they can protect themselves, or until Congress shall regulate their title. The Quartermaster may, on the requisition of the Inspector of Settlements and Plantations, place at the disposal of the Inspector, one or more of the captured steamers, to ply between the settlements and one or more of the commercial points heretofore named in orders, to afford the settlers the opportunity to supply their necessary wants, and to sell the products of their land and labor.

IV. Whenever a negro has enlisted in the military service of the United States, he may locate his family in any one of the settlements at pleasure, and acquire a homestead, and all other rights and privileges of a settler, as though present in person. In like manner, negroes may settle their families and engage on board the gunboats, or in fishing, or in the navigation of the inland waters, without losing any claim to land or other advantages derived from this system. But no one, unless an actual settler as above defined, or unless absent on Government service, will be entitled to claim any right to land or property in any settlement by virtue of these orders.

V. In order to carry out this system of settlement, a general officer will be detailed as Inspector of Settlements and Plantations, whose duty it shall be to visit the settlements, to regulate their police and general management, and who will furnish personally to each head of a family, subject to the approval of the President of the United States, a possessory title in writing, giving as near as possible the description of boundaries; and who shall adjust all claims or conflicts that may arise under the same, subject to the like approval, treating such titles altogether as possessory. The same general officer will also be charged with the enlistment and organization of the negro recruits, and protecting their interests while absent from their settlements; and will be governed by the rules and regulations prescribed by the War Department for such purposes.

VI. Brigadier General R. SAXTON is hereby appointed Inspector of Settlements and Plantations, and will at once enter on the performance of his duties. No change is intended or desired in the settlement now on Beaufort Island, nor will any rights to property heretofore acquired be affected thereby.

BY ORDER OF MAJOR GENERAL W. T. SHERMAN

――――― 5.7 ―――――

'THEY WOULD LIKE TO HAVE LAND — 4 OR 5 ACRES TO A FAMILY'
Establishing the Freedmen's Bureau

Following the Emancipation Proclamation in 1863, the War Department created a commission to study and suggest policy concerning the freed slaves. The American Freedmen's Inquiry Commission held hearings at which Union officers and government officials, as well as emancipated slaves, testified about southern blacks' needs. At the completion of its study, the Commission recommended that the government create a temporary federal agency charged with providing humanitarian assistance to the millions of emancipated men, women, children and families until they were judged capable of self-support. In March 1865, following passage of the 13th Amendment, Congress finally created the Bureau of Refugees, Freedmen, and Abandoned Lands to fulfill that role. It would be one of the most controversial federal agencies in history. The enacting bill built on Sherman's vision of land redistribution, dividing up property abandoned by or confiscated from southern planters into 40 acre plots to be allocated to freed slaves. Two years later, reports from the South of "outrages" committed against freed blacks and Republican whites — violence, harassment, discrimination — would lead Congress to expand the Bureau's power dramatically, into the arena of monitoring and enforcing equal treatment of African Americans by southern whites.

A. Freeman Harry McMillan's testimony before the American Freedmen's Inquiry Commission

Testimony of Harry McMillan. (colored)
Harry McMillan testified —
I am about 40 years of age, and was born in Georgia but came to Beaufort when a small boy. I was owned by General Eustis and lived upon his plantation.
Q. Tell me about the tasks colored men had to do?
A. In old secesh times each man had to do two tasks, which are 42 rows or half an acre, in "breaking" the land, and in "listing" each person had to do a task and a half. In planting every hand had to do an acre a day; in hoeing your first hoeing where you hoe flat was two tasks, and your second hoeing, which is done across the beds, was also two tasks. After going through those two operations you had a third which was two and a half tasks, when you had to go over the cotton to thin out the plants leaving two in each hill.
Q. How many hours a day did you work?
A. Under the old secesh times every morning till night — beginning at daylight and continuing till 5 or 6 at night.
Q. But you stopped for your meals?

A. You had to get your victuals standing at your hoe; you cooked it overnight yourself or else an old woman was assigned to cook for all the hands, and she or your children brought the food to the field.

Q. You never sat down and took your food together as families?

A. No, sir; never had time for it.

Q. The women had the same day's work as the men; but suppose a women was in the family way was her task less?

A. No, sir; most of times she had to do the same work. Sometimes the wife of the planter learned the condition of the woman and said to her husband you must cut down her day's work. Sometimes the women had their children in the field.

Q. Had the women any doctor?

A. No, sir; there is a nurse on the plantation sometimes, — an old midwife who attended them. If a woman was taken in labor in the field some of her sisters would help her home and then come back to the field.

Q. Did they nurse their children?

A. Yes, sir; the best masters gave three months for that purpose.

Q. If a man did not do his task what happened?

A. He was stripped off, tied up and whipped.

Q. What other punishments were used?

A. The punishments were whipping, putting you in the stocks and making you wear irons and a chain at work. Then they had a collar to put round your neck with two horns, like cows' horns, so that you could not lie down on your back or belly. This also kept you from running away for the horns would catch in the bushes. Sometimes they dug a hole like a well with a door on top. This they called a dungeon keeping you in it two or three weeks or a month, and sometimes till you died in there. This hole was just big enough to receive the body; the hands down by the sides. I have seen this thing in Georgia but never here. I know how they whip in the Prisons. They stretch out your arms and legs as far as they can to ring bolts in the floor and lash you till they open the skin and the blood trickles down. ...

Q. What induces a colored man to take a wife?

A. Well; since this affair there are more married than ever I knew before, because they have a little more chance to mind their families and make more money to support their families. In secesh times there was not much marrying for love. A man saw a young woman and if he liked her he would get a pass from his master to go where she was. If his owner did not choose to give him the pass he would pick out another woman and make him live with her, whether he loved her or not.

Q. Colored women have a good deal of sexual passion, have they not — they all go with men?

A. Yes, sir; there is a great deal of that; I do not think you will find five out of a hundred that do not; they begin at 15 and 16.

Q. Do they know any better?

A. They regard it now as a disgrace and the laws of the Church are against it.

Q. They sometimes have children before marriage?

A. Yes, sir; but they are thought less of among their companions, unless they get a husband before the child is born, and if they cannot the shame grows until they do get a husband. Some join a Church when they are 10 years old and some not until they are 30; the girls join mostly before the men, but they are more apt to fall than the men. Whenever a person joins the Church, no matter how low he has been, he is always respected. When the girls join the Church after a while they sometimes become weary and tired and some temptation comes in and they fall. Sometimes the masters, where the mistress was a pious woman, punished the girls for having children before they were married. As a general thing the masters did not care, they liked the colored women to have children.

Q. Suppose a son of the master wanted to have intercourse with the colored women was he at liberty?

A. No, not at liberty; because it was considered a stain on the family, but the young men did it; there was a good deal of it. They often kept one girl steady and sometimes two on different places; men who had wives did it too sometimes; if they could get it on their own place it was easier but they would go wherever they could get it.

Q. Do the colored people like to go to Church?

A. Yes, sir; they are fond of that; they sing psalms, put up prayers, and sing their religious songs.

Q. Did your masters ever see you learning to read?

A. No, sir; you could not let your masters see you read; but now the colored people are fond of sending their children to school.

Q. What is the reason of that?

A. Because the children in after years will be able to tell us ignorant ones how to do for ourselves.

Q. How many children have you known one woman to have?

A. I know one woman who had 20 children. I know too a woman named Jenny, the wife of Dagos, a slave of John Pope, who has had 23 children. In general the women have a great many children — they often have a child once a year. …

Q. Have they any idea of the government of the United States?

A. Yes, sir; they know if the government was not kind to them they could not keep their liberty. When the war began a great many of us believed that the government could not conquer our masters because our masters fooled us. They told us we must fight the Yankees who intended to catch us and sell us to Cuba to pay the expenses of the war. I did not believe it, but a great many did.

Q. What would the colored people like the government to do for them here?

A. They would like to have land — 4 or 5 acres to a family.

Q. How many here could manage and take care of land?

A. A good many. I could take care of 15 acres and would not ask them to do any more for me.

Q. Suppose the government were to give you land, how long would you take to pay for it — five years?

A. I would not take five years; in two years I would pay every cent. The people here would rather have the land than work for wages. I think it would be better to sort out the men and give land to those who have the faculty of supporting their families. Every able bodied man can take care of himself if he has a mind to, but their are bad men who have not the heart or will to do it.

Q. Do you think the colored people would like better to have this land divided among themselves and live here alone, or must they have white people to govern them?

A. They are obliged to have white people to administer the law; the black people have a good deal of sense but they do not know the law. If the government keep the masters away altogether it would not do to leave the colored men here alone; some white men must be here not as masters, but we must take the law by their word and if we do not we must be punished. If you take all the white men away we are nothing. Probably with the children that are coming up no white men will not be needed. They are learning to read and write — some are learning lawyer, some are learning doctor, and some learn minister; and reading books and newspapers they can understand the law; but the old generation cannot understand it. It makes no difference how sensible they are, they are blind and it wants white men for the present to direct them. After five years they will take care of themselves; this generation cannot do it. …

B. Congressional act establishing the Freedmen's Bureau

Be it enacted by the Senate and House of Representatives of the United States of America in Congress assembled, That there is hereby established in the War Department, to continue during the present war of rebellion, and for one year thereafter, a bureau of refugees, freedmen, and abandoned lands, to which shall be committed, as hereinafter provided, the supervision and management of all abandoned lands, and the control of all subjects relating to refugees and freedmen from rebel states, or from any district of country within the territory embraced in the operations of the army, under such rules and regulations as may be prescribed by the head of the bureau and approved by the President. The said bureau shall be under the management and control of a commissioner to be appointed by the President, by and with the advice and consent of the Senate, whose compensation shall be three thousand dollars per annum, and such number of clerks as may be assigned to him by the Secretary of War, not exceeding one chief clerk, two of the fourth class, two of the third class, and five of the first class. And the commissioner and all persons appointed under this act, shall, before entering upon their duties, take the oath of office prescribed in an act entitled "An act to prescribe an oath of office, and for other purposes," approved July second, eighteen hundred and sixty-two, and the commissioner and the chief clerk shall, before entering upon their duties, give bonds to the treasurer of the United States, the former in the sum of fifty thousand dollars, and the latter in the sum of ten thousand dollars, conditioned for the faithful discharge of their duties respectively, with securities to be approved as sufficient by the Attorney-General, which bonds shall be filed in the office of the first comptroller of the treasury, to be by him put in suit for the benefit of any injured party upon any breach of the conditions thereof.

SEC. 2. *And be it further enacted*, That the Secretary of War may direct such issues of provisions, clothing, and fuel, as he may deem needful for the immediate and temporary shelter and supply of destitute and suffering refugees and freedmen and their wives and children, under such rules and regulations as he may direct.

SEC. 3. *And be it further enacted*, That the President may, by and with the advice and consent of the Senate, appoint an assistant commissioner for each of the states declared to be in insurrection, not exceeding ten in number, who shall, under the direction of the commissioner, aid in the execution of the provisions of this act; and he shall give a bond to the Treasurer of the United States, in the sum of twenty thousand dollars, in the form and manner prescribed in the first section of this act. Each of said commissioners shall receive an annual salary of two thousand five hundred dollars in full compensation for all his services. And any military officer may be detailed and assigned to duty under this act without increase of pay or allowances. The commissioner shall, before the commencement of each regular session of congress, make full report of his proceedings with exhibits of the state of his accounts to the President, who shall communicate the same to congress, and shall also make special reports whenever required to do so by the President or either house of congress; and the assistant commissioners shall make quarterly reports of their proceedings to the commissioner, and also such other special reports as from time to time may be required.

SEC. 4. *And be it further enacted*, That the commissioner, under the direction of the President, shall have authority to set apart, for the use of loyal refugees and freedmen, such tracts of land within the insurrectionary states as shall have been abandoned, or to which the United States shall have acquired title by confiscation or sale, or otherwise, and to every male citizen, whether refugee or freedman, as aforesaid, there shall be assigned not more than forty acres of such land, and the person to whom it was so assigned shall be protected in the use and enjoyment of the land for the term of three years at an annual rent not exceeding six per centum upon the value of such land, as it was appraised by the state authorities in the year eighteen hundred and sixty, for the purpose of taxation, and in case no such appraisal can be found, then the rental shall be based upon the estimated value of the land in said year, to be ascertained in such manner as the commissioner may by regulation prescribe. At the end of said term, or at any time during said term, the occupants of any parcels so assigned may purchase the land and receive such title thereto as the United States can convey, upon paying therefor the value of the land, as ascertained and fixed for the purpose of determining the annual rent aforesaid.

SEC. 5. *And be it further enacted*, That all acts and parts of acts inconsistent with the provisions of this act, are hereby repealed.

APPROVED, March 3, 1865.

——— 5.8 ———

RESETTLEMENT AT PORT ROYAL, SOUTH CAROLINA

Freedmen's Bureau records

The federal land redistribution program proceeded quickly to settle black families on abandoned or confiscated plantations in the areas designated under Gen. Sherman's order. The families were encouraged to work the fields and grow crops that could be sold on the market. The system's white promoters saw more than a humanitarian mission at work. They believed that the settlements could prove the viability of free black labor, countering dire predictions from many in the North and South that blacks would be unwilling or unable to produce on their own the sort of crops necessary to jumpstart the southern economy. The resettled plantations of South Carolina's Port Royal Island became the de facto test case for free black labor, and observers around the country anxiously watched how things unfolded. In the report below, the Freedmen's Bureau agent responsible for Port Royal and surrounding islands provides detailed information about the scale of the program and the needs of the nearly 20,000 black refugees who had passed through the area in just the previous eight months.

Office for Freedmen
Beaufort, South Carolina
August 1, 1865
Bvt. Maj. Gen. R. Saxton Asst. Com.
Freedmens Affairs &c
General

In obedience to the requirements of Gen. Order republishing Circular no. 10 I have the honor to submit the following concerning Refugees, Freedmen and Abandoned Lands in the district comprising Port Royal and adjacent Islands and such portion of the abandoned land upon the main extending northwardly from the "Coosa River" as have been visited and inspected.

No census of the Freedmen in this district has been taken since November 1864 and any estimate of the population at any period since "Sherman's Refugees" began so largely to increase the number would necessarily have been unreliable and at best only approximate to fact. From January first to this date nearly seventeen thousand (17000) Freedmen have arrived at Beaufort of whom not exceeding one thousand (1000) now remain this side of the Coosa. 350 of these are staying in the town, more than one half of whom are paupers, with an uncommon proportion of very infirm and aged people. Upon the Island Plantations, sixty-seven (67) of which are being worked to a greater or less extent, the population is not far from five thousand (5000), embracing four hundred and fifty (450) infirm and orphans who have until this time been subsisted by the government. Freedmen and Refugees in Beaufort number twenty two hundred (2200) and on abandoned estates above the "Coosa" six hundred (600) making a total of about seven thousand eight hundred (7800) in the district. The average arrivals of Freedmen in transit from all parts of the state, Georgia, Florida, and North Carolina seeking their relatives and endeavoring to reach their homes have been fifty (50) per day, and twenty one thousand (21000) rations have been issued to such persons during June and July on the ground of absolute destitution and inability to proceed further without such aid; the whole number of rations issued in this district to Freedmen (the Provost Marshal has provided for white refugees) from June first until this date is eighty thousand (80000) of which the value of twenty five thousand seven hundred and fifty four (25754) rations or five thousand one hundred and fifty dollars ($5150.00) has been charged against the consumers and a lien made upon the cotton crop for its payment; it is proper to state that the ration has not included several of the articles enumerated in Circular No. 8, meal and meat being often the only subsistence asked for.

One hundred articles of clothing have been given to Freedmen since June first, the value of which was fifty dollars ($50.00). The whole of it was donated by the Agent of the Sanitary Commission and no supplies distributed from this office have apparently been more needed or better bestowed.

Concerning abandoned lands not yet formally taken possession of by any agent of the Bureau in the district this first report must necessarily be meagre, so little time being given for survey and the gathering of information; herewith is transmitted a sketch of such estates as have been visited and I append estimates of the area of each, with whatever facts have been procured relative to the former owners and a statement of the present condition of each; and I earnestly recommend that all needful steps be speedily taken to secure the entire control to the Bureau of these and still furtheroutlying abandoned properties as they will be needed to furnish homesteads for very many families who will return hither as fast as the way is opened for them; the sketch bears numbers corresponding with those on the subjoined description notes.

No. 1 — Barnwell Island — property of William H. Trescott in the State Dept. at Washington D. C. during the administration of Mr. Buchanan; contains about one thousand (1000) acres of excellent land, two hundred (200) of which are cultivated the present year under the supervision of Miss. Graves who has a school for the children; colored population three hundred (300) mainly old residents or people from Port Royal; the mansion house and fifteen (15) first class cabins are standing and for situation and real value the Island is of importance. Trescott had a command at Hilton Head but his subsequent connexion with the war and his present whereabouts are not known.

No. 2 — Hall Island — comprise the two plantations of Jno. F. Chaplin and Hamilton Fripp, each of which contain six hundred (600) acres of arable land; they have been abandoned until this year when one of

Chaplin's former slaves went back and has induced some twenty seven (27) Chaplin people in all to settle on the place, and on Fripps no dwelling whatever, but the Chaplin place has eighteen (18) cabins. Mr. Chaplin is if living an old man, was prominent in urging the state to "secede" but has not been personally engaged in the war. Fripp has been a private soldier in the Confederate army.

No. 3 to No. 8 — inclusive these six (6) deserted plantations lie along the "Coosa" river eastward from Port Royal ferry and are perfectly desolate, having neither an inhabitant nor a dwelling; they contain variously from three hundred (300) to eight hundred (800) acres each of good land most favorably situated for settlement; the owners were #3 John Chaplin, son of John F., Lieut. in the rebel service, #4 Widow of Edwd. Fripp, #5 Wm. Fripp, heirs unknown, #6 Wm. Adams whose three (3) sons were in the service of the rebel government, #7 John Webb connected in a civil capacity with the Confederate army, #8 Mary Terry present condition or heirs unknown.

No. 9 — Chisholm Island — owned by Robert Chisholm; the father and two (2) sons were engaged during the rebellion as private soldiers in the service of the Confederate government. Forty of the old residents have returned to the farm and with thirty (30) strangers from beyond the "Combahee" are working two hundred (200) acres of fine looking crops; the plantation embraces one thousand five hundred acres including the marsh, a decent mansion house and twenty cabins remain but most of the valuable improvements were burned two (2) years ago by the owner.

No. 10 — Estate of T. H. Span — could not ascertain whether he took part in the rebellion though he is a middle aged man; this place embraces seven hundred (700) to one thousand (1000) acres but includes much marsh, some of which was reclaimed before the war and planted with Rice; the buildings except the mansion house remain and twenty (20) of the freed people are on the place with sixty (60) acres of good crops.

No. 11 — Estate of Hal. Stewart — Lieutenant in the rebel army, the Negroes on his father's, Henry Stewart's, place say that young "mass Hal" was opposed to the war and only went when "he was scripted;" the place is deserted but several tenements are standing in good order, also cotton and gin houses; there are six hundred (600) acres of good land.

No. 12 — "Oak Point" — belonged to Henry Stewart, a "hard master" who promoted the rebellion in every possible way except to take up arms himself. His place is a fine peninsula bounded by Coosa and Bull river; contains six hundred (600) acres and has sufficient houses and other improvements for the present population of sixty (60) Freedmen, only 7 (7) are old residents and about fifty (50) acres are under cultivation.

No. 13 — Lands of Edward Barnwell — about four hundred (400) acres available, remainder marsh; has population of fifteen (15) all old occupants residing in the remaining cabins; they have twenty five (25) acres in provision crops. …

The five plantations 14 to 18 are entirely deserted as they must have been for a long time and together embrace a territory of not less than twenty five hundred (2500) acres without any improvements, even the bridges over ditches and streams being decayed and broken. The arable lands however, are good and fine crops can be realized on them. The owners except Robert and John Barnwell, who were in the Confederate army, are old men, present residence unknown.

No. 19 — Estate of Rafe Elliott — lies south east of Gardners Corners; has no houses or other improvements; comprises eight hundred (800) acres of first quality land. Elliott was a surgeon in the "C. S. A." and was killed early in the war.

No. 20 — Estate of Paul Hamilton — has nothing left upon it but a cotton house; comprises seven hundred (700) acres of good land.

No. 21 — Estate of Dr. Dessaussere v now of Charleston; Grand Master or head of the "Masonic Fraternity" of the state; has three

(300) to four (400) hundred acres unimproved. The Doctor had a son in the "C. S. A."

No. 22 — The John Jenkins Place — lying directly on the "Combahee road" all gone to ruin and everything grown up to weeds — about five hundred (500) acres.

No. 23 — The large estate combining six (6) plantations of Walter Blake — has at least two thousand (2000) acres of arable land, much of it thoroughly reclaimed Rice land; the mansion and Rice mills were burned and only thirty five (35) Negro houses remained; they are now occupied by about one hundred and twenty five (125) of the former residents who have two hundred (200) acres under cultivation mainly corn and rice. Blake was a captain in the rebel army and at one time commanded the district from the Combahee to Pocatotige rivers.

No. 24 — Two Plantations of Henry Middleton — almost surrounded by a bend of the Combahee containing eleven hundred (1100) acres of which one hundred and fifty (150) are rice land. The improvements except a half dozen cabins are all destroyed. Middleton had two (2) sons in the "C. S. A."

No. 25, 26, 27 — "Green Point" "Clay Hall" and "Brantford" — all belonging to the estate of Henry Hayward — lie among the Combahee below the ferry and are fine plantations with an area of fifteen hundred (1500) acres; a few cabins are all that is left of very extensive improvements; these places will be valuable from their location for settlement; one son of Hayward's was in the rebel army.

No. 28 — Estate of Revd. Stephen Elliott — north of Combahee road and west of Walter Blake's place; contains five hundred (500) acres and contains a few Negro cabins — no cultivation — "Parson Elliott" had two (2) sons in the Confederate service, one of whom, Theodore, was Captain, and lost an arm; the other a surgeon who was killed.

No. 29 — Estate of Dr. Thomas Fuller — nearly one thousand (1000) acres; is entirely deserted, apparently for a long time; has a dozen good cabins and a gin house with new engine; cotton gin and corn mill, all in good condition; this place is very desirable, the land being all arable and high.

No. 30 — Estate of Barney, Son of Dr. Fuller — place has no improvements left upon it whatever; comprises seven hundred (700) acres. Barney was a lieutenant in the Confederate army.

No. 31 — Estate of John Chaplin, father of John F.—— contains eight hundred (800) acres without any remaining houses; the land mainly cleared of wood for rebel army use.

No. 32 — Estate of John Rhoades — lies west of Pocotaliga road, contains eleven hundred (1100) acres, everything destroyed, said to be by rebel soldiers two or three years since.

No. 33 — The Yates Plantation — purchased not long before the war by Henry Stewart, is very large and a fine place; seven Negro houses left and no people.

No. 34 — Periclear Place at Port Royal ferry — four hundred (400) acres; was owned by an old man and deserted January 1st, 1865 when the improvements were destroyed by Genl. Stevens.

The summary of the thirty four (34) estates above noted gives twenty five thousand seven hundred (25.700) acres of land or an estimated area of twenty two thousand (22.000) acres available for immediate use and ample in extent for division among six hundred (600) families; the boundaries between plantations are in most cases simple ditches and embankments on three sides, the fourth usually being a highway or river.

Respectfully submitted,

H. G. Judd

Act. Supt. 1st Div.

——— 5.9 ———

'WE ARE LEFT IN A MORE UNPLEASANT CONDITION THAN OUR FORMER'

Freed Blacks of Edisto Island, South Carolina

Andrew Johnson assumed the presidency, following President Lincoln's assassination, in April 1865. Given Johnson's previous stance on the secessionist states, Radical Republicans were thrilled. Surely Johnson's rhet-

oric about being the "Moses" of black people and punishing Confederates — whom he characterized as traitors — would mean a more sweeping socio-political refiguring of the South. They were, however, sorely disappointed. Johnson took a forgiving posture with the southern states that quashed any hope of political or civil rights for blacks in the region and opened the door to another 100 years of state-led racism and discrimination. In late May, he pardoned all southerners who accepted an oath of loyalty to the Union (excepting those with taxable property of over $20,000 in value, who had to appeal individually to him) and restored their former property. Thus ended the Freedmen Bureau's land redistribution schemes.

In August, Johnson ordered Bureau director Oliver Howard to negotiate a return of the land he and Gen. Sherman had distributed and to inform the settlers that they must either accept wage labor from the former owners or depart. Freed blacks were to be encouraged to sign labor contracts spelling out the terms of their service to white planters. Those contracts, such as the one below, typically required blacks to labor for prolonged periods before reaping any benefits. At the time, the Bureau controlled around 850,000 acres of land, most of which had not yet been resettled. But around 40,000 families had built homes — and lives — on the land Sherman granted. Howard, by now a hero among southern blacks, launched a reluctant tour to personally explain what had happened. The black settlers, of course, were outraged, and believed themselves betrayed. The land had never been officially granted as permanent, but the settlers understandably believed it had. In one encounter, at Edisto Island, South Carolina, Howard asked the community to create a board and recommend the best system by which the land could be returned. That board offered the following bitter response, refusing to go quietly back into what they believed was slavery recast.

A. The Edisto Island committee's statement to Howard

General, we want Homesteads, we were promised Homesteads by the government. If it does not carry out the promises its agents made to us, if the government having concluded to befriend its late enemies and to neglect to observe the principles of common faith between its self and us its allies in the war you said was over, now takes away form them all right to the soil they stand upon save such as they can get by again working for *your* late and their *all time* enemies …. we are left in a more unpleasant condition than our former. … You will see this is not the condition of really freemen.

You ask us to forgive the land owners of our island. You only lost your right arm in war and might forgive them. The man who tied me to a tree and gave me 39 lashes and who stripped and flogged my mother and my sister and who will not let me stay in his empty hut except I will do his planting and be satisfied with his price and who combines with others to keep away land from me well knowing I would not have anything to do with him if I had land of my own — that man, I cannot well forgive. Does it look as if he has forgiven me, seeing how he tries to keep me in a condition of helplessness?

B. A Georgia labor contract

State of Georgia
Wilkes County
This agreement entered into this the 9th day of January 1866 between Clark Anderson & Co. of the State of Mississippi, County of (blank) of the first part and the Freedmen whose names are annexed of the State and County aforesaid of the second part. Witnesseth that the said Clark Anderson & Co. agrees to furnish to the Freed Laborers whose names are annexed quarters, fuel and healthy rations. Medical attendance and supplies in case of sickness, and the amount set opposite their respective names per month during the continuation of this contract paying one third of the wages each month, and the amount in full at the end of the year before the final disposal of the crop which is to be raised by them on said Clark Anderson & Co. Plantation in the County of (blank) and State aforesaid. The said Clark Anderson & Co. further agree to give the female laborers one half day in each week to do their washing &c.

The Laborers on their part agree to work faithfully and diligently on the Plantation of

the said Clark Anderson & Co. for six days in the week and to do all necessary work usually done on a plantation on the Sabbath, during this year 1866 commencing with this date and ending 1st January 1867, that we will be respectful and obedient to said Clark Anderson & Co. or their agents, and that we will in all respects endeavor to promote their interests, and we further bind ourselves to treat with humanity and kindness the stock entrusted to our care and will be responsible for such stock as die through our inhumanity or carelessness and we further agree to deduct for time lost by our own fault one dollar per day during the Spring and two dollars during cotton picking season, also that the Father & Mother should pay for board of children, also for lost time by protracted sickness and we further agree to have deducted from our respective wages the expense of medical attendance and supplies during sickness.

——— 5.10 ———

'YOU ENFRANCHISE YOUR ENEMIES, AND DISENFRANCHISE YOUR FRIENDS'

A Confrontation at the White House

In addition to his universal pardon, President Johnson signaled his intent to leave black suffrage out of the Reconstruction equation in late May 1865. He arranged the restoration of North Carolina's full status within the Union, offering voting rights to all those who had been pardoned and enjoyed the right prior to secession. That, of course, excluded African Americans. This was the first in a series of such orders. Further, he went about appointing governors for the southern states who had moderate positions on the terms of Reconstruction. They, in turn, attempted to straddle the delicate political lines of the time by filling their bureaucracies with white aristocrats and former slaveholders. In his seminal study of the period, historian Eric Foner argues that Johnson's motives for taking a soft-line on Reconstruction lay in the same politics as that of his moderate appointees: He knew he needed southern support to be reelected to office, so he softened his previously radical stance.

But moreover, Johnson revealed that he had never really been a supporter of rights for African Americans. He believed that slaves and slaveholders formed two sides of a vice that gripped white yeoman and kept them powerless. His pardon was intended to empower the poor white men of the South, while keeping the aristocratic former slaveholders beholden to him for individually granted pardons. Black suffrage could only complicate efforts to achieve these ends. Finally, Johnson had always been a strict adherent to the principle of states' rights. Secession they had no right to, but the details of voting rights should be left to them.

In a hostile February 1866 meeting with a delegation of blacks, recounted below by the *Washington Morning Chronicle,* Johnson lectured Frederick Douglass and George Downing on these ideas. He focused particularly on his conception of a symbiotic relationship between slaves and slaveholders in which the two sides conspired to keep poor whites as the truly oppressed class.

The President: In reply to some of your inquiries, not to make a speech about this thing, for it is always best to talk plainly and distinctly about such matters, I will say that if I have not given evidence in my course that I am a friend of humanity, and to that portion of it which constitutes the colored population, I can give no evidence here. Everything that I have had, both as regards life an property, has been periled in that cause, and I feel and think that I understand — not to be egotistic — what should be the true direction of this question, and what course of policy would result in the melioration and ultimate elevation, not only of the colored, but of the great mass of people of the United States. ... I have owned slaves and bought slaves, but I never sold one. I might say, however, that practically, so far as my connection with slaves has gone, I have been their slave instead of their being mine. Some have even followed me here, while others are occupying and enjoying my property with my consent. For the colored race my means, my time, my all has been periled; and now at this late day, after giving evidence that is tangible, that is practical, I am free to say to you that I do not like to be arraigned by some who can get up handsomely rounded periods and deal in rhetoric, and talk about abstract

ideas of liberty, who never periled life, liberty or property. ...

I think I know what I say. I feel what I say; and I feel well assured that if the policy urged by some be persisted in, it will result in great injury to the white as well as to the colored man. There is a great deal talk about the sword in one hand accomplishing an end, and the ballot accomplishing another at the ballot-box.

These things all do very well, and sometimes have forcible application. We talk about justice; we talk about right; we say that the white man has been in the wrong in keeping the black man in slavery as long as he has. That is all true. Again, we talk about the Declaration of Independence and equality before the law. You understand all that, and know how to appreciate it. But, now, let us look each other in the face; let us go to the great mass of colored men throughout the slave States; let us take the condition in which they are at present time — and it is bad enough, we all know — and suppose, by some magic touch you could say to every one, "You shall vote to-morrow," how much would that ameliorate their condition at this time?

Now, let us get closer to this subject, and talk about it. (The President here approached very near to Mr. Douglass.) What relation has the colored man and the white man heretofore occupied in the South? I opposed slavery upon two grounds. First, it was a great monopoly, enabling those who controlled and owned it to constitute an aristocracy, enabling the few to derive great profits and rule the many with an iron rod, as it were. And this is one great objection to it in a government, it being a monopoly. I was opposed to it secondly upon the abstract principle of slavery. Hence, in getting clear of a monopoly, we are getting clear of slavery at the same time. So you see there were two right ends accomplished in the accomplishment of one.

Mr. Douglass. Mr. President, do you wish —

The President. I am not quite through yet.

Slavery has been abolished, a great national guarantee has been given, one that cannot be revoked. I was getting at the relation that subsisted between the white man and the colored man. A very small proportion of the white persons compared with the whole number of such owned the colored people of the South. I might instance the State of Tennessee in illustration. There were there twenty-seven non-slaveholders to one slaveholder, and yet the slave power controlled the State. Let us talk about this matter as it is. Although the colored man was in slavery there, and owned as property in the sense and in the language of that locality and of that community, yet, in comparing his condition, and his position there with the non-slaveholder, he usually estimated his importance just in proportion to the number of slaves that his master owned, with the non-slaveholder.

Have you ever lived upon a plantation?

Mr. Douglass. I have, your Excellency.

The President. When you would look over and see a man who had a large family, struggling hard upon a poor piece of land, you thought a great deal less of him than you did of your own master's negro, didn't you?

Mr. Douglass. Not I!

The President. Well, I know such was the case with a large number of you in those sections. Where such is the case we know there is an enmity, we know there is a hate. The poor white man, on the other hand, was opposed to the slave and his master; for the colored man and his master, combined, kept him in slavery, by depriving him of a fair participation in the labor and productions of the rich of land of the country. …

The colored man went into this rebellion a slave; by the operation of the rebellion he came out a freedman — equal to a freeman in any other portion of the country. Then there is a great deal done for him on this point. The non-slaveholder who was forced into the rebellion, who was as loyal as those that lived beyond the limits of the State, but who [was] carried into it, and his property, and in a number of instances, the lives of such were sacrificed, and he who has survived has come out of it with nothing gained but a great deal lost.

Now, upon the principle of justice, should they be placed in a condition different from what they were before? On the one hand, one has gained a great deal; on the other hand, one has lost a great deal, and, in a political view, scarcely stands where he did before. …

Now, where do you begin? Government must have a controlling power; must have a lodgment. For instance, suppose Congress should pass a law authorizing an election to be held at which all over twenty-one years of age, without regard to color, should be allowed to vote, and a majority should decide at such election that the elective franchise should not be universal; what would you do about it? Who would settle it? Do you deny that first great principle of the right of the people to govern themselves? Will you resort to an arbitrary power, and say a majority of the people shall receive a state of things they are opposed to?

Mr. Douglass. That was said before the war.

The President. I am now talking about a principle; not what somebody else said.

Mr. Downing. Apply what you have said, Mr. President, to South Carolina, for instance, where a majority of the inhabitants are colored.

The President. Suppose you go to South Carolina; suppose you go to Ohio. That doesn't change the principle at all. The query to which I have referred still comes up when Government is undergoing a fundamental change. Government commenced upon this principle; it has existed upon it; and you propose now to incorporate into it an element that didn't exist before. I say the query comes up in undertaking this thing, whether we have a right to make a change in regard to the elective franchise in Ohio, for instance, whether we shall not let the people in that State decide the matter for themselves.

Each community is better prepared to determine the depository of its political power than anybody else, and it is for the Legislature, for the people of Ohio to say who shall vote, and not for the Congress of the United States. … It is a fundamental tenet in my creed that the will of the people must be obeyed. Is there anything wrong or unfair in that?

Mr. Douglass (smiling.) A great deal that is wrong, Mr. President, with all respect.

The President. It is the people of the States that must for themselves determine this thing. I do not want to be engaged in a work that will commence a war of races. ...

Mr. Douglass. If the President will allow me, I would like to say one or two words in reply. You enfranchise your enemies and disenfranchise your friends.

The President. All I have done is simply to indicate what my views are, as I supposed you expected me to, from you address.

Mr. Douglass. My own impression is that the very thing that your Excellencey would avoid in the Southern States can only be avoided by the very measure that we propose, and I would state to my brother delegates that because I perceive the President has taken strong ground in favor of a given policy, and distrusting my own ability to remove any of those impressions which he has expressed, I thought we had better end the interview with an expression of thanks. ...

— 5.11 —

'ANY PERSON WHO SHALL SO INTERMARRY ... SHALL BE CONFINED IN THE STATE PENITENTIARY FOR LIFE'
Black Codes

The drastic consequences of President Johnson's hands-off approach to Reconstruction appeared immediately. The new state bureaucracies — in most cases little different in composition from the old ones — began passing laws to suppress their emancipated populations. These laws, known as "Black Codes," essentially reinstated slavery. Though nominally meant to spell out freed blacks' civil rights, they did more to proscribe those rights than anything else. Mississippi's November 1865 codes were, with South Carolina's, among the first. Along with the age-old anti-miscegenation provisions, the laws added clauses designed to retain the white supremacist social hierarchy of slavery by punishing behavior judged disrespectful or insubordinate to whites. The laws banned "malicious mischief" and "insulting gestures" on the part of blacks, for-

bade blacks from carrying firearms and meted out punishments for whites who sold blacks enough liquor to become intoxicated.

The control of black labor was a central component in all states' Black Codes. The "vagrancy" and "civil rights" provisions of the Black Codes mandated that all blacks provide proof of having signed the labor contracts being pushed by the Freedmen's Bureau in the wake of Johnson's return of planter land. Further, they levied punishments for blacks who refused to honor these contracts once it became clear they were unfair, and the codes forbade whites from competing, presumably by offering better contracts, for the labor of a supposedly free black person. The "apprentice" law placed orphaned blacks — or children whose "parents have not the means" to support them — in apprenticeships with court appointed employers, giving the former slave's owner preference in choosing that employer. In effect, black children could be taken from their families and placed in the service of any employer the white administrators chose. The law even went so far as to refer to the youth's employer as a "master." Due to slavery's legacy of divided black families, and the desperate crusades many parents had now launched to find their children, African Americans found the apprentice laws to be the most disheartening of all.

A. Penal code

Section 1. *Be it enacted by the legislature of the state of Mississippi*, that no freedman, free Negro, or mulatto not in the military service of the United States government, and not licensed so to do by the board of police of his or her county, shall keep or carry firearms of any kind, or any ammunition, dirk, or Bowie knife; and, on conviction thereof in the county court, shall be punished by fine, not exceeding $10, and pay the costs of such proceedings, and all such arms or ammunition shall be forfeited to the informer; and it shall be the duty of every civil and military officer to arrest any freedman, free Negro, or mulatto found with any such arms or ammunition, and cause him or her to be committed for trial in default of bail.

Section 2. *Be it further enacted*, that any freedman, free Negro, or mulatto committing riots, routs, affrays, trespasses, malicious mischief, cruel treatment to animals, seditious speeches, insulting gestures, language, or acts, or assaults on any person, disturbance of the peace, exercising the function of a minister of the Gospel without a license from some regularly organized church, vending spirituous or intoxicating liquors, or committing any other misdemeanor the punishment of which is not specifically provided for by law shall, upon conviction thereof in the county court, be fined not less than $10 and not more than $100, and may be imprisoned, at the discretion of the court, not exceeding thirty days.

Section 3. *Be it further enacted*, that if any white person shall sell, lend, or give to any freedman, free Negro, or mulatto any firearms, dirk, or Bowie knife, or ammunition, or any spirituous or intoxicating liquors, such person or persons so offending, upon conviction thereof in the county court of his or her county, shall be fined not exceeding $50, and may be imprisoned, at the discretion of the court, not exceeding thirty days:

Provided, that any master, mistress, or employer of any freedman, free Negro, or mulatto may give to any freedman, free Negro, or mulatto apprenticed to or employed by such master, mistress, or employer spirituous or intoxicating liquors, but not in sufficient quantities to produce intoxication. ...

Section 5. *Be it further enacted*, that if any freedman, free Negro, or mulatto convicted of any of the misdemeanors provided against in this act shall fail — or refuse, for the space of five days after conviction, to pay the fine and costs imposed, such person shall be hired out by the sheriff or other officer, at public outcry, to any white person who will pay said fine and all costs and take such convict for the shortest time.

B. Vagrancy Law

Section 2. *Be it further enacted*, that all freedmen, free Negroes, and mulattoes in this state over the age of eighteen years found on the second Monday in January 1966, or thereafter, with no lawful employment or business, or found unlawfully assembling themselves together either in the day or nighttime, and all white persons so assembling with freedmen, free Negroes, or mulattoes, or usually associating with freedmen, free Negroes, or mulattoes on terms of equality, or living in adultery or fornication with a freedwoman, free Negro, or mulatto, shall be deemed vagrants; and, on conviction thereof, shall be fined in the sum of not exceeding, in the case of a freedman, free Negro, or mulatto, $150, and a white man, $200, and imprisoned at the discretion of the court, the free Negro not exceeding ten days, and the white man not exceeding six months. ...

Section 5. *Be it further enacted*, that all fines and forfeitures collected under the provisions of this act shall be paid into the county treasury for general county purposes; and in case any freedman, free Negro, or mulatto shall fail for five days after the imposition of any fine or forfeiture upon him or her for violation of any of the provisions of this act to pay the same, that it shall be, and is hereby made, the duty of the sheriff of the proper county to hire out said freedman, free Negro, or mulatto to any person who will, for the shortest period of service, pay said fine or forfeiture and all costs:

Provided, a preference shall be given to the employer, if there be one, in which case the employer shall be entitled to deduct and retain the amount so paid from the wages of such freedman, free Negro, or mulatto then due or to become due; and in case such freedman, free Negro, or mulatto cannot be hired out he or she may be dealt with as a pauper. ...

Section 7. *Be it further enacted*, that if any freedman, free Negro, or mulatto shall fail or refuse to pay any tax levied according to the provisions of the 6th Section of this act, it shall be prima facie evidence of vagrancy, and it shall be the duty of the sheriff to arrest such freedman, free Negro, or mulatto, or such person refusing or neglecting to pay such tax, and proceed at once to hire, for the shortest time, such delinquent taxpayer to anyone who will pay the said tax, with accruing costs, giving preference to the employer, if there be one.

C. Civil rights law

Section 1. *Be it enacted by the legislature of the state of Mississippi,* that all freedmen, free Negroes, and mulattoes may sue and be sued, implead and be impleaded in all the courts of law and equity of this state, and may acquire personal property and chose in action, by descent or purchase, and may dispose of the same in the same manner and to the same extent that white persons may:

Provided, that the provisions of this section shall not be construed as to allow any freedman, free Negro, or mulatto to rent or lease any lands or tenements, except in incorporated towns or cities, in which places the corporate authorities shall control the same.

Section 2. *Be it further enacted,* that all freedmen, free Negroes, and mulattoes may intermarry with each other, in the same manner and under the same regulations that are provided by law for white persons:

Provided, that the clerk of probate shall keep separate records of the same.

Section 3. *Be it further enacted,* that all freedmen, free Negroes, and mulattoes who do now and have heretofore lived and cohabited together as husband and wife shall be taken and held in law as legally married, and the issue shall be taken and held as legitimate for all purposes. That it shall not be lawful for any freedman, free Negro, or mulatto to intermarry with any white person; nor for any white person to intermarry with any freedman, free Negro, or mulatto; and any person who shall so intermarry shall be deemed guilty of felony and, on conviction thereof, shall be confined in the state penitentiary for life; and those shall be deemed freedmen, free Negroes, and mulattoes who are of pure Negro blood; and those descended from a Negro to the third generation inclusive, though one ancestor of each generation may have been a white person.

Section 4. *Be it further enacted,* that in addition to cases in which freedmen, free Negroes, and mulattoes are now by law competent witnesses, freedmen, free Negroes, or mulattoes shall be competent in civil cases when a party or parties to the suit, either plaintiff or plaintiffs, defendant or defendants, also in cases where freedmen, free Negroes, and mulattoes is or are either plaintiff or plaintiffs, defendant or defendants, and a white person or white persons is or are the opposing party or parties, plaintiff or plaintiffs, defendant or defendants. They shall also be competent witnesses in all criminal prosecutions where the crime charged is alleged to have been committed by a white person upon or against the person or property of a freedman, free Negro, or mulatto:

Provided, that in all cases said witnesses shall be examined in open court on the stand, except, however, they may be examined before the grand jury, and shall in all cases be subject to the rules and tests of the common law as to competency and credibility.

Section 5. *Be it further enacted,* that every freedman, free Negro, and mulatto shall, on the second Monday of January 1866, and annually thereafter, have a lawful home or employment, and shall have a written evidence thereof, as follows, to wit: if living in any incorporated city, town, or village, a license from the mayor thereof; and if living outside of any incorporated city, town, or village, from the member of the board of police of his beat, authorizing him or her to do irregular and job work, or a written contract, as provided in Section 6 of this act, which licenses may be revoked for cause, at any time, by the authority granting the same.

Section 6. *Be it further enacted,* that all contracts for labor made with freedmen, free Negroes, and mulattoes for a longer period than one month shall be in writing and in duplicate, attested and read to said freedman, free Negro, or mulatto by a beat, city, or county officer, or two disinterested white persons of the county in which the labor is to be performed, of which each party shall have one; and said contracts shall be taken and held as entire contracts; and if the laborer shall quit the service of the employer before expiration of his term of service without good cause, he shall forfeit his wages for that year, up to the time of quitting.

Section 7. *Be it further enacted*, that every civil officer shall, and every person may, arrest and carry back to his or her legal employer any freedman, free Negro, or mulatto who shall have quit the service of his or her employer before the expiration of his or her term of service without good cause, and said officer and person shall be entitled to receive for arresting and carrying back every deserting employee aforesaid the sum of $5, and 10 cents per mile from the place of arrest to the place of delivery, and the same shall be paid by the employer, and held as a setoff for so much against the wages of said deserting employee:

Provided, that said arrested party, after being so returned, may appeal to a justice of the peace or member of the board of police of the county, who, on notice to the alleged employer, shall try summarily whether said appellant is legally employed by the alleged employer and has good cause to quit said employer; either party shall have the right of appeal to the county court, pending which the alleged deserter shall be remanded to the alleged employer or otherwise disposed of as shall be right and just, and the decision of the county court shall be final.

Section 8. *Be it further enacted*, that upon affidavit made by the employer of any freedman, free Negro, or mulatto, or other credible person before any justice of the peace or member of the board of police, that any freedman, free Negro, or mulatto, legally employed by said employer, has illegally deserted said employment, such justice of the peace or member of the board of police shall issue his warrant or warrants, returnable before himself, or other such officer, directed to any sheriff, constable, or special deputy, commanding him to arrest said deserter and return him or her to said employer, and the like proceedings shall be had as provided in the preceding section; and it shall be lawful for any officer to whom such warrant shall be directed to execute said warrant in any county of this state, and that said warrant may be transmitted without endorsement to any like officer of another county, to

be executed and returned as aforesaid, and the said employer shall pay the cost of said warrants and arrest and return, which shall be set off for so much against the wages of said deserter.

Section 9. *Be it further enacted*, that if any person shall persuade or attempt to persuade, entice, or cause any freedman, free Negro, or mulatto to desert from the legal employment of any person before the expiration of his or her term of service, or shall knowingly employ any such deserting freedman, free Negro, or mulatto, or shall knowingly give or sell to any such deserting freedman, free Negro, or mulatto any food, raiment, or other thing, he or she shall be guilty of a misdemeanor; and, upon conviction, shall be fined not less than $25 and not more than $200 and the costs; and, if said fine and costs shall not be immediately paid, the court shall sentence said convict to not exceeding two months' imprisonment in the county jail, and he or she shall moreover be liable to the party injured in damages:

Provided, if any person shall, or shall attempt to, persuade, entice, or cause any freedman, free Negro, or mulatto to desert from any legal employment of any person with the view to employ said freedman, free Negro, or mulatto without the limits of this state, such person, on conviction, shall be fined not less than $50 and not more than $1500 and costs; and, if said fine and costs shall not be immediately paid, the court shall sentence said convict to not exceeding six months' imprisonment in the county jail.

Section 10. *Be it further enacted*, that it shall be lawful for any freedman, free Negro, or mulatto to charge any white person, freedman, free Negro, or mulatto, by affidavit, with any criminal offense against his or her person or property; and, upon such affidavit, the proper process shall be issued and executed as if said affidavit was made by a white person; and it shall be lawful for any freedman, free Negro, or mulatto, in any action, suit, or controversy pending or about to be instituted, in any court of law or equity of this state. to make all needful and lawful affidavits, as shall be necessary for the institution, prosecution, or defense of such suit or controversy.

Section 11. *Be it further enacted*, that the penal laws of this state, in all cases not otherwise specially provided for, shall apply and extend to all freedmen, free Negroes, and mulattoes.

D. Apprentice Law

Section 1. *Be it enacted by the legislature of the state of Mississippi*, that it shall be the duty of all sheriffs, justices of the peace, and other civil officers of the several counties in this state to report to the Probate courts of their respective counties semiannually, at the January and July terms of said courts, all freedmen, free Negroes, and mulattoes under the age of eighteen within their respective counties, beats, or districts who are orphans, or whose parent or parents have not the means, or who refuse to provide for and support said minors; and thereupon it shall be the duty of said Probate Court to order the clerk of said court to apprentice said minors to some competent and suitable person, on such terms as the court may direct, having a particular care to the interest of said minors:

Provided, that the former owner of said minors shall have the preference when, in the opinion of the court, he or she shall be a Suitable person for that purpose. ...

Section 3. *Be it further enacted*, that in the management and control of said apprentices, said master or mistress shall have power to inflict such moderate corporeal chastisement as a father or guardian is allowed to inflict on his or her child or ward at common law:

Provided, that in no case shall cruel or inhuman punishment be inflicted.

Section 4. *Be it further enacted*, that if any apprentice shall leave the employment of his or her master or mistress without his or her consent, said master or mistress may pursue and recapture said apprentice and bring him or her before any justice of the peace of the county, whose duty it shall be to remand said appren-

tice to the service of his or her master or mistress; and in the event of a refusal on the part of said apprentice so to return, then said justice shall commit said apprentice to the jail of said county, on failure to give bond, until the next term of the county court; and it shall be the duty of said court, at the first term thereafter, to investigate said case; and if the court shall be of opinion that said apprentice left the employment of his or her master or mistress without good cause, to order him or her to be punished, as provided for the punishment of hired freedmen, as may be from time to time provided for by law, for desertion, until he or she shall agree to return to his or her master or mistress:

Provided, that the court may grant continuances, as in other cases; and *provided*, further, that if the court shall believe that said apprentice had good cause to quit his said master or mistress, the court shall discharge said apprentice from said indenture and also enter a judgment against the master or mistress for not more than $100, for the use and benefit of said apprentice, to be collected on execution, as in other cases.

Section 5. *Be it further enacted*, that if any person entice away any apprentice from his or her master or mistress, or shall knowingly employ an apprentice, or furnish him or her food or clothing, without the written consent of his or her master or mistress, or shall sell or give said apprentice ardent spirits, without such consent, said person so offending shall be deemed guilty of a high misdemeanor, and shall, on conviction thereof before the county court, be punished as provided for the punishment of persons enticing from their employer hired freedmen, free Negroes, or mulattoes. ...

—— 5.12 ——

THE CIVIL RIGHTS BATTLE OF 1866
U.S. Congress

When the 39th Congress convened in January 1866 the Radical Republicans, led by Senators Charles Sumner of Massachusetts and Thaddeus Stevens of Pennsylvania, were determined to undue what President Johnson had empowered the southern states to accomplish. They refused to recognize southern delegations, which they believed to be illegitimate. And they pushed federal laws forcing more sweeping Reconstruction, including black suffrage. The more compromising tact of moderate Republicans, however, led by Illinois Sen. Lyman Trumbull, prevailed. The Republicans established a Joint Committee on Reconstruction to study what had taken place in the South, and Trumbull introduced two bills designed to set reform apace. One bill expanded the powers and lengthened the mandate of the Freedmen's Bureau. It gave agents authority for oversight and adjudication of disputes, inviting blacks to file complaints about mistreatment and establishing remedies for those complaints. The second bill was to be the nation's first federal civil rights law. Seeking to build on the 13th amendment, the bill defined all persons born in the country as citizens and offered them "full and equal benefit of all laws" regardless of race. Again, it authorized federal agents to provide remedy for individuals whose rights were violated. The southern states had clearly proven they had no intention of moving beyond slavery, even following military defeat, without sustained federal intervention. So, in the name of protecting the freed slaves, Congress sought to expand federal powers over states in unprecedented ways.

Johnson, however, shocked Congress and the nation by vetoing both bills. His veto message for the Freedman's Bureau bill, below, foreshadows arguments against federal support for disadvantaged African Americans for the next century. It not only argues against the bill's particulars, it rejects the entire principle of offering humanitarian support to freed slaves. They have been freed, he argues, and should now become self-reliant like all other Americans. To support them further, moreover, would be an unreasonably expensive drain on federal funds. Johnson's vetoes strengthened the Radical Republicans' hand. An infuriated Congress overrode both vetoes (and, soon thereafter, set out to impeach the president). In an angry speech before the re-passage of the Civil Rights Bill, Trumbull countered Johnson's logic in both veto messages.

A. Johnson's Freedmen's Bureau bill veto message

... If passing from general considerations we examine the bill in detail, it is open to weighty objections. In time of war it was eminently proper that we should provide for those who were passing suddenly from a condition of bondage to a state of freedom; but this bill proposes to make the Freedmen's Bureau, established by the act of 1865, as one of the many great and extraordinary military measures to suppress a formidable rebellion, a permanent branch of the public administration, with its powers greatly enlarged. I have no reason to suppose, and I do not understand it to be alleged, that the act of March, 1865, has proved deficient for the purpose for which it was passed, although at that time, and for a considerable period thereafter, the Government of the United States remained unacknowledged in most of the States whose inhabitants had been involved in the rebellion. The institution of slavery, for the military destruction of which the Freedmen's Bureau was called into existence as an auxiliary, has been already effectually and finally abrogated throughout the whole country by an amendment of the *Constitution* of the United States, and practically, its eradication has received the assent and concurrence of most of those States in which it at any time had an existence. I am not, therefore, able to discern in the condition of the country anything to justify an apprehension that the powers and agencies of the Freedmen's Bureau, which were effective for the protection of freedmen and refugees during the actual continuance of hostilities and of African servitude, will now, in the dawn of peace, and after the abolition of slavery, prove inadequate to the same proper ends. If I am correct in these views, there can be no necessity for the enlargement of the powers of the Bureau for which provision is made in the bill.

The third section of the bill authorizes a general and unlimited grant of support to the destitute and suffering refugees and freedmen, their wives & children. Succeeding sections make provisions for the rent or purchase of landed estates for freedmen, & for the erection for their benefit of suitable buildings for asylums and schools, the expenses to be defrayed from the Treasury of the whole people. The

Congress of the United States has never heretofore thought itself empowered to establish asylums beyond the limits of the District of Columbia, except for the benefit of our disabled soldiers and sailors. It has never founded such schools for any class of our own people, not even for the orphans of those who have fallen in the defence of the Union, but has left the care of education to the much more competent and efficient control of the States, of communities, of private associations and individuals. It has never deemed itself authorized to expend the public money for the rent or purchase of rooms for thousands, not to say millions, of the white race who are honestly toiling from day to day for their subsistence. Asylums for the support of indigent persons in the United States was never contemplated by the authors of the Constitution. Nor can any good reason be adduced why a permanent establishment should be founded for one class of our people more than another. Pending the war, many refugees and freedmen received support from the Government, but it was never intended they should henceforth be fed, clothed, educated, and sheltered by the United States. The idea on which the slaves were assisted to freedom was that on becoming free they would be a self-sustaining population. Any legislation that shall imply that they are expected to attain a self-sustaining condition, must have a tendency injurious alike to their character and their prospects. The appointment of an agent for every county and parish will create an immense patronage, and the expense of the numerous officers and their clerks, to be appointed by the President, will be great in the beginning, with a tendency steadily to increase. The appropriations asked by the Freedmen's Bureau, as now established, for the year 1866, amount to $17,745,000. It may be safely estimated that the cost to be incurred under the pending bill will require double that amount, more than the entire sum expended in any one year under Administration of the second Adams. If the presence of agents in every parish and county is to be considered

as a war measure, opposition, or even resistance might be provoked, so that to give effect to their jurisdiction, troops would have to be stationed within reach of every one of them, and thus, a large standing force would be rendered necessary. Large appropriations would, therefore, be required to sustain and enforce military jurisdiction in every county or parish from the Potomac to the Rio Grande. The condition of our fiscal affairs is encouraging, but in order to sustain the present measure of public confidence, it is necessary we practice, not merely customary economy, but, as far as possible, severe retrenchment.

In addition to the objections already stated, the fifth section of the bill proposes to take away land from its former owners without any legal proceedings being first had, contrary to that provision of the Constitution which declares that no person shall be deprived of life, liberty, or property without due process of law. It does not appear that a part of the lands to which this section refers may not be owned by minors or persons of unsound mind, or by those who have been faithful to all their obligations as citizens of the United States. If any portion of the land is held by such persons, it is not competent for any authority to deprive them of it. If, on the other had, it be found that the property is liable to confiscation, even then it cannot be appropriated to purposes until, by due process of law, it shall have been declared forfeited by the Government. There is still further objection to the bill on grounds seriously affecting the class of persons to whom it is designed to bring relief; it will tend to keep the mind of the freedmen in a state of uncertain expectation and restlessness, while to those among whom he lives it will be a source of constant and vague apprehension. Undoubtedly the freedman should be protected, but he should be protected by the civil authorities, especially by the exercise of all the Constitutional powers of the courts of the United States and of the States. His condition is not so exposed as may at first be imagined. He is in a portion of the country where his labor cannot well be spared.

Competition for his services from planters, those who are constructing or repairing railroads, and from capitalists in his vicinage or from other States, will enable him to command almost his own terms. He also possesses a perfect right to change his place of abode, and if, therefore, he does not find in one community of State a mode of life suited to his desires, or proper remuneration for his labor he can move to one where that labor is more esteemed and better rewarded. In truth, however, each State, induced by its own wants and interests, will do what is necessary and proper to retain within its borders all the labor that is needed for the development of its resources. The laws that regulate, supply and demand, will maintain their force, and the wages of the laborer will be regulated thereby. There is no danger that the exceedingly great demand for labor will not operate in favor of the laborer, neither is sufficient consideration given to the ability of the freedmen to believe that as they have received their freedom with moderation and forbearance, so they will distinguish themselves by their industry and thrift, and soon show the world that in a condition of freedom they are self-sustaining, capable of selecting their own employments and their own places of abode, of insisting for themselves on a proper remuneration, and of establishing and maintaining their own asylums and schools. It is earnestly hoped that instead of wasting away they will by their own efforts, establish for themselves a condition of respectability and prosperity. It is certain that they can attain to that condition only through their own merits and exertions.

In this connection, the query presents itself, whether the system proposed by the bill will not, when put into complete operation, practically transfer the entire care, support and control of four millions of emancipated slaves to agents, overseers, or task-masters, who, appointed at Washington, are to be located in every county and parish throughout the United States containing freedmen and refugees? Such a system would inevitably tend to a concentration of power in the Executive which would enable him, if so disposed, to control the action of this numerous class, and, use them for the attainment of his own political ends. …

B. Civil Rights Act of 1866

Be it enacted, That all persons born in the United States and not subject to any foreign power, excluding Indians not taxed, are hereby declared to be citizens of the United States; and such citizens, of every race and color, without regard to any previous condition of slavery or involuntary servitude, except as a punishment for a crime whereof the party shall have been duly convicted, shall have the same right, in every State and Territory in the United States, to make and enforce contracts, to sue, be parties, and give evidence, to inherit, purchase, lease, sell, hold, and convey real and personal property, and to full and equal benefit of the laws and proceedings for the security of person and property, as is enjoyed by white citizens, and shall be subject to like punishment, pains, and penalties, and to none other, any law, statute, ordinance, regulation, or custom, to the contrary notwithstanding.

Sec. 2. *And be it further enacted*, That any person who, under color of any law, statute, ordinance, regulation, or custom, shall subject, or cause to be subjected, any inhabitant of any State or Territory to the deprivation of any right secured or protected by this act, or to different punishment, pains, or penalties on account of such person having at any time been held in a condition of slavery or involuntary servitude, except as a punishment for any crime whereof the party shall have been duly convicted, or by reason of his color or race, than is prescribed for the punishment of white persons, shall be deemed guilty of a misdemeanor, and, on conviction, shall be punished by fine not exceeding one thousand dollars, or imprisonment not exceeding one year, or both, in the discretion of the court. …

Sec. 4. *And be it further enacted*, That the district attorneys, marshals, and deputy marshals of the United States, the commissioners appointed by the circuit and territorial courts of the United States, with power of arresting, imprisoning, or bailing offenders against the laws of the United States, the officers and agents of the Freedmen's Bureau, and every other officer who may be specially empowered by the President of the United States, shall be, and they are hereby specially authorized and required, at the expense of the United States, to institute proceedings against all and every person who shall violate the provisions of this act, and cause him or them to be arrested and imprisoned, or bailed, as the case may be, for trial before such court of the United States or territorial court as by this act has cognizance of the offense. ...

Sec. 8. *And be it further enacted*, That the whenever the President of the United States shall have reason to believe that offenses have or are likely to be committed against the provisions of this act within any judicial district, it shall be lawful for him, in his discretion, to direct the judge, marshal, and district attorney of such district to attend at such place within the district, and for such time as he may designate, for the purpose of more speedy arrest and trial of persons charged with a violation of this act; and it shall be the duty of every judge or other officer, when any such requisition shall be received by him, to attend at the place and for the time therein designated.

Sec. 9. *And be it further enacted*, That it shall be lawful for the President of the United States, or such person as he may empower for that purpose, to employ such part of the land of naval forces of the United States, or of the militia, as shall be necessary to prevent the violation and enforce the due execution of this act.

Sec. 10. *And be it further enacted*, That upon all questions of law arising in any cause under the provisions of this act a final appeal may be taken to the Supreme Court of the United States.

—————— 5.13 ——————
THE 14TH AMENDMENT
U.S. Congress

The Civil Rights Act created two questions for the Radical Republicans. The first was that of the bill's constitutionality. The second, and more pressing, was its effect on the balance of state representation in congress and the Electoral College. The act, in effect, nullified the "three-fifths clause" of the Constitution by making blacks citizens. As a result, southern states were due massive boosts in national representation. Since it was obvious that they would not allow black suffrage, and congress was not yet prepared to demand it, this meant a sure Democratic sweep in the coming 1868 elections and, thus, a reversal of the new Reconstruction policies. So congress went to work crafting the 14th Amendment to the Constitution. After prolonged and difficult negotiations, senators and representatives agreed on a two-pronged amendment, shepherded through in large part by Radical Republican Rep. Thaddeus Stevens. The first section simply entered the principles of the Civil Rights Act into the nation's founding charter, settling the issue of the bill's constitutionality. The rest of the amendment dealt with the controversial representation issue. It declared that any state that denied males over the age of 21 the right to vote would lose national representation in degrees proportional to the numbers of those disenfranchised. Further, it established a requirement that two-thirds of congress approve any state's representative to national government who had participated in the rebellion.

Many reformers, however, still disliked the amendment. The representation sections were intended to indirectly encourage black suffrage while protecting northern hegemony in congress in the meantime. But some argued the compromise was a weak one, and that the amendment should have protected the new black citizens' right to vote. Further, it indirectly endorsed the ban on women voting by explicitly tying representation to the number of enfranchised males rather than eligible citizens, period. The women's movement was furious, and felt betrayed by abolitionist legislators, such as Sen. Charles Sumner, who had previously supported the cause.

Section 1. All persons born or naturalized in the United States, and subject to the jurisdiction thereof, are citizens of the United States and of the state wherein they reside. No state shall make or enforce any law which shall abridge the privileges or immunities of citizens of the United States; nor shall any state deprive any person of life, liberty, or property, without due process of law; nor deny to any person within its jurisdiction the equal protection of the laws.

Section 2. Representatives shall be apportioned among the several states according to their respective numbers, counting the whole number of persons in each state, excluding Indians not taxed. But when the right to vote at any election for the choice of electors for President and Vice President of the United States, Representatives in Congress, the executive and judicial officers of a state, or the members of the legislature thereof, is denied to any of the male inhabitants of such state, and citizens of the United States, or in any way abridged, except for participation in rebellion, or other crime, the basis of representation therein shall be reduced in the proportion which the number of such male citizens shall bear to the whole number of male citizens twenty-one years of agein such state.

Section 3. No person shall be a Senator or Representative in Congress, or elector of President and Vice President, or hold any office, civil or military, under the United States, or under any state, who, having previously taken an oath, as a member of Congress, or as an officer of the United States, or as a member of any state legislature, or as an executive or judicial officer of any state, to support the Constitution of the United States, shall have engaged in insurrection or rebellion against the same, or given aid or comfort to the enemies thereof. But Congress may by a vote of two-thirds of each House, remove such disability.

Section 4. The validity of the public debt of the United States, authorized by law, including debts incurred for payment of pensions and bounties for services in suppressing insurrection or rebellion, shall not be questioned. But neither the United States nor any state shall assume or pay any debt or obligation incurred in aid of insurrection or rebellion against the United States, or any claim for the loss or emancipation of any slave; but all such debts, obligations and claims shall be held illegal and void.

Section 5. The Congress shall have power to enforce, by appropriate legislation, the provisions of this article.

——————— 5.14 ———————

'IT IS USELESS TO ATTEMPT TO DISGUISE THE HOSTILITY THAT EXIST ... TOWARDS NORTHERN MEN'

New Orleans Riot of 1866

The tensions caused by the ongoing national debates over Reconstruction were best displayed in a riot that erupted in New Orleans during August of 1866. Frustrated with congressional failure to protect black voting rights, angered by the state's Black Codes and doubly insulted by the recent re-election of New Orleans's Confederate mayor, local Radical Republicans decided to reopen the 1864 state constitutional convention. They intended to meet and grant black suffrage, though whether or not such a move would carry any weight was unclear. Nevertheless, when 26 white delegates showed up in New Orleans, met by hundreds of black supporters, a white mob attacked. Reports charged that police, largely ex-Confederate soldiers, not only failed to quell the violence but joined in it. Thirty-four blacks and three whites were murdered, and over a hundred people were injured. President Johnson allowed federal troops to come in to restore peace, and Gen. Philip H. Sheridan filed this report.

... A very large number of colored people marched in procession on Friday night, July 27, and were addressed from the steps of the City Hall by Dr. Dostie, ex- Gov. Hahn, and others.

The speech of Dostie was intemperate in language and sentiment. The speeches of the others, as far as I can learn, were characterized by moderation. I have not given you the words of Dostie's speech, as the version published was denied; but from what I have learned of the man, I believe they were intemperate. The Convention assembled at 12 p.m., on the 30th, the timid members absenting themselves, because of the tone of the general public was ominous of trouble.

I think there were but about 26 members present. In front of the Mechanics' Institute, when the meeting was held, there was assembled some colored men, women, and children, perhaps 18 or 20, and in the Institute a number of colored men, probably 150. Among those outside and inside there might have been a pistol in the possession of every tenth man. About 1 p.m., a procession of say 60 to 130 colored men marched up Burgundy Street and across Canal Street, toward the Convention, carrying an American flag.

These men had about one pistol to every ten men, and canes and clubs in addition. While crossing Canal Street a row occurred. There were many spectators on the streets, and their manner and tone toward the procession unfriendly. A shot was fired, by whom I am not able to state, but believe it to have been by a policeman or some colored man in the procession; this led to other shots, and a rush after the procession.

On arrival at the front of the Institute there was some throwing of brick-brats by both sides. The police, who had been held well in hand, were vigorously marched to the scene of disorder. The procession entered the Institute with the flag, about six or eight remaining outside. A row occurred between a policeman and one of the colored men, and a shot was again fired by one of the parties, which led to an indiscriminate fire on the building through the windows by the policeman.

This had been going on for a short time, when a white flag was displayed from the window of the Institute; whereupon the firing ceased, and *the police rushed into the building. From the testimony of wounded men and others who were inside the building, the policeman opened an indiscriminate fire upon the audience until they had emptied their revolvers, when they retired, and those inside barricaded the doors.*

The door was broken in and the firing again commenced, when many of the colored and white people either escaped through the door or were passed out by the policemen inside, but as they came out, the policemen, who formed the circle nearest the building, fired upon them, and they were again fired upon by the citizens that formed the outer circle.

Many of those wounded and taken prisoners, and others who were prisoners and not wounded, were fired upon by their captors and by citizens. The wounded men were stabbed while lying on the ground and their heads beaten with brick-bats. In the yard of the building, whither some of the colored men had escaped and partially secreted themselves, they were fired upon and killed or wounded by policemen; some men were killed and wounded several squares from the scene. Members of the Convention were wounded by the policeman while their hands as prisoners, some of them mortally.

The immediate cause of this terrible affair was the assembling of this Convention. The remote cause was the bitter and antagonistic feeling which has been growing in this community since the advent of the present Mayor, who, in the organization of his police force, selected many desperate men, and some of them known murderers.

People of clear views were overawed by want of confidence in the Mayor and *fear of the Thugs, many of whom he had selected for his police force.* I have frequently been applied to by prominent citizens on this subject, and have heard them express fear and want of confidence in Mayor Monroe ever since the intimation of the last Convention. I must condemn the course of several of the city papers for supporting, by their articles, the bitter feeling of a bad man. *As to the merciless manner in which the Convention was broken up, I feed obliged to confess a strong repugnance.*

IT IS USELESS TO ATTEMPT TO DISGUISE THE HOSTILITY THAT EXISTS ON THE PART OF A GREAT MANY HERE TOWARD NORTHERN MEN;

AND THIS UNFORTUNATE AFFAIR HAS SO PRECIPITATED MATTERS THAT THERE IS NOW A TEST OF WHAT SHALL BE THE STATUS OF NORTHERN MEN — WHETHER THEY CAN LIVE HERE WITHOUT BEING IN CONSTANT DREAD OR NOT; WHETHER THEY CAN BE PROTECTED IN LIFE AND PROPERTY, AND HAVE JUSTICE IN THE COURTS.

If the matter is permitted to pass over without a thorough and determined prosecution of those engaged in it, *we may look for frequent scenes of the same kind, not only here but in other places.*

No steps have, as yet, been taken by the civil authorities to arrest citizens who were engaged in this massacre, or policeman who perpetrated such cruelties. The members of the Convention have been indicted by the Grand Jury, and many of them arrested and held to bail. As to whether the civil authorities can mete out ample justice to the guilty parties on both sides, I must say it is my opinion, unequivocally, that they cannot. …

——— 5.15 ———

'WE ALWAYS TOLD YOU … THAT IT WOULD BE A GREAT DEAL WORSE FOR YOU WHEN THEY COME'
Freedmen's Bureau Records

A large part of the reason southern whites so despised the Freedmen's Bureau from its outset was that, even before it began adjudicating black complaints against whites, it studiously documented the effort to recreate slavery's social order. The accounts below are excerpted from an 1865 report of the Freedman's Bureau agent in Richmond, Virginia. Blacks testify to arbitrary arrest, violent attacks and myriad forms of harassment at the hands of local officials. A recurring charge is that, as blacks protest the harassment, whites admonish them that they should have known things would get worse once the northerners began meddling in southern affairs.

Statement of Albert Brooks

Albert Brooks a colored man, who paid ($1,100) eleven hundred dollars for his freedom, has kept a livery and hack stable in Richmond more than ten years. At the commencement of the war he and his partner James Turner, owned 10 hacks and 22 horses and were worth more than $10,000 — during the war all their horses were taken by the Rebels, but one, and their hacks destroyed, but three. They have since increased their hacks to five and their horses to ten, with which they are now carrying on their former business. On the arrival of the Federal Army both applied to the Military Authorities for permission to carry on their business, took the oath of allegiance paid $12.50 each for a licence to run five hacks and received "protection" papers. On the 6th of June one of Mayor Major's old policemen, who had known all about me and my business for many years called at my stable and asked me if I had a pass. I showed him all my papers. He said they were no account I must have a pass, and that I must come along with him and go to jail — all niggers that did not have a paper from their master, showing that they were employed, must be taken to jail and hired out for $5.00 per month. He delivered me to a Federal Cavalry soldier and they together took me to the jailor, and he locked me in and they went away. I asked the jailor, the same one who has kept the jail for many years, and who knew all about me and my business, what the law required of us, and what they were going to do with us. He said we are agoing to hire all you niggers out for $5.00 a month, so you will not live on the Government. I said five dollars a month why I now pay four men each $35.00 a month myself. Well all this is done by your Yankee friends, who pretended they was agoing to set all the niggers free — we always told you they was the meanest men in the world, and that it would be a great deal worse for you when they come. Now you have nobody to protect you, and they are agoing to hire you out for $5.00 a month. After a good deal more of the same sort of talk about the Yankees, and

I had remained there an hour or more, one of Mayor's old policemen who was on duty there said Brooks you are a good fellow and I will have you turned out. I asked him what I was to do to prevent being arrested and taken from my business again. He said I must have some white master to give me a pass to show that I was employed. I said if I must have a master, I would have some of these Union men. I went to Asst. Provost Marshal Chas. Warren, 11th C. I. And asked him if he would be my master and give me a pass. He said he would. I asked him if my oath and permit, and licence and the seal of the U. S. were not sufficient — he would not answer. I said don't deceive me again. You told me before that these papers were sufficient — give me something now that will protect me — he than gave me a pass which I am obliged to show to Mayor's police, who stop on nearly every corner of the street and make it nearly impossible for me to carry on my business. I have lived here 40 years, have never received a stripe and was never before arrested, for any cause whatever. I will take oath to the above and can refer to hundreds of the best men in this city who will certify to my good character and voracity.

The above was taken down by me, as related, sentence by sentence.

Attest

signed H. W. Pierson
Richmond, Va.
June 10th 1865 ....

Statement of Wm. Ferguson

Proprietor of the "Shaving Emporium" Exchange Hotel. On the 7th inst. I saw a drunken white man assault a colored boy, for some time the boy made no resistance, but finally seized and threw the white man. A gentleman and myself separated them, and while the boy was hunting his hat, a second attack was made upon him, and they were again separated, and the colored boy retired, but soon after he was arrested and strung up by his arms in front of the Exchange Hotel. I saw him there suspended, and made his case known to two Northern ladies, one of whom went with me to the office of the Provost Marshal where I stated the facts of the case and the boy was released, together with another man who was being punished in a similar manner. Soon after this occurrence, I was talking in the street with Rev. & Mr. Stickney, an U. S. Army Chaplain, when several U. S. Soldiers assaulted me. Mr. Stickney interfered on my behalf & caused the arrest of one of the soldiers, and he was taken before the Provost Marshal, but whether punished or not, I cannot say.

Alex. M. Davis
Richmond, VA
June 9th 1865

In relation to the abuse of colored men by the civil military authorities — also conversation with Genl. Patrick and replies
Office of the Tribune
Richmond, Va., June 9, 1865
Col. O. Brown
Supt. Freedmen's Dept.
Virginia
Sir,
In reference to the wish of a friend, who informs me you are gathering the facts in relation to the condition of the colored people here. I would most respectfully submit the following incident occurring Thursday, June 8th as an indicative of the sentiment of those here having charge.

While standing on the corner of Franklin & 12th Sts. Thursday morning, attracted by the halting, examining and dispatching of colored men, I was somewhat astonished to hear Police officer Cowen make use of the following language to a colored lad formerly free, holding a pass from his employer — also a former freedmen, which pass the officer scrupled to accept, the lad observing "things are worse now than they ever were" to which the reply was "well didn't I tell you so, you damned fool, that when the Yankees came here you'd be a damned sight worse off, here take it," handing back the pass, "and get some white man to endorse it." A little chagrined that such a sentiment was tolerated here, I complained to Genl. Patrick that afternoon, desiring to know if former free Negroes could not give a pass to an employee and if the language cited above was becoming a Policeman in the discharge of his duty, my rebuff was "you had better go about your own business and not meddle with the authorities; there were difficulties enough with putting the Negro up to more; in the carrying out of new orders, abuses would at first exist, but in a time they would all right themselves." I stated "I would desire to have accorded me, while obeying the laws or assisting in their execution the right of protesting" "well, well just go along and you'll have no difficulties, the case of the Negro giving a pass was just decided here it will have to be endorsed by some well known white citizen or Provost Marshal."

The power given the police & guard to inspect the passes of colored men has been the past two days sadly abused, a further continuance is to place a class of our citizens in a state of anarchy and conduce more than any other measure to injure the cause of freedom and union.
Very Respectfully
Alex. M. Davis

——— 5.16 ———

'REBEL STATES SHALL BE DIVIDED INTO MILITARY DISTRICTS'
The Reconstruction Act

Republicans swept the 1866 mid-term elections and reconvened congress emboldened in their intention to reverse President Johnson's initial Reconstruction policies. Members debated a flurry of legislation aiming to overturn Johnson's appointed governments and institute military rule. The goal was to accomplish what the New Orleans Radical Republicans had sought to do before being met with a riot: re-assemble state constitutional conventions and start from scratch, this time keeping avowed Confederates out of government and enfranchising the freed slaves. The Reconstruction Acts of 1867 were the result. The first, passed over Johnson's now routine veto, established military control in all secessionist states and stripped them of national representation. The states could regain it only once they had reopened a constitutional convention of delegates elected by men over the age of 21, regardless of race, and drafted a constitution that conformed with that of the U.S. Additionally, the states would have to agree to the 14th Amendment. Again, many reformers were angered by the bill's failure to force black suffrage into the state constitutions. Congressional Republicans, however, believed they could go no further than forcing integrated conventions. Nevertheless, congress now seemed irreversibly headed down the path to protecting black suffrage.

Whereas no legal State governments or adequate protection for life or property now exists in the rebel States of Virginia, North Carolina, South Carolina, Georgia, Mississippi, Alabama, Louisiana, Florida, Texas and Arkansas; and whereas it is necessary that peace and good order should be enforced in said States until loyal and republican State governments can be legally established: Therefore,

Be it enacted by the Senate and House of Representatives of the United States of America in Congress assembled, That said rebel States shall be divided into military districts and made subject to the military authority of the United States as hereinafter prescribed, and for that purpose Virginia shall constitute the first district; North Carolina and South Carolina the second district; Georgia, Alabama and Florida the third district; Mississippi and Arkansas the fourth district; and Louisiana and Texas the fifth district.

Sec. 2 And be it further enacted, That it shall be the duty of the President to assign to the command of each of the said districts an officer of the army, not below the rank of brigadier-general, and to detail a sufficient military force to enable such officer to perform his duties and enforce his authority within the district to which he is assigned.

Sec. 3 And be it further enacted, That it shall be the duty of each officer assigned as aforesaid, to protect all persons in their rights of person and property, to suppress insurrection, disorder, and violence, and to punish, or cause to be punished, all disturbers of the public peace and criminals; and to this end he may allow local civil tribunals to take jurisdiction of and to try offenders, or, when in his judgment it may be necessary for the trial of offenders, he shall have power to organize military commissions or tribunals for that purpose, and all interference under color of State authority with the exercise of military authority under this act, shall be null and void.

Sec. 4 And be it further enacted, That all persons put under military arrest by virtue of this act shall be tried without unnecessary delay, and no cruel or unusual punishment shall be inflicted, and no sentence of any military commission or tribunal hereby authorized, affecting the life or liberty of any person, shall be executed until it is approved by the officer in command of the district, and the laws and regulations for the government of the army shall not be affected by this act, except in so far as they conflict with its provisions: Provided, That no sentence of death under the provisions of this act shall be carried into effect without the approval of the President.

Sec. 5 And be it further enacted, That when the people of any one of said rebel States shall have formed a constitution of government in conformity with the Constitution of the United States in all respects, framed by a convention of delegates elected by the male citizens of said State, twenty-one years old and upward, of whatever race, color, or previous condition, who have been resident in said State for one year previous to the day of such election, except such as may be disfranchised for participation in the rebellion or for felony at common law, and when such constitution shall provide that the elective franchise shall be enjoyed by all such persons as have the qualifications herein stated for electors of delegates, and when such constitution shall be ratified by a majority of the persons voting on the question of ratification who are qualified as electors for delegates, and when such constitution shall have been submitted to Congress for examina-

tion and approval, and Congress shall have approved the same, and when said State, by a vote of its legislature elected under said constitution, shall have adopted the amendment to the Constitution of the United States, proposed by the Thirty-ninth Congress, and known as article fourteen, and when such article shall have become a part of the Constitution of the United States, said State shall be declared entitled to representation in Congress, and senators and representatives shall be admitted therefrom on their taking the oath prescribed by law, and then and thereafter the preceding sections of this act shall be inoperative in said State: Provided, That no person excluded from the privilege of holding office by said proposed amendment to the Constitution of the United States, shall be eligible to election as a member of the convention to frame a constitution for any of said rebel States, nor shall any such person vote for members of such convention.

Sec. 6 And be it further enacted, That, until the people of said rebel States shall be by law admitted to representation in the Congress of the United States, any civil governments which may exist therein shall be deemed provisional only, and in all respects subject to the paramount authority of the United States at any time to abolish, modify, control, or supersede the same; and in all elections to any office under such provisional governments all persons shall be entitled to vote, and none others, who are entitled to vote under the provisions of the fifth section of this act; and no person shall be eligible to any office under any provisional governments who would be disqualified from holding office under the provisions of the third article of said constitutional amendment.

——— 5.17 ———
'KEEP BRIGHT
THE COUNCIL FIRES'
Union League of Alabama

Black political organizing throughout the Reconstruction era was largely carried out through a network of Union Leagues around the country. Founded during the war, the

Union Leagues maintained a national office in Washington, D.C., but were primarily independent local groups through which blacks joined with southern Unionists and Radical Republicans. In the South, they also served as clearinghouses for information about the unfolding debate over black suffrage and as de facto civic education schools. In small and large meetings, those who were literate read Republican papers and led discussions about the era's fast-moving politics. As a result, the free black population remained engaged, and agitated locally for change (such as in the New Orleans demonstration) — keeping pressure on national politicians to resolve the suffrage issue. Throughout the middle and late 1860s, Republicans particularly leaned on the Union Leagues to rally black and white support for their Reconstruction policies. They issued pamphlets such as the one excerpted below, from Montgomery, Alabama, in 1867, aiming to rally that support and push the state's leadership toward accepting the terms set out in the Reconstruction Acts.

... No word of cheer, however applies to our very properly *unrecognized* State. Alabama.

But for the loyalty before alluded to, which manifests so much power at a distance, the personal safety of the loyal men of Alabama might well be questioned. The late devotees to treason have far too much power to permit a loyal man to be regarded with respect by the masses in their train. The pains taken in all places of public resort to denounce the Government and its defenders; the manner in which a vicious press alludes to our flag; the continual annoyance of those who wear the National uniform in either service; the misrepresentations of a Bureau instituted to secure the colored man justice, and which has not been allowed to secure him that justice; and the ingratitude towards the Government in view of its lavish charity dispensed to suffering whites; all indicate that old things have not yet passed away — that treason is still a power in Alabama.

Here we would gladly pause and dismiss a theme contemplated only with regret. But the interests of humanity demand that the disposition to wrong those who have little, if any, influence in the State, should receive a passing notice, even in our present moderate and con-

servative temper. That freedmen have been defrauded of hard-earned wages justly due — that they have been punished for petty offences as no other class of men has been — that offenders against their persons and property meet with but nominal punishment under a vicious administration of the laws, and are often altogether shielded by a prejudiced public sentiment — and that former owners of minor children have used the State Courts to take them from the custody of guardians and protectors — are facts which must be published. We cannot do less than this. Were we inclined to be vindictive we might say much more, and yet speak but the simple truth. How true it is that the power of treason is thus far only weakened — that the old pro-slavery ideas, in which it had its birth, have still controlling power in the State.

And yet we say to you, our loyal brethren, take courage. The power which has made treason stagger, can make it die.

We desire that you keep bright the council fires, and see that the fact that positive loyalty still exists within our borders, is kept before the people, in season, and when the faint hearted would deem out of season. Teach them that in this whole nation loyalty will take no step backwards. Proclaim that the acceptance of the pending Constitutional amendments, with a rigid adherence to the Test Oath, are the mildest terms that will ever be presented as a basis of peace. — That even these complied with in letter only and not in spirit, will be of no avail. That loyalty, if not met with out-spoken praise, must be respected by the silence of its adversaries.

And brethren, while you do thus, look well unto yourselves, and see that you are true to whole spirit of the times. Meet fully the demands of the present hour. Abolish the spirit of hatred and contempt which makes us unwilling to accord to one class of our fellow citizens their rights as citizens. Let us do with all our might whatever lies in our power to make them competent sovereigns, equally with ourselves, of our free, common country.

In all the nations of the earth we see manifested the workings of an All-wise Providence in behalf of liberty and progress. The Russian Czar continues to execute his promise that, in spirit as well as in name, the serfs shall be free. Hungary again makes her despotic rulers tremble at her demands for a free constitution. Turkey is convulsed by popular uprisings, and her long benighted dependency, Egypt, emerges again into the view of the world with the concessions of suffrage and representation to the people, enslaved for many centuries. Staid old England's titled rulers stagger as they read the un-mistakeable signs of an approaching time in which the people shall rule. But our large slaveholders cling as fondly to the traditions of their favorite institution as the old order of nobles in France did to theirs, and seek to perpetuate their power over the negro by forever retaining him in an object position in our civil and social state. Yet if monarchs are yielding what has been termed a principle, how much easier ought it to be for us to yield a prejudice. It is the cardinal principle of our Government that the people shall rule, and under this principle whether we will it or not, the freedman will soon be recognized as a man, with all the powers and all the rights of every other man under our republican system.

It is your duty then, brethren, in view of this fact — if from no higher consideration — to discard the prejudices of the past against race and color. We would that nobler motives than those of policy might influence you, because even-handed justice is more potent and creditable as an incentive than the lower maxims of the mere politician — But if you will not be constrained by these higher impulses, heed the reasoning of sound policy. In the nature of things, the black man is your friend. In the war, the loyal men of the nation found nothing but kindness and respect on his part. He loved the flag which we love, and he suffered privation and death in behalf of the cause to us so dear. *Shall we have him for our ally or the rebel for our master?*

Trifle not with his friendship by denying him the rights to which he is justly entitled. Accept his proffered assistance, and accord to him the ballot that he may have that hold upon the laws which they have who help make them, and by which he may be shielded from the cruelty, wrong and oppression under which he now suffers. Let us seek to do from a sense of justice what the rebels are ready today to do, were they but convinced that he would use his vote to perpetuate their power.

Be strong, then, in the love of truth. Seek not to increase your numbers unless the numbers can be increased and the principles here enunciated be maintained at the same time.

Do this, and we will shortly be able to prove before the nation the falsity of the charge now made by rebels, that the loyal men of Alabama have not the ability to manage the State.

Do this, and we will be able to show before God and man, that we have not been unfaithful to the high trust committed to our care.

—————— 5.18 ——————

THE 15TH AMENDMENT
U.S. Congress

It has been argued that the 15th Amendment to the Constitution was more significant for what it left out than what it said. Short and relatively vague, the amendment, passed in February 1869, merely forbade the denial of the vote based on "race, color, or previous condition of servitude." Unlike the 14th Amendment, it conspicuously ignored more detailed questions, such as the use of indirect methods to block the vote — from poll taxes to literacy tests. At the time, the Republicans were focused on sealing their victory over southern Reconstruction by forcing the black vote. To do so, they had to protect a consensus within the Party on that point. A broader or more detailed amendment would have opened questions about other disenfranchised groups, such as women or Chinese Americans in the West; there was little agreement in the Party on these issues. Moreover, many reformists, including some well-off blacks and leading Women's Movement advocates such as Elizabeth Stanton, supported literacy tests in order to keep people they believed unprepared to vote disenfranchised. In coming years, the amendment's weakness, coupled with a prevailing view that the "Negro question" had finally been resolved, opened the door for southern politicians to find not-so-subtle routes of keeping blacks from the voting booth. In its immediate aftermath, however, the amendment would spark the election of a wave of black politicians.

Section 1. The right of citizens of the United States to vote shall not be denied or abridged by the United States or by any state on account of race, color, or previous condition of servitude.

Section 2. The Congress shall have power to enforce this article by appropriate legislation.

———— 5.19 ————
THE KU KLUX KLAN
Petitions from African Americans to Congress

The first response of white southerners to their decreased authority and the enfranchisement of blacks was violence. They formed "citizens' councils" and secret societies through which they unleashed reigns of terror on African Americans believed to be challenging the proper social and political order. The Ku Klux Klan, founded in Kentucky in 1866, was the most prominent and widespread of such groups. The organization, believed to have been composed of some of the most prominent members of white southern society, robed itself in secrecy — concealing the faces of members during "night rides" in which they dispensed vigilante justice and conducted lynchings, communicating with secret hand signals and coded language during silent parades, and covering even members' horses in white robes. In addition to concealing the actual membership, these tactics had the added effect of creating fear through mystery. Members were referred to as "ghouls," playing on the self-styled image of the men as avenging ghosts of the Confederacy. The letter to Congress below, from black residents of Frankfort, Kentucky, lists the names of 64 African Americans murdered by the Klan. Appeals such as this led to the Force Act of 1871, in which congress declared armed vigilante mobs equivalent to rebels against the government and granted President Ulysses Grant broad powers in suppressing them. This reaction would ultimately lead to the temporary retreat of Klan groups around the South.

To the Senate and house of Representatives in Congress assembled: We the Colored Citizens of Frankfort and vicinity to this day memorialize your honorable bodies upon the condition of affairs now existing in this the state of Kentucky.

We would respectfully state that life, liberty and property are unprotected among the colored races of this state. Organized Bands of desperate and lawless men mainly composed of soldiers of the late Rebel armies, Armed disciplined and disguised and bound by Oath and secret obligations, have by force terror and violence subverted all civil society among Colored people, thus utterly rendering insecure the safety of persons and property overthrowing all those rights which are the primary basis and objects of the government which are expressly guaranteed to us by the Constitution of the United States as amended; We believe you are not familiar with the description of the Ku Klux Klans riding nightly over the country going from County to County and in the County towns spreading terror wherever they go, by robbing whipping ravishing and killing our people without provocation, compelling Colored people to brake the ice and bathe in the Chilly waters of the Kentucky River.

The Legislature has adjourned; they refused to enact any laws to suppress Ku Klux disorder. We regard them as now being licensed to continue their dark and bloody deeds under cover of the dark night. They refuse to allow us to testify in the state Courts where a white man is concerned. We find their deeds are perpetrated only upon Colored men and white Republicans. We also find that for our services to the Government and our race we have become the special object of hatred and persecution at the hands of the Democratic party. Our people are driven from their homes in great numbers having no redress only the U.S. Courts which is in many cases unable to reach them. We would state that we have been law abiding citizens, pay our tax and in many parts of the state our people have been driven from the poles, refused the right to vote. Many have been slaughtered while attempting to vote, we ask how long is this state of things to last.

We appeal to you as law abiding citizens to enact some laws that will protect us. And that will enable us to exercise the rights of citizens. We see that the senator from this state denies there being organized Bands of desperaders in the state for information we lay before you a number of violent acts occurred during his Administration. Although he [Governor John. W.] Stevenson says half Dozen instances of violence did occur these are not more than one half the acts that have occured. The Democratic party has here a political organization composed only of Democrats not a single Republican can join them where many of these acts have been committed it has been proven that they were the men, done with Armies from the State Arsenal. We pray you will take steps to remedy these evils. Done by a Committee of Grievances appointed at a meeting of all the Colored Citizens of Frankfort & vicinity.

Mar. 25, 1871

Henry Marrs, Teacher colored school

Henry Lynn, Livery stable keeper

N. N. Trumbo, Grocer

Samuel Damsey

B. Smith

B. T. Crampton, Barber

1. A mob visited Harrodsburg in Mercer County to take from jail a man named Robertson, Nov. 14, 1867.

2. Smith attacked and whipped by regulation in Zelun County Nov. 1867.

3. Colored school house burned by incendiaries in Breckinridge Dec. 24, 1867.

4. A Negro Jim Macklin taken from jail in Frankfort and hung by mob January 28, 1868.

5. Sam Davis hung by mob in Harrodsburg May 28, 1868.

6. Wm. Pierce hung by a mob in Christian July 12, 1868.

7. Geo. Roger hung by a mob in Bradsfordville Martin County July 11, 1868.

8. Colored school Exhibition at Midway attacked by a mob July 31, 1868.

9. Seven person ordered to leave their homes at Standford, Ky. Aug. 7, 1868.

10. Silas Woodford age sixty badly beaten by disguised mob. Mary Smith Curtis and Margaret Mosby also badly beaten, near Keene Jessemine County Aug. 1868.

11. Cabe Fields shot — and killed by disguised men near Keene Jessemine County Aug. 3, 1868.

12. James Gaines expelled from Anderson by Ku Klux Aug. 1868.

13. James Parker killed by Ku Klux Pulaski, Aug. 1868.

14. Noah Blankenship whipped by a mob in Pulaski County Aug. 1868.

15. Negroes attacked robbed and driven from Summerville in Green County Aug. 21, 1868.

16. William Gibson and John Gibson hung by a mob in Washington County Aug. 1868.

17. F. H. Montford hung by a mob near Cogers landing in Jessamine County Aug. 28, 1868.

18. Wm. Glasscow killed by a mob in Warren Country Sep. 5, 1868.

19. Negro hung by a mob Sep. 1868.

20. Two Negros beaten by Ku Klux in Anderson county Sept. 11, 1868.

21. Mob attacked house of Oliver Stone in Fayette county Sept. 11, 1868.

22. Mob attacked Cumins house in Pulaski County. Cumins, his daughter and a man named adams killed in the attack Sept. 18, 1868.

23. U. S. Marshall Meriwether attacked captured and beatened with death in Larue County by mob Sept. 1868.

24. Richardson house attacked in Conishville by mob and Crasban killed Sept. 28 1868.

25. Mob attacks Negro cabin at hanging forks in Lincoln County. John Mosteran killed & Cash & Coffey killed Sept. 1869.

26. Terry Laws & James Ryan hung by mob at Nicholasville oct. 26, 1868.

27. Attack on Negro cabin in Spencer County — a woman outraged Dec. 1868.

28. Two negroes shot by Ku Klux at Sulphur Springs in Union County Dec. 1868.

29. Negro shot at Morganfield Union Country, Dec. 1868.

30. Mob visited Edwin Burris house in Mercer County, January, 1869.

31. William Parker whipped by Ku Klux in Lincoln County Jan. 20, 1869.

32. Mob attacked and fired into house of Jesse Davises in Lincoln County Jan. 20, 1868.

33. Spears taken from his room at Harrodsburg by disguise men Jan. 19, 1869.

34. Albert Bradford killed by disguise men in Scott County, Jan. 20, 1869.

35. Ku Klux whipped boy at Standford March 12, 1869.

36. Mob attacked Frank Bournes house in Jessamine County. Roberts killed March 1869.

37. Geo Bratcher hung by mob on sugar creek in Garrard County March 30, 1869.

38. John Penny hung by a mob at Nevada Mercer County May 29, 1869.

39. Ku Klux whipped Lucien Green in Lincoln County June 1869.

40. Miller whipped by Ku Klux in Madison Country July 2d, 1869.

41. Chas Henderson shot and his wife killed by mob on silver creek Madison County July 1869.

42. Mob decoy from Harrodsburg and hangs Geo Bolling July 17, 1869.

43. Disguise band visited home of I. C. Vanarsdall and T. J. Vanarsdall in Mercer County July 18, 1869.

44. Mob attack Ronsey's house in Casey County three men and one woman killed July 1869.

45. James Crowders hung by mob near Lebanon Merion County Aug. 9, 1869

46. Mob tar and feather a citizen of Cynthiana in Harrison County Aug. 1869.

47. Mob whipped and bruised a Negro in Davis County Sept. 1869.

48. Ku Klux burn colored meeting-house in Carrol County Sept. 1869.

49. Ku Klux whipped a negro at John Carmins's farm in Fayette County Sept. 1869.

50. Wiley Gevens killed by Ku Klux at Dixon Webster County Oct. 1869.

51. Geo. Rose killed by Ku Klux near Kirkville in Madison County Oct. 18, 1869.

52. Ku Klux ordered Wallace Sinkhorn to leave his home near Parkville Boyle County Oct. 1869.

53. Man named Shepherd shot by mob near Parksville Oct. 1869.

54. Regulator killed Geo Tanehly in Lincoln County Nov. 2d. 1869.

55. Ku Klux attacked Frank Searcy house in madison County one man shot Nov. 1869.

56. Searcy hung by mob madison County at Richmond Nov. 4th, 1869.

57. Ku Klux killed Robt. Mershon daughter shot Nov. 1869.

58. Mob whipped Pope Hall and Willett in Washington County Nov. 1869.

59. Regulators whipped Cooper in Pulaski County Nov. 1869.

60. Ku Klux ruffians outraged negroes in Hickman County Nov. 20, 1869.

61. Mob take two Negroes from jail Richmond Madison County one hung one whipped Dec. 12, 1869.

62. Two Negroes killed by mob while in civil custody near Mayfield Graves County Dec. 1869.

63. Allen Cooper killed by Ku Klux in Adair County Dec. 24th, 1869.

64. Negroes whipped while on Scott's farm in Franklin County Dec. 1869.

——— 5.20 ———

THE NEW BLACK LAWS
Benjamin W. Arnett

The 1870s saw a series of Supreme Court rulings that slowly eroded the relevance of the post-war constitutional amendments. In 1873, the court ruled the 14th Amendment didn't completely remove the states' right to establish citizenship. Three years later it declared the 15th Amendment only articulated the manner in which the franchise could not be withheld. These rulings, combined with new laws that blocked the black vote indirectly — such as poll taxes and literacy tests that only applied to voters who registered after 1865 — brought southern Democrats back to power. With the nation's attention turned from race relations to economic revival, and Ku Klux Klan activity heighten, racial tensions all over the country, life for African Americans quickly worsened at the end of the century.

Although the immediate post-war Black Codes of the South did not survive Reconstruction, southern legislatures did not give up their efforts to legally re-impose the racial hierarchy of slavery. By the late 1870s, "Jim Crow" laws were reappearing throughout the South and North, separating people by race in transportation, housing, public accommodations, education and nearly every other sphere of society. Social support for these laws was driven by overt appeals to racist beliefs in the innate criminality of African Americans, particularly black men. In an 1886 speech before the Ohio House of Representatives, black legislator Benjamin Arnett, advocating a bill to repeal Ohio's Jim Crow laws, offered a testimony and critique of the civil and social attack on blacks that could have applied almost anywhere in the country.

… The denial of our civil rights in this and other States is a subject of public notoriety, denied by none but acknowledged by all to be wrong and unjust; yet, in traveling in the South we are compelled to feel its humiliating effects. It is written over the door of the waiting room, "For Colored Persons;" and in that small, and frequently dirty and dingy room, you have to go or stand on the platform and wait for the train. In Georgia they have cars marked "For Colored Passengers." There is one railroad in Alabama that has a special car for colored persons. They will not allow a white man to ride in that car; and many other roads allow the lower classes to ride in the car set apart for "Colored Persons."

One would think that at this time of our civilization, that character, and not color, would form the line of distinction in society, but such is not the case. It matters not what may be the standing or intelligence of a colored man or woman, they have to submit to the wicked laws and the more wicked prejudice of the people. It is not confined to either North or South. It is felt in this State to some extent; we feel it in the hotels, we feel it in the opera house. There are towns in this State where respectable ladies and gentlemen have been denied hotel accommodations, but such places

are diminishing daily, under the growing influences of equal laws.

In the city of Cincinnati there are places where a colored man cannot get accommodations for love nor money; there was a man who started an equal rights house; the colored people patronized him; his business increased; he made money. He has closed his house against his former patrons, and will not accommodate them.

Members will be astonished when I tell them that I have traveled in this free country for twenty hours without anything to eat; not because I had no money to pay for it, but because I was colored. Other passengers of a lighter hue had breakfast, dinner and supper. In traveling we are thrown in "jim crow" cars, denied the privilege of buying a berth in the sleeping coach. This monster caste stands at the doors of the theatres and skating rinks, locks the doors of the pews in our fashionable churches, closes the mouths of some of the ministers in their pulpits which prevents the man of color from breaking the bread of life to his fellow men.

This foe of my race stands at the school house door and separates the children, by reason of *color*, and denies to those who have a visible admixture of African blood in them the blessings of a graded school and equal privileges. We propose by this bill to knock this monster in the head and deprive him of his occupation, for he follows us all through life; and even some of our graveyards are under his control. The colored dead are denied burial. We call upon all friends of *Equal Rights* to assist in this struggle to secure the blessings of untrammeled liberty for ourselves and prosperity. …

We are willing to bear our equal burden, and assist in developing the resources of the country. We are willing to go to the corn-field or to the cotton-field, and there do our duty as men. We have toiled in the canebrakes of Alabama, and waded in the rice swamps of the Carolinas; we have dug in the lead mines of Missouri without pay or hope of reward. But now we have the same aspirations that other men have. If they live in the city, so can we. If they prosper on the farm so can we. If they hold office, so can we, if we get *roles enough*. If they go to church, so will we. If they are on the grand or petit jury, one of us will be there to find a true bill or to bring in a verdict. If they go to the workhouse, they will have company in breaking stone. Whether in good or bad society, in doing right or wrong, we are bound together as one. We are united in life, and shall not be separated in death.

Seeing, then, that we are so intimately connected with each other as men and citizens, what wicked prejudice it is to have laws separating our children while learning their duty to themselves, their neighbor, to society, to country and their God; let us do our duty, and in doing this the walls of separation will crumble and fall.

—————— 5.21 ——————

BEHIND THE SCENES
Elizabeth Keckley

When she moved into Washington, D.C., new First Lady Mary Todd Lincoln hired noted black dressmaker Elizabeth Keckley. Keckley remained at Mrs. Lincoln's side throughout her time in the White House and became a confidant. In 1868, she catapulted to fame with her version of the now-routine Washington, D.C., "tell-all" book. In *Behind the Scenes*, she offered the nation an intimate look at the Lincoln family as it navigated the dramatic personal and political turns of Lincoln's tenure as president, a technique that has been used by many intimate associates-cum-writers since. The book was roundly derided as the lies and fantasies of an ignorant black woman, and ultimately withdrawn from the shelves. Keckley, previously a well-respected service-provider to D.C.'s upper crust, was shunned and driven out of business. In the passage below, she quotes Mrs. Lincoln chiding the president about what she feels is poor judgment in selecting political and military associates.

… Mrs. Lincoln prided herself upon her ability to read character. She was shrewd and far-seeing, and had no patience with the frank, confiding nature of the President.

When Andrew Johnson was urged for military Governor of Tennessee, Mrs. Lincoln bitterly opposed the appointment.

"He is a demagogue," she said, almost fiercely, "and if you place him in power, Mr. Lincoln, mark my words, you will rue it some day."

General McClellan, when made Commander-in-Chief, was the idol of the soldiers, and never was a general more universally popular: "He is a humbug," remarked Mrs. Lincoln one day in my presence.

"What makes you think so, mother?" good-naturedly inquired the President.

"Because he talks so much and does so little. If I had the power I would very soon take off his head, and put some energetic man in his place."

"But I regard McClellan as a patriot and an able soldier. He has been much embarrassed. The troops are raw, and the subordinate officers inclined to be rebellious. There are too many politicians in the army with shoulder-straps. McClellan is young and popular, and they are jealous of him. They will kill him off if they can."

"McClellan can make plenty of excuse for himself, therefore he needs no advocate in you. If he would only do something, and not promise so much, I might learn to have a little faith in him. I tell you he is a humbug, and you will have to find some man to take his place, that is, if you wish to conquer the South."

Mrs. Lincoln could not tolerate General Grant. "He is a butcher," she would often say, "and is not fit to be at the head of an army."

"But he has been very successful in the field," argued the President.

"Yes, he generally manages to claim a victory, but such a victory! He loses two men to the enemy's one. He has no management, no regard for life. If the war should continue four years longer, and he should remain in power, he would depopulate the North. I could fight an army as well myself. According to his tactics, there is nothing under the heavens to do but to march a new line of men up in front of the rebel breastworks to be shot down as fast as they take their position, and keep marching until the enemy grows tired of the slaughter. Grant, I repeat, is an obstinate fool and a butcher."

"Well, mother, supposing that we give you command of the army. No doubt you would do much better than any general that has been tried." There was a twinkle in the eyes, and a ring of irony in the voice.

I have often heard Mrs. Lincoln say that if Grant should ever be elected President of the United States she would desire to leave the country, and remain absent during his term of office.

─────── 5.22 ───────
IOLA LEROY
Frances Ellen Watkins Harper

While the political outlook for African Americans began bottoming out in the late 19th century, black culture was about to explode onto the mainstream. From literature to music to journalism to academia, African Americans would take the nation by storm as it headed into the 20th century. And in the last 10 to 15 years of the 1800s, black women writers would particularly blossom. Francis Harper is perhaps the best-known example.

Having begun her writing career back in 1846 (see Chapter Three), Harper was actually a veteran among the new black women writers at the end of the 19th century. Nevertheless, it wasn't until this time, in 1892, that she published her best-known work. For most of the 20th century, her novel *Iola Leroy: or, Shadows Uplifted* was considered the first published by a black woman. (Scholar Henry Louis Gates, Jr., discovered Harriet Wilson's earlier work, *Our Nig*, in 1983. See Chapter Four.) It is still believed to be only the second novel published by an African-American woman. It tells the story of a mixed-race young woman, Iola Leroy, navigating the racism, sexism and classism of the Civil War and Reconstruction eras. In the excerpt below, the light-skinned Iola struggles trying to find work in the North. As long as she allows people to believe she's white, she has no problem. But her conscience does not allow it, and she gets fired. "Passing," as it was called, was common among light-skinned African Americans from the abolitionist era all the way to the end of the Civil Rights movement.

"Uncle Robert," said Iola, after she had been North several weeks, "I have a theory that every woman ought to know how to earn her own living. I believe that a great amount of sin and misery springs from the weakness and inefficiency of women."

"Perhaps that's so, but what are you going to do about it?"

"I am going to join the great rank of bread-winners. Mr. Waterman has advertised for a number of saleswomen, and I intend to make application."

"When he advertises for help he means white women," said Robert.

"He said nothing about color," responded Iola.

"I don't suppose he did. He doesn't expect any colored girl to apply."

"Well, I think I could fill the place. At least I should like to try. And I do not think when I apply that I am in duty bound to tell him my great-grand-mother was a negro."

"Well, child, there is no necessity for you to go out to work. You are perfectly welcome here, and I hope that you feel so."

"Oh, I certainly do. But still I would rather earn my own living."

That morning Iola applied for the situation, and, being prepossessing in her appearance, she obtained it.

For awhile everything went as pleasantly as a marriage bell. But one day a young colored lady, well-dressed and well-bred in her manner, entered the store. It was an acquaintance which Iola had formed in the colored church which she attended. Iola gave her a few words of cordial greeting, and spent a few moments chatting with her. The attention of the girls who sold at the same counter was attracted, and their suspicion awakened. Iola was a stranger in that city. Who was she, and who were her people? At last it was decided that one of the girls should act as a spy, and bring what information she could concerning Iola.

The spy was successful. She found out that Iola was living in a good neighborhood, but that none of the neighbors knew her. The man of the house was very fair, but there was an old woman whom Iola called "Grandma," and she was unmistakably colored. The story was sufficient. If that were true, Iola must be colored, and she should be treated accordingly.

Without knowing the cause, Iola noticed a chill in the social atmosphere of the store, which communicated itself to the cash-boys, and they treated her so insolently that her situation became very uncomfortable. She saw the proprietor, resigned her position, and asked for and obtained a letter of recommendation to another merchant who had advertised for a saleswoman.

In applying for the place, she took the precaution to inform her employer that she was colored. It made no difference to him; but he said: —

"Don't say anything about it to the girls. They might not be willing to work with you."

Iola smiled, did not promise, and accepted the situation.

She entered upon her duties, and proved quite acceptable as a saleswoman.

One day, during an interval in business, the girls began to talk of their respective churches, and the question was put to Iola: —

"Where do you go to church?"

"I go," she replied, "to Rev. River's church, corner of Eighth and L Streets."

"Oh, no; you must be mistaken. There is no church there except a colored one."

"That is where I go."

"Why do you go there?"

"Because I liked it when I came here, and joined it."

"A member of a colored church? What under heaven possessed you to do such a thing?"

"Because I wished to be with my own people."

Here the interrogator stopped, and looked surprised and pained, and almost instinctively moved a little farther from her. After the store was closed, the girls had an animated discussion, which resulted in the information being sent to Mr. Cohen that Iola was a colored girl, and that they protested against her being continued in his employ. Mr. Cohen yielded to the pressure, and informed Iola that her services were no longer needed.

When Robert came home in the evening, he found that Iola had lost her situation, and was looking somewhat discouraged.

"Well, uncle," she said, "I feel out of heart. It seems as if the prejudice pursues us through every avenue of life, and assigns us the lowest places."

"That is so," replied Robert, thoughtfully. ...

--------- 5.23 ---------

THE HEZELEY FAMILY
Amelia Etta Johnson

Amelia Etta Johnson was one of the late 19th century's blossoming black female writers. Johnson, born in Canada to parents who fled slavery in Maryland, was one of the first African Americans to write children's stories. In 1888, she founded *Ivy*, a black children's monthly newspaper. A devout Baptist, she contributed children's stories and poems to denominational publications as well. In 1892, she published the first of three children's novels, each with a white main character. The first, *The Hazeley Family*, excerpted below, tells the story of a 16-year-old young woman named Flora who sets out to do good and bring her family closer together. As with her other books, the story is meant to show children how to lead proper lives.

BREAKFAST over, and the dishes cleared away, Flora looked about, wondering what else there was for her to do. Her father was reading a paper, and the boys had gone away. She went to the window where Lottie's potato stood in its jar. The sight of it carried her thoughts back so vividly to the old days, that she half resolved to look at it no more.

She felt dull and spiritless to-day; it was no wonder, for there was little to make her feel otherwise. At Aunt Bertha's, every one had been accustomed to attend church, and Flora remained to Sunday-school. She had been converted and received into the church about a year before her aunt's death. Her sudden sorrow, her hasty trip from Brinton, and her unfamiliar surroundings in her new home, caused her to feel as if she had been removed to a heathen land.

None of the Hazeley household attended church, and Flora knew of no place to which she could go, for all was so new and strange to her, and being somewhat timid, she would not go alone.

Still standing at the window, and looking drearily out on the quiet street, she saw Ruth and little Jem passing, on their way to church. When they saw Flora they stopped, and she, glad to see a friendly face, hastened to open the door.

"Would you not like to come with us to church, this morning?" asked Ruth.

"Indeed I should," replied Flora. "I was just wondering what I was going to do with myself to day. Wait a minute; I will be ready in a very short time."

As good as her word, she was soon ready. "I am so glad that you stopped for me, Ruth," said she, as they walked along. "I know nothing about the churches here, and no one goes from our house."

"That is too bad," returned Ruth, sympathizingly.

Flora was indeed glad that she had come when, as they ascended the church steps, she heard the deep tones of the organ pealing out a welcome to all who entered. As they walked up the aisle, it seemed as if the sweet notes of the music twined around them, as though enfolding them in a loving embrace. A feeling of quiet content filled the heart of the young girl, and for a time the realities were forgotten in the soothing sense of rest that stole over her. Nor did she attempt to arouse herself until the opening services were ended, and the minister arose to announce his text.

In clear, distinct tones he read: "Whatsoever thy hand findeth to do, do it with thy might." Twice he slowly read the words, until Flora thought he surely must have pressed them right into her brain, for she felt that they were indelibly imprinted on her memory. Whether the sermon was intended especially for young people, or not, she did not know, but she felt that it was peculiarly adapted to herself. I have no doubt that the older folks felt the same with regard to themselves. It was one of those texts and sermons that suit everybody.

"I wonder how many of my hearers can say truthfully that they have done with their might 'whatsoever' their hands found to do," said the minister, looking, as Flora thought, directly at her.

She dropped her eyes uneasily to the floor, and mentally admitted, "I, for one, have not, unless it was to grumble and fret with all my might. I have done that, but nothing else, at least since I came home."

"I am sure you cannot say that your hand has found nothing to do. You can perhaps say that your hand has not found what you wished it to do; but that is not what the words of the text teach. It says *whatsoever* thy hand finds to do.' Then too, it is to be done 'with thy might'; not half-heartedly."

"Oh," commented Flora to herself, "why *should* he talk so straight at me? If he is not describing Flora Hazeley, I am mistaken."

"Did you ever notice," the minister continued, "that when you did a thing heartily, even though it was not the most agreeable occupation to you, it became more easy and pleasant to you?"

Flora thought of the little help she had voluntarily given her mother the previous evening, and again inwardly agreed with the speaker. The minister said a great many things that morning, some of which had never entered Flora's mind, and they made her very thoughtful; so thoughtful that she paid but little attention to the strains of the organ that accompanied her out of the church. She remembered he had spoken of many kinds of work the hands might find to do, and which were to be done faithfully and heartily. Perhaps it would be church work; perhaps professional work; perhaps mechanical work; and perhaps house-work and home-work. The last two, he thought, ought to go together, as neither could do very well without the other, although each differed in character. "House-work," he said, "as all knew, was sweeping, dusting, cooking, and the other duties connected with caring for the house; but home-work was the making and keeping a home;

helping those in it to be contented and happy; brightening and making it cheery by both word and deed; shedding a healthful and inspiring influence, so that those around us may be the better for our presence."

"According to that, we all have a 'whatsoever,'" said Flora, emphatically to herself; "and the sooner I decide to start on my own part, the better it will be for me."

With her mind busy with many things, Flora was very quiet on her way home. The sermon to which they had listened was plain and practical. It was not brilliant, but it was helpful. The ideas were not necessarily new, but the words fell upon at least one heart already prepared and softened by circumstances to receive and profit by them. To Flora they were seed, falling upon the prepared ground of her heart, and in due time the fruit came forth. Most of the suggestions were new to her, for never before had she viewed them in this particular light.

Ruth respected her friend's silence, for she saw that she was busy with her thoughts, and guessing something of what they were, she was also quiet. Jem was unaffected by the silence of her elders. She walked along at Ruth's side, with her hand closely holding her sister's. Her happy life caused her every now and then to lapse from her dignified walk, and give a little jump and a skip. A continual volley of questions was thrown at Ruth, whose replies were not always as obvious as occasion demanded.

Jem's quick retort, "No, it isn't, Ruth," brought her to a realization of her abstractedness, and she resolved to be more attentive.

They left Flora at her door, Ruth asking if she had enjoyed the service, and added:

"Will you not come to Sunday-school with us this afternoon?"

"I did enjoy the sermon very much," Flora replied, "and I shall be pleased to go to Sunday-school. If you will call for me, Ruth, I will be ready when you come." A number of things grew out of Flora's experience on this Sunday. Its influence stayed with her, and had no small part in shaping her future life. She soon became an earnest worker to make the world better for

her living in it; striving patiently and faithfully to render her daily life a power for good to those around her. How she succeeded our story will tell. Last, but not least, a strong affection sprang up between Ruth and herself, which proved a blessing to both. …

——— 5.24 ———

VIOLETS

Alice Ruth Moore (Alice Dunbar-Nelson)

One of the best-known black woman writers of the turn of the century is Alice Ruth Moore, who later married famed black poet Paul Lawrence Dunbar. The New Orleans native was known for her multiple talents and pursuits — teaching, music, stenography, activism and writing of all sorts. She was a poet, essayist, critic and novelist. Her first acclaimed work was the 1895 collection of poems and short stories *Violets and Other Tales*, published three years after she graduated from Dillard University (then Straight College). Her writing addressed many of the social issues involving race and gender that she became involved with politically. But it also covered a range of other topics, including love. The title story of her first collection is a bittersweet take on past romances.

I.

"And she tied a bunch of violets with a tress of her pretty brown hair."

She sat in the yellow glow of the lamplight softly humming these words. It was Easter evening, and the newly risen spring world was slowly sinking to a gentle, rosy, opalescent slumber, sweetly tired of the joy which had pervaded it all day. For in the dawn of the perfect morn, it had arisen, stretched out its arms in glorious happiness to greet the Saviour and said its hallelujahs, merrily trilling out carols of bird, and organ and flower-song. But the evening had come, and rest.

There was a letter lying on the table, it read:

"Dear, I send you this little bunch of flowers as my Easter token. Perhaps you may not be able to read their meanings, so I'll tell you. Violets, you know, are my favorite flowers. Dear, little, human-faced things! They seem always as if about to whisper a love-word; and then they signify that thought which passes always between you and me. The orange blossoms — you know their meaning; the little pinks are the flowers you love; the evergreen leaf is the symbol of the endurance of our affection; the tube-roses I put in, because once when you kissed and pressed me close in your arms, I had a bunch of tube-roses on my bosom, and the heavy fragrance of their crushed loveliness has always lived in my memory. The violets and pinks are from a bunch I wore to-day, and when kneeling at the altar, during communion, did I sin, dear, when I thought of you? The tube-roses and orange-blossoms I wore Friday night; you always wished for a lock of my hair, so I'll tie these flowers with them — but there, it is not stable enough; let me wrap them with a bit of ribbon, pale blue, from that little dress I wore last winter to the dance, when we had such a long, sweet talk in that forgotten nook. You always loved that dress, it fell in such soft ruffles away from the throat and blossoms, — you called me your little forget-me-not, that night. I laid the flowers away for awhile in our favorite book, — Byron — just at the poem we loved best, and now I send them to you. Keep them always in remembrance of me, and if ought should occur to separate us, press these flowers to your lips, and I will be with you in spirit, permeating your heart with unutterable love and happiness."

II.

It is Easter again. As of old, the joyous bells clang out the glad news of the resurrection. The giddy, dancing sunbeams laugh riotously in field and street; birds carol their sweet twitterings everywhere, and the heavy perfume of flowers scents the golden atmosphere with inspiring fragrance. One long, golden sunbeam steals silently into the white-curtained window of a quiet room, and lay athwart a sleeping face. Cold, pale, still, its fair, young face pressed against the stain-lined casket. Slender, white fingers, idle now, they that had never

known rest; locked softly over a bunch of violets; violets and tube-roses in her soft, brown hair, violets in the bosom of her long, white gown; violets and tube-roses and orange-blossoms banked everywhere, until the air was filled with the ascending souls of the human flowers. Some whispered that a broken heart had ceased to flutter in that still, young form, and that it was a mercy for the soul to ascend on the slender sunbeam. To-day she kneels at the throne of heaven, where one year ago she had communed at an earthly altar.

III.

Far away in a distant city, a man, carelessly looking among some papers, turned over a faded bunch of flowers tied with a blue ribbon and a lock of hair. He paused meditatively awhile, then turning to the regal-looking woman lounging before the fire, he asked:

"Wife, did you ever send me these?"

She raised her great, black eyes to his with a gesture of ineffable disdain, and replied languidly:

"You know very well I can't bear flowers. How could I ever send such sentimental trash to anyone? Throw them into the fire."

And the Easter bells chimed a solemn requiem as the flames slowly licked up the faded violets. Was it merely fancy on the wife's part, or did the husband really sigh, — a long, quivering breath of remembrance?

––––––––– 5.25 –––––––––

OAK AND IVY
Paul Lawrence Dunbar

Paul Lawrence Dunbar was perhaps the first major figure in African-American history born after the Civil War. From a humble beginning as the self-published "elevator boy poet," he rose to become one of the most acclaimed poets in the literary history of not only African America, but America at large.

Growing up in Dayton, Ohio, Dunbar was the star of his high school — despite being the only black student in his class. He edited the school's paper, was elected class president and composed the class song — one of his earliest works of poetry. Despite these achievements, Dunbar was unable to find professional work in Dayton upon graduating, and took a job as an elevator boy. The poems and short stories he wrote while operating the lift earned him his early moniker. Encouraged by one of his high school teachers, Dunbar read his work before a writers' convention that met in Dayton in 1892. He was a hit, and word quickly spread around the country about the talented 20-year-old. The following year, he published his first book of poems, *Oak and Ivy*, excerpted below.

A. "Welcome Address"

TO THE WESTERN ASSOCIATION
OF WRITERS.

"Westward the course of empire takes its
    way," —
So Berkeley said, and so to-day
The men who know the world still say.
The glowing West, with bounteous hand,
Bestows her gifts throughout the land,
And smiles to see at her command
Art, science, and the industries,
New fruits of new Hesperides.
So, proud are you who claim the West
As home land; doubly are you blest
To live where liberty and health
Go hand in hand with brains and wealth.
So here's a welcome to you all,
Whate'er the work your hands let fall,
To you who trace on history's page
The footprints of each passing age;
To you who tune the laureled lyre
To songs of love or deeds of fire;
To you before whose well-wrought tale
The cheek doth flush or brow grow pale;
To you who bow the ready knee
And worship cold philosophy,
A welcome warm as Western wine,
And free as Western hearts, be thine.
Do what the greatest joy insures,
The city has no will but yours!
                June 27, 1892.

B. "The Old Tunes"

You kin talk about yer anthems
    An' yer arias an' sich,
An' yer modern choir singin'
    That you think so awful rich;
But you orter heerd us youngsters
    In the times now far away,
A singin' o' the ol' tunes
    In the ol'-fashioned way.

There was some o' us sung treble,
    An' a few o' us growled bass,
An' the tide o' song flowed smoothly
    With its complement o' grace;
There was spirit in that music,
    An' a kind o' solemn sway,
A singin' o' the old tunes
    In the ol'-fashioned way.

I remember oft o' standin'
    In my homespun pantaloons,
On my face the bronze an' freckles
    O' the suns o' youthful Junes,
Thinkin' that no mortal minstrel
    Ever chanted sich a lay
As the ol' tunes we was singin'
    In the ol'-fashioned way.

The boys 'ud always lead us,
    An' the girls 'ud all chime in,
Till the sweetness o' the singin'
    Robbed the list'nin' soul o' sin;
An' I ust to tell the parson
    'Twas as good to sing as pray,
When the people sung the ol' tunes
    In the ol'-fashioned way.

How I long agin to hear it,
    Pourin' forth from soul to soul,
With the treble high an' meller,
    An' the bass's mighty roll;
But the times is very diff'rent,
    An' the muslc heerd to-day
Ain't the singin' o' the ol' tunes
    In the ol'-fashioned way.

Little screechin' by a Woman,
 Little squawkin' by a man,
Then the organ's twiddle-twaddle,
 Jest the empty space to span,
An' ef you should even think it,
 'Tisn't proper fur to say
That you want to hear the ol' tunes
 In the ol'-fashioned way.

But I think that some bright mornin',
 When the toils of life is o'er,
An' the sun o' heaven arisin'
 Glads with light the happy shore,
I shall hear the angel chorus,
 In the realms o' endless day,
A singin' o' the ol' tunes
 In the ol'-fashioned way.

C. "To Miss Mary Britton."

When the legislature of Kentucky was discussing the passage of a separate-coach bill, Miss Mary Britton, a teacher in the Schools of Lexington, Kentucky, went before them, and in a ringing speech protested against the passage of the bill. Her action was heroic, though it proved to be without avail.

God of the right, arise
 And let thy pow'r prevail;
Too long thy children mourn
 In labor and travail.
Oh, speed the happy day
 When waiting ones may see
The glory-bringing birth
 Of our real liberty!

Grant thou, O gracious God,
 That not in word alone
Shall freedom's boon be ours,
 While bondage-galled we moan!
But condescend to us
 In our o'erwhelming need;
Break down the hind'ring bars,
 And make us free indeed.

Give us to lead our cause
 More noble souls like hers,
The memory of whose deed
 Each feeling bosom stirs;
Whose fearless voice and strong
 Rose to defend her race,
Roused Justice from her sleep,
 Drove Prejudice from place.

Let not the mellow light
 Of Learning's brilliant ray
Be quenched, to turn to night
 Our newly dawning day.
To that bright, shining star
 Which thou didst set in place,
With universal voice
 Thus speaks a grateful race:

Not empty words shall be
 Our offering to your fame;
The race you strove to serve
 Shall consecrate your name
Speak on as fearless still;
 Work on as tireless ever;
And your reward shall be
 Due meed for your endeavor.

————— 5.26 —————
'WE WEAR THE MASK'
Paul Lawrence Dunbar

A favorable 1896 *Harper's Weekly* review of his work, by noted white novelist and critic William Dean Howells, cemented Paul Lawrence Dunbar's broad fame. But it was a compromised victory for Dunbar. White America, by and large, adored his use of southern slave dialect. But African Americans, and Dunbar himself, believed his best work was that done in standard English. Later in his career, Dunbar would express frustration with being pigeonholed as a dialect poet by white critics and admirers.

In his relatively short career, Dunbar published 12 poetry collections, five novels, four books of short stories and a play. He is remembered most for his poetry. While his dialect poems shared the southern obsession with romanticizing and simplifying slave life rather than commenting on its reality, his other work often addressed contemporary issues of race. The poems below, two of his most famous, are examples in which he subtly expresses the pain caused by racism. The first, "We Wear the Mask," is perhaps a commentary on his own role as a minstrel poet. The second, "Sympathy," inspired the title of Maya Angelou's Pulitzer Prize–winning biography (see Chapter Eight).

Dunbar died early, at age 33, after his painful divorce from fellow-poet Alice Ruth Moore led him into a spiral of depression and alcohol abuse. He developed a tuberculosis infection — treatment for which, in part, accelerated his alcohol dependency — that ultimately took his life in 1906.

A. "We Wear the Mask"

WE wear the mask that grins and lies,
It hides our cheeks and shades our eyes —
This debt we pay to human guile;
With torn and bleeding hearts we smile
And mouth with myriad subtleties,

Why should the world be over-wise,
In counting all our tears and sighs?
Nay, let them only see us, while
We wear the mask.

We smile, but oh great Christ, our cries
To Thee from tortured souls arise.
We sing, but oh the clay is vile
Beneath our feet, and long the mile,
But let the world dream otherwise,
We wear the mask!

B. "Sympathy"

I KNOW what the caged bird feels, alas!
　　When the sun is bright on the
　　　　upland slopes;
When the wind stirs soft through the
　　　　springing grass,
And the river flows like a stream of glass;
　　When the first bird sings and the first
　　　　bud opes,
And the faint perfume from its chalice steals —
I know what the caged bird feels!

I know why the caged bird beats his wing
　　Till its blood is red on the cruel bars;
For he must fly back to his perch and cling
When he fain would be on the bough
　　　　a-swing;
　　And a pain still throbs in the old, old scars
And they pulse again with a keener sting —
I know why he beats his wing!

I know why the caged bird sings, ah me,
　　When his wing is bruised and his
　　　　bosom sore, —
When he beats his bars and he would be free;
It is not a carol of joy or glee,
　　But a prayer that he sends from his
　　　　heart's deep core,
But a plea, that upward to Heaven he flings —
I know why the caged bird sings!

———— 5.27 ————

THE LYNCH MOB'S 'THREAD-BARE LIE'
Ida B. Wells

By the time Ida Bell Wells-Barnett took up the cause of exposing the lies and horrors of lynching, she had already fought several hard battles. She was orphaned at age 14, when her parents died in a yellow fever epidemic, and started working to support herself and her sisters. But she was eventually fired from her teaching job in Memphis, Tennessee, because of an editorial she wrote accusing the school board of neglecting black students. Later, she lost a state Supreme Court case in which she sued a railroad company for refusing to allow her to sit in a section reserved for white passengers. Two years after that, in 1889, she became editor of the city's black newspaper, the *Free Speech and Appeal*. There, in 1892, Wells launched her career as a moral voice against lynching.

After two black businessmen, friends of Wells, were brutally lynched, the budding journalist became disgusted with mainstream news coverage and popular perception the event. As usual, the victims were portrayed as violent criminals. Wells knew otherwise, and penned a series of blistering editorials not only setting the record of this particular case straight but challenging the pervasive racist assumptions of black guilt that underpinned cultural acceptance of lynching. She spent the following months investigating lynching cases around the south, and writing still more pieces exposing distortions in how the stories had been reported. In the editorial below, her most provocative, Wells directly challenged the oft-repeated charge of rape used to justify lynching black men. Calling such charges a "thread-bare lie," she suggested that interracial sexual relationships that do occur are consensual. That week, a mob burnt down the paper's office and chased Wells and her staff out of Memphis.

Eight negroes lynched since last issue of the 'Free Speech' one at Little Rock, Ark., last Saturday morning where the citizens broke (?) into the penitentiary and got their man; three near Anniston, Ala., one near New Orleans; and three at Clarksville, Ga., the last three for killing a white man, and five on the same old racket — the new alarm about raping white women. The same programme of hanging, then shooting bullets into the lifeless bodies was carried out to the letter.

Nobody in this section of the country believes the old thread bare lie that Negro men rape white women. If Southern white men are not careful, they will over-reach themselves and public sentiment will have a reaction; a conclusion will then be reached which will be very damaging to the moral reputation of their women.

─────── 5.28 ───────
'A NEGROE'S LIFE IS A VERY CHEAP THING IN GEORGIA'
Ida B. Wells

Ida B. Wells considered herself an answer to the supposed objectivity with which mainstream news sources covered lynchings. By and large, white reporters presumed the guilt of the black victims, who were usually accused of sexual misconduct or violence directed at whites. Journalists "balanced" their stories by playing up that guilt as a counter to their descriptions of a lynch mob's excessive violence in news reports. In the worst cases, mainstream newspapers incited the lynchings and brazenly served as a vehicle for coordinating statewide lynching efforts.

As a reporter, first for the *New York Age* and then the *Chicago Conservator*, both black papers, Wells tracked down case after case and uncovered facts showing that lynching victims had committed no crimes at all. She published pamphlets, largely consumed by African Americans, detailing her investigations and offering her theories on the economic tensions motivating lynch mob justice. Her work won international acclaim from some, but merely hatred from mainstream journalists. *The New York Times* dismissed her reporting as overly emotional and biased, calling her a "slanderous and nasty-minded mulattress."

In the pamphlet excerpted below, Wells reports the findings of a detective she sent to Georgia to investigate a recent series of lynchings. The victims had not committed the crimes they were accused of and never were tried for. Here, she challenges the notion that only the "lowest and lawless class" of southern whites were involved in lynchings, by detailing the manner in which the *Atlanta Constitution* and *Atlanta Journal* incited these cases. The community's leaders, she argues, are just as culpable. The pamphlet gives a chilling account of the manner in which a broad swath of white society meticulously prepared for and carried out the lynching of innocent men.

CONSIDER THE FACTS.

During six weeks of the months of March and April just past, twelve colored men were lynched in Georgia, the reign of outlawry culminating in the torture and hanging of the colored preacher, Elijah Strickland, and the burning alive of Samuel Wilkes, alias Hose, Sunday, April 23, 1899.

The real purpose of these savage demonstrations is to teach the Negro that in the South he has no rights that the law will enforce. Samuel Hose was burned to teach the Negroes that no matter what a white man does to them, they must not resist. Hose, a servant, had killed Cranford, his employer. An example must be made. Ordinary punishment was deemed inadequate. This Negro must be burned alive. To make the burning a certainty the charge of outrage was invented, and added to the charge of murder. The daily press offered reward for the capture of Hose and then openly incited the people to burn him as soon as caught. The mob carried out the plan in every savage detail.

Of the twelve men lynched during that reign of unspeakable barbarism, only one was even charged with an assault upon a woman. Yet Southern apologists justify their savagery on the ground that Negroes are lynched only because of their crimes against women.

The Southern press champions burning men alive, and says, "Consider the facts." The colored people join issue and also say, "Consider the facts." The colored people of Chicago employed a detective to go to Georgia, and his report in this pamphlet gives the facts. We give here the details of the lynching as they were reported in the Southern papers, then follows the report of the true facts as to the cause of the lynchings, as learned by the investigation. We submit all to the sober judgment of the Nation, confident that, in this cause, as well as all others, "Truth is mighty and will prevail."

IDA B. WELLS-BARNETT.
2939 Princeton Avenue, Chicago,
June 20, 1899. ...

TORTURED AND BURNED ALIVE.

The burning of Samuel Hose, or, to give his right name, Samuel Wilkes, gave to the United States the distinction of having burned alive seven human beings during the past ten years. The details of this deed of unspeakable barbarism have shocked the civilized world, for it is conceded universally that no other nation on earth, civilized or savage, has put to death any human being with such atrocious cruelty as that inflicted upon Samuel Hose by the Christian white people of Georgia.

The charge is generally made that lynch law is condemned by the best white people of the South, and that lynching is the work of the lowest and lawless class. Those who seek the truth know the fact to be, that all classes are equally guilty, for what the one class does the other encourages, excuses and condones.

This was clearly shown in the burning of Hose. This awful deed was suggested, encouraged and made possible by the daily press of Atlanta, Georgia, until the burning actually occurred, and then it immediately condoned the burning by a hysterical plea to "consider the facts."

Samuel Hose killed Alfred Cranford Wednesday afternoon, April 12, 1899, in a dispute over the wages due Hose. The dispatch which announced the killing of Cranford stated that Hose had assaulted Mrs. Cranford and that bloodhounds had been put on his track.

The next day the Atlanta Constitution, in glaring double headlines, predicted a lynching and suggested burning at the stake. This it repeated in the body of the dispatch in the following language:

"When Hose is caught he will either be lynched and his body riddled with bullets or he will be burned at the stake." And further in the same issue the Constitution suggests torture in these words: "There have been whisperings of burning at the stake and of torturing the fellow low, and so great is the excitement, and so high the indignation, that this is among the possibilities." ...

REPORT OF DETECTIVE LOUIS P. LEVIN.

The colored citizens of Chicago sent a detective to Georgia, and his report shows that Samuel Hose, who was brutally tortured at Newman, Ga., and then burned to death, never assaulted Mrs. Cranford and that he killed Alfred Cranford in self-defense.

The full text of the report is as follows:

... Sam left and went to Atlanta to better his condition. He secured work near Palmetto for a man named Alfred Cranford, and worked for him for about two years, up to the time of the tragedy. I will not call it a murder, for Samuel Wilkes killed Alfred Cranford in self-defense. The story you have read about a Negro stealing into the house and murdering the unfortunate man at his supper has no foundation in fact. Equally untrue is the charge that after murdering the husband he assaulted the wife. The reports indicated that the murderer was a stranger, who had to be identified. The fact is he had worked for Cranford for over a year.

Was there a murder? That Wilkes killed Cranford there is no doubt, but under what circumstances can never be proven. I asked many white people of Palmetto what was the motive. They considered it a useless question. A "nigger" had killed a white man, and that was enough. Some said it was because the young "niggers" did not know their places, others that they were getting too much education, while others declared that it was all due to the influence of the Northern "niggers." W.W. Jackson, of Newman, said: "If I had my way about it I would lynch every Northern 'nigger' that comes this way. They are at the bottom of this." John Low of Lincoln, Ala., said: "My negroes would die for me simply because I keep a strict hand on them and allow no Northern negroes to associate with them."

Upon the question of motive there was no answer except that which was made by Wilkes himself. The dispatches said that Wilkes confessed both to the murder and the alleged assault upon Mrs. Cranford. But neither of these reports is true. Wilkes did say that he killed Mr. Cranford, but he did not at any time admit that he assaulted Mrs. Cranford. This he denied as long as he had breath.

After the capture Wilkes told his story. He said that his trouble began with Mr. Cranford a week before. He said that he had word that his mother was much worse at home, and that he wanted to go home to visit his mother. He told Mr. Cranford and asked for some money. Cranford refused to pay Wilkes, and that provoked hard words. Cranford was known to be a man of quick temper, but nothing had occurred that day. The next day Cranford borrowed a revolver and said that if Sam started any more trouble he would kill him.

Sam, continuing his story, said that on the day Cranford was killed he (Sam) was out in the yard cutting up wood; that Cranford came out into the yard, and that he and Cranford began talking about the subject of the former trouble; that Cranford became enraged and drew his gun to shoot, and then Sam threw the ax at Cranford and ran. He knew the ax struck Cranford, but did not know Cranford had been killed by the blows for several days. At the time of the encounter in the yard, Sam said that Mrs. Cranford was in the house, and that after he threw the ax at Cranford he never saw Mrs. Cranford, for he immediately went to the woods and kept in hiding until he reached the vicinity of his mother's home, where he was captured. During all the time Sam was on the train going to the scene of the burning, Sam is said by all I talked with to have been free from excitement or terror. He told his story in a straightforward way, said he was sorry he had killed Cranford and always denied that he had attacked Mrs. Cranford. …

The burning of Wilkes was fully premeditated. It was no sudden outburst of a furious, maddened mob. It was known long before Wilkes was caught that he would be burned. The Cranfords are an old, wealthy and aristocratic family, and it was intended to make an example of the Negro who killed him. What exasperation the killing lacked was supplied by the report of the alleged attack on Mrs. Cranford. And it was not the irresponsible rabble that urged the burning, for it was openly advocated by some of the leading men of Palmetto. E.D. Sharkey, Superintendent Atlanta Bagging Mills, was one of the most persistent advocates of the burning. He claimed that he saw Mrs. Cranford the day after the killing and that she told him that she was assaulted. As a matter of fact, Mrs. Cranford was unconscious at that time. He persistently told the story and urged the burning of Sam as soon as caught.

John Haas, President of the Capitol Bank, was particularly prominent in advocating the burning. People doing business at his bank, and coming from Newman and Griffin, were urged to make an example of Sam by burning him.

W.A. Hemphill, President and business manager, and Clark Howell, editor of the Atlanta Constitution, contributed more to the burning than any other men and all other forces in Georgia. Through the columns of their paper they exaggerated every detail of the killing, invented and published inflammatory descriptions of a crime that was never committed, and by glaring head lines continually suggested the burning of the man when caught. They offered a reward of $500 blood money for the capture of the fugitive, and during all the time of the man-hunt they never made one suggestion that the law should have its course.

The Governor of the State acquiesced in the burning by refusing to prevent it. Sam Wilkes was captured at 9 o'clock Saturday night. He was in Griffin by 9 o'clock Sunday morning. It was first proposed to burn him in Griffin, but the program was changed, and it was decided to take him to Newman to burn him. Governor Candler had ordered that Wilkes should be taken to the Fulton county jail when he was caught. That would have placed him in Atlanta. When Wilkes reached Griffin he was in custody of J.B. Jones, J.L. Jones, R.A. Gordon, William Mattews, P.F. Phelps, Charles Thomas and A. Rogowski. They would not take the prisoner to Atlanta, where the Governor had ordered him to be taken, but arranged to take him to Newman, where they knew a mob of six thousand were waiting to burn him. It is nearer to Atlanta from Griffin than Newman. Besides, there was no train going to Newman that Sunday morning, so the captors of Wilkes were obliged to secure a special train to take the prisoner to the place of burning. This required over two hour's time to arrange so that the special train did not leave Griffin for Newman until 11:40 am.

Meanwhile the news of the capture of Wilkes was known all over Georgia. It was known in Atlanta in the early morning that the prisoner would not be brought to Atlanta, but that he would be taken to Newman to be burned. As soon as this was settled, a special train was engaged as an excursion train, to take people to

the burning. It was soon filled by the criers, who cried out, "Special train to Newman! All aboard for the burning!" After this special moved out, another was made up to accommodate the late comers and those who were at church. In this way more than two thousand citizens of Atlanta were taken to the burning, while the Governor, with all the power of the State at his command, allowed all preparations for the burning to be made during ten hours of daylight, and did not turn his hand to prevent it.

I do not need to give the details of the burning. I mention only one fact, and that is the disappointment which the crowd felt when it could not make Wilkes beg for mercy. During all the time of his torture he never uttered one cry. They cut off both ears, skinned his face, cut off his fingers, gashed his legs, cut open his stomach and pulled out his entrails, then when his contortions broke the iron chain, they pushed his burning body back into the fire. But through it all Wilkes never once uttered a cry or beg for mercy. Only once in a particularly fiendish torture did he speak, then he simply groaned, "Oh Lord Jesus."

Among the prominent men at the burning, and whose identity was disclosed to me, are William Pinton, Clair Owens and William Potts, of Palmetto; W.W. Jackson and H.W. Jackson of Newman; Peter Howson and T. Vaughn, of the same place; John Hazlett, Pierre St. Clair and Thomas Lightfoot, of Griffin. R. J. Williams, ticket agent at Griffin, made up the special Central Georgia Railroad train and advertised the burning at Griffin, while B. F. Wyly and George Smith, of Atlanta, made up two special Atlanta and West Point Railroad trains. All of these gentlemen of eminent respectability could give the authorities valuable information about the burning if called upon.

While Wilkes was being burned the colored people fled terror-stricken to the woods, for none knew where the fury would strike. I talked with many colored people, but all will understand why I can give no names.

The torture and hanging of the colored preacher is everywhere acknowledged to have been without a shadow of reason or excuse. I did not talk with one white man who believed that Strickland had anything to do with Wilkes. I could not find any person who heard Wilkes mention Strickland's name. I talked with men who heard Wilkes tell his story, but all agreed that he said he killed Cranford because Cranford was about to kill him, and that he did not mention Strickland's name. He did not mention it when he was being tortured because he did not speak to anybody. I could not find anybody who could tell me how the story started that Strickland hired Wilkes to kill Cranford.

On the other hand, I saw many who knew Strickland, and all spoke of him in the highest terms. I went to see Mr. Thomas, and he said that Strickland had been about his family for years, and that he never knew a more reliable and worthy man among the colored people. He said that he was always advising the colored people to live right, keep good friends with the white people and earn their respect. He said he was nearly sixty years old and had not had five dollars at one time in a year. He defended the poor old man against the mob for a long time, and the mob finally agreed to put him in jail for a trial, but as soon as they had Strickland in their control they proceeded to lynch him.

The torture of the innocent colored preacher was only a little less than that of Wilkes. His fingers and ears were cut off, and the mob inflicted other tortures that cannot even be suggested. He was strung up three times and let down each time so he could confess. But he died protesting his innocence. He left a wife and five children, all of whom are still on Colonel Thomas' premises.

I spent some time in trying to find the facts about the shooting of the five colored men at Palmetto a few days before Cranford was killed. But no one seemed to be able to tell who accused the men, and as they were not given a trial, there was no way to get at any of the facts. It seems that one or two barns or houses had been burned, and it was reported that the Negroes were setting fire to the build-

ings. Nine colored men were arrested on suspicion. They were not men of bad character, but quite the reverse. They were intelligent, hard-working men, and all declared they could easily prove their innocence. They were taken to a Warehouse to be kept until their trial next day. That night, about 12 o' clock, an armed mob marched to the place and fired three volleys into the line of chained prisoners. They then went away thinking all were dead. All the prisoners were shot. Of these five died. Nothing was done about the killing of these men, but their families were afterward ordered to leave the place, and all have left. Five widows and seventeen fatherless children, all driven from home, constitute one result of the lynching. I saw no one who thought much about the matter. The Negroes were dead, and while they did not know whether they were guilty or not, it was plain that nothing could be done about it. And so the matter ended. With these facts I made my way home, thoroughly convinced that a Negro's life is a very cheap thing in Georgia. LOUIS P. LEVIN.

------------ 5.29 ------------

A BLACK WOMAN OF THE SOUTH
Anna Julia Cooper

Anna Julia Cooper was born a slave in Raleigh, North Carolina. By the time of her death, she would earn an undergraduate and graduate degree from Oberlin College and later become only the fourth African-American woman to earn a Ph.D. — the first to do so at the Sorbonne in Paris. Education was her passion, and she dedicated her life to helping African Americans, particularly black women, gain access to it. She spent many years as an educator in Washington, D.C., teaching at the nation's largest black college preparatory school and administrating an adult night school. She was an original proponent of the utility of adult community colleges to educate black people.

Among her several publications is her 1892 book *A Voice from the South: By a Black Woman of the South*. In it, she argues the importance of access to higher education, in the liberal arts as well as vocational studies, for women. She accepts the importance of marriage, but rejects the idea that education would "ruin" a woman for it. Rather, she writes, the educated woman becomes more selective, and the onus shifts to the man to earn her love. Of her generation's great black male leaders, she wonders aloud how they can be so progressive in thought on so many issues but "when they strike the woman question they drop back into sixteenth century logic." She closes the chapter on higher education by coining the phrase, "Not less for the boys, but more for the girls." The book is considered one of the earliest Black Feminist texts.

… Now I claim that it is the prevalence of the Higher Education among women, the making it a common everyday affair for women to rea-son and think and express their thought, the training and stimulus which enable and encourage women to administer to the world the bread it needs as well as the sugar it cries for; in short it is the transmitting of the poten-tial forces of her soul into dynamic factors that has given symmetry and completeness to the world's agencies. So only could it be consum-mated that Mercy, the lesson she teaches, and Truth, the task man has set himself, should meet together: that righteousness, or *rightness*, man's ideal, — and *peace*, its necessary 'other half,' should kiss each other.

We must thank the general enlightenment and independence of woman (which we may now regard as a *fait accompli*) that both these forces are now at work in the world, and it is fair to demand from them for the twentieth century a higher type of civilization than any attained in the nineteenth. Religion, science, art, economics, have all needed the feminine flavor; and literature, the expression of what is permanent and best in all of these, may be gauged at any time to measure the strength of the feminine ingredient. You will not find the-ology consigning infants to lakes of unquench-able fire long after women have had a chance to grasp, master, and wield its dogmas. You will not find science annihilating personality from the government of the Universe and making of God an ungovernable, unintelligible, blind, often destructive physical force; you will not

find jurisprudence formulating as an axiom the absurdity that man and wife are one, and that one the man — that the married woman may not hold or bequeath her own property save as subject to her husband's direction; you will not find political economists declaring that the only possible adjustment between laborers and capitalists is that of selfishness and rapacity — that each must get all he can and keep all that he gets, while the world cries *laissez faire* and the lawyers explain, "it is the beautiful working of the law of supply and demand"; in fine, you will not find the law of love shut out from the affairs of men after the feminine half of the world's truth is completed.

Nay, put your ear now close to the pulse of the time. What is the key-note of the literature of these days? What is the banner cry of all the activities of the last half decade?" What is the dominant seventh which is to add richness and tone to the final cadences of this century and lead by a grand modulation into the tri-umphant harmonies of the next? Is it not com-passion for the poor and unfortunate, and, as Bellamy has expressed it, "indignant outcry against the failure of the social machinery as it is, to ameliorate the miseries of men!" Even Christianity is being brought to the bar of humanity and tried by the standard of its abil-ity to alleviate the world's suffering and lighten and brighten its woe. What else can be the meaning of Matthew Arnold's saddening protest, "We cannot do without Christianity," cried he, "and we cannot endure it as it is."

When went there by an age, when so much time and thought, so much money and labor were given to God's poor and God's invalids, the lowly and unlovely, the sinning as well as the suffering — homes for inebriates and homes for lunatics, shelter for the aged and shelter for babes, hospitals for the sick, props and braces for the falling, reformatory prisons and prison reformatories, all show that a "mothering" influence from some source is leavening the nation.

Now please understand me. I do not ask you to admit that these benefactions and virtues are the exclusive possession of women, or even that women are their chief and only advocates. It may be a man who formulates and makes them vocal. It may be, and often is, a man who weeps over the wrongs and struggles for the amelioration: but that man has imbibed those impulses from a mother rather than from a father and is simply materializing and giving back to the world in tangible form the ideal love and tenderness, devotion and care that have cherished and nourished the helpless period of his own existence.

All I claim is that there is a feminine as well as a masculine side to truth; that these are related not as inferior and superior, not as better and worse, not as weaker and stronger, but as complements — complements in one necessary and symmetric whole. That as the man is more noble in reason, so the woman is more quick in sympathy. That as he is indefatigable in pursuit of abstract truth, so is she in caring for the interests by the way — striving tenderly and lovingly that not one of the least of these 'little ones' should perish. That while we not unfrequently see women who reason, we say, with the coolness and precision of a man, and men as considerate of helplessness as a woman, still there is a general consensus of mankind that the one trait is essentially masculine and the other as peculiarly feminine. That both are needed to be worked into the training of children, in order that our boys may supplement their virility by tenderness and sensibility, and our girls may round out their gentleness by strength and self-reliance. That, as both are alike necessary in giving symmetry to the individual, so a nation or a race will degenerate into mere emotionalism on the one hand, or bullyism on the other, if dominated by either exclusively; lastly, and most emphatically, that the feminine factor can have its proper effect only through woman's development and education so that she may fitly and intelligently stamp her force on the forces of her day, and add her modicum to the riches of the world's thought. ...

The high ground of generalities is alluring but my pen is devoted to a special cause: and with a view to further enlightenment on the achievements of the century for THE HIGHER EDUCATION OF COLORED WOMEN, I wrote a few days ago to the colleges which admit women and asked how many colored women had completed the B. A. course in each during its entire history. These are the figures returned: Fisk leads the way with twelve; Oberlin next with five; Wilberforce, four; Ann Arbor and Wellesley three each, Livingstone two, Atlanta one, Howard, as yet, none.

I then asked the principal of the Washington High School how many out of a large number of female graduates from his school had chosen to go forward and take a collegiate course. He replied that but one had ever done so, and she was then in Cornell.

Others ask questions too, sometimes, and I was asked a few years ago by a white friend, "How is it that the men of your race seem to outstrip the women in mental attainment?" "Oh," I said, "so far as it is true, the men, I suppose, from the life they lead, gain more by contact; and so far as it is only apparent, I think the women are more quiet. They don't feel called to mount a barrel and harangue by the hour every time they imagine they have produced an idea."

But I am sure there is another reason which I did not at that time see fit to give. The atmosphere, the standards, the requirements of our little world do not afford any special stimulus to female development.

It seems hardly a gracious thing to say, but it strikes me as true, that while our men seem thoroughly abreast of the times on almost every other subject, when they strike the woman question they drop back into sixteenth century logic. They leave nothing to be desired generally in regard to gallantry and chivalry, but they actually do not seem sometimes to have outgrown that old contemporary of chivalry — the idea that women may stand on pedestals or live in doll houses, (if they happen to have them) but they must not furrow their brows with thought or attempt to help men tug at the great questions of the world. I fear the majority of colored men do not yet think it worth while that women aspire to higher education. Not many will subscribe to the "advanced" ideas of Grant Allen already quoted. The three R's, a little music and a good deal of dancing, a first rate dress-maker and a bottle of magnolia balm, are quite enough generally to render charming any woman possessed of tact and the capacity for worshipping masculinity.

My readers will pardon my illustrating my point and also giving a reason for the fear that is in me, by a little bit of personal experience. When a child I was put into a school near home that professed to be normal and collegiate, i. e. to prepare teachers for colored youth, furnish candidates for the ministry, and offer collegiate training for those who should be ready for it. Well, I found after a while that I had a good deal of time on my hands. I had devoured what was put before me, and, like Oliver Twist, was looking around to ask for more. I constantly felt (as I suppose many an ambitious girl has felt) a thumping from within unanswered by any beckoning from without. Class after class was organized for these ministerial candidates (many of them men who had been preaching before I was born). Into every one of these classes I was expected to go, with the sole intent, I thought at the time, of enabling the dear old principal, as he looked from the vacant countenances of his sleepy old class over to where I sat, to get off his solitary pun — his never-failing pleasantry, especially in hot weather — which was, as he called out "Any one!" to the effect that "*any* one" then meant "*Annie* one."

Finally a Greek class was to be formed. My inspiring preceptor informed me that Greek had never been taught in the school, but that he was going to form a class *for the candidates for the ministry*, and if I liked I might join it. I replied — humbly I hope, as became a female of the human species — that I would like very much to study Greek, and that I was thankful for the opportunity, and so it went on. A boy,

however meager his equipment and shallow his pretentions, had only to declare a floating intention to study theology and he could get all the support, encouragement and stimulus he needed, be absolved from work and invested beforehand with all the dignity of his far away office. While a self-supporting girl had to struggle on by teaching in the summer and working after school hours to keep up with her board bills, and actually to fight her way against positive discouragements to the higher education; till one such girl one day flared out and told the principal "the only mission opening before a girl in his school was to marry one of those candidates." He said he didn't know but it was. And when at last that same girl announced her desire and intention to go to college it was received with about the same incredulity and dismay as if a brass button on one of those candidate's coats had propounded a new method for squaring the circle or trisecting the arc.

Now this is not fancy. It is a simple unvarnished photograph, and what I believe was not in those days exceptional in colored schools, and I ask the men and women who are teachers and co-workers for the highest interests of the race, that they give the girls a chance! We might as well expect to grow trees from leaves as hope to build up a civilization or a manhood without taking into consideration our women and the home life made by them, which must be the root and ground of the whole matter. Let us insist then on special encouragement for the education of our women and special care in their training. Let our girls feel that we expect something more of them than that they merely look pretty and appear well in society. Teach them that there is a race with special needs which they and only they can help; that the world needs and is already asking for their trained, efficient forces. Finally, if there is an ambitious girl with pluck and brain to take the higher education, encourage her to make the most of it. Let there be the same flourish of trumpets and clapping of hands as when a boy announces his determination to enter the lists;

and then, as you know that she is physically the weaker of the two, don't stand from under and leave her to buffet the waves alone. Let her know that your heart is following her, that your hand, though she sees it not, is ready to support her. To be plain, I mean let money be raised and scholarships be founded in our colleges and universities for self-supporting, worthy young women, to offset and balance the aid that can always be found for boys who will take theology.

The earnest well trained Christian young woman, as a teacher, as a home-maker, as wife, mother, or silent influence even, is as potent a missionary agency among our people as is the theologian; and I claim that at the present stage of our development in the South she is even more important and necessary.

Let us then, here and now, recognize this force and resolve to make the most of it — not the boys less, but the girls more.

--------- 5.30 ---------
LIFTING AS WE CLIMB
Mary Church Terrell

In the middle to late 19th century local women's clubs, through which activist women would educate themselves and organize their communities for civic and political causes, began to proliferate. As with most things in society, African Americans were not welcomed in the white clubs. And, as a result, a movement of black women's clubs grew as well. By the 1890s, these had spawned to umbrella organizations, which, in 1896 merged into the National Association of Colored Women (NACW). Today, the NACW is the oldest active black political organization. Taking the phrase "Lifting as We Climb" as its motto, the group offered job training for black women, organized community service efforts and advocated on behalf of both women's and African American's political issues broadly. Mary Church Terrell, a prominent black suffragist and educator, was elected the group's first president. In 1898, she delivered this speech, "The Progress of Colored Women," to the National American Women's Suffrage Association, a white group, in which she champions the heroism of black women and highlights the NACW's work.

… Consider if you will, the almost insurmountable obstacles which have confronted colored women in their efforts to educate and cultivate themselves since their emancipation, and I dare assert, not boastfully, but with pardonable pride, I hope, that the progress they have made and the work they have accomplished, will bear a favorable comparison at least with that of their more fortunate sisters, from the opportunity of acquiring knowledge and the means of self-culture have never been entirely withheld. For, not only are colored women with ambition and aspiration handicapped on account of their sex, but they are everywhere baffled and mocked on account of their race. Desperately and continuously they are forced to fight that opposition, born of a cruel, unreasonable prejudice which neither their merit nor their necessity seems able to subdue. Not only because they are women, but because they are colored women, are discouragement and disappointment meeting them at every turn.

Avocations opened and opportunities offered to their more favored sisters have been and are tonight closed and barred against them. While those of the dominant race have a variety of trades and pursuits from which they may choose, the woman through whose veins one drop of African blood is known to flow is limited to a pitiful few. So overcrowded are the avocations in which colored women may engage and so poor is the pay in consequence, that only the barest livelihood can be eked out by the rank and file. And yet, in spite of the opposition encountered, the obstacles opposed to their acquisition of knowledge and their accumulation of property, the progress made by colored women along these lines has never been surpassed by that of any people in the history of the world.

Though the slaves were liberated less than forty years ago, penniless, and ignorant, with neither shelter nor food, so great was their thirst for knowledge and so Herculean were their efforts to secure it, that there are today hundreds of Negroes, many of them women, who are graduates, some of them having taken degrees from the best institutions of the land. From Oberlin, that friend of the oppressed,

Oberlin, my dear alma mater, whose name will always be loved and whose praise will ever be sung as the first college in the country which was just, broad and benevolent enough to open its doors to Negroes and to women on an equal footing with men; from Wellesley and Vassar, from Cornell and Ann Arbor, from the best high schools throughout the North, East and West, Colored girls have been graduated with honors, and have thus forever settled the question of their capacity and worth.

But a few years ago in an examination in which a large number of young women and men competed for a scholarship, entitling the successful competitor to an entire course through the Chicago University, the only colored girl among them stood first and captured this great prize. And so, wherever colored girls have studied, their instructors bear testimony to their intelligence, diligence and success.

With this increase of wisdom there has sprung up in the hearts of colored women an ardent desire to do good in the world. No sooner had the favored few availed themselves of such advantages as they could secure than they hastened to dispense these blessings to the less fortunate of their race. With tireless energy and eager zeal, colored women have, since their emancipation, been continuously prosecuting the work of educating and elevating their race, as though upon themselves alone devolved the accomplishment of this great task.

Of the teachers engaged in instructing colored youth, it is perhaps no exaggeration to say that fully ninety percent are women. In the back-woods, remote from the civilization and comforts of the city and town, on the plantations reeking with ignorance and vice, our colored women may be found battling with evils which such conditions always entail. Many a heroine, of whom the world will never hear, has thus sacrificed her life to her race, amid surroundings and in the face of privations which only martyrs can tolerate and bear. Shirking responsibility has never been a fault with which colored women might be truthfully charged. Indefatigably and conscientiously, in

public work of all kinds they engage, that they may benefit and elevate their race.

The result of this labor has been prodigious indeed. By banding themselves together in the interest of education and morality, by adopting the most practical and useful means to this end, colored women have in thirty short years become a great power for good. Through the National Association of Colored Women, which was formed by the union of two large organizations in July 1896, and which is now the only national body among colored women, much good has been done in the past, and more will be accomplished in the future, we hope. Believing that it is only through the home that a people can become really good and truly great, the National Association of Colored Women has entered that sacred domain. ...

Questions affecting our legal status as a race are also constantly agitated by our women. In Louisiana and Tennessee, colored women have several times petitioned the legislatures of their respective States to repeal the obnoxious "Jim Crow Car" laws, nor will any stone be left unturned until this iniquitous and unjust enactment against respectable American citizens be forever wiped from the statutes of the South. Against the barbarous Convict Lease System of Georgia, of which Negroes, especially the female prisoners, are the principal victims, colored women are waging a ceaseless war. By two lecturers, each of whom, under the Woman's Christian Temperance Union has been National Superintendent of work among colored people, the cause of temperance has for many years been eloquently espoused.

In business, colored women have had signal success. There is in Alabama a large milling and cotton business belonging to and controlled entirely by a colored woman who has sometimes as many as seventy-five men in her employ. In Halifax, Nova Scotia, the principal ice plant of the city is owned and managed by one of our women. In the professions we have dentists and doctors, whose practice is lucrative and large. Ever since the publication, in 1773, of a book entitled "Poems on Various Subjects,

Religious and Moral," by Phyllis Wheatley, negro servant of Mr John Wheatley of Boston, colored women have from time to time given abundant evidence of literary ability. In sculpture we are represented by a woman upon whose chisel Italy has set her seal of approval; in painting, by Bougerean's pupil, whose work was exhibited in the last Paris Salon, and in Music by young women holding diplomas from the first conservatories in the land.

And, finally, as an organization of women nothing lies nearer the heart of the National Association than the children, many of whose lives, so sad and dark, we might brighten and bless. It is the kindergarten we need. Free kindergartens in every city and hamlet of this broad land we must have, if the children are to receive from us what it is our duty to give. Already during the past year kindergartens have been established and successfully maintained by several organizations, from which most encouraging reports have come. May their worthy example be emulated, till in no branch of the Association shall the children of the poor, at least, be deprived of the blessings which flow from the kindergarten alone.

The more unfavorable the environments of children, the more necessary is it that steps be taken to counteract baleful influences on innocent victims. How imperative is it then that as colored women, we inculcate correct principles and set good examples for our own youth, whose little feet will have so many thorny paths of prejudice temptation, and injustice to tread. The colored youth is vicious we are told, and statistics showing the multitudes of our boys and girls who crowd the penitentiaries and fill the jails appall and dishearten us. But side by side with these facts and figures of crime I would have presented and pictured the miserable hovels from which these youth criminals come.

Make a tour of the settlements of colored people, who in many cities are relegated to the most noisome sections permitted by the municipal government, and behold the mites of humanity who infest them. Here are our little ones, the future representatives of the race, fairly drinking in the pernicious example of their elders, coming in contact with nothing but ignorance and vice, till at the age of six, evil habits are formed which no amount of civilizing or Christianizing can ever completely break. Listen to the cry of our children. In imitation of the example set by the Great Teacher of men, who could not offer himself as a sacrifice, until he had made an eternal plea for the innocence and helplessness of childhood, colored women are everywhere reaching out after the waifs and strays, who without their aid may be doomed to lives of evil and shame. As an organization, the National Association of Colored Women feels that the establishment of kindergartens is the special mission which we are called to fulfill. So keenly alive are we to the necessity of rescuing our little ones, whose noble qualities are deadened and dwarfed by the very atmosphere which they breathe, that the officers of the Association are now trying to secure means by which to send out a kindergarten organizer, whose duty it shall be both to arouse the conscience of our women, and to establish kindergartens, wherever the means therefore can be secured.

And so, lifting as we climb, onward and upward we go, struggling and striving, and hoping that the buds and blossoms of our desires will burst into glorious fruition ere long. With courage, born of success achieved in the past, with a keen sense of the responsibility which we shall continue to assume, we look forward to a future large with promise and hope. Seeking no favors because of our color, nor patronage because of our needs, we knock at the bar of justice, asking an equal chance.

———— 5.31 ————

THE 'ATLANTA COMPROMISE'
Booker T. Washington

Of all the issues the African-American community faced at the turn of the century, the one that seemed paramount was education. And it was from the debate over how black people should gain education, and for what purposes, that two of the period's most significant figures arose: Booker T. Washington and W.E.B. DuBois.

Booker Taliaferro Washington was born a slave in Virginia. Freed at the end of the Civil War, he began working and attending school in West Virginia. In 1872, he famously showed up penniless, on foot, at the doors of Virginia's newly established black college, the Hampton Institute. Here he learned the educational philosophy that he would promote throughout his career: that African Americans needed, first and foremost, to learn agricultural and mechanical skills so that they could both achieve independence and contribute to society. Graduating with honors, he eventually became a faculty member. Having won the praise of the schools' influential white president, the 25-year-old Washington was selected to found another black college in 1881 — the Tuskegee Institute in Alabama.

His success in building Tuskegee, with meager resources, into a renowned vocational school graduating 500 students a year by the end of the decade was widely heralded. He became a leading and influential figure in both black and white educational circles. But his national prominence as more than an educator, as an anointed "leader of his race," grew from his speech at the September 1895 Cotton States and International Exposition in Atlanta. Here he made his famous call for blacks to remain in the South, urging "cast down your buckets where you are." He counted inequality and segregation as an unavoidable reality, and, in the tradition of Jupiter Hammon (see Chapters One and Two), implored African Americans to focus on improving themselves rather than worrying about advocating for rights. In Washington's view, the solutions to the black community's problems lay in self-reliance, not civil rights. The speech, dubbed the "Atlanta Compromise" because of its forgiving proposals on discrimination, has been derided by many subsequent black thinkers as representative of an overly accommodationist posture on racism.

One-third of the population of the South is of the Negro race. No enterprise seeking the material, civil, or moral welfare of this section can disregard this element of our population and reach the highest success. I but convey to you, Mr. President and Directors, the sentiment of the masses of my race when I say that in no way have the value and manhood of the American Negro been more fittingly and generously recognized than by the managers of this magnificent Exposition at every stage of its progress. It is a recognition that will do more to cement the friendship of the two races than any occurrence since the dawn of our freedom.

Not only this, but the opportunity here afforded will awaken among us a new era of industrial progress. Ignorant and inexperienced, it is not strange that in the first years of our new life we began at the top instead of at the bottom; that a seat in Congress or the State Legislature was more sought than real estate or industrial skill; that the political convention or stump speaking had more attractions than starting a dairy farm or truck garden.

A ship lost at sea for many days suddenly sighted a friendly vessel. From the mast of the unfortunate vessel was seen a signal: "Water, water; we die of thirst!" The answer from the friendly vessel at once came back: "Cast down your bucket where you are." A second time the signal, "Water, water; send us water!" ran up from the distressed vessel, and was answered: "Cast down your bucket where you are." And a third and fourth signal for water was answered: "Cast down your bucket where you are." The captain of the distressed vessel, at last heeding the injunction, cast down his bucket, and it came up full of fresh, sparkling water from the mouth of the Amazon River. To those of my race who depend on bettering their condition in a foreign land, or who underestimate the importance of cultivating friendly relations with the Southern white man, who is their next door neighbor, I would say: "Cast down your bucket where you are" — cast it down in making friends in every manly way of the people of all races by whom we are surrounded.

Cast it down in agriculture, mechanics, in commerce, in domestic service, and in the professions. And in this connection it is well to bear in mind that whatever other sins the South may be called to bear, when it comes to business, pure and simple, it is in the South that the Negro is given a man's chance in the commercial world, and in nothing is this

Exposition more eloquent than in emphasizing this chance. Our greatest danger is, that in the great leap from slavery to freedom we may overlook the fact that the masses of us are to live by the productions of our hands, and fail to keep in mind that we shall prosper in proportion as we learn to dignify and glorify common labor, and put brains and skill into the common occupations of life; shall prosper in proportion as we learn to draw the line between the superficial and the substantial, the ornamental gewgaws of life and the useful. No race can prosper till it learns that there is as much dignity in tilling a field as in writing a poem. It is at the bottom of life we must begin, and not at the top. Nor should we permit our grievances to overshadow our opportunities.

To those of the white race who look to the incoming of those of foreign birth and strange tongue and habits for the prosperity of the South, were I permitted, I would repeat what I say to my own race, "Cast down your bucket where you are." Cast it down among the 8,000,000 Negroes whose habits you know, whose fidelity and love you have tested in days when to have proved treacherous meant the ruin of your firesides. Cast down your bucket among those people who have, without strikes and labor wars, tilled your fields, cleared your forests, built your railroads and cities, and brought forth treasures from the bowels of the earth, and helped make possible this magnificent representation of the progress of the South. Casting down your bucket among my people, helping and encouraging them as you are doing on these grounds, and, with education of head, hand and heart, you will find that they will buy your surplus land, make blossom the waste place in your fields, and run your factories. While doing this, you can be sure in the future, as in the past, that you and your families will be surrounded by the most patient, faithful, law-abiding, and unresentful people that the world has seen. As we have proved our loyalty to you in the past, in nursing your children, watching by the sick bed of your mothers and fathers, and often following them with tear-dimmed eyes to their graves, so in the future, in our humble way, we shall stand by you with a devotion that no foreigner can approach, ready to lay down our lives, if need be, in defense of yours, interlacing our industrial, commercial, civil, and religious life with yours in a way that shall make the interests of both races one. In all things that are purely social we can be as separate as the fingers, yet one as the hand in all things essential to mutual progress.

There is no defense or security for any of us except in the highest intelligence and development of all. If anywhere there are efforts tending to curtail the fullest growth of the Negro, let these efforts be turned into stimulating, encouraging, and making him the most useful and intelligent citizen. Effort or means so invested will pay a thousand percent interest. These efforts will be twice blessed — "blessing him that gives and him that takes."

There is no escape through law of man or God from the inevitable:

The laws of changeless justice bind
Oppressor with oppressed;
And close as sin and suffering joined
We march to fate abreast.

Nearly sixteen millions of hands will aid you in pulling the load upwards, or they will pull against you the load downwards. We shall constitute one-third and more of the ignorance and crime of the South, or one-third its intelligence and progress; we shall contribute one-third to the business and industrial prosperity of the South, or we shall prove a veritable body of death, stagnating, depressing, retarding every effort to advance the body politic.

Gentlemen of the Exposition, as we present to you humble effort as an exhibition of our progress, you must not expect over much. Starting thirty years ago with ownership here and there in a few quilts and pumpkins and chickens (gathered from miscellaneous sources), remember the path that has led from these to the invention and production of agricultural implements, buggies, steam engines, newspapers, books, statuary, carving, paintings, the management of drug stores and banks, has not been trodden without contact with thorns and thistles. While we take pride in what we exhibit as a result of our independent efforts, we do not for a moment forget that our part in this exhibition would fall far short of your expectations but for the constant help that has come to our educational life, not only from the Southern States, but especially from Northern philanthropists, who have made their gifts a constant stream of blessing and encouragement.

The wisest among my race understand that the agitation of questions of social equality is the extremist folly, and that progress in the enjoyment of all the privileges that will come to us must be the result of severe and constant struggle rather than of artificial forcing. No race that has anything to contribute to the markets of the world is long in any degree ostracized. It is important and right that all privileges of the law be ours, but it is vastly more important that we be prepared for the exercise of those privileges. The opportunity to earn a dollar in a factory just now is worth infinitely more than the opportunity to spend a dollar in an opera house.

In conclusion, may I repeat that nothing in thirty years has given us more hope and encouragement, and drawn us so near to you of the white race, as this opportunity offered by the Exposition; and here bending, as it were, over the altar that represents the results of the struggle of your race and mine, both starting practically empty-handed three decades ago, I pledge that, in your effort to work out the great and intricate problem which God has laid at the doors of the South, you shall have at all times the patient, sympathetic help of my race; only let this be constantly in mind that, while from representations in these buildings of the product of field, of forest, of mine, of factory, letters, and art, much good will come, yet far above and beyond material benefits will be that higher good, that let us pray

God will come, in a blotting out of sectional differences and racial animosities and suspicions, in a determination to administer absolute justice, in a willing obedience among all classes to the mandates of law. This, coupled with our material prosperity, will bring into our beloved South a new heaven and a new earth.

――――― 5.32 ―――――

SEPARATE BUT EQUAL
U.S. Supreme Court

The year after Booker T. Washington forecast the coming together of races, the U.S. Supreme Court issued a ruling that would legally separate them for the next 60 years. The court's 1896 ruling in Plessy v. Ferguson cemented the national racial divide by its legitimization of government-imposed segregation, declaring that laws providing separate accommodations for citizens based on race were perfectly constitutional as long as those accommodations were equal. For all intents and purposes, the ruling invalidated the 14th Amendment as it applied to African Americans.

Four years earlier, a group of black and white citizens in New Orleans launched a plan to challenge Louisiana's law segregating railcars. The 1877 law stated that train companies had to provide "equal but separate accommodations for the white, and colored races." It further imposed a fine on individuals violating this segregation by taking seats "other than the ones assigned to them, on account of the race they belong to." The citizens' group sent Homer Plessy, a light-skinned black man, to defy the law. In a prearranged encounter, Plessy took his seat in the white section, a conductor asked if he was black, Plessy answered in the affirmative, and he was arrested. This set up a challenge to the law as a violation of the 13th and 14th Amendments.

The case made its way up to the Supreme Court, which ruled 7 to 1 that the Louisiana law was constitutional. Justice Henry Brown wrote the majority opinion (in which the infamous phrase "separate but equal" does not actually appear). Brown argued that laws could not, and had not set out to, abolish social distinctions between races, but rather political ones. "If one race be inferior to the other socially," Brown wrote, "the constitution of the United States cannot put them upon the same plane." Justice John Marshall Harland, however, wrote a passionate dissent. A Southerner, Harland argued Jim Crow laws violate everything about the Civil War amendments and the nation's founding principle. "There is no caste here," he wrote. "Our Constitution is color-blind." Dismissing Brown's distinction between political and social rights, Harlan predicted the ruling would set in motion levels of political segregation that, as written in his dissent, sounded fanciful. But the years following the case proved Harlan's warnings all too prescient. At the time of the ruling, over 100,000 African-American Louisianans were registered to vote; less than ten years later, the state boasted barely 1,000 registered black voters.

A. Justice Brown's majority opinion

… The object of the amendment was undoubtedly to enforce the absolute equality of the two races before the law, but, in the nature of things, it could not have been intended to abolish distinctions based upon color, or to enforce social, as distinguished from political, equality, or a commingling of the two races upon terms unsatisfactory to either. Laws permitting, and even requiring, their separation, in places where they are liable to be brought into contact, do not necessarily imply the inferiority of either race to the other, and have been generally, if not universally, recognized as within the competency of the state legislatures in the exercise of their police power. The most common instance of this is connected with the establishment of separate schools for white and colored children, which have been held to be a valid exercise of the legislative power even by courts of states where the political rights of the colored race have been longest and most earnestly enforced. …

It is claimed by the plaintiff in error that, in a mixed community, the reputation of belonging to the dominant race, in this instance the white race, is 'property,' in the same sense that a right of action or of inheritance is property. Conceding this to be so, for the purposes of this case, we are unable to see how this statute deprives him of, or in any way affects his right to, such property. If he be a white man, and assigned to a colored coach, he may have his action for damages against the company for being deprived of his so-called 'property.' Upon the other hand, if he be a colored man, and be so assigned, he has been deprived of no property, since he is not lawfully entitled to the reputation of being a white man.

In this connection, it is also suggested by the learned counsel for the plaintiff in error that the same argument that will justify the state legislature in requiring railways to provide separate accommodations for the two races will also authorize them to require separate cars to be provided for people whose hair is of a certain color, or who are aliens, or who belong to certain nationalities, or to enact laws requiring colored people to walk upon one side of the street, and white people upon the other, or requiring white men's houses to be painted white, and colored men's black, or their vehicles or business signs to be of different colors, upon the theory that one side of the street is as good as the other, or that a house or vehicle of one color is as good as one of another color. The reply to all this is that every exercise of the police power must be reasonable, and extend only to such laws as are enacted in good faith for the promotion of the public good, and not for the annoyance or oppression of a particular class. …

So far, then, as a conflict with the fourteenth amendment is concerned, the case reduces itself to the question whether the statute of Louisiana is a reasonable regulation, and with respect to this there must necessarily be a large discretion on the part of the legislature. In determining the question of reasonableness, it is at liberty to act with reference to the established usages, customs, and traditions of the people, and with a view to the promotion of their comfort, and the preservation of the public peace and good order. Gauged by this standard, we cannot say that a law which authorizes or even requires the separation of the two races in public conveyances is unreasonable, or more obnoxious to the fourteenth amendment than the acts of congress requiring separate schools for colored children in the District of Columbia, the constitutionality of which does not seem to have been questioned, or the corresponding acts of state legislatures.

We consider the underlying fallacy of the plaintiff's argument to consist in the assumption that the enforced separation of the two races stamps the colored race with a badge of inferiority. If this be so, it is not by reason of anything found in the act, but solely because the colored race chooses to put that construction upon it. The argument necessarily assumes that if, as has been more than once the case, and is not unlikely to be so again, the colored race should become the dominant power in the state legislature, and should enact a law in precisely similar terms, it would thereby relegate the white race to an inferior position. We imagine that the white race, at least, would not acquiesce in this assumption. The argument also assumes that social prejudices may be overcome by legislation, and that equal rights cannot be secured to the negro except by an enforced commingling of the two races. We cannot accept this proposition. If the two races are to meet upon terms of social equality, it must be the result of natural affinities, a mutual appreciation of each other's merits, and a voluntary consent of individuals. As was said by the court of appeals of New York in People v. Gallagher: 'This end can neither be accomplished nor promoted by laws which conflict with the general sentiment of the community upon whom they are designed to operate. When the government, therefore, has secured to each of its citizens equal rights before the law, and equal opportunities for improvement and progress, it has accomplished the end for which it was organized, and performed all of the functions respecting social advantages with which it is endowed.' Legislation is powerless to eradicate racial instincts, or to abolish distinctions based upon physical differences, and the attempt to do so can only result in accentuating the difficulties of the present situation. If the civil and political rights of both races be equal, one cannot be inferior to the other civilly or politically. If one race be inferior to the other socially, the constitution of the United States cannot put them upon the same plane.

B. Justice Harlan's dissent

… In respect of civil rights, common to all citizens, the constitution of the United States does not, I think, permit any public authority to know the race of those entitled to be protected in the enjoyment of such rights. Every true man has pride of race, and under appropriate circumstances, when the rights of others, his equals before the law, are not to be affected, it is his privilege to express such pride and to take such action based upon it as to him seems proper. But I deny that any legislative body or judicial tribunal may have regard to the race of citizens when the civil rights of those citizens are involved. Indeed, such legislation as that here in question is inconsistent not only with that equality of rights which pertains to citizenship, national and state, but with the personal liberty enjoyed by every one within the United States. …

It was said in argument that the statute of Louisiana does not discriminate against either race, but prescribes a rule applicable alike to white and colored citizens. But this argument does not meet the difficulty. Every one knows that the statute in question had its origin in the purpose, not so much to exclude white persons from railroad cars occupied by blacks, as to exclude colored people from coaches occupied by or assigned to white persons. Railroad corporations of Louisiana did not make discrimination among whites in the matter of accommodation for travelers. The thing to accomplish was, under the guise of giving equal accommodation for whites and blacks, to compel the latter to keep to themselves while traveling in railroad passenger coaches. No one would be so wanting in candor as to assert the contrary. The fundamental objection, therefore, to the statute, is that it interferes with the personal freedom of citizens. 'Personal liberty,' it has been well said, 'consists in the power of locomotion, of changing situation, or removing one's person to whatsoever places one's own inclination may direct, without imprisonment or restraint, unless by due course of law.' If a white man and a black man choose to occupy the same public conveyance on a public highway, it is their right to do so; and no government, proceeding alone on grounds of race, can prevent it without infringing the personal liberty of each.

It is one thing for railroad carriers to furnish, or to be required by law to furnish, equal accommodations for all whom they are under a legal duty to carry. It is quite another thing for government to forbid citizens of the white and black races from traveling in the same public conveyance, and to punish officers of railroad companies for permitting persons of the two races to occupy the same passenger coach. If a state can prescribe, as a rule of civil conduct, that whites and blacks shall not travel as passengers in the same railroad coach, why may it not so regulate the use of the streets of its cities and towns as to compel white citizens to keep on one side of a street, and black citizens to keep on the other? Why may it not, upon like grounds, punish whites and blacks who ride together in street cars or in open vehicles on a public road or street? Why may it not require sheriffs to assign whites to one side of a court room, and blacks to the other? And why may it not also prohibit the commingling of the two races in the galleries of legislative halls or in public assemblages convened for the consideration of the political questions of the day? Further, if this statute of Louisiana is consistent with the personal liberty of citizens, why may not the state require the separation in railroad coaches of native and naturalized citizens of the United States, or of Protestants and Roman Catholics?

The answer given at the argument to these questions was that regulations of the kind they suggest would be unreasonable, and could not, therefore, stand before the law. Is it meant that the determination of questions of legislative power depends upon the inquiry whether the statute whose validity is questioned is, in the judgment of the courts, a reasonable one, taking all the circumstances into consideration? A statute may be unreasonable merely because a sound public policy forbade its enactment. But I do not understand that the courts have anything to do with the policy or expediency of legislation. A statute may be valid, and yet, upon grounds of public policy, may well be characterized as unreasonable. Mr. Sedgwick correctly states the rule when he says that, the legislative intention being clearly ascertained, 'the courts have no other duty to perform than to execute the legislative will, without any regard to their views as to the wisdom or justice of the particular enactment.' There is a dangerous tendency in these latter days to enlarge the functions of the courts, by means of judicial interference with the will of the people as expressed by the legislature. Our institutions have the distinguishing characteristic that the three departments of government are coordinate and separate. Each much keep within the limits defined by the constitution. And the courts best discharge their duty by executing the will of the law-making power, constitutionally expressed, leaving the results of legislation to be dealt with by the people through their representatives. Statutes must always have a reasonable construction. Sometimes they are to be construed strictly, sometimes literally, in order to carry out the legislative will. But, however construed, the intent of the legislature is to be respected if the particular statute in question is valid, although the courts, looking at the public interests, may conceive the statute to be both unreasonable and impolitic. If the power exists to enact a statute, that ends the matter so far as the courts are concerned. The adjudged cases in which statutes have been held to be void, because unreasonable, are those in which the means employed by the legislature were not at all germane to the end to which the legislature was competent.

The white race deems itself to be the dominant race in this country. And so it is, in prestige, in achievements, in education, in wealth, and in power. So, I doubt not, it will continue to be for all time, if it remains true to its great heritage, and holds fast to the principles of constitutional liberty. But in view of the constitution, in the eye of the law, there is in this country no superior, dominant, ruling class of citizens. There is no caste here. Our constitution is color-blind, and neither knows nor tolerates classes among citizens. In respect of civil rights, all citizens are equal before the law. The humblest is the peer of the most powerful. The law regards man as man, and takes no account of his surroundings or of his color when his civil rights as guarantied by the supreme law of the land are involved. It is therefore to be regretted that this high tribunal, the final expositor of the fundamental law of the land, has reached the conclusion that it is competent for a state to regulate the enjoyment by citizens of their civil rights solely upon the basis of race.

In my opinion, the judgment this day rendered will, in time, prove to be quite as pernicious as the decision made by this tribunal in the Dred Scott Case.

It was adjudged in that case that the descendants of Africans who were imported into this country, and sold as slaves, were not included nor intended to be included under the word 'citizens' in the constitution, and could not claim any of the rights and privileges which that instrument provided for and secured to citizens of the United States; that, at time of the adoption of the constitution, they were 'considered as a subordinate and inferior class of beings, who had been subjugated by the dominant race, and, whether emancipated or not, yet remained subject to their authority, and had no rights or privileges but such as those who held the power and the government might choose to grant them.' The recent amendments of the constitution, it was supposed, had eradicated these principles from our institutions. But it seems that we have yet, in some of the states, a dominant race — a superior class of citizens — which assumes to regulate the enjoyment of civil rights, common to all citizens, upon the basis of race. The present decision, it may well be apprehended, will not only stimulate aggressions, more or less brutal and irritating, upon the admitted rights of colored citizens, but will encourage the belief that

it is possible, by means of state enactments, to defeat the beneficent purposes which the people of the United States had in view when they adopted the recent amendments of the constitution, by one of which the blacks of this country were made citizens of the United States and of the states in which they respectively reside, and whose privileges and immunities, as citizens, the states are forbidden to abridge. Sixty millions of whites are in no danger from the presence here of eight millions of blacks. The destinies of the two races, in this country, are indissolubly linked together, and the interests of both require that the common government of all shall not permit the seeds of race hate to be planted under the sanction of law. What can more certainly arouse race hate, what more certainly create and perpetuate a feeling of distrust between these races, than state enactments which, in fact, proceed on the ground that colored citizens are so inferior and degraded that they cannot be allowed to sit in public coaches occupied by white citizens? That, as all will admit, is the real meaning of such legislation as was enacted in Louisiana.

The sure guaranty of the peace and security of each race is the clear, distinct, unconditional recognition by our governments, national and state, of every right that inheres in civil freedom, and of the equality before the law of all citizens of the United States, without regard to race. State enactments regulating the enjoyment of civil rights upon the basis of race, and cunningly devised to defeat legitimate results of the war, under the pretense of recognizing equality of rights, can have no other result than to render permanent peace impossible, and to keep alive a conflict of races, the continuance of which must do harm to all concerned. This question is not met by the suggestion that social equality cannot exist between the white and black races in this country. That argument, if it can be properly regarded as one, is scarcely worthy of consideration; for social equality no more exists between two races when traveling in a passenger coach or a public highway than when members of the same races sit by each other in a street car or in the jury box, or stand or sit with each other in a political assembly, or when they use in common the streets of a city or town, or when they are in the same room for the purpose of having their names placed on the registry of voters, or when they approach the ballot box in order to exercise the high privilege of voting.

There is a race so different from our own that we do not permit those belonging to it to become citizens of the United States. Persons belonging to it are, with few exceptions, absolutely excluded from our country. I allude to the Chinese race. But, by the statute in question, a Chinaman can ride in the same passenger coach with white citizens of the United States, while citizens of the black race in Louisiana, many of whom, perhaps, risked their lives for the preservation of the Union, who are entitled, by law, to participate in the political control of the state and nation, who are not excluded, by law or by reason of their race, from public stations of any kind, and who have all the legal rights that belong to white citizens, are yet declared to be criminals, liable to imprisonment, if they ride in a public coach occupied by citizens of the white race. It is scarcely just to say that a colored citizen should not object to occupying a public coach assigned to his own race. He does not object, nor, perhaps, would he object to separate coaches for his race if his rights under the law were recognized. But he does object, and he ought never to cease objecting, that citizens of the white and black races can be adjudged criminals because they sit, or claim the right to sit, in the same public coach on a public highway. The arbitrary separation of citizens, on the basis of race, while they are on a public highway, is a badge of servitude wholly inconsistent with the civil freedom and the equality before the law established by the constitution. It cannot be justified upon any legal grounds.

If evils will result from the commingling of the two races upon public highways established for the benefit of all, they will be infinitely less than those that will surely come from state leg-islation regulating the enjoyment of civil rights upon the basis of race. We boast of the freedom enjoyed by our people above all other peoples. But it is difficult to reconcile that boast with a state of the law which, practically, puts the brand of servitude and degradation upon a large class of our fellow citizens — our equals before the law. The thin disguise of 'equal' accommodations for passengers in railroad coaches will not mislead any one, nor atone for the wrong this day done.

––––––––– 5.33 –––––––––

UP FROM SLAVERY
Booker T. Washington

Booker T. Washington published his autobiography *Up From Slavery* in 1901, both capitalizing on and extending his fame. Its popularity surpassed that of his predecessor, Frederick Douglass, as the internationally recognized voice of black America, becoming an instant bestseller. Keeping with his public theme, Washington's tale focuses on the hard work and moral grounding that he employed to pull himself up from life as a Virginia slave to his current prominence. In the closing chapter, he lauds Tuskegee Institute's accomplishments and fully articulates his educational and implied political philosophy on how to chart black America's future. He makes a passing reference to lynching, but Washington's vision of the future is an optimistic one. He notes "the struggle that is constantly going on in the hearts of both the southern white people and their former slaves to free themselves from racial prejudice." While historians have called the time one of the most precarious for African Americans and most tense for race relations nationally, Washington saw it as one typified by healing and common ground.

… Twenty years have now passed since I made the first humble effort at Tuskegee, in a broken-down shanty and an old hen-house, without owning a dollar's worth of property, and with but one teacher and thirty students. At the present time the institution owns twenty-three hundred acres of land, one thousand of which are under cultivation each year, entirely by student labour. There are now upon the grounds, counting large and small, sixty-six buildings; and all except four of these have been almost wholly erected by the labour of our students. While the students are at work upon the land and in erecting buildings, they are taught, by competent instructors, the latest methods of agriculture and the trades connected with building.

There are in constant operation at the school, in connection with thorough academic and religious training, thirty industrial departments. All of these teach industries at which our men and women can find immediate employment as soon as they leave the institution. The only difficulty now is that the demand for our graduates from both white and black people in the South is so great that we cannot supply more than one-half the persons for whom applications come to us. Neither have we the buildings nor the money for current expenses to enable us to admit to the school more than one-half the young men and women who apply to us for admission.

In our industrial teaching we keep three things in mind: first, that the student shall be so educated that he shall be enabled to meet conditions as they exist *now*, in the part of the South where he lives — in a word, to be able to do the thing which the world wants done; second, that every student who graduates from the school shall have enough skill coupled with intelligence and moral character, to enable him to make a living for himself and others; third, to send every graduate out feeling and knowing that labour is dignified and beautiful — to make each one love labour instead of trying to escape it. In addition to the agricultural training which we give to young men, and the training given to our girls in all the usual domestic employments, we now train a number of girls in agriculture each year. These girls are taught gardening, fruit-growing, dairying, bee-culture, and poultry-raising.

While the institution is in no sense denominational, we have a department known as the Phelps Hall Bible Training School, in which a number of students are prepared for the ministry and other forms of Christian work, especially work in the country districts. What is

equally important, each one of these students works half of each day at some industry, in order to get skill and the love of work, so that when he goes out from the institution he is prepared to set the people with whom he goes to labour a proper example in the matter of industry.

The value of our property is now over $700,000. If we add to this our endowment fund, which at present is $1,000,000, the value of the total property is now $1,700,000. Aside from the need for more buildings and for money for current expenses, the endowment fund should be increased to at least $3,000,000. The annual current expenses are now about $150,000. The greater part of this I collect each year by going from door to door and from house to house. All of our property is free from mortgage, and is deeded to an undenominational board of trustees who have the control of the institution.

From thirty students the number has grown to fourteen hundred, coming from twenty-seven states and territories, from Africa, Cuba, Porto Rico, Jamaica, and other foreign countries. In our departments there are one hundred and ten officers and instructors; and if we add the families of our instructors, we have a constant population upon our grounds of not far from seventeen hundred people.

I have often been asked how we keep so large a body of people together, and at the same time keep them out of mischief. There are two answers: that the men and women who come to us for an education are in earnest; and that everybody is kept busy. The following outline of our daily work will testify to this: —

5 A.M., rising bell; 5.50 A.M., warning breakfast bell; 6 A.M., breakfast bell; 6.20 A.M., breakfast over; 6.20 to 6.50 A.M., rooms are cleaned; 6.50, work bell; 7.30, morning study hour; 8.20, morning school bell; 8.25, inspection of young men's toilet in ranks; 8.40, devotional exercises in chapel; 8.55, "five minutes with the daily news;" 9 A.M., class work begins; 12, class work closes; 12.15 P.M., dinner; 1 P.M., work bell; 1.30 P.M., class work begins; 3.30 P.M., class work

ends; 5.30 P.M., bell to "knock off" work; 6 P.M., supper; 7.10 P.M., evening prayers; 7.30 P.M., evening study hour; 8.45 P.M., evening study hour closes; 9.20 P.M., warning retiring bell; 9.30 P.M., retiring bell.

We try to keep constantly in mind the fact that the worth of the school is to be judged by its graduates. Counting those who have finished the full course, together with those who have taken enough training to enable them to do reasonably good work, we can safely say that at least six thousand men and women from Tuskegee are now at work in different parts of the South; men and women who, by their own example or by direct effort, are showing the masses of our race how to improve their material, educational, and moral and religious life. What is equally important, they are exhibiting a degree of common sense and self-control which is causing better relations to exist between the races, and is causing the Southern white man to learn to believe in the value of educating the men and women of my race. Aside from this, there is the influence that is constantly being exerted through the mothers' meeting and the plantation work conducted by Mrs. Washington.

Wherever our graduates go, the changes which soon begin to appear in the buying of land, improving homes, saving money, in education, and in high moral character are remarkable. Whole communities are fast being revolutionized through the instrumentality of these men and women. ...

Nor can I, in addition to making these addresses, escape the duty of calling the attention of the South and of the country in general, through the medium of the press, to matters that pertain to the interests of both races. This, for example, I have done in regard to the evil habit of lynching. When the Louisiana State Constitutional Convention was in session, I wrote an open letter to that body pleading for justice for the race. In all such efforts I have received warm and hearty support from the Southern newspapers, as well as from those in all other parts of the country.

Despite superficial and temporary signs which might lead one to entertain a contrary opinion, there was never a time when I felt more hopeful for the race than I do at the present. The great human law that in the end recognizes and rewards merit is everlasting and universal. The outside world does not know, neither can it appreciate, the struggle that is constantly going on in the hearts of both the Southern white people and their former slaves to free themselves from racial prejudice; and while both races are thus struggling they should have the sympathy, the support, and the forbearance of the rest of the world.

As I write the closing words of this autobiography I find myself — not by design — in the city of Richmond, Virginia: the city which only a few decades ago was the capital of the Southern Confederacy, and where, about twenty-five years ago, because of my poverty I slept night after night under a sidewalk.

This time I am in Richmond as the guest of the coloured people of the city; and came at their request to deliver an address last night to both races in the Academy of Music, the largest and finest audience room in the city. This was the first time that the coloured people had ever been permitted to use this hall. The day before I came, the City Council passed a vote to attend the meeting in a body to hear me speak. The state Legislature, including the House of Delegates and the Senate, also passed a unanimous vote to attend in a body. In the presence of hundreds of coloured people, many distinguished white citizens, the City Council, the state Legislature, and state officials, I delivered my message, which was one of hope and cheer; and from the bottom of my heart I thanked both races for this welcome back to the state that gave me birth.

——— 5.34 ———
'Tuskegee Song'
Paul Lawrence Dunbar

In 1902, Booker T. Washington commissioned Paul Lawrence Dunbar to write a poem to become Tuskegee Institute's school song. Dunbar did so, but Washington was displeased with his work. He objected to the absence of Biblical references, as well as Dunbar's focus on what he called "the industrial idea." Dunbar wrote an indignant and terse letter defending his composition to Washington, but agreeing to make some changes. The song was ultimately adopted, with Dunbar's revisions.

A. Dunbar's revised "Tuskegee Song"
I

Tuskegee, thou pride of the swift growing South
We pay thee our homage today
For the worth of thy teaching, the joy of thy care;
And the good we have known 'neath thy sway.
Oh, long-striving mother of diligent sons
And of daughters whose strength is their pride,
We will love thee forever and ever shall walk
Thro' the oncoming years at thy side.

II

Thy Hand we have held up the difficult steeps,
When painful and slow was the pace,
And onward and upward we've labored with thee
For the glory of God and our race.
The fields smile to greet us, the forests are glad,
The ring of the anvil and hoe
Have a music as thrilling and sweet as a harp
Which thou taught us to hear and to know.

III

Oh, mother Tuskegee, thou shinest today
As a gem in the fairest of lands;
Thou gavest the Heav'n-blessed power to see
The worth of our minds and our hands.
We thank thee, we bless thee, we pray for
thee years
Imploring with grateful accord,
Full fruit for thy striving, time longer to strive,
Sweet love and true labor's reward.

B. Dunbar's letter to Washington

Mr. Booker T. Washington,
Tuskegee, Ala.,
My dear Mr. Washington,
I have your letter and note your objection to the song. In the first place, your objection to the line, "Swift growing South" is not well taken because a song is judged not by the hundred years that it lives but from the time at which it was written, and the "swift growing" only indicates what the South has been, and will contrast with what it may achieve or any failure it may make. The "Star Spangled Banner" was written for the time, and although we may not be watching the stars and stripes waving from ramparts amid shot and shell, the song seems to be going pretty fairly still.

As to emphasizing the industrial idea, I have done merely what the school itself has done, but I will make this concession of changing the fourth line of the third stanza into "Worth of our minds and our hands," although it is not easy to sing.

The Bible I cannot bring in. The exigencies of verse will hardly allow a paraphrase of it, or an auctioneer's list, and so I am afraid that I shall have to disappoint Mr. Penney as to that. I am afraid that I cannot write verse up to Mr. Penney's standard of it but I believe if you will look over "Fair Harvard" you will note that they have not given their curriculum in the song or a list of the geological formation of the country around the school.

Very truly yours,
Paul Lawrence Dunbar

——— 5.35 ———
'Lift Every Voice and Sing'
James Weldon Johnson

Popular understanding of black history has not accorded James Weldon Johnson a level of attention befitting his significance. A poet, essayist, diplomat, investigative journalist and forefather of the Civil Rights Movement, Johnson was at the center of almost every major event for African America during the crucial early 20th century period. He helped build the National Association for the Advancement of Colored People, was among the leadership of the anti-lynching cause and served as a U.S. ambassador in Latin America. His novel *Autobiography of an Ex-Colored Man* is one of the seminal works of black literature, and his anthologies of black poetry and spirituals were among those that helped establish the cultural movement known as the Harlem Renaissance.

While living in Jacksonville, Florida, in the late 1890s, Johnson was already working as a school principle and newspaper publisher when he became the first African American admitted to the Florida bar. In addition to these activities, he and his brother Rosamond collaborated on songs, which became the source of his early recognition. The pair moved to New York City in 1902, where they met cultural and political black leaders of the time, such as Paul Lawrence Dunbar. James's connections involved him in Theodore Roosevelt's presidential campaign, through which he launched his eight-year diplomatic career. But before leaving Jacksonville, the brothers composed a song entitled "Lift Every Voice and Sing," to be performed by a children's choir during a local celebration of Abraham Linclon's birthday. They envisioned the song as a protest to the time's increasing anti-black violence, but it became much more. Its popularity grew over the years and, by mid-century, was widely considered to be the Negro National Anthem, recorded by countless black performers throughout the 20th century.

I.

Lift every voice and sing
Till earth and heaven ring,
Ring with the harmonies of Liberty;
Let our rejoicing rise
High as the listening skies,
Let it resound loud as the rolling sea.

Sing a song full of the faith that the dark past
has taught us,
Sing a song full of the hope that the present has
brought us,
Facing the rising sun of our new day begun
Let us march on till victory is won.

II.

Stony the road we trod,
Bitter the chastening rod,
Felt in the days when hope unborn had died;
Yet with a steady beat,
Have not our weary feet
Come to the place for which our fathers
sighed?
We have come over a way that with tears have
been watered,
We have come, treading our path through the
blood of the slaughtered,
Out from the gloomy past,
Till now we stand at last
Where the white gleam of our bright star is cast.

III.

God of our weary years,
God of our silent tears,
Thou who has brought us thus far on the way;
Thou who has by Thy might
Led us into the light,
Keep us forever in the path, we pray.
Lest our feet stray from the places, Our God,
where we met Thee;
Lest, our hearts drunk with the wine of the
world, we forget Thee;
Shadowed beneath Thy hand,
May we forever stand.
True to our GOD,
True to our native land.

6

Talented Tenth:
THE HARLEM RENAISSANCE AND THE NEW NEGRO

THE SOULS OF BLACK FOLK
W.E.B. DuBois

Booker T. Washington's philosophy did not originally unnerve his fellow black leaders. But with the Supreme Court's Plessy ruling, anti-black violence on a steady rise and Jim Crow laws proliferating, by the end of the 19th century most African Americans realized a starkly different reality from that of Washington's optimism. Not only was there little improvement in race relations, black citizenship was arguably more threatened now than it had been even before the Civil War constitutional amendments. The call for accommodation and cooperation with white America failed to resonate and the voice of radical dissent and confrontation rose to the fore. The loudest and most sustained of those voice was that of William Edward Burghardt DuBois.

A talented scholar, DuBois graduated from Harvard University as the first black American to earn a doctoral degree. His dissertation on the fight against the international slave trade continues to serve as a key resource on the subject. After teaching for a year at the black Wilberforce College in Ohio, he was hired in 1899 by the University of Pennsylvania to conduct a sociological study of Philadelphia's black population, which he later published as a book.

Then, in 1903, DuBois published what many argue remains the most significant work of political thought in black history. In his *The Souls of Black Folk*, DuBois dedicated a full essay to directly attacking Washington's accommodating philosophy. In that essay, he argues that Washington's leadership is unique among black leaders in urging submission rather than self-assertion. The result, he implies, is that African Americans are willingly relegated to "industrial slavery and civic death." DuBois concludes by noting that Washington's greatest fallacy is his assertion that black people, deprived of opportunity, can "strive and strive mightily" to create it for themselves without the aid of the society that first deprived them of it. With this essay, DuBois changed the course of black politics from Washington's accommodation to one of aggressive engagement with the American political system and an appeal to international moral opinion in an effort to gain the black community's civil and social rights.

"Of Mr. Booker T. Washington and Others"

Easily the most striking thing in the history of the American Negro since 1876 is the ascendancy of Mr. Booker T. Washington. It began at the time when war memories and ideals were rapidly passing; a day of astonishing commercial development was dawning; a sense of doubt and hesitation overtook the freedmen's sons, — then it was that his leading began. Mr. Washington came, with a single definite programme, at the psychological moment when the nation was a little ashamed of having bestowed so much sentiment on Negroes, and was concentrating its energies on Dollars. His programme of industrial education, conciliation of the South, and submission and silence as to civil and political rights, was not wholly original; the Free Negroes from 1830 up to wartime had striven to build industrial schools, and the American Missionary Association had from the first taught various trades; and Price and others had sought a way of honorable alliance with the best of the Southerners. But Mr. Washington first indissolubly linked these things; he put enthusiasm, unlimited energy, and perfect faith into this programme, and changed it from a by-path into a veritable Way of Life. And the tale of the methods by which he did this is a fascinating study of human life.

It startled the nation to hear a Negro advocating such a programme after many decades of bitter complaint; it startled and won the applause of the South, it interested and won the admiration of the North; and after a confused murmur of protest, it silenced if it did not convert the Negroes themselves.

To gain the sympathy and cooperation of the various elements comprising the white South was Mr. Washington's first task; and this, at the time Tuskegee was founded, seemed, for a black man, well-nigh impossible. And yet ten years later it was done in the word spoken at Atlanta: "In all things purely social we can be as separate as the five fingers, and yet one as the hand in all things essential to mutual progress." This "Atlanta Compromise" is by all odds the most notable thing in Mr. Washington's career. The South interpreted it in different ways: the radicals received it as a complete surrender of the demand for civil and political equality; the conservatives, as a generously conceived working basis for mutual understanding. So both approved it, and today its author is certainly the most distinguished Southerner since Jefferson Davis, and the one with the largest personal following.

Next to this achievement comes Mr. Washington's work in gaining place and consideration in the North. Others less shrewd and tactful had formerly essayed to sit on these two stools and had fallen between them; but as Mr. Washington knew the heart of the South from birth and training, so by singular insight he intuitively grasped the spirit of the age which was dominating the North. And so thoroughly did he learn the speech and thought of triumphant commercialism, and the ideals of material prosperity that the picture of a lone black boy poring over a French grammar amid the weeds and dirt of a neglected home soon seemed to him the acme of absurdities. One wonders what Socrates and St. Francis of Assisi would say to this.

And yet this very singleness of vision and thorough oneness with his age is a mark of the successful man. It is as though Nature must needs make men narrow in order to give them force. So Mr. Washington's cult has gained unquestioning followers, his work has wonderfully prospered, his friends are legion, and his enemies are confounded. To-day he stands as the one recognized spokesman of his ten million fellows, and one of the most notable figures in a nation of seventy millions. One hesitates, therefore, to criticise a life which, beginning with so little, has done so much. And yet the time is come when one may speak in all sincerity and utter courtesy of the mistakes and shortcomings of Mr. Washington's career, as well as of his triumphs, without being thought captious or envious, and without forgetting that it is easier to do ill than well in the world. ...

Mr. Washington represents in Negro thought the old attitude of adjustment and submission; but adjustment at such a peculiar time as to make his programme unique. This is an age of unusual economic development, and Mr. Washington's programme naturally takes an economic cast, becoming a gospel of Work and Money to such an extent as apparently almost completely to overshadow the higher aims of life. Moreover, this is an age when the more advanced races are coming in closer contact with the less developed races, and the race-feeling is therefore intensified; and Mr.

Washington's programme practically accepts the alleged inferiority of the Negro races. Again, in our own land, the reaction from the sentiment of war time has given impetus to race-prejudice against Negroes, and Mr. Washington withdraws many of the high demands of Negroes as men and American citizens. In other periods of intensified prejudice all the Negro's tendency to self-assertion has been called forth; at this period a policy of submission is advocated. In the history of nearly all other races and peoples the doctrine preached at such crises has been that manly self-respect is worth more than lands and houses, and that a people who voluntarily surrender such respect, or cease striving for it, are not worth civilizing.

In answer to this, it has been claimed that the Negro can survive only through submission. Mr. Washington distinctly asks that black people give up, at least for the present, three things, —

First, political power,

Second, insistence on civil rights,

Third, higher education of Negro youth, — and concentrate all their energies on industrial education, the accumulation of wealth, and the conciliation of the South. This policy has been courageously and insistently advocated for over fifteen years, and has been triumphant for perhaps ten years. As a result of this tender of the palm-branch, what has been the return? In these years there have occurred:

1. The disfranchisement of the Negro.

2. The legal creation of a distinct status of civil inferiority for the Negro.

3. The steady withdrawal of aid from institutions for the higher training of the Negro.

These movements are not, to be sure, direct results of Mr. Washington's teachings; but his propaganda has, without a shadow of doubt, helped their speedier accomplishment. The question then comes: Is it possible, and probable, that nine millions of men can make effective progress in economic lines if they are deprived of political rights, made a servile caste, and allowed only the most meagre

chance for developing their exceptional men? If history and reason give any distinct answer to these questions, it is an emphatic No. And Mr. Washington thus faces the triple paradox of his career:

1. He is striving nobly to make Negro artisans business men and property-owners; but it is utterly impossible, under modern competitive methods, for workingmen and property-owners to defend their rights and exist without the right of suffrage .

2. He insists on thrift and self-respect, but at the same time counsels a silent submission to civic inferiority such as is bound to sap the manhood of any race in the long run.

3. He advocates common-school and industrial training, and depreciates institutions of higher learning; but neither the Negro common-schools, nor Tuskegee itself, could remain open a day were it not for teachers trained in Negro colleges, or trained by their graduates.

This triple paradox in Mr. Washington's position is the object of criticism by two classes of colored Americans. One class is spiritually descended from Toussaint the Savior, through Gabriel, Vesey, and Turner, and they represent the attitude of revolt and revenge; they hate the white South blindly and distrust the white race generally, and so far as they agree on definite action, think that the Negro's only hope lies in emigration beyond the borders of the United States. And yet, by the irony of fate, nothing has more effectually made this programme seem hopeless than the recent course of the United States toward weaker and darker peoples in the West Indies, Hawaii, and the Philippines, — for where in the world may we go and be safe from lying and brute Force?

The other class of Negroes who cannot agree with Mr. Washington has hitherto said little aloud. They deprecate the sight of scattered counsels, of internal disagreement; and especially they dislike making their just criticism of a useful and earnest man an excuse for a general discharge of venom from small-minded opponents. Nevertheless, the questions involved are so fundamental and serious that it is difficult to see how men like the Grimkes, Kelly Miller, J.W.E. Bowen, and other representatives of this group, can much longer be silent. Such men feel in conscience bound to ask of this nation three things.

1. The right to vote.

2. Civic equality.

3. The education of youth according to ability.

They acknowledge Mr. Washington's invaluable service in counselling patience and courtesy in such demands; they do not ask that ignorant black men vote when ignorant whites are debarred, or that any reasonable restrictions in the suffrage should not be applied; they know that the low social level or the mass of the race is responsible for much discrimination against it, but they also know, and the nation knows, that relentless color-prejudice is more often a cause than a result of the Negro's degradation; they seek the abatement of this relic or barbarism, and not its systematic encouragement and pampering by all agencies of social power from the Associated Press to the Church of Christ. They advocate, with Mr. Washington, a broad system of Negro common schools supplemented by thorough industrial training; but they are surprised that a man of Mr. Washington's insight cannot see that no such educational system ever has rested or can rest on any other basis than that of the well-equipped college and university, and they insist that there is a demand for a few such institutions throughout the South to train the best of the Negro youth as teachers, professional men, and leaders.

This group of men honor Mr. Washington for his attitude of conciliation toward the white South; they accept the "Atlanta Compromise" in its broadest interpretation; they recognize, with him, many signs of promise, many men of high purpose and fair judgment, in this section; they know that no easy task has been laid upon a region already tottering under heavy burdens. But, nevertheless, they insist that the way to truth and right lies in straightforward honesty, not in indiscriminate flattery; in praising those of the South who do well and criticising uncompromisingly those who do ill; in taking advantage of the opportunities at hand and urging their fellows to do the same, but at the same time in remembering that only a firm adherence to their higher ideals and aspirations will ever keep those ideals within the realm of possibility. They do not expect that the free right to vote, to enjoy civic rights, and to be educated, will come in a moment; they do not expect to see the bias and prejudices of years disappear at the blast of a trumpet; but they are absolutely certain that the way for a people to gain their reasonable rights is not by voluntarily throwing them away and insisting that they do not want them; that the way for a people to gain respect is not by continually belittling and ridiculing themselves; that, on the contrary, Negroes must insist continually, in season and out of season, that voting is necessary to modern manhood, that color discrimination is barbarism, and that black boys need education as well as white boys.

In failing thus to state plainly and unequivocally the legitimate demands of their people, even at the cost of opposing an honored leader, the thinking classes of American Negroes would shirk a heavy responsibility, — a responsibility to themselves, a responsibility to the struggling masses, a responsibility to the darker races of men whose future depends so largely on this American experiment, but especially a responsibility to this nation, — this common Fatherland. It is wrong to encourage a man or a people in evil-doing; it is wrong to aid and abet a national crime simply because it is unpopular not to do so. The growing spirit of kindliness and reconciliation between the North and South after the frightful difference of a generation ago ought to be a source of deep congratulation to all, and especially to those whose mistreatment caused the war; but if that reconciliation is to be marked by the industrial slavery and civic death of those same black men, with permanent legislation into a position of inferiority, then those black men, if they are really men, are called upon by every consideration of patriotism and loyalty to oppose such a course by all civilized methods, even though such opposition involves disagreement with Mr. Booker T. Washington. We have no right to sit silently by while the inevitable seeds are sown for a harvest of disaster to our children, black and white.

First, it is the duty of black men to judge the South discriminatingly. The present generation of Southerners are not responsible for the past, and they should not be blindly hated or blamed for it. Furthermore, to no class is the indiscriminate endorsement of the recent course of the South toward Negroes more nauseating than to the best thought of the South. The South is not "solid"; it is a land in the ferment of social change, wherein forces of all kinds are fighting for supremacy; and to praise the ill the South is to-day perpetrating is just as wrong as to condemn the good. Discrim-inating and broadminded criticism is what the South needs, — needs it for the sake of her own white sons and daughters, and for the insurance of robust, healthy mental and moral development.

To-day even the attitude of the Southern whites toward the blacks is not, as so many assume, in all cases the same; the ignorant Southerner hates the Negro, the workingmen fear his competition, the money-makers wish to use him as a laborer, some of the educated see a menace in his upward development, while others — usually the sons of the masters — wish to help him to rise. National opinion has enabled this last class to maintain the Negro common schools, and to protect the Negro partially in property, life, and limb. Through the pressure of the money-makers, the Negro is in danger of being reduced to semi-slavery, especially in the country districts; the workingmen, and those of the educated who fear the Negro, have united to disfranchise him, and some have urged his deportation; while the passions of the ignorant are easily aroused to lynch and abuse any black man. To praise this intricate whirl of thought and prejudice is nonsense; to inveigh indiscriminately against "the South" is unjust; but to use the same breath in praising Governor Aycock, exposing Senator Morgan, arguing with Mr. Thomas Nelson Page, and denouncing

Senator Ben Tillman, is not only sane, but the imperative duty of thinking black men.

It would be unjust to Mr. Washington not to acknowledge that in several instances he has opposed movements in the South which were unjust to the Negro; he sent memorials to the Louisiana and Alabama constitutional conventions, he has spoken against lynching, and in other ways has openly or silently set his influence against sinister schemes and unfortunate happenings. Notwithstanding this, it is equally true to assert that on the whole the distinct impression left by Mr. Washington's propaganda is, first, that the South is justified in its present attitude toward the Negro because of the Negro's degradation; secondly, that the prime cause of the Negro's failure to rise more quickly is his wrong education in the past; and, thirdly, that his future rise depends primarily on his own efforts. Each of these propositions is a dangerous half-truth. The supplementary truths must never be lost sight of: first, slavery and race-prejudice are potent if not sufficient causes of the Negro's position; second, industrial and common-school training were necessarily slow in planting because they had to await the black teachers trained by higher institutions, — it being extremely doubtful if any essentially different development was possible, and certainly a Tuskegee was unthinkable before 1880; and, third, while it is a great truth to say that the Negro must strive and strive mightily to help himself, it is equally true that unless his striving be not simply seconded, but rather aroused and encouraged, by the initiative of the richer and wiser environing group, he cannot hope for great success.

In his failure to realize and impress this last point, Mr. Washington is especially to be criticised. His doctrine has tended to make the whites, North and South, shift the burden of the Negro problem to the Negro's shoulders and stand aside as critical and rather pessimistic spectators; when in fact the burden belongs to the nation, and the hands of none of us are clean if we bend not our energies to righting these great wrongs.

The South ought to be led, by candid and honest criticism, to assert her better self and do her full duty to the race she has cruelly wronged and is still wronging. The North — her co-partner in guilt — cannot salve her conscience by plastering it with gold. We cannot settle this problem by diplomacy and suaveness, by "policy" alone. If worse comes to worst, can the moral fibre of this country survive the slow throttling and murder of nine millions of men?

The black men of America have a duty to perform, a duty stern and delicate, — a forward movement to oppose a part of the work of their greatest leader. So far as Mr. Washington preaches Thrift, Patience, and Industrial Training for the masses, we must hold up his hands and strive with him, rejoicing in his honors and glorying in the strength of this Joshua called of God and of man to lead the headless host. But so far as Mr. Washington apologizes for injustice, North or South, does not rightly value the privilege and duty of voting, belittles the emasculating effects of caste distinctions, and opposes the higher training and ambition of our brighter minds, — so far as he, the South, or the Nation, does this, — we must unceasingly and firmly oppose them. By every civilized and peaceful method we must strive for the rights which the world accords to men, clinging unwaveringly to those great words which the sons of the Fathers would fain forget: "We hold these truths to be self-evident: That all men are created equal; that they are endowed by their Creator with certain unalienable rights; that among these are life, liberty, and the pursuit of happiness."

--------- 6.2 ---------
'THE TALENTED TENTH'
W.E.B. DuBois

W.E.B. DuBois's disagreements with Booker T. Washington on political philosophy ran deep. He did not, however, completely discard Washington's educational philosophy of teaching African Americans vocational skills they could use to better themselves and contribute to society. Rather, he argued that, while the masses learn a voca-

tion, a select caste of blacks should be granted access to a broader education.

In a 1903 essay that many observers have since charged reveals a pompous elitism on DuBois's part, he argued that the race's salvation would depend on its investment in the "Talented Tenth." In his vision, the community's best and brightest must first be groomed for professional and intellectual work. Through their success, they could then to take the lead in breaking society open for the masses of black people — who would, in the meantime, toil on in the "industrial slavery" he implied Washington promoted. His central point, however, was simple, and based in his lack of confidence in the white educational system's willingness, and ability, to educate blacks: higher education, beyond vocational schools, needed to open up to blacks and train teachers that could in turn educate everyone else. Without black teachers, he concluded, there could be no black education.

The Negro race, like all races, is going to be saved by its exceptional men. The problem of education, then, among Negroes must first of all deal with the Talented Tenth; it is the problem of developing the Best of this race that they may guide the Mass away from the contamination and death of the Worst, in their own and other races. Now the training of men is a difficult and intricate task. Its technique is a matter for educational experts, but its object is for the vision of seers. If we make money the object of man-training, we shall develop money-makers but not necessarily men; if we make technical skill the object of education, we may possess artisans but not, in nature, men. Men we shall have only as we make manhood the object of the work of the schools — intelligence, broad sympathy, knowledge of the world that was and is, and of the relation of men to it — this is the curriculum of that Higher Education which must underlie true life. On this foundation we may build bread winning, skill of hand and quickness of brain, with never a fear lest the child and man mistake the means of living for the object of life. ...

And so we come to the present — a day of cowardice and vacillation, of strident wide-voiced wrong and faint hearted compromise;

of double-faced dallying with Truth and Right. Who are to-day guiding the work of the Negro people? The "exceptions" of course. And yet so sure as this Talented Tenth is pointed out, the blind worshippers of the Average cry out in alarm: "These are exceptions, look here at death, disease and crime — these are the happy rule." Of course they are the rule, because a silly nation made them the rule: Because for three long centuries this people lynched Negroes who dared to be brave, raped black women who dared to be virtuous, crushed dark-hued youth who dared to be ambitious, and encouraged and made to flourish servility and lewdness and apathy. But not even this was able to crush all manhood and chastity and aspiration from black folk. A saving remnant continually survives and persists, continually aspires, continually shows itself in thrift and ability and character. Exceptional it is to be sure, but this is its chiefest promise; it shows the capability of Negro blood, the promise of black men. Do Americans ever stop to reflect that there are in this land a million men of Negro blood, well-educated, owners of homes, against the honor of whose womanhood no breath was ever raised, whose men occupy positions of trust and usefulness, and who, judged by any standard, have reached the full measure of the best type of modern European culture? Is it fair, is it decent, is it Christian to ignore these facts of the Negro problem, to belittle such aspiration, to nullify such leadership and seek to crush these people back into the mass out of which, by toil and travail, they and their fathers have raised themselves?

Can the masses of the Negro people be in any possible way more quickly raised than by the effort and example of this aristocracy of talent and character? Was there ever a nation on God's fair earth civilized from the bottom upward? Never; it is, ever was and ever will be from the top downward that culture filters. The Talented Tenth rises and pulls all that are worth the saving up to their vantage ground. This is the history of human progress; and the two historic mistakes which have hindered that progress were the thinking first that no more could ever rise save the few already risen; or second, that it would better the uprisen to pull the risen down.

How then shall the leaders of a struggling people be trained and the hands of the risen few strengthened? There can be but one answer: The best and most capable of their youth must be schooled in the colleges and universities of the land. We will not quarrel as to just what the university of the Negro should teach or how it should teach it — I willingly admit that each soul and each race-soul needs its own peculiar curriculum. But this is true: A university is a human invention for the transmission of knowledge and culture from generation to generation, through the training of quick minds and pure hearts, and for this work no other human invention will suffice, not even trade and industrial schools.

All men cannot go to college but some men must; every isolated group or nation must have its yeast, must have for the talented few centers of training where men are not so mystified and befuddled by the hard and necessary toil of earning a living, as to have no aims higher than their bellies, and no God greater than Gold. …

I would not deny, or for a moment seem to deny, the paramount necessity of teaching the Negro to work, and to work steadily and skillfully; or seem to depreciate in the slightest degree the important part industrial schools must play in the accomplishment of these ends, but I do say, and insist upon it, that it is industrialism drunk with its vision of success, to imagine that its own work can be accomplished without providing for the training of broadly cultured men and women to teach its own teachers, and to teach the teachers of the public schools.

But I have already said that human education is not simply a matter of schools; it is much more a matter of family and group life — the training of one's home, of one's daily companions, of one's social class. Now the black boy of the South moves in a black world — a world with its own leaders, its own thoughts, its own ideals. In this world he gets by far the larger part of his life training, and through the eyes of this dark world he peers into the veiled world beyond. Who guides and determines the education which he receives in his world? His teachers here are the group-leaders of the Negro people — the physicians and clergymen, the trained fathers and mothers, the influential and forceful men about him of all kinds; here it is, if at all, that the culture of the surrounding world trickles through and is handed on by the graduates of the higher schools. Can such culture training of group leaders be neglected? Can we afford to ignore it? Do you think that if the leaders of thought among Negroes are not trained and educated thinkers, that they will have no leaders? On the contrary a hundred half-trained demagogues will still hold the places they so largely occupy now, and hundreds of vociferous busy-bodies will multiply. You have no choice; either you must help furnish this race from within its own ranks with thoughtful men of trained leadership, or you must suffer the evil consequences of a headless misguided rabble.

I am an earnest advocate of manual training and trade teaching for black boys, and for white boys, too. I believe that next to the founding of Negro colleges the most valuable addition to Negro education since the war, has been industrial training for black boys. Nevertheless, I insist that the object of all true education is not to make men carpenters, it is to make carpenters men; there are two means of making the carpenter a man, each equally important: the first is to give the group and community in which he works, liberally trained teachers and leaders to teach him and his family what life means; the second is to give him sufficient intelligence and technical skill to make him an efficient workman; the first object demands the Negro college and college-bred men — not a quantity of such colleges, but a few of excellent quality; not too many college-bred men, but enough to leaven the lump, to inspire the masses, to raise the Talented Tenth to leadership; the second object demands a good system of common schools, well-taught, conveniently located and properly equipped. ...

Men of America, the problem is plain before you. Here is a race transplanted through the criminal foolishness of your fathers. Whether you like it or not the millions are here, and here they will remain. If you do not lift them up, they will pull you down. Education and work are the levers to uplift a people. Work alone will not do it unless inspired by the right ideals and guided by intelligence. Education must not simply teach work — it must teach Life. The Talented Tenth of the Negro race must be made leaders of thought and missionaries of culture among their people. No others can do this work and Negro colleges must train men for it. The Negro race, like all other races, is going to be saved by its exceptional men.

———— 6.3 ————

'WE REFUSE TO ALLOW THE IMPRESSION TO REMAIN THAT THE NEGRO-AMERICAN ASSENTS TO INFERIORITY'
The Niagra Movement

To give their new political perspective cohesion and an institutional vehicle, a group of radical politicians who stood in opposition to Booker T. Washington's "accommodationist" position formed the Niagara Movement in 1905. Led by W.E.B. DuBois and William Monroe Trotter, who edited the radical black paper *Boston Guardian*, they held their first convention in Buffalo, New York and drew up a "Declaration of Principles," below. The statement articulates well the difference between the radicals' approach and that of Washington and his supporters. It also provides an early blueprint for the goals of the mid-century Civil Rights Movement. The Niagra Movement would be a short-lived organization, however. It was an exclusively black organization, and its small membership made fundraising difficult.

Progress: The members of the conference, known as the Niagara Movement, assembled in annual meeting at Buffalo, July 11th, 12th and 13th, 1905, congratulate the Negro-Americans on certain undoubted evidences of progress in the last decade, particularly the increase of intelligence, the buying of property, the checking of crime, the uplift in home life, the advance in literature and art, and the demonstration of constructive and executive ability in the conduct of great religious, economic and educational institutions.

Suffrage: At the same time, we believe that this class of American citizens should protest emphatically and continually against the curtailment of their political rights. We believe in manhood suffrage; we believe that no man is so good, intelligent or wealthy as to be entrusted wholly with the welfare of his neighbor.

Civil liberty: We believe also in protest against the curtailment of our civil rights. All American citizens have the right to equal treatment in places of public entertainment according to their behavior and deserts.

Economic opportunity: We especially complain against the denial of equal opportunities to us in economic life; in the rural districts of the South this amounts to peonage and virtual slavery; all over the South it tends to crush labor and small business enterprises; and everywhere American prejudice, helped often by iniquitous laws, is making it more difficult for Negro-Americans to earn a decent living.

Education: Common school education should be free to all American children and compulsory. High school training should be adequately provided for all, and college training should be the monopoly of no class or race in any section of our common country. We believe that, in defense of our own institutions, the United States should aid common school education, particularly in the South, and we especially recommend concerted agitation to this end. We urge an increase in public high school facilities in the South, where the Negro-Americans are almost wholly without such provisions. We favor well-equipped trade and technical schools for the training of artisans, and the need of adequate and liberal endowment for a few institutions of higher education must be patent to sincere well-wishers of the race.

Courts: We demand upright judges in courts, juries selected without discrimination on account of color and the same measure of punishment and the same efforts at reformation for blacks as for white offenders. We need orphanages and farm schools for dependent children, juvenile reformatories for delinquents, and the abolition of the dehumanizing convict-lease system.

Public opinion: We note with alarm the evident retrogression in this land of sound public opinion on the subject of manhood rights, republican government and human brotherhood, and we pray God that this nation will not degenerate into a mob of boasters and oppressors, but rather will return to the faith of the fathers, that all men were created free and equal, with certain unalienable rights.

Health: We plead for health — for an opportunity to live in decent houses and localities, for a chance to rear our children in physical and moral cleanliness.

Employers and Labor Unions: We hold up for public execration the conduct of two opposite classes of men: The practice among employers of importing ignorant Negro-American laborers in emergencies, and then affording them neither protection nor permanent employment; and the practice of labor unions in proscribing and boycotting and oppressing thousands of their fellow-toilers, simply because they are black. These methods have accentuated and will accentuate the war of labor and capital, and they are disgraceful to both sides.

Protest: We refuse to allow the impression to remain that the Negro-American assents to inferiority, is submissive under oppression and apologetic before insults. Through helplessness we may submit, but the voice of protest of ten million Americans must never cease to assail the ears of their fellows, so long as America is unjust.

Color-Line: Any discrimination based simply on race or color is barbarous, we care not how hallowed it be by custom, expediency or prejudice. Differences made on account of ignorance, immorality, or disease are legitimate methods of fighting evil, and against them we have no word of protest; but discriminations based simply and solely on physical peculiarities, place of birth, color of skin, are relics of that unreasoning human savagery of which the world is and ought to be thoroughly ashamed.

"Jim Crow" Cars: We protest against the "Jim Crow" car, since its effect is and must be to make us pay first-class fare for third-class accommodations, render us open to insults and discomfort and to crucify wantonly our manhood, womanhood and self-respect.

Soldiers: We regret that this nation has never seen fit adequately to reward the black soldiers who, in its five wars, have defended their country with their blood, and yet have been systematically denied the promotions which their abilities deserve. And we regard as unjust, the exclusion of black boys from the military and naval training schools.

War Amendments: We urge upon Congress the enactment of appropriate legislation for securing the proper enforcement of those articles of freedom, the thirteenth, fourteenth and fifteenth amendments of the Constitution of the United States.

Oppression: We repudiate the monstrous doctrine that the oppressor should be the sole authority as to the rights of the oppressed. The Negro race in America stolen, ravished and degraded, struggling up through difficulties and oppression, needs sympathy and receives criticism; needs help and is given hindrance, needs protection and is given mob-violence, needs justice and is given charity, needs leadership and is given cowardice and apology, needs bread and is given a stone. This nation will never stand justified before God until these things are changed.

The Church: Especially are we surprised and astonished at the recent attitude of the church of Christ — of an increase of a desire to bow to racial prejudice, to narrow the bounds of human brotherhood, and to segregate black men to some outer sanctuary. This is wrong, unchristian and disgraceful to the twentieth century civilization.

Agitation: Of the above grievances we do not hesitate to complain, and to complain loudly and insistently. To ignore, overlook, or apologize for these wrongs is to prove ourselves unworthy of freedom. Persistent manly agitation is the way to liberty, and toward this goal the Niagara Movement has started and asks the cooperation of all men of all races.

Help: At the same time we want to acknowledge with deep thankfulness the help of our fellowmen from the abolitionist down to those who today still stand for equal opportunity and who have given and still give of their wealth and of their poverty for our advancement.

Duties: And while we are demanding, and ought to demand, and will continue to demand the rights enumerated above, God forbid that we should ever forget to urge corresponding duties upon our people:

The duty to vote.

The duty to respect the rights of others.

The duty to work.

The duty to obey the laws.

The duty to be clean and orderly.

The duty to send our children to school.

The duty to respect ourselves, even as we respect others.

This statement, complaint and prayer we submit to the American people, and Almighty God.

———— 6.4 ————

'SILENCE MEANS APPROVAL'
The National Association for the Advancement of Colored People

The first decade of the 20th century saw terrible escalations in anti-black violence, not only in southern lynchings, but also in race riots around the north. The economic tensions that Ida B. Wells argued as motivators for lynch-mob anger also fueled the rioting. In the summer of 1908, Springfield, Illinois, erupted in a two-day riot in which scores of African Americans were hunted and killed and thousands driven out of the city. National news reports shocked many of the reform-minded white philanthropists who were supporting Booker T. Washington's efforts at the time. One of those people was New York City's Mary White Ovington. Ovington gathered a small group of similarly outraged white colleagues and, on Lincoln's birthday in February of the following year, issued the "call for a national conference on the Negro question," below. Sixty prominent whites signed the call, along with seven blacks (including both Ida B. Wells and W.E.B. DuBois). The meeting, held on May 30 in New York City's Cooper Union, became the first annual conference of the National Association for the Advancement of Colored People (NAACP). DuBois and other radical blacks who had formed the Niagra Movement three years earlier folded their cash-strapped organization into the new group.

The celebration of the Centennial of the birth of Abraham Lincoln, widespread and grateful as it may be, will fail to justify itself if it takes no note of and makes no recognition of the colored men and women for whom the great Emancipator labored to assure freedom. Besides a day of rejoicing, Lincoln's birthday in 1909 should be one of taking stock of the nation's progress since 1865.

How far has it lived up to the obligations imposed upon it by the Emancipation Proclamation? How far has it gone in assuring to each and every citizen, irrespective of color, the equality of opportunity and equality before the law, which underlie our American institutions and are guaranteed by the Constitution?

DISFRANCHISEMENT

If Mr. Lincoln could revisit this country in the flesh, he would be disheartened and discouraged. He would learn that on January 1, 1909, Georgia had rounded out a new confederacy by disfranchising the Negro, after the manner of all the other Southern States. He would learn that the Supreme Court of the United States, supposedly a bulwark of American liberties, had refused every opportunity to pass squarely upon this disfranchisement of millions, by laws avowedly discriminatory and openly enforced in such manner that the white men may vote and that black men be without a vote in their government; he would discover, therefore, that taxation without representation is the lot of millions of wealth-producing American citizens, in whose hands rests the economic progress and welfare of an entire section of the country.

He would learn that the Supreme Court, according to the official statement of one of its own judges in the Berea College case, has laid down the principle that if an individual State chooses, it may make it a crime for white and colored persons to frequent the same market place at the same time, or appear in an assemblage of citizens convened to consider questions of a public or political nature in which all citizens, without regard to race, are equally interested.

In many states Lincoln would find justice enforced, if it at all, by judges elected by one element in a community to pass upon the liberties and lives of another. He would see the black men and women, for whose freedom a hundred thousand of soldiers gave their lives, set apart in trains, in which they pay first-class fares for third-class service, and segregated in railway stations and in places of entertainment; he would observe that State after State declines to do its elementary duty in preparing the Negro through education for the best exercise of citizenship.

SILENCE...MEANS APPROVAL

Added to this, the spread of lawless attacks upon the Negro, North, South and West — even in the Springfield made famous by Lincoln — often accompanied by revolting brutalities, sparing neither sex nor age nor youth, could but shock the author of the sentiment that 'government of the people, by the people, for the people; should not perish from the earth.'

Silence under these conditions means tacit approval. The indifference of the North is already responsible for more than one assault upon democracy, and every such attack reacts as unfavorably upon whites as upon blacks. Discrimination once permitted cannot be bridled; recent history in the South shows that in forging chains for the Negroes the white voters are forging chains for themselves.

'A house divided against itself cannot stand'; this government cannot exist half-slave and half-free any better today than it could in 1861.

Hence we call upon all the believers in democracy to join in a national conference for the discussion of present evils, the voicing of protests, and the renewal of the struggle for civil and political liberty.

This call was signed by: Jane Adams, Chicago; Samuel Bowles (Springfield Republican); Prof. W. L. Bulkley, New York; Harriet Stanton Blatch, New York; Ida Wells Barnett, Chicago; E. H. Clement, Boston; Kate H. Claghorn, New York; Prof. John Dewey, New York; Dr. W. E. B. DuBois, Atlanta; Mary E. Dreier, Brooklyn; Dr. John L. Elliott, New York; Wm. Lloyd Garrison, Boston; Rev Francis J. Grimke, Washington, D.C.; William Dean Howells, New York; Rabbi Emil G. Hirsch, Chicago; Rev. John Haynes Holmes, New York; Prof. Thomas C. Hall, New York; Hamilton Holt, New York; Florence Kelley, New York; Rev. Frederick Lynch, New York; Helen Marot, New York; John E. Milholland, New York; Mary E. McDowell, Chicago; Prof. J. G. Merrill, Connecticut; Dr. Henry Moskowitz, New York; Leonora O'Reilly, New York; Mary W. Ovington, New York; Rev. Dr. Charles H. Parkhurst, New York; Louis F. Post, Chicago; Rev. Dr. John P. Peters, New York; Dr. Jane Robbins, New York; Charles Edward Russell, New York; Joseph Smith, Boston; Anna Garlin Spencer, New York; William M. Salter, Chicago; J. G. Phelps Stokes, New York; Judge Wendell Stafford, Washington; Helen Stokes, Boston; Lincoln Steffens, Boston; President C. F. Thwing, Western Reserve University; Prof. Wi. I. Thomas, Chicago; Oswald Garrison Villard, New York Evening Post; Rabbi Stephen S. Wise, New York; Bishop Alexander Walters, New York; Dr. William H. Ward, New York; Horace White, New York; William English Walling, New York; Lillian D. Wald, New York; Dr. J. Milton Waldron, Washington, D.C.; Mrs. Rodman Wharton, Philadelphia; Susan P. Wharton, Philadelphia; President Mary E. Wooley, Mt. Holyoke College; Prof. Charles Zueblin, Boston.

6.5

'AGITATION IS A NECESSARY EVIL'
NAACP's The Crisis

Plagued by a lack of resources, and seeing an opportunity to be more effective as part of a larger organization, the Niagra Movement's founders joined the NAACP after its first conference. Although the two groups had drastically different racial make-ups, their missions were all but identical. The marriage would never be a completely comfortable one, as questions persisted about how truly radical the NAACP could be with such substantial white involvement and financial backing.

W.E.B. DuBois, then the only black executive officer of the group, took on the job of editing the organization's publication, The Crisis. As he writes in the November 1910 opening issue, DuBois planned to use it as a stage to "agitate" and build the sort of aggressive political movement he called for in The Souls of Black Folk. Indeed, his often-contrary views would eventually conflict with the organization itself, requiring him to resign. But, for nearly 25 years, he published his and others' radical writings in the mouthpiece of the nascent Civil Rights Movement. The journal, moreover, would offer the coming generation of young black artists and intellectuals a vehicle to publish their groundbreaking works, and thereby help launch the Harlem Renaissance.

The object of this publication is to set forth those facts and arguments which show the danger of race prejudice, particularly as manifested today toward colored people. It takes its name from the fact that the editors believe that this is a critical time in the history of the advancement of men. Catholicity and tolerance, reason and forbearance can today make the world-old dream of human brotherhood approach realization while bigotry and prejudice, emphasized race consciousness and force can repeat the awful history of the contact of nations and groups in the past. We strive for this higher and broader vision of Peace and Good Will.

The policy of The Crisis will be simple and well defined:

It will first and foremost be a newspaper; it will record important happenings and movements in the world which bear on the great problem of inter-racial relations, and especially those which affect the Negro-American.

Secondly, it will be a review of opinion and literature, recording briefly books, articles, and important expressions of opinion in the white and colored press on the race problem.

Thirdly, it will publish a few short articles.

Finally, its editorial page will stand for the rights of men, irrespective of color or race, for the highest ideals of American democracy, and for reasonable but earnest and persistent attempt[s] to gain these rights and realize these ideals. The magazine will be the organ of no clique or party and will avoid personal rancor of all sorts. In the absence of proof to the contrary it will assume honesty of purpose on the part of all men, North and South, white and black.

AGITATION

Some good friends of the cause we represent fear agitation. They say: "Do not agitate — do not make noise; work." They add, "Agitation is destructive or at best negative — what is wanted is positive constructive work."

Such honest critics mistake the function of agitation. A toothache is agitation. Is a toothache a good thing? No. Is it therefore useless? No. It is supremely useful, for it tells the body of decay, dyspepsia and death. Without it the body would suffer unknowingly. It would think: All is well, when lo! danger lurks.

The same is true of the Social Body. Agitation is a necessary evil to tell of the ills of the Suffering. Without it many a nation has been lulled to false security and preened itself with virtues it did not possess.

The function of this Association is to tell this nation the crying evil of race prejudice. It is a hard duty but a necessary one — a divine one. It is Pain; Pain is not good but Pain is necessary. Pain does not aggravate disease — Disease causes pain. Agitation does not mean Aggravation — Aggravation calls for Agitation in order that the Remedy may be found.

—— 6.6 ——

'THE TROTTER ENCOUNTER WITH WILSON. TALKS TO PRESIDENT AS ANY AMERICAN SHOULD.'
William Monroe Trotter and Woodrow Wilson at the White House

William Monroe Trotter was among the most outspoken new activists who joined W.E.B. DuBois in his opposition to Booker T. Washington and call for aggressive agitation. A founder of the Niagra Movement, and ultimately a critic of the NAACP because of its bi-racial leadership, Trotter established the *Boston Guardian* as a platform for his own radicalism. In addition to challenging black leaders to push for more, Trotter attacked every U.S. president from Theodore Roosevelt forward for their failures to protect the rights of African Americans. With a storied short temper, one of Trotter's most famous outbursts was directed at the equally volatile President Woodrow Wilson during a 1914 meeting with black leaders — for which he was ejected from the White House.

The black community had met Wilson's administration with a great deal of optimism. His campaign rhetoric implied he would be open to expanding civil rights. But he quickly proved a disappointment, as he segregated federal agencies and failed to protect black soldiers from a wave of violence targeted against them that erupted during his administration. Trotter led a delegation of black leaders who visited the White House in November 1914 to urge Wilson to repeal his segregating order. During this meeting, Trotter and Wilson's shouting match erupted. The nation's leading black newspaper, the *Chicago Defender*, published the account below of the incident.

THE TROTTER ENCOUNTER WITH WILSON TALKS TO PRESIDENT AS ANY AMERICAN SHOULD OTHER RACES DEMAND RIGHTS AND ARE NOT CALLED INSOLENT

Washington, D.C., Nov. 20 — Thursday afternoon of last week President Wilson became indignant when William Monroe Trotter, editor of the Boston *Guardian*, as chairman of a committee of protest from the National Independence Equal Rights League against the segregation of Afro-

American employees in the government departments in Washington, plainly told the nation's chief executive about it.

Waits Two Years

The committee met the president by appointment after waiting a year for a personal interview with him. Mr. Trotter was the spokesman, and in the fervor of his plea for equal rights for his people he forgot the servile manner and speech once characteristic of the Afro-American and he talked to the president as a man to man, addressing the head of the government as any American citizen should especially when discussing a serious matter. But the president did not like Mr. Trotter's attitude and said that if the committee came to him again it would have to get a new chairman. The president added he had not been addressed in such a manner since he entered the White House.

No Discrimination Intended

The delegation charged that Secretary McAdoo and Comptroller Williams in the treasury and Postmaster General Burleson had enforced segregation rules in their offices. The president replied that he had investigated the question and had been assured there had been no discrimination in the comforts and surroundings given to the Afro-American workers. He added he had been informed by officials that the segregation had been started to avoid friction between the races and not with the object of injuring the Afro-American employees.

The president said he was deeply interested in the race and greatly admired its progress. He declared the thing to be sought by the Afro-American people was complete independence of white people, and that he felt the white race was willing to do everything possible to assist them.

Seek Neither Charity Nor Aid

Mr. Trotter and other members at once took issue with the president, declaring the Afro-American people did not seek charity or assistance, but that they took the position that they had equal rights with whites and that those rights should be respected. They denied there had been any friction between the two races before segregation was begun.

The president listened to what they had to say, and then told the delegation that Mr. Trotter was losing control of his temper, and that he (the president) would not discuss the matter further with him.

The president is understood to have told the committee the question was not a political one, and that he would not take it up on political grounds.

The delegation presented a resolution of the Massachusetts legislature and letters from several Massachusetts Democratic members of congress protesting against race segregation in the government departments. ...

Did Not Come as Wards

Mr. Trotter said in his address that the committee did not come "as wards or looking for charity, but as full-fledged American citizens vouchsafed equality of citizenship by the federal constitution.

"Two years ago," said Mr. Trotter, "you were thought to be a second Abraham Lincoln." The president tried to interrupt, asking that personalities be left out of the discussion. Mr. Trotter continued to speak and the president finally told him that if the organization he represented wished to approach him again it must choose another spokesman. The president told Mr. Trotter that he was an American citizen as fully as anybody else, but that he (Trotter) was the only American citizen who had ever come into the White House and addressed the president in such a tone and with such a background of passion.

Denied That He Had Passion

Here Mr. Trotter denied that he had any passion, but the president told him he had spoiled the cause for which he had come, and said he expected those who professed to be Christians to come to him in a Christian spirit.

The spokesman continued to argue that he was merely trying to show how the Afro-American people felt, and asserted that he and others were now being branded as traitors to the race because they advised the people "to support the ticket."

This mention of votes cause the president to say politics must be left out, because it was a form of blackmail. He said he would resent it as quickly from one set of men as from another, and that his auditors could vote as they pleased, it mattered little to him.

——— 6.7 ———

AUTOBIOGRAPHY OF AN EX-COLORED MAN
James Weldon Johnson

James Weldon Johnson's *Autobiography of an Ex-Colored Man* marked the beginning of a long literary exploration of race and identity among black writers. The novel is the fictional confession of a light-skinned, mixed-race man who, through travels around the country and overseas, comes to the decision to live his life "passing" for white. In clean, unadorned prose, Johnson takes the reader through his narrator's winding journey. As a child, encouraged by his mother, he unwittingly passes for white at school, largely unaware of race in any personal way. But he is soon discovered, and reels from the sudden shock of an imposed race-based identity. When tragedy sends him into the world on his own, light enough to be considered white, but actually black, the narrator has the power to choose which world he will claim. He first embraces a black identity, and through his travels tests out black life as a northerner and southerner, both refined and streetwise. But just as he is growing comfortable with his identity, and choosing a life in the South, he witnesses a lynching and, wracked by the shame of blackness, chooses to leave it behind.

… After supper it was not long before everybody was sleepy. I occupied the room with the school teacher. In a few minutes after we got into the room he was in bed and asleep; but I took advantage of the unusual luxury of a lamp which gave light, and sat looking over my notes and jotting down some ideas which were still fresh in my mind. Suddenly I became conscious of that sense of alarm which is always aroused by the sound of hurrying footsteps on the silence of the night. I stopped work, and looked at my watch. It was after eleven. I listened, straining every nerve to hear above the tumult of my quickening pulse. I caught the murmur of voices, then the gallop of a horse, then of another and another. Now thoroughly alarmed, I woke my companion, and together we both listened. After a moment he put out the light, softly opened the window-blind, and we cautiously peeped out. We saw men moving in one direction, and from the mutterings we vaguely caught the rumor that some terrible crime had been committed, murder! rape! I put on my coat and hat. My friend did all in his power to dissuade me from venturing out; but it was impossible for me to remain in the house under such tense excitement. My nerves would not have stood it. Perhaps what bravery I exercised in going out was due to the fact that I felt sure my identity as a colored man had not yet become known in the town.

I went out, and, following the drift, reached the railroad station. There was gathered there a crowd of men, all white, and others were steadily arriving, seemingly from all the surrounding country. How did the news spread so quickly? I watched these men moving under the yellow glare of the kerosene lamps about the station, stern, comparatively silent, all of them armed, some of them in boots and spurs; fierce, determined men. I had come to know the type well, blond, tall and lean, with ragged mustache and beard, and glittering gray eyes. At the first suggestion of daylight they began to disperse in groups, going in several directions. There was no extra noise or excitement, no loud talking, only swift, sharp words of command given by those who seemed to be accepted as leaders by mutual understanding. In fact, the impression made upon me was that everything was being done in quite an orderly manner. In spite of so many leaving, the crowd around the station continued to grow; at sunrise there were a great many women and children. By this time I also noticed some colored people; a few seemed to be going about customary tasks, several were standing on the outskirts of the crowd; but the gathering of Negroes usually seen in such towns was missing.

Before noon they brought him in. Two horsemen rode abreast; between them, half dragged, the poor wretch made his way through the dust. His hands were tied behind him, and ropes around his body were fastened to the saddle horns of his double guard. The men who at midnight had been stern and silent were now emitting that terror instilling sound known as the "rebel yell." A space was quickly cleared in the crowd, and a rope placed about his neck; when from somewhere came the suggestion, "Burn him!" It ran like an electric current. Have you ever witnessed the transformation of human beings into savage beasts? Nothing can be more terrible. A railroad tie was sunk into the ground, the rope was removed and a chain brought and securely coiled around the victim and the stake. There he stood, a man only in form and stature, every sign of degeneracy stamped upon his countenance. His eyes were dull and vacant, indicating not a single ray of thought. Evidently the realization of his fearful fate had robbed him of whatever reasoning power he had ever possessed. He was too stunned and stupefied even to tremble. Fuel was brought from everywhere, oil, the torch; the flames crouched for an instant as though to gather strength, then leaped up as high as their victim's head. He squirmed, he writhed, strained at his chains, then gave out cries and groans that I shall always hear. The cries and groans were choked off by the fire and smoke; but his eyes bulging from their sockets, rolled from side to side, appealing in vain for help. Some of the crowd yelled and cheered, others seemed appalled at what they had done, and there were those who turned away sickened at the sight. I was fixed to the spot where I stood, powerless to take my eyes from what I did not want to see.

It was over before I realized that time had elapsed. Before I could make myself believe that what I saw was really happening, I was looking at a scorched post, a smoldering fire, blackened bones, charred fragments sifting down through coils of chain, and the smell of burnt flesh — human flesh — was in my nostrils.

I walked a short distance away, and sat down in order to clear my dazed mind. A great wave of humiliation and shame swept over me. Shame that I belonged to a race that could be so dealt with; and shame for my country, that it, the great example of democracy to the world, should be the only civilized, if not the only state on earth, where a human being would be burned alive. My heart turned bitter within me. I could understand why Negroes are led to sympathize with even their worst criminals, and to protect them when possible. By all the impulses of normal human nature they can and should do nothing less.

Whenever I hear protests from the South that it should be left alone to deal with the Negro question, my thoughts go back to that scene of brutality and savagery. I do not see how a people that can find in its conscience any excuse whatever for slowly burning to death a human being, or to tolerate such an act, can be entrusted with the salvation of a race. Of course, there are in the South men of liberal thought who do not approve lynching; but I wonder how long they will endure the limits which are placed upon free speech.

They still cower and tremble before "Southern opinion." Even so late as the recent Atlanta riot, those men who were brave enough to speak a word in behalf of justice and humanity felt called upon, by way of apology, to preface what they said with a glowing rhetorical tribute to the Anglo-Saxon's superiority, and to refer to the "great and impassable gulf" between the races "fixed by the Creator at the foundation of the world." The question of the relative qualities of the two races is still an open one. The reference to the "great gulf" loses force in face of the fact that there are in this country perhaps three or four million people with the blood of both races in their veins; but I fail to see the pertinency of either statement, subsequent to the beating and murdering of scores of innocent people in the streets of a civilized and Christian city.

The Southern whites are in many respects a great people. Looked at from a certain point of view, they are picturesque. If one will put himself in a romantic frame of mind, he can admire their notions of chivalry and bravery and justice. In this same frame of mind an intelligent man can go to the theater and applaud the impossible hero, who with his single sword slays everybody in the play except the equally impossible heroine. So can an ordinary peace-loving citizen sit by a comfortable fire and read with enjoyment of the bloody deeds of pirates and the fierce brutality of Vikings. This is the way in which we gratify the old, underlying animal instincts and passions; but we should shudder with horror at the mere idea of such practices being realities in this day of enlightened and humanitarianized thought. The Southern whites are not yet living quite in the present age; many of their general ideas hark back to a former century, some of them to the Dark Ages. In the light of other days, they are sometimes magnificent. To-day they are often ludicrous and cruel.

How long I sat with bitter thoughts running through my mind, I do not know; perhaps an hour or more. When I decided to get up and go back to the house I found that I could hardly stand on my feet. I was as weak as a man who had lost blood. However, I dragged myself along, with the central idea of a general plan well fixed in my mind. I did not find my school teacher friend at home, so did not see him again. I swallowed a few mouthfuls of food, packed my bag, and caught the afternoon train.

When I reached Macon, I stopped only long enough to get the main part of my luggage, and to buy a ticket for New York. All along the journey I was occupied in debating with myself the step which I had decided to take. I argued that to forsake one's race to bet-

ter one's condition was no less worthy an action than to forsake one's country for the same purpose. I finally made up my mind that I would neither disclaim the black race nor claim the white race; but that I would change my name, raise a mustache, and let the world take me for what it would; that it was not necessary for me to go about with a label of inferiority pasted across my forehead. All the while, I understood that it was not discouragement, or fear, or search for a larger field of action and opportunity, that was driving me out of the Negro race. I knew that it was shame, unbearable shame. Shame at being identified with a people that could with impunity be treated worse than animals. For certainly the law would restrain and punish the malicious burning alive of animals.

─────── 6.8 ───────

'ST. LOUIS BLUES'
W.C. Handy

William Christopher Handy has been called the founding father of the blues. The son of a devout Methodist minister, legend has it that after he saved up money to purchase his first guitar as a young man, his father made him return the "devil's plaything." As an adult, Handy toured with the minstrel band Mahara's Minstrels, feeding the growing hunger for black music (though only a caricatured version of it) among white southerners. In 1902 he formed his own band and, ten years later, his own music-publishing company. In 1814, he wrote his best-selling song, "St. Louis Blues." It was one of the biggest hits of the 20th century, recorded and re-recorded by countless artists around the world.

I hate to see the ev'nin' sun go down
Hate to see the ev'nin' sun go down, 'cause my
baby, he done left this town

Feelin' tomorrow like I feel today
Feel tomorrow like I feel today,
I'll pack my trunk, make my getaway
St. Louis woman with her diamond rings
Pulls that man 'round by her apron strings,
't'want for powder and for store-bought hair

The man I love, would not gone nowhere,
got the St. Louis blues just as blue as I can be
That man got a heart like a rock cast in the sea,
or else he wouldn't have gone so far from me

Been to the gypsy to get my fortune told
To the gypsy, to get my fortune told,
'cause I'm most wild about my jelly roll.

Gypsy done told me, "Don't you wear no black"
Yes, she done told me, "Don't you wear no black,
go to St. Louis, you can win him back"

Help me to Cairo, make St. Louis by myself
Gone to Cairo, find my old friend Jeff
Goin' to pin myself close to his side,
if I flag his train, I sure can ride

I love that man like a schoolboy loves his pie
Like a Kentucky Colonel loves his mint and rye
I'll love my baby till the day I die

You ought to see that stovepipe brown of mine,
like he owns the diamond Joseph line
He'd make a cross-eyed old man go stone blind

Blacker than midnight, teeth like flags of truce
Blackest man in the whole St. Louis
Blacker the berry, sweeter is the juice

About a crap game, he knows a powerful lot,
but when work time comes, he's on the dot
Goin' to ask him for a cold ten spot,
what it takes to get it, he's certainly got

A black-headed gal make a freight train jump
    the track
Said a black-headed gal make a freight train
    jump the track
But a redheaded woman makes a preacher
    ball the jack

6.9
'WE PROTEST THE PROPOSITION THAT THE PICTURED SLANDER AND DISPARAGEMENT OF A MINORITY RACE SHALL MAKE LICENSED AMUSEMENT'
Protesting Birth of a Nation

In 1915, the film *Birth of a Nation* debuted. The immensely popular movie, based on a 1905 play *The Clansman*, romanticized southern plantation life during the Civil War and Reconstruction, and depicted northern liberals as fools who destroyed that genteel world. African Americans, portrayed by white actors in black face, were shown as thieves and villains who dreamed of marrying white women. The Ku Klux Klan was lionized as the region's savior.

Many white Americans believed the movie to have set the record straight on the post–Civil War era. President Wilson hailed the production as "like writing history with lightning." But the black community was outraged, and activists around the country protested the film's showing. In Boston, William Monroe Trotter led an effort to have the movie banned. A group with which W.E.B. DuBois was affiliated, called the New Public Opinion Club, sent the petition below to the mayor asking him to bar further viewings. In Ohio, a campaign to have the film banned, reported on below by the *Cleveland Advocate*, a black newspaper, won its effort, as the state board of censors banned the film and the attorney general defended the action against the filmmaker's lawsuit.

A. Boston petition to mayor

Colored Americans assembled under the auspices of the New Public Opinion Club, on Memorial Sunday, to be addressed by W.E.B. DuBois, on "Fifty Years of Negro Freedom" in Faneuil Hall, sacred edifice which, as Boston's mayor rightly says, has ever stood against prejudice, contempt, injustice enslavement of race, petitions the Boston Censor Board to stop the photoplay *Birth of a Nation*, which teaches race prejudice, racial injustice, racial disenfranchisement against colored Americans, falsifying reconstruction.

From Faneuil Hall itself, we protest the proposition that the pictured slander and disparagement of a minority race shall make licensed amusement for the rest of the people. This is but a step from that brutal tyranny when men were slaughtered to make a Roman holiday.

B. *Cleveland Advocate* on Ohio movement to ban the film

Race is Terribly Upset over 'Birth of a Nation'

About 200 Colored people formed at Central Avenue and E. 30th street on Monday night and, marching down to the Opera House, staged a demonstration of protest against the showing of "The Birth of a Nation."

It was originally planned to hold a mammoth parade in which about 3,000 would have participated. But after considering the matter from all angles, those in charge of the plans decided that no demonstration be made. The matter for decision was in the hands of the court, and it was decided to let the law take its course. A number of zealous persons, however, marched to the Opera House. We are pleased to note that there were no arrests.

——— 6.10 ———

STUMPING FOR THE PEANUT
George Washington Carver

The most well-known of Booker T. Washington's Tuskegee educators was agricultural scientist George Washington Carver. Carver took it as his mission to find new, sustainable crops for the South, for the sake of both sale and subsistence. He earned worldwide respect as one of the most talented scientists of the time, and was a prized example for the Washington model of black self-help. Like Washington with Tuskegee Institute as a whole, Carver built his laboratory at the school from virtually nothing and with few resources.

Carver believed southern planters had eroded much of the nutrients in the region's soil by planting the same crop, cotton, year after year. He urged farmers to rotate their crops, and found that the peanut provided an excellent balance to cotton, and relentlessly promoted it. It was a testament to his success that the market became flooded with peanuts, and he had to begin championing a protective tariff on peanut imports in order to help keep the domestic crop competitive. Below, Carver testifies before the U.S. House Ways and Means Committee in 1921 to make the case. The unflappable Carver wows the committee members with all the varied uses for his beloved peanut even as they make light of him and his testimony.

The CHAIRMAN [Joseph W. Fordney, R-Michigan]. All right, Mr. Carver. We will give you 10 minutes.

Mr. CARVER. Mr. Chairman, I have been asked by the United Peanut Growers' Association to tell you something about the possibility of the peanut and its possible extension. I come from Tuskegee, Ala. I am engaged in agricultural research work, and I have given some attention to the peanut, but not as much as I expect to give. I have given a great deal of time to the sweet potato and allied southern crops. I am especially interested in southern crops and their possibilities, and the peanut comes in, I think, for one of the most remarkable crops that we are all acquainted with. It will tell us a number of things that we do not already know, and you will also observe that it has possibilities that we are just beginning to find out.

If I may have a little space here to put these things down, I should like to exhibit them to you. I am going to just touch a few high places here and there because in 10 minutes you will tell me to stop.

This is the crushed cake, which has a great many possibilities. I simply call attention to that. The crushed cake may be used in all sorts of combinations — for flours and meals and breakfast foods and a great many things that I have not time to touch upon just now.

Then we have the hulls, which are ground and made into a meal for burnishing tin plate. It has a very important value in that direction, and more of it is going to be used as the tin-plate manufacturers understand its value.

The CHAIRMAN. If you have anything to drink, don't put it under the table.

Mr. CARVER. I am not ready to use them just now. They will come later if my 10 minutes are extended. [Laughter.]

Now there is a rather interesting confection.

Mr. GARNER [D-Texas]. Let us have order. This man knows a great deal about this business.

The CHAIRMAN. Yes, let us have order in the room.

Mr. CARVER. This is another confection. It is peanuts covered with chocolate. As I passed through Greensboro, S.C., I noticed in one of the stores that this was displayed on the market, and, as it is understood better, more of it is going to be made-up into this form.

Here is a breakfast food. I am very sorry that you cannot taste this, so I will taste it for you. [Laughter.]

Now this is a combination and, by the way, one of the finest breakfast foods that you or anyone else has ever seen. It is a combination of the sweet potato and the peanut, and if you will pardon a little digression here I will state that the peanut and the sweet potato are twin brothers and can not and should not be separated. They are two of the greatest products that God has ever given us. They can be made into a perfectly balanced ration. If all of the other foodstuffs were destroyed — that is, vegetable foodstuffs were destroyed — a perfectly balanced ration with all of the nutriment in it could be made with the sweet potato and the peanut. From the sweet potato we get starches and carbohydrates, and from the peanut we get all the muscle-building properties.

Mr. TILSON [R-Connecticut]. Do you want a watermelon to go along with that?

Mr. CARVER. Well, of course, you do not have to have it. Of course, if you want a desert, that comes in very well, but you know we can get along pretty well without dessert. The recent war has taught us that.

Here is the original salted peanut, for which there is an increasing demand, and here is a very fine peanut bar. The peanut bar is coming into prominence in a way that very few of us recognize, and the manufacturers of this peanut bar have learned that it is a very difficult matter to get a binder for it, something to stick it together. That is found in the sweet potato sirup. The sweet potato sirup makes one of the best binders of anything yet found. So in comes the sweet potato again. …

You know the country now is alive looking for new things that can be put out in the dietary. Here is a meal, No. 1. That is used for very fine cooking and confections of various kinds. I will not attempt to tell you how it is made. …

Here is another type of breakfast food quite as attractive as the other two. It is ready to serve. All that is necessary is to use cream and sugar, and very little sugar, because it is quite sweet enough.

Here is breakfast food No. 5. That contains more protein than any of the others. One of them is a diabetic food. If any of you are suffering from that disease, you will find one of these breakfast foods very valuable, because it contains such a small amount of starch and sugar.

Here is a stock food that is quite as attractive as any now on the market. It consists of a combination of peanut meal and peanut hay, together with molasses, making a sweet food of it, and chinaberries. The chinaberry has a great many medicinal properties, such as saponin and mangrove, and many other of those peculiar complex bodies that make it an especially valuable product that we are going to use as soon as we find out its value. All kinds of stock eat them with relish, and thrive upon them, and when they are added to these other foodstuffs, it makes a tonic stock-food. I have tried that out to a considerable extent on the school grounds, and I find that it is a very fine thing indeed.

Here is another breakfast food that has its value. I will not attempt to tell you, because there are several of these breakfast foods that I will not take the time to describe, because I suppose my 10 minutes' time is about up. Of course I had to lose some time in getting these samples out.

The CHAIRMAN. We will give you more time, Mr. Carver.

Mr. CARVER. Thank you.

Mr. GARNER: Yes. I think this is very interesting. I think his time should be extended. …

Mr. RAINEY. The use of peanuts is increasing rapidly, is it not?

Mr. CARVER. I beg your pardon?

Mr. RAINEY. The varied use of the peanut is increasing rapidly?

Mr. CARVER. Yes, sir.

Mr. RAINEY. It is an exceedingly valuable product, is it not?

Mr. CARVER. We are just beginning to learn the value of the peanut.

Mr. RAINEY. Is it not going to be such a valuable product that the more we have of them here the better we are off?

Mr. CARVER. Well, that depends. It depends upon the problems that these gentlemen have brought before you.

Mr. RAINEY. Could we get too much of them, they being so valuable for stock foods and everything else?

Mr. CARVER. Well, of course, we would have to have protection for them. [Laughter.] That is, we could not allow other countries to come in and take our rights away from us.

I wish to say here in all sincerity that America produces better peanuts than any other part of the world, as far as I have been able to test them out.

Mr. RAINEY. Then we need not fear these inferior peanuts from abroad at all? They would not compete with our better peanuts?

Mr. CARVER. Well, you know that is just about like everything else. You know that some people like oleomargarine just as well as butter, and some people like lard just as well as butter. So sometimes you have to protect a good thing.

Mr. RAINEY. We have not any tariff on oleomargarine.

Mr. CARVER. I just used that as an illustration.

Mr. RAINEY. But to still carry out your illustration further, oleomargarine is in competition with butter.

Mr. CARVER. I believe that the dairy people want it there.

Mr. RAINEY. They never asked for a tariff on oleomargarine.

Mr. OLDFIELD [D-Arkansas]. But they did put a tax on butter.

Mr. GARNER. And they did use the taxing power to put it out of business.

Mr. CARVER. Oh, yes. Yes, sir. That is all the tariff means — to put the other fellow out of business. [Laughter.]

The CHAIRMAN. Go ahead, brother. Your time is unlimited. …

——————— 6.11 ———————

'STAY ON THE SOIL'
The 1917 Tuskegee Conference and northern migration

The deteriorating conditions in the South during the early 20th century — from entrenchment of Jim Crow laws to increasing anti-black violence — sparked the second mass migration of African Americans out of the region. Many had left in the closing days of Reconstruction, as it became clear the old slave-owning class would maintain control of the region. But many stayed, and some even returned to the South to look for opportunities during Booker T. Washington and Tuskegee's height of popularity. This second northward migration began when the Tuskegee Institute's southern blacks pushed not only by the deteriorating social conditions, but also by a series of poor crops caused by flooding and the persistent boll-weevil (a beetle that destroyed cotton crops), began to investigate jobs opening in northern industries as a result of World War I.

Each year since 1891, southern black leaders had gathered at Tuskegee Institute to evaluate their progress in building Washington's vision of a self-reliant community of tradesmen and farmers. At the 1917 meeting, participants focused on the ever-quickening pace of African-American migration out of the South. The delegates issued a plea to their fellow black southerners, urging them to resist the temptation to go north. "These are transitory times," their statement argued. It went on to invoke Washington's "Atlanta Compromise" speech (see Chapter Five), reissuing his famous call for blacks to cast down their buckets where they found themselves. Notably, in contrast to Washington's views three decades earlier, the delegates added a call for civil rights for blacks in the South. Nevertheless, the era when the Tuskegee message could resonate with southern blacks had passed. By the time of the Depression, over a million African Americans had flocked west, largely towards Chicago, and north, largely toward New York City.

The Twenty-Sixth Annual Tuskegee Negro Conference takes this opportunity through these declarations, to send a message to the Negro people of the South. To them the Conference would say, we are in the midst of serious times.

In some sections there is much distress and suffering because of the floods and boll-weevil. On the other hand there is everywhere in the South much unrest because of the opportunities which are being offered our people to go North to work in many industries where there is now a shortage of labor.

The Conference would also say: these are transitory times. We recognize and appreciate the opportunities offered in the North to our people and the necessity which is compelling many of them to go there. Right here in the South, however, are great and permanent opportunities for the masses of our people. This section, we feel, is just entering upon its greatest era of development. There are millions of acres of land yet to be cultivated, cities to be built, railroads to be extended, hundreds of mines to be worked. Here your labor in the future is going to be in still greater demand.

Of still more importance to us, however, is the fact that in the South we have acquired a footing in the soil. It is here that more than 90 percent of all the farms we own are located. It was here in the decade just past that the value of the farm property we own, increased from less than Two Hundred Million Dollars to Five Hundred Million Dollars. The great bulk of all the property we own is here.

Just now the South is the only place where, with little capital, land can be bought. Because of this fact and also on account of the progress we have already made in land ownership, this Tuskegee Negro Conference in the midst of present conditions would again say, stay on the soil. In the language of the great founder of this Conference, "Let down your buckets where you are." Let them down into the ownership of more land, better farming and better homes.

This Conference especially urges upon the farmers of the South not to plant too much cotton another year. Do not be carried away by the high price which it is bringing. Do not depend entirely upon this staple; diversify your crops. Plant corn, oats, velvet beans, peas, peanuts, raise more poultry, hogs and cattle. On the other hand, we urge those farmers in sections where the boll-weevil is and will be, to learn how to raise cotton under boll-weevil conditions.

This Conference, also begs leave to say to the white people of the South a word on behalf of the Negro. We believe that now and in the near future the South will need his labor as she has never needed it before. The disposition of so many thousands of our people to leave is not because they do not love the Southland, but because they believe that in the North, they will have, not only an opportunity to make more money than they are making here, but also that they will there get better treatment, better protection under the law and better schools and facilities for their children. In a word, that they will get more of a square deal than they are now getting in the South.

This Conference finds that one of the chief causes of unrest among the colored people is the lack of adequate protection under the law.

This Conference is pleased to note and takes this occasion to express its appreciation for the strong editorials that have appeared in the leading daily newspapers of Alabama, Georgia, South Carolina, Louisiana, Texas and other sections of the South, concerning the importance of giving better treatment to the colored people, affording them better protection under the law and providing better educational facilities.

We believe that now is the greatest opportunity that the South has ever had for white and black people in the various communities to get together and have a thorough understanding with reference to their common interest, and also to co-operate for the general welfare of all.

We believe that the time has come for the best element of the white people and colored people to unite to protect the interest of both races to the end that more effective work may be done in the up-building of a greater South.

——— 6.12 ———

THE MOST DANGEROUS NEGROES IN THE UNITED STATES

Asa Philip Randolph and Chandler Owen

Asa Philip Randolph was among the southerners who migrated to New York City. He left Jacksonville, Florida, in 1911, after he graduated atop his high school class but was still unable to afford college or find professional work. In New York, he became involved in the newly-blossoming Socialist Party politics and the anti-war cause. In 1917, the president of a hotel worker's union hired Randolph and his friend Chandler Owen, a black migrant

from North Carolina, to edit a newspaper for black hotel workers. But the two quickly angered the group's leadership by publishing an article on internal corruption and were fired. Emboldened by their journalistic success, they founded a black-socialist newspaper, *The Messenger*.

Some historians have characterized *The Messenger* as among the most radical of black papers to date. One particularly biting early editorial mocked the "cheap peanut politics" of black leaders, dismissed patriotism and loyalty as "meaningless," and derided prayer as "nothing more than a fervent wish."

Through *The Messenger* and their soapbox speeches, Randolph and Owen led a relentless attack on the U.S. war effort in Europe, particularly encouraging blacks to refuse to fight. Why should black men risk their lives for "white democracy" they asked? Their rabble-rousing prompted Attorney General A. Mitchell Palmer to call them "the most dangerous Negroes in the United States." And in July 1918, as a result of the article below, the two men joined the hundreds of American anti-war activists arrested under the Espionage Act during World War I. The law forbade interfering with the recruitment of troops.

At a recent convention of the National Association for the Advancement of Colored People (NAACP), a member of the Administration's Department of Intelligence was present. When Mr. Julian Carter of Harrisburg was complaining of the racial prejudice which American white troops had carried into France, the administration representative rose and warned the audience that the Negroes were under suspicion of having been affected by German propaganda.

In keeping with the ultra-patriotism of the oldline type of Negro leaders the NAACP failed to grasp its opportunity. It might have informed the Administration representatives that the discontent among Negroes was not produced by propaganda, nor can it be removed by propaganda. The causes are deep and dark — though obvious to all who care to use their mental eyes. Peonage, disfranchisement, Jim-Crowism, segregation, rank civil discrimination, injustice of legislatures, courts and administrators — these are the propaganda of discontent among Negroes.

The only legitimate connection between this unrest and Germanism is the extensive government advertisement that we are fighting "to make the world safe for democracy," to carry democracy to Germany; that we are conscripting the Negro into the military and industrial establishments to achieve this end for white democracy four thousand miles away, while the Negro at home, through bearing the burden in every way, is denied economic, political, educational and civil democracy.

——— 6.13 ———

THE 24TH COLORED INFANTRY'S HOUSTON UPRISING

The Baltimore Afro-American

Despite the continued segregation of the U.S. Armed Forces and campaigns such as *The Messenger*'s to discourage blacks from fighting, approximately 200,000 African Americans served in Europe during World War I. The overwhelming number of them were relegated to service and labor roles rather than combat. However, two divisions, which America's generals detailed to the French, served with valor. One of them, the 93rd Division's 369th Infantry, fought at the front for a longer stretch than any other American unit.

White Americans inside and outside the service were loath to recognize black troops. The NAACP fought discrimination within the forces, eventually pushing the government to create a black officers' training camp in Iowa. Still, African Americans comprised less than one percent of the U.S. Armed Forces officers during the war.

Black troops also faced harassment and violence from white civilians and soldiers alike. In 1917, the violent attacks led to a race riot in Houston, Texas when black soldiers fought back. The 24th Colored Infantry had been stationed there, despite a history of tension between the local population and black soldiers. Shortly after the 24th Infantry's arrival, the frequency of violent attacks on African Americans—citizens and soldiers alike—increased throughout the state. One soldier, Jesse Washington, was burned alive in Waco. On August 23rd, the regiment heard a rumor that another lynch mob was being formed in town. In an effort to strike first, the

troops stormed the city, and in the ensuing violence 17 whites were killed. It was the first race riot in which more white than black people had been slain. Following a court martial, in which the soldiers' defense was led by an individual with no legal certification, 19 blacks were executed and nearly 100 sentenced to lengthy prison sentences.

In the nationwide outcry that followed the Houston uprising, the black troops were vilified, and the argument against allowing them to serve gained credence. In an open letter to black newspapers, presented below as published by the *Baltimore Afro-American*, Detroit minister Bishop A.C. Smith defends the troops' actions and questions why they had ever been stationed in such a hostile place. A movement to free the jailed soldiers continued for over 20 years, until the final prisoner was released in 1938.

Aroused by the drastic editorials in the white press condemning the members of the 24th Infantry for shooting up Houston, Texas, Bishop A.C. Smith of the A.M.E. Church in Detroit, Michigan has published an open letter on the subject. The Bishop says:

There are so many currents and counter-currents of a disturbing nature in evidence that this is not time for hasty utterances. Public judgment should be suspended until all material facts in the unfortunate and regrettable occurrence have been fully investigated and the result made known by the War Department.

The stories emanating from Houston are one-sided and reflect the prejudices of the dominant element in Houston instead of the facts in the case. A Negro in military uniform is exasperating to the average Texan as is the flaunting of a red flag in the face of an enraged bull.

When the *Titanic* disaster was reported, it is said, Mr. Andrew Carnegie laconically inquired: "What was she doing up there anyway?" It is equally pertinent to inquire, why were the Negro troops sent to Texas anyway, particularly those of the regular army? Has the remembrance of the Brownsville affair entirely faded from the public memory? Is it so soon forgotten that but a few days ago publicity was given to the report that Negro troops were in a clash with the authorities of Waco, Texas?

Two distinct incidents that occurred during the Spanish-American War are still fresh in my memory — the threat to dynamite a train load of Negro regulars by the dominant element of Texarkana, Arkansas, and the merciless assault made on a train load of Negro volunteers at Nashville, Tennessee while en route from Chattanooga to Cincinnati.

Hon. Joe H. Eagle, M.C. for the Houston district in a dispatch to the Secretary of War said: "Without stating who to blame, it is clearly a race riot and is a tragedy sufficient to compel the statement that it is a tragic blunder to send the Negro troops to southern camps."

Who is to blame for this tragic blunder? The Negro troops went to Houston in obedience to the orders of their superiors whose right it is to direct their movements. A race riot? Yes, and that statement coming from a congressman on the ground, and a chose representative of the dominant of Houston, ought to be sufficient to induce the public to suspend judgment for the time being.

President Wilson made a trenchant statement in a speech in Philadelphia to the effect that "A man may be too proud to fight." With equal force it may be said that man may be too manly to continually submit to extreme brutal treatment. Even the patient ox may be goaded to desperation.

The fact is the white race by precipitating a world-war has turned man's earthly abode into a veritable hell, and there is no telling when the fires of damnation will be extinguished or what elements will be consummated while they are waging. If plain speaking is in order, let both sides be heard.

───── 6.14 ─────

'WE ARE COWARDS AND JACKASSES IF NOW THAT THE WAR IS OVER, WE DO NOT ... BATTLE AGAINST THE FORCES OF HELL IN OUR OWN LAND'
The Crisis

By dispatching the black soldiers in Europe to fight in France, America's generals inadvertently offered them an entirely new way to conceive of race. By and large, the French treated black servicemembers equally, both on the battlefield and off. The brief encounter between African Americans and the French sparked a dual fascination between the two cultures that would last for decades. Countless African-American artists and intellectuals flocked to Paris in the post-war years, fueling a new French hunger for black music and literature.

In the immediate aftermath of the war, the thousands of black troops that had served in Europe returned to a heavily-segregated America. Emboldened by their experiences abroad, by the emerging northern black communities and by the deliberately provocative rhetoric of black leaders like W.E.B. DuBois, these returning soldiers heightened the community's growing impatience for justice. A May 1919 editorial in *The Crisis*, titled "Returning Soldiers," was typical of the language black leaders used in trying to capitalize on the troops' return and feed the flames of discontent in black America.

We are returning from a war! The Crisis and tens of thousands of black men were drafted into a great struggle. For bleeding France and what she means and has meant and will mean to us and humanity against the threat of German race arrogance, we fought gladly and to the last drop of blood; for America and here highest ideals, we fought in far-off hope; for the dominant southern oligarchy entrenched in Washington, we fought in bitter resignation. For the America that represents and gloats in lynching, disfranchisement, caste, brutality and devilish insult — for this, in the hateful upturning and mixing of things, we were forced by vindictive fate to fight, also.

But today we return! We return from the slavery of uniform which the world's madness demanded us to don to the freedom of civil garb. We stand again to look America squarely in the face and call a spade a spade. We sing: This country of ours, despite all its better souls have done and dreamed, is yet a shameful land.

It *lynches*.

And lynching is barbarism of a degree of contemptible nastiness unparalleled in human history. Yet for fifty years we have lynched two Negroes a week, and we have kept this up right through the war.

It *disfranchises* its own citizens.

Disfranchisement is the deliberate theft and robbery of the only protection of poor against rich and black against white. The land that disfranchises its citizens and calls itself a democracy lies and knows it lies.

It encourages *ignorance*.

It has never really tried to educate the Negro. A dominant minority does not want Negroes educated. It wants servants, dogs, whores and monkeys. And when this land allows a reactionary group by its stolen power to force as many black folk into these categories as it possibly can, it cries in contemptible hypocrisy: "They threaten us with degeneracy; they cannot be educated."

It *steals* from us.

It organized industry to cheat us. It cheats us out of our land; it cheats us out of our labor. It confiscates our savings. It reduces our wages. It raises our rent. It steals our profit. It taxes us without representation. It keeps us consistently and universally poor, and then feeds us on charity and derides our poverty.

It *insults* us.

It has organized a nation-wide and latterly a world-wide propaganda of deliberate and continuous insult and defamation of black blood wherever found. It decrees that it shall not be possible in travel nor residence, work nor play, education nor instruction for a black man to exist without tacit or open acknowledgement of his inferiority to the dirtiest white dog. And it looks upon any attempt to question or even

discuss this dogma as arrogance, unwarranted assumption and treason.

This is the country to which we Soldiers of Democracy return. This is the fatherland for which we fought! But it is *our* fatherland. It was right for us to fight. The faults of *our* country are *our* faults. Under similar circumstances, we would fight again. But by God of Heaven, we are cowards and jackasses if now that the war is over, we do not marshal every ounce of our brain and brawn to fight a sterner, longer, more unbending battle against the forces of hell in our own land.

We *return*.

We *return from fighting*.

We *return fighting*.

Make way for Democracy! We saved it in France, and by the Great Jehovah, we will save it in the United States of America, or know the reason why.

———— 6.15 ————

THIRTY YEARS OF LYNCHING

The National Association for the Advancement of Colored People

The NAACP ballooned in size in the years immediately following the war's end. Its membership grew tenfold, from around 9,000 to around 90,000, between 1917 and 1919, and it established hundreds of local branches around the nation. Its first major work was in two arenas: pushing lawsuits to challenge the constitutionality of segregation and working to pass a federal anti-lynching bill. Led by white former American Bar Association president Moorfield Storey, the group saw some early success in its legal war. The effectiveness of its anti-lynching effort was less quantifiable, as Congress never passed any law aimed at curtailing lynching. Nevertheless, the NAACP's public education campaign likely helped turn the moral tide against the practice. In 1919, the group published its first statistical report on lynching. *Thirty Years of Lynching in the United States, 1889–1918* found 3,224 people had been lynched in the past three decades — 2,522 blacks and 702 whites. The report spelled out the trifling charges for which these executions were carried out.

It is to be remembered that the alleged offenses given are pretty loose descriptions of the crimes charged against the mob victims, where actual crime was committed. Of the whites lynched, nearly 46 per cent were accused of murder; a little more than 18 per cent were accused of what have been classified as miscellaneous crimes, i.e., all crimes not otherwise classified; 17.4 per cent were said to have committed crimes against property; 8.7 per cent crimes against the person, other than rape, "attacks upon women," and murder; while 8.4 per cent were accused of rape and "attacks upon women."

Among colored victims, 35.8 per cent were accused of murder; 28.4 per cent of rape and "attacks upon women" (19 per cent of rape and 9.4 per cent of "attacks upon women"); 17.8 per cent of crimes against the person (other than those already mentioned) and against property; 12 per cent were charged with miscellaneous crimes and in 5.6 per cent of cases no crime at all was charged. The 5.6 per cent classified under "Absence of Crime" does not include a number of cases in which crime was alleged but in which it was afterwards shown conclusively that no crime had been committed. Further, it may fairly be pointed out that in a number of cases where Negroes have been lynched for rape and "attacks upon white women," the alleged attacks rest upon no stronger evidence than "entering the room of a woman" or brushing against her. In such cases as these latter the victims and their friends have often asserted that there was no intention on the part of the victim to attack a white woman or to commit rape. In many cases, of course, the evidence points to bona fide attacks upon women.

An examination of Table No. 7 shows that the decreases in succeeding five years' periods in the number of victims charged with rape and "attacks upon women" have been more pronounced than for any other alleged cause. The percentage of Negroes lynched for alleged rape and attacks upon white women (compared with the total number of Negroes

lynched for all causes) in the several five years' periods is shown in the following summary:

1889–1893	31.8
1894–1898	30.7
1899–1903	28.1
1904–1908	27
1909–1913	28
1914–1918	19.8

It is apparent that lynchings of Negroes for other causes than the so-called "one crime" have for the whole period been a large majority of all lynchings and that for the past five years, less than one in five of the colored victims have been accused of rape or "attacks upon women" (rape, 11 per cent; attacks upon women, 8.8 per cent; total, 19.8 per cent).

THE STORY OF ONE HUNDRED LYNCHINGS

To give concreteness and to make vivid the facts of lynching in the United States, we give below in chronological order an account of one hundred lynchings which have occurred in the period from 1894 to 1918. These "stories," as they are technically described in newspaper parlance, have been taken from press accounts and, in a few cases, from the reports of investigations made by the National Association for the Advancement of Colored People. Covering twenty-five years of American history, these accounts serve to present a characteristic picture of the lynching sport, as it was picturesquely defined by Henry Watterson.

The last of the "stories" describes one of the rare events in connection with lynchings, that of the conviction of members of a mob involved in such affairs. In this case no lynching was consummated, it having been prevented by the prompt and public spirited action of the mayor of the city (Winston-Salem, North Carolina), and members of the "Home Guard" and Federal troops who defended the ail against a mob. ...

FLORIDA, 1916

Boisy Long, a Negro farmer of Newberry, Fla., was accused by some white farmers of hog stealing. The sheriff came to arrest Long at two o'clock in the morning. With him was another white man, who was supposed to be the owner of the hogs in question, and to have sworn out the warrant. What occurred in the house is not known, but both the white men were shot, the sheriff dying of the wound.

Long escaped, so that when the Newberry people came to get him they took his wife, Stella Long, and a friend of hers, Mrs. Dennis, on the ground that they refused to give information. It is said that they were tortured to get the information.

The citizens of Newberry and Gainesville continued to look for Long. They did not find him but they met James Dennis, and shot him. James Dennis's brother went into Newberry to buy a coffin and they threw him in jail. Then they met Josh Baskin, a neighbor of the Longs and Dennises, and a preacher. They hanged him. Then they went to the jail, brought out the three Negroes already in jail and hanged them. Mary Dennis was the mother of two children and was pregnant. Stella Long had four children.

Boisy Long has been captured and indicted for shooting the sheriff and the other white man. None of the lynchers has been indicted.

Investigation by the National Association for the Advancement of Colored People.

SOUTH CAROLINA, 1916

Anthony Crawford, a wealthy Negro farmer of Abbeville, S. C., came into town to sell a load of cotton and cotton seed. He got into a dispute with a white storekeeper over the price of the cotton seed and cursed him. He was arrested for disorderly conduct and released on $15 bail. A mob, enraged at this miscarriage of justice, pursued him into a cotton gin and in self-defense, he struck the leader with a hammer, crushing his skull but not fatally injuring him. The mob then dragged him out, beat, kicked, stabbed and partially blinded him. He was rescued with

some difficulty by the sheriff and removed to the county jail. The same afternoon the mob broke into the jail, dragged him out through the streets to the fair grounds, hung him to a tree and riddled his body with bullets. Not one of the lynchers was ever indicted.

Roy Nash, *Independent*, Dec. 11, 1916, Investigation by the National Association for the Advancement of Colored People.

TENNESSEE, 1917

On April 80, Antoinette Rappal, a sixteen-year-old white girl, living on the outskirts of Memphis, disappeared on her way to school. On May third her body was found in a river, her head severed from it. On May 6 a Negro woodchopper, Ell Person, was arrested on suspicion. Under third degree methods he confessed to the crime of murder. The Grand jury of Shelby County immediately indicted him for murder in the first degree.

The prisoner was taken secretly to the State penitentiary at Nashville. It was known that he would be brought back for trial to Memphis. Each incoming train was searched, and arrangements were made for a lynching.

On May 15 the sheriff disappeared from Memphis. He returned on May 18, announcing that he was informed that several mobs were between Arlington and Memphis. The men were reported to be drinking. "I didn't want to hurt anybody and I didn't want to get hurt," he said, "so I went South into Mississippi."

The press did nothing to quell the mob spirit, and on May 21 announced that Ell Person would be brought to Memphis that night. Thousands of persons on foot and in automobiles went to the place that had been prepared for the lynching.

With a knowledge of these conditions, Person was brought back from Nashville, guarded only by two deputies. Without difficulty he was taken from the train, placed in an automobile, and driven to the spot prepared for his death.

The Memphis Press reported the lynching in full. We give a few of its statements.

"Fifteen thousand of them — men, women, even little children, and in their midst the black clothed figure of Antoinette Rappal's mother — cheered as they poured the gasoline on the axe fiend and struck the match.

"They fought and screamed and crowded to get a glimpse of him, and the mob closed in and struggled about the fire as the flames flared high and the smoke rolled about their heads. Two of them hacked off his ears as he burned; another tried to cut off a toe but they stopped him.

"The Negro lay in the flames, his hands crossed on his chest. If he spoke no one ever heard him over the shouts of the crowd. He died quickly, though fifteen minutes later excitable persons still shouted that he lived when they saw the charred remains move as does meat on a hot frying pan.

"'They burned him too quick! They burned him too quick!" was the complaint on all sides.

Investigation of the burning of Ell Person at Memphis, by James Weldon Johnson. Published by the National Association for the Advancement of Colored People.

TENNESSEE, 1918

Jim McIlherron, was prosperous in a small way. He was a Negro who resented the slights and insults of white men. He went armed and the sheriff feared him. On February 8 he got into a quarrel with three young white men who insulted him. Threats were made and McIlherron fired six shots, killing two of the men.

He fled to the home of a colored clergyman who aided him to escape, and was afterwards shot and killed by a mob. McIlherron was captured and full arrangements made for a lynching. Men, women and children started into the town of Estill Springs from a radius of fifty miles. A spot was chosen for the burning. McIlherron was chained to a hickory tree while the mob howled about him. A fire was built a few feet away and the torture began. Bars of iron were heated and the mob amused itself by putting them close to the victim, at first without touching him. One bar he grasped and as

it was jerked from his grasp all the inside of his hand came with it. Then the real torturing began, lasting for twenty minutes.

During that time, while his flesh was slowly roasting, the Negro never lost his nerve. He cursed those who tortured him and almost to the last breath derided the attempts of the mob to break his spirit.

Walter F. White, in *The Crisis*, May, 1918.

GEORGIA, 1918

Hampton Smith, a white farmer, had the reputation of ill treating his Negro employees. Among those whom he abused was Sidney Johnson, a Negro peon, whose fine of thirty dollars he had paid when he was up before the court for gaming. After having been beaten and abused, the Negro shot and killed Smith as he sat in his window at home. He also shot and wounded Smith's wife.

For this murder a mob of white men of Georgia for a week, May 17 to 24, engaged in a hunt for the guilty man, and in the meantime lynched the following innocent persons: Will Head, Will Thompson, Hayes Turner, Mary Tamer, his wife, for loudly proclaiming her husband's innocence, Chime Riley and four unidentified Negroes. Mary Tamer was pregnant and was hung by her feet. Gasoline was thrown on her clothing and it was set on fire. Her body was cut open and her infant fell to the ground with a little cry, to be crushed to death by the heel of one of the white men present. The mother's body was then riddled with bullets. The murderer, Sidney Johnson, was at length located in a house at Valdosta.

The house was surrounded by a posse headed by the Chief of Police and Johnson, who was known to be armed, fired until his shot gave out, wounding the Chief. The house was entered and Johnson found dead. His body was mutilated. After the lynching more than 500 Negroes left the vicinity of Valdosta, leaving hundreds of acres of untilled land behind them.

The Lynchings of May, 1918, in Brooks and Lowndes Counties, Georgia, by Walter F.

White. Published by the National Association for the Advancement of Colored People. ...

─────── 6.16 ───────

THE RED SUMMER OF 1919
Chicago Tribune

The summer of 1919 was one of the most violent in American history. Race riots erupted in 26 cities across the South, North and West. The end of the war created the opportunity for conflict in urban areas with increasingly black populations. White men returned to a labor market crowded with ambitious African Americans, who had been emboldened by their travels during the war and by their ever-increasing involvement in the labor movement. Socialist organizers had become particularly active as well, and, with blacks, became a target for hostility. Like dominoes in a row, one city after another deteriorated into mob violence. African-American neighborhoods, where independent black business had begun to flourish, were destroyed. Hundreds of African Americans were killed and injured. The Ku Klux Klan, thought to have been stomped out, reemerged. One of the fastest-growing and most visible urban black communities was in Chicago. On July 27, the city erupted in days of violence. As this *Chicago Tribune* report describes, mobs of whites and blacks stalked one another around the city.

Report Two Killed, Fifty Hurt
Bathing Beach Fight Spreads to Black Belt All Police Reserves Called to Guard South Side

Two colored men are reported to have been killed and approximately fifty whites and Negroes injured, a number probably fatally, in race riots that broke out at the south side beaches yesterday. The rioting spread through the black belt and by midnight had thrown the entire south side into a state of turmoil.

Among the known wounded are four policemen of the Cottage Grove avenue station, two from west side stations, one fireman of engine company No. 9, and three women.

One Negro was knocked off a raft at the Twenty-ninth street beach after he had been stoned by whites. He drowned because whites are said to have frustrated attempts of colored bathers to rescue him. The body was recovered, but could not be identified.

A colored rioter is said to have died from the wounds inflicted by Policeman John O'Brien, who fired into the mob at Twenty-ninth street and Cottage Grove avenue. The body, it is said, was spirited away by colored men.

Drag Negroes from Cars

So serious was the trouble throughout the district that Acting Chief of Police Alcock was unable to place an estimate on the injured. Scores received cuts and bruises from flying stones and rocks, but went to their homes for medical attention.

Minor rioting continued through the night all over the south side. Negroes who were found in the street cars were dragged to the street and beaten.

They were first ordered to the street by white men and if they refused the trolley was jerked off the wires.

Scores of conflicts between the whites and blacks were reported at south side stations and reserves were ordered to stand guard on all important street corners. Some of the fighting took place four miles from the scene of the afternoon riots.

When the Cottage Grove avenue station received a report that several had drowned in the lake during the beach outbreak, Capt. Joseph Mullen assigned policemen to drag the lake with grappling hooks. The body of a colored man was recovered, but was not identified.

Boats Scour Lake

Rumors that a white boy was a lake victim could not be verified. The patrol boats scoured the lake in the vicinity of Twenty-ninth and State streets after he had tried to rescue a fellow cop from a crowd of howling Negroes. Several shots were fired in his direction and he was wounded in his left arm. He pulled his revolver and fired four times into the gathering. Three colored men dropped.

Man Cop Shot Dies

When the police attempted to haul the wounded into the wagon the Negroes made valiant attempts to prevent them. Two were taken to the Michael Reese Hospital, but the third was spirited away by the mob. It was later learned that he died in a drug store a short distance from the shooting.

Fire apparatus from a south side house answered an alarm of fire which was turned in from a drug store at Thirty-fifth and State streets. It was said that more than fifty whites had sought refuge here and that a number of Negroes had attempted to "smoke them out." There was no semblance of a fire when the autos succeeded in brushing through the populated streets.

——— 6.17 ———

'AFRICA FOR THE AFRICANS'
Marcus Garvey

Marcus Garvey arrived in Harlem, New York, from Jamaica in 1917, amidst the rapid migration and restless politics of the time. Three years earlier, he founded his Universal Negro Improvement Association (UNIA) in Kingston. Inspired, ironically, by Booker T. Washington, his organization aimed to train people of African descent in industrial skills that they could use to support themselves. Echoing the sentiments of Paul Cuffe from over 100 years earlier (see Chapter Two), Garvey believed the only true hope for the world's black people was to emigrate back to Africa, expel the white colonists and found a black nation. He established a UNIA branch in Harlem, began giving street-corner speeches and published his *Negro World* journal. In it, while opposing discriminatory laws in the U.S., he argued in support of segregating the races, championing "Europe for the Europeans" and "Africa for the Africans." It was a propitious time for such sentiments among blacks in northern cities, and Garvey's popularity skyrocketed. His organization had 2 million members and 30 U.S. branches by the beginning of the 1920s.

Garvey's U.S.-venture was, however, short lived. He established the multimillion-dollar Black Star Line trading company, purchasing three steam liners with investments from supporters. The aim was to encourage trade between African Americans and Africa and to transport members to a planned new African colony. But financial troubles shut the business down after just a couple of years. Worse, with the support of established black leadership at the NAACP (who distrusted Garvey and cringed at his ideas' growing popularity), the Justice Department charged Garvey with fraud related to the company's stock sales. He was imprisoned for three years before President Calvin Coolidge, under intense pressure led by Garvey's wife, Amy Jacques Garvey, commuted his sentence and deported him to Jamaica.

A. Garvey in the *Negro World*

Fellowmen of the Negro Race, Greeting: —

And now the world is in an upstir! The Universal Negro Improvement Association has succeeded in arousing the sleeping consciousness of millions of Negroes! And that which was thought impossible has now happened. No one thought up to recently that the Negro was capable of striking out of the barriers of racial entanglement to free himself on the great ocean of Truth. This is the age in which truth has a hearing; when men oppressed and men abused are determined that their cause should be heard at the bar of public opinion, and that justice be meted out to them. Among those who are demanding justice at this time are the four [*unreadable*] membership of three million black souls. The world is now in an upstir because this association is about to hold its great convention in New York City, from the 1st to the 31st of August. At this convention, the Magna Charta of Negro rights will be written. A constitution will be given to the world by which the present and future generations of Negroes shall be governed. The constitution to be written in the month of August is one that will be so sacred to the Negro as to cause him to pledge his very life, his very last drop of blood in its defense. As men of other races and nations regard their constitutions with a holy sense of respect, so will Negroes of the world, after the 31st of August, regard the new constitution of the Negro Race as a sacred epistle to be protected by their very life blood.

For thousands of years and within modern times, for hundreds of years, the Negro has been the outcast of the world. He has been the one lone and helpless wanderer who has never found a haven to rest, but today he forms a part of the new world's reorganization. He is determined that he shall play his part in the reorganization of world affairs. He numbers four hundred millions. He realizes that by unity of purpose and of action great good can be accomplished, but with division of interest the race will continue to be at the mercy of the organized races and nations of the world. This is indeed the hour for concentrated action on the part of all of our race, and that is why the Universal Negro Improvement Association calls this great convention to assemble in New York from the 1st to 31st of August. All Negroes who are interested in themselves, in their race, and in future generations will wend their way to New York City to form a part of this great convention assembled. Let no influence out do your determination to be a part of this great convention. Let no business prevent you from being in line with the thousands who will assemble at the great metropolitan city of the United States of America...

Trusting each and every one of you will do your duty by your race and by yourselves, with very best wishes, Yours fraternally, MARCUS GARVEY

B. UNIA's "Declaration of Rights of the Negro Peoples of the World"

... In order to encourage our race all over the world and to stimulate it to overcome the handicaps and difficulties surrounding it, and to push forward to a higher and grander destiny, we demand and insist on the following Declaration of Rights:

1. Be it known to all men that whereas all men are created equal and entitled to the rights of life, liberty and the pursuit of happiness, and because of this we, the duty elected representatives of the Negro peoples of the world, invoking the aid of the just and Almighty God, do declare all men, women and children of our blood throughout the world free denizens, and do claim them as free citizens of Africa, the Motherland of all Negroes.

2. That we believe in the supreme authority of our race in all things racial; that all things are created and given to man as a common possession; that there should be an equitable distribution and apportionment of all such things, and in consideration of the fact that as a race we are now deprived of those things that are morally and legally ours, we believed it right that all such things should be acquired and held by whatsoever means possible.

3. That we believe the Negro, like any other race, should be governed by the ethics of civilization, and therefore should not be deprived of any of those rights or privileges common to other human beings.

4. We declare that Negroes, wheresoever they form a community among themselves should be given the right to elect their own representatives to represent them in Legislatures, courts of law, or such institutions as may exercise control over that particular community.

5. We assert that the Negro is entitled to even-handed justice before all courts of law and equity in whatever country he may be found, and when this is denied him on account of his race or color such denial is an insult to the race as a whole and should be resented by the entire body of Negroes.

6. We declare it unfair and prejudicial to the rights of Negroes in communities where they exist in considerable numbers to be tried by a judge and jury composed entirely of an alien race, but in all such cases members of our race arc entitled to representation on the jury.

7. We believe that any law or practice that tends to deprive any African of his land or the privileges of free citizenship within his country is unjust and immoral, and no native should respect any such law or practice.

8. We declare taxation without representation unjust and tyrannous, and there should be no obligation on the part of the Negro to obey

the levy of a tax by any law-making body from which he is excluded and denied representation on account of his race and color.

9. We believe that any law especially directed against the Negro to his detriment and singling him out because of his race or color is unfair and immoral, and should not be respected.

10. We believe all men entitled to common human respect and that our race should in no way tolerate any insults that may be interpreted to mean disrespect to our race or color.

11. We deprecate the use of the term "nigger, as applied to Negroes, and demand that the word "Negro" be written with a capital "N."

12. We believe that the Negro should adopt every means to protect himself against barbarous practices inflicted upon him because of color.

13. We believe in the freedom of Africa for the Negro people of the world, and by the principle of Europe for the Europeans and Asia for the Asiatics, we also demand Africa for the Africans at home and abroad.

14. We believe in the inherent right of the Negro to possess himself of Africa and that his possession of same shall not be regarded as an infringement on any claim or purchase made by any race or nation.

15. We strongly condemn the cupidity of those nations of the world who, by open aggression or secret schemes, have seized the territories and inexhaustible natural wealth of Africa, and we place on record our most solemn determination to reclaim the treasures and possession of the vast continent of our forefathers. ...

38. We demand complete control of our social institutions without interference by any alien race or races.

39. That the colors, Red, Black and Green, be the colors of the Negro race.

40. Resolved, That the anthem "Ethiopia, Thou Land of Our Fathers etc.," shall be the anthem of the Negro race.

THE UNIVERSAL ETHIOPIAN ANTHEM
Poem By Burrell and Ford.

Ethiopia, thou land of our fathers,
Thou land where the gods loved to be,

As storm cloud at night sudden gathers
Our armies come rushing to thee.
We must in the fight be victorious
When swords are thrust outward to glean;
For us will the victory be glorious
When led by the red, black and green

CHORUS.

Advance, advance to victory,
Let Africa be free;
Advance to meet the foe
With the might
Of the red, the black and the green.

Ethiopia, the tyrant's falling,
Who smote thee upon thy knees
And thy children are lustily calling
From over the distant seas.
Jehovah the Great One has heard us,
Has noted our sighs and our tears,
With His spirit of Love he has stirred us
To be One through the coming years.

CHORUS

O, Jehovah, thou God of the ages
Grant unto our sons that lead
The wisdom Thou gave to Thy sages
When Israel was sore in need.
Thy voice thro' the dim past has spoken,
Ethiopia shall stretch forth her hand,
By Thee shall all fetters be broken
And Heaven bless our dear fatherland.

CHORUS

41. We believe that any limited liberty which deprives one of the complete rights and

prerogatives of full citizenship is but a modified form of slavery.

42. We declare it an injustice to our people and a serious impediment to the health of the race to deny to competent licensed Negro physicians the right to practice in the public hospitals of the communities in which they reside, for no other reason than their race and color. ...

45. Be it further resolved, That we as a race of people declare the League of Nations null and void as far as the Negro is concerned, in that it seeks to deprive Negroes of their liberty.

46. We demand of all men to do unto us as we would do unto them, in the name of justice; and we cheerfully accord to all men all the rights we claim herein for ourselves.

47. We declare that no Negro shall engage himself in battle for an alien race without first obtaining the consent of the leader of the Negro people of the world, except in a matter of national self-defense.

48. We protest against the practice of drafting Negroes and sending them to war with alien forces without proper training, and demand in all cases that Negro soldiers be given the same training as the aliens. ...

53. We proclaim the 31st day of August of each year to be an international holiday to be observed by all Negroes.

54. We want all men to know that we shall maintain and contend for the freedom and equality of every man, woman and child of our race, with our lives, our fortunes and our sacred honor.

———— 6.18 ————
'IF WE MUST DIE'
Claude McKay

In addition to Marcus Garvey, another Caribbean-American immigrant whose work embodied the restlessness and ambition of post-War black America was Claude McKay. When he arrived in Harlem, he was already an acclaimed poet in his home country of Jamaica. Following the Red Summer riots of 1919, McKay wrote his angry sonnet "If We Must Die." The poem, along with his equally fiery sonnet "The Lynching," established McKay as what James Weldon Johnson later called "preeminently the poet of rebellion." Both were later republished in McKay's 1922 volume *Harlem Shadows*. As the first book of poetry published by a black American since Paul Lawrence Dunbar's death, *Harlem Shadows* inaugurated the flowering of black literature and arts known as the Harlem Renaissance.

A. "If We Must Die"

If we must die, let it not be like hogs
Hunted and penned in an inglorious spot,
While round us bark the mad and hungry dogs,
Making their mock at our accursed lot.
If we must die, O let us nobly die,
So that our precious blood may not be shed
In vain; then even the monsters we defy
Shall be constrained to honor us though dead!
O kinsmen we must meet the common foe!
Though far outnumbered let us show us brave,
And for their thousand blows deal one
    deathblow!
What though before us lies the open grave?
Like men we'll face the murderous,
    cowardly pack,
Pressed to the wall, dying, but fighting back!

B. "The Lynching"

His Spirit in smoke ascended to high heaven.
His father, by the cruelest way of pain,
Had bidden him to his bosom once again;
The awful sin remained still unforgiven.
All night a bright and solitary star
(Perchance the one that ever guided him,
Yet gave him up at last to Fate's wild whim)
Hung pitifully o'er the swinging char.
Day dawned, and soon the mixed crowds
    came to view
The ghastly body swaying in the sun
The women thronged to look, but never a one
Showed sorrow in her eyes of steely blue;
And little lads, lynchers that were to be,
Danced round the dreadful thing in
    fiendish glee.

—— 6.19 ——
"T'AINT NOBODY'S BUSINESS"
Bessie Smith

CRAZY BLUES
By PERRY BRADFORD

Get this number for your phonograph on Okeh Record No. 4169

As the 1920s approached, record companies were as yet unconvinced that there was any market in African-American music sung by and sold to black people. Accomplished black composer Perry "Mule" Bradford changed that in 1920 when he convinced Okeh Records to release what has been credited as the first blues record. He recruited black vaudeville singer Mamie Smith to record his "Crazy Blues," with Johnny Dunn on cornet, Dope Andrews on trombone, Leroy Parker on violin, and Willie Smith on piano. It was an unprecedented hit, selling over a million copies in its first year. Perhaps the most significant point about Smith's album was its packaging and marketing. The company put her picture on the record cover and played up the fact that she was performing uniquely African-American music.

Other record companies rushed to cash in on the new "race" market, falling over themselves to recruit and record black female vocalists singing the blues. The undisputed "Empress" of the blues singers who found new opportunity in this wave was Bessie Smith. The Chattanooga, Tennessee native was already a star among southern blacks by the time she recorded her first song for Columbia Records in 1923. She recorded two songs

that year, one of which was her famous "Down Hearted Blues," that sold nearly a million copies. She would record over 150 songs for Columbia in the next decade, earning her title "Empress of the Blues."

If Claude McKay embodied the time's impatience with white hegemony, Smith symbolized the new-found individuality running throughout black America in the 1920s. The latest generation of African Americans were anxious to claim their own identities and set their own rules, apart from both the dictates of white society and the imposed responsibilities of black leaders of any political philosophy. Smith, openly bisexual, flaunted her sexuality, refused to demure as a "proper" black woman and challenged anyone who she believed had crossed her. She angered white society and earned the adoration of many blacks. Smith's strident individuality came through in her work, and her most celebrated song, "T'aint Nobody's Business If I Do," best explains her bold approach to the world.

A. "T'ain't Nobody's Business if I Do"

There ain't nothing I can do, or nothing I
    can say
That folks don't criticize me
But I'm goin' to, do just as I want to anyway
And don't care if they all despise me

If I should take a notion
To jump into the ocean
T'ain't nobody's bizness if I do, do, do do

If I go to church on Sunday
Then just shimmy down on Monday
Ain't nobody's bizness if I do, if I do

If my friend ain't got no money
And I say "Take all mine, honey"
T'ain't nobody's bizness if I do, do, do do

If I give him my last nickel
And it leaves me in a pickle
T'ain't nobody's bizness if I do, if I do

Well I'd rather my man would hit me,
than to jump right up and quit me
T'ain't nobody's bizness if I do, do, do do

I swear I won't call no copper
If I'm beat up by my papa
T'ain't nobody's bizness if I do, if I do

B. Smith's mythical death by racism

In 1937, Smith had a car accident while driving with her boyfriend of the time, Richard Morgan. The car rear-ended a truck, and Smith died of blood loss before reaching the hospital. The following week, John Hammond, the Okeh Records executive who produced her songs (as well as that of countless premier blues and jazz artists, black and white) wrote an article in *Downbeat*, a prominent jazz magazine, claiming she died because a Mississippi hospital refused her treatment. The allegation was false, but it created an urban legend that many still accept as fact today.

New York, N.Y. — Bessie Smith was killed during this last week in September, and perhaps the greatest and least appreciated artist in American jazz is gone. My own admiration for her has been expressed too often to warrant repeating here again, but I feel like kicking myself for not having done more to make her art known to thousands who might really have appreciated her had they only had the opportunity.

A particularly disagreeable story as to the details of her death has just been received from members of Chick Webb's orchestra, who were in Memphis soon after the disaster. It seems that Bessie was riding in a car which crashed into a truck parked along the side of the road. One of her arms was nearly severed, but aside from that there was no other serious injury, according to these informants. Some time elapsed before a doctor was summoned to the scene, but finally she was picked up by a medico and driven to the leading Memphis hospital. On the way this car was involved in some minor mishap, which further delayed medical attention. When she finally did arrive she was refused treatment because of her color and bled to death while waiting for attention.

TALES MAY BE MAGNIFIED
Realizing that such tales can be magnified greatly in the telling, I would like to get confir-

mation from some Memphis citizens who were on the spot at the time. If the story is true, it is but another example of disgraceful conditions in a certain section of our country already responsible for Scottsboro, the Shoemaker flogging, and the killing and maiming of legitimate union organizers. Of the particular city of Memphis I am prepared to believe almost anything, since its mayor and chief of police publicly urged the use of violence against organizers of the CIO a few weeks ago.

Be that as it may, the UHCA is busy sponsoring a special Bessie Smith memorial album containing twelve of her most inspired blues, with accompaniment by Louis Armstrong, Fletcher Henderson, Joe Smith, Coleman Hawkins, Buster Bailey, Charlie Green, Jimmy Johnson, a few other great artists. The album will be released by Brunswick-Columbia around the middle of November with pictures of the performers and details about each one of the discs. Take it from one who cherished all the records that this will be the best buy of the year in music.

——— 6.20 ———
'TAKE THE "A" TRAIN'
Duke Ellington and Billy Strayhorn

Composer Fletcher Henderson may have been responsible for melding the New Orleans roots of jazz into the swing era, but Duke Ellington is still the undisputed father of the genre. Today considered one of, if not the, greatest American composers, Ellington and his orchestra dominated jazz for decades. As the times and tastes changed,

Ellington struggled to remain relevant, but always managed to do so. For years, his confidant and co-composer Billy Strayhorn, an openly gay black man, was overlooked as just another member of his staff. Recent studies and testimonials from Ellington and Strayhorn's colleagues reveal that the pair, in fact, worked so closely in writing the orchestra's songs that their contributions are indistinguishable.

The Duke Ellington Orchestra's popularity reached its zenith during the 1930s and '40s. The group played the all-white Cotton Club in Harlem from 1927 to 1931, achieving popularity there and among African Americans. With his 1932 "It Don't Mean a Thing (If It Ain't Got That Swing)," Ellington drew national, and eventually international, acclaim. At the end of the decade, he met Strayhorn, who would write the equally famous "Take the 'A' Train" (about traveling to Harlem on the New York City subway) in 1941.

A. "It Don't Mean A Thing"

Wat-dat-to,
Wat-dat-to,
Wat-dat-to,
Wat-dat-to, dat dat do, da da do.

It don't mean a thing if it ain't got that swing,
It don't mean a thing, all you've got to do is sing,
It makes no difference if it's sweet or hot,
Just keep that rhythm, give it everything
   you've got!
It don't mean a thing if it ain't got that swing!

Wa da da do,
Wa da da do, da doh,
Whup de dittle ittle up,
Dat dat dat doh!

It don't mean a thing if it ain't got that swing!

B. "Take the 'A' Train"

You must take the "A" train
To go to Sugar Hill way up in Harlem
If you miss the "A" train

You'll find you missed the quickest way
   to Harlem
Hurry, get on, now it's coming
Listen to those rails a-thrumming
All aboard, get on the "A" train
Soon you will be on Sugar Hill in Harlem

——— 6.21 ———
'A FORM THAT IS FREER AND LARGER'
James Weldon Johnson

What started off as a scattered explosion of new black literature became a more conscious socio-political movement in Harlem in the 1920s. By this time, the area had been anointed the "Negro Capital of the World," as migration had brought to New York City politicians, business people, laborers, religious leaders, hustlers, artists and performers of all sorts, and every stripe of black America conceivable. When the burgeoning bohemian arts and politics movement led white society to take notice of the cultural revolution unfolding in Harlem, black political leaders realized an opportunity had presented itself. People like W.E.B. DuBois and the National Urban League's Charles Johnson believed accomplishments in the field of arts could help push for social and political equality. They began actively encouraging Harlem artists, publishing them in their journals and promoting their work to the white world.

In this vein, in 1922, James Weldon Johnson published the first edition of his influential *Book of American Negro Poetry*. It showcased the poetic works of "New Negroes" such as Claude McKay, Fenton Johnson and William Stanley Braithwaite. In his lengthy introduction, Johnson articulates the black leadership's goals in promoting these new artists. And in a section discussing the poets' retreat from the "long convention" of dialect, he provides one of the most definitive explanations of black America's cultural shift, exemplified by Renaissance writers, away from externally imposed racial identities.

There is, perhaps, a better excuse for giving an Anthology of American Negro Poetry to the public than can be offered for many of the anthologies that have recently been issued. The public, generally speaking, does not know that there are American Negro poets — to supply this lack of information is, alone, a work worthy of somebody's effort.

Moreover, the matter of Negro poets and the production of literature by the colored people in this country involves more than supplying information that is lacking. It is a matter which has a direct bearing on the most vital ofAmerican problems.

A people may become great through many means, but there is only one measure by which its greatness is recognized and acknowledged. The final measure of the greatness of all peoples is the amount and standard of the literature and art they have produced. The world does not know that a people is great until that people produces great literature and art. No people that has produced great literature and art has ever been looked upon by the world as distinctly inferior.

The status of the Negro in the United States is more a question of national mental attitude toward the race than of actual conditions. And nothing will do more to change that mental attitude and raise his status than a demonstration of intellectual parity by the Negro through the production of literature and art.

Is there likelihood that the American Negro will be able to do this? There is, for the good reason that he possesses the innate powers. He has the emotional endowment, the originality and artistic conception, and, what is more important, the power of creating that which has universal appeal and influence. …

It may be surprising to many to see how little of the poetry being written by Negro poets today is being written in Negro dialect. The newer Negro poets show a tendency to discard dialect; much of the subject-matter which went into the making of traditional dialect poetry, 'possums, watermelons, etc., they have discarded altogether, at least, as poetic material. This tendency will, no doubt, be regretted by the majority of white readers; and, indeed, it would be a distinct loss if the American Negro poets threw away this quaint and musical folk speech as a medium of expression. And yet, after all, these poets are working through a problem not realized by the reader, and, perhaps, by many of these poets themselves not realized consciously. They are trying to break away from, not Negro dialect itself, but the limitations on Negro dialect imposed by the fixing effects of long convention.

The Negro in the United States has achieved or been placed in a certain artistic niche. When he is thought of artistically, it is as a happy-go-lucky, singing, shuffling, banjo-picking being or as a more or less pathetic figure. The picture of him is in a log cabin amid fields of cotton or along the levees. Negro dialect is naturally and by long association the exact instrument for voicing this phase of Negro life; and by that very exactness it is an instrument with but two full stops, humor and pathos. So even when he confines himself to purely racial themes, the Aframerican poet realizes that there are phases of Negro life in the United States which cannot be treated in the dialect either adequately or artistically. Take, for example, the phrases rising out of life in Harlem, that most wonderful Negro city in the world. I do not deny that a Negro in a log cabin is more picturesque than a Negro in a Harlem flat, but the Negro in the Harlem flat is here, and he is but part of a group growing everywhere in the country, a group whose ideals are becoming increasingly more vital than those of the traditionally artistic group, even if its members are less picturesque.

What the colored poet in the United States needs to do is something like what Synge did for the Irish; he needs to find a form that will express the racial spirit by symbols from within rather than by symbols from without, such as the mere mutilation of English spelling and pronunciation. He needs a form that is freer and larger than dialect, but which will still hold the racial flavor; a form expressing the imagery, the idioms, the peculiar turns of thought, and the distinctive humor and pathos, too, of the Negro, but which will also be capable of voicing the deepest and highest emotions and aspirations, and allow of the widest range of subjects and the widest scope of treatment.

Negro dialect is at present a medium that is not capable of giving expression to the varied conditions of Negro life in America, and much less is it capable of giving the fullest interpretation of Negro character and psychology. This is no indictment against the dialect as dialect, but against the mold of convention in which Negro dialect in the United States has been set. In time these conventions may become lost, and the colored poet in the United States may sit down to write in dialect without feeling that his first line will put the general reader in a frame of mind which demands that the poem be humorous or pathetic. In the meantime, there is no reason why these poets should not continue to do the beautiful things that can be done, and done best, in the dialect.

In stating the need for Aframerican poets in the United States to work out a new and distinctive form of expression I do not wish to be understood to hold any theory that they should limit themselves to Negro poetry, to racial themes; the sooner they are able to write American poetry spontaneously, the better. Nevertheless, I believe that the richest contribution the Negro poet can make to the American literature of the future will be the fusion into it of his own individual artistic gifts. …

I offer this collection without making apology or asking allowance. I feel confident that the reader will find not only an earnest for the future, but actual achievement. The reader cannot but be impressed by the distance already covered. It is a long way from the plaints of George Horton to the invectives of Claude McKay, from the obviousness of Frances Harper to the complexness of Anne Spencer. Much ground has been covered, but more will yet be covered. It is this side of prophecy to declare that the undeniable creative genius of the Negro is destined to make a distinctive and valuable contribution to American poetry. …

——— 6.22 ———

'THE NEGRO SPEAKS OF RIVERS'

Langston Hughes

Langston Hughes, perhaps the name most popularly identified with the Harlem Renaissance, was still a teenager when he published his first poems in the NAACP's *The Crisis*. Throughout his prolific career, Hughes wrote in many voices and forms, from poetry to short story to novel to play to essay. His work in each has been celebrated as among the best in both African-American and American literary history. Hughes credited his writing style to the influence of jazz, which blossomed alongside him during the Renaissance. In his rhythmic voice, he explored race and its impact on the personal identities and the worldviews of both blacks and whites. Hughes also often employed the street vernacular of Harlem, which further emphasized his poetry's rhythmic feel, as in the title poem to his first collection *The Weary Blues*, published in 1926. In other works, he subtly expressed the emotional toll taken on his characters as they navigated race in America. His writing stretches from 1921, when one of his best-known works, "The Negro Speaks of Rivers," was published in *The Crisis* as a tribute to W.E.B. DuBois, through the 1960s. His 1951 collection *Montage of a Dream Deferred*, containing his signature poem "Harlem" (also known as "A Dream Deferred"), is counted as one of the most significant in black literature. If the Harlem Renaissance had a single poet laureate, it was Langston Hughes.

A. "The Negro Speaks of Rivers"

I've known rivers:
I've known rivers ancient as the world and older than the flow of human blood in human veins.

My soul has grown deep like the rivers.

I bathed in the Euphrates when dawns
    were young.
I built my hut near the Congo and it lulled
    me to sleep.
I looked upon the Nile and raised the pyramids
    above it.

I heard the singing of the Mississippi when
    Abe Lincoln went down to New Orleans,
    and I've seen its muddy bosom turn all
    golden in the sunset.

I've known rivers:
Ancient, dusky rivers.

My soul has grown deep like the rivers.

B. "The Weary Blues"

Droning a drowsy syncopated tune,
Rocking back and forth to a mellow croon,
    I heard a Negro play.
Down on Lenox Avenue the other night
By the pale dull pallor of an old gas light
    He did a lazy sway....
    He did a lazy sway....
To the tune o' those Weary Blues.
With his ebony hands on each ivory key
He made that poor piano moan with melody.
    O Blues!
Swaying to and fro on his rickety stool
He played that sad raggy tune like a musical fool.
    Sweet Blues!
Coming from a black man's soul.
    O Blues!
In a deep song voice with a melancholy tone
I heard that Negro sing, that old piano moan —
    "Ain't got nobody in all this world,
    Ain't got nobody but ma self.
    I's gwine to quit ma frownin'
    And put ma troubles on the shelf."
Thump, thump, thump, went his foot on
    the floor.
He played a few chords then he sang
    some more —
    "I got the Weary Blues
    And I can't be satisfied.
    Got the Weary Blues
    And can't be satisfied —
    I ain't happy no mo'
    And I wish that I had died."
And far into the night he crooned that tune.
The stars went out and so did the moon.
The singer stopped playing and went to bed

While the Weary Blues echoed through his head.
He slept like a rock or a man that's dead.

C. "Harlem" (also known as "A Dream Deferred")

What happens to a dream deferred?

Does it dry up
like a raisin in the sun?
Or fester like a sore —
And then run?
Does it stink like rotten meat?
Or crust and sugar over —
like a syrupy sweet?

Maybe it just sags
like a heavy load.
Or does it explode?

6.23
'YET I DO MARVEL'
Countee Cullen

Rising alongside Langston Hughes in the early 1920s was Countee Cullen, a young New York University student-poet. He was first published in *The Crisis* and the National Urban League's *Opportunity*, but Cullen's poetry hit mainstream magazines early in his career. He had already established a national reputation by the time his first collection, *Color*, was published in 1923. It contained one of his most famous works, "Yet I Do Marvel," and cemented his as another premier Renaissance voice. He became an editor at the *Opportunity*, where he wrote a critic's column. But Cullen's second book of poetry, *Copper Sun* in 1927, stained him with controversy that still lingers today. Critics grumbled about Cullen's move away from racial topics and explicitly black characters. While many of his poems, such as his famous "Heritage," discussed race and his personal identification as a black man, Cullen sought to move beyond classification as a "race" poet. Many black leaders felt betrayed by that sentiment.

A. "Yet Do I Marvel"

I doubt not God is good, well-meaning, kind
And did He stoop to quibble could tell why

The little buried mole continues blind,
Why flesh that mirrors Him must some day die,
Make plain the reason tortured Tantalus
Is baited by the fickle fruit, declare
If merely brute caprice dooms Sisyphus
To struggle up a never-ending stair.
Inscrutable His ways are, and immune
To catechism by a mind too strewn
With petty cares to slightly understand
What awful brain compels His awful hand.
Yet do I marvel at this curious thing:
To make a poet black, and bid him sing!

B. "To A Brown Boy"

That brown girl's swagger gives a twitch
    To beauty like a queen;
Lad, never dam your body's itch
    When loveliness is seen.

For there is ample room for bliss
    In pride in clean, brown limbs,
And lips know better how to kiss
    Than how to raise white hymns.

And when your body's death gives birth
    To soil for spring to crown,
Men will not ask if that rare earth
    Was white flesh once, or brown.

——— 6.24 ———
'HOW IT FEELS TO BE COLORED ME'
Zora Neale Hurston

Another pioneer among the "New Negro" artists of the Harlem Renaissance was Zora Neale Hurston. Hurston arrived in New York in 1925, pursuing her real passion, the study of folklore. Having grown up in the all-black town of Eatonville, Florida, southern black folklore would permeate her life and work for the next several decades. In addition to her three works of anthropology, Hurston wrote fiction set in southern black towns and largely infused with black folklore. Her 1925 short story "Spunk," below, provides an example. She rose to fame in the Renaissance following its publication, for which she won one of the National Urban League's inaugural *Opportunity* Awards.

But Hurston's contrarian attitude on race would ultimately damage her reputation among the black leaders orchestrating the New Negro movement. Hurston did not seek integration with white society, and derided the political leaders who did. In her 1928 essay "How it Feels to Be Colored Me," she explained that she did not belong to "the sobbing school of Negrohood," that she was not "tragically colored." In fact, she did not even "always feel colored," Hurston wrote, because when happily ensconced in black environments, she could discard what she saw as an externally imposed racial identity. Slavery and its evils were behind her, with her ancestors, and now it was time for her to go about living the life they fought to give her. She acknowledged discrimination, but dismissed it as a trifle. Her life was hers, she concluded, above taint by the seemingly insignificant actions of white people. But black critics retorted that Hurston's stance was unrealistic. Society's racism, they argued, made her race-free existence untenable.

A. "Spunk"

I

A Giant of a brown-skinned man sauntered up the one street of the village and out into the palmetto thickets with a small pretty woman clinging lovingly to his arm.

"Looka theah, folkses!" cried Elijah Mosley, slapping his leg gleefully, "Theah they go, big as life an' brassy as tacks."

All the loungers in the store tried to walk to the door with an air of nonchalance but with small success.

"Now pee-eople!" Walter Thomas gasped. "Will you look at 'em!"

"But that's one thing Ah likes about Spunk Banks — he ain't skeered of nothin' on God's green foot stool — *nothin'*! He rides that log down at saw-mill jus' like he struts 'round wid another man's wife — jus' don't give a kitty. When Tes' Miller got cut to giblets on that circle-saw, Spunk steps right up and starts ridin'. The rest of us was skeered to go near it."

A round-shouldered figure in overalls much too large came nervously in the door and the talking ceased. The men looked at each other and winked.

"Gimme some soda-water. Sass'prilla Ah reckon," the newcomer ordered, and stood far down the counter near the open pickled pig-feet tub to drink it.

Elijah nudged Walter and turned with mock gravity to the new-comer.

"Say, Joe, how's everything up yo' way? How's yo' wife?"

Joe started and all but dropped the bottle he held in his hands. He swallowed several times painfully and his lips trembled.

"Aw 'Lige, you oughtn't to do nothin' like that," Walter grumbled. Elijah ignored him.

"She jus' passed heah a few minutes ago goin' thata way," with a wave of his hand in the direction of the woods.

Now Joe knew his wife had passed that way. He knew that the men lounging in the general store had seen her, moreover, he knew that the men knew *he* knew. He stood there silent for a long moment staring blankly, with his Adam's apple twitching nervously up and down his throat. One could actually *see* the pain he was suffering, his eyes, his face, his hands and even the dejected slump of his shoulders. He set the bottle down upon the counter. He didn't bang it, just eased it out of his hand silently and fiddled with his suspender buckle.

"Well, Ah'm goin' after her to-day. Ah'm goin' an fetch her back. Spunk's done gone too fur."

He reached deep down into his trouser pocket and drew out a hollow ground razor, large and shiny, and passed his moistened thumb back and forth over the edge.

"Talkin' like a man, Joe. 'Course that's yo' fambly affairs, but Ah like to see grit in anybody."

Joe Kanty laid down a nickel and stumbled out into the street.

Dusk crept in from the woods. Ike Clarke lit the swinging oil lamp that was almost immediately surrounded by candleflies. The men laughed boisterously behind Joe's back as they watched him shamble woodward.

"You oughtn't to said whut you did to him, Lige — look how it worked him up," Walter chided.

"And Ah hope it did work him up. Tain't even decent for a man to take and take like he do."

"Spunk will sho' kill him."

"Aw, Ah doan' know. You never kin tell. He might turn him up an' spank him fur gettin' in the way, but Spunk wouldn't shoot no unarmed man. Dat razor he carried outa heah ain't gonna run Spunk down an' cut him, an' Joe ain't got the nerve to go up to Spunk with it knowing he totes that Army .45. He makes that break outa heah to bluff us. He's gonna hide that razor behind the first palmetto root an' sneak back home to bed. Don't tell me nothin' 'bout that rabbit-foot colored man. Didn't he meet Spunk an' Lena face to face one day las' week an' mumble sumthin' to Spunk 'bout lettin' his wife alone?"

"What did Spunk say?" Walter broke in — "Ah like him fine but tain't right the way he carries on wid Lena Kanty, jus' cause Joe's timid 'bout fightin'."

"You wrong theah, Walter. Tain't 'cause Joe's timid at all, it's 'cause Spunk wants Lena. If Joe was a passle of wile cats Spunk would tackle the job just the same. He'd go after anything he wanted the same way. As Ah wuz sayin' a minute ago, he tole Joe right to his face that Lena was his. 'Call her and see if she'll come. A woman knows her boss an' she answers when he calls.' 'Lena, ain't I yo' husband?' Joe sorter whines out. Lena looked at him real disgusted but she don't answer and she don't move outa her tracks.

Then Spunk reaches out an' takes hold of her arm an' says: 'Lena, youse mine. From now on ah works for you an' fights for you an' Ah never wants you to look to nobody for a crumb of bread, a stitch of close or a shingle to go over yo' head, but *me* long as Ah live. Ah'll git the lumber foh owah house to-morrow. Go home an' git yo' things together!' 'Thass mah house,' Lena speaks up. 'Papa gimme that.' 'Well,' says Spunk, 'doan give up whut's yours, but when youse inside doan forgit youse mine, an' let no other man git outa his place wid you!'"

"Lena looked up at him with her eyes so full of love that they wuz runnin' over, an' Spunk seen it an' Joe seen it too, and his lip started to tremblin' and his Adam's apple was galloping up and down his neck like a race horse. Ah bet he's wore out half a dozen Adam's apples since Spunk's been on the job with Lena. That's all he'll do. He'll be back heah after while swallowin' en' workin' his lips like he wants to say somethin' an' can't."

"But didn't he do nothin' to stop 'em?"

"Nope, not a frazzlin' thing — jus' stood there. Spunk took Lena's arm and walked off jus' like nothin' ain't happened and he stood there gazin' after them till they was outa sight. Now you know a woman don't want no man like that. I'm jus' waitin' to see whut he's goin' to say when he gits back."

II

But Joe Kanty never came back, never. The men in the store heard the sharp report of a pistol somewhere distant in the palmetto thicket and soon Spunk came walking leisurely, with his big black Stetson set at the same rakish angle and Lena clinging to his arm, came walking right into the general store. Lena wept in a frightened manner.

"Well," Spunk announced calmly, "Joe come out there wid a meat axe an' made me kill him."

He sent Lena home and led the men back to Joe — crumpled and limp with his right hand still clutching his razor.

"See mah back? Mah close cut clear through. He sneaked up en' tried to kill me from the back, but Ah got him, an' got him good, first shot," Spunk said.

The men glared at Elijah, accusingly.

"Take him up an' plant him in Stony Lonesome," Spunk said in a careless voice. "Ah didn't wanna shoot him but he made me do it. He's a dirty coward, jumpin' on a man from behind."

Spunk turned on his heel and sauntered away to where he knew his love wept in fear for him and no man stopped him. At the general store later on, they all talked of locking him up until the sheriff should come from Orlando, but no one did anything but talk.

A clear case of self-defense, the trial was a short one, and Spunk walked out of the court house to freedom again. He could work again, ride the dangerous log-carriage that fed the singing, snarling, biting circle-saw; he could stroll the soft dark lanes with his guitar. He was free to roam the woods again; he was free to return to Lena. He did all of these things.

III

"Whut you reckon, Walt?" Elijah asked one night later. "Spunk's gittin' ready to marry Lena!"

"New! Why, Joe ain't had time to git cold yit. Nohow Ah didn't figger Spunk was the marryin' kind."

"Well, he is," rejoined Elijah. "He done moved most of Lena's things — and her along wid'em — over to the Bradley house. He's buying it. Jus' like Ah told yo' all right in heah the night Joe wuz kilt. Spunk's crazy 'bout Lena. He don't want folks to keep on takin' 'bout her — thass reason he's rushin' so. Funny thing 'bout that bob-cat, wasn't it?"

"What bob-cat, 'Lige? ah ain't heered 'bout none."

"Ain't cher? Well, night befo' las' was the fust night Spunk an' Lena moved together an' just then as they was goin' to bed, a big black bob-cat, black all over, you hear me, black, walked round and round that house and howled like forty, an' when Spunk got his gun an' went to the winder to shoot it, he says it stood right still an' looked him in the eye, an' howled right at him. The thing got Spunk so nervoused up he couldn't shoot. But Spunk says twan't no bob-cat nohow. He says it was Joe done sneaked back from Hell!"

"Humph!" sniffed Walter, "he oughter be nervous after what he done. Ah reckon Joe come back to dare him to marry Lena, or to come out an' fight. Ah bet he'll be back time and again, too. Know what Ah think? Joe wuz a braver man than Spunk."

There was a general shout of derision from the group.

"Thass a fact," went on Walter. "Lookit whut he done; took a razor an' went out to fight a man he knowed toted a gun an' wuz a crack shot, too; 'nother thing Joe wuz skeered of Spunk, skeered plumb stiff! But he went jes' the same. It took him a long time to get his nerve up. Tain't nothin' for Spunk to fight when he ain't skeered of nothin'. Now, Joe's done come back to have it out wid the man that's got all he ever had. Y'all know Joe ain't never had nothin' or wanted nothin' besides Lena. It musta been a h'ant cause ain't nobody never seen no black bob-cat."

"Nother thing," cut in one of the men, "Spunk wuz cussin' a blue streak to-day 'cause he 'lowed dat saw wuz wobblin' — almos' got 'im once. The machinist come, looked it over an' said it wuz alright. Spunk musta been leanin' t'wards it some. Den he claimed somebody pushed 'im but twan't nobody close to 'im. Ah wuz glad when knockin' off time come. I'm skeered of dat man when he gits hot. He'd beat you full of button holes as quick as he's look etcher."

IV

The men gathered the next evening in a different mood, no laughter. No badinage this time.

"Look, 'Lige, you goin' to set up wid Spunk?"

"New, Ah reckon not, Walter. Tell yuh the truth, Ah'm a li'l bit skittish, Spunk died too wicket — died cussin' he did. You know he thought he was done outa life."

"Good Lawd, who'd he think done it?"

"Joe."

"Joe Kanty? How come?"

"Walter, Ah b'leeve Ah will walk up thata way an' set. Lena would like it Ah reckon."

"But whut did he say, 'Lige?"

Elijah did not answer until they had left the lighted store and were strolling down the dark street.

"Ah wuz loadin' a wagon wid scantlin' right near the saw when Spunk fell on the carriage but 'fore Ah could git to him the saw got him in the body — awful sight. Me an' Skint Miller got him off but it was too late. Anybody could see that. The fust thing he said wuz: 'He

pushed me, 'Lige — the dirty hound pushed me in the back!' — he was spittin' blood at ev'ry breath. We laid him on the sawdust pile with his face to the east so's he could die easy. He helt mah hen' till the last, Walter, and said: 'It was Joe, 'Lige... the dirty sneak shoved me... he didn't dare to come to mah face... but Ah'll git the son-of-a-wood louse soon's Ah get there an' make Hell too hot for him. ... Ah felt him shove me... !' Thass how he died."

"If spirits kin fight, there's a powerful tussle goin' on somewhere ovah Jordan 'cause Ah b'leeve Joe's ready for Spunk an' ain't skeered any more — yas, Ah b'leeve Joe pushed 'im mahself.'"

They had arrived at the house. Lena's lamentations were deep and loud. She had filled the room with magnolia blossoms that gave off a heavy sweet odor. The keepers of the wake tipped about whispering in frightened tones. Everyone in the Village was there, even old Jeff Kanty, Joe's father, who a few hours before would have been afraid to come within ten feet of him, stood leering triumphantly down upon the fallen giant as if his fingers had been the teeth of steel that laid him low.

The cooling board consisted of three sixteen-inch boards on saw horses, a dingy sheet was his shroud.

The women ate heartily of the funeral baked meats and wondered who would be Lena's next. The men whispered coarse conjectures between guzzles of whiskey.

B. "How it Feels to Be Colored Me"

I am colored but I offer nothing in the way of extenuating circumstances except the fact that I am the only Negro in the United States whose grandfather on the mother's side was *not* an Indian chief.

I remember the very day that I became colored. Up to my thirteenth year I lived in the little Negro town of Eatonville, Florida. It is exclusively a colored town. The only white people I knew passed through the town going to or coming from Orlando. The native whites rode dusty horses, the Northern tourists chugged down the sandy village road in automobiles. The town knew the Southerners and never stopped cane chewing when they passed. But the Northerners were something else again. They were peered at cautiously from behind curtains by the timid. The more venturesome would come out on the porch to watch them go past and got just as much pleasure out of the tourists as the tourists got out of the village.

The front porch might seem a daring place for the rest of the town, but it was a gallery seat for me. My favorite place was atop the gatepost. Proscenium box for a born first-nighter. Not only did I enjoy the show, but I didn't mind the actors knowing that I liked it. I usually spoke to them in passing. I'd wave at them and when they returned my salute, I would say something like this: "Howdy-do-well-I-thank-you-where-you-goin'?" Usually automobile or the horse paused at this, and after a queer exchange of compliments, I would probably "go a piece of the way" with them, as we say in farthest Florida. If one of my family happened to come to the front in time to see me, of course negotiations would be rudely broken off. But even so, it is clear that I was the first "welcome-to-our-state" Floridian, and I hope the Miami Chamber of Commerce will please take notice.

During this period, white people differed from colored to me only in that they rode through town and never lived there. They liked to hear me "speak pieces" and sing and wanted to see me dance the parse-me-la, and gave me generously of their small silver for doing these things, which seemed strange to me for I wanted to do them so much that I needed bribing to stop. Only they didn't know it. The colored people gave no dimes. They deplored any joyful tendencies in me, but I was their Zora nevertheless. I belonged to them, to the nearby hotels, to the county — everybody's Zora.

But changes came in the family when I was thirteen, and I was sent to school in Jacksonville. I left Eatonville, the town of the oleanders, as Zora. When I disembarked from the river-boat at Jacksonville, she was no more. It seemed that I had suffered a sea change. I was not Zora of Orange County any more, I was now a little colored girl. I found it out in certain ways. In my heart as well as in the mirror, I became a fast brown — warranted not to rub nor run.

But I am not tragically colored. There is no great sorrow dammed up in my soul, nor lurking behind my eyes. I do not mind at all. I do not belong to the sobbing school of Negrohood who hold that nature somehow has given them a lowdown dirty deal and whose feelings are all hurt about it. Even in the helter-skelter skirmish that is my life, I have seen that the world is to the strong regardless of a little pigmentation more or less. No, I do not weep at the world — I am too busy sharpening my oyster knife.

Someone is always at my elbow reminding me that I am the granddaughter of slaves. It fails to register depression with me. Slavery is sixty years in the past. The operation was successful and the patient is doing well, thank you. The terrible struggle that made me an American out of a potential slave said "On the line!" The Reconstruction said "Get set!"; and the generation before said "Go!" I am off to a flying start and I must not halt in the stretch to look behind and weep. Slavery is the price I paid for civilization, and the choice was not with me. It is a bully adventure and worth all that I have paid through my ancestors for it. No one on earth ever had a greater chance for glory. The world to be won and nothing to be lost. It is thrilling to think — to know that for any act of mine, I shall get twice as much praise or twice as much blame. It is quite exciting to hold the center of the national stage, with the spectators not knowing whether to laugh or weep.

The position of my white neighbor is much more difficult. No brown specter pulls up a chair beside me when I sit down to eat. No dark ghost thrusts its leg against mine in bed. The game of keeping what one has is never so exciting as the game of getting.

I do not always feel colored. Even now I often achieve the unconscious Zora of Eatonville before the Hegira. I feel most colored when I am thrown against a sharp white background.

For instance at Barnard. "Beside the waters of the Hudson" I feel my race. Among the thousand white persons, I am a dark rock surged upon, and overswept, but through it all, I remain myself. When covered by the waters, I am; and the ebb but reveals me again.

Sometimes it is the other way around. A white person is set down in our midst, but the contrast is just as sharp for me. For instance, when I sit in the drafty basement that is The New World Cabaret with a white person, my color comes. We enter chatting about any little nothing that we have in common and are seated by the jazz waiters. In the abrupt way that jazz orchestras have, this one plunges into a number. It loses no time in circumlocutions, but gets right down to business. It constricts the thorax and splits the heart with its tempo and narcotic harmonies. This orchestra grows rambunctious, rears on its hind legs and attacks the tonal veil with primitive fury, rending it, clawing it until it breaks through to the jungle beyond. I follow those heathen — follow them exultingly. I dance wildly inside myself; I yell within, I whoop; I shake my assegai above my head, I hurl it true to the mark *yeeeeooww*! I am in the jungle and living in the jungle way. My face is painted red and yellow and my body is painted blue. My pulse is throbbing like a war drum. I want to slaughter something — give pain, give death to what, I do not know. But the piece ends. The men of the orchestra wipe their lips and rest their fingers. I creep back slowly to the veneer we call civilization with the last tone and find the white friend sitting motionless in his seat, smoking calmly.

"Good music they have here," he remarks, drumming the table with his fingertips.

Music. The great blobs of purple and red emotion have not touched him. He has only heard what I felt. He is far away and I see him but dimly across the ocean and the continent that have fallen between us. He is so pale with his whiteness then and I am *so* colored.

At certain times I have no race, I am *me*. When I set my hat at a certain angle and saunter down Seventh Avenue, Harlem City, feeling as snooty as the lions in front of the Forty-Second Street Library, for instance. So far as my feelings are concerned, Peggy Hopkins Joyce on the Boule Mich with her gorgeous raiment, stately carriage, knees knocking together in a most aristocratic manner, has nothing on me. The cosmic Zora emerges. I belong to no race nor time. I am the eternal feminine with its string of beads.

I have no separate feeling about being an American citizen and colored. I am merely a fragment of the Great Soul that surges within the boundaries. My country, right or wrong.

Sometimes, I feel discriminated against, but it does not make me angry. It merely astonishes me. How *can* any deny themselves the pleasure of my company? It's beyond me.

But in the main, I feel like a brown bag of miscellany propped against a wall. Against a wall in company with other bags, white, red and yellow. Pour out the contents, and there is discovered a jumble of small things priceless and worthless. A first-water diamond, an empty spool, bits of broken glass, lengths of string, a key to a door long since crumbled away, a rusty knife-blade, old shoes saved for a road that never was and never will be, a nail bent under the weight of things too heavy for any nail, a dried flower or two still a little fragrant. In your hand is the brown bag. On the ground before you is the jumble it held — so much like the jumble in the bags, could they be emptied, that all might be dumped in a single heap and the bags refilled without altering the content of any greatly. A bit of colored glass more or less would not matter. Perhaps that is how the Great Stuffer of Bags filled them in the first place — who knows?

—— 6.25 ——

'SMOKE, LILIES AND JADE'
Richard Bruce Nugent

Decades before America's sexual revolution, the "Negro Capitol" allowed a sexual liberation unprecedented in American history. Gay men, lesbians, bisexual people and transgender men and women all moved with ease through Harlem's social circles. Many formed exclusive cliques, but they were by no means secretive. Several nightclubs were known as popular among the gay Harlemites, and parties at which revelers experimented with and blurred the boundaries of sexuality and gender were renowned — particularly among whites seeking a safe place, removed from their own worlds, where they could explore otherwise taboo sex.

A number of the Harlem Renaissance's New Negro artists were sexual minorities. Modern historians have argued that luminaries such as Langston Hughes, Zora Neale Hurston, Countee Cullen, Claude McKay and Alain Locke were all bisexual or homosexual, and open about it at least within their own social circles. But speculation aside, some of their closest friends and colleagues were, and expressed as much in their work. Richard Bruce Nugent is perhaps the best known. In 1926, Nugent and Hughes pulled together several New Negro writers to establish the journal *Fire!*. All of the time's soon-to-be-famous writers joined its editorial board: Hughes, Hurston, Cullen, Arna Bontemps, Gwendolyn Bennett and others. Another openly gay black man, Wallace Thurman, served as the managing editor. However, financial difficulty, and criticism from leaders such as W.E.B. DuBois, who called the collection "self-indulgent," limited its publication to one issue in November of that year.

Nugent's contribution to the volume, the narrative poem "Smoke, Lilies and Jade," excerpted below, was the first work of black literature centered on homosexuality. Later in the era, in 1932, Thurman wrote the novel *Infants of the Spring*, a self-satirizing commentary on the artists of the Harlem Renaissance in which he featured an eccentric gay character reportedly inspired by his friend Nugent.

the street was so long and narrow ... so long and narrow ... and blue ... in the distance it reached the stars ... and if he walked long enough ... far enough ... he could reach the stars too ... the narrow blue was so empty ...

quiet ... Alex walked music ... it was so nice to walk in the blue after a party ... Zora had shone again ... her stories ... she always shone ... and Monty was glad ... everyone was glad when Zora shone ... he was glad he had gone to Monty's party ... Monty had a nice place in the village ... nice lights ... and friends and wine ... mother would be scandalized that he could think of going to a party ... without a copper to his name ... but then mother had never been to Monty's ... and mother had never seen the street seem long and narrow and blue ... Alex walked music ... the click of his heels kept time with a tune in his mind ... he glanced into a lighted café window ... inside were people sipping coffee ... men ... why they sit there in the loud light ... didn't they know that outside the street ... the narrow blue street met the stars ... that if they walked long enough ... fare enough ... Alex walked and the click of his heels sounded ... and had an echo ... sound being tossed back and forth ... someone was approaching ... and their echoes mingled ... and gave the sound of castanets ... Alex liked the sound of the approaching man's footsteps ... he walked music also ... he knew the beauty of the narrow blue ... Alex knew that by the way their echoes mingled ... he wished he could speak ... but strangers don't speak at four o'clock in the morning ... at least if they did he couldn't imagine what would be said ... maybe ... pardon me but are you walking toward the stars ... yes, sir, and if you walk long enough ... then may I walk with you I want to reach the stars too ... perdone me senor tiene ud. Fosforo ... Alex was glad he had been addressed in Spanish ... to have been asked for a match in English ... or to have been addressed in English at all ... would have been blasphemy just then ... Alex handed him a match ... he glanced at his companion apprehensively in the match glow ... he was afraid that his appearance would shatter the blue thoughts ... and stars ... ah ... his face was a perfect compliment to his voice ... and the echo of their steps mingled ... they walked in silence ... the castanets of their heels clicking perfect accompaniment ... the stranger inhaled deeply and with a not of content and smile ... blew a cloud of smoke ... Alex felt like singing ... the stranger knew the magic of blue smoke also ... they continued in silence ... the castanets of their heels clicking rhythmically ... Alex turned in his doorway ... up the stairs and the stranger waited for him to light the room ... no need for words ... they had always known each other ... as they undressed by the pale blue dawn ... Alex knew he had never seen a more perfect human being ... his body was all symmetry and music ... and Alex called him Beauty ... long they lay ... blowing smoke and exchanging thoughts ... and Alex swallowed with difficulty ... he felt a glow of tremor ... and they talked ... and ... slept ...

Alex wondered more and more why he liked Adrian so ... he liked many people ... Wallie ... Zora ... Clement ... Gloria ... Langston ... John ... Gwenny ... oh many people ... and they were friends ... but Beauty ... it was different ... once Alex had admired Beauty's strength ... and Beauty's eyes had grown soft ... and he had said ... I like you more than anyone Dulce ... Adrian always called him Dulce ... and Alex had become confused ... was it that he was so susceptible to beauty that Alex like Adrian so much ... but no ... he knew other people who were beautiful ... Fania and Gloria ... Monty and Bunny ... but he was never confused before them ... while Beauty ... Beauty could make him believe in Buddha ... or imps ... and no one else could do that ... that is no one but Melva ... but then he was in love with Melva ... and that explained that ... he would like Beauty to know Melva ... they were both so perfect ... such compliments ... yes he would like Beauty to know Melva because he was in love with both ... there he had thought it ... actually dared to think it ... but Beauty must never know ... Beauty couldn't understand ... Alex couldn't understand ... and it had pained him ... almost physically ... and tired his mind ... Beauty ... Beauty was in the air ... the smoke ... Beauty ... Melva ... Beauty ... Melva ... Alex slept ... and dreamed ...

6.26

THE NEW NEGRO
Alain Leroy Locke

In 1926, as part of the black political leaders' efforts to promote New Negro artists, the National Urban League's Charles Johnson organized a gala dinner to acquaint his white philanthropist associates with some of Harlem's young artists. Following that event, Paul Kellogg recruited black critic and Howard University philosophy professor Alain Leroy Locke to guest edit a special issue of his sociology journal *Survey Magazine*. The March 1925 issue, along with the *New Negro* anthology Locke later turned it into, now stands as the definitive collection of Harlem Renaissance writings. In his opening essay, Locke summarizes the cultural and political import of the era for black Americans. His most astute observation may be his assertion of the Renaissance's psychological impact on African Americans. Prior to this period, he writes, "The chief bond between them has been that of a common condition rather than a common consciousness; a problem in common rather than a life in common." As a result of the Harlem Renaissance, Locke concludes, black people crafted their own individual and collective racial identities. True or false, his essay's message is the essence of what black leaders of the time hoped the Renaissance would mean.

If we were to offer a symbol of what Harlem has come to mean in the short span of twenty years it would be another statue of liberty on the landward side of New York. It stands for a folk-movement which in human significance can be compared only with the pushing back of the western frontier in the first half of the last century, or the waves of immigration which have swept in from overseas in the last half. Numerically far smaller than either of these movements, the volume of migration is such none the less that Harlem has become the greatest Negro community the world has known — without counterpart in the South or in Africa. But beyond this, Harlem represents the Negro's latest thrust towards Democracy.

The special significance that today stamps it as the sign and center of the renaissance of a people lies, however, layers deep under the

Harlem that many know but few have begun to understand. Physically Harlem is little more than a note of sharper color in the kaleidoscope of New York. The metropolis pays little heed to the shifting crystallizations of its own heterogeneous millions. Never having experienced permanence, it has watched, without emotion or even curiosity, Irish, Jew, Italian, Negro, a score of other races drift in and out of the same colorless tenements.

So Harlem has come into being and grasped its destiny with little heed from New York. And to the herded thousands who shoot beneath it twice a day on the subway, or the comparatively few whose daily travel takes them within sight of its fringes or down its main arteries, it is a black belt and nothing more. The pattern of delicatessen store and cigar shop and restaurant and undertaker's shop which repeats itself a thousand times on each of New York's long avenues is unbroken through Harlem. Its apartments, churches and storefronts antedated the Negroes and, for all New York knows, may outlast them there. For most of New York, Harlem is merely a rough rectangle of common-place city blocks, lying between and to east and west of Lenox and Seventh Avenues, stretching nearly a mile north and south — and unaccountably full of Negroes.

Another Harlem is savored by the few — a Harlem of racy music and racier dancing, of cabarets famous or notorious according to their kind, of amusement in which abandon and sophistication are cheek by jowl — a Harlem which draws the connoisseur in diversion as well as the undiscriminating sightseer. This Harlem is the fertile source of the "shuffling " and "rollin'" and "runnin' wild" revues that establish themselves season after season in "downtown" theaters. It is part of the exotic fringe of the metropolis.

Beneath this lies again the Harlem of the newspapers — a Harlem of monster parades and political flummery, a Harlem swept by revolutionary oratory or draped about the mysterious figures of Negro "millionaires," a Harlem pre-occupied with naive adjustments to a white world — a Harlem, in short, grotesque with the distortions of journalism.

Yet in final analysis, Harlem is neither slum, ghetto, resort or colony, though it is in part all of them. It is — or promises at least to be — a race capital. Europe seething in a dozen centers with emergent nationalities, Palestine full of a renascent Judaism — these are no more alive with the spirit of a racial awakening than Harlem; culturally and spiritually it focuses a people. Negro life is not only founding new centers, but finding a new soul. The tide of Negro migration, northward and city-ward, is not to be fully explained as a blind flood started by the demands of war industry coupled with the shutting off of foreign migration, or by the pressure of poor crops coupled with increased social terrorism in certain sections of the South and Southwest. Neither labor demand, the boll-weevil nor the Ku Klux Klan is a basic factor, however contributory any or all of them may have been. The wash and rush of this human tide on the beach line of the northern city centers is to be explained primarily in terms of a new vision of opportunity, of social and economic freedom of a spirit to seize, even in the face of an extortionate and heavy toll, a chance for the improvement of conditions. With each successive wave of it, the movement of the Negro migrant becomes more and more like that of the European waves at their crests, a mass movement toward the larger and the more democratic chance — in the Negro's case a deliberate flight not only from countryside to city, but from medieval America to modern.

The secret lies close to what distinguishes Harlem from the ghettos with which it is sometimes compared. The ghetto picture is that of a slowly dissolving mass, bound by ties of custom and culture and association, in the midst of a freer and more varied society. From the racial standpoint, our Harlems are themselves crucibles. Here in Manhattan is not merely the largest Negro community in the world, but the first concentration in history of so many diverse elements of Negro life. It has attracted the African, the West Indian, the Negro American; has brought together the Negro of the North and the Negro of the South; the man from the city and the man from the town and village; the peasant, the student, the business man, the professional man, artist, poet, musician, adventurer and worker, preacher and criminal, exploiter and social outcast. Each group has come with its own separate motives and for its own special ends, but their greatest experience has been the finding of one another. Proscription and prejudice have thrown these dissimilar elements into a common area of contact and interaction. Within this area, race sympathy and unity have determined a further fusing of sentiment and experience. So what began in terms of segregation becomes more anymore, as its elements mix and react, the laboratory of a great race-welding. Hitherto, it must be admitted that American Negroes have been a race more in name than in fact, or to be exact, more in sentiment than in experience. The chief bond between them has been that of a common condition rather than a common consciousness; a problem in common rather than a life in common. In Harlem, Negro life is seizing upon its first chances for group expression and self-determination. That is why our comparison is taken with those nascent centers of folk-expression and self-determination which are playing a creative part in the world today. Without pretense to their political significance, Harlem has the same role to play for the New Negro as Dublin has had for the New Ireland or Prague for the New Czechoslovakia.

It is true the formidable centers of our race life, educational, industrial, financial, are not in Harlem, yet here, nevertheless, are the forces that make a group known and felt in the world. The reformers, the fighting advocates, the inner spokesmen, the poets, artists and social prophets are here, and pouring in toward them are the fluid ambitious youth and pressing in upon them the migrant masses. The professional observers, and the enveloping communities as well, are conscious of the physics of this stir and movement, of the cruder and more obvious facts of a ferment and a migration. But they are as yet largely unaware of the psychology of it, of the galvanising shocks and reactions, which mark the social awakening and internal reorganization which are making a race out of its own disunited elements.

A railroad ticket and a suitcase, like a Bagdad carpet, transport the Negro peasant from the cotton-field and farm to the heart of the most complex urban civilization. Here in the mass, he must and does survive a jump of two generations in social economy and of a century and more in civilisation. Meanwhile the Negro poet, student, artist, thinker, by the very move that normally would take him off at a tangent from the masses, finds himself in their midst, in a situation concentrating the racial side of his experience and heightening his race-consciousness. These moving, half-awakened newcomers provide an exceptional seed-bed for the germinating contacts of the enlightened minority. And that is why statistics are out of joint with fact in Harlem, and will be for ageneration or so.

Harlem, I grant you, isn't typical — but it is significant, it is prophetic. No sane observer, however sympathetic to the new trend, would contend that the great masses are articulate as yet, but they stir, they move, they are more than physically restless. The challenge of the new intellectuals among them is clear enough — the "race radicals" and realists who have broken with the old epoch of philanthropic guidance, sentimental appeal and protest. But are we after all only reading into the stirrings of a sleeping giant the dreams of an agitator? The answer is in the migrating peasant. It is the "man farthest down" who is most active in getting up. One of the most characteristic symptoms of this is the professional man himself migrating to recapture his constituency after a vain effort to maintain in some Southern corner what for years back seemed an established living and clientele. The clergyman following his errant flock, the physician or lawyer trailing his clients, supply the true clues. In a real sense it is the rank and file who are leading, and the leaders who are following. A transformed and transforming psychology permeates the masses.

When the racial leaders of twenty years ago spoke of developing race-pride and stimulating race-consciousness, and of the desirability of race solidarity, they could not in any accurate degree have anticipated the abrupt feeling that has surged up and now pervades the awakened centers. Some of the recognized Negro leaders and a powerful section of white opinion identified with "race work" of the older order have indeed attempted to discount this feeling as a "passing phase," an attack of "race nerves," so to speak, an "aftermath of the war," and the like. It has not abated, however, if we are to gauge by the present tone and temper of the Negro press, or by the shift in popular support from the officially recognized and orthodox spokesmen to those of the independent, popular, and often radical type who are unmistakable symptoms of a new order. It is a social disservice to blunt the fact that the Negro of the Northern centers has reached a stage where tutelage, even of the most interested and well-intentioned sort, must give place to new relationships, where positive self-direction must be reckoned with in ever increasing measure.

As a service to this new understanding, the contributors to this Harlem number have been asked, not merely to describe Harlem as a city of migrants and as a race center, but to voice these new aspirations of a people, to read the clear message of the new conditions, and to discuss some of the new relationships and contacts they involve. First, we shall look at Harlem, with its kindred centers in the Northern and Mid-Western cities, as the way mark of a momentous folk movement; then as the center of a gripping struggle for an industrial and urban foothold. But more significant than either of these, we shall also view it as the stage of the pageant of contemporary Negro life. In the drama of its new and progressive aspects, we may be witnessing the resurgence of a race; with our eyes focussed on the Harlem scene we may dramatically glimpse the New Negro.

———— 6.27 ————
'WHAT I WANT FROM LIFE'
Paul Robeson

From the very beginning of his career Paul Robeson placed himself at the center of national and international controversy with his refusal to remain silent in the face of anything he considered oppressive. Ultimately, his outspoken political agitation would cost him his career and place him under the constant surveillance of the Federal Bureau of Investigation.

In his 1924 stage debut, Robeson and white actress Mary Blair portrayed an interracial couple in Eugene O'Neill's *All God's Chillun Got Wings*. Whites were furious and threatened to bomb the Greenwich Village theater. Nevertheless, the play went on. The following year Robeson skyrocketed to fame as a vocalist when he gave the first-ever concert of spirituals, and went on to record four albums. His 1928 rendition of "Ol' Man River" in the London production of *Show Boat* cemented his international fame. From that public platform, Robeson vocally protested American racism and Spanish fascism. After making his first trip to the Soviet Union in 1934, he returned regularly and became an outspoken fan of what he perceived as the equality of Soviet society.

Throughout the 1930s, Robeson made his home in London and there, he wrote, he discovered a love for Africa and a spiritual quest to regain his own African heritage. In this 1935 essay in the *Royal Screen Pictorial* magazine, he urged all black Americans to do the same.

I am a Negro. The origin of the Negro is African. It would, therefore seem an easy matter for me to assume African nationality. Instead, it is an extremely complicated matter, fraught with the gravest importance to me and some million of colored folk.

Africa is a Dark Continent, not merely because its people are dark-skinned or by reason of its extreme impenetrability, but because its history is lost. We have an amazingly vivid reconstruction of the culture of ancient Egypt, but the roots of almost the whole remainder of Africa are buried in antiquity.

They are, however, rediscoverable, and they will in time be rediscovered.

I am confirmed in this faith by recent researches linking the culture of the Negro with that of many peoples of the East.

Let us consider for a moment the problem of my people — the African Negroes in the Occident, and particularly in America.

We are now fourteen million strong — though perhaps "strong" is not the apt word; for nearly two and a half centuries we were in chains, and although today we are technically free and officially labelled "American Citizen," we are at a great economic disadvantage, most trades and many professions being practically barred us and social barriers inexorably raised.

Consequently the American Negro in general suffers from an acute inferiority complex; it has been drummed into him that the white man is the Salt of the Earth and the Lord of Creation, and as a perfectly natural result his ambition is to become as nearly like a white man as possible.

He is that tragic creature, a man without a nationality. He claims to be American, to be British, to be French — but you cannot assume a nationality as you would a new suit of clothes.

In the country of his adoption, or the country that ruthlessly adopted his forefathers, he is an alien; but therein lies the tragedy. He believes himself to have broken away from his true origins; he has, he argues, nothing whatever in common with the inhabitant of Africa today — and that is where I believe he is wrong. ...

At present the younger generation of Negroes in America looks towards Africa and asks, "What is there *there* to interest me? What of value has Africa to offer that the Western world cannot give me?" At first glance the question seems unanswerable. He sees only the Africa of savagery, squalor, devil-worship, witch-doctors, voo-doo, ignorance, and darkness taught in American schools.

Where these exist, he is holding at the broken remnants of what was, in its day, a mighty thing — something which perhaps has not been destroyed, but only driven underground, leaving ugly scars upon the earth's surface to mark the place of its ultimate reappearance. ...

Mankind is gradually feeling its way back to a more fundamental, more primitive, but perhaps truer religion; and religion, the orientation of man to God or forces greater than himself, must be the basis, of all culture.

This religion, this basic culture, has its roots in the Far East, and in Africa.

What links the American Negro to this culture? It would take a psycho-anthropologist to give it a name; but its nature is obvious to any earnest inquirer.

Its manifestation occurs in his forms of religion and of art. It has recently been demonstrated beyond a possibility of doubt that the dances, the songs, and the worship perpetuated by the Negro in America are identical with those of his cousins hundreds of years removed in the depths of Africa, of whom he is only dimly aware.

His peculiar sense of rhythm alone would stamp him indelibly as African; and a slight variation of this same rhythm-consciousness is to be found among the Tartars and Chinese, to whom he is much more nearly akin than he is to the Arab, for example.

Not long ago I learned to speak Russian, since, the Russians being so closely allied through the Tartars to the Chinese, I expected to find myself more in sympathy with that language than with English, French or German. I was not disappointed; I found that there were Negro concepts which I could express much more readily in Russian than in other languages.

I would rather sing Russian folk songs than German grand opera — not because it is necessarily better music, but because it is more instinctive and less reasoned music. It is in my blood.

The pressing need of the American Negro is an ability to set his own standards. At school, it didn't matter to me whether white students passed me or I passed them. What mattered was, if I got 85 marks, *why didn't I get 100*? If I got 99, *why didn't I get a 100*? "To thine own self be true" is a sentiment sneered at today as merely Victorian — but upon its observance may well depend the future of nations.

It is, of course, useful and even necessary from an economic and social standpoint for the Negro to understand Western ideas and culture, for he will gain nothing by further isolating himself, and I would emphasize that his mere physical return to his place of origin is not the essential condition of his regeneration. In illustration of this, take the parallel position of the Jews.

They, like a vast proportion of Negroes, are a race without a nation; but, far from Palestine, they are indissolubly bound by their ancient religious practices — *which they recognize as such.* I emphasize this in contradistinction to the religious practices of the American Negro, which, from the snake-worship practiced in the deep South to the Christianity of the revival meeting, are patently survivals of the earliest African religions; and he does not recognize them as such.

Their acknowledgment of their common origin, species, interest and attitudes binds Jew to Jew; a similar acknowledgment will bind Negro to Negro.

I realize that this will never be accomplished by viewing from afar the dark rites of the witch doctor — a phenomenon as far divorced from fundamental reality as are the petty bickerings over altar decorations and details of vestment from the intention of Christ.

It may be accomplished, or at least furthered, by patient inquiry. To this end I am learning Swahili, Tivi, and other African dialects which come easily to me because their rhythm is the same as that employed by the American Negro in speaking English; and when the time is ripe, I propose to investigate on the spot the possibilities of such a regeneration as I have outlined.

Meanwhile, in my music, my plays, my films, I want to carry always this central idea — to be African.

Multitudes of men have died for less worthy ideals; it is even more eminently worth living for.

6.28

CRITICISM OF NIGGER HEAVEN
W.E.B. DuBois

Eventually, white society's notice of Harlem reached beyond the bounds black leaders had hoped for, and turned in the direction of the neighborhood's seedier side. Harlem's nightlife was a vibrant mix of refined entertainment and pool-hall hustling. Its cabarets and parties were renowned, and the area soon developed a reputation as the white liberal's playground. White novelist Carl Van Vechten built on, and perpetuated, that sentiment with his 1926 novel *Nigger Heaven*, which portrayed Harlem as a sleezy underworld. Van Vechten was one of the white artists who had been underwriting and promoting the Renaissance, as well as one of the gay men who reveled in its sexual liberation. As a result, he had close ties to many Harlemites, who felt betrayed by his book. Some, such as James Weldon Johnson and many of the younger New Negro writers, praised Van Vechten. But most black observers, including Alain Locke and W.E.B. DuBois, assailed him. To DuBois, *Nigger Heaven* was the worst kind of slander, and bad art at that. He railed against the book in the December 1926 *The Crisis*.

Carl Van Vechten's "Nigger Heaven" is a blow in the face. It is an affront to the hospitality of black folk and to the intelligence of white. First, as its title: my objection is based on no provincial dislike of the nickname. "Nigger" is an English word of wide use and definite connotation. As employed by Conrad, Sheldon, Allen and even Firbanks, its use was justifiable. But the phrase, "Nigger Heaven," as applied to Harlem is a misnomer. "Nigger Heaven" does not mean, as Van Vechten once or twice intimates, (pages 15, 199) a haven for Negroes — a city of refuge for dark and tired souls; it means in common parlance, a nasty, sordid corner into which black folk are herded, and yet a place which they in crass ignorance are fools enough to enjoy. Harlem is no such place as that, and no one knows this better than Carl Van Vechten.

But after all, a title is only a title, and a book must be judged eventually by its fidelity to truth and its artistic merit. I find this novel neither truthful nor artistic. It is not a true picture of Harlem life, even allowing for some justifiable impressionistic exaggeration. It is a caricature. It is worse than untruth because it is a mass of half-truths. Probably some time and somewhere in Harlem every incident of the book has happened; and yet the resultant picture built out of these parts is ludicrously out of focus and undeniable misleading.

The author counts among his friends numbers of Negroes of all classes. He is an authority on dives and cabarets. But he masses this knowledge without rule or reason and seeks to express all of Harlem life in its cabarets. To him the black cabaret is Harlem; around it all his characters gravitate. Here is their stage of action. Such a theory of Harlem is nonsense. The overwhelming majority of black folk there never go to cabarets. The average colored man in Harlem is an everyday laborer, attending church, lodge and movie and as conservative and as conventional as ordinary working folk everywhere.

Something they have which is racial, something distinctively Negroid can be found; but it is expressed by subtle, almost delicate nuance, and not by the wildly, barbaric drunken orgy in whose details Van Vechten revels. There is laughter, color and spontaneity at Harlem's core, but in the current cabaret, financed and supported largely by white New York, no one but a fool could mistake it for the genuine exhibition of the spirit of the people. …

––––––– 6.29 –––––––
'THE NEGRO ARTIST AND THE RACIAL MOUNTAIN'
Langston Hughes

Carl Van Vecthen's *Nigger Heaven* came at a tenuous time in the Renaissance. Many of the New Negro artists who drove it were beginning to wince under the weight placed on them, and their art, by political leaders. W.E.B. DuBois had just written an essay in *The Crisis* in which he declared art without a political purpose irrelevant. All white art, he argued, had always doubled as subtle "pro-

paganda," and black art needed to do the same. But Renaissance writers grew increasingly annoyed with this imposition. In a June 1926 essay in the *Nation*, Langston Hughes defended his and other black artists' right to independent expression. In the essay, "The Negro Artist and the Racial Mountain," Hughes rejects the demands of either white benefactors or black leaders, arguing that black artists can and must comment on race in any way they are moved to. To Hughes, demands that he portray only the positive parts of black life, in an effort to win America's approval, were nothing more than orders to ape white society. He and his ilk would take their inspiration from wherever it came, be it the university or the street corner. "If white people are pleased," he concludes, "we are glad. If they are not, it doesn't matter. We know we are beautiful. And ugly too."

One of the most promising of the young Negro poets said to me once, "I want to be a poet — not a Negro poet," meaning, I believe, "I want to write like a white poet"; meaning subconsciously, "I would like to be a white poet"; meaning behind that, "I would like to be white." And I was sorry the young man said that, for no great poet has ever been afraid of being himself. And I doubted then that, with his desire to run away spiritually from his race, this boy would ever be a great poet. But this is the mountain standing in the way of any true Negro art in America — this urge within the race toward whiteness, the desire to pour racial individuality into the mold of American standardization, and to be as little Negro and as much American as possible.

But let us look at the immediate background of this young poet. His family is of what I suppose one would call the Negro middle class: people who are by no means rich yet never uncomfortable nor hungry — smug, contented, respectable folk, members of the Baptist church. The father goes to work every morning. He is the chief steward at a large white club. The mother sometimes does fancy sewing or supervises parties for the rich families of the town. The children go to a mixed school. In the home they read white papers and magazines. And the mother often says, "Don't be like niggers" when the children are bad. A frequent phrase from the father is, "Look how well a white man does things." And so the word white comes to be unconsciously a symbol of all the virtues. It holds for the children beauty, morality, and money. The whisper of "I want to be white" runs silently through their minds. This young poet's home is, I believe, a fairly typical home of the colored middle class. One sees immediately how difficult it would be for an artist born in such a home to interest himself in interpreting the beauty of his own people. He is never taught to see that beauty. He is taught rather not to see it, or if he does, to be ashamed of it when it is not according to Caucasian patterns.

For racial culture the home of a self-styled "high-class" Negro has nothing better to offer. Instead there will be perhaps more aping of things white than in a less cultured or less wealthy home. The father is perhaps a doctor, lawyer, landowner, or politician. The mother may be a social worker, or a teacher, or she may do nothing and have a maid. Father is often dark but he has usually married the lightest woman he could find. The family attend a fashionable church where few really colored faces are to be found. And they themselves draw a color line. In the North they go to white theaters and white movies. And in the South they have at least two cars and a house "like white folks." Nordic manners, Nordic faces, Nordic hair, Nordic art (if any), and an Episcopal heaven. A very high mountain indeed for the would-be racial artist to climb in order to discover himself and his people.

But then there are the low-down folks, the so-called common element, and they are the majority — may the Lord be praised! The people who have their nip of gin on Saturday nights and are not too important to themselves or the community, or too well fed, or too learned to watch the lazy world go round. They live on Seventh Street in Washington or State Street in Chicago and they do not particularly care whether they are like white folks or anybody else. Their joy runs, bang! into ecstasy.

Their religion soars to a shout. Work maybe a little today, rest a little tomorrow. Play awhile. Sing awhile. O, let's dance! These common people are not afraid of spirituals, as for a long time their more intellectual brethren were, and jazz is their child. They furnish a wealth of colorful, distinctive material for any artist because they still hold their own individuality in the face of American standardization. And perhaps these common people will give to the world its truly great Negro artist, the one who is not afraid to be himself. Whereas the better-class Negro would tell the artist what to do, the people at least let him alone when he does appear. And they are not ashamed of him — if they know he exists at all. And they accept what beauty is their own without question.

Certainly there is, for the American Negro artist who can escape the restrictions the more advanced among his own group would put upon him, a great field of unused material ready for his art. Without going outside his race, and even among the better classes with their "white" culture and conscious American manners, but still Negro enough to be different, there is sufficient material to furnish a black artist with a lifetime of creative work. And when he chooses to touch on the relations between Negroes and whites in this country with their innumerable overtones and undertones, surely, and especially for literature and the drama, there is an inexhaustible supply of themes at hand. To these the Negro artist can give his racial individuality, his heritage of rhythm and warmth, and his incongruous humor that so often, as in the Blues, becomes ironic laughter mixed with tears. But let us look again at the mountain.

A prominent Negro clubwoman in Philadelphia paid eleven dollars to hear Raquel Meller sing Andalusian popular songs. But she told me a few weeks before she would not think of going to hear "that woman," Clara Smith, a great black artist, sing Negro folk songs. And many an upper-class Negro church, even now, would not dream of employing a spiritual in its services. The drab melodies in white folks' hymnbooks are much to be preferred. "We want to worship the Lord correctly and quietly. We don't believe in 'shouting.' Let's be dull like the Nordics," they say, in effect.

The road for the serious black artist, then, who would produce a racial art is most certainly rocky and the mountain is high. Until recently he received almost no encouragement for his work from either white or colored people. The fine novels of Chestnutt go out of print with neither race noticing their passing. The quaint charm and humor of Dunbar's dialect verse brought to him, in his day, largely the same kind of encouragement one would give a sideshow freak (A colored man writing poetry! How odd!) or a clown (How amusing!).

The present vogue in things Negro, although it may do as much harm as good for the budding colored artist, has at least done this: it has brought him forcibly to the attention of his own people among whom for so long, unless the other race had noticed him beforehand, he was a prophet with little honor. I understand that Charles Gilpin acted for years in Negro theaters without any special acclaim from his own, but when Broadway gave him eight curtain calls, Negroes, too, began to beat a tin pan in his honor. I know a young colored writer, a manual worker by day, who had been writing well for the colored magazines for some years, but it was not until he recently broke into the white publications and his first book was accepted by a prominent New York publisher that the "best" Negroes in his city took the trouble to discover that he lived there. Then almost immediately they decided to give a grand dinner for him. But the society ladies were careful to whisper to his mother that perhaps she'd better not come. They were not sure she would have an evening gown.

The Negro artist works against an undertow of sharp criticism and misunderstanding from his own group and unintentional bribes from the whites. "O, be respectable, write about nice people, show how good we are," say the Negroes. "Be stereotyped, don't go too far, don't shatter our illusions about you, don't

amuse us too seriously. We will pay you," say the whites. Both would have told Jean Toomer not to write "Cane." The colored people did not praise it. The white people did not buy it. Most of the colored people who did read "Cane" hated it. They are afraid of it. Although the critics gave it good reviews the public remained indifferent. Yet (excepting the work of DuBois) "Cane" contains the finest prose written by a Negro in America. And like the singing of Robeson, it is truly racial.

But in spite of the Nordicized Negro intelligentsia and the desires of some white editors we have an honest American Negro literature already with us. Now I await the rise of the Negro theater. Our folk music, having achieved world-wide fame, offers itself to the genius of the great individual American Negro composer who is to come. And within the next decade I expect to see the work of a growing school of colored artists who paint and model the beauty of dark faces and create with new technique the expressions of their own soul-world. And the Negro dancers who will dance like flame and the singers who will continue to carry our songs to all who listen — they will be with us in even greater numbers tomorrow.

Most of my own poems are racial in theme and treatment, derived from the life I know. In many of them I try to grasp and hold some of the meanings and rhythms of jazz. I am sincere as I know how to be in these poems and yet after every reading I answer questions like these from my own people: Do you think Negroes should always write about Negroes? I wish you wouldn't read some of your poems to white folks. How do you find any thing interesting in a place like a cabaret? Why do you write about black people? You aren't black. What makes you do so many jazz poems?

But jazz to me is one of the inherent expressions of Negro life in America: the eternal tom-tom beating in the Negro soul — the tom-tom of revolt against weariness in a white world, a world of subway trains, and work, work, work; the tom-tom of joy and laughter, and pain swallowed in a smile. Yet the Philadelphia clubwoman is ashamed to say that her race created it and she does not like me to write about it. The old subconscious "white is best" runs through her mind. Years of study under white teachers, a lifetime of white books, pictures, and papers, and white manners, morals, and Puritan standards made her dislike the spirituals. And now she turns up her nose at jazz and all its manifestations — likewise almost everything else distinctly racial. She doesn't care for the Winold Reiss portraits of Negroes because they are "too Negro." She does not want a true picture of herself from anybody. She wants the artist to flatter her, to make the white world believe that all Negroes are as smug and as near white in soul as she wants to be. But, to my mind, it is the duty of the younger Negro artist, if he accepts any duties at all from outsiders, to change through the force of his art that old whispering "I want to be white," hidden in the aspirations of his people, to "Why should I want to be white? I am a Negro — and beautiful!"

So I am ashamed for the black poet who says, "I want to be a poet, not a Negro poet," as though his own racial world were not as interesting as any other world. I am ashamed, too, for the colored artist who runs from the painting of Negro faces to the painting of sunsets after the manner of the academicians because he fears the strange un-whiteness of his own features. An artist must be free to choose what he does, certainly, but he must also never be afraid too what he might choose.

Let the blare of Negro jazz bands and the bellowing voice of Bessie Smith singing Blues penetrate the closed ears of the colored near-intellectuals until they listen and perhaps understand. Let Paul Robeson singing Water Boy, and Rudolph Fisher writing about the streets of Harlem, and Jean Toomer holding the heart of Georgia in his hands, and Aaron Douglas drawing strange black fantasies cause the smug Negro middle class to turn from their white, respectable, ordinary books and papers to catch a glimmer of their own beauty. We younger Negro artists who create now intend to express our individual dark-skinned selves without fear or shame. If white people are pleased we are glad. If they are not, it doesn't matter. We know we are beautiful. And ugly too. The tom-tom cries and the tom-tom laughs. If colored people are pleased, we are glad. If they are not, their displeasure doesn't matter either. We build our temples for tomorrow, strong as we know how, and we stand on top of the mountain, free within ourselves.

─────── 6.30 ───────
'THE CREATION'
James Weldon Johnson

James Weldon Johnson's own contribution to the literary canon of the Harlem Renaissance is his 1927 collection of poem-sermons *God's Trombones*. Johnson spent most of the era working within the NAACP, and from there promoting other Renaissance writers. When afforded time, he composed the series of sermons that comprised *God's Trombones*, the most celebrated of which, "The Creation," was originally published years earlier. Through the collection, Johnson hoped to revive the fading reverence within the community for both African-American spirituals and the southern black preachers associated with them. Without employing the dialect he had criticized at the decade's outset, Johnson managed to bring the southern preacher and his sermons to life for northerners, both black and white.

And God stepped out on space,
And he looked around and said:
I'm lonely —
I'll make me a world.

And far as the eye of God could see
Darkness covered everything,
Blacker than a hundred midnights
Down in a cypress swamp.
Then God smiled,
And the light broke,
And the darkness rolled up on one side,
And the light stood shining on the other,
And God said: That's good!

Then God reached out and took the light in
    his hands,
And God rolled the light around in his hands
Until he made the sun;
And he set that sun a-blazing in the heavens.
And the light that was left from making the sun
God gathered it up in a shining ball
And flung it against the darkness,
Spangling the night with the moon and stars.
Then down between
The darkness and the light
He hurled the world;
And God said: That's good!

Then God himself stepped down —
And the sun was on his right hand,
And the moon was on his left;
The stars were clustered about his head,
And the earth was under his feet.
And God walked, and where he trod
His footsteps hollowed the valleys out
And bulged the mountains up.

Then he stopped and looked and saw
That the earth was hot and barren.
So God stepped over to the edge of the world
And he spat out the seven seas —
He batted his eyes, and the lightnings flashed —
He clapped his hands, and the thunders rolled —
And the waters above the earth came down,
The cooling waters came down.

Then the green grass sprouted,
And the little red flowers blossomed,
The pine tree pointed his finger to the sky,
And the oak spread out his arms,
The lakes cuddled down in the hollows of the
    ground,
And the rivers ran down to the sea;
And God smiled again,
And the rainbow appeared,
And curled itself around his shoulder.

Then God raised his arm and he waved his
    hand
Over the sea and over the land,
And he said: Bring forth! Bring forth!

And quicker than God could drop his hand,
Fishes and fowls
And beasts and birds
Swam the rivers and the seas,
Roamed the forests and the woods,
And split the air with their wings.
And God said: That's good!

Then God walked around,
And God looked around
On all that he had made.
He looked at his sun,
And he looked at his moon,
And he looked at his little stars;
He looked on his world
With all its living things,
And God said: I'm lonely still.

Then God sat down —
On the side of a hill where he could think;
By a deep, wide river he sat down;
With his head in his hands,
God thought and thought,
Till he thought: I'll make me a man!

Up from the bed of the river
God scooped the clay;
And by the bank of the river
He kneeled him down;
And there the great God Almighty
Who lit the sun and fixed it in the sky,
Who flung the stars to the most far corner of
    the night,
Who rounded the earth in the middle of
    his hand;
This Great God,
Like a mammy bending over her baby,
Kneeled down in the dust
Toiling over a lump of clay
Till he shaped it in his own image;

Then into it he blew the breath of life,
And man became a living soul.
Amen. Amen.

--------- 6.31 ---------
'STRANGE FRUIT'
Billie Holiday

Billie Holiday, born Eleanor Holiday in Philadelphia, started her career singing jazz and blues songs in Harlem nightclubs and speakeasies, where she eventually met Okeh Records' John Hammond and jazz band leader Benny Goodman. Hammond recorded her first songs in 1933. In the coming years she recorded and played in clubs with Teddy Wilson, receiving limited recognition but largely laboring as a second-tier vocalist. She toured with Count Basie's band later in the decade, before connecting with white band leader Artie Shaw. After a bitter break with Shaw, Holiday went solo as a performer in a new integrated club started by Hammond and Goodman in New York's Sheridan Square — the Café Society. Holiday headlined the club's launch, where she put a haunting poem by Lewis Allen to song. Performed in her throaty, sultry voice, "Strange Fruit" catapulted Holiday to fame. Its unsettling description of a lynched black body "swinging in the southern breeze" continues to spark commentary today. Despised by many white audiences, African Americans and liberal whites turned it into an anthem for the Civil Rights Movement. That same year she debuted another of her signature tunes, "God Bless the Child."

A. "Strange Fruit"

Southern trees bear strange fruit,
Blood on the leaves and blood at the root,
Black bodies swinging in the southern breeze,
Strange fruit hanging from the poplar trees.
Pastoral scene of the gallant south,
The bulging eyes and the twisted mouth,
Scent of magnolias, sweet and fresh,
Then the sudden smell of burning flesh.

Here is fruit for the crows to pluck,
For the rain to gather, for the wind to suck,
For the sun to rot, for the trees to drop,
Here is a strange and bitter cry.

B. "God Bless the Child"

Them that's got shall get
Them that's not shall lose

So the Bible said and it still is news
Mama may have, Papa may have
But God bless the child that's got his own
That's got his own

Yes, the strong gets more
While the weak ones fade
Empty pockets don't ever make the grade
Mama may have, Papa may have
But God bless the child that's got his own
That's got his own

Money, you've got lots of friends
Crowding round the door
When you're gone, spending ends
They don't come no more
Rich relations give
Crust of bread and such
You can help yourself
But don't take too much
Mama may have, Papa may have
But God bless the child that's got his own
That's got his own

Mama may have, Papa may have
But God bless the child that's got his own
That's got his own
He just worry 'bout nothin'
Cause he's got his own

--------- 6.32 ---------
FIGHTING FOR SEGREGATION OR INTEGRATION?
W.E.B. DuBois

Thirty years after W.E.B. DuBois led the last strategic shift in the movement for equality, a shift that had thus far defined the 20th century for African Americans, he again declared it was time to change tack. In the early 1930s, he grew dissatisfied with the effort to win acceptance into American society. Despite the black leaders' strikingly successful efforts to introduce America to the community's artistic talent — to its "Talented Tenth" — segregationists had not budged. Disenchanted by this continued rejection, DuBois became convinced that segregation could not be defeated through negotiation with white America. It was going to take a long and arduous fight. So the black community, he argued, should, in effect, withdraw, regroup and focus on building its own self-sufficient institutions. Continue protesting and objecting to white hegemony, sure, but concentrate more closely on establishing better black schools, churches, businesses and civic organizations. If blacks were to be segregated, their walled-off world should at least be superior.

The NAACP's leaders objected to DuBois's new logic, which they considered an abandonment of the battle against Jim Crow. The organization was founded to fight for integration, not segregation, and that it would continue to do. DuBois pushed the issue in the pages of *The Crisis*, and in June 1934 published the essay below, articulating his final stance on the matter. Later that month, he quit the group and moved to Atlanta University.

Counsels of Despair

Many persons have interpreted my reassertion of our current attitude toward segregation as a counsel of despair. We can't win, therefore, give up and accept the inevitable. Never, and nonsense. Our business in this world is to fight and fight again, and never to yield. But after all, one must fight with his brains, if he has any. He gathers strength to fight. He gathers knowledge, and he raises children who are proud to fight and who know what they are fighting about. And above all, they learn what they are fighting for is the opportunity and the chance to know and associate with black folk. They are not fighting to escape themselves. They are fighting to say to the world: the opportunity of knowing Negroes is worth so much to us and is so appreciated, that we want you to know them too.

Negroes are not extraordinary human beings. They are just like other human beings, with all their foibles and ignorance and mistakes. But they are human beings, and human nature is always worth knowing, and withal, splendid in its manifestations. Therefore, we are fighting to keep open the avenues of human contact; but in the meantime, we are taking every advantage of what opportunities of contact are already open to us, and among those opportunities which are open, and which are splendid and inspiring, is the opportunity of Negroes to work together in the twentieth century for the uplift and development of the Negro race. It is no counsel of despair to emphasize and hail the opportunity for such work.

Surely then, in this period of frustration and disappointment, we must turn from negation to affirmation, from the ever-lasting "No" to the ever-lasting "Yes." Instead of sitting, sapped of all initiative and independence; instead of drowning our originality in mediocre white folks; instead of being afraid of ourselves and cultivating the art of skulking to escape the Color Line; we have got to renounce a program that always involves humiliating self-stultifying scrambling to crawl somewhere where we are not wanted; where we crouch panting like a whipped dog. We have got to stop this and learn that on such a program they cannot build manhood. No, by God, stand erect in a mud-puddle and tell the white world to go to hell, rather than lick boots in a parlor.

Affirm, as you have a right to affirm, that the Negro race is one of the great human races, inferior to none in its accomplishment and in its ability. Different, it is true, and for most of the difference, let us reverently thank God. And this race, with its vantage grounds in modern days, can go forward of its own will, of its own power, and its own initiative. It is led by twelve million American Negroes of average modern intelligence; three or four million educated African Negroes are their full equals, and several million Negroes in the West Indies and South America. This body of at least twenty-five million modern men are not called upon to commit suicide because somebody doesn't like their complexion or their hair. It is their opportunity and their day to stand up and make themselves heard and felt in the modern world.

Indeed, there is nothing else we can do. If you have passed your resolution, "No segregation,

Never and Nowhere," what are you going to do about it? Let me tell you what you are going to do. You are going back to continue to make your living in a Jim-Crow school; you are going to dwell in a segregated section of the city; you are going to pastor a Jim-Crow Church; you are going to occupy political office because of Jim-Crow political organizations that stand back of you and force you into office. All these things and a thousand others you are going to do because you have got to.

If you are going to do this, why not say so? What are you afraid of? Do you believe in the Negro race or do you not? If you do not, naturally, you are justified in keeping still. But if you do believe in the extraordinary accomplishment of the Negro church and the Negro college, the Negro school and the Negro newspaper, then say so and say so plainly, not only for the sake of those who have given their lives to make these things worthwhile, but for those young people whom you are teaching, by that negative attitude, that there is nothing that they can do, nobody that they can emulate, and no field worthwhile working in. Think of what Negro art and literature has yet to accomplish if it can only be free and untrammeled by the necessity of pleasing white folks! Think of the splendid moral appeal that you can make to a million children tomorrow, if once you can get them to see the possibilities of the American Negro today and now, whether he is segregated or not, or in spite of all possible segregation...

A Dream No Longer Deferred:
THE CIVIL RIGHTS
MOVEMENT

─────── 7.1 ───────

'A CALL TO NEGRO AMERICA'

Asa Philip Randolph

When President Franklin D. Roosevelt prepared America to join in World War II, A. Philip Randolph got ready for his own fight: a rematch of his World War I battle over the mistreatment of blacks in the armed services and employment discrimination in the booming defense industry. Working from his post as head of the Brotherhood of Sleeping Car Porters — the black labor union for the nation's largest employer of African Americans, the Pullman Company — Randolph began hounding Roosevelt to do something about both issues. When Roosevelt proved unresponsive, Randolph threatened a march on Washington, D.C. Both the NAACP and the National Urban League lent their support to the effort. Randolph told the president that unless he issued an executive order addressing discrimination in the defense industries and the armed forces, civil rights leaders would bring tens of thousands of black laborers to protest in front of the Lincoln Memorial. To show he meant business, he published the following "Call to Negro America to March on Washington" in the Brotherhood's *Black Worker* (the successor to the *Messenger*; see Chapter Six) and scheduled the march for July 1, 1941.

We call upon you to fight for jobs in National Defense.

We call upon you to struggle for the integration of Negroes in the armed forces, such as the Air Corps, Navy, Army and Marine Corps of the Nation.

We call upon you to demonstrate for the abolition of Jim-Crowism in all Government departments and defense employment.

This is an hour of crisis. It is a crisis of democracy. It is a crisis of minority groups. It is a crisis of Negro Americans.

What is this crisis?

To American Negroes, it is the denial of jobs in Government defense projects. It is racial discrimination in Government departments. It is widespread Jim-Crowism in the armed forces of the Nation.

While billions of the taxpayers' money are being spent for war weapons, Negro workers are being turned away from the gates of factories, mines and mills — being flatly told, "nothing doing." Some employers refuse to give Negroes jobs when they are without "union cards," and some unions refuse Negro workers union cards when they are "without jobs."

What shall we do?

What a dilemma!

What a runaround!

What a disgrace!

What a blow below the belt!

'Though dark, doubtful and discouraging, all is not lost, all is not hopeless. 'Though battered and bruised, we are not beaten, broken or bewildered.

Verily, the Negroes' deepest disappointments and direst defeats, their tragic trials and outrageous oppressions in these dreadful days of destruction and disaster to democracy and freedom, and the rights of minority peoples, and the dignity and independence of the human spirit, is the Negroes' greatest opportunity to rise to the highest heights of struggle for freedom and justice in Government, in industry, in labor unions, education, social service, religion and culture.

With faith and confidence of the Negro people in their own power for self-liberation, Negroes can break down the barriers of discrimination against employment in National Defense. Negroes can kill the deadly serpent of race hatred in the Army, Navy, Air and Marine Corps, and smash through and blast the Government, business and labor-union red tape to win the right to equal opportunity in vocational training and re-training in defense employment.

Most important and vital to all, Negroes, by the mobilization and coordination of their mass power, can cause President Roosevelt to issue an executive order abolishing discriminations in all government departments, Army, Navy, Air corps and National Defense jobs.

Of course, the task is not easy. In very truth, it is big, tremendous and difficult.

It will cost money.

It will require sacrifice.

It will tax the Negroes' courage, determination and will to struggle. But we can, must and will triumph.

The Negroes' stake in national defense is big. It consists of jobs, thousands of jobs. It may represent millions, yes, hundreds of millions of dollars in wages. It consists of new industrial opportunities and hope.

This is worth fighting for.

But to win our stakes, it will require an "all-out," bold and total effort and demonstration of colossal proportions.

Negroes can build a mammoth machine of mass action with a terrific and tremendous driving and striking power that can shatter and crush the evil fortress of race prejudice and hate, if they will only resolve to do so and never stop, until victory comes.

Dear fellow Negro Americans, be not dismayed in these terrible times. You possess power, great power. Our problem is to harness and hitch it up for action on the broadest, most daring and most gigantic scale.

In this period of power politics, nothing counts but pressure, more pressure, and still more pressure, through the tactic and strategy of broad, organized, aggressive mass action behind the vital and important issues of the Negro. To this end, we propose that ten thousand Negroes march on Washington for jobs in National Defense and equal integration in the fighting forces of the United States.

An "all-out" thundering march on Washington, ending in a monster and huge demonstration at Lincoln's Monument will shake up white America.

It will shake up official Washington.

It will give encouragement to our white friends to fight all the harder by our side, with us, for our righteous cause.

It will gain respect for the Negro people.

It will create a new sense of self-respect among Negroes.

But what of national unity?

We believe in national unity which recognizes equal opportunity of black and white citizens to jobs in national defense and the armed forces, and in all other institutions and endeavors in America. We condemn all dictatorships, Fascist, Nazi and Communist. We are loyal, patriotic Americans, all.

But, if American democracy will not defend its defenders; if American democracy will not protect its protectors; if American democracy will not give jobs to its toilers because of race or color; if American democracy will not insure equality of opportunity, freedom and justice to its citizens, black and white, it is a hollow mockery and belies the principles for which it is supposed to stand.

To the hard, difficult and trying problem of securing equal participation in national defense, we summon all Negro Americans to march on Washington. We summon Negro Americans to form committees in various cities to recruit and register marchers and raise funds through the sale of buttons and other legitimate means for the expenses of marchers to Washington by buses, train, private automobiles, trucks, and on foot.

We summon Negro Americans to stage marches on their City Halls and Councils in their respective cities and urge them to memorialize the President to issue an executive order to abolish discrimination in the Government and national defense.

However, we sternly counsel against violence and ill-considered and intemperate action and the abuse of power. Mass power, like physical power, when misdirected is more harmful than helpful.

We summon you to mass action that is orderly and lawful, but aggressive and militant, for justice, equality and freedom.

Crispus Attucks marched and died as a martyr for American independence. Nat Turner, Denmark Vesey, Gabriel Prosser, Harriet Tubman and Frederick Douglass fought, bled and died for the emancipation of Negro slaves and the preservation of American democracy.

Abraham Lincoln, in times of the grave emergency of the Civil War, issued the Proclamation of Emancipation for the freedom of Negro slaves and the preservation of American democracy.

Today, we call upon President Roosevelt, a great humanitarian and idealist, to follow in the footsteps of his noble and illustrious predecessor and take the second decisive step in this world and national emergency and free American Negro citizens of the stigma, humiliation and insult of discrimination and Jim-Crowism in Government departments and national defense.

The Federal Government cannot with clear conscience call upon private industry and labor unions to abolish discrimination based upon race and color as long as it practices discrimination itself against Negro Americans.

―――― 7.2 ――――

EXECUTIVE ORDER 8802
Franklin D. Roosevelt

President Roosevelt held two White House meetings with Randolph and the other civil rights groups asking them to call off their threatened march. He explained that, while he sympathized with their cause, if he issued the orders they wanted, it would prompt other groups to come in and demand all sorts of new orders from him. He couldn't set the precedent. Moreover, Roosevelt urged the civil rights groups to understand that this sort of issue could not be "settled with a sledge hammer." But Randolph refused to back down this time; the march would happen if the president didn't act. So, eventually, Roosevelt relented in part. On June 25, 1941, barely a week before the planned march, he issued Executive Order 8802 banning discrimination based on race in defense industry companies contracting with the federal government and establishing the Fair Employment Practices Committee to monitor compliance. In exchanged, Randolph aborted the march.

WHEREAS it is the policy of the United States to encourage full participation in the national defense program by all citizens of the United States, regardless of race, creed, color, or national origin, in the firm belief that the democratic way of life within the Nation can be defended successfully only with the help and support of all groups within its borders; and

WHEREAS there is evidence that available and needed workers have been barred from employment in industries engaged in defense production solely because of considerations of race, creed, color, or national origin, to the detriment of workers' morale and of national unity;

NOW THEREFORE, by virtue of the authority vested in me by the Constitution and the statutes, and as prerequisite to the successful conduct of our national defense production effort, I do hereby reaffirm the policy of the United States that there shall be no discrimination in the employment of workers in defense industries or government because of race, creed, color, or national origin, and I do hereby declare that it is the duty of employees and of labor organizations, in furtherance of said policy and of this order, to provide for the full and equitable participation of all workers in defense industries, without discrimination because of race, creed, color, or national origin;

And it is hereby ordered as follows:

1. All departments and agencies of the Government of the United States concerned with vocational and training programs for defense production shall take special measures appropriate to assure that such programs are administered without discrimination because of race, creed, color, or national origin;

2. All contracting agencies of the Government of the United States shall include in all defense contracts hereafter negotiated by them a provision obligating the contractor not to discriminate against any worker because of race, creed, color, or national origin;

3. There is established in the Office of Production Management a Committee on Fair Employment Practice, which shall consist of a chairman and four other members to be appointed by the President. The chairman and members of the Committee shall serve as such without compensation but shall be entitled to actual and necessary transportation, subsistence and other expenses incidental to performance of their duties. The Committee shall receive and investigate complaints of discrimination in violation of the provisions of this order and shall take appropriate steps to redress grievances which it finds to be valid. The Committee shall also recommend to the several departments and agencies of the Government of the United States and to the President all measures which may be deemed by it necessary or proper to effectuate the provisions of this order.

––––––– 7.3 –––––––
'NONVIOLENCE VS. JIM CROW'
Bayard Rustin

Bayard Rustin's long civil rights career, and close association with A. Philip Randolph, began when he served as a youth coordinator for the March on Washington Movement.

That same year, Rustin, a Quaker, had been appointed the Race Relations Secretary for the Fellowship of Reconciliation, a pacifist group promoting non-violent resistance to social injustice. From then forward, operating largely behind the scenes, Rustin would be involved in almost every major decision and development in the Civil Rights Movement. In many ways its philosophical architect, the activist-intellectual was a confidant and advisor first to Randolph and later to Martin Luther King, Jr. He counseled King during the Montgomery Bus Boycott, organized the 1963 March on Washington and penned countless essays and articles articulating and guiding the movement's strategies. Significantly, Rustin was openly gay, a point that largely contributed to his role being limited to behind-the-scenes strategizing.

Rustin's activism stretched beyond civil rights to a range of progressive causes, including draft resistance during the war. In one example of Rustin's tireless activism, he organized inmate demonstrations against segregation in prisons while jailed as a conscientious objector in 1943. His passionate belief in tactics of non-violent social change helped drive the Civil Rights Movement's use of them. He articulated the doctrine's utility in this July 1942 *Journal of the Fellowship of Reconciliation* essay.

Recently I was planning to go from Louisville to Nashville by bus. I bought my ticket, boarded the bus, and, instead of going to the back, sat down in the second seat. The driver saw me, got up, and came toward me.

"Hey, you. You're supposed to sit in the back seat."

"Why?"

"Because that's the law. Niggers ride in back."

I said, "My friend, I believe that is an unjust law. If I were to sit in the back I would be condoning injustice."

Angry, but not knowing what to do, he got out and went into the station. He soon came out again, got into his seat, and started off.

This routine was gone through at each stop, but each time nothing came of it. Finally the driver, in desperation, must have phoned ahead, for about thirteen miles north of Nashville I heard sirens approaching. The bus came to an abrupt stop, and a police car and two motorcycles drew up beside us with a flourish. Four policemen got into the bus, consulted shortly with the driver, and came to my seat.

"Get up, you ——— nigger!"

"Why?" I asked.

"Get up, you black ———!"

"I believe that I have a right to sit here," I said quietly. "If I sit in the back of the bus I am depriving that child — " I pointed to a little white child of five or six — "of the knowledge that there is injustice here, which I believe it is his right to know. It is my sincere conviction that the power of love in the world is the greatest power existing. If you have a greater power, my friend, you may move me."

How much they understood of what I was trying to tell them I do not know. By this time they were impatient and angry. As I would not move, they began to beat me about the head and shoulders, and I shortly found myself knocked to the floor. Then they dragged me out of the bus and continued to kick and beat me.

Knowing that if I tried to get up or protect myself in the first heat of their anger, they would construe it as an attempt to resist and beat me down again, I forced myself to be still and wait for their kicks, one after another. Then I stood up, spreading out my arms parallel to the ground, and said, "There is no need to beat me. I am not resisting you."

At this three white men, obviously Southerners by their speech, got out of the bus and remonstrated with the police. Indeed, as one of the policemen raised his club to strike me, one of them, a little fellow, caught hold of it and said, "Don't you do that!" A second policeman raised his club to strike the little man, and I stepped between them, facing the man, and said, "Thank you, but there is no need to do that. I do not wish to fight. I am protected well."

An elderly gentlemen, well dressed and also a Southerner, asked the police where they were taking me.

They said, "Nashville."

"Don't worry, son," he said to me. "I'll be there to see that you get your justice."

I was put into the back seat of the police car, between two policemen. Two others sat in front. During the thirteen-mile ride to town they called me every conceivable name and said anything they could think of to incite me to violence. I found that I was shaking with nervous strain, and to give myself something to do, I took out a piece of paper and a pencil, and began to write from memory a chapter from one of Paul's letters.

When I had written a few sentences, the man on my right said, "What're you writing?" and snatched the paper from my hand. He read it, then crumpled it into a ball and pushed it in my face. The man on the other side gave me a kick.

A moment later I happened to catch the eye of the young policeman in the front seat. He looked away quickly, and I took renewed courage from the realization that he could not meet my eyes because he was aware of the injustice being done. I began to write again, and after a moment I leaned forward and touched him on the shoulder. "My friend," I said, "how do you spell 'difference'?"

He spelled it for me — incorrectly — and I wrote it correctly and went on.

When we reached Nashville, a number of policemen were lined up on both sides of the hallway down which I had to pass on my way to the captain's office. They tossed me from one to another like a volleyball. By the time I reached the office, the lining of my best coat was torn, and I was considerably rumpled. I straightened myself out as best I could and went in. They had my bag, and went through it and my papers, finding much of interest, especially in the *Christian Century* and *Fellowship*.

Finally the captain said, "Come here, nigger."

I walked directly to him. "What can I do for you?" I asked.

"Nigger," he said menacingly, "you're supposed to be scared when you come in here!"

"I am fortified by truth, justice, and Christ," I said. "There's no need for me to fear."

He was flabbergasted and, for a time, completely at a loss for words. Finally he said to another officer, "I believe the nigger's crazy!"

They sent me into another room and went into consultation. The wait was long, but after an hour and a half they came for me and I was taken for another ride, across town. At the courthouse, I was taken down the hall to the office of the assistant district attorney, Mr. Ben West. As I got to the door I heard a voice, "Say, you colored fellow, hey!" I looked around and saw the elderly gentlemen who had been on the bus.

"I'm here to see that you get justice," he said.

The assistant district attorney questioned me about my life, the *Christian Century*, pacifism, and the war for half an hour. Then he asked the police to tell their side of what had happened. They did, stretching the truth a good deal in spots and including several lies for seasoning. Mr. West then asked me to tell my side.

"Gladly," I said, "and I want *you*," turning to the young policeman who had sat in the front seat, "to follow what I say and stop me if I deviate from the truth in the least."

Holding his eyes with mine, I told the story exactly as it had happened, stopping often to say "Is that right?" or "Isn't that what happened?" to the young policeman. During the whole time he never once interrupted me, and when I was through I said, "Did I tell the truth just as it happened?" and he said, "Well…"

Then Mr. West dismissed me, and I was sent to wait alone in a dark room. After an hour, Mr. West came in and said, very kindly, "You may go, *Mister* Rustin."

I left the courthouse, believing all the more strongly in the nonviolent approach. I am certain that I was addressed as "Mister" (as no Negro is ever addressed in the South), that I was assisted by those three men, and that the elderly gentleman interested himself in my predicament because I had, without fear, faced the four policemen and said, "There is no need to beat me. I offer you no resistance."

—————— 7.4 ——————
NATIVE SON
Richard Wright

Richard Wright moved North from Mississippi while still in high school. He migrated towards Chicago, where he worked odd jobs and became active in the Communist Party, an organization he would later disavow for its failure to fully embrace a Civil Rights Movement. In 1938, after years of contributing to Communist and leftist publications, Wright published a collection of stories about growing up in the South called *Uncle Tom's Children*. As with all of his subsequent writing, Wright sought to portray the way American racism destroyed the souls of both black and white people. The collection was well received, but Wright's renown as black America's most disaffected and volatile voice began with his first novel, *Native Son*, published in 1940. Picking up on the theme began in his previous stories, in *Native Son* Wright shows readers his vision of the people hundreds of years of systematic dehumanization in America has created. The story unapologetically presents Bigger Thomas, a young black man who accidentally kills the leftist daughter of a white family he is working for. Rather than regretting the mistake or fearing the consequences, Bigger finds the whole experience liberating. For once, he has set the terms of his interaction with the world. Critics praised Wright for his ability to depict such a damnable character in a way that the reader nonetheless empathizes with his plight. In the excerpt below, Bigger reflects on his new perspective over breakfast the morning after he has murdered the young woman.

… Gus and G.H. and Jack seemed far away to Bigger now, in another life, and all because he had been in Dalton's home for a few hours and had killed a white girl. He looked round the room, seeing it for the first time. There was no rug on the floor and the plastering on the walls and ceiling hung loose in many places. There were two worn iron beds, four chairs, an old dresser, and a drop-leaf table on which they ate. This was much different from Dalton's home. Here all slept in one room; there he would have a room for himself alone. He smelt food cooking and remembered that one could not smell food cooking in Dalton's home; pots could not be heard rattling all over the house. Each person lived in one room and had a little world of his own. He hated this room and all the people in it, including himself. Why did he and his folks have to live like this? What had they ever done? Perhaps they had not done anything. Maybe they had to live this way precisely because none of them in all their lives had ever done anything, right or wrong, that mattered much.

"Fix the table, Vera. Breakfast's ready," the mother called. "Yessum."

Bigger sat at the table and waited for food. Maybe this would be the last time he would eat here. He felt it keenly and it helped him to have patience. Maybe some day he would be eating in jail. Here he was sitting with them and they did not know that he had murdered a white girl and cut her head off and burnt her body. The thought of what he had done, the awful horror of it, the daring associated with such actions, formed for him for the first time in his fear-ridden life a barrier of protection between him and a world he feared. He had murdered and had created a new life for himself. It was something that was all his own, and it was the first time in his life he had had anything that others could not take from him. Yes; he could sit here calmly and eat and not be concerned about what his family thought or did. He had a natural wall from behind which he could look at them. His crime was an anchor weighing him safely in time; it added to him a certain confidence which his gun and knife did not. He was outside of his family now, over and beyond them; they were incapable of even thinking that he had done such a deed. And he had done something which even he had not thought possible.

Though he had killed by accident, not once did he feel the need to tell himself that it had been an accident. He was black and he had been alone in a room where a white girl had been killed; therefore he had killed her. That was what everybody would say anyhow, no matter what he said. And in a certain sense he knew that the girl's death had not been accidental. He had killed many times before, only on those other times there had been no handy victim or circumstance to make visible or dramatic his will to kill. His crime seemed natural; he felt that all of his life had been leading to something like this. It was no longer a matter of dumb wonder as to what would happen to him and his black skin; he knew now. The hidden meaning of his life — a meaning which others did not see and which he had always tried to hide — had spilled out. No; it was no accident, and he would never say that it was. There was in him a kind of terrified pride in feeling and thinking that some day he would be able to say publicly that he had done it. It was as though he had an obscure but deep debt to fulfill to himself in accepting the deed.

Now that the ice was broken, could he not do other things? What was there to stop him? While sitting there at the table waiting for his breakfast, he felt that he was arriving at something which had long eluded him. Things were becoming clear; he would know how to act from now on. The thing to do was to act just like others acted, live like they lived, and while they were not looking, do what you wanted. They would never know. He felt in the quiet presence of his mother, brother, and sister a force, inarticulate and unconscious, making for living without thinking, making for peace and habit, making for a hope that blinded. He felt that they wanted and yearned to see life in a certain way; they needed a certain picture of the world; there was one way of living they preferred above all others; and they were blind to what did not fit. They did not want to see what others were doing if that doing did not feed their own desires. All one had to do was be bold, do something nobody thought of. The whole thing came to him in the form of a powerful and simple feeling; there was in everyone a great hunger to believe that made him blind, and if he could see while others were blind, then he could get what he wanted and never be caught at it. Now, who on earth would think that he, a black timid Negro boy, would murder and burn a rich white girl and would sit and wait for his breakfast like this? Elation filled him.

He sat at the table watching the snow fall past the window and many things became plain. No, he did not have to hide behind a wall or a curtain now; he had a safer way of being safe, an easier way. What he had done last night had proved that. Jan was blind. Mary had been blind. Mr. Dalton was blind. And Mrs. Dalton was blind; yes, blind in more ways than one. Bigger smiled slightly. Mrs. Dalton had not known that Mary was dead while she had stood over the bed in that room last night. She had thought that Mary was drunk, because she was used to Mary's coming home drunk. And Mrs. Dalton had not known that he was in the room with her; it would have been the last thing she would have thought of. He was black and would not have figured in her thoughts on such an occasion. Bigger felt that a lot of people were like Mrs. Dalton, blind. ...

——— 7.5 ———
INVISIBLE MAN
Ralph Ellison

Following his third year at Tuskegee Institute, young Ralph Ellison, unable to afford tuition, took what he thought was a break from school and moved to New York City. A music professor at Tuskegee had introduced him to Alain Locke, who in turn plugged him into the city's black literary scene. Ellison would never return to school, instead entering into the tutelage of Richard Wright and Langston Hughes. Critics, including Wright, would later say his writing style owed too much to Wright's.

Like many black writers of the era, Ellison worked in President Roosevelt's Federal Writer's Project, published book reviews for a number of leftist journals and eventually wrote a handful of short stories. Then, in 1952, he wrote *Invisible Man*. The book met with immediate and sustained critical acclaim, and many still call it one of the greatest American novels of the 20th century.

Invisible Man is the story of a black man who has been driven out of society and literally underground. Ellison never gives the character a name, but rather lets him narrate the tragic tale of how he ended up where he

is. Starting as a promising high school graduate, the narrator is manipulated by one person after another, black and white. Unconcerned about and unaware of his individual identity, he time and again places his trust in someone who sees him as just another black face and who uses him as a weapon in his or her own battle in the race war. He doesn't realize the pattern, or his role in allowing it, until the story's climax. By then his life has already been destroyed, and he is forced to withdraw from society. The novel's message — the social erasure of its narrator — continues to offer a poignant commentary even today on the manner in which American racism pushes black people, both physically and emotionally, to the margins of society. In fact, the narrator's expression of his invisibility in the story's prologue, excerpted below, would be echoed by urban hip-hop artists decades later.

I am an invisible man. No, I am not a spook like those who haunted Edgar Allan Poe; nor am I one of your Hollywood-movie ectoplasms. I am a man of substance, of flesh and bone, fiber and liquids — and I might even be said to possess a mind. I am invisible, understand, simply because people refuse to see me. Like the bodiless heads you see sometimes in circus sideshows, it is as though I have been surrounded by mirrors of hard, distorting glass. When they approach me they see only my surroundings, themselves, or figments of their imagination — indeed, everything and anything except me.

Nor is my invisibility exactly a matter of a biochemical accident to my epidermis. That invisibility to which I refer occurs because of a peculiar disposition of the eyes of those with whom I come in contact. A matter of construction of the inner eyes, those eyes with which they look through their physical eyes upon reality. I am not complaining, nor am I protesting either. It is sometimes advantageous to be unseen, although it is most often rather wearing on the nerves. Then, too, you're constantly being bumped against by those of poor vision. Or again, you doubt if you really exist. You wonder whether you aren't simply a phantom in other people's minds. Say, a figure in a nightmare which the sleeper tries with all his strength to destroy. It's when you feel like this that, out of resentment, you begin to bump people back. And, let me confess, you feel that way most of the time. You ache with the need to convince yourself that you do exist in the real world, that you're a part of all the sound and anguish, and you strike out with your fists, you curse and you swear to make them recognize you. And, alas, it's seldom successful.

One night I accidentally bumped into a man, and perhaps because of the near darkness he saw me and called me an insulting name. I sprang at him, seized his coat lapels and demanded that he apologize. He was a tall blond man, and as my face came close to his he looked insolently out of his blue eyes and cursed me, his breath hot in my face as he struggled. I pulled his chin down sharp upon the crown of my head, butting him as I had seen the West Indians do, and I felt his flesh tear and the blood gush out, and I yelled, "Apologize! Apologize!" But he continued to curse and struggle, and I butted him again and again until he went down heavily, on his knees, profusely bleeding. I kicked him repeatedly, in a frenzy because he still uttered insults though his lips were frothy with blood. Oh yes, I kicked him! And in my outrage I got out my knife and prepared to slit his throat, right there beneath the lamplight in the deserted street, holding him in the collar with one hand, and opening the knife with my teeth — when it occurred to me that the man had not seen me, actually; that he, as far as he knew, was in the midst of a walking nightmare! And I stopped the blade, slicing the air as I pushed him away, letting him fall to the street. I stared at him hard as the lights of a car stabbed through the darkness. He lay there, moaning on the asphalt; a man almost killed by a phantom. It unnerved me. I was both disgusted and ashamed. I was like a drunken man myself, wavering about on weakened legs. Then I was amused: Something in this man's thick head had sprung out and beaten him within an inch of his life. I began to laugh at this crazy discov-

ery. Would he have awakened at the point of death? Would Death himself have freed him for wakeful living? But I didn't linger. I ran away into the dark, laughing so hard I feared I might rupture myself. The next day I saw his picture in the *Daily News*, beneath a caption stating that he had been "mugged." Poor fool, poor blind fool, I thought with sincere compassion, mugged by an invisible man!

Most of the time (although I do not choose as I once did to deny the violence of my days by ignoring it) I am not so overtly violent. I remember that I am invisible and walk softly so as not to awaken the sleeping ones. Sometimes it is best not to awaken them; there are few things in the world as dangerous as sleepwalkers. I learned in time that it is possible to carry on a fight against them without their realizing it. For instance, I have been carrying on a fight with Monopolated Light & Power for some time now. I use their service and pay them nothing at all, and they don't know it. Oh, they suspect that power is being drained off, but they don't know where. All they know is that according to the master meter there in their power station a hell of a lot of free current is disappearing somewhere into the jungle of Harlem. The joke, of course, is that I don't live in Harlem but in a border area. Several years ago (before I discovered the advantages of being invisible) I went through the routine process of buying service and paying their outrageous fees. But no more. I gave up all that, along with my apartment, and my old way of life: That way based upon the fallacious assumption that I, like other men, was visible. Now, aware of my invisibility, I live rent-free in a building rented strictly to whites, in a section of the basement that was shut off and forgotten during the nineteenth century, which I discovered when I was trying to escape in the night from Ras the Destroyer. But that's getting too far ahead of the story, almost to the end, although the end is in the beginning and lies far ahead. ...

──────── 7.6 ────────

'I'M A BELIEVER IN FAIRY TALES NOW'
Jackie Robinson

On October 23, 1945, Brooklyn Dodger owner Branch Rickey made Major League Baseball (MLB) the first integrated American institution of significance since *Plessy* (see Chapter Five). The black press had been hounding MLB to open its doors to Negro League players for years. Rickey was among the few people inside MLB who agreed that it should happen, and launched a covert plan to recruit black players for his team. Claiming he was establishing a new black league, Rickey scouted the Negro Leagues for the right person and settled on Kansas City Monarch Jackie Robinson. Robinson signed a contract on October 23 and went to play for the Dodgers' farm team, the Montreal Royals. Two years later, in April 1947, he donned number 42 and took the field for the Dodgers. Wendell Smith, a reporter for the black newspaper *Pittsburgh Courier*, had been among the most vocal in demanding that MLB integrate. His enthusiastic coverage of Robinson's first game as a Dodger, in which he scored the winning run, is below. Robinson, who had begun writing a regular sports column for the *Courier*, remarked in his submission the next day, "I'm a believer in fairy tales now."

Robinson went on to win the National League Most Valuable Player award in 1949, leading the league with a .342 batting average and 37 stolen bases. During his career, he would play in six World Series and rack up a .311 career batting average. His fame soared among black and white baseball fans, despite difficult early years in which he was harassed — often violently — on and off the field. He used his fame to push for desegregation in other sectors of society, and was actively involved in the Civil Rights Movement throughout his career. But his import to black Americans was his symbolism. Like turn of the century boxing great Jack Johnson's defeat of "the Great White Hope," Jim Jeffries, Robinson's success gave the lie to the white supremacy that justified segregation.

A. Wendell Smith's report on the first game

Robbie's Bunt Turns
By WENDELL SMITH, Courier Sports Editor
PRESS BOX, Ebbets Fields, Brooklyn, N.Y. —

Playing his first big league game of the 1947 National League season, Jackie Robinson came romping home from second base here Tuesday afternoon with what proved to be the Brooklyn Dodgers's winning run while 26,623 fans roared hilariously and the Boston Braves went down to defeat, 5 to 3.

Playing in perfect baseball weather and before a colorful opening day crowd, Robinson made his major league debut at first base and in the seventh inning was responsible for the play that upset Pitcher Johnny Sain and paved the way for a hard-earned and well-deserved victory.

The big play came in the seventh inning. At that point, the "Bums" were tailing the Braves, 3 to 2. Ed Stanky started the fireworks by walking. Robinson then strolled to the plate and the applause from his loyal fans here had hardly died when he laid down a tantalizing bunt along the first base line. Stanky was off like a flash for second as Sain charged in to get the ball. Robinson was in high gear, zooming down the first base line. The frantic Sain grabbed the ball and threw.

Robinson and the ball arrived at first approximately at the same time. First baseman Torgeson was apparently confused as Robinson came storming in his direction. In the confusion, Torgeson missed the throw and the ball rolled into foul territory along the right field line. Stanky kept right on to third and Robinson high-tailed it to a second.

Then little Pete Reiser put the game on ice by slapping one of Sain's fast balls high up on the right field screen, scoring Stanky with the tying run and Robinson with the fourth and the winning marker. Reiser eventually scored, too, but the damaging run as far as the Braves were concerned was that run carried across the platter by Brooklyn's bronze-colored first baseman.

Jackie was at bat officially three times. And, although he failed to come through with a base hit, he looked good at the plate. He was also "on the job" in the field, handling eleven chances perfectly as the "Bums" started the long grind up the pennant road.

B. Jackie Robinson's column following his first major league game

Jackie Robinson Says:

By Jackie Robinson

BROOKLYN, N.Y. — Next time I go to a movie and see a picture of a little ordinary girl become a great star, I'll believe it.

And whenever I heard my wife read fairy tales to my little boy, I'll listen.

I know that dreams do come true.

I know because I am now playing with the Brooklyn Dodgers in the big leagues!

I always dreamed about playing for the Dodgers, but, honestly, I always had my doubts. I used to tell myself: 'Something will happen. It just isn't in the books for your to play in the majors. You're a Negro. Negroes haven't been in the big leagues. Some day they will be. But you won't be the lucky guy."

Then last Thursday, Mr. Rickey called me to his office. He said: "Jackie you're a big leaguer now. You're going to play with the Dodgers and we're announcing it to the world today."

IN A TRANCE

I walked out of his office in a trance. I went from there to Ebbetts Field to play my last game with Montreal against Brooklyn. I don't think I was too impressive in that last game with Montreal. But that was because, I guess, I couldn't keep my mind on the game all the time. Every time I'd look at Pee Wee Reese or Bruce Edwards, I'd start thinking.

"Just think," I'd say to myself, "tomorrow I'll be with them. I'll be wearing a Brooklyn uniform. And then I'd look at the big park and realize that I would be here this year — playing in a major league park before big crowds and fighting for a pennant.

At noon Friday, I walked into the Brooklyn clubhouse. When I opened that door I walked into the major leagues, and a few minutes later I was dressing with big league players and getting ready to play against the famous Yankees.

Then we went out on the field. Gee it seemed big. Twice as big as the day before. I sat down in the Brooklyn dugout and started to think all over again. The game started and I found myself at first base. I was the Brooklyn first baseman. The day before, I had been Montreal's first baseman. "What a difference a day makes," I said to myself.

When the umpire said: "Play ball!" I finally started thinking baseball. I finally realized that I was a member of the Brooklyn Dodgers; that I had made the big leagues.

REALIZED RESPONSIBILITY

When I realized that, the thrill was gone. I knew that from then on I'll have to play like the very devil. So now I'm trying my best, I don't know how successful I'll be, but you can bet that I'll give my level best. I think I can do good enough job to stay up here and face such teams as the Cardinals, Pirates, Giants and the rest. I'm new and have a lot to learn, but I've found out that there are fellows on the club willing to help me. Ed Stanky, a great ball player, helped me the first day. Others have advised me and coached me since. I know by that experience that I'm not alone. I also know by the applause that I've received in these first games that the public is for me and wants to see me make good.

I will never stop trying. I hope that I'll get better and better every day and help bring a pennant and world series to Brooklyn.

Being up here is absolutely wonderful. That's why I'm a believer in fairy tales now. You see, it actually happened to me.

—————— 7.7 ——————

'EQUALITY OF TREATMENT AND OPPORTUNITY FOR ALL THOSE WHO SERVE IN OUR COUNTRY'S DEFENSE'
Harry Truman

When President Harry Truman announced the establishment of a peacetime draft, Randolph and other civil rights leaders saw their chance to push for the final desegregation of U.S. armed forces. Truman was relatively friendly to civil rights and had reached out to black leaders. But when they appealed to him to include a provision integrating the services in the bill creating a draft, he resisted. Randolph warned that he would lead a movement of black draft resisters and organize a campaign of nonviolent civil disobedience if a segregated draft went forward.

Pressure built from within the administration as well. In 1946, following a high profile hate crime in which two black veterans were murdered with their wives in Georgia, Truman had established his President's Committee on Civil Rights. In May 1947, the Committee issued its historic report "To Secure These Rights," recommending a sweeping civil rights agenda, including the integration of the armed forces. Political advisor Clark Clifford chimed in with dire warnings that the northern black vote would be crucial to Truman's reelection in the upcoming 1948 presidential contest. At the July 1948 Democratic National Convention, delegates vetoed a proposed platform that excluded a call to integrate the forces.

With all of this as backdrop, on July 26, 1948, Truman signed Executive Order 9981, ordering the branches of the forces to integrate and establishing the Fahy Committee (named after chair Charles Fahy) to monitor compliance. It was the first major victory of the new Civil Rights Movement. For the next two years, the service branches balked at the order, particularly the Army. The Fahy Committee, backed by Truman, hounded each until it instituted an acceptable integration plan. The Army, still reluctant, was forced to integrate as rising numbers of both black recruits and white casualties during the Korean War made segregation practically impossible to maintain.

A. 'To Secure These Rights'

The Record: Short of the Goal

THE HERITAGE which we have reviewed has been forged by many men through several centuries. In that time the face of our nation has changed almost beyond recognition. New lands, new peoples, new institutions have brought new problems. Again and again the promise of freedom and equality has found new forms of expression, new frameworks of meaning. The goal still remains clear although it is yet to be reached.

The record is neither as black as our detractors paint it, nor as white as people of good will would like it to be. To a large extent the light and dark shades in the picture are a reflection of the nature of our people. The phrase, "civil rights", is an abbreviation for a whole complex of relationships among individuals and among groups. We cannot properly understand the American civil rights record without giving attention to the composition of the American people. ...

THE RIGHT TO BEAR ARMS

Underlying the theory of compulsory wartime military service in a democratic state is the principle that every citizen, regardless of his station in life, must assist in the defense of the nation when its security is threatened. Despite the discrimination which they encounter in so many fields, minority group members have time and again met this responsibility. Moreover, since equality in military service assumes great importance as a symbol of democratic goals, minorities have regarded it not only as a duty but as a right.

Yet the record shows that the members of several minorities, fighting and dying for the survival of the nation in which they met bitter prejudice, found that there was discrimination against them even as they fell in battle. Prejudice in any area is an ugly, undemocratic phenomenon; in the armed services, where all men run the risk of death, it is particularly repugnant. ...

However, despite the lessons of the war and the recent announcement of these policies, the records of the military forces disclose many areas in which there is a great need for further remedial action. Although generally speaking, the basis of recruitment has been somewhat broadened, Negroes, for example, are faced by an absolute bar against enlistment in any branch of the Marine Corps other than the steward's branch, and the Army cleaves to a ceiling for Negro personnel of about ten percent of the total strength of the service.

There are no official discriminatory requirements for entrance into the Navy and the Coast Guard, but the fact that Negroes constitute a disproportionately small part of the total strength of each of these branches of service

(4.4 and 4.2 percent, respectively) may indicate the existence of discrimination in recruiting practices.

Within the services, studies made within the last year disclose that actual experience has been out of keeping with the declarations of policy on discrimination. In the Army, less than one Negro in 70 is commissioned, while there is one white officer for approximately every seven white enlisted men. In the Navy, there are only two Negro officers in a ratio of less than one to 10,000 Negro enlisted men; there are 58,571 white officers, or one for every seven enlisted whites. The Marine Corps has 7,798 officers, none of whom is a Negro, though there are 2,190 Negro enlisted men. Out of 2,981 Coast Guard officers, one is a Negro; there are 910 Negro enlisted men. The ratio of white Coast Guard commissioned to enlisted personnel is approximately one to six.

Similarly, in the enlisted grades, there is an exceedingly high concentration of Negroes in the lowest ratings, particularly in the Navy, Marine Corps, and Coast Guard. Almost 80 percent of the Negro sailors are serving as cooks, stewards, and steward's mates; less than two percent of the whites are assigned to duty in the same capacity. Almost 15 percent of all white enlisted marines are in the three highest grades; less than 2 1/2 percent of the Negro marines fall in the same category. The disparities in the Coast Guard are similarly great. The difference in the Army is somewhat smaller, but still significant: Less than nine percent of the Negro personnel are in the first three grades, while almost 16 percent of the whites hold these ranks. …

B. Executive Order 9981

WHEREAS it is essential that there be maintained in the armed services of the United States the highest standards of democracy, with equality of treatment and opportunity for all those who serve in our country's defense:

NOW THEREFORE, by virtue of the authority vested in me as President of the United States, by the Constitution and the statutes of the United States, and as Commander in Chief of the armed services, it is hereby ordered as follows:

1. It is hereby declared to be the policy of the President that there shall be equality of treatment and opportunity for all persons in the armed services without regard to race, color, religion or national origin. This policy shall be put into effect as rapidly as possible, having due regard to the time required to effectuate any necessary changes without impairing efficiency or morale.

2. There shall be created in the National Military Establishment an advisory committee to be known as the President's Committee on Equality of Treatment and Opportunity in the Armed Services, which shall be composed of seven members to be designated by the President.

3. The Committee is authorized on behalf of the President to examine into the rules, procedures and practices of the Armed Services in order to determine in what respect such rules, procedures and practices may be altered or improved with a view to carrying out the policy of this order. The Committee shall confer and advise the Secretary of Defense, the Secretary of the Army, the Secretary of the Navy, and the Secretary of the Air Force, and shall make such recommendations to the President and to said Secretaries as in the judgment of the Committee will effectuate the hereof.

4. All executive departments and agencies of the Federal Government are authorized and directed to cooperate with the Committee in its work, and to furnish the Committee such information or the services of such persons as the Committee may require in the performance of its duties.

5. When requested by the Committee to do so, persons in the armed services or in any of the executive departments and agencies of the Federal Government shall testify before the Committee and shall make available for use of the Committee such documents and other information as the Committee may require.

6. The Committee shall continue to exist until such time as the President shall terminate its existence by Executive order.

7.8

'WE REAL COOL'
Gwendolyn Brooks

Chicago poet Gwendolyn Brooks was the first African American to win a Pulitzer Prize with her 1949 collection *Annie Allen*. A native of Topeka, Kansas, she moved to Chicago's black South Side as a child and spent her entire life there. Encouraged by James Weldon Johnson and Langston Hughes, she had been published in the *Chicago Defender* by age 16 and by 1934 had published nearly 100 poems in the paper. Brooks released her first book of poetry, *A Street in Bronzeville*, in 1945 to wide critical acclaim. *Annie Allen* was her second work, for which she would win the 1950 Pulitzer. But her best-known work comes not from those volumes, but instead from a collection published in 1960, including her most famous poem, "We Real Cool," an indictment of the romanticized street life of black hustlers.

Brooks won a host of honors beyond the Pulitzer. She was nominated Poet Laureate of Illinois in 1968, named a poetry consultant to the Library of Congress in the 1980s and selected as the National Endowment of Arts' Jefferson Lecturer (the NEH's highest honor) in 1994. In the late 1960s, Brooks was a leading voice in the Black Arts Movement.

A. "The Sonnet-Ballad," from *Annie Allen*

Oh mother, mother, where is happiness?
They took my lover's tallness off to war,
Left me lamenting. Now I cannot guess
What I can use an empty heart-cup for.
He won't be coming back here any more.
Some day the war will end, but, oh, I knew
When he went walking grandly out that door
That my sweet love would have to be untrue.
Would have to be untrue. Would have to court
Coquettish death, whose impudent and strange
Possessive arms and beauty (of a sort)
Can make a hard man hesitate — and change.
And he will be the one to stammer, "Yes."
Oh mother, mother, where is happiness?

B. "We Real Cool," from *The Bean Eaters*

We real cool. We
Left school. We

Lurk late. We
Strike straight. We

Sing sin. We
Thin gin. We

Jazz June. We
Die soon.

7.9

GO TELL IT ON THE MOUNTAIN
James Baldwin

James Baldwin was a product of the Harlem Renaissance. Born and raised in 1920s and 30s Harlem, much of his fiction is autobiographical and based upon the experiences of that childhood. His political essays are informed by the Renaissance's legacy of aggressive confrontation with Jim Crow and active construction of racial identity. As a teenager he was torn between a burgeoning literary career and his brief stint as a child preacher in his stepfather's storefront church. However, influenced by luminaries in New York's black literature scene, such as Richard Wright, he decided to pursue writing. By the time Baldwin left for Paris in 1948, he was a recognized essayist.

As an openly gay man, living in self-imposed exile most of his career, Baldwin's position outside of both American and African American cultural bounds seemed to grant him unusual clarity in deconstructing race and racism, sex and sexuality in both worlds. His political writings on race have often been called prophetic.

Meanwhile, Baldwin's fiction explored both race and sexuality as they influence the individual psyche more than society at large. He preferred this sort of subtle critique of racism to the angry assaults of Richard Wright's *Native Son*, which he derided in the 1949 essay "Everybody's Protest Novel," causing a bitter rift in their friendship. Baldwin's approach is perhaps best displayed in his 1953 debut novel, *Go Tell It on the Mountain*. The autobiographical story opens in Harlem on 14-year-old John's birthday, as he realizes his dual sin of homosexuality and hatred for his preacher father. John struggles with his competing desires to keep the faith in order to please his father and to strike out on a secular life. The story unfolds into a series of "prayers," in which each of his family members reveal their own original sins and struggles. Though not a book *about* race or sexuality, both, as they impact each character, permeate the story.

… John's birthday fell on a Saturday in March, in 1935. He awoke on his birthday morning with the feeling that there was menace in the air around him — that something irrevocable had occurred in him. He stared at a yellow stain on the ceiling just above his head. Roy was still smothered in the bedclothes, and his breath came and went with a small, whistling sound. There was no other sound anywhere; no one in the house was up. The neighbor's radios were all silent, and his mother hadn't yet risen to fix his father's breakfast. John wondered at his panic, then wondered about the time; and then (while the yellow stain on the ceiling slowly transformed itself into a woman's nakedness) he remembered that it was his fourteenth birthday and that he had sinned.

His first thought, nevertheless, was: "Will anyone remember?" For it had happened, once or twice, that his birthday had passed entirely unnoticed, and no one had said "Happy Birthday, Johnny," or given him anything — not even his mother.

Roy stirred again and John pushed him away, listening to the silence. On other mornings he heard his father in the bedroom behind him grunting and muttering prayers to himself as he put on his clothes; hearing, perhaps, the chatter of Sarah and the squalling of Ruth, and the radios, the clatter of pots and pans, and the voices of all the folk nearby. This morning not even the cry of a bed-spring disturbed the silence, and John seemed, therefore, to be listening to his own unspeaking doom. He could believe, almost, that he had awakened late on that great getting-up morning; that all the saved had been transformed in the twinkling of an eye, and had risen to meet Jesus in the clouds, and that he was left, with his sinful body, to be bound in hell a thousand years.

He had sinned. In spite of the saints, his mother and his father, the warnings he had heard from his earliest beginnings, he had sinned with his hands a sin that was hard to forgive. In the school lavatory, alone, thinking of the boys, older, bigger, braver, who made bets with each other as to whose urine could arch higher, he had watched in himself a transformation of which he would never dare to speak.

And the darkness of John's sin was like the darkness of the church on Saturday evenings; like the silence of the church while he was there alone, sweeping, and running water into the great bucket, and overturning the chairs, long before the saints arrived. It was like his thoughts as he moved about the tabernacle in which his life had been spent; the tabernacle that he hated, yet loved and feared. It was like Roy's curses, like the echoes of these curses raised in John: he remembered Roy, on some rare Saturday when he had come to help John clean the church, cursing in the house of God, and making obscene gestures before the eyes of Jesus. It was like all this, and it was like the walls that witnessed and the placards on the walls which testified that the wages of sin was death. The darkness of his sin was in the hardheartedness with which he resisted God's power; in the scorn that was often his while he listened to the crying, breaking voices, and watched the black skin glisten when they lifted up their arms and fell on their faces before the Lord. For he had made his decision. He would not be like his father, or his father's father. He would have another life. …

There had been a time, before John was born, when his father had also been in the field; but now, having to earn for his family their daily bread, it was seldom that he was able to travel further away than Philadelphia, and then only for a very short time. His father no longer, as he had once done, led great revival meetings, his name printed large on placards that advertised the coming of a man of God. His father had once had a mighty reputation; but all this, it seemed, had changed since he had left the South. Perhaps he ought now to have a church of his own — John wondered if his father wanted that; he ought, perhaps, to be leading, as Father James now led, a great flock to the Kingdom. But his father was only a caretaker in the house of God. He was responsible for the replacement of burnt-out light bulbs, and for the cleanliness of the church, and the care of the Bibles, and the hymn-books, and the placards on the walls. On Friday night he conducted the Young Ministers' Service and preached with them. Rarely did he bring the message on a Sunday morning; only if there was no one else to speak was his father called upon. He was kind of a fill-in speaker, a holy handyman.

Yet he was treated, so far as John could see, with great respect. No one, none of the saints in any case, had ever reproached or rebuked his father, or suggested that his life was anything but spotless. Nevertheless, this man, God's minister, had struck John's mother, and John had wanted to kill him — and wanted to kill him still.

John had swept one side of the church and the chairs were still piled in the one space before the altar when there was a knocking at the door. When he opened the door he saw that it was Elisha, come to help him.

"Praise the Lord," said Elisha, standing on the doorstep, grinning.

"Praise the Lord," said John. This was the greeting always used among the saints.

Brother Elisha came in, slamming the door behind him and stamping his feet. He had probably just come from a basketball court; his forehead was polished with recent sweat and his hair stood up. He was wearing his woolen sweater, on which was stamped the letter of his high school, and his shirt was open at the throat.

"You ain't cold like that??" John asked, staring at him.

"No, little brother, I ain't cold. You reckon everybody's frail like you?"

"It ain't only the little ones gets carried to the graveyard," John said. He felt unaccustomedly bold and lighthearted: the arrival of Elisha had caused his mood to change.

Elisha, who had started down the aisle toward the back room, turned to stare at John with astonishment and menace. "Ah," he said, "I see you fixing to be sassy with Brother Elisha tonight — I'm going to have to give you a little correction. You just wait till I wash my hands."

"Ain't no need to wash your hands if you come here to work. Just take hold of that mop and put some soap and water in the bucket."

"Lord," said Elisha, running water into the sink, and talking, it seemed, to the water, "that sure is a sassy nigger out there. I sure hope he don't get hisself hurt one of these days, running his mouth thataway. Look like he won't stop till somebody busts him in the eye."

He sighed deeply, and began to lather his hands. "Here I come running all the way so he wouldn't bust a gut lifting one of them chairs, and all he got to say is 'put some water in the bucket.' Can't do nothing with a nigger nohow." He stopped and turned to face John. "Ain't you got no manners, boy? You better learn how to talk to old folks."

"You better get out here with that mop and pail. We ain't got all night."

"Keep on," said Elisha. "I see I'm going to have to give you your lumps tonight."

He disappeared. John heard him in the toilet, and then over the thunderous water he heard him knocking things over in the back room.

"Now what you doing?"

"Boy, you leave me alone. I'm fixing to work."

"It sure sounds like it." John dropped his broom and walked into the back. Elisha had knocked over a pile of camp chairs, folded in the corner, and stood over them angrily, holding the mop in his hand.

"I keep telling you not to hide that mop back there. Can't nobody get at it."

"I always get at it. Ain't everybody as clumsy as you."

Elisha let fall the stiff gray mop and rushed at John, catching him off balance and lifting him from the floor. With both arms tightening around John's waist he tried to cut John's breath, watching him meanwhile with a smile that, as

John struggled and squirmed, became a set, ferocious grimace. With both hands John pushed and pounded against the shoulders and biceps of Elisha, and tried to thrust with his knees against Elisha's belly. Usually such a battle was soon over, since Elisha was so much bigger and stronger and as a wrestler so much more skilled; but tonight John was filled with determination not to be conquered, or at least to make the conquest dear. With all the strength that was in him he fought against Elisha, and he was filled with a strength that was almost hatred. He kicked, pounded, twisted, pushed, using his lack of size to confound and exasperate Elisha, whose damp fists joined at the small of John's back, soon slipped. It was a deadlock; he could not tighten his hold, John could not break it. And so they turned, battling in the narrow room, and the odor of Elisha's sweat was heavy in John's nostrils. He saw the veins rise on Elisha's forehead and in his neck; his breath became jagged and harsh, and the grimace on his face became more cruel; and John, watching these manifestations of power, was filled with a wild delight. They stumbled against the folding-chairs, and Elisha's foot slipped and his hold broke. They stared at each other, half grinning. John slumped to the floor, holding his head between his hands.

"I didn't hurt you none, did I?" Elisha asked.

John looked up. "Me? No, I just want to catch my breath."

Elisha went to the sink, and splashed some cold water on his face and neck. "I reckon you going to let me work now," he said.

"It wasn't *me* that stopped you in the first place." He stood up. He found that his legs were trembling. He looked at Elisha, who was drying himself on the towel. "You teach me wrestling one time, okay?"

"No, boy," Elisha said, laughing, "I don't want to wrestle with *you*. You too strong for me." And he began to run hot water in the great pail.

John walked past him to the front and picked up his broom. In a moment Elisha followed and began mopping near the door. John had finished sweeping, and he now mounted to the pulpit to dust the three thronelike chairs, purple, with white linen squares for the headpieces and for the massive arms. It dominated all, the pulpit: a wooden platform raised above the congregation, with a high stand in the center for the Bible, before which the preacher stood. There faced the congregation, flowing downward from this height, the scarlet altar cloth that bore the golden cross and legend: JESUS SAVES. The pulpit was holy. None could stand so high unless God's seal was on him.

He dusted the piano and sat down on the piano stool to wait until Elisha had finished mopping one side of the church and he could replace the chairs. Suddenly Elisha said, without looking at him:

"Boy, ain't it time you was thinking about your soul?"

"I guess so," John said with a quietness that terrified him.

"I know it looks hard," said Elisha, "from the outside, especially when you young. But you believe me, boy, you can't find no greater joy than you find in the services of the Lord."

John said nothing. He touched a black key on the piano and it made a dull sound, like a distant drum. ...

——— 7.10 ———

'SEPARATE CANNOT BE EQUAL'
Brown v. Board of Education

Throughout the NAACP's first years the organization's legal battle against Jim Crow laws had mixed success. On one hand, the group won a number of legal cases forcing southern school systems to live up to the "separate but equal" doctrine by improving their infamously neglected black schools. But, on the other hand, the NAACP had not even confronted the larger issue of reversing the *Plessy* decision. In the 1930s, Charles Houston, head of the legal team, did two things to change course. One, he recruited Howard University law student Thurgood Marshall. Two, he began challenging inequality in segregated state universities. His strategy was to force states to choose between the ridiculous expense of building universities for blacks, equal to those for whites, or integrating the existing ones.

Marshall took over the legal effort in 1939, and in the coming years began challenging segregation itself in higher education, arguing that it was impossible to create equal yet separate facilities. Then, in 1949, he accepted five grade school cases in which he directly challenged segregation. Packaged together as *Brown v. Board of Education*, the case came before the Supreme Court in December, 1953. In his briefs, Marshall employed the research of sociologist Kenneth Clark, whose studies showed black children, when presented with white and black dolls, chose the white ones and associated them with positive characteristics. In 1954, led by newly appointed Chief Justice Earl Warren, the Supreme Court ruled that "separate but equal" was not sustainable and a violation of the 14th Amendment. The ruling cited Clark's research.

A. Justice Marshall's oral argument

… JUSTICE FRANKFURTER: But the point is important whether we are to decide that the facilities are equal or whether one says that is an irrelevant question, because you cannot apply that test between white and black.

MR. MARSHALL: In this case it is irrelevant —

JUSTICE FRANKFURTER: All right.

MR. MARSHALL: (continuing) — for two reasons: one, it is not in the case because, we have agreed that equality is outside the case, and our argument is deliberately broad enough to encompass a situation regardless of facilities, and we issue about it.

JUSTICE FRANKFURTER: I understand that, but that will be a ground on which the series of cases in the McLaurin case — the point of my question is that I think we are dealing with two different legal propositions; McLaurin is one and what you are tendering to the Court is another.

MR. MARSHALL: The questions raised by this Court in June, as we understand it, requested us to find out as to whether or not class litigation and, specifically segregation, whether or not it, in and of itself, with nothing else, violated the 14th Amendment.

We addressed ourselves to that in this brief, and we are convinced that the answer is that any segregation, which is for the purpose of setting up either class or caste legislation, is in and of itself a violation of the Fourteenth Amendment, with the only proviso that normally, in normal judicial proceedings, there must be a showing of injury or what have you. That is our position and that is up —

JUSTICE REED: That is solely on the equal protection clause?

MR. MARSHALL: Solely on the equal protection clause…

JUSTICE FRANKFURTER: Your argument comes down to this: If in one of the states in which there is a large percentage of Negro voters, a preponderance, where we get a situation where X state has preponderance of Negro voters who are actually going to the polls, and actually assert their preponderance and install a Negro governor to the extent that more money is spent for Negro education, better housing, better schools, more highly paid teachers, where teachers are more attracted, better maps, better schoolbooks, better everything than the white children enjoy — and I know I am making a fantastic, if you will, assumption —

MR. MARSHALL: Yes.

JUSTICE FRANKFURTER: (continuing) — and yet there is segregation you would come here and say that they cannot do that?

MR. MARSHALL: If it is done by the state, the state has been deprived of —

JUSTICE FRANKFURTER: That is your position; that is the legal —

MR. MARSHALL: I think, Sir, that is our flat legal position, that if it involves class or caste legislation —

JUSTICE FRANKFURTER: That is the antitheses of the McLaurin and the Gaines doctrine.

MR. MARSHALL: Well, of the Gaines case, certainly so, sir, because I, for one, do not believe that the language used by Chief Justice Hughes was — I mean, just do not consider it as dictum when he said that they operated under a doctrine, the validity of which had been supported.

I think that Gaines was interpreted within the "separate but equal" doctrine.

I think Sipuel was, with the addition of "you have to do it now."

I think that Sweatt and McLaurin, if I could disagree for a moment, are moving between the two; that is the way I look at it.

FRANKFURTER: My only purpose is to try to see these things clearly without a simplifying darkness, and to try to see, it clearly. …

JUSTICE FRANKFURTER: I did not suppose that you would say that we had to open this case, that they were not equal, whether psychologically, whether buildings, whether they spent X million dollars for white, or X minus Y for the black, that does not open any doctrine?

MR. MARSHALL: No, sir; and the Delaware case, if I can go to that without going outside of the record, demonstrates a situation more so than it does in South Carolina, because in Delaware so long as the schools are unequal, okay. And then the schools are made equal, and if I understand the procedure, you move the Negroes back to the colored school, and then next year you put ten more books in the white school, and the colored school is unequal, and I do not see how that point would ever be adequately decided, and in truth and in fact, there are no two equal schools, because there are no two equal faculties in the world in any schools.

They are good as individuals, and one is better than the other, but to just — that is the trouble with the doctrine of "separate but equal"; the doctrine of "separate but equal" assumes that two things can be equal.

JUSTICE REED: There is not absolute equality, but substantially equal, in the terms of our cases.

MR. MARSHALL: Yes, sir; starting with Plessy the word "substantial" and we say in our brief — I mean we are absolutely serious about it — that the use of the word "substantial" emphasizes that those cases in truth and in fact amend the Fourteenth Amendment by saying that equal protection can be obtained in a substantially equal fashion, and there is nothing in the debates that will hint in the slightest that

they did not mean complete equality — they said so — to raise the Negro up into the status of complete equality with the other people. That is language they used.

"Substantial" is a word that was put into the Fourteenth Amendment by Plessy v. Fergusson, and I cannot find it, and it cannot be found in any place in debates. …

B. Chief Justice Warren's opinion

… In the instant cases, that question is directly presented. Here, unlike Sweatt v. Painter, there are findings below that the Negro and white schools involved have been equalized, or are being equalized, with respect to buildings, curricula, qualifications and salaries of teachers, and other "tangible" factors. Our decision, therefore, cannot turn on merely a comparison of these tangible factors in the Negro and white schools involved in each of the cases. We must look instead to the effect of segregation itself on public education.

In approaching this problem, we cannot turn the clock back to 1868 when the Amendment was adopted, or even to 1896 when Plessy v. Ferguson was written. We must consider public education in the light of its full development and its present place in American life throughout the Nation. Only in this way can it be determined if segregation in public schools deprives these plaintiffs of the equal protection of the laws.

Today, education is perhaps the most important function of state and local governments. Compulsory school attendance laws and the great expenditures for education both demonstrate our recognition of the importance of education to our democratic society. It is required in the performance of our most basic public responsibilities, even service in the armed forces. It is the very foundation of good citizenship. Today it is a principal instrument in awakening the child to cultural values, in preparing him for later professional training, and in helping him to adjust normally to his environment. In these days, it is doubtful that any child may reasonably be expected to succeed in life if he is denied the opportunity of an education. Such an opportunity, where the state has undertaken to provide it, is a right which must be made available to all on equal terms.

We come then to the question presented: Does segregation of children in public schools solely on the basis of race, even though the physical facilities and other "tangible" factors may be equal, deprive the children of the minority group of equal educational opportunities? We believe that it does.

In Sweatt v. Painter, supra, in finding that a segregated law school for Negroes could not provide them equal educational opportunities, this Court relied in large part on "those qualities which are incapable of objective measurement but which make for greatness in a law school." In McLaurin v. Oklahoma State Regents, supra, the Court, in requiring that a Negro admitted to a white graduate school be treated like all other students, again resorted to intangible considerations: "... his ability to study, to engage in discussions and exchange views with other students, and, in general, to learn his profession." Such considerations apply with added force to children in grade and high schools. To separate them from others of similar age and qualifications solely because of their race generates a feeling of inferiority as to their status in the community that may affect their hearts and minds in a way unlikely ever to be undone. The effect of this separation on their educational opportunities was well stated by a finding in the Kansas case by a court which nevertheless felt compelled to rule against the Negro plaintiffs:

"Segregation of white and colored children in public schools has a detrimental effect upon the colored children. The impact is greater when it has the sanction of the law; for the policy of separating the races is usually interpreted as denoting the inferiority of the negro group. A sense of inferiority affects the motivation of a child to learn. Segregation with the sanction of law, therefore, has a tendency to [retard] the educational and mental development of negro children and to deprive them of some of the benefits they would receive in a racial[ly] integrated school system."

Whatever may have been the extent of psychological knowledge at the time of Plessy v. Ferguson, this finding is amply supported by modern authority. Any language in Plessy v. Ferguson contrary to this finding is rejected.

We conclude that in the field of public education the doctrine of "separate but equal" has no place. Separate educational facilities are inherently unequal. Therefore, we hold that the plaintiffs and others similarly situated for whom the actions have been brought are, by reason of the segregation complained of, deprived of the equal protection of the laws guaranteed by the Fourteenth Amendment. This disposition makes unnecessary any discussion whether such segregation also violates the Due Process Clause of the Fourteenth Amendment.

――――――― 7.11 ―――――――
'THERE COMES A TIME'
Martin Luther King, Jr.

On December 1, 1955, Montgomery, Alabama police arrested a respected local civil rights activist named Rosa Parks for refusing to relinquish her seat to a white man on a segregated public bus. The Women's Political Council organized a one-day bus boycott for the day of her trial on December 5. A number of black ministers, led by Rev. E. D. Nixon, met and planned a rally for the night of the trial as well. When Parks was convicted, the organizers decided to extend the boycott. At the rally that night, 26-year-old local pastor Dr. Martin Luther King, Jr., after having about 30 minutes to prepare his remarks, addressed a crowd of thousands at Holt Street Baptist Church urging them to throw down the gauntlet and stick to the boycott. Most count the sermon as the inaugural address of a decade of nonviolent direct action that would finally sweep away Jim Crow. It was the first in a series of sermons delivered by King at weekly mass meetings during the Montgomery boycott. The sermons are credited with holding the community together in both its boycott and its commitment to nonviolence.

Despite arrests on farcical charges and violent harassment by both white citizens and police,

Montgomery's black community boycotted the buses for over a year. Ultimately, the NAACP would take Parks's case to the Supreme Court and have segregation in public transportation declared unconstitutional. And King, selected as the leader of the Montgomery Improvement Association, which was established to direct the boycott, would reach international fame as the spokesperson for the Civil Rights Movement.

King had studied the Gandhian philosophy of nonviolent resistance while in seminary school, and urged the Montgomery movement to embrace it in the face of white violence. King and Nixon's houses were bombed, and threats of further violence escalated by the day. Fellowship of Reconciliation activist Bayard Rustin, a specialist in nonviolent resistance, came to Montgomery and advised King on how to practically implement the doctrine. (While King embraced Rustin, other movement leaders eventually chased him out of Montgomery because his gay identity and association with socialist causes were deemed liabilities.) The boycotters' resolve and their nonviolent posture even when confronted with violent harassment drew international attention, catapulting the Civil Rights Movement onto the world stage. When the Supreme Court's ruling desegregating public transportation came into effect on December 20, 1956, an interracial group of ministers, led by King, boarded the Montgomery buses. Two years later King published his account of the saga, *Stride Towards Freedom*.

A. King's December 5, 1955, speech launching the prolonged boycott

My friends, we are certainly very happy to see each of you out this evening. We are here this evening for serious business. We are here in a general sense because first and foremost we are American citizens, and we are determined to apply our citizenship to the fullness of its meaning. We are here also because of our love for democracy, because of our deep-seated belief that democracy transformed from thin paper to thick action is the greatest form of government on earth.

But we are here in a specific sense because of the bus situation in Montgomery. We are here because we are determined to get the situation corrected. This situation is not at all new.

The problem has existed over endless years. For many years now, Negroes in Montgomery and so many other areas have been inflicted with the paralysis of crippling fear on buses in our community. On so many occasions, Negroes have been intimidated and humiliated and oppressed because of the sheer fact that they were Negroes. I don't have time this evening to go into the history of these numerous cases. Many of them now are lost in the thick fog of oblivion, but at least one stands before us now with glaring dimensions.

Just the other day, just last Thursday to be exact, one of the finest citizens in Montgomery — not one of the finest Negro citizens, but one of the finest citizens in Montgomery — was taken from a bus and carried to jail and arrested because she refused to get up to give her seat to a white person. Now the press would have us believe that she refused to leave a reserved section for Negroes, but I want you to know this evening that there is no reserved section. The law has never been clarified at that point. Now I think I speak with legal authority — not that I have any legal authority, but I think I speak with legal authority behind me — that the law, the ordinance, the city ordinance has never been totally clarified.

Mrs. Rosa Parks is a fine person. And, since it had to happen, I'm happy that it happened to a person like Mrs. Parks, for nobody can doubt the boundless outreach of her integrity. Nobody can doubt the height of her character, nobody can doubt the depth of her Christian commitment and devotion to the teachings of Jesus. And I'm happy, since it had to happen, it happened to a person that nobody can call a disturbing factor in the community. Mrs. Parks is a fine Christian person, unassuming, and yet there is integrity and character there. And just because she refused to get up, she was arrested.

And you know, my friends, there comes a time when people get tired of being trampled over by the iron feet of oppression. There comes a time, my friends, when people get tired of being plunged across the abyss of humiliation, where they experience the bleakness of nagging despair. There comes a time when people get tired of being pushed out of the glittering sunlight of life's July and left standing amid the piercing chill of an alpine November. There comes a time.

We are here, we are here this evening because we are tired now. And I want to say that we are not here advocating violence. We have never done that. I want it to be known throughout Montgomery and throughout this nation that we are Christian people. We believe in the Christian religion. We believe in the teachings of Jesus. The only weapon that we have in our hands this evening is the weapon of protest. That's all.

And certainly, certainly, this is the glory of America, with all of its faults. This is the glory of our democracy. If we were incarcerated behind the iron curtains of a Communistic nation, we couldn't do this. If we were dropped in the dungeon of a totalitarian regime, we couldn't do this. But the great glory of American democracy is the right to protest for right. My friends, don't let anybody make us feel that we are to be compared in our actions with the Ku Klux Klan or with the White Citizens Council. There will be no crosses burned at any bus stops in Montgomery. There will be no white persons pulled out of their homes and taken out on some distant road and lynched for not cooperating. There will be nobody among us who will stand up and defy the Constitution of this nation. We only assemble here because of our desire to see right exist. My friends, I want it to be known that we're going to work with grim and bold determination to gain justice on the buses in this city.

And we are not wrong; we are not wrong in what we are doing. If we are wrong, the Supreme Court of this nation is wrong. If we are wrong, the Constitution of the United States is wrong. If we are wrong, God Almighty is wrong. If we are wrong, Jesus of Nazareth was merely a utopian dreamer that never came down to Earth. If we are wrong, justice is a lie, love has no meaning. And we are determined here in Montgomery to work and

fight until justice runs down like water, and righteousness like a mighty stream.

I want to say that in all of our actions, we must stick together. Unity is the great need of the hour, and if we are united we can get many of the things that we not only desire but which we justly deserve. And don't let anybody frighten you. We are not afraid of what we are doing, because we are doing it within the law. There is never a time in our American democracy that we must ever think we are wrong when we protest. We reserve that right. When labor all over this nation came to see that it would be trampled over by capitalistic power, it was nothing wrong with labor getting together and organizing and protesting for its rights. We, the disinherited of this land, we who have been oppressed so long, are tired of going through the long night of captivity. And now we are reaching out for the daybreak of freedom and justice and equality.

May I say to you, my friends, as I come to a close, and just giving some idea of why we are assembled here, that we must keep — and I want to stress this, in all of our doings, in all of our deliberations here this evening and all of the week and while, — whatever we do — , we must keep God in the forefront. Let us be Christian in all of our actions. But I want to tell you this evening that it is not enough for us to talk about love, love is one of the pivotal points of the Christian faith. There is another side called justice. And justice is really love in calculation. Justice is love correcting that which revolts against love.

The Almighty God himself is not only, not the God just standing out saying through Hosea, "I love you, Israel." He's also the God that stands up before the nations and said: "Be still and know that I'm God, that if you don't obey me I will break the backbone of your power and slap you out of the orbits of your international and national relationships." Standing beside love is always justice, and we are only using the tools of justice. Not only are we using the tools of persuasion, but we've come to see that we've got to use the tools of coercion. Not only is this thing a process of education, but it is also a process of legislation.

And as we stand and sit here this evening and as we prepare ourselves for what lies ahead, let us go out with the grim and bold determination that we are going to stick together. We are going to work together. Right here in Montgomery, when the history books are written in the future, somebody will have to say, "There lived a race of people, a black people, 'fleecy locks and black complexion', a people who had the moral courage to stand up for their rights. And thereby they injected a new meaning into the veins of history and of civilization." And we're going to do that. God grant that we will do it before it is too late. As we proceed with our program, let us think of these things.

B. "The Violence of Desperate Men," from *Stride Towards Freedom*

In his autobiographical account of the Montgomery boycott, King describes the violent harassment he and his family endured and explains how it strengthened the movement.

After the "get-tough" policy failed to stop the movement the diehards became more desperate, and we waited to see what their next move would be. Almost immediately after the protest started we had begun to receive threatening telephone calls and letters. Sporadic in the beginning, they increased as time went on. By the middle of January, they had risen to thirty and forty a day.

Postcards, often signed "KKK," said simply "get out of town or else." Many misspelled and crudely written letters presented religious half-truths to prove that "God do not intend the White People and the Negro to go to gather if he did we would be the same." Others enclosed mimeographed and printed materials combining anti-Semitic and anti-Negro sentiments. One of these contained a hand-written postscript: "You niggers are getting your self in a bad place. The Bible is strong for segregation as of the jews con-cerning other races. It is even for segregation between the 12 tribes of Israel. We need and will have a Hitler to get our country straightened out." Many of the letters were unprintable catalogues of blasphemy and obscenity.

Meanwhile the telephone rang all day and most of the night. Often Coretta was alone in the house when the calls came, but the insulting voices did not spare her. Many times the person on the other end simply waited until we answered and then hung up. A large percentage of the calls had sexual themes. One woman, whose voice I soon came to recognize, telephoned day after day to hurl her sexual accusations at the Negro. Whenever I tried to answer, as I frequently did in an effort to explain our case calmly, the caller would cut me off. Occasionally, we would leave the telephone off the hook, but we could not do this for long because we never knew when an important call would come in. …

One night toward the end of January I settled into bed late, after a strenuous day. Coretta had already fallen asleep and just as I was about to doze off the telephone rang. An angry voice said, "Listen, nigger, we've taken all we want from you; before next week you'll be sorry you ever came to Montgomery." I hung up, but I couldn't sleep. It seemed that all of my fears had come down on me at once. I had reached the saturation point.

I got out of bed and began to walk the floor. Finally, I went to the kitchen and heated a pot of coffee. I was ready to give up. With my cup of coffee sitting untouched before me I tried to think of a way to move out of the picture without appearing a coward. In this state of exhaustion, when my courage had all but gone, I decided to take my problem to God. With my head in my hands, I bowed over the kitchen table and prayed aloud. The words I spoke to God that midnight are still vivid in my memory. "I am here taking a stand for what I believe is right. But now I am afraid. The people are looking to me for leadership, and if I stand before them without strength and courage, they too will falter. I am at the end of my powers. I have nothing left. I've come to the point where I can't face it alone."

At that moment I experienced the presence of the Divine as I had never experienced Him before. It seemed as though I could hear the quiet assurance of an inner voice saying: "Stand up for righteousness, stand up for truth; and God will be at your side forever." Almost at once my fears began to go. My uncertainty disappeared. I was ready to face anything.

Three nights later, on January 30, I left home a little before seven to attend our Monday evening mass at the First Baptist Church. A member of my congregation, Mrs. Mary Lucy Williams, had come to the parsonage to keep my wife company in my absence. After putting the baby to bed, Coretta and Mrs. Williams went to the living room to look at the television. About nine-thirty they heard a noise in front that sounded as though someone had thrown a brick. In a matter of seconds an explosion rocked the house. A bomb had gone off on the porch. ...

When the opposition discovered that violence could not block the protest, they resorted to mass arrests. As early as January 9, a Montgomery attorney had called the attention of the press to an old state law against boycotts. He referred to Title 14, Section 54, which provides that when two or more persons enter into a conspiracy to prevent the operation of a lawful business, without just cause of legal excuse, they shall be guilty of a misdemeanor. On February 13 the Montgomery County Grand Jury was called to determine whether Negroes who were boycotting the buses were violating this law. After about a week of deliberations, the jury, composed of seventeen whites and one Negro, found the boycott illegal and indicted more than one hundred persons. My name, of course, was on the list. ...

I left the courtroom with my wife at my side and a host of friends following. In front of the courthouse hundreds of Negroes and whites, including television cameramen and photographers, were waiting. As I waved my hand, they shouted: "God bless you," and began to sing, "We ain't gonna ride the buses no more."

Ordinarily, a person leaving a courtroom with a conviction behind him would wear a somber face. But I left with a smile. I knew that I was a convicted criminal, but I was proud of my crime. It was the crime of joining my people in a nonviolent protest against injustice. It was the crime of seeking to instill within my people a sense of dignity and self-respect. It was the crime of desiring for my people the unalienable rights of life, liberty, and the pursuit of happiness. It was above all the crime of seeking to convince my people that noncooperation with evil is just as much a moral duty as is cooperation with good.

So ended another effort to halt the protest. Instead of stopping the movement, the opposition's tactics had only served to give it greater momentum, and to draw us closer together. What the opposition failed to see was that our mutual sufferings had wrapped us all in a single garment of destiny. What happened to one happened to all.

On that cloudy afternoon in March, Judge Carter had convicted more than Martin Luther King, Jr., Case No. 7399; he had convicted every Negro in Montgomery. It is no wonder that the movement couldn't be stopped. Its links were too well bound together in a powerfully effective chain. There is amazing power in unity. When there is true unity, every effort to disunite only serves to strengthen the unity. This is what the opposition failed to see.

The members of the opposition have also revealed that they did not know the Negroes with whom they were dealing. They thought they were dealing with a group who could be cajoled or forced to do whatever the white man wanted them to do. They were not aware that they were dealing with Negroes who had been freed from fear. And so every move they made proved to be a mistake. It could not be otherwise, because their methods were geared to the "old Negro," and they were dealing with a "new Negro."

—————— 7.12 ——————
'MAYBELLENE'
Chuck Berry

Chuck Berry started playing guitar at age 14, while growing up in a middle class black neighborhood of St. Louis.
In and out of trouble as a rambunctious teen, he finally
started to play professionally in 1952 with a group led by
his friend Johnnie Johnson. The group was the house band
at an East St. Louis club, playing primarily blues. But
Berry mixed in some tongue-in-cheek hillbilly numbers,
and drew large crowds. Three years later, he traveled to
Chicago, where he met his idol Muddy Waters. Waters connected him with Chess Records, and that same year he
recorded his first single, "Maybellene." The tune hit number one on *Billboard*'s R&B charts and eventually sold over
a million records. Berry would wow audiences with his
popular rebellious teen anthems for the next two decades.
Countless rock and roll legends have since credited him as
their inspiration and the father of the musical genre.

As I was motivatin' over the hill
I saw Maybellene in a coup de ville.
A Cadillac a-rollin' on the open road,
nothin' will outrun my V8 Ford.
The Cadillac doin' 'bout ninety-five,
she's bumper to bumber rollin' side by side.

Maybellene, why can't you be true?
Oh Maybellene, why can't you be true?
You've started back doing the things you
        used to do.

Pink in the mirror on top of the hill,
it's just like swallowin' up a medicine pill.
First thing I saw that Cadillac grille
doin' a hundred and ten gallopin' over that hill.
Offhill curve, a downhill stretch,
me and that Cadillac neck by neck.

Maybellene, why can't you be true?
Oh Maybellene, why can't you be true?
You've started back doing the things you
        used to do.

The Cadillac pulled up ahead of the Ford,
the Ford got hot and wouldn't do no more.

It then got cloudy and it started to rain,
I tooted my horn for a passin' lead
the rain water blowin' all under my hood,
I knew that was doin' my motor good.

Maybellene, why can't you be true?
Oh Maybellene, why can't you be true?
You've started back doing the things you
        used to do.

The motor cooled down, the heat went down
and that's when I heard that highway sound.
The Cadillac a-sittin' like a ton of lead
a hundred and ten a half a mile ahead.
The Cadillac lookin' like it's sittin' still
and I caught Maybellene at the top of the hill.

Maybellene, why can't you be true?
Oh Maybellene, why can't you be true?
You've started back doing the things you
        used to do.

—————— 7.13 ——————
A RAISIN IN THE SUN
Lorraine Hansberry

Lorraine Hansberry's brief career provided one of American
history's most memorable plays. Hansberry grew up in a
prominent black family in Chicago, where as a child she
met luminaries such as Paul Robeson and Langston
Hughes. After high school and a brief stint in college, she
moved to New York City. There she married a white song-
writer and worked for Robeson's radical journal *Freedom*
while working on her play. In 1957 she opened *A Raisin in
the Sun*, the story of a struggling black family in Chicago
that integrates a white neighborhood. After the father's
death, the family faces hard times and tough decisions
about what to do with his life insurance money. Eventually,
they decide to buy a house in a white neighborhood, and
the son, Walter Lee, soon faces a moral dilemma when
whites try to pay him off to keep the family from moving
in. Ultimately, he opts to save his family's dignity and
rejects the offer. Audiences and critics alike loved the play,
and Hansberry became the first African American to win
the New York Drama Critics' Circle Award for best play of
the year. She used her fame to advocate for civil rights and
women's rights and to oppose colonialism in Africa.

Hansberry's career all-but ended with *Raisin in the Sun*. She wrote another play, but it flopped, closing on the night she died of cancer at a mere 34 years old. Through Hansberry's correspondence with the lesbian publication *The Ladder*, historians have since learned that she privately identified as a lesbian and articulated the need for rights for gay women.

… MAMA Where you been, son?

WALTER (Breathing hard) Made a call.

MAMA To who, son?

WALTER To The Man. (He heads for his room)

MAMA What man, baby?

WALTER (Stops in the door) The Man, Mama. Don't you know who The Man is?

RUTH Walter Lee?

WALTER The Man. Like the guys in the streets say — The Man. Captain Boss — Mistuh Charley... Old Cap'n Please Mr. Bossman...

BENEATHA (Suddenly) Lindner!

WALTER That's right! That's good. I told him to come right over.

BENEATHA (Fiercely, understanding) For what? What do you want to see him for!

WALTER (Looking at his sister) We going to do business with him.

MAMA What you talking 'bout, son?

WALTER Talking 'bout life, Mama. YOU all always telling me to see life like it is. Well — I laid in there on my back today — and I figured it out. Life just like it is. Who gets and who don't get. (He sits down with his coat on and laughs) Mama, you know it's all divided up. Life is. Sure enough. Between the takers and the "tooken." (He laughs) I've figured it out finally. (He looks around at them) Yeah. Some of us always getting "tooken." (He laughs) People like Willy Harris, they don't never get "tooken." And you know why the rest of us do? 'Cause we all mixed up. Mixed up bad. We get to looking 'round for the right and the wrong; and we worry about it and cry about it and stay up nights trying to figure out 'bout the wrong and the right of things all the time. … And all the time, man, them takers is

out there operating, just taking and taking. Willy Harris? Shoot — Willy Harris don't even count. He don't even count in the big scheme of things. But I'll say one thing for old Willy Harris ... he's taught me something. He's taught me to keep my eye on what counts in this world. Yeah — (Shouting out a little) Thanks, Willy.

RUTH What did you call that man for, Walter Lee?

WALTER Called him to tell him to come on over to the show. Gonna put on a show for the man. Just what he wants to see. You see, Mama, the man came here today and he told us that them people out there where you want us to move — well they so upset they willing to pay us not to move! (He laughs again) And — and oh, Mama — you would of been proud of the way me and Ruth and Bennie acted. We told him to get out. ... Lord have mercy! We told the man to get out! Oh, we was some proud folks this afternoon, yeah. (He lights a cigarette) We were still full of that old-time stuff —

RUTH (Coming toward him slowly) You talking 'bout taking them peoples money to keep us from moving in that house?

WALTER I ain't just talking 'bout it, baby — I'm telling you that's what's going to happen!

BENEATHA Oh, God! Where is the bottom! Where is the real honest-to-God bottom so he can't go any farther!

WALTER See — that's the old stuff. You and that boy that was here today. You all want everybody to carry a flag and a spear and sing some marching songs, huh? You wanna spend your life looking into things and trying to find the right and the wrong part, huh? Yeah. You know what's going to happen to that boy someday — he'll find himself sitting in a dungeon, locked in forever — and the takers will have the key! Forget it, baby! There ain't no causes — there ain't nothing but taking in this world, and he who takes most is smartest — and it don't make a damn bit of difference how.

MAMA You making something inside me cry, son. Some awful pain inside me.

WALTER Don't cry, Mama. Understand. That

white man is going to walk in that door able to write checks for more money than we ever had. It's important to him and I'm going to help him — I'm going to put on the show, Mama.

MAMA Son — I come from five generations of people who was slaves and sharecroppers — but ain't nobody in my family never let nobody pay 'em no money that was a way of telling us we wasn't fit to walk the earth. We ain't never been that poor. (Raising her eyes and looking at him) We ain't never been that — dead inside.

BENEATHA Well — we are dead now. All the talk about dreams and sunlight that goes on in this house. It's all, dead now.

WALTER What's the matter with you all? I didn't make this world! It was give to me this way! Hell, yes, I want me some yachts someday! Yes, I want to hang some real pearls 'round my wife's neck. Ain't she supposed to wear no pearls? Somebody tell me — tell me, who decides which women is suppose to wear pearls in this world. I tell you I am a man — and I think my wife should wear some pearls in this world! (This last line hangs a good while and WAL-TER begins to move about the room. The word "Man" has penetrated his consciousness; he mumbles it to himself repeatedly between strange agitated pauses as he moves about)

MAMA Baby, how you going to feel on the inside?

WALTER Fine! ... Going to feel fine... a man...

MAMA You won't have nothing left then, Walter Lee. ...

TRAVIS Grandmama — the moving men are downstairs! The truck just pulled up.

MAMA (Turning and looking at him) Are they, baby? They downstairs?

(She sighs and sits. LINDNER appears in the doorway. He peers in and knocks lightly, to gain attention, and comes in. All turn to look at him)

LINDNER (Hat and briefcase in hand) Uh-hello ... (RUTH crosses mechanically to the bedroom door and opens it and lets it swing open freely and slowly as the lights come up on WALTER within, still in his coat, sitting at the far corner of the room. He looks up and out through the room to LINDNER)

RUTH He's here.

(A long minute passes and WALTER slowly gets up)

LINDNER (Coming to the table with efficiency, putting his briefcase on the table and starting to unfold papers and unscrew fountain pens) Well, I certainly was glad to hear from you people. (WALTER has begun the trek out of the room, slowly and awkwardly, rather like a small boy, passing the back of his sleeve across his mouth from time to time) Life can really be so much simpler than people let it be most of the time. Well — with whom do I negotiate? You, Mrs. Younger, or your son here? (MAMA sits with her hands folded on her lap and her eyes closed as WALTER advances. TRAVIS goes closer to LINDNER and looks at the papers curiously) Just some official papers, sonny.

RUTH Travis, you go downstairs —

MAMA (Opening her eyes and looking into WALTER's) No. Travis, you stay right here. And you make him understand what you doing, Walter Lee. You teach him good. Like Willy Harris taught you. You show where our five generations done come to. (WALTER looks from her to the boy, who grins at him innocently) Go ahead, son — (She folds her hands and closes her eyes) Go ahead.

WALTER (At last crosses to LINDNER, who is reviewing the contract) Well, Mr. Lindner. (BENEATHA turns away) We called you — (There is a profound, simple groping quality in his speech) — because, well, me and my family (He looks around and shifts from one foot to the other) Well — we are very plain people...

LINDNER Yes —

WALTER I mean — I have worked as a chauffeur most of my life-and my wife here, she does domestic work in people's kitchens. So does my mother. I mean — we are plain people.

LINDNER Yes, Mr. Younger.

WALTER (Really like a small boy, looking down at his shoes and then up at the man)

And-uh-well, my father, well, he was a laborer most of his life —

LINDNER (Absolutely confused) Uh, yes — yes, I understand. (He turns back to the contract)

WALTER (A beat, staring at him) And my father (With sudden intensity) My father almost beat a man to death once because this man called him a bad name or something, you know what I mean?

LINDNER (Looking up, frozen) No, no, um afraid I don't —

WALTER (A beat. The tension hangs; then WALTER steps back from it) Yeah. Well — what I mean is that we come from people who had a lot of pride. I mean — we are very proud people. And that's my sister over there and she's going to be a doctor-and we are very proud —

LINDNER Well — I am sure that is very nice, but —

WALTER What I am telling you is that we called you over here to tell you that we are very proud and that this ... (Signaling to TRAVIS) Travis, come here. (TRAVIS crosses and WALTER draws him before him facing the man) This is my son, and he makes the sixth generation our family in this country. And we have all thought about your offer —

LINDNER Well, good... good —

WALTER And we have decided to move into our house because my father — my father — he earned it for us brick by brick. (MAMA has her eyes closed and is rocking back and forth as though she were in church, with her head nodding the Amen yes) We don't want to make no trouble for nobody or fight no causes, and we will try to be good neighbors. And that's all we got to say about that. (He looks the man absolutely in the eyes) We don't want your money. (He turns and walks away) ...

——— 7.14 ———

'I stand upon the Fifth Amendment'
Paul Robeson

As the Cold War heated up, Paul Robeson's outspoken distaste for American inequality and love of the Soviet Union put him at the center of the period's anti-Communist "Red Scare." He was not a member of the Communist Party of America, but was closely affiliated with it. The Federal Bureau of Investigation had been monitoring him for years by the time he made his infamous remarks at the 1949 World Peace Conference in Paris. There, he called it "unthinkable" that African Americans would fight in a war against the Soviet Union, given the difference between how the American and Soviet societies treated blacks. His remarks not only angered his detractors, but put off his supporters in the Civil Rights Movement as well — who were increasingly skittish about links to the Communist Party. That year a mob stormed one of his performances in Peekskill, New York. The State Department repealed his passport and barred him from international travel. Record companies, television producers and movie executives blackballed him. And finally, in 1956, the House Committee on Un-American Activities summoned him to testify.

Robeson was recalcitrant and combative in his testimony. He refused to answer whether or not he was a Communist Party member, refused to name any members he knew, refused to relent on his vocal praise for the Soviet Union and launched his own critique of American racial injustice. Robeson's career never recovered, and he remained largely isolated from black leaders and the entertainment industry for the remainder of his life.

A. Robeson's testimony before the House Committee on Un-American Activities

... Robeson: Just a minute. Do I have the privilege of asking whom I am addressing and who is addressing me?

Arens: I am Richard Arens.

Robeson: What is your position?

Arens: I am Director of the Staff.

Robeson: I see.

Arens: Of the Committee on Un-American

Activities. You are appearing today in response to a subpoena served upon you by this committee?

Robeson: Oh, yes.

Arens: The subpoena which requires your presence here today contains a provision commanding you to produce certain documents including all the U.S. passports issued to you for travel outside the continental limits of the U.S. Do you have these documents?

Robeson: No. There are several in existence, but I have moved several times in the last year, and I just moved recently to Jumel Terrace and I could not put my hands on them. They probably could be produced. And I also lived in Connecticut and we have got a lot of stuff still packed, and if they are unpacked I will be glad to send them to you.

Arens: Now, during the course of the process in which you were applying for this passport, in July 1954, were you requested to submit a non-Communist affidavit?

Robeson: We had a long discussion with my counsel who is in the room, Mr. Boudin, with the State Department, about just such an affidavit and I was very precise not only in the application but with the State Department headed by Mr. Henderson and Mr. McLeod, that under no conditions would I think of signing any such affidavit, that it is a complete contradiction of the rights of American citizens. It is my own feeling that when this gets to the Supreme Court, that it is unthinkable that now this has been applied to any American who wants a passport.

Arens: Did you comply with the requests?

Robeson: I certainly did not and I will not. That is perfectly clear.

Arens: Are you now a member of the Communist Party?

Robeson: Oh please, please, please.

Scherer: Please answer, will you, Mr. Robeson?

Robeson: What is the Communist Party? What do you mean by that?

Scherer: I ask that you direct the witness to answer the question.

Robeson: What do you mean by the Communist Party? As far as I know it is a legal party like the Republican Party and the Democratic Party. Do you mean — which, belonging to a Party of Communists or belonging to a party of people who have sacrificed for my people and for all Americans and workers, that they can live in dignity? Do you mean that Party?

Arens: Are you now a member of the Communist Party?

Robeson: Would you like to come to the ballot box when I vote and take out the ballot and see?

Arens: Mr. Chairman, I respectfully suggest that the witness be ordered and directed to answer that question.

Chairman: You are directed to answer the question.

Robeson: I stand upon the Fifth Amendment. …

Arens: Do you honestly apprehend that if you told this committee truthfully whether you are presently —

Robeson: I have no desire to consider anything. I invoke the Fifth Amendment and it is none of your business what I would like to do, and I invoke the Fifth Amendment, and forget it.

Arens: I respectfully suggest the witness be ordered and directed to answer the question as to whether or not he honestly apprehends that if he gave us a truthful answer to this last principal question he would be supplying information which might be used against him in a criminal proceeding.

Chairman: You are directed to answer that question, Mr. Robeson.

Robeson: Gentlemen, in the first place, wherever I have been in the world, and I have been many places, Scandinavia, England and many places, the first to die in the struggle against Fascism were the Communists and I laid many wreaths upon the graves of Communists. It is not criminal and the Fifth Amendment has nothing to do with criminality. The Chief Justice of the Supreme Court Warren, has been very clear on that in many speeches that the Fifth Amendment does not have anything to do with the inference of criminality. I invoke the Fifth Amendment. …

Robeson: I would say that in Russia I felt for the first time like a full human being, and no color prejudice like in Mississippi and no color prejudice like in Washington and it was the first time I felt like a human being, where I did not feel the pressure of color as I feel in this committee today.

Scherer: Why did you not stay in Russia?

Robeson: Because my father was a slave, and my people died to build this country and I am going to stay here and have a part of it just like you. And no fascist-minded people will drive me from it. Is that clear? ...

Scherer: The reason you are here is because you are promoting the Communist cause in this country.

Robeson: I am here because I am opposing the neo-fascist cause which I see arising in these committees. You are like the Alien and Sedition Act, and Jefferson could be sitting here, and Frederick Douglass could be sitting here, and Eugene Debs could be here.

Arens: ... Now I would invite your attention, if you please, to the Daily Worker of June 29, 1949, with reference to a get-together with you and Ben Davis. Do you know Ben Davis?

Robeson: One of my dearest friends, one of the finest Americans you can imagine, born of a fine family, who went to Amherst and is a great man.

Chairman: The answer is yes.

Robeson: And a very great friend and nothing could make me prouder than to know him.

Chairman: That answers the question.

Arens: Did I understand you to laud his patriotism?

Robeson: I say that he is as patriotic an American as there can be. and you gentlemen belong to the Alien and Sedition Acts, and you are the non-patriots, and you are the un-Americans and you ought to be ashamed of yourselves.

Chairman: Now just a minute, the hearing is now adjourned.

Robeson: I should think it would be.

Chairman: I have endured all of this that I can.

Robeson: Can I read my statement?

Chairman: You cannot read that stuff. The meeting is adjourned.

Robeson: I think it should be and you should adjourn this forever, that is what I would say.

B. Robeson's undelivered statement on appearing before the committee, which he was not allowed to read

It is a sad and bitter commentary on the state of civil liberties in America that the very forces of reaction, typified by Representative Francis Walter and his Senate counterparts, who have denied me access to the lecture podium, the concert hall, the opera house, and the dramatic stage, now have me before a committee of inquisition in order to hear what I have to say. It is obvious that those who are trying to gag me here and abroad will scarcely grant me the freedom to express myself fully in a hearing controlled by them.

It would be more fitting for me to question Walter, Eastland and Dulles than for them to question me, for it is they who should be called to account for their conduct, not I. Why does Walter not investigate the truly "un-American" activities of Eastland and his gang, to whom the Constitution is a scrap of paper when invoked by the Negro people and to whom defiance of the Supreme Court is a racial duty? And how can Eastland pretend concern over the internal security of our country while he supports the most brutal assaults on fifteen million Americans by the white citizens councils and the Klu Klux Klan? When will Dulles explain his reckless, irresponsible "brink of war" policy by which the world might have been destroyed.

And specifically, why is Dulles afraid to let me have a passport, to let me travel abroad to sing, to act, to speak my mind? This question has been partially answered by State Department lawyers who have asserted in court that the State Department claims the right to deny me a passport because of what they called my "recognized status as a spokesman for large sections of Negro Americans" and because I have "been for years extremely active in behalf of independence of colonial peoples of Africa." The State Department has also based its denial of a passport to me on the fact that I sent a message of greeting to the Bandung Conference, convened by Nehru, Sukarno and other great leaders of the colored peoples of the world. Principally, however, Dulles objects to speeches I have made abroad against the oppression suffered by my people in the United States.

I am proud that those statements can be made about me. It is my firm intention to continue to speak out against injustices to the Negro people, and I shall continue to do all within my power in behalf of independence of colonial peoples of Africa. It is for Dulles to explain why a Negro who opposes colonialism and supports the aspirations of Negro Americans should for those reasons be denied a passport.

My fight for a passport is a struggle for freedom — freedom to travel, freedom to earn a livelihood, freedom to speak, freedom to express myself artistically and culturally. I have been denied these freedoms because Dulles, Eastland, Walter and their ilk oppose my views on colonial liberation, my resistance to oppression of Negro Americans, and my burning desire for peace with all nations. But these are views which I shall proclaim whenever given the opportunity, whether before this committee or any other body. ...

──── 7.15 ────
'GIVE US THE BALLOT'
Martin Luther King, Jr.

Following the Montgomery movement, King and the southern ministers around him sought to capitalize on the moment, and created an organization through which they could further push their civil rights goals. Teamed with northern activists Bayard Rustin, Ella Baker and Stanley Levinson, they called for a conference in Atlanta on nonviolent direct action in opposition to segregation. From that gathering the Southern Christian Leadership Conference was born. King was elected president, and his activism for the remainder of his life would stem from that office. The ministers set up an Atlanta office and planned the Prayer Pilgrimage for Freedom in

Washington, D.C. The rally was designed to pressure Eisenhower into more actively enforcing the 1954 *Brown* decision and defending African Americans' right to vote. Rustin, Baker and Levinson organized the affair, bringing in a host of prominent black leaders to speak, along with singers such as Mahalia Jackson and Harry Belafonte to entertain. On May 17, 1957, the three-year anniversary of the *Brown* decision, an estimated 20,000 people (a lower turnout than they hoped for) gathered in front of the Lincoln Memorial. King gave the keynote address.

Mr. Chairman, distinguished platform associates, fellow Americans. Three years ago the Supreme Court of this nation rendered in simple, eloquent, and unequivocal language a decision which will long be stenciled on the mental sheets of succeeding generations. For all men of goodwill, this May seventeenth decision came as a joyous daybreak to end the long night of human captivity. It came as a great beacon light of hope to millions of disinherited people throughout the world who had dared only to dream of freedom.

Unfortunately, this noble and sublime decision has not gone without opposition. This opposition has often risen to ominous proportions. Many states have risen up in open defiance. The legislative halls of the South ring loud with such words as "interposition" and "nullification."

But even more, all types of conniving methods are still being used to prevent Negroes from becoming registered voters. The denial of this sacred right is a tragic betrayal of the highest mandates of our democratic tradition. And so our most urgent request to the president of the United States and every member of Congress is to give us the right to vote.

Give us the ballot, and we will no longer have to worry the federal government about our basic rights.

Give us the ballot, and we will no longer plead to the federal government for passage of an anti-lynching law; we will by the power of our vote write the law on the statute books of the South and bring an end to the dastardly acts of the hooded perpetrators of violence.

Give us the ballot, and we will transform the salient misdeeds of bloodthirsty mobs into the calculated good deeds of orderly citizens.

Give us the ballot, and we will fill our legislative halls with men of goodwill and send to the sacred halls of Congress men who will not sign a "Southern Manifesto" because of their devotion to the manifesto of justice.

Give us the ballot, and we will place judges on the benches of the South who will do justly and love mercy, and we will place at the head of the southern states governors who will — who have felt not only the tang of the human, but the glow of the Divine.

Give us the ballot, and we will quietly and nonviolently, without rancor or bitterness, implement the Supreme Court's decision of May 17th, 1954.

In this juncture of our nation's history, there is an urgent need for dedicated and courageous leadership. If we are to solve the problems ahead and make racial justice a reality, this leadership must be fourfold.

First, there is need for strong, aggressive leadership from the federal government. So far, only the judicial branch of the government has evinced this quality of leadership. If the executive and legislative branches of the government were as concerned about the protection of our citizenship rights as the federal courts have been, then the transition from a segregated to an integrated society would be infinitely smoother. But we so often look to Washington in vain for this concern. In the midst of the tragic breakdown of law and order, the executive branch of the government is all too silent and apathetic. In the midst of the desperate need for civil rights legislation, the legislative branch of the government is all too stagnant and hypocritical.

This dearth of positive leadership from the federal government is not confined to one particular political party. Both political parties have betrayed the cause of justice. The Democrats have betrayed it by capitulating to the prejudices and undemocratic practices of the southern Dixiecrats. The Republicans have betrayed it by capitulating to the blatant hypocrisy of right wing, reactionary northerners. These men so often have a high blood pressure of words and an anemia of deeds.

In the midst of these prevailing conditions, we come to Washington today pleading with the president and members of Congress to provide a strong, moral, and courageous leadership for a situation that cannot permanently be evaded. We come humbly to say to the men in the forefront of our government that the civil rights issue is not an ephemeral, evanescent domestic issue that can be kicked about by reactionary guardians of the status quo; it is rather an eternal moral issue which may well determine the destiny of our nation in the ideological struggle with communism. The hour is late. The clock of destiny is ticking out. We must act now, before it is too late.

A second area in which there is need for strong leadership is from the white northern liberals. There is a dire need today for a liberalism which is truly liberal. What we are witnessing today in so many northern communities is a sort of quasi-liberalism which is based on the principle of looking sympathetically at all sides. It is a liberalism so bent on seeing all sides, that it fails to become committed to either side. It is a liberalism that is so objectively analytical that it is not subjectively committed. It is a liberalism which is neither hot nor cold, but lukewarm. We call for a liberalism from the North which will be thoroughly committed to the ideal of racial justice and will not be deterred by the propaganda and subtle words of those who say: "Slow up for a while; you're pushing too fast."

A third source that we must look to for strong leadership is from the moderates of the white South. It is unfortunate that at this time the leadership of the white South stems from the close-minded reactionaries. These persons gain prominence and power by the dissemination of false ideas and by deliberately appealing to the deepest hate responses within the human mind. It is my firm belief that this close-minded, reactionary, recalcitrant group constitutes a numerical minority. There are in the white South more open-minded moderates than appears on the surface. These persons are silent today because of fear of social, political and economic reprisals. God grant that the white moderates of the South will rise up courageously, without fear, and take up the leadership in this tense period of transition.

I cannot close without stressing the urgent need for strong, courageous and intelligent leadership from the Negro community. We need a leadership that is calm and yet positive. This is no day for the rabble-rouser, whether he be Negro or white. We must realize that we are grappling with the most weighty social problem of this nation, and in grappling with such a complex problem there is no place for misguided emotionalism. We must work passionately and unrelentingly for the goal of freedom, but we must be sure that our hands are clean in the struggle. We must never struggle with falsehood, hate, or malice. We must never become bitter. I know how we feel sometime. There is the danger that those of us who have been forced so long to stand amid the tragic midnight of oppression — those of us who have been trampled over, those of us who have been kicked about — there is the danger that we will become bitter. But if we will become bitter and indulge in hate campaigns, the old, the new order which is emerging will be nothing but a duplication of the old order.

We must meet hate with love. We must meet physical force with soul force. There is still a voice crying out through the vista of time, saying: "Love your enemies, bless them that curse you, pray for them that despitefully use you." Then, and only then, can you matriculate into the university of eternal life. That same voice cries out in terms lifted to cosmic proportions: "He who lives by the sword will perish by the sword." And history is replete with the bleached bones of nations that failed to follow this command. We must follow nonviolence and love. ...

I conclude by saying that each of us must keep faith in the future. Let us not despair. Let us realize that as we struggle for justice and

freedom, we have cosmic companionship. This is the long faith of the Hebraic-Christian tradition: that God is not some Aristotelian Unmoved Mover who merely contemplates upon Himself. He is not merely a self-knowing God, but an other-loving God forever working through history for the establishment of His kingdom.

And those of us who call the name of Jesus Christ find something of an event in our Christian faith that tells us this. There is something in our faith that says to us, "Never despair; never give up; never feel that the cause of righteousness and justice is doomed." There is something in our Christian faith, at the center of it, which says to us that Good Friday may occupy the throne for a day, but ultimately it must give way to the triumphant beat of the drums of Easter. There is something in our faith that says evil may so shape events that Caesar will occupy the palace and Christ the cross, but one day that same Christ will rise up and split history into A.D. and B.C., so that even the name, the life of Caesar must be dated by his name. There is something in this universe which justifies Carlyle in saying: "No lie can live forever." There is something in this universe which justifies William Cullen Bryant in saying: "Truth crushed to earth will rise again." There is something in this universe which justifies James Russell Lowell in saying:

Truth forever on the scaffold,
Wrong forever on the throne.
Yet that scaffold sways the future,
And behind the dim unknown
Stands God, within the shadow,
Keeping watch above His own.

Go out with that faith today. Go back to your homes in the Southland to that faith, with that faith today. Go back to Philadelphia, to New York, to Detroit and Chicago with that faith today: that the universe is on our side in the struggle. Stand up for justice. Sometimes it gets hard, but it is always difficult to get out of Egypt, for the Red Sea always stands before you with discouraging dimensions. And even after you've crossed the Red Sea, you have to move through a wilderness with prodigious hilltops of evil and gigantic mountains of opposition. But I say to you this afternoon: Keep moving. Let nothing slow you up. Move on with dignity and honor and respectability.

I realize that it will cause restless nights sometime. It might cause losing a job; it will cause suffering and sacrifice. It might even cause physical death for some. But if physical death is the price that some must pay to free their children from a permanent life of psychological death, then nothing can be more Christian. Keep going today. Keep moving amid every obstacle. Keep moving amid every mountain of opposition. If you will do that with dignity, when the history books are written in the future, the historians will have to look back and say, "There lived a great people. A people with 'fleecy locks and black complexion,' but a people who injected new meaning into the veins of civilization; a people which stood up with dignity and honor and saved Western civilization in her darkest hour; a people that gave new integrity and a new dimension of love to our civilization." When that happens, "the morning stars will sing together, and the sons of God will shout for joy."

——— 7.16 ———
'THEM AIN'T LOCAL LITTLE ROCK NIGGERS'
Ted Poston

"Separate but equal" public education became a dead legal doctrine with the 1954 *Brown v. Board of Education* Supreme Court ruling, but it lived on for many years in the real lives of black and white students all over the country. Indeed, racially segregated schools remain a reality in public education decades later, in 2008. Immediately after the ruling, southern states began scheming ways to delay complying with it. The court had ordered states to integrate schools "with all deliberate speed"—an imprecise statement that many exploited. Small battles raged from state to state and school system to school system as each decided how far they'd push the boundaries of defiance.

But the most dramatic confrontation came three years after the ruling, when Arkansas Governor Orval Faubus forced what civil rights historian Taylor Branch called "the most severe test of the Constitution since the Civil War."

As the 1957 school year began, white supremacist parents in Little Rock, Arkansas, petitioned Faubus and the local courts to stop their school district's remarkably gradual integration plan—allowing less than a dozen black students to transfer into the white high school—which was set to begin that year. The parents won an injunction in local courts, but a federal judge overrode it. Unable to win in the courts, local segregationists turned to threats of violence. Two days before the school year began, Faubus shocked most observers by stepping in on the segregationists' side. On Labor Day, he ordered the Arkansas National Guard to barricade Little Rock's Central High School and prevent the nine black students who had enrolled there from entering, nominally to prevent violence. After weeks of tense negotiations, President Eisenhower federalized the Guard and sent the 101st Airborne into Little Rock to ensure the nine black students could attend school safely.

The standoff sparked a frenzy of media coverage. TV reporters pioneered live, onsite broadcasting while covering Little Rock—in an unprecedented act, CBS interrupted regular daytime programming eight times on the day the 101st Airborne arrived; NBC eight times. It became the definitive civil rights story for mainstream media, and marked the beginning of the end of the black press' ability to dominate the beat. But black reporters both in the African-American press and the mainstream press continued to offer an entirely more nuanced and human perspective of race in America. Only one mainstream reporter, for instance, bothered to meaningfully consider the nine black students at the center of the Little Rock storm. Ted Poston, an award-winning journalist who was one of the first African Americans to work in mainstream newspapers, covered the drama for the *New York Post*. Poston had been a columnist and editor for two titans of the black press—the *Pittsburgh Courier* and the *New York Amsterdam News*—before working as an advisor to President Roosevelt and, ultimately, making history by becoming a staff reporter for the *Post*. Among his many groundbreaking civil rights stories at the *Post* was a massive, 11-part series profiling each of the black families involved in Little Rock and describing the ordeal from their perspectives. While many other news reports weren't even bothering to spell the students' names correctly, Poston brought them to life as not just brave heroes but everyday teenagers.

NINE KIDS WHO DARED...
The Human Drama in Little Rock

Article I

Little Rock, Oct. 21 — Who are the nine Negro children whose historic roles here at Central High School have electrified most of America and much of the world?

How were they able to inspire President Eisenhower to write their parents, as he did last Oct. 4:

"America's heart goes out to you and your children in your present ordeal. In the course of our country's progress toward equality of opportunity, you have shown dignity and courage in circumstances which would daunt citizens of lesser faith."

What inner resources sustained Elizabeth Ann Eckford, then only 15, as she stood between a jeering mob and a hostile cordon of militia and twice tried to enter a school from which Gov. Faubus had barred her?

What deep restraint contained husky Melba Patillo, also 15, when she was struck in the face by an enraged but smaller white girl? How could she smile and murmur:

"Thank you. I'll take that too."

And what adult wit was concealed in the wry observation of Jefferson Thomas, just turned 15, that:

"President Eisenhower should have federalized the Arkansas navy also. Because Gov. Faubus may bring it steaming up the Arkansas river any day now."

I have tried to find the answers to these and related questions on this first attempt at public school integration in this outwardly placid Southern city of 125,000.

I have lived with these children and their parents, supped at their tables, worshipped at their churches and spent long hours with their mentor, Mrs. Daisy Bates, president of the Arkansas NAACP.

Who Are They?

What are these children like?

They are like teen-agers everywhere—spirited, fun-loving, uninhibited and with sharply contrasting personalities.

In temperament, they range from the genuinely shy and retiring Elizabeth to an irrepressible extrovert like Melba. From talkative Minnie Jean Brown, 16, to quiet, imitative little Gloria Ray, also just turned 15.

Then there is the highly self-confident Ernest Green, 16, who has enjoyed every moment of his tension-packed attendance at Central. He is the model for little Jefferson Thomas and Terrance Roberts, also 15, who have not had Ernest's smooth sailing in the school.

And between the extremes fall shy little Thelma Masterhead, 16, with her slanted glasses and sly humor; and even young Carlotta Walls, 14, the baby of the group.

Only casual friends last year when they attended the all-Negro Horace Mann High School and Dunbar Junior High School here, they are now boon companions and nearly inseparable.

Every morning they assemble at Ernest's house for their jeep-escorted ride to Central and greet each other as if they had been separated for years.

Laughing and joking, they ride to the school and laughing and joking they return to the Green home for a more restrained discussion of the day's happenings and for a talk with Mrs. Bates or Clarence Laws, the NAACP's Southwest regional director who was sent here from New Orleans to help the beleaguered Mrs. Bates.

Laws, at first, was a little disconcerted at the daily jollity of the group.

"When are they going to settle down and be serious about this thing?" he asked earlier. And Frank Smith, the former school teacher who is now executive secretary of the Arkansas NAACP, said:

"Don't let their horseplay fool you. Those kids are more serious about this than either you or I. They just aren't going to let it break their spirit."

And there have been many moments in which spirits—and bodies—might have been broken.

There was that mistaken moment, for instance, when Maj. Gen. Walker, commander of the 101st Airborne Division, placed members of the federalized Arkansas Guard inside the school building.

Several of the Negro children were jostled, struck and insulted as the guardsmen watched and made no attempt to aid them. School books were knocked from their arms, pencils and other small objects were thrown at them.

Jefferson and Terrance were roughed up in front of their lockers by several white students who ended their boycott of the school for just that purpose.

Gov. Faubus could not have known it, but he was closer to partial victory that day than he will probably ever be again—if victory constitutes the withdrawal of the Negro kids from Central.

For both Jefferson and Terrance decided that day that they had had enough. And they were probably not alone. Only the supreme personal confidence of Ernest and the persuasive rationalizations of Mrs. Bates restored their determination to continue.

Moments of Crisis

And even though tough-minded members of the 101st Airborne immediately replaced the negligent guardsmen inside the building, the petty persecutions continue. For there are little things that even the federal troops can't always see.

Jefferson Thomas was taking a shower after gym class the other day, for instance. One of the student segregationists slipped up to his stall and turned the hot water on full force—scalding him.

The jostling continues in the hallways whenever a trooper's back is turned. One day last week, Elizabeth Eckford got her first touch of petty violence. She was walking down the hallway between classes when suddenly a shower of

sharpened pencils rained upon her. Two pencils struck her in the back of the head, but she walked on—head high and never looking back.

School officials are aware of these minor incidents and are anxious to apprehend the very small band of wrong-doers who carry on their undercover campaign.

Repeatedly they urged the Negro students to report the incidents and identify the offencers. They promise to keep such reports secret.

But the Negro students rejected the offer.

"It's nothing we can't handle," one remarked the other day. "We'll take care of the matter our own way. And we're making more friends than enemies every day we remain in Central." ...

Contrary to the repeated contentions of the Capital White Citizens Council and the pro-segregationist Mothers League of Central High, the nine were not "handpicked" by the NAACP or anyone else.

In fact, they picked themselves—with an assist from Little Rock School Superintendent Virgil Blossom. It worked like this:

The Little Rock school board decided last May, after losing a three-year fight to the NAACP, to embark on its 11-year program of gradual desegregation (over NAACP objections). Blossom ordered Dr. L.M. Christophe, principal of Horace Mann, and Prof. Edwin Hawkins, Dunbar's head, to ascertain how many Negro students lived in the Central HS district and to inform them of their right to enroll this fall in the once all-white high school.

No rigid quota was set, but it was felt in responsible Negro circles that Blossom would be happy if not more than 20 Negro students decided to transfer.

Time of Decision

A survey revealed that more than 200 students in the two all-Negro schools were eligible, but only 60-odd expressed a desire to register at Central. The records of these three score students were assembled and each was called in for personal interviews by Christophe, Hawkins or their staffs.

"We discussed the matter seriously with each student who applied," a teacher who participated told *The Post*. "We pointed out what was involved, possible difficulties and obvious advantages in some cases.

"We told each one frankly that although we preferred 'A' students to be the first, scholarship alone was not the only factor to be considered. There was the question of character, ability to get along with other students or teachers. We pointed out that a student who had behavior problems at Dunbar or Horace Mann would undoubtedly have greater problems at Central. But no one was told flatly that he couldn't transfer."

So, among themselves and their parents, the 60-odd Negro students made their decision. When the final list was compiled, there were 10 applicants. And the 10 were notified by Blossom (who had addressed some 300 civic groups in preparing the community for the step) that they would enroll at Central in the fall. …

9 KIDS WHO DARED
Melba Patillo

Article II

Little Rock, Oct. 22—Melba Patillo is, at 15, already something of a legend at Central High School. Well, if not a legend, a myth, anyway.

And the Capital White Citizens Council and spokeswoman for the Mother's League of Central High School cite the myth as one of their principal arguments against the court-ordered integration of the once all-white high school.

"Them ain't local Little Rock Niggers they put in that school," one of the racist orators charged at a meeting. "They imported them smart niggers from somewhere up North. Why, you only have to listen to that plump one. You can see that she talks just like a damn Yankee."

Yes, the myth began with Melba's speech. Her enunciation is perfect and there is not a trace of the Southern drawl or accent.

And before the flu forced her temporary absences from Central, she was annoyed each day by an incredulous white student who accosted her every time she came into a hall.

"Is you sho you was bone down here?" he asked each time. "Now say something so these people can see you was bone up Nawth."

And when the pretty young girl would murmur, "Pardon me, I'm late for class," or "I'm sure I don't know what you're talking about," her interrogator would nod his head in confirmation to anyone present, and say: "Didn't Ah tell you so? Ain't that Yankee talk?"

Mrs. Lois Patillo, who both in face and form is an older edition of Melba, was highly amused when the myth was discussed the other night in her well-appointed home at 1121 Cross St.

Melba was up and around but still unable to return to Central. But her younger brother, Conrad, 13, a student at the Negro Dunbar HS, was still bedded with flu.

As Melba went into the music room right off the entrance lobby to put some albums on her new hi-fi set, Mrs. Patillo tried to talk above the 21-inch TV which her daughter had forgotten to turn off.

"I guess I should regard it as a compliment," she said. "You see, I teach English over at the (Negro) Jones High School in North Little Rock. I once taught French also.

"But I have never gone along with the much-publicized popularity of the Southern drawl. There is no reason why anyone shouldn't speak properly, and I've impressed this on Melba from the moment she learned to talk."

She hesitated and laughed.

"Well, if they want to say she was 'bone' in the North, they may be correct. She was born right across the river in '*North*' Little Rock, and we've lived in this corner house here for 12 of her 15 years."

And Melba yelled from the music room:

"Well, this shift to Central is making it pretty tough. Don't get me wrong: I love my new classmates. But some of the accents I have to hear over there daily makes it pretty hard to remember all you've taught me."

And then she called out:

"They can say I came here from the North. I did do that on Labor Day. We'd been way up North to Cincinnati where we spent our summer vacation."

But there was little levity later when Lois Patillo relived the ordeal of a Negro mother whose child was inside Central on the day that a mob rioted outside and radio announcers mistakenly broadcast that the Negro children were being bloodied up inside.

For Lois and Melba Patillo are unusually close, even for mother and daughter.

"We never get enough of talking to each other," the mother confided at one point. "We always seem to be like we are visiting."

So there was strain on the mother's face when Melba rather laughingly recalled that first morning when white mothers were milling in Central's hallways, taking their children out and yelling at the colored ones:

"Why don't you niggers go back to your own high school?"

It was then that a small, enraged white girl slapped Melba in the face, and the larger Negro girl smiled and said:

"Thank you, I can take that too."

Melba doesn't recall now what the girl looked like so she hasn't recognized her since among her white schoolmates. …

Because of the unusual family name, the Patillos were easily spotted in the telephone book and have been one of the main targets of the anonymous racists who ring their phone at all hours of the day and night.

"I admit that the early obscene calls used to frighten me at first," Mrs. Patillo said, "but finally I got over it."

"Now they just make me angry but even anger fades when you realize that such things are only symbolic of the ignorance of the caller."

Last week, while Melba was out of school with the flu, the phone rang and her grandmother answered.

"This is the principal of Central High School," the caller said. "You'd better come over here right away. They're killing that uppity little granddaughter of yours."

The grandparent hung up the phone without comment.

But Lois Patillo remembers most vividly that day when the racists rioted outside Central, beat and kicked Negro newspaper men and forced panicky city officials to spirit the nine Negro students out of the school.

"I had kept my portable radio on my desk over at Jones all that morning," she recalled, "and then I heard the announcer say that the Negro children were being bloodied up inside Central.

"I could just see Melba hurt or being chased down the halls all bloody and maybe fatally injured. Finally I couldn't take it any longer.

"I tried to get the rest of the day off. But my friends knew that I was planning to get into my car and drive right straight to Central to bring my child out of there. So they persuaded the principal not to let me go. I think tried to get off on sick leave—and I really was sick by that time—but they dissuaded me."

A shadow moves fleetingly across Melba's face as she recalls that day also.

"I was in class and trying to concentrate on my lesson," she said, "when I heard the crowd yelling outside. There seemed to be an animal quality in the voices. I tried to look out of the window but I couldn't see them.

"But after a while I just put it out of my mind. It didn't affect me much. I just went on with my lesson.

"But in a few minutes the assistant principal came in and took me to the principal's office where the rest of the kids were. They told us they were going to take us home. And they took us out the side door away from the mob."

Melba also recalls another bad day—that morning when members of the federalized National Guard replaced the tough members of the 101st Airborne Division who had been maintaining order inside the school's hallways.

"I was changing classes," she said, "and one of the boys came up behind me and pushed me so hard I almost fell on my face. One of the Arkansas Guardsmen was standing right there and saw it all, and he didn't do a thing but turn back as they shoved me again."

(Jefferson Thomas, 15, another of the nine Negro kids, recalls that same day that the young white hoodlums were yelling loudly: "Two, four, six, eight. We ain't going to integrate."

("But we were saying just as determinedly under our breath," Jefferson recalled, "that 'eight, six, four, two. Ten to one, we bet you do.'")

The petty persecutions continue daily, even though the 101st has again replaced the local Guardsmen in the hallways. And Melba is not at all sanguine about what will happen when the federal troops are finally withdrawn.

Asked what she thought would happen if the troops were withdrawn today, she smiled mischievously and said:

"For publication, I should say that I know that the good people of Little Rock would see that nothing happened; that we all believe in law and order; that I pray each night for those who persecute me, and that everything will be all right."

And then she stopped smiling and looked soberly at her visitor.

"If you want to know what I really think about it, it's this—they'll kill us."

But like the eight other Negro kids, Melba has not let his dreary prospect alter her teen-age life and her overweening desire to be an actress or a professional entertainer—a desire which is warmly nurtured by her mother.

"From the time she could think of things," the mother said, "we've both known that was what she wanted to do. So I saw to it that she got ballet lessons, singing lessons, music lessons, and anything she wanted in that line.

"Maybe as a mother I shouldn't say it. But you are going to be reading about this child. She's really going places."

Melba not only sings, dances and plays the piano, but she also composes. She is now waiting for a copyright on two numbers, "Teen-Age Dreams," and "Let's Make Up Or Break-Up," and hopes to record one of the songs for a Kansas City company.

Her brother, Conrad, plays the clarinet, but he has no aspirations in that direction. He wants to be a doctor.

"And he'll be a good one," says Lois Patillo. But back to Central:

Melba knows that she has made a number of casual white friends there, but none that she would call "bosom friends."

"But the first Saturday after she'd entered Central," Mrs. Patillo recalls, "one of her little white classmates called me and asked if she and her boy friends couldn't come by and drive Melba to the football game that night.

"I thanked her, but decided against it. Maybe, when things are more normal, I'll let her do it."

Melba observed:

"Most of the kids are all right. But there's a hard core out there that's really making it tough for us. It is bad enough transferring to a new school anyway, to any school. But when you have to put up with that bunch, well it's rough."

But, in spite of her apprehensions, Melba is sure of one thing.

"The only way they'll get me out of Central now," she says firmly, "is to take me out—feet first. And I intend to keep on standing on my feet."

—————— 7.17 ——————

'THROUGH NONVIOLENCE, COURAGE DISPLACES FEAR'
The Student Sit-Ins of 1960–61

As SCLC ministers deliberated how to guide the Civil Rights Movement forward at the end of the 1950s, four freshmen at the University of North Carolina A&T, an African-American school, lit a fire that changed everything. On February 1, 1960, Ezell Blair, Jr., Franklin McCain, Joseph McNeill and David Richmond (McCain's name is misspelled in some reports, including the one below), walked into F.W. Woolworth's in Greensboro, North Carolina, sat down at a segregated lunch counter, and refused to move until served. Everyone was caught off guard by the explosive act—including what was by then a large cohort of full-time civil rights reporters at major news organizations around the country. The university's intrepid student newspaper, *The Register*, was the only media to fully reconstruct that first day's events. The manager originally tried to ignore the students. But SCLC's Ella

Baker and the Congress of Racial Equality's Gordon Carey spread the word to other college campuses, and within a year there were ongoing department store sit-ins in over 100 cities around the South. For two years, black college students all over the nation protested by refusing to leave whites-only businesses, braving arrests and answering physical attacks with nonviolent resistance.

The originally spontaneous sit-in movement gave birth to the Student Nonviolent Coordinating Committee (SNCC, popularly known as "snick"). A few months after the movement began, in April 1960, Ella Baker, worried that her SCLC and other black groups weren't addressing the concerns of a radicalized black student population, organized a conference of student activists in Raleigh. There, she urged the formation of a new organization for student activists. King and other mainstream leaders thought it unwise, and urged the students to instead form a caucus within the SCLC or NAACP. In May, under the leadership of future Washington, D.C. mayor Marion Barry, the Raleigh conference activists instead officially formed SNCC, embracing King's philosophy of nonviolent direct action.

As a result of the protests, stores in one city after another agreed to integrate. Nashville businesses were the first to give in, integrating their stores following an agreement with the student activists in May, 1960. Woolworth's integrated nationally in July.

A. *The Register's* coverage of the Greensboro, N.C., sit-in

Students Hit Woolworth's For Lunch Service
Freshmen Group Stages Sitdown
Demonstration For Food in Dime Store
By Albert Rozier, Jr.

Four freshman students of this institution started Monday afternoon what they termed a "passive demand for service" at the lunch counter of a downtown five and dime store.

According to Ezell Blair, leader of the group, he and three other students—Franklin McClain, David Richmond, and Joseph McNeill—went into the store at approximately 4:30 p.m. on Monday, purchased small articles from a counter near the lunch bar and took seats at the lunch counter.

Talk with Waitress

Following is a dialogue of the initial conversation between Blair and the waitress behind the lunch counter:

Blair: "I'd like a cup of coffee, please."

Waitress: "I'm sorry. We don't serve colored here."

Blair: "I beg to disagree with you. You just finished serving me at a counter only two feet from here."

Waitress: "Negroes eat on the other end."

Blair: "What do you mean? This is a public place, isn't it? If it isn't, then why don't you sell membership cards? If you do that, then I'll understand that this is a private concern."

Waitress: "Well you won't get any service here!"

After this conversation, said Blair, the waitress left them and went to the other end of the counter.

Immediately following this conversation, however, he stated that a Negro girl, a helper on the counter, confronted them, saying, "You are stupid, ignorant! You're dumb! That's why we can't get anywhere today. You know you are supposed to eat at the other end."

Group Ignored

After this brief encounter, the students said they were completely ignored. When they asked questions, they were not answered.

"I told the waitress we'd sit there until we were served," said McNeill. She said nothing.

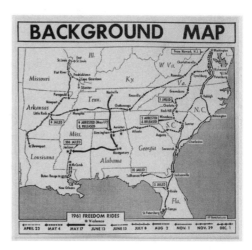

Policemen came in and stared at us and walked up and down the aisle, but said nothing to us. We figured it was an effort on their part to frighten us away, but we stayed until 5:30, when the store closed," he continued.

The group said they tried to talk to the manager of the lunch counter and when they were refused audience, asked to speak with the manager of the store, but were denied this, too. They said that during the entire time they have been there, they have not so much as seen the manager.

Others Join In

The next morning, Tuesday, February 3, a group of approximately twenty students—including the freshman initiators of the demonstration—returned and took seats at the counter.

They entered the store at 10:30 a.m. and remained throughout the day. They were not served, the waitress stating that "it's a store regulation—a custom."

Blair stated that the demonstration was originally planned for two or three weeks; but that now, "We are preparing to continue to sit for as long as is necessary—until we're served."

B. Founding resolution of SNCC

Carrying out the mandate of the Raleigh Conference to write a statement of purpose for the movement, the Temporary Student Nonviolent Coordinating Committee submits for careful consideration the following draft. We urge all local, state or regional groups to examine it closely. Each member of our movement must work diligently to understand the depths of nonviolence.

We affirm the philosophical or religious ideal of nonviolence as the foundation of our purpose, the pre-supposition of our faith, and the manner of our action. Nonviolence as it grows from Judaic-Christian traditions seeks a social order of justice permeated by love. Integration of human endeavor represents the crucial first step towards such a society.

Through nonviolence, courage displaces fear; love transforms hate. Acceptance dissipates prejudice; hope ends despair. Peace dominates war; faith reconciles doubt. Mutual regard cancels enmity. Justice for all overthrows injustice. The redemptive community supersedes systems of gross social immorality.

Love is the central motif of nonviolence. Love is the force by which God binds man to himself and man to man. Such love goes to the extreme; it remains loving and forgiving even in the midst of hostility. It matches the capacity of evil to inflict suffering with an even more enduring capacity to absorb evil, all the while persisting in love.

By appealing to conscience and standing on the moral nature of human existence, nonviolence nurtures the atmosphere in which reconciliation and justice become actual possibilities.

--------- 7.18 ---------

'WE HAVE BEEN COOLING OFF FOR 350 YEARS. IF WE COOL OFF ANY MORE, WE'LL BE IN A DEEP FREEZE'

The Freedom Rides

On May 4, 1960, an interracial group of CORE members boarded public buses in Washington, D.C. intending to ride all the way through the South to New Orleans without obeying segregation policies. They were testing a recent Supreme Court decision, *Boyton v. Virginia*, that ruled segregation in interstate travel facilities unconstitutional, and the mettle of newly elected President John Kennedy, who had professed support for the Civil Rights Movement. When they reached Alabama, the violence began. One bus was firebombed in Anniston. Another, upon arrival in Birmingham, was attacked by a mob of whites just blocks from the sheriff's department, which provided no protection. Alabama Gov. John Patterson defended the failure of duty by explaining, "You just can't guarantee the safety of a fool." Attorney General Robert Kennedy's Justice Department had to intervene and evacuate the riders.

U.S. Rep. John Lewis, a SNCC leader, refused to back down, and SNCC sent in volunteers to reinforce him and continue the ride. Upon arriving in Montgomery, the riders were attacked by hundreds of whites and viciously beaten.

Kennedy sent in federal marshals, and Gov. Patterson declared martial law. The Kennedy administration, through Martin Luther King, Jr., asked the Freedom Riders to call off the ride after Montgomery. CORE organizer James Farmer, who originally conceived of the rides, sent back the famous message, "Please tell the Attorney General that we have been cooling off for 350 years. If we cool off any more, we'll be in a deep freeze. The freedom ride will go on."

When they reached Jackson, Mississippi, the riders were peacefully arrested, owing to an arrangement between Robert Kennedy and Mississippi Senator James Eastland. The mob violence had been largely orchestrated by white leaders, in and out of government, and Eastland agreed to suppress it in Jackson if Kennedy kept his federal marshals out and allowed the riders to be arrested. Reinforcements kept showing up to continue the rides, and officials continued to put them in jail. Hundreds were sent to Mississippi jails in the summer of 1961, and that fall Kennedy's Interstate Commerce Commission issued a ruling finally outlawing segregation in interstate travel facilities.

An Associated Press reporter published the retrospective on the Freedom Rides below, along with a map detailing the routes taken by the several spin-off rides around the country, the location and numbers of arrests and the location of related violence.

Last year's freedom rides traveled a highway cobbled with blood and violence. What has come of the troubled injury? Will there be more?

Scores were injured in attempts to integrate Southern bus terminals. Hundreds were jailed. But, some nine months later, a growing number of terminals have been desegregated.

Asst. Atty. Gen. Burke Marshall said in Washington last week:

"The problem of segregation in bus and rail terminals is largely behind us as a nation and as a region. I have no doubt that where there is a problem — which, there is in a few cities in Mississippi and a few in Louisiana — we are going to resolve the problem. But I'm really quite hopeful we're going to be able to clean up the problem without litigation."

The Congress of Racial Equality (CORE), which organized the freedom rides, reports its teams have recently been served in 85 terminals across the South. These tests followed the ruling by the Interstate Commerce Commission last Nov. 1 forbidding segregation in interstate bus and rail stations.

Marshall said eight or nine committee members in Mississippi and less than eight in Louisiana have not fully complied with the order. He also said he expects desegregation of airport terminals to be aided by a federal court injunction against segregated air facilities in Montgomery, Ala. ...

The first Freedom ride occurred in April, 1947 in the wake of a Supreme Court decision forbidding segregated seating on buses in interstate travel. Eight persons were jailed and four others arrested but later released in the trip through Virginia and North Carolina.

Then on Dec. 5, 1960 the Court ruled against segregated facilities in interstate bus terminals. This decision came in the so-called Boynton Case and the freedom rides of 1961 were made to test its effectiveness.

The first ride, on April 22nd, was from East St. Louis, Ill., to Sikeston, Mo. Twenty-two persons were arrested at Sikeston but charges were dismissed (see map).

On May 4 a freedom ride bus travelling from Washington, D.C., to New Orleans was burned near Anniston, Ala.

There were riots in Birmingham, Ala., which recurred on another ride two weeks later, spreading to Montgomery. On May 20 Atty. Gen. Robert Kennedy sent 400 federal marshals to Montgomery. For a time Alabama Gov. John Patterson threatened to arrest any marshal who interfered but none was.

On May 21, a troup of Nashville students arrived in the Mississippi state capital at Jackson to test segregation. About 306 were jailed as volunteers poured into the city, including a son-in-law of New York Gov. Nelson Rockefeller.

On June 13 four rabbis, seven white and seven Negro ministers staged a freedom ride from Washington to Tallahassee, Fla. Ten were jailed in Tallahassee after they were refused service at an airport restaurant. After they were tried, the restaurant agreed to desegregate its lunch counter and was closed down by the city.

There was another ride July 8 from St. Louis to Shreveport, La., in which four persons were jailed at Little Rock, Ark.

Then, on Aug. 2, a group of freedom riders took a bus from Newark, N.J. to Little Rock. For the first time there was no violence, no arrests.

Other rides (see map) into the deep South brought renewed violence in the fall, particularly at McComb, Miss. Since the Nov. 1 ICC ruling, CORE members have been riding across the South, compiling a growing list of terminals that have desegregated.

These are all noted at New York headquarters, a musty suite of rooms near the Wall Street area.

There Farmer directs CORE's operations from his office. On the wall is a large watercolor done by a youth sentenced to a road gang as a sit-in. Also on the wall is a framed certificate of arrests from Hinds County, Miss., certifying that Farmer, not one to let others do all the work, has been an inmate there during the rides.

──────── 7.19 ────────

LOBBYING KENNEDY
NAACP

The election of President John F. Kennedy created excitement among civil rights leaders, particularly in the NAACP. Kennedy had reached out to blacks during his campaign, and the NAACP's Washington lobbying arm believed the new president would push a bill through Congress dismantling segregation. Kennedy, preoccupied with an escalating Cold War and unnerved by southern legislators, was slow to act. The NAACP, led by Roy Wilkins, chose the path of engagement. While students sat-in and southern ministers boycotted, Wilkins worked the halls of power — becoming the consummate D.C. lobbyist. In this April letter to Kennedy's civil rights advisor and liaison to the black community, Harris Wofford, Wilkins chides the administration for not yet taking up the legislative battle but praises it for "going in the right direction."

Dear Harris:

I have read with much interest your speech before the Nation Civil Liberties Clearing House on March 23rd. Since it is a very smooth (but unmistakable) elaboration of the inept message of Andy Hatcher to our District of Columbia Branch earlier, I would be more or less correct, I assume, in labeling the sentiments the "official line."

It may be that the Kennedy Administration proceeded into other fields as it did in civil rights, but I would be inclined to doubt it. I will believe until shown otherwise that in any important field, labor, agriculture, industry, finance, housing, health, the leading figures were called in and told, in one way or another, what the Administration had in mind. Whether they cooperated on all phases or on only part of them, they at least knew where they stood.

In civil rights, the information on what the Administration had in mind (I do not count too much the campaign utterances) came through columnists, "dope" stories by favorably inclined writers, hints by "those close" etc.

I may be in error, but at no time were the responsible Negro civil rights leaders called in and told formally what the Administration planned to do.

Obviously, if such a sharp departure as proposing no legislative action were in the plans, the civil rights leaders not only were entitled to be told, but to be told, in more or less precise terms, what substitute action, on what levels, the government planned.

Armed with the information, the concerned organizations could then have chosen a course. Without it, they did not feel, perhaps, that they could abandon their usual procedures. Could they tell their boards or their membership that they had switched their emphasis without being able to say what dividends the switch might produce?

I don't believe any knowledgeable person in this field, anyone with more than a year's experience, adheres to the theory of opposition for opposition's sake.

For as long as I can remember, the NAACP (commonly thought of as the opposers, the protesters) has been seeking something far beyond opposition. It was a pioneer in trying to be "in better gear with the Government." Its trademark, almost, has been "the use of the law and of government to fulfill the promise of the Constitution."

The Kennedy Administration has done with Negro citizens what it has done with a vast number of Americans: it has charmed them. It has intrigued them. Every seventy-two hours it has delighted them. On the Negro question it has smoothed Unguentine on a stinging burn even though for a moment (or for perhaps a year) it cannot do anything about a broken pelvis. It has patted a head even though it cannot bind a joint.

All this is good, not only because people like to have their immediate hurts noticed and attended to, but because the attention to them helps create a useful moral (and political) climate.

Experienced observers know that snags have developed, that changes have had to be ordered, that some obeisance to pressures has had to be made. This is politics.

The point is not so much whether we have come out thus far with all we were due (we have not), but whether the lines have been set in such a way that we cannot later recover our proper share.

It is plain why the civil rights legislative line was abandoned, but nothing was accomplished by the maneuver. It did not save the minimum wage bill from gutting and it will not save other legislation. The Southerners and their Northern satellites, Haleck, Mundt, Bennett, Saltonstall and Company, function whether a civil rights bill is proposed or withheld.

An administration gets as much by whacking them as by wooing them. JFK might as well have had a civil rights bill in the hopper; he might as well have won the Senate rules fight (he could have) so he would have a procedure open when he *does* decide to get behind a civil rights bill.

I don't suppose we have a quarrel. We do have a difference with the Kennedy Administration and perhaps that difference is rooted in the purpose of the NAACP as contrasted with the purpose of the government of all the people in a time of world crisis. We are concerned

(as much as our financial and personnel resources will permit) with Big Integration, but we must, because of the very nature of the domestic scene and of our *raison d'etre*, be concerned with Little Integration.

The Negro engineers now employed by IBM and Eastman Kodak and General Electric are a part of Big Integration, but the sore-thumb fact of 2,500,000 Negro youngsters still in segregated schools seven years after 1954 is Little Integration. So are police dog attacks in Mississippi. We do not appreciate the world stage, but we cannot omit East Texas, the citrus belt of Florida, Alabama or the state of John Bell Williams.

As I have indicated, JFK has started well and appears to be going in the right direction. I hope we can be indulged if we stick to our knitting. We may drop a stitch now and then and not match up to the border here and there and, while we must keep in mind a relationship between us and the country as a whole, we concentrate in one area. Of course, we risk a stigmatism, but wide-angle vision has its drawbacks as well.

——— 7.20 ———

HOW THE 'BLUE-EYED DEVIL' RACE WAS CREATED
Malcolm X

In 1952, a Detroit hustler named Malcolm Little left prison, where he had converted to Islam, and joined a 20-year-old black nationalist sect called the Nation of Islam (NOI). Founded in 1930 by Wali Farad, the NOI taught that Africans and people of African descent were God's chosen people. First Farad, and then his successor Elijah Muhammed, were said to be the prophets sent to lead that people out of bondage and restore them as the rulers of the world. The NOI slowly built a following in black urban areas, but never reached wide popularity until Little joined, changed his name to Malcolm X and became its prime public proponent.

Malcolm rose quickly through the ranks of the NOI. A master communicator, he went on national speaking tours and earned appointment as the minister of the important Harlem Mosque No. 7. He dismissed Christianity as an enslaving tool and scoffed at the efforts of civil rights leaders to integrate with a damned society. Black people, he argued, should follow the prophet Elijah Muhammed, learn their glorious history and return to Africa to live among their people as kings. His popularity, and that of the NOI, among young urban blacks skyrocketed. White liberals and black civil rights leaders were terrified by the way the NOI message resonated — and its success convinced many that if they did not ratchet up their movement for integration they would lose supporters to black separatist leaders. In this December, 1962 speech, "The Black Man's History," Malcolm X explains the creation story offered by the NOI as a counter to that of Christianity. In it, he describes the birth of the white race of "blue-eyed devils" and their science of "tricknology."

The only thing that puts you and me at a disadvantage is our lack of knowledge concerning history. So one of the reasons, one of the missions, one of the objectives of The Honorable Elijah Muhammad here in America is not only to teach you and me the right religions but to teach you and me history. In fact, do you know that if you and I know history we know the right religion? The only way that you can become confused, that you can become mixed up and not know which religion belongs to God, is if you don't know history. In fact, you have to know history to know something about God. …

Who is the seed of Abraham? Is it this blue-eyed, blond-haired, pale-skinned Jew? Or is it the so-called Negro — you? Who is it? And what makes it so pitiful, many of our people would rather believe that the Jews are God's Chosen People than to believe that they are God's Chosen People. They would rather believe that the Jew is better than anybody else. This is a Negro. Nobody else would put everybody else above him but the Negro. I mean the American Negro. Remember, God said that the people would be strangers. The Jews aren't strangers. The Jews know their history, the Jews know their culture, the Jews know their language; they know everything there is to know about themselves. They know how to rob you, they know how to be your landlord, they know how to be your grocer, they know how to be your lawyer, they know how to join the NAACP and become the president — right or wrong? They know how to control everything you've got. You can't say they're lost. But the poor so-called Negro, he doesn't control the NAACP, he can't control the Urban League, he can't control his own schools, he can't control his own businesses in his own community. He can't even control his own mind. He's lost and lost control of himself and gone astray. …

The so-called Negro are childlike people — you're like children. No matter how old you get, or how bold you get, or how wise you get, or how rich you get, or how educated you get, the white man still calls you what? Boy! Why, you are a child in his eyesight! And you are a child. Anytime you have to let another man set up a factory for you and you can't set up a factory for yourself, you're a child; anytime another man has to open up businesses for you and you don't know how to open up businesses for yourself and your people, you're a child; anytime another man sets up schools and you don't know how to set up your own schools, you're a child. Because a child is someone who sits around and waits for his father to do for him what he should be doing for himself, or what he's too young to do for himself, or what he is too dumb to do for himself. So the white man, knowing that here in America all the Negro has done — I hate to say it, but it's the truth — all you and I have done is build churches and let the white man build factories.

You and I build churches and let the white man build schools. You and I build churches and let the white man build up everything for himself. Then after you build the church you have to go and beg the white man for a job, and beg the white man for some education. Am I right or wrong? Do you see what I mean? It's too bad but it's true. And it's history. So it shows that these childlike people — people who would be children, following after the white man — it says in the last day that God will raise up Elijah, and Elijah's job will be to turn the hearts of these children back toward their fathers. Elijah will come and change our minds; he'll teach us something that will turn us completely around. When Elijah finds us we'll be easy to lead in the wrong direction but hard to lead in the right direction. But when Elijah gets through teaching the Lost Sheep, or the Lost People of God, he'll turn them around, he'll change their minds, he'll put a board in their back, he'll make them throw their shoulders back and stand upright like men for the first time. It says he'll turn the hearts of these children toward their fathers and the hearts of the fathers toward the children. This is something that The Honorable Elijah Muhammad is doing here in America today. You and I haven't thought in terms of our forefathers. We haven't thought of our fathers. Our fathers, brothers, are back home. Our fathers are in the East. We're running around here begging the Great White Father. You never hear of black people in this country talking or speaking or thinking in terms of connecting themselves with their own kind back home. They are trying to make contact with the white man, trying to make a connection with the white man, trying to connect, trying to make a connection with a kidnapper who brought them here, trying to make a connection with, actually, the man who enslaved them. You know that's a shame — it's pitiful — but it's true. ...

You know, I'm thankful to Allah for raising up The Honorable Elijah Muhammad and making us see these things that we could never see before. The birth of the white race has always been a secret. The Honorable Elijah Muhammad says that the birth of the white race is shrouded in the story of Adam. The story of Adam hides the birth of the white race, and because you and I have never been taught to look into a thing and analyze a thing we took the story of Adam exactly as it was. We thought that God made a man named Adam six thousand years ago. But today The Honorable Elijah Muhammad teaches us that man, Adam, was a white man; that before Adam was made the black man was already here. The white man will even tell you that, because he refers to Adam as the first one. He

refers to the Adamites as those who came from that first one. He refers to the pre-Adamites as those who were here before Adam. Right or wrong? Those people who were here before Adam. And he always refers to these people as "aborigines," which means what? BLACK FOLK!!!! You never find a white aborigine. Aborigines are called natives, and they're always dark-skinned people. You and I are aborigines. But you don't like to be called an aborigine; you want to be called an American. Aborigine actually means, "from the beginning." It's two Latin words, "ab" meaning "from"; "origine" meaning "the beginning"; and aborigine is only the term applied to those dark-skinned people who have been on this earth since the beginning of the universe. ...

Now then, where does this white man come in?

The Honorable Elijah Muhammad says that the wise black man who was a master of science never wrote his history like it is written today, of the past. The wise black man in that day wrote his history in the future. The Honorable Elijah Muhammad says that the circumference of the Earth is 24,896 miles, approximately 25,000 miles. So when he says the wise black man of the East writes history a year of every mile, he writes history to last for 25,000 years — not in the past, but in the future. He says that on this Earth there are wise black men who can tune in and tell what's going to happen in the future just as clear — they can see ahead just as clear — as they can see in the past. And every 25,000 years he says that civilization reaches its peak, or reaches its perfection. At this time the wise black man can hear a pin drop anywhere on the planet Earth. And they sit down and write history to last for 25,000 years. After this history expires they put it in a vault at the Holy City, Mecca, and write a new history. This has been going on and on and on. So, in the year one of the cycle in which we now live, he says that in the East there are twenty-four wise men. They're spoken of in the Bible as twenty-four elders or twenty-four prophets or twenty-four scientists or twenty-four imams. Twelve of them are major and twelve of them are minor. So The Honorable Elijah Muhammad says that these twenty-three men are called together by this one, which makes twenty-four. And these twenty-four, these twenty-three presided over by the twenty-fourth, are spoken of in the Book of Revelation where John said he had a vision in heaven where there was a throne, and around the throne were twenty-four seats and on the seats sat twenty-four elders. These twenty-four elders are called angels. They are actually twenty-four wise black men who live right here on this Earth, but no one knows who they are. At the end of every 25,000 years this one calls all of them into conference, and they sit down at the Holy City, Mecca, and he informs them that the history of the past 25,000 years has expired and it's time to write a new history. So these twenty-four, these scientists, begin to tune in on the population of the planet Earth and he says that back in his day — at that time there were five billion people on this Earth — all of them black, not a white man in sight — five billion people — not a white man in sight, so he says that when these twenty-four scientists begin to tune in, they look down through the wheel of time. They can tell not only what the people on this Earth are thinking, but they can tell what their children are thinking, what the unborn children's children are thinking. They can look right down through the wheel of time and tell minute-by-minute, hour-by-hour, day-by-day, week-by-week, month-by-month, year-by-year, for 25,000 years exactly what is going to take place. And they discovered that in the year 8400 to come it would register that among five billion black people, seventy percent would be satisfied and thirty percent would be dissatisfied. And out of that thirty percent would be born a wise black scientist name Yacub, and Yacub would teach among these thirty percent dissatisfied from whom he would come, and create a new race, start a new world, and a new civilization that would rule this Earth for six thousand years to come. So they brought these findings back to the king and they were put in a book. And by the way, that which is written to last 25,000 years is called the Holy Koran.

The Honorable Elijah Muhammad said that this was put into the history and then when the year 8400 came, Yacub was born. When Yucab reached the age of six years he was playing in the sand one day with two pieces of metal, two pieces of steel, at which time he discovered what is known as the law of magnetism: that unlike attracts and like repels. Two objects that are alike repel each other like two women repel each other, but man and woman attract each other. Unlike attracts and like repels. Yacub discovered this. So Yacub knew that all he had to do was make a man unlike any other man on this Earth and because he would be different he would attract all other people. Then he could teach this man a science called tricknology, which is a science of tricks and lies, and this weak man would be able to use that science to trick and rob and rule the world. So Yacub turned to his uncle and said, "When I grow up I'm going to make a man who will rule you." And Yacub's uncle said, "What can you make other than that which will cause bloodshed and wickedness in the land?" And Yacub pointed to his head and said," I know that which you know not." Yacub was born with a determined idea to make this man because it had been predicted 8400 years prior to his birth that he would be born to do this work. So he was born with this idea in him, and when his uncle realized that this was he about whom it had been prophesied his uncle submitted. The Honorable Elijah Muhammad said that Yacub went to school in the East; he studied the astronomical sciences, mathematical sciences, and the germination of man. He discovered that in the black man there are two germs. In the black man there's a brown man. In the black man, or the black germ, which is a strong germ, there's a weak germ, a brown germ. Yacub was the first one to discover this and Yacub knew that by separating that brown one from the black one, and then by grafting the brown one from the black one so that it became lighter and lighter, it would eventually reach it s lightest stage which is known as white. And when it got to that stage it would be weak, and because it was weak it would be susceptible to wickedness. And then Yacub could take that weak man that he made and teach him how to lie and rob and cheat and thereby become the ruler of all the rest of the world.

So The Honorable Elijah Muhammad teaches us that Yacub began to preach at the age of sixteen. He began to preach all over Arabia in the East. He preached among the thirty percent who were dissatisfied and got many of them to follow him. As they began to listen to Yacub's teachings and believe them, his teachings spread, his followers grew, and it created confusion in the land. So The Honorable Elijah Muhammad says that so much confusion came into existence over there that they threw Yacub's followers in jail, and as fast as they would throw them in jail they taught more people. So the teachings spread in jail. Finally Yacub was put in jail, under an alias. And one day, The Honorable Elijah Muhammad says, the thing began to get out of hand and the authorities went to the king and told him that they couldn't control these people, but that they had the leader of the people in jail right now, and the king said, "Take me to him."

And when the king went to the jail where Yacub was, he greeted Yacub with "Al-Salaam Alaikum, Mr. Yacub" — I know you're Mr. Yacub — and Yacub said, "Wa Alaikum Salaam" — I am Yacub! And the king said, "Look, I came to make an agreement with you. I know that you are the one that it is written or predicted would be on the scene in this day and would create a new race, ant there is nothing we can do to stop you. But in order for us to have peace we want to make an agreement with you. In order to stop the confusion and for there to be some peace in the land, we want you to agree to take all who will follow you and exile yourselves out on an island in the Aegean Sea."

Yacub told them, "I'll go. But you've got to give me everything that I will need to bring into existence a new civilization. You've got to give me everything I'll need. You've got to supply me with everything I need for the next twenty years." ...

The Honorable Elijah Muhammad says that Yacub took 59,999 of his followers down to the seaside, with himself making 60,000. He piled them in boats and took them out to an island in the Aegean Sea called Pelan. In the Bible it's called Patmos. When you read in the Book of Revelation where John, on the island of Patmos, heard the word of the Lord, that is Yacub. What was John doing on the island of Patmos? John was Yacub. John was out there getting ready to make a new race, he said, for the word of the Lord. What was the word of the Lord? The word was that in the year 8400 a new man would be made, a new race would be made. And when Yacub and his followers got out there his followers realized that Yacub was wiser than any man of his day, and they recognized him as a god; he was a god to them. So when you get to the place in the Bible where it says, "And God said, 'Let us make man,'" that was Yacub too, not the Supreme Being. It wasn't the Supreme Being who made the sun who said, "Let us make man." When the Supreme Being made the sun he said, "Let t here be light." He said He was supreme, He was independent, He needed no help, no associates. But when it came to making a man, that god said, "Let us make man." He didn't speak with independence, because there were two different gods. God the Supreme Being made the light. His word is "be"; that's how He makes things. But Yacub, who was lesser god, said to 59,999 of his followers, "Let us make man, let us make a man in our image, in our likeness. We're going to make a white man." It was Yacub talking: "Make him in our image and in our likeness, and give him dominion over the fowl of the air and the fish of the sea and the creatures of the land. And we'll call him Adam." It's only a name for the white man. The white man has taken mastery over the air, his airplanes rule the sky, his submarines and ships rule the sea, his armies rule the land. This was the man that was made six thousand years ago and the purpose for making him was so he could rule the world for six thousand years. That's the white man.

The Honorable Elijah Muhammad says that first thing Yacub did was to get his ministers, doctors, nurses, and cremators together. He gave them the laws because he had to set up a birth control law. He told the doctors whenever two black ones come to him to get married to stick a needle in their veins, take some blood, and go back and tell them that their blood doesn't match so that they can't marry. He also said when a black one and a brown one come, let them get married, or if two brown ones come let them get married. Then he told the nurse nine months after they're married, when you're ready to deliver their child, if it's a black child, put a needle in its brain and feed it to a wild animal or give it to the cremator. Let it be destroyed. But if it's a brown child, take that child to the mother and tell her that this is going to be a great man when he grows up because he's lighter than that the others. Tell her that the child you destroyed was an angel baby and it went up to heaven to prepare a place for her when she dies. Same old lie they tell you today — when a little baby dies he goes to the same place a man goes when he dies — right down into the ground. Is that right or wrong? So The Honorable Elijah Muhammad has taught us that Yacub right there set up his birth control law. Within two hundred years they had killed off all of the black babies on the island. Everything black on the island had been destroyed. And then Yacub only lived 150 years. But he left laws and rules and regulations behind, for his followers to go by. And after they had destroyed all of the black on the island of Pelan, they began to work on the brown germ. They saved the yellow and destroyed the brown, because you see in the black there's brown and in the brown there's yellow. Can you see how it goes? The darkest one always has a lighter one in it. So in the black man there's a brown man, in the brown man there's a yellow man, in the yellow man there's what? A white

man. Oh yes. Getting weaker all the time. So it took two hundred years to destroy the black. And then they worked on the brown for two hundred years. And in two hundred years all the brown was destroyed and all they had on the island of Pelan was a yellow or mulatto-looking civilization. And then they went to work on it and began to destroy it. So that after six hundred years of destruction on the island of Pelan, they had grafted away the black, grafted away the brown, grafted away the yellow, so that all they had left was a pale-skinned, blue-eyed, blonde-haired thing that you call a man. But actually the Bible calls him the devil. That's the devil that the Bible is talking about: old Lucifer, Satan, or the serpent. Because the lighter they got, the weaker they got. As they began to get lighter and lighter they grew weaker and weaker. Their blood became weaker, their bones became weaker, their minds became weaker, their morals became weaker. They became a wicked race; by nature wicked. Why by nature?

The Book says concerning the devil: "He was conceived in inequity and born in sin." What does this mean? At the outset the nurses had to kill the little black babies, but after a while it got so that the mother, having been brainwashed, hated that black one so much she killed it herself. Killed it herself, and saved the light one. And right on down for six hundred years. In order for the white one to come into existence, the darker one was always murdered, murdered, MURDERED! This went right in to the nature of the child that was being born. The mother wanted a light baby when the child was being conceived. This went right into the baby. The mother hated black when the child was being conceived. This went right into the baby. So that at the end of the six hundred years, after planting the seed of inequity right into the brain, right into the mind, right into the heart, right into the nature of these people, by the time they got the white man, they had someone who by nature hated everything that was darker than he was. Why, they had to murder off the black to get to the brown. They had to murder off the brown to get to the yellow. They had to murder off the black, brown, and yellow in order to get to the white. And right to this very day the white man by nature wants to murder off the black, brown, and yellow. You don't have to teach him to kill the black man. He does it for sport. He does it for kicks. He does it because it's his nature to do it. Do you understand that?

So in six hundred years now they got a devil in the scene, a blue-eyed devil, bond-haired. Oh yes, they were out here on the island of Pelan. Yacub was dead. Yacub was their father but he never saw them. They never saw him. Yacub was their god. When the Bible says no man has seen God, that's what it means. No white man has seen their god. None of them saw Yacub because Yacub only lived to be 150 years old. This doesn't mean that no man can see God the Supreme Being. Why, the Book of Revelation says when He comes every eye will see Him. So The Honorable Elijah Muhammad says after these devils got grafted — now we're not going to call them white any more. We call them what they are. White, that's their color, but devil, that's what they are. These aren't white people. You're not using the right language when you say the white man. You call it the devil. When you call him the devil you're calling him by his name — serpent; another name — snake; another name — beast. All these names are in the Bible for the white man. Another name — Pharaoh; another name — Caesar; another name — France; French; Frenchman; Englishman; American; all those are just names for the devil. ...

So, brothers and sisters, my time has expired. I just wanted to point out that the white man, a race of devils, was made six thousand years ago. This doesn't mean to tell you that this implies any kind of hate. They're just a race of devils. They were made six thousand years ago, they were made to rule for six thousand years, and their time expired in the year 1914. The only reason God didn't remove them then was because you and I were here in their clutches and God gave them an extension of time — not them an extension of time, but

they received an extension of time to give the wise men of the East the opportunity to get into this House of Bondage and "awaken" the Lost Sheep. Once the American so-called Negroes have been awakened to a knowledge of themselves and of their own God and of the white man, then they're on their own. Then it'll be left up to you and me whether we want to integrate into this wicked race or leave them and separate and go to our own. And if we integrate we'll be destroyed along with them. If we separate then we have a chance for salvation. So on then note, in the name of Allah, and His Messenger The Honorable Elijah Muhammad, I bring my talk to a close, "Al-Salaam Alaikum." With your hands outstretched in this manner, follow silently in the closing Muslim prayer: In the name of Allah, the Beneficent, the Merciful, All praise is due to Allah, the Lord of the Worlds, The Beneficent, the Merciful, Master of this Day of Judgment in which we now live, Thee do we serve and Thee do we beseech for thine aid. Guide us on the right path, The path upon which Thou hast bestowed favors, Not the path upon which Thy wrath is brought down, Nor of those who go astray after they have heard Thy teaching. Say: He Allah is one God Allah is He upon whom nothing is independent but Upon whom we all depend. He neither begets nor is He begotten and none is like Him. I bear witness there is none to be served but Allah, And I bear witness that The Honorable Elijah Muhammad is His True Servant and Last Apostle... Amen.

--------- 7.21 ---------

'I AIN'T NO ENTERTAINER, AND AIN'T TRYING TO BE ONE'

Miles Davis

Miles Davis was playing trumpet in East St. Louis clubs when he was still a teenager. In the mid-1940s, he went off to the Juilliard School of Music as a way of moving to New York City. He never graduated, spending his time playing in Harlem jazz clubs instead. In 1947, he joined

Charlie Parker's band and became a driving force in bebop jazz. Two years later, he led the first of several innovations in jazz with his *Birth of Cool* recordings. His style has been called "cool jazz" since — a restrained, fluid method marked by intricate harmonic structures and carefully controlled ensemble playing. In the late fifties, Davis again presided over a new style, when his *Kind of Blue* brought in "modal jazz"—an outgrowth of cool jazz based on a limited number of modes (or musical scales), as opposed to music marked by progressions of changing chords. *Kind of Blue* is still considered by many to be his most significant album.

As much as for his music, Davis sparked conversation for his unapologetic bad-guy persona. Critics loved to comment on his bad temper, and Davis loved to comment back. In a lengthy and revealing interview with Alex Haley, published in *Playboy* in September 1962, Davis remarks on his reputation, his thoughts on race and racism, and the music business. But, more than anything, Davis has race on his mind. No matter what Haley asks, Davis returns to the subject of what it means to be a black musician — or just a black person — in America in 1962.

Playboy: Linked with your musical renown is your reputation for bad temper and rudeness to your audiences. Would you comment?

Davis: Why is it that people just have to have so much to say about me? It bugs me because I'm not that important. Some critic that didn't have nothing else to do started this crap about I don't announce numbers, I don't look at the audience, I don't bow or talk to people, I walk off the stage, and all that.

Look, man, all I am is a trumpet player. I only can do one thing—play my horn—and that's what's at the bottom of the whole mess. I ain't no entertainer, and ain't trying to be one. I am one thing, a musician. ...

Anybody wants to believe all this crap they hear about me, it's their problem, not mine. Because, look, man, I like people. I love people! I'm not going around telling everybody that. I try to say that my way—with my horn. Look, when I was a boy, 10 years old, I got a paper route and it got bigger than I could handle because my customers liked me so much. I just delivered papers the best I could and minded my business, the same way I play my horn now. But a lot of the people I meet now make me sick.

Playboy: What types of people do you find especially irritating?

Davis: ... I'm mad every time I run into the Jim Crow scene, I don't care what form it takes. You can't hardly play anywhere you don't run into some of these cats full of prejudice. I don't know how many I've told, "Look, you want me to talk to you and you're prejudiced against me and all that. Why'n't you go on back where you're sitting and be prejudiced by yourself and leave me alone?" I have enough problems without trying to make them feel better. Then they go off and join the rest saying I'm such a big bastard.

I've got no plans of changing what I think. I don't dig people in clubs who don't pay the musicians respect. The average jazz musician today, if he's making it, is just as trained as classical musicians. You ever see anybody go up bugging the classical musicians when they are on the job and trying to work? Even in jazz— you look at the white bandleaders—if they don't want anybody messing with them when they are working, you don't hear anybody squawking. It's just if a Negro is involved that there's something wrong with him. My troubles started when I learned to play the trumpet and hadn't learned to dance.

Playboy: You feel that the complaints about you are because of your race?

Davis: I know damn well a lot of it is race. White people have certain things they expect from Negro musicians—just like they've got labels for the whole Negro race. It goes clear back to the slavery days. That was when Uncle Tomming got started because white people demanded it. Every little black child grew up seeing that getting along with white people meant grinning and acting clowns. It helped white people to feel easy about what they had done, and were doing, to Negroes, and that's carried right on over to now. You bring it down to musicians, they want you to not only play your instrument, but to entertain them, too, with grinning and dancing. ...

Playboy: Are there any particular places or clubs that you don't like to play?

Davis: … I won't play nowhere I know has the kind of audiences that you waste your breath to play for. I'm talking about them expense-account ofays that use music as a background for getting high and trying to show off to the women they brought. They ain't come to hear good music. They don't even know how to enjoy themselves. They drink too much, they get loud, they got to be seen and heard. They'll jump up and dance jigs and sing. …

I told you I ain't going to play nowhere in the South that Negroes can't come. But I ain't going to play nowhere in the North that Negroes don't come. It's one of two reasons they won't, either because they know they ain't wanted, or because they don't like the joint's regular run of music. Negroes ain't got as much money to throw away in night clubs as white people. So a club that Negroes patronize, you can figure that everybody that goes there comes expecting to hear good music. …

——— 7.22 ———

LETTER FROM A BIRMINGHAM JAIL
Martin Luther King, Jr.

In March 1963, at the urging of local pastor Rev. Fred Shuttlesworth, the SCLC launched a drive to desegregate Birmingham, Alabama's stores. The larger goal was to dramatize Jim Crow laws in the national press, thereby strengthening the NAACP's hand in conversations with President Kennedy over a suggested sweeping civil rights bill. With Andrew Young as the negotiator, and Martin Luther King, Jr. as the spokesperson, the group began a boycott designed to impact the crucial Easter buying season. Organizers planned a series of sit-ins and marches to supplement the boycott.

Birmingham had a long history of deep racial tension, and its white community reacted to the boycott with unprecedented resolve, and violence. White leaders were determined not to budge. Each day a new crop of black citizens would march towards city hall, and be arrested before they even arrived. Eventually, the city got a state court injunction against demonstrations, setting the stage for confrontation. In response to the injunction, King led a defiant Good Friday march that he hoped would lead to footage of himself being arrested on the holiday. He was not disappointed, as Police Commissioner Eugene "Bull" Connor ordered an aggressive response. King and others were roughed up and arrested. And when Young and the organizers again led a march on Easter Sunday, Connor pinned the crowd of thousands in at Kelly Ingram Park and turned fire hoses and police dogs on them. News outlets broadcast images of black children in their Easter clothes being attacked by police dogs. The violent nature of southern racism was laid bare before the nation and the world. As Young later wrote, the Birmingham movement "truly broke the back of segregation."

Earlier that weekend, local white ministers wrote to the *Birmingham News* condemning King and his movement. Appalled, King sat down in jail and, on scraps of paper and in margins of old newspaper, wrote a response — his "Letter from a Birmingham Jail."

MY DEAR FELLOW CLERGYMEN:

While confined here in the Birmingham city jail, I came across your recent statement calling my present activities "unwise and untimely." Seldom do I pause to answer criticism of my work and ideas. If I sought to answer all the criticisms that cross my desk, my secretaries would have little time for anything other than such correspondence in the course of the day, and I would have no time for constructive work. But since I feel that you are men of genuine good will and that your criticisms are sincerely set forth, I want to try to answer your statements in what I hope will be patient and reasonable terms.

I think I should indicate why I am here in Birmingham, since you have been influenced by the view which argues against "outsiders coming in." I have the honor of serving as president of the Southern Christian Leadership Conference, an organization operating in every southern state, with headquarters in Atlanta, Georgia. We have some eighty-five affiliated organizations across the South, and one of them is the Alabama Christian Movement for Human Rights. Frequently we share staff, educational and financial resources with our affiliates. Several months ago the affiliate here in Birmingham asked us to be on call to engage in a nonviolent direct-action program if such were deemed necessary. We readily consented, and when the hour came we lived up to our promise. So I, along with several members of my staff, am here because I was invited here. I am here because I have organizational ties here.

But more basically, I am in Birmingham because injustice is here. Just as the prophets of the eighth century B.C. left their villages and carried their "thus saith the Lord" far beyond the boundaries of their home towns, and just as the Apostle Paul left his village of Tarsus and carried the gospel of Jesus Christ to the far corners of the Greco-Roman world, so am I compelled to carry the gospel of freedom beyond my own home town. Like Paul, I must constantly respond to the Macedonian call for aid.

Moreover, I am cognizant of the interrelatedness of all communities and states. I cannot sit idly by in Atlanta and not be concerned about what happens in Birmingham. Injustice anywhere is a threat to justice everywhere. We are caught in an inescapable network of mutuality, tied in a single garment of destiny. Whatever affects one directly, affects all indirectly. Never again can we afford to live with the narrow, provincial "outside agitator" idea. Anyone who lives inside the United States can never be considered an outsider anywhere within its bounds.

You deplore the demonstrations taking place in Birmingham. But your statement, I am sorry to say, fails to express a similar concern for the conditions that brought about the demonstrations. I am sure that none of you would want to rest content with the superficial kind of social analysis that deals merely with effects and does not grapple with underlying causes. It is unfortunate that demonstrations are taking place in Birmingham, but it is even more unfortunate that the city's white power structure left the Negro community with no alternative.

In any nonviolent campaign there are four basic steps: collection of the facts to determine whether injustices exist; negotiation; self-purification; and direct action. We have gone through all of these steps in Birmingham. There can be no gainsaying the fact that racial injustice engulfs this community. Birmingham is probably the most thoroughly segregated city in the United States. Its ugly record of brutality is widely known. Negroes have experienced grossly unjust treatment in the courts. There have been more unsolved bombings of Negro homes and churches in Birmingham than in any other city in the nation. These are the hard, brutal facts of the case. On the basis of these conditions, Negro leaders sought to negotiate with the city fathers. But the latter consistently refused to engage in good-faith negotiation.

Then, last September, came the opportunity to talk with leaders of Birmingham's economic community. In the course of the negotiations, certain promises were made by the merchants — for example, to remove the stores' humiliating racial signs. On the basis of these promises, the Reverend Fred Shuttlesworth and the leaders of the Alabama Christian Movement for Human Rights agreed to a moratorium on all demonstrations. As the weeks and months went by, we realized that we were the victims of a broken promise. A few signs, briefly removed, returned; the others remained.

As in so many past experiences, our hopes had been blasted, and the shadow of deep disappointment settled upon us. We had no alternative except to prepare for direct action, whereby we would present our very bodies as a means of laying our case before the conscience of the local and the national community. Mindful of the difficulties involved, we decided to undertake a process of self-purification. We began a series of workshops on nonviolence, and we repeatedly asked ourselves: "Are you able to accept blows without retaliating?" "Are you able to endure the ordeal of jail?" We decided to schedule our direct-action program for the Easter season, realizing that except for Christmas, this is the main shopping period of the year. Knowing that a strong economic withdrawal program would be the by-product of direct action, we felt that this would be the best time to bring pressure to bear on the merchants for the needed change.

Then it occurred to us that Birmingham's mayoralty election was coming up in March, and we speedily decided to postpone action until after election day. When we discovered that the Commissioner of Public Safety, Eugene "Bull" Connor, had piled up enough votes to be in the run-off we decided again to postpone action until the day after the run-off so that the demonstrations could not be used to cloud the issues. Like many others, we waited to see Mr. Connor defeated, and to this end we endured postponement after postponement. Having aided in this community need, we felt that our direct-action program could be delayed no longer.

You may well ask: "Why direct action? Why sit-ins, marches and so forth? Isn't negotiation a better path?" You are quite right in calling for negotiation. Indeed, this is the very purpose of direct action. Nonviolent direct action seeks to create such a crisis and foster such a tension that a community which has constantly refused to negotiate is forced to confront the issue. It seeks to so dramatize the issue that it can no longer be ignored. My citing the creation of tension as part of the work of the nonviolent resister may sound rather shocking. But I must confess that I am not afraid of the word "tension." I have earnestly opposed violent tension, but there is a type of constructive, nonviolent tension which is necessary for growth. Just as Socrates felt that it was necessary to create a tension in the mind so that individuals could rise from the bondage of myths and half-truths to the unfettered realm of creative analysis and objective appraisal, must we see the need for nonviolent gadflies to create the kind of tension in society that will help men rise from the dark depths of prejudice and racism to the majestic heights of understanding and brotherhood.

The purpose of our direct-action program is to create a situation so crisis-packed that it will inevitably open the door to negotiation. I therefore concur with you in your call for negotiation. Too long has our beloved Southland been bogged down in a tragic effort to live in monologue rather than dialogue.

One of the basic points in your statement is that the action that I and my associates have taken in Birmingham is untimely. Some have asked: "Why didn't you give the new city administration time to act?" The only answer that I can give to this query is that the new Birmingham administration must be prodded about as much as the outgoing one, before it will act. We are sadly mistaken if we feel that the election of Albert Boutwell as mayor will bring the millennium to Birmingham. While Mr. Boutwell is a much more gentle person than Mr. Connor, they are both segregationists, dedicated to maintenance of the status quo. I have hope that Mr. Boutwell will be reasonable enough to see the futility of massive resistance to desegregation. But he will not see this without pressure from devotees of civil rights. My friends, I must say to you that we have not made a single gain in civil rights without determined legal and nonviolent pressure. Lamentably, it is an historical fact that privileged groups seldom give up their privileges voluntarily. Individuals may see the moral light and voluntarily give up their unjust posture; but, as Reinhold Niebuhr has reminded us, groups tend to be more immoral than individuals.

We know through painful experience that freedom is never voluntarily given by the oppressor; it must be demanded by the oppressed. Frankly, I have yet to engage in a direct-action campaign that was "well timed" in the view of those who have not suffered unduly from the disease of segregation. For years now I have heard the word "Wait!" It rings in the ear of every Negro with piercing familiarity. This "Wait" has almost always meant "Never." We must come to see, with one of our distinguished jurists, that "justice too long delayed is justice denied."

We have waited for more than 340 years for our constitutional and God-given rights. The nations of Asia and Africa are moving with jet-like speed toward gaining political independence, but we still creep at horse-and-buggy pace toward gaining a cup of coffee at a lunch counter. Perhaps it is easy for those who have never felt the stinging dark of segregation to say, "Wait." But when you have seen vicious mobs lynch your mothers and fathers at will and drown your sisters and brothers at whim; when you have seen hate-filled policemen curse, kick and even kill your black brothers and sisters; when you see the vast majority of your twenty million Negro brothers smothering in an airtight cage of poverty in the midst of an affluent society; when you suddenly find your tongue twisted and your speech stammering as you seek to explain to your six-year-old daughter why she can't go to the public amusement park that has just been advertised on television, and see tears welling up in her eyes when she is told that Funtown is closed to colored children, and see ominous clouds of inferiority beginning to form in her little mental sky, and see her beginning to distort her personality by developing an unconscious bitterness toward white people; when you have to concoct an answer for a five-year-old son who is asking: "Daddy, why do white people treat colored people so mean?"; when you take a cross-country drive and find it necessary to sleep night after night in the uncomfortable corners of your automobile because no motel will accept you; when you are humiliated day in and day out by nagging signs reading "white" and "colored"; when your first name becomes "nigger," your middle name becomes "boy" (however old you are) and your last name becomes "John," and your wife and mother are never given the respected title "Mrs."; when you are harried by day and haunted by night by the fact that you are a Negro, living constantly at tiptoe stance, never quite knowing what to expect next, and are plagued with inner fears and outer resentments; when you go forever fighting a degenerating sense of "nobodiness" then you will understand why we find it difficult to wait. There comes a time when the cup of endurance runs over, and men are no longer willing to be plunged into the abyss of despair. I hope, sirs, you can understand our legitimate and unavoidable impatience.

You express a great deal of anxiety over our willingness to break laws. This is certainly a legitimate concern. Since we so diligently urge people to obey the Supreme Court's decision of 1954 outlawing segregation in the public schools, at first glance it may seem rather paradoxical for us consciously to break laws. One may want to ask: "How can you advocate breaking some laws and obeying others?" The answer lies in the fact that there are two types of laws: just and unjust. I would be the first to advocate obeying just laws. One has not only a legal but a moral responsibility to obey just laws. Conversely, one has a moral responsibility to disobey unjust laws. I would agree with St. Augustine that "an unjust law is no law at all"

Now, what is the difference between the two? How does one determine whether a law is just or unjust? A just law is a man-made code that squares with the moral law or the law of God. An unjust law is a code that is out of harmony with the moral law. To put it in the terms of St. Thomas Aquinas: An unjust law is a human law that is not rooted in eternal law and natural law. Any law that uplifts human personality is just. Any law that degrades human personality is unjust. All segregation statutes are unjust because segregation distorts the soul and damages the personality. It gives the segregator a false sense of superiority and the segregated a false sense of inferiority. Segregation, to use the terminology of the Jewish philosopher Martin Buber, substitutes an "I-it" relationship for an "I-thou" relationship and ends up relegating persons to the status of things. Hence, segregation is not only politically, economically and sociologically unsound, it is morally wrong and awful. Paul Tillich said that sin is separation. Is not segregation an existential expression of man's tragic separation, his awful estrangement, his terrible sinfulness? Thus it is that I can urge men to obey the 1954 decision of the Supreme Court, for it is morally right; and I can urge them to disobey segregation ordinances, for they are morally wrong.

Let us consider a more concrete example of just and unjust laws. An unjust law is a code that a numerical or power majority group compels a minority group to obey but does not make binding on itself. This is difference made legal. By the same token, a just law is a code that a majority compels a minority to follow and that it is willing to follow itself. This is sameness made legal.

Let me give another explanation. A law is unjust if it is inflicted on a minority that, as a result of being denied the right to vote, had no part in enacting or devising the law. Who can say that the legislature of Alabama which set up that state's segregation laws was democratically elected? Throughout Alabama all sorts of devious methods are used to prevent Negroes from becoming registered voters, and there are some counties in which, even though Negroes constitute a majority of the population, not a single Negro is registered. Can any law enacted under such circumstances be considered democratically structured?

Sometimes a law is just on its face and unjust in its application. For instance, I have been arrested on a charge of parading without a permit. Now, there is nothing wrong in having an ordinance which requires a permit for a parade. But such an ordinance becomes unjust when it is used to maintain segregation and to deny citizens the First Amendment privilege of peaceful assembly and protest.

I hope you are able to ace the distinction I am trying to point out. In no sense do I advocate evading or defying the law, as would the rabid segregationist. That would lead to anarchy. One who breaks an unjust law must do so openly, lovingly, and with a willingness to accept the penalty. I submit that an individual who breaks a law that conscience tells him is unjust and who willingly accepts the penalty of imprisonment in order to arouse the conscience of the community over its injustice, is in reality expressing the highest respect for law.

Of course, there is nothing new about this kind of civil disobedience. It was evidenced sublimely in the refusal of Shadrach, Meshach and Abednego to obey the laws of Nebuchadnezzar, on the ground that a higher moral law was at stake. It was practiced superbly by the early Christians, who were willing to face hungry lions and the excruciating pain of chopping blocks rather than submit to certain unjust laws of the Roman Empire. To a degree, academic freedom is a reality today because Socrates practiced civil disobedience. In our own nation, the Boston Tea Party represented a massive act of civil disobedience.

We should never forget that everything Adolf Hitler did in Germany was "legal" and everything the Hungarian freedom fighters did in Hungary was "illegal." It was "illegal" to aid and comfort a Jew in Hitler's Germany. Even so, I am sure that, had I lived in Germany at the time, I would have aided and comforted my Jewish brothers. If today I lived in a Communist country where certain principles dear to the Christian faith are suppressed, I would openly advocate disobeying that country's antireligious laws.

I must make two honest confessions to you, my Christian and Jewish brothers. First, I must confess that over the past few years I have been gravely disappointed with the white moderate. I have almost reached the regrettable conclusion that the Negro's great stumbling block in his stride toward freedom is not the White Citizen's Counciler or the Ku Klux Klanner, but the white moderate, who is more devoted to "order" than to justice; who prefers a negative peace which is the absence of tension to a positive peace which is the presence of justice; who constantly says: "I agree with you in the goal you seek, but I cannot agree with your methods of direct action"; who paternalistically believes he can set the timetable for another man's freedom; who lives by a mythical concept of time and who constantly advises the Negro to wait for a "more convenient season." Shallow understanding from people of good will is more frustrating than absolute misunderstanding from people of ill will. Lukewarm acceptance is much more bewildering than outright rejection.

I had hoped that the white moderate would understand that law and order exist for the purpose of establishing justice and that when they fan in this purpose they become the dangerously structured dams that block the flow of social progress. I had hoped that the white moderate would understand that the present tension in the South is a necessary phase of the transition from an obnoxious negative peace, in which the Negro passively accepted his unjust plight, to a substantive and positive peace, in which all men will respect the dignity and worth of human personality. Actually, we who engage in nonviolent direct action are not the creators of tension. We merely bring to the surface the hidden tension that is already alive. We bring it out in the open, where it can be seen and dealt with. Like a boil that can never be cured so long as it is covered up but must be opened with all its ugliness to the natural medicines of air and light, injustice must be exposed, with all the tension its exposure creates, to the light of human conscience and the air of national opinion before it can be cured.

In your statement you assert that our actions, even though peaceful, must be condemned because they precipitate violence. But is this a logical assertion? Isn't this like condemning a robbed man because his possession of money precipitated the evil act of robbery? Isn't this like condemning Socrates because his unswerving commitment to truth and his philosophical inquiries precipitated the act by the misguided populace in which they made him drink hemlock? Isn't this like condemning Jesus because his unique God-consciousness and never-ceasing devotion to God's will precipitated the evil act of crucifixion? We must come to see that, as the federal courts have consistently affirmed, it is wrong to urge an individual to cease his efforts to gain his basic constitutional rights because the quest may precipitate violence. Society must protect the robbed and punish the robber.

I had also hoped that the white moderate would reject the myth concerning time in relation to the struggle for freedom. I have just received a letter from a white brother in Texas. He writes: "All Christians know that the col-ored people will receive equal rights eventually, but it is possible that you are in too great a religious hurry. It has taken Christianity almost two thousand years to accomplish what it has. The teachings of Christ take time to come to earth." Such an attitude stems from a tragic misconception of time, from the strangely rational notion that there is something in the very flow of time that will inevitably cure all ills. Actually, time itself is neutral; it can be used either destructively or constructively. More and more I feel that the people of ill will have used time much more effectively than have the people of good will. We will have to repent in this generation not merely for the hateful words and actions of the bad people but for the appalling silence of the good people. Human progress never rolls in on wheels of inevitability; it comes through the tireless efforts of men willing to be co-workers with God, and without this hard work, time itself becomes an ally of the forces of social stagnation. We must use time creatively, in the knowledge that the time is always ripe to do right. Now is the time to make real the promise of democracy and transform our pending national elegy into a creative psalm of brotherhood. Now is the time to lift our national policy from the quicksand of racial injustice to the solid rock of human dignity.

You speak of our activity in Birmingham as extreme. At fist I was rather disappointed that fellow clergymen would see my nonviolent efforts as those of an extremist. I began thinking about the fact that I stand in the middle of two opposing forces in the Negro community. One is a force of complacency, made up in part of Negroes who, as a result of long years of oppression, are so drained of self-respect and a sense of "somebodiness" that they have adjusted to segregation; and in part of a few middle class Negroes who, because of a degree of academic and economic security and because in some ways they profit by segregation, have become insensitive to the problems of the masses. The other force is one of bitterness and hatred, and it comes perilously close to advocating violence.

It is expressed in the various black nationalist groups that are springing up across the nation, the largest and best-known being Elijah Muhammad's Muslim movement. Nourished by the Negro's frustration over the continued existence of racial discrimination, this movement is made up of people who have lost faith in America, who have absolutely repudiated Christianity, and who have concluded that the white man is an incorrigible "devil."

I have tried to stand between these two forces, saying that we need emulate neither the "do-nothingism" of the complacent nor the hatred and despair of the black nationalist. For there is the more excellent way of love and nonviolent protest. I am grateful to God that, through the influence of the Negro church, the way of nonviolence became an integral part of our struggle.

If this philosophy had not emerged, by now many streets of the South would, I am convinced, be flowing with blood. And I am further convinced that if our white brothers dismiss as "rabble-rousers" and "outside agitators" those of us who employ nonviolent direct action, and if they refuse to support our nonviolent efforts, millions of Negroes will, out of frustration and despair, seek solace and security in black-nationalist ideologies, a development that would inevitably lead to a frightening racial nightmare.

Oppressed people cannot remain oppressed forever. The yearning for freedom eventually manifests itself, and that is what has happened to the American Negro. Something within has reminded him of his birthright of freedom, and something without has reminded him that it can be gained. Consciously or unconsciously, he has been caught up by the Zeitgeist, and with his black brothers of Africa and his brown and yellow brothers of Asia, South America and the Caribbean, the United States Negro is moving with a sense of great urgency toward the promised land of racial justice. If one recognizes this vital urge that has engulfed the Negro community, one should readily understand why public demonstrations are taking place. The Negro has many pent-up resentments and latent frustrations, and he must release them. So let him march; let him make prayer pilgrimages to the city hall; let him go on freedom rides — and try to understand why he must do so. If his repressed emotions are not released in nonviolent ways, they will seek expression through violence; this is not a threat but a fact of history. So I have not said to my people: "Get rid of your discontent." Rather, I have tried to say that this normal and healthy discontent can be channeled into the creative outlet of nonviolent direct action. And now this approach is being termed extremist.

But though I was initially disappointed at being categorized as an extremist, as I continued to think about the matter I gradually gained a measure of satisfaction from the label. Was not Jesus an extremist for love: "Love your enemies, bless them that curse you, do good to them that hate you, and pray for them which despitefully use you, and persecute you." Was not Amos an extremist for justice: "Let justice roll down like waters and righteousness like an ever-flowing stream." Was not Paul an extremist for the Christian gospel: "I bear in my body the marks of the Lord Jesus." Was not Martin Luther an extremist: "Here I stand; I cannot do otherwise, so help me God." And John Bunyan: "I will stay in jail to the end of my days before I make a butchery of my conscience." And Abraham Lincoln: "This nation cannot survive half slave and half free." And Thomas Jefferson: "We hold these truths to be self-evident, that all men are created equal..." So the question is not whether we will be extremists, but what kind of extremists we will be. Will we be extremists for hate or for love? Will we be extremists for the preservation of injustice or for the extension of justice? In that dramatic scene on Calvary's hill three men were crucified. We must never forget that all three were crucified for the same crime — the crime of extremism. Two were extremists for immorality, and thus fell below their environment. The other, Jesus Christ, was an extremist for love, truth and goodness, and thereby rose above his environment. Perhaps the South, the nation and the world are in dire need of creative extremists.

I had hoped that the white moderate would see this need. Perhaps I was too optimistic; perhaps I expected too much. I suppose I should have realized that few members of the oppressor race can understand the deep groans and passionate yearnings of the oppressed race, and still fewer have the vision to see that injustice must be rooted out by strong, persistent and determined action. I am thankful, however, that some of our white brothers in the South have grasped the meaning of this social revolution and committed themselves to it. They are still too few in quantity, but they are big in quality. Some — such as Ralph McGill, Lillian Smith, Harry Golden, James McBride Dabbs, Ann Braden and Sarah Patton Boyle — have written about our struggle in eloquent and prophetic terms. Others have marched with us down nameless streets of the South. They have languished in filthy, roach-infested jails, suffering the abuse and brutality of policemen who view them as "dirty nigger lovers." Unlike so many of their moderate brothers and sisters, they have recognized the urgency of the moment and sensed the need for powerful "action" antidotes to combat the disease of segregation.

Let me take note of my other major disappointment. I have been so greatly disappointed with the white church and its leadership. Of course, there are some notable exceptions. I am not unmindful of the fact that each of you has taken some significant stands on this issue. I commend you, Reverend Stallings, for your Christian stand on this past Sunday, in welcoming Negroes to your worship service on a non segregated basis. I commend the Catholic leaders of this state for integrating Spring Hill College several years ago.

But despite these notable exceptions, I must honestly reiterate that I have been disappointed with the church. I do not say this as one of those negative critics who can always find something wrong with the church. I say this as a minister of the gospel, who loves the church; who was nurtured in its bosom; who has been sustained by its spiritual blessings and who will remain true to it as long as the cord of Rio shall lengthen.

When I was suddenly catapulted into the leadership of the bus protest in Montgomery, Alabama, a few years ago, I felt we would be supported by the white church. I felt that the ministers, priests and rabbis of the South would be among our strongest allies. Instead, some have been outright opponents, refusing to understand the freedom movement and misrepresenting its leaders; all too many others have been more cautious than courageous and have remained silent behind the anesthetizing security of stained-glass windows.

In spite of my shattered dreams, I came to Birmingham with the hope that the white religious leadership of this community would see the justice of our cause and, with deep moral concern, would serve as the channel through which our just grievances could reach the power structure. I had hoped that each of you would understand. But again I have been disappointed.

I have heard numerous southern religious leaders admonish their worshipers to comply with a desegregation decision because it is the law, but I have longed to hear white ministers declare: "Follow this decree because integration is morally right and because the Negro is your brother." In the midst of blatant injustices inflicted upon the Negro, I have watched white churchmen stand on the sideline and mouth pious irrelevancies and sanctimonious trivialities. In the midst of a mighty struggle to rid our nation of racial and economic injustice, I have heard many ministers say: "Those are social issues, with which the gospel has no real concern." And I have watched many churches commit themselves to a completely other worldly religion which makes a strange, un-Biblical distinction between body and soul, between the sacred and the secular.

I have traveled the length and breadth of Alabama, Mississippi and all the other southern states. On sweltering summer days and crisp autumn mornings I have looked at the South's beautiful churches with their lofty spires pointing heavenward. I have beheld the impressive outlines of her massive religious-education buildings. Over and over I have found myself asking: "What kind of people worship here? Who is their God? Where were their voices when the lips of Governor Barnett dripped with words of interposition and nullification? Where were they when Governor Wallace gave a clarion call for defiance and hatred? Where were their voices of support when bruised and weary Negro men and women decided to rise from the dark dungeons of complacency to the bright hills of creative protest?"

Yes, these questions are still in my mind. In deep disappointment I have wept over the laxity of the church. But be assured that my tears have been tears of love. There can be no deep disappointment where there is not deep love. Yes, I love the church. How could I do otherwise? I am in the rather unique position of being the son, the grandson and the great-grandson of preachers. Yes, I see the church as the body of Christ. But, oh! How we have blemished and scarred that body through social neglect and through fear of being non-conformists.

There was a time when the church was very powerful — in the time when the early Christians rejoiced at being deemed worthy to suffer for what they believed. In those days the church was not merely a thermometer that recorded the ideas and principles of popular opinion; it was a thermostat that transformed the mores of society. Whenever the early Christians entered a town, the people in power became disturbed and immediately sought to convict the Christians for being "disturbers of the peace" and "outside agitators.'" But the Christians pressed on, in the conviction that they were "a colony of heaven," called to obey God rather than man. Small in number, they were big in commitment. They were too God intoxicated to be "astronomically intimidated." By their effort and example they brought an end to such ancient evils as infanticide and gladiatorial contests.

Things are different now. So often the contemporary church is a weak, ineffectual voice with an uncertain sound. So often it is an archdefender of the status quo. Far from being disturbed by the presence of the church, the power structure of the average community is consoled by the church's silent and often even vocal sanction of things as they are.

But the judgment of God is upon the church as never before. If today's church does not recapture the sacrificial spirit of the early church, it will lose its authenticity, forfeit the loyalty of millions, and be dismissed as an irrelevant social club with no meaning for the twentieth century. Every day I meet young people whose disappointment with the church has turned into outright disgust.

Perhaps I have once again been too optimistic. Is organized religion too inextricably bound to the status quo to save our nation and the world? Perhaps I must turn my faith to the inner spiritual church, the church within the church, as the true ecclesia and the hope of the world. But again I am thankful to God that some noble souls from the ranks of organized religion have broken loose from the paralyzing chains of conformity and joined us as active partners in the struggle for freedom. They have left their secure congregations and walked the streets of Albany, Georgia, with us. They have gone down the highways of the South on tortuous rides for freedom. Yes, they have gone to jail with us. Some have been dismissed from their churches, have lost the support of their bishops and fellow ministers. But they have acted in the faith that right defeated is stronger than evil triumphant. Their witness has been the spiritual salt that has preserved the true meaning of the gospel in these troubled times. They have carved a tunnel of hope through the dark mountain of disappointment.

I hope the church as a whole will meet the challenge of this decisive hour. But even if the church does not come to the aid of justice, I have no despair about the future. I have no fear about the outcome of our struggle in Birmingham, even if our motives are at present misunderstood. We will reach the goal of freedom in Birmingham and all over the nation, because the goal of America is freedom. Abused and scorned though we may be, our destiny is tied up with America's destiny. Before the pilgrims landed at Plymouth, we were here. Before the pen of Jefferson etched the majestic words of the Declaration of Independence across the pages of history, we were here. For more than two centuries our forebears labored in this country without wages; they made cotton king; they built the homes of their masters while suffering gross injustice and shameful humiliation — and yet out of a bottomless vitality they continued to thrive and develop. If the inexpressible cruelties of slavery could not stop us, the opposition we now face will surely fail. We will win our freedom because the sacred heritage of our nation and the eternal will of God are embodied in our echoing demands.

Before closing I feel impelled to mention one other point in your statement that has troubled me profoundly. You warmly commended the Birmingham police force for keeping "order" and "preventing violence." I doubt that you would have so warmly commended the police force if you had seen its dogs sinking their teeth into unarmed, nonviolent Negroes. I doubt that you would so quickly commend the policemen if you were to observe their ugly and inhumane treatment of Negroes here in the city jail; if you were to watch them push and curse old Negro women and young Negro girls; if you were to see them slap and kick old Negro men and young boys; if you were to observe them, as they did on two occasions, refuse to give us food because we wanted to sing our grace together. I cannot join you in your praise of the Birmingham police department.

It is true that the police have exercised a degree of discipline in handing the demonstrators. In this sense they have conducted themselves rather "nonviolently" in public. But for what purpose? To preserve the evil system of segregation. Over the past few years I have consistently preached that nonviolence demands that the means we use must be as pure as the ends we seek. I have tried to make clear that it is wrong to use immoral means to attain moral ends. But now I must affirm that it is just as wrong, or perhaps even more so, to use moral means to preserve immoral ends. Perhaps Mr. Connor and his policemen have been rather nonviolent in public, as was Chief Pritchett in Albany, Georgia but they have used the moral means of nonviolence to maintain the immoral end of racial injustice. As T. S. Eliot has said: "The last temptation is the greatest treason: To do the right deed for the wrong reason."

I wish you had commended the Negro sitinners and demonstrators of Birmingham for their sublime courage, their willingness to suffer and their amazing discipline in the midst of great provocation. One day the South will recognize its real heroes. There will be the James Merediths, with the noble sense of purpose that enables them to face jeering and hostile mobs, and with the agonizing loneliness that characterizes the life of the pioneer. There will be the old, oppressed, battered Negro women, symbolized in a seventy-two-year-old woman in Montgomery, Alabama, who rose up with a sense of dignity and with her people decided not to ride segregated buses, and who responded with ungrammatical profundity to one who inquired about her weariness: "My feets is tired, but my soul is at rest." There will be the young high school and college students, the young ministers of the gospel and a host of their elders, courageously and nonviolently sitting in at lunch counters and willingly going to jail for conscience's sake. One day the South will know that when these disinherited children of God sat down at lunch counters, they were in reality standing up for what is best in the American dream and for the most sacred values in our Judaeo-Christian heritage, thereby bringing our nation back to those great wells of democracy which were dug deep by the founding fathers in their formulation of the Constitution and the Declaration of Independence.

Never before have I written so long a letter. I'm afraid it is much too long to take your precious time. I can assure you that it would have been much shorter if I had been writing from a comfortable desk, but what else can one do when he is alone in a narrow jail cell, other than write long letters, think long thoughts and pray long prayers?

If I have said anything in this letter that overstates the truth and indicates an unreasonable impatience, I beg you to forgive me. If I have said anything that understates the truth and indicates my having a patience that allows me to settle for anything less than brotherhood, I beg God to forgive me.

I hope this letter finds you strong in the faith. I also hope that circumstances will soon make it possible for me to meet each of you, not as an integrationist or a civil rights leader but as a fellow clergyman and a Christian brother. Let us all hope that the dark clouds of racial prejudice will soon pass away and the deep fog of misunderstanding will be lifted from our fear-drenched communities, and in some not too distant tomorrow the radiant stars of love and brotherhood will shine over our great nation with all their scintillating beauty.

Yours for the cause of Peace and Brotherhood,
Martin Luther King, Jr.

--------- 7.23 ---------
'WE SHALL OVERCOME'
Freedom Songs

Throughout all of the demonstrations and marches of the Civil Rights Movement, spirituals adapted to become Freedom Songs were invoked as a way to both build and display unity of purpose. The mass meetings that organized each of the movements — in Birmingham, Albany, Selma, Jackson, Montgomery — where thousands would gather to hear Martin Luther King, Jr. and other ministers speak, opened and closed with the singing of these Freedom Songs. In street demonstrations, marchers locked arms and responded to racist and demeaning taunts from white onlookers with the Freedom Songs. They were such a powerful organizing tool that almost all subsequent movements for social change, in all corners of the globe, would invoke them at mass demonstrations.

A. 'We Shall Overcome'

We shall overcome
We shall overcome
We shall overcome some day

[Chorus]
Oh deep in my heart
I do believe
We shall overcome some day

We'll walk hand in hand
We'll walk hand in hand
We'll walk hand in hand some day

[Chorus]

We shall all be free
We shall all be free
We shall all be free some day

[Chorus]

We are not afraid
We are not afraid
We are not afraid some day

[Chorus]

We are not alone
We are not alone
We are not alone some day

[Chorus]

The whole wide world around
The whole wide world around
The whole wide world around some day

[Chorus]

We shall overcome
We shall overcome
We shall overcome some day

B. 'Oh, Freedom'

O freedom, O freedom,
O freedom after a while,
And before I'd be a slave, I'd be buried
in my grave,
And go home to my Lord and be free.

There'll be no more moaning, no more
moaning,
No more moaning after a while

No more weeping, no more crying,
No more weeping after a while

There'll be no more kneeling, no more bowing,
No more kneeling after a while

There'll be shouting, there'll be shouting,
There'll be shouting after a while

——— 7.24 ———
'THE TIME HAS COME FOR
THIS NATION TO FULFILL
ITS PROMISE'
John F. Kennedy

On June 11, 1963, the night of Medgar Evers's assassination, President Kennedy finally announced his intention to follow through on his campaign promises to the civil rights leaders. Having helped negotiate the Birmingham movement's resolution, and faced down Alabama Governor George Wallace (Wallace had refused to allow black students to enter the University of Alabama, prompting Kennedy to federalize the Alabama national guard and intervene), Kennedy addressed the nation on the topic of civil rights. His address was an unequivocal rejection of segregation. He appealed for understanding, declaring, "We face … a moral crisis as a country and as a people." He echoed Martin Luther King, Jr.'s "Letter from a Birmingham Jail" by declaring that the nation could not ask African Americans to wait any longer. Steps should be taken to protect their constitutionally granted equality immediately — *legislative* steps. The following week, Kennedy requested Congress pass a sweeping civil rights bill dismantling Jim Crow nationwide.

Good evening my fellow citizens. This afternoon, following a series of threats and defiant statements, the presence of Alabama National Guardsmen was required on the University of Alabama to carry out the final and unequivocal order of the United States District Court of the Northern District of Alabama. That order called for the admission of two clearly qualified young Alabama residents who happened to have been born Negro.

That they were admitted peacefully on the campus is due in good measure to the conduct of the students of the University of Alabama, who met their responsibilities in a constructive way.

I hope that every American, regardless of where he lives, will stop and examine his conscience about this and other related incidents. This nation was founded by men of many nations and backgrounds. It was founded on the principle that all men are created equal, and that the rights of every man are diminished when the rights of one man are threatened.

Today we are committed to a worldwide struggle to promote and protect the rights of all who wish to be free. And when Americans are sent to Vietnam or West Berlin, we do not ask for whites only. It ought to be possible, therefore, for American students of any color to attend any public institution they select without having to be backed up by troops.

It ought to be possible for American consumers of any color to receive equal service in places of public accommodation, such as hotels and restaurants and theaters and retail stores, without being forced to resort to demonstrations in the street, and it ought to be possible for citizens of any color to register and to vote in a free election without interference or fear of reprisal.

It ought to be possible, in short, for every American to enjoy the privileges of being American without regard to his race or his color. In short, every American ought to have the right to be treated as he would wish to be treated, as one would wish his children to be treated. But this is not the case.

The Negro baby born in America today, regardless of the section of the nation in which he is born, has about one-half as much chance of completing high school as a white baby born in the same place on the same day, one-third as much chance of completing college, one-third as much chance of becoming a professional man, twice as much chance of becoming unemployed, about one-seventh as much chance of earning $10,000 a year, a life expectancy which is seven years shorter, and the prospects of earning only half as much.

This is not a sectional issue. Difficulties over segregation and discrimination exist in every city, in every state of the union, producing in many cities a rising tide of discontent that threatens the public safety. Nor is this a partisan issue. In a time of domestic crisis men of good will and generosity should be able to unite regardless of party or politics. This is not even a legal or legislative issue alone. It is better to settle these matters in the courts than on the streets, and new laws are needed at every level, but law alone cannot make men see right.

We are confronted primarily with a moral issue. It is as old as the scriptures and is as clear as the American Constitution.

The heart of the question is whether all Americans are to be afforded equal rights and equal opportunities, whether we are going to treat our fellow Americans as we want to be treated. If an American, because his skin is dark, cannot eat lunch in a restaurant open to the public, if he cannot send his children to the best public school available, if he cannot vote for the public officials who represent him, if, in short, he cannot enjoy the full and free life which all of us want, then who among us would be content to have the color of his skin changed and stand in his place?

Who among us would then be content with the counsels of patience and delay? One hundred years of delay have passed since President Lincoln freed the slaves, yet their heirs, their grandsons, are not fully free. They are not yet freed from the bonds of injustice. They are not yet freed from social and economic oppression. And this nation, for all its hopes and all its boasts, will not be fully free until all its citizens are free.

We preach freedom around the world, and we mean it, and we cherish our freedom here at home, but are we to say to the world and, much more importantly, to each other that this is a land of the free except for the Negroes; that we have no second-class citizens except Negroes; that we have no class or caste system, no ghettos, no master race except with respect to Negroes?

Now the time has come for this nation to fulfill its promise. The events in Birmingham and elsewhere have so increased the cries for equality that no city or state or legislative body can prudently choose to ignore them. The fires of frustration and discord are burning in every city, North and South, where legal remedies are not at hand. Redress is sought in the streets, in demonstrations, parades and protests which create tensions and threaten violence and threaten lives.

We face, therefore, a moral crisis as a country and as a people. It cannot be met by repressive police action. It cannot be left to increased demonstrations in the streets. It cannot be quieted by token moves or talk. It is a time to act in the Congress, in your state and local legislative body and, above all, in all of our daily lives. It is not enough to pin the blame on others, to say this is a problem of one section of the country or another, or deplore the fact that we face. A great change is at hand, and our task, our obligation, is to make that revolution, that change, peaceful and constructive for all. Those who do nothing are inviting shame as well as violence. Those who act boldly are recognizing right as well as reality.

Next week I shall ask the Congress of the United States to act, to make a commitment it has not fully made in this century to the proposition that race has no place in American life or law. The federal judiciary has upheld that proposition in a series of forthright cases.

The executive branch has adopted that proposition in the conduct of its affairs, including the employment of federal personnel, the use of federal facilities, and the sale of federally financed housing.

But there are other necessary measures which only the Congress can provide, and they must be provided at this session. The old code of equity law under which we live commands for every wrong a remedy, but in too many communities, in too many parts of the country, wrongs are inflicted on Negro citizens and there are no remedies at law. Unless the Congress acts, their only remedy is in the street. I am, therefore, asking the Congress to enact legislation giving all Americans the right to be served in facilities which are open to the public — hotels, restaurants, theaters, retail stores, and similar establishments. This seems to me to be an elementary right. Its denial is an arbitrary indignity that no American in 1963 should have to endure, but many do.

I have recently met with scores of business leaders urging them to take voluntary action to end this discrimination and I have been encouraged by their response, and in the last two weeks over 75 cities have seen progress made in desegregating these kinds of facilities. But many are unwilling to act alone, and for this reason, nationwide legislation is needed if we are to move this problem from the streets to the courts.

I am also asking Congress to authorize the federal government to participate more fully in lawsuits designed to end segregation in public education. We have succeeded in persuading many districts to desegregate voluntarily. Dozens have admitted Negroes without violence. Today a Negro is attending a state-supported institution in every one of our 50 states, but the pace is very slow. Too many Negro children entering segregated grade schools at the time of the Supreme Court's decision nine years ago will enter segregated high schools this fall, having suffered a loss which can never be restored. The lack of an adequate education denies the Negro a chance to get a decent job.

The orderly implementation of the Supreme Court decision, therefore, cannot be left solely to those who may not have the economic resources to carry the legal action or who may be subject to harassment.

Other features will be also requested, including greater protection for the right to vote. But legislation, I repeat, cannot solve this problem alone. It must be solved in the homes of every American in every community across our country.

In this respect, I want to pay tribute to those citizens North and South who have been working in their communities to make life better for all. They are acting not out of a sense of legal duty but out of a sense of human decency. Like our soldiers and sailors in all parts of the world they are meeting freedom's challenge on the firing line, and I salute them for their honor and their courage. My fellow Americans, this is a problem which faces us all — in every city of the North as well as the South. Today there are Negroes unemployed, two or three times as many compared to whites, inadequate in education, moving into the large cities, unable to find work, young people particularly out of work without hope, denied equal rights, denied the opportunity to eat at a restaurant or lunch counter or go to a movie theater, denied the right to a decent education, denied almost today the right to attend a state university even though qualified. It seems to me that these are matters which concern us all, not merely presidents or congressmen or governors, but every citizen of the United States.

This is one country. It has become one country because all of us and all the people who came here had an equal chance to develop their talents. We cannot say to 10 percent of the population that you can't have that right; that your children cannot have the chance to develop whatever talents they have; that the only way that they are going to get their rights is to go into the streets and demonstrate. I think we owe them and we owe ourselves a better country than that. Therefore, I am asking for your help in making it easier for us to move ahead and to provide the kind of equality of treatment which we would want ourselves; to give a chance for every child to be educated to the limit of his talents. As I have said before, not every child has an equal talent or an equal ability or an equal motivation, but they should have the equal right to develop their talent and their ability and their motivation, to make something of themselves. We have a right to expect that the Negro community will be responsible, will uphold the law, but they have a right to expect that the law will be fair, that the Constitution will be color blind, as Justice Harlan said at the turn of the century.

This is what we are talking about and this is a matter which concerns this country and what it stands for, and in meeting it I ask the support of all our citizens.

Thank you very much.

——————— 7.25 ———————
'I HAVE A DREAM'
Martin Luther King, Jr.

As the events of 1963 unfolded, Bayard Rustin and A. Philip Randolph organized a "march" on Washington, D.C. Like the 1957 Prayer Pilgrimage, it was to be a rally, with speeches and entertainment, on the steps of the Lincoln Memorial.

But the growing movement had begun to fracture. Randolph originally intended the event as a measure to focus the nation on economic inequality. King, however, who was reluctant to participate in a northern-led effort in the first place, wanted a civil rights focus. To compromise, the event was dubbed the March on Washington for Jobs and Freedom. The National Urban League and the NAACP, for their part, already hostile to new-kid-on-the-block King as well as the student activists, refused to participate in anything that involved demonstrations in the nations' capital such as those unfolding throughout the South. They agreed with President Kennedy, who despised the idea because he believed it would jeopardize delicate Congressional support for his bill. Meanwhile, the students of SNCC, and King as well, were outraged at the notion that demonstrations would be left off the agenda. And the suppression of their wishes at the march would be the beginning of a permanent rift between SNCC and the mainstream civil rights groups. Finally, NAACP head Roy Wilkins did not like the fact that Rustin, an openly gay man with a socialist and anti-war past, would be in charge. As in Montgomery, Rustin was asked to remain behind the throne.

The infighting that plagued the March on Washington's planning did not recede once it was underway. The line-up of speakers Bayard Rustin put together completely overlooked black women activists. Not even Dorothy Height, head of the National Council of Negro Women, got a turn at the dias. But perhaps more volatile at the time was SNCC leader John Lewis's speech. Lewis and CORE leader James Forman had written a scathing attack on all political leaders from Kennedy to southern legislators for their failure to protect blacks' rights. NAACP head Roy Wilkins threatened to pull out if Lewis was allowed to deliver it. And, in another compromise, A. Philip Randolph convinced Lewis to tone down his language.

Despite these difficulties, Rustin and Randolph managed to pull the march off. Over a quarter of a million people gathered on the National Mall on August 28, 1963. It was the largest peacetime gathering in national history. At the day's conclusion, King delivered what may be the most recognizable speech in American history.

I am happy to join with you today in what will go down in history as the greatest demonstration for freedom in the history of our nation.

Five score years ago, a great American, in whose symbolic shadow we stand today, signed the Emancipation Proclamation. This momentous decree came as a great beacon light of hope to millions of Negro slaves who had been seared in the flames of withering injustice. It came as a joyous daybreak to end the long night of captivity.

But one hundred years later, we must face the tragic fact that the Negro is still not free. One hundred years later, the life of the Negro is still sadly crippled by the manacles of segregation and the chains of discrimination. One hundred years later, the Negro lives on a lonely island of poverty in the midst of a vast ocean of material prosperity. One hundred years later, the Negro is still languishing in the corners of

American society and finds himself an exile in his own land. So we have come here today to dramatize an appalling condition.

In a sense we have come to our nation's capital to cash a check. When the architects of our republic wrote the magnificent words of the Constitution and the Declaration of Independence, they were signing a promissory note to which every American was to fall heir. This note was a promise that all men would be guaranteed the inalienable rights of life, liberty, and the pursuit of happiness.

It is obvious today that America has defaulted on this promissory note insofar as her citizens of color are concerned. Instead of honoring this sacred obligation, America has given the Negro people a bad check which has come back marked "insufficient funds." But we refuse to believe that the bank of justice is bankrupt. We refuse to believe that there are insufficient funds in the great vaults of opportunity of this nation. So we have come to cash this check — a check that will give us upon demand the riches of freedom and the security of justice. We have also come to this hallowed spot to remind America of the fierce urgency of now. This is no time to engage in the luxury of cooling off or to take the tranquilizing drug of gradualism. Now is the time to rise from the dark and desolate valley of segregation to the sunlit path of racial justice. Now is the time to open the doors of opportunity to all of God's children. Now is the time to lift our nation from the quicksands of racial injustice to the solid rock of brotherhood.

It would be fatal for the nation to overlook the urgency of the moment and to underestimate the determination of the Negro. This sweltering summer of the Negro's legitimate discontent will not pass until there is an invigorating autumn of freedom and equality. Nineteen sixty-three is not an end, but a beginning. Those who hope that the Negro needed to blow off steam and will now be content will have a rude awakening if the nation returns to business as usual. There will be neither rest nor tranquility in America until the Negro is granted his citi-

zenship rights. The whirlwinds of revolt will continue to shake the foundations of our nation until the bright day of justice emerges.

But there is something that I must say to my people who stand on the warm threshold which leads into the palace of justice. In the process of gaining our rightful place we must not be guilty of wrongful deeds. Let us not seek to satisfy our thirst for freedom by drinking from the cup of bitterness and hatred.

We must forever conduct our struggle on the high plane of dignity and discipline. We must not allow our creative protest to degenerate into physical violence. Again and again we must rise to the majestic heights of meeting physical force with soul force. The marvelous new militancy which has engulfed the Negro community must not lead us to distrust of all white people, for many of our white brothers, as evidenced by their presence here today, have come to realize that their destiny is tied up with our destiny and their freedom is inextricably bound to our freedom. We cannot walk alone.

And as we walk, we must make the pledge that we shall march ahead. We cannot turn back. There are those who are asking the devotees of civil rights, "When will you be satisfied?" We can never be satisfied as long as our bodies, heavy with the fatigue of travel, cannot gain lodging in the motels of the highways and the hotels of the cities. We cannot be satisfied as long as the Negro's basic mobility is from a smaller ghetto to a larger one. We can never be satisfied as long as a Negro in Mississippi cannot vote and a Negro in New York believes he has nothing for which to vote. No, no, we are not satisfied, and we will not be satisfied until justice rolls down like waters and righteousness like a mighty stream.

I am not unmindful that some of you have come here out of great trials and tribulations. Some of you have come fresh from narrow cells. Some of you have come from areas where your quest for freedom left you battered by the storms of persecution and staggered by the winds of police brutality. You have been the veterans of creative suffering. Continue to work with the faith that unearned suffering is redemptive.

Go back to Mississippi, go back to Alabama, go back to Georgia, go back to Louisiana, go back to the slums and ghettos of our northern cities, knowing that somehow this situation can and will be changed. Let us not wallow in the valley of despair.

I say to you today, my friends, that in spite of the difficulties and frustrations of the moment, I still have a dream. It is a dream deeply rooted in the American dream.

I have a dream that one day this nation will rise up and live out the true meaning of its creed: "We hold these truths to be self-evident: that all men are created equal."

I have a dream that one day on the red hills of Georgia the sons of former slaves and the sons of former slave owners will be able to sit down together at a table of brotherhood.

I have a dream that one day even the state of Mississippi, a desert state, sweltering with the heat of injustice and oppression, will be transformed into an oasis of freedom and justice.

I have a dream that my four children will one day live in a nation where they will not be judged by the color of their skin but by the content of their character.

I have a dream today.

I have a dream that one day the state of Alabama, whose governor's lips are presently dripping with the words of interposition and nullification, will be transformed into a situation where little black boys and black girls will be able to join hands with little white boys and white girls and walk together as sisters and brothers.

I have a dream today.

I have a dream that one day every valley shall be exalted, every hill and mountain shall be made low, the rough places will be made plain, and the crooked places will be made straight, and the glory of the Lord shall be revealed, and all flesh shall see it together.

This is our hope. This is the faith with which I return to the South. With this faith we will be able to hew out of the mountain of despair a stone of hope. With this faith we will be able to transform the jangling discords of our nation into a beautiful symphony of brotherhood. With this faith we will be able to work together, to pray together, to struggle together, to go to jail together, to stand up for freedom together, knowing that we will be free one day.

This will be the day when all of God's children will be able to sing with a new meaning, "My country, 'tis of thee, sweet land of liberty, of thee I sing. Land where my fathers died, land of the pilgrim's pride, from every mountainside, let freedom ring."

And if America is to be a great nation this must become true.

So let freedom ring from the prodigious hilltops of New Hampshire.

Let freedom ring from the mighty mountains of New York.

Let freedom ring from the heightening Alleghenies of Pennsylvania!

Let freedom ring from the snowcapped Rockies of Colorado!

Let freedom ring from the curvaceous peaks of California!

But not only that; let freedom ring from Stone Mountain of Georgia!

Let freedom ring from Lookout Mountain of Tennessee!

Let freedom ring from every hill and every molehill of Mississippi.

From every mountainside, let freedom ring.

When we let freedom ring, when we let it ring from every village and every hamlet, from every state and every city, we will be able to speed up that day when all of God's children, black men and white men, Jews and Gentiles, Protestants and Catholics, will be able to join hands and sing in the words of the old Negro spiritual, "Free at last! free at last! thank God Almighty, we are free at last!"

7.26

'IN ANSWER TO SENATOR THURMOND'

Bayard Rustin

Roy Wilkins' warnings about Bayard Rustin's liability to the march proved to be prophetic, as did his and President Kennedy's prediction that southern legislators would use the event to rally opposition to a civil rights bill. South Carolina Senator Strom Thurmond led the attack, and opened up with both barrels on Rustin. He maligned Rustin as a draft-dodging, communist homosexual. But Rustin had already proven his immense organizing abilities to even Wilkins, and the civil rights leaders stood behind him. Rustin responded to the charges for himself in an August 12, 1963, statement to the press. He called Thurmond's remarks "a disgrace to the United States Senate and a measure of the desperation of the segregationist cause." Rustin focused on clarifying his anti-war and socialist beliefs, stating on the issue of his homosexuality, "I am disinclined to put myself in the position of having to defend my own moral character."

I wish to comment on two charges leveled against me by Senator Strom Thurmond.

The first charge is that I was a draft dodger during World War II. This is demonstrably false. As a Quaker, I refused to participate in World War II on grounds of conscientious objection. I notified my draft board accordingly. When I was sentenced to twenty-eight months in prison, the judge was sufficiently impressed with the sincerity of my pacifist convictions to allow me three weeks, without bail, to complete my work for the Congress of Racial Equality (CORE) before serving my sentence.

My activities in the pacifist and Quaker organizations are well known. My adherence to nonviolence in the civil rights movement is an outgrowth of the philosophical pacifism I came to accept in the course of those activities. One may quarrel with the conscientious objector, but it is neither fair nor accurate to call him a draft dodger. I did not dodge the draft. I openly and vigorously opposed it. Twenty-eight months' imprisonment was the price I willingly paid for my convictions.

Senator Thurmond charges me with communism. I am not now and never have been a member of the Communist party. More than twenty years ago, while a student at the City College of New York, I was a member of the Young Communist League. I joined the YCL in 1938, just prior to the Hitler-Stalin pact, when communist organizations appeared genuinely interested in peace and in racial justice, and, as a consequence, pacifists could feel relatively comfortable in YCL. In 1941, after Hitler attacked the Soviet Union, the YCL line changed overnight. The fight for peace and for civil rights was declared subordinate to the defense of the Soviet Union. The league instructed me to stop agitating for integration of the armed forces on the grounds that this impaired the war effort.

I have never been willing to subordinate the just demands of my people to the foreign or domestic policy of any nation. I did not then, and I do not now, consider acquiescence in injustice the road to any kind of true democracy. Accordingly, I left the YCL in 1941.

Even before that year, my Quaker beliefs had conflicted with the basic aims and practices of the YCL. Those beliefs, strengthened over the years, remain incompatible with communism. In recent years I have served as executive secretary of the War Resisters' League, of which Albert Einstein was honorary chairman. I am also an editor of a monthly magazine, *Liberation*. In both positions I have given abundant and public demonstration of my opposition to totalitarianism and undemocratic elements everywhere — in Russia as well as in South Carolina.

The Senator alleges that I visited the Soviet Union. In fact, I have never been to the Soviet Union in my life. Mr. Thurmond stated that my imaginary visit to Moscow occurred in connection with the famous San Francisco to Moscow Peace Walk. He forgot to mention that the participants went to Red Square and distributed leaflets, in Russian, condemning nuclear testing by the Soviet government. He also failed to mention that the leaders of the walk spoke at the University of Moscow, where they denounced the absence of political democracy in the Soviet Union. When Communist politicians tried to halt the meeting, the students' heated protests prolonged it for another hour.

I would have been proud to participate in both incidents, whose extraordinary effect in reaching the Russian people with the message of democracy was amply described in *The New York Times* and other publications with which members of the United States Senate are presumed to be familiar. As it was, my role in the project was confined to London, from which city I negotiated with various European governments for passage for the walkers.

I am not the first of my race to have been falsely attacked by the spokesmen for the Confederacy. But even from them a minimal regard for the facts should be expected. Senator Thurmond's remarks were a disgrace to the United States Senate and a measure of the desperation of the segregationist cause.

With regard to Senator Thurmond's attack on my morality, I have no comment. By religious training and fundamental philosophy, I am disinclined to put myself in a position of having to defend my own moral character. Questions in this area should properly be directed to those who have entrusted me with my present responsibilities.

--- 7.27 ---

'THE CHICKENS COME HOME TO ROOST'
Malcolm X

Following the March on Washington, on December 4, 1963, Malcolm X gave his stinging response. The whole affair, he charged, had been a farce. The late President Kennedy (assassinated on November 22) had used the supposed civil rights leaders as puppets in putting on a show designed to placate the increasingly angry black masses. Malcolm launched an unrelenting attack on the march's black leaders, white liberal supporters and Kennedy, warning that "the hour of judgment and doom" had come for white America, and the nation would soon have to pay for

its sins against black people. After the speech, a reporter asked what he thought of Kennedy's assassination, and Malcolm made the fateful remark that he believed it an example of "the chickens coming home to roost." He had gone too far. The Nation of Islam withdrew him from the spotlight, ordering him to cease speaking publicly.

The Honorable Elijah Muhammad teaches us that as it was the evil sin of slavery that caused the downfall and destruction of ancient Egypt and Babylon, and of ancient Greece, as well as ancient Rome, so it was the evil sin of colonialism (slavery, nineteenth-century European style) that caused the collapse of the white nations in present-day Europe as world powers. Unbiased scholars and unbiased observers agree that the wealth and power of white Europe has rapidly declined during the nineteen-year period between World War II and today.

So we of this present generation are also witnessing how the enslavement of millions of black people in this country is now bringing white America to her hour of judgment, to her downfall as a respected nation. And even those Americans who are blinded by childlike patriotism can see that it is only a matter of time before white America too will be utterly destroyed by her own sins, and all traces of her former glory will be removed from this planet forever. …

The hour of judgment and doom is upon White America for the evil seeds of slavery and hypocrisy she has sown; and God himself has declared that no one shall escape the doom of this Western world, except those who accept Allah as God, Islam as his only religion, and The Honorable Elijah Muhammad as his Messenger to the twenty-two million ex-slaves here in America, twenty-two million "Negroes" who are referred to in the symbolism of the Scriptures as the Lost Sheep, the Lost Tribes, or the Lost People of God.

White America is doomed! God has declared that The Honorable Elijah Muhammad is your only means of escape. When you reject The Honorable Elijah Muhammad, when you refuse to hear his message or heed his warning you are closing your only door of escape. When you cut yourself off from him, you cut yourself off from your only way out of the divine disaster that is fast approaching White America.

Before your pride causes you to harden your heart and further close your ears, and before your ignorance provokes laughter, search the Christian Scriptures. Search even the histories of other nations that sat in the same positions of wealth, power, and authority that these white Americans now hold ... and see what God did to them. If God's unchanging laws of justice caught up with every one of the slave empires of the past, how dare you think White America can escape the harvest of unjust seeds planted by her white forefathers against our black forefathers here in the land of slavery! ...

Pharaoh's wealth and power made him too proud to listen to the little inarticulate ex-slave named Moses. He ridiculed Moses' lack of eloquence. White America's attitude today is the same toward The Honorable Elijah Muhammad. They ridicule him because of his lack of education and his cotton-field origin in Georgia. White America chooses to listen to the Negro civil rights leaders, the Big Six. Six puppets who have been trained by the whites in white institutions and then placed over our people by these same whites as "spokesman" for our people. These handpicked "spokesmen" do nothing but parrot for the whites exactly what they know the whites want to hear.

Pharaoh used this same strategy to oppose Moses. Pharaoh also set up puppet-magicians to parrot his lies and to deceive the Hebrew slaves into thinking that Moses was a hate-teacher, and extremist, who was advocating violence and racial supremacy simply because Moses was trying to restore unto his people their own lost culture, their lost identity, their lost racial dignity — the same as The Honorable Elijah Muhammad is trying to do among the twenty-two million "Negro" slaves here in this modern House of Bondage today.

By opposing Moses, Pharaoh was actually opposing Moses' God; thus that same God (Jehovah) was forced to drown Pharaoh in the Red Sea, destroy his slave empire, and remove the Egyptian influence from the face of this earth.

History is repeating itself today. American faces the same fate at the hands of Almighty God. That same divine handwriting is now on he walls of this modern American House of Bondage. ...

Pharaoh hired Hebrew magicians to try and fool their own people into thinking they would soon be integrated into the mainstream of that country's life. Pharaoh didn't want the Hebrews to listen to Moses' message of separation. Even in that day separation was God's solution to the "slave's problem." By opposing Moses, the magicians were actually choosing sides against the God of their own people.

In like manner, modern Negro magicians are hired by the American government to oppose The Honorable Elijah Muhammad today. They pose as Negro "leaders." They have been hired by this white government (white so-called liberals) to make our people think that integration into this doomed white society will soon solve our problem.

The Honorable Elijah Muhammad warns us daily: The only permanent solution to America's race problem is the complete separation of these twenty-two million ex-slaves from our white slave master, and the return of these ex-slaves to our own land, where we can then live in peace and security among our people.

The Honorable Elijah Muhammad warns us daily: The American government is trying to trick her twenty-two million ex-slaves with promises that she never intends to keep. The crooked politicians in the government are working with the Negro civil rights leaders, but not to solve the race problem. The greedy politicians who run this government give lip service to the civil rights struggle only to further their own selfish interests. And their main interest as politicians is to stay in power.

In this deceitful American game of power politics, the Negroes are nothing but tools, used by one group of whites called Liberals against another group of whites called

Conservatives, either to get into power or to remain in power.

Among whites here in America, the political teams are no longer divided into Democrats and republicans. The whites who are now struggling for control of the American political throne are divided into "liberal" and "conservative" camps. The white liberals from both parties cross party lines to work together toward the same goal, and white conservatives from both parties do likewise.

The white liberal differs from the white conservative only in one way: the liberal is more deceitful than the conservative. The liberal is more hypocritical than the conservative.

Both want power, but the white liberal is the one who has perfected the art of posing as the Negro's friend and benefactor; and by winning the friendship, allegiance, and support of the Negro, the white liberal is able to use the Negro as a pawn or tool in this political football game that is constantly raging between the white liberals and white conservatives.

Politically the American Negro is nothing but a football and the white liberals control this mentally dead ball through tricks of tokenism: false promises of integration and civil rights. In this profitable game of deceiving and exploiting the political politician of the American Negro, those white liberals have the willing cooperation of the Negro civil rights leaders. These "leaders" sell out our people for just a few crumbs of token recognition and token gains. These "leaders" are satisfied with token victories and token progress because they themselves are nothing but token leaders. ...

Let us examine briefly some of the tricky strategy used by white liberals to harness and exploit the political energies of the Negro.

The crooked politicians in Washington, D.C., purposely make a big noise over the proposed civil rights legislation. By blowing up the civil rights issue they skillfully add false importance to the Negro civil rights "leaders." Once the image of these Negro civil rights "leaders" has been blown up way beyond its proper proportion, these same Negro civil rights "leaders"

are then used by white liberals to influence and control the Negro voters, all for the benefit of the white politicians who pose as liberals, who pose as friends of the Negro.

The white conservatives aren't friends of the Negro either, but they at least don't try to hide it. They are like wolves; they show their teeth in a snarl that keeps the Negro always aware of where he stands with them. But the white liberals are foxes, who also show their teeth to the Negro but pretend that they are smiling. The white liberals are more dangerous than the conservatives; they lure the Negro, and as the Negro runs from the growling wolf, he flees into the open jaws of the smiling fox.

The job of the Negro civil rights leader is to make the Negro forget that the wolf and the fox both belong to the same family. Both are canines; and no matter which one of them the Negro places his trust in, he never ends up in the White House, but always in the doghouse.

The white liberals control the Negro and the Negro vote by controlling the Negro civil rights leaders. As long as they control the Negro civil rights leaders, they can also control and contain the Negro's struggle, and they can control the Negro's so-called revolt.

The Negro "revolution" is controlled by these foxy white liberals, by the government itself. But the black revolution is controlled only by God.

The black revolution is the struggle of the nonwhites of this earth against their white oppressors. The black revolution has swept white supremacy out of Africa, out of Asia, and is getting ready to sweep it out of Latin America. Revolutions are based upon land. Revolutionaries are the landless against the landlord. Revolutions are never peaceful, never loving, never nonviolent. Nor are they ever compromising. Revolutions are destructive and bloody. Revolutionaries don't compromise with the enemy; they don't even negotiate. Like the flood in Noah's day, revolution drowns all opposition, or like the fire in Lot's day, the black revolution burns everything that gets in its path. ...

Can we prove that the Negro revolution is controlled by white liberals? Certainly!

Right after the Birmingham demonstrations, when the entire world had seen on television screens the police dogs, police clubs, and fire hoses brutalizing defenseless black women, children, and even babies, it was reported on page twenty-six in the May 15 issue of *The New York Times*, that the late President Kennedy and his brother, Attorney General Robert Kennedy, during a luncheon conference with several newspaper editors form the State of Alabama, had warned these editors that they must give at least some token gains to the moderate Negro leaders in order to enhance the image of these moderate Negro leaders in the eyesight of the black masses; otherwise the masses of Negroes might turn in the direction of Negro extremists. And the late President named the Black Muslims as being foremost among the Negro extremist groups that he did not want Negroes to turn toward.

In essence, the late President told these southern editors that he was trying to build up the weak image of the Negro civil rights leaders, in order to offset the strong religious image of the Muslim leader, The Honorable Elijah Muhammad. He wasn't giving these Negro leaders anything they deserved; but he was confessing the necessity of building them up, and propping them up, in order to hold the black masses in check, keep them in his grasp, and under his control.

The late President knew that once Negroes hear The Honorable Elijah Muhammad the white liberals will never influence or control or misuse those Negroes for the benefit of the white liberals any more. So the late President was faced with a desperate situation.

Martin Luther King's image had been shattered the previous year when he failed to bring about desegregation in Albany, Georgia. The other civil rights leaders had also become fallen idols. The black masses across the country at the grass roots level had already begun to take their cases to the streets on their own. The government in Washington knew that something had to be done to get the rampaging Negroes back into the corral, back under the control of the white liberals.

The government propaganda machine began encouraging Negroes to follow only what it called "responsible" Negro leaders. The government actually meant, Negro leaders who were responsible to the government, and who could therefore be controlled by the government, and be used by that same government to control their impatient people.

The government knows that The Honorable Elijah Muhammad is responsible only to God and can be controlled only by God. But this white government of America doesn't believe in God! ...

When the late President had learned that he couldn't stop the march, he not only joined it himself but he encouraged all of his political bedfellows to join it. This is the way the white liberals took over the March on Washington, weakened its impact, and changed its course; by changing the participants and the contents, they were able to change the very nature of the march itself.

Example: If I have a cup of coffee that is too strong for me because it is too black, I weaken it by pouring cream into it. I integrate it with cream. If I keep pouring enough cream in the coffee, pretty soon the entire flavor of the coffee is changed; the very nature of the coffee is changed. If enough cream is poured in, eventually you don't even know that I had coffee in this cup. This is what happened with the March on Washington. The whites didn't integrate it; they infiltrated it. Whites joined it; they engulfed it; they became so much a part of it, it lost its original flavor. It ceased to be a black march; it ceased to be militant; it ceased to be angry; it ceased to be impatient. In fact, it ceased to be a march. It became a picnic, an outing with a festive, circus-like atmosphere — CLOWNS AND ALL.

The government had learned that in cases where the demonstrators are predominantly black, they are extremely militant, and oft-times very violent. But to the same degree that whites participate, violence most times is decreased. The government knew that in cases wherein blacks were demonstrating all by themselves, those blacks are so dissatisfied, disenchanted, and angry at the white man that they will oft-times strike back violently regardless of the odds or the consequences. The white government had learned that the only way to hold these black people in check is by joining them, by infiltrating their ranks disguised as integrationist; by integrating their marches and all their demonstrations, and weakening them: In this way only could they be held in check.

The government told the marchers what time to arrive in Washington, where to arrive, and how to arrive. The government then channeled them from the arrival point to the feet of a dead President, George Washington, and then let them march from there to the feet of another dead President, Abraham Lincoln.

The original black militants had planned to march on the White House, the Senate, and the Congress and to bring all political traffic on Capitol Hill to a halt, but the shrewd politicians in Washington, realizing that those original black militants could not be stopped, joined them. By joining the marchers, the white liberals were able to lead the marchers away from the White House, the Senate, the Congress, Capitol Hill, and away from victory. By keeping them marching from the Washington Monument to the Lincoln Monument, marching between the feet of two dead Presidents, they never reached the White House to see the then living President.

The entire march was controlled by the late president. The government in Washington had told the marchers what signs to carry, what songs to sing, what speeches to make, and what speeches not to make, and then told the marchers to be sure to get out of town by sundown.

One of the Big Six leaders, John Lewis, chairman of the Student Non-Violent Coordinating Committee, was prevented from making a very militant speech. He wanted to attack the Kennedy administration for its hypocrisy on civil rights.

The speech was censored by the Rt. Rev. Patrick O'Boyle, the Catholic Archbishop of Washington, D.C. This was a case in which the Catholic Church itself, for whom Rev. O'Boyle speaks, put itself in the position of censoring the legitimate opinion of one of the Big Six Negro civil rights leaders.

The late President's shrewd strategy was: If you can't beat them, join them. The Catholic President placed his Catholic bishop in a strategic position to exercise censorship over any one of the Big Six Negro leaders who tried to deviate from the script in this great "extravaganza" called the March on Washington which the government had controlled right from the very beginning.

So, in the final analysis of the march: It would have to be classified as the best performance of the year; in fact it was the greatest performance of this century. It topped anything that Hollywood could have produced.

If we were going to give out Academy Awards in 1963, we would have to give the late President an Oscar for the "Best Producer of the Year"; and to the four white liberals who participated should go an Oscar as the "Best Actors of the Year," because they really acted like sincere liberals and fooled many Negroes. And to the six Negro civil rights leaders should go an Oscar for the "Best Supporting Cast," because they supported the late President in his entire act, and in his entire program.

Now that the show is over, the black masses are still without land, without jobs, and without homes — their Christian churches are still being bombed, their innocent little girls murdered. So what did the March on Washington accomplish? Nothing! …

How can America atone for her crimes? The Honorable Elijah Muhammad teaches us that a desegregated theater or lunch counter won't solve our problems. Better jobs won't even solve our problems. An integrated cup of coffee isn't sufficient pay for four hundred years of slave labor, and a better job in the white man's factory or position in his business is, at best, only a temporary solution. The only lasting or permanent solution is complete separation on some land that we can call our own.

The Honorable Elijah Muhammad teaches us that the race problem can easily be solved, just by sending these twenty-two million ex-slaves back to our own homeland where we can live in peace and harmony with our own kind. But this government should provide the transportation, plus everything else we need to get started again in our own country. This government should provide everything we need in machinery, materials, and finance; enough to last us for from twenty to twenty-five years, until we can become an independent people in our own country.

If this white government is afraid to let her twenty-two million ex-slaves go back to our country and to our own people, then America must set aside some separate territory here in the Western Hemisphere, where the two races can live apart from each other, since we certainly don't get along peacefully while we are here together.

The size of the territory can be judged according to our own population. If our people number one-seventh of America's total population, then give us one-seventh of this land. We don't want any land in the desert, but where there is rain and much mineral wealth.

We want fertile, productive land on which we can farm and provide our own people with sufficient food, clothing, and shelter. This government must supply us with the machinery and other tools needed to dig into the earth. Give us everything we need for them for from twenty to twenty-five years, until we can produce and supply our own needs.

If we are a part of America, then part of what she is worth belongs to us. We will take our share and depart, then this white country can have peace. What is her net worth? Give us our share in gold and silver and let us depart and go back to our homeland in peace.

We want no integration with this wicked race that enslaved us. We want complete sepa-ration from this race of devils. But we should not be expected to leave America and go back to our homeland empty-handed. After four hundred years of slave labor, we have some back pay coming, a bill owed to us that must be collected.

If the government of White America truly repents of its sins against our people, and atones by giving us our true share, only then can America save herself!

But if America waits for Almighty God himself to step in and force her into a just settlement, God will take this entire continent away from her; and she will cease to exist as a nation. Her own Christian Scriptures warn her that when God comes He can give the "entire Kingdom to whomsoever He will" ... which only means that the God of Justice on Judgment Day can give this entire continent to whomsoever He wills!

White America, wake up and take heed, before it is too late!

--------- 7.28 ---------

THE CIVIL RIGHTS ACT OF 1964
U.S. Congress

After President Kennedy's assassination, new President Lyndon Johnson pledged to continue down the path to integration. But where Kennedy had led a moral crusade, Johnson, a shrewd politician and former master legislator from a southern state, is credited with having the know-how to get the civil rights bill passed. In February 1964, the civil rights bill passed the House 290-130. In the Senate, things were not as smooth. Southern legislators, again led by Strom Thurmond, sought to delay the vote. But Johnson wrestled the bill free by instigating a massive lobbying campaign by the civil rights leaders and, perhaps more so, with his famous powers of "persuasion" in one-on-one meetings with Senators. The bill passed the Senate in June and Johnson signed it into law on July 2, 1964. It was a broad and thorough attack on segregation, outlawing discrimination based on race in education, public accommodations, employment and any federally-funded program. It also addressed schemes used in southern states to indirectly disenfranchise African Americans and created the Equal Employment Opportunity Commission to enforce the employment law.

An Act

To enforce the constitutional right to vote, to confer jurisdiction upon the district courts of the United States to provide injunctive relief against discrimination in public accommodations, to authorize the Attorney General to institute suits to protect constitutional rights in public facilities and public education, to extend the Commission on Civil Rights, to prevent discrimination in federally assisted programs, to establish a Commission on Equal Employment Opportunity, and for other purposes.

Be it enacted by the Senate and House of Representatives of the United States of America in Congress assembled, That this Act may be cited as the "Civil Rights Act of 1964".

TITLE I — VOTING RIGHTS

SEC. 101. ...

(2) No person acting under color of law shall —

(A) in determining whether any individual is qualified under State law or laws to vote in any Federal election, apply any standard, practice, or procedure different from the standards, practices, or procedures applied under such law or laws to other individuals within the same county, parish, or similar political subdivision who have been found by State officials to be qualified to vote;

(B) deny the right of any individual to vote in any Federal election because of an error or omission on any record or paper relating to any application, registration, or other act requisite to voting, if such error or omission is not material in determining whether such individual is qualified under State law to vote in such election; or

(C) employ any literacy test as a qualification for voting in any Federal election unless (i) such test is administered to each individual and is conducted wholly in writing, and (ii) a certified copy of the test and of the answers given

by the individual is furnished to him within twenty-five days of the submission of his request made within the period of time during which records and papers are required to be retained and preserved pursuant to title III of the Civil Rights Act of 1960. ...

TITLE II — INJUNCTIVE RELIEF AGAINST DISCRIMINATION IN PLACES OF PUBLIC ACCOMMODATION

SEC. 201. (a) All persons shall be entitled to the full and equal enjoyment of the goods, services, facilities, and privileges, advantages, and accommodations of any place of public accommodation, as defined in this section, without discrimination or segregation on the ground of race, color, religion, or national origin.

(b) Each of the following establishments which serves the public is a place of public accommodation within the meaning of this title if its operations affect commerce, or if discrimination or segregation by it is supported by State action:

(1) any inn, hotel, motel, or other establishment which provides lodging to transient guests, other than an establishment located within a building which contains not more than five rooms for rent or hire and which is actually occupied by the proprietor of such establishment as his residence;

(2) any restaurant, cafeteria, lunchroom, lunch counter, soda fountain, or other facility principally engaged in selling food for consumption on the premises, including, but not limited to, any such facility located on the premises of any retail establishment; or any gasoline station;

(3) any motion picture house, theater, concert hall, sports arena, stadium or other place of exhibition or entertainment; and

(4) any establishment (A)(i) which is physically located within the premises of any establishment otherwise covered by this subsection, or (ii) within the premises of which is physically located any such covered establishment, and (B) which holds itself out as serving patrons of such covered establishment. ...

SEC. 204. (a) Whenever any person has engaged or there are reasonable grounds to believe that any person is about to engage in any act or practice prohibited by section 203, a civil action for preventive relief, including an application for a permanent or temporary injunction, restraining order, or other order, may be instituted by the person aggrieved and, upon timely application, the court may, in its discretion, permit the Attorney General to intervene in such civil action if he certifies that the case is of general public importance. Upon application by the complainant and in such circumstances as the court may deem just, the court may appoint an attorney for such complainant and may authorize the commencement of the civil action without the payment of fees, costs, or security. ...

SEC. 206. (a) Whenever the Attorney General has reasonable cause to believe that any person or group of persons is engaged in a pattern or practice of resistance to the full enjoyment of any of the rights secured by this title, and that the pattern or practice is of such a nature and is intended to deny the full exercise of the rights herein described, the Attorney General may bring a civil action in the appropriate district court of the United States. ...

TITLE 7 — EQUAL EMPLOYMENT OPPORTUNITY ...

SEC. 703. (a) It shall be an unlawful employment practice for an employer —

(1) to fail or refuse to hire or to discharge any individual, or otherwise to discriminate against any individual with respect to his compensation, terms, conditions, or privileges of employment, because of such individual's race, color, religion, sex, or national origin; or

(2) to limit, segregate, or classify his employees in any way which would deprive or tend to deprive any individual of employment opportunities or otherwise adversely affect his status as an employee, because of such individual's race, color, religion, sex, or national origin.

(b) It shall be an unlawful employment practice for an employment agency to fail or refuse to refer for employment, or otherwise to discriminate against, any individual because of his race, color, religion, sex, or national origin, or to classify or refer for employment any individual on the basis of his race, color, religion, sex, or national origin.

(c) It shall be an unlawful employment practice for a labor organization —

(1) to exclude or to expel from its membership, or otherwise to discriminate against, any individual because of his race, color, religion, sex, or national origin;

(2) to limit, segregate, or classify its membership, or to classify or fail or refuse to refer for employment any individual, in any way which would deprive or tend to deprive any individual of employment opportunities, or would limit such employment opportunities or otherwise adversely affect his status as an employee or as an applicant for employment, because of such individual's race, color, religion, sex, or national origin; or

(3) to cause or attempt to cause an employer to discriminate against an individual in violation of this section.

(d) It shall be an unlawful employment practice for any employer, labor organization, or joint labor-management committee controlling apprenticeship or other training or retraining, including on-the-job training programs to discriminate against any individual because of his race, color, religion, sex, or national origin in admission to, or employment in, any program established to provide apprenticeship or other training.

8

Say It Loud:

BLACK POWER AND BEYOND

──── 8.1 ────

'THE BALLOT OR THE BULLET'
Malcolm X

Following his silencing by the Nation of Islam, Malcolm X's suspicions of a plot against him within the organization intensified, leading him to quit the group and found his own organization. He had long been uncomfortable with the official NOI policy of staying out of politics; his new group would do no such thing. In the spring of 1964, as the Senate debate over the Civil Rights Act dragged on, Malcolm X built on his warnings of violent unrest among urban blacks. He began urging African Americans to abandon both the fight for civil rights and nonviolent disobedience. Rather, he said, blacks should appeal to the world stage, via the United Nations, for *human* rights. And in the process, whenever they were approached with violence, or whenever the government failed to protect them from violence, they should take whatever steps necessary to protect themselves. His philosophy, articulated in this April 1964 speech, would be the foundation for the coming black nationalist movement of the late 1960s. And his words foreshadowed violent uprisings in black cities around the country during the summer of 1965.

Mr. Moderator, Brother Lomax, brothers and sisters, friends and enemies: I just can't believe everyone in here is a friend and I don't want to leave anybody out. The question tonight, as I understand it, is "The Negro Revolt, and Where Do We Go From Here?" or "What Next?" In my little humble way of understanding it, it points toward either the ballot or the bullet. ...

If we don't do something real soon, I think you'll have to agree that we're going to be forced either to use the ballot or the bullet. It's one or the other in 1964. It isn't that time is running out — time has run out! 1964 threatens to be the most explosive year America has ever witnessed. The most explosive year. Why? It's also a political year. It's the year when all of the white politicians will be back in the so-called Negro community jiving you and me for some votes. The year when all of the white political crooks will be right back in your and my community with their false promises, building up our hopes for a letdown, with their trickery and their treachery, with their false promises which they don't intend to keep. As they nourish these dissatisfactions, it can only lead to one thing, an explosion; and now we have the type of black man on the scene in America today — I'm sorry, Brother Lomax — who just doesn't intend to turn the other cheek any longer.

Don't let anybody tell you anything about the odds are against you. If they draft you, they send you to Korea and make you face 800 million Chinese. If you can be brave over there, you can be brave right here. These odds aren't as great as those odds. And if you fight here, you will at least know what you're fighting for.

I'm not a politician, not even a student of politics; in fact, I'm not a student of much of anything. I'm not a Democrat, I'm not a Republican, and I don't even consider myself an American. If you and I were Americans, there'd be no problem. Those Hunkies that just got off the boat, they're already Americans; Polacks are already Americans; the Italian refugees are already Americans. Everything that came out of Europe, every blue-eyed thing, is already an American. And as long as you and I have been over here, we aren't Americans yet.

Well, I am one who doesn't believe in deluding myself. I'm not going to sit at your table and watch you eat, with nothing on my plate, and call myself a diner. Sitting at the table doesn't make you a diner, unless you eat some of what's on that plate. Being here in America doesn't make you an American. Being born here in America doesn't make you an American. Why, if birth made you American, you wouldn't need any legislation, you wouldn't need any amendments to the Constitution, you wouldn't be faced with civil-rights filibustering in Washington, D.C., right now. They don't have to pass civil-rights legislation to make a Polack an American. …

So, where do we go from here? First, we need some friends. We need some new allies. The entire civil-rights struggle needs a new interpretation, a broader interpretation. We need to look at this civil-rights thing from another angle — from the inside as well as from the outside. To those of us whose philosophy is black nationalism, the only way you can get involved in the civil-rights struggle is give it a new interpretation. That old interpretation excluded us. It kept us out. So, we're giving a new interpretation to the civil-rights struggle, an interpretation that will enable us to come into it, take part in it. And these handkerchief-heads who have been dillydallying and pussyfooting and compromising — we don't intend to let them pussyfoot and dilly-dally and compromise any longer.

How can you thank a man for giving you what's already yours? How then can you thank him for giving you only part of what's already yours? You haven't even made progress, if what's being given to you, you should have had already. That's not progress. And I love my Brother Lomax, the way he pointed out we're right back where we were in 1954. We're not even as far up as we were in 1954. We're behind where we were in 1954. There's more segregation now than there was in 1954. There's more racial animosity, more racial hatred, more racial violence today in 1964, than there was in 1954. Where is the progress?

And now you're facing a situation where the young Negro's coming up. They don't want to hear that "turn the-other-cheek" stuff, no. In Jacksonville, those were teenagers, they were throwing Molotov cocktails. Negroes have never done that before. But it shows you there's a new deal coming in. There's new thinking coming in. There's new strategy coming in. It'll be Molotov cocktails this month, hand grenades next month, and something else next month. It'll be ballots, or it'll be bullets. It'll be liberty, or it will be death. The only difference about this kind of death — it'll be reciprocal. You know what is meant by "reciprocal"? That's one of Brother Lomax's words, I stole it from him. I don't usually deal with those big words because I don't usually deal with big people. I deal with small people. I find you can get a whole lot of small people and whip hell out of a whole lot of big people. They haven't got anything to lose, and they've got everything to gain. And they'll let you know in a minute: "It takes two to tango; when I go, you go." …

I might stop right here to point out one thing. Whenever you're going after something that belongs to you, anyone who's depriving you of the right to have it is a criminal. Understand that. Whenever you are going after something that is yours, you are within your legal rights to lay claim to it. And anyone who puts forth any effort to deprive you of that which is yours, is breaking the law, is a criminal. And this was pointed out by the Supreme Court decision. It outlawed segregation. Which means segregation is against the law. Which means a segregationist is breaking the law. A segregationist is a criminal. You can't label him as anything other than that. And when you demonstrate against segregation, the law is on your side. The Supreme Court is on your side.

Now, who is it that opposes you in carrying out the law? The police department itself. With police dogs and clubs. Whenever you demonstrate against segregation, whether it is segregated education, segregated housing, or anything else, the law is on your side, and anyone who stands in the way is not the law any longer. They are breaking the law, they are not representatives of the law. Any time you demonstrate against segregation and a man has the audacity to put a police dog on you, kill that dog, kill him, I'm telling you, kill that dog. I say it, if they put me in jail tomorrow, kill that dog. Then you'll put a stop to it. Now, if these white people in here don't want to see that kind of action, get down and tell the mayor to tell the police department to pull the dogs in. That's all you have to do. If you don't do it, someone else will.

If you don't take this kind of stand, your little children will grow up and look at you and think "shame." If you don't take an uncompromising stand — I don't mean go out and get violent; but at the same time you should never be nonviolent unless you run into some nonviolence. I'm nonviolent with those who are nonviolent with me. But when you drop that violence on me, then you've made me go insane, and I'm not responsible for what I do. And that's the way every Negro should get. Any time you know you're within the law, within your legal rights, within your moral rights, in accord with justice, then die for what you believe in. But don't die alone. Let your dying be reciprocal. This is what is meant by equality. What's good for the goose is good for the gander.

When we begin to get in this area, we need new friends, we need new allies. We need to expand the civil-rights struggle to a higher level — to the level of human rights. Whenever you are in a civil-rights struggle, whether you know it or not, you are confining yourself to the jurisdiction of Uncle Sam. No one from the outside world can speak out in your behalf as long as your struggle is a civil-rights struggle. Civil rights comes within the domestic affairs of this country. All of our African brothers and our Asian brothers and our Latin-American brothers cannot open their mouths and interfere in the domestic affairs of the United States. And as long as it's civil rights, this comes under the jurisdiction of Uncle Sam.

But the United Nations has what's known as the charter of human rights, it has a committee that deals in human rights. You may wonder why all of the atrocities that have been committed in Africa and in Hungary and in Asia and in Latin America are brought before the UN, and the Negro problem is never brought before the UN. This is part of the conspiracy. This old, tricky, blue eyed liberal who is supposed to be your and my friend, supposed to be in our corner, supposed to be subsidizing our struggle, and supposed to be acting in the capacity of an adviser, never tells you anything about human rights. They keep you wrapped up in civil rights. And you spend so much time barking up the civil-rights tree, you don't even know there's a human-rights tree on the same floor. ...

When you take your case to Washington, D.C., you're taking it to the criminal who's responsible; it's like running from the wolf to the fox. They're all in cahoots together. They all work political chicanery and make you look like a chump before the eyes of the world. Here you are walking around in America, getting ready to be drafted and sent abroad, like a tin soldier, and when you get over there, people ask you what are you fighting for, and you have to stick your tongue in your cheek. No, take Uncle Sam to court, take him before the world. ...

So, you're dealing with a man whose bias and prejudice are making him lose his mind, his intelligence, every day. He's frightened. He looks around and sees what's taking place on this earth, and he sees that the pendulum of time is swinging in your direction. The dark people are waking up. They're losing their fear of the white man. No place where he's fighting right now is he winning. Everywhere he's fighting, he's fighting someone your and my complexion. And they're beating him. He can't win any more. He's won his last battle. He failed to win the Korean War. He couldn't win it. He had to sign a truce. That's a loss. Any time Uncle Sam, with all his machinery for warfare, is held to a draw by some rice eaters, he's lost the battle. He had to sign a truce. America's not supposed to sign a truce. She's supposed to be bad. But she's not bad any more. She's bad as long as she can use her hydrogen bomb, but she can't use hers for fear Russia might use hers. Russia can't use hers, for fear that Sam might use his. So, both of them are weaponless. They can't use the weapon because each's weapon nullifies the other's. So the only place where action can take place is on the ground. And the white man can't win another war fighting on the ground. Those days are over. The black man knows it, the brown man knows it, the red man knows it, and the yellow man knows it. So they engage him in guerrilla warfare. That's not his style. You've got to have heart to be a guerrilla warrior, and he hasn't got any heart. I'm telling you now.

I just want to give you a little briefing on guerrilla warfare because, before you know it, before you know it. ... It takes heart to be a guerrilla warrior because you're on your own. In conventional warfare you have tanks and a whole lot of other people with you to back you up, planes over your head and all that kind of stuff. But a guerrilla is on his own. All you have is a rifle, some sneakers and a bowl of rice, and that's all you need — and a lot of heart. The Japanese on some of those islands in the Pacific, when the American soldiers landed, one Japanese sometimes could hold the whole army off. He'd just wait until the sun went down, and when the sun went down they were all equal. He would take his little blade and slip from bush to bush, and from American to American. The white soldiers couldn't cope with that. Whenever you see a white soldier that fought in the Pacific, he has the shakes, he has a nervous condition, because they scared him to death.

The same thing happened to the French up in French Indochina. People who just a few years previously were rice farmers got together and ran the heavily-mechanized French army out of Indochina. You don't need it — modern warfare today won't work. This is the day of the guerrilla. They did the same thing in Algeria. Algerians, who were nothing but Bedouins, took a knife and sneaked off to the hills, and de Gaulle and all of his highfalutin' war machinery couldn't defeat those guerrillas. Nowhere on this earth does the white man win in a guerrilla warfare. It's not his speed. Just as guerrilla warfare is prevailing in Asia and in parts of Africa and in parts of Latin America, you've got to be mighty naive, or you've got to play the black man cheap, if you don't think some day he's going to wake up and find that it's got to be the ballot or the bullet. ...

So I say, in spreading a gospel such as black nationalism, it is not designed to make the black man re-evaluate the white man — you know him already — but to make the black man re-evaluate himself. Don't change the white man's mind — you can't change his mind, and that whole thing about appealing to the moral conscience of America — America's conscience is bankrupt. She lost all conscience a long time ago. Uncle Sam has no conscience. They don't know what morals are. They don't try and eliminate an evil because it's evil, or because it's illegal, or because it's immoral; they eliminate it only when it threatens their existence. So you're wasting your time appealing to the moral conscience of a bankrupt man like Uncle Sam. If he had a conscience, he'd straighten this thing out with no more pressure being put upon him. So it is not necessary to change the white man's mind. We have to change our own mind. You can't change his mind about us. We've got to change our own minds about each other. We have to see each other with new eyes. We have to see each other as brothers and sisters. We have to come together with warmth so we can develop unity and harmony that's necessary to get this problem solved ourselves. How can we do this?

How can we avoid jealousy? How can we avoid the suspicion and the divisions that exist in the community? I'll tell you how.

I have watched how Billy Graham comes into a city, spreading what he calls the gospel of Christ, which is only white nationalism. That's what he is. Billy Graham is a white nationalist; I'm a black nationalist. But since it's the natural tendency for leaders to be jealous and look upon a powerful figure like Graham with suspicion and envy, how is it possible for him to come into a city and get all the cooperation of the church leaders? Don't think because they're church leaders that they don't have weaknesses that make them envious and jealous — no, everybody's got it. It's not an accident that when they want to choose a cardinal as Pope over there in Rome, they get in a closet so you can't hear them cussing and fighting and carrying on.

Billy Graham comes in preaching the gospel of Christ, he evangelizes the gospel, he stirs everybody up, but he never tries to start a church. If he came in trying to start a church, all the churches would be against him. So, he just comes in talking about Christ and tells everybody who gets Christ to go to any church where Christ is; and in this way the church cooperates with him. So we're going to take a page from his book. Our gospel is black nationalism. We're not trying to threaten the existence of any organization, but we're spreading the gospel of black nationalism. Anywhere there's a church that is also preaching and practicing the gospel of black nationalism, join that church. If the NAACP is preaching and practicing the gospel of black nationalism, join the NAACP. If CORE is spreading and practicing the gospel of black nationalism, join CORE. Join any organization that has a gospel that's for the uplift of the black man. And when you get into it and see them pussyfooting or compromising, pull out of it because that's not black nationalism. We'll find another one.

And in this manner, the organizations will increase in number and in quantity and in quality, and by August, it is then our intention to have a black nationalist convention which will consist of delegates from all over the country who are interested in the political, economic and social philosophy of black nationalism. After these delegates convene, we will hold a seminar, we will hold discussions, we will listen to everyone. We want to hear new ideas and new solutions and new answers. And at that time, if we see fit then to form a black nationalist party, we'll form a black nationalist party. If it's necessary to form a black nationalist army, we'll form a black nationalist army. It'll be the ballot or the bullet. It'll be liberty or it'll be death. ...

Last but not least, I must say this concerning the great controversy over rifles and shotguns. The only thing that I've ever said is that in areas where the government has proven itself either unwilling or unable to defend the lives and the property of Negroes, it's time for Negroes to defend themselves. Article number two of the constitutional amendments provides you and me the right to own a rifle or a shotgun. It is constitutionally legal to own a shotgun or a rifle. This doesn't mean you're going to get a rifle and form battalions and go out looking for white folks, although you'd be within your rights — I mean, you'd be justified; but that would be illegal and we don't do anything illegal. If the white man doesn't want the black man buying rifles and shotguns, then let the government do its job. That's all. And don't let the white man come to you and ask you what you think about what Malcolm says — why, you old Uncle Tom. He would never ask you if he thought you were going to say, "Amen!" No, he is making a Tom out of you. So, this doesn't mean forming rifle clubs and going out looking for people, but it is time, in 1964, if you are a man, to let that man know. If he's not going to do his job in running the government and providing you and me with the protection that our taxes are supposed to be for, since he spends all those billions for his defense budget, he certainly can't begrudge you and me spending $12 or $15 for a single-shot, or double-action. I hope you understand. Don't go out shooting people, but any time, brothers and sisters, and especially the men in this audience — some of you wearing Congressional Medals of Honor, with shoulders this wide, chests this big, muscles that big — any time you and I sit around and read where they bomb a church and murder in cold blood, not some grownups, but four little girls while they were praying to the same god the white man taught them to pray to, and you and I see the government go down and can't find who did it. Why, this man — he can find Eichmann hiding down in Argentina somewhere. Let two or three American soldiers, who are minding somebody else's business way over in South Vietnam, get killed, and he'll send battleships, sticking his nose in their business. He wanted to send troops down to Cuba and make them have what he calls free elections — this old cracker who doesn't have free elections in his own country. No, if you never see me another time in your life, if I die in the morning, I'll die saying one thing: the ballot or the bullet, the ballot or the bullet.

If a Negro in 1964 has to sit around and wait for some cracker senator to filibuster when it comes to the rights of black people, why, you and I should hang our heads in shame. You talk about a march on Washington in 1963, you haven't seen anything. There's some more going down in '64. And this time they're not going like they went last year. They're not going singing "We Shall Overcome." They're not going with white friends. They're not going with placards already painted for them. They're not going with round-trip tickets. They're going with one-way tickets.

And if they don't want that non-nonviolent army going down there, tell them to bring the filibuster to a halt. The black nationalists aren't going to wait. Lyndon B. Johnson is the head of the Democratic Party. If he's for civil rights, let him go into the Senate next week and declare himself. Let him go in there right now and declare himself. Let him go in there and denounce the Southern branch of his party. Let him go in there right now and take a moral stand — right now, not later. Tell him, don't

wait until election time. If he waits too long, brothers and sisters, he will be responsible for letting a condition develop in this country which will create a climate that will bring seeds up out of the ground with vegetation on the end of them looking like something these people never dreamed of. In 1964, it's the ballot or the bullet. Thank you.

8.2

LETTER FROM MECCA
El-Hajj Malik El-Shabazz
(Malcolm X)

In April 1964, Malcolm X followed the Islamic ritual of making a spiritual pilgrimage to Mecca. His experiences with Muslims from around the world and in the Arab World radically changed his outlook on race and race relations. As he states in his *Autobiography of Malcolm X*, his life had always been one of adapting to the new realities presented. And thus he adapted now. He no longer believed the white race to be devils or the rift between white and black in America to be unbridgeable. To the contrary, he became convinced that belief in the "Oneness of God" would do just that. He remained a black nationalist, focused on the community's uplift through unity and self-love, but he set out to reverse the "'hate' image of Malcolm X." In a letter sent first to his family and friends, and then to the press, he announced his change of heart.

Never have I witnessed such sincere hospitality and the overwhelming spirit of true brotherhood as practiced by people of all colors and races here in this Ancient Holy Land, the home of Abraham, Muhammad and all other prophets of the Holy Scriptures. For the past week, I have been utterly speechless and spellbound by the graciousness I see displayed all around me by people of all colors.

I have been blessed to visit the Holy City of Mecca. I have made my seven circuits around the Ka'ba, led by a young Mutawaf named Muhammad. I drank water from the well of Zem Zem. I ran seven times back and forth between the hills of Mt. Al-Safa and Al-Marwah. I have prayed in the ancient city of Mina, and I have prayed on Mt. Arafat.

There were tens of thousands of pilgrims, from all over the world. They were of all colors, from blue-eyed blonds to black skin Africans. But we were all participating in the same rituals, displaying a spirit of unity and brotherhood that my experiences in America had led me to believe never could exist between the white and non-white.

America needs to understand Islam, because this is the one religion that erases from its society the race problem. Throughout my travels in the Muslim world, I have met, talked to, and even eaten with people who in America would have been considered 'white' — but the 'white' attitude was removed from their minds by the religion of Islam. I have never before seen sincere and true brotherhood practiced by all colors together, irrespective of their color.

You may be shocked by these words coming from me. But on this pilgrimage, what I have seen, and experienced, has forced me to rearrange much of my thought-patterns previously held, and to toss aside some of my previous conclusions. This was not too difficult for me. Despite my firm convictions, I have always been a man who tries to face facts, and to accept the reality of life as new experiences and new knowledge unfolds it. I have always kept an open mind, which is necessary to the flexibility that must go hand in hand with every form of intelligent search for truth.

During the past eleven days here in the Muslim world, I have eaten from the same plate, drunk from the same glass, and slept in the same bed, (or on the same rug) — while praying to the same God — with fellow Muslims, whose eyes were the bluest of blue, whose hair was the blondest of blond, and whose skin was the whitest of white. And in the same words and in the actions and in the deeds of the 'white' Muslims, I felt the same sincerity that I felt among the black African Muslims of Nigeria, Sudan and Ghana.

We were truly all the same (brothers) — because their belief in one God had removed the 'white' from their minds, the 'white' from their behavior, and the 'white' from their attitude.

I could see from this, that perhaps if white Americans could accept the Oneness of God, then perhaps, too, they could accept in reality the Oneness of Man — and cease to measure, and hinder, and harm others in terms of their differences in color.

With racism plaguing America like an incurable cancer, the so-called 'Christian' white American heart should be more receptive to a proven solution to such a destructive problem. Perhaps it could be in time to save America from imminent disaster — the same destruction brought upon Germany by racism that eventually destroyed the Germans themselves.

Each hour here in the Holy Land enables me to have greater spiritual insights into what is happening in America between black and white. The American Negro never can be blamed for his racial animosities — he is only reacting to four hundred years of conscious racism of the American whites. But as racism leads America up the suicide path, I do believe, from the experience that I have had with them, that the whites of the younger generation, in the colleges and universities, will see the handwriting on the wall and many of them will turn to the spiritual path of truth — the only way left to America to ward off the disaster that racism inevitably must lead to.

Never have I been so highly honored. Never have I been made to feel more humble and unworthy. Who would believe the blessings that have been heaped upon an American Negro? A few nights ago, a man who would be called in America a 'white' man, a United Nations diplomat, an ambassador, a companion of kings, gave me his hotel suite, his bed. By this man, His Excellency Prince Faisal, who rules this Holy Land, was made aware of my presence here in Jedda. The very next morning, Prince Faisal's son, in person, informed me that by the will and decree of his esteemed father, I was to be a State Guest.

The deputy Chief of Protocol himself took me before the Hajj Court. His Holiness Sheikh Muhammad Harkon himself okayed my visit to Mecca. His Holiness gave me two books on

Islam, with his personal seal and autograph, and he told me that he prayed that I would be a successful preacher of Islam in America. A car, a driver, and a guide, have been placed at my disposal, making it possible for me to travel about this Holy Land almost at will. The government provides air conditioned quarters and servants in each city that I visit. Never would I have even thought of dreaming that I would ever be a recipient of such honors — honors that in America would be bestowed upon a King — not a Negro.

All praise is due to Allah, the Lord of all the Worlds.

Sincerely,

El-Hajj Malik El-Shabazz (Malcom X)

——— 8.3 ———

THE GREATEST OF ALL TIME
Muhammad Ali (Cassius Clay) with Alex Haley

Early in 1964, Olympic Gold Medalist Cassius Clay announced to the world he would knock out Heavyweight Champion Sonny Liston. What he said was stunningly cocky for such a heavy underdog, but what was cockier still was the way he said it. At the weigh-in and in statements to the press Clay put on flamboyant shows, taunting Liston and declaring his certain victory in impromptu poems. His fight strategy, he said, would be to "float like a butterfly, sting like a bee." On February 25, he made good. Liston, previously considered invincible, failed to come out of his corner for the eighth round, claiming a shoulder injury.

But Clay wasn't finished shocking the world. Following the fight, he announced that he was joining the controversial Nation of Islam and changing his name to Muhammad Ali. The nation went into uproar. The World Boxing Association considered revoking his title, and even black civil rights leaders distanced themselves from the young champ. The NOI, throngs of young black Americans and even Africans who followed his progress in the press, however, adored Ali. In October, journalist Alex Haley interviewed him for *Playboy* magazine. Ali candidly discusses his rationale for "bigmouthing" before the Liston fight, explains his poetry and defends his conversion to Islam.

Playboy: After you had scored victories over Archie Moore, Charley Powell, Doug Jones and Henry Cooper, how did you go about your campaign to get a match with Liston?

Clay: Well, the big thing I did is that until then, I had just been loudmouthing mostly for the public to hear me, to build up the gates for my fights. I hadn't never been messing personally with whoever I was going to fight – and that's what I started when it was time to go after Liston. ... I mean I set out to make him think what I wanted him thinking: that all I was was some clown, and that he never would have to give a second thought to me being able to put up any real fight when we got to the ring. The more out of shape and overconfident I could get him to be, the better. The press, everybody – I didn't want nobody thinking nothing except that I was a joke. Listen here, do you realize that of all them ring "experts" on the newspapers, wasn't hardly one that wasn't as carried away with Liston's reputation as Liston was himself? You know what everybody was writing? Saying I had been winning my fights, calling the rounds, because I was fighting "nothing" fighters. Like I told you already, even with people like Moore and Powell and Jones and Cooper, the papers found some excuse: it never was that maybe I could fight. And when it come to Liston, they was all saying it was the end of the line for me. I might even get killed in there; he was going to put his big fist in my big mouth so far they was going to have to get doctors to pull it out, stuff like that. You couldn't read noting else. That's how come, later on, I made them reporters tell me I was the greatest. ...

He spent more time at them Las Vegas gambling tables than he did at the punching bag. He was getting fatter and flabbier every day, and I was steady hollering louder to keep him that way: "I'm going to skin the big bear!" ... "I'm the greatest!" ... "I'm so pretty I can't hardly stand to look at myself!" Like that. People can't stand a blowhard, but they'll always listen to him. ...

Playboy: Don't you feel that whites have some

reason for concern that the heavyweight champion belongs to an organization that is alleged to teach hatred of whites?

Clay: Look, the black man that's trying to integrate, he's getting beat up and bombed and shot. But the black man that says he don't want to integrate, he gets called a "hate teacher." Looka-here, now Chubby Checker is catching hell with a white woman. And I'm catching hell for not wanting a white woman. The followers of Mr. Elijah Muhammad, we're not trying to marry no white man's sisters and daughters. We're not trying to force our way in to no white neighborhoods. It look like to me that the white people who are so against integrated schools and hotels ought to be glad about what Mr. Muhammad is teaching his followers. The only way for peace between the races is separation of the races. ...

Playboy: What do you have to say about the fact that many Negroes, including several Negro leaders, have said that they have no desire to be identified with a heavyweight champion who is a Black Muslim?

Clay: It's ridiculous for Negroes to be attacking somebody trying to stand up for their own race. People are always telling me "what a good example I could set for my people" if I just wasn't a Muslim. I've heard over and over how come I couldn't have been like Joe Louis and Sugar Ray. Well, they're gone now, and the black man's condition is just the same, ain't it? We're still catching hell. The fact is that my being a Muslim moved me from the sports pages to the front pages. I'm a whole lot bigger man than I would be if I was just a champion prizefighter. Twenty-four hours a day I get offers – to tour somewhere overseas, to visit colleges, to make speeches. Places like Harvard and Tuskegee, television shows, interviews, recordings. I get letters from all over. They are addressed to me in ways like "The Greatest Boxer in the World, U.S.A." and they come straight to me wherever they're mailed from. People want to write books about me. And I ought to have stock in Western Union and cable companies, I get so many of them. I'm

trying to show you how I been elevated from the normal stature of fighters to being a world figure, a leader, a statesman. ...

——— 8.4 ———

'AND I SAID "I WANT YOU TO KNOW SOMETHING," I SAID, "IF I LIVE I WILL BECOME A REGISTERED VOTER."'

Fannie Lou Hammer

Medgar Evers was not the first person murdered in Mississippi while advocating for civil rights, and he wouldn't be the last. Mississippi was as hostile as Alabama to the ongoing changes in the South. But SNCC activists refused to shy away from it. Even after the Civil Rights Act, securing blacks' right to vote in Mississippi and other southern states was difficult. Rigged "literacy" tests allowed white registrars subjective power in deciding who could and could not register to vote, while selectively enforced "poll taxes" kept many blacks from voting once registered. In 1964, SNCC and CORE set out to challenge the practice and register scores of black voters for the upcoming presidential election. It became known as the Freedom Summer. They founded the Mississippi Freedom Democratic Party (MFDP), intending to challenge the all-white Mississippi delegation to the Democratic National Convention.

On June 21, one black and two white volunteers — Michael Schwerner, Andrew Goodman, and James Chaney — were arrested for speeding. The police claimed to have later released them, but, as was all too common when blacks fell into the hands of white law enforcement in Mississippi, the men were never seen again. On August 4, little more than two days before the Democratic convention, their bodies were found — they had been shot in the back and dumped in a reservoir. The body of the black volunteer, Chaney, showed signs of having been brutally beaten. MFDP's already growing support base among Democrats increased following the murders, and the emboldened activists demanded that their 68 delegates be seated rather than the illegally-elected white ones.

With the national news cameras rolling, Fannie Lou Hammer led the party's cause in testimony before the convention's credentials committee, chaired by Minnesota Attorney General Walter Mondale, detailing voting irregularities in the state. With the help of the NAACP, Senator Hubert Humphrey brokered a compromise that would have kept the white delegation in place if they pledged allegiance to the Democratic Party platform — which the bulk refused to do, forfeiting their seats. MFDP had never agreed to the compromise in the first place, and when the white delegates left their seats vacant, Mississippi activists filled the gaps. Convention organizers had them thrown out and removed the empty chairs from the floor. But the MFDP activists came back the next day and, standing in the back, sang Freedom Songs throughout the proceedings.

During the following summer, Stanford University radio station KZSU conducted a series of lengthy interviews with activists and citizens in Mississippi. Below are excerpts from the station's conversation with Hammer, in which she explains how she became involved in voter registration efforts, and the tactics used by Mississippi law enforcement officials to harass blacks in the movement.

... So in 1962 in the 14th day of August the Student Nonviolent Coordinating Committee came into Rulesville. That Monday night after the 14th I went over here, right around the corner here to this church, William Chapel and the pastor announced at the end of the service that there would be a mass meeting that night, that Monday night following that Sunday. So I didn't understand what that mass meeting was, I didn't know what it was 'cause I'd never gone to a mass meeting. So on Monday night my husband drove me from out in the rural area where I had been working to the church. And when we got there, Bob Moses, Lawrence Guyot, Regie Robertson, James Bevel and Jim Forman. And James Bevel preached from the twelve chapters of St. Luke describing the signs of the times. Then Jim Forman from SNCC got up and explained how it was our constitutional rights to register to vote, and how it could change ... the different laws like if we didn't want a law in the town or what was going on we could vote it out. So that I thought it was the most remarkable thing that could happen in the state of Miss. So then they ask who would go down on Friday which was the 31st to try and register. So I went down, I was one

of the persons who said I would go to register on the 31st. So then on the 31st there was 18 of us who went 26 miles to the country court house in Indianola to try to register. And we had this long literacy test that we'd never seen before but when we walked in the office the registrar asked us what we want and we told him we was there to try to register to vote. And he said, "All of you can't stay in here now, get out. All but two." Well I was one of the two persons who stayed in the registrar's office and Ernest Davis was the other person. So we filled out this literacy test as best we could — it was very complicated. I don't know whether you've seen one or not. But anyway we filled it out as best we could and after we had finished the other people went in. And it was about 4 o'clock before we had a chance — to get back on the bus to come back. During the time I was in the registrar's office he made a long distance call to call the police dept. in Cleveland, Miss. And I saw so many people around that day with their guns and different things and dogs, and I really didn't understand ... that they didn't want us to register. So when we started back to Rulesville we were stopped by one of the same highway patrolmen that I'd seen cruising around the bus that the Negro fellow had drove down there to carry us to Indianola. He lived in Bolivar Co. and this bus had been used — year after year to carry people to farm work, chopping and picking cotton and then he would use it to Florida every winter. Well when we got ready to come back we noticed while we were on the bus before the others got on that this state highway patrolman and a city police — just kept cruising backwards and forth past the bus. Then finally they were going out of town but we didn't know exactly what was happening. So then when all of us got on the bus and started to Rulesville we were stopped by this same highway patrolman and city police. And they ordered us to get off the bus and we got off and then they ordered us to get back on the bus. We got back on the bus and they told us to turn around and go back to Indianola. When we got back to Indianola the bus driver was charged with driving a bus the wrong color. They first charged $100 and then they cut down from $100 to $50. And from fifty to $30. Well, by the time they go to thirty, the eighteen of us — had enough to pay this fine. We came on to Rulesville. And when I got to Rulesville then Rev. Jeff Sunny carried me out to the rural area where I had worked 18 yrs. as a timekeeper and sharecropper. So when I got out of his car the kids met me — and my oldest girl was very upset. She told me that this man was very mad 'cause I'd gone to Indianola — and tried to register. So I went in the house because it was — disturbing to me as why he didn't want me to register and I was trying to register for myself. So then my husband came and he start telling me about — Mr. Marlow was mad and he said if I didn't go back to Indianola and withdraw I was going to have to leave. So hehadn't finished talking about it for three or four minutes — till Mr. Marlow came. And I had gone in the house and taken a seat on my little girl's bed and he asked my husband said, "Is Fannie Lou come home yet?" And he said, "Yes sir." And he said, "Well did you tell her what I said?" So I got up then and walked out on the screen porch just like this. And when I walked out he said, "Fannie Lou did Pat tell you what I said?" I said, "Yes sir." He said, "Well I mean that so you will have to go back and withdraw or you will have to leave here." And I didn't say anything. He said, "I'm waiting for your answer, yeh or nay." So I said, "Mr. Marlow I didn't go to Indianola to register for you. I went to Indianola because I was trying to register for myself." So I had to leave that same night, that was on the 31st of August in 1962. The 10th of Sept. is when 16 bullets was fired into the house. You can see it and I'd like for you to see it right back of this house. They shot in that house 16 times — to kill me. And that night, that same night, they shot two girls, one right down the street from that house where they shot in for me. Then they shot in Mr. MacDonald's house. ... The 10th of Dec. 1962 I went back to Indianola to take this literacy test again. So again I was met by the registrar —

he wanted to know — what did I want. So I told him I was there again to take the literacy test to register. And I said "I want you to know something," I said, "If I live I will become a registered voter." I said, "You can't have me fired any more because you had me fired at the beginning." I said, "I won't have to move because I'm not living in a white man's house." I said, "You'll see me every thirty days until I become a registered voter." So that was my second test and I passed that literacy test then on the 10th of Jan. 1963. My husband was arrested in 1963 when I went to the City Hall — they uses so many different tactics — to harass us and we have to pay five and six dollars for water that was impossible for us to use. So this time we was charged with using 9,000 gallons of water. I don't have a sink, no running water in the house, just a commode. And I went up there to tell the lady at the City Hall. I said, "I want you to know that I know better but I'll pay you." I said, "But I want you to know that I know it's impossible for me to use 9,000 gallons of water. I don't have a sink in the house. I don't have anything but a commode and my kids go to school everyday. My husband hunt and I'm working" — I was doing voter registration work. My husband was arrested and carried to jail because of that and fined $100. Later on my daughter was arrested in Cleveland and then the 9th of June I was arrested in Winona and I was beaten in jail until my body was just as hard as metal. I'm suffering now with the blood clot in the artery to my left eye and a permanent kidney injury on the right side and people don't know what it's like to have to listen to phone calls when you're being threatened — people telling you what they gonna come do. But I'm determined to bring a change in the state of Miss. because — all my life as long as I can remember I was just fed up and tired of what was going on here — and I just mean to work, if it means dying I know there is a part of me that will keep on living because the people that know that I work hard, that part will give them strength to keep goin'. ...

——— 8.5 ———

BLOODY SUNDAY

The movement in Selma

At the end of 1964 and beginning of 1965 the Civil Rights Movement's attention turned to Selma, Alabama. SNCC had been working in Selma for two years, where national director John Lewis had recently launched an aggressive voter registration drive. The SCLC was on the hunt for someplace that would dramatize voting irregularities in the way Birmingham had done for segregation, and Selma activists convinced the organizers to choose their city. The heart of their campaign was a series of marches to the registrar's office, where they would attempt to register black voters. Sheriff Jim Clark reacted in much the same way as Birmingham's "Bull" Conner, with mass arrests and violence, at one point striking one of the female organizers in front of national news cameras. In February 1965, officers shot and killed Jimmy Lee Jackson while breaking up a march. In response, organizers staged a 54-mile march from Selma to Montgomery, the state capital.

On March 7, now known as "Bloody Sunday," a group of 500 people began their march to Montgomery, with John Lewis, Amelia Boynton and Hosea Williams at the head. But they were met by 200 police officers on the Edmund Pettus Bridge, at the entrance to Selma. The officers rode on horseback into the crowd from either side of the bridge, wielding batons. Lewis, Boynton and Williams were beaten badly. Again, national television news featured graphic footage of the violence of southern racism. That Tuesday, following a repeat march, a white northern minister was murdered. A few days later, President Lyndon Johnson, who thus far had been reluctant to push a voting rights bill through Congress, gave an address to a joint session of Congress announcing his bill. Famously, in his deep Texas drawl, he declared, "We shall overcome." Some historians count it as Johnson's most impressive speech.

On March 21, 3,500 people from around the country set out on a third march, this time armed with a court order allowing the demonstration. On the last leg of the five-day sojourn several black ministers dressed identically and lined up across the front, due to Justice Department reports that a sniper was waiting in Montgomery to shoot Martin Luther King, Jr. The event closed with one of King's most stirring speeches. Standing on the steps of the Alabama state capital, King shouted the now signature phrase, "How long? Not long."

A. President Johnson's speech to Congress

I speak tonight for the dignity of man and the destiny of democracy.

I urge every member of both parties, Americans of all religions and of all colors, from every section of this country, to join me in that cause.

At times history and fate meet at a single time in a single place to shape a turning point in man's unending search for freedom. So it was at Lexington and Concord. So it was a century ago at Appomattox. So it was last week in Selma, Alabama.

There, long-suffering men and women peacefully protested the denial of their rights as Americans. Many were brutally assaulted. One good man, a man of God, was killed.

There is no cause for pride in what has happened in Selma. There is no cause for self-satisfaction in the long denial of equal rights of millions of Americans. But there is cause for hope and for faith in our democracy in what is happening here tonight.

For the cries of pain and the hymns and protests of oppressed people have summoned into convocation all the majesty of this great Government — the Government of the greatest Nation on earth.

Our mission is at once the oldest and the most basic of this country: to right wrong, to do justice, to serve man.

In our time we have come to live with moments of great crisis. Our lives have been marked with debate about great issues; issues of war and peace, issues of prosperity and depression. But rarely in any time does an issue lay bare the secret heart of America itself. Rarely are we met with a challenge, not to our growth or abundance, our welfare or our security, but rather to the values and the purposes and the meaning of our beloved Nation.

The issue of equal rights for American Negroes is such an issue. And should we defeat every enemy, should we double our wealth and conquer the stars, and still be unequal to this issue, then we will have failed as a people and as a nation.

For with a country as with a person, "What is a man profited, if he shall gain the whole world, and lose his own soul?"

There is no Negro problem. There is no Southern problem. There is no Northern problem. There is only an American problem. And we are met here tonight as Americans — not as Democrats or Republicans — we are met here as Americans to solve that problem.

This was the first nation in the history of the world to be founded with a purpose. The great phrases of that purpose still sound in every American heart, North and South: "All men are created equal" — "government by consent of the governed" — "give me liberty or give me death." Well, those are not just clever words, or those are not just empty theories. In their name Americans have fought and died for two centuries, and tonight around the world they stand there as guardians of our liberty, risking their lives.

Those words are a promise to every citizen that he shall share in the dignity of man. This dignity cannot be found in a man's possessions; it cannot be found in his power, or in his position. It really rests on his right to be treated as a man equal in opportunity to all others. It says that he shall share in freedom, he shall choose his leaders, educate his children, and provide for his family according to his ability and his merits as a human being.

To apply any other test — to deny a man his hopes because of his color or race, his religion or the place of his birth — is not only to do injustice, it is to deny America and to dishonor the dead who gave their lives for American freedom.

Our fathers believed that if this noble view of the rights of man was to flourish, it must be rooted in democracy. The most basic right of all was the right to choose your own leaders. The history of this country, in large measure, is the history of the expansion of that right to all of our people.

Many of the issues of civil rights are very complex and most difficult. But about this there can and should be no argument. Every American citizen must have an equal right to vote. There is no reason which can excuse the denial of that right. There is no duty which weighs more heavily on us than the duty we have to ensure that right.

Yet the harsh fact is that in many places in this country men and women are kept from voting simply because they are Negroes.

Every device of which human ingenuity is capable has been used to deny this right. The Negro citizen may go to register only to be told that the day is wrong, or the hour is late, or the official in charge is absent. And if he persists, and if he manages to present himself to the registrar, he may be disqualified because he did not spell out his middle name or because he abbreviated a word on the application.

And if he manages to fill out an application he is given a test. The registrar is the sole judge of whether he passes this test. He may be asked to recite the entire Constitution, or explain the most complex provisions of State law. And even a college degree cannot be used to prove that he can read and write.

For the fact is that the only way to pass these barriers is to show a white skin.

Experience has clearly shown that the existing process of law cannot overcome systematic and ingenious discrimination. No law that we now have on the books — and I have helped to put three of them there — can ensure the right to vote when local officials are determined to deny it.

In such a case our duty must be clear to all of us. The Constitution says that no person shall be kept from voting because of his race or his color. We have all sworn an oath before God to support and to defend that Constitution. We must now act in obedience to that oath.

Wednesday I will send to Congress a law designed to eliminate illegal barriers to the right to vote.

The broad principles of that bill will be in the hands of the Democratic and Republican leaders tomorrow. After they have reviewed it, it will come here formally as a bill. I am grateful for this opportunity to come here tonight at the invitation of the leadership to reason with my friends, to give them my views, and to visit with my former colleagues. …

To those who seek to avoid action by their National Government in their own communities; who want to and who seek to maintain purely local control over elections, the answer is simple:

Open your polling places to all your people.

Allow men and women to register and vote whatever the color of their skin.

Extend the rights of citizenship to every citizen of this land.

There is no constitutional issue here. The command of the Constitution is plain.

There is no moral issue. It is wrong — deadly wrong — to deny any of your fellow Americans the right to vote in this country.

There is no issue of States rights or national rights. There is only the struggle for human rights.

I have not the slightest doubt what will be your answer.

The last time a President sent a civil rights bill to the Congress it contained a provision to protect voting rights in Federal elections. That civil rights bill was passed after eight long months of debate. And when that bill came to my desk from the Congress for my signature, the heart of the voting provision had been eliminated.

This time, on this issue, there must be no delay, no hesitation and no compromise with our purpose.

We cannot, we must not, refuse to protect the right of every American to vote in every election that he may desire to participate in.

And we ought not and we cannot and we must not wait another eight months before we get a bill. We have already waited a hundred years and more, and the time for waiting is gone.

So I ask you to join me in working long hours — nights and weekends, if necessary — to pass this bill. And I don't make that request lightly. For from the window where I sit with

the problems of our country I recognize that outside this chamber is the outraged conscience of a nation, the grave concern of many nations, and the harsh judgment of history on our acts.

But even if we pass this bill, the battle will not be over. What happened in Selma is part of a far larger movement which reaches into every section and State of America. It is the effort of American Negroes to secure for themselves the full blessings of American life.

Their cause must be our cause too. Because it is not just Negroes, but really it is all of us, who must overcome the crippling legacy of bigotry and injustice.

And we shall overcome.

As a man whose roots go deeply into Southern soil I know how agonizing racial feelings are. I know how difficult it is to reshape the attitudes and the structure of our society.

But a century has passed, more than a hundred years, since the Negro was freed. And he is not fully free tonight.

It was more than a hundred years ago that Abraham Lincoln, a great President of another party, signed the Emancipation Proclamation, but emancipation is a proclamation and not a fact.

A century has passed, more than a hundred years, since equality was promised. And yet the Negro is not equal.

A century has passed since the day of promise. And the promise is unkept.

The time of justice has now come. I tell you that I believe sincerely that no force can hold it back. It is right in the eyes of man and God that it should come. And when it does, I think that day will brighten the lives of every American.

For Negroes are not the only victims. How many white children have gone uneducated, how many white families have lived in stark poverty, how many white lives have been scarred by fear, because we have wasted our energy and oursubstance to maintain the barriers of hatred and terror?

So I say to all of you here, and to all in the Nation tonight, that those who appeal to you to hold on to the past do so at the cost of denying you your future.

This great, rich, restless country can offer opportunity and education and hope to all: black and white, North and South, sharecropper and city dweller. These are the enemies: poverty, ignorance, disease. They are the enemies and not our fellow man, not our neighbor. And these enemies too, poverty, disease and ignorance, we shall overcome. ...

My first job after college was as a teacher in Cotulla, Texas, in a small Mexican-American school. Few of them could speak English, and I couldn't speak much Spanish. My students were poor and they often came to class without breakfast, hungry. They knew even in their youth the pain of prejudice. They never seemed to know why people disliked them. But they knew it was so, because I saw it in their eyes. I often walked home late in the afternoon, after the classes were finished, wishing there was more that I could do. But all I knew was to teach them the little that I knew, hoping that it might help them against the hardships that lay ahead.

Somehow you never forget what poverty and hatred can do when you see its scars on the hopeful face of a young child.

I never thought then, in 1928, that I would be standing here in 1965. It never even occurred to me in my fondest dreams that I might have the chance to help the sons and daughters of those students and to help people like them all over this country.

But now I do have that chance — and I'll let you in on a secret — I mean to use it. And I hope that you will use it with me.

This is the richest and most powerful country which ever occupied the globe. The might of past empires is little compared to ours. But I do not want to be the President who built empires, or sought grandeur, or extended dominion.

I want to be the President who educated young children to the wonders of their world. I want to be the President who helped to feed the hungry and to prepare them to be taxpayers instead of taxeaters.

I want to be the President who helped the poor to find their own way and who protected the right of every citizen to vote in every election.

I want to be the President who helped to end hatred among his fellow men and who promoted love among the people of all races and all regions and all parties.

I want to be the President who helped to end war among the brothers of this earth.

And so at the request of your beloved Speaker and the Senator from Montana; the majority leader, the Senator from Illinois; the minority leader, Mr. McCulloch, and other Members of both parties, I came here tonight — not as President Roosevelt came down one time in person to veto a bonus bill, not as President Truman came down one time to urge the passage of a railroad bill — but I came down here to ask you to share this task with me and to share it with the people that we both work for. I want this to be the Congress, Republicans and Democrats alike, which did all these things for all these people.

Beyond this great chamber, out yonder in 50 States, are the people that we serve. Who can tell what deep and unspoken hopes are in their hearts tonight as they sit there and listen. We all can guess, from our own lives, how difficult they often find their own pursuit of happiness, how many problems each little family has. They look most of all to themselves for their futures. But I think that they also look to each of us.

Above the pyramid on the great seal of the United States it says — in Latin — "God has favored our undertaking."

God will not favor everything that we do. It is rather our duty to divine His will. But I cannot help believing that He truly understands and that He really favors the undertaking that we begin here tonight.

B. King's speech on the steps of the Alabama state capital

... They told us we wouldn't get here. And there were those who said that we would get here only over their dead bodies, but all the world today knows that we are here and we are standing before the forces of power in the state of Alabama saying, "We ain't goin' let nobody turn us around."

Now it is not an accident that one of the great marches of American history should terminate in Montgomery, Alabama. Just ten years ago, in this very city, a new philosophy was born of the Negro struggle. Montgomery was the first city in the South in which the entire Negro community united and squarely faced its age-old oppressors. Out of this struggle, more than bus desegregation was won; a new idea, more powerful than guns or clubs was born. Negroes took it and carried it across the South in epic battles that electrified the nation and the world.

Yet, strangely, the climactic conflicts always were fought and won on Alabama soil. After Montgomery's, heroic confrontations loomed up in Mississippi, Arkansas, Georgia, and elsewhere. But not until the colossus of segregation was challenged in Birmingham did the conscience of America begin to bleed. White America was profoundly aroused by Birmingham because it witnessed the whole community of Negroes facing terror and brutality with majestic scorn and heroic courage. And from the wells of this democratic spirit, the nation finally forced Congress to write legislation in the hope that it would eradicate the stain of Birmingham. The Civil Rights Act of 1964 gave Negroes some part of their rightful dignity, but without the vote it was dignity without strength.

Once more the method of nonviolent resistance was unsheathed from its scabbard, and once again an entire community was mobilized to confront the adversary. And again the brutality of a dying order shrieks across the land. Yet, Selma, Alabama, became a shining moment in the conscience of man. If the worst in American life lurked in its dark streets, the best of American instincts arose passionately from across the nation to overcome it. ...

Toward the end of the Reconstruction era,

something very significant happened. That is what was known as the Populist Movement. The leaders of this movement began awakening the poor white masses and the former Negro slaves to the fact that they were being fleeced by the emerging Bourbon interests. Not only that, but they began uniting the Negro and white masses into a voting bloc that threatened to drive the Bourbon interests from the command posts of political power in the South.

To meet this threat, the southern aristocracy began immediately to engineer this development of a segregated society. I want you to follow me through here because this is very important to see the roots of racism and the denial of the right to vote. Through their control of mass media, they revised the doctrine of white supremacy. They saturated the thinking of the poor white masses with it, thus clouding their minds to the real issue involved in the Populist Movement. They then directed the placement on the books of the South of laws that made it a crime for Negroes and whites to come together as equals at any level. And that did it. That crippled and eventually destroyed the Populist Movement of the nineteenth century.

If it may be said of the slavery era that the white man took the world and gave the Negro Jesus, then it may be said of the Reconstruction era that the southern aristocracy took the world and gave the poor white man Jim Crow. He gave him Jim Crow. And when his wrinkled stomach cried out for the food that his empty pockets could not provide, he ate Jim Crow, a psychological bird that told him that no matter how bad off he was, at least he was a white man, better than the black man. And he ate Jim Crow. And when his undernourished children cried out for the necessities that his low wages could not provide, he showed them the Jim Crow signs on the buses and in the stores, on the streets and in the public buildings. And his children, too, learned to feed upon Jim Crow, their last outpost of psychological oblivion.

Thus, the threat of the free exercise of the

ballot by the Negro and the white masses alike resulted in the establishment of a segregated society. They segregated southern money from the poor whites; they segregated southern mores from the rich whites; they segregated southern churches from Christianity; they segregated southern minds from honest thinking; and they segregated the Negro from everything. That's what happened when the Negro and white masses of the South threatened to unite and build a great society: a society of justice where none would pray upon the weakness of others; a society of plenty where greed and poverty would be done away; a society of brotherhood where every man would respect the dignity and worth of human personality.

We've come a long way since that travesty of justice was perpetrated upon the American mind. James Weldon Johnson put it eloquently. He said:

We have come over a way
That with tears hath been watered.
We have come treading our paths
Through the blood of the slaughtered.
Out of the gloomy past,
Till now we stand at last
Where the white gleam
Of our bright star is cast.

Today I want to tell the city of Selma, today I want to say to the state of Alabama, today I want to say to the people of America and the nations of the world, that we are not about to turn around. We are on the move now.

Yes, we are on the move and no wave of racism can stop us. We are on the move now. The burning of our churches will not deter us. The bombing of our homes will not dissuade us. We are on the move now. The beating and killing of our clergymen and young people will not divert us. We are on the move now. The wanton release of their known murderers would not discourage us. We are on the move now. Like an idea whose time has come, not even the marching of mighty armies can halt us. We are moving to the land of freedom.

Let us therefore continue our triumphant march to the realization of the American dream. Let us march on segregated housing until every ghetto or social and economic depression dissolves, and Negroes and whites live side by side in decent, safe, and sanitary housing. Let us march on segregated schools until every vestige of segregated and inferior education becomes a thing of the past, and Negroes and whites study side-by-side in the socially-healing context of the classroom.

Let us march on poverty until no American parent has to skip a meal so that their children may eat. March on poverty until no starved man walks the streets of our cities and towns in search of jobs that do not exist. Let us march on poverty until wrinkled stomachs in Mississippi are filled, and the idle industries of Appalachia are realized and revitalized, and broken lives in sweltering ghettos are mended and remolded.

Let us march on ballot boxes, march on ballot boxes until race-baiters disappear from the political arena.

Let us march on ballot boxes until the salient misdeeds of bloodthirsty mobs will be transformed into the calculated good deeds of orderly citizens.

Let us march on ballot boxes until the Wallaces of our nation tremble away in silence.

Let us march on ballot boxes until we send to our city councils, state legislatures, and the United States Congress, men who will not fear to do justly, love mercy, and walk humbly with thy God.

Let us march on ballot boxes until brotherhood becomes more than a meaningless word in an opening prayer, but the order of the day on every legislative agenda.

Let us march on ballot boxes all over Alabama God's children will be able to walk the earth in decency and honor.

There is nothing wrong with marching in this sense. The Bible tells us that the mighty men of Joshua merely walked about the walled city of Jericho and the barriers to freedom came tumbling down. I like that old Negro spiritual, "Joshua Fit the Battle of Jericho." In its simple, yet colorful, depiction of that great moment in biblical history, it tells us that:

Joshua fit the battle of Jericho,
Joshua fit the battle of Jericho,
And the walls come tumbling down.
Up to the walls of Jericho they marched,
    spear in hand.
"Go blow them ramhorns," Joshua cried,
"'Cause the battle am in my hand."

These words I have given you just as they were given us by the unknown, long-dead, dark-skinned originator. Some now long-gone black bard bequeathed to posterity these words in ungrammatical form, yet with emphatic pertinence for all of us today.

The battle is in our hands. And we can answer with creative nonviolence the call to higher ground to which the new directions of our struggle summons us. The road ahead is not altogether a smooth one. There are no broad highways that lead us easily and inevitably to quick solutions. But we must keep going.

In the glow of the lamplight on my desk a few nights ago, I gazed again upon the wondrous sign of our times, full of hope and promise of the future. And I smiled to see in the newspaper photographs of many a decade ago, the faces so bright, so solemn, of our valiant heroes, the people of Montgomery. To this list may be added the names of all those who have fought and, yes, died in the nonviolent army of our day: Medgar Evers, three civil rights workers in Mississippi last summer, William Moore, as has already been mentioned, the Reverend James Reeb, Jimmy Lee Jackson, and four little girls in the church of God in Birmingham on Sunday morning. But in spite of this, we must go on and be sure that they did not die in vain. The pattern of their feet as they walked through Jim Crow barriers in the great stride toward freedom is the thunder of the marching men of Joshua, and the world rocks beneath their tread.

My people, my people, listen. The battle is in our hands. The battle is in our hands in Mississippi and Alabama and all over the United States. I know there is a cry today in Alabama, we see it in numerous editorials: "When will Martin Luther King, SCLC, SNCC, and all of these civil rights agitators and all of the white clergymen and labor leaders and students and others get out of our community and let Alabama return to normalcy?"

But I have a message that I would like to leave with Alabama this evening. That is exactly what we don't want, and we will not allow it to happen, for we know that it was normalcy in Marion that led to the brutal murder of Jimmy Lee Jackson. It was normalcy in Birmingham that led to the murder on Sunday morning of four beautiful, unoffending, innocent girls. It was normalcy on Highway 80 that led state troopers to use tear gas and horses and billy clubs against unarmed human beings who were simply marching for justice. It was normalcy by a cafe in Selma, Alabama, that led to the brutal beating of Reverend James Reeb.

It is normalcy all over our country which leaves the Negro perishing on a lonely island of poverty in the midst of a vast ocean of material prosperity. It is normalcy all over Alabama that prevents the Negro from becoming a registered voter. No, we will not allow Alabama to return to normalcy.

The only normalcy that we will settle for is the normalcy that recognizes the dignity and worth of all of God's children. The only normalcy that we will settle for is the normalcy that allows judgment to run down like waters, and righteousness like a mighty stream. The only normalcy that we will settle for is the normalcy of brotherhood, the normalcy of true peace, the normalcy of justice.

And so as we go away this afternoon, let us go away more than ever before committed to this struggle and committed to nonviolence. I must admit to you that there are still some difficult days ahead. We are still in for a season of suffering in many of the black belt counties of Alabama, many areas of Mississippi, many areas of Louisiana. I must admit to you that there are still jail cells waiting for us, and dark and difficult moments. But if we will go on with the faith that nonviolence and its power can transform dark yesterdays into bright tomorrows, we will be able to change all of these conditions.

And so I plead with you this afternoon as we go ahead: remain committed to nonviolence. Our aim must never be to defeat or humiliate the white man, but to win his friendship and understanding. We must come to see that the end we seek is a society at peace with itself, a society that can live with its conscience. And that will be a day not of the white man, not of the black man. That will be the day of man as man.

I know you are asking today, "How long will it take?" Somebody's asking, "How long will prejudice blind the visions of men, darken their understanding, and drive bright-eyed wisdom from her sacred throne?" Somebody's asking, "When will wounded justice, lying prostrate on the streets of Selma and Birmingham and communities all over the South, be lifted from this dust of shame to reign supreme among the children of men?" Somebody's asking, "When will the radiant star of hope be plunged against the nocturnal bosom of this lonely night, plucked from weary souls with chains of fear and the manacles of death? How long will justice be crucified, and truth bear it?"

I come to say to you this afternoon, however difficult the moment, however frustrating the hour, it will not be long, because "truth crushed to earth will rise again."

How long? Not long, because "no lie can live forever."

How long? Not long, because "you shall reap what you sow."

How long? Not long:

Truth forever on the scaffold,
Wrong forever on the throne,
Yet that scaffold sways the future,
And, behind the dim unknown,
Standeth God within the shadow,
Keeping watch above his own.

How long? Not long, because the arc of the moral universe is long, but it bends toward justice.

How long? Not long, because:

Mine eyes have seen the glory of the coming
    of the Lord;
He is trampling out the vintage where
    the grapes of wrath are stored;
He has loosed the fateful lightning of his
    terrible swift sword;
His truth is marching on.
He has sounded forth the trumpet that
    shall never call retreat;
He is sifting out the hearts of men before His
    judgment seat.
O, be swift, my soul, to answer Him!
Be jubilant my feet!
Our God is marching on.
Glory, hallelujah! Glory, hallelujah!
Glory, hallelujah! Glory, hallelujah!
His truth is marching on.

——— 8.6 ———
VOTING RIGHTS ACT OF 1965
U.S. Congress

President Johnson signed the Voting Rights Act into law on August 6, 1965. The bill largely restated the 15th Amendment, but also addressed the tactics used in southern precincts to circumvent that amendment. It all but federalized the registration process in certain states, temporarily banning all literacy tests, appointed federal "examiners" to monitor the voting process in those states, and forbade them from creating new registration procedures without federal clearance. By the end of the year over a quarter of a million blacks registered to vote, one-third of whom were registered by the federal examiners.

AN ACT To enforce the fifteenth amendment to the Constitution of the United States, and for other purposes.

Be it enacted by the Senate and House of Representatives of the United States of America in Congress assembled, That this Act shall be known as the "Voting Rights Act of 1965." ...

SEC. 2. No voting qualification or prerequisite to voting, or standard, practice, or procedure shall be imposed or applied by any State or political subdivision to deny or abridge the right of any citizen of the United States to vote on account of race or color.

SEC. 3. (a) Whenever the Attorney General institutes a proceeding under any statute to enforce the guarantees of the fifteenth amendment in any State or political subdivision the court shall authorize the appointment of Federal examiners by the United States Civil Service Commission in accordance with section 6 to serve for such period of time and for such political subdivisions as the court shall determine is appropriate to enforce the guarantees of the fifteenth amendment (1) as part of any interlocutory order if the court determines that the appointment of such examiners is necessary to enforce such guarantees or (2) as part of any final judgment if the court finds that violations of the fifteenth amendment justifying equitable relief have occurred in such State or subdivision: Provided, That the court need not authorize the appointment of examiners if any incidents of denial or abridgement of the right to vote on account of race or color (1) have been few in number and have been promptly and effectively corrected by State or local action, (2) the continuing effect of such incidents has been eliminated, and (3) there is no reasonable probability of their recurrence in the future. ...

SEC. 4. (a) To assure that the right of citizens of the United States to vote is not denied or abridged on account of race or color, no citizen shall be denied the right to vote in any Federal, State, or local election because of his failure to comply with any test or device in any State with respect to which the determinations have been made under subsection (b) or in any political subdivision with respect to which such determinations have been made as a separate unit, unless the United States District Court for the District of Columbia in an action for a declaratory judgment brought by such State or subdivision against the United States has determined that no such test or

device has been used during the five years preceding the filing of the action for the purpose or with the effect of denying or abridging the right to vote on account of race or color: Provided, That no such declaratory judgment shall issue with respect to any plaintiff for a period of five years after the entry of a final judgment of any court of the United States, other than the denial of a declaratory judgment under this section, whether entered prior to or after the enactment of this Act, determining that denials or abridgments of the right to vote on account of race or color through the use of such tests or devices have occurred anywhere in the territory of such plaintiff. ...

SEC. 5. Whenever a State or political subdivision with respect to which the prohibitions set forth in section 4(a) are in effect shall enact or seek to administer any voting qualification or prerequisite to voting, or standard, practice, or procedure with respect to voting different from that in force or effect on November 1, 1964, such State or subdivision may institute an action in the United States District Court for the District of Columbia for a declaratory judgment that such qualification, prerequisite, standard, practice, or procedure does not have the purpose and will not have the effect of denying or abridging the right to vote on account of race or color, and unless and until the court enters such judgment no person shall be denied the right to vote for failure to comply with such qualification, prerequisite, standard, practice, or procedure: Provided, That such qualification, prerequisite, standard, practice, or procedure may be enforced without such proceeding if the qualification, prerequisite, standard, practice, or procedure has been submitted by the chief legal officer or other appropriate official of such State or subdivision to the Attorney General and the Attorney General has not interposed an objection within sixty days after such submission, except that neither the Attorney General's failure to object nor a declaratory judgment entered under this section shall bar a subsequent action to enjoin enforcement of such qualification, prerequisite, standard, practice, or procedure. Any action under this section shall be heard and determined by a court of three judges in accordance with the provisions of section 2284 of title 28 of the United States Code and any appeal shall lie to the Supreme Court.

--------- 8.7 ---------

A EULOGY FOR MALCOLM X

Ossie Davis

After Malcolm X (now El-Hajj Malik El-Shabazz) left the Nation of Islam, a bitter public feud began between him and the group. His fears of an assassination plot against him grew, and in February 1965, his house was fire-bombed. He had already begun to speak publicly about threats on his life, saying he knew of five NOI men who were slated to kill him. Days later, on Sunday, February 21, feeling tired and beleaguered, he stood to give a speech at the Audubon Ballroom in Harlem. Three men rose in the front row and, firing simultaneously, shot Malcolm X 16 times, killing him. Distinguished black actor and writer Ossie Davis delivered this eulogy at Malcolm X's funeral. Responding to subsequent questions as to why he, an active participant in the nonviolent Civil Rights Movement, would eulogize a man who relentlessly criticized the cause, Davis wrote, "It was impossible to remain defensive or apologetic about being a Negro in his presence."

Here — at this final hour, in this quiet place — Harlem has come to bid farewell to one of its brightest hopes — extinguished now, and gone from us forever. For Harlem is where he worked and where he struggled and fought — his home of homes, where his heart was, and where his people are — and it is, therefore, most fitting that we meet once again — in Harlem — to share these last moments with him.

For Harlem has ever been gracious to those who have loved her, have fought for her, and have defended her honor even to the death. It is not in the memory of man that this beleaguered, unfortunate, but nonetheless proud community has found a braver, more gallant young champion than this Afro-American who lies before us — unconquered still. I say the word again, as he would want me to: Afro-American — Afro-American Malcolm, who was a master, was most meticulous in his use of words. Nobody knew better than he the power words have over minds of men. Malcolm had stopped being a 'Negro' years ago. It had become too small, too puny, too weak a word for him. Malcolm was bigger than that. Malcolm had become an Afro-American and he wanted — so desperately — that we, that all his people, would become Afro-Americans too.

There are those who will consider it their duty, as friends of the Negro people, to tell us to revile him, to flee, even from the presence of his memory, to save ourselves by writing him out of the history of our turbulent times. Many will ask what Harlem finds to honor in this stormy, controversial and bold young captain — and we will smile. Many will say turn away — away from this man, for he is not a man but a demon, a monster, a subverter and an enemy of the black man — and we will smile. They will say that he is of hate — a fanatic, a racist — who can only bring evil to the cause for which you struggle! And we will answer and say to them:

Did you ever talk to Brother Malcolm? Did you ever touch him, or have him smile at you? Did you ever really listen to him? Did he ever do a mean thing? Was he ever himself associated with violence or any public disturbance? For if you did you would know him. And if you knew him you would know why we must honor him: Malcolm was our manhood, our living, black manhood!

This was his meaning to his people. And, in honoring him, we honor the best in ourselves. Last year, from Africa, he wrote these words to a friend:

"My journey," he says, "is almost ended, and I have a much broader scope than when I started out, which I believe will add new life and dimension to our struggle for freedom and honor and dignity in the States. I am writing these things so that you will know for a fact the tremendous sympathy and support we have among the African States for our Human Rights struggle.

The main thing is that we keep a United Front wherein our most valuable time and energy will not be wasted fighting each other."

However we may have differed with him — or with each other about him and his value as a man — let his going from us serve only to bring us together, now. Consigning these mortal remains to earth, the common mother of all, secure in the knowledge that what we place in the ground is no more now a man — but a seed — which, after the winter of our discontent, will come forth again to meet us.

And we will know him then for what he was and is — a Prince — our own black shining Prince! — who didn't hesitate to die, because he loved us so.

————— 8.8 —————
'"GET WHITEY," SCREAM BLOOD-HUNGRY MOBS'
Watts Riots of 1965

On August 11, 1965, six days after President Johnson signed the Voting Rights Act into law, two white California Highway Patrol officers pulled over a black motorist they suspected of being intoxicated. A crowd formed, and, it was alleged, someone in the crowd spit on the police. One of the officers stormed into the crowd swinging his nightstick. Tension between the all-white police force and the black community was already high, and this relatively minor incident pushed things over the brink. Thousands of young African Americans rioted for six days, focusing their rage on police and white-owned businesses. Thirty-five people were killed and hundreds injured. Rioters destroyed an estimated $40 million-worth of property. Along with a series of less-dramatic race riots around the country that summer, Watts was a wake-up call to both black civil rights leaders and the nation at-large that the South had no monopoly on racial tension. And it was an ominous foreshadowing of the unrest in black urban neighborhoods that would soon dominate discussions about race in America. The Los Angeles Times quoted black Watts residents explaining their outrage at police conduct in their neighborhoods. In a separate, more sensational, story, a black Times sales representative gave a horrified and indignant account of violence against whites during the riot.

A. Watts residents speak to *Los Angeles Times*

Residents Put Blame on Police for Uproar
By Charles Hillinger and Jack Jones
Times Staff Writers
Knots of Negro residents stood among the shattered glass residue of a hot August night's violence on Avalon Blvd. Thursday and their words were those of anger, frustration and resentment.

An 18-year old girl admitted:

"I threw bricks and rocks and anything I could get my hands on … to hurt them. We were throwing at anything white. Why not do it to you guys? You're doing it to us."

Here and there, a small group of Negroes would break off their conversation to watch silently the approach of white newspapermen, trying to piece together the reasons for the emotional explosion that erupted from the arrest of three Negroes by highway patrolmen at 116th and Avalon.

Blame Police
Those who overcame their suspicions enough to talk about it, told basically the same story: the police handled it all wrong.

The bitterness wasn't exclusive to teen-agers giving vent to pent-up anger.

"I have lived in this city for 17 years and consider myself a responsible person," said Mrs. Ovelmar Bradley, 40, of 1806 W. 131st St., a mother of seven children. "But I have never heard the policeman talk like they did last night. I have never seen anything like this happen here."

Sirens Whining
Mrs. Bradley, arrived with her husband, Henry, to visit a relative in the Avalon area, getting there shortly after the initial flareup over the arrest by the two patrolmen.

Things had quieted momentarily, she said, when 25 or 30 police cars went through the neighborhood with sirens wailing.

"If the police hadn't come in like that," she said, "people wouldn't all have come running out fo their houses to see what was going on.

"My husband and I saw 10 cops beating one man. My husband told the officers, 'You've got him handcuffed.' One of the officers answered, 'Get out of here, nigger. Get out of here, all you niggers!"

She said a few obscenities were added.

Witness Arrest

Richard Brice, 30, who operates a small corner grocery store at 11701 S. Avalon Blvd., recalled that he had just closed up and was walking out into the muggy heat when he saw the initial incident of the drunken arrest.

"This officer had this man handcuffed in the car and the man was trying to fight," said Brice. "The officer took his club and kept jamming it into his stomach. When that happened, all the people standing around got mad. I got mad."

"Everybody got excited and started shouting."

The storekeeper shook his head and added, "Maybe the officer had a reason to do what he was doing. It's just too bad he couldn't have driven away and then struck the man. His action was breeding violence."

'Got Us Calmed'

Another young girl who would not give her name said:

"There was one Negro officer there. He was trying to talk to us. He got us calmed down. Then all these white cops came. They pulled out their shotguns and clubs and the whole thing started again."

Bobby Daniels, 23, a maintenance man of 852 1/2 W 61st Street, who was with his wife, Bertha, 21, was just returning from fishing and stopped by to see what the commotion was about.

"We got out of the car and these 15 officers ran up to us. They jabbed us in the back with clubs and told us to get off the street. They pushed us down and jumped on us, laughing about it."

Resident after resident of the scarred neighborhood, while complaining that the police triggered the eruption, admitted, "Both sides were wrong. This doesn't make us look good."

The Rev. F. Douglas Ferrell, state assemblyman and pastor of Tabernacle of Faith Baptist Church in the neighborhood, who had visited the scene of the rioting, commented:

"A lot of newcomers to California. They bring their hatred and pent-up emotions with them. But interspersed are many good people who are ashamed and sorry about this."

A Negro civil rights leader who tried unsuccessfully to disperse the rioters said he had been "expecting this to happened for two years because the police have no communication with the Negro community."

Robert Hall, co-chairman of the Volunteer Non-Violent Action Committee, said police could have avoided the disturbance to some extent if they had moved out after answering the original trouble call.

Seeking Accord

There were attempts Thursday, by area leaders and social workers to ease the tensions.

Archie W. Hardwicke, 31-year-old Negro director of the Westminster Neighborhood Assn., Inc., a community action agency with support of United Way the Presbyterian Church, said his organization was trying to set up mass meetings — hopefully, with members of the police department — to build some sort of understanding.

"It's a lack of communication between the police and the people of the community," said Hardwicke. "They just don't understand the people here. They came into the area like an army of occupation."

He pointed out that in the neighborhood 34% of the adults are unemployed and 60% of the total population are on some sort of welfare aid.

B. *Times* offers shocked first person account from "a Negro"

EYEWITNESS ACCOUNT
'Get Whitey,' Scream Blood-Hungry Mobs
BY ROBERT RICHARDSON

(Robert Richardson, 24, a Negro, is an advertising salesman for The Times. He witnessed the rioting in South Los Angeles for nearly eight hours Thursday night — Ed.)

It was the most terrifying thing I've ever seen in my life.

I went along with the mobs, just watching, listening.

It's a wonder anyone with white skin got out of there alive.

I saw people with guns. The cry went up several times — "Let's go to Lynwood!" (an all-white neighborhood) whenever there weren't enough whites around.

Racial Word Spreads

Every time a car with whites in it entered the area the word spread like lightening down the street:

"Here comes Whitey, get him!"

The older people would stand in the background, egging on the teen-agers and the people in their early 20s. Then the young men and women would rush in and pull the white people from their cars and beat them and try to set fire to their cars.

One white couple, in their 60s, happened to be driving along Imperial before the blockades were put up. They were beaten and kicked until their faces, hands and clothing were bloody. I thought they were going to be killed. How they survived I don't know. Those not hitting and kicking the couple were standing there shouting, "Kill! Kill!"

Finally they turned them loose and an ambulance was called and they were taken away.

Two white men driving down Avalon Blvd. ducked when rocks bombarded their car. When they ducked they hit a car with Negroes.

They were beaten so badly one man's eye was hanging out of the socket. Some Negro ministers made their way through the crowd and carried both men into an apartment building and called an ambulance.

The crowd called the ministers hypocrites. They cussed them and spit on them. Some

Negro officers tried to disperse the crowd, but they were jeered at, sworn at, called traitors and stoned.

Negro Officers Periled

The Negro officers were given a worse time than the white officers.

Light-skinned Negroes such as myself were targets of rocks and bottles until someone standing nearby would shout, "He's blood," or "He's a brother — lay off!"

As some areas were blockaded during the night, the mobs would move outside, looking for more cars with whites. When they were no more whites they started throwing rocks and bottles at Negro cars. Then near midnight they began looting stores owned by whites.

Everybody got in the looting — children, grownups, old men and women, breaking windows and going into stores.

Then everybody started drinking — even little kids 8 or 9 years old. That's when the cry started. "Let's go where Whitey lives!" that's when I began to see guns.

I believe the mobs would have moved into white neighborhoods, but it was getting late and many of them had to go to work Friday morning.

But some said, "Wait till tonight and Saturday. We'll really rollover the weekend. We'll really get Whitey then!"

They knew they had the upper hand. They seemed to sense that the police nor anyone else could stop them.

I heard them say, "Just wait till one of the blood gets shot — then heads will really roll. Then Whitey will get his!"

--------- 8.9 ---------

A 'DOMESTIC MARSHALL PLAN'
Whitney Young

The Watts riots crystallized a growing feeling among civil rights leaders that all of their work in the South had meant little to those in northern ghettos. For the activists who came to civil rights from labor and economic equality movements, the fact was clear: civil rights were meaningless to poor urban blacks who couldn't afford to exercise them. In a 1964 essay essentially declaring victory over segregation, Bayard Rustin wryly asked, "What is the value of winning access to public accommodations for those who lack money to use them?" But National Urban League head Whitney Young made the loudest call for attention to the needs of poor urban blacks. Two years before Watts, Young published a book of essays entitled *To Be Equal* in which he argued that to level the inequality slavery and segregation created, America would need to invest millions of dollars towards giving blacks the skills to compete in a modern economy. This call for a "domestic Marshall Plan" was the intellectual forefather of today's affirmative action, and it was attacked immediately. Critics — the movement's liberal white supporters foremost among them — asserted that America was not founded on unfair preferences. Young disagreed, arguing that the last two centuries had granted whites exactly that.

To most white Americans the headlines, reporting the crescendo of victories against discriminatory practices, are clear evidence that the Negro citizen is on the threshold of equal participation in American life. This observation is, unfortunately, inaccurate. For at this moment in history, if the United States honestly drops legal, practical, and subtle racial barriers to employment, housing, education, public accommodations, health and welfare facilities and services, the American Negro still will not achieve full equality in our lifetime.

The reason is that the "discrimination gap" caused by more than three centuries of abuse, humiliation, segregation, and bias has burdened the Negro with a handicap that will not automatically slip from his shoulders as discriminatory laws and practices are abandoned. The situation is much like that of two men running the mile in a track meet. One is well-equipped, wears track shoes and runs on cinders. The other is barefoot and runs in sand. Seeing that one runner is outdistancing the other with ease, you then put track shoes on the second fellow and place him on the cinder track also. Seconds later it should surprise no one to see that the second runner is still yards behind and will never catch up unless something else is done to even the contest.

The discrimination gap is real and is explosive. It must be recognized that our Negro citizens, after only grudgingly receiving the barest minimum in health, education, welfare, housing, economic, and cultural opportunities cannot conceivably compete equally for, or share in, the full rewards and responsibilities of our society simply by an announcement, with impressive flourishes, that now a state of equal opportunity exists. Equal opportunity, if it is to be more than a hollow mockery, must also mean the opportunity to be equal; to be given a fair chance to achieve equality. Anything less is simply the exercise by the white majority of a concern that all too clearly is only skin deep. For the individual it represents a shallow attempt to salve one's conscience and remove the symbols that disturb. ...

What I have described in barest outline is a study in inhumanity. In the economic area, it is a disaster — and not just for the Negroes. For the Negro, the situation is far worse than a recession — it constitutes a condition paralleling the Great Depression of the thirties in its pervasive impact. If these conditions affected most Americans to a similar degree, we would be witnessing not peaceful protests but a shooting revolution.

The basic issue here is one of simple logic and fairness. The scales of justice have been heavily weighted against the Negro for over three hundred years and will not suddenly in 1964 balance themselves by applying equal weights. In this sense, the Negro is educationally and economically malnourished and anemic. It is not "preferential treatment" but simple decency to provide him for a brief period with special vitamins, additional food, and blood transfusions.

This is a situation which clearly calls for emergency action on a broad scale in urban communities across the land. Fact-finding committees, pilot projects, tokenism and half-hearted, one-dimensional small-scale efforts will not suffice. This nation and the world need a demonstration that we can bridge the social, economic and educational gap that separates American Negroes from their fellow citizens. It is mandatory that a broad-spectrum, intensive program be launched in the United States, a program that will bring the majority of American Negroes to the point at which they can compete on an equal basis in the nation's increasingly complex and fast-moving industrial economy.

That is why the National Urban League and I, together, have called for an unprecedented domestic "Marshall Plan" approach to these problems. We urgently recommend cooperative special efforts by private, public, and voluntary organizations in a massive "crash" attack on the complete range of economic and social ills involved. …

This special effort program that we recommend should phase out as need for it diminishes over the next decade. It will not be cheap. But it will prove to be an invaluable investment that will reap great returns. Its cost must be viewed in the same terms as programs of preventive medicine. What were the savings from smallpox vaccine? From a polio shot? Or from economic infusions such as the Marshall Plan and our other foreign aid projects? Although the Marshall Plan cost us more than $17 billion, what price can we honestly put on saving Western Europe from being overrun by Communism, on building healthy economies across a war-ravaged continent and strengthening nations in other corners of the world?

--------- 8.10 ---------
'THE DETERIORATION OF THE NEGRO FAMILY'
The Moynihan Report

In early summer 1965, Assistant Secretary of Labor Daniel Patrick Moynihan, a sociologist, published an internal administration memo entitled "The Negro Family: The Call to National Action," since known as the "Moynihan Report." Moynihan argued that all the civil rights gains in the world would only do so much to help African Americans because the root problem the community faced was the "deterioration of the Negro family." The report cited statistics showing the unarguably dire state of black families, particularly in urban areas: over a quarter of black women, once married, no longer lived with their husbands, almost a quarter of all births were "illegitimate" (Moynihan's phrase for children born to unmarried couples), almost half of all black children would receive federal aid at some point in their lives. The report assigned the blame for this deterioration to centuries of oppression and urged a national movement to correct it.

In June, President Lyndon Johnson delivered a major civil rights policy speech at Howard University. Johnson said what many black leaders were then saying — that civil rights without economic empowerment were meaningless — but offered no prescription for dealing with the problem. Rather, he echoed Moynihan's report, discussing the internal social problems of the black community as the core problem at hand. As did the report, he made a vague call to repair the torn black social fabric.

Black leaders of all stripes were outraged. They wanted to talk about rights and about policies reversing the American government's past wrongs. The vehemence of the black leaders' anger at a document that mirrored what many of them were saying themselves is a testament to their heightened impatience with any form of equivocation from the government.

Nevertheless, in effect, the administration had turned from a discussion about the limiting legacy of American racism and discrimination to one about limitations within the black community. The solution to the former would be the sort of "compensatory" programs Whitney Young was promoting; the solution to the latter would be black self-improvement and white assistance that would come and go with the nation's level of sympathy for blacks.

A. The Moynihan Report

At the heart of the deterioration of the fabric of Negro society is the deterioration of the Negro family.

It is the fundamental source of the weakness of the Negro community at the present time.

There is probably no single facet of Negro American life so little understood by whites. The Negro situation is commonly perceived by whites in terms of the visible manifestations of discrimination and poverty, in part because Negro protest is directed against such obstacles, and in part, no doubt, because these are facts which involve the actions and attitudes of the white community as well. It is more difficult, however, for whites to perceive the effect that three centuries of exploitation have had on the fabric of Negro society itself. Here the consequences of the historic injustices done to Negro Americans are silent and hidden from view. But here is where the true injury has occurred: unless this damage is repaired, all the effort to end discrimination and poverty and injustice will come to little.

The role of the family in shaping character and ability is so pervasive as to be easily overlooked. The family is the basic social unit of American life; it is the basic socializing unit. By and large, adult conduct in society is learned as a child.

A fundamental insight of psychoanalytic theory, for example, is that the child learns a way of looking at life in his early years through which all later experience is viewed and which profoundly shapes his adult conduct.

It may be hazarded that the reason family structure does not loom larger in public discussion of social issues is that people tend to assume that the nature of family life is about the same throughout American history. The mass media and the development of suburbia have created an image of the American family as a highly standardized phenomenon. It is therefore easy to assume that whatever it is that makes for differences among individuals or groups of individuals, it is not a different family structure

There is much truth to this; as with any other nation, Americans are producing a recognizable family system. But that process is not completed by any means. There are still, for example, important differences in family patterns surviving from the age of the great European migration to the United States, and these variations account for notable differences in the progress and assimilation of various eth-

nic and religious groups. A number of immigrant groups were characterized by unusually strong family bonds; these groups have characteristically progressed more rapidly than others.

But there is one truly great discontinuity in family structure in the United States at the present time: that between the white world in general and that of the Negro American.

The white family has achieved a high degree of stability and is maintaining that stability.

By contrast, the family structure of lower class Negroes is highly unstable, and in many urban centers is approaching complete breakdown. …

B. President Johnson's Howard University speech

… The voting rights bill will be the latest, and among the most important, in a long series of victories. But this victory — as Winston Churchill said of another triumph for freedom — "is not the end. It is not even the beginning of the end. But it is, perhaps, the end of the beginning."

That beginning is freedom; and the barriers to that freedom are tumbling down. Freedom is the right to share, share fully and equally, in American society — to vote, to hold a job, to enter a public place, to go to school. It is the right to be treated in every part of our national life as a person equal in dignity and promise to all others.

But freedom is not enough. You do not wipe away the scars of centuries by saying: Now you are free to go where you want, and do as you desire, and choose the leaders you please.

You do not take a person who, for years, has been hobbled by chains and liberate him, bring him up to the starting line of a race and then say, "you are free to compete with all the others," and still justly believe that you have been completely fair.

Thus it is not enough just to open the gates of opportunity. All our citizens must have the ability to walk through those gates.

This is the next and the more profound

stage of the battle for civil rights. We seek not just freedom but opportunity. We seek not just legal equity but human ability, not just equality as a right and a theory but equality as a fact and equality as a result.

For the task is to give 20 million Negroes the same chance as every other American to learn and grow, to work and share in society, to develop their abilities — physical, mental and spiritual, and to pursue their individual happiness.

To this end equal opportunity is essential, but not enough, not enough. Men and women of all races are born with the same range of abilities. But ability is not just the product of birth. Ability is stretched or stunted by the family that you live with, and the neighborhood you live in — by the school you go to and the poverty or the richness of your surroundings. It is the product of a hundred unseen forces playing upon the little infant, the child, and finally the man.

This graduating class at Howard University is witness to the indomitable determination of the Negro American to win his way in American life.

The number of Negroes in schools of higher learning has almost doubled in 15 years. The number of nonwhite professional workers has more than doubled in 10 years. The median income of Negro college women tonight exceeds that of white college women. And there are also the enormous accomplishments of distinguished individual Negroes — many of them graduates of this institution, and one of them the first lady ambassador in the history of the United States.

These are proud and impressive achievements. But they tell only the story of a growing middle class minority, steadily narrowing the gap between them and their white counterparts.

But for the great majority of Negro Americans — the poor, the unemployed, the uprooted, and the dispossessed — there is a much grimmer story. They still, as we meet here tonight, are another nation. Despite the court orders and the laws, despite the legislative victories and the speeches, for them the walls are rising and the gulf is widening. …

We are not completely sure why this is. We know the causes are complex and subtle. But we do know the two broad basic reasons. And we do know that we have to act.

First, Negroes are trapped — as many whites are trapped — in inherited, gateless poverty. They lack training and skills. They are shut in, in slums, without decent medical care. Private and public poverty combine to cripple their capacities.

We are trying to attack these evils through our poverty program, through our education program, through our medical care and our other health programs, and a dozen more of the Great Society programs that are aimed at the root causes of this poverty.

We will increase, and we will accelerate, and we will broaden this attack in years to come until this most enduring of foes finally yields to our unyielding will.

But there is a second cause — much more difficult to explain, more deeply grounded, more desperate in its force. It is the devastating heritage of long years of slavery; and a century of oppression, hatred, and injustice.

For Negro poverty is not white poverty. Many of its causes and many of its cures are the same. But there are differences — deep, corrosive, obstinate differences — radiating painful roots into the community, and into the family, and the nature of the individual.

These differences are not racial differences. They are solely and simply the consequence of ancient brutality, past injustice, and present prejudice. They are anguishing to observe. For the Negro they are a constant reminder of oppression. For the white they are a constant reminder of guilt. But they must be faced and they must be dealt with and they must be overcome, if we are ever to reach the time when the only difference between Negroes and whites is the color of their skin.

Nor can we find a complete answer in the experience of other American minorities. They made a valiant and a largely successful effort to emerge from poverty and prejudice. The Negro, like these others, will have to rely mostly upon his own efforts. But he just cannot do it alone. For they did not have the heritage of centuries to overcome, and they did not have a cultural tradition which had been twisted and battered by endless years of hatred and hopelessness, nor were they excluded — these others — because of race or color — a feeling whose dark intensity is matched by no other prejudice in our society.

Nor can these differences be understood as isolated infirmities. They are a seamless web. They cause each other. They result from each other. They reinforce each other.

Much of the Negro community is buried under a blanket of history and circumstance. It is not a lasting solution to lift just one corner of that blanket. We must stand on all sides and we must raise the entire cover if we are to liberate our fellow citizens.

One of the differences is the increased concentration of Negroes in our cities. More than 73 percent of all Negroes live in urban areas compared with less than 70 percent of the whites. Most of these Negroes live in slums. Most of these Negroes live together — a separated people.

Men are shaped by their world. When it is a world of decay, ringed by an invisible wall, when escape is arduous and uncertain, and the saving pressures of a more hopeful society are unknown, it can cripple the youth and it can desolatethe men.

There is also the burden that a dark skin can add to the search for a productive place in our society. Unemployment strikes most swiftly and broadly at the Negro, and this burden erodes hope. Blighted hope breeds despair. Despair brings indifferences to the learning which offers a way out. And despair, coupled with indifferences, is often the source of destructive rebellion against the fabric of society.

There is also the lacerating hurt of early collision with white hatred or prejudice, distaste or condescension. Other groups have felt similar intolerance. But success and achievement could wipe it away. They do not change the color of a man's skin. I have seen this uncomprehending pain in the eyes of the little, young Mexican-American schoolchildren that I taught many years ago. But it can be overcome. But, for many, the wounds are always open.

Perhaps most important — its influence radiating to every part of life — is the breakdown of the Negro family structure. For this, most of all, white America must accept responsibility. It flows from centuries of oppression and persecution of the Negro man. It flows from the long years of degradation and discrimination, which have attacked his dignity and assaulted his ability to produce for his family.

This, too, is not pleasant to look upon. But it must be faced by those whose serious intent is to improve the life of all Americans.

Only a minority — less than half — of all Negro children reach the age of 18 having lived all their lives with both of their parents. At this moment, tonight, little less than two-thirds are at home with both of their parents. Probably a majority of all Negro children receive federally-aided public assistance sometime during their childhood.

The family is the cornerstone of our society. More than any other force it shapes the attitude, the hopes, the ambitions, and the values of the child. And when the family collapses it is the children that are usually damaged. When it happens on a massive scale the community itself is crippled.

So, unless we work to strengthen the family, to create conditions under which most parents will stay together — all the rest: schools, and playgrounds, and public assistance, and private concern, will never be enough to cut completely the circle of despair and deprivation. ...

——— 8.11 ———
BLACK POWER
Stokely Carmichael

The persistent dissatisfaction with the more mainline civil rights groups that permeated SNCC finally boiled over in 1965. A faction of the group had long been annoyed with the idea of lying down for beatings by white cops and the overall strategy of appealing to white America's moral conscience. In May, that wing of the group took over when members elected Stokely Carmichael president over John Lewis. Lewis was a devotee of nonviolent direct action; Carmichael believed blacks should strike back. He picked up where Malcolm X left off, criticizing civil rights leaders as begging for crumbs from their Democrat bosses. He told African Americans to meet violence with violence — thereby wholly redefining an organization that had declared nonviolent social change its founding purpose (see Chapter Seven). And he molded the black nationalist sentiments that had floated on the margins of civil rights circles for decades into a force that would leave a permanent imprint on American politics and culture — the Black Power movement. Others had used the phrase in the past, but Carmichael popularized it in a series of speeches throughout 1966 that he closed by leading a "Black Power" chant.

In the 1966 SNCC pamphlet below, Carmichael attempts to define Black Power. The old civil rights movement was largely "adapted to an audience of middle-class whites," he explains, and had served as a "buffer zone" between them and the growing anger and impatience of young blacks in urban areas, both northern and southern. Black Power does not shield society from that black rage, but rather harnesses it as a tool to wrestle free African Americans' liberty. The first step in that process is unity among black people. Further, he writes, blacks cannot afford to live by the doctrine of nonviolence. To affectively respond to white oppression, American racists had to know that their brutality would be met head on, that they were all in the same boat.

One of the tragedies of the struggle against racism is that up to now there has been no national organization which could speak to the growing militancy of young black people in the urban ghetto. There has been only a civil rights movement, whose tone of voice was adapted to an audience of liberal whites. It served as a sort of buffer zone between them and angry young blacks. None of its so-called leaders could go into a rioting community and be listened to. In a sense, I blame ourselves, together with the mass media, for what has happened in Watts, Harlem, Chicago, Cleveland, Omaha. Each time the people in those cities saw Martin Luther King get slapped, they became angry; when they saw four little black girls bombed to death, they were angrier; and when nothing happened, they were steaming. We had nothing to offer that they could see, except to go out and be beaten again. We helped to build their frustration.

An organization which claims to speak for the needs of a community, as does the Student Nonviolent Coordinating Committee, must speak in the tone of that community, not as somebody else's buffer zone. This is the significance of black power as a slogan. For once, black people are going to use the words they want to use, not just the words whites want to hear. And they will do this no matter how often the press tries to stop the use of the slogan by equating it with racism or separatism.

An organization which claims to be working for the needs of a community, as SNCC does, must work to provide that community with a position of strength from which to make its voice heard. This is the significance of black power beyond the slogan.

Black power can be clearly defined for those who do not attach the fears of white America to their questions about it. We should begin with the basic fact that black Americans have two problems: they are poor and they are black. All other problems arise from this two-sided reality: lack of education, the so-called apathy of black men. Any program to end racism must address itself to that double reality.

Almost from its beginning SNCC sought to address itself to both conditions with a program aimed at winning political power for impoverished Southern blacks. We had to begin with politics because black Americans are a propertyless people in a country where property is valued above all. We had to work for power, because this country does not function by morality, love, and nonviolence, but by power. Thus we determined to win political power, with the idea of moving on from there into activity that would have economic effects. With power, the masses could make or participate in making the decisions which govern their destinies, and thus create basic change in their day-to-day lives.

But if political power seemed to be the key to self-determination, it was also obvious that the key had been thrown down a deep well many years earlier. Disenfranchisement, maintained by racist terror, makes it impossible to talk about organizing for political power in 1966. The right to vote had to be won, and SNCC workers devoted their energies to this from 1961 to 1965. They set up voter registration drives in the Deep South. They created pressure for the vote by holding mock elections in the Mississippi Freedom Democratic Party (MFDP) in 1964. That struggle was eased, though not won, with the passage of the 1965 Voting Rights Act. SNCC workers could then address themselves to the question: "Who can we vote for, to have our needs met, how do we make our vote meaningful?" . . .

In Lowndes County, Alabama, black power will mean that if a Negro is elected sheriff, he can end police brutality. If a black man is elected tax assessor, he can collect and channel funds for the building of better roads and schools serving black people, thus advancing the move from political power into the economic arena. In such areas as Lowndes, where black men have a majority, they will attempt to use it to exercise control. This is what they seek: control. Where Negroes lack a majority, black power means proper representation and sharing of control. It means the creation of power bases from which black people can work to change statewide or nationwide patterns of oppression through pressure from strength, instead of weakness. Politically, black power means what it has always meant to SNCC: the coming-together of black people to elect representatives and to force those representatives to speak to their needs. It does not mean merely putting black faces into office. A man or woman who is black and from the slums cannot be automatically expected to speak to the needs of black people. Most of the black politicians we see around the country today are not what SNCC means by black power. The power

must be that of a community and emanate from there. . . .

Ultimately, the economic foundations of this country must be shaken if black people are to control their lives. The colonies of the United States, and this includes the black ghettoes within its borders, north and south, must be liberated. For a century, this nation has been like an octopus of exploitation, its tentacles stretching from Mississippi and Harlem to South America, the Middle East, southern Africa, and Vietnam; the form of exploitation varies from area to area but the essential result has been the same, a powerful few have been maintained and enriched at the expense of the poor and voiceless colored masses. This pattern must be broken. As its grip loosens here and there around the world, the hopes of black Americans become more realistic. For racism to die, a totally different America must be born.

This is what the white society does not wish to face; this is why that society prefers to talk about integration. But integration speaks not at all to the problem of poverty, only to the problem of blackness. Integration today means the man who "makes it," leaving his black brothers behind in the ghetto as fast as his new sports car will take him. It has no relevance to the Harlem wino or to the cotton-picker making three dollars a day. As a lady I know in Alabama once said, "The food that Ralph Bunche eats doesn't fill my stomach."

Integration, moreover, speaks to the problem of blackness in a despicable way. As a goal, it has been based on complete acceptance of the fact that in order to have a decent house or education, blacks must move into a white neighborhood or send their children to a white school. This reinforces, among both black and white, the idea that "white" is automatically better and "black" is by definition inferior. This is why integration is a subterfuge for the maintenance of white supremacy. It allows the nation to focus on a handful of Southern children who get into white schools, at great price, and to ignore the 94 percent who are left behind in unimproved all-black schools. Such situations will not change until black people have power, to control their own school boards, in this case. Then Negroes become equal in a way that means something, and integration ceases to be a one-way street. Then integration doesn't mean draining skills and energies from the ghetto into white neighborhoods; then it can mean white people moving from Beverly Hills into Watts, white people joining the Lowndes County Freedom Organization. Then integration becomes relevant. ...

The need for psychological equality is the reason why SNCC today believes that blacks must organize in the black community. Only black People can convey the revolutionary idea that black people are able to do things themselves. Only they can help create in the community an amused and continuing black consciousness that will provide the basis for political strength. In the past, white allies have furthered white supremacy without the whites involved realizing it, or wanting it, I think. Black People must do things for themselves. ...

When we urge that black money go into black pockets, we mean the communal pocket. We want to see money go back into the community and used to benefit it. We want to see the cooperative concept applied in business and banking. We want to see black ghetto residents demand that an exploiting landlord or store keeper sell them, at minimal cost, a building or a shop that they will own and improve cooperatively; they can back their demand with a rent strike, or a boycott, and a community so unified behind them that no one else will move into the building or buy at the store. The society we seek to build among black people, then, is not a capitalist one. It is a society in which the spirit of community and humanistic love prevail. The word love is suspect; black expectations of what it might produce have been betrayed too often. But those were expectations of a response from the white Community, which failed us. The love we seek to encourage is within the black community, the only American community where men call each other "brother" when they meet. We can build a community of love only where we have the ability and power to do so: among blacks.

As for white America, perhaps it can stop crying out against "black supremacy," "black nationalism," "racism in reverse," and begin facing reality. The reality is that this nation, from top to bottom, is racist; that racism is not primarily a problem of "human relations" but of an exploitation maintained, either actively or through silence, by the society as a whole. Camus and Sartre have asked, can a man condemn himself? Can whites, particularly liberal whites, condemn themselves? Can they stop blaming us, and blame their own system? Are they capable of the shame which might become a revolutionary emotion?

We have found that they usually cannot condemn themselves, and so we have done it. But the rebuilding of this society, if at all possible, is basically the responsibility of whites: not blacks.

We won't fight to save the present society, in Vietnam or anywhere else. We are just going to work, in the way we see fit, and on goals we define, not for civil rights but for all our human rights.

--------- 8.12 ---------

KWANZAA
Maulana Karenga

In 1966, black nationalist Maulana Karenga, who led a southern California organization called Us, created the holiday season of Kwanzaa. Karenga and his colleagues urged black Americans to return, spiritually, to their African roots. He stressed unity, pride and self-determination for black communities around the world. The holiday is designed to spiritually focus black people on these ideas and their African heritage. To that end, the seven-day ritual revolves around the seven principles below. Each day focuses on a different principle. Ironically, Karenga and his supporters had a bitter conflict with the Black Panther Party over ideologies of black nationalism. The conflict led to a gun battle in 1969.

Umoja (Unity)

To strive for and maintain unity in the family, community, nation and race.

Kujichagulia (Self-Determination)

To define ourselves, name ourselves, create for ourselves and speak for ourselves.

Ujima (Collective Work and Responsibility)

To build and maintain our community together and make our brother's and sister's problems our problems and to solve them together.

Ujamaa (Cooperative Economics)

To build and maintain our own stores, shops and other businesses and to profit from them together.

Nia (Purpose)

To make our collective vocation the building and developing of our community in order to restore our people to their traditional greatness.

Kuumba (Creativity)

To do always as much as we can, in the way we can, in order to leave our community more beautiful and beneficial than we inherited it.

Imani (Faith)

To believe with all our heart in our people, our parents, our teachers, our leaders and the righteousness and victory of our struggle.

——— 8.13 ———

'WE BELIEVE THIS RACIST GOVERNMENT HAS ROBBED US'

The Black Panther Party

In October 1966, as Stokely Carmichael was articulating the ideology of Black Power for the nation, six black men in Oakland, California, started a group that gave it form. Bobby Seale and Huey Newton led the foundation of the Black Panther Party for Self Defense (later shortened to Black Panther Party), designed as a sort of black citizens' militia. They roamed the streets of Oakland aiming to protect black residents from the rampant police brutality and harassment that had set off rioting the previous year. Later, they set up free breakfast programs for school children and health clinics in black neighborhoods. They urged unity among poor black people and criticized

middle-class African Americans for abandoning its lower classes. The Party was not racially exclusive, however, as SNCC was becoming, and reached out to white revolutionary movements of the time. Its founding platform offered an action plan based on Black Power principles. It stated that, if white society refused to give blacks their due rights, blacks should take them. It demanded the release of all black prisoners, arguing none could have had a fair trial. It demanded exemption for black men from military service. And it urged all black people to arm themselves so as to be prepared to strike in self-defense when necessary. Pointedly, the Platform closed by quoting the Declaration of Independence.

A. Black Panther Party Platform and Program

What We Want
What We Believe

1. We want freedom. We want power to determine the destiny of our Black Community.

We believe that black people will not be free until we are able to determine our destiny.

2. We want full employment for our people.

We believe that the federal government is responsible and obligated to give every man employment or a guaranteed income. We believe that if the white American businessmen will not give full employment, then the means of production should be taken from the businessmen and placed in the community so that the people of the community can organize and employ all of its people and give a high standard of living.

3. We want an end to the robbery by the white man of our Black Community.

We believe that this racist government has robbed us and now we are demanding the overdue debt of forty acres and two mules. Forty acres and two mules was promised 100 years ago as restitution for slave labor and mass murder of black people. We will accept the payment as currency which will be distributed to our many communities. The Germans are now aiding the Jews in Israel for the genocide of the Jewish people. The Germans murdered six million Jews. The American racist has taken part in the slaughter of over twenty million black people; therefore, we feel that this is a modest demand that we make.

4. We want decent housing, fit for shelter of human beings.

We believe that if the white landlords will not give decent housing to our black community, then the housing and the land should be made into cooperatives so that our community, with government aid, can build and make decent housing for its people.

5. We want education for our people that exposes the true nature of this decadent American society. We want education that teaches us our true history and our role in the present-day society.

We believe in an educational system that will give to our people a knowledge of self. If a man does not have knowledge of himself and his position in society and the world, then he has little chance to relate to anything else.

6. We want all black men to be exempt from military service.

We believe that black people should not be forced to fight in the military service to defend a racist government that does not protect us. We will not fight and kill other people of color in the world who, like black people, are being victimized by the white racist government of America. We will protect ourselves from the force and violence of the racist police and the racist military, by whatever means necessary.

7. We want an immediate end to police brutality and murder of black people.

We believe we can end police brutality in our black community by organizing black self-defense groups that are dedicated to defending our black community from racist police oppression and brutality. The Second Amendment to the Constitution of the United States gives a right to bear arms. We therefore believe that all black people should arm themselves for self-defense.

8. We want freedom for all black men held in federal, state, county and city prisons and jails.

We believe that all black people should be released from the many jails and prisons because they have not received a fair and impartial trial.

9. We want all black people when brought to trial to be tried in court by a jury of their peer group or people from their black communities, as defined by the Constitution of the United States.

We believe that the courts should follow the United States Constitution so that black people will receive fair trials. The 14th Amendment of the U.S. Constitution gives a man a right to be tried by his peer group. A peer is a person from a similar economic, social, religious, geographical, environmental, historical and racial background. To do this the court will be forced to select a jury from the black community from which the black defendant came. We have been, and are being tried by all-white juries that have no understanding of the "average reasoning man" of the black community.

10. We want land, bread, housing, education, clothing, justice and peace. And as our major political objective, a United Nations-supervised plebiscite to be held throughout the black colony in which only black colonial subjects will be allowed to participate for the purpose of determining the will of black people as to their national destiny.

When in the course of human events, it becomes necessary for one people to dissolve the political bands which have connected them with another, and to assume, among the powers of the earth, the separate and equal station to which the laws of nature and nature's God entitle them, a decent respect to the opinions of mankind requires that they should declare the causes which impel them to the separation.

We hold these truths to be self evident, that all men are created equal; that they are endowed by their Creator with certain unalienable rights; that among these are life, liberty, and the pursuit of happiness. That, to secure these rights, governments are instituted among men, deriving their just powers from the consent of the governed; that, whenever any form of government becomes destructive of these ends, it is the right of the people to alter or to abolish it, and to institute a new government, laying its foundation on such principles, and organizing its powers in such form, as to them shall seem most likely to effect their safety and happiness. Prudence, indeed, will dictate that governments long established should not be changed for light and transient causes; and accordingly, all experience hath shown, that mankind are more disposed to suffer, while evils are sufferable, than to right themselves by abolishing the forms to which they are accustomed. But, when a long train of abuses and usurpations, pursuing invariable the same object, evinces a design to reduce them under absolute despotism, it is their right, it is their duty, to throw off such government, and to provide new guards for their future security.

B. Black Panther National Anthem
In April, 1967, Elaine Brown wrote the
Party's anthem.

Yes — He turned and he walked
Past the eyes of my life.
And, he nodded and sang without sound.
And his face had the look
Of a man who knew strife
And a feeling familiarly came around.
I said,

Man, where have you been for all these years
Man, where were you when I sought you
Man, do you know me as I know you
Man, am I coming through
And, he spoke in a voice
That was centuries old.
And, he smiled in a way that was strange.
And, his full lips of night
Spoke about our people's plight
And a feeling familiarly came around.
And, we sat and we talked
About freedom and things.
And, he told me about what he dreamed.
But I knew of that dream
Long before he had spoke
And a feeling familiarly came around.

—— 8.14 ——
EXECUTIVE MANDATE
NUMBER ONE
Bobby Seale

The Black Panther Party exploded onto the national scene in May 1967, when they marched on the California state capitol building, armed with guns. The legislature was holding hearings on a proposed gun control bill, and the Panthers came to Sacramento to protest it. Twenty-six members stood clad in Panther black, wearing berets and toting loaded weapons. Bobby Seale read "Executive Mandate Number One," below, to the press. They then marched into the capitol where the police arrested them. As Huey Newton had predicted, the story played sensationally around the nation, and the Party's membership and local chapters blossomed as the tale spread through black communities.

The Black Panther Party for Self-Defense calls upon the American People in general and the Black People in particular to take careful note of the racist California Legislature, which is now considering legislation aimed at keeping the Black People disarmed and powerless at the very same time that racist police agencies throughout the country are intensifying the terror, brutality, murder and repression of Black People.

At the same time that the American Government is waging a racist war of genocide in Vietnam the concentration camps in which the Japanese Americans were interned during World War II are being renovated and expanded. Since America has historically reserved its most barbaric treatment for non-White people, we are forced to conclude that these concentration camps are being prepared for Black people who are determined to gain their freedom by any means necessary. The enslavement of Black people at the very founding of this country, the genocide practiced on the American Indians and the confinement of the survivors on reservations, the savage lynching of thousands of Black men and women, the dropping of atomic bombs on Hiroshima and

Nagasaki, and now the cowardly massacre in Vietnam all testify to the fact that toward people of color the racist power structure of America has but one policy: repression, genocide, terror, and the big stick.

Black people have begged, prayed, petitioned and demonstrated, among other things, to get the racist power structure of America to right the wrongs which have been historically perpetuated against Black people. All of these efforts have been answered by more repression, deceit, and hypocrisy. As the aggression of the racist American Government escalates in Vietnam, the police agencies of America escalate the repression of Black people throughout the ghettos of America. Vicious police dogs, cattle prods, and increased patrols have become familiar sights in Black communities. City Hall turns a deaf ear to the pleas of Black people for relief from this increasing terror.

The Black Panther Party for Self-Defense believes that the time has come for Black people to arm themselves against this terror before it is too late. The pending Mulford Act brings the hour of doom one step nearer. A people who have suffered so much for so long at the hands of a racist society must draw the line somewhere. We believe that the Black communities of America must rise up as one man to halt the progression of a trend that leads inevitably to their total destruction.

------- 8.15 -------

VIETNAM: 'A TIME COMES WHEN SILENCE IS BETRAYAL'
Martin Luther King, Jr.

Intense African-American community opposition to the Vietnam War existed long before any civil rights leaders, or even the anti-war movement, began loudly protesting it. Black men were being drafted and killed in disproportionate numbers, and families and communities knew it. But black leaders were reluctant to criticize the Johnson administration on what they then believed to be an issue unrelated to race. They had enough on their plate without taking on Vietnam. But in April 1967, Martin Luther King,

Jr., decided he could no longer "divide my conscience." A few weeks before participating in an anti-war rally in New York, he gave this address. It was one of King's most "progressive" speeches. Associating the war with the "triplets of racism, materialism, and militarism" that he argued America was spreading around the globe, he urged young men to become conscientious objectors.

Other black leaders, including the NAACP's Roy Wilkins and the National Urban League's Whitney Young, blasted King for speaking out against Johnson. The press followed suit, and the speech sparked weeks of controversy. Johnson, of course, was irate. Nevertheless, King would now begin to speak of the war as a civil rights issue, directly damaging the black community, and an example of America's failure to respect the independent rights of people at home and around the world.

I come to this magnificent house of worship tonight because my conscience leaves me no other choice. I join with you in this meeting because I am in deepest agreement with the aims and work of the organization which has brought us together: Clergy and Laymen Concerned about Vietnam. The recent statement of your executive committee are the sentiments of my own heart and I found myself in full accord when I read its opening lines: "A time comes when silence is betrayal." That time has come for us in relation to Vietnam.

The truth of these words is beyond doubt but the mission to which they call us is a most difficult one. Even when pressed by the demands of inner truth, men do not easily assume the task of opposing their government's policy, especially in time of war. Nor does the human spirit move without great difficulty against all the apathy of conformist thought within one's own bosom and in the surrounding world. Moreover when the issues at hand seem as perplexed as they often do in the case of this dreadful conflict we are always on the verge of being mesmerized by uncertainty; but we must move on.

Some of us who have already begun to break the silence of the night have found that the calling to speak is often a vocation of agony, but we must speak. We must speak with all the humility that is appropriate to our limited vision, but we must speak. And we must rejoice as well, for surely this is the first time in our nation's history that a significant number of its religious leaders have chosen to move beyond the prophesying of smooth patriotism to the high grounds of a firm dissent based upon the mandates of conscience and the reading of history. Perhaps a new spirit is rising among us. If it is, let us trace its movement well and pray that our own inner being may be sensitive to its guidance, for we are deeply in need of a new way beyond the darkness that seems so close around us.

Over the past two years, as I have moved to break the betrayal of my own silences and to speak from the burnings of my own heart, as I have called for radical departures from the destruction of Vietnam, many persons have questioned me about the wisdom of my path. At the heart of their concerns this query has often loomed large and loud: Why are *you* speaking about war, Dr. King? Why are *you* joining the voices of dissent? Peace and civil rights don't mix, they say. Aren't you hurting the cause of your people, they ask? And when I hear them, though I often understand the source of their concern, I am nevertheless greatly saddened, for such questions mean that the inquirers have not really known me, my commitment or my calling. Indeed, their questions suggest that they do not know the world in which they live.

In the light of such tragic misunderstandings, I deem it of signal importance to try to state clearly, and I trust concisely, why I believe that the path from Dexter Avenue Baptist Church — the church in Montgomery, Alabama, where I began my pastorate — leads clearly to this sanctuary tonight. …

I wish not to speak with Hanoi and the NLF, but rather to my fellow Americans, who, with me, bear the greatest responsibility in ending a conflict that has exacted a heavy price on both continents.

Since I am a preacher by trade, I suppose it is not surprising that I have seven major rea-

sons for bringing Vietnam into the field of my moral vision. There is at the outset a very obvious and almost facile connection between the war in Vietnam and the struggle I, and others, have been waging in America. A few years ago there was a shining moment in that struggle. It seemed as if there was a real promise of hope for the poor — both black and white — through the poverty program. There were experiments, hopes, new beginnings. Then came the buildup in Vietnam and I watched the program broken and eviscerated as if it were some idle political plaything of a society gone mad on war, and I knew that America would never invest the necessary funds or energies in rehabilitation of its poor so long as adventures like Vietnam continued to draw men and skills and money like some demonic destructive suction tube. So I was increasingly compelled to see the war as an enemy of the poor and to attack it as such.

Perhaps the more tragic recognition of reality took place when it became clear to me that the war was doing far more than devastating the hopes of the poor at home. It was sending their sons and their brothers and their husbands to fight and to die in extraordinarily high proportions relative to the rest of the population. We were taking the black young men who had been crippled by our society and sending them eight thousand miles away to guarantee liberties in Southeast Asia which they had not found in southwest Georgia and East Harlem. So we have been repeatedly faced with the cruel irony of watching Negro and white boys on TV screens as they kill and die together for a nation that has been unable to seat them together in the same schools. So we watch them in brutal solidarity burning the huts of a poor village, but we realize that they would never live on the same block in Detroit. I could not be silent in the face of such cruel manipulation of the poor.

My third reason moves to an even deeper level of awareness, for it grows out of my experience in the ghettoes of the North over the last three years — especially the last three summers. As I have walked among the desperate, rejected and angry young men I have told them that Molotov cocktails and rifles would not solve their problems. I have tried to offer them my deepest compassion while maintaining my conviction that social change comes most meaningfully through nonviolent action. But they asked — and rightly so — what about Vietnam? They asked if our own nation wasn't using massive doses of violence to solve its problems, to bring about the changes it wanted. Their questions hit home, and I knew that I could never again raise my voice against the violence of the oppressed in the ghettos without having first spoken clearly to the greatest purveyor of violence in the world today — my own government. For the sake of those boys, for the sake of this government, for the sake of hundreds of thousands trembling under our violence, I cannot be silent. ...

Finally, as I try to delineate for you and for myself the road that leads from Montgomery to this place I would have offered all that was most valid if I simply said that I must be true to my conviction that I share with all men the calling to be a son of the living God. Beyond the calling of race or nation or creed is this vocation of sonship and brotherhood, and because I believe that the Father is deeply concerned especially for his suffering and helpless and outcast children, I come tonight to speak for them.

This I believe to be the privilege and the burden of all of us who deem ourselves bound by allegiances and loyalties which are broader and deeper than nationalism and which go beyond our nation's self-defined goals and positions. We are called to speak for the weak, for the voiceless, for victims of our nation and for those it calls enemy, for no document from human hands can make these humans any less our brothers.

And as I ponder the madness of Vietnam and search within myself for ways to understand and respond to compassion my mind goes constantly to the people of that peninsula. I speak now not of the soldiers of each side, not of the junta in Saigon, but simply of the peo-

ple who have been living under the curse of war for almost three continuous decades now. I think of them too because it is clear to me that there will be no meaningful solution there until some attempt is made to know them and hear their broken cries.

They must see Americans as strange liberators. The Vietnamese people proclaimed their own independence in 1945 after a combined French and Japanese occupation, and before the Communist revolution in China. They were led by Ho Chi Minh. Even though they quoted the American Declaration of Independence in their own document of freedom, we refused to recognize them. Instead, we decided to support France in its reconquest of her former colony.

Our government felt then that the Vietnamese people were not "ready" for independence, and we again fell victim to the deadly Western arrogance that has poisoned the international atmosphere for so long. With that tragic decision we rejected a revolutionary government seeking self-determination, and a government that had been established not by China (for whom the Vietnamese have no great love) but by clearly indigenous forces that included some Communists. For the peasants this new government meant real land reform, one of the most important needs in their lives. ...

The only change came from America as we increased our troop commitments in support of governments which were singularly corrupt, inept and without popular support. All the while the people read our leaflets and received regular promises of peace and democracy — and land reform. Now they languish under our bombs and consider us — not their fellow Vietnamese — the real enemy. They move sadly and apathetically as we herd them off the land of their fathers into concentration camps where minimal social needs are rarely met. They know they must move or be destroyed by our bombs. So they go — primarily women and children and the aged.

They watch as we poison their water, as we kill a million acres of their crops. They must weep as the bulldozers roar through their areas preparing to destroy the precious trees. They wander into the hospitals, with at least twenty casualties from American firepower for one "Vietcong"-inflicted injury. So far we may have killed a million of them — mostly children. They wander into the towns and see thousands of the children, homeless, without clothes, running in packs on the streets like animals. They see the children, degraded by our soldiers as they beg for food. They see the children selling their sisters to our soldiers, soliciting for their mothers.

What do the peasants think as we ally ourselves with the landlords and as we refuse to put any action into our many words concerning land reform? What do they think as we test our latest weapons on them, just as the Germans tested out new medicine and new tortures in the concentration camps of Europe? Where are the roots of the independent Vietnam we claim to be building? Is it among these voiceless ones?

We have destroyed their two most cherished institutions: the family and the village. We have destroyed their land and their crops. We have cooperated in the crushing of the nation's only non-Communist revolutionary political force — the unified Buddhist church. We have supported the enemies of the peasants of Saigon. We have corrupted their women and children and killed their men. What liberators! …

At this point I should make it clear that while I have tried in these last few minutes to give a voice to the voiceless on Vietnam and to understand the arguments of those who are called enemy, I am as deeply concerned about our troops there as anything else. For it occurs to me that what we are submitting them to in Vietnam is not simply the brutalizing process that goes on in any war where armies face each other and seek to destroy. We are adding cynicism to the process of death, for they must know after a short period there that none of the things we claim to be fighting for are really involved. Before long they must know that their government has sent them into a struggle

among Vietnamese, and the more sophisticated surely realize that we are on the side of the wealthy and the secure while we create hell for the poor.

Somehow this madness must cease. We must stop now. I speak as a child of God and brother to the suffering poor of Vietnam. I speak for those whose land is being laid waste, whose homes are being destroyed, whose culture is being subverted. I speak for the poor of America who are paying the double price of smashed hopes at home and death and corruption in Vietnam. I speak as a citizen of the world, for the world as it stands aghast at the path we have taken. I speak as an American to the leaders of my own nation. The great initiative in this war is ours. The initiative to stop it must be ours. …

There is something seductively tempting about stopping there and sending us all off on what in some circles has become a popular crusade against the war in Vietnam. I say we must enter the struggle, but I wish to go on now to say something even more disturbing. The war in Vietnam is but a symptom of a far deeper malady within the American spirit, and if we ignore this sobering reality we will find ourselves organizing clergy- and laymen-concerned committees for the next generation. They will be concerned about Guatemala and Peru. They will be concerned about Thailand and Cambodia. They will be concerned about Mozambique and South Africa. We will be marching for these and a dozen other names and attending rallies without end unless there is a significant and profound change in American life and policy. Such thoughts take us beyond Vietnam, but not beyond our calling as sons of the living God.

In 1957 a sensitive American official overseas said that it seemed to him that our nation was on the wrong side of a world revolution. During the past ten years we have seen emerge a pattern of suppression which now has justified the presence of U.S. military "advisors" in Venezuela. This need to maintain social stability for our investments accounts for the counter-revolutionary action of American forces in Guatemala. It tells why American helicopters are being used against guerrillas in Colombia and why American napalm and green beret forces have already been active against rebels in Peru. It is with such activity in mind that the words of the late John F. Kennedy come back to haunt us. Five years ago he said, "Those who make peaceful revolution impossible will make violent revolution inevitable."

Increasingly, by choice or by accident, this is the role our nation has taken — the role of those who make peaceful revolution impossible by refusing to give up the privileges and the pleasures that come from the immense profits of overseas investment.

I am convinced that if we are to get on the right side of the world revolution, we as a nation must undergo a radical revolution of values. We must rapidly begin the shift from a "thing-oriented" society to a "person-oriented" society. When machines and computers, profit motives and property rights are considered more important than people, the giant triplets of racism, materialism, and militarism are incapable of being conquered. ...

A true revolution of values will soon look uneasily on the glaring contrast of poverty and wealth. With righteous indignation, it will look across the seas and see individual capitalists of the West investing huge sums of money in Asia, Africa and South America, only to take the profits out with no concern for the social betterment of the countries, and say: "This is not just." It will look at our alliance with the landed gentry of Latin America and say: "This is not just." The Western arrogance of feeling that it has everything to teach others and nothing to learn from them is not just. A true revolution of values will lay hands on the world order and say of war: "This way of settling differences is not just." This business of burning human beings with napalm, of filling our nation's homes with orphans and widows, of injecting poisonous drugs of hate into veins of people normally humane, of sending men home from dark and bloody battlefields physi-

cally handicapped and psychologically deranged, cannot be reconciled with wisdom, justice and love. A nation that continues year after year to spend more money on military defense than on programs of social uplift is approaching spiritual death. ...

We are now faced with the fact that tomorrow is today. We are confronted with the fierce urgency of now. In this unfolding conundrum of life and history there is such a thing as being too late. Procrastination is still the thief of time. Life often leaves us standing bare, naked and dejected with a lost opportunity. The "tide in the affairs of men" does not remain at the flood; it ebbs. We may cry out deperately for time to pause in her passage, but time is deaf to every plea and rushes on. Over the bleached bones and jumbled residue of numerous civilizations are written the pathetic words: "Too late." There is an invisible book of life that faithfully records our vigilance or our neglect. "The moving finger writes, and having writ moves on..." We still have a choice today; nonviolent coexistence or violent co-annihilation. ...

——— 8.16 ———
'I AIN'T GOT NO QUARREL WITH THEM VIET CONG'
Muhammad Ali

In early 1967, Muhammad Ali's name came up for the draft. News reporters contacted him in February, upon hearing the news of his "1A" classification, hounding him for a comment. Ali refused to entertain the idea of fighting — as a Muslim, he was a conscientious objector. He gave reporters the quick, classic Ali poem below to explain his feelings on the matter. That May, the World Boxing Association stripped him of his title and suspended his boxing license. Soon thereafter, he was sentenced to five years imprisonment for draft evasion. Already despised by many white Americans, Ali had become ostracized by almost all of mainstream society. He spent the next three years in exile from boxing, appealing his sentence and touring the country, speaking as a Muslim. In 1971, the Supreme Court tossed the conviction out, ruling that he should have been exempted from service on religious grounds. That same year, after regaining his boxing license in 1970, Ali took the ring for the "Fight of the Century" against heavyweight champion Joe Frazier. Frazier won the bout in a decision, after knocking Ali down in the 15th round.

Keep asking me, no matter how long
On the war in Viet Nam, I sing this song
I ain't got no quarrel with them Viet Cong.

——— 8.17 ———
SOUL ON ICE
Eldridge Cleaver

Among the men who joined Bobby Seale and Huey Newton's Black Panther Party in 1966 was Eldridge Cleaver. An ex-con who had spent most of his prior life in and out of prison, Cleaver felt the sort of restless alienation that Black Panther ideology sought to answer among urban blacks. He became the Party's minister of information.

While he was still in prison, Cleaver wrote a series of essays that discussed his troubled past and outlined his thoughts on American society. Published in 1968 as Soul on Ice, the collection stands as one of the most controversial books ever published. Cleaver sows the seeds of modern black homophobia when, in attacking the writings of James Baldwin, he lashes into black gay men who "want to have a baby by a white man." Noting he has parted with a violent past, he nevertheless describes his former logic for raping white women, assaults he says he launched to punish them for their whiteness. At the end, he proffers a theory on how American society got to a place where it devalues black men as stupid and black women as ugly while it uplifts white women as the ideal of femininity and white men as society's ruler.

... I became an extreme iconoclast. Any affirmative assertion made by anyone around me became a target for tirades of criticism and denunciation.

This little game got good to me and I got good at it. I attacked all forms of piety, loyalty, and sentiment: marriage, love, God, patriotism, the Constitution, the founding fathers, law, concepts of right-wrong-good-evil, all forms of ritualized and conventional behavior. As I pranced about, club in hand, seeking new idols to smash, I encountered really for the first

time in my life, with any seriousness, The Ogre, rising up before me in a mist. I discovered, with alarm, that The Ogre possessed a tremendous and dreadful power over me and I didn't understand this power or why I was at its mercy. I tried to repudiate The Ogre, root it out of my heart as I had done God, Constitution, principles, morals, and values — but The Ogre had its claws buried in the core of my being and refused to let go. I fought frantically to be free, but The Ogre only mocked me and sank its claws deeper into my soul. I knew then that I had found an important key, that if I conquered The Ogre and broke its power over me I would be free. But I also knew that it was a race against time and that if I did not win I would certainly be broken and destroyed. I, a black man, confronted The Ogre — the white woman. ...

From our discussion, which began that evening and has never yet ended, we went on to notice how thoroughly, as a matter of course, a black growing up in America is indoctrinated with the white race's standard of beauty. Not that the whites made a conscious, calculated effort to do this, we thought, but since they constituted the majority the whites brainwashed the blacks by the very processes the whites employed to indoctrinate themselves with their own group standards. It intensified my frustrations to know that I was indoctrinated to see the white woman as more beautiful and desirable than my own black woman. It drove me into books seeking light on the subject. In Richard Wright's *Native Son*, I found Bigger Thomas and a keen insight into the problem. ...

Somehow I arrived at the conclusion that, as a matter of principle, it was of paramount importance for me to have an antagonistic, ruthless attitude toward white women. The term outlaw appealed to me and at the time my parole date was drawing near, I considered myself to be mentally free — I was an "outlaw." I had stepped outside of the white man's law, which I repudiated with scorn and self-satisfaction. I became a law unto myself — my own legislature, my own supreme court, my own executive. At the moment I walked out of the prison gate, my feelings toward white women in general could be summed up in the following lines:

TO A WHITE GIRL

I love you
Because you're white,
Not because you're charming
Or bright.
Your whiteness
Is a silky thread
Snaking through my thoughts
In redhot patterns
Of lust and desire.

I hate you
Because you're white.
Your white meat
Is nightmare food.
White is
The skin of Evil.
You're my Moby Dick,
White Witch,
Symbol of the rope and hanging free,
Of the burning cross.

Loving you thus
And hating you so,
My heart is torn in two.
Crucified.

I became a rapist. To refine my technique and Modus operandi, I started out by practicing on black girls in the ghetto — in the black ghetto where dark and vicious deeds appear not as aberrations or deviations from the norm, but as part of the sufficiency of the Evil of a day — and when I considered myself smooth enough, I crossed the tracks and sought out white prey. I did this consciously, deliberately, willfully, methodically — though looking back I see that I was in a frantic, wild, and completely abandoned frame of mind.

Rape was an insurrectionary act. It delighted me that I was defying and trampling upon the white man's law, upon his system of values, and that I was defiling his women and this point, I believe, was the most satisfying to me because I was very resentful over the historical fact of how the white man has used the black woman. I felt I was getting revenge. From the site of the act of rape, consternation spreads outwardly in concentric circles. I wanted to send waves of consternation throughout the white race. Recently, I came upon a quotation from one of LeRoi Jones' poems, taken from his book *The Dead Lecturer:*

A cult of death need of the simple striking arm under the street lamp. The cutters from under their rented earth. Come up, black dada nihilismus. Rape the white girls. Rape their fathers. Cut the mothers' throats.

I have lived those lines and I know that if I had not been apprehended I would have slit some white throats. There are, of course, many young blacks out there right now who are slitting white throats and raping the white girl. They are not doing this because they read LeRoi Jones' poetry, as some of his critics seem to believe. Rather, LeRoi is expressing the funky facts of life.

After I returned to prison, I took a long look at myself and, for the first time in my life, admitted that I was wrong, that I had gone astray — astray not so much from the white man's law as from being human, civilized — for I could not approve the act of rape. Even though I had some insight into my own motivation I did not feel justified. I lost my self-respect. My pride as a man dissolved and my whole fragile moral structure seemed to collapse, completely shattered.

That is why I started to write. To save myself. ...

—— 8.18 ——

'HOW MANY WHITE FOLKS YOU KILL TODAY?'

H. Rap Brown

In October 1967, Huey Newton was arrested following a gun battle with police in Oakland in which one officer was killed and both Newton and another officer were injured. The Black Panther Party decided to use his imprisonment as their rallying cause, setting him up as a martyr. Stokely Carmichael left SNCC to aid the campaign, led largely by Eldridge Cleaver, that became known as the "Free Huey" movement. The movement was immensely popular among white radicals of the time — which the Black Panther Party always reached out to as fellow revolutionaries — and helped build the Party's popularity among young blacks nationally, as well. In February 1968, the Free Huey movement prompted a faltering SNCC to merge with the Party. The Oakland rally at which this merger was announced was one of the largest Free Huey rallies of the period.

H. Rap Brown was among those who addressed the gathering in Oakland. Brown had taken over SNCC the previous year, and become a leading Black Power and violence-for-self-defense spokesperson. When a riot broke out a few hours following one of his speeches in Cambridge, Maryland, Governor Spiro Agnew had him arrested for inciting the riot. After that arrest, Brown's rhetoric intensified, and he began regularly referring to President Johnson as a "white honky cracker." In the speech below, Brown advocates offensive violence against whites in the name of revolution, asking the crowd, "How many white folks you kill today?"

First of all, I'd like to start out by thanking brother Cleaver and the Black Panther Party for Self Defense. See, unlike America would have us believe, the greatest problem confronting this country today is not pollution and bad breath. It's black people. It's black people. See, that's just one of the big lies that America tells you and that you go for 'cause you chumps. You go for it. One of the lies that we tell ourselves is that we're making progress; but Huey's chair's empty. We're not making progress. We tend to equate progress with concessions. We can no longer make that mistake. You see, when they gave us that nigger astronaut, you say we were making progress, but I told you they were going to lose him in space. He didn't get that far. They gave you Thurgood Marshall, and you said we were making progress. Thurgood Marshall is a tom of the highest order. Anybody who sits down before — anybody who sits before James O. Eastland — a camel-breath, peckerwood nasty honkey from Mississippi — and lets James O. Eastland subject him to the type of questioning that he did, he's a strange breed of man. You put Adam Clayton Powell in office and you couldn't keep him; what you think they gonna do with Thurgood Marshall when they get tired of him? They gave you Walter Washington, of Washington DC, and you said we were making progress; that's not progress. See, it's no in between: you're either free or you're a slave. There's no such thing as second-class citizenship. That's like telling me you can be a little bit pregnant.

The only politics in this country that's relevant to black people today is the politics of revolution ... none other. There is no difference between the Democratic and Republican party. The similarities are greater than the difference of those parties. What's the difference between Lyndon Johnson and Goldwater? None! But a lot of you running around talking about you Democrats, and the Democrats got you in the biggest trick going. They tell you, "It ain't our fault, it's the Dixiecrats." No such thing as a Dixiecrat. The only difference between George Wallace and Lyndon Johnson is one of them's wife's got cancer. That's the only difference. But you go for it! You go for it because you chumps! You go for it! The only thing that's going to free Huey is gun powder. Black powder. Huey Newton is the only living revolutionary in this country today. He has paid his dues! He paid his dues!

How many white folks you kill today? But you revolutionaries! You are revolutionaries! Che Guevara says they only two ways to leave the battlefield: victorious or dead. Huey's in jail! That's no victory, that's a concession. When black people become serious about the revolutionary struggle that they are caught up in, whether they recognize it or not — when they begin to go down and knock off people who are oppressing them, and begin to render these people impotent, that's when the revolutionary struggle unfolds — not until.

See, I want to develop upon what Bobby was talking about about green power, because green power is a myth. No such thing as green power as long as that honky got the power to change the color of money. It's white power that controls this country. To show you America's wanton use and abuse of power in connection with money. Internationally, America changed the international monetary standard from gold to paper gold. Her gold reserve had dwindled from 13.7 billion dollars. France had 12.9. That's why DeGaulle was raising all that hell. DeGaulle says, "I got almost as much gold as you! So how you gonna have more votes than me in the monetary system?" United States got slick cause they got power. They changed it to something they got an abundance of — paper gold. Paper gold. You see, black folks are chumps. If America were to tell you to bring all the rocks in this country to her, and she'll give you a million dollars for it, you'd do it! And the next day she'll telling you, "We using rocks for currency, chump!" You'd go for it because you enjoy being lied to. You enjoy being lied to. You find your security in the lies white America tells you. For four hundred years she taught you white nationalism and you lapped it up. You taught it to your children. You had your children thinking that everything black was bad. Black cows don't give good milk. Black hens don't lay eggs. Black for funerals, white for weddings. You see, everything black is bad. The only black biblical character you knew was Judas. That's all. Syrup of black draught bad. That's white nationalism. Santa Claus: a white honky who slides down a black chimney and comes out white. Flesh-colored band-aids: they had a brother who put one on and thought something was wrong with his skin. That's cause you chumps. You go for it! You enjoy white nationalism! Huntley and Brinkley. Black

folks got more confidence in Huntley and Brinkley than Catholics got in the Pope. They believe anything. According to Huntley and Brinkley, we through fighting in Vietnam. We through killing the enemy; we shooting trees. But you go for it. That's what you want to hear. And you say that you revolutionaries. Well, if you are revolutionaries, you must assume the revolutionary posture. Chairman Mao says power comes from the barrel of a gun. …

In terms of the revolution, I believe that the revolution will be a revolution of dispossessed people in this country: that's the Mexican American, the Puerto Rican American, the American Indian, and black people. We happen to be the vanguard of that revolutionary struggle because we are the most dispossessed. An old African leader says about leadership, he says that leadership should never be shared; it should always remain in the hands of the dispossessed people. We will lead the revolution.

I want to end, because brother Carmichael has a message for you. I'm sure he has a lot to tell you about his revolutionary struggle, about the revolutionary struggle. [Cheers] OK, you asked for it, brothers. OK, we going to talk about law and order versus justice in America, then. You see, Lyndon Johnson can always sit up and talk about — he can always raise an argument about law and order, because he never talks about justice. But black people fall for that same argument, and they go around talking about lawbreakers. We did not make the laws in this country. We are neither morally nor legally confined to those laws. Those laws that keep them up keep us down. We got to begin to understand that. See, justice is a joke in this country, and it stinks of its hypocrisy. Johnson is Hitler's illegitimate child, and J. Edgar Hoover is his half-sister. And we must conduct our struggle on this level. We are fighting enemies of the people! …

8.19

'THE DUTCHMAN'

Amiri Baraka (Leroi Jones)

Much like the New Negro movement of the early 20th century, the Black Power movement spawned a cultural wing. Amiri Baraka is widely considered the father of what came to be known as the Black Arts Movement — a loosely-related group of primarily performance artists in the middle-to-late 1960s. The works that typify Black Arts share an emphasis on African-American unity and empowerment, along with a strong personal pride in being black.

In 1964, Baraka, then still going by his original name LeRoi Jones, debuted his play *The Dutchman*. He had been associated with the Beat poets and other leftist white circles up until this point, but as he began to embrace Black Power politics of the time, his artistic focus shifted as well. *Dutchman* tells the story of a reserved black college student who meets a liberal white woman on a city train. Their conversation leads to her taunting his reserve as a sign of his being an "Uncle Tom." The student, Clay, finally erupts in a monologue on white liberals and their failure to understand black people. The play then closes as the woman, in apparent conspiracy with the other white passengers on the train, kills Clay and discards his body out the window. Clay's angry but resigned monologue is one of the founding literary passages in the Black Arts Movement. The same year *The Dutchman* opened, Baraka launched the Black Arts Reparatory Theater in Harlem, which served as a breeding ground for movement artists.

... CLAY. Now you shut the hell up. [Grabbing her shoulders] Just shut up. You don't know what you're talking about. You don't know anything. So just keep your stupid mouth closed.

LULA. Uncle Tom

CLAY. [Slaps her as hard as he can, across the mouth. Lula's bead bangs against the back of the seat. When she raises it again, Clay slaps her again] Now shut up and let me talk.

[He turns toward the other riders, some of whom are sitting on the edge of their seats. The drunk is on one knee, rubbing his head, and singing softly the same song. He shuts up too when be sees Clay watching him. The others go back to newspapers or stare out the windows]

Shit, you don't have any sense, Lula, nor feelings either. I could murder you now. Such a tiny ugly throat. I could squeeze it flat, and watch you turn blue, on a humble. For dull kicks. And all these weak-faced ofays squatting around here, staring over their papers at me. Murder them too. Even if they expected it. That man there ... [Points to well-dressed man] I could rip that Times right out of his hand, as skinny and middle-classed as I am, I could rip that paper out of his hand and just as easily rip out his throat. It takes no great effort. For what? To kill you soft idiots? You don't understand anything but luxury.

LULA. You fool!

CLAY. [Pushing her against the seat] I'm not telling you again, Tallulah Bankhead! Luxury. In your face and your fingers. You telling me what I ought to do. [Sudden scream frightening the whole coach] Well, don't! Don't you tell me anything! If I'm a middle class fake white man ... let me be. And let me be in the way I want. [Through his teeth] I'll rip your lousy breasts off! Let me be who I feel like being. Uncle Tom. Thomas. Whoever. It's none of your business. You don't know anything except for what's there for you to see. An act. Lies. Device. Not the pure heart, the pumping black heart. You don't ever know that. And I sit here, in this buttoned-up suit, to keep myself from cutting all your throats. I mean wantonly. You great liberated whore! You fuck some black man, and right away you're an expert on black people. What a lotta shit that is. The only thing you know is that you come if he bangs you hard enough. And that's all. The belly rub? You wanted to do the belly rub? Shit, you don't even know how. You don't know how. That ol' dipty-dip shit you do, rolling your ass like an elephant. That's not my kind of belly rub. Belly rub is not Queens. Belly rub is dark places, with big hats and overcoats held up with one arm. Belly rub hates you. Old bald-headed four-eyed ofays popping their fingers ... and don't know yet what they're doing. They say, "I love Bessie Smith." And don't even understand that Bessie Smith is saying, "Kiss my ass, kiss my black unruly ass." Before love, suffering, desire, anything you can explain, she's saying, and very plainly, "Kiss my black ass." And if you don't know that, it's you that's doing the kissing.

Charlie Parker? Charlie Parker. All, the hip white boys scream for Bird. And Bird saying, "Up your, ass, feeble-minded ofay! Up your ass." And they sit there talking about the tortured genius of Charlie Parker. Bird would've played not a note of music if he just walked up to East Sixty-seventh Street and killed the first ten white people he saw. Not a note! And I'm the great would-be poet. Yes. That's right! Poet. Some kind of bastard literature ... all it needs is a simple knife thrust. Just let me bleed you, you loud whore, and one poem vanished. A whole people of neurotics, struggling to keep from being sane. And the only thing that would cure the neurosis would be your murder. Simple as that. I mean if I murdered you, then other white people would begin to understand me. You understand? No. I guess not. If Bessie Smith had killed some white people she wouldn't have needed that music. She could have talked very straight and plain about the world. No metaphors. No grunts. No wiggles in the dark of her soul. Just straight two and two are four. Money. Power. Luxury. Like that. All of them. Crazy niggers turning their backs on sanity. When all it needs is that simple act. Murder. Just murder! Would make us all sane. [Suddenly weary] Ahhh. Shit. But who need it? I'd rather be a fool. Insane. Safe with my words, and no deaths, and clean, hard thoughts urging me to new conquests. My people's madness. Hah! That's a laugh. My people. They don't need me to claim them. They got legs and arms of their own. Personal insanities. Mirrors. They don't need all those words. They don't need any defense. But listen, though, one more thing. And you tell this to your father, who's probably the kind of man who needs to know at once. So he can plan ahead. Tell him not to preach so much rationalism and cold logic to these niggers. Let them alone. Let them sing curses at you in code and see your filth as simple lack of style. Don't make the mistake, through some

irresponsible surge of Christian charity, of talking too much about the advantages of Western rationalism, or the great intellectual legacy of the white man, or maybe they'll begin to listen. And then, maybe one day, you'll find they actually do understand exactly what you are talking about, all these fantasy people. All these blues people. And on that day, as sure as shit, when you really believe you can "accept" them into your fold, as half-white trusties late of the subject peoples. With no more blues, except the very old ones, and not a watermelon in sight, the great missionary heart will have triumphed, and all of those ex-coons will be stand-up Western men, with eyes for clean, hard useful lives, sober, pious and sane, and they'll murder you. They'll murder you, and have very rational explanations. Very much like your own. They'll cut your throats, and drag you out to the edge of your cities so the flesh can fall away from your bones, in sanitary isolation.

LULA. [Her voice takes on a different, more businesslike quality] I've heard enough.

CLAY. [Reaching for his books] I bet you have. I guess I better collect my stuff and get off this train. Looks like we won't be acting out that little pageant you outlined before.

LULA. No. We won't. You're right about that, at least. [She turns to look quickly around the rest of the car] All right! [The others respond]

CLAY. [Bending across the girl to retrieve his belongings] Sorry, baby, I don't think we could make it.

[As he is bending over her, the girl brings up a small knife and plunges it into Clay's chest. Twice. He slumps across her knees, his mouth working stupidly]

LULA. Sorry is right. [Turning to the others in the car who have already gotten up from their seats] Sorry is the rightest thing you've said. Get this man off me! Hurry, now!

[The others come and drag Clay's body down the aisle]

Open the door and throw his body out.

[They throw him off]

And all of you get off at the next stop.

[Lula busies herself straightening her things.

Getting everything in order. She takes out a notebook and makes a quick scribbling note. Drops it in her bag. The train apparently stops and all the others get off, leaving her alone in the coach.]

——— 8.20 ———

THE *CRISIS OF THE NEGRO INTELLECTUAL*
Harold Cruse

Harold Cruse joined Amiri Baraka as one of the cultural figures promoting the idea of a new renaissance of black art, based in Black Power ideology. His 1967 study, *Crisis of the Negro Intellectual*, is today considered one of the most insightful and thorough analyses of the development of black political thought ever written. Cruse traces black intellectual leadership from its earliest stages through Black Power. He argues that, in their zeal to win integration into American society, contemporary black intellectuals neglected the crucial first step of fostering a truly black culture. Bourgeois thinkers and artists, with their minds trained on white culture, no longer have any grounding in the real black world, he writes. Thus, their thought and art is not truly black. But neither are they grounded in white culture, as integration is unattainable. As a result they have become a "rootless class of displaced persons." Moreover, he argues, no culture can win anything in American society that does not have its own distinct base. As a result, the "refugee" intellectuals' ill-fated attempt to integrate has been and will be a failure.

... Today, Afro-American Nationalism is not Garveyism; it poses an American problem growing out of a specific American historical condition — involving three racial stocks — the white, the black and the red. The problem will be solved under specifically American conditions or it will never be solved, for Afro-American Nationalism is basically a black reflection of the unsolved American nationality question. American culture is sick not just because it is discriminatory, but because it reflects a psychological malaise that grows out of the American identity problem. As long as the Negro intellectual is beset with his own cultural identity problem, his attacks on American culture, as discriminatory, become hollow. Two cultural negatives cannot possibly add up to a cultural positive in society at large. Every single American political, social and cultural trend has contributed its bit of illusion to the total Americanization fantasy. Insofar as the Negro intellectual has accommodated this grand myth, his acquiescence must be examined critically before one can dispel the myth. Then, one is on clear ground, the better to deal with the realities of America.

In the effort to clear this ground it has been necessary to review a whole gamut of thinking on various topics: ethnic community; multi-group America; the political leftwing; nationalism vs. integrationism; Negro creative artists as thinkers and spokesmen; aesthetics; Negroes and the theater; individual vs. group roles in society; white liberalism and Negro intellectuals; culture and integrationism; culture and nationalism; literary, dramatic and social criticism; the Negro writer as revolutionary, and so on. ...

The tentative acceptance the Negro intellectual finds in the predominantly white intellectual world, allows him the illusion that integration is real — a functional reality for himself, and a possibility for all Negroes. Even if a Negro intellectual does not wholly believe this, he must give lip service to the aims of racial integration, if only to rationalize his own status in society.

This integrated status is not threatened or challenged; it is even championed, just so long as the black world is on the move in the struggle for integration. But when voices from the black world begin to raise doubts about the meaning, the aims, and the real possibilities of integration, the Negro intellectual is forced to question his own hard-won status. At the same time, those black Doubting Thomases begin to question the status of the Negro intellectual — "What is he doing out there?" "What is his function in relation to us?"

Such questions as these arise only because the social role of the Negro intellectual has never really been defined at all. For the most part, the Negro intellectual has been a rather free agent in the black and white scheme of things. Inasmuch as the support, patronage and prestige of the Negro intellectual come from the white world and its cultural apparatus, his creative and cultural achievements have been seen by the black world as Ebony magazine and *Jet* see them. That is to say, such Negroes have achieved something, they have "made it." They have scored in the white world and are now recognized. It is not necessary to consider how they managed to score, the important thing is that they did. In this way, the Negro creative intellectual has never really been held accountable to the black world for his social role. If he scores, well and good. If he doesn't, that's unfortunate, but it will pass unnoticed and no one will care. This tacit agreement between the Negro intellectual and the black world has prevailed because it is understood that the black world cannot and does not, support the Negro creative intellectual. The black bourgeoisie does not publish books, does not own and operate theaters or music halls. It plays no role to speak of in Negro music, and is remote from the living realities of the jazz musician who plays out his nights in the effete and soulless commercial jungles of American white middle class cafe culture.

Add to the Negro intelligentsia, who have no firm cultural base in the reality of either the black world or the white (even when they have achieved recognition), a large fluctuating contingent who make up the bulk of new aspirants to integrated cultural achievement. The result: a rootless class of displaced persons who are refugees from the social poverty of the black world. At one time, the black world was rich in the pristine artistic essentials for new forms in music, dance, song, theater and even language; then, the black ethnic identity was seen as a unique advantage. But today the style has become a negation of that identity, in pursuit of cultural integration or assimilation. Today the failure of the black bourgeoisie as a class, to play any social role as patron or sponsor of the arts, is all the more glaring. For now the new Negro

cultural aspirants are making vocal and specified demands for integration in cultural fields where the black bourgeoisie has never paid the piper, and therefore can call no tunes. ...

———— 8.21 ————
'NIKKI-ROSA'
Nikki Giovanni

Nikki Giovanni's is one of the most recognizable names of the Black Arts Movement. From her debut collection in 1968, *Black Talk*, through the end of the decade, Giovanni's poetry spoke lyrically but angrily about revolution, black pride and disregard for conventions of American society. She was renowned for her fierce readings of her work as much as for its composition. As her work mellowed in the 1970s, she still confronted gender issues within the black community, exploring relationships between black men and women.

A. "My Poem"

i am 25 years old
black female poet
wrote a poem asking
nigger can you kill
if they kill me
it won't stop
the revolution

i have been robbed
it looked like they knew
that i was to be hit
they took my tv
my two rings
my piece of african print
and my two guns
if they take my life
it won't stop
the revolution

my phone is tapped
my mail is opened
they've caused me to turn
on all my old friends
and all my new lovers
if i hate all black

people
and all negroes
it won't stop
the revolution

if i never write
another poem
or short story
if i flunk out
of grad school
if my car is reclaimed
and my record player
won't play
and if i never see
a peaceful day
or do a meaningful
black thing
it won't stop
the revolution

the revolution
is in the streets
and if i stay
on the fifth floor
it will go on
if i never do
anything
it will go on

B. "Nikki Rosa"

childhood rememberances are always a drag
if you're Black
you always remember things like living in
Woodlawn
with no inside toilet
and if you become famous or something
they never talk about how happy you were to
have your mother
all to yourself and
how good the water felt when you got your
bath from one of those
big tubs that folk in chicago barbeque in
and somehow when you talk about home
it never gets across how much you
understood their feelings

as the whole family attended meetings about
Hollydale
and even though you remember
your biographers never understand
your father's pain as he sells his stock
and another dream goes
And though you're poor it isn't poverty that-
concerns you
and though they fought a lot
it isn't your father's drinking that makes any
difference
but only that everybody is together and you
and your sister have happy birthdays and very
good
Christmasses
and I really hope no white person ever has cause
to write about me
because they never understand
Black love is Black wealth and they'll
probably talk about my hard childhood
and never understand that
all the while I was quite happy

C. "Kidnap Poem"

Ever been kidnapped
by a poet
if I were a poet
I'd kidnap you
put you in my phrases and meter
you to my jones beach
or maybe coney island
or maybe just to my house
lyric you in lilacs
dash you in the rain
blend into the beach
to complement my see
play the lyre for you
ode you with my love song
anything to win you
wrap you in the red Black green
show you off to mama
yeah if I were a poet i'd kid
nap you

——— 8.22 ———
'SAY IT LOUD (I'M BLACK AND I'M PROUD!)'
James Brown

On the popular end of the Black Arts Movement lay funk music — in particular that of James Brown. Brown's 1960s soul records set the stage for the distinctive funk sound that he and bands like Sly and the Family Stone developed in the 1970s. Beginning in the late 1960s, Brown and subsequent funk performers infused Black Pride notions into their song lyrics. Some argue that the style of the music — harder, more expressive and "in-your-face" than the soul of the early 1960s — was itself an outgrowth of Black Pride. Certainly, Brown's 1968 song "Say it Loud (I'm Black and I'm Proud!)" was and is the most identifiable popular culture expression of the political movement.

Uh! Your bad self!
Say it loud! — I'm black and I'm proud
Say it louder! — I'm black and I'm proud

Some people say we got alot of malice
Some say it's a lotta nerve
But I say we won't quit movin' until we get what we deserve
We've been buked and we've been scourned
We've been treated bad, talked about
As sure as you're born
But just as sure as it take two eyes to make a pair — huh!
Brother we can't quit until we get our share

Say it loud — I'm black and I'm proud
Say it loud — I'm black and I'm proud
One more time, say it loud — I'm black and I'm proud
I've worked on jobs with my feet and my hands
But all the work I did was for the other man
And now we demands a chance to do things for ourselves
We tired of beatin' our head against the wall
And workin' for someone else

Say it loud! — I'm black and I'm proud
Say it loud! — I'm black and I'm proud
Say it loud! — I'm black and I'm proud
Say it loud! — I'm black and I'm proud — oow!

Ooo-wee, you're killin' me
Alright, uh! you're out of sight!
Alright, so tough you're tough enough!
Ooowee uh! you're killin' me! oow!

Say it loud! — I'm black and I'm proud
Say it louder! — I'm black and I'm proud

Now we demand a chance to do things for ourselves
We tired of beatin' our heads against the wall
And workin' for someone else
A-look-a-here
There's one thing more I got to say right here
Now, now we're people, we're like the birds and the bees
We rather die on our feet than keep livin' on our knees

Say it loud — I'm black and I'm proud huh!
Say it loud — I'm black and I'm proud huh!
Say it loud — I'm black and I'm proud Lord-a-Lord-a-Lord-a
Say it loud — I'm black and I'm proud — oooh!

Now we can say we do the Funky Broadway
Now we can do huh!
Sometimes we dance we sing and we talk
You know I do like to do the camel walk
Alright now huh! alright-alright now ha!

Say it loud — I'm black and I'm proud
Say it louder — I'm black and I'm proud — let me hear ya'
Say it louder — I'm black and I'm proud
Say it louder — I'm black and I'm proud

Now we's demands a chance to do things for ourselves
We tired of beatin' our heads against the wall

And workin' for someone else huh!
Now we our people too!
We're like the birds and the bees
But we'd rather die on our feet
Than keep a livin' on our knees

Say it louder — I'm black and I'm proud
Say it louder — I'm black and I'm proud
Let me hear ya', huh! say it loud! — I'm black
and I'm proud — huh!
Say it louder — I'm black and I'm proud
Say it louder — I'm black and I'm proud

——— 8.23 ———

DIVIDE AND CONQUER
Federal Bureau of Investigation

J. Edgar Hoover's Federal Bureau of Investigation had long been involved in spying on and actively interfering with the activism and personal lives of civil rights leaders. But the Black Panther Party and other black nationalist groups caused the FBI much greater concern. Hoover wrote in 1968 that he believed the Party to be the nation's biggest threat. The FBI's primary strategy was to sow divisiveness among black nationalist groups. In this, Hoover was largely successful. One of the FBI memos below discusses the agency's plan to divide the SNCC-Black Panther alliance. Similar efforts were carried out
     to heighten tensions between the Black Panthers and Maulana Karenga's Us organization. Ultimately, through these tactics, combined with raids that led to gun battles, the FBI had arrested or driven underground all of the leading Black Power figures by 1970. Eldridge Cleaver fled the country to avoid charges of murdering a police officer in 1969. H. Rap Brown, Bobby Seale and others retreated from politics as the organization dispersed.

A. Memo directing offices to target black nationalists

COUNTERINTELLIGENCE PROGRAM
BLACK NATIONALIST — HATE GROUPS
INTERNAL SECURITY

Offices receiving copies of this letter are instructed to immediately establish a control file, captioned as above, and to assign responsibility for following and coordinating this new counterintelligence program to an experienced and imaginative Special Agent well versed in investigations related to black nationalist, hate-type organizations. The field office control file used under this program may be maintained in a pending inactive status until such time as a specific operation or technique is placed under consideration for implementation.

     The purpose of this new counterintelligence endeavor is to expose, disrupt, misdirect, discredit, or otherwise neutralize the activities of black nationalist, hate-type organizations and groupings, their leadership, spokesmen, membership and supporters, and to counter their propensity for violence and civil disorder. The activities of all such groups of intelligence interest to this Bureau must be followed on a continuous basis so we will be in a position to promptly take advantage of all opportunities for counterintelligence and to inspire action in instances where circumstances warrant. The pernicious background of such groups, their duplicity, and devious manouvers must be exposed to public scrutiny where such publicity will have a neutralizing effect. Efforts of the various groups to consolidate their forces or to recruit new or youthful adherents must be frustrated. No opportunity should be missed to exploit through counterintelligence techniques the organizational and personal conflicts of the leaderships of the groups and where possible an effort should be made to capitalize upon existing conflicts between competing black nationalist organizations. When an opportunity is apparent to disrupt or neutralize black nationalist, hate-type organizations through the cooperation of established local news media contacts or through such contact with sources available to the Seat of the Government, in every instance careful attention must be given to the proposal to insure the targeted group is disrupted, ridiculed, or discredited through the publicity and not merely publicized. Consideration should be given to techniques to preclude violence-prone or rabble-rouser leaders of hate groups from speaking their philosophy publicly or through various mass communications available.

Many individuals currently active in black nationalist organizations have backgrounds of immorality, subversive activity, and criminal records. Through your investigation of key agitators, you should endeavor to establish their unsavory backgrounds. Be alert to determine evidence of misappropriation of funds or other types of personal misconduct on the part of militant nationalist leaders so any practical or warranted counter intelligence may be instituted.

Intensified attention under this program should be afforded to the activities of such groups as the Student Nonviolent Coordinating Committee, the Southern Christian Leadership Conference, Revolutionary Action Movement, the Deacons for Defense and Justice, Congress of Racial Equality, and the Nation of Islam. Particular emphasis should be given to extremists who direct the activities and policies of revolutionary or militant groups such as Stokely Carmichael, H. "Rap" Brown, Elijah Mohammed, and Maxwell Stanford.

B. Memo suggesting tactic to divide SNCC and Black Panthers

SUBJECT: COUNTERINTELLIGENCE PROGRAM
BLACK NATIONALIST — HATE GROUPS
RACIAL INTELLIGENCE
(BLACK PANTHER PARTY)

PURPOSE:
To recommend attached items be given news media sources on confidential basis as counterintelligence measure to help neutralize extremist Black Panthers and foster split between them and Student Nonviolent Coordinating Committee (SNCC).

BACKGROUND:
There is a feud between the two most prominent black nationalist extremist groups, The Black Panthers and SNCC. Attached item

notes that the feud is being continued by SNCC circulating the statement that:

"According to zoologists, the main difference between a panther and other large cats is that the panther has the smallest head."

This is biologically true. Publicity to this effect might help neutralize Black Panther recruiting efforts.

ACTION:
That attached items, captioned "Panther Pinheads," be furnished a cooperative news media source by the Crime Records Division on a confidential basis. We will be alert for other ways to exploit this item

—————— 8.24 ——————
'TWO SOCIETIES, ONE BLACK, ONE WHITE'
Kerner Commission Report

The Black Panther Party's popularity stemmed from its coincidence with a time of unprecedented agitation and frustration in cities with large African-American communities. The violence that exploded in Watts in 1965 marked the front end of a storm of unrest in cities with large black populations over the next few years. Summer after summer, conflict between blacks and police flared up, often leading to riots. The summer of 1967 was a particularly brutal one, the occasion of at least 75 riots. Blacks in at least 20 cities had rioted the previous year. The Johnson administration appointed a National Advisory Committee on Civil Disobedience, chaired by Illinois Governor Otto Kerner. Their report, known as the Kerner Commission Report, was released in the spring of 1968. The report declared America a nation divided. The country, it stated, held "two societies, one black, one white, separate and unequal." Segregation remained a reality, rooted in economic inequality. Blacks were cordoned off in rotting urban ghettos, as whites retreated to the suburbs, content in the lie that they weren't implicated in the violence and poverty unfolding on their television screens. Moreover, the report predicted, the problem was sure to get worse in coming years.

The summer of 1967 again brought racial disorders to American cities, and with them shock, fear and bewilderment in the nation.

The worst came during a two-week period in July, first in Newark and then in Detroit. Each set off a chain reaction in neighboring communities.

On July 28, 1967, the President of the United States established this Commission and directed us to answer three basic questions:

What happened?

Why did it happen?

What can be done to prevent it from happening again?

To respond to these questions, we have undertaken a broad range of studies and investigations. We have visited the riot cities; we have heard many witnesses; we have sought the counsel of experts across the country.

This is our basic conclusion: Our nation is moving toward two societies, one black, one white — separate and unequal.

Reaction to last summer's disorders has quickened the movement and deepened the division. Discrimination and segregation have long permeated much of American life; they now threaten the future of every American.

This deepening racial division is not inevitable. The movement apart can be reversed. Choice is still possible. Our principal task is to define that choice and to press for a national resolution.

To pursue our present course will involve the continuing polarization of the American community and, ultimately, the destruction of basic democratic values.

The alternative is not a blind repression or capitulation to lawlessness. It is the realization of common opportunities for all within a single society.

This alternative will require a commitment to national action — compassionate, massive and sustained, backed by the resources of the most powerful and the richest nation on this earth. From every American it will require new attitudes, new understanding, and, above all, new will.

The vital needs of the nation must be met; hard choices must be made, and if necessary, new taxes enacted.

Violence cannot build a better society. Disruption and disorder nourish repression, not justice. They strike at the freedom of every citizen. The community cannot — it will not — tolerate coercion and mob rule.

Violence and destruction must be ended — in the streets of the ghetto and in the lives of people.

Segregation and poverty have created in the racial ghetto a destructive environment totally unknown to most white Americans.

What white Americans have never fully understood — but what the Negro can never forget — is that white society is deeply implicated in the ghetto. White institutions created it, white institutions maintain it, and white society condones it.

————— 8.25 —————

'WE DON'T HAVE NO LEADER. WE LOST OUR LEADER'

The Washington Post on Martin Luther King's assassination and the 1968 Riots

On the evening of April 4, 1968, Martin Luther King was shot by a sniper while standing on a hotel balcony in Memphis, Tennessee. In the years leading up to 1968, King had directed his SCLC's attention towards the economic issues faced by northern blacks. But the southern ministers were on new and unfamiliar turf, and their efforts had not resonated in the way those of the black nationalists' had. Nevertheless, news of King's murder touched off the worst urban rioting yet. By nightfall, riots were raging in cities all over the country. They would ultimately flare up in over 100 cities. The damage done to black neighborhoods was severe, and in many cases lasting.

As detailed in the *Washington Post* report below, one of the most devastating uprisings was in Washington, D.C., where many civil rights organizers were stationed at the time, preparing for the SCLC's Poor People's Campaign, to be launched in a demonstration on the National Mall later that month. What started as a SNCC-led march to close down the city's businesses in honor of King, developed into a riot. Police first contained rioters inside the city's large and vibrant black business and nightlife district along 14th Street and U Street, leaving the frustrated masses to burn much of the neighborhood to the ground. Later, after nightfall, police moved in and confronted the throngs of people. Efforts to rebuild the neighborhood continued into the late 1990s.

KING ASSASSINATED IN MEMPHIS
Shouting Crowds Smash Stores in District
14th Street Sealed Off; Fires Set

Tense, milling crowds of Negroes — angered by the slaying of the Rev. Dr. Martin Luther King — swarmed along 14th Street's inner-city strip last night and early today, wrecking and looting stores and heckling policemen.

Hundreds of people in clusters, at first embittered, moved haphazardly through the area and baited police into the use of tear gas at one major fire. It started as a parade that Stokely Carmichael and others began and later could not control.

At 12:30 a.m. four to five hours after it began, Public Safety Director Patrick V. Murphy reported "some success in urging people to go home ... the officers are talking to as many people as possible telling them to go home."

Serious fires broke out in at least six areas, the worst a blaze shortly after 2 a.m. in the 2600 block of 14th Street that burned out the interior of the Empire Supermarket at 2601 14th and an adjacent building before firemen arrived.

The flames licked their way along the block to a third building before the fire was brought under at least temporary control by firemen.

The count of arrests at 2:30 a.m. stood at 85 persons.

By 12:45 a.m. police had closed 14th Street from Spring Road to N Street.

A major confrontation between police and a crowd developed shortly before 1 a.m., when a large fire broke out at Steelman's Liquors, 2746 14th St. nw.

A fresh wave of heckling people pelted firefighters, and gas-masked police released tear gas and pulled out their night sticks and pistols to move the crowd down the block away from the flames. ...

About midnight, the 8 a.m. to 4 p.m. shift of policemen was called to duty, putting all three shifts on the street.

Five policemen and one fireman were reported to have suffered minor injuries during the course of the night. Fifty civilians were treated for minor injuries.

The night's raucous activity — neither under control nor completely our of hand — was contained largely by police in a 19 block strip along 14th Street.

Police worked to seal off the area from Park Road to R Street and from 14th to 18th Streets nw.

An informal command post was set up at the 13th Precinct station house, with Mayor Walter E. Washington, Murphy, Licenses and Inspections Chief Julian R. Dugas, Police Chief John B. Layton, the Rev. Walter E. Fauntroy, vice chairman of the City Council, and Clinton Mitchell of the city's Human Relations Council in constant conference.

Shortly before 3 a.m., Mayor Washington issued a report on what he termed "considerable damage to one large neighborhood" and praised police and firemen on behalf of all the city's residents.

"I commend those hundreds of thousands of our citizens who responded to our calls for calm and cooperation," the Mayor added.

The incidents began to erupt shortly after the news of Dr. King's assassination spread through the streets, by radio and word of mouth. A group of about 15 people gathered at Student Nonviolent Coordinating Committee headquarters, 2208 14th St. nw.

At first there were tears, and Lester McKinnie, local SNCC leader called quickly for "a period to react to this great tragedy."

Carmichael burst in to suggest that the group close down the area's stores out of respect for Dr. King. "If Kennedy had died, all these stores would have closed," he said. "Martin Luther King is our leader and we are going to show him some respect."

As the small band began shouting its request to store owners along the way — and many answered them quickly by turning off lights and closing doors — the number of people began to swell.

As it did, quiet respect and polite requests turned to angry shouts, broken windows, more looting and calls for extra policemen to handle an uglier mood that began to overtake the impromptu march.

As windows of stores cracked and TV stets and other appliances were yanked out of stores, Carmichael shouted, "No, no! Not now, not now!" He ordered the looters he saw to "Go home, go home."

Near 14th and W Streets, Mr. Fauntroy appeared and attempted to persuade the people to break it up. "This is not the way to do it, Stokely, this is not the way," he said, gently holding Carmichael's arm.

But Carmichael pulled away and continued the zig-zagging parade, yelling at more store owners to close down.

As the group moved down from 14th and Clifton Streets back toward SNCC, two gunshots were fired, and Carmichael grabbed on gun from a man, saying, "None of this, none of this."

At one point, he pulled out a gun himself, waved it, told the people he was ready but they were not and not to do anything until they were, to wait through the night, to go home.

Someone in the cluster yelled back, "We don't have no leader. We lost our leader."

"You won't get one like this," Carmichael yelled back. "You'll just get shot."

Among stores in the 2000 block of 14th Street that were damaged were a carryout, a TV repair shop, a hardware store, and a dress shop.

Police initially stayed clear of the immediate area, following Murphy's on-the-street order to "keep cool" and pull away from any imminent confrontation.

At 10:40 p.m., police moved to detour northbound traffic around the area where the crowd had gathered, sending cars west on R Street. Sporadically, windows of cars were cracked by flying debris.

At about 11:10 p.m. police, including the Civil Disturbance Unit, were ordered to begin

moving in and disperse the crowd and make arrests, if necessary. The command came as a steady rain began.

By then, about 40 stores had been reported looted, ranging from the 1900 block to the 2400 block of 14th Street, and some side streets.

A car in a lot at 14th and Chapin Streets nw., was set afire.

As the milling continued in the rain, Mr. Fauntroy traveled form one television station to another, appealing for calm, asking "black brother and sisters" to "handle our grief in the spirit of nonviolence."

He implored people to stay home and pray.

McKinnie issued a call for a general strike today "of all black people."

In this way, he declared "we can all begin to analyse what this racist, imperialist country is doing to us.

"We are urging all SNCC offices throughout the country to encourage general strikes in their areas that we may grieve the tragedy of Dr. King's death, because he is flesh of our blood and blood of our blood."

By 11:15, Layton advised Mayor Washington that the incidents had localized in the hub of 14th and U Streets and he felt the situation was coming under control. ...

——— 8.26 ———

'NIGGERS ARE SCARED OF REVOLUTION'
The Last Poets

The spoken word performance group The Last Poets represent a bridge between the Black Arts Movement and the broadly defined hip hop movement of the 1980s and '90s. Three friends who met in prison — Jalal Mansur Nuriddin, Omar Ben Hassan and Abiodun Oyewole — launched the group in 1969 at a Harlem celebration of Malcolm X's birthday. The following year, their debut album, *The Last Poets*, hit the Top 10 on the album charts. They recited their poetry over music, discussing basic Black Power themes. Hip hop scholars count the group as among the founding fathers of rap. After a follow-up album in 1972, and some experimental jazz albums in the next few years, the group receded until rap exploded in a proliferation of artists in the late 1970s. One of their most famous early pieces chastises blacks who don't get involved in the empowerment movement.

Niggers are scared of revolution
Niggers are scared of revolution but niggers shouldn't be scared of revolution because revolution is nothing but change, and all niggers do is change.
Niggers come in from work and change into pimping clothes to hit the street and make some quick change. Niggers change their hair from black to red to blond and hope like hell their looks will change.
Niggers kill others just because one didn't receive the correct change.

Niggers always going through bullshit changes. But when it comes for a real change Niggers are scared of revolution.

Niggers fuck.
Niggers fuck fuck fuck.
Niggers love the word fuck.
They think they're fucking cute.
They fuck you around.
The first thing they say when they're mad is "fuck it."
You play a little too much with them they say "fuck you."
Try to be nice to them they fuck you over.
When it's time to TCB niggers are somewhere fucking.
Niggers don't realize while they're doing all this fucking they're getting fucked around.
But when they do realize it's too late, so all niggers do is just get fucked ... up!

Niggers talk about fucking ... Fucking that ... Fucking this ... Fucking yours ... Fucking my sis.
Not knowing what they fucking for.
Ain't fucking for love and appreciation.
Just fucking to be fucking.
Niggers fuck white thighs, brown thighs, yellow thighs.

Niggers fuck ankles when they run out of thighs.
Niggers fuck Sally, Linda and Sue.
And if you don't watch out niggers will fuck you ...
Niggers would fuck fuck if it could be fucked.
But when it comes to fucking for revolutionary causes Niggers say FUCK! ... revolution.

Niggers are scared of revolution.

——————— 8.27 ———————
A CAGED BIRD SINGING
Maya Angelou

Like her elder contemporary James Baldwin, much of poet and author Maya Angelou's work is autobiographical. She tells her life story over the course of five of these autobiographies. The first of which, *I Know Why the Caged Bird Sings*, is the story of Angelou's troubled but heroic childhood. Published in 1970, it is still her most famous work. It begins with Angelou's early years in Stamps, Arkansas, living with her brother, in whom she confides all, and her grandmother. When their divorced parents, who had abandoned the children years earlier, suddenly show up, the pair go to live with their mother in St. Louis. But the mother's boyfriend molests and rapes young Angelou. The assault sets off a series of tragic events in her life, including five years in which she would not speak to anyone other than her brother. Ultimately, however, Angelou overcomes the pain and moves into her teens, world-weary but resilient.

The book created an image of Angelou — as a woman who has every reason to retreat from the world, yet continues to bravely, and gracefully, confront it — that follows her still today. Angelou reinforced that image through subsequent work, such as the title poem of her third book of poetry, *And Still I Rise*, published in 1978. As is particularly the case with this poem, many readers consider the first person in her work to represent not just herself, but black women as a whole.

A. *I Know Why the Caged Bird Sings*

On a late spring Saturday, after our chores (nothing like those in Stamps) were done, Bailey and I were going out, he to play baseball and I to the library. Mr. Freeman said to me, after Bailey had gone downstairs, "Ritie, go get some milk for the house."

Mother usually brought milk when she came in, but that morning as Bailey and I straightened the living room her bedroom door had been open, and we knew that she hadn't come home the night before.

He gave me money and I rushed to the store and back to the house. After putting the milk in the icebox, I turned and had just reached the front door when I heard, "Ritie." He was sitting in the big chair by the radio. "Ritie, come here." I didn't think about the holding time until I got close to him. His pants were open and his "thing" was standing out of his britches by itself.

"No, sir, Mr. Freeman." I started to back away. I didn't want to touch that mushy-hard thing again, and I didn't need him to hold me anymore. He grabbed my arm and pulled me between his legs. His face was still and looked kind, but he didn't smile or blink his eyes. Nothing. He did nothing, except reach his left hand around to turn on the radio without even looking at it. Over the noise of music and static, he said, "Now, this ain't gonna hurt you much. You liked it before, didn't you?"

I didn't want to admit that I had in fact liked his holding me or that I had liked his smell or the hard heart-beating, so I said nothing. And his face became like the face of one of those mean natives the Phantom was always having to beat up.

His legs were squeezing my waist. "Pull down your drawers." I hesitated for two reasons: he was holding me too tight to move, and I was sure that any minute my mother or Bailey or the Green Hornet would bust in the door and save me.

"We was just playing before." He released me enough to snatch down my bloomers, and then he dragged me closer to him. Turning the radio up loud, too loud, he said, "If you scream, I'm gonna kill you. And if you tell, I'm gonna kill Bailey." I could tell he meant what he said. I couldn't understand why he wanted

to kill my brother. Neither of us had done anything to him. And then.

Then there was the pain. A breaking and entering when even the senses are torn apart. The act of rape on an eight year-old body is a matter of the needle giving because the camel can't. The child gives, because the body can, and the mind of the violator cannot.

I thought I had died — I woke up in a white-walled world, and it had to be heaven. But Mr. Freeman was there and he was washing me. His hands shook, but he held me upright in the tub and washed my legs. "I didn't mean to hurt you, Ritie. I didn't mean it. But don't you tell ... Remember, don't you tell a soul." ...

The court was filled. Some people even stood behind the churchlike benches in the rear. Overhead fans moved with the detachment of old men. Grandmother Baxter's clients were there in gay and flippant array. The gamblers in pin-striped suits and their makeup-deep women whispered to me out of blood-red mouths that now I knew as much as they did. I was eight, and grown. Even the nurses in the hospital had told me that now I had nothing to fear. "The worst is over for you," they had said. So I put the words in all the smirking mouths.

I sat with my family (Bailey couldn't come) and they rested still on the seats like solid, cold gray tombstones. Thick and forevermore unmoving.

Poor Mr. Freeman twisted in his chair to look empty threats over to me. He didn't know that he couldn't kill Bailey and Bailey didn't lie ... to me.

"What was the defendant wearing?" That was Mr. Freeman's lawyer.

"I don't know."

"You mean to say this man raped you and you don't know what he was wearing?" He snickered as if I had raped Mr. Freeman. "Do you know if you were raped?"

A sound pushed in the air of the court (I was sure it was laughter). I was glad that Mother had let me wear the navy-blue winter coat with brass buttons. Although it was too short and the weather was typical St. Louis hot, the coat was a friend that I hugged to me in the strange and unfriendly place.

"Was that the first time the accused touched you?" The question stopped me. Mr. Freeman had surely done some thing very wrong, but I was convinced that I'd helped him to do it. I didn't want to lie, but the lawyer wouldn't let me think, so I used silence as a retreat.

"Did the accused try to touch you before the time he or rather you say he raped you?"

I couldn't say yes and tell them how he had loved me once for a few minutes and how he had held me close before he thought I had peed in the bed. My uncles would kill me and Grandmother Baxter would stop, speaking as she often did when she was angry. And all those people in the court would stone me as they had stoned the harlot in the Bible. And Mother, who thought I was such a good girl, would be so disappointed. But most important, there was Bailey. I had kept a big secret from him.

"Marguerite, answer the question. Did the accused touch you before the occasion on which you claim he raped you?"

Everyone in the court knew that the answer had to be No. Everyone except Mr. Freeman and me. I looked at his heavy face trying to look as if he would have liked me to say No. I said No.

The lie lumped in my throat and I couldn't get air. How I despised the man for making me lie. Old, mean, nasty thing. Old, black, nasty thing. The tears didn't soothe my heart as they usually did. I screamed, "Ole, mean, dirty thing, you. Dirty old thing." Our lawyer brought me off the stand and to my mother's arms. The fact that I had arrived at my desired destination by lies made it less appealing to me.

Mr. Freeman was given one year and one day, but he never got a chance to do his time. His lawyer (or someone) got him released that very afternoon.

In the living room, where the shades were drawn for coolness, Bailey and I played Monopoly on the floor. I played a bad game because I was thinking how I would be able to

tell Bailey how I had lied and, even worse for our relationship, kept a secret from him. Bailey answered the doorbell, because Grandmother was in the kitchen. A tall white policeman asked for Mrs. Baxter. Had they found out about the lie? Maybe the policeman was coming to put me in jail because I had sworn on the Bible that everything I said would be the truth, the whole truth, so help me God. The man in our living room was taller than the sky and whiter than my image of God. He just didn't have the beard.

"Mrs. Baxter, I thought you ought to know. Freeman's been found dead on the lot behind the slaughterhouse."

Softly, as if she were discussing a church program, she said, "Poor man." She wiped her hands on the dishtowel and just as softly asked, "Do they know who did it?"

The policeman said, "Seems like he was dropped there. Some say he was kicked to death."

Grandmother's color only rose a little. "Tom, thanks for telling me. Poor man. Well, maybe it's better this way. He was a mad dog. Would you like a glass of lemonade? Or some beer?"

Although he looked harmless, I knew he was a dreadful angel counting out my many sins.

"No, thanks, Mrs. Baxter. I'm on, duty. Gotta be getting back."

"Well, tell your ma that I'll be over when I take up my beer and remind her to save some kraut for me."

And the recording angel was gone. He was gone, and a man was dead because I lied. Where was the balance in that? One lie surely wouldn't be worth a man's life. Bailey could have explained it all to me, but I didn't dare ask him. Obviously I had forfeited my place in heaven forever, and I was as gutless as the doll I had ripped to pieces ages ago. Even Christ Himself turned His back on Satan. Wouldn't He turn His back on me? I could feel the evilness flowing through my body and waiting, pent up, to rush off my tongue if I tried to open my mouth. I clamped my teeth shut, I'd hold it in. If it escaped, wouldn't it flood the world and all the innocent people?

Grandmother Baxter said, "Ritie and junior, you didn't hear a thing. I never want to hear this situation nor that evil man's name mentioned in my house again. I mean that." She went back into the kitchen to make apple strudel for my celebration.

Even Bailey was frightened. He sat all to himself, looking at a man's death — a kitten looking at a wolf. Not quite understanding it but frightened all the same.

In those moments I decided that although Bailey loved me he couldn't help. I had sold myself to the Devil and there could be no escape. The only thing I could do was to stop talking to people other than Bailey. Instinctively, or somehow, I knew that because I loved him so much I'd never hurt him, but if I talked to anyone else that person might die too. Just my breath, carrying my words out, might poison people and they'd curl up and die like the black fat slugs that only pretended.

I had to stop talking.

B. "And Still I Rise"

You may write me down in history
With your bitter, twisted lies,
You may trod me in the very dirt
But still, like dust, I'll rise.
Does my sassiness upset you?
Why are you beset with gloom?
'Cause I walk like I've got oil wells
Pumping in my living room.

Just like moons and like suns,
With the certainty of tides,
Just like hopes springing high,
Still I'll rise.

Did you want to see me broken?
Bowed head and lowered eyes?
Shoulders falling down like teardrops.
Weakened by my soulful cries.

Does my haughtiness offend you?
Don't you take it awful hard
'Cause I laugh like I've got gold mines
Diggin' in my own back yard.
You may shoot me with your words,
You may cut me with your eyes,
You may kill me with your hatefulness,
But still, like air, I'll rise.

Does my sexiness upset you?
Does it come as a surprise
That I dance like I've got diamonds
At the meeting of my thighs?

Out of the huts of history's shame
I rise
Up from a past that's rooted in pain
I rise I'm a black ocean, leaping and wide,
Welling and swelling I bear in the tide.

Leaving behind nights of terror and fear
I rise
Into a daybreak that's wondrously clear
I rise
Bringing the gifts that my ancestors gave,
I am the dream and the hope of the slave.
I rise

I rise I rise.

——————— 8.28 ———————
'ABC'
Jackson Five

A family group of young vocalists from Gary, Indiana, got their big break in 1967 when they took first place at an amateur night performance at Harlem's Apollo Theater. Two years later the Jackson Five recorded its first single for Motown records. Barry Gordy had snatched the brothers up, styled their flashy outfits and choreography and put young Michael, still a pre-teen, in the limelight. His recipe was a phenomenal success. The brothers' singles were number one hits from the beginning. The second of them, "ABC," released in 1970, is among the most famous the group would record over the next decade-plus of recording and touring. Throughout the 1970s, they split off on solo projects as well, with Michael continuing to draw the most attention. He, of course, would reach unprecedented recording fame as a soloist in the early 1980s.

You went to school to learn girl
things you never knew before
like "I" before "E" except after "C"
and why 2 plus 2 makes 4
now, now, now
I'm gonna teach you, teach you, teach you
all about love girl, all about love
sit yourself down, take a seat
all you gotta do is repeat after me

A B C, it's easy as
1 2 3, as simple as
do re mi, A B C, 1 2 3
baby, you and me girl

Come on and love me just a little bit
I'm gonna teach you how to sing it out
come on, come on, come on
let me tell you what it's all about
reading, writing, arithmatic
are the branches of the learning tree
but without the roots of love every day girl
your education ain't complete
teacher's gonna show you (she's gonna show you)
how to get an "A" (na, na, na, na, na, na)
how to spell "me", "you", add the two
listen to me baby that's all you got to do

Oh,
A B C, it's easy as
1 2 3, as simple as
do re mi, A B C, 1 2 3
baby you and me girl
A B C it's easy, it's like counting up to 3
singing simple melodies
that's how easy love can be
singing simple melodies
1 2 3 baby you and me

Sit down girl, I think I love ya'
No, get up girl, show me what you can do
Shake it, shake it baby, come on now
Shake it, shake it baby, oooh, oooh
Shake it, shake it baby, yeah

1 2 3 baby, oooh oooh
A B C baby, ah, ah
do re mi baby, wow
thats how easy love can be
A B C it's easy, it's like counting up to 3
singing simple melodies
that's how easy love can be
teacher's gonna teach you how to
sing it out, sing it out, sing it out baby

——— 8.29 ———
'I AM SOMEBODY!'
Jesse L. Jackson

After Martin Luther King, Jr.'s death, the SCLC ministers struggled amongst themselves to find both a mission and a leader. King had launched a poverty campaign in Chicago that was plagued by one problem after another, all stemming from the fact that the southern ministers and the northern urban community they were trying to serve had little in common. But following King's death, the new program, called Operation Breadbasket, took off under the leadership of a young, brash SCLC operative named Jesse Jackson. Breadbasket's success strained the ongoing personality conflict between Jackson and Rev. Ralph Abernathy, King's successor atop the group. Eventually, when Abernathy charged Jackson with hoarding funds in Chicago that had been raised for the national organization, Jackson decided to go it on his own. In 1971, he founded Operation PUSH (People United to Save Humanity), which was primarily a political advocacy organization focusing on economic uplift in black communities and empowerment of black business. Throughout the decade, the organization offered Jackson a platform from which he defined himself as the new voice of national black politics. Following in King's tradition, he molded southern Baptist sermons into political speeches, captivating followers with his seemingly bottomless reservoir of catch phrases. Perhaps the most recognizable was his call and response poem, "I Am Somebody." The stanzas are interchangeable and often adapted to fit the particular audience or occasion, but the signature line is always the same.

I am
Somebody
I am

Somebody
I may be poor
But I am
Somebody
I may be young
But I am
Somebody
I may be on welfare
But I am
Somebody
I may have curly hair
I may have straight hair
But I am
Somebody
My clothes are different
My face is different
My hair is different
But I am
Somebody
I am black, brown, white
I speak a different language
But I must be respected
Protected
Never rejected
I am God's child
I am
Somebody

——— 8.30 ———
THE TUSKEGEE SYPHILIS STUDY
Associated Press

In 1972, the Associated Press broke what may be the biggest public health story in black history. In 1932, AP reported, the U.S. Health Service began monitoring 600 poor black men from Macon County, Georgia, at a clinic in Tuskegee's Veteran's Administration hospital, as part of a syphilis study. The government doctors informed the 399 largely poor and uneducated men who were infected with syphilis that they could opt out of the study and receive treatments for the disease. (The other 200 men in the study formed an uninfected control group.) But treatments available at the time were largely considered ineffective and potentially damaging themselves. Weighed against incentives such as free medicine for non-syphilitic ailments and free burial services upon their death, the men agreed to participate. However, ten years later, while the study was still going on, doctors began widely and safely treating syphilis with antibiotics. These treatments were never offered to the men in the study or to their family members, who had likely contracted the highly contagious disease by that time.

Before 1932, the Health Service had been conducting a larger study of syphilis. But budget cutbacks associated with the Depression derailed it, and the Tuskegee study was planned as a temporary replacement, intended to last about six months. It went on, with few efforts to conceal it, until a Health Service employee finally leaked the news to an Associated Press reporter forty years after the study began.

Its legacy continues to haunt public health officials and community health advocates working among African Americans. The black community has long led the nation in a host of chronic and debilitating health problems. At the same time, countless studies have shown widespread distrust of health advice and services involving the government — an important component in public health for resource-poor neighborhoods. Those studies have also consistently found that distrust is directly linked to knowledge of the Tuskegee experiment. Over the years, as the story has mutated to blur the line between history and urban legend, many African Americans have come to believe the government actually infected the men involved in the Tuskegee study with syphilis.

Syphilis Victims in U.S. Study Went Untreated for 40 Years
By Jean Heller
The Associated Press

WASHINGTON, July 25 — For 40 years the United States Public Health Service has conducted a study in which human beings with syphilis, who were induced to serve as guinea pigs, have gone without medical treatment for the disease and a few have died of its late effects, even though an effective therapy was eventually discovered.

The study was conducted to determine from autopsies what the disease does to the human body.

Officials of the health service who initiated the experiment have long since retired. Current officials, who say they have serious doubts about the morality of the study, also say that it is too late to treat the syphilis in any surviving participants.

Doctors in the service say they are now rendering whatever other medical services they can give to the survivors while the study of the disease's effects continues.

Dr. Melvin K. DuVal, Assistant Secretary of Health, Education and Welfare for Health and Scientific Affairs, expressed shock on learning of the study. He said that he was making an immediate investigation.

The experiment, called the Tuskegee Study, began in 1932 with about 600 black men, mostly poor and uneducated, from Tuskegee, Ala., an area that had the highest syphilis rate in the nation at the time.

Four hundred of the group had syphilis and never received deliberate treatment for the venereal infection. A control group of 200 had no syphilis and did not receive any specific therapy.

Some subjects were added to the study in its early years to replace men who dropped out of the program, but the number added is not known. At the beginning of this year, 74 of those who received no treatment were still alive.

As incentives to enter the program, the men were promised free transportation to and from hospitals, free hot lunches, free medicine for any disease other than syphilis and free burial after autopsies were performed.

Could Have Been Helped

The Tuskegee Study began 10 years before penicillin was found to be a cure for syphilis and 15 years before the drug became widely available. Yet, even after penicillin became common, and while its use probably could have helped or saved a number of the experiment subjects, the drug was denied them, Dr. J.D. Millar says.

Dr. Millar is chief of the venereal disease branch of the service's Center for Disease Control in Atlanta and is now in charge of what remains of the Tuskegee Study. He said in an interview that he has serious doubts about the program.

Dr. Millar said that "a serious moral problem" arose when penicillin therapy, which can cure syphilis in its early stages, became available in the late nineteen-forties and was withheld from the patients in the syphilis study. Penicillin therapy became, Dr. Millar said, "so much more effective and so much less dangerous" than pre-existing therapies.

"The study began when attitudes were much different on treatment and experimentation," Dr. Millar said. "At this point in time, with our current knowledge of treatment and the disease and the revolutionary change in approach to human experimentation, I don't believe the program would be undertaken."

Members of Congress reacted with shock to the disclosure today that the syphilis experimentation on human guinea pigs had taken place.

'A Moral Nightmare'

Senator William Proxmire, Democrat of Wisconsin, a member of the Senate Appropriations subcommittee that oversees Public Health Service budgets, called the study "a moral and ethical nightmare."

Syphilis is a highly contagious infection spread by sexual contact. If untreated, it can cause bone and dental deformations, deafness, blindness, heart disease and deterioration of the central nervous system.

No figures were available as to when the last death in the program occurred. One official said that no conscious effort was apparently made to halt the program after it got under way.

A 1969 study of 276 untreated syphilitics who participated in the Tuskegee Study showed that seven had died as a direct result of syphilis. The 1969 study was made by the Atlanta center, whose officials said they could not determine at this late date how many additional deaths had been caused by syphilis.

However, of the 400 men in the original syphilitic group, 154 died of heart disease that officials in Atlanta said was not specifically related to syphilis. Dr. Millar said that this rate was identical with the rate of cardio-vascular deaths in the control, or non-syphilis, group.

Dr. Millar said that the study was initiated in 1932 by Dr. J.R. Heller, assistant surgeon general in the service's venereal disease section, who subsequently became division chief.

Of the decision not to give penicillin to the untreated syphilitics once it became widely available, Dr. Millar said, "I doubt that it was a one-man decision. These things seldom are. Whoever was director of the VD section at that time, in 1946 or 1947, would be the most logical candidate if you had to pin it down."

'Never Clandestine'

The syphilis study "was never clandestine" and 15 scientific reports were published in the medical literature, Dr. Millar said in a telephone interview yesterday from Atlanta.

Officials who initiated the study in 1932 had informed the syphilis victims that they could get treatment for the infection at any time, Dr. Millar said.

"Patients were not denied drugs," Dr. Millar stressed. Rather, they were not offered drugs.

When the study began, doctors could offer only what is now regarded as poor therapy — injections of metals like bismuth, arsenic and mercury. Such treatments were known to be toxic.

Many doctors, Dr. Millar said, then thought "it better not to treat syphilis cases because of the mortality from" the metal therapies.

The critical period in ethics was in the late nineteen-forties and early nineteen-fifties when antibiotics could have been but were not prescribed for the syphilis patients.

<hr>

— 8.31 —
'PERHAPS THAT 18TH CENTURY CONSTITUTION SHOULD BE ABANDONED TO A 20TH CENTURY PAPER SHREDDER'
Barbara Jordan

With the nation rocked by the Watergate scandal, its faith in elected leaders shaken, all eyes looked to Capital Hill for justice during the 1974 hearings on the impeachment of President Richard Nixon. The eyes fell upon one of the most lasting images from the Watergate affair: Texas Democratic Rep. Barbara Jordan delivering her stirring statement at the opening of the House Judiciary Committee's hearing. Jordan was already considered a dynamic woman in American politics and a symbol of the impact that the Voting Rights Act had had on the South. In 1966, she was the first African American elected to the Texas State Senate since the Reconstruction era. In 1972, she became the first black woman to represent a southern state in Congress. During the Watergate hearings, she was a lead Democratic advocate for President Nixon's impeachment. The symbolic weight of her role was not lost on Jordan, as she remarked in discussing her journey from being barely a citizen to becoming an "inquisitor" of the president.

Mr. Chairman, I join my colleague Mr. Rangel in thanking you for giving the junior members of this committee the glorious opportunity of sharing the pain of this inquiry. Mr. Chairman, you are a strong man, and it has not been easy but we have tried as best we can to give you as much assistance as possible.

Earlier today we heard the beginning of the Preamble to the Constitution of the United States, *We, the people*. It is a very eloquent beginning. But when that document was completed, on the seventeenth of September in 1787, I was not included in that *We, the people*. I felt somehow for many years that George Washington and Alexander Hamilton just left me out by mistake. But through the process of amendment, interpretation, and court decision I have finally been included in *We, the people*.

Today I am an inquisitor. I believe hyperbole would not be fictional and would not overstate the solemness that I feel right now. My faith in the Constitution is whole, it is complete, it is total. I am not going to sit here and be an idle spectator to the diminution, the subversion, the destruction of the Constitution.

"Who can so properly be the inquisitors for the nation as the representatives of the nation themselves? The subject of its jurisdiction are those offenses which proceed from the misconduct of public men." That is what we are talking about. In other words, the jurisdiction comes from the abuse of violation of some public trust. It is wrong, I suggest, it is a misreading of the Constitution for any member here to assert that for a member to vote for an article of impeachment means that that member must be convinced that the president should be removed from office. The Constitution doesn't say that. The powers relating to impeachment are an essential check in the hands of this body, the legislature, against and upon the encroachment of the executive. In establishing the division between the two branches of the legislature, the House and the Senate, assigning to the one the right to accuse and to the other the right to judge, the framers of this Constitution were very astute. They did not make the accusers and the judges the same person. ...

Common sense would be revolted if we engaged upon this process for insurance, campaign finance reform, housing, environmental protection, energy sufficiency, mass transportation. Pettiness cannot be allowed to stand in the face of such overwhelming problems. So today we are not being petty. We are trying to be big because the task we have before us is a big one.

This morning, in a discussion of the evidence, we were told that the evidence which purports to support the allegations of misuse of the CIA by the president is thin. We are told that that evidence is insufficient. What that recital of the evidence this morning did not include is what the president did know on June 23, 1972. The president did know that it was

Republican money, that it was money from the Committee for the Re-Election of the President, which was found in the possession of one of the burglars arrested on June 17.

What the president did know on June 23 was the prior activities of E. Howard Hunt, which included his participation in the break-in of Daniel Ellsberg's psychiatrist, which included Howard Hunt's participation in the Dita Beard ITT affair, which included Howard Hunt's fabrication of cables designed to discredit the Kennedy administration.

We were further cautioned today that perhaps these proceedings ought to be delayed because certainly there would be new evidence forthcoming from the president. The committee subpoena is outstanding, and if the president wants to supply that material, the committee sits here.

The fact is that yesterday, the American people waited with great anxiety for eight hours, not knowing whether their president would obey an order of the Supreme Court of the United States.

At this point I would like to juxtapose a few of the impeachment criteria with some of the president's actions.

Impeachment criteria: James Madison, from the Virginia ratification convention. "If the president be connected in any suspicious manner with any person and there be grounds to believe that he will shelter him, he may be impeached."

We have heard time and time again that the evidence reflects payment to the defendants of money. The president had knowledge that these funds were being paid and that these were funds collected for the 1972 presidential campaign.

We know that the president met with Mr. Henry Petersen twenty-seven times to discuss matters related to Watergate and immediately thereafter met with the very persons who were implicated in the information Mr. Petersen was receiving and transmitting to the president. The words are "if the president be connected in any suspicious manner with any person and there be grounds to believe that he will shelter that person, he may be impeached."

Justice Story: "Impeachment is intended for occasional and extraordinary cases where a superior power acting for the whole people is put into operation to protect their rights and rescue their liberties from violations."

We know about the Huston plan. We know about the break-in of the psychiatrist's office. We know that there was absolute complete direction in August 1971 when the president instructed Ehrlichman to "do whatever is necessary." This instruction led to a surreptitious entry into Dr. Fielding's office.

"Protect their rights." "Rescue their liberties from violation."

The South Carolina ratification convention impeachment criteria: those are impeachable "who behave amiss or betray their public trust."

Beginning shortly after the Watergate break-in and continuing to the present time, the president has engaged in a series of public statements and actions designed to thwart the lawful investigation by government prosecutors. Moreover, the president has made public announcements and assertions bearing on the Watergate case which the evidence will show he knew to be false.

These assertions, false assertions, impeachable, those who misbehave. Those who "behave amiss or betray their public trust."

James Madison again at the Constitutional Convention: "A president is impeachable if he attempts to subvert the Constitution."

The Constitution charges the president with the task of taking care that the laws be faithfully executed, and yet the president has counseled his aides to commit perjury, willfully disregarded the secrecy of grand jury proceedings, concealed surreptitious entry, attempted to compromise a federal judge while publicly displaying his cooperation with the processes of criminal justice.

"A president is impeachable if he attempts to subvert the Constitution." If the impeachment provision in the Constitution of the United States will not reach the offenses charged here, then perhaps that eighteenth century Constitution should be abandoned to a twentieth-century paper shredder. Has the president committed offenses and planned and directed and acquiesced in a course of conduct which the Constitution will not tolerate? That is the question. We know that. We know the question. We should now forthwith proceed to answer the question. It is reason, and not passion, which must guide our deliberations, guide our debate, and guide our decision.

8.32

'WHAT IS SPECIAL? I, BARBARA JORDAN, AM A KEYNOTE SPEAKER'
Barbara Jordan

In 1976, Barbara Jordan gave the keynote address at the Democratic National Convention. She was the first African American to do so. Her speech was the first in a series of memorable oratories by black Americans at Democratic Party conventions. She, in fact, addressed the Party again at the 1992 convention. Again, as in the impeachment hearings, Jordan notes her awareness that she is making history as she speaks. Ever the Democratic stalwart, she hailed the Party's inclusive and forward-looking beliefs. Then she elaborates her idea of America in search of a "national community."

One hundred and forty-four years ago, members of the Democratic Party first met in convention to select a Presidential candidate. Since that time, Democrats have continued to convene once every four years and draft a party platform and nominate a Presidential candidate. And our meeting this week is a continuation of that tradition.

But there is something different about tonight. There is something special about tonight. What is different? What is Special? I, Barbara Jordan, am a keynote speaker.

A lot of years passed since 1832, and during that time it would have been most unusual for any national political party to ask that a Barbara Jordan deliver a keynote address —

but tonight here I am. And I feel that notwithstanding the past that my presence here is one additional bit of evidence that the American Dream need not forever be deferred.

Now that I have this grand distinction what in the world am I supposed to say?

I could easily spend this time praising the accomplishments of this party and attacking the Republicans, but I don't choose to do that.

I could list the many problems which Americans have. I could list the problems which cause people to feel cynical, angry, frustrated. Problems which include lack of integrity in government; the feeling that the individual no longer counts; the reality of material and spiritual poverty; the feeling that the grand American experiment is failing or has failed. I could recite these problems and then I could sit down and offer no solutions. But I don't choose to do that either.

The citizens of America expect more. They deserve and they want more than a recital of problems.

We are a people in a quandary about the present. We are a people in search of our future. We are a people in search of a national community.

We are a people trying not only to solve the problems of the present — unemployment, inflation. But we are attempting on a larger scale to fulfill the promise of America. We are attempting to fulfill our national purpose, to create and sustain a society in which all of us are equal. ...

And now we must look to the future. Let us heed the voice of the people and recognize their common sense. If we do not, we not only blaspheme our political heritage, we ignore the common ties that bind all Americans.

Many fear the future. Many are distrustful of their leaders, and believe that their voices are never heard. Many seek only to satisfy their private work wants. To satisfy private interests.

But this is the great danger America faces. That we will cease to be one nation and become instead a collection of interest groups: city against suburb, region against region, individual against individual. Each seeking to satisfy private wants.

If that happens, who then will speak for America?

Who then will speak for the common good?

This is the question which must be answered in 1976.

Are we to be one people bound together by common spirit sharing in a common endeavor or will we become a divided nation?

For all of its uncertainty, we cannot flee the future. We must not become the new puritans and reject our society. We must address and master the future together. It can be done if we restore the belief that we share a sense of national community, that we share a common national endeavor. It can be done.

There is no executive order; there is no law that can require the American people to form a national community. This we must do as individuals and if we do it as individuals, there is no President of the United States who can veto that decision.

As a first step, we must restore our belief in ourselves. We are a generous people so why can't we be generous with each other? We need to take to heart the words spoken by Thomas Jefferson:

Let us restore to social intercourse the harmony and that affection without which liberty and even life are but dreary things.

A nation is formed by the willingness of each of us to share in the responsibility for upholding the common good.

A government is invigorated when each of us is willing to participate in shaping the future of this nation.

In this election year we must define the common good and begin again to shape a common good and begin again to shape a common future. Let each person do his or her part. If one citizen is unwilling to participate, all of us are going to suffer. For the American idea, though it is shared by all of us, is realized in each one of us.

And now, what are those of us who are elected public officials supposed to do? We call ourselves public servants, but I'll tell you this:

We as public servants must set an example for the rest of the nation. It is hypocritical for the public official to admonish and exhort the people to uphold the common good. More is required of public officials than slogans and handshakes and press releases. More is required. We must hold ourselves strictly accountable. We must provide the people with a vision of the future.

If we promise as public officials, we must deliver. If we as public officials propose, we must produce. If we say to the American people it is time for you to be sacrificial; sacrifice. If the public official says that, we (public officials) must be the first to give. We must be. And again, if we make mistakes, we must be willing to admit them. We have to do that. What we have to do is strike a balance between the idea, the belief, that government ought to do nothing. Strike a balance.

Let there be no illusions about the difficulty of forming this kind of a national community. It's tough, difficult, not easy. But a spirit of harmony will survive in America only if each of us remembers that we share a common destiny.

I have confidence that we can form this kind of national community.

I have confidence that the Democratic Party can lead the way. I have confidence. We cannot improve on the system of government handed down to us by the founders of the Republic. There is no way to improve upon that. But what we can do is to find new ways to implement that system and realize our destiny.

Now, I began this speech by commenting to you on the uniqueness of a Barbara Jordan making the keynote address. Well I am going to close my speech by quoting a Republican President and I ask you that as you listen to these words of Abraham Lincoln, relate them to the concept of national community in which every last one of us participates: As I would not be a slave, so I would not be a master. This expresses my idea of Democracy. Whatever differs from this, to the extent of the difference is no Democracy.

--------- 8.33 ---------
ROOTS
Alex Haley

By the 1970s, Alex Haley had already served as the sound-board for many of the most significant personalities in black history. A scrapping freelance journalist, he got his break when he landed an interview with Miles Davis in *Playboy* magazine (see Chapter Seven) — it was the first of the magazine's notoriously candid and immensely popular interviews with national, and international, movers and shakers. *Playboy* later hired him to sit down with both Muhammad Ali and Malcolm X. The Malcolm X interview led the two to collaborate on the *Autobiography of Malcolm X*, published in 1965. After completing that project, Haley labored away for the next 12 years in genealogy research, trying to trace his maternal lineage back to Africa. In 1977, based on that research, he published *Roots*. Part fact, part fiction, *Roots* is the story of a young African man named Kunta Kinte who is captured and sold into slavery in America. The young man despises his bondage and refuses to accept it passively. His repeated attempts to escape lead to brutal scenes of punishment, such as the one below. The book was a huge hit, spawning an equally popular television miniseries.

One cold afternoon almost a moon later — the sky bleak and slaty — Kunta was on his way across one of the fields to help another man repair a fence when to his astonishment, what looked like salt began to fall from the sky, at first lightly, then more rapidly and thickly. As the salt became a flaky whiteness, he heard the blacks nearby exclaiming, "Snow!" and guessed that was what they called it. When he bent down to pick some of it up, it was cold to his touch — and even colder, when he licked it off a finger with his tongue. It stung, and it had no taste whatever. He tried to smell it, but not only did there seem to be no odor either, it also disappeared into watery nothingness. And wherever he looked on the ground was a whitish film.

But by the time he reached the other side of the field, the "snow" had stopped and even begun to melt away. Hiding his amazement, Kunta composed himself and nodded silently to his black partner, who was waiting by the broken fence. They set to work — Kunta helping the other man to string a kind of metal twine that he called "wire." After a while they reached a place almost hidden by tall grass, and as the other man hacked some of it down with the long knife he carried, Kunta's eyes were gauging the distance between where he stood and the nearest woods. He knew that Samson was nowhere near and the "oberseer' was keeping watch in another field that day. Kunta worked busily, to give the other man no suspicion of what was in his mind. But his breath came tensely as he stood holding the wire tight and looking down on the head of the man bent over his work. The knife had been left a few steps behind them, where the- chopping of the brush had stopped.

With a silent prayer to Allah, Kunta clasped his hands together, lifted them high, and brought them down across the back of the man's neck with all the violence of which his slight body was capable. The man crumpled without a sound, as if he had been poleaxed. Within a moment, Kunta had bound the man's ankles and wrists with the wire. Snatching up the long knife, Kunta suppressed the impulse to stab him — this was not the hated Samson — and went running toward the woods, bent over almost double. He felt a lightness, as if he were running in a dream, as if this weren't really happening at all.

He came out of it a few moments later — when he heard the man he had left live yelling at the top of his lungs. He should have killed him, Kunta thought furious with himself, as he tried to run yet faster. Instead of fighting his way deeply into the underbrush when he reached the woods, he skirted it this time. He knew that he had to achieve distance first, then concealment. If he got far enough fast enough, he would have time to find a good place to hide and rest before moving on under cover of the night.

Kunta was prepared to live in the woods as the animals did. He had learned many things about this toubob land by now, together with what he already knew from Africa. He would capture rabbits and other rodents with snare traps and cook them over a fire that wouldn't smoke. As he ran, he stayed in the area where the brush would conceal him but wasn't thick enough to slow him down.

By nightfall, Kunta knew that he had run a good distance. Yet he kept going, crossing gullies and ravines, and for quite a way down the bed of a shallow stream. Only when it was completely dark did he allow himself to stop, hiding himself in a spot where the brush was dense but from which he could easily run if he had to. As he lay there in the darkness, he listened carefully for the sound of dogs. But there was nothing but stillness all around him. Was it possible? Was he really going to make it this time?

Just then he felt a cold fluttering on his face, and reached up with his hand. "Snow" was falling again! Soon he was covered — and surrounded — by whiteness as far as he could see. Silently it fell, deeper and deeper, until Kunta began to fear he was going to be buried in it; he was already freezing. Finally he couldn't stop himself from leaping up and running to look for better cover.

He had run a good way when he stumbled and fell; he wasn't hurt, but when he looked back, be saw with horror that his feet had left a trail in the snow so deep that a blind man could follow him. He knew that there was no way he could erase the tracks, and he knew that the morning was now not far away. The only possible answer was more distance. He tried to increase his speed, but be had been running most of the night, and his breath was coming in labored gasps. The long knife had begun to feel heavy; it would cut brush, but it wouldn't melt "snow." The sky was beginning to lighten in the east when he heard, far behind him, the faint sound of conch horns. He changed course in the next stride. But he had the sinking feeling that there was nowhere he could find to rest safely amid this blanketing whiteness.

When he heard the distant baying of the dogs, a rage flooded up in him such as he had never felt before. He ran like a hunted leopard, but the barking grew louder and louder, and finally, when he glanced back over his shoulder for the tenth time, he saw them gaining on him. The men couldn't be far behind. Then he heard a gun fire, and somehow it propelled him forward even faster than before. But the dogs caught up with him anyway. When they were but strides away, Kunta whirled and crouched down, snarling back at them. As they came lunging forward with their fangs bared, he too lunged at them, slashing open the first dog's belly with a single sideways swipe of the knife; with another blur of his arm, he hacked the blade between the eyes of the next one.

Springing away, Kunta began running again. But soon he heard the men on horses crashing through the brush behind him, and he all but dove for the deeper brush where the horses couldn't go. Then there was another shot and another — and he felt a flashing pain in his leg. Knocked down in a heap, he had staggered upright again when the toubob shouted and fired again, and he heard the bullets thud into trees by his head. Let them kill me, thought Kunta; I will die as a man should. Then another shot hit the same leg, and it smashed him down like a giant fist. He was snarling on the ground when he saw the "oberseer" and another toubob coming toward him with their guns leveled and he was about to leap up and force them to shoot him again and be done with it, but the wounds in his leg wouldn't let him rise.

The other toubob held his gun at Kunta's head as the "oberseer" jerked off Kunta's clothing until he stood naked in the snow, the blood trickling down his leg and staining the whiteness at his feet. Cursing with each breath, the "oberseer" knocked Kunta all but senseless with his fist; then both of them tied him facing a large tree, with his wrists bound on the other side.

The lash began cutting into the flesh across Kunta's shoulders and back, with the "oberseer" grunting and Kunta shuddering under the force of each blow. After a while Kunta couldn't stop himself from screaming with the pain, but the beating went on until his sagging body pressed against the tree. His shoulders and back were covered with long, half-opened bleeding welts that in some places exposed the muscles beneath. He couldn't be sure, but the next thing Kunta knew he had the feeling he was falling. Then he felt the coldness of the snow against him and everything went black.

He came to in his hut, and along with his senses, pain returned excruciating and enveloping. The slightest movement made him cry out in agony; and he was back in chains. But even worse, his nose informed him that his body was wrapped from feet to chin in a large cloth soaked with grease of the swine. When the old cooking woman came in with food, he tried to spit at her, but succeeded only in throwing up. He thought he saw compassion in her eyes.

Two days later, he was awakened early in the morning by the sounds of festivities. He heard black people outside the big house shouting "Christmas gif', Massa!", and he wondered what they could possibly have to celebrate. He wanted to die, so that his soul could join the ancestors; he wanted to be done forever with misery unending in this toubob land, so stifling and stinking that he couldn't draw a clean breath in it. He boiled with fury that instead of beating him like a man, the toubob had stripped him naked. When he became well, he would take revenge — and he would escape again. Or he would die. …

8.34

RACE AS A FACTOR, BUT NO 'QUOTAS'

Regents of University of California v. Bakke

The Johnson administration accepted and pushed forward Whitney Young's call for a domestic Marshall Plan for black America. The first legal use of the term "affirmative action" came in President Johnson's 1965 executive order mandating that contractors with the federal government "take affirmative action to ensure that applicants are employed, and that employees are treated during employment, without regard to their race, creed, color, or national origin." Subsequently, a series of court decisions held that Title VII of the Civil Rights Act and Title IX of the 1972

Education Amendments Act compelled, or at least permitted, educational institutions receiving federal funds to similarly take affirmative action to overcome past disparities in opportunity. Throughout the decade, the principle spread through the private sector, leading most schools and companies to, at least in name, embrace efforts to recruit minority and female applicants.

The original white liberal unease with the idea spread to overt hostility from conservatives. Opponents argued that white men of today had nothing to do with the sins of the past and should not be "penalized" by losing their opportunity for jobs or education to what they argued were less-qualified minority and female applicants. Turning the civil rights movement on its head, in court they argued that affirmative action programs violated the equal protection clause of the Constitution by unduly considering race as a factor. Supporters responded that white male applicants were not being "penalized" but, rather, were finally forced to compete with all Americans on an equal playing field, one that considered more than the traditional standards of qualification that minorities and women had been systematically denied access to.

The dispute boiled up to the Supreme Court in 1978. Its divisive nature could be seen among the judges, as well, who split 4-4 on the constitutionality of a racial affirmative action system set up by the University of California. Justice Lewis Powell cast the deciding vote — though his written opinion settled very little in the debate. Powell's opinion embraced most of the arguments of those opposing affirmative action, and declared that the university's system was in fact unconstitutional, so long as it set aside a fixed number of seats for candidates of a given race. However, he qualified, race was a valid and constitutional consideration in judging applicants as long as it was one among other varied factors. This, he wrote, was in the interest of free speech, not civil rights. It had very little to do with race, and certainly not the reversal of past limitations. Rather, Powell said, the issue at hand was a university's right to create a "robust exchange of ideas" on campus. The opinion raised as many questions as it answered, and the debate about affirmative action would only intensify in coming years.

However, Powell's decision did mark a significant change in the national perception of affirmative action's purpose. Over a decade earlier, the Moynihan Report had moved the federal government from a position of taking steps to correct its past wrongs to offering sympathetic help to African Americans' efforts to fix their own problems. Now, the nation had again moved from Johnson's effort to repair the damage caused by a government-led system of slavery and Jim Crow to offering aid to blacks as an incidental consequence of protecting the free speech of white institutions.

… The parties fight a sharp preliminary action over the proper characterization of the special admissions program. Petitioner prefers to view it as establishing a "goal" of minority representation in the Medical School. Respondent, echoing the courts below, labels it a racial quota.

This semantic distinction is beside the point: The special admissions program is undeniably a classification based on race and ethnic background. To the extent that there existed a pool of at least minimally qualified minority applicants to fill the 16 special admissions seats, white applicants could compete only for 84 seats in the entering class, rather than the 100 open to minority applicants. Whether this limitation is described as a quota or a goal, it is a line drawn on the basis of race and ethnic status.

The guarantees of the Fourteenth Amendment extend to all persons. Its language is explicit: "No State shall … deny to any person within its jurisdiction the equal protection of the laws." It is settled beyond question that the "rights created by the first section of the Fourteenth Amendment are, by its terms, guaranteed to the individual. The rights established are personal rights." The guarantee of equal protection cannot mean one thing when applied to one individual and something else when applied to a person of another color. If both are not accorded the same protection, then it is not equal.

Nevertheless, petitioner argues that the court below erred in applying strict scrutiny to the special admissions program because white males, such as respondent, are not a "discrete and insular minority" requiring extraordinary protection from the majoritarian political process. This rationale, however, has never been invoked in our decisions as a prerequisite to subjecting racial or ethnic distinctions to strict scrutiny. Nor has this Court held that discreteness and insularity constitute necessary preconditions to a holding that a particular classification is invidious. ... Racial and ethnic distinctions of any sort are inherently suspect and thus call for the most exacting judicial examination. ...

Over the past 30 years, this Court has embarked upon the crucial mission of interpreting the Equal Protection Clause with the view of assuring to all persons "the protection of equal laws," in a Nation confronting a legacy of slavery and racial discrimination. Because the landmark decisions in this area arose in response to the continued exclusion of Negroes from the mainstream of American society, they could be characterized as involving discrimination by the "majority" white race against the Negro minority. But they need not be read as depending upon that characterization for their results. It suffices to say that "over the years, this Court consistently repudiated 'distinctions between citizens solely because of their ancestry' as being 'odious to a free people whose institutions are founded upon the doctrine of equality.'" Petitioner urges us to adopt for the first time a more restrictive view of the Equal Protection Clause and hold that discrimination against members of the white "majority" cannot be suspect if its purpose can be characterized as "benign." The clock of our liberties, however, cannot be turned back to 1868. It is far too late to argue that the guarantee of equal protection to all persons permits the recognition of special wards entitled to a degree of protection greater than that accorded others. "The 14th Amendment is not directed solely against discrimination due to a 'two-class theory' — that is, based upon differences between 'white' and Negro."

Once the artificial line of a "two-class theory" of the 14th Amendment is put aside, the difficulties entailed in varying the level of judicial review according to a perceived "preferred" status of a particular racial or ethnic minority are intractable. The concepts of "majority" and "minority" necessarily reflect temporary arrangements and political judgments. As observed above, the white "majority" itself is composed of various minority groups, most of which can lay claim to a history of prior discrimination at the hands of the State and private individuals. Not all of these groups can receive preferential treatment and corresponding judicial tolerance of distinctions drawn in terms of race and nationality, for then the only "majority" left would be a new minority of white Anglo-Saxon Protestants. There is no principled basis for deciding which groups would merit "heightened judicial solicitude" and which would not. Courts would be asked to evaluate the extent of the prejudice and consequent harm suffered by various minority groups. Those whose societal injury is thought to exceed some arbitrary level of tolerability then would be entitled to preferential classifications at the expense of individuals belonging to other groups. Those classifications would be free from exacting judicial scrutiny. As these preferences began to have their desired effect, and the consequences of past discrimination were undone, new judicial rankings would be necessary. The kind of variable sociological and political analysis necessary to produce such rankings simply does not lie within the judicial competence — even if they otherwise were politically feasible and socially desirable.

Moreover, there are serious problems of justice connected with the idea of preference itself. First, it may not always be clear that a so-called preference is in fact benign. Courts may be asked to validate burdens imposed upon individual members of particular groups in order to advance the group's general interest. Nothing in the Constitution supports the notion that individuals may be asked to suffer otherwise impermissible burdens in order to enhance the societal standing of their ethnic groups. Second, preferential programs may only reinforce common stereotypes holding that certain groups are unable to achieve success without special protection based on a factor having no relationship to individual worth.

Third, there is a measure of inequity in forcing innocent persons in respondent's position to bear the burdens of redressing grievances not of their making. By hitching the meaning of the Equal Protection Clause to these transitory considerations, we would be holding, as a constitutional principle, that judicial scrutiny of classifications touching on racial and ethnic background may vary with the ebb and flow of political forces. Disparate constitutional tolerance of such classifications well may serve to exacerbate racial and ethnic antagonism rather than alleviate them. Also, the mutability of a constitutional principle, based upon shifting political and social judgments, undermines the chances for consistent application of the Constitution from one generation to the next, a critical feature of its coherent interpretation. …

The fourth goal asserted by petitioner is the attainment of a diverse student body. This clearly is a constitutionally permissible goal for an institution of higher education. Academic freedom, though not a specifically enumerated constitutional right, long has been viewed as a special concern of the First Amendment. The freedom of a university to make its own judgments as to education includes the selection of its student body. Thus, in arguing that its university must be accorded the right to select those students who will contribute the most to the "robust exchange of ideas," petitioner invokes a countervailing constitutional interest, that of the First Amendment. In this light, petitioner must be viewed as seeking to achieve a goal that is of paramount importance in the fulfillment of its mission. It may be argued that there is greater force to these views at the undergraduate level than in a medical school where the training is centered primarily on professional competency. But even at the graduate level, our tradition and experience lend support to the view that the contribution of diversity is substantial. Physicians serve a heterogeneous population. An otherwise qualified medical student with a particular background — whether it be ethnic, geographic, culturally advantaged or disadvantaged — may bring to a professional school of medicine experiences, outlooks and ideas that enrich the training of its student body and better equip its graduates to render with understanding their vital service to humanity. …

In summary, it is evident that the Davis special admissions program involves the use of an explicit racial classification never before countenanced by the Court. It tells applicants who are not Negro, Asian, or "Chicano" that they are totally excluded from a specific percentage of the seats in an entering class. No matter how strong their qualifications, quantitative and extracurricular, including their own potential for contribution to educational diversity, they are never afforded the chance to compete with applicants from the preferred groups for the special admissions seats. At the same time, the preferred applicants have the opportunity to compete for every seat in the class. The fatal flaw in petitioner's program is its disregard of individual rights as guaranteed by the 14th Amendment. Such rights are not absolute. But when a State's distribution of benefits or imposition of burdens hinges on the color of a person's skin or ancestry, that individual is entitled to a demonstration that the challenged classification is necessary to promote a substantial state interest. Petitioner has failed to carry this burden. For this reason, that portion of the California court's judgment holding petitioner's special admissions program invalid under the 14th Amendment must be affirmed.

In enjoining petitioner from ever considering the race of any applicant, however, the courts below failed to recognize that the State has a substantial interest that legitimately may be served by a properly devised admissions program involving the competitive consideration of race and ethnic origin. For this reason, so much of the California court's judgment as enjoins petitioner from any consideration of the race of any applicant must be reversed.

——— 8.35 ———

BLACK MACHO AND THE MYTH OF THE SUPERWOMAN
Michelle Wallace

Michelle Wallace's 1979 retrospective on the Black Power movement thrust into public discourse the seething anger many black women associated with the movement had felt for years. To Wallace, the movement's legacy for black woman was, in a word, betrayal. Her compelling treatise argues that the primary motive of most Black Power leaders was to restore the masculinity of the much-maligned black male. American racism had hounded, objectified and vilified the black male's sexuality, robbing him of his "right" to head a family, leaving in its wake "castrated black men hanging by their necks from trees." But, Wallace wrote, black women in the civil rights era began to believe they were culpable for the black man's castration as well. That somehow, through standing on their own individual strength in the face of racism rather than lifting up the man as their protector, they had conspired to emasculate their fathers, brothers and lovers. So, Wallace argues, as the Black Power movement blossomed, women such as herself "stood by silently as he became a 'man.'" But, she continues, black men did not keep their end of the bargain by letting black women then grow as well. Rather, they rejected their black sisters for doting white women and insisted that African-American women go on fulfilling their silent, subservient responsibilities to the movement. Wallace's stinging critique was not a lone one, and the writings, speeches and actions of Black Power movement leaders are in and of themselves damning evidence in support of her argument. Ultimately, Wallace concludes, the failure of both black men and women to support one another's joint quests for full humanity destroyed the Black Power movement.

… There was a misunderstanding between the black man and the black woman, a misunderstanding as old as slavery; the I.O.U. was finally being called in. Apart from some occasional drunken ranting on a street corner, the black man had held his silence admirably for centuries. The Moynihan Report, as preposterous a document as it was, combined with the heady atmosphere of the times to loosen the black man's tongue. The Moynihan Report said that the black man was not so much a victim of white institutional racism as he was of an abnormal family structure, its main feature being an employed black woman. This report did not create hostility. It merely helped to bring the hostility to the surface. The result was a brain shattering explosion upon the heads of black women, the accumulation of over three hundred years of rage. The black woman did not, could not, effectively fight back. No one had written a report for her. It was a man's world. And guilt had silenced her. What could she say when the black man cried that the black woman bad never believed in him, had bated him in fact? It wasn't entirely untrue. She could not completely deny it. And even her response that she was his mother, that she had made his survival possible, was made to sound feeble and was turned against her.

Now that freedom, equality, rights, wealth, power were assumed to be on their way, she had to understand that manhood was essential to revolution — unquestioned, unchallenged, unfettered manhood. Could you imagine Che Guevara with breasts? Mao with a vagina? She was just going to have to get out of the way. She had had her day. Womanhood was not essential to revolution. Or so everyone thought by the end of the 1960s.

I am saying, among other things, that for perhaps the last fifty years there has been a growing distrust, even hatred, between black men and black women. It has been nursed along not only by racism on the part of whites but also by an almost deliberate ignorance on the part of blacks about the sexual politics of their experience in this country.

As the Civil Rights Movement progressed, little attention was devoted to an examination of the historical black male/female relationship, except for those aspects of it that reinforced the notion of the black man as the sexual victim of "matriarchal" tyranny. The result has been calamitous. The black woman has become a social andintellectual suicide; the black man, unintrospective and oppressive.

It is from this perspective that the black man and woman faced the challenge of the Black Revolution — a revolution subsequently dissipated and distorted by their inability to see each other clearly through the fog of sexual myths and fallacies. …

Though originally it was the white man who was responsible for the black woman's grief, a multiplicity of forces act upon her life now and the black man is one of the most important. The white man is downtown. The black man lives with her. He's the head of her church and may be the principal of her local school or even the mayor of the city in which she lives.

She is the workhorse that keeps his house functioning, she is the foundation of his community, she raises his children, and she faithfully votes for him in elections, goes to his movies, reads his books, watches him on television, buys in his stores, solicits his services as doctor, lawyer, accountant.

She has made it quite clear that she has no intention of starting a black woman's liberation movement. One would think she was satisfied, yet she is not. The black man has not really kept his part of the bargain they made when she agreed to keep her mouth shut in the sixties. When she stood by silently as he became a "man," she assumed that he would subsequently grant her her long overdue "womanhood," that he would finally glorify and dignify black womanhood just as the white man had done for the white woman. But he did not. He refused her. His involvement with white women was only the most dramatic form that refusal took. He refused her across the board. He refused her because be could not do anything else. He refused her because the assertion of his manhood required something quite different of him. He refused her because it was too late to carbon-copy the traditional white male/female relationships. And he refused her because he felt justified in his anger. He claimed that she had betrayed him. And she believed that, even as she denied it. She too was angry, but paralyzed by the feeling that she had no right to be.

Therefore her strange numbness, her determination, spoken or unspoken, to remain basically unquestioning of the black man's authority and thereby seemingly supportive of all he has done, even that which has been abusive of her. She is in the grip of Black Macho and it has created within her inestimable emotional devastation.

The black woman's silence is a new silence. She knows that. Not so long ago it would have been quite easy to find any number of black women who would say with certainty, "A nigga man ain't shit." Perhaps more to the point, there has been from slavery until the Civil Rights Movement a thin but continuous line of black women who have prodded their sisters to self-improvement. These women were of the opinion that being a woman did not exempt one from responsibility. Just like a man, a woman had to struggle to deliver the race from bondage and uplift it. In their time a woman's interest in herself was not automatically interpreted as hostile to men and their progress, at least not by black people. Day to day these women, like most women, devoted their energies to their husbands and children. When they found time, they worked on reforms in education, medicine, housing, and their communities through their organizations and churches. Little did they know that one day their activities would be used as proof that the black woman has never known her place and has mightily battled the black man for his male prerogative as head of the household.

The American black woman is haunted by the mythology that surrounds the American black man. It is a mythology based upon the real persecution of black men: castrated black men hanging by their necks from trees; the carcasses of black men floating face down in the Mississippi; black men with their bleeding genitals jammed between their teeth; black men shining shoes; black men being turned down for jobs time and time again; black men watching helplessly as their women go to work to support the family; black men behind bars, persecuted by prison guards and police; jobless black men on street corners, with needles in their arms, with wine bottles in their hip pockets; black men being pushed out in front to catch the enemy's bullets in every American war since the Revolution of 1776 — these ghosts, rendered all the more gruesome by their increasing absence of detail, are crouched in the black woman's brain. Every time she starts to wonder about her own misery, to think about reconstructing her life, to shake off her devotion and feeling of responsibility to everyone but herself, the ghosts pounce. She is stopped cold. The ghosts talk to her. "*You* crippled the black man. *You* worked against him. *You* betrayed him. *You* laughed at him. *You* scorned him. *You* and the white man." …

Soul on Ice was a book that appealed to the senses. Cleaver was violent and advocated violence. Cleaver was macho and the sixties were years in which macho heroism was highly exalted and taken seriously by many people of all sorts of political and intellectual persuasions (whites did not scorn Jones's macho but his racism, assuming it is possible to separate the two). People yearned for the smell of blood on a page and Cleaver provided it.

If one is to take Cleaver at his word, the black homosexual is counterrevolutionary (1) because he's being fucked and (2) because he's being fucked by white man. By so doing he reduces himself to the status of our black grandmothers who, as everyone knows, were fucked by white men all the time.

However, it would follow that if a black man were doing the fucking and the one being fucked were a white man, the black male homosexual would be just as good a revolutionary as a black heterosexual male, if not a better one. Black Macho would have to lead to

this conclusion. If whom you fuck indicates your power, then obviously the greatest power would be gained by fucking a white man first, a black man second, a white woman third and a black woman not at all. The most important rule is that *nobody* fucks you.

Finally, if homosexuals are put down, even though they're males, because they get fucked, where does that leave women in terms of revolution? Black Macho allowed for only the most primitive notion of women — women as possessions, women as the spoils of war, leaving black women with no resale value. As a possession, the black woman was a symbol of defeat, and therefore of little use to the revolution except as the performer of drudgery (not unlike her role in slavery).

The white man had offered white women privilege and prestige as accompaniments to his power. Black women were offered no such deal, just the same old hard labor, a new silence, and more loneliness. The patriarchal black macho of Malcolm X might have proven functional — black women might have suffered their oppression for years in comparative bliss — but black men were blinded by their resentment of black women, their envy of white women, and their irresistible urge to bring white women down a peg. With patriarchal macho it would have taken black men years to avenge themselves. With the narcissistic macho of the Black Movement, the results were immediate.

And when the black man went as far as the adoration of his own genitals could carry him, his revolution stopped. A big Afro, a rifle, and a penis in good working order were not enough to lick the white man's world after all.

9

Learning to Talk of Race:
THE MODERN ERA

'RAPPER'S DELIGHT'
Sugar Hill Gang

Just as Black Power grew out of the restless anger of urban black America in the late 1960s, the cultural movement known broadly as hip hop was initiated in the neglected cities of the 1970s. As the Kerner Commission report had warned (see Chapter Eight), money hemorrhaged out of city centers and into suburbia during the 1970s and '80s as a result of "white flight," and the subsequent government neglect of black metropolises. Walled off, and feeling such, black youth developed culture and art that expressed and reflected their disaffection. The Bronx in New York City was among the most economically depressed of those urban areas, and it was there that hip hop started, among the young revelers at neighborhood dance parties. Rather than patronize clubs, Bronx teenagers flocked to these informal events thrown by local DJs turned party promoters, who simply set up massive sound systems in parks and warehouses. The DJs prided themselves on keeping their guests excited and dancing as long as possible. Eventually, pioneering DJs such as Grand Master Flash started altering the records they played at the parties, running one song into another, and scratching and mixing the discs to make entirely new, improvised songs. Next they recruited vocalists to "rap" over their mixes, and hip hop music as we know it was born. It wasn't long, of course, before the compositions starting getting recorded. What many consider the first true rap album was released in 1979 by the independent label Sugar Hill Records. "Rapper's Delight," by the Sugar Hill Gang, was a smash hit and sent the new music onto the national stage.

I said a hip hop the hippie the hippie
To the hip hip hop, a you don't stop
The rock it to the bang bang boogie say up jumped the boogie
To the rhythm of the boogie, the beat
Now what you hear is not a test — I'm rappin' to the beat
And me, the groove, and my friends are gonna try to move your feet
See I am Wonder Mike and I'd like to say hello
To the black, to the white, the red, and the brown, the purple and yellow
But first I gotta bang bang the boogie to the boogie
Say up jump the boogie to the bang bang boogie
Let's rock, you don't stop
Rock the riddle that'll make your body rock
Well so far you've heard my voice but I brought two friends along
And next on the mike is my man Hank
Come on, Hank, sing that song

Check it out, I'm the c-a-s-an-the-o-v-a
And the rest is f-l-y
Ya see I go by the code of the doctor of the mix
And these reasons I'll tell ya why
Ya see, I'm six foot one and I'm tons of fun
And I dress to a T
Ya see, I got more clothes than Muhammad Ali
and I dress so viciously
I got bodyguards, I got two big cars
That definitely ain't the wack
I got a Lincoln Continental and a sunroof Cadillac

So after school, I take a dip in the pool
Which really is on the wall
I got a color TV so I can see
The Knicks play basketball
Hear me talkin' 'bout checkbooks, credit cards
More money than a sucker could ever spend
But I wouldn't give a sucker or a bum from the
rucker
Not a dime 'til I made it again
And everybody go hotel motel whatcha gonna
do today (say what)
Ya say I'm gonna get a fly girl gonna get some
spankin'
Drive off in a def OJ
Everybody go, hotel, motel, Holiday Inn
Say if your girl starts actin' up, then you take
her friend
Master Gee, am I mellow
It's on you so, what you gonna do

Well it's on 'n on 'n on 'n on
The beat don't stop until the break of dawn
I said m-a-s, t-e-r, a-g with a double e
I said I go by the unforgettable name
Of the man they call the Master Gee
Well, my name is known all over the world
By all the foxy ladies and the pretty girls
I'm goin' down in history
As the baddest rapper there could ever be
Now I'm feelin' the highs and ya feelin' the lows
The beat starts getting' into your toes
Ya start poppin' ya fingers and stompin' your feet
And movin' your body while you're sittin' in
your seat
And then damn ya start doin' the freak
I said damn, right outta your seat
Then ya throw your hands high in the air
Ya rockin' to the rhythm, shake your derriere
Ya rockin' to the beat without a care
With the sureshot MCs for the affair
Now, I'm not as tall as the rest of the gang
But I rap to the beat just the same
I got a little face and a pair of brown eyes
All I'm here to do ladies is hypnotize
Singin' on 'n on 'n on 'n on
The beat don't stop until the break of dawn
Singin' on 'n on 'n on 'n on

Like a hot buttered a pop da pop da pop dib-
bie dibbie
Pop da pop pop ya don't dare stop
Come alive y'all, gimme what ya got
I guess by now you can take a hunch
And find that I am the baby of the bunch
But that's okay, I still keep in stride
Cause all I'm here to do is just wiggle your
behind
Singin on 'n 'n on 'n on 'n on
The beat don't stop until the break of dawn
Singin on 'n 'n on 'n on on 'n on
Rock rock y'all, throw it on the floor
I'm gonna freak ya here I'm gonna feak ya there
I'm gonna move you outta this atmosphere
Cause I'm one of a kind and I'll shock your
mind
I'll put t-t-tickets in your behind
I said 1-2-3-4, come on girls, get on the floor
A-come alive, y'all a-gimme what ya got
Cause I'm guaranteed to make you rock
I said 1-2-3-4, tell me Wonder Mike what are
you waitin' for?

I said a hip hop
The hippie to the hippie
The hip hip hop, a you don't stop
The rock it to the bang bang boogie say up
jumped the boogie
To the rhythm of the boogie, the beat
Skiddlee beebop a we rock a scoobie doo
And guess what America? We love you
Cause ya rock and ya roll with so much soul
You could rock till you're a hundred and one
years old
I don't mean to brag, I don't mean to boast
But we like hot butter on our breakfast toast
Rock it up, baby bubbah
Baby bubbah to the boogie da bang bang da
boogie
To the beat beat, it's so unique
Come on everybody and dance to the beat

A hip hop the hippie the hippie
To the hip hip hop, a you don't stop
Rock it out baby bubbah to the boogie da bang
bang

The boogie to the boogie da beat
I said I can't wait 'til the end of the week
When I'm rappin' to the rhythm of a groovy beat
And attempt to raise your body heat
Just blow your mind so that you can't speak
And do a thing but a rock and shuffle your feet
And let it change up to a dance called the freak
And when ya finally do come in to your rhythmic beat
Rest a little while so ya don't get weak
I know a man named Hank
He has more rhymes than a serious bank
So come on Hank sing that song
To the rhythm of the boogie da bang bang da bong

Well, I'm imp the dimp, the ladies' pimp
The women fight for my delight
But I'm the grandmaster with the three MCs
That shock the house for the young ladies
And when you come inside, into the front
You do the freak, spank, and do the bump
And when the sucker MCs try to prove a point
We're treacherous trio, we're the serious joint
A from sun to sun and from day to day
A sit down and write a brand new rhyme
Because they say that miracles never cease
I've created a devastating masterpiece
I'm gonna rock the mike till you can't resist
Everybody, I say it goes like this
Well I was comin' home late one dark afternoon
A reporter stopped me for a interview
She said she's heard stories and she's heard fables
That I'm vicious on the mike and the turntables
This young reporter I did adore
So I rocked a vicious rhyme like I never did before
She said, "Damn fly guy I'm in love with you
The casanova legend must have been true"
I said by the way baby what's your name
Said, "I go by the name of Lois Lane
And you could be my boyfriend you surely can
Just let me quit my boyfriend called Superman"

I said he's a fairy, I do suppose
Flyin' through the air in pantyhose
He may be very sexy or even cute
But he looks like a sucker in a blue and red suit
I said you need a man who's got finesse
And his whole name across his chest
He may be able to fly all through the night
But can he rock a party till the early light
He can't satisfy you with his little worm
But I can bust you out with my super sperm
I go do it, I go do it, I go do it, do it, do it
An I'm here an I'm there, I'm big bang Hank, I'm everywhere
Just throw your hands up in the air
And party hardy like you just don't care
Let's do it, don't stop y'all, a tick a tock y'all you don't stop
Go hotel, motel, what you gonna do today (say what)
I'm gonna get a fly girl gonna get some spank drive off in a def OJ
Everybody go hotel, motel, Holiday Inn
You say if your girl starts actin' up, then you take her friend
I say skip, dive, what can I say
I can't fit 'em all inside my OJ
So I just take half and bust them out
I give the rest to Master Gee so he could shock the house

It was twelve o'clock one Friday night
I was rockin' to the beat, feelin' all right
Everybody was dancin' on the floor
Doin' all the things they never did before
And then this fly fly girl with a sexy lean
She came into the bar, she came into the scene
As she traveled deeper inside the room
All the fellas checked out her white Sasoons
She came up to the table, looked into my eyes
Then she turned around and shook her behind
So I said to myself, its time for me to release
My vicious rhyme I call my masterpiece
And now people in the house this is just for you
A little rap to make you boogaloo
Now the group ya hear is called Phase Two
And let me tell ya somethin', we're a helluva crew

Once a week we're on the street
Just to cut in the jams and look at your feet
For you to party, got to have the moves
So we'll get right down and get you a groove
For you to dance you gotta get hype
For we'll get right down for you tonight
Now the system's on and the girls are there
Ya definitely have a rockin' affair
But let me tell ya somethin', there's still one fact
That to have a party, got to have a rap
So when the party's over you're makin' it home
And tryin' to sleep before the break of dawn
And while ya sleepin' ya start to dream
And thinkin' how ya danced on the disco scene
My name appears in your mind
Yeah, a name you know that was right on time
It was Phase Two just a doin' a do
Rockin ya down cause ya know we cool
To the rhythm of the beat that makes ya freak
Come alive girls get on your feet
To the rhythm of the beat to the beat the beat
To the double beat beat that makes ya freak
To the rhythm of the beat that says ya go on
On 'n on into the break of dawn
Now I got a man comin' on right now
He's guaranteed to throw down
He goes by the name of Wonder Mike
Come on Wonder Mike, do what ya like

I say a can of beer that's sweeter than honey
Like a millionaire that has no money
Like a rainy day that is not wet
Like a gamblin' fiend that does not bet
Like Dracula without his fangs
Like the boogie to the boogie without the boogie bang
Like collard greens that don't taste good
Like a tree that's not made out of wood
Like goin' up and not comin' down
Is just like the beat without the sound no sound
To the beat beat, ya do the freak
Everybody just rock and dance to the beat
Have you ever went over a friend's house to eat
And the food just ain't no good?
I mean the macaroni's soggy, the peas are mushed

And the chicken tastes like wood
So you try to play it off like you think you can
By sayin' that you're full
And then your friend says, "Momma he's being polite
He ain't finished uh uh that's bull"
So your heart starts pumpin' and you think of a lie
And you say that you already ate
And your friend says, "Man there's plenty of food"
So you pile some more on your plate
While the stinky food's steamin' your mind starts to dreamin'
Of the moment that it's time to leave
And then you look at your plate and your chickens slowly rottin'
Into something that looks like cheese
Oh so you say that's it I got to leave this place
I don't care what these people think
I'm just sittin' here makin' myself nauseous
With this ugly food that stinks
So you bust out the door while its still closed
Still sick from the food you ate
And then you run to the store for quick relief
From a bottle of Kaopectate
And then you call your friend two weeks later
To see how he has been
And he says, "I understand about the food
Baby bubbah but we're still friends"
With a hip hop the hippie to the hippie
The hip hip a hop a you don't stop the rockin'
To the bang bang boogie
Say up jump the boogie to the rhythm of the boogie the beat
I say Hank can ya rock
Can ya rock to the rhythm that just don't stop
Can ya hip me to the shoobie doo
I said come on make the make the people move

I go to the halls and then ring the bell
Because I am the man with the clientele
And if ya ask me why I rock so well
A big bang, I got clientele
And from the time I was only six years old
I never forgot what I was told
It was the best advice that I ever had

It came from my wise dear old dad
He said, "Sit down punk I wanna talk to you
And don't say a word until I'm through
Now there's a time to laugh a time to cry
A time to live and a time to die
A time to break and a time to chill
To act civilized or act real ill
But whatever ya do in your lifetime
Ya never let a MC steal your rhyme"
So from six to six 'til this very day
I'll always remember what he had to say
So when the sucker MCs try to chump my style
I let them know that I'm versatile
I got style finesse and a little black book
That's filled with rhymes and I know you
wanna look
But there's a thing that separates you from me
And that is called originality
Because my rhymes are on, from what you heard
I didn't even bite and not a goddamn word
And I say a little more later on tonight
So the sucker MCs can bite all night
A tick a tock y'all, a beat beat y'all
A let's rock y'all ya don't stop
Ya go hotel, motel, whatcha gonna do today
(say what)
Ya say I'm gonna get a fly girl gonna get some
spankin
Drive off in a def OJ
Everybody go hotel, motel, Holiday Inn
Ya say if your girl starts actin' up then you take
her friends
A like that ya'll, to the beat y'all
Beat beat ya'll ya dont stop
A Master Gee am I mellow?
It's on you so whatcha gonna do
Well like Johnny Carson on the late show
A like Frankie Croker in stereo
Well like the Barkays singin' "Holy Ghost"
The sounds to throw down they're played the
most
It's like my man Captain Sky
Whose name he earned with his super sperm
We rock and we don't stop
Get off y'all I'm here to give you whatcha got
To the beat that it makes you freak
And come alive girl get on your feet

A like a Perry Mason without a case
Like Farrah Fawcett without her face
Like the Barkays on the mike
Like gettin' right down for you tonight
Like movin' your body so ya don't know how
Right to the rhythm and throw down
Like comin' alive to the Master Gee
The brother who rocks so viciously
I said the age of one my life begun
At the age of two I was doin' the do
At the age of three it was you and me
Rockin' to the sounds of the Master Gee
At the age of four I was on the floor
Givin' all the freaks what they bargained for
At the age of five I didn't take no jive
With the Master Gee it's all the way live
At the age of six I was a pickin' up sticks
Rappin' to the beat my stick was fixed
At the age of seven I was rockin' in heaven
Dontcha know I went off
I gotta run on down to the beat you see
Gettin right on down, makin' all the girls
Just take of their clothes to the beat the beat
To the double beat beat that makes you freak
At the age of eight I was really great
Cause every night you see I had a date
At the age of nine I was right on time
Cause every night I had a party rhyme
Goin on 'n n on 'n on on 'n on
The beat don't stop until the break of dawn
A sayin' on 'n 'n on 'n on on 'n on ...
Like a hot buttered de pop de pop de
popcorn ...

———— 9.2 ————

'I KNOW WHAT IT MEANS
TO BE CALLED A NIGGER. I
KNOW WHAT IT MEANS TO
BE CALLED A FAGGOT.'
Melvin Boozer

In 1980, Melvin Boozer, an openly gay black man, was nominated vice president at the Democratic National Convention in a symbolic campaign led by the Lesbian and Gay Caucus of the Democratic Party. As a result, Boozer addressed the convention, becoming the first openly gay person to do so. He urged the Party's continued and heightened support for a gay rights agenda, comparing the burgeoning movement's goals to that of the civil rights movement. It's an assertion that earned him criticism then, and would be a recurring sore point between black civil rights activists and gay rights activists in the future. Boozer, then-head of Washington, D.C.'s Gay Activists Alliance, was a vocal advocate not just for gay rights but specifically for recognition of lesbian and gay African Americans within both the larger gay and black communities.

Mr. Chairman, I rise in grateful appreciation of more than 400 delegates at this convention who gladly signed the petition to place my name in nomination, and in appreciation of those who wanted to sign but were not able to, and for the 77 women and men in the lesbian and gay caucus who have worked day and night to circulate the petition.

I rise in proud recognition of the Mayor of the District of Columbia, Mr. Marion Barry, and the entire delegation of the District of Columbia who have supported me and encouraged me in this effort.

I rise in thankful recognition of the citizens of the District of Columbia who voted for me to come here knowing that I am gay, and who continue to labor and live in a city which has no voice in determining how it shall be taxed and which has no power to effect the decisions which affect the quality of our lives.

And finally, Mr. Chairman and members of the convention, I rise in anguished recognition of more than 20 million Americans who love this country and who long to serve this country in the same freedom that others take for granted, 20 million lesbian and gay Americans whose lives are blighted by a veil of ignorance and misunderstanding.

For more than 200 years a majority of Americans waited to be admitted to the institutions of our nation on an equal footing. This struggle has led us successfully through the abolition of slavery, the movement for universal suffrage, the civil rights movement, the continuing movements to include the elderly, the physically challenged, and the economically disadvantaged. And now the same vision which has guided the first two centuries of our existence compels us to pass the Equal Rights Amendment so that women and men can share equally in that vision and in our continuing struggle to make that vision a reality for all Americans.

But this same struggle which has animated our greatest leaders and our most loyal citizens is far from over. Mr. Chairman, members of the convention, today across our land more than 20 million Americans hide in the twilight of fear and oppression. Lesbians and gay men throughout this country are daily forced to choose between a life of service and labor to their communities without identity, or an identity which would deprive them of any opportunity to serve and work at all.

Mr. Chairman, we have come to the Democratic Party, as others have come before us, to appeal to the vision of equal justice, the belief in fair play, and the sense of compassion which are the bedrock upon which the greatness of our nation is founded.

We believe that now more than ever fairness, equal justice and compassion are under attack by the forces of the extreme right, but we also believe that the ideals embedded in our Constitution by the founders of our republic are alive and well in the Democratic Party.

Mr. Chairman, we come from towns and cities where our friends are jailed and beaten on the slightest pretext. We come from churches which have been burned to the ground because they admit us to worship. We come from families which have been torn apart because we have lost our jobs, and we have lost our good names which have been slandered by false accusations, myths, and lies.

Mr. Chairman, the leadership of the Democratic Party has called upon us to be responsive to the plight of all oppressed groups. Governor Brown has declared that lesbians and gay men have a right to a job without reprisals and a right to serve in the highest capacities of civil government.

Representative Dellums of California has affirmed that lesbians and gay men are entitled to the same rights as all other Americans. Senator Kennedy has declared that it is the responsibility of government to protect the rights of all American citizens, including lesbians and gay men. And President Carter, before he became President, declared that lesbians and gay citizens should not be subjected to arbitrary discrimination because of their sexual orientation.

Members of the convention, we are pleased that the charter of our party now bans discrimination on the basis of sexual orientation. We are pleased that the charter and the platform ban discrimination. Yet, today the suffering continues across our land by those who are willing to hold us up as scapegoats to the extreme right for all the ills which beset our society.

But why should so many men and women continue to suffer from arbitrary discrimination? Why must we be denied a fair chance to participate in the American life which we have contributed to as much as anyone else? Why must we be subjected to harassment and intimidation and ridicule when the Constitution of this great nation has already provided that all citizens shall enjoy the equal protection of the law?

Members of the Democratic Convention, there can be no justification, no defense for social injustice. The Constitution does not make exception. We who have waited patiently to be admitted to the vision of the Constitution know the consequences of prejudice. We have felt the sting of ignorance, and we have come to the Democratic Party seeking new hope which this party has always represented.

Over and over again the Democratic Party has insisted that in our society there can be no haven for discrimination. Is this not the same party which has championed the cause of every minority which has come before us? Is this not the same party which has sought to include women on an equal footing? Is this not the same party which has led the battle for civil rights for black Americans?

Would you ask me how I'd dare to compare the civil rights struggle with the struggle for lesbian and gay rights? I can compare, and I do compare them. I know what it means to be called a nigger. I know what it means to be called a faggot. And I can sum up the difference in one word: none. Bigotry is bigotry. I have been booed before. Discrimination is discrimination. It hurts just as much. It dishonors our way of life just as much, and it betrays a common lack of understanding, fairness and compassion.

I know I am an American. I know not because of my birth certificate, but because when Old Glory is unfurled and the Anthem is played, my heart is warmed and my eyes are watered. I love this country as much as anyone in this hall. I am thankful in my prayers for the privilege of being a citizen of this nation.

I believe that there is no power on this earth that can defeat the American people as long as we remain true to the values which have made us great.

Equal justice, fair play and compassion are the true sources of our greatness. I shudder to contemplate how we waste the energy and devotion of more than 20 million lesbian and gay Americans who remain shackled by degradation and isolation. And I am astonished by the longing and pleading of my gay brothers and sisters whose faith in this Party, in this country, and the democratic process has not been defeated, and will not be defeated by the falsehoods and fears of all those who would oppress us.

Like them, I have faith in this nation and in its people, and in this Party. I believe that when the American people have heard the facts, when they have seen us as we truly are, then they will insist that we not be abandoned to the prejudices and the caprices of the ignorant.

So, my fellow Democrats, I appeal to you to search your hearts and minds and recall that you, too, have wanted the right to work as long as you could do so competently; and you, too, have sought the right to live and seek your own happiness, as long as you did not interfere with the right of other people to do the same. And I beg you to recall that most of you in this hall who now take those same rights for granted have had to struggle to overcome suspicion and fear and prejudice in order to achieve them.

So now, we, too, appeal to you to acknowledge for ourselves the same rights, and together to continue the struggle to expand the vision so that no American can ever again be subjected to abuse and harassment.

And so, my fellow Democrats, in keeping with the faith which has made this nation great, in keeping with the promise of the American vision, and in keeping with the belief that we are all equal Americans, I respectfully withdraw my nomination.

Thank you.

--------- 9.3 ---------

'THE IMPERIALISM OF PATRIARCHY'
bell hooks

bell hooks began writing her first book, *Ain't I a Woman: Black women and feminism*, in 1974, when she was 19 years old. She didn't publish it until 1981, when it became the first in her series of missives on black women and their relation to society. hooks, who de-capitalizes her assumed name to emphasize her ideas over herself, is one of the modern era's leading black feminist voices. Building on Michelle Wallace's 1979 critique of the Black Power movement (see Chapter Eight), hooks takes aim at black male leadership, going back to early slavery. She argues that, from the first, black men have sought to express their own freedom by demanding their access to America's patriarchy. As African Americans made progress in liberating themselves, black men, and women, measured that liberation by the degree to which the community's male was empowered to rule the home and "control his woman."

"The Imperialism of Patriarchy"

When the contemporary movement toward feminism began, there was little discussion of the impact of sexism on the social status of black women. The upper and middle class white women who were at the forefront of the movement made no effort to emphasize that patriarchal power, the power men use to dominate women, is not just the privilege of upper and middle class white men, but the privilege of all men in our society regardless of their class or race. White feminists so focused on the disparity between white male/white female economic status as an indication of the negative impact of sexism that they drew no attention to the fact that poor and lower-class men are as able to oppress and brutalize women as any other group of men in American society. The feminist tendency to make synonymous male possession of economic power with being an oppressor caused white men to be labeled "the" enemy. The labeling of the white male patriarch as "chauvinist pig" provided a convenient scapegoat for black male sexists. They could join with white and black women to protest against white male oppression and divert attention away from their sexism, their support of patriarchy, and their sexist exploitation of women. Black leaders, male and female, have been unwilling to acknowledge black male sexist oppression of black women because they do not want to acknowledge that racism is not the only oppressive force in our lives. Nor do they wish to complicate efforts to resist racism by acknowledging that black men can be victimized by racism but at the same time act as sexist oppressors of black women. Consequently there is little acknowledgement of sexist oppression in black male/female relationships as a serious problem. Exaggerated emphasis on the impact of racism on black men has evoked an image of the black male as effete, emasculated, crippled. And so intensely does this image dominate American thinking that people are absolutely unwilling to admit that the damaging effects of racism on black men neither prevents them from being sexist oppressors nor excuses or justifies their sexist oppression of black women. …

Many black men who express the greatest hostility toward the white male power structure are often eager to gain access to that power. Their expressions of rage and anger are less a critique of the white male patriarchal social order and more a reaction against the fact that they have not been allowed full participation in the power game. In the past, these black men have been most supportive of male subjugation of women. They hoped to gain public recognition of their "manhood" by demonstrating that they were the dominant figure in the black family.

Just as 19th century black male leaders felt that it was important that all black men show themselves willing to be protectors and providers of their women as a sign to the white race that they would tolerate no more denial of their masculine privilege, 20th century black male leaders used this same tactic. Marcus Garvey, Elijah Muhammed, Malcolm X, Martin Luther King, Stokely Carmichael, Amiri Baraka and other black male leaders have righteously supported patriarchy. They have all argued that it is absolutely necessary for black men to relegate black women to a subordinate position both in the political sphere and in home life.

——— 9.4 ———

THE COLOR PURPLE
Alice Walker

The growing chorus of black women intellectuals and artists commenting on the community's misogyny finally sparked vocal backlash when Alice Walker published her Pulitzer Prize–winning novel *The Color Purple* in 1982. Walker had already published volumes of poetry and prose and worked as an editor at *Ms.* magazine during the 1970s, but the novel is responsible for catapulting her to mainstream fame. It sparked heated protest from African-American men, who argued that her novel presented an overly critical and negative image of the black man.

The Color Purple tells the story of Celie, a young black woman growing up in the turn-of-century South. The man she believes to be her father sells her into marriage with a cruel neighbor who drives away her sister — the only person she loves. Beaten down by racism and domineering men, Celie sees little value in herself or her life, until she meets her husband's vibrant and independent mistress, Shug. Shug teaches Celie to love herself — to love her womanhood — and to rebel against the abuse of the men in her life. The two fall in love and, eventually, Celie escapes through her. The central male figures who lord over Celie's life are never given names. Many black men

pointed to this sort of aggressive effort to de-emphasize their significance as proof that the novel was a "man-hating" treatise. The lesbian love affair at the novel's core (largely removed in the subsequent motion picture), which was the impetus for Celie's reawakening, was also the source of much backlash to the book. In the excerpt below, Shug explains to Celia where she finds strength to overcome barriers to her independence and self-respect as a black woman.

Dear Nettie,
I don't write to God no more, I write to you.

What happened to God? ast Shug.

Who that? I say.

She look at me serious.

Big a devil you is, I say, you not worried bout no God, surely.

She say, Wait a minute. Hold on just a minute here. Just because I don't harass it like some people us know don't mean I ain't got religion.

What God do for me? I ast.

She say, Celie! Like she shock. He gave you life, good health, and a good woman that love you to death.

Yeah, I say, and he give me a lynched daddy, a crazy mama, a lowdown dog of a step pa and a sister I probably won't ever see again. Anyhow, I say, the God I been praying and writing to is a man. And act just like all the other mens I know. Trifling, forgitful and lowdown.

She say, Miss Celie, You better hush. God might hear you.

Let 'im hear me, I say. If he ever listened to poor colored women the world would be a different place, I can tell you.

She talk and she talk, trying to budge me way from blasphemy. But I blaspheme much as I want to.

All my life I never care what people thought bout nothing I did, I say. But deep in my heart I care about God. What he going to think. And come to find out, he don't think. Just sit up there glorying in being deaf, I reckon. But it ain't easy, trying to do without God. Even if you know he ain't there, trying to do without him is a strain.

I is a sinner, say Shug. Caus I was born. I don't deny it. But once you find out what's out there waiting for us, what else can you be?

Sinners have more good times, I say.

You know why? she ast.

Cause you ain't all the time worrying about God, I say.

Naw, that ain't it, she say. Us worry bout God a lot. But once us feel loved by God, us do the best us can to please him with what us like.

You telling me God love you, and you ain't never done nothing for him? I mean, not go to church, sing in the choir, feed the preacher and all like that?

But if God love me, Celie, I don't have to do all that. Unless I want to. There's a lot of other things I can do that I speck God likes.

Like what? I ast.

Oh, she say. I can lay back and just admire stuff. Be happy. Have a good time.

Well, this sound like blasphemy sure nuff.

She say, Celie, tell the truth, have you ever found God in church? I never did. I just found a bunch of folks hoping for him to show. Any God I ever felt in church I brought in with me. And I think all the other folks did too. They come to church to *share* God, not find God.

Some folks didn't have him to share, I said. They the ones didn't speak to me while I was there struggling with my big belly and Mr.___ children.

Right, she say.

Then she say: Tell me what your God look like, Celie.

Aw naw, I say. I'm too shame. Nobody ever ast me this before, so I'm sort of took by surprise. Besides, when I think about it, it don't seem quite right. But it all I got. I decide to stick up for him, just to see what Shug say.

Okay, I say. He big and old and tall and graybearded and white. He wear white robes and go barefooted.

Blue eyes? she ast.

Sort of bluish-gray. Cool. Big though. White lashes, I say.

She laugh.

Why you laugh? I ast. I don't think it so funny. What you expect him to look like, Mr.___?

That wouldn't be no improvement, she say. Then she told me this old white man is the same God she used to see when she prayed. If you wait to find God in church, Celie, she say, that's who is bound to show up, cause that's where he live.

How come? I ast.

Cause that's the one that's in the white folks' white bible.

Shug! I say. God wrote the bible, white folks had nothing to do with it.

How come he look just like them, then? she say. Only bigger? And a heap more hair. How come the bible just like everthing else they make, all about them doing on thing and another, and all the colored folks doing is gitting cursed?

I never thought bout that.

Nettie say somewhere in the bible it say Jesus' hair was like lamb's wool, I say.

Well, say Shug, if he came to any of these churches we talking bout he'd have to have it conked before anybody paid him any attention. The last thing niggers want to think about they God is that his hair kinky.

That's the truth, I say.

Ain't no way to read the bible and not think God white, she say. Then she sigh. When I found out I thought God was white, and a man, I lost interest. You mad cause he don't seem to listen to your prayers. Humph! Do the mayor listen to anything colored say? Ask Sofia, she say.

But I don't have to ast Sofia. I know white people never listen to colored, period. If they do, they only listen long enough to be able to tell you what to do.

Here's the thing, say Shug. The thing I believe. God is inside you and inside everybody else. You come into the world with God. But only them that search for it inside find it. And sometimes it just manifest itself even if you not looking, or don't know what you looking for. Trouble do it for most folks, I think. Sorrow, lord. Feeling like shit.

It? I ast.

Yeah, It. God ain't a he or she, but a It.

But what do it look like? I ast.

Don't look like nothing, she say. It ain't a picture show. It ain't something you can look at apart from anything else, including yourself. I believe God is everything, say Shug. Everything that is or ever was or ever will be. And when you can feel that, and be happy to feel that, you've found It.

Shug a beautiful something, let me tell you. She frown a little, look out cross the yard, lean back in her chair, look like a big rose.

She say, My first step from the old white man was trees. Then air. Then birds. Then other people. But one day when I was sitting quiet and feeling like a motherless child, which I was, it come to me: that feeling of being part of everything, not separate at all. I knew that if I cut a tree, my arm would bleed. And I laughed and I cried and I run all around the house. I knew just what it was. In fact, when it happen, you can't miss it. It sort of like you know what, she say, grinning and rubbing high up on my thigh.

Shug! I say.

Oh, she say. God love all them feelings. That's some of the best stuff God did. And when you know God loves 'em you enjoys 'em a lot more. You can just relax, go with everything that's going, and praise God by liking what you like.

God don't think it dirty? I ast.

Naw, she say. God made it. Listen, God love everything you love — and a mess of stuff you don't. But more than anything else, God love admiration.

You saying God vain? I ast.

Naw, she say. Not vain, just wanting to share a good thing. I think it pisses God off if you walk by the color purple in a field somewhere and don't notice it.

What it do when pissed off? I ast.

Oh, it make something else. People think pleasing God is all God care about. But any fool living in the world can see it always trying to please us back.

Yeah? I say.

Yeah, she say. It always making little surprises and springing them on us when us least expect.

You mean it want to be loved, just like the bible say.

Yes, Celie, she say. Everything want to be loved. Us sing and dance, make faces and give flower bouquets, trying to be loved. You ever notice that trees do everything to git attention we do, except walk?

Well, us talk and talk bout God, but I'm still adrift. Trying to chase that old white man out of my head. I been so busy thinking bout him I never truly notice nothing God make. Not a blade of corn (how it do that?) not the color purple (where it come from?). Not the little wildflowers. Nothing.

Now that my eyes opening, I feels like a fool. Next to any little scrub of a bush in my yard, Mr.___'s evil sort of shrink. But not altogether. Still, it is like Shug says, You have to git man off your eyeball, before you can see anything a'tall.

Man corrupt everything, say Shug. He on your box of grits, in your head, and all over the radio. He try to make you think he everywhere. Soon as you think he everywhere, you think he God. But he ain't. Whenever you trying to pray, and man plop himself on the other end of it, tell him to git lost, say Shug. Conjure up flowers, wind, water, a big rock.

But this hard work, let me tell you. He been there so long, he don't want to budge. He threaten lightening, floods and earthquakes. Us fight. I hardly pray at all. Every time I conjure up a rock, I throw it.

Amen

——— 9.5 ———
'WOMANIST' DEFINED
Alice Walker

Following *The Color Purple*, Alice Walker published a book of essays entitled *In Search of Our Mother's Garden*. The collection is best known for introducing the term "womanist." As Walker defines it, womanist is a feminist of color. A womanist is "willful," rejects her assigned role as a silent server of men, appreciates and prefers woman's culture, loves other women "sexually and/or nonsexually," and rejects artificial racial categories. Literary scholars note that the Shug character in *The Color Purple* is Walker's archetype womanist.

Womanist 1. From *womanish*. (Opp. of "girlish", i.e., frivolous, irresponsible, not serious.) A black feminist or feminist of color. From the black folk expression of mothers to female children, "You acting womanish," i.e., like a woman. Usually referring to outrageous, audacious, courageous or *willful* behavior. Wanting to know more and in greater depth than is considered "good" for one. Interested in grown-up doings. Acting grown up. Being grown up. Interchangeable with another black folk expression: "You trying to be grown." Responsible. In charge. *Serious.*

2. *Also*: A woman who loves other women, sexually and/or nonsexually. Appreciates and prefers women's culture, women's emotional flexibility (values tears as natural counter-balance of laughter), and women's strength. Sometimes loves individual men, sexually and/or nonsexually. Committed to survival and wholeness of entire people male *and* female. Not a separatist, except periodically, for health. Traditionally universalist, as in: "Mama, why are we brown, pink and yellow, and our cousins are white, beige and black?" Ans.: "Well, you know the colored race is just like a flower garden, with ever color flower represented. Traditionally capable, as in: "Mama, I'm walking to Canada and I'm taking you and a bunch of other slaves with me." Reply: "It wouldn't be the first time."

3. Loves music. Loves dance. Loves the moon. *Loves* the Spirit. Loves love and food and roundness. Loves struggle. Loves the Folk. Loves herself. *Regardless.*

4. Womanist is to feminist as purple is to lavender.

9.6

'GOD BLESS YOU JESSE JACKSON'
The Rescue of Lt. Robert Goodman

In 1983, Jesse Jackson shocked the country by announcing his candidacy for the Democratic presidential nomination. He would be the first, and still the only, African American to mount a serious presidential campaign. He campaigned on a "rainbow coalition" platform, pledging to bring the nation's minorities and economically disadvantaged communities together. He reached out to rural whites, particularly small farmers who were being increasingly squeezed out of business. Progressive Democrats enthusiastically embraced Jackson's campaign, popularizing the "Run, Jesse, Run!" slogan.

During the campaign, in January 1984, Jackson began establishing his career as a freelance diplomat and negotiator with rogue states. Lt. Robert Goodman, a black Navy pilot, was being held hostage by the Syrian government as part of a stand-off with the Reagan administration. Repeated diplomatic efforts failed, and Jackson announced his intention to resolve the situation. On January 3, 1984, he brought Lt. Goodman home. The nation was shocked, and, as reported in the *Washington Post* account of Jackson and Goodman's homecoming ceremonies below, African Americans claimed ownership of the victory. One observer, a Jackson confidant, argued it was the first time the American government took Jackson seriously. A few years earlier, in 1979, Jackson had drawn criticism at home for his professed support of the Palestinian Liberation Organization. That had been his first real foray into U.S. foreign policy, and earned him high standing among Arab leaders in the Middle East. Some commentators believe this affinity, combined with the Syrian government's desire to embarrass President Reagan, was the secret to Jackson's success.

The Homecoming;
Early Risers Cheer Jackson, Goodman at Andrews

When the military airplane carrying U.S. Navy Lt. Robert O. Goodman Jr. and Jesse L. Jackson landed at Andrews Air Force Base early yesterday morning, a sleepy-eyed crowd of several hundred persons was waiting to witness a moment that some said they would remember for the rest of their lives.

"We feel that history is being made here," said Kim Y. Williams of Southeast Washington. "As black people, we have been a part of it and we feel it is our duty to be here. I feel that Jackson has made a mark and shown that anyone with strong enough feelings and convictions can accomplish something."

Many of the people who gathered at the air base came in groups on buses provided by local churches. Some said they got up at 4 a.m. to get to Andrews in time for the arrival, which occurred shortly before 7.

Etta Gibson, who came with members of First Rising Mount Zion Baptist Church — which is led by her husband, the Rev. Ernest R. Gibson, head of the Council of Churches of Greater Washington — said she was not discouraged by the early hour.

"I just wanted to look back and be able to say that I was here," she said.

"This is something people will want to tell their children about. Right now, we're here to let the world know that we are proud."

The airport welcome was the first in a series of events put on by District residents and government officials to applaud the successful negotiations that Jackson, a Democratic presidential candidate, conducted to secure the release of Goodman from the Syrian government.

Those who joined the day-long celebration cheered wildly each time Jackson appeared. They interrupted his comments with applause. They prayed for him and with him. Some were overcome with emotion and cried.

Jackson's biggest reception came last night at a rally where a capacity crowd of more than 1,000 filled the pews and lined up against the walls at Shiloh Baptist Church in Northwest Washington. The crowd waited for an hour and 45 minutes to hear Jackson speak.

It all began at Andrews. As the airplane's door opened, several dozen D.C. government officials and dignitaries scurried for good positions. In the background, a high school band

lined up. People quickly hoisted black-and-white posters with such slogans as "Goodman's Release: A Giant Step For Peace" and "God Bless You Jesse Jackson." In an effort to get a better view, some of the crowd squeezed into the section designated for the 240 reporters and photographers who came to record the event.

The Rev. Rodney Young was surrounded by reporters who fumbled with pens that refused to work in the cold morning air and camera crews pleading for someone to shift equipment that blocked their best shots.

"I got up this morning at 4 a.m. and I drove here alone," said Young. "This is a moment for the nation and I felt that it was important enough to get here."

At least one city official who joined the crowd at the airport made a special effort to get there on time. Mayor Marion Barry, a strong Jackson supporter, cut short a Barbados vacation to meet Jackson.

After flying to New York, Barry had to take a bus to Washington and arrived at 5 a.m., according to his press spokesman.

When Goodman and Jackson finally emerged from the plane, they stood side by side and waved as loud cheers rose from the crowd.

In brief remarks, Goodman said that while in captivity he thought daily about his training to withstand the prisoner-of-war experience. He added a flourish: "God bless America."

Jackson thanked Syrian President Hafez Assad for helping "to chart a new course in Middle East foreign policy," and President Reagan for not using the authority of his office to stop Jackson's trip. "This mission was a political risk but not a moral risk. It was the right thing to do," Jackson said.

After leaving Andrews, Goodman was taken to Bethesda Naval Hospital for a physical examination while Jackson went to New Bethel Baptist Church at Ninth and S streets NW, which is led by D.C. Del. Walter E. Fauntroy, for an ecumenical prayer service.

As ministers took turns praying for the Goodman family, for Jackson, for those who are suffering in the Middle East and for world peace, Syrian Ambassador Rafic Jouejati wiped away tears.

When Jouejati stood to address the audience, he was greeted with thunderous applause and a standing ovation. He said he had been impressed by Jackson's actions and was convinced that Jackson was "a dedicated servant of God."

Muslim leader Louis Farrakhan drew loud cheers from the crowd when he repeatedly pointed to Jackson as a person who illustrates the belief that God can be seen in man.

"As Jesse handled the press with such skill, I didn't see Jesse. I saw God," said Farrakhan. "When he pleaded a case before the president of Syria, Hafez Assad, we didn't see Jesse, we saw God. ... Jesse Jackson is a merciful message from God to this country. You should hurry and see God working in one of the children of the slaves."

Barry, who also attended the prayer service, said later that although Jackson was on a moral mission, he will reap political benefits as well from his trip to Syria. While Jackson has not been very successful in raising money for his political campaign, he is now getting something that is as good as money, Barry said.

"This gesture demonstrates to the American people that Jackson is probably more qualified than anybody to be president," Barry said. "It is going to negate our lack of money because he's got all the publicity and he's able to articulate his foreign policy in action."

Last night at the Shiloh Baptist Church, a soloist sang "I'm climbing up the rough side of the mountain" as Jackson, smiling, entered the church amidst a crowd of people who clapped their hands and stomped their feet to the music.

But by 9:15 p.m., when Jackson began to address the crowd, he downplayed his Syrian mission and stressed his political campaign. A collection was taken before Jackson spoke, and he talked at length about future fund-raising drives.

Acknowledging that he was a bit tired, Jackson launched into a defense of his mission as a presidential candidate. He said his candi-

dacy is not about a private effort to jockey for political position, but about "a public negotiation for parity and justice. ..."

"Our mission is to change the face of American politics," he said. "Whenever we feel the restrictions, we react. "

The crowd at Shiloh was made up largely of Jackson supporters, who said they came to honor him for his accomplishments. Pauline and Kenneth Chapman of Southeast Washington said they skipped dinner and arrived at Shiloh two hours before the rally was scheduled to begin at 7:30 p.m., to be certain to get a good seat.

"All day long I had this beautiful feeling," said Pauline Chapman. "It's like Jesse Jackson is a prophet. I'm so filled up I can barely talk about it."

——————— 9.7 ———————

'THE CONTROVERSY OVER JACKSON'S REMARKS MIGHT HAVE BEEN MUCH EASIER FOR MANY BLACKS TO ACCEPT HAD THE MESSENGER BEEN WHITE'
Milton Coleman and the 'Hymietown' story

In February 1984, just one month after his triumphant mission to Syria, Jesse Jackson's skyrocketing presidential campaign hit turbulence, as he was forced to answer for a remark that continues to color his difficult relationship with the Jewish community. Jackson was already facing heavy criticism from many for his refusal to break ties with and publicly repudiate Nation of Islam leader Louis Farrakhan, whose organization had (and has) a long history of proffering anti-Semitic ideas. But the real damage came when black *Washington Post* reporter Milton Coleman contributed to a story charging Jackson with calling New York City "Hymietown." In a conversation Jackson believed to be off-the-record — a point about which Coleman disagrees — Jackson reportedly told Coleman, "Let's talk black talk." He then proceeded to rant about what he felt was a disproportionate concern with Israel in American politics, declaring "every time you go to Hymietown, that's all they want to talk about."

Jackson at first balked at demands that he apologize for the remark, but ultimately appeared before a New Hampshire synagogue and delivered a tearful apology. In many ways he never recovered from the remark. He continues to face charges of anti-Semitism today.

Coleman met with his own critics. Many black Americans felt he had betrayed Jackson, and Farrakhan went so far as to publicly threaten the reporter. That April, Coleman published the following essay in the *Post's* Sunday editorial section, explaining why his journalistic ethics required him to break the story.

There were only 18 words, a single sentence that appeared two-thirds of the way down in a long story published Feb. 13 in The Washington Post. The subject of the article was the strain in relations between Jesse Jackson, the Democratic presidential candidate, and American Jews:

"In private conversations with reporters, Jackson has referred to Jews as 'Hymie' and to New York as 'Hymietown.'"

The controversy sparked by those words is now more than seven weeks old. It has variously been a sideshow, a backdrop or a main event in the campaign for the Democratic nomination. It has been cited as the cause of heightened tensions between blacks and Jews and of embarrassment, disillusion and infighting among blacks. It has forged divisions among journalists, black and white. It has brought strident threats of harassment, punishment, humiliation and death against me and my family.

The accuracy of that sentence is not in question. Jackson acknowledged six weeks ago that the statement is true. The ugly aftermath has yet to end, however. It has developed a life of its own.

Professionally, as the journalist responsible for its publication, I never realized and certainly never hoped that reporting the remark would lead to all of this. As a person, I wish the process had not been so painful for all. But I am convinced that I did the right thing and that I acted on principles and stuck to them firmly. The cost has been exceedingly high. ...

On Jan. 25, Jackson was scheduled to depart the Butler Aviation Terminal at National Airport for a campaign swing through South Carolina, Alabama and North Carolina. I was one of the reporters covering the trip.

I had not seen or talked to Jackson in a month. When a campaign aide informed me that Jackson would be going next door to have breakfast first, I decided to go also. Time with the candidate is important. A reporter from *The New York Times* followed me.

Jackson invited both of us to the table where he was sitting. We started with small talk and a pair of invitations that I had been asked to pass on to him. Benjamin C. Bradlee, executive editor of *The Washington Post*, was having a reception at his home in Georgetown for Harold Evans, former editor of *The Times* of London. All the presidential candidates were invited, including Jackson. Secondly, the national editors of *The Post* wanted Jackson to meet with them and reporters over breakfast, lunch or a conference table.

Earlier, on Nov. 9, Jackson had come to breakfast at The Post. Much of the discussion that day concerned Jackson's criticism of delegate selection rules for the Democratic National Convention. At the end he said he was surprised no one had asked him about Israel.

Between that breakfast and this campaign swing, Jackson had gone to Syria and won the release of captured Navy pilot Lt. Robert O. Goodman Jr. His homecoming remarks on foreign policy and the Third World had piqued the interest of Post editors, including Peter Silberman, assistant managing editor for national news. "Tell him this time I will ask him some questions about Israel," Silberman had told me. I passed on the message.

Jackson said he would be glad to come to discuss foreign policy, including Israel and the Middle East. He would not be "intimidated," he said, he would answer all the questions, and he would ask in rebuttal why so much time had been spent discussing 4 million people. That is part of Jackson's general assertion that U.S. policy in the Middle East is tilted unfairly toward Israel at the expense of America's own best interests. There is something wrong, he usually says, with a policy that "excites one nation" — Israel — "and incites 23 others" — the Arab world.

Then came a statement that has evolved as a central part of the "Hymie" controversy: "Let's talk black talk," Jackson said.

That is a phrase that Jackson often uses to talk on what reporters call "background," one of several mechanisms used when sources want or are willing to tell something to a reporter but don't want to be identified. In print, those comments come out as information from an unnamed source, the pronouncements of a "senior official" or as "private conversation." But the assumption on both sides, unless some other arrangement is made explicitly clear, is that the substance of the conversation will someday find its way into print.

I don't know what Jackson says to white reporters when he wants to talk on background. But with me and other blacks, he has placed it in a racial context: "Let's talk black talk." I understood that to mean background, and I assumed that Jackson, an experienced national newsmaker now running for president, knew that no amnesia rule would apply. I signaled him to go on.

Jackson then talked about the preoccupation of some with Israel. He said something to the effect of the following: That's all Hymie wants to talk about is Israel; every time you go to Hymietown, that's all they want to talk about. The conversation was not tape recorded, and I did not take notes. But I am certain of the thrust of his remarks and the use of the words, "Hymie" and "Hymietown." I had not heard him use them before. I made a mental note of the conversation.

I did not write a memo to myself shortly afterward, as reporters sometimes do. Nor did I write a story immediately afterward or tell my editors. It seemed clear that the context suggested at worst an ethnic slur, though not one as blatant as calling a Jew a "kike," or a stereotyping, like referring to Hispanics as "Jose." I also felt that to rush it into print would have

amounted to a sort of "gee-whiz journalism" on which I frown. As Jackson often says of isolated statements, "Text without context is pretext."

In the days that followed, the same words came up in casual conversations with other reporters on the campaign. Two or three mentioned that they, too, had heard Jackson use the words.

The next week, there were reports in The New York Times concerning contributions to Jackson-affiliated organizations from the Arab League, and within a few days a colleague at The Post, reporter Rick Atkinson, called me in New Hampshire. Atkinson had been assigned to write a story on Jackson's views on foreign policy in the Third World, especially in the Middle East, and the political ramifications here. In other words, I said, a story on Jesse and the Jews? Right, Atkinson responded. ...

Back in Washington the following week, Atkinson showed me a draft of his story. I made two suggestions. One was that he include a view offered by Don Rose, a writer and political consultant in Chicago, on the problems that Jackson's views on Israel posed for black politicians, including Jackson, who sought support from white liberals. Many liberals are Jews and are reluctant to line up with Jackson because of his views on the Middle East. I had interviewed Rose for a profile I did on Jackson in January but had not used the material. Rick did.

My other suggestion concerned Jackson's use of the words "Hymie" and "Hymietown." The subject of the story was Jackson's conflict with Jews on domestic and foreign policy issues. It talked about threats on his life by radical Jewish groups, longstanding problems between blacks and Jews, statements by Jackson that offended Jews, Jackson's responses to all of that and some of his other views. In that story, I thought, Jackson's use of "Hymie" and "Hymietown" was germane.

Moreover, Jackson was running for president of the United States. Even in context, even in "private" among reporters, even "off the record," the remarks suggested an insensitivity to those he referred in the sense that he believed that in unguarded moments with other blacks or with disarmed reporters it was acceptable to make such references.

At the time I was aware of one similar situation. Earl Butz, as secretary of agriculture in the Ford administration, had, in the private company of a reporter on assignment, told a joke that demeaned blacks. The reporter reported it, and Butz was forced to resign. Jackson's remarks, I decided, were in the same general category.

I explained the circumstances surrounding the statements to Atkinson and to Leonard Downie Jr., the national editor. I also told Atkinson that he had to call Jackson before he used the material and gave him Jackson's home number.

Four days later, on Feb. 13, the story appeared under Atkinson's byline prominently displayed on the front page under a three column headline. The story was 52 paragraphs long and quoted Jackson at length. The 37th and 38th paragraphs read:

"In private conversations with reporters, Jackson has referred to Jews as 'Hymie' and to New York as 'Hymietown.'" ...

For more than a week, Jackson insisted that he had no recollection of making the remarks and that such statements would be out of character for him as a human rights advocate. He asked the accuser to come forth, even after he had been told in a meeting that I was the source of the report. Requests for a straight yes or no answer dogged him throughout New Hampshire and sandbagged his performance in the crucial debates five days before the primary.

On the Sunday night before the election, he made a dramatic appearance at Temple Adath Yeshurun in Manchester:

"I was shocked and astonished that this ethnic characterization made in a private conversation apparently was overheard by a reporter," Jackson said. "I am dismayed that a subject so small has become so large that it threatens relationships long in the making, and those relationships must be protected. However innocent and unintentional, the remark was insensitive and it was wrong. In part, I am to blame and for that I am deeply distressed. I categorically deny that this in any way reflects my basic attitude towards Jews or Israel."

Now, let's talk black talk.

The controversy over Jackson's remarks might have been much easier for many blacks to accept had the messenger been white. It certainly would have been neat and easy. But it didn't happen that way. It rarely does.

This is the first time so many blacks have played major roles in such a high-level drama as the presidential campaign and a flawless performance would have been nice. But the glitches here have nothing to do with race. They are part of the process.

When Jackson agreed to run for president, when Farrakhan chose to openly support him and when I agreed to cover the campaign for The Post, we all undertook to take the bitter with the sweet. I am moved by Jackson's campaign. Almost anyone black would be, and it is much easier to be moved by it when you trek across the nation with Jackson, stopping at some of the shrines that were only faraway places of heroic struggle when I was growing up — Selma, Montgomery, Birmingham, Atlanta.

Sometimes, in stories designed to capture mood and color, my heart creeps into print. That is natural and proper. A reporter gauges the mood of the audience from what he hears and sees and how he filters it through the lens of his own experience. No reporter is a robot.

But when it comes to the facts of the campaign, I have to throw personality aside. I cannot openly support any candidate. The others wouldn't stand for it. I cannot covertly support any candidate. My ethics wouldn't stand for it.

At the time Jackson's remarks were inserted into Atkinson's story, I knew they would become controversial — though I couldn't guess how controversial. I continue to think that the controversy caused by their simple publication has been greatly aggravated by the fact that, for 13 days at every opportunity

Jackson was given to explain the remarks, he denied them instead.

These were especially sensitive remarks because they involved blacks and Jews, who, despite the unity of the civil rights days, also have longstanding differences that are still not resolved. What better way to destroy Jackson, the argument goes, than to give "those Jews" ammunition to shoot him down.

If I knew that publication of the remarks would cause trouble for Jackson, why did I disclose them? That is simple. It is not my job to avoid controversy for Jackson. His aides have that job. Reporters do not try to help or hurt the candidates they cover. They just cover them.

There are some reporters who pull punches to curry favor with those they cover. Those people should not be categorized as white racist reporters protecting white candidates. Those are bad reporters. They come in all colors.

And in a presidential campaign, reporters don't often gain access just because of their vaunted closeness to the source or their friendship with the candidate. It helps, but to the disappointment of our egos, access is often determined by the second line on the press tags dangling around our necks — CBS News, *The Washington Post, The New York Times.*

Jackson has perhaps given me access to him because I'm black. But he also gives it to most of my colleagues at this paper: he knows when he's talking to *The Washington Post.*

A week before he announced his candidacy he met with a group of black reporters here and said he would keep us posted on his plans. A week later he announced his candidacy to "brother" Mike Wallace on CBS's "60 Minutes," one of the most widely watched television programs in the nation.

Other reporters have said they heard Jackson's remarks but they have not reported them. One told editors of the remarks but the editors were not interested in printing the story. All of these people must speak for themselves.

Jackson himself has dozens of phrases that describe this painful process we all are going through. "Moving from the Harlem Globetrotters to the NBA" and "Play the game by one set of rules" are two of the most appropriate.

Black people have never asked not to be told the down sides of their heroes, and the vote for Jackson in primaries and caucuses since publication of his remarks indicates that his political ship has not sprung massive leaks among blacks, though his "rainbow coalition" has yet really to develop.

When I first began reporting on the *Milwaukee Courier*, a black weekly, I explained to my friends that I was going into journalism to help blacks get the information needed to make intelligent decisions affecting their lives. I still believe in doing that, even though I am working for a vastly different newspaper with a much wider audience.

A friend has followed me through my 15 years as a short-term black activist and ideologue, as a movement newspaperman and into the mainstream at *The Washington Post.* We were together in the movement and now have pursued separate careers, but we have always been the best of friends.

The friend, too, was puzzled and deeply disturbed by my reporting of Jackson's remarks, but last week, after countless conversations, we reached an understanding.

Now I realize what you did and why you did it, the friend said. I think you acted in line with your ideals and it was the right thing to do. I could not have done it. I would not have done it, the friend said. I could never be a reporter.

--------- 9.8 ---------

'OUR TIME HAS COME!'
Jesse Jackson

Despite the setbacks from his anti-Semitic remarks, Jesse Jackson's campaign garnered far more votes in the Democratic primary than anyone had expected. He had mounted a legitimate challenge, and the Party had to take him seriously. Nominee Walter Mondale adapted his message to reach out to Jackson supporters, and Jackson was offered a prime time slot to speak at the Democratic National Convention in San Francisco. His July 17 address is counted as one of the greatest in American political history. Thirty-three million television viewers tuned in for it, the audience growing as the 50-minute speech went along. Responding to fears that his campaign had torn the Party apart and risked the election, Jackson put forth a call for unity. He addressed questions of his own anti-Semitism with a moving passage on the historic bond between African Americans and Jews. And he declared victory for the progressive coalition in American politics, shouting his now signature phrase, "Our time has come!" Jackson had stolen the show, and, moreover, cemented himself as an indispensable coalition partner in any future national Democratic election.

Tonight we come together bound by our faith in a mighty God, with genuine respect and love for our country, and inheriting the legacy of a great party, the Democratic Party, which is the best hope for redirecting our nation on a more humane, just and peaceful course.

This is not a perfect party. We are not a perfect people. Yet, we are called to a perfect mission: our mission to feed the hungry; to clothe the naked; to house the homeless; to teach the illiterate; to provide jobs for the jobless; and to choose the human race over the nuclear race.

We are gathered here this week to nominate a candidate and adopt a platform which will expand, unify, direct and inspire our Party and the Nation to fulfill this mission.

My constituency is the desperate, the damned, the disinherited, the disrespected, and the despised. They are restless and seek relief. They've voted in record numbers. They have invested faith, hope and trust that they have in us. The Democratic Party must send them a signal that we care. I pledge my best to not let them down. ...

I've had the rare opportunity to watch seven men, and then two, pour out their souls, offer their service and heal — and heed the call of duty to direct the course of our Nation. There is a proper season for everything. There is a time to sow, a time to reap. There is a time to compete, and a time to cooperate.

I ask for your vote on the first ballot as a vote for a new direction for this Party and this

Nation. A vote of conviction, a vote of conscience.

But I will be proud to support the nominee of this convention for the Presidency of the United States of America.

I have watched the leadership of our party develop and grow. My respect for both Mr. Mondale and Mr. Hart is great. I have watched them struggle with the crosswinds and crossfires of being public servants, and I believe they will both continue to try to serve us faithfully.

I am elated by the knowledge that for the first time in our history a woman, Geraldine Ferraro, will be recommended to share our ticket.

Throughout this campaign, I've tried to offer leadership to the Democratic Party and the Nation. If in my high moments, I have done some good, offered some service, shed some light, healed some wounds, rekindled some hope, or stirred someone from apathy and indifference, or in any way along the way helped somebody, then this campaign has not been in vain.

For friends who loved and cared for me, and for a God who spared me, and for a family who understood, I am eternally grateful.

If, in my low moments, in word, deed or attitude, through some error of temper, taste or tone, I have caused anyone discomfort, created pain or revived someone's fears, that was not my truest self. If there were occasions when my grape turned into a raisin and my joy bell lost its resonance, please forgive me. Charge it to my head and not to my heart. My head — so limited in its finitude; my heart, which is boundless in its love for the human family. I am not a perfect servant. I am a public servant doing my best against the odds. As I develop and serve, be patient. God is not finished with me yet.

This campaign has taught me much; that leaders must be tough enough to fight, tender enough to cry, human enough to make mistakes, humble enough to admit them, strong enough to absorb the pain and resilient enough to bounce back and keep on moving.

For leaders, the pain is often intense. But you must smile through your tears and keep moving with the faith that there is a brighter side somewhere.

I went to see Hubert Humphrey three days before he died. He had just called Richard Nixon from his dying bed, and many people wondered why. I asked him. He said, "Jesse, from this vantage point, with the sun setting in my life, all of the speeches, the political conventions, the crowds and the great fights are behind me now. At a time like this you are forced to deal with your irreducible essence, forced to grapple with that which is really important to you. And what I have concluded about life," Hubert Humphrey said, "When all is said and done, we must forgive each other, and redeem each other, and move on."

Our party is emerging from one of its most hard fought battles for the Democratic Party's presidential nomination in our history. But our healthy competition should make us better, not bitter.

We must use the insight, wisdom, and experience of the late Hubert Humphrey as a balm for the wounds in our Party, this Nation and the world. We must forgive each other, redeem each other, regroup and move one.

Our flag is red, white and blue, but our nation is a rainbow — red, yellow, brown, black and white — and we're all precious in God's sight.

America is not like a blanket — one piece of unbroken cloth, the same color, the same texture, the same size. America is more like a quilt — many patches, many pieces, many colors, many sizes, all woven and held together by a common thread. The white, the Hispanic, the black, the Arab, the Jew, the woman, the native American, the small farmer, the businessperson, the environmentalist, the peace activist, the young, the old, the lesbian, the gay and the disabled make up the American quilt.

Even in our fractured state, all of us count and all of us fit somewhere. We have proven that we can survive without each other. But we have not proven that we can win and progress without each other. We must come together.

From Fannie Lou Hamer in Atlantic City in

1964 to the Rainbow Coalition in San Francisco today; from the Atlantic to the Pacific, we have experienced pain but progress as we ended American apartheid laws, we got public accommodation, we secured voting rights, we obtained open housing, as young people got the right to vote. We lost Malcolm, Martin, Medgar, Bobby, John and Viola. The team that got us here must be expanded, not abandoned. Twenty years ago, tears welled up in our eyes as the bodies of Schwerner, Goodman and Chaney were dredged from the depths of a river in Mississippi. Twenty years later, our communities, black and Jewish, are in anguish, anger and pain. Feelings have been hurt on both sides.

There is a crisis in communications. Confusion is in the air. But we cannot afford to lose our way. We may agree to agree; or agree to disagree on issues; we must bring back civility to these tensions.

We are co-partners in a long and rich religious history — the Judeo-Christian traditions. Many blacks and Jews have a shared passion for social justice at home and peace abroad. We must seek a revival of the spirit, inspired by a new vision and new possibilities. We must return to higher ground.

We are bound by Moses and Jesus, but also connected with Islam and Mohammed. These three great religions, Judaism, Christianity and Islam, were all born in the revered and holy city of Jerusalem.

We are bound by Dr. Martin Luther King Jr. and Rabbi Abraham Heschel, crying out from their graves for us to reach common ground. We are bound by shared blood and shared sacrifices. We are much too intelligent; much too bound by our Judeo-Christian heritage; much too victimized by racism, sexism, militarism and anti-Semitism; much too threatened as historical scapegoats to go on divided one from another. We must turn from finger pointing to clasped hands. We must share our burdens and our joys with each other once again. We must turn to each other and not on each other and choose higher ground.

Twenty years later, we cannot be satisfied by

just restoring the old coalition. Old wine skins must make room for new wine. We must heal and expand. The Rainbow Coalition is making room for Arab Americans. They, too, know the pain and hurt of racial and religious rejection. They must not continue to be made pariahs. The Rainbow Coalition is making room for Hispanic Americans who this very night are living under the threat of the Simpson-Mazzoli bill. And farm workers from Ohio who are fighting the Campbell Soup Company with a boycott to achieve legitimate workers' rights.

The Rainbow is making room for the Native American, the most exploited people of all, a people with the greatest moral claim amongst us. We support them as they seek the restoration of their ancient land and claim amongst us. We support them as they seek the restoration of land and water rights, as they seek to preserve their ancestral homelands and the beauty of a land that was once all theirs. They can never receive a fair share for all they have given us. They must finally have a fair chance to develop their great resources and to preserve their people and their culture.

The Rainbow Coalition includes Asian Americans, now being killed in our streets, scapegoats for the failures of corporate, industrial and economic policies.

The Rainbow is making room for the young Americans. Twenty years ago, our young people were dying in a war for which they could not even vote. Twenty years later, young America has the power to stop a war in Central America and the responsibility to vote in great numbers. Young America must be politically active in 1984. The choice is war or peace. We must make room for young America.

The Rainbow includes disabled veterans. The color scheme fits in the Rainbow. The disabled have their handicap revealed and their genius concealed; while the able-bodied have their genius revealed and their disability concealed. But ultimately, we must judge people by their values and their contribution. Don't leave anybody out. I would rather have Roosevelt in a wheelchair than Reagan on a horse.

The Rainbow includes small farmers. They have suffered tremendously under the Reagan regime. They will either receive 90 percent parity or 100 percent charity. We must address their concerns and make room for them.

The Rainbow includes lesbians and gays. No American citizen ought to be denied equal protection from the law.

We must be unusually committed and caring as we expand our family to include new members. All of us must be tolerant and understanding as the fears and anxieties of the rejected and of the party leadership express themselves in so many different ways. Too often what we call hate — as if it were some deeply rooted philosophy or strategy — it is simply ignorance, anxiety, paranoia, fear and insecurity.

To be strong leaders, we must be long-suffering as we seek to right the wrongs of our Party and our Nation. We must expand our Party, heal our Party and unify our Party. That is our mission in 1984.

We are often reminded that we live in a great nation — and we do. But it can be greater still. The Rainbow is mandating a new definition of greatness. We must not measure greatness from the mansion down, but from the manger up.

Jesus said that we should not be judged by the bark we wear but by the fruit that we bear. Jesus said that we must measure greatness by how we treat the least of these.

President Reagan says the nation is in recovery. Those 90,000 corporations that made a profit last year but paid no Federal taxes are recovering. The 37,000 military contractors who have benefited from Reagan's more than doubling of the military budget in peacetime, surely they are recovering.

The big corporations and rich individuals who received the bulk of a three-year, multibillion tax cut from Mr. Reagan are recovering. But no such recovery is under way for the least of these. Rising tides don't lift all boats, particularly those stuck at the bottom.

For the boats stuck at the bottom there's a

misery index. This Administration has made life more miserable for the poor. Its attitude has been contemptuous. Its policies and programs have been cruel and unfair to working people. They must be held accountable in November for increasing infant mortality among the poor. In Detroit — in Detroit, one of the great cities in the western world, babies are dying at the same rate as Honduras, the most underdeveloped nation in out hemisphere. This Administration must be held accountable for policies that have contributed to the growing poverty in America. There are now 34 million people in poverty, 15 percent of our Nation. Twenty-three million are White, eleven million Black, Hispanic, Asian and others. By the end of this year, there will be 41 million people in poverty. We cannot stand idly by. We must fight for change now.

Under this regime, we look at Social Security. The 1981 budget cuts included nine permanent Social Security benefit cuts totaling $20 billion over five years.

Small businesses have suffered on the Reagan tax cuts. Only 18 percent of total business tax cuts went to them, 82 percent to big businesses.

Health care under Mr. Reagan has already been sharply cut. Education under Mr. Reagan has been cut 25 percent. Under Mr. Reagan there are now 9.7 million female-head families. They represent 16 percent of all families. Half of all of them are poor. Seventy percent of all poor children live in a house headed by a woman, where there is no man.

Under Mr. Reagan, the Administration has cleaned up only six of 546 priority toxic waste dumps.

Farmers' real net income was only about half its level in 1979.

Many say that the race in November will be decided in the South. President Reagan is depending on the conservative South to return him to office. But the South, I tell you, is unnaturally conservative. The South is the poorest region in our nation and, therefore, the least to conserve. In his appeal to the South,

Mr. Reagan is trying to substitute flags and prayer cloths for food, and clothing, and education, health care and housing.

Mr. Reagan will ask us to pray, and I believe in prayer. I have come to this way by power of prayer. But then, we must watch false prophecy. He cuts energy assistance to the poor, cuts breakfast programs from children, cuts lunch programs from children, cuts job training from children, and then says to an empty table, "Let us pray." Apparently he is not familiar with the structure of prayer. You thank the Lord for the food that you are about to receive, not the food that just left. I think that we should pray, but don't pray for the food that left. Pray for the man that took the food — to leave.

We need a change. We need a change in November.

Under Mr. Reagan, the misery index has risen for the poor. The danger index has risen for everybody. Under this administration, we have lost the lives of our boys in Central America and Honduras, in Grenada, in Lebanon, in a nuclear standoff in Europe. Under this Administration, one-third of our children believe they will die in a nuclear war. The danger index is increasing in this world.

All the talk about the defense against Russia; the Russian submarines are closer, and their missiles more accurate. We live in a world tonight more miserable and a world more dangerous. While Reaganomics and Reaganism is talked about often, so often we miss the real meaning. Reaganism is a spirit, and Reaganomics represents the real economic facts of life.

In 1980, Mr. George Bush, a man with reasonable access to Mr. Reagan, did an analysis of Mr. Reagan's economic plan. Mr. George Bush concluded that Reagan's plan was "voodoo economics." He was right.

Third-party candidate John Anderson said "a combination of military spending, tax cuts and a balanced budget by 1984 would be accomplished with blue smoke and mirrors." They were both right.

Mr. Reagan talks about a dynamic recovery.

There's some measure of recovery. Three and a half years later, unemployment has inched just below where it was when he took office in 1981. There are still 8.1 million people officially unemployed, 11 million working only part-time. Inflation has come down, but let's analyze for a moment who has paid the price for this superficial economic recovery.

Mr. Reagan curbed inflation by cutting consumer demand. He cut consumer demand with conscious and callous fiscal and monetary policies. He used the Federal budget to deliberately induce unemployment and curb social spending. He then weighed and supported tight monetary policies of the Federal Reserve Board to deliberately drive up interest rates, again to curb consumer demand created through borrowing. Unemployment reached 10.7 percent. We experienced skyrocketing interest rates. Our dollar inflated abroad. There were record bank failures; record farm foreclosures; record business bankruptcies; record budget deficits; record trade deficits.

Mr. Reagan brought inflation down by destabilizing our economy and disrupting family life. He promised — he promised in 1980 a balanced budget. But instead we now have a record toward a billion dollar budget deficit. Under Mr. Reagan, the cumulative budget deficit for his four years is more than the sum total of deficits from George Washington through Jimmy Carter combined.

I tell you, we need a change. …

This consumer-led but deficit-financed recovery is unbalanced and artificial. We have a challenge as Democrats to point a way out. Democracy guarantees opportunity, not success. Democracy guarantees the right to participate, not a license for a majority to dominate. The victory for the Rainbow Coalition in the Platform debates today was not whether we won or lost, but that we raised the right issues.

We could afford to lose the vote; issues are non-negotiable. We could not afford to avoid raising the right questions. Our self-respect and our moral integrity were at stake. Our heads are perhaps bloody, but not bowed. Our back is straight. We can go home and face our people. Our vision is clear.

When we think, on this journey from slaveship to championship, that we have gone from the planks of the Boardwalk in Atlantic City in 1964 to fighting to help write the planks in the platform in San Francisco in 1984 there is a deep and abiding sense of joy in our souls in spite of the tears in our eyes. Though there are missing planks, there is a solid foundation upon which to build. Our party can win, but we must provide hope, which will inspire people to struggle and achieve; provide a plan that shows a way out of our dilemma and then lead the way.

In 1984, my heart is made to feel glad because I know there is a way out — justice. The requirement for rebuilding America is justice. The linchpin of progressive politics in our nation will not come from the North, they in fact will come from the South.

That is why I argue over and over again. We look from Virginia around to Texas, there's only one black Congress person out of 115. Nineteen years later, we're locked out of the Congress, the Senate and the Governor's mansion.

What does this large black vote mean? Why do I fight to win second primaries and fight gerrymandering and annexation and at-large elections? Why do we fight over that? Because I tell you, you cannot hold someone in the ditch unless you linger there with them. Unless you linger there.

If you want a change in this nation, you enforce that Voting Rights Act. We'll get 12 to 20 Black, Hispanic, female and progressive congresspersons from the South. We can save the cotton, but we have got to fight the boll weevils. We have got to make a judgment. We have got to make a judgment.

It is not enough to hope that ERA will pass. How can we pass ERA? If Blacks vote in great numbers, progressive Whites win. It is the only way progressive Whites win. If Blacks vote in great numbers, Hispanics win. When Blacks, Hispanics and progressive Whites vote, women win. When women win, children win. When women and children win, workers win. We must all come together. We must come together.

I tell you, in all our joy and excitement, we must not save the world and lose our souls. We should never short-circuit enforcing the Voting Rights Act at every level. When one of us rises, all of us will rise. Justice is the way out. Peace is the way out. We should not act as if nuclear weaponry is negotiable and debatable.

In this world in which we live, we dropped the bomb on Japan and felt guilty, but in 1984 other folks have also got bombs. This time, if we drop the bomb, six minutes later we, too, will be destroyed. It is not about dropping the bomb on somebody. It is about dropping the bomb on everybody. We must choose to develop minds over guided missiles, and then think it out and not fight it out. It is time for a change. ...

There is one way out, jobs. Put America back to work.

When I was a child growing up in Greenville, South Carolina, the Reverend Sample used to preach every so often a sermon relating to Jesus and he said, "If I be lifted up, I will draw all men unto me." I didn't quite understand what he meant as a child growing up, but I understand a little better now. If you raise up truth, it is magnetic. It has a way of drawing people.

With all this confusion in this Convention, the bright lights and parties and big fun, we must raise up the single proposition: If we lift up a program to feed the hungry, they will come running; if we lift up a program to start a war no more, our youth will come running; if we lift up a program to put America back to work, and an alternative to welfare and despair, they will come running.

If we cut that military budget without cutting our defense, and use that money to rebuild bridges and put steel workers back to work, and use that money and provide jobs for our cities, and use that money to build schools and pay teachers and educate our children, and build hospitals, and train doctors and train nurses, the whole nation will come running to us.

As I leave you now, we vote in this convention and get ready to go back across this nation in a couple of days, in this campaign I tried to be faithful to my promise. I lived in old barrios, ghettos and in reservations and housing projects.

I have a message for our youth. I challenge them to put hope in their brains and not dope in their veins. I told them that like Jesus, I, too, was born in the slum, and just because you're born in a slum does not mean the slum is born in you and you can rise above it if your mind is made up. (Applause) I told them in every slum there are two sides. When I see a broken window that's the slummy side. Train some youth to become a glazier; that is the sunny side. When I see a missing brick, that is the slummy side. Let that child in a union and become a brick mason and build; that is the sunny side. When I see a missing door, that is the slummy side. Train some youth to become a carpenter, that is the sunny side. When I see the vulgar words and hieroglyphics of destitution on the walls, that is the slummy side. Train some youth to be a painter and artist, that is the sunny side. We leave this place looking for the sunny side because there's a brighter side somewhere. I am more convinced than ever that we can win. We will vault up the rough side of the mountain. We can win. I just want young America to do me one favor, just one favor.

Exercise the right to dream. You must face reality, that which is. But then dream of a reality that ought to be, that must be. Live beyond the pain of reality with the dream of a bright tomorrow. Use hope and imagination as weapons of survival and progress. Use love to motivate you and obligate you to serve the human family.

Young America, dream. Choose the human race over the nuclear race. Bury the weapons and don't burn the people. Dream — dream of a new value system. Teachers who teach for life and not just for a living; teach because they can't help it. Dream of lawyers more concerned about justice than a judgeship. Dream of doctors more concerned about public health than personal wealth. Dream of preachers and priests who will prophesy and not just profiteer. Preach and dream! Our time has come. Our time has come.

Suffering breeds character. Character breeds faith, and in the end faith will not disappoint. Our time has come. Our faith, hope and dreams have prevailed. Our time has come. Weeping has endured for nights but that joy cometh in the morning.

Our time has come. No grave can hold our body down. Our time has come. No lie can live forever. Our time has come. We must leave the racial battle ground and come to the economic common ground and moral higher ground. America, our time has come.

We come from disgrace to amazing grace. Our time has come. Give me your tired, give me your poor, your huddled masses who yearn to breathe free and come November, there will be a change because our time has come.

Thank you and God bless you.

9.9
'THRILLER'
Michael Jackson

Throughout the 1970s Michael Jackson's popularity as a soloist grew. Though still a member of the Jackson Five's collective effort, he, as had his brothers, branched off to record on his own, releasing several hit singles. In 1982, Jackson released a solo album that would not only redefine his career, but would also make him one of the biggest worldwide celebrities in history. The album, *Thriller*, sold nearly 50 million copies, making it the best-selling record of all time. Songs like "Beat It," "Billy Jean" and the title track, below, came to define a generation of American teens. Jackson's spectacular stage performances and style spawned an entire pop culture, as fans mimicked his clothing and dance.

It's close to midnight, and something evil's lurking in the dark
Under the moonlight, you see a sight that almost stops your heart
You try to scream, but terror takes the sound before you make it

You start to freeze, as horror looks you right between the eyes
You're paralyzed

'Cause this is thriller, thriller night
And no one's gonna save you from the beast about to strike
You know it's thriller, thriller night
You're fighting for your life inside a killer, thriller tonight

You hear the door slam, and realize there's nowhere left to run
You feel the cold hand, and wonder if you'll ever see the sun
You close your eyes, and hope that this is just imagination
But all the while, you hear the creature creepin' up behind
You're out of time

'Cause this is thriller, thriller night
There ain't no second chance against the thing with forty eyes
You know it's thriller, thriller night
You're fighting for your life inside a killer, thriller tonight

Night creatures call, and the dead start to walk in their masquerade
There's no escapin', the jaws of the alien this time
(They're open wide)
This is the end of your life
They're out to get you, there's demons closing in on every side
They will possess you, unless you change the number on your dial
Now is the time, for you and I to cuddle close together
All thru the night, I'll save you from the terror on the screen,
I'll make you see

That this is thriller, thriller night
'Cause I can thrill you more than any ghost would dare to try

Girl, this is thriller, thriller night
So let me hold you tight and share a killer,
diller, chiller, thriller
Here tonight
(Rap Performed By Vincent Price)
Darkness Falls Across The Land
The Midnite Hour Is Close At Hand
Creatures Crawl In Search Of Blood
To Terrorize Y'awl's Neighbourhood
And Whosoever Shall Be Found
Without The Soul For Getting Down
Must Stand And Face The Hounds Of Hell
And Rot Inside A Corpse's Shell
The Foulest Stench Is In The Air
The Funk Of Forty Thousand Years
And Grizzy Ghouls From Every Tomb
Are Closing In To Seal Your Doom
And Though You Fight To Stay Alive
Your Body Starts To Shiver
For No Mere Mortal Can Resist
The Evil Of The Thriller

--------- 9.10 ---------
'SUCKER MCs'
Run-DMC

The hip hop craze that started off as an urban ghetto cultural movement, primarily limited to the boroughs of New York City, burst into the pop culture mainstream in the middle-1980s. Rap artists such as Kurtis Blow, the Fat Boys and Kool Moe Dee recorded albums that found wide commercial success and radio play. But rap, and Hip hop culture with it, truly caught national attention with the "cross-over" success of Run-DMC. Their first album, *Sucker MCs*, was released in 1984. The title track, below, hit first, and the record went on to outsell any rap album thus far. The trio appeared regularly on MTV and on both white and black radio stations. Their music and the content of their rhymes appealed to teenage white listeners just as much as it did to rap's black fan base. Cognizant of that appeal, the group fused rap with elements of rock, incorporating electric guitar and driving beats. Subsequent records, with more explicit rock fusion — including a collaboration with legendary rock-n-roll supergroup Aerosmith — were commercial blockbusters as well. More than anyone else, Run-DMC was responsible for the early mainstreaming of hip hop.

Two years ago a friend of mine
Asked me to say some MC rhymes
So I said this rhyme I'm about to say
The rhyme was def a then it went this way
Took a test to become an MC
And Orange Krush became amazed at me
So Larry put me inside his Cadillac
The chauffeur drove off and we never came back
Dave cut the record down to the bone
And now they got me rockin' on the microphone
And then we talkin' autograph, and here's the laugh
Champagne caviar, and bubble bath
But see ahh, ah that's the life, ah that I lead
And you sucker MCs is who I please
So take that and move back catch a heart attack
Because there's nothin' in the world, that Run'll ever lack
I cold chill at a party in a b-boy stance
And rock on the mic and make the girls wanna dance
Fly like a dove, that come from up above
I'm rockin' on the mic and you can call me Run-Love
I got a big long Caddy not like a Seville
And written right on the side it reads 'Dressed to Kill'
So if you see me cruisin' girls just a-move or step aside
There ain't enough room to fit you all in my ride
It's on a, ah first come, first serve basis
Coolin' out girl, take you to the def places
One of a kind and for your people's delight
And for you sucker MC, you just ain't right
Because you're bitin all your life, you're cheatin' on your wife
You're walkin round town like a hoodlum with a knife
You're hangin' on the Ave, chillin' with the crew
And everybody know what you've been through

Ah with the one two three, three to two one
My man Larry Larr, my name DJ Run
We do it in the place with the highs and the bass
I'm rockin' to the rhythm won't you watch it on my face
Go Uptown and come down to the ground
You sucker MC's, you bad face clown
You five dollar boy and I'm a million dollar man
You'se a sucker MC, and you're my fan
You try to bite lines, but rhymes are mine
You'se a sucker MC in a pair of Calvin Klein
Comin' from the wackest part of town
Tryin' to rap up but you can't get down
You don't even know your English, your verb or noun
You're just a sucker MC you sad face clown
So DMC and if you're ready
The people rockin' steady
You're drivin' big cars get your gas from Getty

I'm DMC in the place to be
I go to St. John's University
And since kindegarten I acquired the knowledge
And after 12th grade I went straight to college
I'm light skinned, I live in Queens
And I love eatin' chicken and collard greens
I dress to kill, I love the style
I'm an MC you know who's versatile
Say I got good credit in your regards
Got my name not numbers on my credit cards
I go uptown, I come back home
With who, me, myself and my microphone
All my rhymes are sweet delight
So here's another one for y'all to bite
When I rhyme, I never quit
And if I got a new rhyme I'll just say it
Cause it takes a lot, to entertain
And sucker MC's can be a pain
You can't rock a party with the hip in hop
You gotta let 'em know you'll never stop
The rhymes have to make (a lot of sense)
You got to know where to start (when the beats come in ...)

——— 9.11 ———

'IT IS RACIST TO SUGGEST THAT THE SERIES IS MERELY *FATHER KNOWS BEST* IN BLACKFACE'

Alvin Poussaint on The Cosby Show

On September 20, 1984, the floundering NBC premiered *The Cosby Show*. ABC had passed on the sitcom, and NBC executives worried about black comedian Bill Cosby's past television flops. But the show immediately proved everyone's concerns misplaced. It finished third in ratings in its first year, and first each of the next four. America loved it; black America wasn't sure what to make of it. The show, guided by Cosby and black psychiatrist Alvin Poussaint, depicted the lives of an upper-middle class black family in Brooklyn. It was pointedly counter to the black television of the 1970s, in that the family was stable, traditional, affluent and classically educated. Many African Americans adored the new "positive" portrayal of blacks. But just as many called it a whitewash — a 1950s conservative white family remade to be black. Critics complained that, at a time when conservative national leaders were scapegoating poor blacks for the nation's problems, Cosby failed to present a realistic and challenging portrait of black America. But Cosby believed this, too, was part of black America, a much-overlooked part in those times that the world needed to see. In the October, 1988 Ebony essay below, Poussaint makes that argument as well. A shrewd businessman, Cosby parlayed the show into Hollywood clout. He hired black actors, underwrote other black art, and aggressively promoted black colleges and universities. African Americans continue to debate whether or not The Cosby Show represents a triumph of black entrepreneurship and popular culture representation or a sell-out to the conservative values of 1980s America.

The most popular program on television for all four years of its existence, *The Cosby Show* has been a spectacular success among both Black and White Americans — and people in many foreign countries as well. The Huxtable family projects universal values so appealing that viewers from a wide range of ethnic and social backgrounds can identify with the problems and triumphs of this lovable, but admittedly make-believe, upper-middle-class Black family.

The questions often asked are: Just how "make-believe" is this affluent household? How much is fact and how much is fantasy? Many people, including those who watch and enjoy the show, doubt that Black families like the Huxtables really exist, and they wonder if *Cosby* has created a new myth about the Black experience in America. Critics express their skepticism by asking, rhetorically, "The Huxtables don't represent a typical Black family, do they?" they answer is, "Of course not"; they are not a "typical" Black family, because this dual-career couple — physician-husband and lawyer-wife — represent only a small, but growing, segment of the Black population.

However, there are families like the Huxtables in many communities; in the past several decades, the number of Black professionals in America has more than tripled, and the Black middle class has grown significantly larger. Even though the characters are idealized, many two-career professional families, and many more average middle-class families, feel they have a lot in common with the Huxtables. In that sense, *The Cosby Show* does depict one aspect of Black "reality."

It surprises me when Black people claim that families who talk and act like the Huxtables do not exist. They probably mean that they personally do not know any such families. It is unfortunately true that upper-income families — Black and White — have little or no social contact with families of lower socioeconomic levels. This division is accentuated by the physical distance between poor and affluent neighborhoods, which weakens the cohesion of the Black community. In addition, the Black upper middle class is seldom described in the media, because journalists have a tendency to focus on the problems of the poor Black community, which is understandable, and to describe images they feel are "authentically Black" — that is, stereotypes of the underclass — which is less understandable.

Most TV sitcoms about Black families, like *Good Times*, *That's My Mama*, and *The Jeffersons*, portray characters from poor- or lower-middle-class backgrounds, using the shuckin' and jivin', street-wise styles that the general public associates with Blacks. Even dated clichés — for example, "Give me five!" and "Hey, man, wha's happenin'?" — are still mouthed by many Black television characters. It is naïve, at the very least, to suppose that all, or even most, Blacks talk that way. White people should know this, and Black people certainly should. As opportunities for Blacks expand, it is reasonable to expect that certain styles and actions, which might have typified past Black behavior, will change and vary widely in the future.

The Cosby Show is delivering this message to the American and world public. Despite its limitations as a half-hour sitcom, it has dramatically altered the image of Blacks as poor, downtrodden, yet happy-go-lucky clowns. The Huxtable family is helping to dispel old stereotypes and to move its audience toward more realistic perceptions. Like Whites, Blacks on television should be portrayed in a full spectrum of roles and cultural styles, and no one should challenge the existence of such an array of styles within a pluralistic society.

The Huxtables, representing only one facet of the Black community, cannot possibly depict the full range of reality within Black family life and they don't even try. For example, the show has not fully explored some of the problems confronting two-career families: these parents always seem to be at home and available to the children, and the house is spotless with no evidence of anyone's having cleaned it. Such dramatic license is a hallmark of TV comedies. The sitcom formula also limits the range of what are considered appropriate story lines; audiences tune in to be entertained, not to be confronted with social problems. Critical social disorders, like racism, violence and drug abuse, rarely lend themselves to comic treatment; trying to deal with them on a sitcom could trivialize issues that deserve serious, thoughtful treatment.

It is certainly a compliment to *The Cosby Show* that people expect much more from it than they do from other TV programs. But no one expects other sitcoms, Black or White, to examine social problems and offer profound solutions to the audience. Television should indeed address the full range of the Black experience in America, but that should be accomplished through a drama series or by having existing programs confront Black issues along with those pertinent to other ethnic groups. Unfortunately, one legacy of racism is that only comic series have been deemed to be appropriate starring vehicles for Black actors; we need to pressure network executives to provide a wider variety of Black culture.

It should be apparent by now that *The Cosby Show* presents a high level of positive images that are far ahead of other Black sitcoms, and it is racist to suggest that the series is merely *Father Knows Best* in blackface. The Black style of the characters is evident in their speech, intonations and nuances; Black art, music and dance are frequently displayed; Black authors and books are often mentioned; Black colleges and other institutions have been introduced on the show, perhaps for the first time on network television.

There is ample evidence to suggest that as the show has raised Blacks' self-esteem, it has simultaneously lessened stereotypical views of Blacks among Whites. It is even possible that *The Cosby Show* will produce changes in American attitudes that are not yet apparent. But no one should suppose that because families like the Huxtables exist there are not at the same time many families who endure oppressive experiences in America; the evils of poverty and racism still trap millions of Blacks. The ongoing struggle against these conditions should not be diminished because of the affluence of Bill Cosby's television family.

The happy message of *The Cosby Show*, if anything, should raise the level of Black expectations and strengthen our determination to achieve full participation in the American Dream for all.

9.12
BELOVED
Toni Morrison

Toni Morrison was already an accomplished and prolific writer and professor by the time she published her 1986 novel *Beloved*. But the Pulitzer Prize–winning book stands out as her most impressive and memorable work. In *Beloved*, Morrison tells the story of Sethe, an escaped slave living in post–Civil War Ohio. Sethe has fled bondage, but she cannot leave the emotional scars of slavery behind. The novel turns on her singular obsession with protecting her children from the horrors she has endured. To do so, just after she escapes, she kills her baby daughter rather than allow slave catchers to reclaim her. Years later, after she's been freed from jail and the war's ended, that daughter comes back as a ghost named Beloved. Sethe sets to showing Beloved how deep her love is, and explaining why she had to kill her, so that they may move into the future together. Beloved, however, has not come to bring future joy, but rather to haunt the family with its past pain. Sethe's struggle is universal for African Americans. She is free physically, but remains bound by the ghosts of slavery. In the excerpt below, she seeks to explain her actions to Paul D — her current lover and friend from the plantation upon which she lived.

Among Morrison's countless awards was the 1993 Nobel Prize for Literature.

… Perhaps it was the smile, or maybe the ever-ready love she saw in his eyes — easy and upfront, the way colts, evangelists and children look at you: with love you don't have to deserve — that made her go ahead and tell him what she had not told Baby Suggs, the only person she felt obliged to explain anything to. Otherwise she would have said what the newspaper said she said and no more. Sethe could recognize only seventy-five printed words (half of which appeared in the newspaper clipping), but she knew that the words she did not understand hadn't any more power than she had to explain. It was the smile and the upfront love that made her try.

"I don't have to tell you about Sweet Home — what it was — but maybe you don't know what it was like for me to get away from there."

Covering the lower half of her face with her palms, she paused to consider again the size of the miracle; its flavor.

"I did it. I got us all out. Without Halle too. Up till then it was the only thing I ever did on my own. Decided. And it came off right, like it was supposed to. We was here. Each and every one of my babies and me too. I birthed them and I got em out and it wasn't no accident. I did that. I had help, of course, lots of that, but still it was me doing it; me saying *Go on*, and *Now*. Me having to look out. Me using my own head. But it was more than that. It was a kind of selfishness I never knew nothing about before. It felt good. Good and right. I was big, Paul D, and deep and wide and when I stretched out my arms all my children could get in between. I was *that* wide. Look like I loved em more after I got here. Or maybe I couldn't love em proper in Kentucky because they wasn't mine to love. But when I got here, when I jumped off that wagon — there wasn't nobody in the world I couldn't love if I wanted to. You know what I mean?"

Paul D did not answer because she didn't expect or want him to, but he did know what she meant. Listening to the doves in Alfred, Georgia, and having neither the right nor the permission to enjoy it because in that place mist, doves, sunlight, copper dirt, moon — everything belonged to the men who had the guns. Little men, some of them, big men too, each one of whom he could snap like a twig if he wanted to. Men who knew their manhood lay in their guns and were not even embarrassed by the knowledge that without gunshot fox would laugh at them. And these "men" who made even vixen laugh could, if you let them, stop you from hearing doves or loving moonlight. So you protected yourself and loved small. Picked the tiniest stars out of the sky to own; lay down with head twisted in order to see the loved one over the rim of the trench before you slept. Stole shy glances at her between the trees at chain-up. Grass blades, salamanders, spiders, woodpeckers, beetles, a kingdom of ants. Anything bigger wouldn't do.

A woman, a child, a brother — a big love like that would split you wide open in Alfred, Georgia. He knew exactly what she meant: to get to a place where you could love anything you choose — not to need permission for desire — well now, *that* was freedom.

Circling, circling, now she was gnawing something else instead of getting to the point.

"There was this piece of goods Mrs. Garner gave me. Calico. Stripes it had with little flowers in between. 'Bout a yard — not enough for more 'n a head tie. But I had been wanting to make a shift for my girl with it. Had the prettiest colors. I don't even know what you call that color: a rose but with yellow in it. For the longest time I been meaning to make it for her and do you know like a fool I left it behind? No more than a yard, and I kept putting it off because I was tired or didn't have the time. So when I got here, even before they let me get out of bed, I stitched her a little something from a piece of cloth Baby Suggs had. Well, all I'm saying is that's a selfish pleasure I never had before. I couldn't let all that go back to where it was, and I couldn't let her nor any of em live under schoolteacher. That was out."

Sethe knew that the circle she was making around the room, him, the subject, would remain one. That she could never close in, pin it down for anybody who had to ask. If they didn't get it right off — she could never explain again. Because the truth was simple, not a long-drawn-out record of flowered shifts, tree cages, selfishness, ankles ropes and wells. Simple: she was squatting in the garden and when she saw them coming and recognized schoolteacher's hat, she heard wings. Little hummingbirds stuck their needle beaks right through her headcloth into her hair and beat their wings. And if she thought anything, it was No. No. Nono. Nonono. Simple. She just flew. Collected every bit of life she had made, all the parts of her that were precious and fine and beautiful, and carried, pushed, dragged them through the veil, out, away, over there where no one could hurt them. Over there. Outside this place, where they would be safe.

And the hummingbird wings beat on. Sethe paused in her circle again and looked out the window. She remembered when the yard had a fence with a gate that somebody was always latching and unlatching in the time when 124 was busy as a way station. She did not see the white boys who pulled it down, yanked up the posts and smashed the gate leaving 124 desolate and exposed at the very hour when everybody stopped dropping by. The shoulder weeds of Bluestone Road were all that came toward the house.

When she got back from the jail house, she was glad the fence was gone. That's where they had hitched their horse — where she saw, floating above the rail as she squatted in the garden, schoolteacher's hat. By the time she faced him, looked him dead in the eye, she had something in her arms that stopped him in his tracks. He took a backward step with each jump of the baby heart until finally there were none.

"I stopped him," she said, staring at the place where the fence used to be. "I took and put my babies where they'd be safe."

The roaring in Paul D's head did not prevent him from hearing the pat she gave the last word, and it occurred to him that what she wanted for her children exactly what was missing in 124: safety. Which was the very first message he got the day he walked through the door. He thought he had made it safe, had gotten rid of the danger; beat the shit out of it; run it off the place and showed it and everybody else the difference between a mule and a plow. And because she had not done it before he got there her own self, he thought it was because she could not do it. That she lived with 124 in helpless, apologetic resignation because she had no choice; that minus husbands, sons, mother-in-law, she and her slow-witted daughter had to live there all alone making do. The prickly, mean-eyed Sweet Home girl he knew as Halle's girl was obedient (like Halle), shy (like Halle), and work-crazy (like Halle). He was wrong. This here Sethe was new. The ghost in her house didn't bother her for the very same reason a room-and-board witch with other new shoes was welcome. This here Sethe talked about love like any other woman; talked about baby clothes like any other woman, but what she meant could cleave the bone. This here Sethe talked about safety with a handsaw. This here new Sethe didn't know where the world stopped and she began. Suddenly he saw what Stamp Paid wanted him to see: more important than what Sethe had done was what she claimed. It scared him.

"Your love is too thick," he said, thinking, That bitch is looking at me; she is right over my head looking down through the floor at me.

"Too thick?" she said, thinking of the clearing where Baby Suggs's commands knocked the pods off horse chestnuts. "Love is or it ain't. Thin love ain't love at all."

"Yeah. It didn't work, did it? Did it work?" he asked.

"It worked," she said.

"How? Your boys gone and you don't know where. One girl dead, the other won't leave the yard. How did it work?"

"There ain't a sweet home. Schoolteacher ain't got em."

"Maybe there's worse."

"It ain't my job to know what's worse. It's my job to know what is and to keep them away from what I know is terrible. I did that."

"What you did is wrong, Sethe."

"I should have gone on back there? Taken my babies back there?"

"There could have been a way. Some other way."

"What way?"

"You got two feet, Sethe, not four," he said, and right then a forest sprang up between them; trackless and quiet.

Later he would wonder what made him say it. The calves of his youth? Or the conviction that he was being observed through the ceiling? How fast he had moved from his shame to hers. From this cold-house secret straight to her too-thick love.

Meanwhile the forest was locking the distance between them, giving it shape and heft.

He did not put his hat on right away. First

he fingered it, deciding how this was going to be, how to make it an exit not an escape. And it was very important not to leave without looking. He stood up, turned and looked up the white stairs. She was there all right. Standing straight as a line with her back to him. He didn't rush to the door. He moved slowly and when he got there he opened it before asking Sethe to put supper aside for him because he might be a little late getting back. Only then did he put on his hat.

Sweet, she thought. He must think I can't bear to hear him say it. That after all I have told him and after telling me how many feet I have, "goodbye" would break me to pieces. Ain't that sweet.

"So long," she murmured from the far side of the trees.

——— 9.13 ———
'LEN BIAS IS DEAD ... TRACES OF COCAINE FOUND IN SYSTEM'
Washington Post

Crime and drugs had been running rampant in American cities for years by 1986, and the Reagan administration, backed by both parties in Congress, had determined to get tough on it. Sentencing laws were being rewritten, and a debate about the delicate balance between judicial discretion and mandatory sentencing minimums was underway. Then it happened: University of Maryland basketball superstar Len Bias was found dead in the Washington, D.C., suburb of College Park — just two days after he had signed a contract with the Boston Celtics. Bias had been a media darling, and the last person expected to be a drug user. But investigators found traces of cocaine in his system and ultimately linked the drug to his sudden death. Bias's death had ramifications far beyond basketball. The shocking news sparked widespread outrage about what the nation perceived to be unprecedented increases in drug use, and hardened both citizens and policy makers' opinions about how to fight the escalating "war on drugs." In its wake, federal and state drug policy would stiffen dramatically — and in a way that many now argue led to a dramatic rise in the number of young black men incarcerated for petty crimes.

Maryland Basketball Star Len Bias Is Dead at 22
Traces of Cocaine Found in System
By Keith Harriston and Sally Jenkins
Washington Post Staff Writers
June 20, 1986

University of Maryland all-America basketball player Len Bias collapsed in his dormitory suite early yesterday morning and two hours later was pronounced dead of cardiac arrest at Leland Memorial Hospital in Riverdale.

Evidence of cocaine was found in a urine sample taken at the hospital as an emergency medical team labored from 6:50 to 8:50 a.m. to revive him, police sources said. Maj. James Ross, head of criminal investigations for Prince George's County police, said even if cocaine had been detected, it would not be possible to tell if that had contributed to Bias' death without further tests.

Medical experts said sudden cardiac arrest in a 22-year-old in apparent top physical shape could have been caused by cocaine, by a heart ailment that even frequent examinations might have missed, or by a combination of the two.

Sources said Bias passed a physical — including a urinalysis to test for drugs — administered May 27 by the Boston Celtics, who Tuesday made him the No. 2 overall pick in the National Basketball Association draft. Bias showed no sign of a heart ailment in yearly team physicals, including a special study to look for hidden heart disease, and no evidence of drug use in urine tests late last season, according to University of Maryland physicians.

From interviews with Bias' family, teammates and friends, a picture of his last hours emerges: He flew in from Boston with his father, went to the family home in Landover about 11 p.m., arrived at College Park around midnight, ate crabs in his dormitory suite with teammates and a member of the football team until about 2 a.m., drove off alone and was seen at an off-campus gathering, and returned to his dorm about 3 a.m. He collapsed some time after 6 a.m., while talking with teammate Terry Long.

Bias was unconscious and was not breathing when county ambulance attendants arrived at his dormitory suite at 6:36 a.m. — four minutes after they were called and six minutes before a mobile intensive care unit arrived — and he never regained consciousness nor breathed on his own, said Dr. Edward Wilson, chief emergency room physician at Leland Memorial.

Bias's body was taken to the state medical examiner's office in Baltimore yesterday for an autopsy. Dr. John E. Smialek, Maryland's chief medical examier, said it would be seven to 10 days before complete autopsy results are obtained.

"We are not releasing any preliminary results,' said Smialek. "We will wait until everything is properly evaluated."

The county's homicide unit is investigating, as is routine, but a spokesman said no foul play is suspected. All five teammates who shared the suite with Bias will be questioned, Detective Paul Noblitt said. Keith Gatlin was taken in shortly after 11 o'clock last night.

Bias' sister Michelle said she was told her brother was talking with Long on a couch in their dormitory suite in Washington Hall when he collapsed. A fire department spokesman, Maj. Thomas Brinkley, said Long was administering cardiopulmonary resuscitation when the county ambulance arrived. It could not be determined who placed the call for assistance.

"He was sitting on the couch with Terry Long," said Michelle Bias, who was not at the dorm, "and he laid back like he was going to sleep and he started to have a seizure."

Details of what Bias did between midnight and 6:30 a.m. were vague. His sister said Bias and their father, James, flew in from Boston and drove directly to their home in Landover. "He (Bias) left home at 11:30 p.m. to go back to the dorm," Michelle Bias said.

Keeta Covington, a defensive back on the Maryland football team, said he was in the dorm suite when Bias arrived. Covington said he, Long, Bias and basketball players Gatlin, David Gregg and Jeff Baxter ate crabs and talked about the Celtics and Bias' future until about 2 a.m. at which point Bias left. ...

David Driggers, a friend with whom Bias often played pickup basketball games, said he saw Bias at a small gathering on Cherry Hill just off campus. "He stopped by and said how excited he was and talked for a while," Driggers said.

Driggers said there was no alcohol or drugs at the gathering. "Just soda," he said.

Driggers placed Bias at the party "around 2, 2:30," and Covington was quoted as saying Bias returned to campus about an hour after his departure — which would have been about 3 a.m.

What happened between then and the time of Bias' collapse in the suite (shared by him, Baxter, Long, Gatlin, Gregg and teammate Phil Nevin) could not be determined. Long was not available to comment and Gregg declined to discuss it.

Nevin said he was out for most of the night and early morning, and when he returned he immediately went to bed, without seeing anyone. He said he awoke when the paramedics were taking Bias out.

Asked if he had seen any evidence of drug use, Nevin said, "I didn't see anything, but the police are going through it (the suite) with a fine-tooth comb."

Baxter and Gatlin both said they fell asleep earlier in the evening, and Gatlin said when he awoke he saw Bias on the floor and paramedics in attendance.

"I was in a state of shock," Gatlin said. "I was worried about Lenny, he was on the floor. All my teammates and I just rushed up, got dressed, shorts or anything, and followed him to the hospital. I called his mother and just told her that Len had a seizure and they were taking him to the hospital, and she said, 'Okay, I'm going.'" ...

In the medical examiner's office in Baltimore, Smialek said only the "initial phase" of the postmortem was completed.

Smialek said he had heard reports the hospital had found traces of cocaine in Bias' urine, but refused to say whether the medical examiner's office had found anything to suggest drug involvement.

"We obtained some of the urine sample that the hospital got and we are in the process of testing it, along with other samples obtained during the autopsy," said Smialek. "I'm not going to give any preliminary indication of anything so there are no misconceptions."

--------- 9.14 ---------

THE WAR ON DRUGS
Mandatory Minimum Sentences

At the time of Len Bias's death, the media had begun to notice the existence of a new drug in black ghettos in Los Angeles and New York City. The drug was described as a potent "rock" of cocaine, known as "crack." Because it sold for far cheaper than powdered cocaine, the drug became the primary product for urban gangs leading the domestic narcotics trade. The massive infusion of cash it provided was one of the main factors in the dramatic increase in gang activity and associated violence throughout the 1980s in large cities with sizable black populations. Police forces, particularly in Los Angeles, responded by upping the ante with their own heavier artillery and increasingly heavy-handed tactics to break up gangs and close down the "rock houses" where they sold crack. The "war on drugs" had begun in earnest.

With the public in an increasing frenzy about crack, Congress leapt into action. Within weeks, Congressional hearings were underway, and Bias's death had been transformed into a "crack cocaine overdose" in Senate hearings. That session, Congress passed the first Anti-Drug Abuse Act, setting mandatory prison sentences for first-time offenders on drug trafficking charges. The sentences were to be triggered when convicted traffickers were in possession of a certain quantity and type of drug, including "cocaine base," or crack. It was the first legislative mention of crack cocaine.

But two years later, Congress returned to the issue to attack crack specifically. The 1988 version of the drug abuse law made crack the first drug ever to trigger a mandatory prison sentence for *possession* rather than dealing. Possession of just five grams of "cocaine base" triggered a mandatory five years imprisonment. For sec-

ond-time offenders, possession of three grams mandated the five-year sentence, and just one gram for third time offenders. With crack use running rampant in poor black neighborhoods, the ranks of imprisoned African Americans skyrocketed. Today, critics argue this law unfairly targets poor, black drug users, who are in need of treatment, not jail. They point out that the more expensive powdered versions of cocaine popular among white college students and business people did not receive the same scrutiny from Congress.

A. *United Press International* **report on Los Angeles police efforts to stop gangs and "rock houses"**

Jagged red, blue and brown lines on a white police map mark the boundaries of South Los Angeles' war zone, where gangs have names like Bloods and Crips and Rolling 60s, where murder is a game and rite of passage, and the night belongs to teen-age warlords.

America's second-largest city accounts for the largest number of street gangs in the nation, about 150 cliques that have evolved from loose-knit neighborhood clubs into packs of drug dealers and killers.

It is an area where standing on a street corner can justify a bullet in the back, where drug houses are protected with armor plates, and where the knives and chains of "West Side Story" have given way to Uzi submachine guns.

"I have talked to one youngster who bragged about the 13 homicides he committed," said Police Lt. Sam Dacus, who commands the city's largest gang detail. "I believed him."

Battle Lines Drawn

The jagged lines describe a graffiti-scarred area of mostly blacks and Latinos south of downtown and east of the Harbor Freeway. By day they are neighborhoods of palm-lined streets and modest homes, but at night they become a violent no man's land.

Red lines on the map show Bloods' territory, blue lines mark off the Crips' zone and brown lines mark sectors controlled by Latino gangs.

Four pins stuck in the Rolling 60s ground stand for the four gang killings committed there in the last several months. Three pins mark deaths in the Gangster Crips territory, four more highlight the area controlled by the Inglewood Family Bloods, another four mark attacks in Broadway-Hoover Gangster Crips territory and one pin sits on the border dividing the 18th Street Gang and the Al Capones.

Automobile Ambush

Cruising gangs ambush rivals from the safety of passing cars. Bystanders are routinely gunned down, sometimes by accident, sometimes by mistake, and sometimes for the fun of it. Ambulance sirens wail through the night.

Dacus is convinced that gang members are beginning to arm themselves with high-powered weapons.

"I think we only had one cutting death last year," he said. "The rest is guns. We've only seized shot guns and handguns, but I have heard about the purchase of Uzis and military assault rifles. I have no doubt there are gang members armed with them. The days of knives, chains and clubs are over."

The number of gang-related deaths has dropped since hitting a peak of 192 in 1980, but the ferocity of gang crime has increased the level of fear among people trying to lead normal lives.

Every time there is a gang killing, officers from Dacus' Community Resources Against Street Gangs and Hoodlums (CRASH) squad investigates. The police team cleans up the blood, talks to grieving relatives and tries to interview terrified witnesses.

"I was supposed to come to this unit on loan," said Detective Ray Paik, a veteran investigator assigned to CRASH after five teen-agers were gunned down on 54th Street last October.

"The loan is indefinite and I can see this area of the city is where the need for detectives is the greatest."

At the scene of a recent killing, Paik and his partner lit 108th Street with powerful spotlights, searching the grit for bullet casings.

Bright red road flares burned in the street and yellow tape marked off the area where Bloods member Donnie Newton hit the ground. The 15-year-old was taken to Martin Luther King Jr. Hospital, where he died from a chest wound.

"I have a 14-year-old," Paik shook his head. "I can't imagine dying at such a young age."

A few feet away, Sgt. Tom Jones, the crime scene supervisor, coaxed leads from a crowd of young spectators wearing identical baseball caps.

"I can't be seen talking to you, man," one youth said. "They'll call me a snitch."

"We're going to talk to everybody," Jones soothed. "You can't snitch if you don't know who did it. You just have to tell us what you saw."

The killing began like a bizarre child's game, with Bloods chasing a youth — a member of the Crips, police think — down the street, throwing rocks and sticks at him. The youth returned about an hour later and gunned down their friend.

The last words Donnie Newton heard were, "Hey, Cuz, I got ya."

The killer escaped in a green 1967 Chevy.

"This happens every Friday night," one officer said, watching traffic slowly move around the flares. "The news would be if it didn't happen."

Inaccurate Image

Jones, 33, a 12-year department veteran, hates the romantic "player and gambler" image that gang members exude with their sporty clothes, tattoos and exotic nicknames. Like most gang detail officers, he hates identifying the groups for the news media because the gangs crave attention. "They're little thugs," he said. "Not all kids are in the gangs. A lot of them aren't. You don't have to be in a gang.

"They've created divisions in a community that didn't need any more divisions. They're a subculture that's creating division. It's worse than five years ago. In 1979, the gangs were here, but now every neighborhood has its own little gang.

"They're probably our primary crime problem in Los Angeles. They do more crime than any other group. They've specialized and diversified into burglary, robbery and drugs."

A few blocks away a series of shots are fired in rapid sequence.

"That one was a 9-millimeter," one officer said.

Revenge a Motive

"These kids have no conception of their own mortality," Jones said. "It accounts for their selfishness. All they'll be talking about now (after the night's killing) is pay-back."

Poverty and the absence of jobs are often given as reasons for gang membership and frustration that leads to violence, but Dacus said the presence and activity of sophisticated drug pushers represents a greater danger.

Among other distinctions, Los Angeles is the only city where police have employed a tank-like vehicle to batter down the walls of steel-fortified homes known as "rock houses." The homes are where drug dealers do business, protected by armed gang members. The houses got their name from their fortress-like modifications and the "rocks" — crystallized cocaine most often peddled from them.

"The gang members are not running the drug traffic," Dacus said. "But for the pushers to operate in the area, they have to employ the gangs. We know who a lot of the dealers are. Some we don't. There are a lot of independents and a lot who we find in the morgue."

Task Force Needed

Studies have failed to show that more police mean less crime, but Dacus is confident that the concentrated effort in South Los Angeles helps. "We have to go in almost like an occupation (force) and run it like the old foot beat," he said. Solutions to the root of the problem are more elusive.

"I was at a United Way meeting and someone told me we've got to come up with jobs, and that may be the case," he said. "But what we have to do first is remove a $200-a-day

source of income that a young person can make in drug activity. Then those $4-an-hour jobs may mean something."

Drug dealers in South Los Angeles use gang members as their troops, so Dacus says more narcotics enforcement is needed to weaken the gang structure. In the past, gangs were mostly the province of teen-agers, but now he says older members are staying on because of drug money.

Will Take Time

Cmdr. Lorne Kramer, assigned by Police Chief Daryl F. Gates to "eradicate" gangs in the aftermath of the 54th Street killings, does not predict a quick solution.

Kramer recently told the Police Commission that more coordination is needed with city, state and federal agencies. He added, almost as an afterthought, that more officers are needed.

Police are hopeful that the broad number of agencies working on the problem can turn the tide.

"I've been on 20 years and I know that to be effective, you've got to be persistent," Dacus said. "I think we can win it. I've never before seen so many organizations focused on the problem.

"Either we're going to do something this time or we'll have to fold up our tents and go home."

B. 1988 mandatory minimum sentencing law

U.S. Code
Title 21
Sec. 844. Penalties for simple possession
(a) Unlawful acts; penalties
… a person convicted under this subsection for the possession of a mixture or substance which contains cocaine base shall be imprisoned not less than 5 years and not more than 20 years, and fined a minimum of $1,000, if the conviction is a first conviction under this subsection and the amount of the mixture or substance exceeds 5 grams, if the conviction is after a prior conviction for the possession of such a mixture or substance under this subsection becomes final and the amount of the mixture

or substance exceeds 3 grams, or if the conviction is after 2 or more prior convictions for the possession of such a mixture or substance under this subsection become final and the amount of the mixture or substance exceeds 1 gram. ...

--------- 9.15 ---------
'FUCK THA POLICE'
Niggaz With Attitude (N.W.A.)

By the end of the 1980s, the violent tensions of urban black neighborhoods had once again peaked. The drug trade and its associated gang violence, combined with aggressive police activity (largely stemming from the new drug laws) put many American cities under siege. Hip hop culture soon began to reflect that reality. In 1988, a new rap group from Compton, California, introduced the country to "gangsta-rap" with its debut album *Straight Outta Compton*. Niggaz With Attitude, or N.W.A., struck a nerve. Many young blacks felt the group's celebration of gang culture and open hostility to law enforcement articulated their own feelings. Among their most popular songs was the defiant "Fuck Tha' Police," in which they express resentment at the tactics police often used in the "war on drugs." National politicians and law enforcement officials were appalled by this and other songs, and they vocally condemned the group. Nevertheless, N.W.A.'s enormous popularity gave birth to a new wing of hip hop music and culture, which today continues to be associated with its West Coast roots. Its "thug" style and often-violent tone has proven to be extremely successful commercially — ironically, driven in part by its simultaneous appeal to disaffected suburban white teenagers.

— Right about now, NWA Court is in full effect
Judge Dre presidin'
In the case of NWA versus the police department
The prosecuting attorneys are M.C. Ren, Ice Cube, and Eazy motherfuckin' E
— Order, order order
Ice Cube, take the motherfuckin' stand
Do you swear to tell the truth, the whole truth and nothin' but the truth, so help yo' black ass?
— "You're goddamned right!"
Why dontcha tell everybody what the fuck you gotta say?

Fuck tha police comin' straight from the underground
A young nigger got it bad 'cause I'm brown
And not the other color
So police think
They have the authority to kill a minority
Fuck that shit 'cause I ain't the one
For a punk motherfucker with a badge and a gun
To be beatin' on and thrown in jail
We can go toe to toe in the middle of a cell
Fuckin' with me 'cause I'm a teenager
With a little bit of gold and a pager
Searchin' my car, lookin' for the product
Thinkin' every nigger is sellin' narcotics
You'd rather see me in the pen
Than me and Lorenzo rollin' in a Benz-o
Beat up police, out of shape
And when I'm finished, bring the yellow tape
To tape off the scene of the slaughter
Still can't swallow bread and water
I don't know if they fags or what
Search a nigger down and grabbin' his nuts
And on the other hand
Without a gun, they can't get none
But don't let it be a black and a white one
'Cause they'll slam ya down to the street top
Black police showin' out for the white cop
Ice Cube will swarm
On any motherfucker in a blue uniform
Just 'cause I'm from the C-P-T
Punk police are afraid of me, huh
A young nigger on the warpath
And when I finish, it's gonna be a bloodbath
Of cops dyin' in L.A.
Yo, Dre, I got something to say

Fuck tha police!
Fuck tha police!
Fuck tha police!
Fuck tha police!

Sample Scene One:
— Pull your goddamn ass over right now
— Aw, shit, and what the fuck you pullin' me over for?
— 'Cause I feel like it, just sit your ass on the curb and shut the fuck up

— Man, fuck this shit
— All right smartass, I'm takin' your black ass to jail

M.C. Ren, will you please give your testimony to the jury about this fucked up incident?

Fuck tha police and Ren said it with authority
Because the niggers on the street is a majority
A gang — that's with whoever I'm steppin'
And a motherfuckin' weapon is kept in
A stash spot for the so-called law
Wishin' Ren was a nigger that they never saw
Lights all flashin' behind me
But they're scared of a nigger so they mace me to blind me
But that shit don't work, I just laugh
Because it gives 'em a hint not to step in my path
To police, I'm sayin', "Fuck you punk"
Readin' my rights and shit — it's all junk
Pullin' out a silly club so you stand
With a fake-assed badge and a gun in your hand
But take off the gun so you can see what's up
And we'll go at it, punk, and I'm 'a fuck you up
Make you think I'm 'a kick your ass
But drop your gat and Ren's gonna blast
I'm sneaky as fuck when it comes to crime
But I'm 'a smoke 'em now and not next time
Smoke any motherfucker that sweats me
Or any asshole that threatens me
I'm a sniper with a hell of a scope
Takin' out a cop or two that can't cope with me
The motherfuckin' villain that's mad
With potential to get bad as fuck
So I'm 'a turn it around
Put in my clip, yo
And this is the sound
[Boom-Boom]
Yeah, somethin' like that
But it all depends on the size of the gat
Takin' out a police would make my day
But a nigger like Ren don't give a fuck to say

Fuck tha police!
Fuck tha police!

Fuck tha police!
Fuck tha police!

— Yo, man, watchya need?
— Police, open now (Oh shit), we have a warrant for Eazy E's arrest
— Oh shit
— Get down and put your hands up where I can see 'em!
— Man, what did I do?
— Just shut the fuck up and get yo' motherfuckin' ass on the floor
— But I didn't do shit
— Man just shut the fuck up

Eazy E, why don't you step up to the stand and tell the jury how you feel about this bullshit?

I'm tired of the motherfuckin' jackin'
Sweatin' my gang while I'm chillin' in the shack an'
Shinin' the light in my face and for what?
Maybe it's because I kick so much butt
I kick ass, or maybe it's 'cause I blast
On a stupid-assed nigger when I'm playin' with the trigger
Of an Uzi or an AK
'Cause the police always got somethin' stupid to say
They put up my picture with silence
'Cause my identity by itself causes violence
The E with the criminal behavior
Yeah, I'm a gangster, but still I got flavor
Without a gun and a badge, what do you got?
A sucker in a uniform waitin' to get shot
By me or another nigger
And with a gat, it don't matter if he's smaller or bigger
(Size don't mean shit, he's from the old school, fool)
And as you all know, E's here to rule
Whenever I'm rollin', keep lookin' in the mirror
And ears on cue, yo, so I can hear a
Dumb motherfucker with a gun
And if I'm rollin' off the eight, he'll be the one
That I take out and then get away
While I'm drivin' off laughin', this is what I'll say

Fuck tha police!
Fuck tha police!
Fuck tha police!
Fuck tha police!

The verdict:
— The jury has found you guilty of being a red-neck, white-bread, chicken-shit mother-fucker
— "That's a lie! That's a god damn lie!"
— Get him out of here!
— "I want justice!"
— Get him the fuck out my face
— "I want justice!"
— Get him the fuck out my face
— Out right now!
"Fuck you, you black motherfuckker-rrrrrrrrrrr!"

Fuck tha police!
Fuck tha police!
Fuck tha police!

———— 9.16 ————
'DON'T BELIEVE THE HYPE'
Public Enemy

In addition to gangsta-rap, late 1980s hip hop also developed a more deliberately political wing. Artists such as KRS-One and Public Enemy wrote lyrics intended as lessons for listeners, delivering the "truths" about American politics and culture — truths that had been hidden from black people. The archetype of this style of hip hop music is Public Enemy's 1987 song "Don't Believe the Hype," off of the group's second album, *It Takes a Nation of Millions*. Public Enemy, as their name suggests, styled themselves as harbingers of black revolution — in true Black Arts movement form. Indeed, later politically charged hip hop bands would stress Afrocentric ideology and explicitly invoke Black Power leaders as their intellectual and cultural predecessors. Public Enemy front man Chuck D himself became involved in political causes, and continues to be an activist today.

Back — caught you lookin' for the same thing
It's a new thing — check out this I bring

Uh-oh, the roll below the level
'Cause I'm livin' low
Next to the bass (c'mon)
Turn up the radio
They claim that I'm a criminal
By now I wonder how
Some people never know
The enemy could be their friend, guardian
I'm not a hooligan
I rock the party and
Clear all the madness, I'm not a racist
Preach to teach to all
('Cause some they never had this)
Number one, not born to run
About the gun
I wasn't licensed to have one
The minute they see me, fear me
I'm the epitome — a public enemy
Used, abused without clues
I refused to blow a fuse
They even had it on the news
Don't believe the hype

Yes — was the start of my last jam
So here it is again, another def jam
But since I gave you all a little something
That we knew you lacked
They still consider me a new jack
All the critics you can hang 'em
I'll hold the rope
But they hope to the pope
And pray it ain't dope
The follower of Farrakhan
Don't tell me that you understand
Until you hear the man
The book of the new school rap game
Writers treat me like Coltrane, insane
Yes to them, but to me I'm a different kind
We're brothers of the same mind, unblind
Caught in the middle and
Not surrenderin'
I don't rhyme for the sake of riddlin'
Some claim that I'm a smuggler
Some say I never heard of ya
A rap burglar, false media
We don't need it do we?
(It's fake, that's what it be to ya, dig me?)

Yo, Terminator X, step up on the stand and
show the people what time it is, boyyyyy!)

Don't believe the hype

Don't believe the hype — its a sequel
As an equal, can I get this through to you
My 98's boomin' with a trunk of funk
All the jealous punks can't stop the dunk
Comin' from the school of hard knocks
Some perpetrate, they drink Clorox
Attack the Black, cause I know they lack exact
The cold facts, and still they try to Xerox
The leader of the new school, uncool
Never played the fool, just made the rules
Remember there's a need to get alarmed
Again I said I was a time bomb
In the daytime the radio's scared of me
'Cause I'm mad, 'cause I'm the enemy
They can't come on and play me in primetime
'Cause I know the time, plus I'm gettin' mine
I get on the mix late in the night
They know I'm livin' right, so here go the
mike, psych
Before I let it go, don't rush my show
You try to reach and grab and get elbowed
Word to herb, yo if you can't swing this
Learn the words, you might sing this
Just a little bit of the taste of the bass for you
As you get up and dance at the LQ
When some deny it, defy it, I swing bolos
Then they clear the lane I go solo
The meaning of all of that
Some media is the whack
You believe it's true, it blows me through the
roof
Suckers, liars, get me a shovel
Some writers I know are damn devils
For them I say, "Don't believe the hype"
(Yo Chuck, they must be on a pipe, right?)
Their pens and pads I'll snatch
'Cause I've had it
I'm not an addict fiendin' for static
I'll see their tape recorder and grab it
(No, you can't have it back, silly rabbit)
I'm going' to my media assassin
Harry Allen, I gotta ask him

Yo Harry, you're a writer, are we that type?
Don't believe the hype
(Now, here's what I want y'all to do for me)
Don't believe the hype
I got flavor and all those things you know
(Yeah boy, part two bum rush the show)
Yo Griff, get the green, black, red, and
Gold down, countdown to Armageddon
'88 you wait the S-One's will
Put the left in effect and I still will
Rock the hard jams, treat it like a seminar
Reach the bourgeois, and rock the boulevard
Some say I'm negative
But they're not positive
But what I got to give
(The media says this)
Red black and green
Know what I mean
(Yo, don't believe the hype)

——— 9.17 ———
'KEEP HOPE ALIVE!'
Jesse Jackson

Jesse Jackson mounted a second campaign for the Democratic presidential nomination in 1988. No longer as fanciful as it was in 1984, Jackson's campaign again energized the Party's progressive wing. He built on the same "rainbow coalition" concept he started in 1984 (which he had turned into a new organization named after the phrase), and appealed to minority women and working class voters. He came to the convention a contender, with 1,200 delegates and having finished second to Michael Dukakis. Again, Jackson had asserted his relevance within the Party. And again he took the podium for a prime-time address. Observers continue to debate whether his 1984 or this, his 1988 address, is the best ever delivered at a political convention.

Tonight, we pause and give praise and honor to God for being good enough to allow us to be at this place, at this time. When I look out at this convention, I see the face of America: Red, Yellow, Brown, Black and White. We are all precious in God's sight — the real rainbow coalition.

All of us — all of us who are here think that

we are seated. But we're really standing on someone's shoulders. Ladies and gentlemen, Mrs. Rosa Parks. The mother of the civil rights movement. (Parks is honored.) …

We meet tonight at the crossroads, a point of decision. Shall we expand, be inclusive, find unity and power; or suffer division and impotence?

We've come to Atlanta, the cradle of the old South, the crucible of the new South. Tonight, there is a sense of celebration, because we are moved, fundamentally moved from racial battlegrounds by law, to economic common ground. Tomorrow we will challenge to move to higher ground.

Common ground! Think of Jerusalem, the intersection where many trails met. A small village that became the birthplace for three religions — Judaism, Christianity and Islam. Why was this village so blessed? Because it provided a crossroads where different people met, different cultures, different civilizations could meet and find common ground. When people come together, flowers always flourish — the air is rich with the aroma of a new spring.

Take New York, the dynamic metropolis. What makes New York so special? It's the invitation of the Statue of Liberty, "Give me your tired, your poor, your huddled masses who yearn to breathe free." Not restricted to English only. Many people, many cultures, many languages — with one thing in common, they yearn to breathe free. Common ground!

Tonight in Atlanta, for the first time in this century, we convene in the South; a state where Governors once stood in schoolhouse doors; where Julian Bond was denied a seat in the State Legislature because of his conscientious objection to the Vietnam War; a city that, through its five Black Universities, has graduated more black students than any city in the world. Atlanta, now a modern intersection of the new South.

Common ground! That's the challenge of our party tonight. Left wing. Right wing.

Progress will not come through boundless liberalism nor static conservatism, but at the critical mass of mutual survival. It takes two wings to fly. Whether you're a hawk or a dove, you're just a bird living in the same environment, in the same world.

The Bible teaches that when lions and lambs lie down together, none will be afraid and there will be peace in the valley. It sounds impossible. Lions eat lambs. Lambs sensibly flee from lions. Yet even lions and lambs will find common ground. Why? Because neither lions nor lambs can survive nuclear war.

If lions and lambs can find common ground, surely we can as well — as civilized people.

The only time that we win is when we come together. In 1960, John Kennedy, the late John Kennedy, beat Richard Nixon by only 112,000 votes — less than one vote per precinct. He won by the margin of our hope. He brought us together. He reached out. He had the courage to defy his advisors and inquire about Dr. King's jailing in Albany, Georgia. We won by the margin of our hope, inspired by courageous leadership.

In 1964, Lyndon Johnson brought wings together — the thesis, the antithesis, and the creative synthesis — and together we won.

In 1976, Jimmy Carter unified us again, and we won. When do we not come together, we never win.

In 1968, division and despair in July led to our defeat in November. In 1980, rancor in the spring and the summer led to Reagan in the fall.

When we divide, we cannot win. We must find common ground as the basis for survival and development and change, and growth.

Today when we debated, differed, deliberated, agreed to agree, agreed to disagree, when we had the good judgment to argue a case and then not self-destruct, George Bush was just a little further away from the White House and a little closer to private life.

Tonight I salute Governor Michael Dukakis. He has run — he has run a well-managed and a dignified campaign. No matter how tired or how tried, he always resisted the temptation to stoop to demagoguery.

I've watched a good mind fast at work, with

steel nerves, guiding his campaign out of the crowded field without appeal to the worst in us. I have watched his perspective grow as his environment has expanded. I've seen his toughness and tenacity close up. I know his commitment to public service. Michael Dukakis' parents were a doctor and a teacher; my parents a maid, a beautician and a janitor. There's a great gap between Brookline, Massachusetts and Haney Street in the Fieldcrest Village housing projects in Greenville, South Carolina.

He studied law; I studied theology. There are differences of religion, region, and race; differences in experiences and perspectives. But the genius of America is that out of the many we become one.

Providence has enabled our paths to intersect. His foreparents came to America on immigrant ships; my foreparents came to America on slave ships. But whatever the original ships, we're in the same boat tonight. Our ships could pass in the night — if we have a false sense of independence — or they could collide and crash. We could lose our passengers. But we can seek a high reality and a greater good.

Apart, we can drift on the broken pieces of Reagonomics, satisfy our baser instincts, and exploit the fears of our people. At our highest we can call upon noble instincts and navigate this vessel to safety. The greater good is the common good.

As Jesus said, "Not My will, but Thine be done." It was his way of saying there's a higher good beyond personal comfort or position.

The good of our Nation is at stake. It's commitment to working men and women, to the poor and the vulnerable, to the many in the world.

With so many guided missiles, and so much misguided leadership, the stakes are exceedingly high. Our choice? Full participation in a democratic government, or more abandonment and neglect. And so this night, we choose not a false sense of independence, and our capacity to survive and endure. Tonight we choose interdependency, and our capacity to act and unite for the greater good.

Common good is finding commitment to new priorities to expansion and inclusion. A commitment to expanded participation in the Democratic Party at every level. A commitment to a shared national campaign strategy and involvement at every level.

A commitment to new priorities that insure that hope will be kept alive. A common ground commitment to a legislative agenda for empowerment, for the John Conyers bill — universal, on-site, same-day registration everywhere. A commitment to D.C. statehood and empowerment — D.C. deserves statehood. A commitment to economic set-asides, commitment to the Dellums bill for comprehensive sanctions against South Africa. A shared commitment to a common direction.

Common ground! Easier said than done. Where do you find common ground? At the point of challenge. This campaign has shown that politics need not be marketed by politicians, packaged by pollsters and pundits. Politics can be a moral arena where people come together to find common ground.

We find common ground at the plant gate that closes on workers without notice. We find common ground at the farm auction, where a good farmer loses his or her land to bad loans or diminishing markets. Common ground at the schoolyard where teachers cannot get adequate pay, and students cannot get a scholarship, and can't make a loan. Common ground at the hospital admitting room, where somebody tonight is dying because they cannot afford to go upstairs to a bed that's empty waiting for someone with insurance to get sick. We are a better nation than that. We must do better.

Common ground. What is leadership if not present help in a time of crisis? So I meet you at the point of challenge. In Jay, Maine, where paper workers were striking for fair wages; in Greenville, Iowa, where family farmers struggle for a fair price; in Cleveland, Ohio, where working women seek comparable worth; in McFarland, California, where the children of Hispanic farm workers may be dying from poisoned land, dying in clusters with cancer; in an

AIDS hospice in Houston, Texas, where the sick support one another, too often rejected by their own parents and friends.

Common ground. America is not a blanket woven from one thread, one color, one cloth. When I was a child growing up in Greenville, South Carolina my grandmama could not afford a blanket, she didn't complain and we did not freeze. Instead she took pieces of old cloth — patches, wool, silk, gabardine, crockersack — only patches, barely good enough to wipe off your shoes with. But they didn't stay that way very long. With sturdy hands and a strong cord, she sewed them together into a quilt, a thing of beauty and power and culture. Now, Democrats, we must build such a quilt.

Farmers, you seek fair prices and you are right — but you cannot stand alone. Your patch is not big enough. Workers, you fight for fair wages, you are right — but your patch of labor is not big enough. Women, you seek comparable worth and pay equity, you are right — but your patch is not big enough.

Women, mothers, who seek Head Start, and day care and prenatal care on the front side of life, relevant jail care and welfare on the backside of life — you are right — but your patch is not big enough. Students, you seek scholarships, you are right — but your patch is not big enough. Blacks and Hispanics, when we fight for civil rights, we are right — but our patch is not big enough.

Gays and lesbians, when you fight against discrimination and a cure for AIDS, you are right — but your patch is not big enough. Conservatives and progressives, when you fight for what you believe, right wing, left wing, hawk, dove, you are right from your point of view, but your point of view is not enough.

But don't despair. Be as wise as my grandmama. Pull the patches and the pieces together, bound by a common thread. When we form a great quilt of unity and common ground, we'll have the power to bring about health care and housing and jobs and education and hope to our Nation.

We, the people, can win!

We stand at the end of a long dark night of reaction. We stand tonight united in the commitment to a new direction. For almost eight years we've been led by those who view social good coming from private interest, who view public life as a means to increase private wealth. They have been prepared to sacrifice the common good of the many to satisfy the private interests and the wealth of a few.

We believe in a government that's a tool of our democracy in service to the public, not an instrument of the aristocracy in search of private wealth. We believe in government with the consent of the governed, "of, for and by the people." We must now emerge into a new day with a new direction.

Reaganomics. Based on the belief that the rich had too little money and the poor had too much. That's classic Reaganomics. They believe that the poor had too much money and the rich had too little money so they engaged in reverse Robin Hood — took from the poor and gave to the rich, paid for by the middle class. We cannot stand four more years of Reaganomics in any version, in any disguise.

How do I document that case? Seven years later, the richest 1 percent of our society pays 20 percent less in taxes. The poorest 10 percent pay 20 percent more. Reaganomics.

Reagan gave the rich and the powerful a multibillion-dollar party. Now the party's over, he expects the people to pay for the damage. I take this principal position, convention, let us not raise taxes on the poor and the middle-class, but those who had the party, the rich and the powerful must pay for the party.

I just want to take common sense to high places. We're spending $150 billion a year defending Europe and Japan 43 years after the war is over. We have more troops in Europe tonight than we had seven years ago. Yet the threat of war is ever more remote.

Germany and Japan are now creditor nations; that means they've got a surplus. We are a debtor nation. It means we are in debt. Let them share more of the burden of their own defense. Use some of that money to build decent housing. Use some of that money to educate our children. Use some of that money for long-term health care. Use some of that money to wipe out these slums and put America back to work!

I just want to take common sense to high places. If we can bail out Europe and Japan; if we can bail out Continental Bank and Chrysler — and Mr. Iaccoca makes $8,000 an hour — we can bail out the family farmer.

I just want to make common sense. It does not make sense to close down 650,000 family farms in this country while importing food from abroad subsidized by the U.S. Government. Let's make sense.

It does not make sense to be escorting all our tankers up and down the Persian Gulf paying $2.50 for every $1 worth of oil we bring out, while oil wells are capped in Texas, Oklahoma and Louisiana. I just want to make sense.

Leadership must meet the moral challenge of its day. What's the moral challenge of our day? We have public accommodations. We have the right to vote.

We have open housing. What's the fundamental challenge of our day? It is to end economic violence. Plant closings without notice — economic violence. Even the greedy do not profit long from greed — economic violence.

Most poor people are not lazy. They are not black. They are not brown. They are mostly white and female and young. But whether white, black or brown, a hungry baby's belly turned inside out is the same color — color it pain, color it hurt, color it agony.

Most poor people are not on welfare. Some of them are illiterate and can't read the want-ad sections. And when they can, they can't find a job that matches the address. They work hard everyday. I know, I live amongst them. They catch the early bus. They work every day. They raise other people's children. They work every day.

They clean the streets. They work every day. They drive dangerous cabs. They change the beds you slept in in these hotels last night and can't get a union contract. They work every day.

No, no, they're not lazy. Someone must defend them because it's right and they cannot speak for themselves. They work in hospitals. I know they do. They wipe the bodies of those who are sick with fever and pain. They empty their bedpans. They clean out their commodes. No job is beneath them, and yet when they get sick they cannot lie in the bed they made up every day. America, that is not right. We are a better nation than that!

We need a real war on drugs. You can't "just say no." It's deeper than that. You can't just get a palm reader or an astrologer. It's more profound than that.

We are spending $150 billion on drugs a year. We've gone from ignoring it to focusing on the children. Children cannot buy $150 billion worth of drugs a year; a few high-profile athletes — athletes are not laundering $150 billion a year — bankers are.

I met the children in Watts who unfortunately, in their despair, their grapes of hope have become raisins of despair, and they're turning on each other and they're self-destructing. But I stayed with them all night long. I wanted to hear their case.

They said, "Jesse Jackson, as you challenge us to say no to drugs, you're right; and to not sell them, you're right; and to not use these guns, you're right." And by the way, the promise of CETA; they displaced CETA — they did not replace CETA. "We have neither jobs nor houses nor services nor training; no way out."

"Some of us take drugs as anesthesia for our pain. Some take drugs as a way of pleasure, good short-term pleasure and long-term pain. Some sell drugs to make money. It's wrong, we know, but you need to know that we know. We can go and buy the drugs by the boxes at the port. If we can buy the drugs at the port, don't you believe the Federal government can stop it if they want to?"

They say, "We don't have Saturday night specials anymore." They say, "We buy AK47's and Uzi's, the latest make of weapons. We buy them across the street, along these boulevards."

You cannot fight a war on drugs unless until

you're going to challenge the bankers and the gun sellers and those who grow them. Don't just focus on the children, let's stop drugs at the level of supply and demand. We must end the scourge on the American culture!

Leadership. What difference will we make? Leadership. We cannot just go along to get along. We must do more than change presidents. We must change direction.

Leadership must face the moral challenge of our day. The nuclear war build-up is irrational. Strong leadership cannot desire to look tough and let that stand in the way of the pursuit of peace. Leadership must reverse the arms race. At least we should pledge no first use. Why? Because first use begets first retaliation. And that's mutual annihilation. That's not a rational way out.

No use at all. Let's think it out and not fight it out because it's an unwinnable fight. Why hold a card that you can never drop? Let's give peace a chance.

Leadership. We now have this marvelous opportunity to have a breakthrough with the Soviets. Last year 200,000 Americans visited the Soviet Union. There's a chance for joint ventures in space — not Star Wars and war arms escalation but a space defense initiative. Let's build in space together and demilitarize the heavens. There's a way out.

America, let us expand. When Mr. Reagan and Mr. Gorbachev met there was a big meeting. They represented together one-eighth of the human race. Seven-eighths of the human race was locked out of that room. Most people in the world tonight — half are Asian, one-half of them are Chinese. There are 22 nations in the Middle East. There's Europe; 40 million Latin Americans next door to us; the Caribbean; Africa — a half-billion people.

Most people in the world today are yellow or brown or black, non-Christian, poor, female, young and don't speak English in the real world.

This generation must offer leadership to the real world. We're losing ground in Latin America, Middle East, South Africa because we're not focusing on the real world. That's the real world. We must use basic principles, support international law. We stand the most to gain from it. Support human rights; we believe in that. Support self-determination, we're built on that. Support economic development, you know it's right. Be consistent and gain our moral authority in the world. I challenge you tonight, my friends, let's be bigger and better as a Nation and as a Party!

We have basic challenges — freedom in South Africa. We have already agreed as Democrats to declare South Africa to be a terrorist state. But don't just stop there. Get South Africa out of Angola; free Namibia; support the front line states. We must have a new humane human rights consistent policy in Africa.

I'm often asked, "Jesse, why do you take on these tough issues? They're not very political. We can't win that way."

If an issue is morally right, it will eventually be political. It may be political and never be right. Fanny Lou Hamer didn't have the most votes in Atlantic City, but her principles have outlasted the life of every delegate who voted to lock her out. Rosa Parks did not have the most votes, but she was morally right. Dr. King didn't have the most votes about the Vietnam War, but he was morally right. If we are principled first, our politics will fall in place. "Jesse, why do you take these big bold initiatives?" A poem by an unknown author went something like this: "We mastered the air, we conquered the sea, annihilated distance and prolonged life, but we're not wise enough to live on this earth without war and without hate."

As for Jesse Jackson: "I'm tired of sailing my little boat, far inside the harbor bar. I want to go out where the big ships float, out on the deep where the great ones are. And should my frail craft prove too slight for waves that sweep those billows o'er, I'd rather go down in the stirring fight than drowse to death at the sheltered shore."

We've got to go out, my friends, where the big boats are. …

Why can I challenge you this way? "Jesse

Jackson, you don't understand my situation. You be on television. You don't understand. I see you with the big people. You don't understand my situation."

I understand. You see me on TV, but you don't know the me that makes me, me. They wonder, "Why does Jesse run?" because they see me running for the White House. They don't see the house I'm running from.

I have a story. I wasn't always on television. Writers were not always outside my door. When I was born late one afternoon, October 8th, in Greenville, South Carolina, no writers asked my mother her name. Nobody chose to write down our address. My mama was not supposed to make it, and I was not supposed to make it. You see, I was born of a teen-age mother, who was born of a teen-age mother.

I understand. I know abandonment, and people being mean to you, and saying you're nothing and nobody and can never be anything.

I understand. Jesse Jackson is my third name. I'm adopted. When I had no name, my grandmother gave me her name. My name was Jesse Burns until I was 12. So I wouldn't have a blank space, she gave me a name to hold me over. I understand when nobody knows your name. I understand when you have no name.

I understand. I wasn't born in the hospital. Mama didn't have insurance. I was born in the bed at the house. I really do understand. Born in a three-room house, bathroom in the backyard, slop jar by the bed, no hot and cold running water.

I understand. Wallpaper used for decoration? No. For a windbreaker. I understand. I'm a working person's person. That's why I understand you whether you're black or white.

I understand work. I was not born with a silver spoon in my mouth. I had a shovel programmed for my hand.

My mother, a working woman. So many of the days she went to work early, with runs in her stockings. She knew better, but she wore runs in her stockings so that my brother and I could have matching socks and not be laughed at at school. I understand.

At 3 o'clock on Thanksgiving Day, we couldn't eat turkey because momma was preparing somebody else's turkey at 3 o'clock. We had to play football to entertain ourselves. And then around 6 o'clock she would get off the Alta Vista bus and we would bring up the leftovers and eat our turkey — leftovers, the carcass, the cranberries — around 8 o'clock at night. I really do understand.

Every one of these funny labels they put on you, those of you who are watching this broadcast tonight in the projects, on the corners, I understand. Call you outcast, low down, you can't make it, you're nothing, you're from nobody, subclass, underclass; when you see Jesse Jackson, when my name goes in nomination, your name goes in nomination.

I was born in the slum, but the slum was not born in me. And it wasn't born in you, and you can make it.

Wherever you are tonight, you can make it. Hold your head high, stick your chest out. You can make it. It gets dark sometimes, but the morning comes. Don't you surrender. Suffering breeds character, character breeds faith. In the end faith will not disappoint.

You must not surrender. You may or may not get there but just know that you're qualified. And you hold on, and hold out. We must never surrender. America will get better and better.

Keep hope alive!

Keep hope alive!

Keep hope alive!

On tomorrow night and beyond, keep hope alive! I love you very much. I love you very much.

——— 9.18 ———

BLACKS THREE TIMES AS LIKELY AS WHITES TO CONTRACT AIDS
U.S. Centers for Disease Control

From the very beginning of the Acquired Immune Deficiency Syndrome (AIDS) epidemic, African Americans were disproportionately impacted. The nation's attention focused mainly on the disease's effect on gay men, ignoring the fact that a greatly disproportionate number of those men were African Americans. Along with them, injection drug users — another high-risk group for contracting HIV, the virus that causes AIDS — were largely black. But while the white gay community rallied to fight the epidemic, mainstream black organizations and leaders, with the notable exception of Jesse Jackson, paid scant attention to the virus. With resources dwindling, and drugs and gang violence plaguing black cities, those leaders either were unable or unwilling to see AIDS as the looming threat it was; ironically, public health officials now agree that the epidemic's rampant spread in the black community was largely an outgrowth of the drug and poverty problems of the 1980s. The U.S. Centers for Disease Control, meanwhile, tracked the epidemic's attack on African Americans. In October 1986, in its regular report on disease in the country, the CDC published shocking statistics about the spread of AIDS beyond gay men and drug users. Black women, it said, accounted for half of all AIDS cases among women. Blacks and Latinos in general were three times as likely to contract the virus as were whites. It was only the beginning. By the end of the century, the CDC would estimate 1 in 50 black men and 1 in 160 black women were HIV positive.

In the period June 1, 1981-September 8, 1986, physicians and health departments in the United States notified CDC of 24,576 patients meeting the AIDS case definition for national reporting. Of these, 6,192 (25%) were black and 3,488 (14%) were Hispanic, whereas these groups represent only 12% and 6%, respectively, of the U.S. population. The proportion of cases by racial/ethnic group has remained relatively constant over time, but the number of reported cases of AIDS among persons of all racial and ethnic backgrounds continues to rise.

Adult Patients. The race and ethnicity was known for 24,102 adult AIDS patients greater than or equal to 15 years of age; 14,554 (60%) of these patients were non-Hispanic whites; 5,988 (25%), blacks; 3,411 (14%), Hispanics; and 149 (1%), members of other racial/ethnic groups. The overall cumulative incidences for black and Hispanic adults were 3.1 and 3.4 times, respectively, that for whites.

Black and Hispanic adults with AIDS were more likely than white adult AIDS patients to reside in New York, New Jersey, or Florida: 62% and 65% of the black and Hispanic patients, respectively, resided in these three states, as did 33% of white patients. Cumulative incidences in these states for blacks and Hispanics were from 2.5 to 9.0 times those for whites. Of the black and Hispanic patients from New York and New Jersey, approximately half were intravenous (IV) drug abusers. Of the black patients from Florida, 40% were born in Haiti.

Among men, blacks and Hispanics accounted for 23% and 14%, respectively, of the 22,468 male AIDS patients. However, among women, blacks and Hispanics accounted for 51% and 21%, respectively, of the 1,634 female patients. Cumulative incidences for black and Hispanic women were 13.3 and 11.1 times, respectively, the incidence for white women.

The distribution of AIDS cases by race/ethnicity differed by recognized transmission categories for AIDS. Homosexual or bisexual men who had AIDS and patients who acquired AIDS from blood or blood products were predominately white, whereas patients with a history of IV drug abuse or heterosexual contact with persons at increased risk for acquiring AIDS, and persons with no identified mode of transmission were predominately black or Hispanic. The proportion of blacks or Hispanics with AIDS was relatively high (in terms of their proportions in the overall U.S. population) in all transmission categories with the exception of hemophilia.

The racial/ethnic distribution of homosexual/ bisexual patients differed from that of heterosexual patients. Among homosexual/bisexual male AIDS patients, 16% were black; 11%, Hispanic; and 73%, white. Among heterosexual AIDS patients in all other transmission categories, 50% were black; 25%, Hispanic; and 25%, white.

Pediatric Patients. Of the 350 AIDS patients who were children (i.e., 15 years of age) and whose race/ethnicity was known, 204 (58%) were black and 77 (22%) were Hispanic. The overall cumulative incidences for black and Hispanic children were 15.1 and 9.1 times, respectively, the incidence for white children.

As with black and Hispanic adult AIDS patients, black and Hispanic children with AIDS were more likely than white children with AIDS to reside in New York, New Jersey, or Florida. Of the black and Hispanic children with AIDS, 73% and 70%, respectively, lived in New York, New Jersey, or Florida. Of the 68 white children with AIDS, 40% also lived in one of those three states.

The distribution of pediatric AIDS cases by race/ethnicity varied by transmission category. Ninety percent of the children with perinatally acquired AIDS compared with 42% of the children with hemophilia- or transfusion-associated AIDS were black or Hispanic. The observation that children with perinatally acquired AIDS (mother-to-infant transmission) were predominately black or Hispanic is consistent with the high proportion (75%) of heterosexual adults who are black or Hispanic. As with adults, the proportion of pediatric patients who were black or Hispanic was highest in the transmission categories associated with IV drug abuse by at least one of the parents. Reported by AIDS Program, Center for Infectious Diseases, CDC.

—————— 9.19 ——————

COMING OUT

Linda Villarosa

In 1991, *Essence* magazine senior editor Linda Villarosa published an article in which she came out to readers as a lesbian. *Essence* was and is one of only a few national black magazines, and is considered one of the era's most significant black publications. The essay ran in the magazine's Mother's Day issue, and Villarosa's mother, Clara, penned a companion essay on her own journey to acceptance of her daughter's sexuality. The magazine reportedly received more letters on this story than any it had run to date, primarily supportive and positive. At a time when the African-American community boasted few openly gay public figures, the article was a bold stroke. It challenged the widespread notion within the community that sexual identity was an issue relevant only to white people. Further, the article reflected the widening scope of what the black community deemed "acceptable," a widening that had begun in the Harlem Renaissance. Decades later, African Americans, from feminists to conservatives to gays and lesbians, were still debating, and allowing for varied definitions of, blackness.

THE MODEL DAUGHTER: *Linda*
Growing up, I was what you'd call a "good girl." I minded my parents, sent Hallmark cards to all my great-aunts on their birthdays, said the Pledge of Allegiance and never got into trouble. Other kids probably thought I was nauseating.

In high school I was a cheerleader, the president of the senior class, captain of the track team, an honor student and a prom-queen candidate, and I still managed to work evenings and weekends. I had a nice boyfriend, and I wanted to marry him, have two children, live near my parents and have a career as a lawyer or writer, or maybe even a social worker like my mother.

I seemed just like all the other girls I knew who were my age — only more of a goody-goody. But somehow deep inside I suspected I was different.

BECOMING A MOTHER: *Clara*
At 3 P.M. on January 9, 1959, the doctor smiled at me and said, "You have a beautiful baby girl." And beautiful my baby was, dainty and small, a cute little thing I could dress up, play with and read to. Her father and I named her Linda, which in Spanish means pretty. In my life, all was well. I had completed my master's in psychiatric social work. I had worked for five years before having the baby, so that I could stay at home with her once I had her. Three years later, just as we'd planned, I had another baby.

As Linda grew up she remained petite and feminine. Whenever we went out, people remarked on her beauty and grace. She had large hazel eyes that stared both knowingly and inquisitively, and I enjoyed dressing her up in frilly dresses and fixing her hair in two bouncy ponytails. She loved little girl activities, like having tea parties and playing house with real chores. When she was older she modeled in fashion shows, demonstrating poise and confidence.

Linda dated in high school, and by that time I was back at work, surrounded by friends. The highlight of those years for me was Linda's senior prom. I made her a beautiful peach-colored dress, and that prom night, when her steady boyfriend picked her up, I was so proud of my beautiful daughter. As I watched her leave, I fantasized about her being happily married, a mother, with me a happy grandmother.

I used to think of Linda as my "normal" child. That turned out to be totally unrealistic, because all the other parents were having problems with their adolescents. But Linda was so good.

FACING UP TO IT: *Linda*

Even in high school I was attracted to other girls. I loved slumber parties, cheerleading practice, basketball and track workouts and other all-girl activities. Sometimes I assumed my feelings were normal, just another one of those adolescent things you don't really understand, you're ashamed of and don't tell a soul.

By the time I reached my sophomore year in college, my high school boyfriend and I had broken up. It was very difficult for me for a few months because he had been my first love and we had been — and remain — good friends. We had also fumbled through losing our virginity together, and he was a loving, caring and creative sexual partner and I liked having sex with him. I continued to date men. The men I dated were handsome and outgoing and my parents approved of them. I felt that I was sleepwalking, though, going through the motions. One of my boyfriends was really cute but he was boring. All he talked about was his fraternity. But I wanted to have a boyfriend so I could be like everybody else. I wasn't very attentive, I didn't dress up or wear makeup and I wasn't particularly excited about sex. And of course this lackadaisical atti-

tude made me more attractive because guys thought I was a challenge.

Then everything changed. I became increasingly attracted to Laura, one of my female instructors. She was bright and funny and she listened with interest to everything I said. Eventually I admitted to myself that I was attracted to this woman. Finally, after I had spent five months worshiping her in the classroom, we spent a day together. After that I realized I was in love. That realization was all at once frightening, horrifying, gratifying and relieving. At that point I began to think of myself as bisexual, something that seemed cool and hip. I didn't think about what this might mean to my life, I didn't wonder why I was this way, I didn't contemplate whether gay people were good or bad or would go to heaven or be sweating it out in hell. All I could think of was how nice it felt to truly love someone and admit it.

SUSPICION: *Clara*

Once Linda got to college, I began to notice that she didn't have much romantic interest in men. I would frequently ask about any man that she mentioned even casually, but she never really seemed to care. Nor did she seem to care about clothes and makeup. I tried not to get upset, thinking that she didn't have much time to date or worry about her appearance because she was too busy with her classes and her job.

By her second year in college, I had gone from being quietly worried to being truly panicked about Linda. She spoke about men only in platonic ways, and I noticed that an inordinate amount of her conversation focused on one of her female instructors, Laura. Linda brought Laura to dinner, and my suspicions were heightened because Laura appeared more "butch" than feminine. The way the two interacted and the things they talked about made it clear to me that they were spending a lot of time together. My husband and I exchanged looks across the dinner table. After they left, I just had to say it. I turned to my husband and asked, "Did you see it?," He said yes. I said,

"Do you think Laura is gay?!" He did. Finally we spoke the unspeakable: Could our daughter be a lesbian? …

TRYING TO COME OUT OF HIDING: *Linda* …

After I realized I was gay, I had to reinvent myself and the image of my life. I had to let go of everything I thought I was supposed to have, such as a beautiful wedding. I had to figure out who I was apart from the straight world I no longer felt I belonged in. This was a very difficult and lonely period because I couldn't tell anyone. Finally, after two years, I told my best friend.

I didn't know any other gay women besides my lover and a few of her friends. And like everybody else I had been brought up on a steady diet of antigay stereotypes. I felt like one of society's outcasts. I no longer fit into heterosexual society, and I didn't want to fit into the gay community — whatever and wherever it was. I assumed there were only a handful of other lesbians in the world, all short, fat, unattractive women with bad haircuts. All they did was play softball and go to feminist group meetings and try to hide who they were from their coworkers, friends and family. It went without saying that they all hated men. There was a reason these girls didn't have a man. Because I wasn't like this, I wasn't too sure who I was.

So unsure of myself, I was deathly afraid of rejection. I just kept my mouth shut about my sexuality and quietly locked myself away in the closet. I tried to straddle both worlds, happy with my lover and pretending to be accepting of my new life, but secretly scared and insecure. Like one of those tragic mulattoes of the past, I was passing but always petrified that someone would uncover my secret. I didn't stop hanging with my friends, I simply stopped talking about myself and steered clear of any personal questions. I listened to dyke and fag jokes and sometimes even laughed along. I went to weddings and would cry, always attributing it to happiness, not loss.

FEELING THE PAIN: *Clara*

Despite my hopes, the nightmare was not ending. And the more Linda began to try to explore herself and identity as a lesbian, the angrier I got, and now not at Laura anymore, but at her. How could my daughter do this to me? I was so embarrassed. I was paranoid, thinking that everyone in my community knew and that they were laughing at me, at my failure as a parent. It was doubly humiliating for me — trained as an adolescent therapist — to have raised a daughter who had "gone wrong."

I was devastated and blamed myself. I searched through the past to determine what I had done to make this happen to her. At this point I was in the middle of a divorce. I was also searching for my purpose in life, but I wasn't finding it. People had said I have an aggressive personality, and I wondered if Linda was a lesbian because of my behavior. Maybe I gave her the impression that I hated men. I felt my whole world collapsing.

RESOLUTION AND ACCEPTANCE: *Linda*

… It has been important for me, too, to realize that being gay is not a curse; in fact, it's been an awakening. I've become more introspective and tolerant of people who are different. Before I "came out," I had always tried to do everything right, everything according to plan — society's plan and my parents' plan — but not my own plan because I didn't really have one. And that behavior — be a good girl, go to college, get married, have a child — was valued by society. So when I turned out to be different, I assumed something was wrong with me. I had no reason to question the world I was brought up in, much less to try to understand anyone who wasn't thinking and behaving exactly the way I was. When I realized I wasn't going to live in the suburbs, I was free to forge my own path and not get stuck in a Black society thing — wearing nice shoes and going to club meetings.

But having felt like an outcast, separate from everyone Black and white, has made me empathize with others who have felt the same way for whatever reason.

Most important, I've also stopped being so afraid of being rejected by people who find out I'm gay. The closet is dark and lonely and not somewhere I plan to hide away. The most important people in my life already know, and they still accept me. No matter how disappointed and angry my mother felt, she never stopped loving me. She and the rest of my family made it okay for me to be me. ...

——— 9.20 ———

'I WILL NOT PROVIDE THE ROPE FOR MY OWN LYNCHING'

Clarence Thomas and Anita Hill

In September 1991, President George Bush appointed District Court Judge Clarence Thomas to fill retiring Supreme Court Justice Thurgood Marshall's seat. Marshall, the first and only black justice, was a bastion of liberal thought, a living embodiment of the Civil Rights Movement's legal battles. Thomas was fiercely conservative. Despite having led the Equal Employment Opportunity Commission, he fervently opposed affirmative action and a host of other federal Civil Rights programs. But, he was black. His confirmation, therefore, was expected to be a formality. Then news leaked that a former employee named Anita Hill had charged Thomas with sexual harassment when interviewed by agents conducting his background check. The ensuing Senate Judiciary Committee hearings were bitter and divisive. Television networks broadcast them in primetime, and the country was gripped in one of its first national conversations about sexual harassment. Opinion, both in the public and on Capitol Hill, remained split down the party line. And many who supported Thomas believed Hill to be a traitor or a liar or both. As is frequently the case in sexual harassment charges, she often found herself deflecting attacks on her behavior rather than focusing on that of Thomas. Thomas, meanwhile, handled the hearings masterfully. He painted himself as a victim and, ironically, appealed to the nation's moral consensus against racial prejudice by calling the hearings a lynching. Ultimately, Thomas was confirmed by a party-line vote.

A. Clarence Thomas's statement in response to the charges

Mr. Chairman, Senator Thurmond, members of the committee. As excruciatingly difficult as the last two weeks have been, I welcome the opportunity to clear my name today. No one other than my wife and Senator Danforth, to whom I read this statement at 6:30 a.m. has seen or heard this statement. No handlers, no advisors. first I learned of the allegations by Professor Anita Hill was on September 25, 1991, when the FBI came to my home to investigate her allegations. When informed by the FBI agent of the nature of the allegations and the person making them, I was shocked, surprised, hurt and enormously saddened. I have not been the same since that day.

For almost a decade my responsibilities included enforcing the rights of victims of sexual harassment. As a boss, as a friend, and as a human being I was proud that I had never had such an allegation leveled against me, even as I sought to promote women and minorities into non-traditional jobs.

In addition, several of my friends who are women have confided in me about the horror of harassment on the job or elsewhere. I thought I really understood the anguish, the fears, the doubts, the seriousness of the matter. But since September 25th, I have suffered immensely as these very serious charges were leveled against me. I have been racking my brains and eating my insides out trying to think of what I could have said or done to Anita Hill to lead her to allege that I was interested in her in more than a professional way and that I talked with her about pornographic or X-rated films.

Contrary to some press reports, I categorically denied all of the allegations and denied that I ever attempted to date Anita Hill when first interviewed by the FBI. I strongly reaffirm that denial. ...

At EEOC, our relationship was more distant and our contacts less frequent as a result of the increased size of my personal staff and the dramatic increase and diversity of my day-to-day responsibilities. Upon reflection, I recall that she seemed to have had some difficulty adjusting to this change in her role. In any case, our relationship remained both cordial and professional.

At no time did I become aware, either directly or indirectly, that she felt I had said or done anything to change the cordial nature of our relationship. I detected nothing from her or from my staff, or from Gil Hardy, our mutual friend, with whom I maintained regular contact. I am certain that had any statement or conduct on my part been brought to my attention I would remember it clearly because of the nature and seriousness of such conduct, as well as my adamant opposition to sex discrimination and sexual harassment. But there were no such statements.

In the spring of 1983, Mr. Charles Kothe contacted me to speak at the Law School at Oral Roberts University in Tulsa, Oklahoma. Anita Hill, who is from Oklahoma, accompanied me on that trip. It was not unusual that individuals on my staff would travel with me occasionally. Anita Hill accompanied me on that trip primarily because this was an opportunity to combine business and a visit to her home.

As I recall, during our visit at Oral Roberts University, Mr. Kothe mentioned to me the possibility of approaching Anita Hill to join the faculty at Oral Roberts University Law School. I encouraged him to do so and noted to him, as I recall, that Anita Hill would do well in teaching. I recommended her highly and she eventually was offered a teaching position. …

Throughout the time that Anita Hill worked with me I treated her as I treated my other special assistants. I tried to treat them all cordially, professionally, and respectfully and I tried to support them in their endeavors and be interested in and supportive of their success. I had no reason or basis to believe my relationship with Anita Hill was anything but this way until the FBI visited me a little more than two weeks ago.

I find it particularly troubling that she never raised any hint that she was uncomfortable with me. She did not raise or mention it when considering moving with me to EEOC from the Department of Education, and she'd never raised it with me when she left EEOC and was moving on in her life. And, to my fullest knowledge, she did not speak to any other women working with or around me who would feel comfortable enough to raise it with me, especially Diane Holt, to whom she seemed closest on my personal staff. Nor did she raise it with mutual friends such as Linda Jackson and Gil Hardy.

This is a person I have helped at every turn in the road since we met. She seemed to appreciate the continued cordial relationship we had since day one. She sought my advice and counsel, as did virtually all of the members of my personal staff.

During my tenure in the executive branch as a manager, as a policymaker, and as a person, I have adamantly condemned sex harassment. There is no member of this Committee or this Senate who feels stronger about sex harassment than I do. As a manager, I made every effort to take swift and decisive action when sex harassment raised or reared its ugly head. The fact that I feel so very strongly about sex harassment and spoke loudly at EEOC has made these allegations doubly hard on me. I cannot imagine anything that I said or did to Anita Hill that could have been mistaken for sexual harassment.

But with that said, if there is anything that I have said that has been misconstrued by Anita Hill or anyone else to be sexual harassment, then I can say that I am so very sorry and I wish I had known. If I did know, I would have stopped immediately and I would not, as I've done over the past two weeks, have to tear away at myself, trying to think of what I could possibly have done. But I have not said or done the things that Anita Hill has alleged. God has gotten me through the days since September 25th, and he is my judge.

Mr. Chairman, something has happened to me in the dark days that have followed since the FBI agents informed me about these allegations. And the days have grown darker as this very serious, very explosive, and very sensitive allegation — or these sensitive allegations were selectively leaked in a distorted way to the media over the past weekend. As if the confidential allegations themselves were not enough, this apparently calculated public disclosure has caused me, my family, and my friends enormous pain and great harm. I have never in all my life felt such hurt, such pain, such agony. My family and I have been done a grave and irreparable injustice.

During the past two weeks, I lost the belief that if I did my best all would work out. I called upon the strength that helped me get here from Pin Point, and it was all sapped out of me. It was sapped out of me because Anita Hill was a person I considered a friend whom I admired and thought I had treated fairly and with the utmost respect. Perhaps I could have been — better weathered this if it was from someone else. But here was someone I truly felt I had done my best with. Though I am by no means a perfect person, no means, I have not done what she has alleged, and I still don't know what I could possibly have done to cause her to make these allegations.

When I stood next to the President in Kennebunkport being nominated to the Supreme Court of the United States, that was a high honor; but as I sit here before you 103 days later, that honor has been crushed. From the very beginning, charges were leveled against me from the shadows, charges of drug abuse, anti-Semitism, wife beating, drug use by family members, that I was a quota appointment, confirmation conversion, and much, much more. And now, this.

I have complied with the rules. I responded to a document request that produced over 30,000 pages of documents, and I have testified for five full days under oath. I have endured this ordeal for 103 days. Reporters sneaking into my garage to examine books I read. Reporters and interest groups swarming over divorce papers looking for dirt. Unnamed people starting preposterous and damaging rumors. Calls all over the country specifically requesting dirt.

This is not American; this is Kafkaesque. It has got to stop. It must stop for the benefit of future nominees and our country. Enough is enough.

I'm not going to allow myself to be further humiliated in order to be confirmed. I am here specifically to respond to allegations of sex harassment in the workplace. I am not here to be further humiliated by this committee or anyone else, or to put my private life on display for prurient interests or other reasons. I will not allow this committee or anyone else to probe into my private life. This is not what America is all about. To ask me to do that would be to ask me to go beyond fundamental fairness.

Yesterday I called my mother. She was confined to her bed, unable to work and unable to stop crying. Enough is enough.

Mr. Chairman, in my 43 years on this earth I have been able with the help of others and with the help of God to defy poverty, avoid prison, overcome segregation, bigotry, racism and obtain one of the finest educations available in this country, but I have not been able to overcome this process. This is worse than any obstacle or anything that I have ever faced.

Throughout my life I have been energized by the expectation and the hope that in this country I would be treated fairly in all endeavors. When there was segregation I hoped there would be fairness one day or some day. When there was bigotry and prejudice, I hoped that there would be tolerance and understanding some day.

Mr. Chairman, I am proud of my life, proud of what I have done and what I have accomplished, proud of my family and this process, this process is trying to destroy it all. No job is worth what I have been through, no job. No horror in my life has been so debilitating. Confirm me if you want. Don't confirm me if you are so led, but let this process end. Let me and my family regain our lives.

I never asked to be nominated. It was an honor. Little did I know the price, but it is too high.

I enjoy and appreciate my current position and I am comfortable with the prospect of returning to my work as a judge on the US Court of Appeals for the DC Circuit and to my friends there. Each of these positions is public service and I have given at the office. I want my life and my family's life back, and I want them returned expeditiously.

I have experienced the exhilaration of new heights from the moment I was called to Kennebunkport by the President to have lunch and he nominated me. That was the high point. At that time, I was told eye-to-eye that, "Clarence, you made it this far on merit. The rest is going to be politics." And it surely has been.

There have been other highs. The outpouring of support from my friends of long standing; a bonding like I have never experienced with my old boss, Senator Danforth; the wonderful support of those who have worked with me. There have been prayers said for my family and me by people I know and people I will never meet, prayers that were heard and that sustained not only me, but also my wife and my entire family.

Instead of understanding and appreciating the great honor bestowed upon me, I find myself here today defending my name, my integrity, because somehow select portions of confidential documents dealing with this matter were leaked to the public.

Mr. Chairman, I am a victim of this process. My name has been harmed. My integrity has been harmed. My character has been harmed. My family has been harmed. My friends have been harmed. There is nothing this committee, this body, or this country can do to give me my good name back. Nothing.

I will not provide the rope for my own lynching or for further humiliation. I am not going to engage in discussions nor will I submit to roving questions of what goes on in the most intimate parts of my private life or the sanctity of my bedroom. These are the most intimate parts of my privacy, and they will remain just that, private.

B. Anita Hill's opening statement

… In 1981, I was introduced to now Judge Thomas by a mutual friend. Judge Thomas told me that he was anticipating a political appointment, and he asked if I would be interested in working with him. He was, in fact, appointed as Assistant Secretary of Education for Civil Rights. After he had taken that post, he asked if I would become his assistant, and I accepted that position.

In my early period there, I had two major projects. The first was an article I wrote for Judge Thomas' signature on the education of minority students. The second was the organization of a seminar on high-risk students which was abandoned because Judge Thomas transferred to the EEOC where he became the chairman of that office.

During this period at the Department of Education, my working relationship with Judge Thomas was positive. I had a good deal of responsibility and independence. I thought he respected my work and that he trusted my judgment. After approximately three months of working there, he asked me to go out socially with him.

What happened next and telling the world about it are the two most difficult things — experiences of my life. It is only after a great deal of agonizing consideration and sleepless number — a great number of sleepless nights that I am able to talk of these unpleasant matters to anyone but my close friends.

I declined the invitation to go out socially with him and explained to him that I thought it would jeopardize what at the time I considered to be a very good working relationship. I had a normal social life with other men outside of the office. I believed then, as now, that having a social relationship with a person who was supervising my work would be ill-advised. I was very uncomfortable with the idea and told him so.

I thought that by saying no and explaining my reasons my employer would abandon his social suggestions. However, to my regret, in the following few weeks, he continued to ask me out on several occasions. He pressed me to justify my reasons for saying no to him. These incidents took place in his office or mine. They were in the form of private conversations which would not have been overheard by anyone else.

My working relationship became even more strained when Judge Thomas began to use work situations to discuss sex. On these occasions, he would call me into his office for reports on education issues and projects, or he might suggest that, because of the time pressures of his schedule, we go to lunch to a government cafeteria. After a brief discussion of work, he would turn the conversation to a discussion of sexual matters.

His conversations were very vivid. He spoke about acts that he had seen in pornographic films involving such matters as women having sex with animals and films showing group sex or rape scenes. He talked about pornographic materials depicting individuals with large penises or large breasts involved in various sex acts. On several occasions, Thomas told me graphically of his own sexual prowess.

Because I was extremely uncomfortable talking about sex with him at all and particularly in such a graphic way, I told him that I did not want to talk about these subjects. I would also try to change the subject to education matters or to nonsexual personal matters such as his background or his beliefs. My efforts to change the subject were rarely successful.

Throughout the period of these conversations, he also from time to time asked me for social engagements. My reaction to these conversations was to avoid them by eliminating opportunities for us to engage in extended conversations. This was difficult because at the time I was his only assistant at the Office of Education — or Office for Civil Rights.

During the latter part of my time at the Department of Education, the social pressures and any conversation of his offensive behavior ended. I began both to believe and hope that our working relationship could be a proper, cordial, and professional one.

When Judge Thomas was made chair of the EEOC, I needed to face the question of whether to go with him. I was asked to do so, and I did. The work itself was interesting, and at that time it appeared that the sexual overtures which had so troubled me had ended. I also faced the realistic fact that I had no alternative job. While I might have gone back to private practice, perhaps in my old firm or at another, I was dedicated to civil rights work, and my first choice was to be in that field. Moreover, the Department of Education itself was a dubious venture. President Reagan was seeking to abolish the entire department.

For my first months at the EEOC, where I continued to be an assistant to Judge Thomas, there were no sexual conversations or overtures. However, during the fall and winter of 1982, these began again. The comments were random and ranged from pressing me about why I didn't go out with him to remarks about my personal appearance. I remember his saying that some day I would have to tell him the real reason that I wouldn't go out with him.

He began to show displeasure in his tone and voice and his demeanor and his continued pressure for an explanation. He commented on what I was wearing in terms of whether it made me more or less sexually attractive. The incidents occurred in his inner office at the EEOC.

One of the oddest episodes I remember was an occasion in which Thomas was drinking a Coke in his office. He got up from the table at which we were working, went over to his desk to get the Coke, looked at the can and asked, "Who has put pubic hair on my Coke?" On other occasions, he referred to the size of his own penis as being larger than normal, and he also spoke on some occasions of the pleasures he had given to women with oral sex.

At this point, late 1982, I began to feel severe stress on the job. I began to be concerned that Clarence Thomas might take out his anger with me by degrading me or not giving me important assignments. I also thought that he might find an excuse for dismissing me.

In January of 1983, I began looking for another job. I was handicapped because I feared that, if he found out, he might make it difficult for me to find other employment and I might be dismissed from the job I had. Another factor that made my search more difficult was that there was a period — this was during a period of a hiring freeze in the government. In February of 1983, I was hospitalized for five days on an emergency basis for acute stomach pain which I attributed to stress on the job.

Once out of the hospital, I became more committed to find other employment and sought further to minimize my contact with Thomas. This became easier when Allison Duncan became office director, because most of my work was then funneled through her and I had contact with Clarence Thomas mostly in staff meetings.

In the spring of 1983, an opportunity to teach at Oral Roberts University opened up. I participated in a seminar — taught an afternoon session and seminar at Oral Roberts University. The dean of the university saw me teaching and inquired as to whether I would be interested in furthering — pursuing a career in teaching, beginning at Oral Roberts University. I agreed to take the job in large part because of my desire to escape the pressures I felt at the EEOC due to Judge Thomas.

When I informed him that I was leaving in July, I recall that his response was that now I would no longer have an excuse for not going out with him. I told him that I still preferred not to do so. At some time after that meeting, he asked if he could take me to dinner at the end of the term. When I declined, he assured me that the dinner was a professional courtesy only and not a social invitation. I reluctantly agreed to accept that invitation, but only if it was at the very end of a working day.

On, as I recall, the last day of my employment at the EEOC in the summer of 1983, I did have dinner with Clarence Thomas. We went directly from work to a restaurant near the office. We talked about the work I had done, both at education and at the EEOC. He told me that he was pleased with all of it except for an article and speech that I had done for him while we were at the Office for Civil Rights. Finally, he made a comment that I will vividly remember. He said that if I ever told anyone of his behavior that it would ruin his career. This was not an apology, nor was it an explanation. That was his last remark about the possibility of our going out or reference to his behavior. …

It is only after a great deal of agonizing consideration that I am able to talk of these unpleasant matters to anyone except my closest friends. As I've said before, these last few days have been very trying and very hard for me and it hasn't just been the last few days this week. It has actually been over a month now that I have been under the strain of this issue.

Telling the world is the most difficult experience of my life, but it is very close to having to live through the experience that occasioned this meeting. I may have used poor judgment early on in my relationship with this issue. I was aware, however, that telling at any point in my career could adversely affect my future career. And I did not want early on to burn all the bridges to the EEOC.

As I said, I may have used poor judgment. Perhaps I should have taken angry or even militant steps, both when I was in the agency, or after I left it. But I must confess to the world that the course that I took seemed the better as well as the easier approach.

I declined any comment to newspapers, but later when Senate staff asked me about these matters I felt I had a duty to report. I have no personal vendetta against Clarence Thomas. I seek only to provide the committee with information which it may regard as relevant.

It would have been more comfortable to remain silent. I took no initiative to inform anyone. But when I was asked by a representative of this committee to report my experience, I felt that I had to tell the truth. I could not keep silent.

—— 9.21 ——

'I FELT EACH ONE OF THOSE NOT GUILTYS'

Assault on Rodney King and 1992 Riots

On March 3, 1991, four Los Angeles Police Department officers pulled over Rodney King, an African-American man, for speeding and driving erratically. According to the officers, King appeared to be on drugs and resisted arrest. Therefore, they later testified, they had to shock him repeatedly with a stun gun and deliver between 53 and 56 blows with their nightsticks, fists and feet in order to subdue him. An area resident, George Holliday, happened to be nearby with a home video recorder and caught the entire incident on film. Within days, the tape had been broadcast throughout the world. African Americans nationwide were outraged. King's eye-socket bone, along with 11 others at the base of his skull, was broken. In his report on the incident, unaware of the videotape, ranking officer Sgt. Stacey Koon noted King suffered injuries "of a minor nature. … Subject oblivious to pain." LAPD Chief Daryl Gates, who had presided over the department's 1980s escalation in its campaign to fight gangs and drugs, stood behind Koon and the other officers.

In Los Angeles, blacks believed it was finally proof to the world that their decades-old charges of rampant anti–black and Latino police brutality were true. Below is the transcript of police radio conversations just prior to and following the beating, published in the *Los Angeles Times* two weeks after it took place. In it, two of the officers involved, Laurence Powell and Timothy Wind, refer to a domestic dispute between two African Americans, the scene of which they had just left, as "right out of Gorillas in the Mist." The unidentified respondent then answers in mocking black vernacular. Given that the conversation was over a monitored police radio, it seemed to be proof of widespread and accepted racism in the department.

A. Transcript of police conversation

The following is the transcript of computer transmissions between squad cars and the watch commander's office of the Los Angeles Police Department's Foothill Division beginning at 12:29 a.m. and ending at 1:17 a.m. on March 3 — the morning Rodney King was beaten by officers at a traffic stop.

12:29 a.m. From unidentified foot patrol officers in Sunland-Tujunga to Officers Laurence M. Powell and Timothy Wind: "What are you up to? … We are up on the rock with [cars] L170, 82 and A89 on top of some abandon house with narco and BFMV [burglary from motor vehicle] suspects in it. … We are waiting for them to hit some places."

12:31 a.m. From Powell and Wind to the foot patrol officers: " … Sounds almost exciting as our last call. … It was right out of 'Gorillas in the Mist.'"

12:32 a.m. From the foot patrol officers to Powell and Wind: " … Ha ha ha ha. … Let me guess who be the parties."

12:32 a.m. From Powell and Wind to the foot patrol officers: " … I'm just trying to get through the night cause then I'm off for six, count them six, days. … Time for some serious bike riding."

12:32 a.m. From Powell and Wind to the foot patrol officers: " … Good guess."

12:34 a.m. From the foot patrol officers to Powell and Wind: " … You can't even get out of bed in the morning let alone bike ride. … I'll believe that when I see it. … I have one more then I'm off for four."

12:36 a.m. From Powell and Wind to the foot patrol officers: " … That's where your wrong. … I was up at 12:30 today. … I can't sleep that's the problem. … I need to get worn out."

12:43 a.m. From the foot patrol officer to Powell and Wind: " … But can you keep up. … Ha ha ha ha … People better know we are talking about bicycling and not something else or they will begin to wonder what these messages are about … Ha ha ha ha."

12:45 a.m. From Powell and Wind to the foot patrol officer: "Oh bicycling. … Of course."

12:47 a.m. From emergency board operator to all units: "CHP [California Highway Patrol] advises their officers are in pursuit of a vehicle failing to yield southbound Paxton-Foothill. … Vehicle is white Hyundai, license 2KFM102, now approaching Glenoaks. … Vehicle is now southbound Glenoaks-Paxton. ... Now passing Sylmar. ... Vehicle is now northbound Van Nuys-Bordon. ... Foothill RTO [radio-telephone operator] is taking over the broadcasting of the pursuit [car] 16A23 [Powell and Wind] is the primary unit. ... Now eastbound Van Nuys at Fulton. ... Stopped at a light southbound Van Nuys at Foothill. ... Two male black occupants. ... Vehicle still refusing to yield now eastbound Foothill at Osborne ..." Powell and Wind then got out of their car to investigate on Foothill east of Osborne. One of them subsequently broadcast a Code 4, meaning sufficient units were on scene and suspects were in custody at 12:59.

12:56 a.m. From Sgt. Stacy C. Koon to Foothill watch commander's office: " ... You just had a big time use of force ... tased and beat the suspect of CHP pursuit, big time."

12:57 a.m. From watch commander's office to Koon: "Oh well ... I'm sure the lizard didn't deserve it. ... Ha ha, I'll let them know, O.K."

1:11 a.m. From Koon to watch commander's office: " ... I'm gonna drop by the station for a fresh taser and darts ... please have desk have one ready."

1:11 a.m. From watch commander's office to Koon: "Okey doke on the ACC desk. ... You want extra darts??? It's got two."

1:12 a.m. From Powell and Wind to the foot patrol officer: " ... Ooops."

1:12 a.m. From the foot patrol to Powell and Wind: "Oops, what?"

1:13 a.m. From Powell and Wind to the foot patrol: "I haven't beaten anyone this bad in a long time."

1:15 a.m. From the foot patrol to Powell and Winds: "Oh not again. ... Why for you do that. ... I thought you agreed to chill out for awhile. ... What did he do? ..."

1:16 a.m. From Powell and Wind to the foot patrol: "I think he was dusted. ... Many broken bones later. ... After the pursuit ..."

1:17 a.m. From the foot patrol to Powell and Wind: "What pursuit? ..."

B. The Riots

Rodney King sued, and the officers were brought up on several charges. But on April 29, a predominantly white jury (there were no black members) acquitted all four officers, accepting the argument that they acted judiciously in self-defense. Commentators have debated hotly whether it was the correct verdict. But for black America, and particularly for blacks in Los Angeles, the point is moot. The tape proved true a widespread belief that law enforcement was there to contain, harass and abuse them rather than serve them. When the legal system still refused to believe that assertion, it lost its legitimacy altogether. Los Angeles Mayor Tom Bradley, an African American and former civil rights activist, summed up that feeling in the Los Angeles Times story below, stating, "The jury's verdict will never blind the world to what we saw on the videotape." Within hours of the verdict, some of the worst rioting in the past century erupted in Los Angeles. Several smaller riots flared up around the country.

All 4 in King Beating Acquitted
Violence Follows Verdicts
Guard Called Out
Trial: Governor deploys troops at mayor's request after arson, looting erupt. Ventura County jury apparently was not convinced that videotape told the whole story.
By: RICHARD A. SERRANO and TRACY WILKINSON
TIMES STAFF WRITERS
SIMI VALLEY — Four Los Angeles police officers won acquittals Wednesday in their trial for the beating of black motorist Rodney G. King, igniting renewed outrage over a racially-charged case that had triggered a national debate on police brutality. Hours after the verdicts were announced, angry demonstrators torched buildings, looted stores and assaulted passersby as civic leaders pleaded for calm. Gov. Pete Wilson deployed the National Guard at the request of Mayor Tom Bradley, who warned residents to "stay off the streets."

Bradley, in a late-night televised address to the city, said a curfew may be imposed tonight if the violence continues. Wilson's decision to send in the National Guard came after rioters touched off more than 150 fires, stormed police headquarters and trashed numerous downtown buildings. Sporadic gunfire flared in the streets, and heavy smoke rising from the fires forced the authorities to reroute landing patterns for aircraft at Los Angeles International Airport.

By late Wednesday night, authorities had linked four deaths and 106 injuries to the violence. Some people were pulled from their cars and beaten.

It was the largest rioting to erupt in Los Angeles since the Watts riots of 1965. ...

A visibly angry [Mayor] Bradley said he was left "speechless" by the "senseless" verdicts and urged the city to refrain from violence.

"The jury's verdict will never blind the world to what we saw on the videotape," Bradley said.

The not guilty verdicts by a Ventura County Superior Court jury — which included no blacks — were reached after seven days of deliberations. For three days, the jury forewoman said, the panel focused exclusively on a single count of assault against one of the officers. With the jury unable to reach a consensus, a mistrial was declared on that count by Judge Stanley M. Weisberg.

Except for the single deadlocked count, all four defendants, who are white, were acquitted on all counts. The unresolved count is an assault charge against Powell; prosecutors will announce May 15 whether they will retry the officer.

Upon hearing the verdicts, Briseno — who had testified that he believed his fellow officers were "out of control" when they beat and stomped King — leaped to his feet and hugged his attorney. Powell and his attorney, Michael Stone, hugged each other.

"I'm very happy," Powell told reporters. "But it's hard to be surprised. I felt all along that I was innocent. Now I know I'm innocent."

Attorney Darryl Mounger, who defended Koon, said he believed the verdict turned on "truth."

"He (Koon) wasn't doing anything but making an arrest."

Mounger added that the trial represented a "no-win" situation for all concerned. "Nobody wins," he said. "These officers have been punished enough. Rodney King got out of jail, where he should be, and instead he's going to win a million dollars (in a civil lawsuit)."

As Koon left the courthouse, angry bystanders shouted "Guilty!" and scuffled briefly with sheriff's deputies flanking the sergeant. Powell was greeted by a similar crowd that hurled rocks at him as he left.

The prosecutors, who had stared silently at their table during the reading of the verdicts, hung their heads and marched out of the courtroom.

"My reaction is shock first, then disappointment," said Deputy Dist. Atty. Terry White, the lead prosecutor in the case. "Obviously we feel the evidence warranted a conviction of the defendants and the jury disagreed with us."

The defense strategy turned on persuading the jury that King was a combative suspect who did not comply with officers' orders. Evidently, it worked.

"He refused to get out of the car," said one juror who was interviewed by *The Times*. "His two companions got out of the car and complied with all the orders and he just continued to fight. So the Police Department had no alternative. He was obviously a dangerous person. ... Mr. King was controlling the whole show with his actions."

Extraordinary secrecy measures surrounded the jury, which was sequestered throughout its deliberations. Members refused to talk to reporters after the verdicts were read in a packed, silent courtroom at the East County Courthouse.

"This experience has been an extremely difficult and stressful one, one that we have all agonized over a great deal," said a statement prepared by the jury forewoman, a 64-year-old military contracts manager. "We feel we have done the best job we could have done."

The statement was read by a court official after the jurors were whisked away in a Ventura County Sheriff's Department bus to a nearby

Travelodge where they had been sequestered during their deliberations.

There, they were escorted to pick up their bags, some of which had masking tape placed on tags to conceal their names and addresses.

The four defendants were acquitted on one count of assault with a deadly weapon. All except Powell were acquitted of assault under the color of authority; the jury deadlocked 8 to 4 favoring acquittal on this count for Powell. He may face a new trial on that count.

Powell and Koon were acquitted of filing a false police report. Koon also was found not guilty of acting as an accessory after the fact. King's attorney, Steve Lerman, was furious with the verdicts.

"It says it's OK to beat somebody on the ground and beat the crap out of him," Lerman said. "They (the jurors) chose to ignore and disregard the fundamental issue: The issue of brutal, vicious felonious assault against this man. There is nothing Rodney King did to deserve this fate, and (the defendants) are walking out as heroes.

"The fact that maybe 12 white jurors are not going to convict four white cops, it may be as basic as that." …

Throughout Los Angeles on Wednesday, residents who sat glued to their television sets to watch the delivering of the verdicts expressed astonishment.

"The jury apparently didn't see and hear the same trial I heard," said Inglewood resident Terry Coleman, 49, a former police officer who estimates that he saw 95% of the trial on television. "The verdict's just as racist as what happened that night. I'm ashamed to be from Los Angeles. I'm happy I don't have a uniform anymore.

"I feel like I did when I heard that Martin Luther King died," added Coleman, who is black. "I felt each of those not guiltys — each one of them." …

—————— 9.22 ——————
'LEARNING TO TALK OF RACE'
Cornel West

Then-Princeton University Director of African-American Studies and cultural critic Cornel West responded to the Rodney King riots by offering a redefinition of what took place. In a *New York Times Magazine* essay published a few months after the affair, West argued that the riots were neither traditional race riots nor directly related to Rodney King. Both racial animosity and King's assault, he writes, were merely triggers to unleash a larger rage stemming from the tensions associated with life in post-industrial cities. America's inability to either understand or confront those tensions, however, is a result of its failure to confront its racism. A massive social divide remains because, rather than approach race with an intent to deal with white society's deficiencies, the nation has collectively chosen to address the problems presented by black people — problems such as riots. To West, that divide is America's intellectual barrier to understanding, itself. West is a luminary among the contemporary crop of black intellectuals, and his observations on race in America often echo the crux of this piece: America has never confronted the profound impact race and racism have had, and continue to have, on its cultural and political makeup. Until it does, the nation will struggle to understand itself and its challenges.

What happened in Los Angeles this past April was neither a race riot nor a class rebellion. Rather, this monumental upheaval was a multiracial, trans-class and largely male display of justified social rage. For all its ugly, xenophobic resentment, its air of adolescent carnival and its downright barbaric behavior, it signified the sense of powerlessness in American society. Glib attempts to reduce its meaning to the pathologies of the black underclass, the criminal actions of hoodlums or the political revolt of the oppressed urban masses miss the mark. Of those arrested, only 36 percent were black, more than a third had full-time jobs and most claimed to shun political affiliation. What we witnessed in Los Angeles was the consequence of a lethal linkage of economic decline, cultural decay and political lethargy in American life. Race was the visible catalyst, not the underlying cause.

The meaning of the earthshaking events in Los Angeles is difficult to grasp because most of us remain trapped in the narrow framework of the dominant liberal and conservative views of race in America, which with its worn-out vocabulary leaves us intellectually debilitated, morally disempowered and personally depressed. The astonishing disappearance of the event from public dialogue is testimony to just how painful and distressing a serious engagement with race is. Our truncated public discussions of race suppress the best of who and what we are as a people because they fail to confront the complexity of the issue in a candid and critical manner. The predictable pitting of liberals against conservatives, Great Society Democrats against self-help Republicans, reinforces intellectual parochialism and political paralysis.

The liberal notion that more government programs can solve the problems is simplistic — precisely because it focuses solely on the economic dimension. And the conservative idea that what is needed is a change in the moral behavior of poor black urban dwellers (especially poor black men, who, they say, should stay married, support their children and stop committing so much crime) highlights immoral actions while ignoring public responsibility for the immoral circumstances that haunt our fellow citizens.

The common denominator of these views of race is that each still sees black people as a "problem people," in the words of Dorothy Height, president of the National Council of Negro Women, rather than as fellow American citizens with problems. Her words echo the poignant "unasked question" of W. E. B. Du Bois, who wrote: "They approach me in a half-hesitant sort of way, eye me curiously or compassionately, and then instead of saying directly, How does it feel to be a problem? they say, I know an excellent colored man in my town. ... Do not these Southern outrages make your blood boil? At these I smile, or am interested, or reduce the boiling to a simmer, as occasion may require. To the real question, How does it feel to be a problem? I answer seldom a word." Nearly a century later, we confine discussions about race in America to the "problems" black people pose for whites rather than considering what this way of viewing black people reveals about us as a nation.

This paralyzing framework encourages liberals to relieve their guilty consciences by supporting public funds directed at "the problems"; but at the same time, reluctant to exercise principled criticism of black people, they deny them the freedom to err. Similarly, conservatives blame the "problems" on black people themselves — and thereby render black social misery invisible or unworthy of public attention.

Hence, for liberals, black people are to be "included" and "integrated" into "our" society and culture, while for conservatives they are to be "well behaved" and "worthy of acceptance" by "our" way of life. Both fail to see that the presence and predicaments of black people are neither additions to nor defections from American life but rather constitutive elements of that life.

To engage in a serious discussion of race in America, we must begin not with the problems of black people but with the flaws of American society — flaws rooted in historic inequalities and longstanding cultural stereotypes. How we set up the terms for discussing racial issues shapes our perception and response to these issues. As long as black people are viewed as a "them," the burden falls on blacks to do all the "cultural" and "moral" work necessary for healthy race relations. The implication is that only certain Americans can define what it means to be American — and the rest must simply "fit in."

The emergence of strong black-nationalist sentiments among blacks, especially young people, is a revolt against this sense of having to "fit in." The variety of black nationalist ideologies, from the moderate views of Supreme Court Justice Clarence Thomas in his youth to those of Louis Farrakhan today, rest upon a fundamental truth: white America has been historically weak-willed in insuring racial justice and has continued to resist accepting fully the humanity of blacks. As long as double standards and differential treatment abound — as long as the rap performer Ice T is harshly condemned while former Los Angeles Police Chief Daryl F. Gates's anti-black comments are received in polite silence, as long as Dr. Leonard Jeffries's anti-Semitic statements are met with vitriolic outrage while Presidential candidate Patrick J. Buchanan's are received with a genteel response — black nationalisms will thrive.

Afrocentrism, a contemporary species of black nationalism, is a gallant yet misguided attempt to define an African identity in a white society perceived to be hostile. It is gallant because it puts black doings and sufferings, not white anxieties and fears, at the center of discussion. It is misguided because — out of fear of cultural hybridization, silence on the issue of class, retrograde views on black women, homosexuals and lesbians and a reluctance to link race to the common good — it reinforces the narrow discussions about race

To establish a new framework, we need to begin with a frank acknowledgment of the basic humanness and Americanness of each of us. And we must acknowledge that as a people — E Pluribus Unum — we are on a slippery slope toward economic strife, social turmoil and cultural chaos. If we go down, we go down together. The Los Angeles upheaval forced us to see not only that we are not connected in ways we would like to be but also, in a more profound sense, that this failure to connect binds us even more tightly together. The paradox of race in America is that our common destiny is more pronounced and imperiled precisely when our divisions are deeper. The Civil War and its legacy speak loudly here. Eighty-six percent of white suburban Americans live in neighborhoods that are less than 1 percent black, meaning that the prospects for the country depend largely on how its cities fare in

the hands of a suburban electorate. There is no escape from our interracial interdependence, yet enforced racial hierarchy dooms us as a nation to collective paranoia and hysteria, the unmaking of any democratic order.

The verdict that sparked the incidents in Los Angeles was perceived to be wrong by the vast majority of Americans. But whites have often failed to acknowledge the widespread mistreatment of black people, especially black men, by law-enforcement agencies, which helped ignite the spark. The Rodney King verdict was merely the occasion for deep-seated rage to come to the surface. This rage is fed by the "silent" depression ravaging the country — in which real weekly wages of all American workers since 1973 have declined nearly 20 percent, while at the same time wealth has been upwardly distributed.

The exodus of stable industrial jobs from urban centers to cheaper labor markets here and abroad, housing policies that have created "Chocolate cities and vanilla suburbs "(to use the popular musical artist George Clinton's memorable phrase), white fear of black crime and the urban influx of poor Spanish speaking and Asian immigrants — all have helped erode the tax-base of American cities just as the Federal Government has cut its supports and programs. The result is unemployment, hunger, homelessness and sickness for millions.

Driving that rage is a culture of hedonistic self-indulgence and narcissistic self-regard. This culture of consumption yields coldhearted and mean-spirited attitudes and actions that turn poor urban neighborhoods into military combat zones and existential wastelands.

And the pervasive spiritual impoverishment grows. The collapse of meaning in life, the eclipse of hope and absence of love of self and others, the breakdown of family and neighborhood bonds leads to the social deracination and cultural denudement of urban dwellers, especially children. We have created rootless, dangling people with little link to the supportive networks — family, friends, school — that sustain some sense of purpose in life. We have witnessed the collapse of the spiritual communities that help us face despair, disease and death and that transmit through the generations dignity and decency, excellence and elegance.

The result is lives of what we might call "random nows," of fortuitous and fleeting moments preoccupied with "getting over" — with acquiring pleasure, property and power by any means necessary. (This is not what Malcolm X meant by this famous phrase.) Post-modern culture is more and more a market culture dominated by gangster mentalities and self-destructive wantoness. This culture engulfs all of us — yet its impact on the disadvantaged is devastating, resulting in extreme violence in everyday life. Sexual violence against women and homicidal assaults by young black men on one another are only the most obvious signs of this empty quest for pleasure, property and power.

Lastly, this rage is fueled by a political atmosphere in which images, not ideas, dominate, where politicians spend more time raising money than issues. The functions of parties have been displaced by public polls, and politicians behave less as thermostats that determine the climate of opinion than as thermometers registering the public mood. American politics has been rocked by an unleashing of greed among opportunistic public officials following the lead of their counterparts in the private sphere, where, as of 1989, 1 percent of the population owned 37 percent of the wealth leading to a profound cynicism and pessimism among the citizenry.

And given the way in which the Republican Party since 1968 has appealed to popular xenophobic images — playing the black, female and homophobic cards and realigning the electorate along race, sex and sexual orientation lines — it is no surprise that the notion that we are all part of one garment of destiny is discredited. Appeals to special interests rather than public interests reinforce this polarization. The Los Angeles upheaval was an expression of utter fragmentation by a powerless citizenry that includes not just the poor but all of us. ...

——— 9.23 ———
'THE INAUGURAL POEM'
Maya Angelou

When Arkansas Governor Bill Clinton won the presidential election of 1992, he invited Maya Angelou to read a poem at his inauguration. By this point, she had cemented herself as the poet laureate of the black community, and an elder stateswoman of American arts. That she would be only the second poet to compose and read verse for the presidential inauguration seemed fitting. She wrote the poem below, entitled "On the Pulse of Morning: The Inaugural Poem."

A rock, A river, A tree
Hosts to species long since departed,
Marked the mastodon.
The dinosaur, who left dry tokens
Of their sojourn here
On our planet floor,
Any broad alarm of their
Hastening doom
Is lost in the gloom of dust and ages. ...

Each of you a bordered country,
Delicate and strangely made proud.
Yet thrusting perpetually under siege.
Your armed struggles for profit
Have left collars of waste upon
My shore, currents of debris upon my breast.
Yet, today I call you to my riverside,
If you will study war no more. Come,
Clad in peace and I will sing the songs
The Creator gave to me when I and the
Tree and the stone were one.

Before cynicism was a bloody scar across your
Brow and when you yet knew you still
Knew nothing.
The River sings and sings on.

There is a true yearning to respond to
The singing River and the wise Rock.
So say the Asian, the Hispanic, the Jew
The African and Native American, the Sioux,
The Catholic, the Muslim, the French, the Greek
The Irish, the Rabbi, the Priest, the Sheikh,

The Gay, the Straight, the Preacher, the Teacher.
They hear. They all hear
The speaking of the Tree.

Today, the first and last of every Tree
Speaks to humankind. Come to me,
here beside the River
Plant yourself beside me, here beside
the River.

Each of you, descendant of some passed
On traveler, has been paid for.
You, who gave me my first name, you
Pawnee, Apache and Seneca, you
Cherokee Nation, who rested with me, then
Forced on bloody feet, left me to the employ-
ment of
Other seekers — desperate for gain,
Starving for gold.
You, the Turk, the Swede, the German, the
Scot ...
You the Ashanti, the Yoruba, the Kru, bought,
Sold, stolen, arriving on a nightmare
Praying for a dream.
Here, root yourselves beside me.
I am the Tree planted by the River,
Which will not be moved.
I, the Rock, I the River, I the Tree

I am yours — your Passages have been paid.
Lift up your faces, you have a piercing need
For this bright morning dawning for you.
History, despite its wrenching pain,
Cannot be unlived, and if faced
With courage, need not be lived again.

Lift up your eyes upon
The day breaking for you.
Give birth again
To the dream.

Women, children, men,
Take it into the palms of your hands.
Mold it into the shape of your most
Private need. Sculpt it into
The image of your most public self.
Lift up your hearts

Each new hour holds new chances
For new beginnings.
Do not be wedded forever
To fear, yoked eternally
To brutishness.

The horizon leans forward.
Offering you space to place new steps of change.
Here, now the pulse of this fine day
You may have the courage
To look up and out upon me, the
Rock, the River, the Tree, your country.
No less to Midas than the mendicant.
No less to you now than the mastodon then.
Here on the pulse of this new day
You may have the grace to look up and out
And into your sister's eyes, into
Your brother's face, your country
And say simply
Very simply
With hope
Good morning.

——————— 9.24 ———————

WAITING TO EXHALE
Terry McMillan

Novelist Terry McMillan's first novel, *Mama*, published in 1987, was a hit only because she marketed it herself. The book, as with her subsequent work, was written expressly for a black female audience. Publishers didn't believe that audience bought books; McMillan's *Mama* began to counter that prejudice. But the real proof was her third novel, 1992's *Waiting to Exhale*. The book, a portrait of a group of black female friends who find love among themselves and within themselves, resonated with middle-class African American women. Much like Alice Walker's *The Color Purple* ten years earlier, however, the book also sparked criticism from black men, who protested that they had been portrayed in an overly negative light. Following the book's commercial success, publishers have raced to replicate the formula — though often in form more than substance. Contemporary black authors express frustration, for instance, that their publishers insist they replicate McMillan's signature colorful book jackets, regardless of the book's theme.

BACK TO LIFE

Bernadine sat at her desk, pretending to move her fingers on the adding machine keys. Her phone rang. Finally. She prayed to God it was her lawyer. She'd been waiting all morning to hear from her.

"Well," Jane Milhouse said, "it's over."

Bernadine's heart was pounding so hard she thought it was going to explode. She took a deep breath. "And?"

"How does nine hundred sixty-four thousand sound to you?"

Bernadine exhaled. Her hands fell on top of the keys. "Did you say nine hundred and sixty-four thousand dollars?"

"That's what I said."

"That's almost a million dollars!"

"That it is," Jane said.

"John must be in his grave by now," she said.

"He could be, but that's not our problem, now is it?"

"No, it isn't," Bernadine said, and swallowed hard. "And you're absolutely, positively sure about this?"

"I just left his lawyer's office."

"Was John there?"

"No, he wasn't."

"Nine hundred sixty what?"

"Nine hundred sixty-four thousand. You'll also be entitled to half of his pension when he retires. And since you're already aware of our legal fees, we can talk more about the details of the settlement later."

"Thank you," Bernadine said. "Really."

"You're quite welcome. Now. When would you like to come in?"

"You tell me."

"Well, they've got twenty-four hours to deliver a certified check to my office. How's day after tomorrow?"

"I'll be there," she said. "And thank you again."

Bernadine hung up and immediately called Savannah. After she told her the good news, she asked Savannah if she could meet her, Gloria, and Robin for dinner the next day. She wanted to take everybody out to celebrate. Much to Bernadine's surprise, Savannah said she had a date. "A what?"

"You heard me. A date."

"With who?"

"This painter I met."

"Where'd you meet him?"

"At that new black gallery that just opened."

"Any potential?"

"Girl, I'm not even going to guess. Let's just say he's nice. But I'll cancel. For you."

Bernadine was flattered. "And you're still not smoking?"

"Hell no. Whatever was in those needles worked. I lost the craving. But I won't lie. I did go back for a booster, just in case." Bernadine laughed. Savannah was the most resilient woman she knew.

"Do you need anything?" Bernadine asked.

"Like what?"

"Anything?"

"I can't think of anything."

"Stop lying, bitch," Bernadine said. "After all we've been through, we both could use a vacation. And you know what? We're spending New Year's in London. And don't argue with me either. Didn't you always say you wanted to go to London?" She didn't give Savannah a chance to answer. "You tell those folks down at Drum Beat or whatever the name of that show's called — tell 'em you're going to see the queen of fucking England. It is time," she said. "It is time."

"You're crazy," Savannah said. "But I'll start packing tonight. They've got the best hats in the world in London. And I'll buy as many as I can squeeze in the overhead compartment."

"Speaking of hats. Let's all wear one tomorrow, Savannah. And put on your best shit. Nothing glittery, but do get clean. Remember when we said we'd have our own Sisters' Nite Out?"

"Yeah."

"Well, it is time."

"I hear you," Savannah said.

"What you doing for Christmas?"

"Spending it with you and the kids."

"Don't forget James," Bernadine added.

"Oh, shit. I forgot. I don't have to stay all day. I'll drop the kids' presents off, have some eggnog, and make like a banana and split."

"Savannah, give me a fucking break, would you? I want you to spend the damn night. Help me play Santa Claus. Shit, help me cook. James is a real man, girl. Nothing like John. So bring your flannel jammies."

"I'll do that," Savannah said. "A million fucking dollars, huh?"

"And that's the truth, Ruth. Bye." Bernadine blurted out: "I love you, girl."

Next she called Robin. After Bernadine told her the good news, she gave Robin the same instructions for dinner, right on down to the dress code. Robin was so excited for her she said she was going to pee on herself. "I don't have any hats," she said.

"Well, buy one," Bernadine said. "Seriously, Robin. How's everything going?"

"Everything's fine, girl. I'm sick as a dog, though. Eating crackers like it's going out of style."

"How's your mother?"

"She's doing good. Got me down here making quilts again."

"Good. Keep your ass out of trouble. Any word from Russell?"

"Yeah. You want to hear what that bastard said?"

"What?"

"He said how's he know this baby's his."

"No, he didn't."

"Girl, I'm not thinking about Russell."

"Well, fuck him," Bernadine said. "Me, Gloria, and Savannah'll help you do everything but breast-feed the little rug rat when it's born. And for your information, when you get closer to your due date, I'm giving you the biggest goddamn baby shower in history. Now get your pregnant ass in the car and drive on up here tomorrow. And don't forget to wear a hat."

"What's with the hats, Bernie?"

"Because we're stepping out, that's why. And it is time," Bernadine said again. "And

speaking of time, have your black ass at my house on time. Seven o'clock sharp, Robin. No bullshit."

"I will I will I will," she said. "Bye, you rich bitch!"

Bernadine was still laughing when she called Gloria. By now, of course, Savannah had already called and told her Bernadine's news. "Savannah's got a big mouth," Bernadine said. "So, Glo. Tell me. Do you need any extra cash for Tarik?"

"Nope," Gloria said. "We've got everything under control. He's working his behind off. Cleaning up people's yards, painting fences, you name it."

"Gloria, the boy is going around the god-damn world."

"I know that! But I'll tell you something, since you're in such a generous mood. You could send Phillip a few dollars."

"Consider it done. Just give me his address. How's he doing anyway?"

"He's much better. He's not doing as much hair as he hoped. He'd really appreciate it. Especially coming from you. Phillip always liked you."

"You don't think he'd be offended, do you?"

"No."

"Did you ever get anybody to replace Desiree?"

"Miss Black America came back on her hands and knees. Begging me for her job back." Gloria was clearly being sarcastic.

"Did you slap her for old time's sake?"

"No," Gloria said, laughing. "I told her to go ahead and set up her station, whip that hair out of her plastic bag, and get busy. As long as we don't say too much to each other, we'll get along fine."

"You sure you don't need anything, Gloria?"

"I've got everything I need."

"Meaning what?"

"Well, me and Marvin've got a 'thang' going on," Gloria said, and was actually giggling.

"You mean to tell me you finally did the nasty?" Bernadine said.

"No. We haven't done the nasty yet," Gloria

said. "I'm still recuperating, girl. But he did kiss me."

"Kissed you?" Bernadine moaned.

"Yeah. A kiss is worth a whole lot. He's being so good to me. Ain't nothing in this house broke anymore. When I'm fully recovered, don't worry, we'll do the nasty, and I'll call you up while we're doing it, to let you know how it's going. How's that?"

"Fuck you, Gloria."

"You ought to stop saying that word so much. It doesn't become you."

"Fuck you, Gloria. Do you think you could possibly squeeze me in tomorrow? I need to get my hair done bad. Maybe get some of those acrylic nails too. Wait. Never mind. I'm wearing a hat, shit. And forget about the nails. I won't be needing anybody's long fingernails for what I'm about to do," she said.

"Which is what?"

"You'll see soon enough," she said. "Don't forget, Gloria. Wear a hat. You're a churchgoing woman, so I know you've got a closetful. Just don't come out looking like Sister Monroe."

"Fuck you, Bernie."

After she hung up, Bernadine knew her girlfriends were just as elated about her settlement as she was. She could hear it in their voices. Hell, they'd been waiting as long as she had. Now it seemed as if they'd all won the lottery. And as far as Bernadine was concerned, they had.

She looked at the control sheets spread out on her desk, then glanced down at the adding machine. Bernadine was trying to remember where she'd left off. It was damn near impossible. She couldn't wait to get home to tell the kids. But what would she tell them? She hadn't figured that out yet. And then a light went on in her head. She'd tell them their daddy wanted to be extra nice, so he gave her a little extra money. Out of habit, Bernadine reached for a cigarette, then she shook her head. She inhaled deeply. Then slowly exhaled.

Now that she thought about it, Bernadine herself owned only one decent hat. She'd stop by the mall on the way home. After she picked up the kids. No. She couldn't do that. She'd promised she'd take them to see Home Alone tonight. She'd broken enough promises. The hat she had would have to do.

Bernadine sat there a few more minutes, drumming a pencil on her desk. She was thinking. About all this. She could definitely quit this damn job. But not until after the first of the year. If she quit now, she'd leave them in a bind. That wouldn't be right. Like Robin always said, good karma was a good thing to have. She'd finally be able to spend more time with her kids, which made Bernadine smile. She'd be the first mother there after school. Every single day. She'd sit in her Cherokee, listening to George Winston, long before that bell rang. No more rushing in rush hour. No more leaving at dawn, getting home when it was dark.

She also wouldn't have to worry about selling the house now. But Bernadine wasn't taking that fucker off the market. She'd drop the price. And she'd send a nice check to the United Negro College Fund, something she'd always wanted to do. She'd help feed some of those kids in Africa she'd seen on TV at night. She'd call that toll free number she'd written down on a piece of paper that was stuck under a magnet on the refrigerator. Maybe she'd send some change to the Urban League and the NAACP, and she'd definitely help out some of those programs that BWOTM had been trying to get off the ground for the last hundred years. At the rate she was going, Bernadine had already given away over a million dollars. But she sat there, still trying to think of who else might need her help.

And James. The man had backed up everything he said, and then some. Bernadine was still love-struck. And planned to stay that way. He'd be there for Christmas. He'd already found an apartment. His next step was setting up his law practice here. James said he wanted to see what he could do to help get the King referendum passed in this racist state. Once and for all. He'd already joined a coalition to stop the liquor board from allowing so many liquor stores in the black community. Savannah was even planning to do a show on it. The man was for real. James promised he wouldn't rush her. That he'd be patient. But now, Bernadine wanted to be rushed. She wanted to get this show on the road. Hell, she had her life back. The one she'd lost eleven years ago.

And now that she'd have the money to start her catering business, Bernadine didn't want to be bothered. She'd had a better dream. One that would see the light. Since these white folks were making a fortune selling these damn chocolate chip cookies, she'd open up her own little shop. Sell nothing but sweets, the kind black folks ate: blackberry cobbler, peach cobbler, sweet potato pie, bread pudding, banana pudding, rice pudding, lemon meringue pie, and pound-cake. She'd put it in the biggest mall in Scottsdale. Serve the finest gourmet coffee she could find: cappuccino and all those other ridiculous coffees everybody couldn't live without these days. She already had the name picked: Bernadine's Sweet Tooth. That sounded good. Yeah, she thought. It's got a real nice ring to it.

——— 9.25 ———

'PLEASE THINK OF THE REAL O.J.'

O.J. Simpson

On June 13, 1994, Los Angeles police officers discovered the slain body of Nicole Brown Simpson, the white wife of black National Football League superstar O.J. Simpson, murdered alongside family friend Ron Goldman. Over the next few days, police came to the conclusion that Simpson was the primary suspect, and reports of Simpson's past physical abuse of his wife resurfaced. On June 17, police issued a warrant for his arrest. That evening marked the beginning of the world's enduring infatuation with the mystery of who killed Nicole Brown Simpson and Ron Goldman, and the nagging question of O.J. Simpson's guilt or innocence. It started in properly dramatic fashion, as an emotionally unwound Simpson led police on a two-hour low-speed chase through suburban Los Angeles. Television cameras trained on his now notorious white Bronco as it cruised along; commentators speculated on whether or not Simpson would go through with his rumored plot to commit suicide, as he states in the note below. When Simpson finally turned

himself in, it was hardly the end. The 34-week trial that began in January, 1995 forever altered the way television news does business. Stations covered the trial gavel to gavel and examined the case in excruciating detail. It became a nationally watched soap opera, as lawyers and judges and expert witnesses became celebrity personalities.

Opinions about the case split down racial lines: Whites, by and large, believed Simpson to be guilty and longed for him to face the full weight of the law; African Americans, on the other hand, saw a classic example of an "uppity black man" being put in his place. He had grown too big, he had married a white woman, and now the infamous Los Angeles Police Department and its justice system were taking him down. Simpson's defense team argued that Detective Mark Furhman, who gathered the evidence on which the prosecution's case stood, was a blatant racist. They produced a recording of an interview he conducted with a screenwriter in which he used the word "nigger" 41 times and discussed planting evidence on suspects. When Simpson was ultimately found not guilty, many Los Angeles blacks said they felt the ruling was a vindication of their charges three years previous, in the Rodney King affair, that the LAPD was aggressively racist and regularly conspired to harass, abuse and jail African Americans.

To Whom It May Concern:
First, everyone understand. I have nothing to do with Nicole's murder. I loved her; always have and always will. If we had a problem, it's because I loved her so much.

Recently, we came to the understanding that for now we were not right for each other, at least for now. Despite our love, we were different and that's why we mutually agreed to go our separate ways.

It was tough splitting for a second time, but we both knew it was for the best. Inside, I had no doubt that in the future we would be close friends or more. Unlike what has been written in the press, Nicole and I had a great relationship for most of our lives together. Like all long-term relationships, we had a few downs and ups.

I took the heat New Year's 1989 because that's what I was supposed to do. I did not plead no contest for any other reason but to protect our privacy and was advised it would end the press hype.

I don't want to belabor knocking the press, but I can't believe what is being said. Most of it is totally made up. I know you have a job to do, but as a last wish, please, please, please, leave my children in peace. Their lives will be tough enough.

I want to send my love and thanks to all my friends. I'm sorry I can't name every one of you, especially A.C. Man, thanks for being in my life. The support and friendship I received from so many: Wayne Hughes, Lewis Marks, Frank Olson, Mark Packer, Bender, Bobby Kardashian. I wish we had spent more time together in recent years. My golfing buddies: Hoss, Alan Austin, Mike, Craig, Bender, Wyler, Sandy, Jay, Donnie, thanks for the fun.

All my teammates over the years: Reggie, you were the soul of my pro career. Ahmad, I never stopped being proud of you. Marcus, you've got a great lady in Catherine, don't mess it up. Bobby Chandler, thanks for always being there. Skip and Kathy, I love you guys. Without you, I never would have made it through this far.

Marguerite, thanks for the early years. We had some fun. Paula, what can I say? You are special. I'm sorry I'm not going to have, we're not going to have, our chance. God brought you to me, I now see. As I leave, you'll be in my thoughts.

I think of my life and feel I've done most of the right things. So why do I end up like this? I can't go on. No matter what the outcome, people will look and point. I can't take that. I can't subject my children to that. This way, they can move on and go on with their lives.

Please, if I've done anything worthwhile in my life, let my kids live in peace from you, the press.

I've had a good life. I'm proud of how I lived. My mama taught me to do unto others. I treated people the way I wanted to be treated. I've always tried to be up and helpful. So why is this happening?

I'm sorry for the Goldman family. I know how much it hurts.

Nicole and I had a good life together. All this press talk about a rocky relationship was no more than what every long-term relationship experiences. All her friends will confirm that I have been totally loving and understanding of what she's been going through.

At times, I have felt like a battered husband or boyfriend, but I loved her; make that clear to everyone. And I would take whatever it took to make it work.

Don't feel sorry for me. I've had a great life, great friends. Please think of the real O.J. and not this lost person.

Thanks for making my life special. I hope I helped yours.

Peace and love, O.J.

--------- 9.26 ---------
THE MILLION MAN MARCH
Louis Farrakhan

Nation of Islam Minister Louis Farrakhan's crowning achievement in American politics must be said to be the Million Man March. The event grew from his idea of creating a "Day of Atonement," in which the black community would stop and consider the continued crippling of African-American men — and what their resulting economic and social impotence means for the community as a whole. He wanted black men, and black men only, to come to Washington, D.C., for a mass vigil on their behalf.

From the start, many were uncomfortable with participating in an event led by Farrakhan and the Nation of Islam, given the charges of anti-Semitism and misogyny that had plagued his group for years. But, with the help of former NAACP head Benjamin Chavis, who largely organized the event, Farrakhan was able to build a coalition of supporters that crossed the spectrum of black culture and politics. The event's message — that the black man is in dire straights, and nobody can save him but himself — resonated deeply within the community. One person after another declared that he might have issues with the organizer, but the cause mandated he attend. Ultimately, the attendance numbers are in dispute. However many were there, it was by far the largest gathering of African Americans to date, as well as the largest gathering of any sort on the National Mall. Speakers ranged from Maya Angelou to Jesse Jackson, and Farrakhan delivered a lengthy keynote address in which he urged black men to take responsibility for turning their lives around and assuming leadership in their families and communities. The speech is excerpted below as reported by Cable News Network. Many black women responded by noting that the event promoted more of the same sort of cult of masculinity they objected to in previous community movements.

... Now, why have you come today?

You came not at the call of Louis Farrakhan, but you have gathered here at the call of God. For it is only the call of Almighty God, no matter through whom that call came, that could generate this kind of outpouring. God called us here to this place, at this time, for a very specific reason.

And now, I want to say, my brothers — this is a very pregnant moment. Pregnant with the possibility of tremendous change in our status in America and in the world. And although the call was made through me, many have tried to distance the beauty of this idea from the person through whom the idea and the call was made.

Some have done it mistakenly. And others have done it in a malicious and vicious manner. Brothers and sisters, there is no human being through whom God brings an idea that history doesn't marry the idea with that human being, no matter what defect was that human being's character.

You can't separate Newton from the law that Newton discovered, nor can you separate Einstein from the theory of relativity. It would be silly to try to separate Moses from the Torah or Jesus from the Gospel or Muhammad from the Koran.

When you say Farrakhan, you ain't no Moses, you ain't no Jesus, and you're not no Muhammad. You have a defect in your character.

Well, that certainly may be so, however, according to the way the Bible reads, there is no profit of God written of in the Bible that did not have a defect in his character. But, I have never heard any member of the faith of Judaism separate David from the Psalms, because of what happened in David's life and you've never separated Solomon from the building of the Temple because they say he had

a thousand concubines, and you never separated any of the Great Servants of God.

So today, whether you like it or not, God brought the idea through me and he didn't bring it through me because my heart was dark with hatred and anti-Semitism, he didn't bring it through me because my heart was dark and I'm filled with hatred for white people and for the human family of the planet. If my heart were that dark, how is the message so bright, the message so clear, the response so magnificent? ...

And now, in spite of all that division, in spite of all that divisiveness, we responded to a call and look at what is present here today. We have here those brothers with means and those who have no means. Those who are light and those who are dark. Those who are educated, those who are uneducated. Those who are business people, those who don't know anything about business. Those who are young, those who are old. Those who are scientific, those who know nothing of science. Those who are religious and those who are irreligious. Those who are Christian, those who are Muslim, those who are Baptist, those who are Methodist, those who are Episcopalian, those of traditional African religion. We've got them all here today.

And why did we come? We came because we want to move toward a more perfect union. And if you notice, the press triggered every one of those divisions. You shouldn't come, you're a Christian. That's a Muslim thing. You shouldn't come, you're too intelligent to follow hate! You shouldn't come, look at what they did, they excluded women, you see? They played all the cards, they pulled all the strings.

Oh, but you better look again, Willie. There's a new Black man in America today. A new Black woman in America today. Now Brothers, there's a social benefit of our gathering here today. That is, that from this day forward, we can never again see ourselves through the narrow eyes of the limitation of the boundaries of our own fraternal, civic, political, religious, street organization or professional organization. We are forced by the magnitude of what we see here today, that whenever you return to your cities and you see a Black man, a Black woman, don't ask him what is your social, political or religious affiliation, or what is your status? Know that he is your brother.

You must live beyond the narrow restrictions of the divisions that have been imposed upon us. Well, some of us are here because it's history-making. Some of us are here because it's a march through which we can express anger and rage with America for what she has and is doing to us. So, we're here for many reasons, but the basic reason why this was called was for atonement and reconciliation. So, it is necessary for me, in as short of time as possible, to give as full an explanation of atonement as possible. ...

I heard my brother from the West Coast say today, I atone to the mothers for the death of the babies caused by our senseless slaughter of one another. See, when he feels sorry deep down inside, he's going to make a change.

That man has a change in his mind. That man has a change in his heart. His soul has been unburdened and released from the pain of that sin, but you got to go one step further, because after you've acknowledged it, confessed it, repented, you've come to the fifth stage. Now, you've got to do something about it.

Now, look brother, sisters. Some people don't mind confessing. Some people don't mind making some slight repentance. But, when it comes to doing something about the evil that we've done we fall short.

But, atonement means satisfaction or reparation for a wrong or injury. It means to make amends. It means penance, expiation, compensation and recompense made or done for an injury or wrong.

So, atonement means we must be willing to do something in expiation of our sins. So we can't just have a good time today, and say we made history in Washington. We've got to resolve today that we're going back home to do something about what's going on in our lives and in our families and in our communities.

Now, we all right? Can you hang with me a few more? Now, brothers and sisters, if we make atonement it leads to the sixth stage. And the sixth stage is forgiveness. Now, so many of us want forgiveness, but we don't want to go through the process that leads to it. And so, when we say we forgive, we forgive from our lips, but we have never pardoned in the heart.

So, the injury still remains. My dear family, my dear brothers, we need forgiveness. God is always ready to forgive us for our sins. Forgiveness means to grant pardon for, or remission of, an offense or sin. It is to absolve, to clear, to exonerate and to liberate. Boy, that's something!

See, you're not liberated until you can forgive. You're not liberated from the evil effect of our own sin until we can ask God for forgiveness and then forgive others, and this is why in the Lord's Prayer you say, forgive us our trespasses as we forgive those who trespass against us.

So, it means to cease, to feel offense and resentment against another for the harm done by an offender. It means to wipe the slate clean. And then, that leads to the seventh stage. You know, I like to liken this to music. Because in music, the seventh note is called a leading tone. Do, re, me, fa, so, la, te — You can't stop there. te. It leaves you hung up, te. What you got to get back to? Do. So, whatever you started with when you reach the eight note, you're back to where you started only at a higher vibration. Now, look, at this. The seventh tone, the leading tone that leads to the perfect union with God is reconciliation and restoration. Because after forgiveness, now, we are going to be restored to what? To our original position. To restore, to reconcile means to become friendly, peaceable again, to put hostile persons into a state of agreement or harmony, to make compatible or to compose or settle what it was that made for division.

It means to resolve differences. It can mean to establish or re-establish a close relationship between previously hostile persons. So, restoration means the act of returning something to an original or un-impaired condition. Now, when you're backed to an impaired position, you have reached the eighth stage, which is perfect union. And when we go through all these steps, there is no difference between us that we can't heal. There's a balm in Gilead to heal the sin-sick soul. There is a balm in Gilead to make the wounded whole. …

Black men, you're the descendants of the builders of the pyramids. But you have amnesia now. You can't remember how you did it. But the Master has come. You know, pastors, I love that scripture where Jesus told his disciples, go there and you'll see an ass and a colt tied with her. Untie them and bring them to me. If anybody ask you what you're doing, because it may look like you're stealing and you know they are going to accuse you of stealing, tell them the Master got need of these. And Jesus rode into Jerusalem on an ass.

The Democratic Party has for its symbol, a donkey. The donkey stands for the unlearned masses of the people. But the Democratic Party can't call them asses no more. You got them all tied up, but you're not using. The donkey is tied up. But can you get off today? No, I can't get off, I'm tied up. Somebody on your donkey? Well, yeah. I got a master. He rides me like the Master rode Balem's ass, you know. But, hail, the ass is now talking with a man's voice. And the ass wants to throw the rider off, because he got a new rider today.

If anybody ask you, tell them the Master has need. Look at you. Oh, I don't know what the number is. It's too much for me to count. But I think they said it's a million and a half, or two. I don't know how many. But you know, I called for a million. When I saw the word go out my mouth, I looked at it. I said, oh my God! It just came out of my mouth. I didn't know. And after it came out, I said, well I got to go with it. And, I'm so glad I did. People told me you better change that figure to one more realistic. And I should have changed it to the Three Million Man March. …

Now brothers, sisters, I want to close this lecture with a special message to our President and to the Congress. There is a great divide, but the real evil in America is not white flesh, or black flesh. The real evil in America is the idea that undergirds the set up of the western world. And that idea is called white supremacy.

Now wait, wait, wait. Before you get angry. Those of you listening by television. You don't even know why you behave the way you behave.

I'm not telling you I'm a psychiatrist, but I do want to operate on your head. White supremacy is the enemy of both white people and black people because the idea of white supremacy means you should rule because you're white, that makes you sick. And you've produced a sick society and a sick world. The founding fathers meant well, but they said, "toward a more perfect union." So, the Bible says, we know in part, we prophesy in part, but when that which is perfect is come, that which is in part shall be done away with.

So either, Mr. Clinton, we're going to do away with the mind-set of the founding fathers. You don't have to repudiate them like you've asked my brothers to do me. You don't have to say they were malicious, hate filled people. But you must evolve out of their mind-set. You see their minds was limited to those six European nations out of which this country was founded. But you've got Asians here. How are you going to handle that? You've got children of Africa here. How are you going to handle that?

You've got Arabs here. You've got Hispanics here. I know you call them illegal aliens, but hell, you took Texas from them by flooding Texas with people that got your mind. And now they're coming back across the border to what is Northern Mexico, Texas, Arizona, New Mexico, and California. They don't see themselves as illegal aliens. I think they might see you as an illegal alien. You have to be careful how you talk to people. You have to be careful how you deal with people. The Native American is suffering today. He's suffering almost complete extinction. Now, he learned about bingo. You taught him. He learned about black jack. You taught him. He learned about playing roulette. You taught him. Now, he's making a lot of money. You're upset with him because he's adopted your ways. What makes you like this? See, you're like this because you're not well. You're not well. And in the light of today's global village, you can never harmonize with the Asians. You can't harmonize with the islands of the Pacific. You can't harmonize with the dark people of the world who out number you 11 to one, if you're going to stand in the mind of white supremacy. White supremacy has to die in order for humanity to live.

Now, oh, I know. I know. I know it's painful, but we have to operate now, just, just take a little of this morphine and you won't feel the pain as much. You just need to bite down on something, as I stop this last few minutes, just bite down on your finger. Listen, listen, listen, listen, white supremacy caused you all, not you all, some white folk, to try to rewrite history and write us out. White supremacy caused Napoleon to blow the nose off of the Sphinx because it reminded you too much of the Black man's majesty.

White supremacy caused you to take Jesus, a man with hair like lamb's wool and feet like burnished brass and make him White. So that you could worship him because you could never see yourself honoring somebody black because of the state of your mind. You see, you, you really need help. You'll be all right. You'll be all right. You will be all right. Now, now, now, you painted the Last Supper, everybody there white.

My mother asked the man that came to bring her the Bible. He said, look there, the pictures in the Bible. You see, Jesus and all his disciples are at the Last Supper — my mother in her West Indian accent — said, you mean ain't nobody black was at the Last Supper? And the man said, yes, but they was in the kitchen. So now you've whitened up everything.

Any great invention we made you put white on it, because you didn't want to admit that a black person had that intelligence, that genius. You try to color everything to make it satisfactory to the sickness of our mind.

So you whitened up religion, Farrakhan didn't do that. You locked the bible from us, Farrakhan didn't do that. Your sick mind wouldn't even let you bury us in the same ground that both of us came out of. We had to be buried somewhere else, that's sick. Some of us died just to drink water out of a fountain marked white. That's sick. Isn't it sick?

You poisoned religion. And in all the churches, until recently, the master was painted white. So, you had us bowing down to your image. Which ill-effected our minds. You gave us your version of history. And you whitened that up. Yes, you did. Yes, you did.

You are a white Shriner. The black Shriner don't integrate the shrine. Why don't you black Shriners integrate the shrine? Because in the shrine, you are the essence of the secret. They don't want you there. They'll have to tell the world, it's you we been thinking about all along.

Now, white folks, see the reason you could look at the O.J. Simpson trial in horror, and the reason black folks rejoiced, had nothing to do with the horror of the tragedy. Black folk would never rejoice over the slaughter of Ron Goldman and Nicole Brown Simpson.

Black folk saw that with compassion. Many black folk grieve over that reality. You say, "O.J. sold out." No, he didn't sell out. He was drawn out.

Black folk that got talent, they all grow up in the "hood." When we first sing, we sing in these old raunchy night clubs in the "hood." When we play sandlot ball, we play it in the "hood." But when you spot us, you draw us out. You say "that Negro can run. Look at how high he jumps." So you give us a scholarship to your university. But the blacks who are in college, who play basketball for you, who play football for you, who run track for you, you disallow them to get involved with black students and the suffering of black students on all white campuses. You hide them away. Give them privileges. Then they find themselves with your daughter.

Then you take them into the NBA, the NFL, and they become megastars. Or in the entertainment field and when they become megastars, their association is no longer black. They may not have a black manager, a black agent, a black accountant. They meet in parties, in posh neighborhoods that black folk don't come into. So their association becomes white women, white men, and association breeds assimilation. And if you have a slave mentality, you feel you have arrived now because you can jump over cars, running in airports, playing in films.

I'm not degrading my brother, I love him. But he was drawn out. He didn't sell out, he was drawn out. Michael Jackson is drawn out. Most of our top stars are drawn out. And then, when you get them, you imprison them with fear and distrust. You don't want them to speak out on the issues that are political, that are social. They must shut their mouths or you threaten to take away their fame, take away their fortune, because you're sick. And the president is not gonna point this out. He's trying to get well. But he's a physician that can't heal himself.

I'm almost finished. White supremacy has poisoned the bloodstream of religion, education, politics, jurisprudence, economics, social ethics and morality. And there is no way that we can integrate into white supremacy and hold our dignity as human beings because, if we integrate into that, we become subservient to that. And to become subservient to that is to make the slave master comfortable with his slave. So, we got to come out of here my people. Come out of a system and a world that is built on the wrong idea. An idea that never can create a perfect union with God.

The false idea of white supremacy prevents anyone from becoming one with God. White people have to come out of that idea, which has poisoned them into a false attitude of superiority based on the color of their skins. The doctrine of white supremacy disallows whites to grow to their full potential. It forces white people to see themselves as the law or above the law. And that's why Furhman could say that he is like a god. See, he thinks like that, but that idea is pervasive in police departments across the country. And it's getting worse and not better because white supremacy is not being challenged.

And I say to all of us who are leaders, all of us who are preachers, we must not shrink from the responsibility of pointing our wrong, so that we can be comfortable and keep white people comfortable in their alienation from God. And so, white folks are having heart attacks today because their world is coming down. And if you look at the Asians, the Asians have the fastest growing economies in the world. The Asians are not saying, bashing white people. You don't find the Asians saying the white man is this, the white man is that, the white man is the other.

He don't talk like that. You know what he does? He just relocates the top banks from Wall Streets to Tokyo. He don't say, I'm better than the white man. He just starts building his world and building his economy and challenging white supremacy. …

So, my beloved brothers and sisters, here's what we would like you to do. Everyone of you, my dear brothers, when you go home, here's what I want you to do. We must belong to some organization that is working for and in the interest of the uplift and the liberation of our people.

Go back, join the NAACP if you want to, join the Urban league, join the All African People's Revolutionary Party, join us, join the Nation of Islam, join PUSH, join the Congress of Racial Equality, join SCLC — the Southern Christian Leadership Conference, but we must become a totally organized people and the only way we can do that is to become a part of some organization that is working for the uplift of our people.

We must keep the local organizing committees that made this event possible, we must keep them together. And then all of us, as leaders, must stay together and make the National African American Leadership Summit inclusive of all of us.

I know that the NAACP did not officially endorse this march. Neither did the Urban League. But, so what? So what? Many of the members are here anyway. I know that Dr. Lyons, of the National Baptist Association

USA did not endorse the march, nor did the Reverend Dr. B.W. Smith, nor did Bishop Chandler Owens, but so what? These are our brothers and we're not going to stop reaching out for them simply because we feel there was a misunderstanding. We still want to talk to our brothers because we cannot let artificial barriers divide us. Remember the letter of Willie Lynch and let's not let Willie Lynch lynch our new spirit and our new attitude and our new mind.

No, we must continue to reach out for those that have condemned this, and make them to see that this was not evil, it was not intended for evil, it was intended for good. Now, brothers, moral and spiritual renewal is a necessity. Every one of you must go back home and join some church, synagogue or temple or mosque that is teaching spiritual and moral uplift. I want you, brothers, there's no men in the church, in the mosque.

The men are in the streets and we got to get back to the houses of God. But preachers we have to revive religion in America. We have to revive the houses of God that they're not personal thiefdoms of those of us who are their preachers and pastors. But we got to be more like Jesus, more like Mohammed, more like Moses and become servants of the people in fulfilling their needs.

Brothers, when you go home, we've got to register eight million, eligible but unregistered brothers, sisters. So you go home and find eight more like yourself. You register and get them to register. I register as Democrat. Should I register as a Republican? Should I register as independent?

If you're an independent, that's fine. If you're a Democrat, that's fine. If you're a Republican, that's OK. Because in local elections you have to do that which is in the best interest of your local community. But what we want is not necessarily a third party, but a third force.

Which means that we're going to collect Democrats, Republicans and independents around an agenda that is in the best interest of our people. And then all of us can stand on that agenda and in 1996, whoever the standard bearer is for the Democratic, the Republican, or the independent party should one come into existence. They've got to speak to our agenda.

We're no longer going to vote for somebody just because they're black. We tried that. We wish we could. But we got to vote for you, if you are compatible with our agenda.

Now many of the people that's in this House right here are put there by the margin of the black vote. So, in the next election we want to see, who's in here do we want to stay and who in here do we want to go? And we want to show them that never again will they ever disrespect the black community. We must make them afraid to do evil to us and think they can get away with it.

We must be prepared to help them if they are with us or to punish them if they're against us. And when they are against us, I'm not talking about color. I'm talking about an agenda that's in the best interest of the black, the poor and the vulnerable in this society.

Now atonement goes beyond us. I don't like this squabble with the members of the Jewish community. I don't like it. The honorable Elijah Muhammad said in one of his writings that he believed that we would work out some kind of an accord. Maybe so. Reverend Jackson has talked to the 12 presidents of Jewish organizations and perhaps in the light of what we see today, maybe it's time to sit down and talk. Not with any preconditions. You got pain. Well, we've got pain, too. You hurt. We hurt, too.

The question is: if the dialogue is proper then we might be able to end the pain. And ending the pain may be good for both and ultimately good for the nation. We're not opposed to sitting down. And I guess if you can sit down with Arafat where there are rivers of blood between you — why can't you sit down with us and there's no blood between us? It don't make sense not to dialogue. It doesn't make sense. ...

Take this pledge with me. Say with me please, I, say your name, pledge that from this day forward I will strive to love my brother as I love myself. I, say your name, from this day forward will strive to improve myself spiritually, morally, mentally, socially, politically, and economically for the benefit of myself, my family, and my people. I, say your name, pledge that I will strive to build business, build houses, build hospitals, build factories, and then to enter international trade for the good of myself, my family, and my people. I, say your name, pledge that from this day forward I will never raise my hand with a knife or a gun to beat, cut, or shoot any member of my family or any human being, except in self-defense.

I, say your name, pledge from this day forward I will never abuse my wife by striking her, disrespecting her, for she is the mother of my children and the producer of my future. I, say your name, pledge that from this day forward I will never engage in the abuse of children, little boys, or little girls for sexual gratification. But I will let them grow in peace to be strong men and women for the future of our people. I, say your name, will never again use the B word to describe my female, but particularly my own black sister.

I, say your name, pledge from this day forward that I will not poison my body with drugs or that which is destructive to my health and my well-being. I, say your name, pledge from this day forward, I will support black newspapers, black radio, black television. I will support black artists, who clean up their acts to show respect for themselves and respect for their people, and respect for the ears of the human family.

I, say your name, will do all of this so help me God. ...

—————— 9.27 ——————

'THIRTEEN WAYS OF LOOKING AT A BLACK MAN'

Henry Louis Gates, Jr.

Henry Louis Gates, Jr., Harvard University Director of African-American Studies, has risen to fame as the reigning intellectual of black America at the turn of the 21st century. It was fitting then that, following the string of high-profile events testing America's racial divide in the early and middle 1990s, Gates would pen a definitive piece summing them up. In the October 1995 issue of *The New Yorker*, to which Gates is a regular contributor, he took the Simpson verdict as his starting point for a discussion about black perception of the world and white reaction to that perception. Part essay and part survey of the opinions of celebrity African Americans, the piece argues the subjectivity of truth, particularly as it relates to race and gender in America, and then offers a litany of the versions of truth black and white people can and have drawn from the Simpson case, the Million Man March, the Clarence Thomas hearings and the Rodney King beating. Those versions, he says, too often end up on a binary track of white reaction and black counter-reaction, substituting a cycle of blame for a meaningful conversation about race. America was gripped by the Simpson case, he concludes, because it was the perfect "empty vessel" — as a courtroom drama, involving an interracial couple — for this confining debate.

"Every day, in every way, we are getting meta and meta," the philosopher John Wisdom used to say, venturing a cultural counterpart to Emile Coué's famous mantra of self-improvement. So it makes sense that in the aftermath of the Simpson trial the focus of attention has been swiftly displaced from the verdict to the reaction to the verdict, and then to the reaction to the reaction to the verdict, and, finally, to the reaction to the reaction to the reaction to the verdict — which is to say, black indignation at white anger at black jubilation at Simpson's acquittal. It's a spiral made possible by the relay circuit of race. Only in America.

An American historian I know registers a widespread sense of bathos when he says, "Who would have imagined that the Simpson trial would be like the Kennedy assassination — that you'd remember where you were when the verdict was announced?" But everyone does, of course. The eminent sociologist William Julius Wilson was in the red-carpet lounge of a United Airlines terminal, the only black in a crowd of white travelers, and found himself as stunned and disturbed as they were. Wynton Marsalis, on tour with his band in California, recalls that "everybody was acting like they were above watching it, but then when it got to be ten o'clock — zoom, we said, 'Put the verdict on!'" Spike Lee was with Jackie Robinson's widow, Rachel, rummaging through a trunk filled with her husbands belongings, in preparation for a bio-pic he's making on the athlete. Jamaica Kincaid was sitting in her car in the parking lot of her local grocery store in Vermont, listening to the proceedings on National Public Radio, and she didn't pull out until after they were over. I was teaching a literature seminar at Harvard from twelve to two, and watched the verdict with the class on a television set in the seminar room. That's where I first saw the sort of racialized response that itself would fill television screens for the next few days: white students looked aghast, and black students cheered. "Maybe you should remind the students that this is a case about two people who were brutally slain, and not an occasion to celebrate" my teaching assistant, a white woman, whispered to me.

The two weeks spanning the O. J. Simpson verdict and Louis Farrakhan's Million Man March on Washington were a good time for connoisseurs of racial paranoia. As blacks exulted at Simpson's acquittal, horrified whites had a fleeting sense that this race thing was knottier than they'd ever supposed — that, when all the pieties were cleared away, blacks really *were* strangers in their midst. (The unspoken sentiment: *And I thought I knew these people.*) There was the faintest tincture of the Southern slaveowner's disquiet in the aftermath of the bloody slave revolt led by Nat Turner — when the gentleman farmer was left to wonder which of his smiling, servile retainers would have slit his throat if the rebellion had spread as was intended, like fire on parched thatch. In the day or so following the verdict, young urban professionals took note of a slight *froideur* between themselves and their nannies and babysitters — the awkwardness of an unbroached subject. Rita Dove, who recently completed a term as the United States Poet Laureate, and who believes that Simpson was guilty, found it "appalling that white peo-

ple were so outraged — more appalling than the decision as to whether he was guilty or not." Of course, it's possible to overstate the tensions. Marsalis invokes the example of team sports, saying, "You want your side to win, whatever the side is going to be. And the thing is, we're still at a point in our national history where we look at each other as sides." …

For white observers, what's even scarier than the idea that black Americans were plumping for the villain, which is a misprision of value, is the idea that black Americans didn't recognize him as the villain, which is a misprision of fact. How can conversation begin when we disagree about reality? To put it at its harshest, for many whites a sincere belief in Simpson's innocence looks less like the culture of protest than like the culture of psychosis.

Perhaps you didn't know that Liz Claiborne appeared on "Oprah" not long ago and said that she didn't design her clothes for black women — that their hips were too wide. Perhaps you didn't know that the soft drink Tropical Fantasy is manufactured by the Ku Klux Klan and contains a special ingredient designed to sterilize black men. (A warning flyer distributed in Harlem a few years ago claimed that these findings were vouchsafed on the television program "20/20.") Perhaps you didn't know that the Ku Klux Klan has a similar arrangement with Church's Fried Chicken — or is it Popeye's?

Perhaps you didn't know these things, but a good many black Americans think they do, and will discuss them with the same intentness they bring to speculations about the "shadowy figure" in a Brentwood driveway. Never mind that Liz Claiborne has never appeared on "Oprah," that the beleaguered Brooklyn company that makes Tropical Fantasy has gone as far as to make available an F.D.A. assay of its ingredients, and that those fried chicken franchises pose a threat mainly to black folks' arteries. The folklorist Patricia A. Turner, who has collected dozens of such tales in an invaluable 1993 study of rumor in African-American culture, "I Heard It Through the Grapevine," points out the patterns to be found here: that these stories encode regnant anxieties, that they take root under particular conditions and play particular social roles, that the currency of rumor flourishes where "official" news has proved untrustworthy.

Certainly the Fuhrman tapes might have been scripted to confirm the old saw that paranoids, too, have enemies. If you wonder why blacks seem particularly susceptible to rumors and conspiracy theories, you might look at a history in which the official story was a poor guide to anything that mattered much, and in which rumor sometimes verged on the truth. Heard the one about the L.A. cop who hated interracial couples, fantasized about making a bonfire of black bodies, and boasted of planting evidence? How about the one about the federal government's forty-year study of how untreated syphilis affects black men? For that matter, have you ever read through some of the F.B.I.'s COINTELPRO files? ("There is but one way out for you," an F.B.I. scribe wrote to Martin Luther King, Jr., in 1964, thoughtfully urging on him the advantages of suicide. "You better take it before your filthy, abnormal, fraudulent self is bared to the nation.")

People arrive at an understanding of themselves and the world through narratives — narratives purveyed by schoolteachers, newscasters, "authorities," and all the other authors of our common sense. Counternarratives are, in turn, the means by which groups contest that dominant reality and the fretwork of assumptions that supports it. Sometimes delusion lies that way, sometimes not. There's a sense in which much of black history is simply counternarrative that has been documented and legitimatized, by slow, hard-won scholarship. …

Another barrier to interracial comprehension is talk of the "race card" — a phrase that itself infuriates many blacks. Judge Higginbotham, who pronounces himself "not uncomfortable at all" with the verdict, is uncomfortable indeed with charges that Johnnie Cochran played the race card. "This whole point is one hundred per cent inaccurate," Higginbotham says. "If you

knew that the most important witness had a history of racism and hostility against black people, that should have been a relevant factor of inquiry even if the jury had been all white. If the defendant had been Jewish and the police officer had a long history of expressed anti-Semitism and having planted evidence against innocent persons who were Jewish, I can't believe that anyone would have been saying that defense counsel was playing the anti-Semitism card." Angela Davis finds the very metaphor to be a problem. "Race is not a card," she says firmly. "The whole case was pervaded with issues of race."

Those who share her view were especially outraged at Robert Shapiro's famous post-trial rebuke to Cochran — for not only playing the race card but dealing it "from the bottom of the deck." Ishmael Reed, who is writing a book about the case, regards Shapiro's remarks as sheer opportunism: "He wants to keep his Beverly Hills clients — a perfectly commercial reason." In Judge Higginbotham's view, "Johnnie Cochran established that he was as effective as any lawyer in America, and though whites can tolerate black excellence in singing, dancing, and dunking, there's always been a certain level of discomfort among many whites when you have a one-on-one challenge in terms of intellectual competition. If Edward Bennett Williams, who was one of the most able lawyers in the country, had raised the same issues, half of the complaints would not exist."

By the same token, the display of black prowess in the courtroom was heartening for many black viewers. Cornel West says, "I think part of the problem is that Shapiro — and this is true of certain white brothers — has a profound fear of black-male charisma. And this is true not only in the law but across the professional world. You see, you have so many talented white brothers who deserve to be in the limelight. But one of the reasons they are not in the limelight is that they are not charismatic. And here comes a black person who's highly talented but also charismatic and therefore able to command center stage. So you get a very real visceral kind of jealousy that has to do with sexual competition as well as professional competition."

Erroll McDonald touches upon another aspect of sexual tension when he says, "The so-called race card has always been the joker. And the joker is the history of sexual racial politics in this country. People forget the singularity of this issue — people forget that less than a century ago black men were routinely lynched for merely glancing at white women or for having been thought to have glanced at a white woman." He adds, with mordant irony, "Now we've come to a point in our history where a black man could, potentially, have murdered a white woman and thrown in a white man to boot — and got off. So the country has become far more complex in its discussion of race." This is, as he appreciates, a less than perfectly consoling thought. ...

Of course, the popular trial of Nicole Brown Simpson — one conducted off camera, in whispers — has further occluded anything recognizable as sexual politics. When Anita Hill heard that O. J. Simpson was going to be part of the Million Man March on Washington, she felt it was entirely in keeping with the occasion: a trial in which she believed that matters of gender had been "bracketed" was going to be succeeded by a march from which women were excluded. And, while Minister Louis Farrakhan had told black men that October 16th was to serve as a "day of atonement" for their sins, the murder of Nicole Brown Simpson and Ronald Goldman was obviously not among the sins he had in mind. bell hooks argues, "Both O.J.'s case and the Million Man March confirm that, while white men are trying to be sensitive and pretending they're the new man, black men are saying that patriarchy must be upheld at all costs, even if women must die." She sees the march as a congenial arena for Simpson in symbolic terms: "I think he'd like to strut his stuff, as the patriarch. He is the dick that stayed hard longer." ("The surprising thing is that you won't see Clarence Thomas going on that March," Anita Hill remarks of another icon of patriarchy.) Farrakhan himself prefers metaphors of

military mobilization, but the exclusionary politics of the event has clearly distracted from its ostensible message of solidarity. "First of all, I wouldn't go to no war and leave half the army home," says Amiri Baraka, the radical poet and playwright who achieved international renown in the sixties as the leading spokesman for the Black Arts movement. "Logistically, that doesn't make sense." He notes that Martin Luther King's 1963 March on Washington was "much more inclusive," and sees Farrakhan's regression as "an absolute duplication of what's happening in the country," from Robert Bly on: the sacralization of masculinity.

Something like that dynamic is what many white feminists saw on display in the Simpson verdict; but it's among women that the racial divide is especially salient. The black legal scholar and activist Patricia Williams says she was "stunned by the intensely personal resentment of some of my white women friends in particular." Stunned but, on reflection, not mystified. "This is Greek drama," she declares. "Two of the most hotly contended aspects of our lives are violence among human beings who happen to be police officers and violence among human beings who happen to be husbands, spouses, lovers." Meanwhile, our attention has been fixated on the rhetorical violence between human beings who happen to disagree about the outcome of the O. J. Simpson trial. ...

"Trials don't establish absolute truth; that's a theological enterprise," Patricia Williams says. So perhaps it is appropriate that a religious leader, Louis Farrakhan, convened a day of atonement; indeed, some worry that it is all too appropriate, coming at a time when the resurgent right has offered us a long list of sins for which black men must atone. But the crisis of race in America is real enough. And with respect to that crisis a mass mobilization is surely a better fit than a criminal trial. These days, the assignment of blame for black woes increasingly looks like an exercise in scholasticism; and calls for interracial union increasingly look like an exercise in inanity. ("Sorry for the Middle Passage, old chap. I don't know *what* we were thinking." "Hey, man, forget it — and here's your wallet back. No, really, I want you to have it.") The black economist Glenn Loury says, "If I could get a million black men together, I wouldn't march them to Washington, I'd march them into the ghettos."

But because the meanings of the march are so ambiguous, it has become itself a racial Rorschach — a vast ambulatory allegory waiting to happen. The actor and director Sidney Poitier says, "If we go on such a march to say to ourselves and to the rest of America that we want to be counted among America's people, we would like our family structure to be nurtured and strengthened by ourselves and by the society, that's a good point to make." He sees the march as an occasion for the community to say, "Look, we are adrift. Not only is the nation adrift on the question of race — we, too, are adrift. We need to have a sense of purpose and a sense of direction." Maya Angelou, who agreed to address the assembled men, views the event not as a display of male self-affirmation but as a ceremony of penitence: "It's a chance for African-American males to say to African-American females, 'I'm sorry. I am sorry for what I did, and I am sorry for what happened to both of us.'" But different observers will have different interpretations. Mass mobilizations launch a thousand narratives — especially among subscribers to what might be called the "great event" school of history. And yet Farrakhan's recurrent calls for individual accountability consort oddly with the absolution, both juridical and populist, accorded O. J. Simpson. Simpson has been seen as a symbol for many things, but he is not yet a symbol for taking responsibility for one's actions.

All the same, the task for black America is not to get its symbols in shape: symbolism is one of the few commodities we have in abundance. Meanwhile, DuBois's century-old question "How does it feel to be a problem?" grows in trenchancy with every new bulletin about crime and poverty. And the Simpson trial spurs us to question everything except the way that the discourse of crime and punishment has enveloped, and suffocated, the analysis of race and poverty in this country. For the debate over the rights and wrongs of the Simpson verdict has meshed all too well with the manner in which we have long talked about race and social justice. The defendant may be free, but we remain captive to a binary discourse of accusation and counter-accusation, of grievance and counter-grievance, of victims and victimizers. It is a discourse in which O. J. Simpson is a suitable remedy for Rodney King, and reductions in Medicaid are entertained as a suitable remedy for O. J. Simpson: a discourse in which everyone speaks of payback and nobody is paid. The result is that race politics becomes a court of the imagination wherein blacks seek to punish whites for their misdeeds and whites seek to punish blacks for theirs, and an infinite regress score-settling ensues — yet another way in which we are daily becoming meta and meta. And so an empty vessel like O. J Simpson becomes filled with meaning, and more meaning — more meaning than any of us can bear. No doubt it is a far easier thing to assign blame than to render justice. But if the imagery of the court continues to confine the conversation about race, it will really be a crime.

——— 9.28 ———

'GOVERNMENT-SPONSORED RACIAL DISCRIMINATION BASED ON BENIGN PREJUDICE IS JUST AS NOXIOUS AS DISCRIMINATION INSPIRED BY MALICIOUS PREJUDICE'
Justice Clarence Thomas

Throughout the 1980s and 1990s, the backlash to affirmative action swelled. By the close of the 20th century, the future of both federal and state level programs, in the public as well as the private sector, was in question. Politically, affirmative action came under attack most heavily in California, where the state university system dumped all such efforts in hiring and admissions in

1995. The following year voters passed Proposition 209, which blocked racial considerations in any state-funded program. Around the country, conservative legal activists systematically attacked affirmative action programs in an effort to establish their unconstitutionality based on a web of court rulings striking them down. As a testimony to that effort's success, in 1996 the 5th U.S. Circuit Court ruled that the University of Texas Law School could not consider race in hiring and admissions, contradicting the 1978 Supreme Court ruling in *Bakke* (see Chapter Eight). But the most significant legal development came in the Supreme Court's 1995 ruling in *Adarand v. Pena*. The case examined a Small Business Administration regulation that required that a percentage of federal highway construction contracts go to small businesses owned by "socially and economically disadvantaged individuals," which it defined as racial and ethnic minorities.

Writing for the majority, Justice Sandra Day O'Connor argued that the rule violated the constitutional guarantee to due process before the law, just as any other race-based consideration by the government would. The Court declared that, in order to consider race and ethnicity in federal contracts, the government must be able show both a "compelling interest" and that their solution to the problem at hand is "narrowly tailored." This represented the application of "strict scrutiny," the most stringent legal standard of proof, to the defense of affirmative action. Justices John Paul Stevens and Ruth Bader Ginsberg dissented, arguing, in Stephens' words, "There is no moral or constitutional equivalence between a policy that is designed to perpetuate a caste system and one that seeks to eradicate racial subordination. Invidious discrimination is an engine of oppression, subjugating a disfavored group to enhance or maintain the power of the majority. Remedial race-based preferences reflect the opposite impulse: a desire to foster equality in society." Justice Clarence Thomas responded to that dissent, articulating his own distaste for affirmative action, a feeling shared by many conservative African Americans.

I agree with the majority's conclusion that strict scrutiny applies to all government classifications based on race. I write separately, however, to express my disagreement with the premise underlying JUSTICE STEVENS' and JUSTICE GINSBURG'S dissents: that there is a racial paternalism exception to the principle of equal protection. I believe that there is a "moral [and] constitutional equivalence," between laws designed to subjugate a race and those that distribute benefits on the basis of race in order to foster some current notion of equality. Government cannot make us equal; it can only recognize, respect, and protect us as equal before the law.

That these programs may have been motivated, in part, by good intentions cannot provide refuge from the principle that under our Constitution, the government may not make distinctions on the basis of race. As far as the Constitution is concerned, it is irrelevant whether a government's racial classifications are drawn by those who wish to oppress a race or by those who have a sincere desire to help those thought to be disadvantaged. There can be no doubt that the paternalism that appears to lie at the heart of this program is at war with the principle of inherent equality that underlies and infuses our Constitution.

These programs not only raise grave constitutional questions, they also undermine the moral basis of the equal protection principle. Purchased at the price of immeasurable human suffering, the equal protection principle reflects our Nation's understanding that such classifications ultimately have a destructive impact on the individual and our society. Unquestionably, "[i]nvidious [racial] discrimination is an engine of oppression." It is also true that "[r]emedial" racial preferences may reflect "a desire to foster equality in society." But there can be no doubt that racial paternalism and its unintended consequences can be as poisonous and pernicious as any other form of discrimination. So-called "benign" discrimination teaches many that because of chronic and apparently immutable handicaps, minorities cannot compete with them without their patronizing indulgence. Inevitably, such programs engender attitudes of superiority or, alternatively, provoke resentment among those who believe that they have been wronged by the government's use of race. These programs stamp minorities with a badge of inferiority and may cause them to develop dependencies or to adopt an attitude that they are "entitled" to preferences. Indeed, JUSTICE STEVENS once recognized the real harms stemming from seemingly "benign" discrimination. (Noting that "remedial" race legislation "is perceived by many as resting on an assumption that those who are granted this special preference are less qualified in some respect that is identified purely by their race.")

In my mind, government-sponsored racial discrimination based on benign prejudice is just as noxious as discrimination inspired by malicious prejudice. In each instance, it is racial discrimination, plain and simple.

————— 9.29 —————
'WHAT THE UNITED STATES GOVERNMENT DID WAS SHAMEFUL, AND I AM SORRY'
President Bill Clinton

Among the actions that made President Bill Clinton one of the most popular presidents among African Americans was his historic 1997 apology for the Tuskegee syphilis experiments (see Chapter Eight). By the end of the Tuskegee project in 1972, 28 of the men involved had died of syphilis, 40 of their wives had been infected and 19 of their children had been born with the virus. Black leaders and public health officials had urged the White House to do something to counter the lingering distrust in government-related health-care initiatives. As a community, African Americans struggle with some of the worst health problems in the nation. From AIDS to asthma to heart disease, blacks have consistently ranked as most at-risk. And efforts to turn that trend around have been hampered by the distrust stemming from, among other things, the legacy of Tuskegee. Clinton agreed. And on May 16, 1997, flanked by 94-year-old Herman Shaw, a survivor of the experiments, Clinton issued the apology below. In a passionate speech, he called the endeavor "shameful" and "clearly racist." The impact of such a seemingly simple statement is a testament to Cornel West's assertions that the nation has never dealt with its racial history.

Ladies and gentlemen, on Sunday, Mr. Shaw will celebrate his 95th birthday. I would like to recognize the other survivors who are here today and their families: Mr. Charlie Pollard is here. Mr. Carter Howard. Mr. Fred Simmons. Mr. Simmons just took his first airplane ride, and he reckons he's about 110 years old, so I think it's time for him to take a chance or two. I'm glad he did. And Mr. Frederick Moss, thank you, sir.

I would also like to ask three family representatives who are here — Sam Doner is represented by his daughter, Gwendolyn Cox. Thank you, Gwendolyn. Ernest Hendon, who is watching in Tuskegee, is represented by his brother, North Hendon. Thank you, sir, for being here. And George Key is represented by his grandson, Christopher Monroe. Thank you, Chris.

I also acknowledge the families, community leaders, teachers and students watching today by satellite from Tuskegee. The White House is the people's house; we are glad to have all of you here today. ...

The eight men who are survivors of the syphilis study at Tuskegee are a living link to a time not so very long ago that many Americans would prefer not to remember, but we dare not forget. It was a time when our nation failed to live up to its ideals, when our nation broke the trust with our people that is the very foundation of our democracy. It is not only in remembering that shameful past that we can make amends and repair our nation, but it is in remembering that past that we can build a better present and a better future. And without remembering it, we cannot make amends and we cannot go forward.

So today America does remember the hundreds of men used in research without their knowledge and consent. We remember them and their family members. Men who were poor and African American, without resources and with few alternatives, they believed they had found hope when they were offered free medical care by the United States Public Health Service. They were betrayed.

Medical people are supposed to help when we need care, but even once a cure was discovered, they were denied help, and they were lied to by their government. Our government is supposed to protect the rights of its citizens; their rights were trampled upon. Forty years, hundreds of men betrayed, along with their wives and children, along with the community in Macon County, Alabama, the City of Tuskegee, the fine university there, and the larger African American community.

The United States government did something that was wrong — deeply, profoundly, morally wrong. It was an outrage to our commitment to integrity and equality for all our citizens.

To the survivors, to the wives and family members, the children and the grandchildren, I say what you know: No power on Earth can give you back the lives lost, the pain suffered, the years of internal torment and anguish. What was done cannot be undone. But we can end the silence. We can stop turning our heads away. We can look at you in the eye and finally say on behalf of the American people, what the United States government did was shameful, and I am sorry.

The American people are sorry — for the loss, for the years of hurt. You did nothing wrong, but you were grievously wronged. I apologize and I am sorry that this apology has been so long in coming.

To Macon County, to Tuskegee, to the doctors who have been wrongly associated with the events there, you have our apology, as well. To our African-American citizens, I am sorry that your federal government orchestrated a study so clearly racist. That can never be allowed to happen again. It is against everything our country stands for and what we must stand against is what it was.

So let us resolve to hold forever in our hearts and minds the memory of a time not long ago in Macon County, Alabama, so that we can always see how adrift we can become when the rights of any citizens are neglected, ignored and betrayed. And let us resolve here and now to move forward together.

The legacy of the study at Tuskegee has reached far and deep, in ways that hurt our progress and divide our nation. We cannot be one America when a whole segment of our nation has no trust in America. An apology is the first step, and we take it with a commitment to rebuild that broken trust. We can begin by making sure there is never again another episode like this one. We need to do more to ensure that medical research practices are sound and ethical, and that researchers work more closely with communities.

Today I would like to announce several steps to help us achieve these goals. First, we will help to build that lasting memorial at Tuskegee. The school founded by Booker T. Washington, distinguished by the renowned scientist George Washington Carver and so many others who advanced the health and well-being of African Americans and all Americans, is a fitting site. The Department of Health and Human Services will award a planning grant so the school can pursue establishing a center for bioethics in research and health care. The center will serve as a museum of the study and support efforts to address its legacy and strengthen bioethics training.

Second, we commit to increase our community involvement so that we may begin restoring lost trust. The study at Tuskegee served to sow distrust of our medical institutions, especially where research is involved. Since the study was halted, abuses have been checked by making informed consent and local review mandatory in federally-funded and mandated research.

Still, 25 years later, many medical studies have little African-American participation and African-American organ donors are few. This impedes efforts to conduct promising research and to provide the best health care to all our people, including African Americans. So today, I'm directing the Secretary of Health and Human Services, Donna Shalala, to issue a report in 180 days about how we can best involve communities, especially minority communities, in research and health care. You must — every American group must be involved in medical research in ways that are positive. We have put the curse behind us; now we must bring the benefits to all Americans.

Third, we commit to strengthen researchers' training in bioethics. We are constantly working on making breakthroughs in protecting the health of our people and in vanquishing diseases. But all our people must be assured that their rights and dignity will be respected as new drugs, treatments and therapies are tested and used. So I am directing Secretary Shalala to work in partnership with higher education to prepare training materials for medical researchers. They will be available in a year. They will help researchers build on core ethical principles of respect for individuals, justice and informed consent, and advise them on how to use these principles effectively in diverse populations.

Fourth, to increase and broaden our understanding of ethical issues and clinical research, we commit to providing postgraduate fellowships to train bioethicists especially among African Americans and other minority groups. HHS will offer these fellowships beginning in September of 1998 to promising students enrolled in bioethics graduate programs.

And, finally, by executive order I am also today extending the charter of the National Bioethics Advisory Commission to October of 1999. The need for this commission is clear. We must be able to call on the thoughtful, collective wisdom of experts and community representatives to find ways to further strengthen our protections for subjects in human research.

We face a challenge in our time. Science and technology are rapidly changing our lives with the promise of making us much healthier, much more productive and more prosperous. But with these changes we must work harder to see that as we advance we don't leave behind our conscience. No ground is gained and, indeed, much is lost if we lose our moral bearings in the name of progress.

The people who ran the study at Tuskegee diminished the stature of man by abandoning the most basic ethical precepts. They forgot their pledge to heal and repair. They had the power to heal the survivors and all the others

and they did not. Today, all we can do is apologize. But you have the power, for only you — Mr. Shaw, the others who are here, the family members who are with us in Tuskegee — only you have the power to forgive. Your presence here shows us that you have chosen a better path than your government did so long ago. You have not withheld the power to forgive. I hope today and tomorrow every American will remember your lesson and live by it.

Thank you, and God bless you.

——————— 9.30 ———————
'I RISE TO OBJECT!'
Congressional Black Caucus

The presidential election of 2000 was the closest in modern history. Following an epic election night, when both candidates thought they had won at one time or another, the election evolved into a legal battle over the vote count in Florida. The Democratic nominee, Vice President Al Gore, had narrowly won the popular vote nationally. But, without Florida's 25 electoral votes, he would lose the contest in the Electoral College. Bush appeared to have won those votes, but thousands of popular votes — deemed unreadable by mechanical vote counters or ineligible because of voter error — had not been counted. Most observers believed those discarded votes would have swung the state — and the election — in Gore's favor. Gore's camp filed a number of lawsuits to get them counted, launching tortured legal arguments as to why the state's refusal to recognize them was illegal. He did not, however, argue that there had been widespread voting irregularities based on race in Florida. Black political leaders did, and were furious.

Ultimately, the Supreme Court settled the matter, clearing Florida election officials to certify Bush's victory. National politicians, including Gore, called for healing and urged America to accept the legitimacy of Bush's victory. Black leaders in and out of government pointedly refused. The voting irregularities uncovered during the controversy in Florida smacked of age-old Jim Crow tactics. The NAACP and the Congressional Black Caucus (CBC) began inquiries, and in county after county where there was a majority black population, voting irregularities were reported. Haitians had been refused translators. Confused voters had been turned away from the polls and lied to about the proper procedures for casting a vote.

Technology had been unevenly distributed, neglecting predominantly black districts.

When Congress met in January 2001 to certify the election, despite the calls for unity, the CBC objected. Rules required any objection to be signed by at least one senator, but none would join the CBC campaign. So, unable to file a formal objection, when the Electoral College votes were presented — with Gore, as sitting vice president, presiding — one CBC member after another rose to voice their protests. The Congressional Record transcript of the proceedings is excerpted below.

(Ms. WATERS asked and was given permission to address the House for 1 minute.)

Ms. WATERS. Mr. Speaker, let the record show that on today, Saturday, January 6, I am present on the floor of the House of Representatives prepared to object to the electoral vote count for the State of Florida at the proceedings that will take place at 1 o'clock.

Let the record show that the rules require all objections to be submitted in writing and signed by a Member of the House and a Member of the Senate. As of 11:00 today, I have not been able to identify any U.S. Senator prepared to sign any objections; therefore, all attempts to object may be denied. However, I am voicing my objections to the electoral votes submitted by Florida.

Mr. Speaker, I believe these electoral votes to be illegitimate and unrepresentative of the true popular vote in Florida. Vice President Gore is leading in popular votes in excess of 500,000 votes in this country, and all of Florida's vote recounts are not yet tabulated. The recounts will document that Gore won Florida, despite voter fraud, despite voter intimidation, despite the butterfly ballots, despite the criminal recording of ID numbers on absentee ballots. History will record what really took place in this election. ...

The VICE PRESIDENT. For what purpose does the gentlewoman from California (Ms. WATERS) rise?

Ms. WATERS. Mr. Vice President, I rise to object to the fraudulent 25 Florida electoral votes.

The VICE PRESIDENT. Is the objection in writing and signed by a Member of the House and a Senator?

Ms. WATERS. The objection is in writing, and I do not care that it is not signed by a Member of the Senate.

The VICE PRESIDENT. The Chair will advise that the rules do care, and the signature of a Senator is required. The Chair will again put that part of the question: Is the objection signed by a Senator?

Ms. WATERS. Mr. Vice President, there are gross violations of the Voting Rights Act from Florida, and I object; and it is not signed by a Senator.

The VICE PRESIDENT. The Chair thanks the gentlewoman from California. On the basis previously stated, the objection may not be received.

For what purpose does the gentlewoman from California (Ms. LEE) rise?

Ms. LEE. Mr. President, I have an objection.

The VICE PRESIDENT. Is the objection in writing and signed by a Member of the House of Representatives and a Senator?

Ms. LEE. Mr. President, it is in writing and signed by myself on behalf of many of the diverse constituents in our country, especially those in the Ninth Congressional District and all American voters who recognize that the Supreme Court, not the people of the United States, decided this election.

The VICE PRESIDENT. Is the objection signed by a Senator?

Ms. LEE. Unfortunately, Mr. President, it is not signed by one single Senator.

The VICE PRESIDENT. On the basis previously stated, the objection may not be received. The Chair thanks the gentlewoman from California.

For what purpose does the gentlewoman from Georgia (Ms. MCKINNEY) rise?

Ms. McKINNEY. Mr. President, I have an objection at the desk to Florida's 25 electoral votes.

The VICE PRESIDENT. Is the objection in writing and signed by a Member of the House of Representatives and a Senator?

Ms. McKINNEY. Mr. President, it is in writing and it is signed by my Congressional Black Caucus colleagues, my House colleagues and myself; but it is not signed by one single Senator.

The VICE PRESIDENT. The Chair thanks the gentlewoman from Georgia. On the basis previously stated, the objection may not be received.

For what purpose does the gentlewoman from Hawaii (Mrs. MINK) rise?

Mrs. MINK of Hawaii. Mr. President, I want to voice my objection.

The VICE PRESIDENT. Is the objection in writing and signed by a Member of the House of Representatives and a Senator?

Mrs. MINK of Hawaii. Mr. President, it is in writing, and I have signed it on behalf of not only myself and other colleagues of the House but my constituents. Unfortunately, I have no authority over the United States Senate and no Senator has signed.

The VICE PRESIDENT. The Chair thanks the gentlewoman from Hawaii. On the basis previously stated, the objection may not be received.

For what purpose does the gentlewoman from North Carolina (Mrs. CLAYTON) rise?

Mrs. CLAYTON. Mr. President, I rise in objection to the Florida electoral votes, and I rise to object to the process that, indeed, that voters do count, the essence of democracy demands that we speak to it.

The VICE PRESIDENT. Is the objection in writing and is it signed by a Member of the House of Representatives and a Senator?

Mrs. CLAYTON. Mr. President, it is in writing and it is signed by more than 10 of my Members in the House.

The VICE PRESIDENT. Is the objection signed by a Senator?

Mrs. CLAYTON. Unfortunately, it is not.

The VICE PRESIDENT. On the basis previously stated, the objection may not be received. The Chair thanks the gentlewoman from North Carolina. …

Ms. WATERS. Mr. Speaker, I rise to address the House for 5 minutes to speak about what took place here in joint session today and to talk about what has led us to this point.

Today, here in this Chamber, we had a joint session to count the electoral votes; and, of course, there were some of us, mostly represented by Members from the Congressional Black Caucus, who chose to come to the floor in an attempt to object to the acceptance of the electoral votes from Florida. We did that, despite the fact we understood the rules. We knew that in order to object, we had to have in writing the objection, signed by both a House Member and a Member of the Senate.

We did not have one Member of the Senate who had signed any objection, but we came to the floor of this House and we said to the Vice President, who presided over the joint session, each time that we objected we said that, no, we did not have a signature from a United States Senator, that we only had our signatures, we had the signatures of some of our colleagues, and we had the support of our constituents.

It was important for us to do this. It was important because we have just experienced one of the most traumatizing and devastating elections, particularly as it played out in Florida, that this country has ever been involved with.

I would like to cite to you some of what happened in Florida that has caused us so much concern. I am going to quote from an article that was done by Laura Flanders. I will not be quoting all of the article, but I will be submitting the rest of this for inclusion in the record.

On day one after the election, there was a story in the Florida papers about an unauthorized police roadblock, stopping cars not a mile from a black church-turned-polling-booth. NAACP volunteers reported being swamped with complaints from registered voters who found it impossible to vote. They heard stories of intimidation at and around polling places; demands for superfluous ID; people complained about a pattern of singling out black men and youth for criminal background checks, and in call after call, would-be voters complained they had been denied language interpretation and other help at the polls.

By now it is clear that overwhelmed election workers made a mass of mistakes, but those mistakes were laced through with some clear intent to suppress some votes.

A full three weeks after the election, *The New York Times* finally took a serious look and reported that, anticipating a large turnout in a tight race, Florida election officials had given laptop computers to precinct workers so they would have direct access to the State's voter rolls, but the computers only went to some precincts and only one went to a precinct whose people were predominantly black. The technology gap in the no-laptop precincts forced the workers there to rely on a few phone lines to the head office. Voters whose names did not appear on the rolls were held up, while workers tried to get through on the phone, for hours, or until they gave up.

For those who voted, there was another technology glitch. Mr. Speaker, 185,000 Floridians cast votes that did not count. Theirs were the ballots that had been punched too few or too many times, or were otherwise flawed. Flaws too, seem to have followed race lines. In an election that turned on a few hundred votes, Floridians whose ballots failed to register a mark for President were much more likely to have voted with computer punch cards than optical scanning machines. In Miami Dade, the county with the most votes cast, predominantly black precincts saw their votes thrown out at 4 times the rate of white precincts. According to the Times, one out of 11 ballots in predominantly black precincts were rejected, a total of 9,904.

Urban, multi-racial Palm Beach, home of the infamous butterfly ballot and Duval, where candidates' names were spread across 2 pages despite what the published ballot had shown, produced 31 percent of Florida's discarded ballots, but only 12 percent of the total votes cast. In Duval, which has one of the highest illiteracy rates in the Nation, more than 26,000

votes were rejected, 9,000 from precincts that were predominantly black.

Many Floridians who found themselves "scrubbed" off the voting rolls were not purged accidentally, reports Gregory Palast for Salon.com. Florida Secretary of State Katherine Harris paid a private firm, ChoicePoint, $4 million to cleanse the voting rolls, and the firm used the State's felon-ban to exclude 8,000 voters who had never committed a felony. ChoicePoint is a Republican outfit. Board members include former New York Police Commissioner Howard Safir, and billionaire Ken Langone, chair of the fund-raising committee for Mayor Giuliani's aborted New York Senate bid.

I cannot complete all of what I would like to share, but I will be submitting this for the record. Let the record show that we were here today, that we participated and we voiced our objection, and the fight will continue for justice and equality. People were disenfranchised, and that must be stopped and corrected. ...

────── 9.31 ──────

'AMERICA IS SPECIAL AMONG NATIONS'

Condoleezza Rice

Despite the racially tinged controversy of the 2000 elections, the Bush administration came into office and made history for African Americans with high-level foreign policy appointments. Bush's cabinet included the first black secretary of state, retired General Colin Powell, who had already served as chairman of the Joint Chiefs of Staff and was a well-known and respected figure. But Bush also appointed Condoleezza Rice as his national security advisor, making Rice the highest-ranking black woman to serve in government. Rice had stormed onto the national scene as Bush's foreign policy advisor during the campaign.

Bush ran for the White House as a governor with little world affairs background and battled media speculation he wasn't smart enough for the job. So throughout the campaign he leaned on Rice's glowing credentials as a president of Stanford University and a Russian affairs expert to bolster his own résumé. But her real political payoff came in domestic affairs. The Bush campaign sold a "big tent" vision of the Republican Party, in which divisive social issues played less of a role and conservative blacks and Latinos were welcomed. Rice's speech during the July 2000 party convention—an affair heavily choreographed to showcase the party's diversity—went a long way toward conveying that image to the nation. In it, she articulated the understanding of racial politics and personal identity that had shaped her life. Rice had grown up middle class in black Birmingham, Alabama, and was a young girl at the time of the devastating church bombings. Contrary to what many critics have argued, being black was a central part of her identity, and she did not presume America to be free of racism. But her solution for conquering racism lay in developing a racial identity driven by her individual powers and abilities, not the strength of a larger, racially defined community.

But if the contemporary impact of Rice's speech was that the nation watched a smart black woman proudly articulate why she supported the GOP and Bush, viewed through the lens of history her foreign policy pronouncements appear comically ironic. Bush's presidency was marred by, among other things, a disastrous and wildly unpopular war in Iraq driven by a foreign policy vision quite incongruent with that outlined by Rice. Her tenure as national security advisor was considered at best a disappointment, precisely because she failed to outmaneuver a cabal of neo-conservative hawks who shaped the administration's foreign policy in its first term. She would recoup her reputation in Bush's second term, when she became the first black woman to serve as secretary of state. There, she was widely credited with rebuilding a department that had been marginalized by the neo-cons and successfully reigning in their still expansive vision of America's military as a global sledgehammer for spreading democracy.

… It is fitting that I stand before you to talk about Governor Bush's commitment to America's principled leadership in the world, because that is the legacy and tradition of our party—because our party's principles made me a Republican.

The first Republican I knew was my father and he is still the Republican I most admire. He joined our party because the Democrats in Jim Crow Alabama of 1952 would not register him to vote. The Republicans did. My father has never forgotten that day, and neither have I.

I joined for different reasons. I found a party that sees me as an individual, not as part of a group. I found a party that puts family first. I found a party that has love of liberty at its core. And I found a party that believes that peace begins with strength.

George W. Bush and Dick Cheney live and breathe these Republican principles. They understand what is required for our time, and what is timeless.

It all begins with integrity in the Oval Office. George W. Bush is a man of his word. Friend and foe will know that he tells the truth.

He believes that America has a special responsibility to keep the peace—that the fair cause of freedom depends on our strength and purpose.

He recognizes that the magnificent men and women of America's armed forces are not a global police force. They are not the world's 911.

They are the strongest shield and surest sword in the maintenance of peace. If the time ever comes to use military force, President George W. Bush will do so to win—because for him, victory is not a dirty word.

George W. Bush will never allow America and our allies to be blackmailed. And make no mistake; blackmail is what the outlaw states seeking long-range ballistic missiles have in mind. It is time to move beyond the Cold War. It is time to have a president devoted to a new nuclear strategy and to the deployment of effective missile defenses at the earliest possible date.

George W. Bush knows that America has allies and friends who share our values. As he has said, the president should call our allies when they are not needed, so that he can call upon them when they are needed.

He understands the power of trade to create jobs at home and extend liberty abroad.

The George W. Bush I know is a man of uncommonly good judgment. He is focused and consistent. He believes that we Americans are at our best when we exercise power without fanfare or arrogance. He speaks plainly and with a positive spirit. In the past year, I have had a glimpse of what kind of president he will be.

I traveled with him to Mexico and saw the respect he has gained from its leaders and the affection he has won from its people. When he enters office, he will know more about our neighbor Mexico than any president in our history. He speaks to the Mexican people not just in the language of diplomacy, but in their native tongue.

I have watched him explain America's interests to the Russian foreign minister, while assuring him that a peaceful Russia has nothing to fear from America.

He told the South African president of his hope for peace and prosperity in Africa.

I know that he understands the complexities of our relationship with China. He believes that conflict between our nations is not inevitable. Yet he recognizes the challenge that the Chinese government poses to our interests and values and the irresistible demand for liberty that can be unleashed by freer trade with its people.

And he has joined the bipartisan tradition of support for Israel's quest for enduring peace with its neighbors.

George W. Bush will work with Congress so that America speaks with one voice. He has demonstrated in this campaign that he will never use foreign policy for narrow partisan purposes.

The United States cannot lead unless the President inspires the American people to accept their international responsibilities. George W. Bush will inspire us, because he understands who we are.

He knows that we are an innovative people who find kinship with those in other nations who are entrepreneurial in spirit.

He realizes that we are a nation that has been forged not from common blood but from common purpose—that the faces of America are the faces of the world. It has not been easy for our country to make "We, the people" mean all the people. Democracy in America is a work in progress—not a finished masterpiece.

But even with its flaws, this unique American experience provides a shining beacon to peoples who still suffer in places where ethnic difference is a license to kill.

And George W. Bush understands that America is special among nations. That throughout our history, people everywhere have been inspired to flee tyranny and the constraints of class to gain liberty and pursue happiness in this great land.

In America, with education and hard work, it really does not matter where you came from—it matters where you are going. But that truth cannot be sustained if it is not renewed in each generation—as it was with my grandfather.

George W. Bush would have liked Granddaddy Rice. He was a poor farmer's son in rural Alabama—but he recognized the importance of education. Around 1918, he decided it was time to get book learning, so he asked, in the language of the day, where a colored man could go to college. He was told about little Stillman College, a school about 50 miles away. So Granddaddy saved his cotton for tuition and went off to Tuscaloosa.

After the first year, he ran out of cotton and needed a way to pay for college. Praise be—God gave him one. Grandfather asked how the other boys were staying in school. "They have what's called a scholarship," he was told, "and if you wanted to be a Presbyterian minister, then you could have one, too." Granddaddy Rice said, "That's just what I had in mind." And my family has been Presbyterian and college-educated ever since. This is not just my grandfather's story—it is an American story.

My friends, George W. Bush challenges us to call upon our better selves—to be compassionate toward those who are less fortunate; to cherish and educate every child, descendants of slaves and immigrants alike, and to thereby affirm the American dream for us all.

On that foundation, confident of who we are, we will extend peace, prosperity and liberty beyond our shores.

Elect George W. Bush and Dick Cheney! God bless you and God bless America.

——— 9.33 ———
'GEORGE BUSH DOESN'T CARE ABOUT BLACK PEOPLE'
Kanye West

Early on the morning of August 29, 2005, Hurricane Katrina slammed into the southeast shore of Louisiana. The massive storm had first formed six days previous over the Bahamas, and the nation watched with horror as it barreled toward the mainland of the United States. While over the Gulf of Mexico, it grew to one of the strongest hurricanes on record. But it lost steam as it headed inland, and by the time it reached New Orleans many were breathing a sigh of relief at what was expected to be a severely damaging, but not catastrophic, blow. That reaction proved to be tragically premature. The levees protecting the historic city, built essentially in a basin, gave way and much of New Orleans, particularly the low-income and African-American lower 9th ward, was swept away in putrid, deadly waters.

But more than by the storm itself, the nation was rocked by the Bush administration's slow and inept response to a disaster that became one of the deadliest and costliest in U.S. history. Hour after hour, cable news beamed images of poor African-American survivors trapped on their rooftops. Many who escaped their homes were taken to shelter at the New Orleans Saints' football stadium, the Superdome, only to be stranded in squalor there. And with each day that passed without a federal response, black outrage grew greater. The indignities piled one on top of the next: News media inflamed tensions by repeatedly characterizing black people who were scavenging for survival goods as looters. Many black observers also cringed when commentators referred to the primarily black storm survivors still trapped in the city as "refugees." The term reinforced the idea that black citizenship was of a different quality than that of whites.

Meanwhile, the Bush administration continued to reinforce the impression that it simply couldn't be bothered to help. The president himself offered what would become an iconic symbol of his failure amid this crisis. In a press conference while touring Louisiana's destruction, Bush turned to his by-then widely discredited Federal Emergency Management Agency director, Michael Brown, and opined, "Brownie, you're doing a heck of a job." The

ordeal was five days old and many survivors were still stranded in floodwaters.

With all of this as backdrop, hip-hop star Kanye West provided the moment that ultimately came to represent black America's response to Katrina. On the same day as Bush's remark, the Red Cross and NBC produced a televised benefit concert. During a break in the performances, West and comedian Mike Myers stood together to make a pitch for donations. Behind them, the haunting images of stranded black families continued to show on a large monitor. Myers spoke first, but when West's turn came he departed from the script. Visibly shaken, West let fly a staccato, stream-of-conscious condemnation of the government's response to the crisis. It was a break with decorum so many had longed for over the previous days. Finally, someone had acknowledged the racial elephant in the middle of America's TV screens. When West concluded bluntly, "George Bush doesn't care about black people," the producers cut away.

A. Kanye West at the Red Cross's benefit

West: I hate the way they portray us in the media. You see a black family, it says, "They're looting." You see a white family, it says, "They're looking for food." And, you know, it's been five days because most of the people are black. And even for me to complain about it, I would be a hypocrite, because I've tried to turn away from the TV, because it's too hard to watch. I've even been shopping before even giving a donation. So now I'm calling my business manager right now to see what's—what is the biggest amount I can give. And just to imagine, if I was—if I was down there. And those are—those are my people down there. So anybody out there that wants to do anything that we can help — with the set up, the way America is set up to help, the poor, the black people, the less well-off, as slow as possible. I mean, this is, the Red Cross is doing everything they can. We already realize a lot of people that could help are at war right now, fighting another way — and they've given them permission to go down and shoot us.

Myers: [Pause.] And subtle but even, in many ways, more profoundly devastating is the lasting damage to the survivors' will to rebuild and remain in the area. The destruction of the spirit of the people of southern Louisiana and Mississippi may end up being the most tragic loss of all.

West: George Bush doesn't care about black people.

Myers: Please call—[Producer cuts.]

B. An oral history of Katrina survivor Tysuan Harris, collected by G. R. Anderson, Jr., for the *Minneapolis/St. Paul City Pages.*

People need to understand what happened, once and for all. My name's Tysuan Harris, and I'm from New Orleans, Louisiana, the lower Ninth Ward. My husband and I, I'm just gonna say his name is Moe, been married five months. When the water went through, our house was completely underwater, and my husband had to kick in the door above us. And me, my husband and four of our dogs—we had a pit bull and three puppy pit bulls—stayed up there for two days, in the apartment above us.

We slept up there for two days with two bottles of water and a block of cheese left to eat. We didn't have no power. We was laying in our feces, and also the dog feces. We was burning t-shirts and plastic to get the helicopters to notice us. And when a helicopter did notice us, he flashed his lights on us and kept going. Finally I told my husband I had given up on faith.

His cousin and his girlfriend walked in the water to come save us. They threw a door into the water, and we floated on top of the door to higher ground. The only thing we had was the pajamas on my back. My husband went back in the house to get me some shoes and dry clothes, but he couldn't salvage nothing. We had to leave our four dogs behind. We floated on that until we was able to get into water that was walkable, four blocks from our house. It was about 12 feet high up until then.

We got a boat and we canoed to France and Robertson Street, where we stayed in a two-level house with 20 other people. We had food,

we had water, but we didn't have electricity. No running water for toilets. We took a bath with bottled water, we washed our clothes with bottled water, and we slept in our underwear and wet t-shirts. This was on French Street in the lower Ninth Ward.

My husband and his cousin went out to get us food and water. It was like day four. They got [food and water] from stores that was broken down and stuff. They got anything that wasn't contaminated by the water. When they came back, the Coast Guard came and told us we had to leave because they was gonna open the floodgates to level the water off so the water could go down.

The Coast Guard told us we had to leave. I'm thinking I'm gonna die if nobody's gonna come help us. They didn't help us. They just told us to leave, they was evacuating the whole city. They told us to go to the Convention Center. It took us two days to get there. We walked the water through the darkness, flashing flashlights on each other to make sure nobody drowned. Oh, that water. Gas, oil, brake fluid, chains, bodies, snakes—everything. All kinds of snakes.

When we got to the Convention Center, the first thing I see is six dead bodies. We slept outside. It was like hell. It was like slavery days again. I ain't never been through it, but that's what it felt like. Four of us, two females, two men. Five days we're out there. Everything. Fires to get helicopters' attention. When they came and brought us water and food, it was peaceful for a second. But then agitation stirred up again. We were staying in the River Walk parking lot, that's where we slept for five days. Thousands of people. We [slept on] the grass. We made pallets on the parking lot, on the concrete. We took baths on them, with whatever bottled water we could find. We had candy, but we didn't have food-food, you know.

We tried to walk out once, across the Mississippi River bridge. The military turned us back. They pointed their guns at us and told us to get back down [off] the fucking bridge. Made us feel like shit. Like shit. They told us the only way we could cross was if we had a car. They probably thought if we were gonna walk we was gonna steal. But we just wanted out. Eventually we came across a car that had the keys still in it, and we drove it across the bridge. They let us cross. We got to a pay phone, and we called our cousin Tony, and he drove from Baton Rouge to come get us.

When Bush got off the helicopter, we were standing on the bridge waiting for them to come with a vehicle for us. He got out, and he had the nerve to have the military pointing guns at people who was trying to greet him to let him know we needed help. And I think that was sick of him. Then and when we tried to walk across was the first time in my life I ever had a gun pointed at me.

We stayed in Baton Rouge for four days. Then I had to go to the LSU medical center that they had opened up because I got sick. I have auto-immune hepatitis. I had got sick, and a pastor volunteered to drive us from Baton Rouge to Chicago. From Chicago we drove to Minnesota, and now we're living, nine of us, in a three-bedroom house with my husband's aunt and uncle.

My liver was shutting down on me. I couldn't tolerate food or water. I stayed until they got me stable enough to go for a 16-hour drive. Just to clear up, Jesse Jackson, LSU was not being racist. At all. You cannot say it's a race thing because if the NAACP was worried about us, they could have chartered planes and dropped us food. So if they gonna blame anybody, they might as well blame white and black politics too.

I'm gonna get a house in St. Paul. I ain't got nothing to go back to at all. I was a certified nurse's aide. In New Orleans we made 6 or 7 dollars. Here they pay you 15 and above, plus you get good benefits. I do want to say thank you to everyone in St. Paul, Minnesota, who helped everyone from New Orleans, Louisiana. You all been very, very kind.

Twenty-four years of my life, my whole family's from there. My mama, my daddy, my sister, my whole family's from there. Now my mama's in Texas, my father's in Texas, my little brother's in Alexandria, Louisiana, and my sister's in New York. I don't really get to talk to my sister and my brother. I know that they're all right. Only one I don't know about is my niece DeJhai Campbell. She's two years old and we don't know where she is.

--------- 9.34 ---------

'THIS WAS THE MOMENT ... WHERE AMERICA REMEMBERED WHAT IT MEANS TO HOPE'
Barack Obama

Barack Obama strode onto the national scene with an electrifying performance at the Democratic National Convention during the hotly contested 2004 elections, where he introduced the nation to his compelling articulation of "hope" as a revolutionary act rather than a naïve leap of faith. Democratic candidate John Kerry lost that election to President Bush, but Obama emerged from the campaign with the winds of history at his back. Two years later, when he won the Illinois Senate seat in his first statewide campaign, speculation about his bright future erupted. Commentators of all political stripes mused, improbably, about Obama one day rising to become America's first black president. But going into the 2008 elections, no one considered that more than wistful punditry—Hillary Clinton was the Democrats' presumed nominee, and the neophyte Obama was surely going to wait his turn before trying something so audacious.

But Obama proved to have more audacity than anyone could have imagined. The 48-year-old son of a white mother and black Kenyan father had already lived an unexpected life, having called places ranging from Hawaii to Harvard to the south side of Chicago his home. And he saw something in American political culture that few fully appreciated at the start of 2007: Voters were desperately seeking a dramatic break with the past. With a disastrous war dragging on and middle class families increasingly pinched by everything from a housing market crisis to sky-rocketing gas prices, a candidate that looked and sounded nothing like those they'd seen before held tremendous appeal. Obama stepped in to meet that demand.

He announced his run in February 2007, and plunged into the longest primary season America had ever seen.

The first actual vote wasn't until almost a year later, on January 3, 2008, in the Iowa Democratic caucuses. There, Obama stunned the nation with a commanding victory, and immediately became the party's front-runner for president. His victory speech from Des Moines was a hair-raising political moment in which black oratory—so long the impassioned and eloquent voice of an oppositional, marginalized minority—spoke for the political majority. Obama articulated the core message of his campaign: against all odds, America has the power to change, to become greater than the sum of its too-long-divided parts. He was the ideal carrier for such a message—mixed racial heritage; old enough to be a baby boomer, yet young enough to connect with those born into a post–Jim Crow world; Harvard educated but having spent 20 years in community organizing. His very existence spanned multiple historic lines of division in American culture, and Democratic voters embraced it.

Thank you, Iowa. You know, they said this day would never come. They said our sights were set too high. They said this country was too divided; too disillusioned to ever come together around a common purpose. But on this January night—at this defining moment in history—you have done what the cynics said we couldn't do. You have done what the state of New Hampshire can do in five days. You have done what America can do in this New Year, 2008. In lines that stretched around schools and churches; in small towns and big cities; you came together as Democrats, Republicans and Independents to stand up and say that we are one nation; we are one people; and our time for change has come.

You said the time has come to move beyond the bitterness and pettiness and anger that's consumed Washington; to end the political strategy that's been all about division and instead make it about addition—to build a coalition for change that stretches through "red" states and "blue" states. Because that's how we'll win in November, and that's how we'll finally meet the challenges that we face as a nation.

We are choosing hope over fear. We're choosing unity over division, and sending a powerful message that change is coming to America.

You said the time has come to tell the lobbyists who think their money and their influence speak louder than our voices that they don't own this government, we do; and we are here to take it back.

The time has come for a president who will be honest about the choices and the challenges we face; who will listen to you and learn from you even when we disagree; who won't just tell you what you want to hear, but what you need to know. And in New Hampshire, if you give me the same chance that Iowa did tonight, I will be that president for America.

I'll be a president who finally makes health care affordable and available to every single American the same way I expanded health care in Illinois—by bringing Democrats and Republicans together to get the job done.

I'll be a president who ends the tax breaks for companies that ship our jobs overseas and puts a middle-class tax cut into the pockets of the working Americans who deserve it.

I'll be a president who harnesses the ingenuity of farmers and scientists and entrepreneurs to free this nation from the tyranny of oil once and for all.

And I'll be a president who ends this war in Iraq and finally brings our troops home; who restores our moral standing; who understands that 9/11 is not a way to scare up votes, but a challenge that should unite America and the world against the common threats of the 21st century; common threats of terrorism and nuclear weapons; climate change and poverty; genocide and disease.

Tonight, we are one step closer to that vision of America because of what you did here in Iowa. And so I'd especially like to thank the organizers and the precinct captains; the volunteers and the staff who made this all possible.

And while I'm at it, on "thank yous," I think it makes sense for me to thank the love of my life, the rock of the Obama family, the closer on the campaign trail; give it up for Michelle Obama.

I know you didn't do this for me. You did this because you believed so deeply in the most American of ideas—that in the face of impossible odds, people who love this country can change it. I know this because while I may be standing here tonight, I'll never forget that my journey began on the streets of Chicago doing what so many of you have done for this campaign and all the campaigns here in Iowa — organizing and working and fighting to make people's lives just a little bit better.

I know how hard it is. It comes with little sleep, little pay, and a lot of sacrifice. There are days of disappointment, but sometimes, just sometimes, there are nights like this—a night that, years from now, when we've made the changes we believe in; when more families can afford to see a doctor; when our children—when Malia and Sasha and your children—inherit a planet that's a little cleaner and safer; when the world sees America differently, and America sees itself as a nation less divided and more united; you'll be able to look back with pride and say that this was the moment when it all began.

This was the moment when the improbable beat what Washington always said was inevitable. This was the moment when we tore down barriers that have divided us for too long—when we rallied people of all parties and ages to a common cause; when we finally gave Americans who'd never participated in politics a reason to stand up and to do so. This was the moment when we finally beat back the politics of fear, and doubt, and cynicism; the politics where we tear each other down instead of lifting this country up. This was the moment.

Years from now, you'll look back and you'll say that this was the moment — this was the place — where America remembered what it means to hope.

For many months, we've been teased, even derided for talking about hope. But we always knew that hope is not blind optimism. It's not ignoring the enormity of the task ahead or the roadblocks that stand in our path. It's not sitting on the sidelines or shirking from a fight.

Hope is that thing inside us that insists, despite all evidence to the contrary, that something better awaits us if we have the courage to reach for it, and to work for it, and to fight for it.

Hope is what I saw in the eyes of the young woman in Cedar Rapids who works the night shift after a full day of college and still can't afford health care for a sister who's ill; a young woman who still believes that this country will give her the chance to live out her dreams.

Hope is what I heard in the voice of the New Hampshire woman who told me that she hasn't been able to breathe since her nephew left for Iraq; who still goes to bed each night praying for his safe return.

Hope is what led a band of colonists to rise up against an empire; what led the greatest of generations to free a continent and heal a nation; what led young women and young men to sit at lunch counters and brave fire hoses and march through Selma and Montgomery for freedom's cause.

Hope, hope is what led me here today—with a father from Kenya; a mother from Kansas; and a story that could only happen in the United States of America. Hope is the bedrock of this nation; the belief that our destiny will not be written for us, but by us; by all those men and women who are not content to settle for the world as it is; who have the courage to remake the world as it should be.

That is what we started here in Iowa, and that is the message we can now carry to New Hampshire and beyond; the same message we had when we were up and when we were down; the one that can change this country brick by brick, block by block, calloused hand by calloused hand—that together, ordinary people can do extraordinary things; because we are not a collection of red states and blue states, we are the United States of America; and at this moment, in this election, we are ready to believe again. Thank you, Iowa.

—————— 9.35 ——————

'I CAN NO MORE DISOWN HIM THAN I CAN MY WHITE GRANDMOTHER'

Barack Obama

Barack Obama's primary campaign walked a fine line on race. For months, he managed a remarkable racial juggling act. On one hand, his personal profile as a mixed-race American with a black father helped propel his campaign—he was able to position his own story as an example of America's potential to heal festering wounds that had long divided the nation and, in his estimation, limited the ability to build and sustain a progressive policy agenda. On the other hand, he studiously avoided contentious racial discussions. His campaign's success seemed to rely upon the impression that he had transcended race—as his supporters chanted following his victory in South Carolina's Democratic primary, "Race doesn't matter." It was a balancing act that made many black and progressive watchers uncomfortable. The irrelevance of race was, after all, precisely the line of attack conservatives had used against programs like affirmative action for nearly 30 years.

In March 2008, race finally caught up with Obama. His former Chicago pastor, Reverend Jeremiah Wright, had long been fond of provocative sermons and speeches—though no more so than many mainstream faith leaders in urban, black churches. Wright regularly articulated the frustrations so commonly heard in black oratory and writing, from Frederick Douglass to James Baldwin, and did so with a flair. But once clips from his sermons began circulating on the Internet, white pundits and voters alike were shocked by the anger they directed at white America. Suddenly, they wondered aloud whether Obama was so racially transcendent, after all.

Obama first tried to dismiss the controversy by simply saying he didn't share all of his pastor's views. That was not nearly enough, and the outcry began to appear like the beginning of his downfall. Voters and media demanded to hear more from him. And on March 18, in Philadelphia, Pennsylvania, he finally responded. The deeply personal speech received near universal praise. It not only helped defuse the controversy, it reinforced the notion that he was a substantively different kind of candidate. Rather than simply distance himself from Wright, he passionately explained that he could no more distance himself from his minister than he could his white grandmother. Both, he said, had been deeply scarred by the experience of race in America, but both were nonetheless integral parts of his life. Moreover, he insisted, if America is ever to truly overcome its brutally divisive racial history, it would have to move past demonizing either of them and toward trying to understand them and bring them together. Politics laid to the side, as a rare public exhortation for an honest discussion of race in America, the speech prompted many to wonder aloud whether it would one day be remembered as a turning point in American history. It is fitting, however, that the speech was delayed for 45 minutes as technicians struggled—failingly—to make the microphone work correctly.

"We the people, in order to form a more perfect union."

Two hundred and twenty one years ago, in a hall that still stands across the street, a group of men gathered and, with these simple words, launched America's improbable experiment in democracy. Farmers and scholars; statesmen and patriots who had traveled across an ocean to escape tyranny and persecution finally made real their declaration of independence at a Philadelphia convention that lasted through the spring of 1787.

The document they produced was eventually signed but ultimately unfinished. It was stained by this nation's original sin of slavery, a question that divided the colonies and brought the convention to a stalemate until the founders chose to allow the slave trade to continue for at least twenty more years, and to leave any final resolution to future generations.

Of course, the answer to the slavery question was already embedded within our Constitution—a Constitution that had at is very core the ideal of equal citizenship under the law; a Constitution that promised its people liberty, and justice, and a union that could be and should be perfected over time.

And yet words on a parchment would not be enough to deliver slaves from bondage, or provide men and women of every color and creed their full rights and obligations as citizens of the United States. What would be needed were Americans in successive generations who were willing to do their part — through protests and struggle, on the streets and in the courts, through a civil war and civil disobedience and always at great risk—to narrow that gap between the promise of our ideals and the reality of their time.

This was one of the tasks we set forth at the beginning of this campaign—to continue the long march of those who came before us, a march for a more just, more equal, more free, more caring and more prosperous America. I chose to run for the presidency at this moment in history because I believe deeply that we cannot solve the challenges of our time unless we solve them together—unless we perfect our union by understanding that we may have different stories, but we hold common hopes; that we may not look the same and we may not have come from the same place, but we all want to move in the same direction—towards a better future for our children and our grandchildren.

This belief comes from my unyielding faith in the decency and generosity of the American people. But it also comes from my own American story.

I am the son of a black man from Kenya and a white woman from Kansas. I was raised with the help of a white grandfather who survived a Depression to serve in Patton's Army during World War II and a white grandmother who worked on a bomber assembly line at Fort Leavenworth while he was overseas. I've gone to some of the best schools in America and lived in one of the world's poorest nations. I am married to a black American who carries within her the blood of slaves and slaveowners —an inheritance we pass on to our two precious daughters. I have brothers, sisters, nieces, nephews, uncles and cousins, of every race and every hue, scattered across three continents, and for as long as I live, I will never forget that in no other country on Earth is my story even possible.

It's a story that hasn't made me the most conventional candidate. But it is a story that has seared into my genetic makeup the idea that this nation is more than the sum of its parts—that out of many, we are truly one.

Throughout the first year of this campaign, against all predictions to the contrary, we saw how hungry the American people were for this message of unity. Despite the temptation to view my candidacy through a purely racial lens, we won commanding victories in states with some of the whitest populations in the country. In South Carolina, where the Confederate flag still flies, we built a powerful coalition of African Americans and white Americans.

This is not to say that race has not been an issue in the campaign. At various stages in the campaign, some commentators have deemed me either "too black" or "not black enough." We saw racial tensions bubble to the surface during the week before the South Carolina primary. The press has scoured every exit poll for the latest evidence of racial polarization, not just in terms of white and black, but black and brown as well.

And yet, it has only been in the last couple of weeks that the discussion of race in this campaign has taken a particularly divisive turn.

On one end of the spectrum, we've heard the implication that my candidacy is somehow an exercise in affirmative action; that it's based solely on the desire of wide-eyed liberals to purchase racial reconciliation on the cheap. On the other end, we've heard my former pastor, Reverend Jeremiah Wright, use incendiary language to express views that have the potential not only to widen the racial divide, but views that denigrate both the greatness and the goodness of our nation; that rightly offend white and black alike.

I have already condemned, in unequivocal terms, the statements of Reverend Wright that have caused such controversy. For some, nagging questions remain. Did I know him to be an occasionally fierce critic of American domestic and foreign policy? Of course. Did I ever hear him make remarks that could be considered controversial while I sat in church?

Yes. Did I strongly disagree with many of his political views? Absolutely—just as I'm sure many of you have heard remarks from your pastors, priests, or rabbis with which you strongly disagreed.

But the remarks that have caused this recent firestorm weren't simply controversial. They weren't simply a religious leader's effort to speak out against perceived injustice. Instead, they expressed a profoundly distorted view of this country—a view that sees white racism as endemic, and that elevates what is wrong with America above all that we know is right with America; a view that sees the conflicts in the Middle East as rooted primarily in the actions of stalwart allies like Israel, instead of emanating from the perverse and hateful ideologies of radical Islam.

As such, Reverend Wright's comments were not only wrong but divisive, divisive at a time when we need unity; racially charged at a time when we need to come together to solve a set of monumental problems—two wars, a terrorist threat, a falling economy, a chronic health care crisis and potentially devastating climate change; problems that are neither black or white or Latino or Asian, but rather problems that confront us all.

Given my background, my politics, and my professed values and ideals, there will no doubt be those for whom my statements of condemnation are not enough. Why associate myself with Reverend Wright in the first place, they may ask? Why not join another church? And I confess that if all that I knew of Reverend Wright were the snippets of those sermons that have run in an endless loop on the television and YouTube, or if Trinity United Church of Christ conformed to the caricatures being peddled by some commentators, there is no doubt that I would react in much the same way

But the truth is, that isn't all that I know of the man. The man I met more than twenty years ago is a man who helped introduce me to my Christian faith, a man who spoke to me about our obligations to love one another; to care for the sick and lift up the poor. He is a man who served his country as a U.S. Marine; who has studied and lectured at some of the finest universities and seminaries in the country, and who for over thirty years led a church that serves the community by doing God's work here on Earth—by housing the homeless, ministering to the needy, providing day care services and scholarships and prison ministries, and reaching out to those suffering from HIV/AIDS.

In my first book, *Dreams From My Father*, I described the experience of my first service at Trinity:

"People began to shout, to rise from their seats and clap and cry out, a forceful wind carrying the reverend's voice up into the rafters....And in that single note—hope!—I heard something else; at the foot of that cross, inside the thousands of churches across the city, I imagined the stories of ordinary black people merging with the stories of David and Goliath, Moses and Pharaoh, the Christians in the lion's den, Ezekiel's field of dry bones. Those stories—of survival, and freedom, and hope—became our story, my story; the blood that had spilled was our blood, the tears our tears; until this black church, on this bright day, seemed once more a vessel carrying the story of a people into future generations and into a larger world. Our trials and triumphs became at once unique and universal, black and more than black; in chronicling our journey, the stories and songs gave us a means to reclaim memories that we didn't need to feel shame about...memories that all people might study and cherish—and with which we could start to rebuild."

That has been my experience at Trinity. Like other predominantly black churches across the country, Trinity embodies the black community in its entirety—the doctor and the welfare mom, the model student and the former gang-banger. Like other black churches, Trinity's services are full of raucous laughter and sometimes bawdy humor. They are full of dancing, clapping, screaming and shouting that may seem jarring to the untrained ear.

The church contains in full the kindness and cruelty, the fierce intelligence and the shocking ignorance, the struggles and successes, the love and yes, the bitterness and bias that make up the black experience in America.

And this helps explain, perhaps, my relationship with Reverend Wright. As imperfect as he may be, he has been like family to me. He strengthened my faith, officiated my wedding, and baptized my children. Not once in my conversations with him have I heard him talk about any ethnic group in derogatory terms, or treat whites with whom he interacted with anything but courtesy and respect. He contains within him the contradictions—the good and the bad—of the community that he has served diligently for so many years.

I can no more disown him than I can disown the black community. I can no more disown him than I can my white grandmother—a woman who helped raise me, a woman who sacrificed again and again for me, a woman who loves me as much as she loves anything in this world, but a woman who once confessed her fear of black men who passed by her on the street, and who on more than one occasion has uttered racial or ethnic stereotypes that made me cringe.

These people are a part of me. And they are a part of America, this country that I love.

Some will see this as an attempt to justify or excuse comments that are simply inexcusable. I can assure you it is not. I suppose the politically safe thing would be to move on from this episode and just hope that it fades into the woodwork. We can dismiss Reverend Wright as a crank or a demagogue, just as some have dismissed Geraldine Ferraro, in the aftermath of her recent statements, as harboring some deep-seated racial bias.

But race is an issue that I believe this nation cannot afford to ignore right now. We would be making the same mistake that Reverend Wright made in his offending sermons about America—to simplify and stereotype and amplify the negative to the point that it distorts reality.

The fact is that the comments that have been made and the issues that have surfaced over the last few weeks reflect the complexities of race in this country that we've never really worked through—a part of our union that we have yet to perfect. And if we walk away now, if we simply retreat into our respective corners, we will never be able to come together and solve challenges like health care, or education, or the need to find good jobs for every American.

Understanding this reality requires a reminder of how we arrived at this point. As William Faulkner once wrote, "The past isn't dead and buried. In fact, it isn't even past." We do not need to recite here the history of racial injustice in this country. But we do need to remind ourselves that so many of the disparities that exist in the African-American community today can be directly traced to inequalities passed on from an earlier generation that suffered under the brutal legacy of slavery and Jim Crow.

Segregated schools were, and are, inferior schools; we still haven't fixed them, fifty years after *Brown v. Board of Education*, and the inferior education they provided, then and now, helps explain the pervasive achievement gap between today's black and white students.

Legalized discrimination—where blacks were prevented, often through violence, from owning property, or loans were not granted to African-American business owners, or black homeowners could not access FHA mortgages, or blacks were excluded from unions, or the police force, or fire departments—meant that black families could not amass any meaningful wealth to bequeath to future generations. That history helps explain the wealth and income gap between black and white, and the concentrated pockets of poverty that persists in so many of today's urban and rural communities.

A lack of economic opportunity among black men, and the shame and frustration that came from not being able to provide for one's family, contributed to the erosion of black families—a problem that welfare policies for many years may have worsened. And the lack of basic services in so many urban black neighborhoods—parks for kids to play in, police walking the beat, regular garbage pick-up and building code enforcement—all helped create a cycle of violence, blight and neglect that continue to haunt us.

This is the reality in which Reverend Wright and other African-Americans of his generation grew up. They came of age in the late fifties and early sixties, a time when segregation was still the law of the land and opportunity was systematically constricted. What's remarkable is not how many failed in the face of discrimination, but rather how many men and women overcame the odds; how many were able to make a way out of no way for those like me who would come after them.

But for all those who scratched and clawed their way to get a piece of the American dream, there were many who didn't make it—those who were ultimately defeated, in one way or another, by discrimination. That legacy of defeat was passed on to future generations—those young men and increasingly young women who we see standing on street corners or languishing in our prisons, without hope or prospects for the future. Even for those blacks who did make it, questions of race, and racism, continue to define their worldview in fundamental ways. For the men and women of Reverend Wright's generation, the memories of humiliation and doubt and fear have not gone away; nor has the anger and the bitterness of those years. That anger may not get expressed in public, in front of white co-workers or white friends. But it does find voice in the barbershop or around the kitchen table. At times, that anger is exploited by politicians, to gin up votes along racial lines, or to make up for a politician's own failings.

And occasionally it finds voice in the church on Sunday morning, in the pulpit and in the pews. The fact that so many people are surprised to hear that anger in some of Reverend Wright's sermons simply reminds us of the old truism that the most segregated hour in American life occurs on Sunday morning. That anger is not always productive; indeed, all too often it distracts attention from solving real problems; it keeps us from squarely facing our own complicity in our condition, and prevents the African-American community from forging the alliances it needs to bring about real change. But the anger is real; it is powerful; and to simply wish it away, to condemn it without understanding its roots, only serves to widen the chasm of misunderstanding that exists between the races.

In fact, a similar anger exists within segments of the white community. Most working- and middle-class white Americans don't feel that they have been particularly privileged by their race. Their experience is the immigrant experience—as far as they're concerned, no one's handed them anything, they've built it from scratch. They've worked hard all their lives, many times only to see their jobs shipped overseas or their pension dumped after a lifetime of labor. They are anxious about their futures, and feel their dreams slipping away; in an era of stagnant wages and global competition, opportunity comes to be seen as a zero sum game, in which your dreams come at my expense. So when they are told to bus their children to a school across town; when they hear that an African American is getting an advantage in landing a good job or a spot in a good college because of an injustice that they themselves never committed; when they're told that their fears about crime in urban neighborhoods are somehow prejudiced, resentment builds over time.

Like the anger within the black community, these resentments aren't always expressed in polite company. But they have helped shape the political landscape for at least a generation. Anger over welfare and affirmative action helped forge the Reagan coalition. Politicians routinely exploited fears of crime for their own electoral ends. Talk show hosts and conservative commentators built entire careers unmasking bogus claims of racism while dismissing legitimate discussions of racial injustice and inequality as mere political correctness or reverse racism.

Just as black anger often proved counter-productive, so have these white resentments distracted attention from the real culprits of the middle class squeeze—a corporate culture rife with inside dealing, questionable accounting practices, and short-term greed; a Washington dominated by lobbyists and special interests; economic policies that favor the few over the many. And yet, to wish away the resentments of white Americans, to label them as mis-guided or even racist, without recognizing they are grounded in legitimate concerns—this too widens the racial divide, and blocks the path to understanding.

This is where we are right now. It's a racial stalemate we've been stuck in for years. Contrary to the claims of some of my critics, black and white, I have never been so naïve as to believe that we can get beyond our racial divisions in a single election cycle, or with a single candidacy—particularly a candidacy as imperfect as my own.

But I have asserted a firm conviction—a conviction rooted in my faith in God and my faith in the American people—that working together we can move beyond some of our old racial wounds, and that in fact we have no choice if we are to continue on the path of a more perfect union.

For the African-American community, that path means embracing the burdens of our past without becoming victims of our past. It means continuing to insist on a full measure of justice in every aspect of American life. But it also means binding our particular grievances—for better health care, and better schools, and better jobs—to the larger aspirations of all Americans—the white woman struggling to break the glass ceiling, the white man whose been laid off, the immigrant trying to feed his family. And it means taking full responsibility for our own lives—by demanding more from our fathers, and spending more time with our children, and reading to them, and teaching them that while they may face challenges and

discrimination in their own lives, they must never succumb to despair or cynicism; they must always believe that they can write their own destiny.

Ironically, this quintessentially American—and yes, conservative—notion of self-help found frequent expression in Reverend Wright's sermons. But what my former pastor too often failed to understand is that embarking on a program of self-help also requires a belief that society can change.

The profound mistake of Reverend Wright's sermons is not that he spoke about racism in our society. It's that he spoke as if our society was static; as if no progress has been made; as if this country—a country that has made it possible for one of his own members to run for the highest office in the land and build a coali-tion of white and black; Latino and Asian, rich and poor, young and old—is still irrevocably bound to a tragic past. But what we know—what we have seen—is that America can change. That is the true genius of this nation. What we have already achieved gives us hope—the audacity to hope—for what we can and must achieve tomorrow.

In the white community, the path to a more perfect union means acknowledging that what ails the African-American community does not just exist in the minds of black people; that the legacy of discrimination—and current inci-dents of discrimination, while less overt than in the past—are real and must be addressed. Not just with words, but with deeds—by investing in our schools and our communities; by enforcing our civil rights laws and ensuring fairness in our criminal justice system; by pro-viding this generation with ladders of opportu-nity that were unavailable for previous generations. It requires all Americans to realize that your dreams do not have to come at the expense of my dreams; that investing in the health, welfare, and education of black and brown and white children will ultimately help all of America prosper.

In the end, then, what is called for is noth-ing more, and nothing less, than what all the world's great religions demand—that we do unto others as we would have them do unto us. Let us be our brother's keeper, scripture tells us. Let us be our sister's keeper. Let us find that common stake we all have in one another, and let our politics reflect that spirit as well.

For we have a choice in this country. We can accept a politics that breeds division, and conflict, and cynicism. We can tackle race only as spectacle—as we did in the OJ trial—or in the wake of tragedy, as we did in the aftermath of Katrina—or as fodder for the nightly news. We can play Reverend Wright's sermons on every channel, every day and talk about them from now until the election, and make the only question in this campaign whether or not the American people think that I somehow believe or sympathize with his most offensive words. We can pounce on some gaffe by a Hillary supporter as evidence that she's playing the race card, or we can speculate on whether white men will all flock to John McCain in the general election regardless of his policies.

We can do that.

But if we do, I can tell you that in the next election, we'll be talking about some other distraction. And then another one. And then another one. And nothing will change.

That is one option. Or, at this moment, in this election, we can come together and say, "Not this time." This time we want to talk about the crumbling schools that are stealing the future of black children and white children and Asian children and Hispanic children and Native American children. This time we want to reject the cynicism that tells us that these kids can't learn; that those kids who don't look like us are somebody else's problem. The children of America are not those kids, they are our kids, and we will not let them fall behind in a 21st century economy. Not this time.

This time we want to talk about how the lines in the emergency room are filled with whites and blacks and Hispanics who do not have health care; who don't have the power on their own to overcome the special interests in Washington, but who can take them on if we do it together.

This time we want to talk about the shuttered mills that once provided a decent life for men and women of every race, and the homes for sale that once belonged to Americans from every religion, every region, every walk of life. This time we want to talk about the fact that the real problem is not that someone who doesn't look like you might take your job; it's that the corporation you work for will ship it overseas for nothing more than a profit.

This time we want to talk about the men and women of every color and creed who serve together, and fight together, and bleed together under the same proud flag. We want to talk about how to bring them home from a war that never should've been authorized and never should've been waged, and we want to talk about how we'll show our patriotism by caring for them, and their families, and giving them the benefits they have earned.

I would not be running for president if I didn't believe with all my heart that this is what the vast majority of Americans want for this country. This union may never be perfect, but generation after generation has shown that it can always be perfected. And today, whenever I find myself feeling doubtful or cynical about this possibility, what gives me the most hope is the next generation—the young people whose attitudes and beliefs and openness to change have already made history in this election.

There is one story in particularly that I'd like to leave you with today—a story I told when I had the great honor of speaking on Dr. King's birthday at his home church, Ebenezer Baptist, in Atlanta.

There is a young, twenty-three year old white woman named Ashley Baia who organized for our campaign in Florence, South Carolina. She had been working to organize a mostly African-American community since the beginning of this campaign, and one day she was at a roundtable discussion where everyone went around telling their story and why they were there.

And Ashley said that when she was nine years old, her mother got cancer. And because she had to miss days of work, she was let go and lost her health care. They had to file for bankruptcy, and that's when Ashley decided that she had to do something to help her mom.

She knew that food was one of their most expensive costs, and so Ashley convinced her mother that what she really liked and really wanted to eat more than anything else was mustard and relish sandwiches. Because that was the cheapest way to eat.

She did this for a year until her mom got better, and she told everyone at the roundtable that the reason she joined our campaign was so that she could help the millions of other children in the country who want and need to help their parents too.

Now Ashley might have made a different choice. Perhaps somebody told her along the way that the source of her mother's problems were blacks who were on welfare and too lazy to work, or Hispanics who were coming into the country illegally. But she didn't. She sought out allies in her fight against injustice.

Anyway, Ashley finishes her story and then goes around the room and asks everyone else why they're supporting the campaign. They all have different stories and reasons. Many bring up a specific issue. And finally they come to this elderly black man who's been sitting there quietly the entire time. And Ashley asks him why he's there. And he does not bring up a specific issue. He does not say health care or the economy. He does not say education or the war. He does not say that he was there because of Barack Obama. He simply says to everyone in the room, "I am here because of Ashley."

"I'm here because of Ashley." By itself, that single moment of recognition between that young white girl and that old black man is not enough. It is not enough to give health care to the sick, or jobs to the jobless, or education to our children.

But it is where we start. It is where our union grows stronger. And as so many generations have come to realize over the course of the two-hundred and twenty one years since a band of patriots signed that document in Philadelphia, that is where the perfection begins.

SUGGESTED READING

A would-be student of black history and culture could go a long way by just exploring the works of Carter G. Woodson, the turn of the century African-American scholar credited with founding the study of black history. However, the books listed below offer excellent starting points for those interested in learning more about the contexts from which the documents presented in this collection emerged. A handful of the items listed are multimedia learning tools, designed for classroom as well as individual use.

Anderson, Jervis. *This was Harlem: A Cultural Portrait, 1900–1950*. New York: Farrar, Straus and Giroux, 1982.

Appiah, Kwame Anthony and Gates, Henry Louis, Jr. *Africana: The Encyclopedia of the African American Experience*. New York: Basic Civitas Books, 1999. [Also available on CD-Rom and, in part, online at www.Africana.com.]

Aptheker, Herbert. *American Negro Slave Revolts*. New York: International Publishers, 1974.

Baraka, Amiri (LeRoi Jones). *Blues People: Negro Music in White America*. New York: William Morrow, 1963.

Branch, Taylor. *Parting the Waters: America in the King Years, 1954–63*. New York: Simon & Schuster, 1989.

_____. *Pillar of Fire: America in the King Years, 1963–65*. New York: Simon & Schuster, 1999.

_____. *At Canaan's Edge: America in the King Years, 1965–68*. New York: Simon & Schuster, 2006.

DuBois, W.E.B. *The Suppression of the African Slave Trade to the United States of America, 1683–1870*. New York: Longman Green, 1896.

Foner, Eric. *Reconstruction: America's Unfinished Revolution, 1863–1877*. New York: Harper & Row Publishers, 1988.

Foner, Philip S. *The Life and Writings of Frederick Douglass*. New York: International Publishers, 1950.

Frey, Sylvia and Betty Wood. *Come Shouting to Zion: African American Protestantism in the American South and British Caribbean to 1830*. Chapel Hill: University of North Carolina Press, 1998.

Ham, Debra Newman. *The African-American Mosaic: A Library of Congress resource guide for the study of Black history and culture*. Washington, D.C.: Library of Congress, 1993. [This and other Library of Congress works on African Americans are available, in part, as online exhibits at www.loc.gov/exhibits.]

Haskins, James. *Black Music in America: A History Through its People*. New York: Harper & Row Publishers, 1987.

Johnson, Charles and Patricia Smith. *Africans in America: America's Journey Through Slavery*. New York: Harcourt Brace, 1998. [Also available as a video or CD-Rom set and, in part, online at www.pbs.org/wgbh/aia.]

Johnson, James Weldon. *The Book of American Negro Poetry*. New York: Harcourt Brace Jovanovich, 1931.

Kaplan, Sidney and Emma Nogrady Kaplan. *The Black Presence in the Era of the American Revolution*. Amherst: University of Massachusetts Press, 1989.

Kluger, Richard. *Simple Justice: The History of Brown v. Board of Education and Black America's Struggle for Equality*. New York: Alfred A. Knopf, 1976.

Landers, Jane. *Black Society in Spanish Florida*. Urbana: University of Illinois, 1999.

Lewis, David Levering. *When Harlem was in Vogue*. New York: Vintage Books, 1981.

Reinarman, Craig and Harry Levine. *Crack in America: Demon Drugs and Social Justice*. Berkeley: University of California Press, 1997.

Roberts, Gene and Hank Klibanoff. *The Race Beat: The Press, the Civil Rights Struggle, and the Awakening of a Nation*. New York: Alfred A. Knopf, 2006.

Wood, Peter. *Black Majority: Negroes in Colonial South Carolina from 1670 through the Stono Rebellion*. New York, Alfred A. Knopf: 1974.

Woodson, Carter G. *History of the Negro Church*. Washington, D.C.: The Associated Publishers, 1921.

Woodson, Carter G. *Mis-education of the Negro*. Washington, D.C.: The Associated Publishers, 1933.

———. *The Negro in Our History*. Washington, D.C.: The Associate Publishers, 1922.

PERMISSIONS

Maya Angelou: Excerpt from I KNOW WHY THE CAGED BIRD SINGS by Maya Angelou, copyright © 1969 and renewed 1997 by Maya Angelou. Used by permission of Random House, Inc.

The Associated Press: "Syphillis Victims in U.S. Study Went Untreated for 40 Years" by Jean Heller reprinted with permission of The Associated Press. "Freedom Riders Brought More Than Violence" by Sid Moody, published by the Associated Press on February 8, 1962, reprinted with permission of The Associated Press.

The A&T Register: "Nine Kids Who Dared" by Ted Poston first appeared in the February 5, 1960 issue. Reproduced with permission.

James Baldwin: Excerpt from GO TELL IT ON THE MOUNTAIN by James Baldwin, copyright © 1952, 1953 by James Baldwin. Used by permission of Doubleday, a division of Random House, Inc.

Amiri Baraka: Excerpts from THE DUTCHMAN are reprinted by permission of Sterling Lord Literistic, Inc. Copyright by Amiri Baraka.

Gwendolyn Brooks: "We Real Cool" and "The Sonnet Ballads" copyright © 1991 by Gwendolyn Brooks, published by Third World Press, Chicago. Reprinted by permission of the author.

James Brown: "Say it Loud (I'm Black and I'm Proud)" reprinted by permission of Unichappell.

Cassius Clay: Excerpts from interview with Alex Haley appeared in *Playboy*, October 1964.

Eldridge Cleaver: Excerpt from SOUL ON ICE by Eldridge Cleaver, copyright © 1968 by McGraw-Hill. Reprinted by permission of McGraw-Hill.

Stanley Crouch: Interviewed by David Gergen on the MacNeil/Lehrer Hour on February 22, 1996. Transcript reprinted by permission of the MacNeil/Lehrer Hour.

Harold Cruse: Excerpt from THE CRISIS OF THE NEGRO INTELLECTUAL by HAROLD CRUSE. Copyright © 1967 Harold Cruse. Reprinted by permission of HarperCollins Publishers, Inc.

Countee Cullen: "Yet Do I Marvel" and "To a Brown Boy" copyright © 1925 by Harper & Brothers; copyright renewed 1953 by Ida M. Cullen. Reprinted by permission of GRM Associates, agents for the estate of Ida M. Cullen.

Miles Davis: Excerpts from interview with Alex Haley appeared in *Playboy*, September 1962.

Ossie Davis: Excerpt from speech at the funeral of Malcolm X used by permission of the author.

W.E.B. DuBois: "Criticism of Nigger Heaven" and "Counsels of Despair" from W.E.B. DUBOIS: A READER by David Levering Lewis, © 1995 by David Levering Lewis. Reprinted by permission of Henry Holt and Company LLC.

Bob Dylan: "Only A Pawn in their Game" by Bob Dylan reprinted by permission of Special Writer Music.

Duke Ellington: "It Don't Mean a Thing (If It Ain't Got That Swing)" from SOPHISTICATED LADIES. Words and Music by Duke Ellington and Irving Mills. Copyright © 1932 (Renewed 1959) and Assigned to Famous Music Corporation and EMI Mills Music Inc. in the U.S.A. Rights for the world outside the U.S.A. Controlled by EMI Mills Music Inc. and Warner Bros. Publications Inc. International Copyright Secured. All Rights Reserved.

Ralph Ellison: Excerpt from INVISIBLE MAN by Ralph Ellison, copyright © 1974, 1948, 1952 by Ralph Ellison. Used by permission of Random House, Inc.

Henry Louis Gates, Jr.: "Thirteen Ways of Looking at a Black Man," copyright © 1995 by Henry Louis Gates, Jr., originally appeared in *The New Yorker*. Used by permission of Alfred A. Knopf, a division of Random House, Inc.

Nikki Giovanni: "My Poem," "Kidnap Poem," and "Nikki Rosa" from THE SELECTED POEMS OF NIKKI GIOVANNI by Nikki Giovanni. Compilation copyright © 1996 by Nikki Giovanni. Reprinted by permission of William Morrow, a division of HarperCollins Publishers, Inc.

Alex Haley: Excerpt from ROOTS by Alex Haley, copyright © 1976 by Alex Haley. Used by permission of Doubleday, a division of Random House, Inc.

Fannie Lou Hamer: Excerpt from interview broadcast on KZSU in the summer of 1965 reprinted by permission of KZSU.

Lorraine Hansberry: A RAISIN IN THE SUN by Lorraine Hansberry, copyright © 1958 by Robert Nemiroff, as an unpublished work. Copyright © 1959, 1966, 1984 by Robert Nemiroff. Used by permission of Random House, Inc.

Photography Credits

INDEX

A

"ABC," 601–602

Abernathy, Ralph, 602

abolitionists
  Brown, John, 264
  Fugitive Slave Act of 1850 and, conflicts over, 247–248
  Fugitive Slave Act of 1850 and, criticism of, 232
  violence against, 187–188

abolition movement, 21–22, 128–257
  African-American literature and, 21
  African-American political oratory and, 22
  Amistad Africans and, 173
  Anglican missionaries and, 28
  Atkins in, 41
  convention movement and, 155
  Darien Scots in, 46
  Douglass role in, 159, 193–195
  female role in, 185
  Garrison in, 158–162
  Harper's involvement in, 158
  in literary works, 221–225
  Methodist Church in, 77–78
  mob attacks as result of, 187–188
  morality of slavery and, 35, 45–46
  Pennsylvania Abolition Society and, 112
  Quakers in, 159
  repatriation to Africa within, 134–136
  slave narratives and, role in, 59, 213–221
  Uncle Tom's Cabin influence on, 240
  women's movement and, 185, 211

Acquired Immune Deficiency Syndrome (AIDS), 663–665
  CDC rates for, 663–664

ACS. *See* American Colonization Society

Adams, John, on Attucks, 72–73

Adams, John Quincy, Amistad Africans and, request for legal counsel, 173–174

Adams, Samuel, 70

Adarand v. Pena, 698

'An Address to the Negroes of the State of New York' (Hammon, Jupiter), 106–109

'An Address to the Public' (Franklin), 112

'Address to the Human and Benevolent Inhabitants of the City' (Forten), 134

affirmative action
  "domestic Marshall Plan" as early form of, 567
  legal challenges to, 611–614
  Proposition 209 and, 698
  Regents of University of California v. Bakke and, 611–614
  Thomas as opponent of, 668, 697–699

African-American literature. *See* literature, African-American

African-American poetry. *See* poetry, African-American

African-American political organizations. *See* political organizations, African-American

African-Americans. *See also* employment, for African-Americans; essays by African-Americans, during American Revolution; literature, African-American; military, African-Americans in; music, African-American; newspapers, African-American; poetry, African-American; popular entertainment in 20th century, African-American role in; suffrage rights, for African-Americans; voting rights, for African-Americans
  in American Revolution, 70–71, 82–101
  Baptist faith among, 21, 46
  in Battle of Bunker Hill, 84
  in Battle of Groton Heights, 85
  as British loyalists, 82–84
  Canadian migration of, 155
  as Freemasons, 100
  homosexuality and, 622–625
  medical studies with, 603–605
  Methodist faith among, 21, 46, 77
  in militia, 84
  religious oratorical style of, 19
  during Revolutionary War, 82–92
  under U.S. Constitution, as 'three fifths' of a person, 98
  Vietnam War opposition by, 578–582

African Methodist Episcopal (AME) Church, 21
  Allen and, 117
  church hymns in, 126–127
  sexism within, 180

Agnew, Spiro, 585

AIDS. *See* Acquired Immune Deficiency Syndrome

Ain't I a Woman: Black women and feminism (hooks), 625–626

Alabama. *See* Birmingham, Alabama, store boycott in; Montgomery Bus Boycott; Selma, Alabama

Ali, Muhammad, 550–551, 609
  opposition to Vietnam War, 582–583

Allen, Lewis, 463

Allen, Richard, 21, 116–122, 155–156
  AME Church and, 117
  support for female ministry, 180

All God's Chillun Got Wings (O'Neill), 455

AME. *See* African Methodist Episcopal Church

American Anti-Slavery Society, 162–165, 193

American colonies. *See* Georgia; Maryland; Massachusetts; Pennsylvania; Rhode Island, African-American militia regiments in; South Carolina; Virginia

American Colonization Society (ACS), 134
  congressional power of, 165

Garrison and, 158–160, 165
Liberia and, 136–139, 167–171

American Revolution. *See also* Revolutionary War
  African-American literature during, 88–92, 103–106
  African-Americans and, 70–71, 82–101
  Attucks' role in, 70
  Boston Massacre as impetus for, 70–71, 88

American Society of Free Persons of Color, 155

Amistad Africans, 171–180, 195
  abolitionist support for, 173
  Adams, John Quincy and, request for legal counsel, 173–174
  Barber descriptions of, 175–180
  Spanish response to, 171–172
  before U.S. Supreme Court, 174–175

Andrew, John, 314

Andrews, Dope, 439

And Still I Rise (Angelou), 598, 601

Angelou, Maya, 22, 598–601, 680–681, 686
  "Sympathy" as influence on, 381

Anglican missionaries
  abolition treatises of, 28
  in Barbados, 28
  feelings on slavery, 26

Anglo-African, 318

Anglo-American Magazine, 298–303

Annie Allen (Brooks, Gwendolyn), 479

anti-discrimination laws, in Massachusetts, 331. *See also* desegregation

Anti-Drug Abuse Act, 651

anti-Semitism
  of Jackson, Jesse, 636
  of NOI, 631, 686

Anti-Slavery Burglar, 211–212

Anti-Slavery Convention of American Women, 185, 187

Anti-Slavery Society, 323

Appeal to the Colored Citizens of the World (Walker, David), 144–151
  barbarity of slavery in, 145–151
  Black Power Movement influenced by, 145

"Appeal to the Coloured Citizens of the World" (Walker), 21

armies. *See* military, African-Americans in; Union armies

Arnett, Benjamin, 371–373

Arnold, Benedict, 85

'Ar'n't I a Woman' (Truth), 211–213

Associated Press, 603–605

Atchison, David, 264

Atkins, John, 41–43

"Atlanta Compromise" (Washington, Booker T.), 392–395, 426

Atlanta Constitution, 382

Atlanta Journal, 382

Atlantic Slave Trade, 27–28, 30
  Atkins involvement in, 41–43
  Constitutional Convention and, compromises over, 98–100

ACKNOWLEDGMENTS

This book is built on the work of scores of historians who have dedicated their careers to ecording the lives of African Americans. The scholarship of these men and women makes a collection such as this one possible. Their work provided me with a road map in compiling the documents presented here, and it is to them that I, as a researcher, and indeed all of us, as a community and a nation, owe a great debt. I am further indebted to my editor, Michael Driscoll, and publisher, J.P. Leventhal, for conceiving the book and offering me an opportunity to edit it. Michael's guidance throughout the project has proven invaluable, and his bottomless patience with me has itself been historic. Reeve Chace's work securing permissions was a great help, and Merideth Harte and her colleagues at 27.12 also deserve thanks for the book's wonderful design.

The friends and loved ones who supported me during this adventure are too many to list. However, I am particularly grateful to Stacey Whitmire, who typeset many of the documents in this collection, and Aimee Lessard, who helped me navigate the insufferable world of information technology. Everything I accomplish, including this book, begins with the foundation of self-confidence instilled in me by my family. With their ongoing love and support, anything is achievable. My partner, Mark Bailey, perhaps deserves the greatest acknowledgment. Not only did he graciously allow me to turn our home into a research library, but throughout the process of developing this book Mark jumped in to solve crisis after crisis—from my emotional breakdowns to my planning failures. Without his love, and his unerring eye for solutions, this book would not have been published.

$7.83